The Oxford History *of* WESTERN MUSIC

College Edition

Richard Taruskin
University of California, Berkeley

Christopher H. Gibbs
Bard College, Annandale-on-Hudson, New York

New York Oxford
OXFORD UNIVERSITY PRESS

Oxford University Press, Inc., publishes works that further Oxford University's objective of excellence in research, scholarship, and education.

Oxford New York
Auckland Cape Town Dar es Salaam Hong Kong Karachi
Kuala Lumpur Madrid Melbourne Mexico City Nairobi
New Delhi Shanghai Taipei Toronto

With offices in
Argentina Austria Brazil Chile Czech Republic France Greece
Guatemala Hungary Italy Japan Poland Portugal Singapore
South Korea Switzerland Thailand Turkey Ukraine Vietnam

For titles covered by Section 112 of the US Higher Education Opportunity Act, please visit www.oup.com/us/he for the latest information about pricing and alternate formats.

Published by Oxford University Press, Inc.
198 Madison Avenue, New York, New York 10016
http://www.oup.com

Library of Congress Cataloging-in-Publication Data

Taruskin, Richard.
The Oxford history of Western music / Richard Taruskin ; Christopher Gibbs.—College ed.
p. cm.
Includes bibliographical references and index.
ISBN 978-0-19-509762-7
1. Music—History and criticism. I. Gibbs, Christopher Howard. II. Title.
ML160.T182 2012
780.9—dc23

2011040998

9 8 7 6 5 4 3 2 1
Printed in the United States of America
on acid-free paper

Contents

CHAPTER 19
Romantic Spectacles: From Virtuosos to Grand Opera • 563

CHAPTER 20
Literary Musicians • 588

CHAPTER 21
Music Imported and Exported • 620

The Story of Western Classical Music . . . Told By Today's Outstanding Music Historians

Based on the award-winning six-volume work by Richard Taruskin, *The Oxford History of Western Music,* College Edition, offers a complete package of everything needed to build your understanding and appreciation of the classical canon. The package includes:

- A full text designed to facilitate your exploration of the many facets of the classical repertory.
- Three score anthologies for analyzing the music with introductory essays for each work.
- A three-volume CD set in MP3 format for listening to the music for easy downloading to a portable listening device (as well as a single-volume concise version spanning all eras).
- A companion website including chapter outlines, key terms and definitions, and suggested links to articles from *The New Grove Dictionary of Music and Musicians.* A brief introduction on how to research music history is included for use in preparing term papers.
- Eighteen months' access to *Oxford Music Online,* the definitive resource for conducting further research in the field.

The Most Up-to-Date, Comprehensive History of Western Classical Music Available

Richard Taruskin and Christopher H. Gibbs offer a unique combination of historical knowledge and teaching experience that informs this new survey of Western classical music. Richard Taruskin has demonstrated the special ability to synthesize social and cultural history, a deep understanding and appreciation for the full range of musical expression, and a knowledge of the composers and creators who shaped the development of the greatest music from the Medieval era to modern times. In his monumental six-volume *The Oxford History of Western Music,* Taruskin took on the challenge of telling not only the story of the music but also of the cultural forces that molded our great musical heritage. Christopher H. Gibbs, an expert teacher and renowned scholar, has built on the foundation that Taruskin created to make this history accessible for today's music students. Gibbs has taken Taruskin's themes and woven them into a compelling story of how musicians, living in key places and at important historical moments, were able to create a lasting canon of musical excellence.

Putting People First

While other histories of music focus on musical genres or theories, *The Oxford History of Western Music*, College Edition, foregrounds the people who created, patronized, performed, presented, published, criticized, and heard each era's music. This is not only a story of notes on the page, but a dynamic history of musical sound made by human beings to be heard, enjoyed, and preserved as a key part of cultural expression.

Making Connections Among Musical Works and Across History

Music making does not occur in a vacuum. Just as people create music, the interaction among people, in specific places and times, shapes the music that is made. Where other texts emphasize individual works, *The Oxford History of Western Music*, College Edition, emphasizes the connections among works, both within each cultural era and across time and place. Connections are made between composers, eras, and centers of musical activity so that you can understand the full history of Western music. The discussion of specific musical works, therefore, goes beyond technical analysis of harmony, rhythm, and phrasing to take into account connections with society, politics, and other art forms. This includes considering the genesis of pieces as well as their reception, and ultimately thinking about their meanings.

Improving Critical Thinking

Today, we understand that history is a story also made by people, and that in telling this story certain assumptions are made, with certain composers and works elevated above others. Over time, the story has changed, as new information has been discovered, but also as changing tastes have elevated the works of some composers while leading others to be forgotten. *The Oxford History of Western Music*, College Edition, tells the story of how the history of music has been constructed, asking students to examine basic assumptions and beliefs as part of the process of learning about the music itself. Readers will develop an understanding not just of the facts of music history—of pieces, names, dates, and places—but also cultivate ways of historical and critical thinking.

Building Listening and Analysis Skills

More than ever, students are listening to music as an accompaniment to their day-to-day lives; but are they understanding what they are hearing? The *Oxford History of Western Music*, College Edition, shows students how to build critical listening skills through detailed discussions of classics of the Western tradition. The three-part *Oxford Recorded Anthology of Western Music* draws from the best possible performances offering outstanding interpretations of each work. The three-volume *Oxford Anthology of Western Music* offers the corresponding scores for these works, along with introductory essays that provide models for students about how to conduct musical analysis.

Covering the Story More Completely Than Before

The *Oxford History of Western Music,* College Edition, covers more musical works in more detail than any previous textbook in the field. Every major era is addressed with the full depth and critical complexity that it deserves. Yet there is also an understanding that certain eras demand fuller exploration, based on their impact on the subsequent history of music. The last two hundred years of music history are given enhanced coverage, recognizing that these are the works that are most salient to today's students.

Breaking New Ground

In developing the *Oxford History of Western Music,* College Edition, we called on the expertise of over 60 professors teaching music history across the country. The reviewers were united in their belief that this work would revolutionize the way music history is taught:

- "The *Oxford History of Western Music,* College Edition, has a thrilling sense of wonder and excitement, and conveys a personal sense of engagement with music that I find lacking in the texts we have available now."—Robert Eisenstein, University of Massachusetts, and Mount Holyoke College
- ". . . Fascinating and essential observations that no other survey text includes . . . Without a doubt, the content of this text and its fundamental approach to writing history are superior to all other texts out there."—Julie Hubbert, University of South Carolina
- ". . . It fills all the traditional gaps (Bach family, Chopin, Tchaikovsky, nationalism). The attention to stylistic transitions is remarkably constructed and particularly notable. This text offers a wonderful historical perspective, and in my opinion is really the only book that is truly a history book."—Nora Lewis, Kansas State University

Getting the Most from This Package

The *Oxford History of Western Music*, College Edition makes history come alive through several key textual features.

Marginal links to the print anthologies and the CD sets
Timelines introducing key musical and historical events for every chapter
Musical examples and diagrams illuminate the discussion of key works

2 CHAPTER 1 THE FIRST LITERATE REPERTORY IN WESTERN MUSIC: GREGORIAN CHANT

TIMELINE

ca. 1200 BCE Musical notation inscribed on a Babylonian cuneiform tablet
ca. 800 BCE Homer, *Iliad* and *Odyssey*
ca. 580–500 BCE Pythagoras explores harmonic ratios
ca. 450–325 BCE Socrates, Plato, and Aristotle pose influential ideas on music
ca. 360 BCE Plato, *The Republic*
27 BCE Rome becomes an empire under Augustus
ca. 20 BCE Virgil, *Aeneid*
First century CE *Epitaph of Seikilos*
391 St. Augustine, *De musica*
395 Division of the Roman Empire into East and West
476 Fall of the Roman Empire in the West
ca. 500–10 Boethius, *De institutione musica*
ca. 530 St. Benedict, *Regula monachorum*
754 Pope Stephen II visits King of the Franks, Pepin III, instigating the spread of Roman chant
800 Pope Leo III crowns Charlemagne as Emperor of the Western Roman Empire
ca. 843 Aurelian of Réôme, *Musica disciplina*
ca. 860–900 *Musica enchiriadis*

There are many surviving illustrations of ancient music making found in prehistoric cave paintings, in Egyptian murals, on Greek pottery, and elsewhere that provide further indications of the instruments that were used, if not of the specific music that was produced. Also abundant are written descriptions. The Bible gives some particularly vivid ones. Psalm 150, the climax of the **Psalter** (Book of Psalms), is in fact an account of singing God's praises in the ancient temple. It reads, in part:

Praise him with fanfares on the trumpet,
praise him upon the lute and harp;
praise him with tambourines and dancing,
praise him with flute and strings;
praise him with the clash of cymbals,
praise him with triumphant cymbals;
let everything that has breath praise the LORD!

We will not find such goings-on in any synagogue today. We can read of the chanting of **psalms** and other sacred texts in the synagogue, but no Jewish music was written down exactly until much more modern times.

While some early kinds of musical notation survive to a very limited degree from ancient cultures, the principal challenge has been figuring out how to decode them. In the 1970s scholars managed to transcribe the notation on a cuneiform tablet dating from around 1200 BCE that had been unearthed on the site of the ancient Babylonian city of Ugarit, near Ras-Shamra in modern Syria.[1] The tablet contained a **hymn** to the goddess Nikkal, the wife of the moon god Kushuh (Ex. 1-1). What may be most remarkable is how unremarkable this e… now seems when transcribed into modern notatio… nized as consonant in most Western music today.

Example 1-1 First phrase of Hurrian hymn fron… by Anne Draffkorn Kilmer

Anthology Vol 1-1

The ancient Greeks later developed a pitch-sp… ful of melodies survive, at least partially, in deciphe… two Delphic hymns, pieces praising the god Apollo… what remains are relatively late examples, set down l… losophers and playwrights.[2] One complete "compo… (Ex. 1-2), which probably dates from the first cent… now housed at the National Museum in Copenha… that was discovered in the late nineteenth century d… road in what is modern Turkey. The brief piece sho… important in remembering the dead. The opening l… stone state its purpose: "I am a tombstone, an imag…

266 CHAPTER 7 HUMANISM AND THE BIRTH OF OPERA

It was already considered provocative to display operatic divas (women singers, literally "goddesses") to the public gaze. A notorious Jesuit critic, Giovan Domenico Ottonelli, denounced the theaters of the "money-grubbing musicians" as indulgent and corrupting, in contrast to the edifying spectacles mounted "at the palaces of great princes."[16] But the most significant licenses were as much political as moral. Public opera, as we will see, became a world where satyrs romped and Eros reigned, where servant girls outwitted and chastised their masters, where philandering counts were humiliated, and where—later and more earnestly—rabbles were roused and revolutions were abetted. It is hardly surprising that opera would become the most stringently watched and censored of all forms of art until the twentieth century, when that grim distinction passed to movies. Examples of opera's disruptive and destabilizing possibilities can be drawn from any phase in its history, beginning with the earliest, as we can see by comparing the courtly *L'Orfeo* with the commercial *L'incoronazione di Poppea*.

The Carnival Show: *L'incoronazione di Poppea*

Anthology Vol 1-68a-e
Full CD II, 17–21
Concise CD I, 77–81

In an extraordinary feat of self-rejuvenation, Monteverdi came out of retirement in his seventies and composed a final trio of operas for the Teatro SS. Giovanni e Paolo, one of several competitors that quickly sprang up to challenge San Cassiano, the original Venetian opera house. The first was *Il ritorno d'Ulisse in patria* (Ulysses's Return to His Homeland, 1640), based on Homer's *Odyssey*. The second, now lost, concerned another mythological subject, the wedding of Aeneas, drawn from Virgil's *Aeneid*. The last was *L'incoronazione di Poppea*, not a mythological story but a historical fantasy based on the writings of Tacitus and other Roman historians. The librettist was Giovanni Francesco Busenello (1598–1659), a famous poet who was active in the Accademia degli Incogniti (Academy of the Disguised), a society of libertines and skeptics who dominated the early Venetian commercial theater.

Busenello's libretto celebrates neither the reward of virtue nor the chastisement of vice. It is, rather, a celebration of virtue mocked and vice triumphant. The opera celebrates erotic love as well as the intrigue and betrayal it can entail. Yet the moral …

Paradox and Contradiction: Late Italian Madrigalists 231

air, chimeras founded upon sand, these novelties do not please me; they deserve blame, not praise."[11]

Artusi proceeds to give seven little extracts from *Cruda Amarilli*, each containing some offense against the rules of proper counterpoint as laid down by Zarlino. The most famous infraction is the first, a skip in the most exposed voice, the soprano, from an A that enters as a dissonance against the bass G to an F that is also a dissonance: two sins at a single stroke (Ex. 6-6). What Artusi left out of his discussion, however, is the very thing that motivated the trespasses and that alone can explain them—namely, the text. This testifies either to a devious strategy on the author's part or, more likely, to his inability to comprehend the literary basis of the new style or admit that musical procedures could legitimately rest on textual rather than musical grounds. In advancing such a selectively chosen position he has had successors in every subsequent century, right up to the present. Ignoring the implications of words and dramatic situation has long been a fault of purists who would deny music's fruitful merging with other arts.

Example 6-6 Claudio Monteverdi, *Cruda Amarilli*, mm. 9–14, encompassing the first of Artusi's "spots"

[Cruel Amaryllis,] who, even with your name, teach, alas!, [to love bitterly].

What proved so stimulating to the musical imagination was the new "affective" style in which the poet cast his "pathetic" monologues, that is, the monologues depicting the sentiments of suffering lovers, expressed not only in words but in sighs and tearful exclamations like *ohimè!* ("oh me") and *ahi lasso!* ("ah, weary me," whence "alas")—the very phrase to which Monteverdi's main "transgression" was set. Thus composers were encouraged to develop an "affective" style of their own, analogizing the one that was being developed in literature. The remarkable thing is the way the new musical style came into its own just as—or even because—the poetry was becoming less "articulate" in its eloquence, more given over to elemental

Maps showing key centers of musical activity

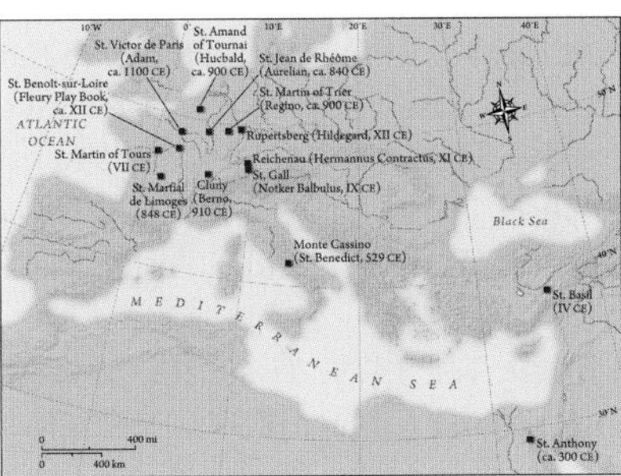

Figure 1-6 Early Christian monastic centers.

reflect the primitive origins of chant, early Christian monophony in fact represents the purposeful rejection of earlier, more elaborate practices, both Judaic and pagan.

The Development of the Liturgy: The Offices

In his book of rules St. Benedict required that the Psalter be recited in a weekly round of services known as the ***Offices***, of which there were eight each day. The greatest single portion went to the Night Office (now called *Matins*), which accounted for more than half of the weekly round of all 150 psalms. The shorter day Offices began at dawn with one of praise (*Lauds*) and continued with four "minor hours" named after the clock hours according to Roman terminology: *Prime* (the first hour), *Terce* (the third hour), *Sext* (the sixth hour), and *None* (the ninth hour). The public liturgical day ended with *Vespers*, which features the psalm-like "Canticle of Mary" (known as the Magnificat, which is its first word).

Anthology Vol 1-64

As Vesta Was from Latmos Hill Descending, Weelkes's delightful contribution to *The Triumphes of Oriana* honoring Elizabeth I, displays an abundance of playful madrigalisms. In his score for six unaccompanied voices, the composer revels in every conceivable chance to have the music illustrate the text. The words "descending" and "ascending" are predictably set to scales going down and up. The idea of everyone "running down" evokes more complex descending passages in imitation. When the "company" assembles, first "two by two," there are just two voices, to which another is added for "three by three," until all six parts sound "together" in a homorhythmic exclamation before Vesta (the goddess of hearth and home) is left "all alone" to the highest soprano. Such "word painting" continues to the end of the piece, with the shouts of "Long live fair Oriana" (here the bass sustains long notes—another musical pun).

If at times, especially in its English realizations, the madrigal seems more amusing than significant, a minor genre, its attention to language and to the music/text relationship was nevertheless momentous. This development led to a new dramatic element—music making a spectacle of itself—subsuming all the novel expressive resources cultivated by the madrigalists, the new mixtures of vocal and instrumental forces in the concertato style, and the new craving for *mimesis* (realistic representation) inspired by the humanist movement. The dramatic sensibility was the great conceptual innovation—the "paradigm shift," as historians of science would later call it—lurking behind all the shocking stylistic novelties that doomed the *ars perfecta* and gave rise to that aggressively exteriorized style conventionally deemed Baroque.

Summary

Changes in musical style in the later sixteenth century came from many directions, including the Protestant Reformation and the Catholic response to it, known as the Counter-Reformation. Some Protestant reformers turned away from complex polyphony, preferring simpler styles of music that allowed for congregational singing. Despite Martin Luther's (1483–1546) admiration for the *ars perfecta*, the Lutheran service music he recommended took the form of chorales, strophic unison hymns derived from Gregorian chant or popular song, which were later harmonized. Chorales formed the basis for polyphonic settings like those of Johann Walther in his *Geystliches gesangk Buchleyn* (Little Sacred Songbook, 1524). Music associated with the more radical reforms of John Calvin (1504–64) consisted of versified translations of the psalms, such as the Geneva Psalter (1543), sung to popular tunes.

Moving in a different direction, some Catholic church music took on a more sensuous and inspirational quality, evident in the increasing number of compositions for multiple choirs, or *cori spezzati*. Polychoral music flourished especially at St. Mark's in Venice. There Andrea Gabrieli (ca. 1532–85) and his nephew Giovanni Gabrieli (ca. 1554/57–1612) wrote works in "concerted," or *concertato*, style, featuring alternation between different combinations of voices and instruments. In their emphasis on short-range contrast rather than long-range continuity, these pieces differed greatly from the *ars perfecta*. The instruments were often specified, marking the beginning of the art of orchestration, as in Giovanni Gabrieli's *In ecclesiis benedicite Domino* ("Bless the Lord in the Churches"). Another element of the new style was the presence of a *basso continuo*, an independent organ part written with one line but with shorthand instructions for realizing the full harmony.

Study Questions

1. Why do you think Josquin de Prez achieved an unprecedented level of fame? What aspects of sixteenth-century society contributed to his reputation? Thinking back to previous chapters, consider how his reputation reflects changing attitudes about the role and status of the individual composer.
2. What evidence do we have of Josquin's reputation among later composers and theorists? Which composers wrote parodies of his works, and how would you characterize them?
3. Explain the various ways that Josquin's setting of *Ave Maria* reflects the declamation, syntax, and semantic content of the words.
4. What is the concept of *ars perfecta*? What are its characteristics, as codified in Gioseffo Zarlino's theoretical writings?
5. Why did Zarlino call Adrian Willaert "the new Pythagoras"?
6. How would you characterize the earliest written instrumental music, as reflected in the works of Jacques Buus?
7. Describe the views about church music articulated by the Council of Trent. In what ways is Giovanni Pierluigi da Palestrina's *Missa Papae Marcelli* consistent with these recommendations?
8. What circumstances gave birth to the myth that Palestrina saved church music? Why do you think people were drawn to this legend in the centuries after Palestrina's death?
9. What stylistic traits in the music of Palestrina came to define the *stile antico*? How does Johann Joseph Fux's *Gradus ad Parnassum* (1725) attest to the continuing importance of this style?
10. Discuss William Byrd's position as a Catholic in Protestant England. How was Byrd's music influenced by his Catholicism, particularly after his retirement from the Chapel Royal?

Key Terms

ars perfecta
contrafactum
cori spezzati
Council of Trent
humanism
imitation Mass
metrical psalm
point of imitation
ricercare
soggetto cavato dalle vocali
stile antico

End-of-chapter summaries of the central issues and music covered, along with lists of key terms and study questions to inspire further reflection on music history

Glossary, bibliography of further readings, and index are included at the end of the book

A Full Package

In addition to the main text, the following material is available for separate purchase.

- *Oxford Anthology of Western Music, Vol. 1: Earliest Notation to Early Eighteenth Century* (David Rothenberg, Case Western Reserve University, and Robert Holzer, Yale School of Music) (9780199768257)
- *Oxford Anthology of Western Music, Vol. 2: Late Eighteenth and Nineteenth Centuries* (Klára Móricz and David Schneider, Amherst College) (9780199768264)
- *Oxford Anthology of Western Music, Vol. 3: The Twentieth Century* (Klára Móricz and David Schneider, Amherst College) (9780199768271)

To accompany the text, the three-volume *Oxford Anthology of Western Music* offers the scores of many of the key works discussed in the book. Introductory essays probe questions of the history and analysis of these compositions to inspire students' own further exploration of this musical repertory. Like the main text, the commentary focuses on how the piece was created and how it relates to other works studied, and gives notes on its performance and interpretation. Translations are offered for foreign language texts to further student understanding.

For a complete list of the contents of these volumes, go to http://www.oup.com/us/taruskin

The Oxford Recorded Anthology of Western Music

- *Oxford Recorded Anthology of Western Music,* Vol. 1 (9780199768288)
- *Oxford Recorded Anthology of Western Music,* Vol. 2 (9780199768295)
- *Oxford Recorded Anthology of Western Music,* Vol. 3 (9780199768301)
- *Oxford Recorded Anthology of Western Music,* Concise (9780199768318)

Recognizing that students often listen to music on portable devices or directly on their computers, we have prepared a three-volume collection of CDs with all of the musical examples in high-quality MP3 files. These files can be downloaded for listening and are compatible with all major playback systems. In addition, for those who do not require the full set of recordings, we have issued a single volume, *Oxford Recorded Anthology of Western Music,* Concise Edition, as a more affordable alternative.

For complete playlists for these sets, go to http://www.oup.com/us/taruskin

Companion Website (http://www.oup.com/us/taruskin)

For students, we have provided a companion website at no additional charge that gives chapter outlines, key terms and definitions, and suggested links to *Grove Music* articles. A brief introduction on how to research music history is included for use in preparing term papers.

Access to Oxford Music Online

Oxford Music Online is the access point for Oxford music reference subscriptions. In addition to free access to *Grove Music* online, the eighteen month subscription includes access to *The Oxford Companion to Music* and *The Oxford Dictionary of Music,* which both supplement Grove's extensive coverage with content geared toward undergraduates.

For The Instructor

Computerized Testbank and Instructor's Resource CD (9780199768240)

A full computerized testbank that may be edited and augmented to create exams is provided for the instructor. Additionally, the Instructor's Resource CD includes a full Instructor's Manual with lecture outlines with teaching strategies and recommended resources, study questions, and links to *Grove's Dictionary of Music* for further assignments and study. Powerpoint slides are provided for use in class or for student review.

Introduction: Reading Music

by Christopher H. Gibbs

Perhaps because I initially came to classical music in high school as an engaged listener rather than fledgling composer or performer, I have always been fascinated by its history, by biographies of musicians, and by the ways music connects with other aspects of life and culture: with politics, the arts, and philosophy. As I majored in music history at college and then went on to graduate school, I was drawn to courses and writings that explored these things and found myself frustrated that surveys and standard histories so often shied away from what I thought were important issues. The emphasis tended to be on compositions in splendid isolation, on formal descriptions and bloodless analysis. The biographical treatment of composers in textbooks was usually relegated to brief sketches in sidebars, and so were illuminating primary source readings such as letters, diaries, and reviews. The college literature classes I took were not spent parsing grammar and sentence structure, but something comparably dull seemed to be the point of too many discussions about music.

So it was with great excitement that, many years later, I anticipated the publication in 2005 of the *Oxford History of Western Music* by Richard Taruskin, a historian known for making connections among music, musicians, and the world. A year later I enthusiastically accepted an offer to transform his six-volume reference work into a textbook. I wanted to share such an outstanding resource with those new to the history of music. I embarked on the daunting task of drastically abridging, extensively reshaping, and judiciously augmenting Taruskin's work with practical considerations in mind: limitations on space, concrete pedagogical aims, and the desire to tell a story. This volume is the result.

I am sometimes asked by students thinking of taking a course with me whether they need to be able to "read music." It is a common enough question for non-music majors to ask but, on reflection, a rather strange one. Students wanting to take art history or literature classes don't ask the professor if they have to be able to draw or write fiction; everyone assumes they can see and read. But with music, the ability to read the notes, to be musically literate, helps shape one's understanding and gives access to compositions that are neither recorded nor performed. It facilitates technical analysis of a descriptive nature. And yet I love having interested students with limited or no musical training in my classes, because I find they often have insights that more advanced music students preoccupied by theoretical issues may miss.

The whole question of reading music is particularly relevant for this book because the study of Western music differs fundamentally from that of the other arts with respect to what has been transmitted from the distant past. We can engage directly with many literary and visual masterpieces dating back thousands of years, see sculptures, walk in and around historic buildings, read classic poems, and experience great dramas. Music does not survive in any comparable manner, not because it did not exist in antiquity but rather because there was no means for preserving it—no adequate notation and, of course, no technological means for audio recording. Rudimentary musical notation only emerged about a thousand years ago in a way that allowed the gradual preservation and spread of a large quantity of music.

While this fact places certain limits on the study of the Western musical tradition, it also opens up an opportunity: the possibility of tracing music as it has been written down from its earliest manifestations to the present day. The sheer abundance and diversity of notated music in the West over the centuries is deserving of critical study—one that does not take literacy for granted, or simply celebrate it as a special Western achievement, but rather considers the consequences. Indeed, Taruskin claims that the literate musical tradition is coherent at least insofar as it has a shape. Its beginnings are known and explicable, as we'll see in Chapter 1, and its end is now foreseeable, and also explicable, as the final chapters explore. The music discussed in the opening chapters is primarily religious, vocal, sung in Latin, and related to the Roman Catholic Church, because that was what was most often written down and therefore survives in the greatest quantity. The music examined in the final chapters is dominated by the interplay of notated classical pieces and unnotated ones, particularly jazz and rock.

No single book, even one as long as this, can cover all the different kinds of music that have been made in Europe and the Americas over the past 1,000 years. Our concern is with what is usually called "art music," "concert music," or "classical music" (for convenience, I use the last term, lower case and without quotes, throughout the book). The treatment of jazz, rock, and other popular twentieth-century musical styles is thus primarily in relation to the interplay and influence—sometimes the enormous influence—these styles have had on the classical tradition. Recent decades have seen an explosion in the serious study of jazz, rock, and world music, which fortunately has led to textbooks and courses specifically dedicated to them.

An important consequence of the focus here on literate music is that the history narrated is that of elite genres: Masses, concertos, operas, symphonies, and many other kinds of pieces. Until recently, and in some ways even up to the present day, literacy has been the privilege—the closely guarded possession—of social elites: ecclesiastical, political, military, hereditary, meritocratic, professional, economic, educational, academic, and fashionable. What else, after all, makes "high art" high? One of the threads woven throughout this book is the tension between music intended for a select few and that meant for a broader audience.

There has been a progressive broadening of access to literacy together with various cultural benefits (the history, as it is sometimes called, of the democratization of taste). This increased access to culture for a larger group of people was met at every turn with a counterforce seeking to redefine elite status ever upward. The cultural goods that we all enjoy—music, art, literature, film, and even sporting events—are a primary means of how we define ourselves. Debates about taste occur across class lines and often pit classical styles against popular ones. This tension is commonly viewed as being relatively recent, but in fact has a much longer and more diverse history in all of the arts. The competing ways in which people view music are crucial to the narrative in this book.

We will encounter a large cast of characters who have played many sorts of roles in musical life over the past thousand years. Most histories of Western music cover the relevant repertoire of musical compositions, but make little effort to explain why and how things happened as they did, or to identify who made them happen in the first place. Musical compositions, however, did not emerge out of thin air and then miraculously influence later pieces. *People* wrote these works; other people patronized, performed, presented, published, criticized, and heard them.

Inevitably composers receive the greatest attention. Relatively little is known about the lives of most musicians discussed in the first third of this book—even about very famous composers as late as Handel and Bach in the early eighteenth century. On the other hand, with the late-eighteenth and nineteenth centuries, in an era of renewed individualism, a profound and much better documented relationship is apparent between composers' lived experiences and the music they created. That Mozart emerges as the first real personality in our story is not just because of the popularity of *Amadeus*, a play from the late 1970s turned into an award-winning movie. As a purely practical matter, a multitude of Mozart's intimate letters survive, many of them written to his ambitious, high-maintenance father, that make for wonderful reading. For Beethoven, Schumann, Wagner, and a host of other prominent nineteenth-century composers, we have access to private lives that seem (perhaps too conveniently) to connect in fascinating ways with their works.

In writing a survey of Western music, authors face hard choices of providing depth versus covering a breadth of material. We could have profiled many other composers and compositions, debates, ideas, genres, and geographical centers of activity, each worthy of attention. We opted instead for a narrative approach, telling stories about different times, people, places, and pieces, all of which takes time to unfold in continuous prose uncluttered by distracting sidebar discussions. But this approach requires some caution because stories themselves have histories. Exploring who tells the tales in history and how they tell them—what is presented, omitted, valued, and discounted—is the concern of *historiography*, the study of the nature of history. All historians have particular (even if not always conscious) interests, concerns, and methods that are never completely objective or comprehensive. You will find spread throughout the book reflections on important historical and methodological issues. These "time outs" are crucial because they encourage reflection on the nature of history itself, on history as a construct. As in every class I teach, I hope that students not only develop a body of cumulative knowledge—of pieces, names, and dates—but also cultivate ways of historical and critical thinking. Ideally (and idealistically), I hope that some of this kind of thinking can extend beyond the arts and into life more generally.

One of the great challenges of the contextual study of music is trying to develop an historical imagination. I know it is not possible to listen with the ears of the past, but it is still worth thinking about the conditions that surrounded the creation of the music we listen to, play, study, and love. I wonder what it must have been like to hear a Mass by Giovanni Pierluigi da Palestrina during the sixteenth century. How did people experience such music in a particular time and space? I try to imagine the sense of awe at entering the Sistine Chapel in Rome, of being in a place that exalted magnificent art and that smelled of incense, a feast for the senses. Or I think about what the listening experience might have been like in the first decades of the nineteenth century, when Beethoven challenged the expectations of audiences with symphonies that were shockingly longer, louder, and more technically difficult than any symphony ever heard before. Indeed, except for sounds such as thunder claps and cannon fire, people in a pre-electronic age rarely heard anything so loud, so intense, as the famous Fifth Symphony.

The discussion of individual compositions in this book therefore goes beyond technical analysis and so-called style criticism, taking into account connections with society, politics, and other art forms, considering how pieces were created as well as their reception, and ultimately thinking about their meanings. It is easier (and safer) to look at music in abstract and isolated ways, to talk just about the notes. But a principal reason music endures is because meaning can be ascribed to it; this is why so many of us are drawn so powerfully to this particular art form. Music historians must try to go beyond their own personal reactions and consider a range of responses over time. The trick is to shift the question from "What does it mean?" to "What has it meant?"

Value judgments—what stacks up as great music over time—also have an honorable place in historical narratives, but they should not merely be the historian's judgment. Musicians who emulate, perform, and promote music that means the most to them establish what endures. No patron or press agent can decree a classic. Beethoven's greatness is "only" an opinion, one widely held by a general public as well as by countless musicians. Beethoven's perceived greatness emerged during the nineteenth century and continues still today. This is what constitutes his commanding authority, which certainly is a historical fact. Without taking Beethoven's stature and influence into account one cannot understand what went on in the world of classical music over the last 200 years. Whether the historian agrees or not with the past critical verdicts on Beethoven has no bearing on the obligation to report them.

As stories tend to do, the narrative here unfolds chronologically. This allows us to discuss the trajectories of musicians' lives as well as the relationships and influences among composers and compositions. As Western music developed over the centuries and became ever more widely disseminated, there were ever more interconnections among works. Composers often modeled pieces on earlier ones; there were frequent contests to outdo the past, all of which helped to establish and maintain dynasties of prestige. Along with connections among compositions, in many instances there was contact between composers, sometimes directly through teaching or mentorship. We will encounter a whole line of celebrated composers who passed the torch to younger ones by bestowing on them some memorable pronouncement of future glory. Even though there is good reason to be skeptical about the authenticity of many of these benedictions, such soundbites nonetheless played an important role in the construction of a musical mainstream, what is known as a *canon*, which we will have many opportunities to explore and question.

Some compositions are treated at considerable length not only because they were so famous but also because they became exemplary and representative. By getting to know well works like Josquin des Prez's motet *Ave Maria*, Richard Wagner's opera *Tristan und Isolde*, and Igor Stravinsky's Octet we are better able to understand subsequent musical developments. These pieces entered a canon of select masterpieces and eventually a sort of aural museum of musical works that lent them ever greater stature and influence.

Specific works (or parts of them) of great historical importance were selected for the anthologies and recordings accompanying this textbook in order for them to be easily available to students. I have not allowed space and other limitations to restrict too much the scope of discussions in this book. Technology today allows easy access to an enormous quantity of music as well as to scores. In the chapter on Beethoven, for example, the primary focus with regard to symphonies concerns the Third, Fifth, and Ninth, but all nine are mentioned and discussion of some distinctive features should encourage students to explore this repertory more on their own. Anyone today interested in hearing the unusual opening of the First Symphony or the witty finale of the Second can do so with just a few clicks on a computer. A few more clicks and the scores can be accessed. I encourage you to experiment and explore.

While at times I expanded the range of references from Taruskin's lengthy history, I have retained the general proportions of his volumes. The coverage of the so-called historical style periods—the all-too-handy Medieval, Renaissance, Baroque, Classic, Romantic, and Modern eras—is unequal in length, with an emphasis on the music of the past two hundred years. To a certain extent this reflects the quantity of the surviving evidence, the duration of the compositions themselves, and the place this repertory continues to hold in musical life today.

The ability to "read music" long separated musicians in classical genres from those who just listened or played "by ear," as is the case with many musicians who specialize in popular music. A common lament these days is that classical music is dying—it is an issue explored in the last chapter—but if this book shows anything it is that music is always changing and adapting. Classical music no longer plays the role it did for elite audiences in Beethoven's time 200 years ago, yet countless more people are exposed to it today than ever were in his day, if only because of technology. The recent and astounding embrace of Western classical music in Asia is yet another indication that far from dying the tradition is in certain ways expanding. The history of this musical tradition—from its birth as a literate art form in the cavernous spaces of Medieval monasteries and cathedrals to its current expansion across the Internet to electronic devices throughout the world—is a story well worth telling.

Acknowledgments

All thanks must commence with Richard Taruskin for the opportunity of transforming his magisterial six-volume *Oxford History of Western Music* into a textbook and for giving me a free hand in doing so. In the original reference work he acknowledged the many people who helped in its preparation and it is now my pleasure to thank the many others who assisted in creating this College Edition.

Foremost, I am grateful to Jan Beatty, the executive music editor in the Higher Education division of Oxford University Press for most of the six years the book was in development. From the day we met in my office at Bard College and she persuaded me to take on such a daunting and fascinating project, Jan provided a keen, dedicated, and strategic guiding hand. I am grateful as well to others at Oxford who helped shepherd the project, including Richard Carlin, Cory Schneider, Nichole LeFebvre, Theresa Stockton, and particularly Lauren Mine, who went well beyond the call of duty in suggesting illustrations and working on other materials.

The editors of the anthologies that accompany this textbook—David Rothenberg (Case Western Reserve University), Robert Holzer (Yale School of Music), David Schneider (Amherst College), and Klára Móricz (Amherst College)—played crucial roles in the planning and in the choice of pieces on which to focus. I am grateful to all the members of the editorial board for assisting in so many ways over the years. In particular, Byron Adams (University of California, Riverside) gave incisive advice at key moments, and Tamara Levitz (University of California, Los Angeles) offered an especially challenging reading of the latter half of the book. My thanks go as well to Rebecca Maloy (University of Colorado) for preparing the preliminary version of the timelines, chapter summaries, and study questions.

Beyond all the generous help from readers official and unofficial, acknowledged and anonymous, two individuals followed the project from start to finish and provided the kind of sensitive editorial comments that authors crave but rarely receive. Christopher Hatch (Columbia University) took time from blissful retirement in Vermont to offer his wisdom. Beth Levy (University of California, Davis) was drawn ever deeper into the project after her initial readings of selected chapters proved so astute. I am very grateful to them both.

An ambitious project such as this invites the opportunity to enlist the advice of colleagues and friends. Many generously answered questions and read chapters related to their areas of expertise, including Peter Bloom (Smith College), Caryl Clark (University of Toronto), Kyle Gann (Bard College), John Halle (Bard College Conservatory of Music), Peter Laki (Bard College), Ralph Locke (University of Rochester), Michael Lorenz (Vienna), Morten Solvik (Institute for the International Education of Students, Vienna), and Wendy Powers (Queens College, CUNY). Sean Colonna, an excellent undergraduate at Bard, assisted with the endnotes. The reader reports Oxford solicited provided helpful suggestions, refinements, and corrections. Thomas Brothers (Duke University), Alice Clark (Loyola University, New Orleans), Daniel Grimley (Oxford University), bruce d. mcclung (University of Cincinnati), and Honey Meconi (Eastman School of Music) read sustained portions of the book and graciously offered detailed comments.

I would also like to thank the following people who helped develop this text by participating in manuscript reviews, focus groups, and in discussions:

Stephen Allen, Rider University
Pedro Aponte, James Madison University
Candace Bailey, North Carolina Central University
Paul T. Barte, Ohio State University
Laura Basini, Sacramento State University
Glen Bauer, Webster University
Matthew Baumer, Indiana University of Pennsylvania
Jonathan Bellman, University of Northern Colorado
John Brobeck, University of Arizona
Lance Brunner, University of Kentucky
Gordon Callon, Acadia University
Charles Carson, University of Delaware
Mel Comberiati, Manhattanville College
Jane Dahlenburg, University of Central Arkansas
Terry Dean, Indiana State University
Silvio dos Santos, University of Florida
Ralph Dudgeon, State University of New York, Cortland
Robert Eisenstein, Mt. Holyoke, University of Massachusetts
Sarah Eyerly, Butler University
Howard Goldstein, Auburn University
David Grayson, University of Minnesota, Twin Cities
Richard Greene, Georgia College & State University
Olga Haldey, University of Maryland
L. Curtis Hammond, Morehead State University
Gregory Harwood, Georgia Southern University
Karl Hinterbichler, University of New Mexico
Julie Hubbert, University of South Carolina
Kevin Karnes, Emory University
Derek Katz, University of California, Santa Barbara
Ben Korstvedt, Clark University
Jonathan Kregor, University of Cincinnati
Jonathan Kulp, University of Louisiana, Lafayette
Zoë Lang, University of South Florida
James Leve, Northern Arizona University
David Levy, Wake Forest University
Nora Lewis, Kansas State University
Melanie Lowe, Vanderbilt University
Gayle Sherwood Magee, University of Illinois, Urbana-Champaign
James Maiello, Vanderbilt University
Peter Marsh, California State University, East Bay

Kerry McCarthy, Duke University
Alyson McLamore, California Polytechnic State University, San Luis Obispo
Stephen Meyer, Syracuse University
Vera Micznik, University of British Columbia
Michael Miranda, Loyola Marymount University
Sharon Mirchandani, Rider University
Simon Morrison, Princeton University
Caroline Polk O'Meara, University of Texas at Austin
Mathew Peattie, University of Cincinnati College Conservatory of Music
Thomas Peattie, Boston University
Elaine Peterson, Mississippi State University
Mark Radice, Ithaca College
Christina Reitz, Western Carolina University
Eric Rice, University of Connecticut
Jerry Rife, Rider University
Kailan Rubinoff, University of North Carolina, Greensboro
Peter Schimpf, Metropolitan State College
David Schulenberg, Wagner College
Douglass Seaton, Florida State University
Jennifer Thomas, University of Florida
Robin Wallace, Baylor University
Sarah F. Williams, University of South Carolina
Stephen A. Willier, Temple University.

Professional and personal gratitude merge in my enormous debt to Leon Botstein, president of Bard College, conductor, and music historian, who enthusiastically supported my involvement with this project from day one. The influence of his thinking about music history resonates in many parts I contributed to the book. The community at Bard College and at the Bard Music Festival offered further stimulus, and I am grateful for the encouragement of James H. Ottaway, Jr., David and Ruth Schwab, Robert C. Edmonds, Felicitas Thorne, Jeanne Donovan Fisher, Anthony and Margo Viscusi, and Denise Simon, and for the support of my colleagues Irene Zedlacher, James Bagwell, Noah Chasin, Deborah Krohn, and Robert Martin. Darrin Britting, associate director of communications for the Philadelphia Orchestra, has been an excellent editor for more than a decade now of my program notes, parts of which I adapted for use here. I am grateful to my family for their patient understanding, to my sister Nancy and her family, to my mother Janet, and especially to my wife Helena Sedláčková Gibbs, for the considerable sacrifices she made all the while offering loving support.

I

The First Literate Repertory in Western Music: Gregorian Chant

Our story begins, as it must, in the middle of things. The advent of music notation coincided with no specific event. Still less did it mark the origin of music or of any particular musical repertory. Yet sometime over a thousand years ago music stopped being an almost exclusively oral tradition and became a partly literate one. The history of written music in the West begins with the music for the services of the Roman Catholic Church. What had previously been transmitted from generation to generation through singing and playing came to be partially written down, preserved, and disseminated. This was an enormously important change. The beginning of music writing gives us access through actual documents to the musical repertories of the past and suddenly raises the curtain, so to speak, on activities that had been going on for many centuries. No matter exactly when, where, and how it happened, we can from this point become witnesses of a sort, able to trace the evolution of music over the past millennium through notated sources.

Music had, of course, already existed for many millennia. The problem is that we know very little about what it actually sounded like. Unlike ancient works of visual art and literature, much of which survived and exerted enormous influence, music works proved ephemeral and disappeared. What abstract knowledge we have about preliterate music, from tens of thousands of years ago, from biblical times, from ancient Greece, and then from the first millennium of the Common Era, can be gleaned from various kinds of visual, descriptive, and physical evidence, including some very early instruments. In 2009, for example, archaeologists in Germany discovered a five-finger flute made of bone from the Stone Age, at least 35,000 years ago (Fig. 1-1).

TIMELINE

ca. 1200 BCE Musical notation inscribed on a Babylonian cuneiform tablet

ca. 800 BCE Homer, *Iliad* and *Odyssey*

ca. 580–500 BCE Pythagoras explores harmonic ratios

ca. 450–325 BCE Socrates, Plato, and Aristotle pose influential ideas on music

ca. 360 BCE Plato, *The Republic*

27 BCE Rome becomes an empire under Augustus

ca. 20 BCE Virgil, *Aeneid*

First century CE ***Epitaph of Seikilos***

391 St. Augustine, *De musica*

395 Division of the Roman Empire into East and West

476 Fall of the Roman Empire in the West

ca. 500–10 Boethius, *De institutione musica*

ca. 530 St. Benedict, *Regula monachorum*

754 Pope Stephen II visits King of the Franks, Pepin III, instigating the spread of Roman chant

800 Pope Leo III crowns Charlemagne as Emperor of the Western Roman Empire

ca. 843 Aurelian of Réôme, *Musica disciplina*

ca. 860–900 *Musica enchiriadis*

There are many surviving illustrations of ancient music making found in prehistoric cave paintings, in Egyptian murals, on Greek pottery, and elsewhere that provide further indications of the instruments that were used, if not of the specific music that was produced. Also abundant are written descriptions. The Bible gives some particularly vivid ones. Psalm 150, the climax of the **Psalter** (Book of Psalms), is in fact an account of singing God's praises in the ancient temple. It reads, in part:

> Praise him with fanfares on the trumpet,
> praise him upon the lute and harp;
> praise him with tambourines and dancing,
> praise him with flute and strings;
> praise him with the clash of cymbals,
> praise him with triumphant cymbals;
> let everything that has breath praise the LORD!

We will not find such goings-on in any synagogue today. We can read of the chanting of **psalms** and other sacred texts in the synagogue, but no Jewish music was written down exactly until much more modern times.

While some early kinds of musical notation survive to a very limited degree from ancient cultures, the principal challenge has been figuring out how to decode them. In the 1970s scholars managed to transcribe the notation on a cuneiform tablet dating from around 1200 BCE that had been unearthed on the site of the ancient Babylonian city of Ugarit, near Ras-Shamra in modern Syria.[1] The tablet contained a **hymn** to the goddess Nikkal, the wife of the moon god Kushuh (Ex. 1-1). What may be most remarkable is how unremarkable this earliest preserved piece of music now seems when transcribed into modern notation: It consists of intervals recognized as consonant in most Western music today.

Example 1-1 First phrase of Hurrian hymn from ancient Ugarit, transcribed by Anne Draffkorn Kilmer

Anthology Vol 1-1
Full CD/Concise CD I, 1

The ancient Greeks later developed a pitch-specific musical notation. A handful of melodies survive, at least partially, in decipherable sources, the earliest being two Delphic hymns, pieces praising the god Apollo, from around 130 BCE. Most of what remains are relatively late examples, set down long after the era of the great philosophers and playwrights. One complete "composition" is the *Epitaph of Seikilos* (Ex. 1-2), which probably dates from the first century of the Common Era and is now housed at the National Museum in Copenhagen. It appears on a tombstone that was discovered in the late nineteenth century during the construction of a railroad in what is modern Turkey. The brief piece shows that to the Greeks music was important in remembering the dead. The opening lines engraved on the memorial stone state its purpose: "I am a tombstone, an image. Seikilos placed me here as an everlasting sign of deathless remembrance." This suggests that Seikilos (whoever he was) may have written the following short epitaph (Greek for "over a tomb," that is, a short memorial poem) and perhaps the melody as well:

> As long as you live, shine
> Grieve you not at all
> Life is of brief duration
> Time demands its end.

The Greeks used letters and symbols to indicate pitch and rhythm. Example 1-2 shows the original notation over a modern transcription, a melody that would be familiar to our ears today.[2] Although this is just a vocal melody, contemporaneous illustrations suggest that sung texts were often accompanied by various kinds of instruments, including the cithara or lyre, plucked string instruments, and the aulos, a wind instrument.

ca. 880 Notker Balbulus, *Liber hymnorum*

997–1006 Winchester Tropers

ca. 1028 Guido of Arezzo, *Micrologus*

1054 Schism between Eastern and Western Christian churches

1066 Norman Conquest

ca. 1150 Hildegard of Bingen, *Symphonia armonie celestium revelationum*

Example 1-2 The Epitaph of Seikilos

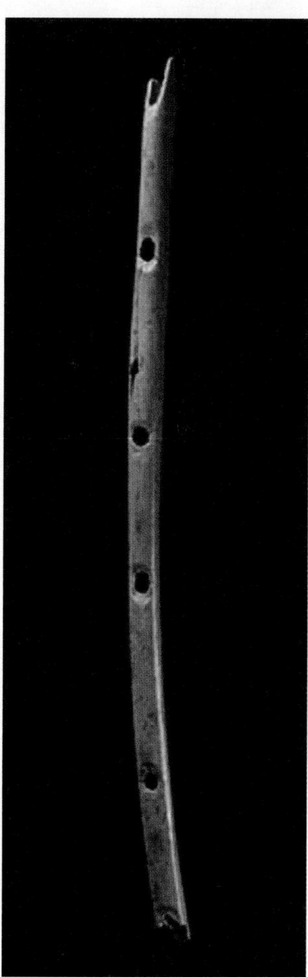

Figure 1-1 Five-finger flute carved from bird bone at least 35,000 years ago and unearthed in a cave in Germany in 2009.

Music played an important role in ancient Greece. It was integral to theater, in which the chorus commented on the action of the drama and in which dance was one of the elements of the total spectacle. Greek philosophers wrote at considerable length about music, specifically about its ethical qualities and what its proper place should be in society. In a famous passage from Plato's *Republic* (written around 360 BCE), Socrates advocated banning most of the musical scales "because more than anything else rhythm and harmony find their way to the inmost soul and take strongest hold upon it."[3] Understandably, the power of music, often associated with bodily and sensual pleasures, has always unsettled those who would seek to control human emotions for religious, political, or cultural reasons. At the

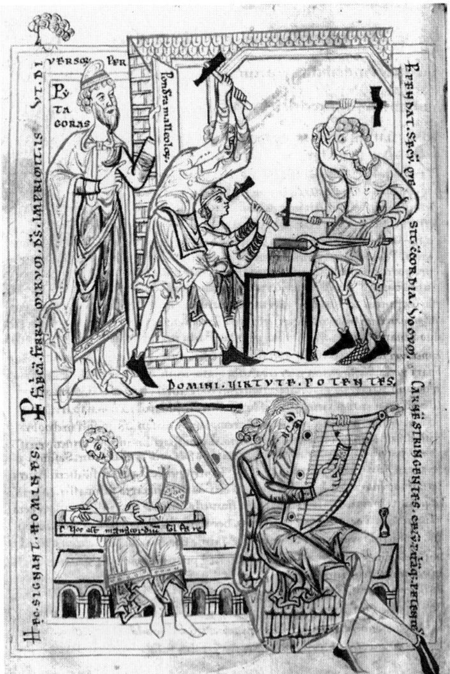

Figure 1-2 Illustration from a thirteenth-century manuscript showing Pythagoras in the blacksmith shop, measuring harmonic consonances.

same time music has long been praised for its healing properties, spiritual effects, and ability to express emotions. Debates about the dangers and benefits of music continue to this day.

Theories of Music

The ancient Greeks wrote about music theory as well, which means that something is known concerning their tuning systems. According to Greek legend, the sixth-century BCE philosopher Pythagoras one day heard beautiful sounds coming unexpectedly out of a blacksmith's shop. Weighing the anvils the smiths were striking, he discovered the harmonic ratios governing the perfect ("Pythagorean") consonances (Ex. 1-3; Fig. 1-2). For many centuries to come, when musicians thought theoretically about music—that is, made systematic generalizations about it—they usually did so in terms of the arts of measurement. What was measurable was what was studied: the pitch ratios we call *intervals* and the durational ratios we call *rhythms*, which were eventually organized into meters (another reference to measuring). One of the most influential treatises was *De musica* (About Music) by St. Augustine (354–430), the greatest of the Fathers of the Christian Church. Completed in 391 CE, the book covers nothing but rhythmic proportions (quantitative metrics) and contains a famous definition of music as "the art of measuring well." It ends with a meditation on the theological significance of harmonious proportions and the way in which they reflect the essential nature of the universe.

Example 1-3 Deduction of the diatonic pitch set from the Pythagorean consonances

Pythagorean harmonies (the four anvils)

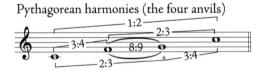

The most-studied treatise was *De institutione musica* (On the Organization of Music), by the Roman statesman and educational reformer Anicius Manlius Severinus Boethius (ca. 480 to ca. 524). It consisted largely of translations from earlier Greek-influenced writers who had lived in the second century CE in Arabia and Egypt. Although by Boethius's time the actual music practiced by the ancient Greeks had fallen into oblivion, his text became the source of Medieval scholars' knowledge of Greek music theory. Accordingly, his treatise concerns not practical music but abstract *musica*, perhaps best translated in this context as "harmony." Boethius inherited two transcendent ideas from followers of Plato: that ***musica*** mirrored the essential harmony of the cosmos and that it therefore had a decisive influence on human health and behavior. This was known as the doctrine of *ethos*, from which the word "ethics" is derived. Audible music (*musica instrumentalis*, "music such as instruments produce") is thus only a gross metaphor for two higher levels. At the top was the harmony of the cosmos (*musica mundana*), and in the intermediate position was the harmony of the human constitution (*musica humana*).

This scheme can be quite effectively seen in a famous manuscript illumination of the thirteenth century, fully 700 years after Boethius (Fig. 1-3). In each of the three panels of this illumination, the personification of *musica* points to a different level of her manifestation. In the top panel she points to a representation of the universe, with its four elements: earth, air, fire (the sun), and water. The sun and moon further represent the periodic movements of the heavens, an aspect of measurable "harmony." In the middle panel she points to four men representing the four "humors," temperaments, or basic personality types—that is, the four types of "human harmony": The "choleric" temperament was ruled by bile, the "sanguine" by blood, the "phlegmatic" by phlegm, and the "melancholic" by black bile. The four humors mirror the four elements; thus, human harmony is a function of the celestial. In the bottom panel we find *musica instrumentalis*, the music that we actually hear, represented by a fiddle player.

Figure 1-3 Frontispiece of a mid-thirteenth-century manuscript representing the musical cosmology described by Boethius in *De institutione musica*.

Historical Imagination

Attempts to decipher some of the notation of antiquity reveal a problem that we will encounter as well in the earliest notated music of the Christian Church. Like the Greek system, it employed what is now often called the "**diatonic** pitch set," the field of pitches and pitch relationships reducible to a specific arrangement of tones and semitones ("whole steps" and "half steps"), of which the major and minor scales are most familiar today. The earliest Christian notation indicated only the contour of melodies, but gradually a system developed that allows us, for the most part, to decipher the exact pitches and thus the specific melody. This early notation, however, conveys little or nothing about meter and rhythm. Notation in the Christian world that indicates measured rhythm emerged in the late twelfth century. For much music of the distant past we know almost nothing about crucial elements that make a particular piece of music distinctive for us today: meter and rhythm, harmony, tempo, dynamics, instrumentation, and so forth. Part of the story we will tell in this book concerns the continuing refinement of notation in an attempt by composers to retain—or assert—ever-greater control over performance. An interesting consequence is that notation itself came to influence what was composed, rather than being only a means of committing compositions to paper.

Most of the music that survives from the Middle Ages is sacred, that is, connected to religion, principally to the Roman Catholic Church, rather than secular, the music of everyday nonreligious life. The earliest music typically comes down to us as monophonic chant, single unaccompanied lines of pure melody, rather than as polyphonic (multivoiced) pieces or pieces played on instruments. Most of the music was sung in Latin rather than in everyday (vernacular) languages. From these facts it would be easy to draw various false conclusions, to assume that in the West there was sacred music before there was secular music, monophonic before there was polyphonic, vocal before there was instrumental. In fact, the chant connected to the Catholic Church was only one of many musical repertories that coexisted in Europe a thousand years ago. Nonetheless, it is the earliest body of music that, thanks to notation, we can study in detail.

In order to appreciate the context of this first great surviving Western repertory of music, what is now commonly called **Gregorian chant**, we need to discuss the organization of religious life, how the days and years and services of the Church worked. We also need to use some historical imagination so as to appreciate how music functioned within religious life. It was meant not to be "performed" for pleasure or entertainment, as is the case for much of the music we will consider, but, rather, to be enacted as one element of a life devoted to God.

For us, Medieval chants have become a form of concert music, which we now experience in new surroundings (concert halls, our homes, our cars, our classrooms) and for new purposes. For example, in the mid-1990s a CD of chants sung by an ensemble of Spanish monks unexpectedly rose to the top of the popular music sales charts. Yet if we imagine ourselves hearing these chants with "medieval ears," in the position of the chants' original contemporaries, we may gain some access to meanings we might otherwise never experience. Perhaps even more importantly, we may achieve a distanced perspective on our own contemporary world, a form of critical awareness we would otherwise never gain. These are among the most potent reasons for studying history.

Christian Beginnings, As Far As We Know Them

The early notation of the few examples mentioned so far fell out of use and in any case was only deciphered in modern times. The first surviving artifact of actual Christian service music is a fragment of a Greek hymn to the Holy Trinity, notated on a papyrus strip during the fourth century CE (Ex. 1-4); some pitches are uncertain. It is the earliest surviving representative, by six or seven centuries, of the Greek-texted music of the Orthodox Church of the Eastern Roman Empire, known as the Byzantine Empire. (Orthodox in Greek means "correctly believing.") Unlike the Western Roman Church, which came to cultivate the traditional prose-poetry of the Psalter as its main sphere of musical creativity, the Eastern Orthodox Church emphasized hymns, newly composed "songs with praise of God" in metrical verse, a repertory known as Byzantine chant. In addition to this chant repertoire in the East, different ones were associated with other locations: Coptic chant in Egypt, Ambrosian in Milan, Mozarabic in Spain, and Gallican in northern Europe. There is a considerable range in style and in the quantity of surviving music for each of these repertories, and much of it was notated only centuries later. Our focus will be on the music of the Roman Church, which has the most extensive written legacy.

Example 1-4 **Fourth verse of a proto-Byzantine Hymn to the Trinity, transcribed by E. Pöhlmann and M. West (opening)**

Hym - noun - ton d' hy - mon pa - te - ra hui - on ha - gi - on pneu - ma Pa - sai dy - na - meis
6
e - pi - pho - noun - ton a - min a - min.

As we hymn the Father, the Son, and the Holy Spirit,
Let all the powers add Amen Amen.

Christianity was initially a persecuted religion that only won broader acceptance after the Roman Emperor Constantine converted to it in 312 CE. During the centuries that followed, Rome emerged as the most powerful seat of the Christian Church, although there were other important (and sometimes competing) centers as well as many smaller and simpler communities, known as monasteries. In 753, Pope Stephen II headed north from Rome, crossed the Alps, and visited the king of the Franks, Pepin III, to gain support for his struggles against the Lombards, a Germanic tribe. Two decades later, Pepin's son and successor, Charles I, known as Charlemagne (Charles the Great, ca. 742–814), once again intervened to help the pope, as he would yet again in 800, when he entered Rome in triumph. On Christmas Day 800 Pope Leo III crowned Charlemagne as secular ruler of the Western Roman Empire (with Leo himself maintaining his role as spiritual ruler). This date is traditionally said to inaugurate what came to be known as the "Holy Roman Empire," which lasted—at least in name—for more than a thousand years. The alliance of imperial and papal authority led to a short period of peaceful stability during which there was a resurgence of learning and creativity known as the Carolingian Renaissance. (Carolingian is a Latinized reference to the noble family that traced its lineage back to Frankish ruler Charles Martel.)

The exporting of the Roman chant to the Frankish lands in the north was one of the facets of that cultural rebirth (Fig. 1-4). A central figure in the process was an English scholar, Alcuin of York (ca. 735–804), who served as Charlemagne's tutor and later advised him in matters of state. He was a great proponent of literacy and instituted one of the earliest educational systems in Europe. The curriculum for higher education was based on the seven "liberal arts" of the ancients: the three arts of language (grammar, logic, and rhetoric), known as the *trivium;* and the four arts of measurement (arithmetic, geometry, astronomy, and music), known as the *quadrivium.* Within the quadrivium, music was conceived in entirely theoretical terms as measurement of harmonic ratios (tunings and intervals) and of rhythmic quantities (poetic meters). This made it possible to study music even in the absence of any form of practical musical notation. Music continued to be studied for centuries in a generalized and speculative way, quite unrelated to actual music making. And yet Alcuin's zealous emphasis on writing things down became a Carolingian obsession that was eventually extended to practical music.

The principal reason the Roman chant needed to be imported was that the Carolingians wanted to centralize authority. The geographical sweep of the Catholic

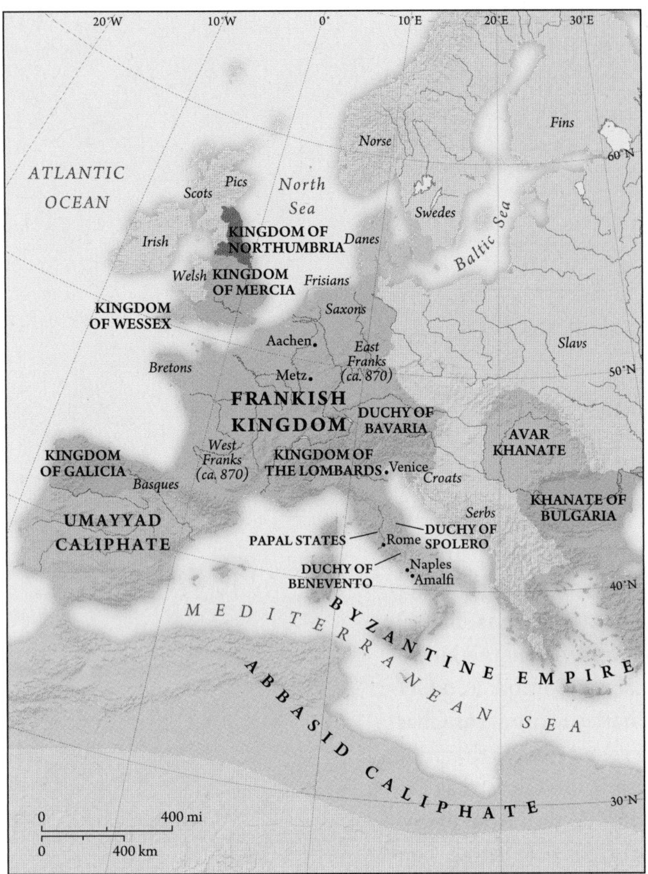

Figure 1-4 Europe in the eighth century, shortly before the earliest notations of Christian chant.

territories was vast, incorporating peoples speaking many languages and including a large assortment of local legal systems and religious practices. With the establishment of the Roman pope as spiritual patron of the Carolingian Empire, the unification of the whole broad realm of religious services according to the Roman practices became necessary. This meant suppressing the so-called Gallican rite in the north (as well as the Ambrosian and Mozarabic, among others) and replacing them with Roman service texts and tunes.

The words of the Roman **liturgy**—the prescribed order for the religious service—could be imported easily enough in books; but without a way to write down the melodies, the only means of conveying the music was to import cantors, that is, ecclesiastical singers, from Rome who could teach their chant by laborious rote to their Frankish counterparts. The fact that eighth-century Roman liturgical song—*cantus* in Latin, from which we get the word "chant"—was singled out for preservation in written form during the Carolingian Renaissance was therefore not because it came first or because it had some uniquely special musical quality. Rather, there was a need for notation because of the aim of the powers in Rome to spread its liturgy and music elsewhere.

The Legend of St. Gregory

From around the time of the advent of chant into written history, it was widely asserted that the entire musical legacy of the Roman Church was the inspired creation of a single man, the sainted Pope Gregory I, who had served as pope from 590 until his death in 604. Yet in Gregory's time there was no way to notate melodies. His contemporary, St. Isidore, Bishop of Seville (ca. 560–636), put it this way: "Unless sounds are held in the memory by man they perish, because they cannot be written down."[4]

By the ninth century the legend was firmly established that Pope Gregory was the composer of what has ever since been known as Gregorian chant. The legend was propagated not only in literary accounts but also in visual tradition (see Fig. 1-5). As the story goes, the pope, while dictating to a scribe his commentary on parts of the Bible, often paused for a long time. Gregory's silences puzzled the scribe, who was separated from him by a screen. Peeping through, he beheld the dove of the Holy Spirit hovering around the head of St. Gregory, who resumed his dictation only when the dove moved away. (It is from such representations of divine inspiration that we get our expression "A little bird told me.") The legend was a propaganda ploy developed to persuade the northern churches that the Roman chant was better than theirs. As a divine creation, mediated through an inspired, canonized human vessel, the Roman chant would have the prestige it needed to triumph eventually over all local opposition. Yet no one person, neither Gregory nor any of his contemporaries, actually composed the "Gregorian" chants. It was a huge collective enterprise that seems to have achieved standardization in Rome by the end of the eighth century.

But what were its origins? Until very recently it was assumed as a matter of course that the origins of Christian liturgical music went back, like the rest of Christian practice and belief, to the "sacred bridge" connecting the Christian religion with Judaism. This would seem a natural connection between Christ, himself a Jew, and the early rise of Christianity. Moreover, the words of Gregorian chants were overwhelmingly psalm verses, and the recitation of psalms, along with other scriptural readings, is to this day a common element of Jewish and Christian worship. But it does not seem now that the Jewish rites were immediately transferred to Christian worship services; that happened to some extent later and in different circumstances. The origins of Christian psalmody lie not in the very public worship of the Jewish temple but, rather, in the secluded services of early Christian ascetics worshiping in monasteries.

Figure 1-5 This illustration, dating from the end of the ninth century, is one of the earliest representations of Pope Gregory I (Saint Gregory the Great), who is receiving the chant from the Holy Spirit in the guise of a dove.

Christian monasticism arose in the fourth century, partly in reaction to the Church's worldly success following its establishment as the official religion of the late Roman Empire (Fig. 1-6). An increasing number of Christian enthusiasts reacted against what they considered the oppressive power structure of the Church and advocated retreat into a simple, solitary life more akin, in their view, to the original teachings of Christ. The communities thus established had various profiles, although most centered around an austere life devoted to prayer and meditation or to ascetic communal living devoted to pious fellowship and productive work. Separate communities were established for women, which were later called convents or nunneries.

The most famous monastery was founded in 529 at Monte Cassino, in central Italy, by St. Benedict of Nursia (480–547). He wrote an influential set of rules, his *Regula monachorum*, that governed daily life in his monastery and that became widely adopted elsewhere as the "Rule of Saint Benedict." The practices of chanting Psalms that gradually developed into Gregorian chant arose in such a communal context. An important aspect of the monastic regimen was staying up at night, a discipline known as the vigil. To help the monks keep awake and to assist their meditations, they would recite constantly, chiefly from the Bible and particularly from the Psalter, in a kind of heightened speech (**cantillation**). Reciting the complete 150 psalms in a ceaseless cycle, somewhat in the manner of a mantra, distracted the mind from physical appetites and was thought to lead to higher levels of consciousness.

Musical metaphors of community and discipline were symbolized by unaccompanied singing in unison. This remained the Gregorian ideal, although the community of worshipers was replaced in the more public services by specially trained choirs. **Monophony** was thus a choice but not a necessity. While it may seem to

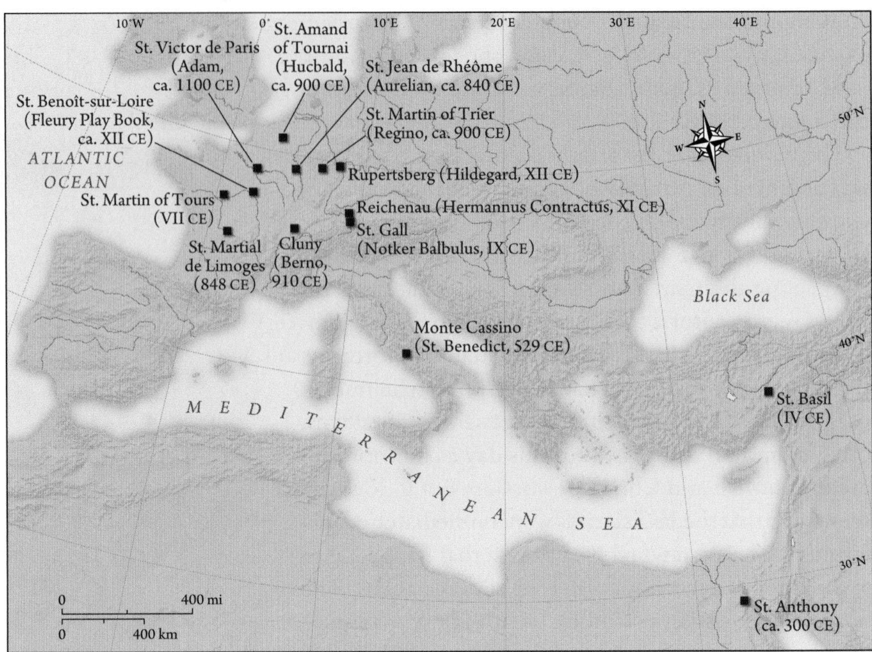

Figure 1-6 Early Christian monastic centers.

reflect the primitive origins of chant, early Christian monophony in fact represents the purposeful rejection of earlier, more elaborate practices, both Judaic and pagan.

The Development of the Liturgy: The Offices

In his book of rules St. Benedict required that the Psalter be recited in a weekly round of services known as the ***Offices***, of which there were eight each day. The greatest single portion went to the Night Office (now called *Matins*), which accounted for more than half of the weekly round of all 150 psalms. The shorter day Offices began at dawn with one of praise (*Lauds*) and continued with four “minor hours” named after the clock hours according to Roman terminology: *Prime* (the first hour), *Terce* (the third hour), *Sext* (the sixth hour), and *None* (the ninth hour). The public liturgical day ended with *Vespers*, which features the psalm-like “Canticle of Mary” (known as the Magnificat, which is its first word). Finally, there was a bedtime service for monks called *Compline* (completion), at which more elaborate chants were sung, especially in the later Middle Ages, to the Blessed Virgin as a plea for her intercession. (Lauds, Vespers, and Compline are services that contain *canticles*—texts from the New Testament that are sung in the manner as psalms.) At a minimum an Office service included a psalm, a scripture reading, and a *hymn*, which was a metrical song of praise derived from Greek pagan practice.

Just as the liturgical day was a cycle of services and the monastic week was a cycle of psalms, so the whole Catholic Church calendar was organized in a yearly cycle of commemorations known as *feasts*. Monks thus lived out their lives according to these nested cycles—wheels within wheels within wheels. The basic annual framework commemorated events in the life of Christ, organized in two great cycles surrounding the two biggest feasts, Christmas (the Birth of Christ) and Easter (the Resurrection of Christ). The Christmas cycle, beginning with four solemn weeks of preparation called Advent and ending with the feast of Epiphany on 6 January, uses the Roman pagan calendar and has the fixed date of 25 December. The Easter cycle, beginning with the forty-day fast called Lent and ending on the fiftieth day after Easter Sunday with the feast of Pentecost, derives from the Jewish calendar. The date of Easter can therefore vary by well more than a month and falls from 22 March to 25 April. The yearly calendar also came to include a cycle of ever-more numerous feasts for the Virgin Mary and saints' commemorations and many other occasions, among them special (so-called *votive*) occasions where prayers and offerings are made, such as weddings, funerals, and memorials.

As official occasions were added to the calendar—and they continue to be added and deleted to this day—they had to be provided with appropriate texts and melodies. Many of the words and melodies were sung only once a year, while others were sung every day. The church therefore needed an enormous quantity of music. The use of words and music often varied from region to region, even from town to town. The veneration of a local "patron saint" (a go-between to God for a particular place or group) demanded more elaborate music than would be sung in places without this special connection. The words of the Book of Psalms were fixed, but additional texts, placed before and after a psalm, would vary so that the meaning of a psalm could be amplified and feasts could be differentiated. These added *antiphons* and *responds* thus became a site of new musical composition. An **antiphon** is a short sentence or verse that is sung before or after a psalm and sometimes between its individual verses, which were sung in alternation by two halves of the choir. A **respond** is the first part of *responsorial* chant, in which the full choir alternates with a soloist singing a verse to follow.

The Order of the Mass

The most elaborate music of the Christian Church is associated with the *Mass*, the central public service of worship. The **Mass** is a reenactment of Christ's Last Supper, the Jewish Passover Seder he held the evening before his crucifixion, when he gathered his disciples together. The opening part of the service, called the *synaxis* ("synagogue," after the Greek for "a meeting or assembly"), consists of prayers, chants, and readings and is open to those who have not yet completed their religious instruction. The often beautiful, elaborate, and awe-inspiring ritual elements—the elegance of the clothes, the allure of the smell of incense, the sweetness of the sounds, the majesty of the physical space—were enticing and impressive. This was meant in part to attract new members to the Church at a time when Christianity was competing for prominence with other religions.

The second part of the Mass, an esoteric service known as the *Eucharist* (from the Greek for "thanksgiving"), is closed to all who have not yet been baptized. It consists of a reenactment of the Last Supper in which the congregation mystically ingests the blood and body of Christ in a form miraculously transformed from wine and bread. As a public service that incorporated a great deal of action, the Mass did not contain full psalms or hymns, with their many stanzas—that would take too long. Instead, it featured short texts set to elaborate music, including words that expressed the "proper" identity of each occasion at which Mass was celebrated—feast, Sunday, or saint's day.

In some sections of the Mass, therefore, the words change from day to day; these sections form the ***Proper*** of the Mass. In other sections the words remain the same day in and day out, and these parts make up the ***Ordinary***. The term "Mass Ordinary" eventually came to mean five unchanging texts sung by the choir: Kyrie, Gloria, Credo, Sanctus, and Agnus Dei. These began to receive significant musical attention in the Carolingian period and centuries later would be set as unified cycles. This later development spawned a tradition of Mass composition to which many famous composers of the standard concert repertory made contributions, including Bach, Haydn, Mozart, and Beethoven.

With the standardization of the Ordinary chants, the Franks thus effected a musical consolidation of the Western Mass that established its form for the next millennium. Their version was reimported back to Rome in the eleventh century and became standard almost everywhere in Europe and the British Isles. The text and chants of the Mass Ordinary developed over centuries, with the Gloria probably being the oldest part and the Agnus Dei the latest addition. Later in this chapter we will go through the individual parts of the Mass, both Proper and Ordinary, sung and recited, in the order they eventually assumed in the service, an assemblage and ordering that likewise took centuries to become standard (Table 1-1).

Writing It Down: Neumes

On a very superficial level the music associated with the Office and Mass services may strike some listeners today as all sounding alike: monophonic melodies chanted in Latin. Its richness and diversity, however, are extraordinary, which should not be surprising given the great span of time and space over which it developed. After we see how the music was eventually written down and learn the rudiments of how to read the notation, we will get a sense of this musical variety by looking at different musical adornments to a single verse of a single psalm.

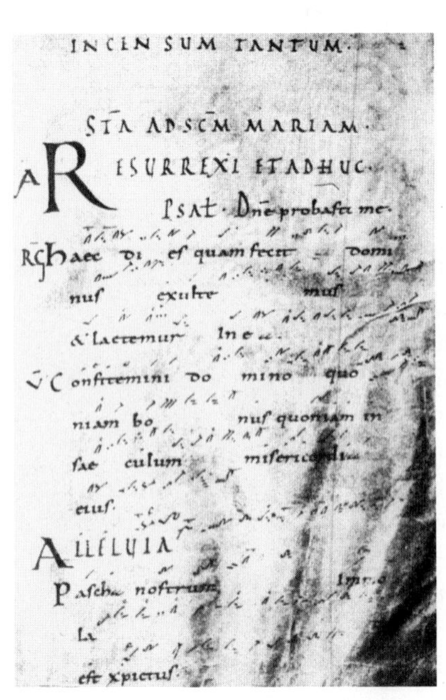

Figure 1-7 Easter Introit, *Resurrexi*, from a soloist's chant book, prepared at the Swiss monastery of St. Gall early in the tenth century.

Chant notation evolved through the invention of so-called ***neumes*** that tracked the relative rise and fall of the melodies and the placement of notes in relation to text syllables (Fig. 1-7). Etymologically, the word *neume*, which comes from the Greek word *pneuma* ("breath," suggesting also vital spirit or soul), referred to a characteristic melodic turn such as may be sung on one breath. Today, however, the word more commonly denotes the written sign that represented such a turn. Some early surviving liturgical books contain neumes, but not before the end of the ninth century, several generations after the Carolingian chant reform had been undertaken. This has led to a great deal of scholarly speculation about the actual origins of the neumes and the date of their earliest use.

Scholars long assumed that the Carolingian neumes were an outgrowth of "prosodic accents," the signs—acute (´), grave (`), circumflex (^), and so forth—that represented the inflection of poetry-recitation in late classical antiquity and that still survive to a certain extent in the writing of modern French and other languages. As originally conceived, the acute accent meant a raising of vocal pitch, the grave a lowering, the circumflex a raising-plus-lowering. Putting such signs over syllables would therefore help remind someone who

Table 1-1 Order of the Western Mass

SUNG (*concentus*)		SPOKEN OR RECITED TO A TONE (*accentus*)	
Proper	**Ordinary**	**Proper**	**Ordinary**
		SYNAXIS	
1. Introit			
	2. Kyrie 3. Gloria (omitted during Lent and Advent)		
		4. Collect (call to prayer) 5. Epistle reading	
6. Gradual (replaced between Easter and Pentecost by an Alleluia) 7. Alleluia (replaced during Lent and Advent by the Tract) 8. Sequence (ubiquitous and fully canonical from the tenth to the sixteenth centuries; only four survived the Counter Reformation)			
		9. Gospel reading [Sermon]	
		EUCHARIST	
	10. Credo		
11. Offertory			
			12. Offertory prayers
		13. Secret (Celebrant's silent prayer) 14. Preface to the Sanctus	
	15. Sanctus		
			16. Canon (Celebrant's Prayer consecrating wine and bread) 17. Lord's Prayer (congregation)
	18. Agnus Dei		
19. Communion			
		20. Postcommunion prayer	
	21. Dismissal (*Ite, missa est*, replaced during Lent and Advent by *Benedicamus Domino*, "Let us bless the Lord"		

already knew a melody about its general contour (that is, whether the tune was going up or down), but the signs would not indicate the precise interval. There are other theories about the origin of neumes, including one that associates them with a system of punctuation signs—functional equivalents of what we know today as commas, colons, question marks, and so on—that break up a written text into easily comprehended bits by governing the reader's vocal inflections.

These explanations assume that the neumes were dependent on some earlier sign-system, and yet we have no evidence to rule out the possibility that the neumes were invented independently in response to the immediate musical purpose at hand. After all, there were much earlier, pre-Christian schemes for graphically representing music that did not reflect melodic contour but were entirely arbitrary written signs that represented melodic formulas by convention, the way alphabet letters represent speech sounds. As we have seen, the ancient Greeks used actual alphabetic signs as musical notation. A more familiar example of special formula-signs for music include the so-called Masoretic accents (*ta'amim*) of Jewish biblical cantillation, which Jewish children are taught to this day in preparation for their rite of passage to adulthood (*bar* or *bat mitzvah*), when they are called to the pulpit to read from scripture.

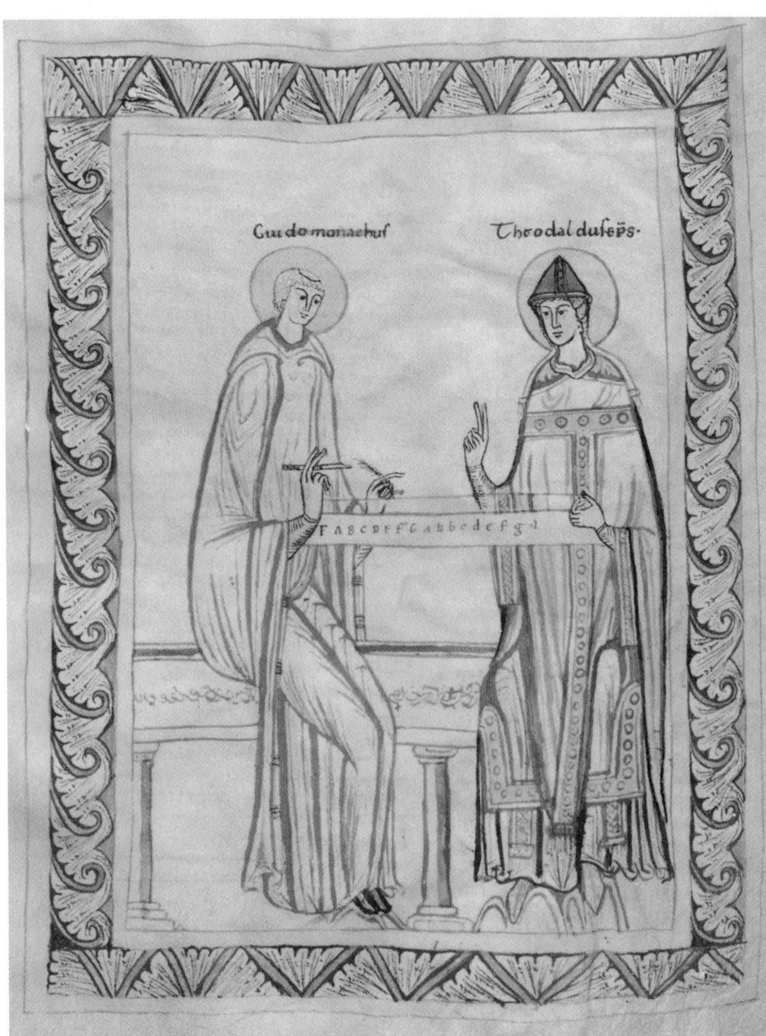

Figure 1-8 Guido of Arezzo showing his pupil Theodal how to calculate the string lengths of the scale using a monochord.

The new contour-based Carolingian neumes that are our concern here follow an entirely different principle of representation, out of which developed the Western notation that is familiar today. Carolingian neumes shared the limitation of all the early neumatic systems: We cannot actually read a melody from them unless we already know the tune. To read a previously unknown melody at sight, we need at a minimum a means of precise intervallic (or relative-pitch) measurement. It was not until the early eleventh century that neumes were "heighted," or arranged *diastematically*, on the lines and spaces of a staff. Only then was it possible to transmit melodies soundlessly, although the notation still did not convey many parameters of how the music actually sounded.

Guido of Arezzo

According to tradition, heighted neumes were the invention of the Italian monk Guido of Arezzo (Fig. 1-8). His *Micrologus* (Little Treatise), a manual on the rudiments of music theory completed around 1028, and another one of his texts included the earliest guide to staff notation. The breakthrough came when neumes were placed on the lines and spaces of a ruled staff to show precisely their relative pitch locations. Special colors, later replaced by alphabet signs, were used to denote the C and F "key" lines—*claves* in Latin—that have half steps below them; these letters survive as our modern "clefs." These innovations made "sight-singing" possible. Most of the Medieval notation we will consider employed four staff lines, not five as used today.

Guido lived from about 990 to about 1033 and specialized for most of his life in the training of choirboys. As a tool he used a hymn called *Ut queant laxis* ("So that tongues might loosen"), in which the tune is so constructed that the first syllable in each half-line of text falls one scale degree higher than the one that precedes it, the entire series tracing out exactly the basic six-note diatonic segment, or ***hexachord***, from C to A (Ex. 1-5). Associating the text syllables with the appropriate pitches gave a syllable name to each degree in the hexachord (*ut–re–mi–fa–sol–la*). Once internalized, the syllables served a double purpose for ear training. Any interval, ascending or descending, could be demonstrated in terms of a syllable combination (thus: ut–re, the whole step; ut–mi, the major third; ut–fa, the perfect fourth; re–fa, the minor third; etc.). Second, the difference between the whole step and the half step could be mastered by drilling the interval mi–fa. The reason it is so important to know where the half step mi–fa is situated is that this is the definer of mode quality (the distribution of half steps and whole steps), or what we now think of as scales.

Example 1-5 Hymn, *Ut queant laxis;* words by Paul the Deacon, music possibly by Guido of Arezzo

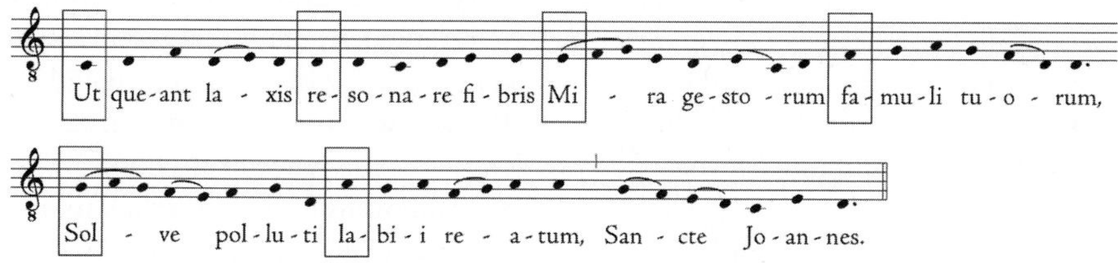

That thy servants may freely proclaim the wonders of thy deeds,
absolve the sins of their unclean lips, O holy John.

Many centuries later the syllable *si* was added by some singing teachers so that a full major scale could be sung with model ("**solmization**") syllables. In modern practice, *si* has been replaced by *ti*, and *ut* has been replaced by *do*. Guido, however, who did not as yet have or need the concept of the major scale, managed to complete the octave by transposing the basic module so that it began on G, the intervals of the hexachord G–E being identical with C–A. In this new placement, the progression *mi–fa* corresponds with the half step B–C. To solmize the full scale from C to C, one mutates at some convenient point, either reinterpreting *sol* as *ut*

or reinterpreting *la* as *re* so that the syllables fill an entire octave. Dashes below denote half steps:

C	D	E	—	F	G	A	B	—	C
ut	re	mi	—	fa	sol	la			
					ut	re	mi	—	fa

To avoid the tritone that arises between F and B, later theorists recognized another transposition of the module, beginning on F, that would place the *mi–fa* pair on A and B♭. The entire range of hexachord transpositions thus achieved, mapping out the musical pitch space within which Gregorian chant was habitually sung, finally looked like Ex. 1-6.

Example 1-6 The gamut, or full range of pitches represented on the Guidonian hand, together with the seven hexachords that are required for its solmization

In order to gain an *ut* at the bottom on which to begin the first set of syllables, Guido placed a G below the A that normally marked the lower end of the modal system, discussed later. This extra G was represented by its Greek equivalent, *gamma*. Its full name within the array was "Gamma ut," which was shortened to *gamut* and became the name of the array itself. (The word "gamut," of course, has entered the common English vocabulary to denote the full range of anything.) The two versions of B (the one sung as *mi* over G, corresponding to our B natural, and the one sung as *fa* over F, corresponding to B♭), were assigned to a single mutable space, whose actual pitch realization would depend on the context. The higher B, known as the hard one (*durus*), was represented by a square-shaped letter that eventually evolved into the modern natural sign (♮). The hexachord containing it was also known as the "hard" hexachord (*hexachordum durum*). The lower one, which softened augmented fourths into perfect ones, was known accordingly as soft (*mollis*) and was represented by a rounded letter that eventually evolved into the modern flat sign (♭). The hexachord containing B♭ was known as the "soft" hexachord; the original module, derived from the hymn, was called the "natural" hexachord.

The once-widespread use of mnemonic devices is still reflected in our daily language by expressions like "rule of thumb" and "at one's fingertips."

As an aid toward memorization, a device was later adopted whereby items to be memorized were mapped in spiral fashion onto the joints of the left palm (Fig. 1-9). The once-widespread use of such mnemonic devices as the "**Guidonian Hand**" is still reflected in our daily language by expressions like "rule of thumb" and "at one's fingertips." Armed with the internalized *gamut*, a singer could parse a written melody into its constituent intervals without hearing

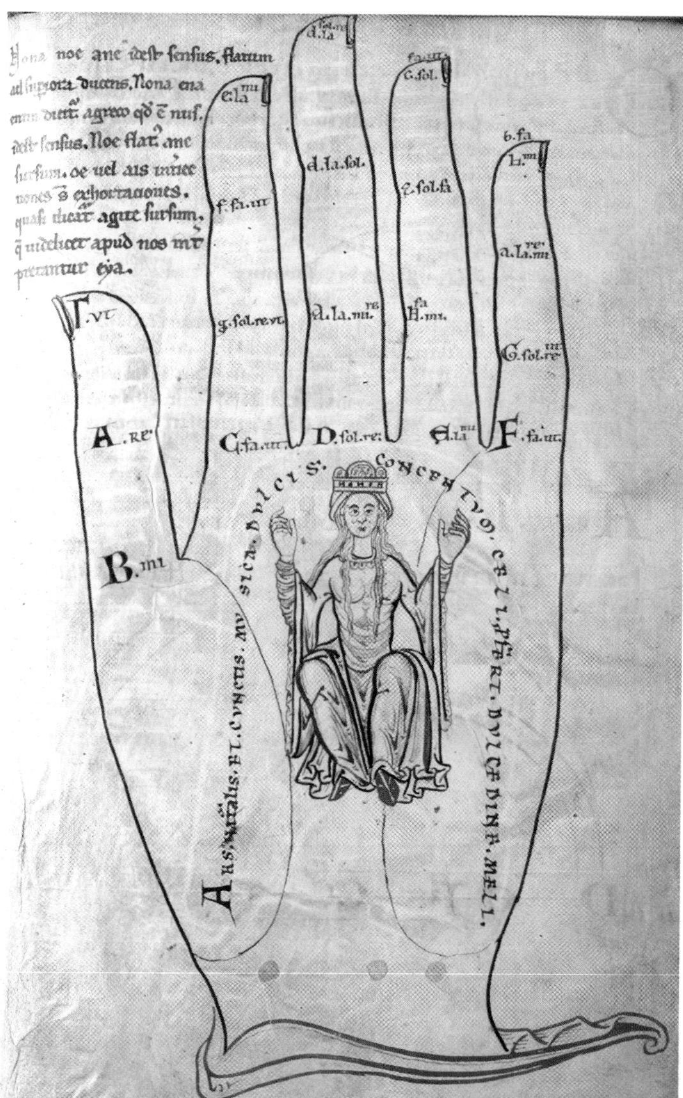

Figure 1-9 The "Guidonian Hand" as represented in a thirteenth-century Bavarian manuscript.

or playing it. A singer could truly sing at sight, or, as Guido put it, "sing an unknown melody."[5]

It took centuries for a more standardized system to develop. In our exploration of early music we will encounter a notation that in the late nineteenth century was called "square" or "quadratic," after the shape of the note heads, adapted from a calligraphic-style handwriting that became prevalent in twelfth-century manuscripts. The notation of Example 1-7a is printed exactly as it is found in the *Liber responsorialis,* a book of Office chants published in 1895 by the monks of the Benedictine Abbey of Solesmes in France. The monks at the Abbey carried out a vast restoration project in which the corpus of Gregorian chant was edited from its original manuscript sources. Many of our examples in this chapter are given in square notation as they are found in the *Liber usualis,* a large anthology of the basic chants for Mass and Office, also issued by the monks of Solesmes. Example 1-7b transcribes part of the antiphon into modern notation.

Example 1-7a ***Justus ut palma*** **as it appears in the** ***Liber responsorialis,*** **a book of Office chants published in 1895 by the monks of the Benedictine Abbey of Solesmes in France**

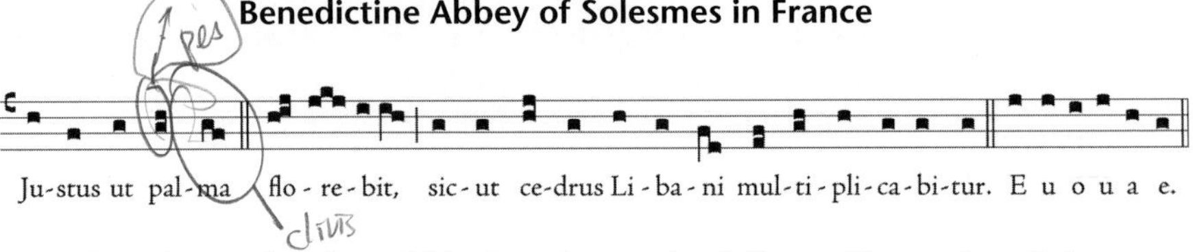

The righteous shall flourish like the palm tree: he shall grow like a cedar in Lebanon.

Example 1-7b ***Justus ut palma*** **as antiphon to Psalm 91**

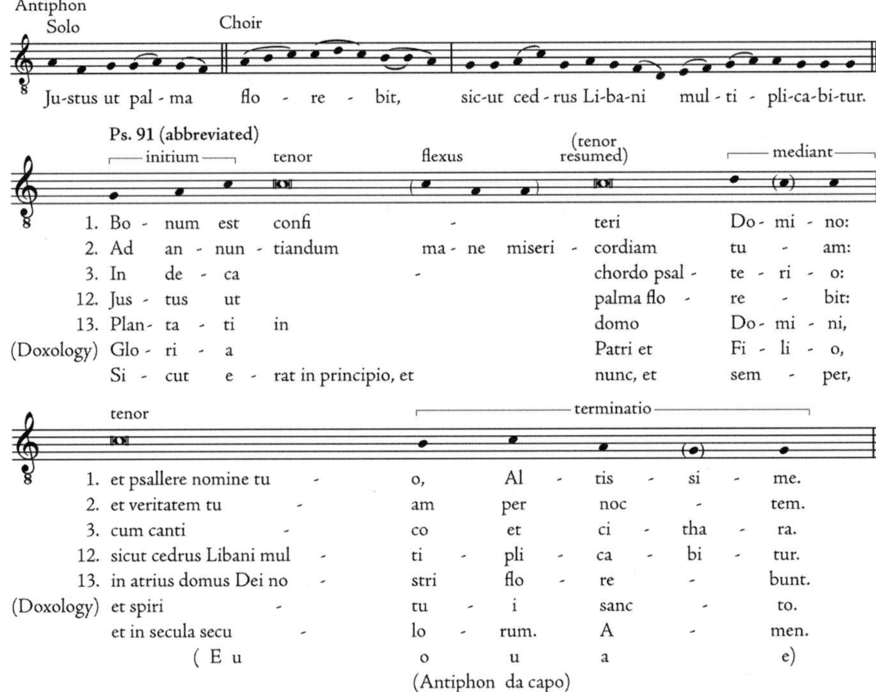

1. It is a good thing to give thanks unto the Lord, and to sing praises unto thy name, O most High:
2. To shew forth thy loving kindness in the morning, and thy faithfulness every night,
3. Upon an instrument of ten strings, and upon the psaltery; upon the harp with a solemn sound.
12. The righteous shall flourish like the palm tree: he shall grow like a cedar in Lebanon.
13. Those that be planted in the house of the Lord shall flourish in the courts of our God.

(Doxology) Glory be to the Father, the Son, and the Holy Spirit.
As it was in the beginning, is now, and ever shall be, world without end. Amen.

As early as the tenth century, neumes were learned from tables in which each shape was given a distinctive name. In Example 1-7a, the two-note ascent over pal-, for example, was called the *pes* (or *podatus*), meaning "foot." Its descending counterpart, over -ma, was called the *clivis* (meaning "sloped"). The three-note neumes were known respectively as the *scandicus* (from scandere, "to climb"), the *torculus* ("a little turn"), and the *trigon* ("a toss"). The motion opposite to the *torculus* (i.e., first down and then up) is shown by the *porrectus* ("stretched"), with its striking oblique stroke: N. The pes, clivis, torculus, and porrectus were the basic shapes, corresponding roughly to the acute, grave, circumflex, and anticircumflex accents, and they were retained in later notational schemes.

Modal Theory

The formula for singing a psalm, called a *psalm tone*, is melody stripped to its minimum functional requirements as a medium for the exaltation of a sacred utterance. Eight **psalm tones** are used in the Latin liturgy, plus one called the *tonus peregrinus* ("migrating tone") because the most prominent pitch of the second half-verse is different from that of the first half. In its earliest usages, the term **mode** is best defined as a fund of shared melodic turns characterizing the chants of a given functional type. While the concept of mode is still prevalent in the Greek Orthodox Church, our more recent concept of mode, based on that of a scale and defined mainly in terms of its final note, fits the Gregorian repertory poorly. Thinking of the modes as a function of scale and final note was originally the product of music theory of the tenth and eleventh centuries, in which an attempt was made to organize the chants of the Roman Church according to the categories of ancient Greek music theory.

In the ninth century there emerged collections of antiphons that were grouped according to the psalm tones with which they were melodically associated. These collections, which came to include all kinds of chants, are known as *tonaries*. These books served an eminently practical purpose, since in every service newly learned antiphons had to be attached appropriately to psalm tones. To achieve this practical goal, large stylistic generalizations had to be made about the antiphons on the basis of observation, with the compiler comparing the beginnings and endings of the antiphons with those of the psalm tones. In effect, a large collection of melodies inherited from the Roman tradition was being compared with, and assimilated to, an abstract classification of melodic turns and functions imported from another tradition (the eight-mode system of the Byzantine Church). The result was something neither Roman nor Greek but specifically Frankish—and tremendously fertile, a triumph of imaginative synthesis.

Antiphons were compared with psalm tones to see how the interval was filled in between their ending note (*finalis*) and the pitch corresponding to the psalm tone's reciting tone (*tenor*), normally a fifth above. There are four ways that the interval of a fifth can be filled in with four tones (T) or semitones (S). In the order of the tonaries these were (1) **TSTT**, (2) **STTT**, (3) **TTTS**, and (4) **TTST**. The ending notes of these four species-defining segments—D, E, F, and G—were named according to their Greek numbers: *protus* (first), *deuterus* (second), *tritus* (third), and *tetrardus* (fourth), respectively.

Better correspondence between the chant classification and the preexisting eightfold system of psalm tones was achieved by invoking the category of *ambitus*, or range. Chants ending on each of the four final notes were therefore further broken down into two classes. Those with the final note at the bottom of their range were said to be in "authentic" modes, while those that extended lower than their final notes, so that the final occurred in the middle of their range, were called "plagal." The four final notes, each governing two modes in both authentic and plagal forms, made for a total of eight, in exact accordance with the configuration of the eightfold

Table 1-2 Modes and Octave Species

MODE		LOWER TETRACHORD	PENTACHORD	UPPER TETRACHORD
Protus (Final D)	Authentic		T–S–T–T	T–S–T
	Plagal	T–S–T	T–S–T–T	
Deuterus (Final E)	Authentic		S–T–T–T	S–T–T
	Plagal	S–T–T	S–T–T–T	
Tritus (Final F)	Authentic		T–T–T–S	T–T–S
	Plagal	T–T–S	T–T–T–S	
Tetrardus (Final G)	Authentic		T–T–S–T	T–S–T
	Plagal	T–S–T	T–T–S–T	

system of psalm tones. Table 1-2 shows the layout of basic pentachord, a scale of five adjacent notes outlining a fifth, and upper and lower tetrachords, outlining the four adjacent notes that complete the octave.

In Example 1-8, Table 1-2 is translated into modern staff notation, giving the full array of so-called Medieval **church modes**. They will henceforth be numbered from 1 to 8, as they are in the later Frankish treatises, and they will be given the Greek names that the Frankish theorists borrowed from Boethius: Dorian, Phrygian, Lydian, Mixolydian. The Greek prefix *hypo-*, attached to the names of the plagal scales, is roughly synonymous with the word *plagal* itself: both mean "lower." Example 1-8 also includes the tenors of the corresponding psalm tones, for these were sometimes claimed by contemporary theorists to pertain to the church modes as well. The tenor of three of the authentic modes lies a fifth above the final note.

Example 1-8 The eight Medieval modes

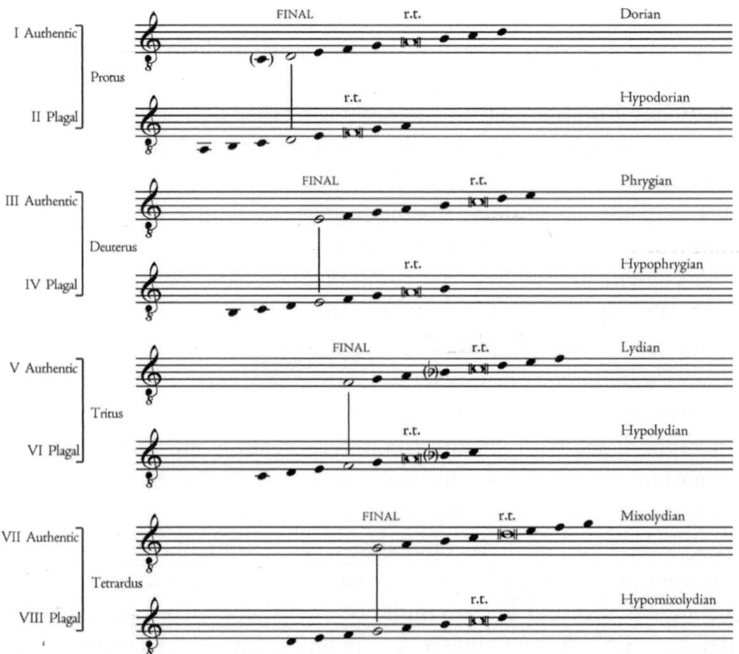

The tenor of a plagal mode lies a third below that of its authentic counterpart. Note that in a psalm tone wherever, according to these rules, the tenor would fall on B, it is changed to C. This was evidently because of an aversion to reciting on the lower note of a semitone pair. Note, too, that the tenor of the fourth tone is A rather than G by the regular application of the rules; it is a third lower than its adjusted counterpart (C in place of B transposes to A in place of G).

It is important to bear in mind that Medieval modal scales do not specify actual pitch frequencies, the way they do in our modern practice. Thus we must try to avoid the common assumption that the Dorian scale represents the piano's white keys from D to D, the Phrygian from E to E, and so on. Rather, the "four finals" and their concomitant scales represent nothing more than the most convenient way of notating patterns of half steps and whole steps.

Psalmody in Practice: The Office and the Mass

It is time now to look closely at some music. We will begin by tracing settings of a single psalm verse through various liturgical habitats in both the Offices and the Mass. The twelfth verse of Psalm 91 was an especially favored one in the liturgy, perhaps owing to its vivid similes, and it invited settings both simple and elaborate. The Latin verse reads: *Justus ut palma florebit, et sicut cedrus Libani multiplicabitur,* translated in the King James Bible as "The righteous shall flourish like the palm tree: he shall grow like a cedar in Lebanon."

Anthology Vol 1-2a
Full CD/Concise CD I, 2

Example 1-7b is the simplest of the settings, indeed barely a melody at all. Singing, however minimal, elevates words out of the context of the everyday. Such a simple kind of chanting is very ancient. Here Psalm 91 is paired with an antiphon consisting of its own twelfth verse, the *Justus ut palma,* used in a service commemorating a martyred saint to whom the sentiments expressed in the text are especially pertinent. Beginning in the ninth century, the refrain sandwiches the entire psalm rather than alternating with every verse.

In Example 1-7b the tone formula is analyzed into its constituent parts, which function very much like punctuation marks. First there is the intonation, given by a soloist to establish the pitch. The intonation formula always ascends to a repeated pitch, called the *reciting tone* or *tenor* (because it is "held," for which the Latin is *tenere*). This pitch is repeated as often as necessary to accommodate the syllables of the text, the number of which can vary considerably from verse to verse. In a long verse there will be many repetitions of the tenor, lending the whole the "monotone" quality often associated with the idea of chanting. The longest verses (here, verses 2, 4, and 5) have a "bend" (*flexus*) as additional punctuation. The end of the first half-verse is sung to a formula known as the *mediant,* which functions as a divider, like the comma or colon in the text. The second half-verse again begins on the tenor, and the whole verse ends with the *termination,* often called the "cadence" because, again as in a declarative sentence, it entails a pitch's lowering or "falling" (for which the Latin is *cadere*).

The relationship between the text and the music in the psalm tone is straightforwardly *syllabic*: one note to each syllable, the reciting tone accommodating most of them. The antiphon is a moderately *neumatic* chant, in which nine of the twenty-one syllables in the text carry two- or three-note neumes. As we see in Examples 1-7a and 1-7b, added to the end of the psalm is the *Doxology* (from the Greek for "words of praise"), the Christianizing tag invoking the Holy Trinity. It is treated simply as an extra pair of psalm verses. In the *Liber usualis* the Doxology is given as a group of six notes set over the space-saving abbreviation "E u o u a e," which are the vowel letters in ". . . seculorum. Amen."

Justus ut palma appears in two more Office services in commemoration of a martyred saint. At Vespers it functions as a psalm antiphon but is sung to a different melody requiring a different psalm tone (Ex. 1-9). At the end of None a really minimal setting of the verse functions as a concluding versicle (from the Latin "little verse"; Ex. 1-10). The extreme simplicity of this versicle reflects the direct connection between the importance of an occasion and the elaborateness of the music that enhances it.

Example 1-9 ***Justus ut palma*** **as a Vespers antiphon**

Ju-stus ut pal - ma flo - re - bit, sic - ut ce-drus Li - ba - ni mul - ti - pli - ca - bi - tur.

Example 1-10 ***Justus ut palma*** **as a versicle**

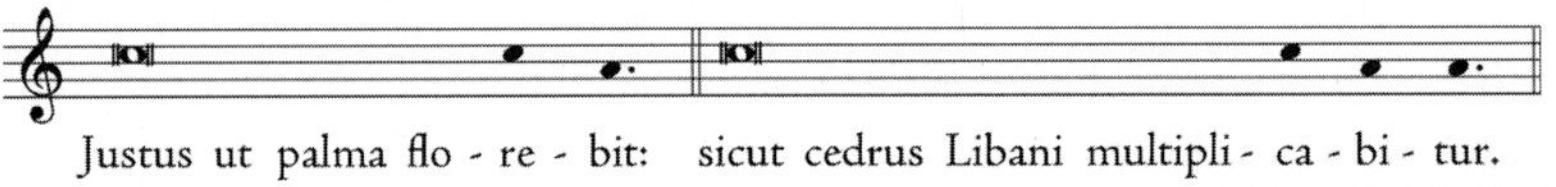
Justus ut palma flo - re - bit: sicut cedrus Libani multipli - ca - bi - tur.

The *Justus ut palma* text appears not just in Office services but also at least four times in the original Gregorian corpus of Mass Propers, the chants for the yearly round of feasts. Their degree of elaborateness varies depending on the occasion and the liturgical function they accompany. Because *Justus ut palma* is a verse about praise, it is particularly suitable for honoring saints. Example 1-11 shows the first part of the chant opening the service, the *Introit.* Being a Mass chant, it is considerably more elaborate than its Office counterparts. There are a few compound neumes, such as the first syllable, which is set to a seven-note complex. This chant possesses the same graceful arc-like shape we have already observed in microcosm in the Office psalm tones.

Anthology Vol 1-2b
Full CD/Concise CD I, 3

Example 1-11 ***Justus ut palma*** **as Introit (opening)**

Ju - stus * ut palma flo-re - bit:

Anthology Vol 1-2c
Full CD/Concise CD I, 4

Our next example is the opening of the Offertory on *Justus ut palma* (Ex. 1-12). This setting is even more ornate than the previous example: There are now many notes assigned to certain single syllables, a style called ***melismatic***, with lengthy ***melismas*** comprising most of the music.

Example 1-12 ***Justus ut palma*** **as Offertory (opening)**

Ju - stus * ut palma flo - re - bit:

Settings of the *Justus ut palma* verse also function as "lesson chants" sung between the scripture readings that cap the first portion of the Mass, at a time when there is little or no liturgical action going on. These are the most florid of all the Mass chants, because more than any other they are meant as listeners' music. The lesson chants are responsorial ones with a soloist alternating with the choir. At the beginning of the Alleluia verse (Ex. 1-13), the soloist sings up to the asterisk; the choir begins again and continues into the fifty-one-note *jubilus*, the long melisma on the last syllable of the word "alleluia." Melismatic singing was held by Christian mystics to be the highest form of religious utterance: "It is a certain sound of joy without words," St. Augustine wrote of such chanting in the fourth century, "the expression of a mind poured forth in joy."[6] The same soloist/choir alternation is indicated in the verse (given mainly to the soloist) by the asterisk before the word *multiplicabitur*. The choral alleluia is repeated after the verse, giving the whole a rounded (ABA) form, showing an apparent concern for musical shaping that is mirrored on a smaller scale by the internal repetitions (representable as aabb) that make up the internal melisma on the word *cedrus*. The repetitions that give the Alleluia setting its striking shape are memorable not just for the listener but also for the singer. Such repeated phrases or formulas served as vital memory aids in an age of oral composition and show the relationship between this extraordinarily ornate, mystically evocative composition and the simple psalm tone with which our survey of chant genres began (cf. Ex. 1-7).

Anthology Vol 1-2d
Full CD/Concise CD I, 5

Example 1-13 ***Justus ut palma*** **as Alleluia**

Al-le - lu - ia. *
℣.Ju - stus ut palma flo - re - bit, et sicut ce -
drus *multi - plica - bi-tur.

Melodic repetitions of this type not only link the parts of individual chants, they link whole chant families as well. Examples 1-14a and 1-14b contain two Graduals, each consisting of a melismatic respond and an even more melismatic verse

Anthology Vol 1-3a
Full CD/Concise CD I, 6

Anthology Vol 1-3b
Full CD/Concise CD I, 7

for a cantor. The respond in the first of them (Ex. 1-14a) is yet another setting of the *Justus ut palma* verse. The second (Ex. 1-14b) is the Easter Gradual *Haec dies,* in which the text consists of two verses from Psalm 117, one functioning as respond, the other as soloist's verse.

Example 1-14a ***Justus ut palma*** **as Gradual**

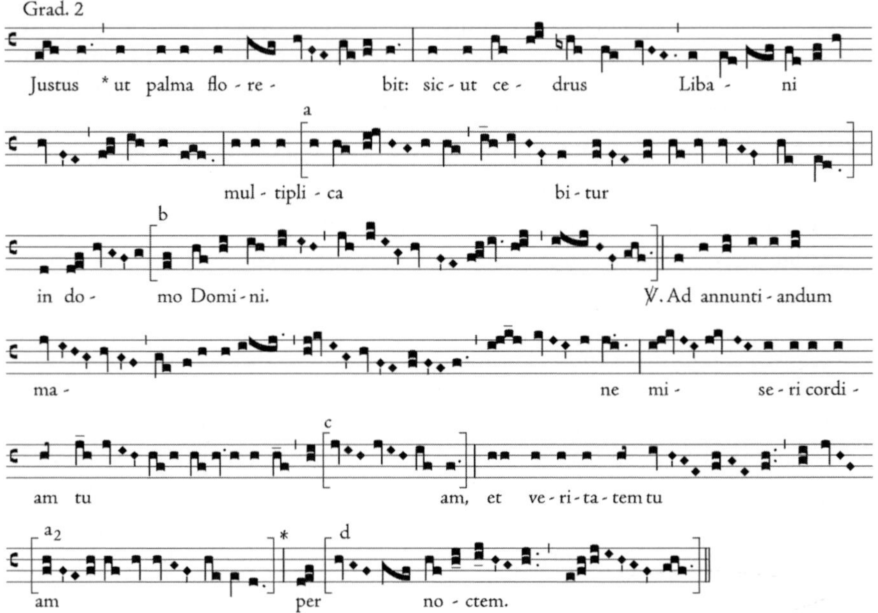

Example 1-14b ***Haec dies*** **(Easter Gradual)**

This is the day which the Lord hath made: we will rejoice and be glad in it (Psalm 117, 24).

O give thanks unto the Lord, for He is good: because his mercy endureth forever (Psalm 117, 1)

As the bracketed sections in these examples show, the two chants draw heavily on a shared fund of melodic turns, and indeed a whole family of Graduals, numbering more than twenty in all, have these formulas in common. The shared formulas are found most frequently at initial and cadential points, and internal repetitions regularly occur to accommodate lengthier texts. Scholars used to think that the large amount of shared material within chant families reflected a "patchwork" process of composition, but more recently some have preferred to consider it a product of an oral composition process in which a body of melodic formulas is flexibly adapted to different texts according to certain rules and customs. The shared formulas seen in these two Graduals, for example, are found only in Graduals. The use of such standard melodic material would have aided in the process of oral composition and made the melodies easier to remember.

The Layout of the Mass Service

Now that we have sampled some of the stylistic variety among chants, we can look at the layout of the Mass service as it was eventually codified with its sung and recited parts, the Ordinary sections, which are the same at every service, and the Proper ones, which change from day to day (cf. Table 1-1). The service begins with a Proper chant, the *Introit,* which is an antiphon plus a verse or two that accompanies the entrance of the celebrants at the start of the service. The first Ordinary chant follows, the *Kyrie eleison,* which has a complex and somewhat puzzling history. Its special status is immediately evident from its language: This is the one Greek survival in the otherwise Latin Mass. *Kyrie eleison* (Greek) means "Lord, have mercy on us," which alternates with the words *Christe eleison* ("Christ, have mercy on us"). By the ninth century, when the Frankish musicians were attempting to standardize chant, the Kyrie had been established as a ninefold entreaty: three times singing Kyrie eleison, three times Christe eleison, and another three times Kyrie eleison. As in the case of the other Ordinary chants, the Kyrie inspired a wide range of musical settings, from quite simple to complex. The more artful Kyrie tunes often reflect the shape of the text they adorn, matching its ninefold elaboration of a three-part text with patterns of repetition like AAA BBB AAA′ or AAA BBB CCC′. (In both cases the last invocation—the A′ or C′—is usually rendered more emphatic than the rest, most typically by inserting or repeating a melisma, which provides a sense of closure.)

Anthology Vol 1-4a
Full CD/Concise CD I, 8

In Anthology Volume 1-4a, the words *Kyrie–Christe–Kyrie* are set to a nonrepeating (ABC) pattern, but the word *eleison* has an aa′b pattern. The retention of the same formula for *eleison* while *Kyrie* changes to *Christe* and back seems to be a vestige of an old congregational refrain. This particular chant dates from the tenth century and is known as Kyrie IV. The identifying number for this and other Ordinary chants is the one assigned to it in modern chant books. Melismatic Kyries were sometimes fitted with other words. Although the Church later purged these added texts, the old opening words (*incipits*) are still used as identification in modern liturgical books, as is the case in Anthology Volume 1-4b called Kyrie IV, *Cunctipotens Genitor Deus.*

Anthology Vol 1-4b
Full CD/Concise CD I, 9

Anthology Vol 1-4c
Full CD/Concise CD I, 10

The second Ordinary section immediately follows the Kyrie. The *Gloria* begins with two verses from the Gospel of St. Luke, quoting the angelic greeting to the shepherds on the night of the Nativity (Ex. 1-15). Next comes a series of praises, then a series of litanies (petitions), and finally a concluding praise song. While its earliest use seems to have been congregational, implying a simple, formulaic style, the Glorias preserved in Frankish manuscripts are usually neumatic chants with occasional melismas. Once past the celebrant's intonation with the words "Gloria in excelsis Deo," they are clearly intended for the clerical or monastic choir. The complete text is as follows:

Gloria in excelsis Deo. Et in terra pax hominibus bonae voluntatis. Laudamus te. Benedicimus te. Adoramus te. Glorificamus te. Gratias agimus tibi propter magnam gloriam tuam.	Glory to God on high. And on earth peace to men of good will. We praise thee, we bless the, we adore thee, we glorify thee. We give thee thanks for thy great glory.
Domine Deus, Rex caelestis, Deus Pater omnipotens. Domine Fili unigenite Jesu Christe. Domine Deus, Agnus Dei, Filius Patris.	O Lord God, King of heaven, God the Father almighty. O Lord, the only begotten Son, Jesus Christ. O Lord God, Lamb of God, Son of the Father.
Qui tollis peccata mundi, Miserere nobis. Qui tollis peccata mundi, suscipe deprecationem nostram. Qui sedes ad dexteram Patris, Miserere nobis.	Thou who takest away the sins of the world, have mercy on us. Thou who takest away the sins of the world, receive our prayer. Thou who sittest at the right hand of the Father, have mercy on us.
Quoniam tu solus sanctus. Tu solus Dominus. Tu solus Altissimus, Jesu Christe.	For thou only art holy, thou only art Lord. Thou only art most high, O Jesus Christ.
Cum Sancto Spiritu, in Gloria Dei Patris. Amen.	With the Holy Ghost, in the glory of God the Father. Amen.

A comparison of the texts of these two opening Ordinary sections reveals something that would have enormous musical consequences. The Kyrie sets just three words (Kyrie, Christe, eleison), although with many repetitions. The text of the Gloria, on the other hand, contains more than a hundred words, virtually without repetition. The obvious result is that Kyrie settings typically have melismatic melodies that linger over the few words. The Gloria, as a wordy section of the Mass, does not invite the luxury of lingering over words or even single syllables, lest the whole section take too long to sing. Melismas therefore tended to be far less common or to be used sparingly to highlight a particular moment in the text. Example 1-15 shows the beginning of a ninth-century Gloria melody, one of the earliest of the forty or so surviving Frankish settings.

Example 1-15 Gloria IV (opening)

Glo - ri - a in excelsis De - o. Et in terra pax ho - mi - ni - bus bonae vo - lunta - tis. Laudamus te.
Bene - di - cimus te. Ado - ra - mus te. Glo - ri - fica - mus te.

Between two readings, or "lessons," (from Paul's Epistles and from the Gospels, respectively) come two Proper chants that tended to be quite elaborate: the *Gradual* (named for the stairs by which the celebrants ascend to the pulpit) and the *Alleluia*, which is replaced during penitential seasons such as Advent and Lent by the *Tract*, a long, sometimes highly melismatic psalm setting.

Anthology Vol 1-4d
Full CD/Concise CD I, 11

Concluding the first part of the Mass is the next Ordinary text: the *Credo*, a setting of the Nicene Creed, the articles of Christian faith from the fourth century. It was adopted by the Franks in 798 and was formally incorporated into the Latin Mass by Pope Benedict VIII in 1014, positioned between the Gospel reading and the Offertory as the divider between the two parts of the service. Despite its late adoption, the formulas to which this venerable text is most often sung are demonstrably archaic and demonstrably Greek. This text is even longer than that of the Gloria and thus again invites syllabic text setting:

Credo in unum Deum, Patrem	I believe in one God, the Father
omnipotentem, factorem caeli et terrae,	almighty, maker of heaven and earth,
visibilium omnium et invisibilium.	and of all things visible and invisible.
Et in unum Dominum Jesum Christum,	And in one Lord Jesus Christ,
Filium Dei unigenitum. Et ex Patre natum	the only-begotten Son of God,
ante omnia saecula.	begotten of his Father before all ages,
Deum de Deo, lumen de lumine, Deum verum	God of God, Light of Light, true God
de Deo vero. Genitum, non factum,	of true God, begotten, not made,
consubstantialem Patri: per quem omnia	being of one substance with the Father,
facta sunt. Qui propter nos homines, et	by whom all things were made; who for
propter nostram salutem descendit	us men and for our salvation descended
de caelis.	from heaven,
Et incarnatus est de Spiritu Sancto	And was incarnated by the Holy Spirit
ex Maria virgine:	through the Virgin Mary,
et homo factus est.	and was made man,
Crucifixus etiam pro nobis sub Pontio	and was crucified for us under Pontius
Pilato: passus, et sepultus est.	Pilate. He suffered and was buried,
Et resurrexit tertia die, secundum scripturas.	and on the third day rose again according to the scriptures,
Et ascendit in caelum, sedet ad	and ascended into heaven, and sits at
dexteram Patris.	the right hand of the Father.
Et iterum venturus est cum gloria judicare	And he shall come again with glory to
vivos et mortuos:	judge both the living and the dead,
cuius regni non erit finis.	he whose kingdom shall have no end.
Et in Spiritum Sanctum Dominum,	And I believe in the Holy Spirit,
et vivificantem: qui ex patre, filioque procedit.	the Lord and giver of life, who proceeds from the Father and the Son,
Qui cum Patre, et Filio simul adoratur,	who with the Father and the Son together
et conglorificatur:	is worshipped and glorified,
qui locutus est per prophetas. Et unam,	who spoke through the prophets. And I
sanctam, catholicam et apostolicam Ecclesiam.	believe in one holy, catholic and apostolic church.
Confiteor unum baptisma in	I acknowledge one baptism for the
remissionem peccatorum. Et exspecto	remission of sins. And I look for the
resurrectionem mortuorum. Et vitam	resurrection of the dead, and the life of
venturi saeculi. Amen.	the world to come. Amen.

The second part of the service, the Eucharist (Fig. 1-10), begins with antiphons that accompany the collection (*Offertory*), one of the Proper chants. The

Anthology Vol 1-4e
Full CD/Concise CD I, 12

next Ordinary section is the *Sanctus*, an acclamation from the Book of Isaiah. (Under its Hebrew name, *Kedusha*, it has been part of the Jewish worship service since ancient times.) In its Latin form, the Sanctus text retains a pair of Hebrew words: *Sabaoth* ("hosts") and *Hosanna* ("save us"). The earliest Frankish settings date from the tenth century. By then, like the Gloria, it was sung not by the entire congregation but by the trained choir. The complete text runs:

Sanctus, Sanctus, Sanctus	Holy, holy, holy, Lord
Dominus Deus Sabaoth.	God of Hosts.
Pleni sunt caeli et terra Gloria tua.	The heavens and earth are full of thy glory.
Hosanna in excelsis.	Hosanna in the highest.
Benedictus qui venit in nomine Domini.	Blessed is he who comes in the name of the Lord.
Hosanna in excelsis.	Hosanna in the highest.

Anthology Vol 1-4f
Full CD/Concise CD I, 13

After the spoken *Canon*, consecrating the bread and the wine, and the Lord's Prayer (*Pater noster*), comes the next Ordinary chant: the *Agnus Dei* (Lamb of God). This was introduced to the Mass in the seventh century to accompany the breaking of bread before communion. At first it was cast as a litany, with an unspecified

Figure 1-10 Ivory book cover from the court of Charles the Bald, Charlemagne's grandson, who ruled the kingdom of the West Franks from 843 to 877. It shows the Eucharist service—the second part of the solemn Mass, in which the wine and host are miraculously transformed.

number of repetitions of the entreaty to the Lamb of God, answered by the congregational prayer, "have mercy on us." The chant was later standardized and abbreviated, limited to three acclamations, and with the third response changed to "grant us peace." The chant for the Agnus Dei is sometimes cast in a rounded "ternary form" (ABA), thus similar to some settings of the opening Kyrie:

Agnus Dei, qui tollis peccata mundi: Miserere nobis.	Lamb of God, who takest away the sins of the world, have mercy on us.
Agnus Dei, qui tollis peccata mundi: Miserere nobis.	Lamb of God, who takest away the sins of the world, have mercy on us.
Agnus Dei, qui tollis peccata mundi: Dona nobis pacem.	Lamb of God, who takest away the sins of the world, grant us peace.

The consummation of the Eucharist (*Communion*) is a psalmodic chant like the Offertory, which is followed by a prayer. Another text that was often included in the early Ordinary formularies was the dismissal versicle (*Ite, missa est*—"Go, it is sent," from which the term *Missa*, for Mass, was adopted) and its response, *Deo gratias* ("Thanks be to God"). During Lent and Advent this is replaced by *Benedicamus Domino* ("Let us bless the Lord").

Frankish Additions to the Chant Repertory

As Franks made their own additions to the Gregorian repertory, the Mass became more elaborate. In the middle of the ninth century Amalar of Metz, an urban cleric who was in the service of Charlemagne, supported the practice of inserting melismas into festive chants. This disciple of Alcuin believed such additions could offer an ecstatic or mystical kind of "understanding" beyond the power of words to convey. Amalar wrote enthusiastically of the Roman practice of replacing the traditional jubilus, the melisma on the "-ia" of "Alleluia," with an even longer melody, which he describes as "a jubilation that the singers call a *sequentia*."[7] Such lengthy additions did not please everyone. Agobard of Lyons, another ecclesiastical observer from the time, condemned what Amalar praised. He complained that sacred singers spent all their time improving their voices instead of their souls, boasted of their virtuosity and their memories, and vied with one another in melismatic contest.

Agobard of Lyons complained that sacred singers spent all their time improving their voices instead of their souls.

The early *sequentia* melismas had many internal phrase repetitions, such as we saw earlier with the two Graduals (cf. Exs. 1-14a and 1-14b), designed to make them easier to memorize. Another memory aid employed by Frankish singers had far-reaching artistic significance: adding words to melismatic chants that turned them, somewhat paradoxically, into syllabic hymns with little prose poems in the manner of the psalms. This led to a fantastic flowering of new devotional song that developed over three centuries and reached its peak in twelfth-century France.

An early witness to the practice of giving syllabic texts to melismatic melodies is Notker Balbulus (Notker the Stammerer, d. 912; Fig. 1-11), a monk who was Charlemagne's first biographer. In the introduction to his *Liber hymnorum* (Book of

Figure 1-11 Notker Balbulus, a ninth-century monk from the Swiss monastery of St. Gall, shown in an illumination from a manuscript probably prepared there some 200 years later. He looks as though he is trying to remember a *longissima melodia* (extra-long melody), as he tells us he did in the preface to his *Liber hymnorum* (Book of Hymns), which contains some early examples of prosulated melismas known as *sequences*.

Hymns), which dates from about 880, Notker recalls that in his youth he learned the practice from a monk who had escaped from an abbey in northwestern France after it had been laid waste by marauding "Normans" (that is, Vikings).[8] This would have been in 852, about twenty years after Amalar had first described the *sequentia* and promoted it among the Franks. The fleeing monk, Notker tells us, had with him a book of antiphons in which some *sequentia* melismas had words added. Notker leapt at this device for making memorable extra-long vocalises, what he calls *longissimae melodiae,* what we now call the ***sequence.***

The opening melodic phrase of Notker's *Rex regum* (Ex. 1-16) is artfully derived from the Alleluia *Justus ut palma* (cf. Ex. 1-13); there are other similarities between the two melodies as well. The sequence may thus have been meant to link up with that particular Alleluia, but there is no reason to suppose it would have been limited to such use. The melodic resemblance is only approximate and thus has the effect of an allusion, like those in the text, that might compliment any distinguished churchman.

Example 1-16 Sequence by Notker Balbulus, *Rex regum* (opening)

King of kings, our God, celebrate!
You guide the Christian army
in the dreadful battle . . .

The sequence, which came to be a syllabically texted chant with a double versicle structure, was one of the indigenous Frankish contributions to the evolving Roman liturgy, on a par with the Alleluia that it followed and the Gospel reading that it preceded. In the sixteenth century, during the reforms of the so-called Counter-Reformation, all but four sequences were eliminated from the service. The fortunate four were those for Easter (*Victimae paschali laudes*), Pentecost (*Veni sancte spiritus*), Corpus Christi (*Lauda Sion*, by St. Thomas Aquinas), and the Requiem Mass (*Dies irae*).

Anthology Vol 1-5a
Full CD/Concise CD I, 14

Anthology Vol 1-5b
Full CD/Concise CD I, 15

Dies irae (Day of Wrath) is an example of a sequence in metrical verse, in this instance rhyming (Ex. 1-17). Settings of such texts, especially rhymed metrical sequences, are often called *versus* to distinguish them from prose settings. *Dies irae* comes from the Mass for the Dead and is probably the most famous of all Medieval liturgical songs. It is a very late one, perhaps even a thirteenth-century composition, for the text, in rhymed three-line stanzas, is attributed to Thomas of Celano (d. ca. 1255). In its full form the *Dies irae* has three paired versicles that repeat like a litany: AABBCC/AABBCC/AABBC, with the last C replaced by a final couplet, to which an additional unrhymed couplet and an Amen were added by an anonymous reviser. (Example 1-17 gives the first versicle.)

Example 1-17 ***Dies irae*** **(Requiem)**

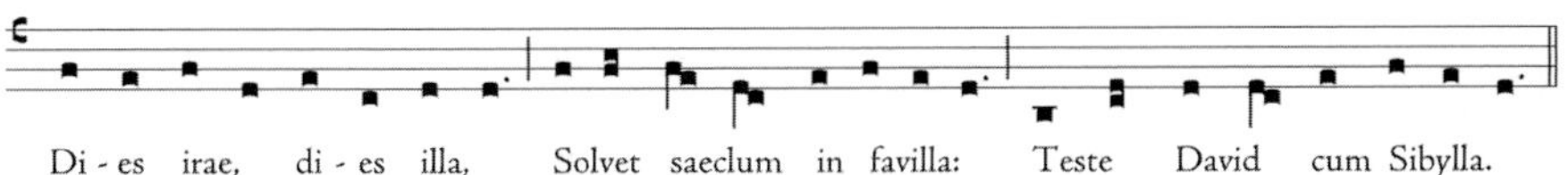
Di - es irae, di - es illa, Solvet saeclum in favilla: Teste David cum Sibylla.

Dreaded day, that day of ire,
When the world shall melt in fire,
Told by Sybil and David's lyre.

Altogether different were the remarkable contemporaneous sequences of Hildegard of Bingen (1098–1179; Fig. 1-12), one of the most formidable figures of the Middle Ages. Because St. Paul had declared that women should remain silent in churches (1 Corinthians 14:34–35), it is hardly surprising that we do not find women writing music for public services. But the secluded life of convents was different. Hildegard was the tenth child of a noble family who lived near the Rhine River. At age eight her parents decided that her life would be devoted to the church, and six years later she entered a Benedictine monastery. Eventually she established her own convent at Rupertsberg in the Rhine Valley near the German city of Trier. As abbess (the head of the convent) she devoted herself not only to guiding this institution but also to a wide range of spiritual and intellectual activities. She wrote on scientific matters and on her own mystic visions. She also produced a large amount of poetry and music, using it to express a visionary "symphony of the harmony of heavenly revelations" (*symphonia armonie celestium revelationum*), as she called her collected works, assembled by the late 1150s. Besides her sequences, the book contains antiphons, responsories, hymns, and Kyries.

Figure 1-12 Hildegard of Bingen, the twelfth-century abbess of Rupertsberg, writing down her visions (or, possibly, her chants). The illustration comes from a manuscript of her treatise *Scivias* ("Know the ways of the Lord") called the *Codex Rupertsberg*. It disappeared during World War II.

Hildegard's melodies often have an extraordinary range from lowest to highest notes, up to two and a half octaves, and sometimes wide leaps of intervals as well. In the sequence *Columba aspexit* ("The dove looked in") for the commemoration feast of St. Maximinus, a local saint of Trier, the versicles are paired in the traditional way, but loosely and not always corresponding in syllable count (Ex. 1-18). Compared with the literal repetition characteristic of the late Medieval sequence, Hildegard's melodic parallelism seems more to resemble a process of variation. The imagery, much of it derived from the Song of Songs, evokes strong sensory impressions, especially implicating the sense of smell. It produces an immensity of feeling we associate with revelation rather than reflection. Hildegard's is a lyricism of mystical immediacy.

Anthology Vol 1-6
Full CD/Concise CD I, 16

Example 1-18 Hildegard of Bingen, *Columba aspexit* (opening)

Co - lum - ba as - pex - it

per can - sel - los fe - nes - tre

u - bi an - te fa - ci - em e - ius

su - dan - do su - dan bal - sa - mum

de lu - ci - do Ma - xi - mi - no.

The dove peered in
through the lattices of the window
where, before its face,
a balm exuded
from incandescent Maximinus.

Hymns, Tropes, and Liturgical Drama

The sequence was only one of many new musical forms with which the Franks amplified the imported Roman chant and made it their own. The strophic Office hymn was another genre avidly cultivated. Hymnody is the apparent antithesis of psalmody. Where psalms are lofty and numinous, inviting spiritual repose and contemplation, hymns are the liturgy's popular songs: markedly rhythmical, strongly profiled in melody, conducive to enthusiasm.

Anthology Vol 1-7a-c
Full CD/Concise CD I, 17–19

Some hymn melodies became very famous and later formed the basis for celebrated polyphonic settings by leading composers. *Ave maris stella* ("Hail, Star of the sea"; Anthology Volume 1-7a) is an acclamation to the Blessed Virgin Mary with a rather decoratively neumatic tune (Ex. 1-19). The words to *Pange lingua gloriosi* ("Sing, O my tongue") were by the greatest Latin hymn writer around the time of Pope Gregory, Venantius Fortunatus (d. ca. 600), whose metrical scheme was widely imitated by later hymn composers. The version given in Anthology Volume 1-7b is not Venantius's original but a reworking by St. Thomas Aquinas (d. 1274), composed for the Office of Corpus Christi (veneration of the body of Christ), so in this case the melody is far older than the words. *Veni creator spiritus* (Anthology Volume 1-7c), the great Pentecost hymn, employs the so-called Ambrosian stanza (four lines of eight syllables each), established by St. Ambrose, the original Latin hymnodist five centuries before; but the dynamically arching melody, its successive phrases marking cadences on what we still identify as "primary" scale degrees, is of exemplary Frankish design.

Example 1-19 ***Ave maris stella***

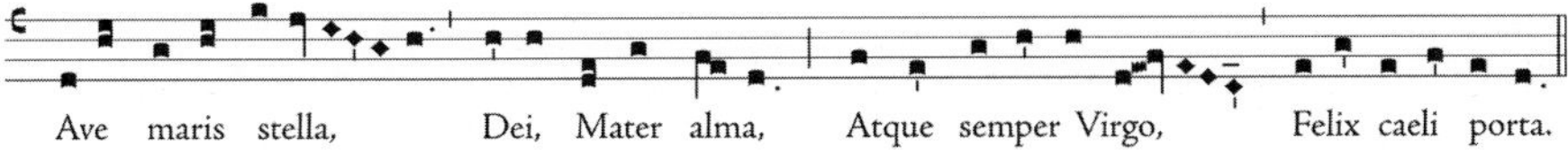
Ave maris stella, Dei, Mater alma, Atque semper Virgo, Felix caeli porta.

Hail, thou Star of the sea, ever Virgin Mother of the Lord most high, portal of the sky.

Sequences and hymns were complete compositions in their own right—freestanding songs, so to speak. Another large category of Frankish compositional innovations consisted of chants that did not stand alone but were attached in various ways to other chants, usually to older, canonical (that is, officially established) ones. This was often accomplished by attaching the new addition as a preface, to amplify and interpret the old one for the benefit of contemporary worshipers. The added material (music, words, or both) was called a ***trope***. Tropes began to be cultivated most intensely in the tenth century and the primary sites of troping were the chants of the Mass Proper. Attached most characteristically to the Introit, the trope became a comment on the Mass as a whole, as if to say, "We are celebrating Mass today, and this is the reason." Tropes were also attached to the other Gregorian chants that accompanied ritual action, especially the Offertory ("We are offering gifts, and this is the reason") and the Communion ("We are tasting the wine and the bread, and this is the reason"). Tropes could be placed in between lines and phrases of a chant or at the end of a chant. Whether they came before, during, or after, the common idea was to enhance and individualize services.

Manuscripts containing tropes, called *tropers*, are particularly associated with two monasteries. One is the East Frankish monastery of St. Gall, where Notker Balbulus played his part in the development of the **sequence** and where the monk Tuotilo (d. 915) may have had a similar hand in the development of the trope. The other is the West Frankish monastery of St. Martial at Limoges in southwestern France, part of the Duchy of Aquitaine.

In the St. Martial tropers we find various tropes that were meant to enlarge on the Introit of the Easter Sunday Mass. The canonical text of the Introit consists of excerpts from three verses of Psalm 138, words that by the ninth century already had a long tradition of Christian doctrinal interpretation. Within the original pre-Christian Psalm, the verse excerpt that opens the Introit—*Resurrexi, et adhuc tecum sum* ("I arose, and am still with thee")—refers to an awakening from sleep. Amalar of Metz was one of the many Christian commentators who interpreted these words as referring prophetically to the event the Easter Mass celebrates: Christ's resurrection from the dead after his crucifixion. One of the functions of the tropes was to confirm this interpretation and make it explicit. The most famous of all tropes are those that recount the visit of the three Marys to Christ's tomb on the morning after his burial (Fig. 1-13) *Quem quaeritis in sepulchro* ("Whom do you seek in the tomb?") is in the form of a dialogue between the women and the angel who announces the Resurrection, thus furnishing a very neat transition into the Introit text (Ex. 1-20). Tropes like this one were the earliest and simplest of what

Anthology Vol 1-8a
Full CD/Concise CD I, 20

Anthology Vol 1-8b
Full CD/Concise CD I, 21

eventually became a large repertory of Latin church plays with music, sometimes called "liturgical dramas."

Example 1-20 Easter dialogue trope (*Quem quaeritis in sepulchro*)

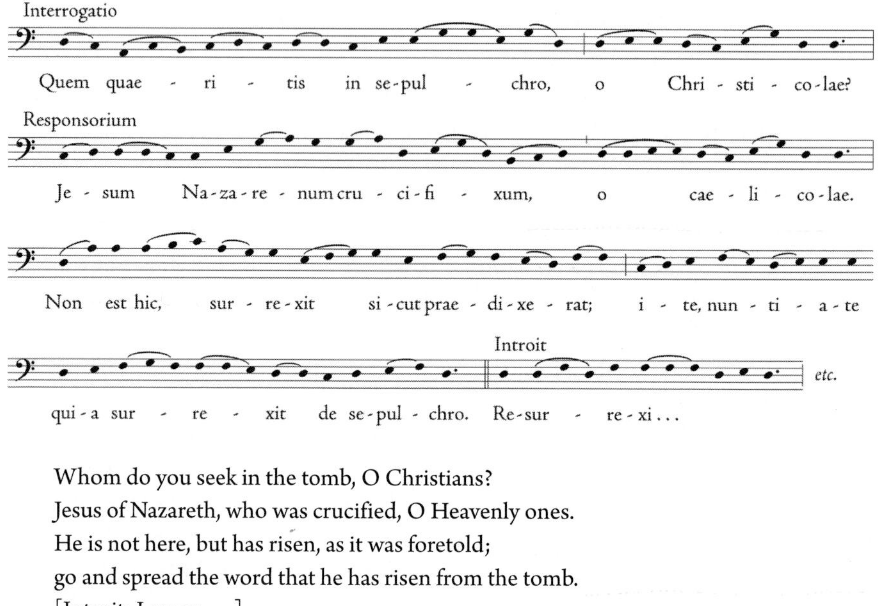

Whom do you seek in the tomb, O Christians?
Jesus of Nazareth, who was crucified, O Heavenly ones.
He is not here, but has risen, as it was foretold;
go and spread the word that he has risen from the tomb.
[Introit: I arose . . .]

Figure 1-13 *Holy Women at the Sepulchre* from the *Armadio degli Argenti* (Silver Chest) painting series by Fra Angelico around 1450.

The sung verse play in Latin was truly a craze in northern Europe and England by the twelfth century, and space in churches was increasingly given over to dramatic representations of various kinds on major festival occasions. Such plays begin to appear in written sources in the tenth century, and it is probably no accident that the earliest ones enact the same episode as the tropes to the Easter and Christmas Introits: the visit of the women (or the Magi, the "three wise men") to Christ's tomb (or his birthplace in a manger) and their meeting with an angel. Like the tropes and sequences, the church plays evolved—between the tenth and twelfth centuries—from a prose into a verse genre. Twelfth-century liturgical dramas were elaborate combinations of newly composed versus, older hymns and sequences, and Gregorian antiphons, these being retained as a kind of scriptural allusion or invocation.

Their subjects also included dramatizations of the risen Christ's appearances to his disciples, shepherds' plays for Christmas, the slaughter of the Holy Innocents (sometimes called the "play of Herod"), the wise and foolish virgins, the raising of Lazarus, the miracles of St. Nicholas, and the so-called play of Daniel. It is clear that such church plays were a part of the same impulse to adorn and amplify the liturgy that produced the sequence, the trope, and all the other specifically Frankish liturgical genres surveyed earlier. A particularly notable example is Hildegard of Bingen's largest work, a play with music called *Ordo virtutum* (The Enactment of the Virtues). In it, the devil and the sixteen virtues do battle for the possession of a Christian soul. It is by far the oldest existing example of what is now called the "morality play," a form of allegorical drama in which the actors personify virtues and vices.

Marian Antiphons

The latest genre of Medieval chant to be incorporated (in some part) into the canonical liturgy was the votive antiphon. Votive antiphons were nonpsalmic antiphons—that is, independent Latin songs—attached to the ends of Office services to honor or appeal to local saints or to the Virgin Mary. As a human chosen by God to bear His son, Mary was thought to mediate between the human and the divine even more powerfully than did the other saints.

One fanciful image casts Mary as the "neck" connecting the Godhead and the body of the Christian congregation. As such she was the natural recipient of personal prayers or devotional vows. From the cult of Mary arose the **Marian antiphon**, or "anthems to the Blessed Virgin Mary." Our English word *anthem*, meaning a song of praise or devotion, now as often patriotic as religious, comes from "antiphon." These ample songs of salutation to the Mother of God appear in great numbers in written sources beginning early in the eleventh century. By the middle of the thirteenth, a few had been adopted for ordinary use in monasteries to conclude the Compline service at the end of the liturgical day. At English cathedrals they enhanced the Evensong service, which lay worshipers attended. It was to keep these prayers for intercession going in perpetuity that the "choral foundations"—endowments to fund the training of choristers—were set up at English cathedrals and university chapels. They have lasted to this day.

At first the Marian antiphons were sung, like the psalms, in a weekly cycle. In the liturgy today, only four remain, and they follow a seasonal round. In winter the anthem is the penitential *Alma Redemptoris Mater* ("Sweet Mother of the Redeemer . . . have pity on us sinners"); in spring it is the panegyric *Ave Regina coelorum* ("Hail, O Queen of the heavens"). For the exultant fifty-day period between Easter and Pentecost, known as Paschal Time, *Regina caeli, laetare* ("O Queen of heaven, rejoice") is the prescribed antiphon; and during the remaining largest portion of the year, encompassing late summer and fall, it is *Salve, Regina* ("Hail, O Queen"), the best known of the Marian antiphons.

Anthology Vol 1-9a-b
Full CD/Concise CD I, 22–23

How to Do Polyphony

To generalize from the fact that all the music we have looked at so far has been monophonic would be very misleading. There has never been a time in the recorded history of European music—or of any music, it seems—when **polyphony** was unknown. Descriptions of music making in ancient Greece and Rome offer tantalizing suggestions about harmonic and contrapuntal practices, and music theory is full of elaborate accounts of harmonic consonances. As soon as the Franks could write down their liturgical music, they illustrated assorted methods of harmonically amplifying that music. We have evidence of polyphonic performance practice for Medieval chant as early as we have written evidence of the chant itself.

Although more is known about sacred music, reports of secular part singing are likewise enticing. In the late twelfth century a Welsh churchman and historian who wrote under the name Giraldus Cambrensis gave this description of his countrymen: "They sing their tunes not in unison, but in parts with many simultaneous modes and phrases. Therefore, in a group of singers you will hear as many melodies as there you will see heads, yet they all accord in one consonant and properly constituted composition." Giraldus also commented enthusiastically on the virtuosity of instrumentalists, specifically ones playing the harp who performed "with such smooth rapidity, such unequaled evenness, such mellifluous harmony throughout the varied tunes and the many intricacies of the part music."[9]

So, written or not, polyphony was always there in the Western musical tradition. As with any other kind of music, its entry into written sources was not any sort of "event" in its history. And by the same token, there is no point at which polyphony completely replaced monophony in the history of Western music. For example, in the middle of the fifteenth century the celebrated composer Guillaume Du Fay wrote elaborate monophonic Office chants, a reminder that the march of musical genres and styles down through the ages in single file is something historians, not composers, have created.[10] Yet even granting all of this, we can still identify the extraordinary twelfth century as the one in which European musical practice took a decisive turn toward polyphonic composition.

If we are interested in isolating the fundamental distinguishing feature of what may be called Western music, this might as well be it. After this turning point, polyphonic composition in the West would be indisputably, increasingly, and characteristically the norm. From then on, stylistic development would essentially mean the development of techniques for polyphonic composition. Training in composition would thenceforth be basically training in polyphony—in harmony and counterpoint, the controlled combination of different pitches in time—and such training would become ever more sophisticated. Combination, the creation of order and expressivity out of diversity, became the very definition of music. During the later

Middle Ages, music was often called the *ars combinatoria* or the *discordia concors*: the "art of combining things" or the "concord of discord." This underscores the new preoccupation with polyphony while reconciling it with older notions of music as an all-embracing cosmic harmony.

So what might be called the polyphonic revolution, while real, should not be mistaken for the beginning or the invention or the discovery of polyphony. It was, rather, the coalescing into compositional procedure of what had always been a performance option. The great spur to this vastly accelerated development of compositional technique was not so much a change in taste as it was a change in educational philosophy. The twelfth century was the century in which the primary place of education shifted first from monasteries to urban cathedral schools and then to new universities. In the course of this shift, Paris emerged as the intellectual center of Europe. The blossoming of polyphonic composition followed the same trajectory. Beginning in monasteries, it reached its first great, transforming culmination in the cathedral schools of Paris, and in a new form it radiated from that cosmopolitan center throughout Western Christendom, finding a special place in the universities.

Symphonia and Its Modifications

Polyphony will therefore be most of our story in the pages to follow. To end this first chapter, let us look at some of the earliest scattered written manifestations. As a performance practice associated with plainchant, polyphony makes its documentary debut in the *Musica enchiriadis* (Handbook of Music), the first surviving Frankish treatise about practical music making, which is thought to date from some time between 860 and 900, and in a longer contemporary commentary to it, called the *Scolica enchiriadis* (Commentary on the Handbook).

There were two basic techniques of embellishing a melody harmonically. One consists of simply accompanying a melody in bagpipe fashion, with a drone on the final note of the mode. That method still survives as a traditional way of performing the Byzantine chant of the Orthodox Church. The other technique consisted of "parallel doubling"—that is, accompanying a melody with a transposition of itself at a constant consonant interval below; this was known by the Greek term *symphonia*. Three intervals were considered eligible for this purpose; they are the ones we still call "perfect" (fourth, fifth, and octave). The combined voices produced what was called ***organum***.

After the extraordinary twelfth century, polyphonic composition in the West would be indisputably, increasingly, and characteristically the norm.

An original chant, the *vox principalis* (principal voice), would be doubled at one or more of those intervals by a lower *vox organalis* (organal voice). As Examples 1-21a and 1-21b show, these simple devices were actually practiced in a complex synthesis requiring considerable artistry—which is why a "how to" treatise needed to be written about them in the first place. The reason why parallel doubling is not acceptable without modification is because of the tritone, a prohibited dissonance. (It was later known as the *diabolus in musica*—the "devil in music.") In an organum, if a given diatonic melody is doubled at a constant fourth or fifth below, then dissonant tritones will emerge whenever the note B has to be doubled at the fourth or the note F at the fifth. Adjustment of the doubling vox organalis at these places eliminates tritones against the original chant.

Example 1-21a Parallel organum at the octave

We who live praise the Lord now and in eternity.

Example 1-21b Parallel organum at the fifth

A compromise between theory and practice was required. The author of the *Scolica enchiriadis* shows a solution when constructing an example to illustrate parallel doubling at the perfect fourth. The two lines end on the same final note, that is, on a unison. In order to meet, of course, they must stop being parallel and instead approach the final note in contrary motion. Such an approach is called an ***occursus***, literally "a meeting." In order to smooth the way to the occursus and to avoid tritones, the vox organalis begins to behave like a drone—or like a sequence of drones. Instead of following the contour of the vox principalis, the vox organalis hugs first the D and then the C, moving from the one to the other when the opportunity presents itself to recover the correct symphonia (perfect fourth) against a repeated note in the vox principalis (Ex. 1-22a). The added voices above and below the vox principalis behave similarly in Example 1-22b, a composite organum simultaneously demonstrating octaves, fifths, and fourths.

Example 1-22a Organum at the fourth

Example 1-22b Composite parallel organum

Nos qui vivimus, benedicimus Do-mi-no, ex hoc nunc et us-que in sae-cu-lum.

When the vox organalis moves in this modified, somewhat independent way, using not just parallel motion in relation to the original chant but oblique (one remaining in place, the other moving) and contrary motion as well, a variety of harmonic intervals are introduced into the texture, and the resulting voice part can be described as a true counterpoint (a word derived from the Latin *punctus contra punctum*, in English "point against point" or "note against note"). The intervals are ordered hierarchically. In addition to the actual symphonia (here the perfect consonance of the fourth), Examples 1-22a and 1-22b contain thirds and unisons. The organum setting of the sequence *Rex caeli* from *Musica enchiriadis* contains actual dissonances (Ex. 1-23; Fig. 1-14). The vox organalis begins with a dronelike stretch against which the vox principalis rises by step from unison until the symphonia, in this case the perfect fourth again, is reached. Its second note, then, forms a "passing" dissonant second against the accompanying voice. The thirds, "imperfect" consonances, are contrapuntally subordinate: a vox organalis can move only to a perfect consonance; the thirds can occur only over a stationary accompaniment. Thus the fourth, being unrestricted in its possible occurrences, is "functionally consonant" according to the style-determining rules here in force, while the third is "functionally dissonant."

Example 1-23 ***Rex caeli Domine*** **from** ***Musica enchiriadis*** **transcribed**

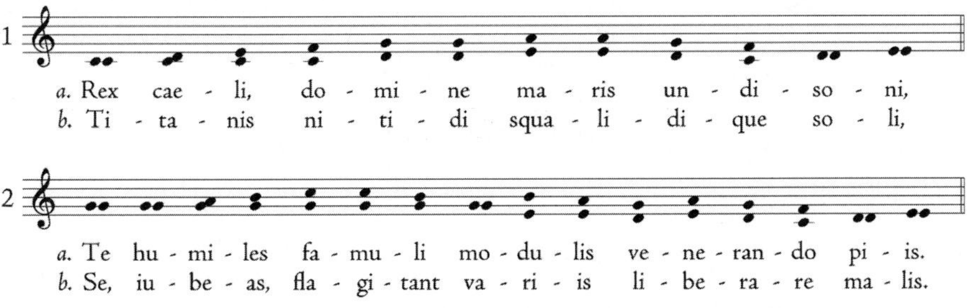

King of heaven, Lord of the wave-sounding sea, of the shining Titan and of the dark earth, Thy humble servants entreat Thee, by worshipping Thee with pious words as Thou hast commanded, to free them from their sundry ills.

Figure 1-14 *Rex caeli Domine*, a sequence-like hymn probably dating from the ninth century.
(a) Its most complete source, a French manuscript from the tenth century written in an alphabetic notation that specifies pitch precisely. (b) Its earliest source, the treatise *Musica enchiriadis*, shows a fragment of it, adapted to illustrate a common practice whereby monophonic chants were amplified polyphonically in performance. This provides evidence of polyphony as early as any evidence of the chant itself.

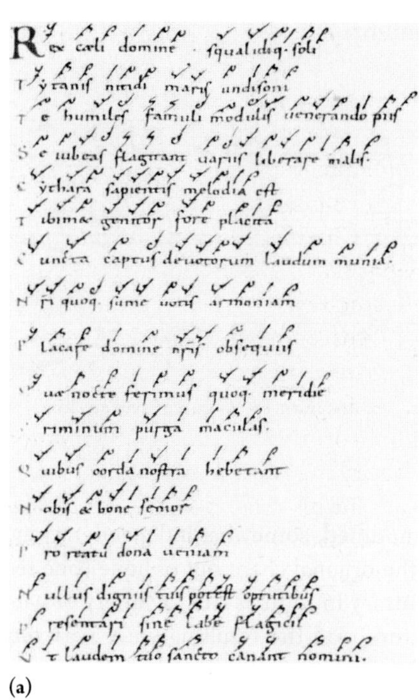

(a)

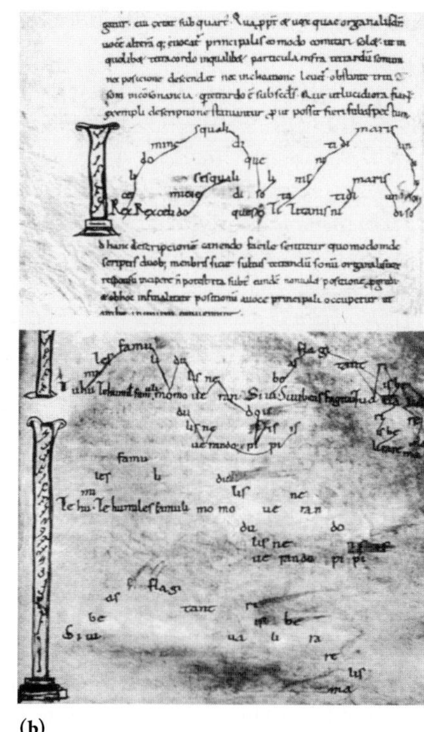

(b)

Organum and Discant

Guido of Arezzo made a decisive contribution to the development of contrapuntal technique. In his *Micrologus*, he devoted one section to a discussion of organum in which he emphasized obtaining maximum variety in interval succession and on fashioning a good occursus. Guido illustrated his points with examples; but he also gave more than one solution to contrapuntal problems, between which the student was invited to choose *ad libitum*, "at pleasure." For instance, Example 1-24 shows two counterpoints to a psalm that produce the same occursus, in one case by direct leap to the final, in the other by the use of a passing tone to smooth the way.

Example 1-24 Guido of Arezzo, *Micrologus*; Two counterpoints to *Jherusalem*

(vox principalis in white noteheads, vox organalis in black)

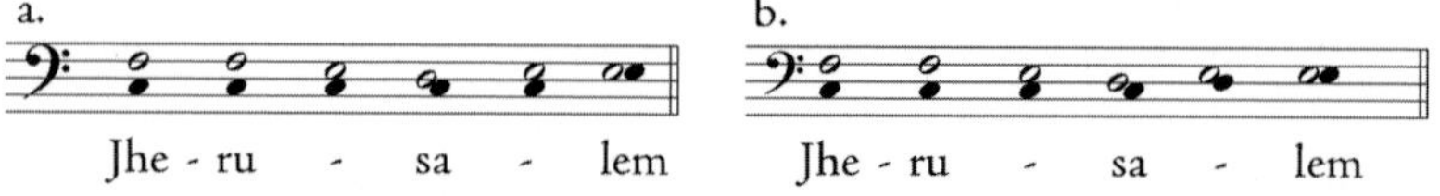

After Boethius's *De institutione musica*, Guido's *Micrologus* was the most widely disseminated book on music theory before the age of printing. Most monastery or cathedral libraries had a copy, and it was used in primary music instruction as late as the fifteenth century. We should not be surprised to discover its influence in the places were polyphonic composition began to flower. One of the earliest was at Winchester, in southeast England, where a huge collection of polyphonic tropes is found in a manuscript copied over a ten-year period ending in 1006. The so-called Winchester Tropers are notated in staffless neumes, showing that the Winchester cantors sang their counterpoints by heart. We cannot decipher them with much precision, but their contours definitely accord with Guidonian preferences regarding voice crossing and occursus.

The earliest fully legible practical source of composed polyphonic music is a late-eleventh-century fragment from the town of Chartres, southwest of Paris, containing Alleluia verses and processional antiphons set in two-part, note-against-note counterpoint. There is virtually no parallel doubling; nor is there much note repetition in the *vox organalis*, even when the original chant has a repeated note. Instead, there is pervasive contrary motion and ceaseless intervallic variety (Ex. 1-25). The style of counterpoint exemplified in the Chartres fragment strikingly resembles the one described by John of Afflighem, a Flemish theorist of the early twelfth century, in his treatise *De musica*. In the later twelfth century this style would become known as *discantus*, or "descant." The Latin word means literally "singing apart," thus "singing in parts." Music historians generally prefer "discant" to "descant" as an English equivalent when referring to Medieval polyphony.

Example 1-25 ***Dicant nunc judei***

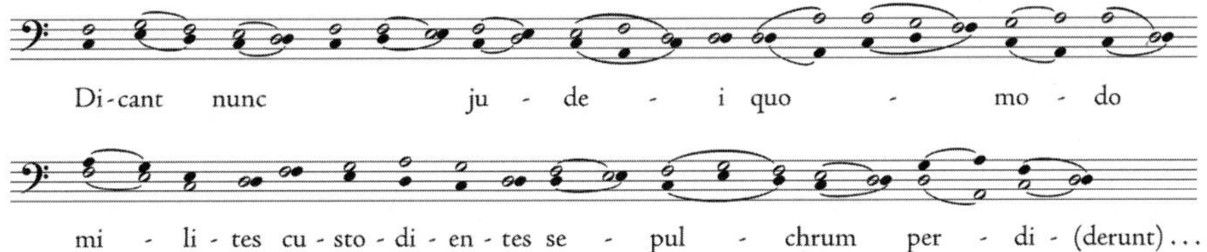

Now the Jews said, "How did the soldiers guarding the tomb lose [the risen Christ]?"

The contrapuntal principles we have observed here remained the bedrock principles of Western polyphonic practice for centuries. The art of counterpoint is most economically defined as the art of balancing normative harmonies ("consonances") and subordinate ones ("dissonances") and elaborating rules for "handling" the latter. The quotes around the terms are a reminder that criteria of consonance and dissonance are culture bound, hence relative and changeable, and are best described not on the basis of their sound as such but on the basis of how they function within a style. The styles we all assimilate today in the process of acculturation as we go from birth onward teach us to hear and to use intervals in a specific way. We have all been trained to "hear" thirds as consonances and fourths as dissonances.

Literate Music and the Persistence of Oral Traditions

It should be emphasized that the instructional examples found in "how to" books are not polyphonic "compositions." Rather, they give some idea of how Medieval church musicians harmonized the chants they sang "by ear." The monks who notated our first examples of polyphony were adapting it from oral practice, very likely connected with secular music making.

This situation may prompt us to ponder what in fact constitutes an actual musical composition, a so-called "piece of music." The answer is not self-evident. We often read great literature in translation and see visual works of art in reproductions, but it is nonetheless pretty clear what a sonnet by Shakespeare is, or a painting by Leonardo da Vinci. But with music there are usually mediating factors that complicate the matter, especially when notation, printing, and sound recording are taken into account. As this book traces the history of literate music in the West we will return to the issue time and time again.

We have all to some degree now fallen prey to the danger about which Plato warned long ago: "If men learn writing, it will implant forgetfulness in their souls."

Our principal concern here is music that has been objectified as "art." This happened in stages, including the crucially momentous one in which music was first written down. With the advent of commercial music printing almost exactly 500 years ago (and thus some 500 years after the introduction of music writing), reproduction became easy and cheap. Music could now be disseminated much more widely than ever before and much more impersonally. Later still, around 1900, the advent of sound recording led to new methods of music preservation, from early phonograph cylinders and 78 rpm records to compact discs and iPods.

While this chapter has concentrated on how the development of musical notation raised the curtain on our knowledge of surviving music beginning about a millennium ago, writing certainly did not end the oral tradition. Manuscripts with unheighted neumes went on being produced in Frankish monastic centers until the fifteenth century, which shows that the transmission of melodies went right on being accomplished by age-old oral/aural methods, that is, by listening, repeating, and memorizing. Most monks still learn their chants that way—as do many churchgoers. Notation did not supersede memory, and it never has. After a thousand years of pitch notation, 500 years of printing, and a couple generations of inexpensive photocopying, Western "art musicians" and music students have become so dependent on written texts that it is hard to imagine minds that could really use their memories—not just to store melodies by the thousand but to create them as well. We have all to some degree now fallen prey to the danger about which Plato warned long ago: "If men learn writing, it will implant forgetfulness in their souls" (*Phaedrus*, 275a).

As is clear from a great amount of music making all over the world today, musical composition in an oral context should not be confused with improvisation. While some forms of orally transmitted music do enlist the spontaneous creative faculty in real time (a good bit of jazz, for example), there have always been musicians who work out compositions without notation yet meticulously, in detail, and in advance (most of today's rock bands). They fix their work in memory in the very act of creating it so that it will be permanent. Every performance is expected more or less to resemble every other one, although this does not preclude spontaneity or improvement over time.

So in no way did literacy suddenly replace orality as a means of musical transmission. Ever since the time of the earliest Carolingian musical manuscripts, the oral and literate means of transmission have coexisted in the West in a complex, ever-evolving symbiosis. There are plenty of familiar tunes that are still transmitted within our culture almost exclusively by oral means: national anthems, patriotic and holiday songs ("America," "Jingle Bells"), songs for occasional use ("Happy Birthday"), folk songs ("Home on the Range"), spirituals ("Amazing Grace"), as well as a vast repertory of children's songs ("It's Raining, It's Pouring"). Yet while almost every reader of this book will be able to sing these songs by heart, very few will have ever seen their "sheet music."

At the same time, the literate Western music most associated with the classical tradition—like sonatas, symphonies, and operas—actually relies for its transmission on a large amount of oral mediation. By aural example teachers demonstrate to their pupils many crucial aspects of performance—such as nuances of dynamics, articulation, phrasing, even rhythmic execution—that are not conveyed by (or are only inadequately conveyed by) even the most detailed notation. Conductors communicate their "interpretations" by singing, shouting, grunting, gesticulating. Not only jazz performers, but classical ones, too, copy the performances of famous artists from recordings as part of their learning process. All of this is just as oral a means of transmission as anything that may have happened in earlier times.

Musical notation is always incomplete and inadequate, despite becoming much more specific over the centuries. We will have many occasions to investigate the consequences of the act of writing music down, of trying to capture a sounding phenomenon as an object. Since the written artifacts of musical notation translate music that unfolds in time into objects that occupy space, we can think of literate musical cultures as cultures that tend conceptually to substitute space for time—that is, to spatialize the temporal.

Summary

The history of written music in the West begins with the music for the services of the Roman Catholic Church. For reasons that were political as much as religious, this chant repertory came to be viewed as an authoritative musical tradition. On Christmas Day in the year 800 Pope Leo III crowned King Charles I, known as Charlemagne, as secular ruler (with Leo himself as spiritual ruler) of the Western Roman Empire. To symbolize the authority of the resulting alliance with Rome, the Carolingian kings mandated that the entire kingdom adopt the Roman order of service (called the liturgy) and the music that was part of that service. This Frankish version of Roman chant, first recorded in notation in the late ninth century, became known as "Gregorian chant" because of a ninth-century legend that Pope Gregory the Great (d. 604) received these chant melodies through the divine intervention of the Holy Spirit. This legend underscored the authority of the Roman chant over other local practices, including the Ambrosian, Mozarabic, and Gallican in other parts of Europe.

Gregorian chant was sung in two types of service, the Mass and the Office. The Office was a series of eight daily prayer services, the most elaborate of which was the night vigil known as Matins. The Mass begins with a series of readings and then proceeds to the Eucharist, reenacting the Last Supper of Jesus and his disciples. In addition to the weekly Mass, other Christian celebrations were organized in a yearly cycle that commemorated events in the life of Christ and certain saints. The full year required the performance of hundreds of chants. One group of Mass texts, known as the Ordinary, had invariable texts that were sung at each service. Another group, known as the Proper, varied according to the yearly cycle. In the Mass, the Proper chants accompanied specific actions of the liturgy, beginning with the entrance chant called the Introit. The Gradual and Alleluia were sung between readings, the Offertory during the preparation of bread and wine, and the Communion at the distribution of bread and wine. Interspersed among these were the Ordinary chants: Kyrie, Gloria, Credo, Sanctus, and Agnus Dei.

Gregorian chant is varied in musical style. Simple melodic formulas for singing psalms, known as psalm tones, were performed with a short section of music called an antiphon. Other chants are much more elaborate. The Gradual and Alleluia, for example, have lengthy, wordless melismas in which a single syllable is stretched through many musical notes or phrases and alternate between a choir and a soloist.

The chant the Franks received from the Romans was an oral tradition. As it gained an authoritative status, the Franks saw a need to systematize and preserve the melodies. For this reason, they invented musical notation and adapted existing music theories to create a system of eight modes. The notational signs known as neumes, which first appear in the ninth century, at first showed the contour of the melodies but not their specific pitches, serving as a memory aid but not as a way to transmit unfamiliar music. Notation became fully pitch-readable in the eleventh century. The church modes arose through a fusion of concepts borrowed from Byzantine chant and ancient Greek modal theory. In its fully developed form, modal theory categorizes each chant by its final pitch, D, E, F, or G, and by its ambitus, or range. Theorists further explained the modes in terms of the interval patterns surrounding each final. To help singers learn where to place the semitones, Guido of Arezzo (ca. 990–1033) invented solmization, a mnemonic device in which intervals were associated with syllables.

Between the ninth and twelfth centuries, the Franks expanded the existing repertory in various ways. New melismas could be added to existing chants, and new texts could be added to existing melismas. A trope was an addition of new words and music to an existing chant, often providing a commentary on its text. The sequence was a newly created poetic text, set in a syllabic style (one note per syllable) and performed after the Alleluia of the Mass. Other new compositions included the hymn, a strophic setting of poetry performed in the Office.

While Gregorian chant was monophonic (consisting of a single line), early polyphony (music combining two or more lines) also began to be written down in the Middle Ages, often reflecting older, previously unwritten practices. The earliest polyphony in the written tradition was formed simply by doubling a chant in parallel motion a fourth, fifth, or octave lower, producing a kind of polyphony called organum. The two voices would come together in unison at the end of a phrase. The earliest manual for creating polyphony, the ninth-century *Musica enchiriadis* (Music Handbook, ca. 860–910), gives extensive instructions for making an added voice that avoids the undesirable interval of the tritone. Over time, an increasingly wide range of intervals was permitted, as attested in Guido of Arezzo's treatise *Micrologus* (Little Treatise, ca. 1028) and in the earliest manuscripts to contain examples of polyphony, such as the Winchester Troper (completed ca. 1006).

Study Questions

1. Describe the role of music in ancient Greek society. How would you characterize Greek attitudes about music? What aspects of Greek musical thought have influenced Western music history?
2. What topics are addressed in Boethius's *De institutione musica*? How does this work reflect ancient Greek and medieval understandings of music?
3. What political circumstances led to the adoption of Roman chant in the Frankish kingdom? Why was the chant attributed to Gregory the Great?
4. Compare and contrast the four different settings of the text *Justus ut palma* discussed in this chapter. What are their main stylistic and formal features, and how might they have been used in context?
5. What do the earliest notations show about a chant melody, and what knowledge must the singer have in order to use the notation?
6. Explain the contributions of Guido of Arezzo to music theory and pedagogy, including solmization, the hexachord, and his theory of organum.
7. Focusing on the Ordinary, briefly describe the origins, text, and music for the chants of the Mass. How did each one fit into the liturgy?
8. Describe the new types of composition that arose between the ninth and eleventh centuries, including the trope, sequence, hymn, and Marian antiphon. What are the main characteristics of these genres, and how did they originate?
9. How did the sequences composed by Hildegard of Bingen compare with other Medieval sequences? In what other areas of musical and religious life was Hildegard active?
10. Explain at least two approaches to making polyphony. How was this taught in the *Musica enchiriadis* and *Scolica enchiriadis*? How did this practice change in the next two centuries?
11. Most of the music studied in this chapter falls on a spectrum between being oral and fully literate. In what ways did oral tradition persist after writing began? How do our assumptions about art and what constitutes a "piece" of music differ from those of the Middle Ages?

Key Terms

antiphon
Cantillation
church modes
diatonic
discant
Gregorian chant
Guidonian Hand
hexachord
hymn, hymnody
liturgy
Marian antiphon
Mass
melisma, melismatic
mode
monophony
musica
neume
occursus
Office
Ordinary
organum
polyphony
Proper
psalm (Psalter)
psalm tone
respond
sequence
solmization
trope

2

Secular and Cathedral Music in the High Middle Ages

One of the lessons we can learn from studying history is to appreciate the problems posed by rigidly oppositional distinctions and to try to resist them. Hard and fast antitheses, often called *binarisms,* tend to be conceptual rather than empirical; that is, they are more likely to be found in the clean laboratories of our minds than in the messy world our bodies inhabit. (And even to say this much is to commit several errors of arbitrary opposition.) One can hardly avoid categories; they simplify experience and, above all, simplify the stories we tell. They make things intelligible. Without them, writing a book like this—let alone reading it—would be virtually impossible. They involve sacrifice, however, as well as gain.

The invention of staff notation, presented in the first chapter as a great victory, is a case in point. The gain in (apparent) precision was accompanied by a definite loss in variety. The staff is nothing if not an instrument for imposing hard distinctions: between A and B, between B and C, and so forth. These distinctions are gross as well as hard; singing from a staff is like putting the frets of a guitar on one's vocal cords. One has only to compare the staffless neumes of early chant manuscripts with the staved notations that emerged to see how much more stylized notation had to become—and how much farther, we must conclude, from the oral practice it purported to transcribe—in order to furnish the precise information about pitch that we now prize. A whole category of ornamental neumes (called *liquescent,* implying fluidity, flexibility of voice, and, most likely, intonation "in the cracks") was sacrificed and eventually lost from practice. No one knows today exactly what they once signified. The precision of staff notation regularized certain aspects of music and made many developments possible. Yet at the same time it foreclosed other aspects and potential developments that other musical cultures have continued to cultivate. Anyone who has heard the classical music of Iran or

India will have an idea of what may have been lost from the European tradition.

At a more conceptual level, consider the binary distinction between sacred and secular. Up to this point only sacred music has figured in our story because only it was available for detailed examination. We are now about to encounter the earliest secular music that was written down in quantity and thus preserved. These are the first musical repertories that were not intended for use in divine worship but were nonetheless deemed worthy of keeping. On the basis of an overly firm distinction between the sacred and the secular (on which, for example, our present-day institutions of government depend), we may tend to assume that secular music will be radically different from sacred. Perhaps some of it was; the writings of the early Church Fathers abound in condemnations of "licentious songs."[1] But unfortunately we do not know those songs. We will never know exactly how much they may have differed from the music of which the Fathers approved, and we may even suspect that what made them objectionable had more to do with their words, the occasions at which they were sung, or the people who sang them than with their actual musical character. "Sacred" and "secular" are not so much styles as uses; we will encounter many fascinating intersections between them.

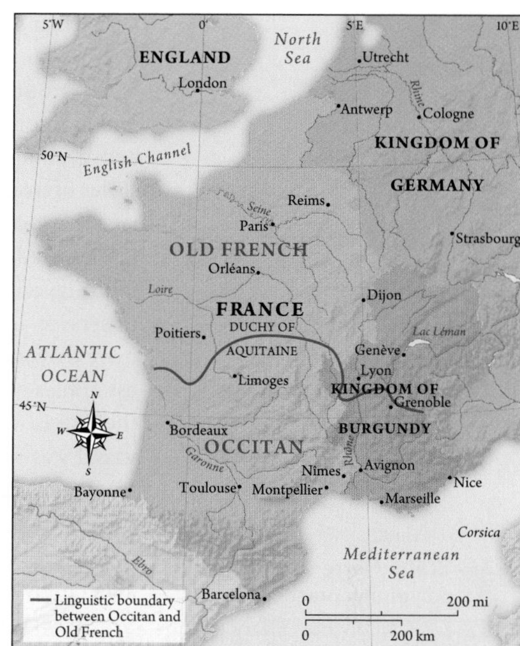

Figure 2-1 The Languedoc region in the twelfth century. Note the close proximity of Limoges, the monastic center, where Latin liturgical poetry to music was composed in profusion; and Poitiers, the center of troubadour activity.

Troubadours

The earliest secular repertories not in Latin of which we have direct knowledge consist of songs (*chansons*) by knightly poets. Stylistically, they are often remarkably like the sacred repertories with which we have been dealing so far. The first written-down knightly songs in a European vernacular (that is, a locally spoken language) originated in Aquitaine, a duchy whose territory occupied parts of what is now southern and south-central France. It had been conquered in the late eighth century by Charlemagne and incorporated into the Carolingian Empire. Over the course of the ninth and tenth centuries, as a result of invasions by Normans on one side and Muslims on the other, royal influence gave way to the dominance of several independent noble families. Eventually the counts of Poitou emerged as the most powerful among these clans and ruled the whole territory, beginning in 973. Later still, the marriage in 1137 of Eleanor of Aquitaine (ca. 1122–1204) to the French King Louis VI joined Aquitaine to France; two months after that marriage was annulled in 1152 (she had produced, not a male heir, but, rather, two daughters), Eleanor married the Norman duke who later became King Henry II of England, which led to a long struggle over the territory that lasted for centuries (Fig. 2-1).

It was during the period of Aquitaine's relative independence at the beginning of the millennium that its courtly poetic and musical traditions arose. William (Guillaume), seventh count of Poitiers and ninth duke of Aquitaine (1071–1126), was the first European vernacular poet whose work has come down to us. Thus the tradition, socially speaking, began right at the top, with all that that implies as to "highness" of style, tone, and diction. The language William IX used was *Provençal,* alias *Occitan,* or *langue d'oc* (from the local word for "yes"). In Provençal, poetry was called *trobar,* meaning words "found," and a poet was called a *trobador,* a "finder" of words. (In English we use the Frenchified form, **troubadour.**) Old French, the

TIMELINE

1088 University of Bologna founded

1096–99 The First Crusade

1100–1200 Troubadour tradition flourishes in southern France

ca. 1100–50 St. Martial polyphony practiced

1128 Cathedral of Santiago de Compostela consecrated in Spain

1137 Eleanor of Aquitaine marries future King Louis VII of France

1150–1250 Notre Dame polyphony practiced

1152 Louis VII divorces Eleanor of Aquitaine, who marries future King Henry II of England

ca. 1160–1300 Trouvère tradition flourishes in northern France

ca. 1160 University of Paris founded

1163 Construction of Notre Dame Cathedral begins

1167 University of Oxford founded

vernacular spoken to the north, was called *langue d'oïl* and was used somewhat later by poet-musicians there who called themselves ***trouvères***.

A troubadour's subject matter was the life he led, viewed in terms of his social and amorous relations, which were ceremonial, idealized, and ritualized to a point approaching the sacred. In keeping with the rarefied subject matter, the genres and styles of troubadour verse were highly formalized. Many songs dealt with feudal service that reflected the hierarchical structure of lords and vassals. Feudalism, arising in unsettled conditions of dispersed or competing claims to power and frequent ruinous invasion, was based on land grants and on contractual, consensual exchanges of service and protection on which everyone's welfare depended. Land was legally owned by the king, who deeded and parceled it out in the form of "fiefs" to the greatest nobles, who in turn deeded it to lesser nobles, and so on down to the barons and their serfs, who worked the soil on the manor estate. The bond between lord and vassal was sealed downright liturgically, in a ritual of homage whereby the vassal, placing his hands in the lord's, swore an oath of loyalty that obliged him to perform certain specified duties, including military service. The lord, in turn, bound himself to protect the vassal. The feudal nobility was thus primarily a military caste system, a hierarchy of knights, or warriors-in-service.

Several kinds of troubadour verse celebrated feudal ideals. There was a song from vassal to lord about knightly service or about some theme of political alliance (*sirventes*), songs complaining about infractions of knightly decorum (*enueg*), songs that glorified one's own exploits or issued a challenge (*gap*). The most serious was the *planh*, a eulogy on the death of a lord. There were also many songs about the Crusades, military campaigns to win control of the Holy Land from Muslim rule. William IX of Aquitaine, our first troubadour, led a Crusade himself in 1101; his unlucky army never reached its distant goal.

The heart of the troubadour legacy was the ***canso***, which means a love song—or, better, perhaps, a song about love. The love celebrated by knightly singers was just as "high," just as formalized and ritualized, as any other theme articulated publicly. Modern scholars have christened the subject of the canso "courtly love" (*amour courtois*); the troubadours themselves called it ***fin' amors***, "refined love." The love songs of the troubadours emphasized service and the idolization of a beloved lady. Courtly love was generally hopeless because the lady outranked her admirer. She was typically married, although often left alone for long periods while her husband was away on military campaigns or Crusades. At such times she was the effective ruler of his domain. Her identity is concealed behind a code name, supposedly known only to the lady and her admirer.

The conventions of courtly love heightened the unavailability of the lady as actual lover and made her an object not of lust but of veneration. The canso was essentially a devotional song and thus a link with the sacred sphere, especially with the burgeoning devotion to the Blessed Virgin. Veneration of the lady, like veneration of Mary, promoted not sensuality but, rather, the sublimation of desire in charity, self-mortification, and acts of virtue. The one type of troubadour love song that did emphasize the joy of consummation was the *alba*, or "dawn song." The lovers, having passed a clandestine night together in oblivious bliss, are awakened—by the sun, by singing birds, by a watchman's cry, or by a confidant—to the breaking day and to the peril of being discovered together.

Anthology Vol 1-10
Full CD/Concise CD I, 24

The poetic and musical style associated with courtly love was self-consciously lofty, as shown by the imagery of the most famous of all cansos, *Can vei la lauzeta mover* ("When I see the lark unfurl his wings for joy") by Bernart de Ventadorn

(d. ca. 1200; Fig. 2-2). This song is in *strophic* form, in which all the stanzas have the same rhyme scheme and are sung to the same music (Ex. 2-1). It begins with an unforgettable metaphor comparing the joy of love to the soaring and swooping of a lark in flight. This is contrasted with the lovesick poet's unhappy state, condemned to adore a cold and unresponsive lady from afar. In Bernart's case it was easy enough for him to feel outranked by the lady; like many of the later troubadours, he appears to have been a commoner who rose to prominence, and received noble patronage, on his merits as a poet. His patron was in fact Eleanor of Aquitaine, with whom he traveled to France after her first marriage and to England after her second, thus spreading his art abroad.

1170 Thomas à Becket murdered in Canterbury Cathedral

ca. 1170s Bernart de Ventadorn, *Can vei la lauzeta mover*

1189 Richard I (Lionheart) becomes King of England

1192 Richard I (Lionheart), *Ja nun hons pris*

ca. 1200 Comtessa de Dia, *A chantar*

1208–29 Albigensian Crusade in southern France

1215 Magna Carta signed

1240s Earliest manuscript sources of Notre Dame polyphony

ca. 1250–1280 *Cantigas de Santa Maria* compiled

1264–73 Thomas Aquinas, *Summa theologiae*

ca. 1270–80 Anonymus IV treatise written

ca. 1280 Franco of Cologne, *Ars cantus mensurabilis*, treatise on mensural notation

ca. 1283 Adam de la Halle, *Le jeu de Robin et Marion*

ca. 1300 Johannes de Grocheio, *Ars musicae*

Example 2-1 **Bernart de Ventadorn, *Can vei la lauzeta mover***

When I see the lark unfurl his wings for joy
against the sun's rays,
and how he lingers and lets himself swoop down
because of the sweetness that floods his heart,
ah! I am filled with such great envy
towards all creatures whom I see rejoice;
I marvel that my heart
does not immediately melt with desire.

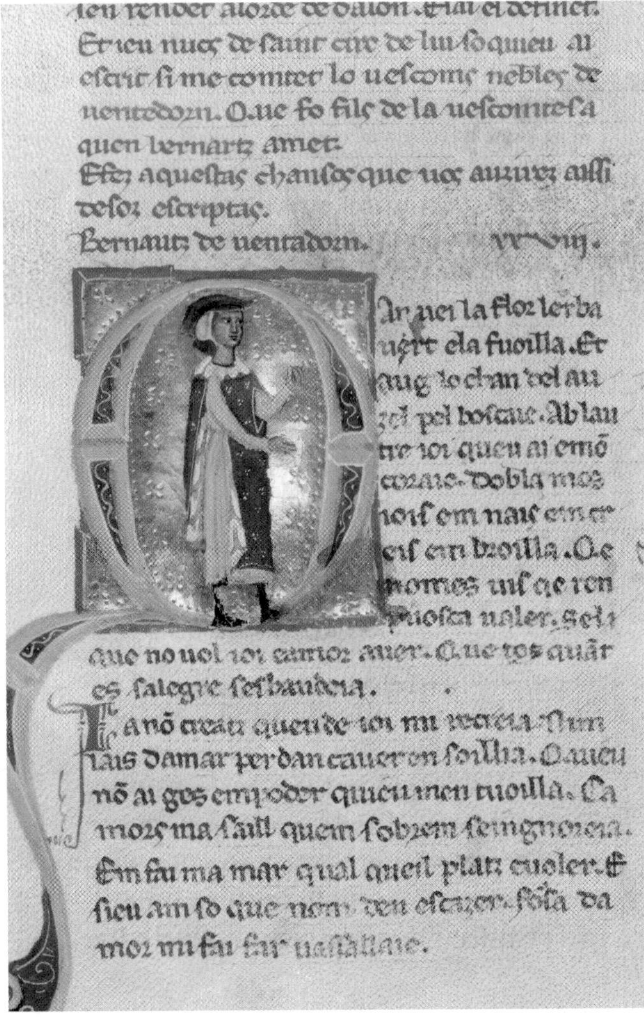

Figure 2-2 Bernart de Ventadorn, from an illumination accompanying his *vida*, the biographical preface to his collected song texts without melodies, in a manuscript copied in Italy in the late thirteenth or early fourteenth century, by which time the Occitan culture of southern France had already been destroyed. (Only five of the thirty-seven manuscripts known to have contained troubadour songs had musical notations.)

Performance and Oral Culture

As with the chant idiom already familiar to us, the notation of the troubadour songs tells us nothing about rhythm. We know some songs were connected to dance and therefore the rhythm in them must be metrical. Clues concerning rhythm can also be based on the meter of the poetry, but as with sacred music this remains a contested issue. The higher the style of a troubadour melody, the more likely it was to have affinities with chant. On the other hand, some troubadour songs effected a mock-popular style that may have drawn stylistically not on chant but on otherwise-unrecorded folk idioms. One such genre was the **pastorela** (or *pastourelle*), in which a knight seduces (or tries to seduce) a shepherdess. The best-known and earliest surviving example of this genre is *L'autrier jost' una sebissa* ("The other day by a hedge row") by Marcabru, an early troubadour who served in his youth at the court of William IX. He memorialized his patron in a Crusader song (*Pax! In nomine Domini*, "Peace! In the name of the Lord") that mixes Latin verses with vernacular ones. Texts that do this are called *macaronic* ("jumbled" like macaroni). In *L'autrier jost' una sebissa*, the flattering knight, determined to seduce the beautiful

Anthology Vol 1-11
Full CD I, 25

Figure 2-3 Manuscript illumination of jongleurs and troubadours from a facsimile of the *Manessa Codex* (ca. 1300).

peasant girl, is both elevated and crude in his entreaties to her but in the end unable to win her over.

While the art of the troubadours was ultimately aristocratic, an art of the castle, it was not an art practiced only by aristocrats. Indeed, the actual performance of the songs was often left to those we now call *minstrels*: professionals of a lower caste, singer-entertainers called ***joglars*** in Provençal (***jongleurs*** in French, both from the Latin *joculatores*, "jokers"), from which we get our word "juggler" (Fig. 2-3). Most of the commoner-troubadours started out as minstrels who learned the work of the noble poets by rote and who later developed creative facility in their own right.

A noble poet would compose a song and teach it to a minstrel, thus sending it out into the oral tradition, from which it might be transcribed, with luck, perhaps a century later. The written documentation of the troubadour art began only when the tradition was already dying; vastly more poems survive alone than they do with music. The manuscripts containing troubadour songs, called *chansonniers* (books of songs), are thus retrospective anthologies prepared beginning in the middle of the thirteenth century. Their purpose was commemorative and decorative; they had little to do with practice or performance. Chansonniers often contained fanciful portraits of the poets as well as biographies, called ***vidas***.

Because the creation of poetry was viewed as a noble pastime rather than a profession, it could be practiced by lords—and by ladies, too. We know of at least twenty lady troubadours (*trobairitz*) who created courtly songs but who apparently did not sing them, at least not in public. Four poems are attributed to the late twelfth-century trobairitz Comtessa de Dia (Countess of Dia), whose brief vida tells us "was the wife of Lord Guillem de Poitou, a beautiful and a good lady. And she fell in love with Lord Raimbaut d'Aurenga and composed many good songs about him."[2] There are historical discrepancies in this account, and her first name and identity remain something of a mystery, although she has often been called Beatriz de Dia. Of the four poems attributed to her only *A chantar m'er de so gu'en no volria* ("I must sing of that which I would rather not") survives with a melody, one that uses a mock-popular style. Its overall structure is that of the regularized or rounded canso with a repeated couplet and final refrain (AB AB CD B); the tune alternates cadences on E and D common in the dances and dance songs of a slightly later period. Such endings would be designated *ouvert* and *clos*—"open" and "shut"—in thirteenth-century dance manuscripts; they prefigure what we would now call half and full cadences.

Anthology Vol 1-12
Full CD I, 26

That the composition of troubadour songs was an oral practice is shown by a revealing anecdote in the vida of the late-twelfth-century troubadour Arnaut Daniel, a great knightly poet known for his exceptional virtuosity in rhyme. Another troubadour had boasted that he could compose a better poem than Arnaut and challenged him to a contest. The king confined the two poets to different rooms in his castle, stipulating that at day's end they were to appear before him and recite their new poems, whereupon the king would determine the winner of the bet. Arnaut's inspiration failed him; but from his room he could hear his rival singing as he composed his song, and he learned it by heart. When the trial began, Arnaut asked to perform first and sang his rival's song, leaving his opponent to look like the imitator.

Like many of the anecdotes in the vidas, this one probably never happened. But, as the Italian proverb has it, *Se non è vero, è ben trovato*: "Even if it isn't true, it's very apt" (literally, "well made-up")—and note how the Italian for "making up" comes from the same root stock as *trobar*. What is so befitting and revealing about it are the points the author of the vida took for granted: first, that a troubadour in the act of composition did not write but sang aloud; and second, that a troubadour could memorize a song at an aural glance. These are the assumptions of an oral culture.

Music for Elites: *Trobar Clus*

There is another important genre of troubadour poetry with music: the ***tenso***, an often-jesting debate song that involves two or more participants and that was sometimes actually a joint composition by two or more poets. The subject matter could be some fine point of feudal service or courtly love (such as "If you love a lady, would it be better to be married to her or to have her love you back?"), or it could be about poetry itself, in which the troubadour addressed his craft directly and self-consciously. The tenso was thus a sort of school for poets that can be extremely instructive for us.

One of the favorite themes for debate was the eternal conflict between what was called at the time ***trobar clus*** and *trobar leu*, that is, between "closed," or difficult, poetry for connoisseurs and "light" poetry designed for immediate pleasure and easy communication. The virtues claimed for the difficult *trobar clus* were its technical prowess, its density of meaning, and the exclusive nature of its appeal, which allowed it to create an elite occasion and foster solidarity among a group of insiders. It promoted a social hierarchy and was therefore an art ultimately expressive of aristocratic values. The virtues claimed for the communicative poetry of the *trobar leu* were its greater technical prowess (or so it was argued, since, as the ancient Roman poet Horace famously remarked, the greatest art is the art that conceals art) and its power to create a sense of community and shared values.

These arguments were given an early, classic exposition in a tenso by Guiraut de Bornelh (ca. 1140 to ca. 1200), a recent convert to *trobar leu*, in mock debate with a fellow troubadour known as Linhaure (probably Raimbaut d'Aurenga), who remained loyal to *trobar clus*. The melody, unfortunately, has not survived. In somewhat abridged translation, the dispute runs as follows:

> *Linhaure*: I should like to know why you keep blaming the obscure style. Tell me if you prize so highly that which is common to all? For then would all be equal.
>
> *Guiraut*: I do not take it to heart if each man composes as he pleases; but judge that song is more loved and prized which is made easy and simple, and do not be vexed at my opinion.
>
> *Linhaure*: I do not like my songs to be so confused, that the base and good, the small and great be appraised alike; my poetry will never be praised by fools, for they have no understanding nor care for what is more precious and valuable.
>
> *Guiraut*: If I work late and turn my rest into weariness to make my songs simple, does it seem that I am afraid of work? Why compose if you do not want all to understand? Song brings no other advantage.
>
> *Linhaure*: Provided that I produce what is best at all times, I care not if it be not so widespread; commonplaces are no good for the appreciative—that is why gold is more valued than salt, and with song it is just the same.[3]

The contest between the obscurely difficult and the more easily communicative will run through this book like a red thread, as the audience for art changes and the gulf between elite and popular music widens over time.

Many troubadours cultivated both styles, depending on the occasion, and saw no compelling reason to choose between them. And yet the debate continues. The contest between the obscurely difficult and the more easily communicative will run through this book like a red thread, steadily gathering force and urgency as the audience for art changes and the gulf between elite and popular music widens over time. For one of the enduring characteristics of "high art," and a perennial source of contention, is that it is produced by and for social and political elites. That, after all, is what makes it "high." The competing values of the *trobar clus* and *trobar leu*, by other names and in other forms, are with us still. Each still has its ardent defenders and its adamant detractors. Their subtexts and agendas are many. There is no more consequential theme in the history of music.

Trouvères

The art of the troubadours lasted about 200 years and then declined, together with the Provençal culture that had sustained it. Some of the later troubadours fled southward, into present-day Spain and Italy, at the time of the so-called Albigensian Crusade (from 1208), a devastating twenty-year war of aggression waged by northern French Catholics to root out perceived heretics. Guiraut Riquier (ca. 1230 to ca. 1300), known as the last of the troubadours, found employment at the court of Alfonso X of Castile, which became a major center of vernacular song, but no longer in the Provençal language. He was not the only troubadour who stimulated the spread of vernacular poetry into other tongues.

The earliest imitations of Provençal lyrics in northern France, by the poet-musicians called trouvères, gathered strength through the thirteenth century as the art of the troubadours declined. One of the main brokers of this northward migration was Eleanor of Aquitaine herself. She was the granddaughter of William IX, the first troubadour, as well as the patron of Bernart de Ventadorn and both mother and great-grandmother of notable trouvères. Her trouvère son, Richard I (Lionheart), though born in England and eventually his father's successor as king (1189–99), lived most of his life in Aquitaine. He never learned English.

Anthology Vol 1-13
Full CD I, 27

His poems are found in both Provençal and French sources; the only one to survive with a melody is in French, *Ja nun hons pris* ("No prisoner will ever speak his mind"), and is not about love but, rather, about honor. The poem laments his famous captivity (1192–94), when his enemy Leopold V of Austria held him for the proverbial "king's ransom," a ruinous levy that was eventually raised by Richard's English subjects. Questionable though it almost surely is, we cannot omit the "well-found" legend that Richard's squire and fellow trouvère, Blondel de Nesle, succeeded in learning the captured king's whereabouts by singing one of Richard's songs within royal earshot and hearing the king respond in turn with the refrain. True or false, the story certainly shows the importance the knight-crusaders attached to their musical activity.

As long as the art of the trouvère remained an art of the castle, it differed little, except in language (*langue d'oïl*), from the art of the troubadour. Yet from the beginning there were some subtle but significant differences, both on the level of form and style and on that of social attitude and practice, which only became more pronounced over time. Narrative genres loomed much larger in the trouvère repertory. The *lai*, an extended song form of changing stanzas held together by a story line, reflects the longstanding popularity in the north of narrative poetry (*romances* and ***chansons de geste***, "songs of deeds"). One of the earliest trouvères, Chrétien de Troyes, active in the latter half of the twelfth century, was much better known for his epic romances, including the original Arthurian legends of Perceval and Lancelot, than for his handful of lyrics.

> ***"I will make a song that is light upon the ear, for it matters to me that all may learn it and willingly sing it."—Conon de Béthune***

New genres of narrative song in a folklike style became popular in thirteenth-century France. One of these, the *chanson de toile*, always reflected the woman's point of view, whatever the gender of the singer. The name of the genre, literally "picture song" (from *toile*, "a canvas"), referred to the opening device of setting a domestic scene, usually of a lovely maiden spinning, weaving, or reading a book—but mainly pining for her lover. Each stanza ended with an exclamatory refrain to underscore the maiden's tender feelings. Refrains lived a life of their own in the works of the trouvères. Detached from their original contexts they circulated like proverbs from song to song, and it became a mark of skill for a trouvère to contrive new settings for familiar tags. Narratives and migrating refrains were both popularizing touches, and so was the general lack of concern among the trouvères for the values of elite *trobar clus*, so beloved of the troubadours. Conon de Béthune (d. 1220), one of the noblest trouvères by birth and also a knight-crusader, put it this way: "I will make a song that is light upon the ear, for it matters to me that all may learn it and willingly sing it."[4] The sentiment would only gain in force as the courtly art he practiced underwent a phenomenal social transformation.

Adam de la Halle and the *Formes Fixes*

After the middle of the thirteenth century, the main site of French musico-literary activity shifted from castle to town, mirroring a general societal movement. Paris, as we shall see, became the great center of activity, but other places also assumed new prominence. By the end of the twelfth century the town of Arras to the north had become an international center of banking and trade, the stronghold of France's emerging class of town-dwelling freemen—*bourgeoisie,* in the original meaning of the term. It was at Paris and Arras that musical activity blossomed and came to be organized along lines comparable in some respects to craft guilds. This tendency was epitomized in the Confrérie des jongleurs et des bourgeois d'Arras (Brotherhood of Minstrels and Townspeople of Arras), nominally a lay religious guild founded near the beginning of the thirteenth century, which became a leading sponsor of musico-poetic pursuits. Audefroi le Bastart, who was active from 1190 to 1230 and a specialist in *chansons de toile,* was a member, as were the three most important trouvères of the thirteenth century: Moniot d'Arras (d. 1239), Jehan Bretel (d. 1272), and Adam de la Halle (d. ca. 1307; Fig. 2-4).

Figure 2-4 Adam de la Halle. Miniature from musical codex.

To Moniot d'Arras, whose pseudonym means "The Little Monk of Arras," belongs the most famous pastourelle in the repertory, *Ce fut en mai* ("It happened in May"). Its text contains a valuable bit of testimony, corroborated by other witnesses, about how such songs were performed: It describes a dance accompanied by a fiddle (*viele*). On the assumption that *Ce fut en mai* is a dance song, it is transcribed in Example 2-2 with a regular alternation of long and short syllables. The musical structure approximates the so-called binary form of later dance styles (AA′ BB′): two phrases of equal length, each repeated with contrasting "open" and "shut" cadences.

Anthology Vol 1-14
Full CD I, 28

Jehan Bretel was the great master of the *jeu-parti* (mock debate), the trouvère equivalent of the troubadour tenso. Although not a nobleman but a wealthy citizen of the town, he won debate contests so often that he was elected a presiding judge, thus putting him out of contention. His elevation was a formal assertion of artistic meritocracy—aristocracy achieved by merit, not birth. Jehan's musical debating partner was often Adam de la Halle, called "Adam le Bossu"—Adam the Hunchback—by his contemporaries ("although I am not one," he complained in one of his poems).

Example 2-2 Moniot d'Arras, *Ce fut en mai* (pastourelle)

Ce fut__ en mai, Au douz_ tens gai Que la__ sai - sons_ est be - le, Main
me__ le - vai, Jo - er__ m'a - lai Lez u - ne fon - te - ne - le. En
un__ ver - gier Clos d'ai - glen - tier O - i___ u - ne vi - e - le; La
vi___ dan - cier Un che - va - lier Et u - ne da - moi - se - le.

It happened in May,
when the heavens laugh,
a lovely time of year.
I got up early
to play at the fountain.
In a garden
surrounded by wild roses
I heard a fiddle playing;
and there I saw a knight
and a girl dancing.

Advanced studies in Paris as a young man had acquainted Adam with the various forms of current "university music" that will be discussed later in this chapter. His education equipped him to compose polyphonic music, and he became the only trouvère we know of to do so. His skills made him famous, and he enjoyed an international career that included time in Italy and England. An entire chansonnier, evidently compiled late in the thirteenth century, is given over almost wholly to a retrospective collection of his works, grouped by genres: first traditional *chansons courtoises,* then the *jeux-partis,* and finally the polyphonic works. This retrospective manuscript of Adam's compositions was not published until the 1870s; nevertheless it made him the earliest Medieval musician whose music was comprehensively recovered in modern times.

Adam's polyphonic pieces are of two kinds. The first consists of French verses, harmonized the way Latin **versus** was often harmonized at the time, in a fairly strict homorhythmic (note-against-note, or "chordal") texture. The second group consists of more complicated polyphonic compositions called ***motets,*** which were, as discussed later in this chapter, one of the most important new polyphonic genres to emerge. Adam's used a new type of notation that fixed the rhythms exactly.

Polyphonic writing was a learned style for a trouvère, so what is especially interesting about Adam's polyphonically set verses is that they are cast in the folksiest (or, rather, the most mock naive) of all quasi-pastoral genres, the dance song called *rondel* (or ***rondeau,*** as it is more commonly called by musicians). These pieces feign naiveté because, for all their rustic pretension, the poems are quite sophisticated. The name of the genre, which connotes "round" or "circular," may originally have stemmed from the nature of the dance it accompanied, but it also well describes the "rounded" form of the poem, in which a "contained refrain" both frames the verse and appears, truncated, within it. Contained refrains are ones that use the same melody as the verse itself. The form of a rondeau can thus be represented with letters as follows: AB a A ab AB. Here the capital letters stand for the refrain text and the lowercase letters for new text, sung to the same tune. The trick was to come up with a poem in which the refrains both rounded the verse and made linear sense when the entire text was presented in sequence, as we can hear in Adam's *Je muir, je muir d'amorete* ("I die, I die of love"; Ex. 2-3).

Anthology Vol 1-15a
Full CD I, 29
Concise CD I, 25

Example 2-3 Adam de la Halle, *Je muir, je muir d'amorete* (Rondeau)

1.4.7. Je muir, je muir d'a - mo - re - te, Las! ai - mi!
3. A pre - miers le vi dou - che - te, Las! ai - mi!
5. D'une a - trai - ant ma - nie - rete A - dont le vi,
2.8. Par de - fau - te d'a - mi - e - te. De mer - chi.
6. Et puis le truis si fie - re - te, Quant li pri.

I die, I die of love, ah weary, ah me,
it is my beloved's want of all mercy!

At first she was demure and attractively docile;
I die, I die of love, ah weary, ah me,

With that catching little way she has, I saw her then;
but since I've found her so proud when I beg for loving.

I die, I die of love, ah weary, ah me,
it is my beloved's want of all mercy!

Beginning with Adam in the late thirteenth century, the rondeau, as well as the other dance songs with refrains (the **ballade** and **virelai**), came into widespread use as a model for composed music. While they differed from one another chiefly in the deployment of their refrains, these three types of song had a lot in common. Take away the refrains from a rondeau—that is, simply take away the capital letters from the alphabet scheme given earlier—and you are left with the long-familiar *chanson courtoise*, the basic stanza in aab form:

<AB> a <A> ab <AB> → aab

Anthology Vol 1-15b
Full CD I, 30
Concise CD I, 26

Add a refrain (not a contained refrain but one with different music) on either side of the basic stanza, and you get the form of Adam's *Dieus soit en cheste maison* ("God be in this house"), which is called a *ballade* (Ex. 2-4):

R aab R <aab R aab R aab R, etc.>

Example 2-4 Adam de la Halle, *Dieus soit en cheste maison* (ballade)

Example 2-4 (continued)

God, be in this house,
And send it wealth and joy.

Lord Christmas
sends us to his friends.
to lovers,
and to the courtly and well-born,
to collect
a Christmas penny

God, be in this house . . .

Our lord is such
that he would beg only against his will,
but to the unworthy,
he sent us to his place,
who are his family
and children.

God, be in this house . . .

Give the refrain the same melody as the nonrepeating line (b) of the stanza so that it is "contained" and you get the form of Adam's *Fines amouretes ai* ("Many fine lovers have I"; Ex. 2-5), a *chanson ballade*, or "danced song," more commonly called a *virelai*, from the Old French verb *virer*, "to turn around":

Anthology Vol 1-15c
Full CD I, 31
Concise CD I, 27

B aab B <aab B aab B aab B, etc.>

Example 2-5 Adam de la Halle, *Fines amouretes ai* (virelai)

Refrain (= b)
Fi - nes a - mou - re - tes _ ai, Dieu! si ___ ne sai, quant les ver - rai.
Fine
Verse
a
a'
1. Or man-de - rai m'a - mi - e - te, Qui est ___ coin - te et jo - li - e - te
2. Et s'ele est de moi en - chain - te, Tost de - ven - ra paile et ___ tain - te;
3. Mieus vaut que je m'en as - tien - gne Et pour _ li jo - li me _ tien - gne

Example 2-5 (continued)

Et ___ s'est si sa - ve - rou - se - te, clas - te - nir ne m'en por - rai.
S'il en _ est es - clan - de - le et _ plain - te, Des - hon - ne - ré - e l'ar - rai.
Et ___ que de li me _ sou - vien - gne Car _ s'on-nour li gar - de - rai.
Back to refrain

I have had fancy love affairs, God knows!
Such that I don't know when I will see the like again.

Now I will send for my little friend,
who is pretty and refined
and so tasty a dish
that I won't be able to hold myself in!
I have had fancy, etc.

But if she should become pregnant by me,
and gets pale and sickly,
and should a scandal and an outcry ensue,
then I shall have dishonored her.
I have had fancy, etc.

It would be better if I abstained,
and, for the pretty one's sake,
contented myself with merely remembering her.
Thus does her honor protect her.
I have had fancy, etc.

Because it is common sense to begin an alphabet scheme with the letter A, the virelai form is almost always given as A bba A, which unfortunately disguises the basic stanza within it. These three forms—rondeau, ballade, and virelai—encompass what would be called the ***formes fixes*** (see Table 2-1), the "fixed forms" in which lyric poetry would continue to be set to increasingly elaborate music over the next two centuries.

The work for which Adam is best known is *Le jeu de Robin et de Marion* (The Play of Robin and Marion; Fig. 2-5), which he wrote during time he spent in Italy. This musical play from the mid-1280s alternated dialogue with sixteen diminutive monophonic dance songs and duets. The work has often been archaically compared with later kinds of musical theater, such as comic opera. More appropriately, it can be described as an acted-out pastourelle, for that is the narrative tradition to which its dramatized plot belongs. Marion, a shepherdess, loves the shepherd Robin, as she tells us in the song; accosted by Sir Aubert, a knight out hunting, she resists; Robin goes to town in search of protection for her; while he is gone Sir Aubert comes back, abducts Marion; Robin, warned by a friend, pursues but is beaten back; Marion escapes anyway; the lovers, reunited, celebrate. Such love stories would become the stuff of musical theater some three centuries later, when opera was invented.

Table 2-1 The *Formes Fixes*

Form	
Ballade: aab[C]	Ballades were usually composed in three stanzas, each of which follows the form shown here. The two "a" sections often end with open and closed cadences. Sometimes the "b" section of each stanza ends with the same bit of text—a refrain, indicated by the capital letter "C."
Rondeau: ABaAabAB	Rondeaux are typically composed in a single stanza. Often the "a" section ends on a note other than the final note, creating an "open" effect. The "b" section, which concludes the form, always ends on the final note, creating a "closed" effect.
Virelai: AbbaA	Virelais typically have numerous stanzas, which proceed A bba A bba A bba A etc. The two "b" sections often end with open and closed cadences.

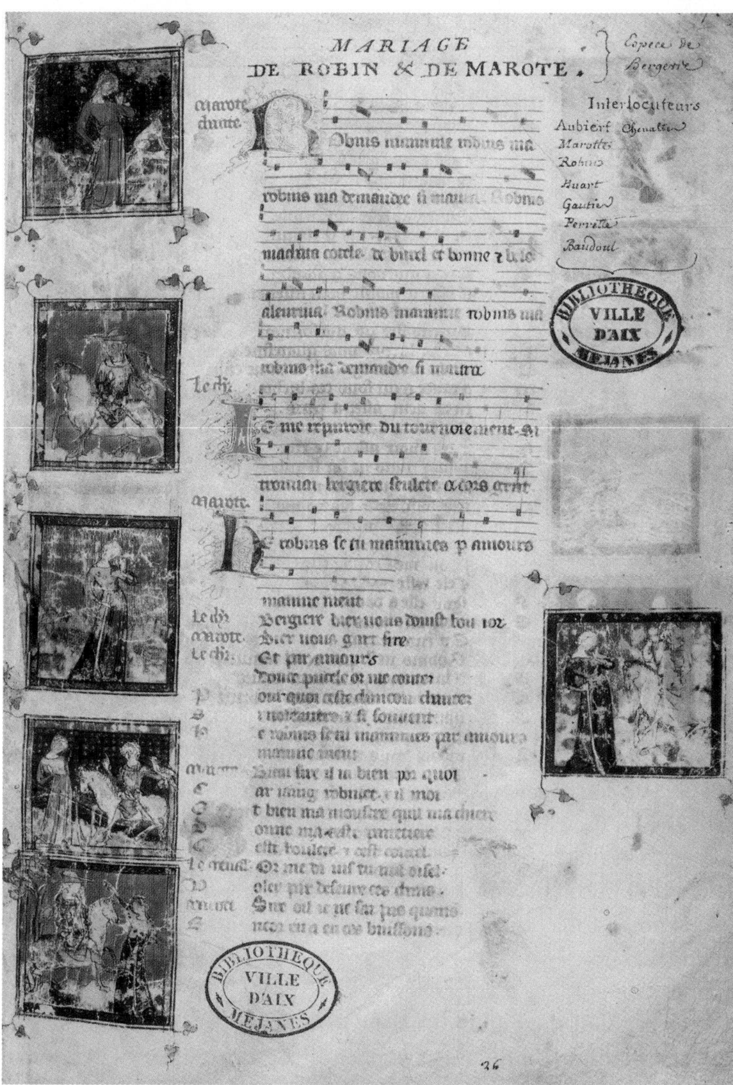

Figure 2-5 Page from the manuscript for *Le jeu de Robin et de Marion* by Adam de la Halle, with notation in neumes and manuscript illuminations, mid-1280s.

Geographical Diffusion

The earliest written vernacular repertories in several other European countries are traceable to the influence of the troubadours and trouvères. Troubadour influence went south into the Iberian and Italian peninsulas (Fig. 2-6). In some parts of what is now Spain, especially at the northwestern court of Castile and León, the troubadours were emulated in the local literary vernacular, Galician-Portuguese. This brief efflorescence left a major musical monument in its wake, the *Cantigas de Santa Maria*, compiled over a period of as much as thirty years (1250–80) under the supervision of King Alfonso X (*el Sabio*, "The Wise"). The word *cantiga* is the equivalent of *canso*: a courtly song in the vernacular. Alfonso's collection of songs expressed loving devotion to the Virgin Mary, once again blurring the line we now insist on drawing between the sacred and the secular.

The earliest surviving genre of vernacular song in the Italian peninsula was cultivated by a very different sort of musician from those we have examined thus far. The thirteenth-century *lauda spirituale* (devotional song of praise) was not a courtly genre but a religious one. Because these pieces were often sung with new words to familiar melodies, they could be characterized as pious pop songs. They were apt to be cast in the popular form of the virelai (A bba A bba A, etc.). Beginning in the fourteenth century, such a song would be called a *ballata*, betraying its descent from dance.

A large body of German courtly song is also traceable to trouvère influence. That eastward migration of the art of *fin' amours* is often said to begin with the wedding, in 1156, of Frederick I (known as Barbarossa, "Red Beard"), the Holy Roman Emperor and King of Germany, to the Duchess Beatrice of Burgundy. The songs were called *Minnelieder*, composed by *Minnesinger*—singers of *Minne*, German for "courtly love." Walther von der Vogelweide (d. ca. 1230) was regarded both by his contemporaries and by his successors as the preeminent master of the ***Minnesang***, the German Medieval lyric.

The knightly Minnesinger cultivated three main genres, all more or less directly adapted from the Romance-language tradition we have just considered. The narrative *Leich* came directly from the French lai. The *Lied* (song) was the equivalent of the *canso* or *chanson courtoise*, and like its counterparts it encompassed an important subgenre, the *Tagelied* (daybreak song), equivalent to the troubadour *alba*. Finally, there was the *Spruch* (saying), a genre that encompassed many of the same topics as did the debating songs. The Minnesang did not use dialogue form but was often a moralizing single stanza that has the character of a sung proverb.

The art of Minnesang underwent a "popularization" over the course of the thirteenth century, first detected in the work of the knight and crusader Neidhardt von Reuenthal (d. ca. 1250). His pieces were exceedingly famous, and some of them became folk songs. That is, they have rejoined the oral tradition and were unwittingly collected many centuries later by the early folklorists of the German Romantic movement. Neidhardt himself became a folk hero, as did other legendary personalities, who are best known today through their nineteenth-century presentations in operas by Richard Wagner.

One of Wagner's operas, *Die Meistersinger von Nürnberg* (The Mastersingers of Nuremberg, 1868), is about the guild musicians who flourished in southern German towns between the fourteenth and seventeenth centuries. Like the very late trouvères, they were craftsmen, not nobles, and their chief activity consisted of

Figure 2-6 Europe in the middle of the eleventh century.

convening assemblies at which song contests were held. A *Meisterlied* (mastersong) was the musical equivalent of a *Meisterstück* (masterpiece, from which we get our English term), the final offering by which an apprentice graduated to the rank of master artisan in a Medieval guild. The pieces were in *bar form* (AAB) having two constituent parts: two *Stollen* (pillars) followed by an *Abgesang* (sing-off). We can hear this lore imparted in Wagner's opera when the shoemaker Hans Sachs, the leader of the Nuremberg mastersingers—an actual historical personage who lived from 1494 to 1576 and whose musical works survive—instructs the entirely fictional hero in the making of a prize song.

A Note on Instruments

One of the glories of the rich thirteenth- and fourteenth-century cantiga manuscripts are the dozens of colored miniatures that decorate them (Fig. 2-7). These little paintings are so detailed and precisely drawn that they are believed in some cases to be portraits of actual people. They show courtiers and minstrels of every stripe—Spanish, Moorish (black North African), Jewish, male and female—all rubbing shoulders at Alfonso's court in Toledo and playing an encyclopedic assortment of instruments (more than forty, from the ever-present minstrel's fiddle to more exotic Moorish instruments, including zithers, bladder pipes, castanets, and hurdy-gurdies). These illustrations inevitably raise more questions than they answer. They stimulate the performer's imagination, but as historical evidence they must be approached with caution, despite their evident realism. We cannot merely

Figure 2-7 Miniatures from the *Cantigas de Santa Maria* manuscript at the Escorial Palace, Madrid, showing various contemporary instruments.

assume that all the instruments so marvelously depicted ever played together or that they played cantigas.

These images also invite us to think more generally about instruments and instrumental music. Just as we should not be misled into thinking there was not much secular music in the Middle Ages because little of it was written down, so too we should not assume that the notation of monophonic (that is, unaccompanied) Medieval songs reflects their actual performance practice. Early written sources such as chansonniers were more often prestige items—"collectibles"—than actual performance materials. And, as we may recall from the first chapter, the strictly unaccompanied unison style of Gregorian chant was regarded as something of a special effect. So there is really no reason to allow the stark appearance of early written music in itself to influence or limit our notion of what it may have sounded like in performance.

On the basis of all the available evidence—contemporary pictures, literary descriptions of performances, the writings of music pedagogues and theorists, archival documents, even some surviving instruments—historians now believe that the use of instruments to accompany Medieval song depended a great deal on genres and their social connotations. The higher the style and the closer its alliance with the ethos of liturgical chant, the more likely it was to be performed by solo voice alone. Among the troubadours, instrumentalists participated in the "lesser" genres, especially dance songs. With the lowering of the social standing of trouvère song and its urbanization in the thirteenth century came a greater participation in it by minstrel instrumentalists, especially fiddlers, who had their own professional guild in Paris.

As the text of Moniot d'Arras's *Ce fut en mai* explicitly informs us, fiddlers had a repertory of their own in the form of dances. The most elaborate dance form was variously called *estampie*, which suggests a heavy and vigorous step. The estampie form was a little like that of the lai or sequence: a series of paired strains with alternately open and shut cadences. The earliest estampies preserved in writing are those in the mid-thirteenth-century *Manuscrit du roi* (King's Manuscript; Fig. 2-8). Their notation is very advanced for the time, for it conveys their rhythm (according to principles discussed later in this chapter), as notated dance music must do when no text is present to suggest meter or accent.

So far the evidence seems to suggest that instrumentalists performed such pieces and accompanied singers where appropriate, predominantly as soloists rather than

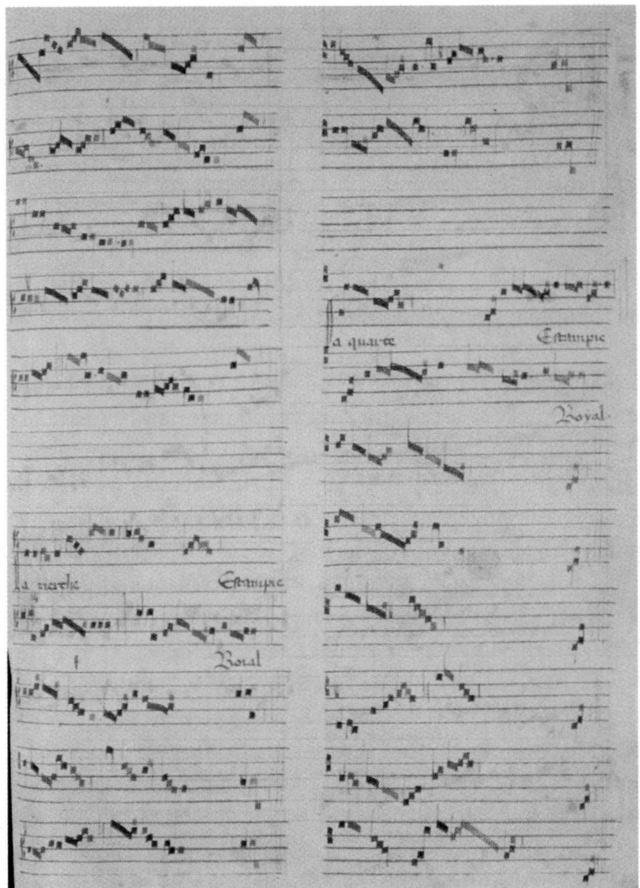

Figure 2-8 Dances from the *Manuscrit du Roi*, a huge codex, copied in the mid-thirteenth century, that contains songs of the troubadours alongside those of the trouvères and even a few items, like these dances, in mensural notation (that is, notation prescribing rhythm).

in groups. Such accompaniments were not necessarily modest or primitive. On the contrary, it seems that Medieval instrumentalists were often extraordinary technicians and that they cultivated techniques of self-accompaniment (drones, doublings, even counterpoint). Evidence of ensemble performance is rare, ambiguous, and often (like the cantiga miniatures) of questionable accuracy. The relationship between the forms and practices that survive in notated sources and those that came and went without a paper trail has been aptly characterized as "the iceberg problem."[5] The written elite dominates our view, but it accounts for only the smallest fraction of what existed at the time. The great vanished mass is what dominated the view—that is, formed the assumptions and the expectations—of contemporaries.

Polyphony in Aquitanian Monastic Centers

Quite near the royal troubadour William IX's seat at Poitiers was Limoges, another Aquitanian town and the site of the Benedictine Abbey of St. Martial. This abbey was the greatest center for the production of Latin versus, on which the troubadours modeled their *vers* (to use the Provençal word for poetry with music). Rhythmically and formally, the Latin versus was just as various and almost as virtuosic as troubadour songs. Actual Provençal words occasionally appear in versus from St. Martial.

Most striking of all, there are subgenres of versus that, like the most elevated troubadour genres, straddle the ambiguous line between the sacred and the secular.

Aquitaine was a center not only for the secular music of the troubadours, but also for an important repertory of early polyphonic composition that survives in manuscripts long kept in the library of the Abbey of St. Martial. "St. Martial" **organum** polyphony is found in four bound volumes comprising nine separate manuscripts, compiled between about 1100 and 1150. (The quotation marks here are a reminder that the music was kept and used at the abbey but not necessarily composed there.) The notation, like that of chant, specifies pitch but not rhythm, reminding us once again that the music was composed, learned, and performed by oral methods.

This poses a particular problem with polyphonic music. We, who must read these texts in order to sing the music that twelfth-century monks knew by heart, are more seriously handicapped by the rhythmic indeterminacy of the notation than we are in the case of monophonic chant, and for a fairly obvious reason. When two parts are sung simultaneously, the singers must know how to "line up." All we have to go on today is the rough vertical alignment of the parts in the manuscript and the rule (already implied as far back as *Musica enchiriadis*) that the sustained part can move only when its motion will create a consonance against the faster-moving part.

The new style of "St. Martial" organum resembles some of the early organum we considered at the end of Chapter 1, in that one voice is relatively stationary while the other moves freely. The great difference is that now the dronelike lower voice is the original chant melody (vox principalis) and the melismatic moving upper voice (vox organalis) is the newly added one. This amounts to standing the previous polyphonic texture on its head: What was top is now bottom; what was mobile is now stationary, and vice versa. Most important from the listener's perspective, the added voice, which had been subordinate, is now dominant. In this new melismatic organum, the chant seems paradoxically to accompany its accompaniment.

In keeping with this changed perspective, a new terminology is warranted. Instead of vox principalis, let us simply call the voice that sustains the long-held notes of the original chant the "holding part." Since the Latin infinitive "to hold" is *tenere*, the chant-bearing part will henceforth be known as the ***tenor***. The word begins appearing in this sense in treatises of the thirteenth century, and, although its connotations have varied over the years, this was its first meaning for polyphonic music: the voice that holds a preexistent melody out in long notes over which another voice sings in florid counterpoint. It was the relegation of the chant melody to the tenor that was the new event, for it inaugurated a texture and a procedure that would last for centuries under the thirteenth-century name ***cantus firmus***, or "fixed tune."

Anthology Vol 1-16
Full CD I, 32
Concise CD I, 28

For a sample of the new texture let us look at organum called *Jubilemus exultemus* (Fig. 2-9). The tenor is in fact a metrical versus composed to adorn the end of Christmas Matins. What is this melismatic organum, then, but an adornment of an adornment, a polyphonic trope? It is a melismatic gloss sung not in place of an older chant or in between its phrases but (imagining two singers now) superimposed on it. "St. Martial"-style polyphony is thus a new kind of trope, simultaneous rather than prefatory; it is a sonic amplification of the liturgy. The notation is vague—a speculative transcription of the beginning of the piece is given as Example 2-6. Here we see anywhere from one to fifteen notes in the upper voice for each of the lower (that is, the original chant). But it is not clear how fast they should move or how the two parts should line up.

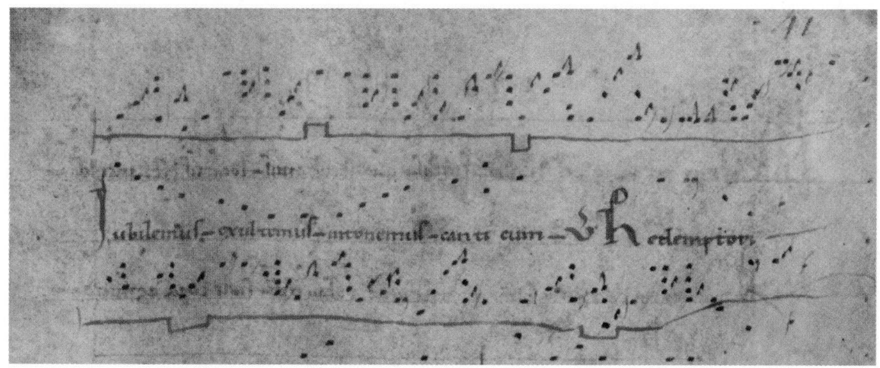

Figure 2-9 Melismatic organum on the versus *Jubilemus, exultemus* from one of the twelfth-century "St. Martial" manuscripts (Paris: Bibliotheque Nationale, Fonds Latins MS 1139, fol. 41).

Example 2-6 Transcription of the beginning of *Jubilemus, exultemus*

Let us rejoice, let us exult, let us sing a song

In some settings the two voices are so intricately (and playfully!) interrelated that it seems clear that the whole texture of the piece must have been conceived simultaneously. We see this in *Ad superni regis* (Ex. 2-7), a versus in which the texture is "neume-against-neume" rather than note-against-note. (The slurs in the example show how the notes in the original notation were joined into neumatic groups, or

Anthology Vol 1-17
Full CD I, 33
Concise CD I, 29

Example 2-7 Versus sung as a prosulated *Benedicamus Domino* response at St. Martial and elsewhere (Paris, BN, LAT. 1139), opening

To the jewel of the king who possesses all things

ligatures—literally, "bindings"—of two, three, four, or more pitches.) This transcription assumes that every neume lasts the same amount of time, represented here as a quarter note's duration. At the beginning of the piece this duration also corresponds to the syllables, but the neumes in the decorative melismas that come at the ends of verses are matched together in the same way.

This particular versus evidently was especially popular. It is found in three of the four "St. Martial" manuscripts containing polyphony, and it is found in another form in the other main source of early-to-mid-twelfth-century polyphonic composition: the so-called Codex Calixtinus, more accurately known as the *Liber sancti Jacobi*, or Book of St. James. (A codex—plural codices—is a thick manuscript consisting of separately sewn component *fascicles* that are bound together.) The Codex Calixtinus is a huge memorial potpourri dedicated to the apostle James the Greater and commissioned, according to myth, by Pope Callistus (Calixtus) II, who reigned from 1119 to 1124. According to tradition, the martyred body of St. James was miraculously transported from Judea to Spain, where he had preached and where he is now venerated (under the Spanish name Sant' Iago, or Santiago) as patron saint. There is a particularly lavish copy of the Codex Calixtinus at St. James's own shrine in the Cathedral of Santiago de Compostela, one of the great pilgrimage spots in late Medieval Europe.

The Codex Calixtinus includes some polyphonic Mass and Office music associated with the special local liturgy of St. James that is in the new organum style, with the original chant as the sustained tenor and an especially florid counterpoint above it. This is cathedral, not monastic, polyphony. The most florid of all the settings is the Kyrie *Cunctipotens genitor* (Fig. 2-10; Ex. 2-8b). Familiar to us already

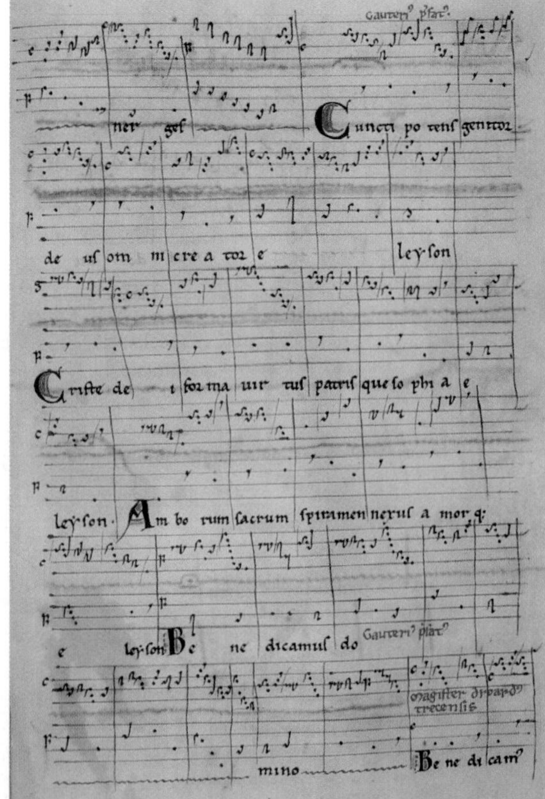

Figure 2-10 *Cunctipotens genitor,* as set melismatically in the Codex Calixtinus, a late-twelfth-century French manuscript now kept at the Cathedral of Santiago de Compostela in Spain. The setting begins halfway through the first system with the ornate capital C and ends at the beginning of the fifth system; the opening is transcribed in Example 2-8b.

as a chant (cf. Anthology Vol 1-4b), it was something of a favorite for polyphonic treatment in the twelfth century. An anonymous treatise from around 1100 called *Ad organum faciendum* (How to Make Organum) had already used it to demonstrate note-against-note **discant** in a rather dogged contrary motion (Ex. 2-8a). That example has its own historical significance because it is one of the earliest settings to give the vox organalis a higher tessitura than the original melody. The placement of the counterpoint above the chant makes a particularly apt comparison with the melismatic setting of the same item in the Codex Calixtinus (Ex. 2-8b). Putting them side by side, we can easily imagine the one, or something like it, turning into the other over time and finally getting written down as a "keeper."

Example 2-8a ***Cunctipotens genitor*** **setting, from** ***Ad organum faciendum*****, opening**

Example 2-8b ***Cunctipotens genitor*** **setting, from Codex Calixtinus, opening**

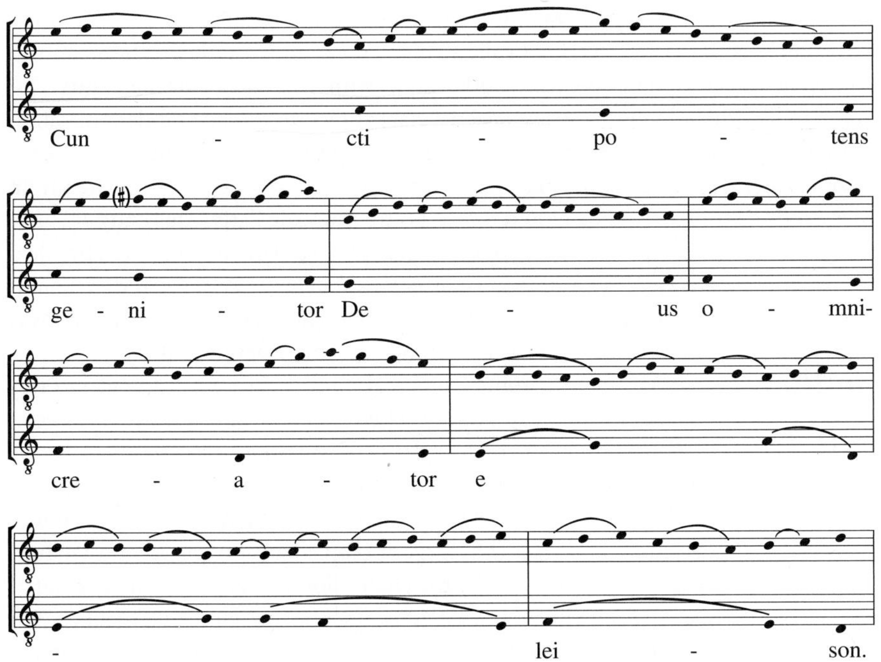

All-powerful father, Lord, creator of all, have mercy upon us

The transcription in Example 2-8b has been spatially laid out so that the notes in the tenor come beneath notes in the vox organalis that form perfect consonances with it. Yet this arrangement corresponds only loosely with the way in which the parts line up in the manuscript. While manuscript alignment may not be the most reliable guide, there were generally held theoretical principles from the time that help us determine which pitches sounded together. Particularly important was the principle mentioned in the previous chapter of occursus, moving to the concluding consonance by contrary motion. The strategic placement of dissonance (or imperfect consonance) immediately before perfect consonance and its "resolution" to the latter by contrary voice leading was regarded as the essential function of discant harmony. It became the primary signal of closure, or phrase ending in polyphonic music, the necessary determiner of cadences, and eventually the primary shaper of musical form. As befits something so important to musical structure and perception, it was eventually standardized in the "laws of counterpoint."

The Cathedral-University Complex

The grandest, most ambitious polyphony originated in the heart of Paris, the grandest, most ambitious city in northern Europe—the intellectual capital of Europe. Urbanization, on the ascent since the eleventh century, had begun to soar. Over the century ending around 1250, Paris doubled in size. Many of its streets were paved and its walls expanded. The first Louvre, a mighty fortress, and several major churches were built; the city's schools were organized into a university.

Urbanization brought about a decline in the importance of monasteries as centers of learning and a swift rise in the prestige of cathedral schools. The enhanced importance of the cathedral churches, which served as administrative centers for a surrounding ecclesiastical territory called a *diocese*, was underscored by the gigantism of their architecture. The so-called Gothic style, with its soaring pillars and huge, hierarchically ordered interior spaces, had its start at this time. The grandeur of cathedrals, their sheer size and beauty, eclipsed every other building and inspired a sense of awe. The cornerstone of the present-day cathedral of Paris, dedicated to the Virgin Mary and affectionately known therefore as Notre Dame de Paris (Our Lady of Paris) or simply as Notre Dame (Fig. 2-11), was laid in 1163 by Pope Alexander III. The altar was consecrated twenty years later, and the building began to function, although the whole enormous structure was not finished until the beginning of the fourteenth century.

The grandest, most ambitious polyphony originated in the heart of Paris, the grandest, most ambitious city in northern Europe—the intellectual capital of Europe.

Within and around the great Gothic cathedrals, the clergy was organized into a community. The resident staff or faculty was sworn to a quasi-monastic regime defined by a *canon*, or consensual law. A full member of the community was called a "canon regular," the group of whom in turn elected the bishop who ruled them. The community of canons, known as the *college* or *chapter*, was organized into a hierarchy of offices overseen by the chancellor or dean, the bishop's chief of staff. They included the *scolasticus* (school director) and the *precentor* (musical director). Much of this vocabulary is now used to designate positions in a university, and that is no coincidence. The university as we know it was a twelfth-century innovation, initially formed by consolidating and augmenting the faculties of cathedral schools. The University of Paris was the first great northern European university, preceded only by the University of Bologna. As a physical campus it grew up alongside the new cathedral; it was fully functioning by around 1170. It later became known as the Sorbonne.

Figure 2-11 Cathedral of Notre Dame in Paris.

This unprecedented royal/papal and educational/ecclesiastical establishment was the environment in which an equally unprecedented music thrived. Our knowledge of it, while extensive, is curiously indirect, pieced together by collating evidence from a few skimpy descriptive accounts, four lengthy musical manuscripts, and half a dozen more or less detailed theoretical treatises. These sources transmit what we now call the "Notre Dame School" of polyphonic composition. The new music associated with Notre Dame was as ambitious as the grand cathedral for which it was composed. The pieces took their stylistic bearings from existing polyphonic repertories but vastly outstripped their predecessors in every dimension—length, range, and number of voices. The music of Notre Dame exemplified St. Augustine's metaphor of "a mind poured forth in joy," but it also accorded with the size of the reverberant spaces it had to fill and with a message of institutional triumph at a time notable for its triumphant institutionalism.

The bulk of the surviving repertoire is found in three service books compiled in Paris in the mid- to late thirteenth century and one compiled in Britain. Although they contain a lot of music, these are not themselves large choir books. The actual written area of a page from the smallest of them measures about 5½ by 2½ inches, while the largest measures only about 6¼ by 4 inches. A musicologist in her study, working at leisure, has to squint to make out the tiny fly specks; such a book could hardly have been used in the act of performing. The assumption has to be, rather, that the Notre Dame cantors and anyone else who sang their music in the dark confines of a Medieval church performed from memory. A codex copied in Paris during the 1240s, now housed in the Medici library in Florence and usually called the "Florence manuscript," is known as Flo or simply as F. Roughly contemporaneous is a manuscript copied in England or Scotland for the Augustinian Abbey of St. Andrews, now the older of two Notre Dame codices kept at the former ducal library in the German town of Wolfenbüttel, for which reason it is known as W_1. Another manuscript, also copied in Paris but about two or three decades later than F, is also now in Wolfenbüttel and known as W_2. In addition to these three sources there is a slightly smaller one called Ma, roughly contemporaneous with W_2, copied for the cathedral at Toledo, and now at the National Library in Madrid.

These four principal Notre Dame sources house a far more imposing body of polyphonic chant settings than the modest repertories of the St. Martial and Compostela manuscripts, just as the great central cathedral-university complex itself stood in relation to the outlying monasteries of an earlier age. The earlier repertories had been primarily local ones, emphasizing patron saints and observances. The new one emphasized the general liturgy, the great yearly feasts, and the largest, musically most elaborate liturgical occasions, such as Christmas and Easter. Where the earlier repertories had consisted, with rare exceptions, of two-part settings that paired the original chant tenor with one added voice, there are Notre Dame settings with two added parts, for a total texture of three voices, and even a few specialty items with three added parts, for an unheard-of complement of four.

The music of Notre Dame exemplified St. Augustine's metaphor of "a mind poured forth in joy."

The earlier repertories had favored two styles: the note-against-note discant and the somewhat more florid organum, with the tenor sustained against short melismatic flights in the added voice. The typical Notre Dame composition alternated these two styles and took both of them to extremes. In the organum sections a single tenor note could last a minute or more, furnishing a series of protracted drones supporting tremendous melismatic outpourings; the discant sections, by contrast, were driven by rhythms that, for the first time, were precisely fixed in the notation.

Works of the Notre Dame composers could be used anywhere the Latin liturgy of the Western Christian Church was employed. The composers aspired to encyclopedic completeness: It is evident that the surviving codices reflect attempts to outfit the entire calendar of feasts with polyphony. Thus, with their works, the musicians of Notre Dame symbolized the strong, united church they served and promoted catholicism in the literal and original sense of the word. We know their program was successful from the dispersion of works in the existing sources. The central Parisian repertory was copied far and wide and sung well beyond its home territory; this repertory lasted for generations after its creators' lives had ended.

Piecing the Evidence Together

Like most manuscripts containing music for ecclesiastical use, the Notre Dame sources carried no attributions of authors' names. Only secular works, such as courtly songs, sometimes included names. Thanks to the alliance of the Church of Notre Dame with the University of Paris, however, we do know the identities of some of the composers as well as something about the history of the repertory and its early development. The information identifies the first "big name" composers in Western music after Hildegard of Bingen, who was active slightly earlier.

Around 1270 or 1280, an English student in Paris wrote approvingly about the music there in a treatise called *De mensuris et discantu* (On Rhythmic Notation and Discant). His account was published some six centuries later, in 1864, as the fourth item in a batch of anonymous Medieval writings on music. Unfortunately, the treatise has been associated ever since with the writer instead of the text. The poor fellow, whomever he was and whatever his real name may have been, is forever known to music history students as "Anonymous Four," after the treatise's nineteenth-century publication as *Anonymus IV* (with the Latin spelling and Roman numeral). In any case, the treatise seems something like a set of university lecture notes. The most famous passage in the treatise honors "Leoninus magister" (Master Leonin), who, "it is said," was the best *organista* (maker of organum). He made a *magnus liber*, a "great book" of about 100 two-voice organa on both Mass and Office chants. That is all we are told about Master Leonin.

Next, the Anonymus IV treatise reports what the lecturer said about *Perotinus magnus* (the great Perotin), who was the best *discantor* (composer of discant) and "better than Leoninus."[6] Perotin is identified first as the reviser of Leonin's work. He also inserted many ***clausulae*** (little discant sections) of his own devising into Leonin's compositions. The revision of the *Magnus liber organi* did not entail the goals that a modern editor might have in establishing an improved, corrected, or definitive text. The aim, rather, seems to have been to make a wealth of interchangeable material available.

The Anonymus IV treatise provides a list—we have no idea how complete—of Perotin's original works, beginning with the real newsmakers: the *quadrupla*, organa in four parts (that is, three parts added above the Gregorian tenor). Two specific titles are given: *Viderunt omnes fines terrae* ("All the ends of the earth have seen") and *Sederunt principes et adversum me loquebantur* ("Princes sat and plotted against me"), both of them Graduals that appear to have been composed at the very end of the twelfth century. Three musicians in all are named in Anonymus IV: besides Leonin and Perotin, there is one Robert de Sabilone, who is lavishly praised but otherwise unidentified and whose name is found nowhere else. Beyond their names we do not know much about who these people actually were, although a number of candidates have been proposed for Leonin. One suggestion is that he was a canon and priest at Notre Dame and St. Victor whose peak of documented activity was reached in the 1180s and 1190s and who died in 1201 or 1202. This Leonin is identified not as a musician but as a poet of considerable renown, best known for his paraphrase of the first eight books of the Old Testament in verse—some 14,000 lines of it![7]

But about Perotin, whom the author of Anonymus IV treatise emphatically insists was the greatest musician of his time, we mainly have a few remarks in a set of lecture notes taken down by a nameless student at least fifty and possibly as many as seventy years after his death. Like the music manuscripts themselves, the surviving documentation of Leonin's and Perotin's existence is fragile and sporadic at best. And yet the very names of these composers give the aura of a "creation myth"—that is, a story that seeks to account for the existence of something wonderful (here, the matchless repertory of polyphonic music at Notre Dame) by supplying it with an origin and an originator. Compare the way the Bible accounts for the existence of music by naming its inventor—Jubal, son of Lamech, "the forerunner of all who play the harp and flute" (Genesis 4:21)—or the way Franz Joseph Haydn was later named the "Father of the Symphony," to say nothing of Saint Gregory and his dove. The author of Anonymus IV is one of the first to give a benediction on a great composer—we will encounter many more in the chapters to come.

Measured Music

The glory of the repertory of Notre Dame polyphony in the eyes of its latter-day practitioners was the fact that it was metrical. That is to say, it managed to incorporate precise time measurement into composition and notation. It accomplished this feat by adapting to musical purposes the principles of versification long familiar from poetry. In a quantitative poetic meter, one assumes at least two abstract durations—one "long" and the other "short." They are related to each other by some simple arithmetic proportion, the simplest being a factor of 2, with a long equaling two shorts. Two note lengths were assumed: a *nota longa* (shortened in normal parlance to *longa,* or, in English, a "long") and a *nota brevis* (*brevis,* or a "breve"). A long was assumed to equal two breves, and the simplest way of turning their relationship into a metrical pattern (called an *ordo,* plural *ordines*) was simply to alternate them: LBLBLBLBLBL . . . ; in effect "tum-ta-tum-ta-tum-ta-tum-ta-tum-ta-tum . . . ," and so on. This was the basic *modus* (or "rhythmic mode" or "way of doing rhythm") in use during Leonin's time.

So the standard musical "foot" (*pes*) was like the "trochee" of classical poetry: a long followed by a short. The difference between a pes (mere building material) and an ordo (an actual "line" of musical poetry) was that the ordo ended with a long at the end of a poetic line, after which a pause could take place for the sake of scansion or simply for a breath. The beautiful elegance in this abstractly conceived "modal" meter was that its notation did not require the invention of any new signs or shapes. The old square chant neumes could be adapted directly to the new purpose. There was no special sign for a long note or for a short one such as we use today in modern notation. There was no need, because the unit of notation was not the individual note but, rather, the ordo, the pattern. The most efficient way of representing such a pattern of measured sounds was by a pattern of familiar neume shapes—that is, ligatures, in which two, three, or more pitches were bound together in a single sign. An ordo was represented by a particular sequence of these shapes. The basic long/short modus was signaled by an initial three-note ligature (*ternaria*) followed by any number of two-note ones (*binariae*) (Ex. 2-9a). If you wanted the opposite metrical arrangement ("iambic" rather than "trochaic" meter), in which the basic foot is BL and the first perfect ordo is BLB, all you had to do was reverse the pattern of ligatures: a series of two-note ligatures followed by a three-note one (Ex. 2-9b). Thus the rhythmic significance of a given neume shape was not absolute but depended on the context. Later, of course, shapes—both of single notes and of ligatures—did acquire inherent meanings.

Example 2-9a Trochaic pattern notated with "modal" ligatures

Example 2-9b Iambic pattern notated with "modal" ligatures

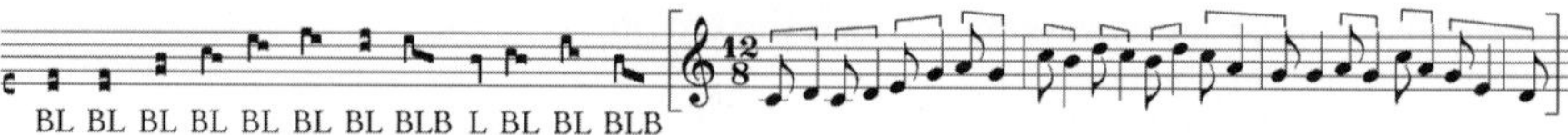

Anthology Vol 1-18
Full CD I, 34
Concise CD I, 30

We can see Notre Dame polyphony in action, rhythm and all, in a two-part setting, an ***organum duplum***, of the kind associated in Anonymus IV with the original "great book" of Leonin. It is a setting of the Gradual *Viderunt omnes*, used variously at Christmas (25 December) and at the Feast of the Circumcision (1 January). This

Gradual opens the *Magnus liber organi* in all its existing sources and received particularly elaborate treatment, beginning with this two-voice setting that was later recomposed for four voices.

The two-voice setting in the Florence manuscript is based on a chant melody that is used as the tenor—the lowest voice (Fig. 2-12a). It is immediately evident that the Notre Dame style gave new meaning to the word melisma. The first syllable of text ("Vi-") carries an outpouring of more than forty notes of **duplum** set against a single note in the tenor. At such a rate, it seems, it might take forever to get through the entire chant; in fact, the organum setting is drastically incomplete. After the opening pair of words, "Viderunt omnes," the organum skips all the way to the words "Notum fecit." The composer took notice of the way the soloist and choir divide up the text in the original responsorial chant and set as organum only the soloist's portion. We might think of the two-voice polyphony, therefore, as representing a multiplied soloist. Polyphony at Notre Dame was an art of virtuoso soloists and something of a counterpart to the rich visual decorations found in the manuscripts. As befits its pride of place, *Viderunt omnes* is decorated in the particularly lavish Florence manuscript with an impressive illuminated capital *V* containing a three-part illustration (Fig. 2-12b).

Comparing the original chant in Figure 2-12a further with the organum in Figure 2-12b, we notice that when the soloist's portion of the chant has its own melismas (at "om-" of *omnes* and especially at "Do-" of *Dominus*), the organum tenor notes at this point are written in clumps, taking up far less space, which means far less time. The primary motivation for hurrying the tenor along at such spots was undoubtedly practical, but what begins in necessity often ends in play—that is, in "art." It was precisely these hurried-along sections of the organum, where the tenor itself is melismatic, that evoked from composers what we would call the greatest artfulness or creativity.

Figure 2-12 (a) The Christmas gradual *Viderunt omnes* as it appears in *Liber usualis*, the standard modern chant book of the Catholic Church (in use from 1903 to 1963). Translation: "All the ends of the earth have seen the salvation of our God; sing joyfully to God, all the earth. The Lord hath made known his salvation; he hath revealed his justice in the sight of the Gentiles" (Psalm 98). (b) *Viderunt omnes* set as organum duplum, perhaps by Leonin, as the first item in *Magnus liber de gradali et antefonario* (Florence, Biblioteca Medica Laurenziana, Plut.29.I, fol. 99-99v).

(a)

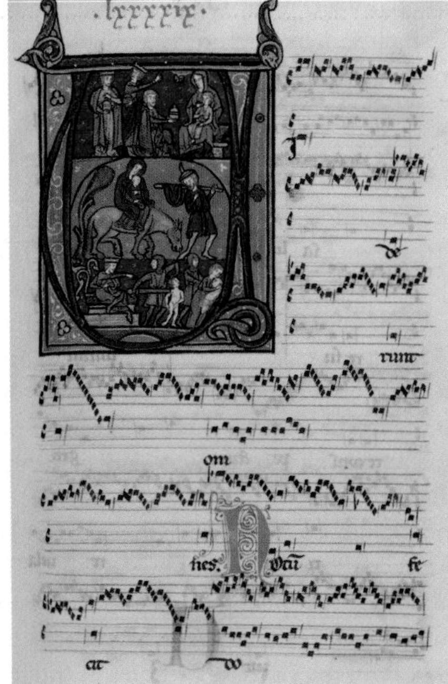

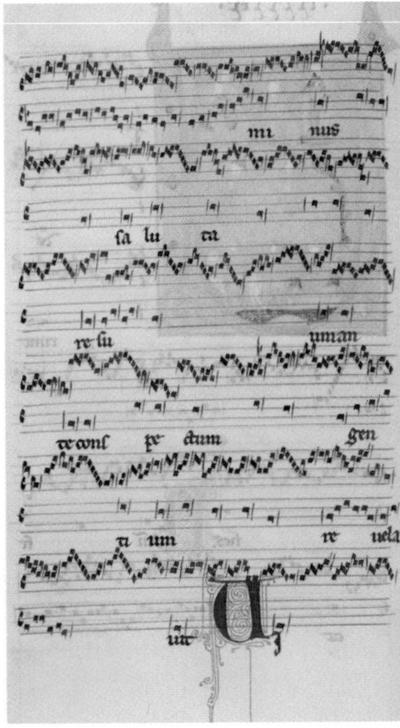

(b)

In a style where free organum sections with a slow tenor and discant sections are so radically contrasted in rhythm, meter, and speed, it is not surprising that there is an intermediate texture as well, called ***copula*** (from the Latin for "something that binds," like a string). In a copula, the duplum usually sings two phrases in regular modal patterns over sustained tenor notes. Here, on the other hand, the ratio of notes in the duplum to notes in the tenor in such sections becomes much closer; we are now obviously dealing with a type of note-against-note discant, or ***clausula***. It is here that we are most apt to find the clear organization of ligatures in the duplum voice into patterns of the so-called rhythmic modes, invoking the metrical schemes described earlier.

In the brief discant sections where the tenor chant moves rapidly against the modal rhythms of the duplum, it too must be organized into notes of determinate length. The usual method was to have each note of the tenor equal a metrical foot in the duplum. Such a note would equal the sum of a long and a breve, and theorists revealingly called this longer note by different names. Some were content to call the three-tempora length a *longa ultra mensuram*, which simply means "a long beyond [normal] measure." Others, however, called it a "perfect" (that is, completed) long, recognizing it as the primary unit, of which the shorter values were now both regarded as subdivisions. Theorists began to speak abstractly of "perfections"—time units measured out in advance, as it were, waiting to be filled. Such a concept corresponds in some ways to our modern idea of a measure.

Organum with Another Voice

As a fully elaborated system of metrics and notation, modal rhythm pertains not to the orally created and rhythmically transmitted music of the Leonin generation but rather to the very intricate and stylized output of the Perotin generation, which is found in all its many sources in essentially one version and which may have been the first musical style in the West that depended on notation for its composition. The major works from Perotin's time differ from those of the previous generation in the fundamental respect that they are written for more than two parts. The presence of the added voice or voices changed everything. These new upper voices moved at the rate of the duplum, not the tenor (so they were called the ***triplum*** and, when present, the *quadruplum*). Two or three parts moving at a similar rate are in effect in discant with one another, and so they had to be notated throughout in strict modal rhythm. Everything now had to move in countable groups, or "perfections."

Anthology Vol 1-19
Full CD I, 35
Concise CD I, 31

For an example at its most luxuriant, we can examine the four-part setting of *Viderunt omnes* attributed to Perotin in Anonymus IV. This was the recognized jewel in the Notre Dame crown and moves throughout in an especially stately version of the trochaic meter we first observed in Leonin's version. The long-held opening note in the duplum, triplum, and quadruplum creates a chord that is a composite of all the perfect consonances (*symphoniae*). There is an octave between the tenor and the triplum, a fifth between the tenor and the duplum (or the quadruplum), a fourth between the duplum and the triplum, and a prime or unison between the duplum and the quadruplum (Ex. 2-10). This harmony—built on the Pythagorean perfect consonances—would be the standard consonance for polyphony in three or more parts until the sixteenth century. Although not every piece made such a spectacular opening display of it as Perotin's *Viderunt omnes*, every piece had to end with it.

Example 2-10 ***Viderunt omnes*** **a 4 (attributed to Perotin), opening**

The perfect long preceding the final consonance is calculated to achieve the maximum possible dissonance (*asymphonia*), both with respect to the tenor and within the upper parts themselves. In making the resolution, every voice proceeds by step. The dissonant second between the triplum and quadruplum arises not out of some "nonharmonic" Medieval way of hearing (as we are sometimes tempted to imagine it) but out of the implied voice-leading rule that dissonance proceeds to consonance by step. We have, in short, the beginnings of a cadential practice here, in which the motions of the individual parts are subordinated to an overall harmonic function (maximum dissonance resolving to maximum consonance). This is the beginning of harmonic tonality (or, if you prefer, of tonal harmony). It exemplifies textural integration, control, and planning.

Throughout the piece Perotin also engages in elaborate voice exchanges by which a passage from one voice moves between and among the upper parts. This procedure begins with part of the triplum in the first ordo moving to the duplum in the second ordo and on further from there. Another device he exploits is the *hoquetus*—"hocket" in English—from the Latin for "hiccup." Here the voice exchanges of notes and rests interrupt the melodic lines like spasms.

The spirit of creative exuberance, of delight in construction, so evident in this magnificent example of four-part polyphony, led inevitably to greater rhythmic variety, such as a new metric foot made up of a long and two breves (LBB). The most authoritative source for our knowledge of the epochal rhythmic practices of the Notre Dame School is the treatise *De mensurabili musica* (On Measured Music), which was long attributed to Johannes de Garlandia, who appears to have updated an earlier anonymous thirteenth-century treatise.

Although the treatise claimed to be based on observation (descriptive rather than speculative), the discussion of the rhythmic modes was in fact not really descriptive—at least not entirely. Rather, it was adopted from the poetic meters listed in an authoritative grammar textbook written a few decades earlier. From this model the author of *De mensurabili musica* took over the six classical poetic meters that were defined in terms of long and short syllables, asserted that there were six rhythmic modes in use in Notre Dame polyphony, and arranged the modes in three symmetrical pairs. Modes 1 and 2 were the trochee (LB) and its reverse, the iamb (BL). Modes 3 and 4 were the dactyl (LBB) and its reverse, the anapest (BBL). Modes 5 and 6 were the spondee (LL), confined to longs, and its conceptual opposite the tribrach (BBB).

Although the second mode (BL) is occasionally found in the earliest layers of the *Magnus liber organi*, at least one of these modes, the fourth (BBL), was pure fiction, which was included in deference to authority. There is not a single practical source that contains music in this mode. Only brief passages in uniform breves, the sixth mode, are found in Notre Dame polyphony. (Sometimes longer notes are "broken up" into extra breves by a process called *fractio modi*, literally "breaking the rhythmic pattern.") Actual rhythmic practice therefore was more or less confined to three patterns corresponding to the odd-numbered modes. The even-numbered trio, put there for the sake of theoretical completeness, was later incorporated to some extent into practice under the influence of the theory. *De mensurabili musica*, which purported to describe a musical practice, thus ended up prescribing one instead. This situation invites us to consider the often-complex relationship between theory and practice. Theory is rarely pure description. It is often a representation not of the world the theorist actually sees but of a more orderly, more perfect, or more easily described world the theorist would like to see.

Conductus at Notre Dame

The remaining polyphonic genre practiced at Notre Dame was the ***conductus***, what we have previously called *versus*. Well over a hundred survive, in two, three, and four voices. Conductus was exceptional among Notre Dame genres in that it was not based on a preexisting chant but was a setting of a contemporary Latin poem, potentially composed from scratch. The texture of a conductus is basically homorhythmic (note-against-note) and syllabically texted. This is significant because it meant the music had to be notated in individual notes rather than in ligatures, and that is significant because ligatures were the available means of indicating rhythm. The conductus therefore exposed the chief shortcoming of the practice of modal rhythm: It was not possible to tell what mode was in play for pieces with words because the notation used individual notes rather than ligatures.

Anthology Vol 1-20
Full CD I, 36
Concise CD I, 32

Considering ligatures nonetheless gives us a possible solution to the problem of rhythm in the four-voice Christmas conductus *Vetus abit littera*. Until the next-to-last syllable of text, the notation consists almost entirely of single notes, but that penultimate syllable then has a sizable melisma in all voices. A concluding melisma, written in ligatures, is a standard feature in Notre Dame conductus settings and is called the ***cauda***, which means literally "the tail." One assumption is that the cauda may indicate the mode of the entire piece and is present not simply for the sake of embellishment. In this instance it could convey the otherwise unconveyable information that the whole piece is to be sung in "first mode," as is assumed in Example 2-11. The problem of *musica cum littera*—"music with letters" (that is, with words)—created the necessity that mothered the invention of an explicit rhythmic notation in which individual notes carried rhythmic information. First described in full in the mid-thirteenth century, it sustained three centuries of development and continues, in a more remote way, to underlie the rhythmic notation we still use today.

Example 2-11 ***Vetus abit littera,*** **transcribed in first mode, opening (mm. 1–4)**

The old world has passed away,
The ancient rite is gone,
The child-bearing virgin gives
To us a new son,
(Trans. Alexander Blachly)

The Motet: Music for an Intellectual and Political Elite

Some of what is known about Parisian musical life around 1300 comes from information provided by a university lecturer named Johannes de Grocheio, who wrote a remarkable treatise variously called *Ars musicae* (The Art of Music) or *De musica* (About Music).[8] What makes this treatise remarkable is its worldly bent. It contains neither cosmic speculation nor nuts-and-bolts theory nor a guide to notation. Instead, it offers a survey of "the music which men in Paris use," classified according to "how men in Paris use it." It is, in a way, the first sociological treatise on music, in which musical genres are defined primarily in terms of their "class" affiliations.

Grocheio's description of how various types of music are used is really a description of how he thought various types of music ought to be used. All the genres we have encountered thus far are given not so much an actual as an ideal place in a utopian depiction of social harmony. Thus epic songs (*chansons de geste*), for example, ought to be provided "for old men, working citizens, and for average people when they rest from their accustomed labor, so that, having heard the miseries and calamities of others, they may more easily bear up under their own, and go about their tasks more gladly," and without threatening the peace with any fresh notions about social justice.[9] "By these means," Grocheio adds, "this kind of music has the power to protect the whole state."

For an example at the other end of the social spectrum, Grocheio says that prize-winning trouvère songs are ordained among kings and nobles in order to "move their souls to audacity and bravery, to magnanimity and liberality,"[10] qualities that also keep society running smoothly. Lower types of secular song, namely, those with refrains, are meant for "the feasts of the vulgar," where they serve a similar edifying purpose, but more artlessly. Chant and organum, its polyphonic offspring, are "sung in churches or holy places for the praise of God and reverence of His high place." Even dance music has its assigned place in a well-ordered society, for it "excites the soul of man to move ornately" and in its more artful forms it "makes the soul of the performer and also the soul of the listener pay close attention and frequently turns the soul of the wealthy from depraved thinking." So despite Grocheio's insistence that he meant only to describe music in the world he knew, his account in the end is quite consistent with that of Plato, the greatest of all utopians and idealists. For both of them, music was a social regulator, a means for organizing and controlling society.

Part of Grocheio's treatise is devoted to the music of his own class, the music he knew best and valued most. It was a new sort of music, one that we have not encountered as yet: the *motet*, derived from French, in which *mot* is the word for "word." The simplest definition of a motet, in its earliest form, would be a texted bit of discant or clausula. Its origins were a syllabic text added to one or more of the upper voices of an organum. Since the duplum in a motet now has a text, it can no longer use the first-mode ligatures of the clausula. It is now a *motellus* (later, and more standardly, a *motetus*), a "texting" or a "part with words." Anyone actually inserting the motetus into the organum would have to know the rhythms of the clausula by heart. So at this early stage a motet had to be notated twice, both times with the tune, but once for the rhythm and again for the text. There was a large supply of clausulae to which composers could add words; the Notre Dame manuscripts feature sizeable sections devoted to these spare parts, today referred to as "substitute clausulae."

For Grocheio, epic songs ought to be provided "for old men, working citizens, and average people so that, having heard the miseries and calamities of others, they may more easily bear up under their own, and go about their tasks more gladly."

We can trace the process of constructing a motet by looking at one of Perotin's clausulae, *Ex semine*, from his three-voice organum *Alleluia Nativitas*. Figure 2-13a shows the clausula in its original notation, and Figure 2-13b shows the duplum from the same clausula with the words of a Latin poem added. This syllabic text honors both the Virgin Mary's birth and that of her son. The newly added poem is a gloss on the text of the *Alleluia Nativitas* in the manner of a trope. A page from a later manuscript containing nothing but motets has the same three-voice clausula on *Ex semine*, but in this case the triplum has another text, also a gloss reflecting on the marvel of the Virgin

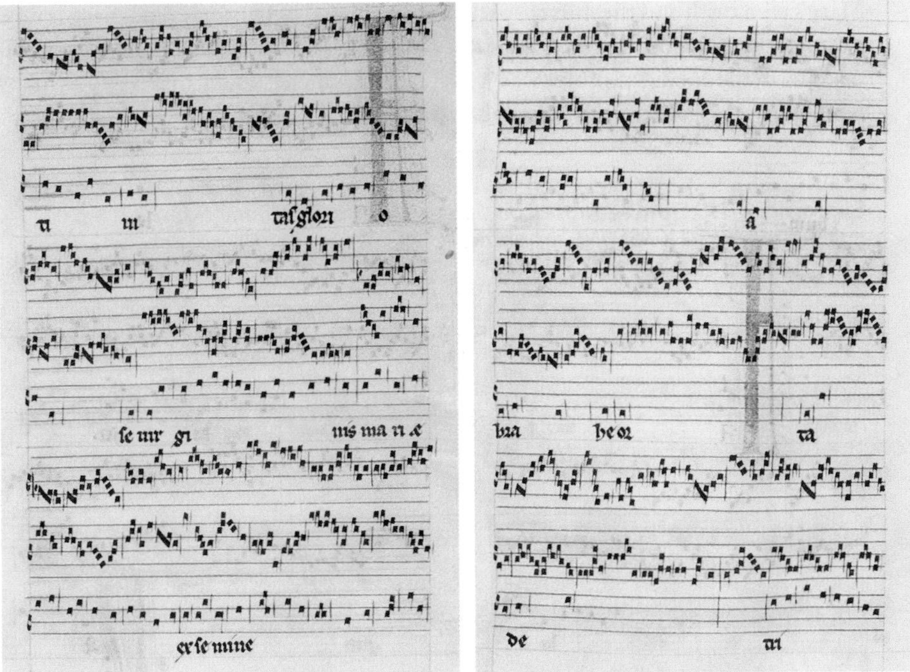

Figure 2-13a *Ex semine* clausula (W_2, fols. 16v–17). It begins halfway through the bottom system on the left.

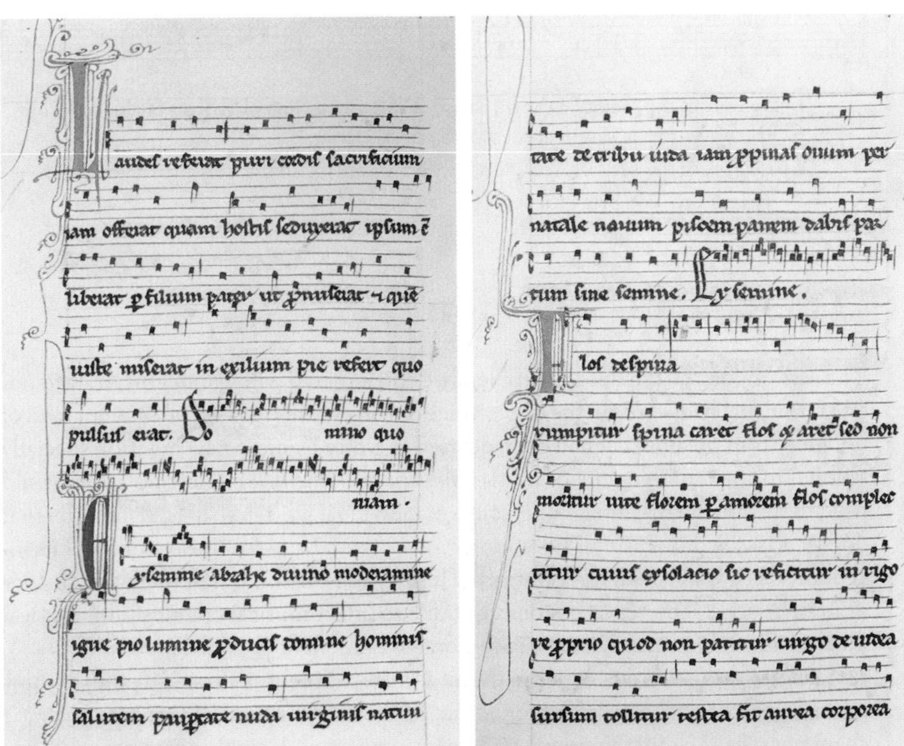

Figure 2-13b Motetus on the same clausula (W_2, fol. 146v–147) as in Figure 2-13a. It begins with the ornate capital E halfway down the left side and ends halfway down the right.

Anthology Vol 1-21
Full CD I, 37
Concise CD I, 33

Mary's own birth and the miracle of the "virgin birth," of her son's. The piece is now a doubly texted clausula, more commonly known as a *double motet*. In its fully developed form the Medieval motet was "polytextual," which is to say that it had as many texts as it had voices over the Gregorian tenor (Ex. 2-12).

Example 2-12 Double motet on *Ex semine rosa/Ex semine Habrahe/ EX SEMINE*, opening

Triplum: From the seed of a thorn, a rose comes forth. The olive fruit is plucked from the olive tree. A Virgin comes forth . . .

Duplum: From the seed of Abraham, by divine control, in the holy fire of your presence, Lord, you bring forth . . .

"Franconian" Notation

The early motet thus shares the problem we encountered with conductus: how to notate music that had words in the upper voice or voices. This required a different kind of notation from the one that had been devised at Notre Dame, a new notation specially tailored to the requirements of motets, *musica cum littera*. The new notation would need to specify the rhythmic significance of individual written shapes. A notation that does this is called "mensural" notation, from *mensura*, Latin for "measurement." Its invention was a watershed, not only in the history of notation but in the wider history of musical style. The repercussions continue to affect musical composition, musical practice, musical attitudes, and musical controversies right up to the present day.

The notation that developed in the mid-thirteenth century to specify the rhythms of the motet was efficiently fashioned out of the existing fund of familiar quadratic chant neumes. The first prerequisite was to come up with single note shapes to represent the long and the short (longa and brevis). The solution will seem obvious to us, who have lived with its consequences since birth, but at the time it was a considerable feat of imagination. Chant notation already possessed two different single-note shapes: the point, or *punctum* (simple square), and the rod, or *virga* (square with tail at right). Whereas these symbols had previously been used to indicate pitch, they were now adapted for duration. Thanks to the explicit differentiation of longs and breves, it now became possible to indicate the trochaic rhythm (LB) of the familiar clausula without the use of ligatures. And there was an additional benefit: Because the individual notes had intrinsic rhythmic values, it was no longer necessary to align the parts in score, which saved valuable space on the page.

The fullest discussion of early **mensural notation** is found in a famous treatise called *Ars cantus mensurabilis* (The Art of Measured Song) by a German writer, Franco of Cologne, whose name has become attached to the notation he described. The principles of "Franconian" notation, first formulated by around 1280 and much modified over the years, were enormously influential. Franco's rhythmic notation did not replace the contextual aspects of "modal" notation; rather, it represented a compromise of sorts between the intrinsic and the contextual. A virga unambiguously represented a long rather than a breve, but that long could be either a perfect (three-tempora) long or an imperfect (two-tempora) long, depending on the context. A punctum unambiguously represented a breve and not a long, but that breve could be a normal one-tempus breve (*brevis recta*) or a two-tempora "altered" breve (*brevis altera*). The contexts, which can be complicated, are partially spelled out in Example 2-13, which outlines some of the basic principles of Franconian notation. The remaining innovation was the division of the breve (or tempus) into semibreves so that three note values were available. For the semibreve, too, an existing musical sign was co-opted. It was represented by the diamond shape that had originally been part of the three-note descending neume in Gregorian chant notation known as the *climacus*.

Example 2-13 Principles of Franconian notation

Three note values:

(long), (breve), (semibreve),

Longs are defined as "perfect" (i.e., containing three breves),

=

unless "imperfected' by a single intervening breve.

=

If two breves intervene between longs, the second is "altered,"

=

unless a "point of division" says otherwise:

=

Semibreves are to breves as breves are to longs.

=

When they come only in pairs they may be presumed equal:

=

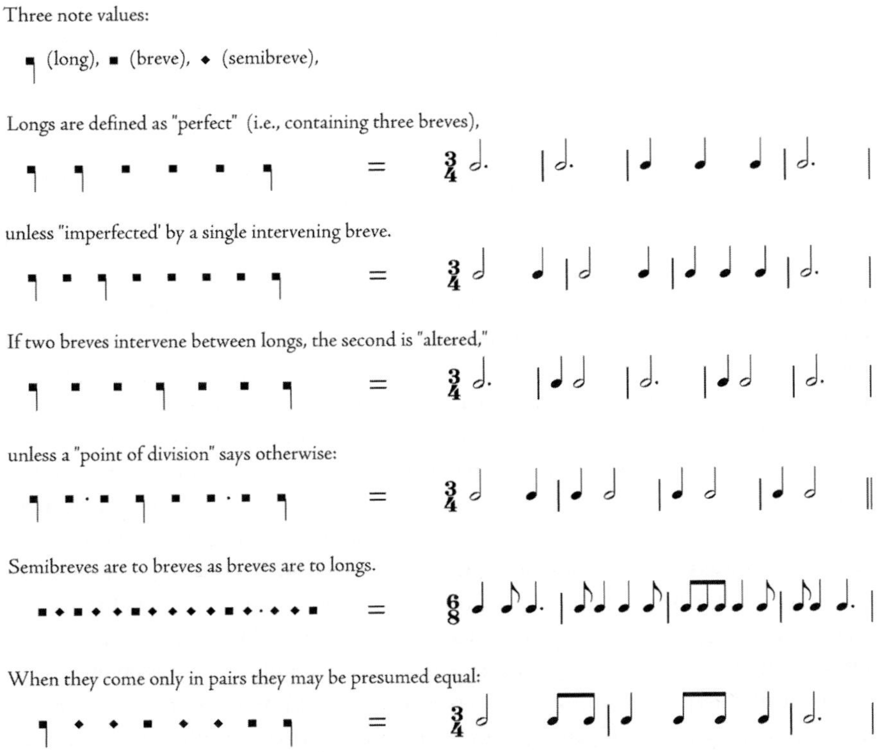

Example 2-13 (continued)

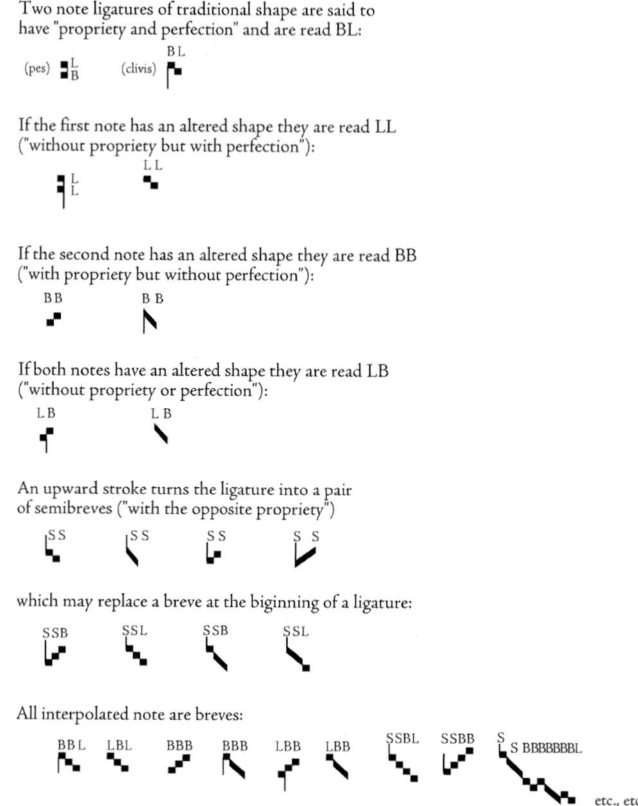

Two note ligatures of traditional shape are said to have "propriety and perfection" and are read BL:
(pes) L B
(clivis) BL
If the first note has an altered shape they are read LL ("without propriety but with perfection"):
L L
LL
If the second note has an altered shape they are read BB ("with propriety but without perfection"):
BB
BB
If both notes have an altered shape they are read LB ("without propriety or perfection"):
LB
LB
An upward stroke turns the ligature into a pair of semibreves ("with the opposite propriety")
SS SS SS SS
which may replace a breve at the biginning of a ligature:
SSB SSL SSB SSL
All interpolated note are breves:
BBL LBL BBB BBB LBB LBB SSBL SSBB S S BBBBBBBL
etc., etc.

The motets derived from a specific clausula-protoype demonstrate the descent of the motet from the liturgical repertory of Notre Dame. That is only half the story, though. There is yet another texting of the same *Ex semine* clausula we have been looking at, which is musically identical if we allow for some minor copying variants. This motet, *Se j'ai ame/EX SEMINE*, thus has the same tune but now with different words, which is called a ***contrafactum***. This motet comes from a Notre Dame source (W_2 fols. 136–136v) and involves a change not only of words but also of language, from Latin to French. The *Ex semine* clausula is effectively transformed into a French song for two voices over a vocalized or instrumental tenor. Its text, skillfully modeled to fit the irregular phrases of the original clausula, begins in translation: "If I have loved/I should not be blamed/Since I am pledged/To the fairest little/creature in Paris town." Allowing for a bit of urbanization ("Paris town"), this is a trouvère poem in all but name.

Recall that the trouvère tradition was in the process of transplantation. Geographically it was moving from its original abode in the aristocratic countryside to the towns of northern France; in terms of genre, its destination was the new motet, the primary site for the production of French "literary song" in the late thirteenth century. The motet in French was thus an interesting hybrid, crossbred from two exceedingly disparate traditions, each of which showed its own overlap between the courtly and the ecclesiastical. We can imagine that city-dwelling clerics, who would have known and valued both the urbanized chanson and the texted organum, would have been the ones most apt to crossbreed the two and arrive at a new music that pleased them particularly.

A New *Trobar Clus*?

By the end of the thirteenth century the motet was becoming increasingly elaborate. People like Grocheio reveled in the complexity of the polytextual motet. An example of the fully evolved, late thirteenth-century French motet is *L'autre jour/ Au tens pascour/IN SECULUM*. The form of the piece is clearly clausula-derived, although there is no known clausula counterpart to it. Two parts in trochaic meter (first mode) are composed against a spondaic (fifth mode) cantus firmus borrowed from a Gregorian melisma we know, the Easter Gradual *Haec dies* (cf. Ex. 1-14b). The motetus and triplum texts are both little pastourelles reminiscent of trouvère poetry, even down to the name of Robin the shepherd and a cliché beginning that goes all the way back to the troubadours: "The other day at morn/down by a valley/ at break of day/I spied a shepherdess/and watched her a while."

Anthology Vol 1-22
Full CD I, 38

Naive and folksy as these texts seem, they are cast in a very urbane musical construction that contradicts their rustic nature. That comic incongruity is already one delightful aspect of *ars combinatoria*, the art of combining things. And it is one reason why Grocheio, the intellectual connoisseur, placed the motet at the summit of Parisian genres, for it was "a song composed of many voices, having many words or a variety of syllables, [but] everywhere sounding in harmony."[11] The harmonization of contrary things (*discordia concors*) encompassed the texts as well as the tunes, even including the unsung, incongruously Latinate and liturgical text of the tenor. The duplum text begins with a reference to Eastertime ("At Eastertime/All the shepherd folk/from one locale/gathered together/at the bottom of a valley"), which obliquely alludes to the source of the Easter chant melisma on which the whole polyphonic superstructure of the motet has been erected. Motets are full of such in-jokes.

But that was not the only reason for Grocheio's devotion to the new genre. As usual, the theorist prescribes as well as describes, and this is his prescription for the motet:

> This kind of song ought not to be propagated among the vulgar, since they do not understand its subtlety nor do they delight in hearing it, but it should be performed for the learned and those who seek after the subtleties of the arts. And it is normally performed at their feasts for their edification, just as the song they call rondeau is performed at the feasts of the vulgar.[12]

And so this song, all about the shepherds and their faithful lassies, is not to be sung before Robin, Roger, and their gang, because they would never understand it. In fact, the complicated polytextual song itself served to mark off the occasion at which it is sung—a university recreation, or, as Grocheio puts it, a "feast of the learned." Such elite occasions allowed the members of Grocheio's new class to demonstrate their superiority to the "vulgar." Now that seems to ring a bell. This is similar to the sentiments we saw in the mock debate between two troubadours over the values of *trobar clus*, the "difficult" poetry of the courtly elite.

Grocheio's praise of exclusionary values on behalf of the motet is an excellent example of the way in which newly emerging elites—in this case the urban and literate elite, many of whose members had been drawn from the lower classes—aspire to the status of an older, established aristocracy. The self-congratulating learned class represented by Grocheio provided an audience that encouraged composers to experiment and vie with one another in the creation of *tours de force*, feats of ingenuity.

As part of this process, the motet became a hotbed of technical innovation and multifaceted adventure.

The most comprehensive and lavishly appointed motet book to survive from the thirteenth century is the so-called Montpellier Codex, which contains more than 300 motets of every description, ranging in date over the whole century. The motets are gathered in eight fascicles; the first six seem to have been compiled around 1280, but the last part dates from the turn of the fourteenth century, Grocheio's time exactly. By now the fun-and-games aspect of *discordia concors* had so grown as to invite free choice of found objects in all parts, the more extravagant the better.

Anthology Vol 1-23
Full CD I, 39
Concise CD I, 34

The anonymous motet *On parole/A Paris/FRESE NOUVELE* is one of those racy things Grocheio particularly recommends for his "feasts of the learned" (Ex. 2-14). Semibreves permeate all parts. The triplum and motetus texts are descriptions of just such Medieval fraternity parties as Grocheio describes, at which young scholars gathered to gorge on food and drink and nuzzle girls and despise manual labor and praise Paris. And the tenor? It consists of a fourfold repetition of a fruit seller's cry—"Fresh strawberries, ripe blackberries!"—possibly drawn directly "from life" as lived on the Parisian streets. A motet like this one, in which both musical and subject matter are entirely urban and entirely secular, no longer has any direct relationship to the courtly and ecclesiastical traditions that historically nourished the genre.

Example 2-14 ***On parole/A Paris/FRESE NOUVELE*, opening**

Triplum: The talk is of threshing and winnowing, of digging and ploughing. Such pastimes are not at all to my liking. For there is nothing like having one's fill . . .
Duplum: Morning and night in Paris there is good bread to be found and good, clear wine, good meat and fish . . .
Tenor: Fresh strawberries! Nice blackberries! Blackberries, nice blackberries!

The "Petronian" Motet

We will close our discussion of the late-thirteenth-century motet by mentioning the one that opens the seventh fascicle of the Montpellier Codex. On the basis of citations by fourteenth-century writers, these motets are attributed to a shadowy but evidently important composer and theorist named Petrus de Cruce (Pierre de la Croix). The motet *Aucun/Lonc tans/ANNUN* (and another half dozen with similar characteristics conjecturally credited to Petrus) is in a very special style that takes the device of rhythmic stratification to the very limit that contemporary notation allowed (Ex. 2-15).

Example 2-15 Petrus de Cruce, *Aucun/Lonc tans/ANNUN,* opening

Its tenor is of a traditional type, borrowed from a Notre Dame organum. The triplum has syllabically texted semibreves, the motetus has semibreves but carries syllables only on longs and breves or their equivalents, and the tenor moves in perfect longs throughout. And yet the sound and style of the piece are very novel indeed, owing to the flexibility with which the triplum part subdivides the basic beat. Petrus marks off the triplum's breve units (*tempora*) with little dots called division points (*puncta divisionis*) that function like modern bar lines, turning the tempora into measures. Between puncta there can be anywhere from two to seven semibreves. Modal rhythm now loses the patterning and governing properties that were its original reason for being. In addition, the exaggerated rhythmic differentiation of the triplum from the supporting voices has moved irrevocably beyond the origin of the motet style in the note-against-note texture of discant composition. While the technical innovations of its notation give such a piece its historical significance, we can see in the words of this motet a last look at the loftiest class of secular chanson, the troubadour and trouvère tradition with which this chapter began. The opening text of the triplum, for example, sounds the familiar theme of refined love:

Aucun ont trouvé chant par usage,	There are men who live by writing songs but I am inspired
Mes a moi en doune ochoison	by a love that so fills my heart with joy
Amours, qui resbaudist mon courage	that I can't stop myself writing a song.
Si que m'estuet faire chançon.	For a fair and lovely lady
Car amer me fait dame bele et sage	of high repute
Et de bon renon;	has made me love her
Et je, qui li ai fait houmage,	And I who am pledged to serve her
Pour li serviir tout mon age,	all my days without thought of betrayal,
De loial cuer sans penser trahison.	shall sing, for from her do I
Chanterai, car de li tieng un si douz heritage	hold such a sweet bequest
Que joie n'ai se de ce non:	that it alone can give me joy.
C'est la pensee que mon douz mal m'asouage	It is this thought that soothes my sweet sorrow
Et fait esperer garrison.	and gives me hope of curing it.

Summary

This chapter traces two interrelated developments: the emergence of new written traditions and the increasing emergence of identifiable composers. The earliest secular music to be written down and preserved was that of the poet-composers known as *troubadours,* who flourished in the twelfth and thirteenth centuries, lived in southern France, and wrote in the romance language known as Provençal. A favored type of song among the troubadours was the *canso,* which expressed the ideal of "courtly" love: devotion to a beloved lady, of higher social rank, who was unavailable and idolized (see Bernart de Ventadorn's *Can vei la lauzeta mover,* "When I see the lark unfurl his wings for joy"). Other genres included songs about a vassal addressing a lord, songs glorifying one's own accomplishments, and laments. Although the troubadours expressed aristocratic values, their songs were performed both by aristocrats and by traveling entertainers of the lower caste, called *joglars.*

In northern France, *troubadour* music and poetry were imitated by the *trouvères,* who flourished in cities such as Arras and Paris in the late twelfth and thirteenth centuries. The trouvères differed from the troubadours in their language—Medieval French rather than Provençal—and in their preference for narrative poetry. Beginning with Adam de la Halle (d. ca. 1307), composers of secular music started to write pieces in various types of refrain forms that became known as the *formes fixes.* In addition to his monophonic songs, Adam also composed polyphonic *rondeaux* that set pastoral poetry to sophisticated music, using music notation that at last specified rhythm.

The twelfth century saw the emergence of a new perspective in sacred polyphony, which survives in manuscripts from St. Martial, a monastery in the southern French city of Limoges. Like earlier polyphony, this practice was based on plainchant, but the chant melody now became the lower voice, allowing the added upper voice to gain a new prominence. The two parts were distinguished by their rate of movement: The chant melody in the lower voice was held out in long notes, hence the name *tenor* (from Latin word meaning "to hold"), whereas the upper part moved at a faster rate. Because the notation used at St. Martial does not indicate rhythm, we do not know precisely how the two parts were coordinated in performance.

During the twelfth century, the focus of learning and intellectual activity moved from the monasteries to the cathedrals of large cities, and the cathedral schools gave birth to the first universities. This development provided the context for a new type of learned polyphony that flourished at the Notre Dame Cathedral in Paris in the years between 1150 and 1250. Much of our historical knowledge about this practice comes from an Englishman studying in Paris, who wrote a treatise known to historians as Anonymus IV. Written in the 1270s, it identifies two composers of the Notre Dame repertory, Leonin and Perotin. In these new sacred repertories, rhythm was notated in a much more precise way. The basic rhythmic principle was the patterned alternation of long and short notes (longs and breves), which produced six different rhythmic patterns called rhythmic modes, corresponding roughly to the meters of poetic verse. When the modes are transcribed into modern notation, they are typically represented in triple meter. Two different musical styles are associated with Notre Dame polyphony. In melismatic organum, the original chant, always in the bottom voice, is set in very long, drawn-out notes in the tenor, above which the upper voices move much more rapidly. In discant style, the voices move together, each in a rhythmic mode. (See the settings of *Viderunt omnes fines terrae*, "All the ends of the earth have seen.")

Other types of music practiced at this time include the conductus and motet. The conductus was a setting of Latin verse that was homorhythmic (note-against-note) and not based on a preexisting chant (see *Vetus abit littera*, "The old world has passed away"). The early motets (from the French word for "word") were formed by adding words, in either Latin or French, to the top voice of a section of discant-style organum. The two upper voices of a discant were often given different texts. The two texts, heard simultaneously, were often on the same theme, providing a kind of commentary on one another. Because the conductus and motet had a syllabic text setting, they could not be notated in the rhythmic modes, which indicated rhythm by associating the long-familiar neumes and ligatures with particular patterns of longs and breves. As a solution, note shapes began to be used to represent duration. This approach, called mensural notation, was most fully described by the theorist Franco of Cologne in a treatise called *Ars cantus mensurabilis* (The Art of Measured Song, ca. 1280).

Study Questions

1. Compare and contrast troubadour and trouvère songs. What are some common topics and poetic genres in each repertory?
2. To what extent was troubadour music an oral style?

3. What is the difference between *trobar clus* and *trobar leu*? How do the debates on the relative merits of the two styles reflect questions about music that continue to be debated in the present day?
4. Discuss the diffusion of secular monophony in Iberia (Spain and Portugal), Italy, and German-speaking regions. What were the main genres?
5. Describe the music of Adam de la Halle. How does it reflect his time and place?
6. What type of polyphony flourished at the abbey of St. Martial in Limoges in the twelfth century?
7. What sources of information do we have about the polyphony that flourished at Notre Dame Cathedral in Paris in the twelfth and thirteenth centuries? How have historians pieced together the surviving bits of evidence?
8. What are the rhythmic modes? How did they originate, and how are they indicated in notation?
9. What is mensural notation? How did it differ from older rhythmic notation?
10. In Chapters 1 and 2, we have seen a progressive move from an oral tradition to a written one, with increasingly precise notation. Trace this change through Gregorian chant, troubadour and trouvère music, and different types of polyphony.
11. What aesthetic values are reflected in the Medieval motet?
12. What does Johannes de Grocheio's treatise *Ars musica* tell us about thirteenth-century musical practice and the social roles of different genres? What was Grocheio's attitude toward the motet, and how does it reflect the growing presence of an intellectual elite in Paris?

Key Terms

ballade
canso
cantus firmus
cauda
chansons de geste
clausula
conductus
contrafactum
copula
discant
duplum
fin' amors **(courtly love)**
formes fixes
joglar (jongleur)
ligature
mensural notation
Minnesang
motet
organum
pastorela
rondeau
tenor
tenso
triplum
trobar clus
troubadour
trouvère
versus
vida
virelai

3

The *Ars Nova*: Musical Developments in the Fourteenth Century

Notational innovations used in the increasingly complex motets we examined at the end of the previous chapter point to some new musical possibilities that blossomed in the fourteenth century. We need to be careful, however, to distinguish between technical progress and stylistic evolution. Technique is an aspect of production, of making art; style is an attribute of the product, and it involves the listener as well. Whereas new techniques can replace or invalidate old ones, new styles do not do this, at least so far as the beholder is concerned. The fact that so many of us still listen to old music as much as (if not more than) to new music is sufficient proof of that.

Seeking style change in the name of progress means merging the concepts of technique and style. To do that required a fundamental shift in the way artists (and not only artists) thought about means and ends. That change began to happen only near the end of the eighteenth century, and so we are a long way from investigating it in this book. But the question needs airing now, because the fourteenth century was without doubt a time of intensive and deliberate technical progress in music with an inevitable enormous change in musical style.

Some of the best evidence we have that fourteenth-century technical progress was a highly self-conscious affair comes from the titles of two important treatises from around 1322–23 and the nature of the debates they sparked: *Ars novae musicae* (The Art of New Music), by Jehan des Murs (alias Johannes de Muris; ca. 1290 to ca. 1350), and the even more bluntly titled ***Ars nova*** (The New Art), a composite of fragments and commentaries based on the teachings of Philippe de Vitry (1291–1361). The authors, both trained at the University of Paris, were mathematicians as well as musicians, not surprising in light of music's traditional place alongside mathematics and astronomy in the liberal arts curriculum.

Although originally spurred by a speculative, mathematical impulse, the notational breakthroughs of Jehan and Philippe had enormous repercussions on the practice of learned music, first displayed in the motet and eventually reaching every genre. So decisive were their contributions that this theoretical tradition has lent its name to an entire era; we often call the music of fourteenth-century France and its cultural colonies the music of the **Ars Nova**. Perhaps neither before nor since has theory ever so clearly and fruitfully conditioned practice, although we will see something similar much later, in the mid-twentieth century.

TIMELINE

ca. 1305 Giotto, frescoes at Scrovegni Chapel, Padua

1307 Dante Alighieri, *The Divine Comedy*

1309 Papal seat moved to Avignon

ca. 1316 ***Roman de Fauvel***

ca. 1322–23 Jehan de Murs, *Ars novae musicae*

ca. 1322–23 *Ars Nova,* treatise attributed to Philippe de Vitry

ca. 1330 Jacobus de Liège, Speculum musicae

1337–1453 Hundred Years War between England and France

1340 Guillaume de Machaut becomes canon of Reims cathedral

ca. 1340–86 Jacopo da Bologna active in Italy

1347–51 The plague, or Black Death, kills a third of Europe's population

1349 Mass of Tournai

1353 Giovanni Boccaccio, *The Decameron*

ca. 1360 Machaut, *Rose, Liz* and *La Messe de Nostre Dame*

1366 Francesco Petrarch, *Canzoniere*

ca. 1370–90 *Ars Subtilior* flourishes

1378–1417 Great Schism

ca. 1387–1400 Geoffrey Chaucer, *The Canterbury Tales*

ca. 1415 Squarcialupi Codex

1436 Guillaume Du Fay, *Nuper rosarum flores*

Music from Mathematics

From a purely mathematical point of view, the Ars Nova innovations were a byproduct of the theory of exponential powers and one of its subtopics, the theory of "harmonic numbers." It was in the fourteenth century that mathematicians began investigating powers beyond those that could be demonstrated by the simple geometry of squares and cubes. As mathematical thinking began to get more complicated, so too did music, its sister discipline.

In the "Petronian" motets written at the turn of the century (and mentioned at the end of the previous chapter), a breve could be divided into anywhere from two to nine semibreves. The obvious way of resolving this ambiguity was to extend the idea of perfection to the semibreve. The shortest Petronian semibreve ($1/9$ of a breve) could be considered an additional—minimal—level of time division, for which the obvious term would be a *minima* (in English, a "minim"), denoted by a semibreve with a tail, thus: ↓. Thus nine minims would equal three perfect semibreves, which in turn would equal a perfect breve. All of this merely carried out at higher levels of division the well-established concept of ternary "perfection," first expressed in the relationship of the breve to the long. On further analogy to the perfect division of the long (but in the other direction, so to speak), three perfect longs could be grouped within a perfect maxima, or *longa triplex*.

We are thus working within a fourfold perfect system expressible by the mathematical term 3^4, "three to the fourth power." The minim is the unit value. Multiplied by 3 (or 3^1) it produces the semibreve, which has three minims. Multiplied by 3×3 (or 3^2) it produces the breve, which has nine minims. Multiplied by $3 \times 3 \times 3$ (or 3^3) it produces the long, which has twenty-seven minims; and multiplied by $3 \times 3 \times 3 \times 3$ (or 3^4) it produces the maxima, which has eighty-one minims. Each of these powers of three constitutes a level of time division. Taking the longest as primary, Jehan des Murs called the levels:

1. *Maximodus* (great mode), describing the division of the maxima into longs;
2. *Modus* (mode), as in the "modal" rhythm of old, describing the division of longs into breves, or tempora;
3. ***Tempus*** (time), describing the division of breves into semibreves; and
4. *Prolatio* (Latin for "extension," usually designated in English by an ad hoc cognate, "**prolation**") describing the division of semibreves into minims.

And he represented it all in a chart (Fig. 3-1), which gives the minim content of every perfect note value in Ars Nova notation.

First degree (Great mode)	81 Maxima	54 Duplex long	27 Long
Second degree (Mode)	27 Perfect long	18 Imperfect long	9 Breve
Third degree (Time)	9 Perfect breve	6 Imperfect breve	3 Semibreve
Fourth degree (Prolation)	3 Perfect semibreve	2 Imperfect semibreve	1 Minim

Figure 3-1 Harmonic proportions according to Jehan des Murs.

And now the stroke of genius: Each level of the fourfold system, involving the very same note values and written symbols, could be divided in half instead of in thirds, predicated on Garlandia's "imperfect" long as well as Franco's "perfect" one. A fourfold imperfect system could be derived. Thus at its perfect and imperfect extremes, the Ars Nova system posits a maximum notatable value that could contain as many as eighty-one minimum values or as few as sixteen. Between these extremes many other values were also possible. The levels of maximodus, modus, tempus, and prolatio were treated as independent variables; each of them could be either perfect or imperfect, yielding on the theoretic level an exhaustive array of "harmonic numbers."

Although this new system clearly offered many possibilities, in actual practice things were not quite so complicated. To begin with, maximodus was pretty much a theoretical level. In practice it was the breve, rather than the maxima or the minim, that functioned as regulator. Its position in the middle of things made calculations much more convenient with lengths thought of as either multiples or divisions of breves. So we are left with the levels of tempus and prolation—that is, the number of semibreves in a breve and of minims in a semibreve. The former level defines the number of beats in a measure, the latter the number of subdivisions in a beat. And that relates rather obviously to the way we still define musical meters today. We thus end up with four basic combinations of tempus (T) and prolation (P):

1. Both perfect (*tempus perfectum, prolatio major*—perfect time, major prolation)
2. T perfect, P imperfect (*tempus perfectum, prolatio minor*—perfect time, minor prolation)
3. T imperfect, P perfect (*tempus imperfectum, prolatio major*—imperfect time, major prolation)
4. Both imperfect (*tempus imperfectum, prolatio minor*—imperfect time, minor prolation).

The first combination, with what we would call three beats in a measure (or bar; there were no bar lines at the time) and three subdivisions in a beat, is comparable to our modern compound triple meter ($^{9}_{8}$). The second, with three beats in a measure and two subdivisions in a beat, is like "simple" (or just plain) triple meter ($^{3}_{4}$). The third, with two beats in a measure and three subdivisions in a beat, resembles

1. ⊙ (tempus perfectum, prolatio major)

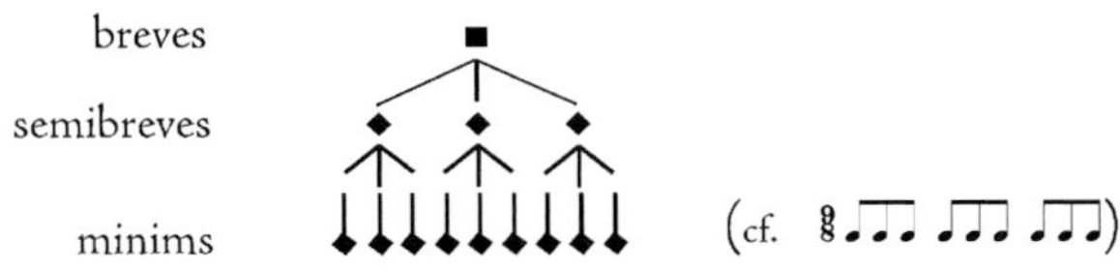

2. O (tempus imperfectum, prolatio minor)

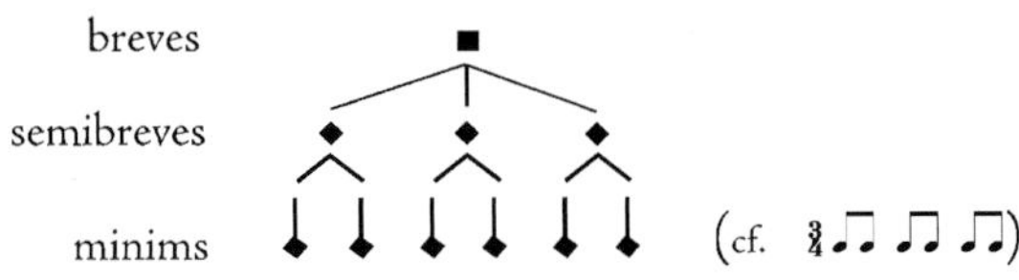

3. Ͼ (tempus imperfectum, prolatio major)

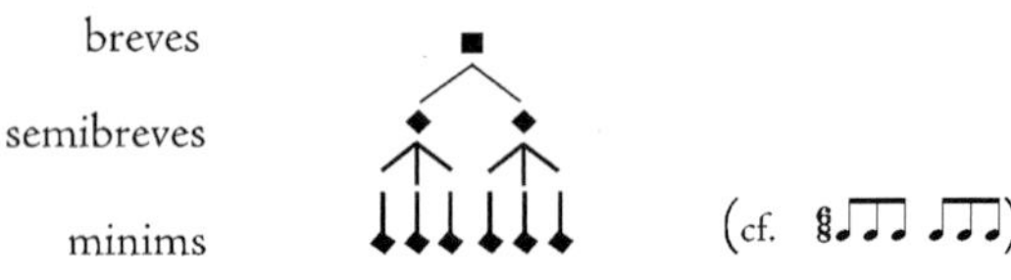

4. C (tempus imperfectum, prolatio minor)

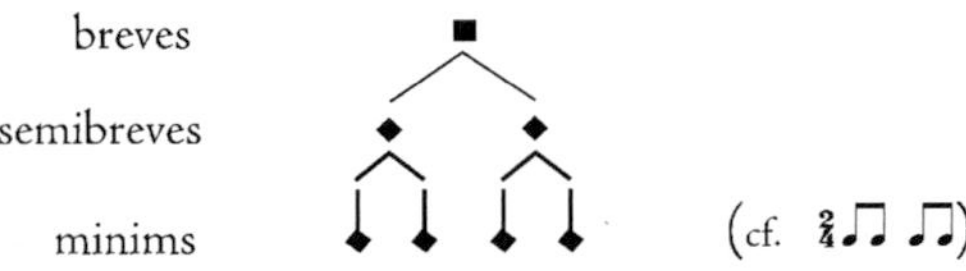

Figure 3-2 Ars Nova notation: the four mensuration schemes.

compound duple meter ($\frac{6}{8}$). And the fourth, with two beats in a measure and two subdivisions in a beat, is like our "simple" (or just plain) duple meter ($\frac{2}{4}$).

In order to distinguish mensural relationships between the familiar shapes of Gregorian quadratic notation, a new set of ancillary signs called time signatures was needed. These signs were adapted directly from existing measuring practices (that is, from daily life) particularly those involving time measurement and business calculations involving weights, measurements, and monetary units.[1] The circle and semicircle were adopted as symbols for the division of the tempus (breves into semibreves) in Ars Nova notation, thus becoming the first standard time signatures used in Western music. The circle stood for *tempus perfectum*—that is, the "whole," or "perfect," breve containing three semibreves—and the semicircle stood, correspondingly, for *tempus imperfectum*, with two semibreves to a breve. Other signs included a point or dot; by the end of the fourteenth century the four tempus-with-prolation combinations or meters listed earlier were represented by four standard time signatures: ⊙, O, Ͼ, C.

Figure 3-2 sums up the relationships specified by the mensural notation that was first employed by the Parisian musicians who promoted the Ars Nova in the early fourteenth century. These relationships remained the basis for musical notation in Europe to almost the end of the sixteenth century. Despite the resemblance between these Ars Nova mensuration schemes and modern meters, note that meter today implies a pattern of accentuation (strong and weak beats), whereas mensuration is only a time measurement. It is also worth mentioning that when modern meters are compared or when passing from one to another, it is usually the "beat" (the counterpart to the semibreve) that is assumed to be constant, whereas in Ars Nova mensuration the assumed constant was either the measure (the breve) or the unit value (the minim). The beat (called the *tactus*, the "felt" pulse) was variable within the Ars Nova mensuration scheme, and, because authorities differed as to whether the measure (*tempus*) was also variable, a serious ambiguity remained at the heart of the system that had to be remedied over the years by various auxiliary rules and signs.

Eventually the whole field became a jungle, and a new notational "revolution" was necessary, which happened around the beginning of the seventeenth century. We are living with its results to this day. Still, the extraordinary advance Ars Nova notation marked over its predecessors in rhythmic versatility and exactness is evident. It unquestionably amounted to technical progress. Everything that was formerly possible to notate was still possible under the new system, but now a great deal more besides. As Jehan des Murs triumphantly observed, as a result of the Ars Nova breakthroughs, "whatever can be sung can [now] be written down."[2]

But let us not confuse progress in notation with progress in music. In particular, let's not think for a moment that duple meter was "invented" in the fourteenth century, as often claimed, just because the means of its notation and its "artful" development now existed—as if two-legged creatures needed the elaborate rationalizations of the Ars Nova in order to make music to accompany marching or working or dancing. The unwritten repertory was then, and has always remained, many times larger than the literate repertories that form the main subject matter of this or any history text. But even if the "imperfect mensuration" of the Ars Nova had its origins in speculation about musical analogues to squares and cubes and ultimately in speculation about how music might best represent God's cosmos, it nevertheless made possible the unambiguous graphic representation of plain old duple meter. Lofty theory had provided the means by which musical art could reflect more directly the music of daily human life.

The circle and semicircle were adopted as symbols for the division of the tempus, becoming the first standard time signatures used in Western music.

The new music didn't please everyone. Just as the technology-minded theorists of the Ars Nova represented the first self-conscious avant-garde faction in European literate music, so they inspired the first conservative backlash. Such is found in the mammoth *Speculum musicae* (The Mirror of Music), completed around 1330 by Jacobus de Liège. The author was a retired University of Paris professor (thus Jehan des Murs's senior colleague) who sought to provide a universal compendium of musical knowledge. The young innovators of the Ars Nova, by extending the boundaries of musical theory, threatened the completeness of Jacobus's account, so he tried to discredit their advance and thus neutralize the threat.

His basic ploy was to dismiss the Ars Nova innovations as so much superfluous complexity. Jacobus reasoned that the music of Ars Nova, by permitting so much "imperfection," was thereby itself made imperfect when compared with what Jacobus called the *Ars Antiqua*, represented at its unsurpassable zenith by Franco of Cologne. The term Ars Antiqua has also entered the conventional vocabulary of music history to denote Parisian music of the thirteenth century. The term is problematic, however, because it has meaning only in connection with its antithesis; using it tends to ratify the notion that not just technique but art itself makes progress. Citing a passage in Jehan des Murs's treatise, in which the author explained the use of the term "perfection" in music by saying that "all perfection does in fact lie in the ternary number" (beginning with the perfection of God Himself, who is single in substance but a Trinity of persons), Jacobus maintained that "the art that uses perfect values more often is, therefore, more perfect" and that "the art that does that is the Ars Antiqua of Master Franco."[3]

Music about Music

The innovations of the Ars Nova were demonstrably a breakthrough and also controversial, but they were not "revolutionary." The granting of full rights to the imperfect was no challenge to the perfect. Rather, it was an attempt to encompass more fully the traditional Medieval objective of translating number into sound, thus more fully realizing the ideal significance of music as cosmic metaphor. By radically increasing the number of disparate elements that could go into its representation of harmony, moreover, the Ars Nova innovations only made more potent the musical representation of *discordia concors,* the divine tuning of the world through the harmonization of oppositions. The earliest genre and the most characteristic one to be affected by the Ars Nova was the motet, already a hotbed of innovation.

In addition to the technical progress of musical notation, there was an increasing self-awareness on the part of composers concerning attitudes toward art in general. Before turning to the most exalted specimens of the Ars Nova, let us explore some of the playful pieces from the early fourteenth century that cast light on the emergence within musical practice of "art" as we know it, that is, as a self-conscious thing, concerned as much with manner as with matter. Its Latin cognate, *ars* (as in Ars Nova) simply means "method" or "way." The title of the treatise attributed to Vitry simply means "a new way [of doing things]." That is the sense of art implied by words like "artful" and "artificial." They mean "full of method," hence "full of skill" and ultimately "full of style." Therefore, what makes an artist, in the familiar, current sense of the word, is high consciousness of style.

What makes an artist, in the familiar, current sense of the word, is high consciousness of style.

The earliest musical compositions that seem to exhibit this awareness on the part of their makers come out of the Ars Nova milieu, although the biographical vidas going back to the troubadours suggest some similar attitudes.

Such self-regard is exemplified in the text to an anonymous motet called *Musicalis sciencia/Sciencie laudabili* (ca. 1325). Here are the words for the triplum and motetus, abridged to eliminate a lengthy honor roll of famous musicians:

> *Triplum*: The science of music sends greetings to her beloved disciples. I desire each one of you to observe the rules and not to offend against rhetoric or grammar by dividing indivisible syllables. Avoid all faults. Farewell in melody.
>
> *Motetus*: Rhetoric sends greetings to learned Music, but complains that many singers make faults in her compositions by dividing simple vowels and making hockets; therefore I request that you remedy this.

Perhaps, needless to say, the composer, while setting these texts, flagrantly commits every one of the "faults" for which singers are berated by Music and by Rhetoric. The piece is a kind of satire, one that requires an attitude of ironic detachment, a consciousness of art as artifice, and a wish to make that artifice the principal focus of attention. These are traits we normally (and perhaps self-importantly) ascribe to the "Modern" temperament, not the "Medieval" one. Only we (we tend to think), with our contemporary notions of psychology and our modern sense of "self," are capable of self-reflection. Only we, in short, can be "artists" as opposed to "craftsmen." Not so.

Establishing the Prototype: The *Roman de Fauvel*

The earliest surviving pieces in which elements of Ars Nova notation are clearly discernable are a group of motets found in a lavish manuscript, compiled in or just after 1316, that contains a lavishly illustrated version of a famous allegorical poem, the *Roman de Fauvel.* The poem, by Gervès de Bus, an official at the French royal court, is also found in about a dozen other sources, but this one provided the poem with a veritable soundtrack consisting of 126 pieces of music, ranging from little snippets of chant through monophonic rondeaux and ballades to twenty-four polyphonic motets. The musical items were meant as accessories to the poem, on a par with its abundant illuminations.

Despite their motley variety of genre, style, language, and date, what links all the musical pieces is their pertinence to the poem's theme: ferocious civil and political satire. The name of the title character, Fauvel, meaning roughly "little deerlike critter" who is *faus* and *de vel* (false and furtive) and of dull fallow hue (*fauve*), is actually an acrostic standing for a whole medley of political vices, apparently modeled on the list of seven deadly sins:

F laterie
A varice
U ilanie (i.e., villainy, U and V being equivalent in Latin spelling)
V ariété (duplicity, "two-facedness")
E nvie
L ascheté (laziness, indolence)

The manuscript illuminations represent Fauvel as something between a fawn and a horse or ass. Indeed, everyone "fawns" over him, from garden-variety nobles and clerics to the pope and the French king. (Our expression "to curry favor" was originally "to curry favel," meaning to flatter Fauvel.) Fauvel is practically omnipotent; his feat of placing the moon above the sun symbolized secularism and the corruption of court and clergy. Now he wants to pay back Dame Fortune for the favors she has granted him and he proposes marriage to her—but this, too, is a trick. Once married to Fortune, Fauvel will become her master as well, and truly all-powerful. Fortune refuses the offer but gives Fauvel the hand of her daughter, Vaine Gloire, through whom he populates the earth with little Fauvels.

Anthology Vol 1-24
Full CD I, 40
Concise CD I, 35

The motet *Tribum/Quoniam/MERITO* appears in the section containing the description of the Fountain of Youth, in which Fauvel, his wife, and his entourage—Carnality, Hatred, Gluttony, Drunkenness, Pride, Hypocrisy, Sodomy, and a host of others just as attractive—bathe on the day following the wedding (Fig. 3-3). The triplum and motetus texts are laden with Fauvel-related allegories, perhaps associated with the fate of Enguerrand de Marigny, the finance minister to French King Philippe IV (Philip the Fair), who was hanged in 1315 following the death of the sovereign. His death is held up as an object lesson concerning the whims of Fortune and the dangers of concentrating political power. The texts thus reflect the interests of the feudal nobility who sought to limit the power of the throne and forced concessions from Philip's successor, Louis X.

Because this motet corresponds so closely to the rhythmic and notational features soon to be set forth in the treatise *Ars Nova* (where a passage from it is actually quoted), the music of this little political tract in tones is thought to be by Philippe de Vitry. Philippe helped establish the fourteenth-century motet as a genre and provided the prototypes for a century of stylistic development. To begin with, the text is in Latin, not French; its tone is admonishing, not confessional; and its subject is public life, not private emotion. The motet repertory would henceforth be dominated by moralizing texts—allegories, sermons, and injunctions. To match and enhance the seriousness of the words, the formal gestures of the motet became increasingly ample, ceremonious, and dramatic.

For example, the fourteenth-century motet sometimes dramatized the tenor entrance; in *Tribum/Quoniam/MERITO* the voices enter one by one, the tenor last. The introductory section preceding the tenor entrance became so standardized that it was given a name, one with which we are familiar in another context: It was called the *introitus*, suggesting that the entering voices formed a procession (Ex. 3-1). And

Figure 3-3 Philippe de Vitry's motet *Tribum/Quoniam/MERITO* in the *Roman de Fauvel* showing an allegory of the fountain of youth (Paris, Bibliotheque Nationale, Fonds Français 146, 42).

just as in the case of the Introit procession at the beginning of the Mass, the most important participant (whether the celebrant or the tenor) enters last. The tenor is the "worthiest part," in the words of one theorist, because it is literally the "fundamental" voice.[4] In fourteenth-century motets it is chosen with care to support and gloss the orations in the upper two voices. In this case the tenor is drawn from a chant sung during Lent, the most penitential season of the church year. Its implied words—*Merito hec patimur* ("It is right that we suffer thus")—are plainly an extra comment on just deserts, and they amplify the severely critical allegories running above on the fate of corrupt politicians.

Isorhythm

In keeping with the belief in a hidden order and unity behind the world's apparent chaos, composers of Ars Nova motets placed particular emphasis on subtle but complex patterning that unified and organized the varied surface of their work. The principal way of doing this was by repeating a pattern, usually in the tenor, of rhythmic values (called the ***talea***, Latin for "measuring rod") and a recurring melodic pattern (called the ***color***).

This method of constructing tenors, in which a predetermined, repeated pitch-succession borrowed from a chant was overlaid on a different but still predetermined, repeated succession of durations, opened up vast new possibilities for intellectual tours de force. Modern scholars use the term ***isorhythm*** (same rhythm) to denote the use of these recurrent patterns, which are often quite long and cunningly constructed. Motets that employ such recurrent patterns are thus known as *isorhythmic motets*. (Despite the Greek derivation of the term, it was coined in only

Example 3-1 Philippe de Vitry, *Tribum/Quoniam/MERITO*, mm. 1–18

Triplum: Furious Fortune did not fear
to turn quickly against the tribe
that did not recoil from a shameless rise [to power]
when she did not spare
the governing leader of the tribe

Motetus: Since with the plots of thieves and the den of shady dealers

Tenor: We suffer this deservedly

the early twentieth century.) As currently used, the term *isorhythm* implies literal rhythmic repetition that, while often coordinated with melodic repetition (chiefly in tenors), is nevertheless organized independently.

The isorhythmic tenor in *Tribum/Quoniam/MERITO*, which is stated twice, is built on two periodic cycles, the talea governing duration, the color governing the pitch. And this implies the separate, hence abstract, conception of rhythmic and melodic successions. In addition, the passages of rhythmic repetition in the tenor in this motet are accompanied by rhythmic recurrences in the upper parts as well, so this particular motet has patches of "pan-isorhythm," in which all the voices are bound periodically into recurrent patterns.

Figure 3-4 Illumination from the largest of the "Machaut manuscripts," showing the poet composing *Les nouveaus dis amoureus* (New Poems in Honor of Love).

Isorhythm was a musical intricacy that served a symbolic purpose, for its periodicities were meant to reflect those of nature, such as celestial orbits, tides, and seasons. The coordination of surface and deeper structure exemplifies an appeal to both sense and reason, which may all be contained under the heading of rhetoric—the art of persuasion. That was the all-encompassing aim to which every detail of the ceremonious late-Medieval motet was geared, whether at the level of grandiose architecture or that of seductive detail.

Guillaume de Machaut: Poet and Musician

Guillaume de Machaut (ca. 1300–77) was considered the greatest poet-musician of mid-fourteenth-century France and the chief extender of the trouvère tradition (Fig. 3-4). He gave that tradition a new lease on life by channeling it into styles and genres that would thrive for over a century. We will consider his amazing accomplishment in a variety of sacred and secular genres, beginning with a motet that combines both realms and that shows how Machaut carried on the tradition of the French love-song motet into the fourteenth century and applied to it all the novel technologies of the Ars Nova, including the use of isorhythm.

The Latin sacred genre that stood closest to the secular tradition of *fin' amors* was the antiphon to the Blessed Virgin Mary. It is not surprising to find that Machaut's grandest, most rigorous essay in the most exalted genre available to him was an appeal to Mary in her role as intercessor between man and God. This lofty, ambitiously structured isorhythmic motet—*Felix virgo/Inviolata genitrix/AD TE SUSPIRAMUS*—is harmonically amplified by the addition of a *contratenor*, a fourth voice composed "against the tenor" and in the same range (Ex. 3-2). In this motet the *color* turns out to be the famous Marian antiphon *Salve Regina*.

Anthology Vol 1-25
Full CD I, 41
Concise CD I, 36

Example 3-2 Guillaume de Machaut, *Felix virgo/Inviolata genitrix/ AD TE SUSPIRAMUS*, mm. 1–40

Example 3-2 (continued)

Motetus: Happy Virgin, Mother of Christ,
Who brought joy to a sad world
By your birth,

Triplum: Inviolate Mother,
Gracious conqueress of pride,
Lacking any peer,
Gatekeeper of the celestial temple,

In such an extremely formalized motet, architectural analogies are virtually inescapable, for the elaborate structures were probably planned in advance. The fourteenth-century isorhythmic motet, perhaps the most hierarchically conceived and rigorously ordered genre in the history of European music, was more concerned than any other to incorporate a representation of the higher "intellectual" elements and their controlling influence, which, being hidden from the senses, were in the most literal and etymological way occult. That is another way of interpreting the enormous value and emphasis that was placed on the structural architecture of the motet.

Musica Ficta

At the same time, this motet has a sensuous surface. What made it so was an extraordinary harmonic idiom that we now call *chromaticism*, known in Machaut's day as ***musica ficta*** (imaginary music) or *musica falsa* (false music). These terms should not be taken too literally. Indeed, Philippe de Vitry himself cautioned that "false music" is not false but real "and even necessary." All that the name *musica ficta* implied was that the altered notes involved were not part of the gamut as defined long ago by Guido of Arezzo and that they had no predefined position within a hexachord. So in order to find a place for them among the *ut–re–mi* vocabulary of traditional sight-singing one had to imagine a hexachord that contained them, one that may have been "fictitious" with respect to the official theory of music but whose sounding contents were fully presentable to the senses and in that respect altogether real.

And also necessary: The principal purpose of chromatically altered notes was to make perfect a diminished fifth or an augmented fourth. As we know, a certain provision of this kind was made by the earliest theorists of harmony, when they incorporated B♭ into the modal system alongside B for use in conjunction with F. But when an E was written against the B♭, one had to go outside the system to harmonize it—that was musica ficta. As most singers thought in terms of solmization, they could make the adjustment without being specifically told to do so and, it follows, without even being aware of the adjustment as "chromaticism." It was not a deviation from a pure diatonic norm; it was a preservation of pure diatonic norms (in particular, perfect fourths and fifths) where they were compromised by a well-known kink in the diatonic system.

Musica ficta adjustments were generally taken for granted—in other words, left to oral tradition—so the term is often loosely (and, technically, wrongly) employed to refer only to the "chromatics" that were unnotated. Contemporary scholars who transcribe early polyphony for singers today usually indicate the adjustments with little accidentals placed above the staff (for instance, measure 4 in Example 3-2). Yet accidentals that are explicitly signed, often very abundant in fourteenth-century music and particularly in Machaut's music, should just as much be considered musica ficta (unless they are B♭). The purpose of the written accidentals, however, was different. Instead of being musica ficta *causa necessitatis* (harmonically necessary adjustments), they represented musica ficta *causa pulchritudinis*—chromatic adjustments made "for the sake of their beauty," that is, for the sensuous enhancement of the music.

The introitus to Machaut's *Felix virgo/Inviolata genitrix/AD TE SUSPIRAMUS* has in the triplum a signed C♯ at the moment when the motetus enters in m. 11. It follows the note D. If it returned to D, then strictly speaking it would not need to be expressly "signed." But it does not return to D; instead, it skips to a wholly unexpected note, G♯. Its purpose is to create a striking effect in the harmony, a sort of heartthrob, expressing love for the Virgin the way so many similar harmonic throbs express love for the lady in Machaut's secular French songs. All of the signed accidentals in the introitus are C♯s or G♯s that demand cadential resolution to crucial scale tones. By evading or delaying that resolution, a harmonic tension is created that will not be fully discharged until the introitus reaches its final cadence.

That cadence incorporates both the C♯ and the G♯, resolving in parallel to D and A, the notes that define the Dorian mode. The defining notes are each thus provided with a leading tone, the strongest possible preparation. For this reason such a cadence has been dubbed the "double leading-tone cadence." However, what gave it that stabilizing and articulating (form-defining) power had only partly to do with the doubled leading tone. One of its central features is the contrary motion between the motetus and the tenor, which move outward from the sixth e/c♯ to the octave d/d′. The coming together of two parts in contrary motion goes back to the earliest days of discant, when cadence was synonymous with occursus. The earliest variation on this was its inversion, in which the two parts moved out to the octave in contrary motion; this endured as the basic cadential frame until the end of the sixteenth century.

Machaut and the Art of Courtly Song

Machaut is often considered the last of the trouvères, his most kindred predecessors. Like them, Machaut belongs as much to literary as he does to musical history. He is regarded by literary historians today as the greatest French poet of his age; his poetry is studied alongside that of Chaucer (whom he knew and influenced) and Dante, although it no longer enjoys a wide general readership.

Machaut spent the first half of his long life chiefly in service as secretary to John of Luxembourg (1296–1346), a son of the Holy Roman Emperor Henry VII, who succeeded his father-in-law, Wenceslaus, as king of Bohemia in 1310. Machaut, who was born around 1300, came from the territory surrounding the cathedral town of Reims in the north of France, not far from Luxembourg. He was in John's service by 1323 and traveled widely with him on campaigns across northern and eastern Europe. After his patron's spectacularly violent death (tied blind to his horse on the battlefield of Crécy), Machaut returned to Reims and lived out his last three decades connected to the cathedral but with few official duties. He was in effect a wealthy man of leisure, free to pursue his artistic callings. He died in 1377, remarkably old for a man who lived during a century of the great plagues that killed millions of people.

As his literary reputation grew, Machaut wrote lengthy allegorical poems to honor several dukes and kings and from whom he probably received some payment. He also supervised the copying of his complete poetical and musical works into rich manuscripts (Fig. 3-5), making him the earliest musical poet whose creations come down to us in what amounts to an authorized collected edition. His longest and most impressive works are extended narrative poems in which the lyric musical compositions served as occasional interpolations.

Figure 3-5 In this miniature from a manuscript prepared late in Machaut's lifetime, Love visits Machaut and introduces his three children, Sweet Thoughts, Pleasure, and Hope.

The first of these grand narratives, *Le Remède de Fortune* (Fortune's Remedy; ca. 1349), contains exemplary specimens of all the main song genres, placed within a story that defines their expressive content and social use. The very plot of the poem is motivated by poetry. The poet anonymously composes a lai in honor of his lady, who discovers it, bids him read it to her, and asks who wrote it. Embarrassed, he flees her presence and addresses a complaint to Love and Fortune. Hope appears and comforts him with two songs in praise of love. The poet expresses his gratitude in a standard ballade. He seeks out his lady, finds her dancing, and accompanies her movements with a virelai. He confesses authorship of the original lai, she receives him as her lover, and, after a day spent together, they exchange rings and he expresses his joy in a rondeau.

This narrative amplified the typical blueprint of a vida, the troubadour and trouvère biographies of old. With it, Machaut deliberately gave the dying art of the knightly poet-lover new life, distinguished especially by the use of polyphonic music in the latest style. While operating on just as lofty and aristocratic a plane, Machaut preferred to compose in the *formes fixes*—that is, the fixed forms of dance songs with refrains. These, we may recall, had originally come into their own when the courtly art of the trouvères had moved from castle to city and become the property of the guilds.

Machaut reinvested the urbanized, popular genres of *fin' amors* with privileged refinement through stylistic renovation. He was able to enhance the style of courtly love poetry, even while retaining its more popular forms, because he possessed a polyphonic craft that went far beyond the attainments of any previous love singer. Of all the formes fixes, the ballade in three stanzas was for Machaut and his followers the most exalted—and musically, therefore, the most elaborate. In the manuscripts Machaut personally oversaw, the section containing ballades was headed, "Here begin the ballades or high song." "Highness" (*hauteur*, whence "haughty") was expressed in the traditional way: by the use of an especially melismatic style.

The Top-Down Style

Machaut's motet *Felix virgo/Inviolata genitrix/AD TE SUSPIRAMUS* is constructed along lines of what might be called "bottom-up" techniques, geared toward erecting highly stratified polyphonic superstructures over artfully elaborated foundations. Those foundations came from cantus firmus melodies most often borrowed from the high-authority repertoire of canonized Church chant. The **chanson** worked differently: while the motet was composed "from the bottom up," the chanson was composed "from the top down."

To appreciate this new way of composing, it is best to begin with a pair of Machaut's virelais, one of them monophonic. In fact, most of his virelais were monophonic, presumably because, of the three main fixed forms, the virelai was the one that continued most often to serve a traditional social function—public dance—and was the one most often performed by minstrels. Particularly well known is the catchy *Douce dame jolie* ("Sweet, pretty lady"). The first three lines of the poem are set to what are in essence three repetitions of a single musical phrase, but each of them is subtly distinguished from the others. The music begins with rests, even though there are no accompanying parts, because without bar lines the only way in which an initial upbeat could be indicated was by showing the silent part of the hypothetical first measure. Like many duple-metered pieces of the time, it especially emphasizes syncopations (Ex. 3-3).

Anthology Vol 1-26a
Full CD I, 42
Concise CD I, 37

Example 3-3 Guillaume de Machaut, *Douce dame jolie* (monophonic virelai)

Example 3-3 (continued)

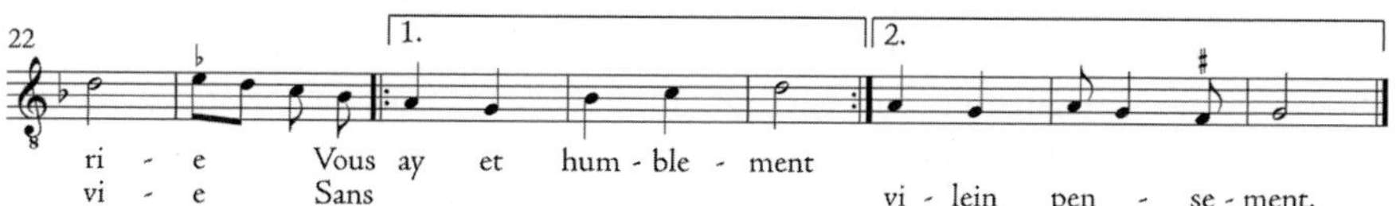
22
1.
2.
ri - e Vous ay et hum - ble - ment
vi - e Sans vi - lein pen - se - ment.

A Fair, sweet lady,
for God's sake do not think
that any woman has mastery
over me other than you alone.

b For without deceit, I have always
held you dear and humbly
b served you all the days of my life,
without any bad thought.
a Alas! I beg
for hope and aid,
and so my joy is ended
if you do not take pity on me.

A Fair, sweet lady . . .

b But your sweet mastery masters
my heart so harshly
b that it torments and blinds it
with such love
a that it desires nothing
other than to be in your power;
and yet your heart
grants it no relief.

A Fair, sweet lady . . .

b And since my malady
will not be cured at all
b without you, sweet enemy,
who are happy about my torment,
a with clasped hands I pray
that your heart, because it forgets me,
might soon kill me,
for I have languished for too long.

A Fair, sweet lady . . .

Machaut's *En mon cuer* ("In my heart"; Ex. 3-4) is a polyphonic virelai with a texted "**cantus**" (song) part and a tenor part without text. The arrangement already suggests that a tenor has been added to a song, or, in other words, that the song existed as a monophonic composition, such as did *Douce dame jolie,* before it was made polyphonic by adding a lower accompanying voice. This was not a preexisting tenor but rather one created from scratch. Adding a tenor to a preexisting cantus was of course the very antithesis of motet composition. Starting "at the top" represented a whole new concept of composing, at least within the literate tradition. The musical and written evidence suggests that any of Machaut's two-part virelais could have started out as monophonic songs, to which tenors were added later. A corollary implication is that monophonic performance was probably a standard option for all his virelais. If Machaut's monophonic melodies had to be eligible for accompaniment by an added tenor in this way, then they had to differ fundamentally from previous monophonic melodies we have encountered so that the new tenor could make correct counterpoint with the tune.

Anthology Vol 1-26b
Full CD I, 43
Concise CD I, 38

Example 3-4 Guillaume de Machaut, *En mon cuer* (virelai a 2), mm. 1–8

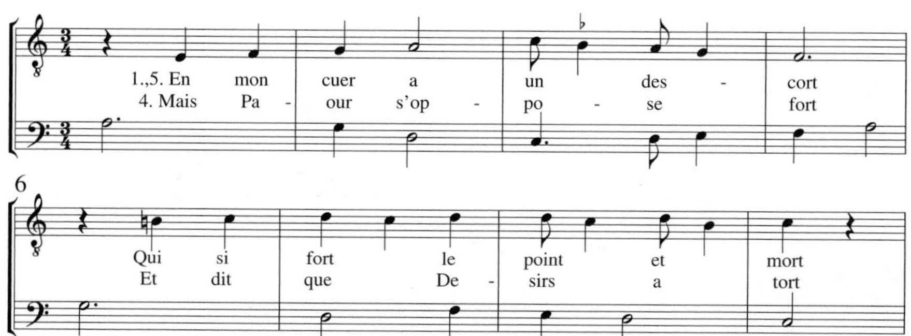
1.,5. En mon cuer a un des - cort
4. Mais Pa - our s'op - po - se fort
6
Qui si fort le point et mort
Et dit que De - sirs a tort

Refrain: There is discord in my heart, which so strongly pierces and wounds it

Both *Douce dame jolie* and the cantus of *En mon cuer* make their cadential approaches not from above but from below, from the leading tone. They are monophonic melodies that were conceived in the context of polyphony, by a composer whose musical imagination had been definitively shaped by polyphony. The new style of song melody, composed with polyphonic accompaniment in mind, was called *cantilena*. By itself the melody was sufficient, making correct cadences and fitting the words. With the addition of a tenor, a two-part discant texture was achieved in which cadences were still correct. With the addition of a third voice, whether a texted triplum in the range of the cantus or an untexted contratenor in the range of the tenor, the two-part structure was sonorously enhanced and the harmonies made "sweet." The most usual way of sweetening the harmony was to amplify the imperfect consonances into full triads; and the most characteristic place to observe this is, again, at cadences, usually with the "double leading-tone."

Anthology Vol 1-26c
Full CD I, 44
Concise CD I, 39

Machaut's *Tres bonne et belle* ("Most good and beautiful lady"; Ex. 3-5) is the only virelai to come down in all its sources as a three-voice composition, this one sporting an added contratenor. Although they occupy exactly the same pitch space, the tenor and contratenor are not equivalent parts. Each of them behaves, so to speak, according to its station within the textural hierarchy. It is the tenor alone that makes the true discant cadence against the cantus. Even if Machaut wrote all the parts in one sitting, he nevertheless provided three grammatically viable performance possibilities. At their most luxuriant, Machaut's textures could in fact accommodate four voices: the "structural" cantus/tenor pair, accompanied by both a triplum and a contratenor. This in effect blended the traditional motet complement (which included a triplum) with the newer cantilena complement (which included a contratenor). It was a rich, all-purpose texture that could be adapted either to motet (as in *Felix virgo/Inviolata genitrix/AD TE SUSPIRAMUS*) or to chanson designs, as in Machaut's rondeau *Rose, liz* ("The rose, the lily").

Anthology Vol 1-27
Full CD I, 45

Example 3-5 **Guillaume de Machaut, *Tres bonne et belle* (virelai a 3), mm. 1–7**

Refrain: Most good and beautiful lady, my eyes find delightful sustenance [in your face]

Machaut's *Messe de Nostre Dame*

Anthology Vol 1-28
Full CD I, 46
Concise CD I, 40

By a curious twist of fate, Guillaume de Machaut—best known in his day as a poet and, secondarily, as a composer of courtly songs—is now known for what seems an entirely uncharacteristic work: a complete polyphonic setting of the Ordinary of the Mass. Machaut's *Messe de Nostre Dame* (Mass of Our Lady) is in fact the earliest such setting to survive from the hand of a single known author. What might seem a liturgical anomaly in an otherwise basically secular career has instead loomed disproportionately large both within Machaut's output and in music historiography itself. This is because it seems to be the first example of the "cyclic Mass Ordinary," which as we will see became the dominant musical genre of the fifteenth and sixteenth centuries. The **cyclic Mass Ordinary** is a setting of the mostly nonconsecutive items of the Ordinary liturgy as a connected musical unit, unified in various ways by motives or modes or other compositional procedures. There has been an understandable temptation for historians to designate Machaut as the inventor of the genre. The actual history of the cyclic Mass is a more complex story than the myth of its single-handed invention by Machaut might suggest.

The rise of polyphonic Ordinaries was in fact a by-product of one of the most turbulent periods in the history of the Roman Catholic Church—the phase during which, briefly, the church was not Roman. In 1309, Pope Clement V, a Frenchman, abandoned Rome at the behest of the French king, Philip the Fair, and moved the papacy to Avignon, a city in the southeastern corner of France (Figs. 3-6 and 3-7). The next six popes were also French and also subservient to their kings. This virtual "capture" of the papacy by the French crown was dubbed the "Babylonian Captivity" by disapproving Italians, including the great fourteenth-century writer Francesco Petrarch. In 1378 Pope Gregory XI was prevailed on to move the papacy back to Rome, touching off what is known as the Great Schism, during which there were competing popes. The French popes continued under royal protection but were later decanonized—ruled "antipopes"—at the Council of Constance, which ended the Schism in 1417 and brought the papacy back exclusively within the Italian orbit.

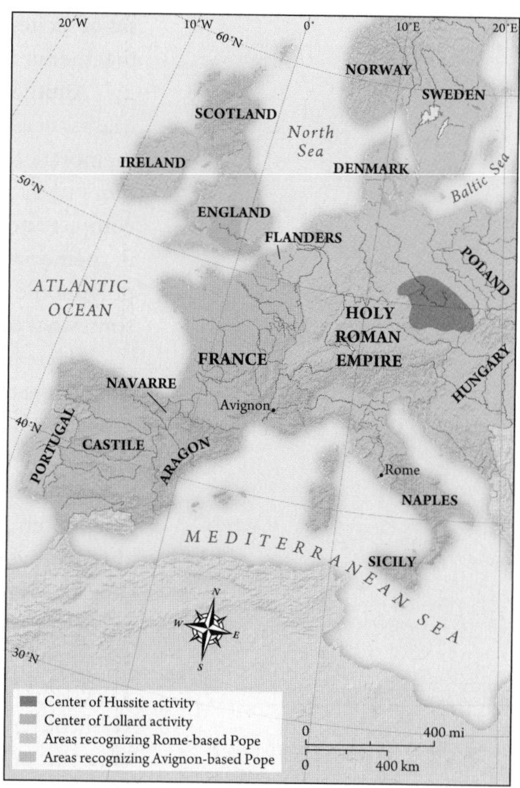

Figure 3-6 The Church during the Great Schism (1378–1417).

It was in Avignon that Mass Ordinary settings began to proliferate. Two surviving late-fourteenth-century manuscripts, known as the Apt and Ivrea Codices (after the towns in which they may have originated), comprise what music remains from the papal liturgical repertory at Avignon. Both codices are full of Ordinary settings that employ textures associated with other genres prevalent in France, perhaps deliberately modeled on them. The most elaborate are in motet style, built up from a cantus firmus that is often isorhythmic, but others use the French cantilena style, composed in the top-down fashion associated with Machaut.

The Apt Codex, which dates from around 1400, consists not of complete or cyclic ordinary settings but of individual items ("movements" as they are sometimes called) and occasional pairs, notably the Gloria and the Credo (the two parts with lengthy prose texts) and the Kyrie and the Agnus Dei (both repetitive petitions or litanies). The earliest polyphonic Ordinaries that survive are thus not unified cyclic compositions but, rather, composites. The most

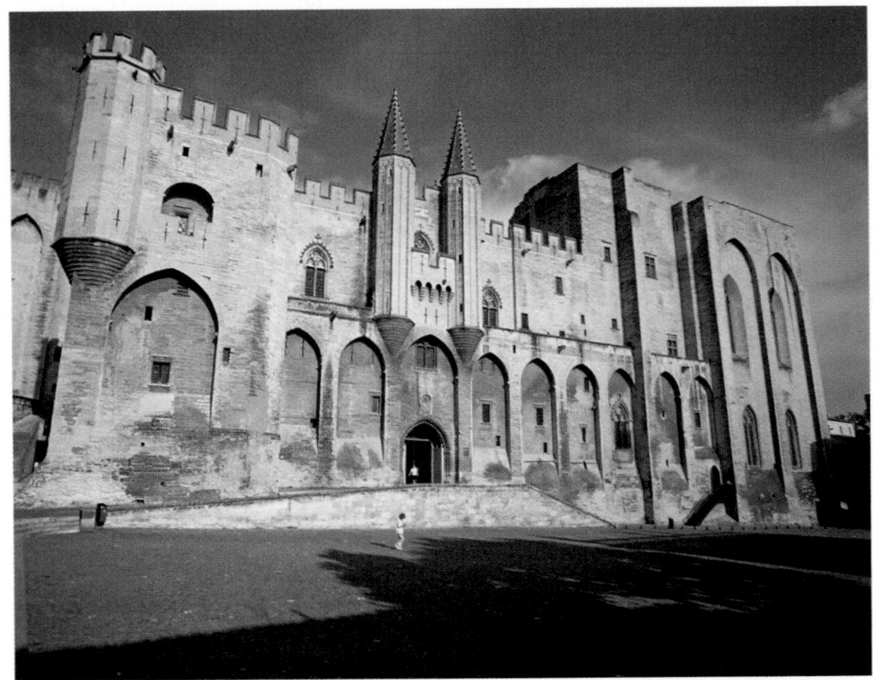

Figure 3-7 Palace of the Popes in Avignon.

complete of them, one that Machaut must surely have known, is the so-called Mass of Tournai, from a cathedral town not far from Machaut's home city of Reims. A full set of six items (it includes a setting of the concluding Ite missa est), it was gathered together in 1349.

Another spur to the composition of Mass Ordinary settings was the growth of Masses celebrated on special occasions, so-called Votive Masses. They might commemorate the dedication of a church or the installation of a bishop or something more personal, marking a birth, marriage, burial, or memorial service. The earliest complete polyphonic Mass Ordinaries were collected in special manuscripts for use in memorial chapels, where votive Masses were offered on behalf of donors. The polyphonic Mass Ordinary, among other things, was one of the finer fruits of a somewhat dubious practice of buying and selling the good graces of the church.

"Here begins the Mass of Our Lady" reads the heading following the motet section in one of Machaut's most awe-inspiring personally supervised manuscripts. His votive Mass was one that the composer endowed with a bequest to serve as a memorial to himself and his brother Jean in the Reims Cathedral of Our Lady (*L'eglise de Notre Dame*). Machaut's *Messe de Nostre Dame* was a hodgepodge of styles: isorhythmic motets, chanson, and conductus. It is modally disparate: The final of the first three "movements" is D (minorish), while that of the last three is F (majorish).

The Kyrie, which uses the *Cunctipotens genitor* melody as its tenor cantus firmus, is composed in four sections, the repetitions of which fill a ninefold scheme: a Kyrie for singing threefold; a Christe for singing threefold; a second Kyrie to be repeated once; and a final, somewhat more elaborate Kyrie to conclude, in a total form that could be represented AAABBBCCD. The most striking rhythmic effect—and a characteristic one—in the Christe is that of wild activity regularly hitting the brick wall of utter stasis. Machaut was not the only composer of his time to revel in this kind of radical contrast, which displays the potentialities of the Ars Nova at maximum strength.

The Gloria and the Credo contrast stylistically with the other movements. The Gloria is a cantilena bordering on homorhythm but with a grand motetlike Amen featuring hockets; the Credo is in a more rigorously homorhythmic style, like a conductus. The punctuation of the text is followed faithfully, each sentence being marked off from the surrounding ones by little textless bridge passages in the two lower voices. The unprecedented four-part chordal textures of the Gloria and Credo explore novel sonorities. The Sanctus and the Agnus Dei form a pair and are stylistically related to the Kyrie—but in a different mode. The response to the Ite missa est is cast as a full-fledged isorhythmic motet over a liturgical cantus firmus.

Machaut's Mass is far more ambitious than earlier ones, which is partly the result of a heightened emphasis he gives to motetlike architectonics: the Kyrie, Sanctus, Agnus Dei, and Ite missa est are all based on isorhythmic tenors derived from canonical plainchant; several subsections, moreover, are pan-isorhythmic, with repeating taleas in all parts. The work is also more sonorous than any of its counterparts, being cast throughout in the luxuriant four-part texture associated with other genres, adding both a high supplementary voice (typical of the motet) and a low one (typical of the cantilena) to round out the essential counterpoint of cantus (here called the *triplum*) and tenor. With four elaborate movements in motet style, one quasi-cantilena, and one quasi-conductus, Machaut's Mass stands as a comprehensive work of contemporary compositional technique. It is nonetheless better viewed as a culmination of a half-century of Avignon-oriented liturgical composition than as a dry run at the fifteenth century's cyclic Masses we will encounter in the next chapter.

Canons

Machaut's art was a connoisseur's art: an art of *literati* whose tastes were flattered by tours de force. He fashioned many complex pieces full of hidden meanings and arcane structural relationships. In this respect we might look on the musico-poetic legacy of the Ars Nova as another resurgence of the trobar clus favored by the noblest troubadours.

Machaut created several works notable for intellectual cleverness and intricacy of detail. Of these the most famous is the rondeau *Ma fin est mon commencement*, the text of which starts: "My end is my beginning and my beginning my end." The whole point of the composition is the strange way in which its first half ("my beginning") relates to its second half ("my end"). The piece is notated in two parts, but the text refers to the "third part," a performance direction (*rubric*) that informs us that a tenor needs to be added to create a three-voice texture. When all is worked out, the highest voice sings its line from beginning to end, the tenor sings the same notes backward, and the added tenor, only half as long, sings half the piece and then doubles back to the start. The result is the sort of thing Machaut would have expected adept musicians to solve directly from his incomplete notation and textual hints. The joy of the piece consists not only in the enjoyment of its pretty sounds but in the triumph over unnecessary but delightful obstacles.

Another word for a rubric, a supplementary guide to performance like the text in this eccentric piece, is ***canon***, which originally meant a stiff, straight rod, by extension to mean a measuring rod, and then anything that sets a standard or imposes a rule. We know the word *canon* best, of course, in a different connection: To us it means a composition in which at least two parts are related by strict melodic imitation. But that modern, familiar musical meaning is actually a direct extension of the earlier meaning, since when two parts are in strict imitation, only one of them need be written down. The other can be deduced with the aid of a rubric or some other sign that directs one performer to sing the same part as another but to enter later or in some other manner, such as at a different interval or speed or backwards. To realize the unnotated part, all you have to do is follow the directions given by the canon.

Anyone reading this book probably has known at least a few simple canons since childhood: "Row, Row, Row Your Boat" or "Frère Jacques." They are the easiest of all polyphonic pieces for a group of children to learn because you only have to learn one melody to sing all the parts. And while they have a definite beginning, they have no end—or rather, no composed ending. (They usually end in giggles or elbows jabbed in ribs rather than in cadences.) Such songs just go round and round—whence their name, of course. (The Latin for a "round" is *rota*; we will encounter a famous example in the next chapter.) Canons came into their own, along with so many other technically impressive genres, precisely in the fourteenth century. The original French name for them was *chace*, and it was a pun. The word is a cognate of the English "chase," which describes the behavior of the successively entering voices, each running after the previous one. The primary French meaning is the "hunt," and it is reflected in the novel subject matter of several chaces and even more so, as we shall see, in the similarly named Italian genre, the *caccia*.

Subtilitas

Another outstanding feature of the newly sophisticated fourteenth-century music is *subtilitas*, the easiest translation of which is the cognate "subtlety." The word literally denotes fineness and delicacy, which are aristocratic values (obvious to anyone who knows the story of "The Princess and the Pea"). From the artistic point of view, it suggests both allusiveness and elusiveness, qualities that point to something easily missed (as when we speak of "subtle wit" or "subtle irony"); or something faint and mysteriously suggestive (as when we speak of "a subtle smile"); or something requiring mental acuteness to perceive (as when we speak of "a subtle point" in argument). In most general terms, the word suggests a focus on the small, on details.

To make these polymeters as unambiguous as possible, Caserta used a variety of bizarre note forms to supplement the standard time signatures. Since the 1960s this style has been called the Ars Subtilior

The *subtilitas* with which Machaut expressed his implicitly aristocratic outlook on art and culture took a somewhat technocratic turn in the work of the generations of poets and musicians who followed him and who looked on him as a creative father. This was the period of the final (some say decadent or "mannerist") phase of the Ars Nova, notable for an explosion of convoluted musical artifice and intricate embellishment that reached a height of sumptuous complexity unrivaled until the twentieth century. The whole explosion of complexity was predicated on the idea of emulation—not just imitation but the effort to surpass. Contests of this sort can be objectively won or lost only on the basis of technique. Technical virtuosity became the primary focus, as manifested in the handling of complex contrapuntal webs, in the contrivance of new rhythmic combinations, and in the invention of new notational devices for representing them. In the name of *subtilitas*, composers at the end of the fourteenth century became involved in a sort of technical arms race.

It was spelled out in a treatise on advanced notation attributed to Philippus de Caserta, an Italian-born composer who worked around 1370–90 at the papal court of Avignon during the time of the divided church. Caserta wanted to go beyond the limits of Philippe de Vitry's practice as set forth in the Ars Nova treatises. Where Vitry had posited his four basic tempus/prolation combinations as alternatives, Caserta wanted to be able to combine them all "vertically," that is, as simultaneous polymeters. To make these polymeters as unambiguous as possible, he used a variety of bizarre note forms to supplement the standard time signatures; his new notation involved two (or even three) ink colors, filled and void note heads, and all kinds of tails and flags, sometimes employed in tandem (one extending upward from the note head, the other down or to the side). He did this, he said, to achieve a *subtiliorem modum*, a way of composing with greater subtlety—with greater refinement, greater decorativeness, greater sophistication, and especially with ever more flamboyant technique. Since the 1960s this style has been called the ***Ars Subtilior*** after Caserta's assertion.

Caserta explicitly cast himself as Machaut's heir by quoting the opening text from one of the older composer's ballades and the refrain of another in his own ballade *En remirant* ("While gazing"; Ex. 3-6). The choice of genre was significant: The grand strophic ballade had replaced the motet as the supreme genre for Ars Subtilior composers. The introductory words of Caserta's ballade were in turn quoted by Johannes Ciconia, whom we will meet later in this chapter and who may have been Caserta's pupil. In such a way composers sought to establish and maintain dynasties of prestige.

Anthology Vol 1-29

Example 3-6 Philippus de Caserta, *En remirant* (ballade), mm. 1–5

Another way to establish musical dynasties, of course, was through the sheer virtuosity of composing, manifested at once in contrapuntal control of very complex rhythmic textures and in notational ingenuity. The original notation of Caserta's ballade is not a particularly outlandish example of Ars Subtilior notation but

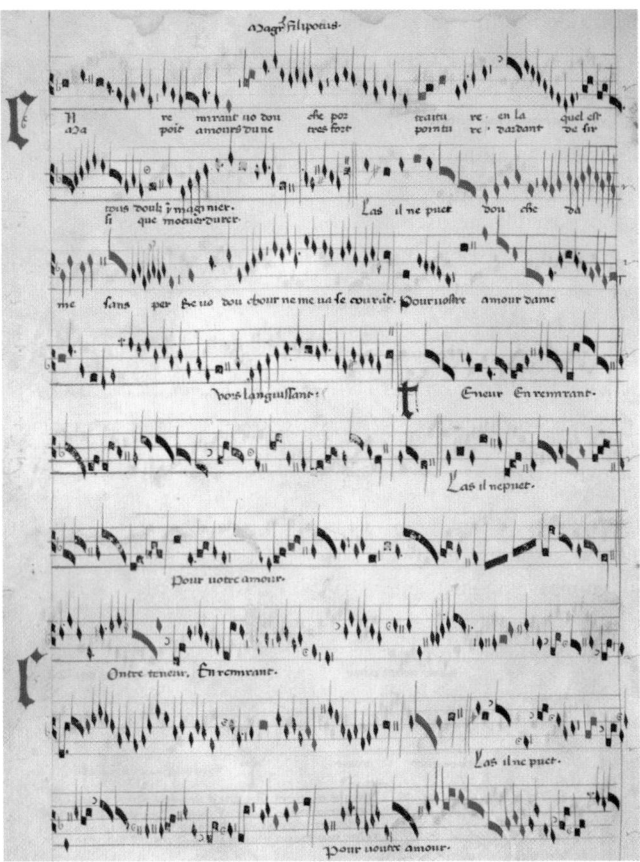

Figure 3-8 Philippus de Caserta's ballade *En remirant*, as notated in Modena, Biblioteca Estense, MS a.M.5.24, copied in Bologna ca. 1410 (fol. 34v).

a representative one (Fig. 3-8). It displays the kinds of rhythmic stunts composers enjoyed contriving. As usual in this style, the tenor plays straight man to the cantus and contratenor, its relatively steady tread supplying an anchor to ground their rhythmic and notational subtleties.

There were four main types of new notational virtuosity in *En remirant*. First, there are lengthy passages in syncopation initiated by little "dots of division," like the one that comes after the second note in the cantus. Second, there is interplay of perfect and imperfect note values, represented by contrasting ink colors, red standing for the opposite of whatever the prevailing mensuration happens to be. This characteristic 3:2 proportion was called *hemiola* (from the Greek) or *sesquialtera* (from the Latin), both meaning "one-and-a-half." Third, there are superimposed and juxtaposed time signatures throughout, both perfect and imperfect, which result in duple and triple meter in transcription. Finally, there are the unusual note shapes without which no self-respecting Ars Subtilior composition would be complete. There are two such shapes in *En remirant*, both borrowed from Italian-style notation we will encounter later in this chapter. One of them—a curious red note with stems both up and down—creates a 4:3 relationship at the level of the minim. The other creates the same 4:3 relationship at the level of the breve.

Ars Subtilior composition was a French phenomenon not exclusively limited to France. The location of the other center of activity may seem surprising: Cyprus, the most easterly of the major Mediterranean islands, off the southern coast of Turkey and the western coast of Syria, which had been conquered during the Third Crusade in 1191 by an army under Richard Lionheart. Because of various political alliances and marriages, the musical chapel in Cyprus was filled with French musicians. The surviving legacy is a huge manuscript, now housed in the National Library of Turin, containing plainchant Masses and Offices and more than 200 polyphonic compositions in every contemporary French genre—Mass Ordinary settings, Latin and French motets, ballades, rondeaux, and virelais. Although produced entirely by imported French musicians, it was a wholly native repertory and, with one exception, a wholly anonymous one. Not a single composition from the Cypriot manuscript turns up in any other source, showing, once again, how extremely fragile and incomplete a picture we gain from those compositions that do survive from the time.

Ars Subtilior composition flourished most of all in the south of France, whose traditions of trobar clus it was in a sense upholding. This region included papal Avignon as well as the duchy of Berry and the county of Foix at the foot of the Pyrenees. The chronicler Jehan Froissart (ca. 1337 to ca. 1405) noted about 1380 that during his lifetime there had been more feats and marvels to relate than in the preceding 300 years of history. The Ars Subtilior is best understood, perhaps, as an expression of that culture of marvels. Marvelous musical feats of syncopation and polymeter are abundantly displayed in a late-fourteenth-century manuscript, itself a phenomenal feat of calligraphy, which is now kept at the Musée Condé in Chantilly. The Chantilly Codex contains several pieces dedicated to Jean, the Duke of Berry, who had a magnificent court located in the city of Bourges. (Jean's sumptuous prayer book, known as the "Très riches heures" after the "hours" of the Office, is a well-known testimony to that magnificence; see Fig. 3-9.)

The poet-composer most closely associated with Jean's court, it appears, was a man named Solage, whose dates and even whose first name are unknown but all ten of whose surviving works are found in the Chantilly Codex. Solage's best-known piece is a bizarre rondeau called *Fumeux fume* ("Smoky smoke"; Ex. 3-7), which stands out from the whole Ars Subtilior repertory for the way its composer makes a tour de force out of chromatic harmony with the same exploratory intensity that drove his contemporaries to their extraordinary rhythmic adventures. Such outlandish chromaticism was another legacy of Machaut, whose style Solage seems deliberately to have copied in several works. The "smoke" connection was another link, although an indirect one, with the earlier master. The *fumeux* were a sort of playful literary guild of whimsical eccentrics that met at least from 1366 to 1381, striving to outdo one another in "smoky," sensational fancies and conceits. Solage, with his smoky harmonies and smokier tessitura, may have outdone them all.

The fumeux were a sort of playful literary guild of whimsical eccentrics, striving to outdo one another in "smoky," sensational fancies and conceits.

Anthology Vol 1-30
Full CD I, 47

Example 3-7 **Solage, *Fumeux fume* (rondeau), mm. 1–9**

Solage's *Fumeux fume* is a rondeau, a fixed form not as exalted as the ballade but not as humble as the virelai. And yet by the last quarter of the fourteenth century, even the lowly virelai, a dance song with refrain that as late as Machaut's time had remained largely monophonic, had begun to put forth some Ars Subtilior plumage. Its subtleties were of a sort that accorded with its content. The virelai became the site of sophisticated, even virtuoso, parodies of rustic and natural music. The genre signals a new artistic outlook that found its most extensive expression in the contemporary vernacular music of Italy.

Figure 3-9 "The Adoration of the Magi," from *Les Très Riches Heures du Duc de Berry* (1416).

"A Pleasant Place": Trecento Vernacular Music

Throughout the fourteenth century composers in Italy portrayed benign nature as something to enjoy rather than stand in awe of. Much of their music celebrated pastoral scenes inherited from the classical authors, such as the "idylls" and "eclogues" of Virgil. It is in such a "pleasant place" (*locus amoenus* in Latin) that pastoral lyrics were set: a stream, a shade tree, flowers in bloom. This is the setting familiar from paintings and tapestries of noble outings, situated around the same noble villas and their grounds where these agreeable songs were generally performed. The human ingredients are likewise idyllic: a beautiful lady, her graceful dance, her sweet song.

We have already seen the rise of European vernacular literatures and song genres, beginning with the troubadours in Aquitaine toward the end of the eleventh century and gradually spreading south and east, reaching Germany by the end of the thirteenth century. Why, then, with the exception of the examples of a pious pop song, the lauda, did Italy wait until the fourteenth century before developing a vernacular literature with its attendant music? The answer seems to be that for a long time the Italian aristocracy preferred their courtly songs in the "original"—that is, Occitan (or, less precisely, Provençal), the language of southern France. Throughout the thirteenth century, various Aquitainian troubadours were officially attached to the feudal courts of northern Italy and to the royal court of Sicily down south. Their work was imitated by local poets who took over not only the subject matter and forms but the language as well. Even the greatest literary genius of his age, Dante Alighieri (1265–1321) tells us that, before making up his mind that it would after all be possible to write poetry of profound intellectual substance in the Tuscan dialect of his native Florence, he had planned to use the internationally prestigious Occitan tongue.

And yet Dante was also among the earliest writers to attempt to separate poetry from music, holding that for stylistically ornate, philosophically weighty "cantos" in high style, the decorative addition of music would only be a distraction. He advocated the creation of special "mediocre" (that is, "in-between") genres of pastoral *poesia per musica* (poetry for music). Such pastoral, descriptive poetry would not be the main attraction, so to speak, but would, rather, furnish an elegant pretext for the creation of a secular music that might itself aim higher than ever, unimpeded by great verse. Thus the Italian song genres, when they were at last established in the fourteenth century, gave rise to a predominantly polyphonic and exceptionally decorative repertory. That repertory had its own notation and its own generic forms, related by a common ancestry to those of contemporary France but nevertheless distinctive and in some ways mysterious.

The characteristic song-poem of the *trecento*—so-called after the Italian word for the 1300s to distinguish it from contemporaneous French Ars Nova developments—was called the *madrigale* (**madrigal**, in English). A trecento madrigal was a vernacular poem that consisted of two or more three-line stanzas called *terzetti* (tercets), which are sung to the same music, and a single concluding one- or two-line "ritornello" (a little something that returns) in a contrasting rhyme scheme or meter. The familiar sonnet form associated with Petrarch and later with Shakespeare is a related one that substitutes quatrains (four-line stanzas) for tercets.

For Dante, the twelfth-century troubadour Arnaut Daniel provided the great model, a supreme forerunner of Italian mother-tongue literature. This is seen in an illustration from a Bolognese legal treatise (Fig. 3-10) showing the three main practitioners of the early madrigal—Giovanni de Cascia, a certain "Maestro Piero," and in the middle, standing on a pedestal with arm raised triumphantly, Jacopo da Bologna (1340 to ca. 1386), the leading musician of his generation.[5] The three madrigalists are flanked, on the right, by a group of chanting monks, and on the left, by Arnaut Daniel. Giovanni, Piero, and Jacopo served side by side during the 1340s and early 1350s at the two richest north Italian courts, that of the Viscontis in Milan and of the Scalas in Verona. Giovanni is shown holding a fiddle (*vielle*), which suggests that these poets may have performed their own songs. The fact that they sometimes set the same texts hints that they competed, as the troubadours had done, for prizes and favors.

The sources of trecento polyphony often look like the big presentation chansonniers that retrospectively preserved the music of the troubadours. This is particularly true of the so-called Squarcialupi Codex (named after an organist who was one of its early owners), a magnificent compendium put together around 1415 as a memorial to the art of the trecento when that art had already faded. Its expensive materials and lavish illuminations make this codex literally priceless. It is priceless in another sense as well: It preserves dozens of compositions that would otherwise have been entirely lost. The contents of the Squarcialupi Codex are organized by author, each section introduced by a portrait of the composer. Nowhere do we get a more vivid sense of how consciously the poet-musicians of the trecento thought of themselves as the inheritors and reanimators of the lost art of Aquitaine.

These Italian composers worked as polyphonists from the beginning and seem to have initially practiced their art largely as an aspect of university culture. The great Jacopo of Bologna came from the most venerable of all the Italian university towns. (The University of Bologna was founded in 1088.) That he wrote a musical treatise suggests he may have actually been a university teacher. The only Italian city to rival Bologna for academic eminence was Padua, site of Italy's second oldest university, founded in 1222. The basic treatise on the theory and notation of trecento music was the work of a Paduan musician, Marchetto of Padua (d. 1326), whose *Pomerium* (The Fruit Tree) contained the "flowers and fruits" of the art of mensural music. It is not clear whether Marchetto actually

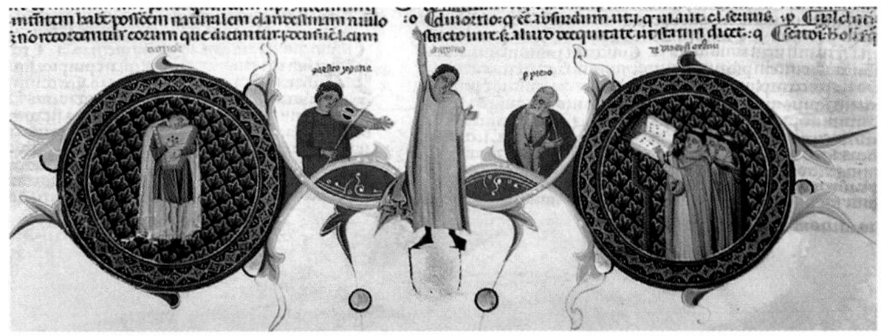

Figure 3-10 The troubadour Arnaut Daniel and his madrigalist offspring, Giovanni da Cascia, Jacopo da Bologna, and Maestro Piero, depicted in a fourteenth-century Bolognese legal treatise now in the Hessian Provincial Library at Fulda, Germany.

invented the notational system he expounded in this text, completed in 1319, or just systematized it.

The considerable differences between the Italian and the French systems of notation may be explained by viewing the Ars Nova as a direct outgrowth of the "Franconian" notation of the thirteenth century, whereas the trecento system refined the somewhat-offbeat "Petronian" tradition—the tradition of Petrus de Cruce, the composer of those late-thirteenth-century motets (like Ex. 2-15) that divided the breve into freely varying groups of semibreves. When it came to varying the rhythms that occurred within a basic meter, the Italian system, which used a wide variety of tailed note shapes, was exceedingly supple and precise. At least one of these special Italian note shapes—the single eighth note with a "flag"—has survived in modern notation. The rarer Italian shapes, as mentioned with regard to Philippus de Caserta's *En remirant,* were a major source for the novel signs used by Ars Subtilior composers. But of course many of those subtle composers, including Caserta, were Italians working in France. They were actually drawing to a large extent on their native traditions. So what modern scholars used to call the "mannered" notation of the late fourteenth century was in fact a fusion of French and Italian practices that widened the possibilities of both.

The "Wild Bird" Madrigals

Anthology Vol 1-31a
Full CD I, 48
Concise CD I, 41

Jacopo da Bologna's madrigal *Osellecto selvaggio* ("A wild bird"; Ex. 3-8a) is a music-about-music piece that casts a fascinating light on fourteenth-century aesthetics. The poem begins as if setting the expected pastoral scene so common to trecento art. The wild songbird is a standard ingredient of "pleasant places." But having introduced the bird, the poet immediately turns it into a metaphor for song itself and proceeds to deliver a little sermon on the art of singing and composing, mentioning three genres (madrigal, motet, and ballata) in which everyone tries to surpass Philippe de Vitry and Marchetto of Padua. By being the medium for a discourse on good singing and composing, Jacopo's music thus becomes "exemplary." The music itself must demonstrate the sweetness and moderation the words proclaim. Therefore it shuns the fancy virtuosity so often found in madrigals.

Example 3-8a Jacopo da Bologna, *Osellecto selvaggio,* set as a madrigal, mm. 1–10

Example 3-8a (continued)

A wild bird [during the season sings sweet lines in a fine style.]

Yet Jacopo set the same poem very differently on another occasion, this time heartily indulging in virtuosity. The text is spat out so quickly that the first tercet (Ex. 3-8b) takes only twelve measures in transcription. This version of *Ogelletto silvagio* is a **caccia**. The word is so clearly a cognate to the French *chace* that we might expect a canon. And a canon it is, albeit with a difference. For Italian poet-musicians the caccia was a type of madrigal, which meant a form in two sections (terzetti and ritornello). Its texture consisted of a cantus (in this case running against itself in canon) over an untexted tenor, which may mean that it was performed by instruments. Like the French word *chace*, the word *caccia* had a built-in "extramusical" association, and its subject matter frequently involved the hunt. The "wild bird" in the context here of a caccia therefore meant not a song, as in Jacopo's madrigal, but, rather, prey.

Anthology Vol 1-31b
Full CD I, 49
Concise CD I, 42

Example 3-8b Jacopo da Bologna, *Ogelletto Silvagio,* set as a caccia, mm. 1–6

Landini and *Ballata* Culture

Besides motets and madrigals, Jacopo mentions a third musico-poetic genre in the *Oselleto salvagio* text—the **ballata** (plural: *ballate*), which gradually stole pride of place from the madrigal. The word comes from the verb "to dance," identifying the genre as a dance song with refrain and thus associating it with the French virelai. The French and Italian dance songs were counterparts, and there is good evidence that as an "art" genre the ballata was directly influenced by the virelai. Unlike the "learned" madrigal, cultivated in universities, the ballata began as a popular genre, that is, as an oral and monophonic one (Table 3-1).

The beginnings of the ballata tradition can be found in the trecento's great prose classic, the *Decameron*, by the writer Florentine Giovanni Boccaccio (1313–75). Like Chaucer's *Canterbury Tales* (for which it served as a model), it is a collection of titillating stories that vividly expose contemporary mores and social attitudes. The setting is Florence in 1348, the year of the so-called Black Death, the great plague that killed a large portion of the European population. A group of seven young ladies and three young gentlemen have fled the infested city to the outskirts of town, where they go from villa to villa, enjoying the countryside pleasures as they wait out the epidemic. On each of ten days each member of the party tells a story, and the day's entertainments are formally concluded with a performance of a ballata accompanied on various instruments.

The last generation of trecento composers cast ballate with their form adapted to the French manner. They did this by means of a "contained" refrain, with open-and-shut cadences for the inner verses, and a three-part texture that included a contratenor. The great master of the genre—regarded by all his contemporaries as the greatest musician of the trecento—was a blind Florentine organist named Francesco Landini (ca. 1325–97; Fig. 3-11). With more than 150 compositions Landini has by far the largest surviving body of works among Italian composers of his century. All but fifteen (twelve madrigals, a caccia, and a couple of miscellaneous songs, one in French) are polyphonic ballate, about a third of those in the French three-part texture. This enormous emphasis on what was originally the humblest and least literary of the trecento genres reflects a changed social setting. Landini wrote music for the Florentine ruling class. His French-influenced ballata style may have reflected the tastes of that elite, which maintained a lively commerce with their French counterparts.

One of the ways we know that Landini's ballata was exceptionally popular is its inclusion in the earliest existing source of music composed or arranged for keyboard instruments.

Like many of the earlier troubadours, Landini was born into the artisan class, which in Florence represented no impediment to social prominence. His father had been a church painter, and he himself earned his living as an organ technician. So it is not surprising that the works of an artisan musician within an urban industrial community should have differed greatly from those composed by university-trained clerics for dynastic courts. Landini's ballate do not so much evoke bountiful pastoral surroundings, extol hedonistic pleasures, or narrate amorous conquests as they communicate personal feeling—often the conventionalized love-longing that by the fourteenth century was more a "bourgeois" affectation than a noble sentiment. Therein lay the difference between the "madrigal culture" of the noble north and the "ballata culture" of the Tuscan trading centers.

Anthology Vol 1-32
Full CD I, 50
Concise CD I, 43

The three-voiced *Non avrà ma' pietà* ("She'll never pity me"), one of Landini's most popular ballate, amply displays the French connection. The texture, with a

Table 3-1 Trecento Song Forms

Form	Comments
Madrigal: aa[a]b	Fourteenth-century madrigals have two distinct musical sections and no refrain. There are two or three "a" sections, called *terzetti,* each of which sets three lines of poetry. These are followed by a single "b" section, called the *ritornello,* which generally sets only two lines of poetry and has a different time signature than the *terzetti.*
Ballata: AbbaA	The fourteenth-century Italian ballata resembles the French virelai very closely. It follows the same form as the virelai, and its two "b" sections also often conclude with open and closed cadences. The chief difference between the ballata and the virelai—other than the language of their texts—is that the ballata usually has only a single stanza.

single-texted cantus accompanied by an untexted tenor and contratenor, is indistinguishable from that of a virelai. The open-and-shut cadences of the middle verses are reminiscent of Machaut. Besides the language of the text, only the "clumping" of the poem's syllables between melismas at the beginnings and ends of lines remains characteristically Italian. Landini's fingerprint is nonetheless unmistakable, owing to the use throughout of a cadential ornament so identified with him as eventually to bear his name. It would become a stylistic commonplace in the thoroughly internationalized music of the fifteenth century. While similar to the "double leading-tone" cadence, the so-called **Landini cadence** or Landini sixth decorated its melodic motion; the note before the final one proceeds down an additional scale step (from the seventh degree above the final to the sixth) before leaping up to the ending note, its behavior resembling what we would now call an "escape tone" (Ex. 3-9).

Example 3-9 Francesco Landini, *Non avrà ma' pietà* (ballata), mm. 1–4

One of the ways we know that Landini's ballata *Non avrà ma' pietà* was exceptionally popular is its inclusion in a north Italian manuscript from about two decades after his death that is the earliest existing source of music composed or arranged for keyboard instruments. The Faenza Codex, named after an Italian town, contains both sacred and secular music. This arrangement (or *intabulation,* as arrangements for keyboard are often called) gives us some idea of what instrumental virtuosos did at a time when practically no instrumental music was written down. Instrumental music, too, started out as an oral culture, based on listening, practicing, and emulating.

Figure 3-11 Francesco Landini wearing a laurel crown, from the Squarcialupi Codex. Although the piece that the portrait illuminates, the three-voiced motetlike madrigal *Musica son* ("Music Am I"), is one of Landini's most complex, the great majority of his works were in the less venerable genre of the dance song (*ballata*).

The Faenza Codex reveals the way in which "standard" or "classic" vocal compositions may have provided highly skilled instrumentalists (like jazz virtuosos) with a repertoire for specialist improvisation. The mixed contents of the Faenza Codex (it contains works by Machaut as well as by Jacopo and Landini) is another indication that Italian and French styles were merging by the end of the fourteenth century. When we remember that Landini was the foremost organist in Italy and that this had been his chief claim to contemporary fame, it is hard not to speculate on the extent to which the keyboard arrangements in Faenza may reflect his own improvisatory skills.

The Motet As Political Show

The gallicization of the Italian style was matched, although a few decades later, by the Italianization of the French, both tendencies converging on an internationalized style that in fact became truly international. That was to be the great musical story of the fifteenth century, as we shall see in the next chapter. International careers and wide dissemination of music (especially after the invention of musical printing in 1501) had important consequences for the style of the grandest genres: the Mass and the motet. So let us conclude this chapter by returning to the motet and to northern musicians.

The crowning period in the history of the Ars Nova motet is best exemplified by works written not in France but in Italy, although by composers who had emigrated there from northern Europe. Italy at the end of the fourteenth century was a checkerboard of city-states, many of them ruled by local despots who had seized power violently and who wished to establish legitimacy by ostentatious displays of power. Milan was controlled by the Sforza family, Florence by the Medici, and Mantua by the Gonzaga. Legitimacy was a major issue for the Church as well, since this was the time of the Great Schism, when rival claimants vied for the papacy. Such a period of political and ecclesiastical chaos proved to be a gold mine for the arts, for the simple reason that one of the chief means of asserting political power has always been lavish arts patronage. Composers trained in the techniques of monumental musical architecture and who could produce works of grandiose design could put on particularly impressive legitimizing political shows for their patrons, and they found a rich market for their skills. Such composers came from the north, the land of the Ars Nova, where the techniques had been chiefly developed, one of the reasons why the best-paid, most sought-after musicians of northern Italy in the fifteenth century were immigrants from France and Flanders.

The first of this distinguished line was Johannes Ciconia, who was born in the Belgian town of Liège during the 1370s and received his basic training there, but by 1401 he was employed by the municipal cathedral in Padua, where he died in 1412. His chief Paduan patron was Francesco Zabarella (1360–1417), the cathedral archpriest and a famous university law professor, who served as a diplomat for Pisan Pope John XXIII and who was later made bishop of Florence and eventually became a cardinal. Zabarella played a major role at the Council of Constance, where the end of the papal schism was brokered. It was he who finally persuaded his own patron, Pope John XXIII, to resign in the interests of church harmony. At the time of his death, Zabarella was widely regarded as being next in line for the papacy.

In honor of this illustrious statesman and churchman, Ciconia composed two exceptionally grand isorhythmic motets in a style clearly influenced by the Italian secular genres we just examined. It has been suggested that *Doctorum principem super ethera/Melodia suavissima cantemus* ("The worthy merits of his virtues/With the sweetest melody, let us sing"), the second and more ample of them, was composed as a send-off from Padua when Zabarella left to assume his post as bishop at Florence. The triplum and motetus texts are of equal length, sung at equal rates, and alternate with one another at times so that the two texts seem to interlock like a hocket in a single address to the honored patron. The tenor layout and the mensural scheme are a virtual summation of Ars Nova practices, and in their combination of diversity and comprehensiveness they symbolize the harmonizing of competing interests—the *discordia concors*—that is the primary undertaking of any diplomat. This motet, then, is emblematic both of its recipient and of the genre itself, especially in this phase of its history, when it had become primarily a political instrument.

Anthology Vol 1-33
Full CD I, 51

Guillaume Du Fay's *Nuper rosarum flores*

To conclude this chapter, let us consider an isorhythmic motet by another northerner in Italy—the great Guillaume Du Fay (ca. 1397–1474), with whom we will spend more time in the next chapter. It is worth considering at least one of his works now, however, in order to appreciate the direct generic and stylistic continuity that linked his creative output with that of his fourteenth-century precursors.

Du Fay's career was much like Philippe de Vitry's a century earlier. He was a university-educated ordained cleric who thought in scholastic terms about his craft but in Platonic terms about the world. For him, no less than for the founders of the Ars Nova, the world was materialized number, and the highest purpose of music was to dematerialize it back to its essence. Mostly likely born near Brussels, Du Fay followed in Ciconia's footsteps to early employment in Italy. He may have first gone down there as a choirboy in the entourage of the local bishop, who attended the Council of Constance. By 1420, when he was about twenty three, Du Fay was employed by the Pesaro branch of the notorious Malatesta family, the despots of the Adriatic coastal cities of west-central Italy. He joined the papal choir in 1428 and evidently formed a close relationship with Gabriele Cardinal Condulmer, who in 1431 became Eugene IV, the second pope to reign over the reunited church.

Du Fay wrote three grandiose motets in honor of Pope Eugene IV. The first, *Ecclesie militantis Roma sedes* ("Rome, seat of the Church militant"), was composed shortly after the pope's election, at a precarious moment for the reclaimed papacy. That motet, expressive of the political conflicts that beset the new pope, is a riot of complexity, with a complement of five polyphonic parts (three of them texted), and a series of no fewer than six mensuration changes. The second motet, *Supremum est mortalibus bonum* ("For mortals the greatest good"), is a celebration of a peace treaty between Pope Eugene IV and Sigismund, the Holy Roman Emperor. It is an epitome of concord, employing only one text and using a novel, sugar-sweet harmonic idiom of which Du Fay was an innovator. Near the end the names of the protagonists of the peace are declaimed in long-sustained consonant chords—concord concretized.

Anthology Vol 1-34
Full CD I, 52
Concise CD I, 44

The third motet, *Nuper rosarum flores* ("Garlands of roses"), is the most famous one because of the way it manipulates symbolic numbers. In 1434, the pope, exiled from Rome by a rebellion, had set up court in Florence, where two years later the cathedral, under construction since 1294, was finally ready for dedication. A magnificent neoclassical edifice, crowned by a glorious dome designed by the great architect Filippo Brunelleschi (1377–1446), the Florence Cathedral was dedicated to the Virgin Mary (Fig. 3-12). Pope Eugene IV performed the dedication ceremony

Figure 3-12 The Cathedral of Florence; dome designed by Filippo Brunelleschi.

himself, and he commissioned a commemorative motet for the occasion from Du Fay. This was to be the musical show of shows.

Nuper rosarum flores is cast in four large musical sections plus a dazzling melismatic "Amen" to conclude. The layout is remarkable for its symmetry. The first and longest section begins with an introitus for the upper (texted) voices lasting twenty-eight tempora. The Gregorian cantus firmus, the fourteen-note incipit of the Introit antiphon for the dedication of a church (*Terribilis est locus iste*, "Awesome is this place"), now enters, carried by a pair of tenors that present it in two seven-note groups. Each of the succeeding sections presents the same 7 + 7 disposition of the tenor and the same balanced alternation of duo and full complement [28 + 28 tempora, or 4 × (7 + 7)]. The pair of tenors is written out only once, with directions to repeat, with each tenor statement cast in a different mensuration: O, C, ¢, and ⦶.

These mensurations stand in a significant proportional relationship to one another. The order in which Du Fay presents them yields the durational proportions 6:4:2:3. As anyone trained in the quadrivium would instantly recognize, these are Pythagorean proportions, which can easily be translated from durations into pitch, for they describe the harmonic ratios of the most consonant intervals. Du Fay's motet embodies a hidden but comprehensive Pythagorean digest of the ways in which music represents the enduringly valid harmony of the cosmos (Ex. 3-10). It is the most complete symbolic summary of its kind in any isorhythmic motet.

Example 3-10 Proportional numbers in *Nuper rosarum flores* represented as pitch intervals

6X
4X
3X
2X
(X)
Perfect concord

But that is not all. The number symbolism in Du Fay's motet also makes contact with a venerable tradition of biblical interpretation that bears directly on the circumstances that inspired the work and the occasion that it adorned.[6] As we read in the first book of Kings, where the building of the great temple of Jerusalem is described, "the house which king Solomon built to the Lord, was three-score cubits in length, and twenty cubits in width, and thirty cubits in height" (1 Kings 6:2); that the inner sanctum, the "Holy of Holies," was forty cubits from the doors of the temple (1 Kings 6:17); and that the feast of dedication lasted "seven days and seven days, that is, fourteen days" (1 Kings 8:65). These, of course, are precisely the numbers that have figured in our structural analysis of Du Fay's motet. The durational proportions of the tenor taleae are precisely those governing the dimensions of Solomon's temple (60:40:20:30 cubits; 6:4:2:3 minims to a breve); and the length and layout of the chant fragment chosen as color correspond to the days of the dedication feast (7 + 7 = 14). The relationship of all of this to the dedication feast for the Florence Cathedral could hardly be more evident—or more favorable, in view of the Christian tradition that cast Rome as the new Jerusalem and the Catholic church as the new temple of God.

And yet there is more. The Florence Cathedral was dedicated to the Virgin Mary, as the motet text affirms. That text is cast in a rare poetic meter, with seven syllables per line. The introitus before the tenor entrance in each stanza lasts 28 (4 × 7) tempora, and the section following the tenor entrance likewise lasts 4 × 7. Seven is the number that mystically represented the Virgin in Christian symbolism, through her sevenfold attributes (her seven sorrows, seven joys, seven acts of mercy, seven virginal companions, and seven years of exile in Egypt). Four is the number that represented the temple, with its four cornerstones, four walls, four corners of the altar, and—when translated into Christian cruciform terms—four points on the cross, the shape of the cathedral floor plan. Four times seven mystically unites the temple with Mary, who through her womb that bore the son of God was also a symbol of Christian sanctuary.

All of this is expressed in the occult substructure of Du Fay's motet, while on the sensuous surface, according to the testimony of the Florentine scholar Giannozzo Manetti, an ear witness,

> all the places of the Temple resounded with the sounds of harmonious symphonies as well as the concords of diverse instruments, so that it seemed not without reason that the angels and the sounds and singing of divine paradise had been sent from heaven to us on earth to insinuate in our ears a certain incredible divine sweetness; wherefore at that moment I was so possessed by ecstasy that I seemed to enjoy the life of the Blessed here on earth.[7]

What could better serve the church, better spiritually nourish its flock, or better assert its authority?

Periodization

The beginning of "The Renaissance," for music, is often placed around the start of the fifteenth century. Constructing such major historiographical divisions can act as barriers, however, sealing off from one another persons and works that happen to fall on opposite sides of the fancied line, no matter how significant their similarities. Not only that, but an appearance of stylistic backwardness—inevitable when sweeping categories like Medieval and Renaissance are too literally believed in—can easily blind us to the value of supreme artistic achievements such as Du Fay's isorhythmic motets. They are not evidence of regressive tendencies but mark a zenith.

With Du Fay we enter a new century and what is traditionally viewed as a new period in music history, when there was a shift from the God-centered worldview of the Middle Ages to the man-centered view of the Renaissance sparked by the humanist revival of classical antiquity. This common historiographical perception raises the larger issue of periodization in general, an issue that will remain relevant for the rest of this book. Artificial conceptual structures such as historical "periods" are necessary for the processing of empirical information. Without them, it would be more difficult to relate observations to one another or assign them any sort of relative weight. All we would be able to perceive would be the daily dribble of existence multiplied by weeks and years and centuries. That is the very antithesis of history. On a more mundane level, we need subdivisions of some kind in our conceptualization of history because subdivisions provide handles by which we can grip the part of the story that interests us at the moment without having to contend at all times with the whole. Without such conceptual subdivisions we would have no way of delimiting fields of research or of dividing a book like this into chapters.

There is always the risk, however, that artificial conceptual subdivisions, hardened into mental habits, will become conceptual walls or blinders. And there is also the related risk that traits originally grouped together for convenience will begin to look as though they are inherent (or immanent, "in-dwelling," to use the philosopher's term for it) in the material being sorted rather than the product of an intellectual act on the part of the sorting historian. When we allow ourselves to be convinced that traits we have adopted as aids in delimiting the Medieval or Renaissance phases of history are in some sense inherent qualities of the Middle Ages or the Renaissance—or, worse, that they express the "spirit" of the Middle Ages or the Renaissance—we have fallen victim to a fallacy.

That fallacy is called the fallacy of "essentialism." When an idea or a style trait has been unwittingly defined not just as a convenient classifying device but as something *essentially* "Medieval" or *essentially* "Renaissance," we are then fated to identify it outside as well as inside the boundaries of the period in question. Stylistic traits are then liable to take on the appearance of "progressive" ones (if they show up, as it were, in advance of their assigned period) or "regressive" ones (if they show up afterward). Du Fay's *Nuper rosarum flores,* for example, might be thought of as both progressive in its harmonic language and regressive in its isorhythmic structure. This confusion of assigned attribute with natural essence contributes to the goal-oriented view of history as a directed march of styles (directed toward what, though, and by whom?). It also reflects values associated with terms like *progressive* and *regressive,* which are borrowed from the language of politics and are not morally neutral.

When periods are essentialized, we may begin seeing objects classed within them in undesirable comparative terms as more or less essentially Medieval, Renaissance, Baroque, Classical, and so forth. We may become burdened with considerations of purity or fidelity to a *Zeitgeist* (a "spirit of the time") that never burdened contemporaries. And that is because, unless we are cautious indeed, we can forget that *Zeitgeist* is a concept that we, not "the time," have constructed. We may then value some objects over others as being better or even as being "the best" expressions of "the spirit of the Middle Ages" or "the spirit of the Renaissance." If this sort of essentialism seems innocuous enough, we might transpose the frame of reference from the chronological to the geographical and reflect on what happens when people become concerned over the purity or genuineness of one's essential Americanism or Africanness or Russianness.

Categories, in short, are necessary but also risky. Historical periodization, while purportedly a neutral—which is to say a "value-free"—conceptual aid, rarely manages to live up to that purpose. Values always seem somehow to get smuggled in. The reason for raising these questions at this juncture is that the fourteenth century, and in particular the Italian trecento, has been a period of contention with respect to musical periodization. In art history and the history of literature, scholars have agreed that the Florentine trecento marks the beginning of the Renaissance ever since the concept of the Renaissance as a historiographical period was formulated in the mid-nineteenth century. For art historians the first Renaissance painter, by long-established convention, is Giotto (ca. 1266–1337), whose primary medium was the church *fresco,* or wall painting. In literature, it is Dante and Boccaccio, also both Florentines, who mark the great Renaissance divide. It is not at all difficult to relate the proto-Renaissance indicators to the music of the trecento. The special relevance of

Unless we are cautious, we can forget that Zeitgeist is a concept that we, not "the time," have constructed.

Landini, the foremost exponent of ballata culture, to Boccaccio's world could hardly be more conspicuous. Moreover, much of trecento music came about in response to the tastes of the Florentine public—an audience of self-made men.

The concept of the Renaissance in general historiography centers on three main related considerations: secularism, humanism, and the rebirth (in French, *renaissance*) of interest in the art and philosophy of pre-Christian antiquity. All three concepts depend on the prior notion of a Medieval world that was sacred and inhuman in its outlook and shut off from the classical past. ("Essential" concepts usually originate as comparative ones: If we did not know "hot," we would not know "cold.") Humanism, which looked to the thinking of classical authors and to a revival of many of their secular ideas and values, was a movement that we will see dominate much of the discussion in the next few chapters.

A preoccupation with the classical past and a striving for its rebirth was complicated, however, in music history by the extreme perishability of music as compared with the other art media and the consequent lack of actual classical models. There could be no revival of a pre-Christian classical past in music, since there was practically nothing left from that vanished musical culture to revive. As a result, the idea arose among musicians and their audience alike that music was an art virtually without a past—or at least without "a usable past." As one German writer, Othmar Luscinius, put it in 1536, at the height of what we call the Renaissance,

> How strange it is that in matters of music we find a situation entirely different from that of the general state of the arts and letters: In the latter whatever comes closest to venerable antiquity receives most praise; in music, he who does not excel the past becomes the laughing stock of all.[8]

Many modern historians prefer to view the beginning of the musical Renaissance somewhere between the beginning and the middle of the fifteenth century, a period from which we have many witnesses testifying to the general perception that music had been reborn. We will sample and evaluate their opinions on the new music in later chapters; here it will suffice to quote the fifteenth-century theorist Johannes Tinctoris's opinion of pre-fifteenth-century music, including trecento music. Such songs, he wrote, were "so ineptly, so stupidly composed that they rather offended than pleased the ear."[9] Indeed Cosimo Bartoli, a Florentine scholar of the sixteenth century, observed that the composers of Tinctoris's time had "rediscovered music, which then was as good as dead."[10]

If we call that "rediscovery" the beginning of the Renaissance period for music, we are using the term in a different way from the way it is used in general history. We are in effect endorsing and perpetuating an undesirable comparison. The term, in such a usage, is not descriptive but honorific, a mark of favorable judgment. The use of the term Renaissance to coincide with what fifteenth-century musicians saw as the birth of their art or its rupture with its past becomes positively paradoxical at the other end of the period, for at the end of the sixteenth century, musicians did in fact try to revive the art of pre-Christian antiquity—not in terms of its style and actual sound (for they could not know what that was) but in terms of its effects as described by classical authors. Only then did music actually join the Renaissance, as the term is understood by general historians. But this belated emulation of antiquity was precisely what led to the overthrow of what music historians now call the Renaissance period and its replacement by the so-called Baroque!

Yet to try and avoid this terminological quagmire merely by pushing the beginning of the Renaissance back a hundred years to the trecento would scarcely help. As we will see in the next chapter, there was indeed a stylistic watershed for music in the fifteenth century, as there was for painting and literature in the fourteenth. If there is to be a periodization, it should not contradict the actual history of styles. As already hinted, the fifteenth-century watershed came about as the result of the internationalization of musical practices—what might be called the musical unification of Europe. But it was not a "Renaissance," and there is no point in calling it that. We may as well admit that the term serves little purpose for music history except to keep music in an artificial lockstep with the other arts—a lockstep for which there is a need only insofar as one needs to construct a *Zeitgeist*, an essential spirit of the age.

Summary

The new musical style that arose in fourteenth-century France has come to be known as *Ars Nova* (The New Art). The primary innovations of the era are rhythmic, pointing to a fundamental concern of the era: the musical representation of numbers. The name derives from a treatise of the same name, based on the teachings of Philippe de Vitry (1291–1361). De Vitry and Jehan des Murs (ca. 1290 to ca. 1350), introduced innovations to rhythmic notation that allowed duple rhythms to be notated. Like our modern notation, Ars Nova notation is based on the division of notes into smaller values. The central innovation was that each rhythmic level could now be divided into either two or three smaller units. A breve, the equivalent of the modern double whole note, could be divided into either two or three semibreves (modern whole notes). The semibreve could be divided into either two or three minims (half notes) and the minim into two or three semiminims (quarter notes). The division of the breve into semibreves, called "time," defines the number of beats in a measure; the division of the semibreve into minims, called "prolation," refers to the number of subdivisions in a beat. There were four different combinations of time and prolation, equivalent to our modern time signatures: $\frac{9}{8}$, $\frac{3}{4}$, $\frac{6}{8}$, and $\frac{2}{4}$.

The earliest surviving pieces in the new style come from a manuscript of the *Roman de Fauvel*, an allegorical poem of political satire copied in 1316 (see *Tribum/Quoniam*/MERITO). The self-consciously artistic and technical aspects of Ars Nova music are evident in the isorhythmic tenors of motets, which use a large-scale repeating rhythmic pattern called a *talea* and a repeating melodic pattern called a *color*. The fourteenth century also saw the expansion of the traditional Medieval gamut through unwritten *musica ficta*. In order to avoid awkward intervals between voices (especially the tritone), singers could adjust individual pitches by adding a sharp or a flat, in effect reinterpreting their solmization on the spot either for contrapuntal necessity or to decorate the musical surface.

The leading composer of the Ars Nova was Guillaume de Machaut (ca. 1300–77). As a renowned poet and the heir of the trouvère tradition, Machaut excelled in writing chansons (songs), using the *formes fixes* (see Chapter 2). His polyphonic chanson differed from previous compositions in that the top voice, called the cantus, was composed first, served as the primary voice, and could sometimes stand alone as a monophonic song. In a two-voice texture, a newly composed tenor was added as the discant voice. In three-voice chansons, a contratenor was added to enhance the texture. Machaut was also known for his isorhythmic motets and contrapuntal tours de force, such as the quasi-palindromic rondeau *Ma fin est mon commencement.*

Another genre that arose in the fourteenth century was the polyphonic Mass Ordinary setting. These movements circulated often in pairs and occasionally in complete compilations. Machaut's *Messe de Nostre Dame* (Mass of Our Lady) is the first complete, cyclic setting of the Mass Ordinary by a single composer. Unlike the earlier composite "Mass of Tournai," all the movements are Machaut's own. The Kyrie, the Sanctus, the Agnus Dei, and the final Ite missa est are isorhythmic, with a chant melody used as a *cantus firmus* in the tenor. The Gloria and the Credo, with their longer texts, are homorhythmic. Altogether Machaut's *Messe de Nostre Dame* brought the genres of fourteenth-century sacred music to new heights.

Yet at the end of the fourteenth century, the complexity of the Ars Nova style was taken to still further extremes in the movement called *Ars Subtilior* (more subtle art). This style, which flourished at the papal court at Avignon from about 1370 to 1390, was marked by chromaticism and the simultaneous use of different meters (see the examples by Philippus de Caserta and Solage).

Music developed along different lines in fourteenth-century Italy. The poets and composers of *trecento* music (from the Italian for "fourteenth century") were active at a time of great cultural exchange between France and the Italian city-states; they thought of themselves as the inheritors of the troubadour tradition. Their music lacked the extreme complexity of Ars Nova and used a different system of notation. The three principal genres were the madrigal, in aab form; the *caccia* (hunt), a genre with its upper two voices in canon; and the *ballata,* a dance song with the same form as the French virelai (AbbaA). The leading composer of the ballata was Francesco Landini, whose name has been attached to a cadential procedure that remained common well into the fifteenth century (with the melody moving 7-6-1) to the close.

The legacy of the Ars Nova continued into the fifteenth century, especially in the isorhythmic motets written for ceremonial occasions. *Nuper rosarum flores* ("Garlands of roses") by Guillaume Du Fay (ca. 1397–1474), written for the dedication of the Florence Cathedral in 1436, shows the continuing symbolic power of numbers. The tenor and contratenor are written out only once but performed four times in different meters, producing a proportion 6:4:2:3. The numbers represent simultaneously the musical consonances and the proportions of the temple of Jerusalem. The number 28 (4 × 7) also figures prominently into the structure of the motet: The number 4 is associated with the temple and 7 with the Virgin Mary. Du Fay's motet is a good reminder that most compositions combine features and procedures that may seem "progressive" (harmonic language) or "regressive" (isorhythm) only in light of what are often artificial categories created by historical periodization.

Study Questions

1. Explain the general principles of the Ars Nova innovations in rhythm and notation.
2. What was the focus of the allegorical poem *Roman de Fauvel?* How does the motet *Tribum/Quoniam/MERITO* fit into this theme?
3. What is isorhythm? Describe how it is used in *Tribum/Quoniam/MERITO* and in Guillaume de Machaut's *Felix virgo/Inviolata genitrix/AD TE SUSPIRAMUS?*
4. Describe the compositional innovations of Machaut's chansons. Which voice was the primary voice? What was the role of the tenor and the contratenor?
5. When did polyphonic settings of the Mass Ordinary begin? Describe the variety of styles and compositional traits in Machaut's *Messe de Nostre Dame.*
6. Describe the Ars Subtilior and its musical characteristics. How are these traits exemplified in Philippus de Caserta's *En remirant* and Solage's *Fumeux fume*?
7. What are the salient characteristics of Italian trecento music? Describe the characteristics of each of the three main genres.
8. Describe the ways in which number symbolism is incorporated into the structure of Du Fay's *Nuper rosarum flores.*

Key Terms

Ars Nova
Ars Subtilior
ballata
caccia
cantus
chanson
color
cyclic Mass
isorhythm
Landini cadence
madrigal
musica ficta
prolation
talea
tempus (time)

4

Island and Mainland: Toward a Pan-European Style

The story of European music in the fifteenth and sixteenth centuries is one of increasing internationalization, with the movement back and forth between Franco-Burgundian musicians in the north and Italian ones in the south. A seeming anomaly, the intense cultivation of Ars Subtilior composition in far-off Cyprus during the early fifteenth century, has shown us that French musicians (and their techniques) were exceptionally mobile and that European politics led to some unusual migrations. We must now expand our scope to consider musical life in the British Isles, which will reveal further fruitful interactions, and indeed decisive ones.

First we need to revisit some developments in English musical life before the fifteenth century. Polyphonic music there pursued a somewhat different line from the one we have traced on the European mainland. It may be tempting to look on England as a sort of musical Australia, an island culture inhabited by its own insular fauna—musical kangaroos and koalas. That, however, would very much exaggerate England's musical isolation and its independence.

The British Isles (Fig. 4-1) were not an isolated territory, but a site of repeated invasion and colonization going back even before the most momentous invasion of all, the Norman Conquest of 1066, which brought the English into an intense, long-lasting, and all-transforming intercourse with the French language and French society. By the late thirteenth century, English and French culture were so thoroughly intermixed that their disentangling was no longer feasible. Nor was their cultural exchange a one-way street. England was politically subject to France, but culturally the shoe was often on the other foot. The English college at the University of Paris in particular thrived around the turn of the thirteenth century—precisely, that is, when the "Notre Dame School" was consolidating. Remember that much of our information about that school came from lecture notes known as "Anonymus IV," written by an Englishman studying in Paris.

Some of the most distinctive stylistic qualities associated with English music can be found quite early in a short composition known as the Sumer Canon (Fig. 4-2; Ex. 4-1). Ever since the 1770s, when the first modern histories of music were written, the Sumer Canon has been the most famous piece of "ancient music" in the Western world (apart from Gregorian chants in daily use). It is found in a manuscript that was probably compiled around the middle of the thirteenth century at the Benedictine Abbey of Reading, a town some fifty miles west of London. The text is in the local dialect and celebrates the arrival of summer: *Sumer is icumen in/Lhude sing cuccu*! In modernized English, it goes like this:

Anthology Vol 1-35
Full CD I, 53
Concise CD I, 45

> Summer has come! Loudly sing cuckoo! Seed is growing, the flowers are blowing in the field, the woods are newly green. The ewe bleats after her lamb, the cow lows after her calf. The bull starts, the buck runs into the brush. Merrily sing cuckoo! That's it, keep it up!

In order to perform the music, you must read a long set of instructions—the rubric—that explains what to do:

> This ***rota*** [round] can be sung by four companions, but not by less than three (or at least two), in addition to the ones on the part marked *pes* ["foot" or "ground"]. Sing it thus: While the rest remain silent, one begins together with the singers of the *pes* [foot], and when he comes to the first note after the cross, another begins, and so on. Pause at the rests, but nowhere else, for the length of one long note.

So this piece is a round, or a canon, a simple kind of imitation familiar today from children's songs like "Row, Row, Row Your Boat." The Sumer Canon has a definite beginning but no specified end. It is to be sung over a fundamental repetitive phrase, which is what *pes* means in this context. The two rounds are directed by their own rubrics to enter together, rather than in sequence, and are sung in perpetual voice exchange: A against B, then B against A, and so on forever. The result is an accompanied round in as many as six separate parts. There is nothing comparable to such a conception in any other manuscript music of this period in any country, and no other six-part composition has been preserved in writing until the latter part of the fifteenth century, some 200 years later.

It is not difficult to see why this little piece has been a celebrity of music history. But just what has made it such a hit? Its "bigness," if we allow ourselves a moment to reflect, is somewhat illusory. A lot of parts get going at once, to be sure, but they are organized according to a very simple pattern, the repetitive pes with its implied harmonic oscillation between the final (F) and its "supertonic" (G)—the very oscillation that has governed the "open/shut" endings of some of the formes fixes we already encountered. That oscillation has a harmonic quality familiar to us

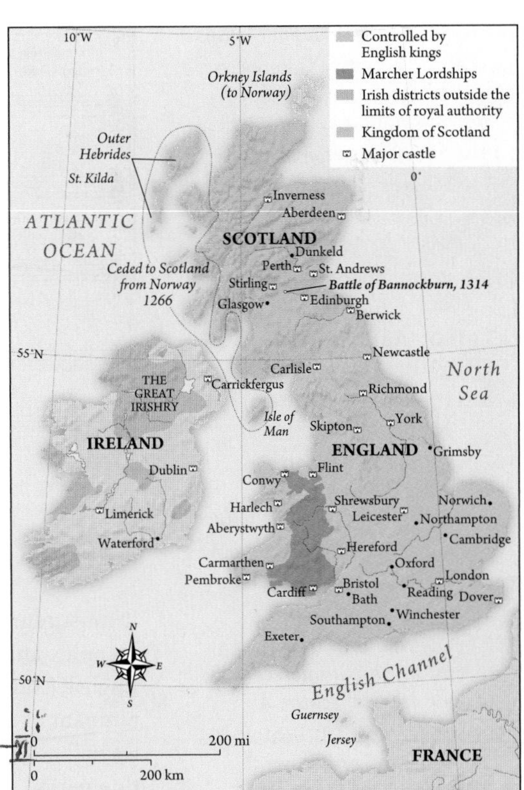

Figure 4-1 The British Isles at the end of the thirteenth century.

today but that we have not yet encountered in Medieval music. Once the second voice has entered, full F-major and G-minor triads sound on practically every beat, creating an abundance of thirds that we will see are especially characteristic of English music.

TIMELINE

ca. 1250 The Sumer Canon
ca. 1400 The Old Hall Manuscript
1415 Henry V of England defeats French at Agincourt
1419–67 Reign of Philip the Good, Duke of Burgundy
ca. 1420 John Dunstable, *Quam pulchra es*
1429 Christine de Pisan, *The Tale of Joan of Arc*
1431 Joan of Arc burned at the stake
1430s Gilles de Bins (Binchois), *Deuil angoisseux*
1430s Guillaume Du Fay, *Ave maris stella*
ca. 1440 Earliest *Caput* Masses
ca. 1450 Johannes Gutenberg develops movable type for printing
1450s Earliest *L'Homme armé* Masses
1453 End of the Hundred Years War
1453 Constantinople falls to the Turks
ca. 1460 Antoine Busnoys, *Missa L'Homme armé*
1460s Jean de Ockeghem, *Ma bouche rit*
1470s Phillipe Basiron, *Salve regina*
1477 Death of Charles the Bold, last of the Burgundian dukes
1478 Beginning of the Spanish Inquisition
1501 Ottaviano Petrucci publishes *Harmonice musices odhecaton A*
1504–05 Jacobus Obrecht at court in Ferrara

Example 4-1 ***Sumer is icumen in,* mm 1–10**

Fragmentary Remains

It must remain an open question to what extent the Sumer Canon is a uniquely complex and innovative musical composition, the product of some anonymous English composer's forward-looking musical genius, or a lucky (for us) written remnant of a widespread but otherwise-unrecorded oral tradition. A major reason we will never know the answer is because so very little English music survives from this period. There was a wholesale destruction of manuscripts containing Latin church music during the course of the Anglican Reformation in the sixteenth century, which proved a great disaster for music history. Between the eleventh century,

Figure 4-2 *Sumer is icumen in* (London, British Library, MS Harley 978).

the time of the staffless Winchester Tropers mentioned in Chapter 1, and the beginning of the fifteenth, sources of English polyphonic music do not survive intact. Rather, what we have are individual pages (or leaves), or bits of them, which for utilitarian purposes had been recycled (as we would now put it). Some had been bound into newer manuscript books as flyleaves (the heavier protective leaves in the front and back of bound volumes) or as stiffeners for the spine. Some had even been rolled up and inserted into organ pipes to stop little leaks that were causing the pipes to sound continuously.

As we can tell from the page (also called *folio* or *leaf*) numbers of what does survive as well as from some tables of contents that have outlived their hosts, many of the original manuscripts were massive tomes, comparable to the famous codices that preserve the French repertory of the thirteenth and fourteenth centuries. Most historians take it as a fact that pre-Reformation Britain produced more manuscripts of polyphonic music than did any other country during those centuries. But all we have to go on now are pitiful fragments from which no more than a few dozen whole pieces or even self-contained sections can be salvaged. Many of the existing manuscript bits originated or at least were used at Worcester Cathedral, a hundred miles northwest of London. In the early part of the twentieth century these various loose leaves were collected and bound into three main codices now known as the "Worcester fragments." About three-quarters of this repertory can be dated to the last third of the thirteenth century.

What in French music is only a sporadic and short-lived device of third consonances became definitive in English music over the course of the thirteenth century.

While the ample texture of the Sumer Canon may be its most immediately striking feature, its use of triadic harmony is ultimately the most distinctive feature of English music. There is the roughly contemporaneous testimony in Anonymus IV that English singers felt that thirds, rather than octaves or fifths, were "the best consonances." It would be a considerable exaggeration to view the English preference for thirds as something altogether alien to continental practice, as if only in remote geographical corners (and behind closed doors, among consenting adults) could harmonies unsanctioned by Pythagoras or the *Musica enchiriadis* be secretly enjoyed.

The English predilection nonetheless seems to have had a particularly long history. In Giraldus Cambrensis' late-twelfth-century observations of contemporary lore he noted that polyphonic folksinging in the British Isles was concentrated in two areas, Wales and the northern territory occupied by the old kingdom of Northumbria. He ventured that "it was from the Danes and the Norwegians, by whom these parts were more frequently invaded and held longer, that they contracted this peculiarity of singing." The Northumbrian style of "symphonious" singing consisted of only two parts, "one murmuring below and the other in a like manner softly and pleasantly above"—that is, "twin song" (*tvisöngur*), to give it its old Scandinavian (or modern Icelandic) name. A late-thirteenth-century manuscript contains a strophic hymn setting of *Nobilis, humilis,* which undoubtedly represents a Nordic style of singing about which virtually nothing else is known (Ex. 4-2). The critical thing to note is the treatment of the third as a primary normative consonance. No matter what the exact origin, this much can be agreed on: What in French music is only a sporadic and short-lived device of third consonances became definitive in English music over the course of the thirteenth century.

Example 4-2 "Hymn to St. Magnus" (*Nobilis, humilis*), mm. 1–4

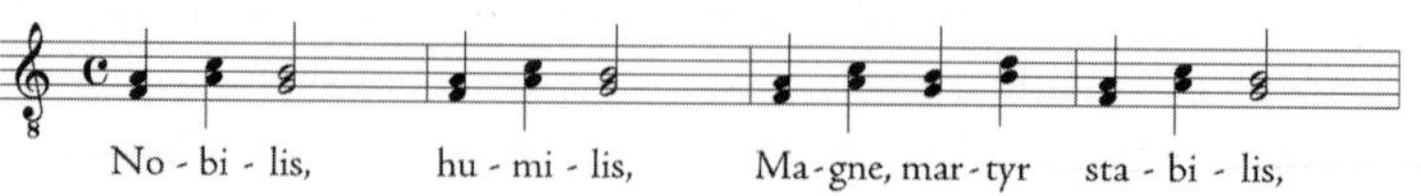
No - bi - lis,
hu - mi - lis,
Ma - gne, mar - tyr
sta - bi - lis,

O noble, humble Magnus, steadfast martyr

Anthology Vol 1-36
Full CD I, 54

We can hear this feature in abundance in the motet *Thomas gemma Cantuariae/ Thomas cesus in Doveria* ("Thomas, jewel of Canterbury/Thomas, slain in Dover"; Ex. 4-3). The piece was discovered accidently during the mid-twentieth century in the flyleaves of a nonmusical fourteenth-century manuscript; its text commemorates two martyrs who died more than a century apart. The motetus celebrates Thomas de la Hale, a Benedictine monk at Dover, the chalk-cliffed English Channel port; he was slain in a French raid that took place in August 1295, prefiguring the protracted conflict that became known as the Hundred Years War. The triplum celebrates another Thomas, the most eminent of all English martyrs: Thomas à Becket (1118–70), known since his canonization in 1173 as St. Thomas of Canterbury, who was murdered in the Canterbury Cathedral at the behest of King Henry II (Fig. 4-3). The texts in conjunction draw parallels between the two martyred Thomases.

Example 4-3 ***Thomas gemma Cantuariae/Thomas cesus in Doveria,*** **mm. 1–10**

As might be guessed, the triplum and motetus, each representing a Thomas, are "twinned," sharing the same range and indulging in frequent voice exchanges and hockets. And they are accompanied by a tenor and a contratenor that are twinned in the same ways, thus producing a double twin-song texture. That is already an English trademark, the first of many. The whole piece is laid out, like the Sumer Canon, as a set of variations over a pes. In this instance the pes is essentially a harmonic rather than a melodic idea. Although never literally restated, its harmonic framework is repeated more than twenty times. That framework oscillates between the final F (the "shut-cadence" note) and its upper neighbor G (the "open-cadence" note) in a regular four-bar pattern, as follows: I/I–ii/ii/ii–I (here "I" means F and "ii" means G).

The reason for using the roman numerals I and ii, reminiscent of modern harmonic analysis, instead of the note names F and G to represent the pes, is that G is

Figure 4-3 The murder of St. Thomas of Canterbury in 1170, from a Latin psalter made in England ca. 1200.

not invariably the lowest note in the "ii" portions. When G is the lowest note, the cadences are of the familiar "double leading tone" type. But sometimes, when one of the twinned tenors has G, the other one takes the C a fifth below, producing a "bass progression" not of ii–I but, rather, of V–I. No one reading this book should fail to take notice of the first occurrence in its narrative of a "V–I" cadential pattern, the most familiar and decisive of all harmonic closes to our modern ears. (What it meant to fourteenth-century ears is unknowable.)

Kings and the Fortunes of War

English composers were well aware of continental developments, and we will see over the course of this chapter the important repercussions of continental composers learning about English music. Note that while for convenience historians often refer to France, Italy, Spain, Germany, and so forth, these lands centuries ago were not constituted as they are today. The Netherlands and Low Countries now are made up of a large part of the Burgundian Lands. Spain had the kingdoms of Navarre, Castile, and Aragon; the Italian peninsula consisted of the Papal States in the middle, Naples to the south, the Duchy of Milan, the republics of Venice and of Florence to the north, as well as smaller city-states (Fig. 4-4).

By the end of the fourteenth century, when evidence of musical activity in the British Isles begins to become much more abundant, it is clear that there were plenty of musicians there who kept well abreast even of the most arcane Ars Subtilior techniques and paraded them proudly in their own work. The earliest English source of decipherable polyphonic church music to come down to us relatively intact is a magnificent codex known as the **Old Hall Manuscript**, which represents the state of English music at or near the end of the fourteenth century. It is now thought to have been copied for the chapel of Thomas, Duke of Clarence, second son of Henry IV and younger brother of Henry V. It consists predominantly of Mass Ordinary settings.

From the historian's point of view the Old Hall Manuscript is truly a feast after a famine. About a hundred of its 147 pieces carry attributions, naming no fewer than twenty-four composers, so that we have more English musical names from this period to conjure with (even if many of them are nothing but names) than we have from any other country. Among all of them one has understandably conjured up special fascination: "Roy Henry," French for "King Henry." A royal composer! But which Henry? Henry IV and Henry V, the father and the brother, respectively, of the manuscript's possible first owner, both reigned during the period of its compiling. Opinions still differ as to which of them may have composed the two works attributed to Roy Henry (and there is no guarantee that

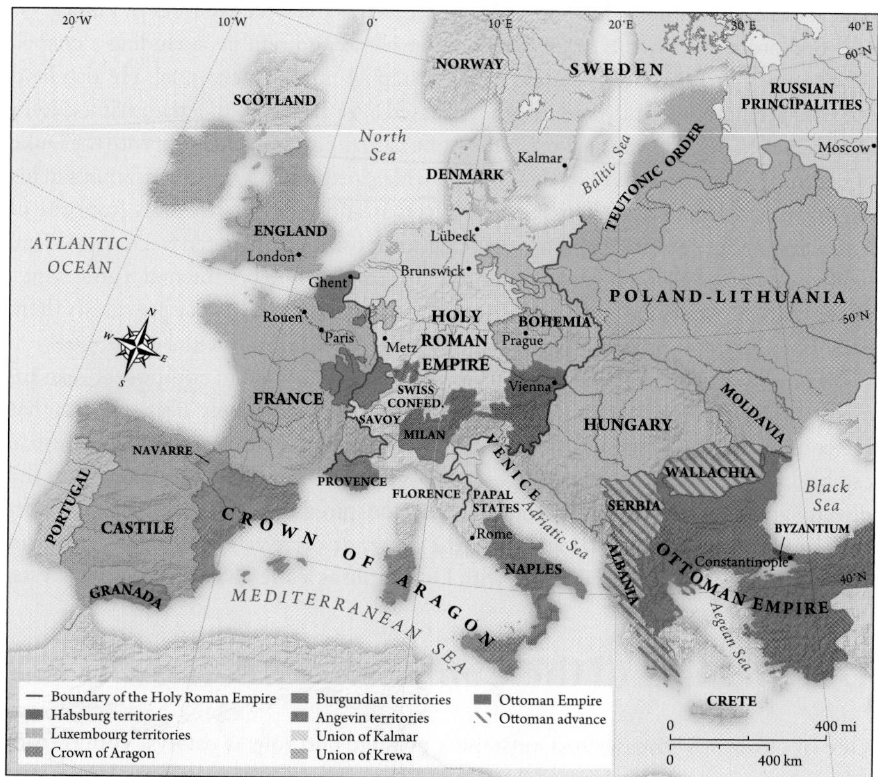

Figure 4-4 Europe ca. 1400.

either attribution is anything but honorific). One of the pieces, a Sanctus setting, stands at the head of its section in the manuscript. Smoothly and skillfully written, maintaining the English predilection for full triadic sonority, it can be taken as representative of "normal" English style just before that style became momentously influential on the continent.

The Old Hall Manuscript is truly a feast after a famine, naming no fewer than twenty-four composers.

Both King Henrys are well known to fans of Shakespeare's history plays, as are the political events around Henry V's career. Particularly notable was his triumph of 25 October 1415, when he and his well-equipped force defeated a much larger French army on the field of Agincourt near Calais. This proved to be the most important English victory in the Hundred Years War, the territorial conflict that actually lasted (off and on) for 116 years, from 1337 to 1453. Henry died in 1422, but the English armies continued to enjoy victories until by 1429 almost all of France north of the Loire River was in their hands. It was at this point that the French rallied under Joan of Arc, and they eventually won back most of their territory for the hereditary French heir, Charles VII.

Important musical repercussions arose from these political events. The English occupation of northern France in the 1420s and early 1430s brought a host of English officials, both military and civil, to French soil. At their head was John of Lancaster, the Duke of Bedford, Henry V's brother. Henry left behind a nine-month-old son and heir, Henry VI, who was also heir by treaty to the French throne. Bedford and his brother were named joint regents until the king came of age. Bedford had primary responsibility for prosecuting the war with France and administering the English occupation, duties that required his continued residence on French soil until his ally the Duke of Burgundy turned against him and made a separate peace with the French heir. From 1422 until his death in 1435, Bedford was the effective ruler of France.

Bedford maintained a regal traveling household and retinue, including a chapel. Based largely in Paris, it was staffed by a substantial musical personnel. He also held many estates in Normandy, one of which passed after his death to a man named John Dunstable (ca. 1390–1453), whose tombstone names him as "a musician with the Duke of Bedford." The man thus rewarded in 1436 with a lordship in France was famous in his day as "an astrologian, a mathematician, a musitian, and what not," to quote from one of his epitaphs. Out of more than fifty surviving compositions attributed to Dunstable (all but five on Latin religious texts), three-fifths are found only in continental manuscripts. This cannot be explained solely by the scarcity of English sources, since previously there had been nothing approaching such an English presence in continental ones.

Dunstable's works had enormous influence on continental composers—an influence enthusiastically acknowledged by a number of witnesses. This suggests that the composer himself spent time in Paris at the head of the Duke of Bedford's musical establishment just as English prestige was at its height. That political prestige, plus the novelty and sheer allure of the English style, conspired to produce a stylistic watershed in European music, after which for the first time there was truly a pan-European musical style for which the English, with Dunstable as leader, had served as catalysts.

Dunstable and the *Contenance Angloise*

One of our best witnesses to Dunstable's prestige and role as catalyst comes from a Burgundian court poet named Martin le Franc (ca. 1410–61), who writes that at the beginning of the fifteenth century there were three great Parisian composers:

Johannes Carmen, Johannes Césaris, and Jean de Noyers, called Jean Tapissier. Their work had astonished Paris and impressed visitors. But they had been eclipsed in recent years by a new generation of French and Burgundian musicians, who "have taken to the English guise [*la contenance angloise*] and followed Dunstable, which has made their song marvelously pleasing, distinguished, and delightful."[1]

Le Franc's vague but eloquent phrase ***la contenance angloise***—one dictionary lists "air, bearing, attitude" as well as "guise"—resists precise translation but gives voice to the conventional wisdom of the day. What contemporaries found so attractive were those features that until the end of the fourteenth century most distinguished English music from that of the continent, features like "major-mode" tonality, full-triadic harmony (or at least a greater reliance on imperfect consonances), and smooth handling of dissonance.

Although he looms large in traditional historiography for his decisive impact on a new generation of continental musicians, Dunstable was at least as much a continuer and an adapter of traditional Medieval genres. He wrote a considerable number of isorhythmic motets; indeed he was particularly expert in this loftiest of genres, as we might fairly expect "an astrologian, a mathematician, a musitian, and what not" to be. Like his contemporaries, Dunstable was still brought up musically in the spirit of the quadrivium, the arts of measurement. But the content with which he invested old forms—the new wine, as the old metaphor has it, that he poured into the old bottles—was indeed something different. Dunstable's music displays an unprecedented smooth technique of part writing; its dissonances are consistently subordinated to consonances in ways that begin to approximate the rules of dissonance treatment still taught today in counterpoint class (passing tones, neighbor notes, and so on).

For a dose of English newness at its most radical, let us consider Dunstable's most famous composition: *Quam pulchra es* ("How beautiful thou art"), a setting from the Song of Songs. Verses from that book of the Bible had become exceedingly popular in England as a result of the burgeoning of votive services addressed to the Virgin Mary, mediator between man and God. The love lyrics attributed to King Solomon, for which a long tradition of allegorical interpretations existed, now came into their own as votive antiphons. The Song of Songs nevertheless remains an erotic poem, and its surface meaning no doubt conditioned the exceedingly sensuous settings its verses received from English composers, starting with the "Old Hall" generation and, through Dunstable and his contemporaries, eventually infiltrating the continent.

Anthology Vol 1-37
Full CD I, 55
Concise CD I, 46

A new style of discant setting that emerged is widely known in the scholarly literature as the "declamation motet," although a better name might be "cantilena motet" because of its similarity to the lyrical texture of the continental courtly chanson. The seductive sweetness of *Quam pulchra es* is largely the result of an extreme control of dissonance. There are only nine dissonant notes (the first one circled in Example 4-4), and they all conform to the highly regulated dissonance treatment still codified in academic rules of counterpoint. Such a refining-out of dissonance requires effort. It is indeed conspicuous and therefore expressive of the text, reminding us that we normally take for granted a much higher level of dissonance as the norm.

No less expressive is the declamation. The homorhythmic texture of the old conductus is here adapted to the actual rhythms of spoken language. The naturalistic declamation is used selectively to spotlight key words and phrases, chiefly terms of endearment and symbols of feminine sexuality. The words singled out include *carissima* ("dearest"), *collum tuum* ("your neck," perhaps not just erotic but also symbolic of Mary as the "neck" between man and God), and *ubera* ("breasts"), the latter emphasized twice, once by the male lover and another time, at the end, by the female. The most dramatically set of all is the female lover's command—*Veni dilecte mi* ("Come, my beloved")—set off by homorhythm, by long note values, and by time-stopping fermatas.

Example 4-4 John Dunstable, *Quam pulchra es,* mm. 1–12

How beautiful thou art, and how graceful,
my dearest in delights.
Your stature I would compare [to the palm tree]

One can well imagine the kind of impression music as voluptuous as this must have made on continental musicians when they finally had an opportunity to hear it. It opened up a whole new world of musical expressivity. The first thing they must have noticed about the "English guise" was its luxuriant saturation with full triads, most conspicuous of all when they came in chains. Those chains had already been a standard feature of some earlier English pieces that had used an English technique of harmonizing chants at sight called ***faburden,*** in which the singing of three-voice parallel chords was realized over a plainchant. In Dunstable's *Quam pulchra es* the triads were absorbed into a more varied and subtly controlled compositional technique. The only kind of parallel voice leading he allowed was the kind that avoided perfect consonances in favor of the more mellifluous, more characteristically English imperfect ones.

Du Fay and Fauxbourdon

The continental response to such exotic euphony came in surprisingly concrete form beginning in the 1420s—right on schedule, as it were, following the Council of Constance in 1417 that ended the Great Schism in the Church and coinciding with the Duke of Bedford's regency in France. A piece like Guillaume Du Fay's

Communion antiphon *Vos qui secuti estis me* ("You who have followed me"), based on a Gregorian chant (the original melody signaled by the little crosses [+] in Example 4-5a), is notated as a "duo" (a piece "for two") but a curious one. The only intervals employed are octaves and sixths, with the octaves at the beginnings and ends of phrases and the sixths dominating in the middles, moving in parallel. Sixths are strange intervals for music in the "mainstream" theoretical tradition; while nominally consonances, they had always been described by theorists as an interval normally avoided. Here, bizarrely, they seem to be the prevalent interval.

Example 4-5a Guillaume Du Fay, *Vos qui secuti estis me* (Communion from *Missa Sancti Jacobi*), as notated (chant notes signaled by +), mm. 1–4

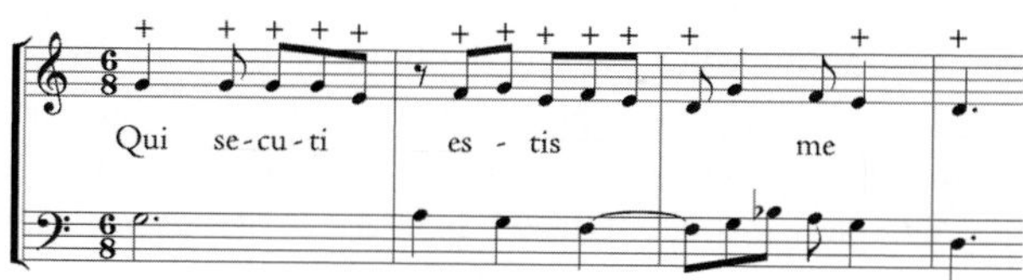

But the duo carries a rubric that says, "If you desire a three-part piece, take the top notes and start with them, but down a fourth." When this is done, fifths are added to the framing octaves, and thirds are added to the sixths to produce a procedure called ***fauxbourdon***, a parallelism of imperfect consonances amounting to a parallelism of triads, voiced for maximum smoothness, with the "hard" and "hollow" perfect fifth avoided. In Example 4-5b, the beginning of the Communion is "realized" according to the given recipe; but any singer who can read the top part can deduce the unnotated middle voice from it by transposition, without any need for a special notation. The technique for deriving three parts from two achieves the *contenance angloise* just the way Martin le Franc jokingly said Du Fay did it: *En fainte, en pause, et en muance*, which means roughly "in faking, in relaxing, and in transposition [i.e., making hexachord mutations]."

Example 4-5b Guillaume Du Fay, *Vos qui secuti estis me* (Communion from *Missa Sancti Jacobi*), first phrase as realized in performance

Also noteworthy is that in this new style the cantus part, not the tenor, carries the original chant. The chant-bearing cantus was adapted by embellishment and rhythmic adjustment to the conventions of the contemporary "top-down" genre, the chanson. Singers seeing the word *fauxbourdon* would know that the cantus part of the piece so labeled had to be doubled at the lower fourth and that the tenor was fashioned so that a voluptuous array of parallel imperfect consonances *à la contenance angloise* would emerge against the doubled line. The technique became understandably popular—faddish, in fact.

It remains mysterious as to just what the word *fauxbourdon* meant etymologically or why it was coined to designate this particular manner of composing or arranging. With only a handful of exceptions, the surviving pieces so labeled are all based on chants that have been transposed and embellished like Du Fay's. If fauxbourdon literally meant *faux bourdon* (false bass), then it might have referred to this transposition, leaving in the bottom voice what was usually found above (that is, a discant to a cantus firmus). The enigma is compounded by the existence of the English term mentioned earlier, *faburden*, which denotes something comparable to fauxbourdon but not identical with it. How (or indeed whether) the two terms and practices are related has been a matter of considerable speculation and debate. In the case of faburden the chant is thought of as the middle voice and the doubling part is above it. In the case of fauxbourdon the chant is thought of as the "cantus" and the doubling part is below. The point of fauxbourdon, as practiced by continental composers, was the transformation of "plainsong" into "fancy song." The raw material of plainchant was processed in this way into the highly refined style of the courtly "art song."

Figure 4-5 Guillaume Du Fay and Gilles Binchois, French followers of Dunstable and the *contenance angloise*, as depicted in a manuscript of Martin le Franc's epic *Le champion des dames*, copied in Arras in 1451.

Du Fay and Binchois

It seems no accident, then, that Du Fay (ca. 1397–1474) and Gilles de Bins, called Binchois (ca. 1400–60), the two most prolific masters of fauxbourdon, were also the leading song composers of their generation (Fig. 4-5). The liturgical genre most characteristically treated in the fauxbourdon manner was the hymn, the most songlike of chant types. What is often viewed as "Renaissance" about Du Fay and Binchois is exactly what Martin le Franc said was "new" about them: that they "have taken to the English guise and followed Dunstable," particularly as regards harmony and part writing. In fact the continental composers invented new ways—clever cookbook recipes—for instantly transforming their style and donning that "English guise."

Du Fay enjoyed a brilliant international career, with phases in Italy (including a stint in the papal choir) and at the court of Savoy before returning to Cambrai, near the present-day border of France and Belgium, serving as a canon at the cathedral. As we saw in the previous chapter with his extraordinary motet *Nuper rosarum flores*, he was an extremely ambitious composer, which is also apparent in many of his other motets and Masses. In addition he composed a large quantity of secular songs in all the formes fixes. He used one of his ballades *Se la face ay pale* ("If my face is pale, love's to blame . . .") as a cantus firmus for his best-known Mass. Du Fay was a pioneer in basing sacred music on secular tenors. Far from a blasphemy, it seems to have worked the other way, as a means of consecrating the secular. His setting of the Marian hymn *Ave maris stella* assimilates a famous chant melody to the style of the courtly chanson and also uses fauxbourdon (Ex. 4-6). Du Fay's chant **paraphrase**, as the technique of embellishing chants is now called, is extremely decorative: The plainchant's opening leap of a fifth is filled in with what amounts to an original melody. The alternation of cadences in the piece creates a bipartite structural symmetry not at all typical of plainchant melodies but typical of courtly songs, whose "fixed forms" always comprised two main sections.

Anthology Vol 1-38
Full CD I, 56
Concise CD I, 47

Example 4-6 Guillaume Du Fay, *Ave maris stella* in fauxbourdon, mm. 1–6

Binchois spent virtually his entire career as a court and chapel musician to Philip the Good, the long-reigning Duke of Burgundy, whose court was widely acknowledged to be the most magnificent in Western Europe at a time when art consumption was a prime measure of courtly magnificence (Fig. 4-6). Binchois wrote more than sixty chansons, and his finest achievements were ballades. By the early fifteenth century, the ballade, the oldest and most distinguished of the courtly song genres, had become a thing of grandeur, associated with special occasions, chiefly commemorative and public.

Among the grandest Franco-Burgundian ballade texts was *Deuil angoisseux* ("Anguished grief") by Christine de Pisan (ca. 1364 to ca. 1430)—one of the outstanding poets of her day—as set to music by Binchois for performance at the court of Burgundy. Pisan's poem was composed in 1390 upon the death of her husband, Etienne Castel, a notary in service to the king of France. Christine remained a quasi-official French court poet and a partisan commentator on the Hundred Years War. It is a bit ironic, then, to find in Binchois's setting of Pisan's early ballade a gorgeous epitome of the *contenance angloise*, the English-influenced style that testified to the musical ascendancy of France's enemy.

Anthology Vol 1-39
Full CD I, 57

Figure 4-6 Detail from the painting depicting the garden of love at the court of Philip the Good, in the gardens of the Chateau de Hesdin in 1431. French School, sixteenth century.

Binchois's *Deuil angoisseux* can tell us an enormous amount about the aesthetics of fifteenth-century courtly art. It is a marvelously effective, even hair-raising outpouring of emotion, and yet it scarcely conforms to our own conventional notions of what makes music sound "sad." Our present-day musical "instincts" demand that laments be set to extra-slow, extra-low music, harmonically dark ("minor") or dissonant. Binchois's setting flatly contradicts these assumptions with its bright F-majorish (English) tonality, its high tessitura, and its wide vocal ranges. Even the tempo contradicts our normal assumptions; the time signature of the song makes for shorter note values that hence move more quickly than normal. What Binchois conveys is not private anguish but a public proclamation of grief, as suggested in the poem itself with a concluding passage addressed to an assembled audience of "princes." The mood is one of elevation in tone, in diction, in delivery, all reflecting the elevated social setting in which the performance took place.

The Internationalism of the Upper Crust

The southward trajectory of Du Fay's career was characteristic, even typical, for the time. The old Frankish territories were still the chief seats of musical learning, but the newly rich Italian courts, avidly competing with one another for the most brilliant artistic personnel, were becoming great magnets for musical talent. Even after impregnation by the English, the basic technique of music remained French; once the northerners began invading the south, however, it became impossible to tell by style where a piece of continental music had been composed. Europe, at least musically, seemed united.

This apparent musical unity should not be read as an indicator of cultural or social unity. Literate musicians, we recall, served a tiny clientele of aristocrats and ecclesiastics. These elite classes did indeed identify with their counterparts throughout the length and breadth of Europe. At less exalted social levels, however, musically and in every other way, Europe was far from united. The minority culture of the literate cannot yet be taken as representative of society as a whole. Owing to the nature of our sources of evidence, the limited remains of elite music tend to hide the rest (which was the bulk) of daily musical life from view. Unless we are careful to remind ourselves, we can easily forget that the vast majority of Europeans lived out their lives in complete ignorance of the music we are investigating even as they made music themselves by continuing oral traditions.

Binchois's* Deuil angoisseux *is a marvelously effective, even hair-raising outpouring of emotion, and yet it scarcely conforms to our own conventional notions of what makes music sound "sad."

We can get some idea of the preeminent elite composers of the day from the writings of Johannes Tinctoris (ca. 1435–1511), a minor composer himself but a theorist of encyclopedic ambition. His dozen treatises attempt collectively to encompass all of contemporary music, its practices, practitioners, and products alike. The composers from whom Tinctoris drew his didactic examples are the ones whose works are found in sources throughout Europe, irrespective of provenance. He called Dunstable the fountainhead of contemporary music and consigned everything earlier to oblivion. He famously announced in 1477 that there was not a single piece of music more than forty years old that is "regarded by the learned as worth hearing" because, as mentioned in the previous chapter, he found the music composed "so ineptly, so stupidly."[2] Tinctoris presented an honor roll of his great contemporaries—bestowing benedictions on a favored few. Pride of place went to Johannes Ockeghem (ca. 1410–97) and Antoine Busnoys (ca. 1430–92), who in their joint preeminence have, much like Leonin and Perotin, like Du Fay and Binchois, haunted historical memory as a pair.

We will increasingly encounter prominent musical lineages, not just personal ones between and among composers but also specific ones between and among compositions. In such lineages later compositions are not so much imitations as they are **emulations**, that is, both an homage and an attempt to surpass. The dynasties of composers and of compositions that so distinguished the fifteenth and sixteenth centuries were dynasties of emulation. Works of high style became models for other works that aspired to highness in a spirit at once of submission to a tradition and mastery of it and in a spirit at once of honoring and vying with one's elders. A composition regarded as especially masterly will come to possess authority (*auctoritas*). It sets a standard of excellence, but at the same time it becomes something to beat. A true emulation will honor the model by conforming to it but will also distinguish itself from the model in a conspicuously clever way.

Ockeghem composed a sung lament—a *déploration*—on the death of Binchois in 1460, which suggests he may have been a pupil of the leading composer to the Burgundian court. Ockeghem came from St. Ghislain in the French-speaking Belgian province of Hainaut. By 1443 he was a singer at the cathedral of Notre Dame in Antwerp, the leading church of Flanders. It was at the court and chapel of the French king, however, that Ockeghem made his real mark, beginning in 1451 (Fig. 4-7). He became a great favorite of Charles VII and his successor, Louis XI, such that by the time of his death he was surely the most socially exalted musician in Europe, and the richest as well. Ockeghem was particularly venerated. By all odds the most beautiful musical manuscript of the fifteenth century is a priceless presentation volume from

Figure 4-7 Illustration from *Chants Royaux sur la Conception Couronnee du Puy de Rouan* (ca. 1520s) depicting the choir singing with Johannes Ockeghem, who stands at the right wearing glasses.

1498 known as the Chigi Codex, which contains the just-deceased Ockeghem's virtually complete collected sacred works and some of Busnoys's as well.

Busnoys was Ockeghem's counterpart (and Binchois's successor) at the court of Burgundy, where he served Charles the Bold (d. 1477), the last of the Burgundian dukes. As Ockeghem may have been a pupil of Binchois, so Busnoys may have received instruction from Ockeghem. He is perhaps the earliest leading composer from whom autograph manuscripts survive, so we know how he personally spelled his surname (often routinely modernized in the scholarly literature to Busnois).

The fifteenth century was one of those times when intellectual attainments and cerebral virtuosity were considered appropriate in an artist. Busnoys put his formidable linguistic, musical, and intellectual skills to work in praise of Ockeghem in motet called *In hydraulis* ("On the water organs"), which compares his great contemporary with the mythic musicians Pythagoras and Orpheus. Ockeghem returned the compliment in the form of an even more elaborate motet called *Ut heremita solus*

("Lonely as a hermit"), whose opening seems to combine a reference to Busnoys's hermit patron saint with an encomium, loneliness often being synonymous with eminence (as in "it's lonely at the top").

Beginning with those composers who were reaching maturity in the 1470s, the generation after that of Ockeghem and Busnoys, residence at the high-paying Italian courts became the rule. Some may have gotten their positions through Ockeghem, who in 1472 received a personal communication from Duke Galeazzo Maria Sforza in Milan requesting help in recruiting French singers for his chapel. Indeed, several important composers of the early sixteenth century had their professional start in the Milanese court chapel choir around this time. The outstanding representative was Jacobus Obrecht (as he was habitually named in Italian sources; ca. 1457–1505; Fig. 4-8), who after a distinguished career in various Dutch and Belgian cities was summoned to the magnificent court of Ercole I, the Duke of Ferrara, where he died of plague.

Figure 4-8 Jacobus Obrecht. Portrait by an anonymous painter, Netherlandish or French, 1496.

The Cyclic Mass

The **cyclic Mass** emerged as the major genre on which composers lavished their great skill, becoming the chief vehicle for their fame and for displaying the most dazzling feats of emulation. The new type of standardized Mass, which may be fairly regarded as the emblem of the era's musical attainments, set as a musical unit the five items from the Ordinary (no longer including the final Ite missa est). It was precisely a musical unit, not a liturgical one, because there is nothing unified about the Kyrie, Gloria, Credo, Sanctus, and Agnus Dei as a set of texts except that they are unchanging. As we know, they have different histories and use different languages; their structures are different, and they serve different functions in the service. Two are prayers, two are acclamations, and one is a profession of faith. Only the Kyrie and the Gloria are consecutive. The other parts of the Mass Ordinary are spread out over the whole length of the service, spaced as much as fifteen or twenty minutes apart, with much intervening liturgical activity, including speaking and other music.

The new unified cyclic Mass Ordinaries were large and impressively complex compositions in multiple parts. Their status as the paramount genre of their day prompts comparison with those that enjoyed comparable standing in other historical periods, particularly the multimovement symphonies of the eighteenth and nineteenth centuries. Yet a moment's reflection will confirm that the constituent sections of the Mass actually have little in common with uninterrupted symphonic movements. That is exactly one of the reasons why the Mass movements were deliberately made to resemble each other as much as possible, often beginning alike with a "head motive," featuring the same foundation melody, and following similar or identical standardized formal schemes that would emphasize unity and could easily be remembered and heard.

Settings of the Ordinary earlier in the fourteenth century, as we saw in the previous chapter, were of individual movements or occasionally of pairs. Complete settings like the Mass of Tournai and Machaut's *Messe de Nostre Dame* were compilations of individual, musically heterogeneous items. Yet now, all of a sudden (or so it seems), the Mass Ordinary emerges as a unified musical genre—covering a longer span and shaped by more purely musical compositional processes than any we have yet encountered. The musically integrated Mass Ordinary setting came to unify the whole service, symbolically integrating a process lasting as much as an hour or more by means of periodic returns to familiar sounds. The interconnections were a potent demonstration of the abstract shaping powers of music and their potential import in mediating between the human and the divine. The musically unified Mass Ordinary quickly acquired enormous prestige as a symbol of ecclesiastical power—the power, let us recall, of a Church that was itself newly restored to unity after the Great Schism.

Mass movements were deliberately made to resemble each other as much as possible, often featuring the same foundation melody that would emphasize unity and could easily be remembered and heard.

The history of the unified Mass, like so much in the history of fifteenth-century music, begins with the English. The device of paired movements based on a common cantus firmus tenor, already found in the Old Hall Manuscript, was expanded to encompass the other parts of the Ordinary. One of the earliest is a Kyrie–Gloria–Credo–Sanctus set, somewhat shakily attributed to Dunstable. It was likely first performed in 1420 at the wedding of Henry V of England to Catherine of Valois and perhaps again at another royal occasion, the Paris coronation of Henry VI in 1431. Use at such events shows another possible purpose of the cyclic organization of the Ordinary: A symbolic or emblematic tenor unites the various sections and renders the Ordinary "proper" to an occasion. A shared cantus firmus, if carefully chosen, could act like a symbolic commentary on the service and could even suggest that there would be no separation between church and state. Another early four-part English Mass is attributed to Leonel Power (d. 1445); it comprises an Ordinary complex based on a tenor derived from the Marian antiphon *Alma Redemptoris Mater*. This composition, found only in northern Italian manuscripts copied around 1430–35, contains some of the best evidence of the prestige of English music and its influence on the continent at the time.

Unifying the sections of Mass cycles on the basis of common tenors meant laying out a foundation in advance and building from the ground up. This architectonic conception had previously been the special distinguishing characteristic of the motet. And indeed, that genre was the source of the idea, even as the motet itself was undergoing change in the fifteenth century, a change that involved a lowering of its style. What happened, in effect, was that the rigidly conceived, highly structured style of the isorhythmic motet—the high style of the fourteenth century—passed from the motet into the domain of the cyclic Mass, which was potentially a kind of isorhythmic motet writ large.

"Caput" and the Beginnings of Four-Part Harmony

Continental composers adopted the cyclic Mass as the standard high genre from the English and further developed its compositional techniques. We can see this in a series of Masses based on the same cantus firmus melody: a supermelisma on *caput* (Latin for "head"), the concluding word of an antiphon, *Venit ad Petrum* ("He came to Peter"), that was sung at England's Salisbury Cathedral for the ceremony of "washing the feet" during Holy Week preceding Easter. "Do not wash only my feet, but also my hands and my *head*," said Peter to Jesus (John 13:9), in the line that became the antiphon whose melodic material became the basis for the so-called **Caput Masses**.

Sometime around 1440, an anonymous English composer turned the fancy "caput" melisma into a cantus firmus to produce a Mass similar to Leonel's Mass on *Alma Redemptoris Mater*, although on a much grander scale. The vastness of the conception in this instance suggests no mere chapel votive service but a cathedral Mass attended by dignitaries, the function that isorhythmic motets used to serve. The cantus firmus, with minor variables such as rests between phrases, serves for all the movements, each of which has the same overall structure articulated through the contrast of perfect and imperfect mensurations. In the first movement, for example, the "Kyrie" is in perfect time and "Christe" in imperfect.

Anthology Vol 1-40
Full CD I, 58

This anonymous English Mass is particularly impressive in its amplified sonorous texture, increased here to four voices and which became the norm. Once something becomes normal it is taken for granted; so let us seize this moment, while things we have long since taken for granted are still in the process of being formed, to witness the birth of familiar "four-part harmony"(Ex. 4-7). Although the sources that include the anonymous *Missa Caput* retain the nomenclature of voice parts with which we are familiar, scribes in the mid-fifteenth century adopted a new one, as shall we from now on. The two contratenors above and below the tenor were called "high" (*altus*) and "low" (*bassus*), which was eventually Anglicized as "alto" and "bass." The highest voice (till now called the cantus or the triplum) became known as the "top voice"—*superius*, from which the word *soprano* is derived. And thus we have our full familiar range of voice parts: soprano, alto, tenor, bass (SATB).

Example 4-7 ***Missa Caput*, Kyrie (sung with prosulas), mm. 11–18**

Also noteworthy is how the bass voice in the *Missa Caput* occupies a pitch space all its own and behaves in a new harmony-defining way. It tends to make disjunct leaps and has a newly standardized role at cadences, often going from the fifth scale degree to the final. This motion, of course, accords with what we are accustomed to calling a V–I, or dominant–tonic, progression. To call it that is to think of the motion of the lowest part as the essential cadential approach and to associate the gesture toward closure with the "dominant" harmony. The question for historians is at what point such a way of conceptualizing cadences matches that of fifteenth-century musicians and listeners. However they were conceptualized, such an approach and such a harmony were perceptually a part of virtually every final cadence from the midcentury on.

Patterns of Emulation

Two leading fifteenth-century composers of different generations of continental musicians, Ockeghem and Obrecht, wrote *Caput* Masses in emulation of the anonymous English one we have been examining, thereby casting themselves into a sort of three-generation dynasty. Ockeghem's Mass is presumed to be a relatively early work, possibly from the 1450s. The original *Caput* Mass set a standard, as can already be seen by comparing its Kyrie with Ockeghem's. As was the English practice, the anonymous *Missa Caput* Kyrie carried an added Latin text that necessitated a very spacious musical treatment. Ockeghem, having only eighteen canonical words to set (3 × Kyrie eleison; 3 × Christe eleison; 3 × Kyrie eleison), streamlined his setting. His way of distinguishing himself was to transpose the tenor down an octave so that it became the effective bass—no doubt originally sung by the composer himself, leading his choir with his famously deep voice.

Anthology Vol 1-41
Full CD I, 59
Concise CD I, 48

Ockeghem's audacity in transposing this particular cantus firmus melody down an octave meant that it begins with the one note—B natural—that normally cannot function as a bass since the diatonic pitch set can offer no perfect fifth above it with which to resonate. He goes ahead and writes an F above the cantus firmus B anyway, which forces alteration of the F to F♯ *causa necessitates* ("by necessity"), producing what we would call a B-minor triad. But the F♯ is immediately contradicted by the superius's F natural against the second cantus firmus note, D, producing what we would call a D-minor triad. This harmonic succession, by virtue of a root progression by thirds and a melodic cross relation, is still odd to the ear even after half a millennium. By harnessing the old devices of music ficta to new effect—a pungent effect implicit in the cantus firmus taken over from an earlier composer but one that the earlier composer had not exploited—Ockeghem announces his emulatory designs on the *Caput* tradition and proclaims himself a worthy heir to his distinguished predecessor.

Now it is time to ask who might this distinguished predecessor have been? Why should an anonymous English Mass have attracted such determined emulation? The likelihood, of course, is that in Ockeghem's day the Mass was not anonymous. He probably knew for a fact something about which we now can only hazard a guess. The gargoylish manuscript illuminations in Figure 4-9 give a subtle hint as to what he knew of the earlier author's identity. They show dragons galore, which any fifteenth-century astrologer or navigator would have associated with the topmost star of the constellation Draco, the ancient polestar. The actual term "Caput Draconis" mysteriously appears at the start of the first appearance of the cantus firmus of the original *Caput* Mass in another manuscript source. For those in the know, what better way could there be than this—a visual pun linking the cantus firmus

Figure 4-9 Opening of Ockeghem's *Missa Caput* from the so-called Chigi Codex.

of this magnificent Mass with a bright heavenly orb—for evoking the great figure known to his contemporaries as "an astrologian, a mathematician, a musitian, and what not"? Because of the astrological reference, scholarly suspicion has begun to fall on none other than John Dunstable as the author of the original *Caput* Mass.[3]

Obrecht further continued the emulatory line in his *Missa Caput* by citing, at the beginning of his Gloria, the phrase that begins every movement of the original English *Caput* Mass. He also showed his awareness of Ockeghem's Mass by carrying farther the special technical maneuver of cantus firmus transposition, transposing it to five different pitch levels (one for each movement of the Mass) and having it migrate through the entire four-part texture.

Such emulations of the original *Caput* Mass, whoever its author may have been, certainly show how some composers of this time were inclined toward tours de force. The most famous tours de force in all of fifteenth-century music, in fact, are a couple of Masses by Ockeghem—works with which his historical reputation, for better or worse, is permanently bound up. One of them is called the *Missa Prolationum*, the "Mass of the Time Signatures." It is sung in four parts but written in two. The peculiar title advertises the fact that each of the two voices carries a double time signature; and when the Mass is actually sung, each of the four voices realizes its note values according to a different mensuration scheme. The other jewel in Ockeghem's crown is the *Missa cuiusvis toni*, the "Mass in Any Mode." It is notated without clefs. The singers can decide on one of four different clef combinations, each of which, when supplied mentally, fixes the notated music on one of the "four finals"—when the final is D, the modal scale will be Dorian; when E, Phrygian; when F, Lydian; and when G, Mixolydian.

To say that Ockeghem's historical reputation rests disproportionately on these Masses "for better or worse" suggests that not everyone is equally impressed by such elaborate technical virtuosity. Charles Burney (1726–1814), a noted English music historian whose testimony we will hear more of in the chapters to come, captured well the appeal of such a difficult and learned style when he wrote of the *Missa Prolationum* that "the performer was to solve canonical mysteries, and discover latent beauties of ingenuity and contrivance, about which the hearers were indifferent, provided the general harmony was pleasing."[4] For Ockeghem's singers, as for all lovers of puzzles (or, more broadly, the members of any in-group), the notational complexities were not perceived as a burden; their solution was a sufficiently satisfying reward. Yet ever since the sixteenth century, when the Swiss music theorist Henricus Glareanus illustrated the composer's work exclusively with these bizarre technical feats, Ockeghem has had a reputation for cold calculation. As long as Ockeghem and his contemporaries were judged by an impressive but unrepresentative sample of their work, the verdict stood. Implicit in the (mis)appraisal is a caution for anyone who would attempt to understand, let alone judge, the past by its fragmentary remains.

The Man at Arms

Anthology Vol 1-42a-b
Full CD I, 60–61
Concise CD I, 49

The most celebrated and extensive dynasty of Masses was the long line based on a cantus firmus derived not from a sacred church chant but from a secular (folk or popular?) song called ***L'Homme armé*** ("The Man at arms"). More than forty such Masses survive by authors of virtually every Western European nationality. The earliest was composed sometime after 1454, and practically every composer mentioned by Tinctoris (including Tinctoris himself) wrote at least one *Missa L'Homme armé*, as did their pupils and their pupils' pupils. The principle of emulation, thus applied on such a massive scale, produced the very summit of fifteenth-century musical art and artifice. The latest composers in the line, Italians who were distant in time and place from the origins of the tradition, probably thought of it as a "purely musical" one involving nothing more than a test piece to establish professional credentials.

The most celebrated and extensive dynasty of Masses was the long line based on a cantus firmus derived not from a sacred church chant but from a secular song called **L'Homme armé.**

The circumstances attending the earliest *L'Homme armé* Masses in the mid-fifteenth century point to the court of Burgundy and in particular to a knightly order founded there. In 1453, Constantinople (now Istanbul in Turkey), the largest city in Europe, capital of the Byzantine Empire, and seat of Greek Christendom, fell after a two-month siege by the Ottoman Sultan, Muhammad II ("The Conqueror"). He made it the capital of his empire, which it remained until 1918, and it has been a Turkish and a Muslim city ever since its conquest. The European response to this stunning event was one of horror and professed resolve but little action. In immediate response to the calamity, Duke Philip the Good of Burgundy vowed to go on a Crusade against the Turks. On 17 February 1454 he convened a great meeting of his knightly retinue, the Order of the Golden Fleece. At this meeting, known as the Banquet of the Oath of the Pheasant, the knights were sworn to the defense of Constantinople.

Descriptions of the proceedings by court chroniclers recount the lavish musical performances that enlivened the banquet. Right before the oath itself was sworn, a giant led in an elephant on whose back was a miniature castle, from which a woman dressed in mourning sang a lament for the fallen city. This gives us some idea of the

Figure 4-10 *L'Homme armé* tune as it is given in its single complete and texted source.

manner in which ceremonial music was "consumed" by the court of Burgundy and the sorts of occasions that the leading musicians of the day were expected to dignify. Much sacred music has been circumstantially associated with the Order of the Golden Fleece, including many of the early *L'Homme armé* Masses. These pieces date from the period when the Order had become at least nominally a crusading order and when Philip the Good's famously belligerent son, Charles the Bold, had become active in it. Charles is already known to us as the patron of Antoine Busnoys, who had entered his service shortly before Charles's accession to the ducal throne in 1467.

The song *L'Homme armé* was a special favorite of Charles, who identified himself with the "Man at Arms" of the title (probably Christ himself, if the connection with Crusades was there from the beginning).[5] The song may even originally have been written for Charles. In any case, we know its music and words thanks to a manuscript containing a cycle of six anonymous *L'Homme armé* Masses that bears a dedication to Charles and carries the original song up front (Fig. 4-10). The tune playfully incorporates a horn call—presented variously in three-note and four-note versions, dropping a fifth after an initial series of repeated notes, a sort of musical tattoo—that was possibly drawn from Burgundian town and castle life.

The cycle of six Masses fits exactly the service requirements of the Sainte Chapelle at Dijon, the official chapel of the Order, where every week six polyphonic Masses and a Requiem were sung.[6] The Masses have a durational structure that is built on the prime number 31: The song is 31 *tempora* (breve-length measures) long, and the subsections of the Mass are likely to be 31 or 62 (31 × 2) or 93 (31 × 3) measures long. Thirty-one was the prescribed number of men-at-arms in the Order and hence symbolized it. Busnoys's *Missa L'Homme armé* seems to have been regarded as a special "classic," especially by contemporary composers (who emulated it with particular zeal and fidelity) and by contemporary theorists (who cited it more often than any other then-current Mass composition).

Among its telling features are the multiple techniques by which Busnoys's Mass is unified in various musical dimensions. Most obvious, of course, is in the use of the *L'Homme armé* melody as the cantus firmus in all five movements. Moreover, all five begin identically, with a head motive consisting of a duo in which the lower part anticipates the cantus firmus tune. If the words were different, the first three measures of the Kyrie could just as easily have been the first three measures of the Gloria, the Credo, the Sanctus, or the Agnus Dei. Table 4-1 sums up the distribution of the cantus firmus in each section and subsection of the Mass. The treatment varies somewhat according to the nature and the length of the various texts, but in all sections the cantus firmus is dramatically deployed in conjunction with the other voices to create a sense of climax, much in the tradition of the isorhythmic motet.

In the Kyrie and Agnus Dei, the single run-through of the cantus firmus is split right down the middle and interrupted by a subsection in which "the tenor is silent." That is the rubric—*tenor tacet*—used in choir books from which such tenorless middle sections as the Christe eleison and the Agnus Dei II get their generic name. Such an

Table 4-1 Deployment of the Cantus Firmus in Busnoys, *Missa L'Homme armé*

MASS SECTION	PORTION OF CANTUS FIRMUS USED
Kyrie	mm. 1–15
Christe	*tenor tacet*
Kyrie II	mm. 16–end
Et in terra	mm. 1–18
Qui tollis	mm. 18–end
Tu solus altissimus	complete
Patrem	mm. 1–15
Et incarnatus est	mm. 16–end
Confiteor	mm. 1–5, 12–27
Sanctus	mm. 1–19
Pleni sunt coeli	*tenor tacet*
Osanna	mm. 20–end
Benedictus	*tenor tacet*
(Osanna)	*ut supra*
Agnus I	mm. 1–15
Agnus II	*tenor tacet*
Agnus III	mm. 16–end

alternation of sections supplies the requisite "A–B–A-ness" to delineate the textual form. Busnoys provides a virtuoso ending for the final Agnus Dei by manipulating the cantus firmus with a jesting puzzle rubric. The tenor appears to carry the tune in its usual form, but the rubric instructs, "Where [the armed man's] scepter is raised, there go lower and vice versa," thus directing the singers to exchange roles with the basses, who sing the cantus firmus not only down an octave but also with all the intervals inverted.

"Pervading Imitation"

The relatively inconspicuous tenor tacet sections of the Kyrie, Sanctus, and Agnus Dei movements represent a new principle of composing—exceptional in Busnoys's time but standard practice a hundred years later. Since these parts are written without a prefabricated tenor, the composer proceeds instead in short spurts of imitative writing similar to what we have encountered in the chace, or caccia. The superius, at the beginning of the Christe eleison (Ex. 4-8), guides the altus strictly for the duration of the first phrase. But the imitation remains strict only as far as the cadence, when it gives way to a conventional close. Then the bassus, entering, guides the superius strictly as far as the next cadence. Finally, all three voices come together for the third phrase; the altus, rejoining the texture, imitates the head motive of the preceding duo, still functioning as a (would-be) guide. The other voices pile in for a "free" discant, significantly the shortest of the sections because it is the one least guided.

Such tenor tacet sections were epoch-makers. Out of earlier techniques of canon and voice exchange the composer has developed a manner of writing that replaces the cantus firmus with a series of "points of imitation," as they have become known after centuries of standardization. Each point corresponds to a discrete portion of the text, the parsing of the words thus acquiring a far more direct role in the shaping of the music than in the sections of the Mass that are built over the cantus firmus. Each point of imitation comes to a full cadential close before proceeding to the next. Beginning with the generation of Obrecht, composers of Masses and motets typically practiced the "pervading imitation" style when not using a cantus firmus. They learned it, directly or indirectly, from Busnoys and his contemporaries.

Example 4-8 Antoine Busnoys, *Missa L'Homme armé,* Christe

Another reason that Busnoys's *Missa L'Homme armé* is emblematic of its genre was one that lay beneath the surface, in the realm of ideal, esoteric, even occult structure. Like the ordering principles governing the isorhythmic motets surveyed in Chapter 3, this impressive numerological feature cannot be heard in performance but can easily be grasped and relished by the rational mind. Amidst Busnoys's play with numbers and Pythagorean proportions a prime number suddenly occurs in the durational plan of the measures that seems to throw it off course right smack in the middle of the middle movement of the Mass (Credo). But that number is 31, symbolizing the Order of the Golden Fleece. So rather than distorting the plan, the existence of 31 as a durational unit provides further evidence that Busnoys attached symbolic significance to durations and planned them out in advance, just as a composer of ceremonial motets might formerly have done.

Many other composers displayed their technique with Masses based on *L'Homme armé*. Du Fay was the oldest and most distinguished to have joined the game, and he produced a true masterpiece that contains the single most complicated passage in all of fifteenth-century choral polyphony: a montage of four different mensurations, one for each voice, at the point in the Credo where the text, referring to God the Father, says "by [Him] all things are made" (*per quem omnia facta sunt*). The last three Latin words can also mean "all things are done," and that is what Du Fay has his chorus do, all at the same time. Once again what may seem to us like nothing more than a pun can be a serious symbol and the pretext for exalted creative play.

For one last and particularly revealing dynastic commentary, let us mention a later stage of the *L'Homme armé* tradition. The composer who headed the next generation after Obrecht and who was as commanding a presence among the musicians of his time as Obrecht had been—or Busnoys and Ockeghem before Obrecht, or Du Fay before Busnoys and Ockeghem, or Dunstable before Du Fay—was Josquin des Prez, whom we will consider at length in the next chapter. It was Josquin's special good fortune to have been the leading figure in one of the great historical turning points for European music, when music printing was invented, causing a revolution that utterly transformed its literate wing. The very first published volume of music devoted to the works of a single composer was a collection of Masses by Josquin, issued by the pioneering Venetian music printer Ottaviano Petrucci in 1502. Of the five Masses the book contained, two of them—the first and the last—were based on *L'Homme armé*. There could be no greater testimony to Josquin's stature than his laying claim in this way to the venerable tradition, and no greater testimony to the potency of that tradition than the way it was spotlighted by Petrucci in opening and closing this noteworthy volume.

The first was called *Missa L'Homme armé super voces musicales*, based on the six solmization syllables of the Guidonian hexachord: *Ut–re–mi–fa–sol–la*. The special unifying tour de force of Josquin's Mass was to begin it with the cantus firmus pitched on C (the "natural" *ut*) for the Kyrie and to have it ascend step by step throughout the Mass so that in the final Agnus Dei, scored for a climactically enlarged five-part chorus, it was pitched on A (the natural *la*). No question, then, that Josquin was still engaging in the process of emulation—the process that continually asked, "Can you top this?"

Yet even as he attempted to top all his predecessors in his manipulation of the age-old cantus firmus, he paid them signal tribute in his head motive. This theme—the opening music, so to speak, in Petrucci's volume of the greatest Masses by the greatest composer of the day—is modeled on the phrase with which Busnoys had set the name of Ockeghem in *In hydraulis* and with which Ockeghem had returned the compliment in *Ut heremita solus*. Josquin, who wrote a lament on Ockeghem's death in which he referred to the older composer as his "bon père," his good (musical) father, was very possibly Ockeghem's pupil. Surely he knew Busnoys's Mass and its special place in the *L'Homme armé* tradition. How better to assert his place in the dynasty of distinguished composers than by making this conspicuous reference to their most directly relevant work? And how better legitimate the "future" of music as a literate tradition—the phase of printed music, which has lasted until today—than by making showy reference to the glories of the immediate past? Josquin's head motive was thus a triple emblem: the emblematic unifier of his Mass, an emblem of his special musical inheritance, and an emblem of the continuing vitality of the dynastic tradition.

Josquin was engaging in the process of emulation—the process that continually asked, "Can you top this?"

High, Middle, and Low

By the early fifteenth century the Mass had clearly emerged as the highest musical genre of the age. As we have begun to see, the quality of "height" was an important determinant of style within an aristocratic culture. It was the yardstick by which subject matter and rhetorical manner had been correlated since pre-Christian times. The classic formulation had been given long ago by Marcus Tullius Cicero (106–43 BCE), the Roman statesman and orator, who sought an ideal union of rhetoric and philosophy to guide human affairs. Cicero distinguished three basic styles of oratory, which he called *gravis*, *mediocris*, and *attenuatus*: weighty, middling, and plain. In the twelfth century this was modified to reflect literary categories. *Humilis* (low) was now associated with the vernacular tongues that had replaced Latin for everyday speech. In arguing later for artistic literature in the vernacular, Dante had set himself the task of proving (on the basis of the troubadours' achievement) that vernacular languages could accommodate all three levels of discourse, identifying them in terms that had even more obvious social connotations: *illustre*, *mediocre*, and *humile* (noble, middling, and lowly). It was Tinctoris in the early 1470s who first applied a variation of this time-honored scheme to music. In his dictionary of terms, he designated three musical styles, calling them *magnus*, *mediocris*, and *parvus*: great (= high-ranking), middle, and small (= low-ranking). He related each to a genre. The small was associated with the vernacular chanson, the middle with the motet, and the great with the Mass.

Over the course of the fifteenth century, the cyclic Mass Ordinary had displaced the motet from its position at the high end of the musical style spectrum. That is one of the reasons why the motet itself underwent a radical transformation during that time. From an isorhythmic, tenor-dominated, polytextual construction, it became a Latin cantilena, a sacred song that served primarily devotional rather than ceremonial purposes. Connection with plainchant was retained but modified. Paraphrase—the technique pioneered in fauxbourdon settings, whereby an old chant was melodically refurbished and turned into a new "cantus"—began to dominate the motet. Textual and expressive factors began to weigh more heavily than before both in the structure and in the detail work of the newly renovated motet. The aim was lowered, so to speak, from the altogether transcendent to somewhere nearer the human plane.

It became all the more fitting, then, that the middle style should continue to address the Virgin Mary, the "middle being" situated between the transcendent and the human. Accordingly, the fifteenth century witnessed the zenith of musical "Mariolatry." Its chief expressive outlet became the polyphonic arrangement of the Marian antiphons. A wonderful introduction to the fifteenth-century Marian motet

Anthology Vol 1-43

is a *Salve Regina* setting by Philippe Basiron (d. 1491). The original melody, signaled by the little crosses (+) in Example 4-9, has been familiar to us since Chapter 1 (c.f. Anthology Vol. 1-9). It resembles a troubadour canso—or, in terms more contemporary with the polyphonic setting, a ballade—in its repeated opening phrase, which is paraphrased in Basiron's superius. This points to his awareness of the melody's resemblance to a secular love song as well as to his wish to preserve that resonant resemblance in his cantilena setting.

Example 4-9 Philippe Basiron, *Salve Regina*, mm. 1–10

Hail, holy Queen, Mother of mercy; Hail, our life, our sweetness, [our hope!].

Basiron builds other generic resonances into his setting as well. The opening line of the chant paraphrase is accompanied by the altus only, creating the kind of duo we often find in older isorhythmic motets that preceded the entrance of the all-important tenor—and, sure enough, the tenor behaves on entering just like a cantus firmus voice, in long note values. The tenor thus seems to impersonate the bearer of the holy relic, the preexisting chant, when all the while the chant-bearing voice is actually the superius. The tenor melody has never been identified and in all likelihood will never be. It is a decoy.

What we have, in short, is a deliberate play on styles and genres by a supremely self-conscious composer: a paraphrase motet disguised as a cantus firmus motet. The disguise is light; by the time the superius has descended its fifth between *sal-* and *-ve* in the first measure, everyone in Basiron's envisaged audience would have surely recognized the most famous melody in all the liturgy. It is just a playful disguise, not meant to deceive but to amuse in an enriching way. The deliberate playfulness—what we might call the "thematization" of genre—has a serious point. Incorporating elements of "low" (the superius in "pseudovernacular" style) and "high" (the tenor in "pseudoplainchant" style), the motet balances itself right in the middle, showing the composer's awareness of the rhetorical categories available to him and his ability to exploit them meaningfully. Basiron's Marian antiphon setting also sounds a personal note that we have not previously encountered in liturgical music. That is another aspect of "middling" tone; but it accords well with the votive aspects of Marian worship, the component of the Christian liturgy that in those days was most intensely personal.

The English Keep Things High

The musical cult of Mary reached its zenith in England where the new-style motet began. As usual, precious little pre-Reformation source material survived the sixteenth-century holy wars, but just as with the Old Hall Manuscript at the beginning of the century, a single enormous volume survives at century's end to tell us about British worship music. That is the so-called **Eton Choir Book**, compiled for Evensong (Vesper) services at Eton College during the reign of Henry VII (1485–1509), the first Tudor king of England, but containing a repertory that had been forming since Dunstable's time. Eton College, founded in 1440, was specifically authorized by its statutes to honor the Blessed Virgin daily by singing a polyphonic votive antiphon. Every evening its illustrious choir was to enter the chapel in formal procession, two by two, sing the Lord's Prayer before the crucifix, and then proceed to the image of the Virgin, there to sing a Marian antiphon "as well as they know how."

It is not surprising therefore that the music in the Eton Choir Book contains a great deal of melismatic virtuosity. The boys in the famous choir needed to be proper vocal athletes to negotiate their passagework in this music, so the college offered, then and now, what amounted to a kind of athletic scholarship for qualified music students. The style of the Eton antiphons is also noteworthy in terms of sheer sonority. The phenomenal upward extension of range in this music testifies to the Eton choirboys' astounding proficiency. Their ample numbers are suggested as well by the augmented complement of voices—five parts being the Eton norm, with several pieces going to six or even more. All that magnificence comes at a price. The Eton music is thoroughly "official," collective, and impersonal. It is institutional devotion par excellence. It makes no concession whatever to the "middling" tone that had long since begun to distinguish a continental votive motet like Basiron's and give it compelling personal urgency.

The very peak of the High Church style came early in the sixteenth century, when English and continental music contrasted even more starkly. By the time of the English Reformation (or, rather, just before it), as we will see in the next chapter, English and continental styles were downright antithetical despite their common ancestry. That musical divergence reflects a larger divergence in ecclesiastical mores. The one cannot be understood historically without taking due account of the other.

The Milanese Go Lower Still

A further step in the continental transformation and stylistic "lowering" of motet style was taken in Milan in the 1470s, when a custom was instituted within the Ambrosian rite of writing cycles of substitute motets for the Mass, known as ***motetti missales***. The most accomplished of these substitute pieces came from Flemish composers employed at the court of the Sforzas (the brazenly self-styled "Usurpers," or "Governors-by-force"), a family of mercenary soldiers who in the middle of the century had suddenly risen from the peasantry to become the ruling family of Milan. Among this clan of ruthless parvenus were some astute and enthusiastic patrons of the arts, notably the despotic Duke Galeazzo Maria Sforza (Fig. 4-11), the temporal ruler of the city from 1466 until his assassination ten years later, and his brother, Cardinal Ascanio Maria Sforza (d. 1505), the city's ecclesiastical dictator.

Galeazzo's chief court-and-chapel composer was a very eminent and influential musician, yet one whose current historical reputation does not adequately reflect his eminence and influence. Gaspar van Weerbeke (ca. 1445 to ca. 1516), a Dutchman, was recruited to lead the Milanese ducal chapel in 1471. His *motetti missales* seem so decisively to reject the lofty tone and the architectural genres of the Franco-Burgundian tradition that his style is often described as having been influenced by Italian popular (hence oral, undocumented) styles and genres. That may be one reason for his comparative neglect by historians and performers, who have understandably tended to find most of interest in the loftiest and the lowest and to take the stylistic middle for granted.

The Sforza dukes managed to recruit future stars at early phases of their careers, including Johannes Martini (d. 1498) and the even more illustrious Frenchman Loyset Compère (d. 1518), who had trained under Weerbeke in Milan during the 1470s. Compère eventually went back home to serve in the court chapel of King Charles VIII in Paris. Weerbeke and his specially crafted Milanese music made the strongest immediate impression on Compère. His Marian pastiche, *Ave Maria*, is about as low in style as a motet can go, leading one to suspect a double purpose, hailing both Maria Virgo and Galeazzo Maria, both Virgin protectress and noble patron. In its patchwork of texts and tunes it is a virtual sendup of the ancient *ars combinatoria*, cast in very up-to-date patter declamation—syllables placed on minims—that renders the texts with a dispatch bordering on flippancy.

Anthology Vol 1-44
Full CD I, 62

In the motet's *prima pars* (first part), a cantus firmus is sneaked into the altus, the least conspicuous voice, and paraphrased in such a way as virtually to disappear amongst the counterpoint. The plainsong original begins with the familiar

Figure 4-11 Galeazzo Maria Sforza kneeling in prayer; below is the coat of arms of the Dukes of Milan; Choir Book, Milanese, 1477.

words of the daily "Hail, Mary!" prayer (Ex. 4-10). As the piece proceeds, the texture changes from the fairly fragmented state of the opening, through structurally paired voices, continuing through an opposition of high and low voices, and ending with an emphatic homorhythm. The *secunda pars* (second part) expands the litany to include a wide variety of patron saints, mirroring the crowd of new names with a pervasively imitative texture in which the order and interval of entries and the rhythmic values are unpredictably varied. The motet explodes at the end into a long and exceptionally virtuosic triple "proportion." This is truly something new: funny church music—funny but still pious. Piety of this kind, though, is "humane"—pitched to the level of its hearers, rather than, as in the English High-Church polyphony, way, way over their heads.

Example 4-10 Loyset Compère, *Ave Maria,* mm. 1–3

Love Songs

The effects of whimsical, humanized religion seem to suggest the influence of the secular, vernacular genres of literate music—the official "low" style, according to Tinctoris. Vernacular genres were also undergoing significant change in the later fifteenth century, in stylistic terms aiming both higher and lower than before, and making many new points of contact across generic and stylistic boundaries. For one thing, there was a new genre on the horizon, called the ***bergerette***. Although its name ("shepherdess") suggests a pastoral style, it originated in French court circles and was a sort of high-toned synthesis of two earlier fixed forms, the rondeau and the virelai.

Anthology Vol 1-45
Full CD I, 63
Concise CD I, 50

An early classic of the genre, probably dating from the 1460s, was Ockeghem's *Ma bouche rit et ma pensée pleure* ("My mouth laughs but my thoughts weep," Ex. 4-11)—a classic by virtue of its wide dissemination in many manuscripts and its later emulation by younger composers. The outstanding textural novelty of *Ma bouche rit* is the use of almost systematic imitation entirely confined to the superius and the tenor, the voices that make up the structural pair. It became a standard practice that typifies the convergence of the middle and low genres—a convergence that, depending on the context (motet or chanson, for example), can be construed as either the lowering of the middle or the raising of the low. In the case of the bergerette, it is clearly a case of raising the low. No less significant is the casting of the music in two absolutely self-contained sections, with the second (here, the *residuum,* "the rest") actually labeled as such. That amounts to mimicry of the musical structure of the motet. In later bergerettes, including those of Busnoys, the *residuum* is often set off from the refrain by the use of a contrasting mensuration, again mimicking the motet.

Example 4-11 Johannes Ockeghem, *Ma bouche rit*

My mouth laughs and my thoughts weep, my glance is gay, but my heart curses the hour

Instrumental Music Is Printed

Popular chansons enjoyed a further life as instrumental arrangements that led in the late fifteenth century to a new, purely instrumental genre. Although without precedent in the literate tradition, it nonetheless probably reflected the longstanding practice of virtuoso improvisers. In his treatise called *De inventione et usu musicae* (On the Invention and Use of Music), Tinctoris described the work of "two blind Flemings," barred by their handicap from involvement in literate repertories, who nevertheless put their learned colleagues to shame with their flamboyant improvisations on standard tunes: "At Bruges I heard Charles take the treble and Jean the tenor in many songs, playing the fiddle (*vielle*) so expertly and with such charm that the fiddle has never pleased me so well."[7]

Virtuoso fiddling on the trebles and tenors of familiar chansons had a long history before its earliest reflections in written sources. There now emerged instrumental arrangements of songs, sometimes very elaborate ones, as well as "how to" treatises that give instructions on writing such works. One of these treatises contains dozens of little problem pieces, mainly in two parts, many of which are known to be by Tinctoris himself. Each one introduces some new difficulty of notation, preparing the way for a three-part monster called *Difficiles alios* (translatable in this context as "The hardest ones of all").[8]

Instrumental arrangements of chansons clearly captured an eager audience. It is no accident that the very earliest printed publication containing polyphonic music was given over largely to textless chanson arrangements. It was brought out in 1501 by Petrucci, the same enterprising Venetian printer who the next year brought out the volume of Josquin Masses mentioned earlier. Its grandiose pseudo-Greek title was *Harmonice musices odhecaton A*, which means, roughly, "A Hundred Pieces of Polyphonic Music, Vol. I." Petrucci knew his market. The next year he issued his second volume, and in 1504 he issued a third, equal in size to the other two combined.

The chanson arrangement was, by Petrucci's time, only one kind of "song without words." Another, equally popular kind consisted of tenor tacet subsections extracted from Masses and motets, sometimes identified as such, more often not. In the tenor tacet sections, we may recall, the cantus firmus–bearing tenor goes silent while the other voices engage in pervasive imitation, a "purely musical" sort of patterning that could sustain a "purely musical" listener's interest even in the absence of text. The final stage consisted of specially composed songs without words in a style adapted from those of chanson arrangements and tenor tacet sections but without recourse to any preexisting material. Such pieces amounted to the earliest repertoire of abstractly conceived chamber music.

The first important contributors to this genre included some of the same composers renowned for the chanson arrangement. The most prolific was Henricus Isaac (ca. 1450–55 to 1517), a Fleming who worked in Florence and then later at the Austrian court of the Holy Roman Emperor Maximilian I. The runners-up were Martini, Josquin, and Alexander Agricola (ca. 1445 to 1506), who wrote his share of Masses, motets, and songs for the courts and churches of Burgundy, France, and Italy but whose chief claim to fame was a whole raft of instrumental songs that eventually found their way to the commercial presses of Petrucci.

Anthology Vol 1-46
Full CD I, 64
Concise CD I, 51

An example of the newly created instrumental song from Petrucci's *Odhecaton* is *La Alfonsina,* a brilliant little piece written by Johannes Ghiselin (alias Verbonnet), a northern French composer who worked in Italy alongside Obrecht and Josquin at the court of Ferrara. The title translates as "Alfonso's little piece," after the composer's patron, Alfonso I d'Este, Duke of Ferrara (and husband of the notorious Lucrezia Borgia). The piece emulates the Benedictus section from a Mass by Isaac. The transfer of imitative texture to the instrumental medium was the real signal of imitation's ascendancy (Ex. 4-12). Imitation was now polyphony's basic method of operation, and so it would remain throughout the sixteenth century, which might appropriately be called the century of imitative polyphony. In any case, as we shall see, the perfection of imitative polyphony in the sixteenth century meant for contemporary musicians the perfection of the art of music itself.

Example 4-12 **Johannes Ghiselin, *La Alfonsina,* mm. 1–11**

The production of printed music books, and the new music-economy thus ushered in, was a crucial stage in the conceptualizing of a "piece" of music as a concrete product that can be sold in a tangible, reproducible form. The commercialization of printed music also required middlemen for its dissemination. The long-range result of this enterprise was a dramatic increase in music literacy. From this time on, music would be defined, at least for the educated, as something that was primarily written: a text. Inconsequential though it was, the printed instrumental chanson arrangement—the mechanized, commercialized, middle-class by-product of the high-purpose, high-class genres of the day, amounting to the bastard offspring of Mass, motet, and chanson—was indirectly of decisive importance to the future of literate music and music making in the West.

Summary

Due to the wholesale destruction of manuscripts containing Latin church music during the Anglican Reformation in the sixteenth century, few examples of earlier English music have survived intact; an innovative example that did is the Sumer Canon from a manuscript compiled about 1250. The influence of English music on the continent in the fifteenth century brought about fundamental changes in musical style. Following Henry V's victory at Agincourt in 1415, the English occupied northern France, bringing with them musicians such as John Dunstable (ca. 1390–1453). With its preference for the interval of a third and its clear text declamation, Dunstable's music contrasts markedly with the *Ars Subtilior* of continental composers (see *Quam pulchra es,* "How beautiful thou art"). The influence of this style on continental composers such as Guillaume Du Fay (ca. 1397–1474) and Gilles de Bins (Binchois) (ca. 1400–60) is evident in their use of *fauxbourdon,* a technique of elaborating plainchant. A voice was written out a sixth below the chant and another was improvised a fourth below, producing a sonic equivalent of parallel 6/3 chords. Similar sonorities could also be heard in the earlier English technique for harmonizing plainchant called *faburden,* which resulted in chains of parallel triads and was partly responsible for contemporary identification of an "English guise" in music (*la contenance angloise*). Du Fay uses fauxbourdon in his *Ave maris stella* ("Hail, star of the sea"), which is based on an elaborated or paraphrased version of plainchant. The English sound also influenced chansons such as Binchois's ballade *Deuil angoisseux* ("Anguished grief"). While originally English, many of these stylistic traits were carried farther south by Franco-Flemish composers who found employment in Italy and took the new style with them.

The most prestigious genre of the fifteenth century was the cyclic Mass, which set the texts for the Ordinary: Kyrie, Gloria, Credo, Sanctus, and Agnus Dei. Although these items had different origins and were separated in time during the service, fifteenth-century composers of cyclic Masses unified the movements with a common cantus firmus in the tenor, thus symbolizing the unity of the service. The cantus firmus Mass became an esteemed tradition in which composers emulated earlier works, both paying homage to them and trying to surpass them. One melody that composers frequently used as a cantus firmus is the "caput" melisma, so called because it comes on the word "caput" in the original chant. The *Missa Caput* by an unknown English composer was circulated widely, prompting

Johannes Ockeghem (ca. 1410–97) and Jacobus Obrecht (ca. 1457–1505) to write their own Caput Masses.

The popular tune *L'Homme armé* ("The Man at Arms") served as the cantus firmus for at least forty different Masses, a respected tradition to which nearly every known fifteenth-century composer contributed. The tune's origin may lie with the Order of the Golden Fleece, founded at the opulent Burgundian court, which vowed to defend Constantinople after it fell to Turkish conquerors in 1453. The "armed man" probably refers to Christ, in connection with the intended but unrealized Crusades against the Turks. In addition to their use of the tune as a cantus firmus, the movements of Antoine Busnoys's *Missa L'Homme armé* are unified by a "head motive" that occurs at the opening of each movement.

The cyclic Mass was the venue for both technical display and stylistic innovation. Ockeghem's *Missa cuiusvis toni* (Mass in Any Mode), for example, is written without clefs and may be performed at any transposition. For his *Missa Prolationum* (Mass of the Time Signatures), Ockeghem wrote two parts, each intended to be realized simultaneously in two different time signatures, creating a four-voice double canon. Another stylistic innovation in the cyclic Mass was the texture of "pervading imitation" in all voices, particularly in sections where the cantus firmus–based tenor drops out.

In the 1470s, the theorist Johannes Tinctoris (ca. 1435–1511) divided the musical genres of his day into high, middle, and low. Highest was the cyclic Mass, with its technical virtuosity. English polyphony of this time maintains a consistently high style, as evidenced in the complex polyphony of the Eton Choir Book. Motets, however, came to be written in a more accessible middle style, adopting the melody-dominated texture that had been associated with secular song. The top voice often consisted of a paraphrased version of the original chant (Philippe Basiron, *Salve regina*, "Hail Queen," Anthology Vol 1-43). A further "lowering" of style is evident in the *motetti missales*, cycles of substitute motets for the Mass, written in Milan in the 1470s and influenced by the popular lauda (e.g., Compère, *Ave Maria*, "Hail Mary"). Tinctoris's low genres consisted of secular music such as the bergerette, a love song related in form to the older virelai but consisting of a single strophe with an ample refrain. Ockeghem's bergerette *Ma bouche rit* ("My mouth laughs") employs some imitation associated with higher styles, attesting to a convergence of different styles. Popular chansons were also arranged for instruments, as were the tenorless (tenor tacet) sections of Masses and motets, in which composers relied on pervading imitation rather than counterpoint against a given cantus firmus. The resulting arrangements became the first polyphonic works to be published when in 1501 the same enterprising Venetian printer, Ottaviano Petrucci, issued his *Harmonice musices odhecaton A*, which means, roughly, "A Hundred Pieces of Polyphonic Music, Vol. I" and which contained Johannes Ghiselin's *La Alfonsina*. Petrucci anticipated and helped shape a new market for newly commodified music.

Study Questions

1. What makes the Old Hall Manuscript such an important document in English music history?
2. What was the *contenance angloise*? How is it exemplified in works such as John Dunstable's *Quam pulchra es?* How does *Quam pulchra es* contrast with the Ars Nova works discussed in Chapter 3?

3. How is the English influence reflected in the works of Guillaume Du Fay and Gilles Binchois?
4. Describe the virtuosic compositional techniques used in cyclic Masses of the fifteenth century. How were the five movements unified, and what was the symbolic value of this unification?
5. What is the *caput* melisma? In what ways do works based on it appear to anticipate a more modern approach to part writing?
6. What is *L'Homme armé?* Describe the cultural milieu in which the tune originated and what its lyrics symbolize.
7. Using either the *Caput* Masses or the *L'Homme armé* Masses, consider the fifteenth-century practice of emulation. How did each composer attempt to honor or surpass the works that had come before?
8. Describe Johannes Tinctoris's division of musical genres into high, middle, and low. How is this division reflected in the works discussed in this chapter? Place the following on Tinctoris's spectrum, and explain your reasons for doing so: (a) the Milanese *motteti missales*; (b) works in the Eton Choir Book; (c) the *bergerette;* (d) the earliest instrumental pieces; (e) the cyclic Mass.

Key Terms

bergerette
Caput Masses
cyclic Mass
emulation
Eton Choir Book
faburden
fauxbourdon
la contenance angloise
L'Homme armé
motetti missales
Old Hall Manuscript
paraphrase
rota, round

5

A Perfected Art: Church Polyphony in the Late Fifteenth and Sixteenth Centuries

Josquin des Prez (ca. 1450–1521; Fig. 5-1) became a legend in his own time, remained a legend throughout the sixteenth century, and reemerged once again when he was discovered by modern historians. His supreme status has made him more intensively studied than any contemporary or predecessor. The Josquin legend itself is worth exploring because in accounting for its formation we may gain some critical insight into momentous changes that took place more generally in the sixteenth century affecting attitudes toward music and its creators. These changes are in large part what led to applying the word "Renaissance" to a new period in music history.

In his unprecedented stature and his undisputed preeminence, Josquin has never failed to remind modern historians of Ludwig van Beethoven (1770–1827), who was similarly regarded three centuries later. Drawing parallels between the two composers is easy, though we should beware of merely trying to cast Josquin as a fifteenth- or sixteenth-century Beethoven, especially if the result is a universalized concept of "essential" musical greatness. The legendary status of both composers can nonetheless tell us a great deal about their respective times. Each composer provided an apt focal point for the crystallization of new attitudes about music and about artistic creation.

Josquin was the first composer to interest his contemporaries and posterity as a personality. By the end of his life he was the subject of gossip and anecdote, and the picture that emerges again resembles the popular conception of Beethoven:

a cantankerous, arrogant, distracted sort of man, difficult in social situations but excused by grace of his transcendent artistic gifts. Josquin was looked on with awe as one marked off from others by divine inspiration—a status formerly reserved for prophets and saints. Among "musicians," the role had been reserved for Pope Gregory alone (at least when his dove was present). This divine inspiration, indeed, is the kernel of our popular conception of musical genius to this day. The humanistic sensibility that elevated Josquin and the Romantic one that elevated Beethoven had an important component in common: a high appreciation of individualism. In each case this stemmed on the one hand from cultural and social conditions and on the other from economic and commercial ones. A similar humanistic celebration of individualism in the work of the great visual artists of Josquin's time, such as Leonardo da Vinci (1452–1519), Michelangelo (1475–1564), and Raphael (1483–1520), is found in Giorgio Vasari's *Le Vite delle più eccellenti pittori, scultori, ed architettori* (Lives of the Most Eminent Painters, Sculptors, and Architects), first published in 1550.

Figure 5-1 Woodcut of Josquin des Prez, 1611, based on an earlier painting, now lost.

On the most practical, worldly level, Josquin was able to achieve an unprecedented reputation thanks to the newly available means of music printing, through which his works achieved an unprecedented circulation. He was the chief beneficiary of the growing "music biz," the dawn of commercial music printing pioneered by the Venetian publisher Ottaviano Petrucci in 1501, and the first composer who made his reputation on the basis of publication. He also became the first musician to be an object of commercial exploitation. One of the chief tasks of modern Josquin scholarship has been trying to weed out the many false attributions made to him by sixteenth-century music publishers who sought to capitalize on his fame by publishing fakes. "Josquin" became music's first big brand name. The section given over to his "Doubtful and Misattributed Works" in the latest edition of *The New Grove Dictionary of Music and Musicians* lists 14 Masses (as against 18 authenticated ones), 7 separate Mass sections (against 7), an astounding 117 motets (against 59), and 36 secular songs or instrumental pieces (against 72). Most of the bogus items were first released in posthumous publications.

Yet that commercial exploitation was unavoidably linked with the loftier aspects of the Josquin legend. The lion's share of the sixteenth-century Josquin trade took place in German-speaking countries, where the music business flourished. Sixteenth-century Germany was both a hotbed of humanistic thought and the cradle of the Protestant Reformation. Both were individualistic movements, and Protestantism placed a high value on the achievement and expression of subjective religious faith. Josquin's music was often interpreted as personally expressive and communicative. Martin Luther, the founder of German Protestantism, famously declared that Josquin alone was "master of the notes: They must do as he wills; as for other composers, they have to do as the notes will."[1]

The qualities humanist thinkers valued so highly in his music were mainly ones we have so far associated with Italy and with the "lowering" of style, such as lucidity of texture, text-based form, and clarity of declamation. Humanists looked to classical antiquity for models of how to think and communicate forcefully, persuasively, and clearly. As these qualities were reinterpreted in the sixteenth century, Josquin seemed to represent a new ordering of aesthetic values. Through the writings of music theorists like Henricus Glareanus (1488–1563), his most enthusiastic booster, his works became the classics on which the new aesthetic rested. Glareanus went so far as to declare Josquin the creator of an *ars perfecta*: a "perfected art" that could never be improved, "to which nothing can be added, after which nothing but decline is to be expected."[2] That is exactly the definition of a classic.

TIMELINE

1501 Ottaviano Petrucci publishes *Harmonice musices odhecaton A*

1502 Josquin des Prez, *Ave Maria . . . virgo serena* is published

1503 Leonardo da Vinci, *Mona Lisa*

1504 Michelangelo, *David*

1515 Antoine de Févin, Mass on *Ave Maria . . . Virgo serena*

1517 Martin Luther posts 95 Theses, leading to Protestant Reformation

1519–22 Ferdinand Magellan voyages around the world

1520s John Taverner, Masses and motets

1527 Adrian Willaert appointed *maestro di cappella* at St. Mark's

1533 Henry VIII of England excommunicated from Roman Catholic Church

1537 Ludwig Senfl, *Ave Maria . . . virgo serena*

1543 Thomas Tallis becomes organist at Chapel Royal

1545–63 Council of Trent

1545 Willaert, *Benedicta es, coelorum regina*

1547 Henricus Glareanus, *Dodecachordon*

1549 First Anglican *Book of Common Prayer*

1553 Mary I becomes Queen of England and restores Catholicism

1558 Gioseffo Zarlino, *Le Istitutioni harmoniche*

1567 Giovanni Pierluigi da Palestrina, *Missa Papae Marcelli*

1575 William Byrd, *Cantiones quae ab argumento sacrae vocantur*

1593–95 Byrd, Masses

1605 Byrd, *Gradualia* volume 1

A Poet Born, Not Made

When Josquin began his long career, sometime during the third quarter of the fifteenth century, music was still traditionally ranked alongside arithmetic, geometry, and astronomy as part of the quadrivium, the arts of measurement (Fig. 5-2). By the time of his death in 1521, music was already more apt to be classed with the arts of rhetoric. Music was now to be regarded as a branch of poetic eloquence, an art of persuasion and disclosure. Although his works were often cited as examples, Josquin was hardly responsible for this change; it was a by-product of classical **humanism**, a renewed interest in the study of ancient texts that informed the ideals of the Renaissance. The rediscovery of old texts, particularly those by Roman orators like Cicero and Quintilian, stressed the correspondence between music and heightened speech and defined its purpose as that of swaying the emotions of listeners.

Josquin was cast by the proponents of musical rhetoric as the chief model for emulation and so treated in various musical textbooks. If music was now to be a form of rhetorical expression—of a text, of emotion, or of a composer's unique spirit or "genius" (which originally meant exactly that: spirit, whence "inspiration")—it could no longer be regarded simply as the application of formal rules. There had to be something more in a composition that moved its hearers—something put there by a faculty that went beyond what could be learned. And that, of course, is our familiar definition of genius—something essentially unteachable yet capable of being developed through education. It is a notion that was given new emphasis by the humanists.

The idea of genius is pre-Christian, an idea recovered from the ancients, and thereby qualifies as a Renaissance idea. It is related to the Platonic notion that artists create not by virtue of rational decision but because they are gifted with "poetic frenzy." The belief that great composers are innately talented can be traced back to an aphorism attributed to the Roman poet Horace: *poeta nascitur non fit*, "a poet is born not made."[3] Josquin was a "born" composer in this new sense. He did not know that he was that, of course. The terms, as well as the humanistic belief system that undergirded them, were applied to him retrospectively, which is to say, anachronistically. But that is just the point. Because he eventually became the emblem of the new discourse about music, Josquin was able to have a posthumous historical influence that conditioned the development of later sixteenth-century music. With few exceptions, the many literary testimonials and benedictions that form our idea of Josquin's personality date, like Luther's, from after the composer's death and more likely reflect the ideas and values of the later writers than they do Josquin's own.

The greatest popularizer of the Josquin legend was someone who was also concerned to popularize his music. This was Glareanus, the author of a treatise that circulated piecemeal in manuscript for decades and was finally published in 1547 under the title *Dodecachordon* (The Twelve-Stringed Lyre). Glareanus was a different sort of theorist from most we have encountered thus far. He was neither a composer nor a practical musician but, rather, an all-round scholar of the purest humanistic type, a disciple of the great Renaissance humanist Desiderius Erasmus of Rotterdam (1466–1536). Glareanus held professorial chairs not in music but in poetry and theology at the University of Freiburg. As a music theorist, he consciously modeled himself on Boethius, the classical prototype of the encyclopedic humanist. But his actual musical views differed radically from everything Boethius had stood for.

Glareanus's main theoretical innovation, reflected in the pseudo-Greek title of his book, lay in the recognition of four additional modes beyond the eight established by earlier theorists of Gregorian chant. These modes, which he christened Ionian and Aeolian (together with their plagal, or "hypo-," forms), had their respective finals on C and A and hence corresponded to what we now know as the major and minor scales. Glareanus illustrated all twelve modes by citing the works of Josquin. While it is questionable whether his novel terms really contributed to the understanding of contemporary music, he certainly did succeed in grounding contemporary music in a discourse of classical authority, turning Josquin into the musical equivalent of a classical master like Horace or Cicero. It was Glareanus, if anyone, who brought "the Renaissance" to music and made Josquin des Prez the great "Renaissance" composer.

Figure 5-2 *Allegory of the Liberal Arts*, painted by Biagio d'Antonio da Firenze. From bottom to top: Priscian or Donatus with Grammar to the left of the gate of Wisdom, Cicero with Rhetoric, Aristotle with Logic, Tubalcain with Music, Ptolemy with Astronomy, Euclid with Geometry, and Pythagoras with Mathematics.

Josquin's Career

According to the most recent scholarly consensus, Josquin was born in or near the town of St. Quentin in Picardy, a northeasterly region of France, about twenty miles south of the cathedral city of Cambrai, where Du Fay had worked and had died (Fig. 5-3). The first document to mention him is a bequest of land from his uncle and aunt, dated December 1466 from the town where they lived, Condé-sur-l'Escaut, in northernmost France, right across the river from Belgium. This deed gives the future composer's name as Jossequin Lebloitte dit Desprez.[4] Only since 1998 has even so basic a fact as his original family name, Lebloitte, been known to modern scholarship. The first documents to mention Josquin as a musician place him, from 1475, at the opposite end of France: in Aix-en-Provence, near the Mediterranean coast, where he served in the chapel choir of René, King of Sicily and Duke of Anjou, who died in 1480. In February 1483 he reappears in Condé to claim the land bequeathed to him nearly two decades earlier. The next year, he entered the service of Cardinal Ascanio Sforza, a Milanese aristocrat and churchman.

Josquin was in his mid- to late thirties when, as a document dated June 1489 attests, he joined the papal chapel choir in Rome. It was here, as a member of the most prestigious musical establishment in Western Christendom, that he began to make his mark as a composer, and his music began to circulate, as we have seen, through the efforts of Petrucci. Petrucci's initial publication was issued in May 1501 and contained six carmina (instrumental pieces based on or in the style of a song) attributed to Josquin. In February 1502 came the first printed music book devoted to a single composer (*Liber primus missarum Josquini*, The First Book of Masses by Josquin), the volume that opened and closed with his Masses based on *L'Homme armé*. The following May Petrucci released a collection of fifty motets in which one by Josquin was given pride of place.

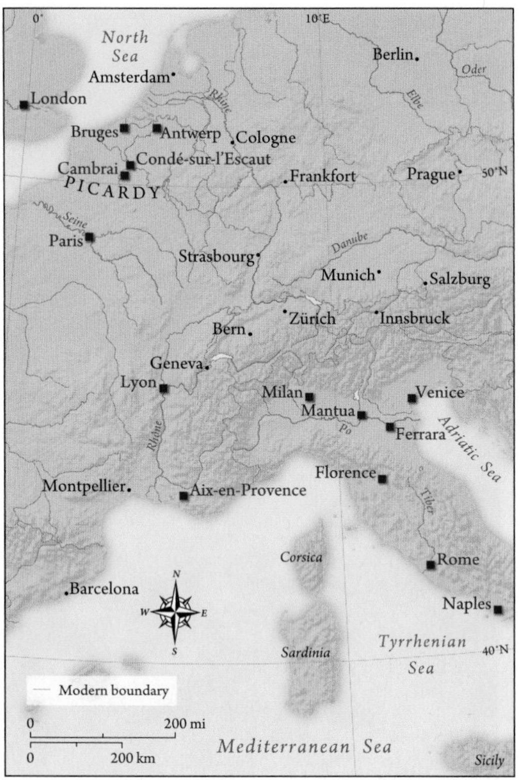

Figure 5-3 Some of the principal locations of musical activity in France and Italy during the Renaissance.

By this time Josquin seems to have left the papal service. In September 1502, an agent from the court of Ercole (Hercules) d'Este, the Duke of Ferrara (Fig. 5-4), advised his employer to hire Henricus Isaac as his music director rather than Josquin, since Isaac is "more sociable" and "composes new things more quickly," while Josquin, though he "composes better," does so "only when he pleases, not when he is requested to, and has demanded 200 ducats in salary, while Isaac is content with 120."[5] The duke ignored the advice and hired Josquin.

The duke has received much praise from historians for showing such keen artistic judgment, but he was probably acting on less lofty impulses. For one thing, there was the lure of conspicuous consumption—the same impulse that today motivates the purchase of expensive designer jeans or luxury cars. Indeed, a rival scout had recommended Josquin to the duke a month earlier, advising him that "there is neither lord nor king who will now have a better chapel than yours if Your Lordship sends for Josquin."[6] This represented a new level of prestige for music itself, and not just for Josquin.

The most immediate evidence of this new prestige was a Mass in which Josquin kept the implied promise to memorialize his patron the way poets and painters had traditionally done in word and image. The work bears the title *Missa Hercules Dux Ferrariae* (The Mass of Hercules, Duke of Ferrara) and was published by Petrucci in his second volume of Josquin Masses (1505); it has kept alive the name of the duke. One of the reasons for the Mass's popularity is the clever way in which Josquin fashioned its cantus firmus out of his patron's name and title. It is what the Italian theorist Gioseffo Zarlino would later call a ***soggetto cavato dalle vocali*** ("theme carved out of the vowels").[7] Here an abstract series of pitches is arrived at by matching solmization syllables to the vowels in the phrase *Hercules, Dux Ferrari(a)e*, thus: HER-CU-LES DUX FER-RA-RI-E = rE-Ut-rE-Ut-rE-fA-mI-rE (Ex. 5-1).

Figure 5-4 Hercules d'Este, Duke of Ferrara, for whom Josquin des Prez composed his *Missa Hercules Dux Ferrariae.*

Example 5-1 "Hercules, Dux Ferrari(a)e" in musical notation

By May 1504, Josquin was associated with the Collegiate Church of Notre Dame in the town of Condé-sur-l'Escaut. There he died on 27 August 1521, probably at about age seventy. He had continued to compose on commission and, at the very end, he also composed for his own purposes. His will contains a provision that after his death the Notre Dame choir was to stop before his house during all festival processions and sing his polyphonic setting of the Lord's Prayer in his memory.[8] Josquin's professional career thus spanned some forty-five busily creative years and yielded a large output. The exasperating fact is that, with only a few exceptions, we cannot correlate his enormous musical legacy with the sketchy biographical framework just outlined, and so we have no reliable chronology of his work. Lacking the evidence on which to base a strictly documentary chronology, historians have had to resort to a stylistic chronology—that is, a chronology based on ideas about the evolution of Josquin's style.

A Model Masterpiece

Anthology Vol 1-47
Full CD I, 65
Concise CD I, 52

Ever since the sixteenth century, the motet *Ave Maria . . . Virgo serena* has been not only Josquin's most famous work but also, in at least two senses, his exemplary one. One meaning of *exemplary* is "representative." On the basis of this motet, generations of musicians, music students, and music lovers have formed their idea of Josquin's methods, his characteristics, and his excellence. Another meaning of *exemplary* is "example-setting." The whole "perfected art" of sixteenth-century sacred music, it sometimes seems, was formed on the example of this single supreme masterpiece. Its stylistic influence was enormous and widely acknowledged. To a degree previously unapproached by any one composition, it was regarded as a timeless standard of perfection, a classic. This is the motet that Petrucci chose in 1502 to open his first motet collection, the earliest such printed collection in history. It was also the basis for many later compositions, including keyboard and lute arrangements. In our time, it has been recorded more often than any other work of Josquin, to say nothing of his contemporaries.

The text combines three different liturgical items: a central votive antiphon to the Blessed Virgin Mary, framed by a prefacing quatrain that quotes both the words and the music of the Gregorian sequence for the Feast of the Annunciation (commemorating the occasion at which the archangel Gabriel uttered the original "Hail, Mary") and by a closing couplet that voices a common prayer formula of the day. The central antiphon is a metrical hymn that echoes Gabriel's "Ave" through five stanzas that recall in turn the five major feasts commemorating events of Mary's life: The Immaculate Conception (December 8), Nativity (September 8), Annunciation (March 25), Purification (February 2), and Assumption (August 15):

Ave Maria,	Hail, Mary,
gratia plena,	full of grace,
Dominus tecum,	the Lord is with thee,
Virgo serena.	virgin serene.
(1) *Ave, cujus CONCEPTIO,*	Hail, thou whose conception,
solemni plena gaudio,	full of solemn joy
coelestia, terrestria,	fills all things in heaven and earth
nova replet laetitia.	with renewed gladness.
(2) *Ave, cujus NATIVITAS*	Hail, thou whose birth
nostra fuit solemnitas,	became our solemn rite,
ut lucifer lux oriens	a light arising like the morning star
verum solem praeveniens.	going before the true sun.
(3) *Ave, pia humilitas,*	Hail true humility,
sine viro fecunditas,	fruitfulness without man,
cujus ANNUNTIATIO	whose annunciation
nostra fuit salvatio.	has become our salvation.
(4) *Ave, vera virginitas,*	Hail, true virginity,
immaculata castitas,	immaculate chastity,

cujus PURIFICATIO	whose purification
nostra fuit purgatio.	has become our cleansing.
(5) *Ave, praeclara omnibus*	Hail, most glorious one
angelicis virtutibus,	in all angelic virtues,
cujus ASSUMPTIO	whose assumption
nostra fuit glorificatio.	has become our glorification.
O mater Dei,	O mother of God,
memento mei. Amen.	remember me. Amen.

Entirely in keeping with the humanist rhetoricians' ideals of clarity and force of expression, Josquin's music is shaped closely around the words, a process that may be observed and described at three distinct levels. The most concrete is that of *declamation,* the fit between notes and syllables. Then there is the level of overall structure, or *syntax,* the ways in which the various parts of the text and those of the music relate to each other and to the whole. Finally, there is the level of textual illustration, the ways in which the music can be made to parallel or underscore the *semantic* content, the meaning, of the words.

All three aspects of these text-music relationships are vividly exemplified by the setting of the opening quatrain, based on the words and melody of the Annunciation sequence (Ex. 5-2a). The preexisting tune is not treated as a traditional tenor cantus firmus, nor is it paraphrased by the superius in cantilena style. Instead, the four phrases of the paraphrased chant melody are each made in turn the basis for a lucid, airy **point of imitation**, so the texture is fully integrated by shared melodic material, and the voices are made functionally equal. Relatively little previous fifteenth-century music unfolds in this way, but in the sixteenth century it became the absolute norm.

The first phrase of the melody is quoted quite literally from the chant, with the declamation nearly syllabic. Thereafter the chant is more or less decoratively paraphrased; melismas tend to come at or near the ends of phrases. Accented syllables are placed on longer note values, all of which help to maintain the intelligibility of the words. The entry of the voices is systematic, from the highest to the lowest. The final entry, in the bassus, is in each case the least adorned and the most straightforwardly declaimed. The fact that voices proceed as identical straightforward descents from top to bottom can be interpreted as an illustration of Gabriel's descent, as divine messenger, from God's abode in heaven to Mary's abode on earth.

Example 5-2a Josquin des Prez, *Ave Maria . . . Virgo serena,* mm. 1–8

Example 5-2a (continued)

As a final remark concerning shaping and Josquin's exemplary craftsmanship, note the difference between the final point of imitation, on "virgo serena," and the three previous ones. What had become predictable is now modified. The order of entries is varied at last; but, more importantly, so is the time interval between the entries, which is subtly tightened, the tenor following the superius after only one beat instead of two, and the four voices all gathering in to sound together for the first time at the cadence. All of these effects, so carefully and subtly planned, serve to mark off the prefatory quatrain from what follows. It is an ideal instance of the way in which the shape of the text governs and is reflected by the shape and syntax of the music.

Every succeeding textual unit is marked off cadentially in similar, but never identical, fashion. And each one is purposefully shaped around its words, often by artful "scoring" devices. The first stanza of the five-stanza votive antiphon ("Ave, cujus conceptio") begins with a homorhythmic superius/altus duo that is immediately imitated by the complementary tenor/bassus pair. After the first two notes, however, the altus slyly joins them in a mock-fauxbourdon texture, so there is not only a "paired" repetition of the opening phrase but also an increase from two voices to three, preparing incrementally for the emphatically homorhythmic four-voice tutti on "solemni plena gaudio," which just happens to coincide with the first "affective," or emotion-laden, word in the text: *gaudio* ("joy"). All three levels of textual shaping have been cunningly made to work in tandem to produce a simple, "natural" rhetorical effect. The full ensemble having been achieved, it is maintained through the full-textured syncopated sequences that dramatize the word *replete* ("fills") and achieve cadential release at a melodic high point coinciding with the next affective word, *laetitia* ("gladness").

The second stanza, beginning "Ave, cujus nativitas," opens with another pair of duos that introduce close imitation at the fifth, and the harmonically richer contrapuntal combination persists through the next tutti ("Ut lucifer"). The third stanza ("Ave, pia humilitas") is foreshortened by splitting the text between rigorously maintained high and low voice pairs, contrasting with the total integration of the lilting fourth stanza ("Ave, vera virginitas"), which moves in dancelike trochees and chordal homorhythm throughout. The fifth, climactic stanza ("Ave, praeclara") is set in the most traditional texture to be found in Josquin's motet: The structural pair, superius and tenor, are in strict imitation throughout, phrase by phrase and at a fixed time interval, while the "nonessential" voices, altus and bassus, supply fanciful nonimitative counterpoints.

The textural intricacy of the climactic stanza offsets the stark homorhythm of the concluding prayer, in which all four parts enter together on an "open" perfect consonance on "O." Everywhere else, four-part homophony implies triadic harmony. Here the four voices are absorbed into the perfect consonance so as to sound like an amplification of a single voice. And, once again, the motivation is textual: For the one and only time in this composite text, the first-person-singular pronoun (*mei*, "of me") replaces the plural (*nostra*, "our"). There can be no question that the composer of this motet saw himself as the "performer" of the words, a musical rhetorician par excellence (Ex. 5-2b).

Example 5-2b Josquin des Prez, *Ave Maria . . . Virgo serena*, mm. 36 to the end

O ma-ter De - i me-men-to me - i. A - men.

O ma-ter De - i me-men-to me - i. A - men.

O ma-ter De - i me-men-to me - i. A - men.

O ma-ter De - i me-men-to me - i. A - men.

Imitations

Josquin's example was supremely valued by many humanist musicians, and they propagated it zealously. Glareanus reproduced the whole motet in his treatise. Glareanus's colleague, the Swiss composer Ludwig Senfl (ca. 1486 to ca. 1543), who had been a pupil of Isaac, created a gigantic reworking of Josquin's motet, in which the younger composer did everything in his considerable power to monumentalize the work and posthumously monumentalize its creator. In his expanded version of *Ave Maria . . . Virgo serena*, published in 1537, Senfl expanded the texture from four voices to six; he tripled the length of the work by means of overlapping imitative repetitions and transpositions of Josquin's melodic motives; and he turned the opening six-note chant-derived motto into one that recurs in the tenor part throughout the piece. The younger composer's resourcefulness is clearly meant both to honor Josquin's genius and to display his own.

Even before Senfl paid his tribute, Josquin's emblematic motet had been reworked into an entire Mass by Senfl's somewhat older contemporary Antoine de Févin (ca. 1470 to ca. 1512). Févin was of aristocratic birth but nevertheless pursued a professional career as a musician, serving as a member of Louis XII's musical establishment at the time when Josquin is commonly supposed to have worked in France. It was on the basis of their presumed relationship that Glareanus called Févin "Josquin's happy follower." Févin's Mass on *Ave Maria . . . Virgo serena*, published by Petrucci in 1515, bears a novel relationship to its musical model, in a manner dictated by the nature of the model. In the new style exemplified by Josquin's motet, the texture is so protean—now imitative, now homorhythmic, now proceeding by one sort of pairing, now by another—that no single voice part has enough self-sufficiency to bear appropriation either as a tenor for cantus firmus treatment or as a melody for paraphrase. Instead, the polyphonic reworking of such a piece has to adopt the whole polyphonic texture as its model. The adaptation consists of a thorough reweaving of the texture, producing a new polyphonic fabric from the same fund of melodic motives (Ex. 5-3).

Anthology Vol 1-48
Full CD I, 66

Example 5-3 **Antoine de Févin, *Missa super Ave Maria*, Kyrie, first section mm. 1–14**

A Mass in such a style is called a *Missa ad imitationem* ("Mass in imitation of") or simply a *Missa super* ("Mass on") followed by the name of the model. Jacob Paix, a fairly obscure late-sixteenth-century German composer in the humanist tradition, published a Mass in this style in 1587 under an affected pseudo-Greek equivalent, *Missa parodia*. Modern scholars for a long time adopted Paix's term for the polyphonic reweaving technique, calling such works "parody Masses" and trying to forget that the term today ordinarily suggests some sort of caricature or lampoon. "**Imitation Masses**" has recently become a more favored designation.

Facts and Myths

Févin was "Josquin's happy follower" chiefly in matters of texture, the texture exemplified in the original motet by its rhetorically supple alternation of pervasive imitation and emphatic chordal declamation. This created a full integration of musical space rather than the hierarchical stratification of parts found in older music. Josquin's treatment of texture implied not only a new technique but a whole new philosophy of composition, in which each part was free to play whatever role a composer might wish to assign it. The ideal of integrated musical texture and the ideal of compositional freedom and mastery in tandem have seemed to many influential modern scholars to be closely allied to notions we now associate with the "Renaissance" mentality, especially as contrasted with that of the "Middle Ages." It became customary to link this with Josquin's *Ave Maria . . . Virgo serena* and therefore, based on style, to assume it was a relatively late work.

And so there was both considerable excitement and consternation when new evidence suggested that *Ave Maria . . . Virgo serena*, this most famous of motets probably dated from earlier in Josquin's career.[9] It seems to have been written before the musical developments it was thought to exemplify. Yet an early date places Josquin's masterpiece in the tradition of the Milanese *motetti missales*, comparable to Compère's *Ave Maria*. In fact, Josquin's opening quatrain is based on the same sequence melody that Compère appropriated in the altus of his litany motet, probably because the tune was a local favorite. We identified the Milanese "ducal motets" in the previous chapter with Galeazzo Maria Sforza, the brother of Ascanio Sforza, Josquin's sometime patron. *Ave Maria . . . Virgo serena* seems to be fully representative of its fifteenth-century parent repertory, even if its artistic quality far outstrips that of its companions. Although exceptionally realized and full of idiosyncratic detail, its style is consistent with its time and place. Both in its avoidance of a cantus-firmus-bearing tenor and in its close-fitting text–music relationship, it resonates less with lofty humanism than with its near opposite, the stylistic "lowering" associated with the influence of local, nonliterate popular genres. This motet survived in print, in memory, and in use. Such a work of art can and often does transcend its time and place of origin (as anyone attending concerts today can attest), and works that have so survived can exert influence at the farthest, most improbable remove of time and place.

There was both considerable excitement and consternation when new evidence suggested* Ave Maria . . . Virgo serena, *this most famous of motets, probably dated from earlier in Josquin's career.

The pervading imitation exemplified in *Ave Maria*, however, did not "emancipate" music or its composers from the tyranny of the cantus firmus. Imitation and older cantus firmus techniques could happily coexist, as can be seen in a later work by Josquin, his motet *Benedicta es, coelorum regina* ("Blessed art thou, O Queen of the

Anthology Vol 1-49
Full CD I, 67

Heavens"). This six-voice motet is based on a chant sequence for the Feast of the Annunciation of the Virgin (March 25) having six verses, paired so as to form three parts (Ex. 5-4). Josquin quotes the entire chant model in his motet but does not follow its formal divisions, opting instead to divide the motet into a prima pars (first part) setting the first two versicle pairs (1a and 1b, 2a and 2b); a secunda pars (second part) setting a single versicle (3a) as a duet; and the tertia pars (third part) setting the last versicle (3b) in an imitative manner. Like so many older musical techniques, cantus firmus writing therefore did not die out completely, but coexisted with imitation, just as, to recall an analogous discussion in Chapter 1, literacy replaced oral practices. The one joined the other, affecting it, to be sure, but never altogether supplanting it.

Example 5-4 Josquin des Prez, *Benedicta es, coelorum regina,* mm. 1–4

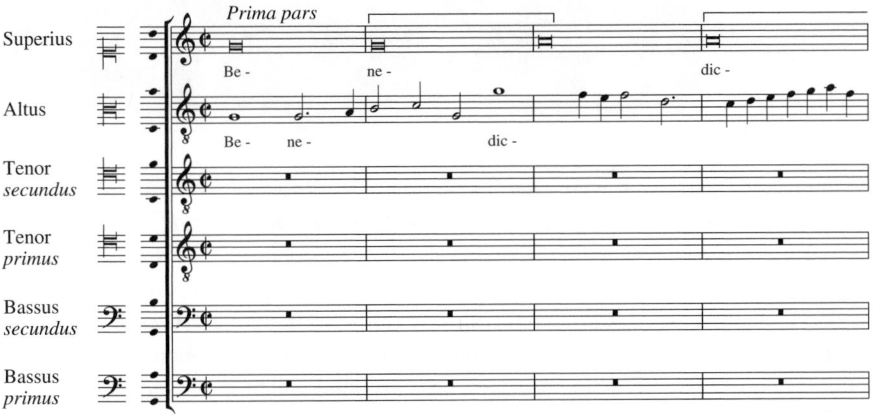

All Is Known

In the sixteenth century there was an enormous striving after an objective standard of perfection across the arts that, once achieved, would remain good for all time. We can see this ideal in the art of Leonardo, Michelangelo, and Raphael and hear it in the music of Josquin and his successors (Fig. 5-5). Many in the latter half of the sixteenth century believed this happy state had been reached in their time. Vasari thought thus about the "Renaissance" art of the time; indeed he was one of the first to use the term *rinascita* (rebirth).

Music was now an *ars perfecta*. After floundering in the "lowest depths" of decay during an age of barbarism (what those who believe in the Renaissance call the Middle Ages), it had rescaled the "heights of perfection" it had known in ancient times.[10] No further technical development was necessary. What was needed was codification: the casting of the perfected style in permanent rules so that its harmony and balance might be preserved and passed along even to those who had not the genius to discover it for themselves. No one needed to rediscover what had already been discovered. All was known. An age of conformity with established excellence had dawned. It was accordingly a great age for theorists.

The outstanding codifier of the *ars perfecta* was Gioseffo Zarlino (1517–90), from whose great treatise *Le istitutioni harmoniche* (1558) the historical judgments in

Figure 5-5 Detail of Raphael's *Parnassus*, a fresco in the Palace of the Vatican showing the god Apollo surrounded by the muses (1511).

the preceding paragraph were taken. The title of Zarlino's four-volume manual was itself a sign of the times. Often translated as "Elements of Harmony" or "Principles of Harmony" or something equally neutral, it more emphatically means "The Established Rules of Harmony." And harmony, both in the narrow musical sense and in the wider aesthetic sense, was what it purported to impart. "If we follow the rules given up to now," Zarlino promised, "our compositions will be free of reprehensible elements, purged of every error and polished, and our harmonies will be good and pleasant."[11]

Zarlino recognized that harmony as it actually functioned in the music of his age was worthy of theoretical attention. For quite some time now—at least since the beginning of the fifteenth century and most likely before that in unwritten repertories—the triad, first imported into continental music from England, had been the de facto normative consonance for all European polyphonic music. Before Zarlino, however, no theorist had recognized it as an entity, given it a name, or legitimized its use. All theory we have studied up to now has been discant theory, in which two voices (the structural pair) define harmonic norms and in which only perfect consonances can by used freely.

Zarlino accepted the triad as a full-fledged consonance and dubbed it the *harmonia perfetta*—the "perfect harmony." He appreciated the sensory pleasure that triadic harmony evoked and its affective qualities. He was the first to come right out and say that "when [in a triad] the major third is below [the minor] the harmony is gay, and when it is above, the harmony is sad."[12] Zarlino called on mathematical theory to justify his claims. The "perfect harmony," he asserted, was the product of the "perfect number," which for him was 6, thus bettering the perfect 4 postulated some 2,000 years earlier by Pythagoras. He felt that a harmonic system that was expanded to embody all the ratios between 1 and 6 would be a perfect harmony and that a music that employed such harmony would be a perfect music. In effect, that meant adding a major third (harmonic ratio 5:4) above the fourth and a minor third (ratio 6:5) above the major third. This produces a sonorous spacing of tones, a kind of ideal doubling of the triad in six voices (three roots, two fifths, one third), as shown in Example 5-5.

Example 5-5 Gioseffo Zarlino's *senaria* (chord of six), based on C

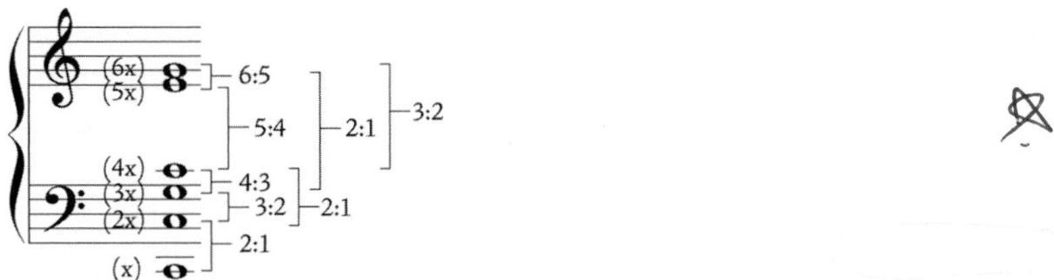

Nowadays this configuration is recognizable as the beginning of the natural harmonic series (or "overtone" series), which since the eighteenth century has been the standard method of explaining the triad and asserting its "naturalness." Zarlino would have jumped for joy to see this confirmation of his rational speculation in the realm of "natural philosophy." But nobody knew about overtones in the sixteenth century. They just thought that when pitches were stacked up in this way they sounded good. In rich textures of five and six voices, which were increasingly common by the late sixteenth century, this ideal spacing was widely practiced, and compositions ended more and more frequently with full triads. Now both of these harmonically enriching practices—larger vocal complements, triadic endings—had a properly "theoretical" support. They were among the finishing touches, so to speak, that defined the *ars perfecta* as the last word in harmony.

The "Post-Josquin" Generation

The other main perfecting touch that distinguished the "classic" polyphony of the mid-sixteenth-century higher genres (Mass and motet) was the codification of dissonance treatment, a polishing process. Zarlino was again the authoritative theorist and confessed his particular indebtedness to his revered teacher, to whom he referred as the "new Pythagoras." We know him as Adrian Willaert (ca. 1490–1562), who in a way was Josquin's creative grandchild, for his primary teacher was Jean Mouton (ca. 1459–1522), who had a special affinity with Josquin.

Two important contemporaries, both slightly younger than Willaert but shorter-lived, further represent the post-Josquin style at its most seamless and luxuriant. The Fleming Nicolas Gombert (ca. 1495 to ca. 1560) was reputed to have been Josquin's pupil, but this is likely just another use of "Josquin" as a brand name.[13] The other was the fantastically prolific Jacobus Clemens (1510–56), jestingly dubbed by his publisher "Clemens non papa" (Clemens not the pope), as if anyone would confuse a Dutch composer with the leader of Western Christendom. The silly nickname, however, has stuck. His sacred music falls into two very different groups. The larger portion consists of roughly 15 Latin Masses and some 233 motets.

The other branch of Clemens's sacred output is at the opposite stylistic extreme. His four volumes of *Souterliedekens* (Little Psalter Songs), published in 1556–57, contain three-voice polyphonic settings of all 150 Psalms paraphrased into Dutch verse. The publication of "**metrical psalms**," as they are generally called, in vernacular languages became a virtual craze in the wake of the Reformation, even in countries that did not immediately participate in the rise of Protestantism. They were meant both for public worship in the form of congregational singing and for home use and proved a bonanza for publishers. The psalm translations Clemens set had first been issued in 1540 by an Antwerp printer named Simon Cock. To make it even more marketable, Cock's book provided popular or folk tunes—love songs, ballads, drinking songs, and familiar hymns—to which each of the metrical paraphrases could be sung. One of these tunes was printed above each psalm. But the whole purpose of their inclusion was that they were widely known by heart.

This kind of appropriation from oral tradition is known in the scholarly literature as ***contrafactum*** (literally, a "makeover" or counterfeit). The idea is to get everyone singing familiar tunes together as quickly as possible, without any special instructions. Accordingly, Clemens did not just set the texts published in the 1540 edition; he also incorporated the well-known tunes, either in the tenor or the superius. The psalms became musically semiliterate, so to speak: still available for unison singing as contrafacta but also available in an elegant harmonization for the literate. The homely domestic psalms are not examples of *ars perfecta* but an alternative to it. This reminds us that the *ars perfecta,* despite Zarlino's claims and the undeniable quality of the music he espoused, was never truly a universal style. It also shows that even as the *ars perfecta* was being perfected, there were forces at work that would compromise and eventually supplant it. The popularization of religious art in the name of reform was only one of these forces.

Adrian Willaert

Born around 1490 in West Flanders (now Belgium), Willaert was one of the last in the line of Flemings and Frenchmen who had dominated Italian court and chapel music since the early fifteenth century. He lived and worked in Italy, at once the focal point of patronage and the center of the burgeoning music business. He was lucky enough to find an admirer in Andrea Gritti, the doge (chief magistrate) of republican Venice, who chose him for one of the most prestigious church posts to which a musician could aspire—*maestro di cappella,* or music director, at the splendid eleventh-century church of St. Mark's (Fig. 5-6), one of Europe's architectural glories. Willaert was installed in 1527, when he was in his middle thirties, and served until his death in 1562. He also struck up a profitable relationship with the local music printers who brought out about two dozen volumes devoted to his Masses, motets, and secular vocal and instrumental music. The man became a one-man music industry.

And yet Willaert's preeminence depended at least in equal part on the specific qualities of his music. His secret, the thing that made him, rather than Gombert or Clemens, the true classic of his time and the arbiter supreme of established excellence, was his stylistic moderation and lack of idiosyncrasy. Moderation and a certain impersonalism are traits commonly correlated with classicism. He achieved the extraordinary balance, clarity, and refinement identified with perfection while avoiding the density and conceits associated with some of his contemporaries. He deliberately restored some basic elements of Josquin's earlier style, as idealized and propagated by the humanists.

Anthology Vol 1-50
Full CD I, 68
Concise CD I, 53

The seamless quality of this music characterized the true art of "perfected" music. Willaert was the supreme technician, and that is why, for Zarlino and all who read his treatise, Willaert was the perfecter of music. His accomplishment can be keenly illustrated by a motet that parallels the famous *Ave Maria* of Josquin. *Benedicta es, coelorum regina,* published in 1545, draws its melodic material from the same Gregorian sequence that had previously served as a source both for motets by both Josquin and Jean Mouton. In Willaert's motet the chant material is thoroughly

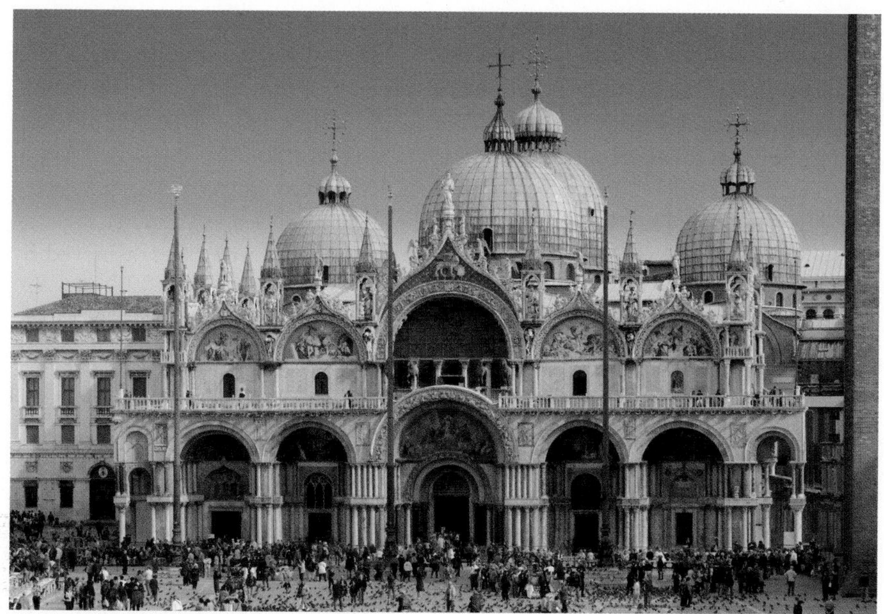

Figure 5-6 Facade of St. Mark's Basilica, Venice.

absorbed into the imitative texture, and there are no essential functional distinctions among the voices, which links it with the opening of Josquin's *Ave Maria*, the model of models. There is the same varied pairing of voices, the same canny deployment of the texture so that tuttis are rare and climactic (Ex. 5-6).

Example 5-6 Adrian Willaert, *Benedicta es, coelorum regina*, mm. 1–15

While Willaert followed Josquin in his attention to declamation and rhetorical use of homorhythm for emphasis, he is nevertheless recognizably a post-Josquin composer in his use of harmony. The obvious giveaway is the final chord of the motet, a full triad approached plagally—even now the most typical sort of "Amen" cadence. By the middle of the century such endings were standard. Another important way in which Willaert's style differs from Josquin's is that he was concerned to maintain a seamless flow of melody, heard in the way he mitigated, elided, or evaded cadences. Willaert's motet is a veritable textbook on cadence avoidance, often achieved by what we still call the "deceptive cadence."

The New Instrumental Music

Because he was so enthusiastically a perfecter of method and because he seems to have had both a flair and a taste for pedagogy, Willaert enjoyed enormous celebrity as a teacher. No previous composer that we know of left behind so distinguished a list of pupils or so explicit a technical legacy. Among his pupils were some famous Flemings, traditionally supposed to include Cipriano de Rore (ca. 1515–65). He was appointed to succeed Willaert as St. Mark's choirmaster, no doubt owing to the lingering preference given northerners.

Partly owing to ill health, de Rore was unsuccessful in the St. Mark's post and withdrew after a couple of years. He died in 1565 and was replaced by Zarlino, a fellow pupil of Willaert but an Italian, who held it until his death in 1590. Afterward the musical leadership at St. Mark's remained in native hands, reflecting a lessened sense that high art music was an imported product. Largely thanks to Willaert, Venice was full of outstandingly learned Italian musicians: Nicola Vicentino, Girolamo Parabosco, Costanzo Porta, and, above all, Andrea Gabrieli, to name only his most famous Italian pupils. It was Willaert's supremacy in Venetian music and his success as a teacher that finally overcame the Franco-Flemish dominance of Italian music. Indeed, by the end of the sixteenth century Italy would become the great training center for musicians in the literate tradition.

Another important Fleming whom Willaert trained or at least decisively affected was the Ghent-born Jacques (Jachet or Jakob) Buus (ca. 1500–65), who in the 1540s worked under Willaert as second organist at St. Mark's and published three books of music for his instrument. The fact that Buus was the first distinguished musician in the literate tradition to be chiefly concerned with instrumental music makes him of considerable historical importance. His main contribution came with the ***ricercare***. The word, etymologically related to our word "research," connotes seeking and finding. That is an old metaphor for what we now think of as artistic "creation," familiar to us at least since the days of the troubadours, the "finders" of courtly love songs.

By the end of the sixteenth century Italy would become the great training center for musicians in the literate tradition.

As Willaert's second organist at St. Mark's, Buus composed *ricercari* for the keyboard in the clean "perfected" style of a Willaert motet—pieces so finely crafted and precisely voiced that they could be published in partbooks and marketed not just for keyboard but as actual ensemble music. This marked a contrast from previous keyboard practice. Buus's keyboard pieces imitated the contrapuntal consistency of contemporary vocal music, which indicated that the perfected style was now held to be a universally valid achievement, whether sung or played. The lengthy fourth item from his 1547 collection of *ricercari* opens like a motet through several points of imitation, each based on a new "subject" (*soggetto*, to use Zarlino's word) as if it were being crafted to fit a new line of text. Every one of its points of imitation is based obsessively on the same five- to seven-note motivic "head," marked in brackets in Example 5-7. While applying a technique that had its origins in text setting, Buus's ricercare has thus clearly transcended those origins and has entered the realm of abstracted technique. His goal was not to match a subject to a phrase of text but to show everything that could be done with a given subject within the technique normally applied to texts. At any rate, the name of the genre, ricercare, seems eminently justified: The composer's aim has indeed been deflected from expression or communication to pure "research." It will not be the last time we see this phenomenon.

Example 5-7 Jacques Buus, Ricercare No. 4, mm. 1–10

Buus was identified as holding the position of "second organist" under Willaert. The term was not solely an indication of rank. St. Mark's Cathedral had two organ lofts, each with its own designated player. It was inevitable that antiphonal music making would be cultivated there, with the cathedral choir split into two groups. Such performances took place primarily at Vespers, the service most associated with psalms, which were antiphonal by biblical tradition. Although not the first *maestro di cappella* to set psalms for ***cori spezzati*** (split choirs), Willaert classicalized the practice. In his settings, the two four-part choirs alternate verse by verse and then come together in eight parts for the concluding doxology, turning a formulaic termination into an impressive musical climax.

In its penetration of the instrumental domain, long the mainstay of the improvised, the unwritten, and the dance-like, the *ars perfecta* can seem to embody a crowning triumph for literacy. All that was preserved, however, was the elite tip of a huge iceberg. The vast majority of instrumentalists continued as before to perform by a combination of ear, hand, and memory. Church organists more often improvised their accompaniments to services than read them off their music rack. And they still do: Organists are perhaps the only literate musicians who still receive training in the art of improvisation in the classical tradition.

Palestrina and the Ecumenical Tradition

The Italian Giovanni Pierluigi da Palestrina (ca. 1525–94; Fig. 5-7) and the English William Byrd (1543–1623) were the outstanding composers of the final generation of musicians who unquestioningly kept the *ars perfecta* faith. Together with Tomás Luis de Victoria (1548–1611), a Spanish organist and composer active for many years in Rome, and Orlando di Lasso (1532–94), whom we will consider in the next chapter, theirs was the last generation who unanimously saw the highest calling of their art in divine service and whose primary social status as artists was defined in relation to the institutions of the Catholic Church.

While Palestrina and Byrd brought the *ars perfecta* to its greatest stylistic heights, even in the period of its cultural decline, their actual relationship to religious authority differed diametrically. Palestrina was the quasi-official musical spokesman of Catholic power at a time when the Church was being challenged by Reformation movements in Germany and elsewhere. Byrd was the Church's clandestine servant in adversity, for he remained Catholic while his country established the Church of England. That great difference is reflected in their music, but that difference found expression within a fundamental stylistic agreement, which after all is what the *ars perfecta* was all about.

Palestrina was born in or near Rome and died there on 2 February 1594, as he approached the age of seventy. By then he had been either directly in the papal service or at the musical helm of one of the major Roman churches for more than forty years. His service began in 1550 with the election of Pope Julius III, and it ended ten popes later, with Clement VIII. That is the central fact of Palestrina's career. He was the pope's composer, a veritable papal institution in his own right.

To do best what everybody does is the aim of a classicist. Practice makes perfect.

That status made him the recipient of a paradoxical commission: In 1577, at the height of his fame, Palestrina was enjoined by Pope Gregory XIII to revise the plainchant that bore the name of the pope's sainted namesake, Gregory I. As we saw in Chapter 1, chant was supposed by long tradition to have been divinely revealed. Yet it was now subjected to a "modern" stylistic and aesthetic critique and, in the spirit of the *ars perfecta*, purged of its "Gothic" impurities. Palestrina did not complete the project, which reached publication only twenty years after his death; indeed it is not known how much of the revision he or his assistant finally accomplished. The result, however, was exactly what one might expect: a simpler, more directed—in short, a more "classic"—melodic line.

Palestrina's status as a virtual musical pope made him the most prolific composer of Masses. Complete settings of the Ordinary securely attributed to him number 104; another dozen or so survive with disputed attributions to the composer,

Figure 5-7 Portrait of Giovanni Pierluigi da Palestrina.

whose fame, like Josquin's earlier, had made him a brand name. Forty-three Masses were published during his lifetime, beginning in 1554, and another forty posthumously. The resurgence of the Mass as the dominant genre testifies to the quasi-official character of Palestrina's activity.

Not that he neglected the motet, with upwards of 400 to his credit, including a celebrated book of fairly lively works based on the Song of Songs and another fifty with Italian rather than Latin texts. Palestrina also composed two ambitious books of service music that sought to outfit the whole church calendar. One was a book of Vespers hymns (1589), the other a complete cycle of Mass Offertories that appeared in the last full year of his life, 1593. Last, and definitely least, come two books of secular part songs (madrigals)—but even in this genre, which Palestrina devalued in his devout maturity and even went so far as to recant, he wrote one indisputable "classic" (*Vestiva i colli*, "The hills are bedecked").

Palestrina's output of Masses is an astonishing and telling achievement. The idea of setting the same text to music over a hundred times is on one level the ultimate stylistic exercise, the supreme expression of the *ars perfecta*. It addresses a ritualized and impersonal attitude toward composing. The aim is not to express or illuminate the words, as one might seek to illustrate the unique text of a votive motet or a secular poem, but, rather, to provide an ideal medium for them. Not only is Palestrina's staggering output in itself exemplary, it also implies a commitment to what has already been identified as the "classical" ideal, that of conformity with established excellence and the refinement of existing standards. To do best what everybody does is the aim of a classicist. Practice makes perfect. Continual striving after the same goal results, at the very least, in facility, which is how one becomes prolific and why certain historical periods (the "classical" ones) are so full of prolific composers. The sixteenth century was the first of them.

Palestrina thus brought the *ars perfecta* to its final pitch with a body of work that constitute a *summa*—an encyclopedic summation of the state of the perfected art. And that seems only right, because no composer ever harbored a more demanding sense of heritage than Palestrina. He practiced the branch of Western musical art that had the longest written tradition and that had just begun to monumentalize its great figures, most notably Josquin. Hence Palestrina was easily the most historically minded composer we have yet encountered. He was the first to do what so many have later done in his name (in counterpoint class)—that is, deliberately master archaic styles as a basis for contemporary composition.

Continuing the Tradition

All but a handful of Palestrina's some hundred Masses are based on preexisting music. That in itself was not remarkable; the polyphonic Mass Ordinary cycle was from the very beginning a cannibalistic genre. But Palestrina also retained an active interest in the techniques of earlier composers whose work he discovered in the manuscripts of the Sistine Chapel. (He was pensioned out of the Sistine Chapel choir in

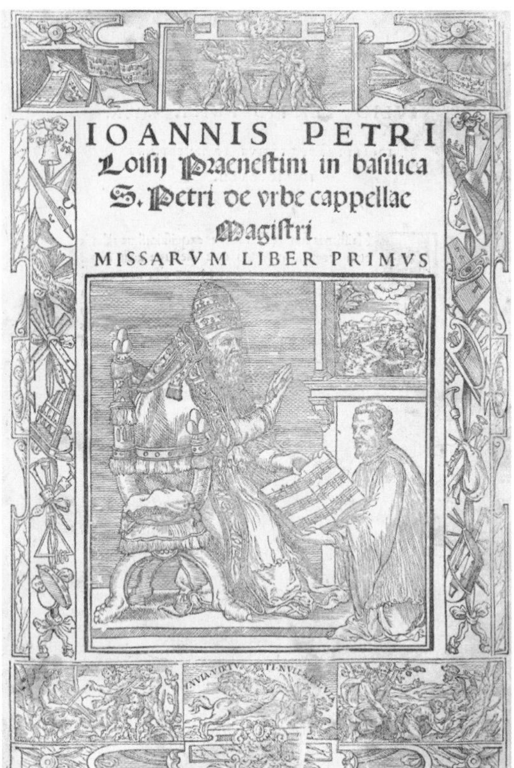

Figure 5-8 Title page of Palestrina, *Missarum liber primus* (Rome, 1554), showing the composer kneeling before Pope Julius III.

1555 owing to Pope Paul IV's decision to enforce the long-dormant rule of celibacy there; Palestrina was one of the three married members who had to be let go.)

His first volume of Masses, released in 1554 (Fig. 5-8), was dedicated to Palestrina's protector, the recently elected Pope Julius III, and opened with one based on the liturgical antiphon *Ecce sacerdos magnus*—"Behold the great priest"—presumably composed in celebration of Julius's ascent. It was an old-fashioned tenor cantus firmus Mass. The final Agnus Dei even has some old-fashioned "poly-mensural" tricks. Palestrina demonstrated his intimate familiarity with the work of Josquin (dead before he was born) by basing a Mass on his motet *Benedicta es, coelorum regina*.

Palestrina often reached even further back for models, rooting himself as deeply as he could in the Franco-Flemish legacy. Sure enough, he wrote a *L'Homme armé* Mass, one of the last contributions to the noble emulatory line. (Palestrina's most recent predecessor had been the Spanish composer Cristóbal de Morales [ca. 1500–53], who had worked before him at the Sistine Chapel and published a pair of *L'Homme armé* Masses in the 1540s.) In so boldly bringing up the rear, so expressly establishing a connection between his work and the half-forgotten wellsprings of the Franco-Flemish art, Palestrina could not have staked his claim on tradition more plainly.

More than thirty of Palestrina's Masses are of the paraphrase type, in which a Gregorian chant is absorbed into a pervadingly imitative texture. But the lion's share, accounting for almost half, is imitation (or parody) Masses, in which the motives of a polyphonic model are exhaustively rewoven into new textures. The sources of these Masses were most often motets by composers whose works were popular in local liturgical use during Palestrina's youth. More than twenty times, though, Palestrina based a Mass on one of his own motets (or even madrigals, including *Vestiva i colli*).

Palestrina's *Missa Papae Marcelli* and the Bishops

Palestrina's Masses were written for "the one holy, catholic and apostolic church" at the very moment when the church, under pressure from the Protestant Reformation to the north, was renewing its age-old mission as the "Church Militant" (*ecclesia militans*) in what came to be known as the Counter-Reformation. As we will see in the next chapter, that rekindled militancy was ultimately subversive of the *ars perfecta*. But in its early stages it created the demand for a new clarity in texture that could be seen as the ultimate refinement—the ultimate perfecting—of the traditional style. Clearly that was how Palestrina saw it. By seizing the opportunity to satisfy that demand, he created prestigious masterworks, an influential style he could call his own, and a durable personal legend.

At least as early as the 1540s and particularly in Roman circles, some churchmen had taken a negative attitude toward the music of the post-Josquin generation, which for all its technical excellence ran counter, they thought, to the proper function of church music. One prime objection was to the increasing use of secular musical styles. There were also objections that the elegant imitative texture that had been so widely adopted was far too artistic. Such music, in its preoccupation with its own beauty of form, exemplified the sin of pride and interfered with the understandability of the sacred texts, to which it was meant to be subordinate. Impressive artistic complexity obscured understanding the holy words.

Such complaints were not new. Made now against the music of the *ars perfecta*, however, the charge carried considerable conviction, because an imitative musical texture was an artistic value first and last and was hardly reconcilable with the demands of intelligibility of the words, no matter how much attention a composer like Willaert paid to correct declamation. As one indignant bishop, Bernardino Cirillo Franco, observed of contemporary composers: "In our times they have put all their industry and effort into the compositions of fugues, so that while one voice says 'Sanctus,' another says 'Sabaoth,' still another 'Gloria tua,' with howling, bellowing, and stammering, so that they more nearly resemble cats in January than flowers in May."[14]

The part about "howling, bellowing, and stammering" was just all-purpose invective, but the remark about imitation was a fair one, and it proceeded, moreover, from a genuine, specifically Italian humanist impulse. English musicians, for example, could be every bit as devout and yet quite indifferent to the matter of textual intelligibility, seeing music as serving another sort of religious purpose that had little to do with humanism. In Italy, however, what had been a grumpy minority opinion in the 1540s had become a concern of powerful "mainstream" Catholics by the middle of the next decade, exactly when Palestrina was beginning to establish himself as a papal musician.

According to Bishop Cirillo Franco himself, writing a quarter of a century later, one of these mainstream figures was his friend Cardinal Marcello Cervini, who was elected pope in 1555 and promised to do something about the problem. The bishop claimed that in due course he received from Rome "a Mass that conformed very closely to what I was seeking."[15] Cardinal Cervini reigned, as Pope Marcellus II, for only twenty days before his sudden death; but there is nevertheless some evidence that corroborates Cirillo Franco's testimony about the pontiff's concern for intelligible church music. The diary of Angelo Massarelli, the pope's private secretary, contains an entry dated Good Friday 1555, the third day of the pontiff's brief reign. Marcellus came down to the Sistine Chapel to hear the choir, of which Palestrina was then a member, sing on that gravest day of the church year. "Yet the music performed," Massarelli noted, "did not suit the solemnity of the occasion. Rather, their many-voiced singing exuded a joyful mood. . . . Accordingly, the pope himself, having beckoned to his singers, directed them to sing with proper restraint, and in such a way that everything was audible and intelligible, as it should be."[16]

"In our times they have put all their industry and effort into the compositions of fugues, so that while one voice says 'Sanctus,' another says 'Sabaoth,' still another 'Gloria tua,' with howling, bellowing, and stammering, so that they more nearly resemble cats in January than flowers in May."
—Bernardino Cirillo Franco

Palestrina was one of the singers who heard this fatherly lecture from the pontiff. His second book of Masses, published in 1567, is prefaced by a letter of dedication in which he testified to his resolve, "in accordance with the views of most serious and most religious-minded men, to bend all my knowledge, effort, and industry toward that which is the holiest and most divine of all things in the Christian religion—that is, to adorn the holy sacrifice of the Mass in a new manner."[17] The final one in the book is entitled *Missa Papae Marcelli* (The Mass of Pope Marcellus). And indeed, it is a Mass that conformed very closely to what was apparently desired by the short-reigned pope, for it set the sacred words "in such a way that everything was audible and intelligible, as it should be."

Was this the same Mass that Bishop Cirillo Franco had received from Pope Marcellus II? To believe that, we would have to imagine Palestrina writing it and then the pope dispatching it, all within seventeen days, which was just the earthly time the pontiff had left. That is not impossible. But by the time of its publication in 1567 the "intelligibility movement" had gathered a powerful impetus, and the dedication to Pope Marcellus II may have been one of commemoration, honoring one whose reign had been so abruptly terminated but who was now looked back on as the spur that had set an important musical reform in motion.

Figure 5-9 Engraving of the Council of Trent, with descriptions of the members of the assembly present, 1545.

That reform had already reached a critical point in the year 1562, when the Nineteenth Ecumenical Council of the Western Church (popularly known as the **Council of Trent**, after the north Italian city where it met), finally got around to considering music. The Council was an emergency legislative body that had convened in 1545 to stem the tide of the Protestant Reformation that was posing such a threat (Fig. 5-9). Music was not terribly high on the Council's agenda, but it, too, could play a part in the general effort to revitalize the Church through modesty and piety, to personalize its religious message, and by so doing to steal some of the Protestants' thunder. Appropriate music could help adjust the traditionally unworldly, impersonal tone of Catholic worship to a point where it might meet the comprehension of the ordinary worshiper halfway.

That was the purpose that motivated the intelligibility crusade, and it was explicitly formulated by the Council in its "Canon on Music to Be Used in the Mass." According to this document, the singing of the Mass should not be an obstacle to the worshipers' involvement but, rather, should allow the Mass and its sacred symbolism "to reach tranquilly into the ears and hearts of those who hear them."[18] Music was not provided in church for the benefit of music lovers: "The whole plan of singing in musical modes should be constituted not to give empty pleasure to the ear, but in such a way that the words be clearly understood by all, and thus the hearts of the listeners be drawn to desire of heavenly harmonies, in the contemplation of the joys of the blessed." It was left to musicians to find the means for implementing these general guidelines, but it was up to the bishops and cardinals to make sure that those means were found. In the years immediately following the Council's charge there were efforts to get composers "to compose a Mass that should be as clear as possible," as Cardinal Carlo Borromeo put it, and then to have it tested.[19]

A Mass by Vincenzo Ruffo (ca. 1508–87), the *maestro di cappella* in Milan, was most likely among those tried out by the Papal Chapel Choir on 28 April 1565. Whether Palestrina's *Missa Papae Marcelli* was also tested on that occasion is a matter of conjecture. The notion is plausible, given the Mass's publication two years later, and the assumption that it was heard that day has formed the basis of one of the most enduring legends in the history of European music. The story exaggerated the event by making the test a public trial, a virtual musical Inquisition, with music coming "very near to being banished from the Holy Church by a sovereign pontiff [Pius IV], had not Giovanni Palestrina found the remedy, showing that the error lay, not with music, but with the composers, and composing in confirmation of this the Mass entitled *Missa Papae Marcelli*."[20]

Those words come from a treatise published in 1607, that is, more than forty years later and a dozen years after Palestrina's death. It is the first account to cast the testing of the Mass in such confrontational terms. It is hard to know whether the author was drawing on oral history, on unsubstantiated rumor, or on pure fantasy. But if this report was the first to cast Palestrina as music's heroic savior, it was certainly not the last. The legend passed from pen to pen throughout the seventeenth and eighteenth centuries, until it reached a peak in 1828 in the first full-length biography of Palestrina, by the priest and papal musician Giuseppe Baini. "Poor Pierluigi!" Baini wrote: "He was placed in the hardest straits of his career. The fate of church music hung from his pen, and so did his own career, at the height of his fame."[21] However unsurpassable Baini's account seemed, it has been outdone many times over in popular history. The nineteenth-century German philosopher Arthur Schopenhauer put it this way: "Church music was saved forever. Italian music was founded at the same time. What if Palestrina had not succeeded? The mind staggers."[22] Such dubious legends are perhaps inevitable when a piece of music becomes so famous; in any case, the *Missa Papae Marcelli* exerted enormous influence and has remained the composer's best-known work.

Freedom and Constraint

Palestrina's third book of Masses, published in 1570, contained complicated works in Netherlandish style. Clearly there was never an actual inquisitorial ban on Catholic worship music imposed by the Council of Trent. Still, the style of the *Missa Papae Marcelli* remains arguably a coerced, official style—not a style, in other words, that Palestrina or Ruffo or any other composer at the time would have adopted spontaneously but, rather, one imposed by an external force. Yet the resulting music could undeniably be very beautiful and moving, a style that later artists found sufficiently inspiring to emulate willingly. It was a tribute to Palestrina's artistic imagination to have found so successful a means of reconciling artistic and ecclesiastical criteria.

As the *Missa Papae Marcelli* shows, Palestrina's post-Council-of-Trent style could be a style of special grandeur, grace, and expressivity. It is a "freely composed" Mass, one of the few by Palestrina not to incorporate preexisting material—or, at least, none that has yet been detected. This makes the composer's shaping hand all the more crucial and gives the Mass a musical shape more elegant than ever, despite (or perhaps because of) the loss of the usual external scaffold.

Anthology Vol 1-51
Full CD I, 69
Concise CD I, 54

The opening idea of the Kyrie is both the subject of the Mass's first point of imitation and the Mass's main melodic building block; it embodies the quintessence of Palestrina's style in what is known as the "recovered leap" (Ex. 5-8). This model motif begins with an ascending leap of a fourth, which is immediately filled in, or "recovered," by descending stepwise motion. It is the double reciprocity—immediate reversal of contour after a leap, the exchange of leaps and steps—that creates the "balanced" design with which the name Palestrina has become synonymous. The wealth of passing tones (many of them accented), guaranteed by the stepwise recovery of skips, gives Palestrina's texture its much-esteemed patina. Otherwise the style of this Kyrie does not differ especially from the *ars perfecta* idiom with which we are familiar, because this movement is a sparsely texted, traditionally melismatic one where textual clarity was not of paramount concern.

Example 5-8 **Giovanni Pierluigi da Palestrina, *Missa Papae Marcelli*, opening Kyrie, mm. 1-6**

Anthology Vol 1-51
Full CD I, 70–71

It is in the "wordy" movements of the Mass—the Gloria and the Credo—that we can see the special qualities dictated by the Council of Trent. The setting of the very first phrase of polyphony in the Credo can serve as paradigm (Ex. 5-9). The bass has the model motif that had opened the Kyrie, its first note repeated twice to accommodate two unaccented syllables. Four of the six voices sing the phrase in choral homorhythm, with melodic decorations taking place only where syllables are held long, so as not to obscure the words. The second phrase of text ("factorem coeli . . .") is scored for a different four-voice sample from the six available parts, chosen for maximum contrast. The two voices that had played the most conspicuous melodic role in the first phrase are silenced and replaced by the two voices that had been silent before. This creates a kind of antiphony within the single choir, a device that will in effect replace imitation as the prime structural principle for the Credo.

Example 5-9 Giovanni Pierluigi da Palestrina, *Missa Papae Marcelli,* Credo, mm. 1–8

We can summarize the structure of the Credo as a strategically planned series of cadential "cells," or "modules," each expressed through a fragment of text declaimed homorhythmically by a portion of the choir in an iridescently shifting succession and rounded off by a beautifully crafted cadence. The movement ends with the full six-part complement in a massive tutti at the final "Amen" that develops the arching "recovery" idea—upward leaps followed by downward scales—into a thrilling peroration. The expressivity of this music arises out of the cadence patterns. It is with Palestrina that we first begin to notice—and, more, to feel the effects of—strategic harmonic delays.

"Stairway to Parnassus"

The final stage in Palestrina's texturally clarified, harmonically saturated, motivically economical *ars perfecta* polyphony is reached in the book of Offertories that he published in the last year of his life. *Tui sunt coeli* ("Thine are the heavens") is the one for Christmas. Compared with the *Missa Papae Marcelli* this pervasively imitative composition might seem like a relapse into the bad old habits "corrected" by the Council of Trent. But this is pervasive imitation with a difference. The points are tightly woven out of laconic motives that are precisely modeled on the pronunciation of the words.

Anthology Vol 1-52
Full CD I, 72
Concise CD I, 55

Many motives ("et tua est terra," "orbem terrarum," etc.) are almost syllabically texted in all parts. Elsewhere, Palestrina deploys the free imitation technique in a way that maximizes intelligibility. The words are concentrated at the heads of the motives, the parts that all the voices have in common. In the first point of imitation, for example, the syllabically texted head coincides exactly with the verbal phrase; everything that follows is freely melismatic. Thus every new entrance stands out from the choral fabric in note lengths, in texting style, and by virtue of its wide skips. The placid river of melismatic notes murmurs in what is definitely the aural background. A similarly hierarchical sense of perspective orders the harmony as well. It is virtually taken for granted by now that imitation will be "tonal" rather than literal. The age of functional tonal harmony, it can be argued, begins with pieces like this, although the full panoply of tonal functions will not come into play until complete diatonic circles of fifths become standard—in about a century's time and also in Italy.

The extraordinary lucidity and rational control that Palestrina achieved in his late work corresponds quite closely with the ideals of the Society of Jesus, popularly known as the Jesuits, a religious order founded by Palestrina's older contemporary Saint Ignatius of Loyola (1491–1556), devoted equally to learning and to the propagation of the faith. The use to which Palestrina's music has been put in educational institutions both sacred and secular substantiates the affinity. The developing tonal functionalism we find in his music seems to have something to do with his being an Italian composer—the first to achieve parity with the northern masters of the literate tradition and, for that reason, an inspiring historical figure for Italian musical nationalists even centuries later.

The relevance of Palestrina's nationality to his tonal practice and the way the latter inflected his style had to do above all with the nonliterate musical culture that surrounded him in his formative years—the art of improvisers, whether poets declaiming their stanzas to stock melodic-harmonic formulas or instrumentalists displaying their virtuosity. The earliest written examples of "part music" to emulate these improvisations were settings of Italian poetry that began appearing near the end of the fifteenth century and that were published in great quantities in the early 1500s by Petrucci and the other early printers. Such a simple part song, called a *frottola,* has long been viewed as a major hotbed of functional, or "tonal," harmony. Palestrina was among the first to transfer something of the tonal regularity of the humble frottola to the loftiest literate genres.

Palestrina is the longest-running composer in Western musical history, the earliest composer whose works have an unbroken tradition in performance from his time to ours.

The technical regularity of Palestrina's music, along with its towering prestige, made him the basis of the most enduring academic style in the history of European music. At first this was a matter of turning the Sistine Chapel—the pope's own parish church in the Vatican—into a musical time capsule, sealing it off from history by decree and freezing the perfected polyphonic art of Palestrina into a timeless dogma, as it were, to join the timeless dogmas of theology. Long after the "concerted" style that mixed separate vocal and instrumental parts (which we will explore in a coming chapter) had become standard for Catholic church music, especially in Italy, the Sistine Chapel maintained a rule that forbade the use of instruments, permitting only voices, and mandated the retention of *ars perfecta* polyphony as its standard repertory. We still talk of vocal pieces being sung *a cappella Sistina* ("in the style of the Sistine Chapel") when sung without instrumental accompaniment.

Palestrina remained the papal staple. He is thus the longest-running composer in Western musical history, the earliest composer whose works have an unbroken tradition in performance from his time to ours. Even more remarkable, composers continued to be trained long after his time to write in the *a cappella, ars perfecta* style (or what was taken as the "Palestrina" style). By the early seventeenth century, two styles were officially recognized by church composers: the *stile moderno*, or "modern style," which kept up with the taste of the times; and the ***stile antico***, or "old style," which was the timelessly embalmed Palestrina style, a style that had in effect stepped out of history and into eternity.

But the *stile antico* lived on longer still and assumed yet another role in Western musical culture. In 1725, an Austrian church composer named Johann Joseph Fux (1660–1741) published a treatise called *Gradus ad Parnassum* (Stairway to Parnassus, that is, to the abode of the muses). Its derivation from Palestrina was emphasized to enhance its prestige value. Indeed, Fux cast the whole treatise in the form of a dialogue between the master "Aloysius" (= Palestrina) and the pupil "Josephus" (= Fux). Either in itself or as absorbed by later writers, Fux's treatise remained current into the twentieth century, when several other major counterpoint texts derived from Palestrina were written, further updating the *stile antico* as a purely pedagogical style.

As the bible of the "strict style," Fux's *Gradus ad Parnassum* became the first "counterpoint text" in the modern sense and the greatest schoolbook in the history of European music. Fux's rationalization of the *stile antico* gave it a new lease on life, not only as an artificially preserved style of Roman Catholic sacred music but also as basic training for composers. His treatise was a brilliantly successful attempt to reduce the *stile antico* to a concise set of rules. Fux divided the realm of old-style polyphony into what he called five "species" of rhythmic relationships, and for each one he also prescribed the appropriate "dissonance treatment":

1. Note against note (or *punctum contra punctum*, whence "counterpoint")
2. Two notes against one in cantus firmus style
3. Three or four notes against one in cantus firmus style
4. Syncopation against a cantus firmus
5. Mixed values ("florid style")

Alternatives to Perfection

We should remember that musical perfection, as a standard, is a matter of attitude and values. The ideals implicit in the *ars perfecta* were not universally shared, as we have only to glance across the English Channel to discover. When last we looked, with music connected to the Eton Choir Book in the latter half of the fifteenth century, English church music had diverged significantly in style from music on the continent, and the stylistic differences, it was already evident, indicated a difference in attitude. This continued with the music of John Taverner (1490–1545), Willaert's great English contemporary. With Taverner the luxuriant melismatic cantus firmus polyphony that characterized the Eton Choir Book antiphons continued its jungle growth. Neither textual declamation nor structural imitation play anything like the role they had long since come to play in the humanistically influenced sacred music of continental Europe.

At the most basic level, it came down to a difference in how music and words were supposed to connect. Where continental musicians strove to make their music reflect both the shape and the meaning of the texts to which it was set, the English remained true to an older attitude, according to which the music contributed something essentially other than what human language could encompass. Their music, aspiring to raise the listener's mind up above the terrestrial, provided a sensory overload: higher treble parts than anywhere else, lower bass parts, and richer harmonies. Motivic imitation—an orderly, rational procedure if ever there was one—is only a sporadic decoration, not a structural frame. The heaviest overload of all came in the guise of length, a heavenly expanse in which the listener is lost, by design. An early Tudor setting like Taverner's of the Mass Ordinary—a text that can be recited in a couple of minutes—will typically last about three-quarters of an hour.

The Recusant William Byrd

William Byrd was two years old when Taverner died in 1545, and he created his far more personal art in a very different English religious and political context. Byrd's musical style was more similar than Taverner's to that of his near contemporary, Palestrina, although Byrd was a more versatile composer than the Italian. He was adept in every contemporary genre, both sacred and secular, and made an important contribution to the early development of instrumental chamber and keyboard music (Fig. 5-10), realms about as far removed from Palestrina's sphere of interest and influence as can be imagined. We will concentrate on the side of Byrd's output that overlapped with Palestrina's and on his position as a late great master of polyphonic service music in the Catholic tradition, of all European musical traditions the most venerable.

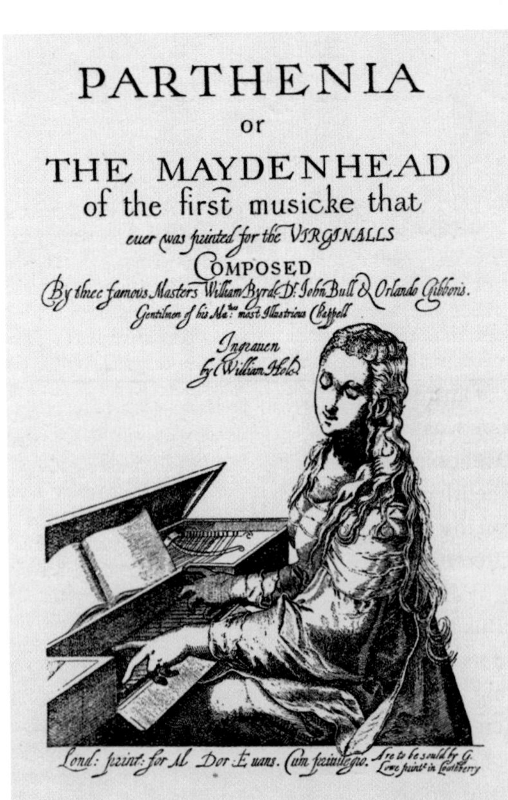

Figure 5-10 Keyboard music by William Byrd, Orlando Gibbons, and John Bull collected under the title *Parthenia* (1612–13).

With Byrd we truly reach the end of the line. His work was never canonized the way Palestrina's was but had to await revival by musical antiquarians in the nineteenth and twentieth centuries. The reason was simple and dramatic: The church he served had also reached the end of the line in England. Far from being the official musical spokesman of established religious power as Palestrina was, Byrd became the musical spokesman of the losing side in a religious war: that of the so-called recusants, loyal Catholics in an England that had cursed the pope and persecuted his followers. Byrd's latest and greatest music was the music of a church gone underground.

The English Reformation was totally unlike the German and Swiss ones, whose musical manifestations we will consider in the next chapter. It was led from above by the monarch and was as much a political as a religious commotion. It began as a quarrel between King Henry VIII (1491–1547; Fig. 5-11a) and Pope Clement VII, who had refused Henry's request for annulment of his marriage to his first wife, Catherine of Aragon, after she failed to produce a male heir. When Henry divorced Catherine in defiance of the church, the pope excommunicated him, and the king retaliated in 1534 with the Act of Supremacy, by which he made himself the head of the Church of England.

This treason against the Catholic Church hierarchy polarized England and had to be enforced by violence. English monasteries, loyal to Rome, were forcibly dissolved. Musical repercussions were inevitable, if not quite immediate. Henry himself was an enthusiastic music lover who played various instruments and even

Figure 5-11 (a) Henry VIII, portrait by Hans Holbein the Younger (1540). (b) Elizabeth I bestriding the map of England, portrait by Marcus Gheerhaerts (1592).

composed in a modest way. He took great pride in the virtuosity of his chapel choir as they sang the works of Taverner and William Cornysh (d. 1523), Henry's own court composer. Except for its repudiation of the pope's authority, the newly established national Church of England did not at first differ much, either doctrinally or liturgically, from the Church of Rome. During the six-year reign of Henry's son, Edward VI, who became king at the age of nine in 1547, the Anglican Church began to show real signs of doctrinal Protestantism. This was thanks to the boy-king's loyal Archbishop of Canterbury, Thomas Cranmer, who now asserted his own objections to the Catholic liturgy. It was largely at his instigation that the notorious search-and-destroy missions mentioned in Chapter 4 took place, thanks to which so little early English polyphony survives.

Cranmer also objected to the overelaborate nature of polyphonic music at the expense of the sacred words. He collaborated with an anti-Catholic composer named John Merbecke (ca. 1505 to ca. 1585) on a new liturgy in English. The Anglican ideal was an austere polyphonic style more radically stripped down than anything ever imagined by the Catholics at the Council of Trent. In 1549, Cranmer had published *The Booke of Common Praier*, a comprehensive translation of the liturgy, followed the next year by *The Booke of Common Praier Noted*, which provided the only legal liturgical music for the Church of England. Not that a style founded on "plain and distinct note, for every syllable one," as Cranmer had insisted, necessarily precluded good music or even masterworks.[23] Pieces by Thomas Tallis (1505–85), the greatest composer in England after the death of Taverner in 1545, who was organist at the Chapel Royal all through the period of reform, show what was still possible to achieve.

The music of the Anglican Church did not develop in any more smooth or orderly fashion than did the Church itself. The boy-king was succeeded in 1553 by his half-sister, Mary I ("Bloody Mary"), Henry VIII's daughter by Catherine of Aragon. She was a loyal Catholic and undid most of the Anglican reforms. What was instituted through violence had to be suppressed through violence. Cranmer was burned at the stake. Protestantism again became an illegal heresy. After Mary died in 1558, the country was brought to the brink of a religious civil war. Her half-sister, the long-reigning Elizabeth I (1533–1603; Fig. 5-11b), ascended the throne and achieved a compromise, known as the Elizabethan Settlement, between the antithetical religious factions. While the Catholic Church remained legally abolished, recusants were not to be subject to legal reprisal, at least for a while.

The First English Cosmopolite

The religious predicaments of the Elizabethan period were epitomized in the recusant William Byrd's long career as the country's foremost musician, a career that spanned virtually the whole of Elizabeth's prominent reign, from 1558 to her death in 1603. At the beginning, Elizabeth's tolerance of elaborate ritual within the Church of England made it possible for a high art of Latin polyphony to flourish again. Yet it was a changed art nevertheless. It had been affected—we might even say contaminated—by continental styles, and proudly so. Byrd was the great protagonist of this change, which in the face of English withdrawal from the universal church might seem a bit paradoxical. Yet it reflected in its particular domain the same heightened cultural commerce with continental Europe that distinguished the Elizabethan age generally.

One famous émigré was Alfonso Ferrabosco (1543–88), a Bolognese composer whom Elizabeth hired in 1562. According to a Venetian intelligence report a dozen years later, Alfonso had become one who "enjoys extreme favour with her Majesty on account of his being an excellent musician."[24] Royal favor meant royal protection, which could be a critical matter for Catholics such as Alfonso, who for some time was able to hold high official positions without converting to the new faith. Despotisms have arbitrary beneficiaries as well as victims.

Byrd's first important publication was a volume of motets called *Cantiones quae ab argumento sacrae vocantur* (Songs that are Called Sacred Because of their Text), which he published jointly with his mentor, Tallis, in 1575, five years after his appointment as organist to the Chapel Royal. Amazingly enough, it was the first book of Latin-texted music ever printed in England, and Tallis and Byrd were themselves literally the publishers, having been granted a patent from the queen giving them a monopoly on English music printing and staved manuscript paper. Dedicated to Elizabeth, the volume opens with a series of prefatory and dedicatory poems that positively trumpet rapprochement between the musicians of England—formerly insular and print-shy but now aggressively modern and entrepreneurial—and the great names of ecumenical Europe, such as Gombert, Clemens, and their ambassador, as it were, to the English, "Alfonso, our Phoenix."[25] The works of Byrd that show Ferrabosco's influence most faithfully were precisely the ones he chose for his debut appearance in print.[26] The Italianate motets in the 1575 *Cantiones*, most of which have liturgical texts, assert Byrd's claim as a composer of great sacred music.

As his career went on, however, Byrd had less and less opportunity to play the role of official church composer in the *ars perfecta* style. There was obviously no room for a Palestrina in England and no chance to make a reputation composing Masses. The range of suitable texts for motets was stringently circumscribed by the narrow limits of Catholic-Anglican overlap (mainly psalms). As life became more difficult for Catholics in England, Byrd withdrew into the closet world of recusancy. He and Palestrina were comparably devoted to the universal church, but where

Palestrina's devotion brought him worldly fame and fortune, Byrd's meant virtually giving up his career. There is not another case like it in the history of Western church music, which, through Byrd, eventually reached a stylistic climax on an agonizing note of personal sacrifice and risk.

The Music of Defiance

Byrd's withdrawal took place in stages. In 1589 and 1591 he published two volumes of *Cantiones sacrae*, motets of a very different sort from the ones in the book of 1575. Their texts, no longer liturgical, were biblical pastiches, mostly of intensely plaintive or penitential character: *O Domine, adjuva me* ("Deliver me, O Lord"), *Tristitia et anxietas* ("Sorrow and distress"), and *Infelix ego* ("Unhappy am I"). Others, with texts lamenting the destruction of Jerusalem and the Babylonian captivity, easily support allegorical readings that may covertly have expressed and sought to comfort the sentiments of the oppressed Catholic minority.

The final stage of Byrd's compositional activity was devoted to the setting of forbidden liturgical texts, coinciding with his effective retirement, at the age of fifty, from the Chapel Royal and his move to a recusant community in the country. It was for such communities that his late work was evidently intended. From 1593 to 1595, Byrd issued three settings of the Mass Ordinary, respectively for four, for three, and for five voice parts. This was music that could only be sung behind closed doors, for use by recusants at home; nonetheless, they were the first Mass Ordinary settings ever printed in England.[27] In 1605 and 1607 Byrd followed up with two volumes of Propers, called *Gradualia*, a comprehensive body of gorgeously fashioned but modestly scaled polyphonic music for the whole liturgical year. Byrd's settings were the concise and tightly woven epitome of a half-century's striving after imitative perfection.

Byrd's preface to the *Gradualia* contains one of the most eloquent descriptions of musical rhetoric ever penned. Sacred words, he wrote, have an *abstrusa et recondita vix* (translatable as "a cryptic and mysterious power"). Yet what Byrd affected to attribute to the words was really the power of his own musical inspiration. "As I have learned by trial," he continued, "the most suitable of all musical ideas occur as of themselves (I know not how) to one thinking upon things divine and earnestly and diligently pondering them, and suggest themselves spontaneously to the mind that is not indolent and inert."[28] It is the consummate balance of distinctive personal enunciation and lucid formal design that is so affecting in Byrd's last works. His way of shaping musical motives—so closely modeled on the precious, threatened Latin words—into contrapuntal structures of such dazzling technical finish sums up the whole notion of the *ars perfecta* and raises it one final, matchless, and unprecedented notch.

"The most suitable of all musical ideas occur to one thinking upon things divine and earnestly and diligently pondering them, and suggest themselves spontaneously to the mind that is not indolent and inert."—William Byrd

In the case of Byrd's Mass Ordinary settings, the works are literally without precedent. The tradition of Mass composition in England was decisively broken by the Reformation. The grandiose festal Masses of Taverner and his generation—implying a secure institutional backing—were not suitable models for Masses that would be sung by undercover congregations using whatever vocal forces it could muster up. Nor is there any indication that much continental Mass music—unprintable stuff in England—could have come Byrd's way. This was a wheel that he would have to reinvent.

He did so on the basis of his own motet-writing experience, in which he had worked out a very personal synthesis of *ars perfecta* imitation and rhetorical homophony. Byrd's Masses are in effect extended, multipartite "freestyle" motets of this kind, affording a whole new way of approaching the text, a manner unprecedented on the continent, where composers wrote their Masses by the dozen. Byrd did not take that text for granted but set it with unparalleled awareness of its semantic content: a very significant awareness, in fact, as befitted his plight and that of his community.[29] Where Palestrina had segregated the two techniques (systematic imitation, declamatory homorhythm), Byrd integrates them with singular terseness and word responsiveness.

Anthology Vol 1-53a
Full CD I, 73
Concise CD I, 56

We can see how Byrd responded differently to the text of the Agnus Dei in his Mass for four parts and the one for five. The Mass in Four Parts, the earliest of three Masses, was composed almost immediately after Byrd's second volume of protest motets was issued, and it retains something of their tortured mood. The astonishing degree of dissonance grates most where it is least expected, in the Agnus Dei, a text outwardly concerned with gentleness, deliverance from sin, and peace. Byrd's setting, unlike practically any continental setting, is one continuous piece, not a triptych. The three invocations of the Lamb, all strictly if concisely imitative in texture, are nevertheless distinguished from one another by the progressive enrichment of their "scoring": the first for a duo, the second for a trio, and the last, with its new words (*dona nobis pacem*, "grant us peace") for the full complement. The dissonance level is unprecedented, both in its sheer sensuous effect and in its exceptional rhetorical complexity. There is irony in it: We are surely meant to sense a contradiction between the meaning of the word "peace" and the extreme tension of Byrd's discords. But the apparent irony is trumped by a naked truth: They only beg for peace who have no peace. Once one has thought of this, one can hardly view this Agnus Dei as anything other than a portrait of the artist as recusant—or, more appropriately perhaps, a portrait of the general mood that reigned where such a Mass as this was sung.

Anthology Vol 1-53b
Full CD I, 74
Concise CD I, 57

The Mass in Five Parts, the last of Byrd's settings, displays a very different "reading" of the same text, yet an interpretation just as complex and profound. Again there is a rhetorical progression of harmonic density that gives shape to the threefold petition, from three parts to four to the full five. The first acclamation uses harmonic color to distinguish Christ's metaphorical name ("Lamb of God") from the actual prayer. The harmonic softening on the word *miserere* can only refer to the act of mercy itself, rather than the petition. The emphasis, therefore, is not on what is lacking (as in the Mass in Four Parts) but on what is given. In the second acclamation, Byrd again makes the point that the Lamb of God will not fail its pious petitioners. The third acclamation is yet something different. The whole choir gathers itself up for a pair of sudden homorhythmic outbursts—literal "calls" to the Lamb of a kind no other composer had thought to make. Again we are reminded of the plight of the persecuted. But this time the leisurely *dona nobis pacem* comes as a relief and an expression of confidence, of faith.

The kind of interpretive analysis these descriptions of Byrd's Agnus Dei settings have attempted is what theologians and literary scholars call *hermeneutics*. Byrd's is among the earliest music—certainly among settings of the Mass Ordinary—to have called forth such interpretations from modern critics, because his music seems to offer rich interpretive readings of their texts. These are the kinds of readings "official" settings like Palestrina's do not encourage, precisely because they are official. Byrd's Masses, because they are written out of a very extreme human situation, open up new levels of musical meaningfulness. They are personal, rather than institutional, statements, a profession of dangerous personal faith.

The Peak (and Limit) of Stylistic Refinement

Byrd, who lived until 1623, was the very last composer for whom the *ars perfecta* was not a *stile antico* but a living style to sustain the best imaginings of the greatest musical minds. Works by Palestrina and Byrd have shown the extraordinary versatility that pliant medium had achieved over the century of its growth since the humanist embrace of Josquin. Why, then, was it abandoned? It is not enough simply to invoke progress (at best) or change (at least) as the general, inevitable condition of human history. We must try to account for changes, especially changes as fundamental as this one, in specific terms, as responses to specific pressures.

Three such pressures will be described in more detail in the next two chapters. We have already begun to see the effects of religious unrest as well as changes brought about by the invention of music printing. There was also the pressure from humanist activities that led to a rethinking of the music/text relationship and to enormously consequential innovations in musical theater—namely, the invention of opera. None of these pressures accomplished their evolutionary work suddenly. To account for each of them it will be necessary once again to step back in time and tell the story of sixteenth-century music from a new perspective. Breaking down a complex story of change into several perspectives is admittedly an artificial analytical technique and one not normally available to those who live through the change in question.

Therein lies both the advantage and the disadvantage of retrospect. We can perform our dissection, if we are lucky, to our satisfaction and persuade ourselves that we understand the change better than those who experienced it. But they are the ones who felt (or resisted) its necessity, suffered the losses, and rejoiced in the gains. Our understanding is rationalized, articulate, and imaginary; theirs was immediate, real, but inarticulable. The reconciliation of the two, as well as the resynthesis of all the different stories our analytical perspectives entail, must take place, however imperfectly, in the reader's mind.

Summary

The sixteenth century saw the emergence of new musical styles and the rise of the music printing industry. The most influential intellectual trend was humanism, a renewed interest in the study of ancient texts that informed the ideals of the Renaissance. In the light of these developments, Josquin des Prez (ca. 1450–1521) achieved a stature and reputation that was unprecedented, emulated by both his contemporaries and his successors. Widely circulated in the sixteenth century by the new printing industry, his music set the standard for a new musical aesthetic based on clear texture, lucid text declamation, and rhetorical expression, all humanistic ideals.

Josquin's most famous work, the motet *Ave Maria . . . Virgo serena* (Hail Mary, serene virgin), exemplifies many distinctive features of his style. His setting of the text reflects the accent patterns of its declamation and its syntax, which is articulated with clear cadences, pauses, and strategic changes in texture. At the opening of the motet, each new verbal phrase is introduced with a new point of imitation, in which the text is announced in one voice and imitated by others and certain passages of text are set in a homorhythmic, declamatory style. Other composers took Josquin's rhetorical techniques, and even his actual compositions, as the basis for their works. Antoine de Févin's *Missa super Ave Maria* borrows and reworks all four voices of Josquin's motet to create a "parody" or "imitation Mass." Somewhat later, Ludwig Senfl reworked Josquin's *Ave Maria,* making it more monumental in texture and contrapuntal artifice.

In the fifteenth century it was believed that the arts had reached a level of perfection, hence the use of the term *ars perfecta* to designate the style. In order to codify this practice, Gioseffo Zarlino (1517–90) created rules of harmony and counterpoint, including the interval of the third as an element of "perfect harmony." Composers in the post-Josquin generation include Adrian Willaert (ca. 1490–1562), Nicolas Gombert (ca. 1495 to ca. 1560), and Jacobus Clemens (1510–56). Willaert's music in particular was seen to represent an exquisite balance, clarity, and refinement. This generation also saw the beginnings of written instrumental music. Jacques Buus (ca. 1500–65), an organist at St. Mark's in Venice (where Willaert was *maestro di cappella),* produced three books of organ works, including many ricercares, a contrapuntal work of instrumental music modeled on the *ars perfecta* vocal style.

The generation of composers who brought the *ars perfecta* style to its height included Giovanni Luigi da Palestrina (ca. 1525–94) and William Byrd (1543–1623). Palestrina, the first composer whose works have been continually performed into the present time, spent his life working in Rome, the seat of Roman Catholic power. Most of his Masses are based on preexisting material, using either paraphrase or parody technique. As early as the 1540s, some church leaders had begun to disparage complex, imitative polyphony because it interfered with the intelligibility of the words and their role as service music. In 1562, the Council of Trent recommended that the liturgical music focus on clear text expression. Palestrina's *Missa Papae Marcelli* (Pope Marcellus Mass), published five years later, seems to resonate so strongly with this directive, particularly in the Gloria and the Credo, that it gave rise to a persistent but unproven legend: that Palestrina was responsible for "saving" church music. In addition to his Masses, Palestrina continued to produce some complex, contrapuntal works and even some lighter ones, including madrigals. The lucid points of imitation in his sacred music became the basis of centuries of instruction in counterpoint, influentially captured in Johann Joseph Fux, *Gradus ad Parnassum* (Stairway to Parnassus).

While Palestrina served the Church in the most public and "official" venues, his fellow Catholic William Byrd faced very different circumstances in England. Although Byrd maintained his Catholic faith through the English Reformation, he served in Elizabeth I's Chapel Royal, composing music for Anglican services. After his retirement, he turned to setting forbidden Catholic liturgical texts for use in the intimate contexts of the persecuted Catholic, or "recusant," services.

Study Questions

1. Why do you think Josquin des Prez achieved an unprecedented level of fame? What aspects of sixteenth-century society contributed to his reputation? Thinking back to previous chapters, consider how his reputation reflects changing attitudes about the role and status of the individual composer.
2. What evidence do we have of Josquin's reputation among later composers and theorists? Which composers wrote parodies of his works, and how would you characterize them?
3. Explain the various ways that Josquin's setting of *Ave Maria* reflects the declamation, syntax, and semantic content of the words.
4. What is the concept of *ars perfecta*? What are its characteristics, as codified in Gioseffo Zarlino's theoretical writings?
5. Why did Zarlino call Adrian Willaert "the new Pythagoras"?
6. How would you characterize the earliest written instrumental music, as reflected in the works of Jacques Buus?
7. Describe the views about church music articulated by the Council of Trent. In what ways is Giovanni Pierluigi da Palestrina's *Missa Papae Marcelli* consistent with these recommendations?
8. What circumstances gave birth to the myth that Palestrina saved church music? Why do you think people were drawn to this legend in the centuries after Palestrina's death?
9. What stylistic traits in the music of Palestrina came to define the *stile antico*? How does Johann Joseph Fux's *Gradus ad Parnassum* (1725) attest to the continuing importance of this style?
10. Discuss William Byrd's position as a Catholic in Protestant England. How was Byrd's music influenced by his Catholicism, particularly after his retirement from the Chapel Royal?

Key Terms

ars perfecta
contrafactum
cori spezzati
Council of Trent
humanism
imitation Mass
metrical psalm
point of imitation
ricercare
soggetto cavato dalle vocali
stile antico

6

After Perfection: Pressures for Change

Perfection cannot change, yet nothing in human history stands still. So it was that the perfected art of Josquin and Willaert, of Palestrina and Byrd, was preserved by sealing it off from history. This was done, but the price was high. The *ars perfecta* still exists, but not in a way that matters much anymore. In the sixteenth century it claimed the greatest musical minds in Catholic Christendom. Later, it was practiced by nonentities, and the Church that maintained its artificial life-support system gradually lost its significance as a creative site for music. The sixteenth century was the last in which the music of the Catholic Church made history. From then on it was history. Great sacred and spiritual music continued to be composed—it still is today—but institutional affiliations weakened, particularly those with the Church of Rome.

The *ars perfecta* came about because musicians had something timeless, universal, and consummate to express: God's perfection as embodied and represented by God's own true Church, the institution that employed them. The doctrines of religion held by believers represented an absolute truth, which in turn mandated an absolute standard of behavior. That standard does not aim to gratify the individual and cannot be altered to suit the purposes of individuals or the changing fashions of secular society. The standards to which musicians serving such institutions aspired transcended matters of personal taste.

Therein lay both the beauty and the despair of the *ars perfecta*. It was the music of Utopia—a term coined in the early sixteenth century by the humanist English statesman Sir Thomas More, whom King Henry VIII beheaded in 1535 for his principled refusal to recognize the king's religious authority. With the world as its enemy, perfection had to be enforced in order to exist at all. And yet music, a human product, did inevitably change. Many deplored the changes. The word eventually used to sum up the new style—"Baroque"—although now regarded as a neutral identifying label like "Renaissance," was originally a term of reproach, employed by jewelers to describe a misshapen pearl or by critics to describe a bombastic utterance. It meant "distorted."

By the second half of the sixteenth century the forces of distortion were rampant, as we have already begun to see, some having arisen from within the Church itself. To this was added the pressure of new markets opened up by the printing of music, which reflected the overall rise of a mercantile (money-based) economy. There were also new literary movements that influenced the ways in which secular poetry was set. And, as we shall examine even more in the next chapter, there was the pressure of humanism, a true Renaissance ideal, which eventually brought about the loss of faith in "Renaissance" styles and ideas, leading to their disintegration and the birth of the Baroque.

By the end of the sixteenth century the *ars perfecta* was only one style among many. In a way its fate mirrored the larger fate of the Roman Catholic Church, which was left by century's end a transformed institution—no longer truly "catholic," but much more truly "Roman." It was no longer truly catholic because it was no longer the undisputedly universal Western church; now it had to compete for adherents with a whole variety of reformed churches that had sprung up to the north (Fig. 6-1) for a variety of reasons, doctrinal (Germany, Switzerland) and political

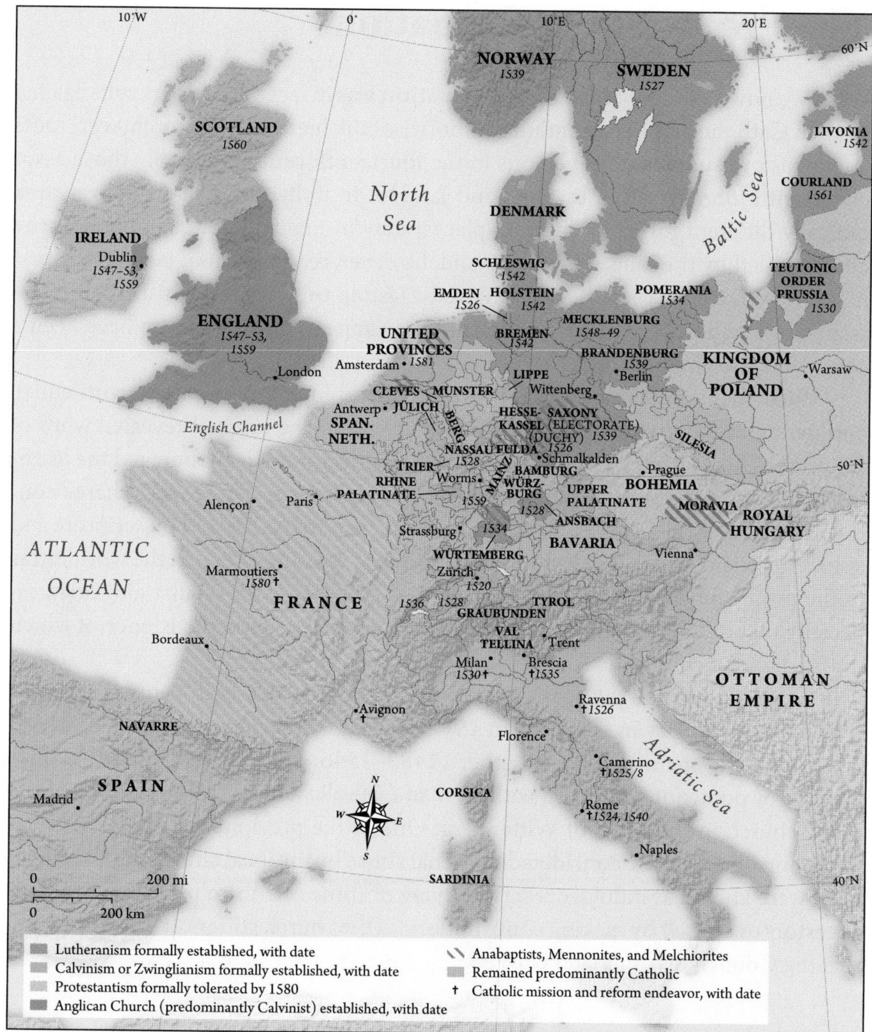

Figure 6-1 Religious divisions in Europe in the sixteenth century.

TIMELINE

1501 Pietro Bembo publishes the complete works of Francesco Petrarch

1504 Ottaviano Petrucci, *Frottole libro primo*

1508–12 Michelangelo, Sistine Chapel paintings

1517 Martin Luther posts his Ninety-Five Theses, leading to Protestant Reformation

1524 Johann Walther, *Geystliches gesangk Buchleyn*

1528 Claudin de Sermisy, *Tant que vivray*, published by Pierre Attaingnant

1528 Clément Janequin, *La Guerre*, published by Attaingnant

1532 François Rabelais, *Pantagruel*

1535 Thomas More beheaded

1539 Jacques Arcadelt, *Il bianco e dolce cigno*

1543 Calvinist Church's Geneva Psalter

1545–63 Council of Trent

1555 Orlando di Lasso, *Je l'ayme bien*

1558–1603 Reign of Elizabeth I in England

1563 Church of England established

1565 Autobiography of St. Teresa of Avila

1566 Andrea Gabrieli appointed organist at St. Mark's Basilica in Venice

1588 Thomas Morley publishes *Musica transalpina*

1594 William Shakespeare, *Romeo and Juliet*

1597 Giovanni Gabrieli publishes *Sacrae symphoniae*

1599 Luca Marenzio, *Solo e pensoso*

(England—where More lost his head). It was much more truly Roman because its power was increasingly concentrated among the Italian bishops and cardinals. The last non-Italian pope before the election of John Paul II in 1978 and Benedict XVI in 2005 was the short-reigned Adrian VI, a Netherlander elected in 1522. For some 450 years the nationality of the Roman pope was basically a foregone conclusion. The same sixteenth-century transfer from Netherlandish to Italian leadership took place in Roman Catholic music.

And yet, in agitating for change, Italy also took the lead. None of these religious, economic, or intellectual pressures for change accomplished their evolutionary work suddenly. To account for each of them it will be necessary to revisit and renarrate the story of sixteenth-century music from a new perspective. Because the music of perfection was most associated with the Roman Catholic Church, we shall first look at the religious unrest, some of it already touched on in the previous chapter, and then examine the pressures of music markets, literary trends, and radical humanism. This exercise entails some time travel back and forth throughout the eventful sixteenth century, between the sacred and the secular, among different countries, interests, and political concerns.

The Protestant Reformation

What we now call the **Protestant Reformation** was in fact a series of revolts against Roman Catholic orthodoxy and the authority of the hierarchical church, with roots going back to suppressed rebellions in the fourteenth century, notably those associated with John Wyclif in England and Jan Hus in Bohemia. The challenges took radically different forms in different places; only in England, for example, was the challenge led by the king. The revolts did, however, reach a shared peak in the first half of the sixteenth century and achieved a lasting rupture in the history of European Christendom, for which reason they now appear in retrospect to have been a concerted movement, which they were not.

What the continental reform movements had in common was an antifeudal, antihierarchical individualism and a zeal to return to the original revealed word of scripture. This in itself was a by-product of humanism, which encouraged the learning of the original scriptural languages, Hebrew and Greek. There was a shared confidence that every believer could find a personal path to truth based on scripture and a shared disdain for formulaic liturgical ritual. The reformers reviled the worldliness of the professionalized Catholic clergy and its collusion with secular authority, especially that of the supranational Holy Roman Empire, the very existence of which testified to that collusion.

What is now thought of as the first overt act of the sixteenth-century religious revolution took place in Germany in 1517, when, as an invitation to debate, an Augustinian monk named Martin Luther (1483–1546; Fig. 6-2) nailed Ninety-Five Theses, or points of difference with Roman Catholic authority, to the door of the castle church in the town of Wittenberg. One of the precipitating causes was Luther's horror at what he considered the venal abuse by the local church authorities of what were known as indulgences: the buying of "time off" from purgatory for one's ancestors or oneself by making contributions to the church coffers. It was something that the Council of Trent later banned.

Music did not rank very high on the Reformation agenda, but the effects of reform were felt very keenly in the musical sphere, for it was a revolt within the very stronghold of cultivated music, the source of most of its richest patronage. Just think how much of the music we have considered thus far has been bound up with the liturgy that was now coming under attack and how much the now-suspect opulence of the Roman Church hierarchy had contributed to the material support of musicians. Under particularly strict reform conditions, music just about disappeared. What the various reform movements shared was a hostility to the pope's music: rich, professionalized, and out of touch with ordinary life—just like the hierarchical clergy itself. What many reformers hated, in other words, was the *ars perfecta*, whose very perfection now came under suspicion. But musical agreement among the reformers ended there. They had no united vision of music's positive place in religion.

ca. 1600 Claudio Monteverdi, *Cruda Amarilli*

1600 John Dowland, *Flow My Tears*

1600 Giovanni Maria Artusi, *Book Concerning the Imperfections of Modern Music*

1601 Morley publishes *The Triumphes of Oriana*

ca. 1605 Gabrieli, *In ecclesiis benedicite Domino*

1611 Carlo Gesualdo, *Moro, lasso*

One of the most negative was John Calvin (1504–64), the Geneva reformer, whose emphasis on austerity and complete rejection of the sacraments left little room for music in his services and none at all for professional music. The only musical artifact of the Calvinist, or Huguenot, Church was the Geneva Psalter (1543), a book of psalms put into metrical verse for singing to the tunes of popular songs. To the extent that music was cultivated as an art, it had no place in the Calvinist Church; to the extent it had a place in church, it was to be uncultivated and unlettered. The same could be said for the Swiss German Reformed Church of Ulrich Zwingli (1484–1531); of all the Protestant churches it was the most hostile to liturgy and sponsored public burnings of organs and liturgical music books. Less extreme but similarly unsupportive attitudes would later be held by the Quakerism of George Fox (1624–91) and by the Puritan tradition in Colonial America.

The great exception to this pervasive music hatred was the largest and most successful of the continental reformed churches, the one named for Luther himself. Although he was by far the most spectacular and theatrical of the reformers, Luther was in some ways the most conservative, retaining a far more regular and organized liturgy than his counterparts and in particular keeping the sacrament of the Eucharist, renamed the Lord's Supper in its modified Lutheran form. Moreover, Luther was personally a fervent music lover who played several instruments, loved to sing, and even composed a bit. He did not fear the seductiveness of melody as did Calvin or Zwingli but, instead, wished to harness and exploit it for his own purposes. His most widely quoted remark on music—"Why should the Devil have all the good tunes?"—speaks directly to this wish.[1] Even more unlike the Swiss reformers, Luther urged the cultivation of polyphonic music for the glorification of God in churches, schools, and homes.

Figure 6-2 Martin Luther, portrait by Lucas Cranach the Elder, 1529

The polyphonic church music he favored, however, was still of a different order from anything we have seen up to now. It was not totally divorced from the *ars perfecta*, since Luther wanted music modeled after that of Josquin des Prez, whose compositions he treasured. Still, he opposed professionalization and hierarchy, seeing his church as a universal priesthood of all believers. The music he wanted was not for a professional choir but for a congregational community. Describing his musical ideals in the preface to a schoolbook issued in 1538 called *Symphoniae jucundae* (Pleasant Polyphonic Pieces), he observed that all men are naturally musical, which means that the Creator wished them to make music. "But," he continued, "what is natural should still be developed into what is artful." With the addition of learning and artifice, "which corrects, develops, and refines the natural music, then at last it is possible to taste with wonder (yet still not comprehend) God's absolute and perfect wisdom in his wondrous work of music. . . . But any who remain unaffected are clodhoppers indeed and are fit to hear only the words of dung-poets and the music of pigs."[2]

The kind of music that Luther is praising here is what modern scholars call a ***Tenorlied*** (tenor song): a polyphonic setting of a lyrical song-melody, placed usually in the tenor. Such a setting of a tenor (or cantus firmus), either traditional or newly composed, by the early sixteenth century would have been considered a fairly dated style in other countries. That is no surprise. We know that Germany also took up the monophonic courtly song later than its western and southern neighbors. Luther proved to be a great devotee of the Tenorlied, which was given a new lease on life by the growth of the printing trade. Next to the divine Josquin, he worshiped its foremost practitioner, Ludwig Senfl, whose expanded version of *Ave Maria . . . Virgo serena* we mentioned in the previous chapter. "I could never compose a motet like Sennfl's [sic], even were I to tear myself to pieces in the attempt," wrote Luther in admiration; "but on the other hand," he could not resist adding, "Sennfl could never preach as well as I."[3]

The Lutheran Chorale

The Tenorlied texture was not only distinctively German but also adaptable to the musical needs of the emerging Lutheran Church. In keeping with the simplified communitarian ideals of the reform, Luther at first advocated full congregational singing in place of the traditional service music that required the use of a professional choir and thus created a musical hierarchy. The lay congregation could become its own choir even as the whole congregation of the faithful, not the minister's ordained authority, now constituted the priesthood.

Congregational singing became the distinctive musical activity of the Lutheran Church, in the form of the strophic unison German hymn known as the *Choral* (**chorale** in English), a term that originally meant "chant." Chorales were intended to take the place of the Gregorian chant, from which many of the earliest ones were in fact adapted. Some were direct translations, such as the Latin Advent hymn *Veni redemptor gentium* ("Come, Redeemer of the Heathen"), which became *Nun komm, der Heiden Heiland*, and the Pentecost favorite, *Veni creator spiritus* ("Come, Creator, Holy Ghost"), which became *Komm, Gott Schöpfer, Heiliger Geist*. There were also freer adaptations, such as the famous Easter hymn *Christ lag in Todesbanden* ("Christ Lay in Death's Bondage"), descended ultimately from *Victimae paschali laudes* ("To the Paschal Victim"), the Latin Easter sequence (Ex. 6-1).

In keeping with the "why should the Devil . . ." theory, many other Lutheran chorales were adapted from secular songs, including one based on *Innsbruck, ich muss dich lassen* ("Innsbruck, I now must leave thee"), a well-known piece composed by Heinrich Isaac. Finally, there were newly composed chorales, but composed as far as possible to resemble traditional melodies. Many of the most famous tunes are attributed to Luther himself, probably as an honorific. The best known one, with an attribution to Luther that dates from within his lifetime and is therefore possibly trustworthy, is *Ein' feste Burg ist unser Gott* ("A Mighty Fortress Is Our God"), a hearty "faith-proclaiming song," as Luther termed it, for which he adapted a text from his own translation of Psalm 46 (Fig. 6-3).

Example 6-1 *Christ lag in Todesbanden* **compared with** *Victimae paschali*

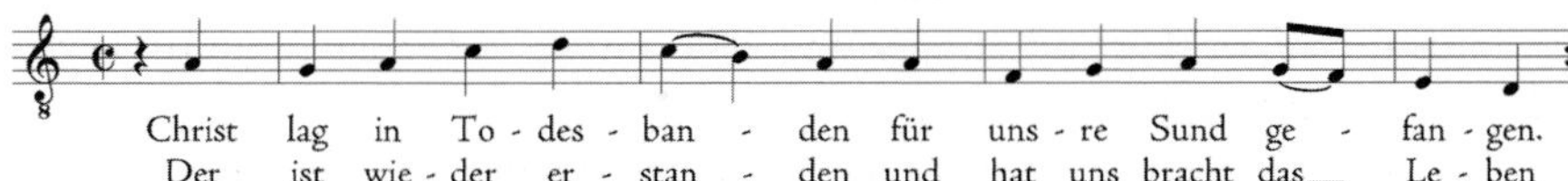

Christ lay in the bonds of death, handed over for our sins.

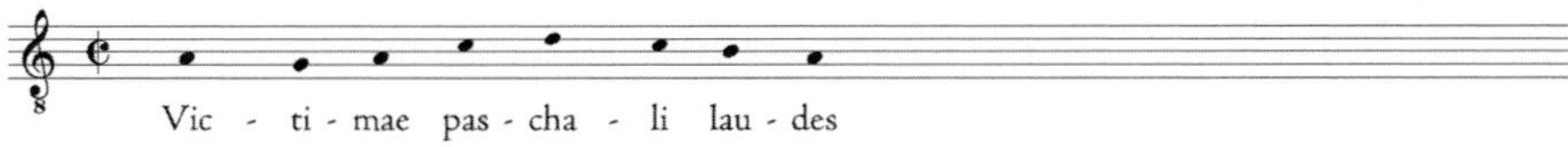

He is risen again, and has brought us life.

The first book of polyphonically arranged chorales appeared in Wittenberg in 1524, the work of Johann Walther (1496–1570), who had become Luther's main musical consultant and assistant. Walther's *Geystliches gesangk Buchleyn* (Little Sacred Songbook) was intended for use chiefly at religious boarding schools so that "young people," as Luther put it in the preface, "who should and must be trained in music and other proper arts, would free themselves from love songs and other carnal music and learn something wholesome instead."[4] The level of musical training at such schools must have been fairly high, to judge by the sophistication of Walther's settings. That of *Christ lag in Todesbanden,* for example, treats the tune to a point of imitation before the tenor enters; and the tenor, when it does come in, comes in as twins: Up to the double bar the setting is canonic, and it remains pretty strictly imitative thereafter. But even at its most elaborate, the Lutheran polyphonic chorale setting was clearly organized around the cantus firmus and dominated by it. The accompanying parts, though provided with text, were often played on the

Anthology Vol 1-54
Full CD I, 75

Figure 6-3 Martin Luther's *Ein' feste Burg* (A Mighty Fortress) as printed by Joseph Klug (*Geistliche Lieder,* 1533).

organ or by ensemble instruments; this set the precedent for the important instrumental genre called **chorale prelude** (*Choralvorspiel*) that kept the traditional art of cantus firmus writing and improvising alive among Lutheran composers well into the eighteenth century.

The melody in chorales soon migrated to the soprano, creating the texture familiar ever since. Four-part chorales have remained standard for congregational singing (as well as for elementary harmony instruction) for centuries—indeed, into our own time. The basic texture of these settings seems to have been adapted from the Calvinist psalters; but by having the melody consistently in the soprano part rather than the tenor, a congregation could more easily sing along by ear. These four-part chorales were the antecedents of the practice that J. S. Bach would bring to its stylistic peak a century and a half later, but they also give some idea of the extreme conservatism of the atmosphere in which Bach would work his compositional miracles.

Even at its fanciest, Lutheran church music was a town music, enhancing and solacing the day-to-day life of students, churchgoers, and families at home.

Rarely do the chorale settings of the first Lutheran century indulge in any semantic play to illustrate the words, nor do they aspire to any startling compositional effect. Most early settings, however artful, remain essentially down-to-earth and stick closely to the traditional tune so that no one could possibly miss it. The art of concealment, so dear to the Netherlanders and even to Josquin, was essentially foreign to the Lutheran ideal. And so were all literary pretensions, radical experiments, or (at least at first) efforts at rhetorical persuasion. A Lutheran musician was an honest tradesman. His aim was not to bowl you over or attempt sublime disclosure but to furnish an attractive, craftsmanly, not overly polished setting for a cherished article of common faith. Even at its fanciest, Lutheran church music was a town music, not a court music, enhancing and solacing the day-to-day life of students, churchgoers, and families at home.

The Catholic Response: The Counter-Reformation

The response of the Catholic Church to the Reformation attacks on its authority took a turn that could never have been predicted at midcentury, when the leading bishops were most concerned about the incursion of secular music on the sacred and finding ways to make sacred words understandable in a service. Those desires, which we saw associated with the Council of Trent and with Palestrina, could be interpreted as an attempt to meet the Lutheran reform musically on its own ground—grounds of modesty. The Council did not threaten the *ars perfecta*; on the contrary, it sought to amend and thus preserve it.

But the Catholic reaction to the Reformation, now known as the **Counter-Reformation**, eventually took on a mystical, enthusiastic, and antirationalist character that spelled fundamental theological change. Along with it, of course, came musical change that did fundamentally threaten the *ars perfecta*. As the Catholic Church turned toward pomp and spectacle and as preaching turned toward emotional oratory, church music began to move toward sensuous opulence and inspirational sublimity meant to instill awe. For the late Counter-Reformation, church music became a kind of aural incense, an overwhelming, mind-expanding drug.

The Spanish theologian St. Ignatius of Loyola, founder of the Society of Jesus, wrote during the 1520s in his *Spiritual Exercises*: "To attain the truth in all things we ought always to be ready to believe that what seems to us white is black, if the Hierarchical Church so defines it."[5] God-given though it was, human reason had its limits. To place excessive trust in it was a hubris on which the Devil could play, if it led proud thinkers away from faith. This aspect of Counter-Reformation teaching was in harmony with the spirit of the Reformation that had spurred it. The huge difference was the source of the faith the two churches espoused. The one placed it in the hands of an infallible Hierarchy, the other in the spirituality of the individual believer. It became the job of the Counter-Reformation to win souls back from Luther by fostering emotional dependency on the Hierarchy, which, like the feudal hierarchy it supported, viewed itself as God's own institution among men.

The highest spiritual premium was placed on a direct and permanently transforming emotional apprehension of the divine presence. The most famous literary description of religious "ecstasy" is from the 1565 autobiography of a Spanish nun, Saint Teresa of Avila, an epileptic whose seizures were accompanied by visions. In one of them, immortalized by the seventeenth-century Italian sculptor Giovanni Bernini, Saint Teresa recounts the visit by a beautiful angel, who "thrust a long dart of gold, tipped with fire, through my heart several times, so that it reached my very entrails. So real was the pain that I was forced to moan aloud, yet it was so surpassingly sweet that I would not wish to be delivered from it. No delight of life can give more content. As the angel withdrew the dart, he left me all burning with a great love of God."[6] There can be little doubt that it was the extravagant sensuality of Saint Teresa's description that made it so famous. At its most potent, Counter-Reformation art frequently reflects such a spiritualized sensuality or sensualized spirituality (Fig. 6-4).

Figure 6-4 Gian Lorenzo Bernini, *The Ecstasy of Saint Teresa of Avila* (1652) at the Church of Santa Maria della Vittoria in Rome.

In music, that sensuality had two main avenues of expression. One involved transferring to the religious domain the techniques of quasi-pictorial illustration and affective, sometimes highly erotic connotation that had been developed in the secular music we will examine later in this chapter. The other was the augmentation of the sheer sound medium and its spectacular deployment so that sound itself became virtually palpable. Magnificent architectural and sculptural projects in Italy, such as those by Michelangelo and Gian Lorenzo Bernini undertaken at St. Peter's in Vatican City, were evidence of a new grandeur. The imposing physical spaces had an impact on the kind of music written to fill them. The *cori spezzati*, pieces for multiple choirs pioneered rather tamely in the first half of the sixteenth century by Willaert and some of his Venetian contemporaries, became a craze by the end of the century—at least in those churches that could afford and accommodate such presentations. Both the spatialized effect and the multiplication of voice parts contributed to the awe-inspiring result, bypassing reason and boosting faith.

Polychoral and "Concerted" Music

The polychoral style and the Counter-Reformation attitudes associated with it reached new heights in Venice. The two musicians who brought Catholic music to its ecstatic pinnacle were from the same family, and both served as organists at St. Mark's Basilica under Zarlino. Andrea Gabrieli (ca. 1532–85) competed successfully, after several failures, for the first organist's position in 1566 and held the post until his death nearly twenty years later. During that period there were several major quasi-secular celebrations held at the cathedral—the most outstanding one followed the naval victory over the Turks in 1571—and Gabrieli's music for these occasions revealed an enormous aptitude for ceremonial splendor. He also furnished music for theatrical presentations, including a set of choruses performed in March 1585 at a gala staging of Sophocles's tragedy *Oedipus Tyrannus*. It is the earliest surviving music specifically composed for a humanist revival of Greek drama.

Behind attacks on new labor-saving devices lay a profound and legitimate concern that unwritten improvisatory traditions were about to be lost to literate habits, which is gradually what happened.

Andrea Gabrieli's collected sacred works, published two years after his death, contain several spectacular Masses and motets that employ larger and more varied forces than any previous written music. Especially indicative of the trend is a Mass for sixteen voices organized into four antiphonally deployed four-part choirs and probably performed in 1585 to welcome a party of visiting Japanese princes. One of the choirs was marked *a cappella*, designating it alone as intended for performance by unaccompanied voices on all four parts. The intended performing medium for the other choirs can be deduced from the title page of the collection, which announces *Concerti* for voices and musical instruments in 6, 7, 8, 10, 12, and 16 parts (Fig 6-5).

Concerti! A momentous word. From this title page one can learn what it originally meant: works expressly combining voices and instruments—written, that is, in what is still sometimes called the "concerted" style—in which the contrast and interplay of timbres are an integral part of the musical conception. From the employment lists at St. Mark's it is possible to infer that these works by Gabrieli mixed and alternated voices with wind instruments on the upper parts (or choirs) and trombones on the lower, with the organ playing along to provide the sonic glue that held things together. Gabrieli's concerted Masses and motets were quickly imitated by others, with the terms *concerto* and *concertato* becoming standard in titles.

In a fairly modest publication published in Venice in 1602 called *Cento concerti ecclesiastici, a una, a due, a tre & a quattro voci* (One Hundred Church Concertos for 1, 2, 3, and 4 Voices) by a north Italian friar named Lodovico Viadana (1560–1627), a streamlined organ part was devised. As the title page advertised, there was a "continuous bass line [*basso continuo*] to play on the organ, a new invention for the convenience of all kinds [i.e., any number] of singers and for the organists." The ***basso continuo***, a term that caught on and has been standard ever since, was an independent organ part written as one line but realized in full harmonies. This extraordinarily important innovation had radical implications: For the first time in "composed" music, the literate tradition we are tracing in this book, chordal harmony functioned as a sonorous filler or background, independent of controlled part writing. In effect, the notated line was to be played by the left hand and the unnotated chords by the right. It was called "continuous" because it played throughout the composition, no matter what went on above it. Such a semi-improvised organ part would later be played by all kinds of keyboard instruments as well as by plucked instruments such as the lute.

CANTO
CONCERTI
DI ANDREA.
ET DI GIO: GABRIELI
ORGANISTI
DELLA SERENISS. SIG. DI VENETIA.
Continenti Musica DI CHIESA. Madrigali, & altro, per voci, & stromenti Musicali; à 6. 7. 8. 10. 12. & 16.
Nouamente con ogni diligentia dati in luce.
LIBRO PRIMO ET SECONDO.
CON PRIVILEGIO.
IN VENETIA.
Appresso Angelo Gardano. 1587.

Figure 6-5 Title page of Andrea Gabrieli's *Concerti* for voices and instruments.

In view of the radical harmonic implications of the new style, it should be reemphasized that Viadana did not suddenly invent any new technique of accompaniment. All he and others at the time did was publish written aids to help organists do what they did anyway by longstanding tradition. From around 1600, though, no music print was complete—or financially competitive—without the helpful provision of a separate organ bass book. Eventually, the most common kind of organ part simply tracked the progress of the lowest-sounding vocal parts from start to finish. By doing so, the organist could accompany the whole ensemble without even seeing the other parts. The introduction of such a laborsaving device inspired a backlash from those proud of their laborious skills. The composer Adriano Banchieri (1568–1634) sneered that "soon we shall have two classes of players: on the one hand Organists, that is to say, those who practice good playing from score and improvisation, and, on the other hand, Bassists who, overcome by sheer laziness, are content with simply playing the Basso Continuo."[7]

Behind such petulant words lay a profound and legitimate concern that unwritten improvisatory traditions were about to be lost to literate habits, which is gradually what happened. The mandate of the marketplace was more compelling than any musician's complaints, and music publications that remained in print had to be fitted out with a basso continuo part to remain viable. Even older music was sometimes renovated in this way. Palestrina's *Missa Papae Marcelli*, the prime embodiment of the earlier, less musically radical phase of the Counter-Reformation and almost from the moment of its creation a revered "classic," was arranged in the early seventeenth century both as a polychoral composition (for two four-part choirs) and as a basso continuo–accompanied one.

The Art of Orchestration Is Born

At the risk of getting too far ahead of our story, we should look at some of the implications of these developments at the start of the next century. Except for the provision of the organ bass part, the early publications did not specify the instrumentation; the voices and instruments had to be assigned for each new performance. The first eminent composer to furnish definite specifications for his concerted works—in other words, the first composer to practice the art of orchestration as we know it—was Andrea Gabrieli's nephew and pupil Giovanni Gabrieli (ca. 1554/57–1657), who took the post of second organist at St. Mark's during the last year of his uncle's life and stayed there for the rest of his own. His concerti would surpass those of his uncle and, through his own pupils, transform church music thoroughly, in the process dealing a body blow to the *ars perfecta,* no less effective for its being unintended.

Besides eleven concerted motets of his own that he published along with his uncle's concerti in 1587, the only volume of music Giovanni Gabrieli saw fit to publish during his lifetime was a book of what he called *Sacrae symphoniae* (1597)—Sacred Symphonies, here adapting the new concerto idea of many-different-things-simultaneously-coordinated to an old word with classy Greek roots that meant "things sounding together in harmony." The second book of *Sacrae symphoniae,* issued posthumously in 1615, was the epoch-maker because of its exact specification of the instrumentation and dynamics.

Anthology Vol 1-55
Full CD I, 76
Concise CD I, 58

In ecclesiis benedicite Domino ("Bless the Lord in the Churches"), probably composed sometime after 1605, shows the younger Gabrieli at the height of his powers. There are fifteen parts in all, deployed in three groups plus an organ part. The three groups are of distinctive, mutually exclusive composition. There are four parts (SATB) labeled *cappella,* standing for the chorus; there are four parts (SATB) labeled *voce,* standing for vocal soloists; and there are six parts assigned to specific instruments. The final part includes three *cornetti* (instruments held and fingered like oboes but played with a brass cup mouthpiece), two trombones, and the *violino,* then a new instrument, making an early appearance in notated music and in this case sounding in the range associated now with the viola. The vocal and instrumental parts are distinct from one another both in style and in function; but so are the choral and solo parts within the vocal contingent. The soloists' parts have a great deal of written embellishment that again probably reflects what was previously the unwritten improvisatory norm.

In ecclesiis builds from a modest opening to a dazzling conclusion. It begins with a single soprano voice supported by an independent organ continuo line. The chorus enters as if in response at *Alleluia,* its music contrasting in every conceivable way with that of the soloist: in texture, in its homorhythmic relationship with the bass, and in its strikingly dancelike triple meter. The soprano soloist, meanwhile, sings in alternation with the chorus, emphasizing the ancient responsorial effect and showing its relationship to the new concerted style. But even more basic to the concertato idea, and its truly subversive aspect from the standpoint of the *ars perfecta,* is the emphasis on short-range contrast rather than long-range continuity. Also new is the "general pause"—the rest in all parts appearing in m. 10. It is not only a rhetorical pause but a pragmatic concession to the reverberant enclosed space that would have originally resonated with Gabrieli's sonic overload. The grand pauses are there to let the echo dissipate—an echo that at St. Mark's lasts a good many seconds when the music is on this grand scale.

Next the bass soloist sings another little "concerto" to the bare organ's support—and now the chorus is back with another *Alleluia* in response. But whereas the bass's music differed from the soprano's, the chorus's responses are both the same. The Alleluias, in other words, are acting as refrains, or, to adopt the newer word Gabrieli would have used, is a ***ritornello*** ("a little something that returns"). The use of a ritornello, a brief recurrent musical strain, is as endemic to the new **concertato style** as is the use of a basso continuo. Where the one anchors the heterogeneous texture, the other anchors the heterogeneous sequence of events.

At this point, after two solo verses and two choral refrains, the instruments interrupt the proceedings for a ceremonial proclamation of their own, marked *Sinfonia* to show that they have the stage, so to speak, all to themselves. After they have shown off their lips and tongues a bit with dotted rhythms and quick upbeat figures in sixteenth notes, the two remaining vocal soloists, alto and tenor, join them for the next verse. Another aspect of concertato writing emerges when the singers begin vying in virtuosity with the cornetti, sixteenth notes and all. The verse is capped, by now predictably, with the choral Alleluia ritornello, but this time the chorus trades off not with one singer but with two, backed up by the full instrumental choir.

The fourth verse ventures yet another combination, pitting soprano against bass over the continuo in a duel of dotted rhythms and sixteenth notes. The chorus enters on schedule with its ritornello. And now, with only one verse to go, Gabrieli pulls out all the stops: The full three-choir ensemble is heard for the first time, and to magnify the sublime effect the composer adds some chromatic harmony. The peak is reached when the vocal soloists pour on the virtuosity atop the massed sound. The final ritornello sustains the full ensemble to the end, reinforcing the sense of arrival by twice repeating the final cadence, capped by the cornetti at the brilliant high end of their range. This expertly constructed music shows the composer's high awareness of himself as orator and rhetorician—that is, as a persuader. If such a music proclaims it, we may very well believe that what seems to us white is black.

To see how far behind Gabrieli has left the *ars perfecta* we need only take note of one amazing fact: From the beginning of this monster motet to the end, there has been not a single point of imitation. There are motives that pass from voice to voice, especially in the vocal soloists' parts, but never are these motives combined into a continuous interwoven fabric; instead, they are forever being tossed back and forth like sonic projectiles, heightening a sense of agitated contrast rather than one of calm commingling. The aspects of spectacle and virtuosity place a new emphasis on the act of performance. In other words, the act of making music has been dramatized and more thoroughly professionalized than ever before. Musical performers would increasingly become public figures on spectacular display, be they

To see how far behind Giovanni Gabrieli has left the* ars perfecta *we need only take note of one amazing fact: From the beginning of this monster motet to the end, there has been not a single point of imitation.

in church, in aristocratic chambers, or—a new venue—in theaters. Anywhere that music was made by virtuosos became, in effect, a theater.

The combination of voices with specific instruments came along with the increasing intrusion of secular influences from such popular fare as battle pieces and from the newly reinvented madrigal, which we will consider later in this chapter. The Council of Trent had tried to ban this creeping secularism at an earlier phase of the Counter-Reformation: "Let nothing profane be intermingled," so the decree read in 1562, "when Masses are celebrated with singing and with organ."[8] That was then. By the turn of the century the Catholic Church had decided it had better pack them in by hook or by crook. A church service that included popular pieces along with concerted motets or psalms or Masses was to all intents and purposes a concert. And indeed, Venetian services at the height of the Counter-Reformation could well be looked on as the earliest public concerts (for a "mass" audience, so to speak). Huge congregations flocked to them, and their fame was spread abroad so that travelers made special journeys to Venice, already a major tourist spot, to hear the music. The most spectacular impression was made not by the singers but by the massed instrumentalists.

As the titles of featured works on display began to show, the word *sonata* was gaining currency alongside *canzona* to designate the newly spectacular instrumental genre. It did not mean anything special as yet; like canzona, it was an abbreviation of the full name of the genre, *canzona per sonare* ("song for playing"), from which came *canzona sonata* ("played song"), and then plain *sonata*—something "played." The word *sonata* still means "something played," of course, but the meaning of the term in question has changed many times since Gabrieli. One of his best-known pieces, and the earliest to indicate dynamics, is called *Sonata pian'e forte*—"piece played soft and loud"—and is symptomatic of the sensuous delight listeners had begun to take in sonic effects and displays of all kinds in this early period of music-as-spectacle. With regard to the consequences of religious unrest, such sonatas by Gabrieli and his contemporaries underscore an irony: What would remain for centuries the elite genre of "absolute" secular instrumental music was born in church.

Music Printers and Their Audiences

Momentous cultural changes brought about by religious unrest were abetted and widely disseminated through the steady expansion of mercantilism—that is, of economic enterprise and money-based trade. Protestantism, capitalism, and incipient nationalism went hand in hand, it has often been observed, and all three renewed Europe in ways that ultimately went far beyond religion. One manifestation of mercantilism was the growth of the printing industry, which not only facilitated the spread of humanistic learning and secular music but also proved crucial in the rapid spread and reach of Protestant ideas. In return, the Reformation provided a large new market for printers.

In the area of music, the innovative Venetian printer Ottaviano Petrucci released his first volumes in 1501, almost fifty years after the German printer Johannes Gutenberg (ca. 1400–68) had invented movable type and issued the first printed books, most famously the "Gutenberg Bible." Music printing took longer to perfect because it was far more complicated and initially required a triple impression. A page was fed to the presses once for the staves, again for the notes, and yet a third time for the words. Alongside the Masses, motets, and instrumentalized chansons for which Petrucci is best remembered, the enterprising Venetian also issued Italian songbooks for the brisk local trade.

The first such book, *Frottole libro primo* (First Book of Frottolas), came out in 1504, the fourth year of his business activity and his seventh publication. A scant decade later, by 1514, Petrucci had released fifteen such volumes, each containing about fifty or sixty songs, which accounted for more than half of his total output. When Petrucci's competitor, the Roman printer Andrea Antico, set up operations in 1510, his cautious maiden outing was also a book of Italian songs: *Canzoni nove* (New Songs). But most of them were not new. They were pirated from Petrucci, whose copyright was good only in Venice. Clearly we are dealing with a demand for printed songs that was created and sustained by the music-printing business. The pieces tended to be relatively conservative, enjoyable music with a broad appeal. This was the first significant instance of commodification in the history of European music: the turning of artworks, through mass reproduction, into tangible articles of trade—items that could be bought, stockpiled, and sold for profit.

Although books of Latin church music and Franco-Flemish court music were Petrucci's and Antico's prestige items, humble vernacular songs were their moneymakers. The same held true in other countries to which music printing soon spread, including Germany and England. In France, music printing got under way when Pierre Attaingnant set up shop in Paris in the mid-1520s. Attaingnant was not just a printer, for he was the inventor of a new labor-saving and cost-cutting method for music typesetting that swept Europe in the 1530s and completely transformed the business, making real mass production and high-volume distribution possible.

The triple impression method employed by Petrucci and the other early Italians produced stunning results—Petrucci's early books were never surpassed as models of printerly art—but the process wasted time and resources and was overly difficult. In Attaingnant's method, every possible note shape and rest shape was cast along with a short vertical fragment of the staff on a single piece of type. When these were placed in a row and printed, the staff-lines joined together or nearly so. Far less elegant than Petrucci's, the result was so much more practical and economical that the older typesetting method could not stand a chance against the new. Attaingnant's technique remained standard as long as typography was the print medium of choice for music—until the eighteenth century, when copperplate engraving came into widespread use (Fig. 6-6).

Petrucci's early volumes, with their cumbersome production methods and handsome appearance, were luxury items, collectibles, items of conspicuous consumption. The trend, however, was toward economy and utility, which is why Attaingnant was so successful. We know from literary accounts that household entertainment was the chief use to which vernacular songbooks were put. There are frequent references from the time to the ritual of passing out part books at social functions or around the table after meals. The ability to sing at sight and play an instrument increasingly became an important social grace, on a par with dancing. One of the main consequences of the music trade was that music traveled faster, farther, and in greater volume than ever before. This was particularly true of Attaingnant's

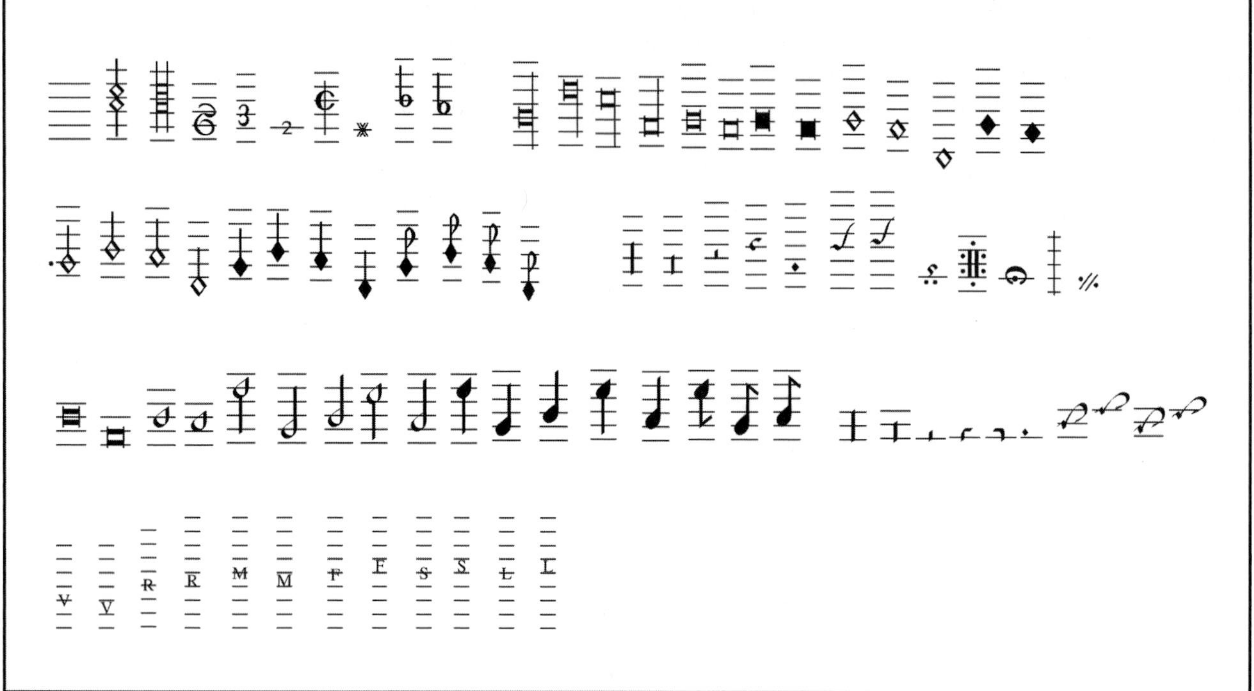

Figure 6-6 Specimens of Pierre Attaingnant's movable music type.

aggressively marketed editions and those of his competitors. As we shall see, this ease of travel facilitated some surprising hybrid styles and genres.

Vernacular Song in Italy

And what characterized the songs that the early printers printed, the early collectors collected, and the early consumers consumed? In contrast to the shared sacred style of the *ars perfecta*, they differed markedly, like their languages, from country to country. At first they reflected the earlier courtly fixed forms in their poetry, but their novel musical textures reflected the new conditions of trade. The Italian ***frottola*** (pl. *frottole*) as published by Petrucci was a lightweight affair; the name was derived from the Latin *frocta,* meaning "a motley group of trifling objects." A whiff of that slightly uncomplimentary nuance clung to the genre. The best translation of frottola might be "a trifling song." The frottola had been around for some time but for want of prestige and noble patronage had not yet managed to establish itself as literate. The sudden explosion of frottola writing was just that: an explosion of *writing,* stimulated by the printing trade.

Oral genres, as we have seen, are usually formulaic, and many a frottola was not so much a song as a kind of matrix for song making, a melodic/harmonic mold into which countless poems could be poured. The song as it appears in print is a sort of transcription from life: a snapshot of an improvisation or of a pattern abstracted from countless improvisations. In Baldesar Castiglione's famous *Book of the Courtier,* the frottola composer Marco Cara (ca. 1465–1525) is described as a renowned "singer to the lute"[9]—that is, a self-accompanied vocal soloist and undoubtedly an improviser. Cara's suave but simple *Mal un muta per effecto* ("One cannot truly change"; Ex. 6-2) was included in Petrucci's seventh book of frottole (1507). Everything about the piece suggests its origin in oral practice. The attractively lilting or dancelike rhythms in Cara's frottole are all stock formulas that were originally devised for the musical recitation of lines of poetry in a popular eight-syllable pattern (*ottonario*) favored by Italian court poets and musicians. The conclusion is virtually inescapable that frottole were originally and primarily solo songs for courtiers and court singers to sing to the lute or other instrumental accompaniment. From this observation it follows that the "monodic revolution" of the early seventeenth century that, as we shall soon see, ushered in the "Baroque" era was no revolution at all.

Anthology Vol 1-56
Full CD I, 77

Example 6-2 Marco Cara, *Mal un muta per effecto*

1. O- gni co - sa sua na - tu - ra Se- gui- tar- e di me- sti - e - ro;
2. L'ar- me- lin per non man-chiar - se Pria al ne- mi - co vien in ma - no;
3. Or- na ben di sel - la e fre - no Las- si nel mi - se- ro e vi - le,
(Altus, Tenor, Bassus)

Everything follows its own nature
And performs its own task.

The ermine, to avoid being marked,
Comes into hand when faced with its enemy.

A bejeweled saddle and bridle
Are miserable and vile shackles

Cara was one of the two leading frottolists employed at the smallish court of Mantua in the north-central Italian area known as Lombardy. The mistress of that court was the duchess Isabella d'Este (Fig. 6-7), the daughter of Hercules I of Ferrara, famous in music history as the patron whose name Josquin des Prez turned into a Mass tenor. Isabella, who probably would have hired famous Flemings if she could have afforded them, instead became the patroness who oversaw—through Cara and his colleague Bartolomeo Tromboncino—the rebirth of Italian song as a literate tradition.

The frottola was the first literate musical genre since the fourteenth century to be produced by Italians for Italians. Its style was so different from that of the northerners, the *oltremontani* (from "over the mountains") in Italy who furnished the wealthier Italian courts and churches with polyphonic music, that we sense a deliberate opposition of taste, one that was maintained all through the fifteenth century. Only in the sixteenth century did crossovers begin to occur. The Italian pupils of Willaert and others of their generation eventually took over the *ars perfecta* genres, as we have seen. Crossover in the opposite direction was much rarer.

Figure 6-7 Isabella d'Este, portrait by Titian (ca. 1535).

The "Parisian" Chanson and the Music of Description

During the fifteenth century, the chanson had become an international courtly style. A French song in a fixed form might be written anywhere in Europe, by a composer of any nationality whether at home or abroad. The age of printing in the sixteenth century brought a change: a new style of French chanson that was distinctively French, the way the Tenorlied was German and the frottola Italian. Its centers were the printing capitals: Paris to the north and Lyons to the south, with Paris sufficiently out in front that the genre is generally known as the "Parisian" chanson (Fig. 6-8). Its great master was Claudin de Sermisy (ca. 1490–1562), who served King Francis I as music director of the Chapel Royal.

Anthology Vol 1-57
Full CD I, 78
Concise CD I, 59

Attaingnant's very first songbook, the *Chansons nouvelles en musique* (New Songs with Music) of 1528, opens with a run of eight by Claudin, the second of which, *Tant que vivray* ("As long as I live") to a text by Francis I's court poet Clément Marot, has always been *the* textbook example of the new chanson because of its memorable, very strongly harmonized tune. The humanistic poetic idiom of Marot and his literary contemporaries proved to be a crucial generative influence on the new **chanson** style. Claudin's chanson clothes the syllabification of its poem in a musical scansion that seems as strict and formulaic as those in the frottola.

A new sort of literary music came into being when, later in 1528, Attaingnant brought out a slim volume devoted to the works of a single composer. The title page read *Chansons de maistre Clement Janequin*, and it contained only five items. Those five, however, took up as much space as fifteen had occupied in Attaingnant's first collection because of their greater ambition. Four of them became famous and vastly influential all over Europe and, most amazingly of all, remained in print for almost a century. The composer, Clément Janequin (ca. 1485–1558), was a provincial priest from Bordeaux, who despite his clerical calling was almost exclusively a chanson specialist. He wrote more than 250 of them, many broadly humorous or racy or downright lewd. When thinking of Janequin it is hard not to recall his near-exact contemporary, François Rabelais (ca. 1494–1553), the novel-writing monk whose name became synonymous with gross drollery. It was Janequin who gave the "Rabelaisian" mood its musical embodiment.

The age of printing in the sixteenth century brought a change: a new style of French chanson that was distinctively French, the way the Tenorlied was German and the frottola Italian.

The four big chansons of 1528 define the Rabelaisian genre at extraordinary length. And what were the texts for such chansons? Things get even more curious, because if "text" is taken to mean something meaningful written in French words, then these colossal pieces have hardly any text at all. *La guerre* ("The war") is a 234-measure monster that commemorates the Battle of Marignano, the Milanese conquest of 1515. Its text, once past the opening salute ("Hear ye, gentlemen of France, of our noble King François"), consists almost entirely of vocal imitation of battle sounds: guns and cannon fire, bugles, war whoops, and laments for the fallen. (It must have been written much earlier than its publication date, since by 1528 Francis had been defeated, captured, ransomed, and forced to give up all his Italian territorial claims.) The following three chansons are likewise descriptive: *La chasse* ("The chase") is a hunting piece full of horn calls and barking dogs; *L'alouette* ("The lark") invokes

Figure 6-8 *Concert of Women* (ca. 1520) by the Master of the Female Half-Lengths. Three women play a chanson by Claudin de Sermisy—one sings, the others play a flute and a six-string lute.

birdsong but is overshadowed in ornithological frenzy by *Le chant des oyseux* ("The song of the birds").

These orgies of imitative and expressive sounds and sheer imaginative play amount at times to long stretches of what might best be described as pure texture. The beginning of the second part of *La guerre* (quaintly listed in 1528 by its incipit, "Fan frere le le lan fan"), which depicts the height of battle, holds a single chord for a veritable eternity. The singers have nothing resembling a tune to sing and nothing resembling words to say, just a concatenation of lingual sound effects—a virtuoso turn for performer and composer alike. As befits such a stunning tour de force, it inspired emulation on a grand scale, beginning with Philippe Verdelot (ca. 1480 to ca. 1530), a French composer active in Italy, who skillfully added a fifth voice to the piece (Ex. 6-3). To call a piece like Janequin's *La guerre* "literary" is to interpret the word a little loosely. It would make no sense to say that such a work "expresses" its text, for how do we express "fan frere le le lan fan"? Rather, the text and the music work together to evoke the sounds of the world at large.

Example 6-3 Clément Janequin, *La guerre*, a 5, with Philippe Verdelot's extra voice (secunda pars, mm. 1–5)

Orlando di Lasso: The Cosmopolite Supreme

Real literary music—indeed a virtual literary revolution in music—is looming on our horizon, but before immersing ourselves in it and becoming absorbed in its consequences, there is a loose end to tie up. "Loose end" hardly does justice to a composer thought by many of his contemporaries to be the most brilliant musician alive, but Orlando di Lasso (1532–94) is an unclassifiable figure who sits uncomfortably in any slot. It was his unparalleled versatility, the very quality that makes him retrospectively a loose end, that made him such a paragon in his day.

One of the last of the great wandering Netherlanders, Lasso was born in Mons, now an industrial town in southern Belgium, probably in 1532. His baptismal name was Roland de Lassus, but by the age of twelve he was already a professional chorister in the service of the Duke of Mantua, where he adopted the Italian name by which he remains best known. From 1556 until his death in 1594, Lasso served faithfully as court and chapel musician to the Dukes of Bavaria in Munich. Thus he was born a French speaker, educated in Italy, and reached his creative maturity in Germany, making him the very model of the cosmopolitan musician of his age. But whereas the earlier cosmopolitan ideal—the ideal of the *ars perfecta*, brought to its peak by his Roman-based contemporary Palestrina—had been ecumenical, that is, reflective of religious universalism and hence nation-transcending, Lassus was brought up in the age of music-printing and was an ambitious child of the burgeoning age of worldly music commerce. His brand of cosmopolitanism was not ecumenical but widely diverse. He and Palestrina were complementary figures—they died the same year—and in many respects incommensurable ones; between them they summed up the contradictory ideals and leanings of a musical world in transition.

Lasso's appointments were secular, though they did entail the writing of huge quantities of service music, and his allegiance was always a dual one: to his patrons and to his many publishers. During his lifetime a staggering seventy-nine printed volumes of his music were issued, a total that leaves his nearest competitors far behind. His output covered every viable sacred and secular genre of continental Europe, written in all the languages he spoke. His work has never been published in its entirety; his sons tried to issue his entire backlog after his death but gave up in despair.

From this vast assortment any selection at all would be unrepresentative, but to sample the range of his secular work, which was unique, let us mention a single piece in each of four languages, illustrating this cagey chameleon-composer's bent for witty mixtures, juxtapositions of styles, and awareness of the possibilities of a kind of musical rhetoric. The chanson *Je l'ayme bien* ("I love her") is from Lasso's very first publication, published in Antwerp in 1555, when the composer was twenty-three years old. The Parisian chanson style, by then a quarter-century old, has been elegantly reconciled to the *ars perfecta* in Lasso's setting.

Anthology Vol 1-58a
Full CD I, 79
Concise CD I, 60

Matona mia cara ("My lady, my darling") was printed rather late in Lasso's career, in a 1581 volume of low-style Italian songs published in Paris, although it was probably written much earlier. There could be no better emblem of Lasso's cosmopolitanism than this silly Italian song, written by a Fleming in imitation of a clumsy German soldier of fortune, who as a suitor barely speaks his lady's language. The genre to which it belongs, called *villanelle*, or town songs (or, more precisely, a *todesca*, meaning a villanella with a ridiculous German accent), was a strophic song with refrains and hence the direct descendant of the trifling frottola. The refrains are usually nonsensical or onomatopoetic; here, it takes the form of the lovesick suitor's feeble attempts to serenade his lady on the lute. Another comical piece by Lasso is *Audite nova* ("Hear the news!"), written in the solemn manner of a Latin motet that quickly shifts to a preposterous tale about a dimwitted farmer ("Der Bawr von Eselskirchen," literally "The Farmer from Ass-Church") and his honking goose, the latter rendered musically in the manner one might expect.

Anthology Vol 1-58b
Full CD I, 80
Concise CD I, 61

Anthology Vol 1-58c
Full CD I, 81

Finally, as if to atone for representing so imposing and varied an output as Lasso's with fluff, albeit the kind of fluff no one else could have composed, we can consider a serious Latin setting. But here, too, there were genres in which Lasso stood virtually alone by virtue of his wit and intellectual élan. He was much drawn to classical texts and themes; his most notorious work in this category was the *Prophetiae Sibyllarum* ("The Sibylline prophecies"), published posthumously in 1600 but perhaps written as early as 1560. In antiquity, the sibyls were specially gifted prophetic women; in the Christian tradition the twelve sibyls were assimilated to be connected with biblical prophecy and are best known today from Michelangelo's renderings on the ceiling of the Sistine Chapel (Fig. 6-9).

Anthology Vol 1-58d
Full CD I, 82
Concise CD I, 62

The twelve anonymous prophetic poems Lasso set to music are quasi-pagan mystical texts that demanded some form of unusual musical treatment to present

Figure 6-9 View of the ceiling fresco by Michelangelo Buonarroti at the Sistine Chapel (the Creation, Prophets and Sibyls, Ancestors of Christ), 1508–12.

their mysterious contents. Drawing on a kind of humanistic musical speculation that was just then emerging in Italy, Lasso adopted a style of extreme, tonally disorienting chromaticism, coupled with a starkly homorhythmic, vehemently declamatory manner that brought out the weird words and the weirder harmonies with a rhetorical urgency. The result is hair-raising, not only as an expression of religious mysticism but as the revelation, so to speak, of an alternative path for music that challenged the absolute validity of the *ars perfecta*.

The Literary Revolution and the Return of the Madrigal

Although musically intelligible, such an eerily astonishing and extreme style as Lasso's is not easily explained on purely musical grounds. That is, it would be hard to account for Lasso's musical decisions or their motivation without taking the text into consideration. Are the motivations then "extramusical"? Is the result "literary"?

Do such motivations or such results make the product artistically impure? And is artistic impurity an artistic vice? These questions have been debated, and no matter what we may agree on among ourselves, they will go on being debated for centuries, for the question behind them is a fundamental one of values. The best we can do is to try to understand the various positions that have been taken, including our own, in their historical context.

In the sixteenth century the dispute was between the proponents of the *ars perfecta*, a musical style founded on a specific musical history and valued for its universality, and the proponents of stylistic mixture in the name of expression, which implicitly denied universal or autonomous musical values. Many composers, Lasso included, saw no need to choose between the two principles but adapted their style according to functional and textual requirements. Partisan positions were more apt to be espoused by theorists and patrons than by composers themselves. Still, even within the relativist camp distinctions and nuances can be observed. Even Lasso's Sibylline style was addressed more to the overall character of the text—its supernatural origin, its quality as mysterious utterance—than to the specifics of its semantic content, to the exact meaning of the words. Larger moods are expressed over time more than specific words at a given point in time. Indeed, when it came to the mechanics of the word–music relationship, Lasso came down in his *Sibylline Prophecies* on the side of rhetorical declamation, just like the chanson composers. If "literary" music means music that embodies or is responsive to meaning, Lasso's Sibylline motets do not qualify.

But a great deal of sixteenth-century music did qualify, and it is to that style, to the reinvented genre of the **madrigal**, that we will now turn. The revolutionary movement that supported the madrigal transformed music fundamentally and irrevocably.[10] One impetus was the "Petrarchan movement," a literary revival of fourteenth-century poetic genres associated with the eminent writer and humanist Francesco Petrarch (1304–74). The influence of the Petrarchan revival is already suggested by the revival of the word *madrigal* to identify the new style of Italian verse setting. There is no musical connection at all between the sixteenth-century madrigal and its trecento forebear, which we examined in Chapter 3. The latter, a strophic piece in AAB form, had died out and long been forgotten. The new form was continuous, with music changing to reflect the meaning of the text. Another influence was the application to settings of Italian texts of styles and techniques previously associated with "northern" polyphony, both sacred (Latin motets) and secular (Franco-Flemish chansons). The first sixteenth-century madrigalists of note were not Italians but *oltremontani*, northerners who had found gainful employment in Italy.

The protagonists of the literary revolution in its earliest phases were the humanist scholar (and later cardinal) Pietro Bembo (1470–1547) and the composers Verdelot and Jacques Arcadelt (d. 1568), a Walloon or French-speaking Fleming. Verdelot's first book of madrigals was published in 1533, although he was active mainly in the 1520s. Arcadelt published five books of madrigals between 1539 and 1544, by which time the madrigal had been established as the dominant musical genre for Italian poetry. It would retain its supremacy for over a century, although with many modifications along the way to accommodate changing styles and social functions. By the end of the sixteenth century, moreover, madrigals were an international craze, both in the sense that Italian madrigals were eagerly imported and performed abroad and in the sense that they inspired emulations in other countries and other languages, particularly English.

The revolutionary movement that supported the madrigal transformed music fundamentally and irrevocably.

Bembo's revival of Petrarch was a watershed for Italian poetry and for the reestablishment of the Florentine or Tuscan dialect as a standard literary language. He published an edition of Petrarch's complete works in 1501. Four years later, he published a dialogue on courtly love that included a selection of illustrative verses of his own composition in the style of Petrarch, demonstrating what Bembo took to be the great poet's essential devices and themes. The most famous part of the book was the chapter devoted to lovers in conflict, in which the device of antithesis—the immediate confrontation of words, feelings, and ideas with their opposites—was exploited in spectacular fashion. In a later work, *Prose della volgar lingua* (Writings on the Vulgar Language, 1525), Bembo drew out of Petrarch the idea of an antithesis of styles as well. His polar categories—*gravità* (gravity or dignity) and *piacevolezza* (pleasingness or charm)—were to be realized technically by the mechanics of the verse: phonology, rhyme scheme, and meter.

Arcadelt's* Il bianco e dolce cigno *was possibly the century's most famous single piece of art music, one that many knew by heart.

These theories were enormously stimulating to musicians. Bembo's poems and eventually those of Petrarch himself became a much used source for composers of madrigals, who began to specialize in the expression of violent emotional contrasts that could be effectively linked with musical contrasts: high/low, fast/slow, up/down, consonant/dissonant, major/minor, diatonic/chromatic, and homorhythmic/imitative—as suggestive of meaning. Musical tones all by themselves may not possess much in the way of semantic reference; they may not *denote* objects or ideas with much precision. But antithetical relationships between tones and tone constructs can *connote* plenty, as in the predictable "descendit/ascendit" (descended/ascended) contrasts in settings of the Credo of the Mass describing Christ's coming down from heaven and ascending to it.

Anthology Vol 1-59
Full CD II, 1
Concise CD I, 63

An ideal starting point for observing the growth of literary music through the madrigal and its growing antagonism to the impersonal universalism of the *ars perfecta* is *Il bianco e dolce cigno* ("The white delightful swan"), the opening item in Arcadelt's first book of madrigals (1539), the most frequently reprinted music book of the whole sixteenth century. This madrigal was possibly the century's most famous single piece of art music, one that many knew by heart. As is typical for madrigal poems, the text of Arcadelt's swan song consists of a single stanza in lines of varying length, without refrain or any other obvious formal scheme. The music does not impose one either, and thus it differs from most other vernacular genres of the time. Most of these were in some sort of fixed form. To those already mentioned we could add the Spanish *villancico*, a dance-descended song.

A madrigalist went after content and its maximal musical representation. Madrigal composers of Arcadelt's generation and especially *oltremontani* tended to present the poem fairly straightforwardly, aiming at a general mood of gravity or charm. Their settings are mild compared to what came later. But even Arcadelt's swan poem is built à la Petrarch around an antithesis (the swan's sad death, the poet's happy "death" in love), and the composer gives two vivid hints of the particularizing impulse that would later become such a fetish among madrigalists. The first high-powered affective word, *piangendo* (weeping), receives the first chromatic harmony. There is nothing intrinsically weepy about the chord itself—just another major triad—but in context it contrasts with the diatonic norm, which gives it prominence (Ex. 6-4). As to the second hint, there could be nothing more ordinary or less particularly expressive in music of the sixteenth century than a point of imitation. Yet Arcadelt's imitative setting of the thrice-repeated last line, by standing out from the homorhythmic norm, is emphasized and therefore illustrative of the sense of the line, which refers to a multiple, repetitive act—and underscores the double entendre: *Lo piccolo morte* ("the little death") was the standard Italian euphemism for the climax of the sexual act.

Example 6-4 Jacques Arcadelt, *Il bianco e dolce cigno*, mm. 1–10

The white and sweet swan
dies singing. And I,
weeping, come to the end
of my life.

Because it so privileged the humanistic axiom that music should be the servant of the sense of the poetry and therefore imitate it, the madrigal became a hotbed of musical radicalism and experimentation, especially at those moments in the text where what came to be called "**madrigalisms**" and "word painting" could provide a textual excuse to do almost anything. Because of its "literary" premises, the madrigal was tolerant of audacities that in any other genre would have been thought blunders or lapses of style. The meaning of the words thus became the excuse for breaking the rules and for flights of imagination beyond perfection. This latter feature might be considered analogous to the wildly imaginative depictions of hell in the visual arts. Whereas painters, for example, had rather limited options perfectly depicting Madonna and child, when confronted with the challenge of imaging eternal damnation they could do almost anything and break almost any rule. Some artists from around the same time as the early madrigalists, most notoriously Hieronymus Bosch

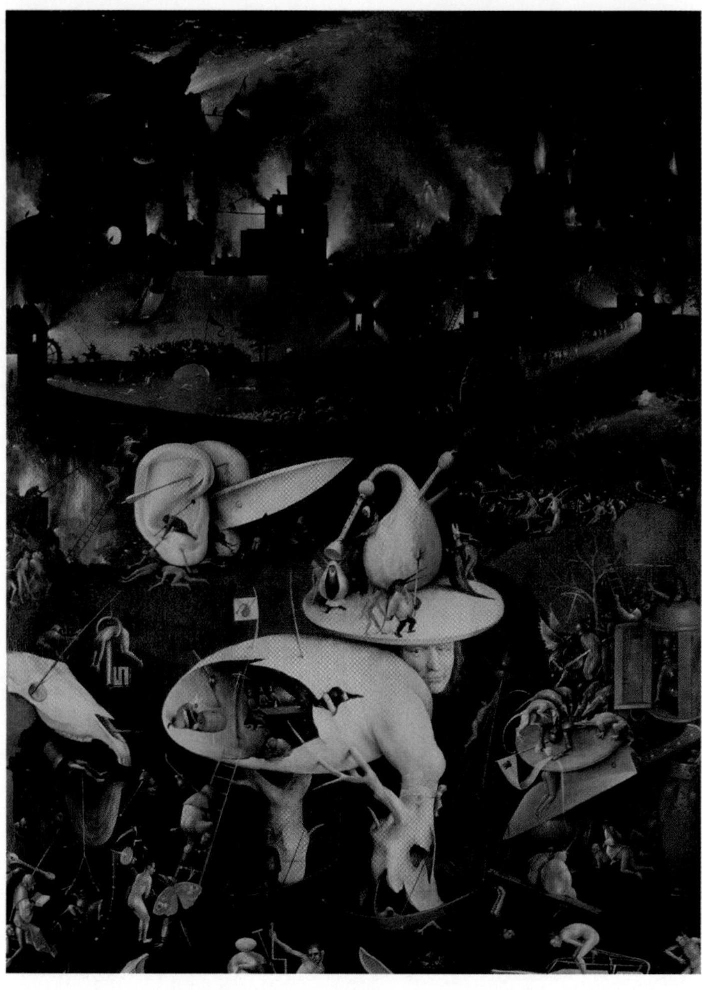

Figure 6-10 *Hell*, right panel of *The Garden of Earthly Delights*, triptych by Hieronymus Bosch, ca. 1500.

(ca. 1450–1516), made lucrative careers by creating fantastic hellish representations rather than conventional heavenly ones (Fig. 6-10).

Anthology Vol 1-60
Full CD II, 2
Concise CD I, 64

Real affronts to musical perfection started to emerge in the 1560s, beginning with the madrigals of Cipriano de Rore (1516–65), the Flemish associate and pupil of Willaert. The whole poem of his *Da le belle contrade d'oriente* ("From the fair regions of the east") consists of one sustained, multileveled antithesis: Recollections of physical pleasures placed at the beginning and the end are juxtaposed with a sudden outpouring of emotional anguish in the middle, expressed in direct speech. The multiple contrast is expressed with unprecedented violence in the music. The narrative portions at the two ends are full of delightful descriptive effects: the rocking rhythms where the poet speaks of enjoying bliss in his lover's arms ("fruiva in braccio . . ."), the intricate imitative polyphony where the intertwining of the lovers' limbs is compared with the snaky growth of vines.

In contrast, the middle section of de Rore's madrigal has a serious tone and agonized mood. The composer adopts a wholly different approach by imitating the actual quoted speech of the disconsolate lady, including sniffles and sobs, especially poignant when, after an unexpected rest representing a sigh, she blurts out her harmonically wayward, syncopated curse on Eros ("Ahi, crudo Amor"/"Ah, cruel love"). It is a supremely calculated effect, needless to say, but it is fashioned to resemble a spontaneous outburst, following an old theory of Aristotle's that, speech being the outward expression of emotion, imitation of speech is equal to the direct imitation of emotion (Ex. 6-5).

Example 6-5 **Cipriano de Rore, *Da le belle contrade d'oriente*, mm. 36–48**

What will become of me here, gloomy and sad?
Alas, cruel love, how false and brief
Are your pleasures

The direct imitation of tortured speech, evoking a single subject's extreme personal feeling by the use of extreme musical relationships, is as far from the aims of the *ars perfecta* as can be imagined. The musical means employed, judged from the standpoint of the *ars perfecta*, are full of bombastic exaggeration and distortion—in a word, they are "Baroque." But Rore's exaggerations and distortions only begin to suggest the assault that the last generations of madrigalists, working around the turn of the century, would wreak on the consummate musical idiom their fathers had perfected.

Paradox and Contradiction: Late Italian Madrigalists

As in the realm of Catholic sacred music, where the imported generation of Willaert gave way to that of homegrown Palestrina, so it was in the realm of the madrigal: Native Italian talent gradually took possession of the elite genres from the northerners. The first of the great Italian-born madrigalists was Luca Marenzio (ca.1554–99), who spent most of his career in Rome. *Solo e pensoso* ("Alone and distracted"), from Marenzio's ninth and last book of madrigals (1599), sets a famous poem by Petrarch himself. The ingenious rendering of the opening couplet illustrates another possibility for painting a text musically. Music moves, and in its movements it can analogize physical movement, even physical space. The opening image of the poem is that of numbly wandering "with slow and halting steps." The steady tread of whole notes in the accompanying voices suggests those steps. They accompany a soprano voice moving in whole notes through what is perhaps the first complete chromatic scale in the history of European art music, ascending through fifteen half-step progressions and then descending through eight. What better way to indicate unpremeditated movement through deserted fields, parts unknown?

Anthology Vol 1-61
Full CD II, 3

The elevated poetry and formal freedom of the Italian madrigal invited harmonic experimentation. The most celebrated example, because it led to a famous debate, was *Cruda Amarilli* ("Cruel Amaryllis"), which opens the fifth madrigal book by Claudio Monteverdi (1567–1643; Fig. 6-11). The long-lived and celebrated Monteverdi had a multifaceted career that included pioneering work in genres that properly belong to the seventeenth century; we will review his biography and survey his output, notably as the first great composer of opera, in the next chapter. Here we will mention him exclusively as a late madrigalist, who attracted hostile attention from proponents of the *ars perfecta* who saw him as a particular threat precisely because his work was so persuasive.

Anthology Vol 1-62
Full CD II, 4
Concise CD I, 65

Figure 6-11 Claudio Monteverdi, painting by Bernardo Strozzi, 1630.

Cruda Amarilli became a cause célèbre when it was angrily attacked by Giovanni Maria Artusi (1540–1613), a pupil of Zarlino's and a latter-day proponent of the *ars perfecta*, in a treatise published in 1600 and pointedly titled *L'Artusi, overo Delle imperfettioni della moderna musica* (Artusi's Book Concerning the Imperfections of Modern Music). Like most treatises of this period, it is in dialogue form. Artusi puts his criticisms in the mouth of a wise old monk, Signor Vario, to whom the other character, Signor Luca, has brought the unnamed Monteverdi's latest work. "It pleases me, at my age," says Signor Vario, "to see a new method of composing, though it should please me much more if I saw that these passages were founded upon some reason which could satisfy the intellect. But as castles in the air, chimeras founded upon sand, these novelties do not please me; they deserve blame, not praise."[11]

Artusi proceeds to give seven little extracts from *Cruda Amarilli*, each containing some offense against the rules of proper counterpoint as laid down by Zarlino. The most famous infraction is the first, a skip in the most exposed voice, the soprano, from an A that enters as a dissonance against the bass G to an F that is also a dissonance: two sins at a single stroke (Ex. 6-6). What Artusi left out of his discussion, however, is the very thing that motivated the trespasses and that alone can explain them—namely, the text. This testifies either to a devious strategy on the author's part or, more likely, to his inability to comprehend the literary basis of the new style or admit that musical procedures could legitimately rest on textual rather than musical grounds. In advancing such a selectively chosen position he has had successors in every subsequent century, right up to the present. Ignoring the implications of words and dramatic situation has long been a fault of purists who would deny music's fruitful merging with other arts.

Example 6-6 **Claudio Monteverdi, *Cruda Amarilli*, mm. 9–14, encompassing the first of Artusi's "spots"**

[Cruel Amaryllis,] who, even with your name,
teach, alas!, [to love bitterly].

What proved so stimulating to the musical imagination was the new "affective" style in which the poet cast his "pathetic" monologues, that is, the monologues depicting the sentiments of suffering lovers, expressed not only in words but in sighs and tearful exclamations like *ohimè!* ("oh me") and *ahi lasso!* ("ah, weary me," whence "alas")—the very phrase to which Monteverdi's main "transgression" was set. Thus composers were encouraged to develop an "affective" style of their own, analogizing the one that was being developed in literature. The remarkable thing is the way the new musical style came into its own just as—or even because—the poetry was becoming less "articulate" in its eloquence, more given over to elemental plaintive sounds, rhetorical "music." The two arts seemed to be converging, meeting in the middle, each giving something up (stylistic perfection, exalted diction), each gaining something else (heightened expressivity). Out of that nexus a momentous style transformation was bound to occur.

The ultimate madrigalian stage was reached by Carlo Gesualdo (1560–1613), the Prince of Venosa, near Naples in southern Italy. Gesualdo was a colorful figure, himself a nobleman in no need of patronage and with a biography rich in lurid anecdote as only a nobleman's could be. His reputation derives equal notoriety from his having ordered the murder of his unfaithful first wife and from his astonishing musical compositions. It would be the wiser course, perhaps, to resist the temptation to link the two sides of his fame, but there is no gainsaying his music's lurid aspect, reported in his day as being an art "full of attitudes."[12]

Anthology Vol 1-63
Full CD II, 5
Concise CD I, 66

Gesualdo brought to its peak the tradition of chromatic artifice initiated fifty years earlier by Lasso, and he applied it to the new, supercharged vein of erotic love poetry, as in *Moro, lasso* ("I shall die, O miserable me"), which comes from his sixth and last book, published in 1611. Gesualdo's harmonic progressions, more fully saturated than any predecessor's with true chromatic voice leading, often in two, sometimes even three voices at once, has frequently been compared with much later music. Those inclined to make such comparisons—such as Igor Stravinsky, who became fascinated with Gesualdo in the 1950s and even orchestrated three of his madrigals—are also inclined to look on Gesualdo as a "prophetic" composer, someone so far ahead of his time that it took two and a half centuries for the rest of the world to catch up with him. The later understanding of Gesualdo was motivated, however, by new interests and a different intellectual climate, and the passage of years or centuries irrevocably altered the context in which he was perceived.

Music for the Eyes

The great popularity of madrigals point to a music that was largely social, a kind of vocal chamber music intended more to delight those singing than to entertain people listening. Part of the fun, of course, was discovering the ingenious ways composers had devised for the music to reflect the meaning of the words. Some of what composers did was not (or not only) an audible effect but, instead, a visual one—or, rather, a literary pun based on the visual appearance of the notated music. The Germans have a word for this sort of thing: ***Augenmusik***, meaning "eye music." It may seem a trivial variety of madrigalism, but it carries an important cultural message. Composers who indulge in Augenmusik give clear evidence of regarding the notation as being a part of the music along with performance. The music becomes indelibly associated with its written embodiment, yet another repercussion of the rise of print culture in the sixteenth century. Musicians who think this way have come to regard music as being a primarily literate, secondarily oral medium rather than the other way around.

Augenmusik is also intimately connected with issues of musical symbolism and hidden meaning. Sometimes aural and visual madrigalisms are connected. When a composer sets the Italian word *onde* (wave) with a wavelike musical passage, the effect is both seen and heard. Marenzio, a composer particularly given to eye music, does this in his madrigal *Già torna a rallegrar l'aria e la terra* ("Now turneth to former joys"). But more often there is no direct relation between sight and sound. By making use of certain notational conventions, a composer could convey meanings of which only he and the performers would be aware. One example is the use of notational coloration—white and black notes—to express a text, for example, about night and day, or coloring all the notes black in a lament or funeral piece. Other instances in Marenzio's madrigals indicate objects, as in a depiction of a string of five pearls (*di cinque perle*) by use of a string of five whole notes in *O bella man che mi distringi il core* (Ex. 6-7). Also popular among madrigalists was setting the word *occhi*—"eyes"—as two whole notes on the same pitch side by side, each representing an eye. In these cases the device is a delightful visual pun—eyes that only the eyes of the performer will see (Ex. 6-8).

Example 6-7 Luca Marenzio, *O bella man che mi distringi il core*

Example 6-8 Luca Marenzio, *Occhi sereni e chiari*

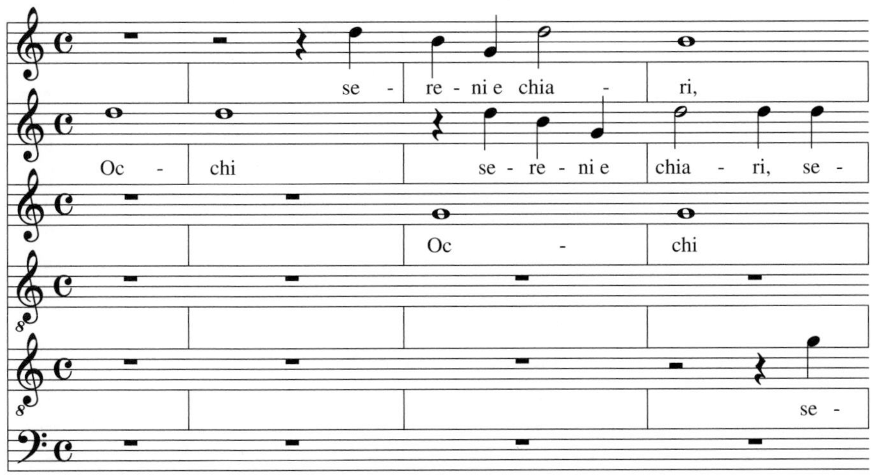

Back over the Mountains: The English Madrigal

Both the music-printing business and the cultivation of vernacular art music had a relatively slow start in England. William Byrd, who with Thomas Tallis received monopoly rights on music printing, turned out to be an ineffectual businessman. Some music circulated in manuscript during the sixteenth century, but little of the English song literature was set for vocal ensembles as on the continent. It consisted, rather, of instrumentally accompanied solo "ayres," either with "consorts" of viols (bowed string instruments) or alternatively with lute. The accompaniments were often contrapuntally intricate, the texts melancholy, the music respectful of the structure of the poem in a way that the madrigal was not.

The most important late-sixteenth-century composer of English verse settings untouched by madrigalian influence was the lutenist John Dowland (1563–1626), like Byrd a recusant Catholic. A supreme virtuoso of his instrument, Dowland could write for it in a very strict contrapuntal style, which made it easy for him to arrange his lute ayres for publication as vocal ensembles after the madrigal had caught on in England. But much of his work belongs to the earlier tradition, a tradition that goes back to the strophic dance song. Most of Dowland's ayres are cast in the form of one of the two main ballroom dances of the time: the stately duple-metered *pavan* and the lively triple-metered *galliard*. The most famous of all pavans, Dowland's song *Flow My Tears* (1600), is a model of English musical prosody (Ex. 6-9).

Example 6-9 John Dowland, "Flow My Tears," first strain

The musical situation in Elizabethan England changed rather abruptly in 1588, the year of the great sea battle with the Spanish Armada, hence a year usually associated in English history with victory and conquest. In music it went the other way. It was the English who were conquered by the Italians. As translator, as arranger, as monopolistic publisher, and as literary propagandist, Thomas Morley (1557–1602) deserves most of the credit for the English craze for Italian music that flared up after the publication of the first volume of *Musica transalpina* in 1588. This was a large anthology of fifty-seven mainly Italian madrigals for four, five, and six voices, with their texts translated into English by a London music lover named Nicholas Yonge. Yonge had long made it a hobby to sing Italian madrigals in his home and to translate their texts for his friends, knowing that so literary a genre as the madrigal will only be sung "with little delight" by those ignorant of the language.

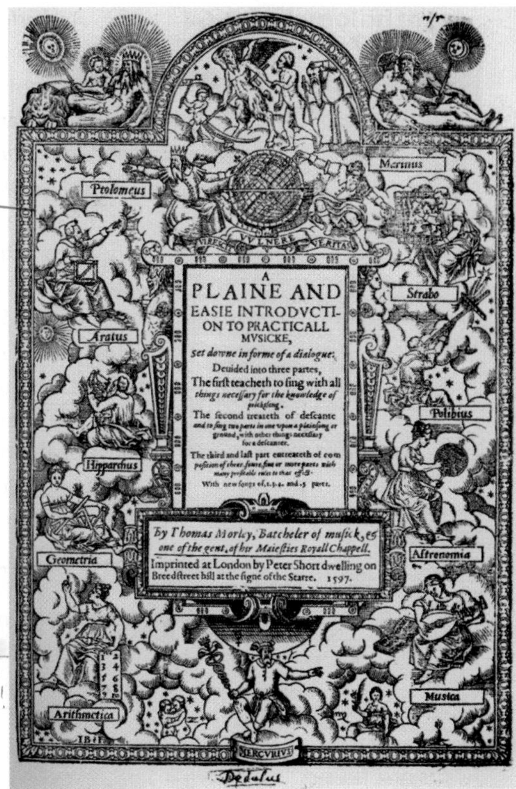
A PLAINE AND EASIE INTRODVCTION TO PRACTICALL MVSICKE, Set downe in forme of a dialogue: Deuided into three partes, The first teacheth to sing with all things necessary for the knowledge of pricksong. The second treateth of descante and to sing two parts in one upon a plainsong or ground, with other things necessary for a descanter. The third and last part entreateth of composition of three, foure, fiue or more parts with many profitable rules to that effect. With new songs of .2.3.4. and .5 parts.

By Thomas Morley, Batcheler of musick, & one of the gent. of her Maiesties Royall Chappell.

Imprinted at London by Peter Short dwelling on Breedstreet hill at the signe of the Starre. 1597.

Figure 6-12 Thomas Morley's book *A Plaine and Easie Introduction to Practicall Musicke,* facsimile of original frontispiece (London, 1597).

Yonge's bestseller was followed two years later by poet Thomas Watson's *The First Sett of Italian Madrigalls Englished,* containing mainly works by Marenzio. Next it was Morley's turn to make a killing. Aiming for the widest possible appeal, he concentrated at first on the lighter Italian genres that had descended from dance songs: the *canzonet* (little homorhythmic song), the *ballet* (little dance), and the like (Fig. 6-12), based most directly on works by Giovanni Gastoldi (d. 1622). These are the genres that have the *fa-la-la* nonsense refrains, which parody solmization syllables and have become firmly associated with English madrigals as commonly defined. Their continued popularity among glee clubs and singing groups goes all the way back to Morley's popularizing efforts.

Once Morley got the commercial ball rolling, there was no stopping it, or so it seemed. Between the mid-1590s, when he began, and the early 1620s, when Thomas Tomkins (1572–1656) published his last madrigal book, about fifty prints containing madrigals were issued, by almost as many composers, some of whom were remarkable musicians indeed. Emblematic of the whole movement was a collection Morley published in 1601: *The Triumphes of Oriana,* consisting of madrigals by some two dozen composers, all in praise of Queen Elizabeth and all ending with a common refrain, "Long live fair Oriana." Thus nationalism, public relations, and entrepreneurship conjoined to turn the century's most quintessentially Italian musical genre, or at least a lightened variant of it, into a genre the English accepted as their own.

Among the most eminent English madrigalists were the three W's: John Ward (1571–1638), John Wilbye (1574–1638), and Thomas Weelkes (1576–1623). They combined the kind of musico-literary imagination that marked the best of the Italian madrigalists with outstanding contrapuntal techniques, making them absolutely the last composers whose work exemplified the sixteenth-century polyphonic style as a living, rather than an embalmed, tradition. Compared to the Italians, the English madrigalists deliberately curbed emotional intensity and avoided any but jocular references to sex. In other words, what had fueled the most powerful moments in the most serious Italian madrigals and in particular provided the impetus for the most extreme chromatic experiments was politely relegated in England to a lighter vein. While the Italians capitalized on the great poetic heritage of Petrarch and Dante and on contemporary writers such as Torquato Tasso (1544–95) and Giovanni Battista Guarini (1538–1612), the English tended to set more trivial texts and have more silly fun with them.

Anthology Vol 1-64
Full CD II, 6
Concise CD I, 67

As Vesta Was from Latmos Hill Descending, Weelkes's delightful contribution to *The Triumphes of Oriana* honoring Elizabeth I, displays an abundance of playful madrigalisms. In his score for six unaccompanied voices, the composer revels in every conceivable chance to have the music illustrate the text. The words "descending" and "ascending" are predictably set to scales going down and up. The idea of everyone "running down" evokes more complex descending passages in imitation. When the "company" assembles, first "two by two," there are just two voices, to which another is added for "three by three," until all six parts sound "together" in a homorhythmic exclamation before Vesta (the goddess of hearth and home) is left "all alone" to the highest soprano. Such "word painting" continues to the end of the piece, with the shouts of "Long live fair Oriana" (here the bass sustains long notes—another musical pun).

If at times, especially in its English realizations, the madrigal seems more amusing than significant, a minor genre, its attention to language and to the music/text relationship was nevertheless momentous. This development led to a new dramatic element—music making a spectacle of itself—subsuming all the novel expressive resources cultivated by the madrigalists, the new mixtures of vocal and instrumental forces in the concertato style, and the new craving for *mimesis* (realistic representation) inspired by the humanist movement. The dramatic sensibility was the great conceptual innovation—the "paradigm shift," as historians of science would later call it—lurking behind all the shocking stylistic novelties that doomed the *ars perfecta* and gave rise to that aggressively exteriorized style conventionally deemed Baroque.

Summary

Changes in musical style in the later sixteenth century came from many directions, including the Protestant Reformation and the Catholic response to it, known as the Counter-Reformation. Some Protestant reformers turned away from complex polyphony, preferring simpler styles of music that allowed for congregational singing. Despite Martin Luther's (1483–1546) admiration for the *ars perfecta,* the Lutheran service music he recommended took the form of chorales, strophic unison hymns derived from Gregorian chant or popular song, which were later harmonized. Chorales formed the basis for polyphonic settings like those of Johann Walther in his *Geystliches gesangk Buchleyn* (Little Sacred Songbook, 1524). Music associated with the more radical reforms of John Calvin (1504–64) consisted of versified translations of the psalms, such as the Geneva Psalter (1543), sung to popular tunes.

Moving in a different direction, some Catholic church music took on a more sensuous and inspirational quality, evident in the increasing number of compositions for multiple choirs, or *cori spezzati.* Polychoral music flourished especially at St. Mark's in Venice. There Andrea Gabrieli (ca. 1532–85) and his nephew Giovanni Gabrieli (ca. 1554/57–1612) wrote works in "concerted," or *concertato,* style, featuring alternation between different combinations of voices and instruments. In their emphasis on short-range contrast rather than long-range continuity, these pieces differed greatly from the *ars perfecta.* The instruments were often specified, marking the beginning of the art of orchestration, as in Giovanni Gabrieli's *In ecclesiis benedicite Domino* ("Bless the Lord in the Churches"). Another element of the new style was the presence of a *basso continuo,* an independent organ part written with one line but with shorthand instructions for realizing the full harmony.

Popular genres in vernacular languages flourished in the sixteenth century. Fueled in part by the proliferation of music publishing, these works were intended for domestic use. The *frottola,* based on an oral tradition of self-accompanied solo song, was a syllabic and homophonic work produced by Italian composers such as Marco Cara (ca. 1465–1525). While the chansons of Claudin de Sermisy (ca. 1490–1562) provided a French equivalent to the frottola, those of Clément Janequin (1485–1558) consisted of colorful onomatopoeia that evoked sounds of battles, hunting, and birdsong (e.g., *La guerre* ["The war"]). Later, the Franco-Flemish composer Orlando di Lasso (1532–94) mastered not just the Parisian chanson and low-style songs in German and Italian, but also sacred works in the *ars perfecta* style.

The sixteenth-century madrigal marked a turn toward a more literary kind of music, influenced by the "Petrarchan movement" in poetry. In their imitations of the fourteenth-century Italian scholar and writer Petrarch, poets focused on the principle of contrasting styles and emotions. Madrigal composers such as Jacques Arcadelt (d. 1568) likewise depicted the meaning of the text with contrasts between high and low registers, consonance and dissonance, imitation and homophony, and diatonic and chromatic passages. Middle- and late-period madrigalists such as Cipriano de Rore (1516–65), Luca Marenzio (1553–99), and Claudio Monteverdi (1567–1643) developed a radically new style contrary to the *ars perfecta,* depicting the text in the most literal way (called "madrigalism" or "word painting") and using these depictions as justification for breaking conventional rules of counterpoint and dissonance treatment. Beginning with the collection *Musica transalpina* (1588), the Italian madrigal was imported into England, inspiring English madrigalists such as Thomas Morley (1557–1602), John Wilbye (1574–1638), and Thomas Weelkes (1576–1623).

Study Questions

1. Explain the impact of the Protestant Reformation on sacred music. What were the underlying theological reasons that many reformers preferred congregational hymns and chorales to complex polyphony?
2. What features characterized the music of the Counter-Reformation in the decades following the Council of Trent? Considering the events discussed in this chapter and in Chapter 5, describe how the history of music was shaped by the religious divisions of the sixteenth century.
3. Contrast Giovanni Gabrieli's *In ecclesiis* with a typical work in the *ars perfecta* style, such as Josquin's *Ave Maria . . . virgo serena* (Chapter 5). How does Gabrieli's work differ from these works in terms of musical conception, instrumentation, compositional technique, and demands made on performers?
4. Discuss music publishing and the resulting consumer culture of music. Who were the primary musical publishers in the sixteenth century? How did they impact the production and consumption of music?
5. Describe the new genres of popular music in Italy and France during the sixteenth century. What are their salient traits, and how are they reflected in the works of Marco Cara, Claudin de Sermisy, and Clément Janequin?

6. In what ways was Orlando di Lasso a cosmopolitan composer? How is this reflected in the different types of music he composed?
7. What was the Petrarchan movement? How is it tied to the origins of the madrigal?
8. What were the central features of the Italian madrigal? How do the works of Jacques Arcadelt and Cipriano de Rore reflect new relationships between music and text?
9. In what ways did the madrigals of Luca Marenzio, Claudio Monteverdi, and Carlo Gesualdo violate the norms of *ars perfecta*?
10. What criticisms were leveled against the new style by the critic Giovanni Maria Artusi? How do Monteverdi and Artusi represent contrasting musical values, and how are similar debates played out in our own time?
11. How did the Italian madrigal change as it was imported into England?

Key Terms

Augenmusik
basso continuo
chanson
chorale
Chorale prelude
concertato style
Counter-Reformation
frottola
madrigal
madrigalism
Protestant Reformation
ritornello
Tenorlied

7

Humanism and the Birth of Opera

The central irony of the Renaissance, as the term is traditionally applied to music, is the way in which the Greek revivalism that motivated the "rebirth" of the other arts and of philosophy actually undermined the dominant Renaissance musical style, the *ars perfecta*. At a time, for example, when fifteenth-century thought, literature, and architecture had found a source of renewal in Greek antiquity, music was much less affected, remaining principally beholden to the perfected art that came to be exemplified by Josquin. The influence of the Greek past on music emerged later, when the Renaissance in the other arts was already old news. The word **"Baroque"** was apparently first applied to a musical composition (Jean-Philippe Rameau's opera *Hippolyte et Aricie*) in 1734, as an insult. A generation later, in his *Dictionnaire de musique* (1768), French philosopher Jean-Jacques Rousseau asserted that "a baroque music is that in which the harmony is confused, charged with modulations and dissonances, the melody is harsh and little natural, the intonation difficult, and the movement constrained."[1] *Baroque* eventually became another of the handy labels historians used, in this case to encompass the music of the period from roughly around 1600 to 1750, that is, from the time of the first operas to the death of J. S. Bach. A principal use of the word today seems to be as a commercial logo for a brand of classical music that record companies and radio stations market as sonic wallpaper.

So what shall we call the music conventionally called Baroque—the repertory that arose in Italy at the end of the sixteenth century and died out in Germany some time in the middle third of the eighteenth? We could simply call this the Italian age, since most of the musical innovations during that time took place in Italy and radiated out to other parts of Europe. There were pockets of resistance, to be sure, but conscious resistance is an acknowledgment of dominion.

TIMELINE

1573 **Girolamo Mei completes *On the Musical Modes of the Ancients***

1586 El Greco, *The Burial of Count Orgaz*

1589 Princess Christine of Lorraine marries the Grand Duke Ferdinando de' Medici of Tuscany

1597–98 **Jacopo Peri's *La Dafne* performed in Florence**

1600 Henry IV of France marries Marie de' Medici

1600 **Emilio de' Cavalieri, *Rappresentatione di Anima et di Corpo***

1601 **Peri, *Euridice,* and Giulio Caccini, *Euridice***

1601 William Shakespeare, *Hamlet*

1602 **Caccini, *Le nuove musiche***

1605 Miguel de Cervantes, *Don Quixote*

1607 **Claudio Monteverdi, *L'Orfeo***

1607 Jamestown, Virginia, becomes first permanent English colony in the New World

1611 Publication of King James Version of the Bible

1613 **Monteverdi moves to Venice**

If politics defines an age, then this was one of Absolutism, when a commanding figure such as the French King Louis XIV (1638–1715) ruled with an absolute authority that had a powerful effect on the arts. If we want to emphasize scientific and philosophical thought, we could call this the *Galilean period,* after Galileo Galilei (1564–1642), the great astronomer and pioneering experimental scientist. Along with the discoveries of Nicolaus Copernicus (1473–1543), Johannes Kepler (1571–1630), and, later, Sir Isaac Newton (1642–1727), the view of the place of the earth in the grand scheme of the universe fundamentally changed. Secular thought and art reached decisive ascendancy in the West, which gives the story of Galileo's persecution by the Roman Inquisition in the 1630s mythic stature. We might do even better to call it the *Cartesian period,* after René Descartes (1596–1650), the philosophical founder of empirical science, whose extreme mind/matter dualism made possible the idea of objective knowledge and representation. A great deal of seventeenth- and early-eighteenth-century music seeks to represent objects, including objectified emotions, rationally, systematically, and accurately and to formulate rules for doing so. We should note here an important word, one that already cropped up in the previous chapter: "affection." Representing, evoking, and moving the "affections," particular expressive and emotional states, emerged as primary concerns in music.

If we want to spotlight genre, we could call this period the *theatrical age.* Music theater as we know it today was born at the turn of the seventeenth century, precisely under the influence of the neoclassical revival. But we could just as well call it the *instrumental age,* for large, purely instrumental forms were also an innovation of the seventeenth century. It was a great time of instrumental virtuosity—which is to say, instrumental music made theatrical—but both music theater and instrumental music, not to mention virtuosity, are very much still with us and therefore not uniquely defining characteristics of this era.

If we want to keep the emphasis on musical technique, then the obvious name for the period—and perhaps the best one—would be the *continuo age.* The basso continuo as a virtually obligatory aspect of any musical performance that was not a keyboard solo originated around the turn of the seventeenth century, as we learned in the previous chapter, and it died out before the end of the eighteenth. Clearly the presence of the basso continuo as a constant factor throughout this period, and its failure to survive, in some sense defines the period. And that sense has to do with harmony itself, reconceived and newly emphasized as a driving force in music. It was the development of harmony as an independent shaping factor and its deployment over larger and larger temporal spans that made possible the development of abstract musical forms.

In short, there are many ways to characterize the period conveniently known as the Baroque. But what were the connections among the ideological, the aesthetic, and the technical? Were there affinities binding the neoclassical impulse, the theatrical impulse, and the rise of the continuo? In fact there were, and to locate them we must turn our attention to the Florentine academies of the late sixteenth century and to the writings of a remarkable scholar, Girolamo Mei (1519–94).

The Pressure of Humanism

The original ancient Greek Academy was founded by Plato early in the fourth century BCE. The revival of the term "academy" in the late fifteenth century to designate an association of artists and thinkers was one of the most self-conscious, programmatic acts of the humanist rebirth of learning. This began with the Accademia Platonica, an informal circle led by a noted humanist, Marsilio Ficino, that met at the palace of Lorenzo de Medici in Florence during the 1470s and '80s. The Medici family, which dominated Florentine politics and culture for more than three centuries, emerged as the dominant patrons of music.

During the sixteenth century, *Accademie*—literary and artistic circles supported by noble patronage—flourished in many Italian cities, but Florence remained the center. The most prestigious one, the Accademia degli Umidi (Academy of the Wet Ones), later the Accademia Fiorentina, was founded in 1540. Mei, at age twenty-one the youngest charter member of this group, initially wrote treatises devoted to Italian literature before turning to Greek music as his main subject. In 1573 he completed a four-volume treatise entitled *De modis musicis antiquorum* (On the Musical Modes of the Ancients). This scholarly dissertation, which draws on classical writers and also summarizes modern mode theory, deals both with the tuning and structure of the modes and with their expressive and ethical effects.

Mei concludes with a discussion, influenced strongly by Aristotle, on the uses of the modes in education, therapy, poetry, and drama. In ancient times, he asserted, poems and plays were always sung—and always monophonically, whether by soloists or by the chorus, whether unaccompanied or doubled by instruments. For all its wealth of information, however, Mei's treatise provides no actual examples of Greek music beyond the late Delphic hymns mentioned in Chapter 1. Mei thus presents everything anyone might have wanted to know about Greek music except an idea of what it actually sounded like. And that, paradoxically, is exactly why his treatise became an important influence on the course of contemporary music. There was no musical evidence to contradict Mei's impressive assertions about what Greek music could do and why the music of his own day could no longer equal its effects.

1616 Death of Shakespeare
1618 **Death of Caccini**
1622 Peter Paul Rubens, *The Medici Cycle*
1633 **Death of Peri**
1633 **Inquisition tries Galileo Galilei for his theory that the earth revolves around the sun**
1637 René Descartes, *Discourse on Method*
1637 **Teatro San Cassiano opens in Venice**
1638 **Monteverdi, *Madrigali guerrieri et amorosi***
1642 **Monteverdi, *L'incoronazione di Poppea***
1643 **Death of Monteverdi**

Even if Mei did not know what Greek music sounded like, he knew (or thought he knew) what it did *not* sound like. It was not full of counterpoint, in which many simultaneous melodies "convey to the soul of the listener at the same time diverse and contrary affections."[2] It was partly because their music was monophonic, Mei believed, that the ancient Greeks were able to achieve miracles of *ethos*, or moral influence through music. He looked with some envy at the power, artistic as well as ethical, that Greek music was said to have possessed and sought in vain to find its contemporary equivalent amid the contrapuntal complexities of the *ars perfecta*. Mei argued that it would be necessary to go back to monophonic basics for a neoclassical revival.

The revival of the term "academy" in the late fifteenth century to designate an association of artists and thinkers was one of the most self-conscious, programmatic acts of the humanist rebirth of learning.

Mei's researches became familiar to a group of Florentine humanists known as the **Camerata**. In the 1570s and '80s they met at the home of Count Giovanni de' Bardi, a favorite courtier of Grand Duke Francesco I of Tuscany, for whom Mei had the job of organizing court entertainments, often including musical spectacles. It was in this latter capacity that Bardi became interested in theatrical music and began to correspond with Mei about the music of the Greek tragedies and comedies. Bardi also put Mei in touch with Vincenzo Galilei (late 1520s–1591), a lutenist-singer, the best-trained musician in his inner circle, and father of the scientist Galileo. Galilei had already published a treatise on arranging polyphonic music for solo voice accompanied by lute and had begun a gloss on his teacher Zarlino's *Le istitutioni harmoniche,* supplemented with information on

Figure 7-1 Title page of Vincenzo Galilei's *Dialogo della musica antica et della moderna* (Florence, 1581).

ancient music theory as it was being disseminated among humanists. Mei's research had revealed the differences between the ancient system of modes and tunings and the modern, thus contradicting Zarlino's assertion that the one had grown directly out of the other.

Galilei's challenge to the historical legitimacy of the *ars perfecta* estranged him from his former teacher. It became his mission to effect a true reconciliation of ancient theory and modern practice. This Galilei never achieved; indeed such a thing was scarcely achievable. But his communications with Mei won him over to the view that the *ars perfecta*, far from the ultimate perfection of music, was a frivolous deviation from the true meaning and purpose of music as practiced by the ancients. He further came to believe that the only way of restoring to music the ethical and expressive powers of which the ancients wrote would be to strip away the purely sensuous adornments of counterpoint and return to an art truly founded on the imitation of nature. Galilei cast this inflammatory thesis into the suitably Platonic form of a dialogue: the *Dialogo della musica antica et della moderna* (Dialogue on Music Ancient and Modern; Fig. 7-1), published in 1581. His scientist son would adopt a similar strategy with his groundbreaking *Dialogo sopra i due massimi sistemi del mondo* (Dialogue Concerning the Two Chief World Systems, 1632), which opposed the older geocentric Ptolemaic system with the new Copernican system, in which the earth and the other planets orbit around the sun.

Vincenzo Galilei reserved his strongest invective for the madrigalists. Although he had himself published a book of madrigals seven years earlier (and would another six years later), he rejected the madrigalists' claim that they were already the humanist reformers of music, imitating nature in their works. He condemned the trivial word games he believed they played in their pieces. Galilei had a certain point in ridiculing "madrigalisms," which are indirect and artificial imitations. They are like plays on words, puns, and wit. We often react to a madrigalism, even a serious one, the way we do to a joke: We are satisfied when we "get it." Galilei sneered:

> Our practicing contrapuntists [will say] that they have imitated the words, each time they set to music a sonnet, a madrigal, or other poem in which one finds verses that say, for example, "Bitter heart and fierce, cruel desire," which happens to be the first line of one of Petrarch's sonnets, and they see to it that between the parts that sing it are many sevenths, fourths, seconds, and major sixths, and that by means of these they have made a rough, bitter, grating sound in their listeners' ears. Another time they will say they have imitated the words when among the ideas in the text are some that have the meaning "to flee," or "to fly." These will be declaimed with such speed and so little grace as can hardly be imagined. As for words like "to vanish," "to swoon," "to die," they will make the parts fall silent so abruptly that far from inducing any such effect, they will move their listeners to laughter, or else to indignation, should they feel they are being mocked. . . . Finding words denoting contrasts of color, like "dark" versus "light hair," and the like, they will set them to black and white notes, respectively, to express their meaning most astutely and cleverly, they say; never mind that they have altogether subordinated

the sense of hearing to accidents of form and color which are properly the domain of vision and touch. Another time, they will have a verse like this: "He descended into Hell, into the lap of Pluto," and they will make one of the parts descend so that the singer sounds to the listener more like someone moaning to frighten and terrify little girls than like someone singing something sensible. And where they find the opposite—"He doth aspire to the stars"—they will have it declaimed in such a high register that no one screaming in pain has ever equaled it.

Unhappy men, they do not realize that if any of the famous orators of old had ever once declaimed two words in such a fashion they would have moved their hearers to laughter and contempt at once, and would have been ridiculed and despised by them as stupid, abject, and worthless men.[3]

The Representational Style

The question is: Are there any real structural correspondences between music and nature? There is one, Galilei contended, if by *nature* we mean human nature, and that is speech. Plato himself had accounted for the *ethos* of the modes—their ability to influence the soul—for the same reason. For Galilei what mattered was not just the literal meaning of words but also the intonation, pitch, tone of voice, and every other aspect of speech that also communicates. These features are the so-called paralexical ones, and sometimes, as in instances of contradiction or irony, they are to be trusted over semantics, the overt meaning.

Following Plato, Galilei argued that music could be an art of persuasion. He suggested that when musicians go to the theater they should "observe in what manner the actors speak, in what range, high or low, how loudly or softly, how rapidly or slowly they enunciate their words, when one gentleman converses quietly with another." Such observations should extend to considering human speech in the rest of everyday life. He counsels musicians to pay close attention to the way that a gentleman addresses his servants, a prince his subjects, to how lovers speak with one another and how people inflect their voices when they are happy, sad, frightened, and so forth: "From these diverse observations, if they are carried out attentively and considered with care, one can deduce the way that best suits the expression of whatever meanings or emotion may come to hand."[4]

What musicians stood to gain, in Galilei's opinion, was a true ***stile rappresentativo***: a "representational style." Such a thing was not unknown to the madrigalists. We have already observed some pretty accurate imitation of speech in the middle section of Cipriano de Rore's *Da le belle contrade d'oriente* (see Ex. 6-5). But even in the most rigorously representational polyphonic setting, there is a fundamental contradiction between the singleness of the expressive poetic text and the multiplicity of actual singing voices. The solution Galilei proposed was a return not to literal monophony but to what he called *monodia*, or **"monody"**—namely, a single voice accompanied by the lute, likened in this context to Apollo's lyre. In this way expressive harmony could be retained without violating the demands of representation.

Thus what had long been just one performance option among many, one rarely committed to writing, now became a high cause. The vocal style advocated was new, in that, even more than the polyphonic madrigal's, it took its bearings from actual, enacted, enunciated speech rather than from the formal arrangements of verse. Galilei made a setting of some verses from Dante's *Inferno* and performed them for Bardi's Camerata as a demonstration of the new monodic style. Neither these nor any other monodic compositions by Galilei have survived, however; the kind of music Galilei imagined on the basis of Mei's research can only be inferred from the work of others.

Intermedii

One early practical demonstration of the new humanist aesthetic came in 1589, when Count Bardi was asked to organize the entertainment for the wedding between Princess Christine of Lorraine and Grand Duke Ferdinando de' Medici of Tuscany, the younger brother and successor (some say the murderer) of Bardi's original patron, Francesco I (Fig. 7-2). Seizing the opportunity, he put his friends to work on a colossally extravagant set of ***intermedii***, allegorical pageants with music to be performed between the acts of a spoken comedy, *La pellegrina* (The Pilgrim Girl).

Such added entertainments were a central Italian theatrical specialty. Their original purpose was utilitarian and the music correspondingly modest. Since the curtain was not lowered at performances, divisions of the play were signaled by musical interludes, often instrumental ones played from the wings. Particularly in Florence and especially at court celebrations, the *intermedii* became increasingly lavish and costly, meant to impress invited guests. Their height was reached at Medici family weddings, each successive one striving to outdo the last. The music for the first

Figure 7-2 Ventura Salimbeni, *Wedding of Ferdinando de' Medici and Christine of Lorraine* (1589). This was an occasion for which members of the Florentine Camerata devised their *intermedii*.

of the occasions, in 1518, no longer exists, but it does for the wedding of Cosimo I in 1539. Only a very small fraction of *intermedio* music has survived from the next fifty years, although souvenir books contain extensive descriptions of the action, sets, and costumes and their allegorical significance, from which we can get an idea of the imposing scale on which the musical entertainments were cast.

Ferdinando's wedding in 1589 was the most lavish of the Medici extravaganzas. Texts for some of the six *intermedii* were by the famous poet Ottavio Rinuccini (1562–1621), and the staging was by Emilio de' Cavalieri (ca. 1550–1602), who had been director of music for Ferdinando during the latter's years as a cardinal in Rome. The big concerted numbers—for up to thirty voices in seven choirs, often fitted out with instrumental ritornellos—were mainly the work of the great madrigalist Luca Marenzio and of Cristofano Malvezzi, the organist of the Medici chapel.

Figure 7-3 Jacopo Peri as Arion, singing his own compositions in the fifth intermedio of 1589 (costume design by Bernardo Buontalenti).

Bardi also worked in a few numbers by his younger friends, musicians who frequented the meetings of his Camerata. Giulio Caccini (1551–1618), a well-established singer at the Medici court, later claimed that he learned more from the "savant speeches" of the poets and philosophers who met at Bardi's "than I had in over thirty years' study of counterpoint."[5] Jacopo Peri (1561–1633), technically an aristocratic dilettante but a highly accomplished musician, sang his own pieces, accompanying himself on a specially constructed type of lute called a *chitarrone*, after the Greek *kithara*, or lyre (Fig. 7-3).

The Monodic Revolution

The arias by Caccini and Peri are evidence of a blossoming of monody usually dated a decade later, around 1600. What actually happened at the turn of the century was no sudden musical revolution but, rather, the emergence into print of musical practices that had been in the process of formation for some decades in genres like the frottola. These practices had been given an additional impetus by the recent humanist revival, with all its attendant neoclassical theorizing, and by the backing of prestigious patrons. They now made their print debuts in four noteworthy releases.

First to appear was Cavalieri's *Rappresentatione di Anima, et di Corpo* (The Representation of Soul and Body), a sacred play designed, according to the title page, *per recitar cantando*, "for recitation in singing," or, more literally, "to recite singingly" (Fig. 7-4). It was first performed in Rome at the Oratorio di Santa Maria in Vallicella. We should note the name of the venue, for it eventually named a genre—the oratorio. Cavalieri's sacred play was produced in February 1600, fully staged, which tended not to happen with later oratorios. The Soul (a soprano) and the Body (a tenor), each with teams of allegorical supporters, advisers, and tempters, struggle

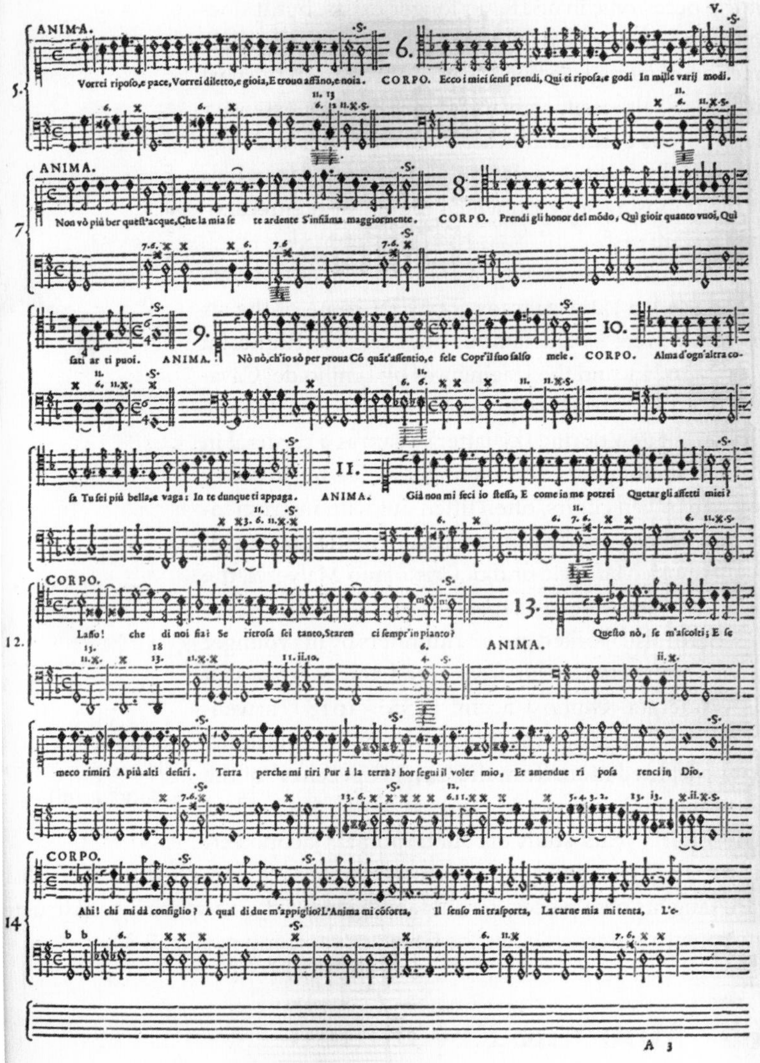

Figure 7-4 Dialogue of Body (Corpo) and Soul (Anima) over a figured bass (the first to be printed), in Emilio de' Cavalieri's *Rappresentatione di Anima, et di Corpo* (Rome, 1600).

against the blandishments of worldly delights. They ultimately succeed, and the work ends with spectacular visions of hell and heaven.

While the *Rappresentatione* was not all that different from the Florentine *intermedii*, it was much more modest. In one ongoing dramatic whole rather than half a dozen loosely connected episodes, the solo music consisted of a string of little songs connected by musicalized prose recitations of the sort that would later be called **recitative**. It is notated in score over what was the earliest printed ***figured bass***—that is to say, a continuous bass line in which the harmonies to be filled in by the performer are indicated by little numbers representing intervals. The figures show what pitches in a chord could not be taken for granted.

In early 1601 (or, by the Florentine calendar of the time, late 1600), two different musical settings of the same mythological story were printed. The authors were Peri and Caccini, who had become jealous rivals. The play was a pastoral drama by Rinuccini called *Euridice*, after the myth of Orpheus and Eurydice as told by the ancient Roman poet Ovid in his *Metamorphoses*. The story proved a perfect subject for musical representation, and not only because it was based on a classical myth. Orpheus is the supreme lyric artist, a musician who can move heaven and earth (and enter hell) through the power of his music making. He is a figure who attracted not only the first composers of musical dramas around 1600 but many later ones as well. Although the basic story exists in various versions, at its core is Orpheus winning the lovely Eurydice as his wife but all too soon learning of her death from a snakebite. He descends to the Underworld to plead for her return. The gods allow him to bring her back from the dead, but only on the condition that he not look at or talk to Eurydice until they have returned home safely. When she begs for his attention, however, Orpheus glances back and she dies a second death. Sources and operatic treatments differ considerably as to the ending—there are both tragic and happy versions.

Peri's was the earlier setting. It was performed (with some interpolations by Caccini, at the latter's insistence) on 6 October 1600 at the Palazzo Pitti in Florence as part of the festivities of another Medici marriage, in this instance of Maria de' Medici, daughter of Francesco I, to the King of France, Henri IV. As befits such a happy occasion, all ends well in this version—Euridice is restored to Orpheus without any conditions; there is no second death, no second loss. Peri's version remains within the boundaries of the dramatized *favola pastorale,* the pastoral play, a light genre that did not exist in classical antiquity. The music for both Peri's version and Caccini's (which was only later performed in its entirety) was similar in design to that of Cavalieri's *Rappresentatione,* except that it had far more recitative. Dramatic continuity was given greater emphasis than spectacle.

Early in 1602, Caccini issued a book of solo songs with figured bass called *Le nuove musiche*. That title has been one of the most oversold in all of music history. All it means is "new songs" or "new musical pieces," but it has been invested with a much deeper significance by those who have seen in it the proclamation of a "new music" or the dawn of a new musical epoch. Such propaganda must partly account for the inflation of the volume's reputation, but surely even more critical was its appearance at the turn of a century. The influence of the calendar—or just the decimal system, really—on our sense of history should never be underestimated, as most recently happened with the millennial frenzies of the year 2000. Artists have long made money on such auspicious dates, such as German artist Albrecht Dürer did with a famous apocalyptic series of woodcuts just before 1500 (Fig. 7-5).

Caccini's* Le nuove musiche *means "new songs" or "new musical pieces," but has been invested with a much deeper significance by those who have seen in it the proclamation of a "new music" or the dawn of a new musical epoch.

This cluster of turn-of-the-century publications by Cavalieri, Peri, and Caccini—plus Lodovico Viadana's *Cento concerti ecclesiastici* of 1602, which amounted to "nuove musiche" set to sacred Latin texts—brought the monodic style into the authoritative medium of print. Print spread it far and wide. Adding to this was the prestige of high aristocratic patronage behind the publication of the *Euridice* settings, which now have the reputation of being the first operas, even if the same can been claimed for Cavalieri's oratorio. The wide dissemination in print and the high prestige of patronage meant that performance practices that had been cooking in Italy for many decades could now become standard compositional practices all over Europe.

And that, in fact, was a revolution. It was not, however, a revolution brought about singlehandedly by a determined composer or band of composers. That is how traditional historiography—bourgeois historiography, we should not forget—tends

Figure 7-5 Woodcut by Albrecht Dürer showing the first four seals and the four horsemen of the Apocalypse. Edition of 1498.

to represent and celebrate change. Whether in the arts or elsewhere, change is usually explained in such narratives by the heroic efforts of superior, visionary, revolutionary individuals. In fact, the monodic revolution was the slowly evolving and overlapping work of various performers, arrangers, patrons, churchmen, scholars, teachers, composers, and printers. The only sudden role was that of the printers and that is what made the difference.

Madrigals and Arias Revisited

For a closer look at some of the early printed artifacts of the revolution, the most expedient way to proceed will be not in strictly chronological order but, rather, in order of increasing size and complexity of genre. Caccini's *Le nuove musiche,* which contains songs that may have been composed (or, possibly, first improvised) decades earlier at meetings of the Camerata, amounts to a sort of showcase displaying the basic elements out of which the early continuously musical plays were fashioned. Indeed, it contains bits of Caccini's own larger spectacles, including four arias and two choruses from a musical play after Ovid called *Il rapimento di Cefalo* (The Abduction of Cephalus), which had furnished the main entertainment for the same Medici wedding that witnessed the unveiling of Peri's *Euridice*.

The larger part of *Nuove musiche* is given over to individual songs and to a preface that instructs the singer on the properly aristocratic way of tossing them off—with great artfulness but with what Caccini characterized as *una certa nobile sprezzatura di canto* ("a certain noble nonchalance in song"). His songs are of two basic types, both familiar to us from previous incarnations. A strophic one, based on repetition, is an *aria*, or air. The other kind—in a single stanza that is composed straight through without repeating stanzas—is a madrigal. A madrigal therefore is no longer necessarily a multivoice piece. Any setting of a single stanza in a word-sensitive style that employs no formulaic repetitions or refrains could go by the name. With this fact in mind, we have a new way of understanding the importance Caccini attached to his experimental madrigals. In them he developed a style that, better than any other, could "move the soul's affection," or, as we might put it now, move the listener emotionally.[6] So Caccini himself boasted in the preface, where he says the great discovery had taken place some fifteen years earlier, in the mid-1580s. His claim of priority was hotly disputed by Cavalieri and need not detain us, since Galilei was probably there first anyway. But Caccini's madrigals are indeed the place to look first to see "monody" in action.

Anthology Vol 1-65
Full CD II, 7
Concise CD I, 68

Amarilli mia bella has a text by Alessandro Guarini (ca. 1565–1636), whose father, Giambattista, was one of the finest and most frequently set poets of the late sixteenth century (Ex. 7-1). Caccini's setting was an attempt to show that only monody could really do a madrigal's job. And yet this is a madrigal without obvious pictorial "madrigalisms." There is no rapid scale to show the arrow's flight. There is no thumping throb to show the beating heart. Rather, the concentration is on speech, delivered at something close to normal speech tempo and restricted to something like normal speech range so that the words can be understood. The whole vocal part is confined to a range of a ninth but really an octave, since the high note is reached only once, near the end—an obvious correlation of range with rhetorical emphasis. That rhetorical emphasis is the principal purpose of the song. Everything is correlated with it, including the harmonies specified by the figured bass (Fig. 7-6).

The most obvious rhetorical effect—borrowed from the polyphonic madrigal but vastly augmented—is the textual repetition. Where polyphonic madrigalists liked to repeat the last line or couplet to make the final cadence stick, Caccini repeats the beloved's name four times to conclude. But what is so rhetorical about literal repetition? Such a procedure might diminish rather than enhance expression. And so it certainly would if it really were literal, but it is not. It just looks literal in the score, warning us yet again that music cannot be judged only by the way it is notated. There is still an oral practice to consider, one to which Caccini devoted a lengthy illustrated discussion in the preface to *Le nuove musiche*. What this revealing document introduces, as far as we are concerned, is not a book of songs but the whole practice of rhetorical embellishment, a constant oral factor in almost every musical performance that took place during the seventeenth and eighteenth centuries but one that left little visible trace in the notated musical sources. The four repetitions in *Amarilli mia bella* should sound very different from one another in performance because of the way they are ornamented on the spot by the singer.

Example 7-1 Giulio Caccini, *Amarilli mia bella,* transcription of opening of Figure 7-6, mm. 1–10

Amaryllis, my fair one,
do you not believe, o my
heart's sweet delight,
that you are my love?

In the preface, Caccini, himself a virtuoso singer, divulges his whole bag of singerly tricks, called *gorgia,* or throat music, already a clue to its production. He provides the first systematic survey of the methods by which solo performers were expected to enhance the notes and a chastening reminder of how much is lost from any performing repertoire that survives only in written form. (Just think how much would be missing if all we knew about most jazz and popular music today came from notated sources rather than from recordings and performances.)

Figure 7-6 Giulio Caccini, *Amarilli mia bella* (*Le nuove musiche*, 1601). The opening is transcribed in Example 7-1.

Caccini's rhetorical embellishments included some that divided the written notes in fancy passagework, fast runs, and the like. Others were calculated to imitate, or, rather, to stylize, various tones of voice, or rhetorical "manners of speaking," that give evidence of strong emotion. The very word Caccini chose for one of them—*esclamazione* (exclamation), described as "the foundation of passion"—shows the directness with which the emotions were to be physically portrayed.[7] It consists of a gradual crescendo in the voice, transforming a long note into an outcry, made more artful by first diminishing the volume before beginning the increase—"reversed hairpins," musicians familiar with modern crescendo/decrescendo marks would say.

Caccini then proceeds to describe techniques for mimicking unsteady speech—tremblings and catchings of the throat. The artfully simulated vocal tremble or shake, involving the rapid alternation of contiguous notes of the scale, he calls the *gruppo* (note group), what we would call a trill, starting on the main note. Caccini's *trillo* is something else: It is the increasingly rapid, controlled repetition of a single pitch. Finally, Caccini lists some "graces," ways of modifying a melodic line to heighten the effect of "speaking in harmony" and "neglecting the music," which mainly involve little rhythmic liberties that put the singer "out of sync" with the bass.

Favola in Musica

The style developed by Caccini did not stay long in private chambers but was immediately returned to the theater. The monodist's objective, after all, was to recapture the emotional and ethical power of the ancient Greek poet-musicians, to resurrect Athenian drama as reimagined by Mei. The birth of new music out of the spirit of old drama was, like everything else that seems sudden in history, a gradual thing, with phases unrepresented in written sources and that therefore left few traces. Moreover, the ancients could not provide an actual model, since their music did not survive. "I would not dare affirm this to be the song used in Greek and Roman plays," Peri wrote, although their ideals inspired him to forge a new music that lay between speech and song.[8]

Although there were undoubtedly earlier precedents, the first existing songs that were performed in the course of a stage spectacle were the ones in the 1589 Medici wedding *intermedii* celebrating the dynastic alliance between Florence and Lorraine. In the late fifteenth century we find accounts of musicalized dramatic presentations at the central Italian courts. A *Fabula di Orfeo* (Tale of Orpheus), based on the same mythological story from Ovid's *Metamorphoses* that would form the basis of the earliest published musical plays, was composed by the Medici court poet Angelo Poliziano and performed, at least partly sung, during the carnival season in Mantua over a century earlier. Between the 1589 Florentine *intermedii* that Cavalieri masterminded and his own Roman *Rappresentatione di Anima, et di Corpo* of 1600, he produced a number of sung pastorals in Florence, with texts by the noblewoman poet Laura Guidiccioni (1550 to ca. 1597). According to Peri's generous remark in the Preface to *Euridice*, Cavalieri's pastorals were the first stage works to put the ***stile recitativo*** into practice.

***Cavalieri's pastorals do not survive, just as, apart from a few fragments, we do not know what is often called the first true opera: Peri's* La Dafne.**

But they do not survive, just as, apart from a few fragments, we do not know what is often called the first true opera: *La Dafne*. This tale, also based on Ovid, relates how the nymph Daphne, pursued by the god Apollo, is transformed into a laurel tree. Rinuccini provided the poem and Peri wrote the music, with some advice from Jacopo Corsi, a noble dilettante who supported neoclassical musico-dramatic experimentation. The first performance of *La Dafne* took place, with Peri himself in the role of Apollo, during the Florence carnival season of 1597–98. After several revivals, the libretto was set again in 1608, by Marco da Gagliano (1582–1643), perhaps the consummate Florentine musician of the early seventeenth century. The preface to the published score of Gagliano's version provides most of what we know about the original *La Dafne*, for he acknowledges the novelty of Peri's and Rinuccini's spectacle. This testimony has led to its being accorded the exalted position it now occupies in history as the first opera, in preference to Cavalieri's pastorals or any previous ***favola in musica*** (musical tale), to use Gagliano's expression.

"The pleasure and amazement produced in the audience by this novel spectacle cannot be described," Gagliano reports. "Suffice it to say that each of the many times it was performed it generated the same admiration and the same delight." Then comes a significant remark: "This experiment having taught Signor Rinuccini how well singing was suited to the expression of every sort of affection, and that it not only afforded no tediousness (as many might perchance have presumed) but indeed incredible delight, he composed his *Euridice*, dilating somewhat more in the dialogues."[9] The comment shows increasing emphasis on the dialogue-music, as opposed to the song-and-dance music, and thus greater emphasis on music that imitated speech, as opposed to the music that functioned primarily as musical entertainment.

Operatic Conventions: Heard and Unheard Music

Audiences had to learn to accept such speech-music—the *stile recitativo*—as dramatically viable. To believe in speaking from the stage delivered in song required an imaginative leap that not everyone was prepared to take. Some resist to this very day. Peri himself put the aesthetic problem in a nutshell when he wrote in the preface to the printed edition of *Euridice* of his paradoxical aim "to imitate with singing whoever speaks (and without doubt no one ever spoke singing)."[10]

These early operas begin a line that connects them with us, for **opera** is the first large-scale secular genre we have encountered in this book that has persisted in an apparently unbroken tradition to the present day. As we shall see, however, the apparent continuity may initially be somewhat misleading; and perhaps we should even resist using the word "opera" for a while in favor of calling them "musical tales," as Peri, Caccini, Gagliano, and Monteverdi themselves did. In any case, what made the Florentine musical tales operatic was not the mere fact that they were sung continuously. So were Cavalieri's pastorals and perhaps other earlier works. The novelty, rather, was that they accentuated the dialogue of the drama, representing all of it through singing.

The essential operatic move was the insistence that music function on two levels: as representing music and also as representing speech, which meant that some of the music was coded one way for the characters onstage and another way for the audience. On the one hand, there was music that both the audience and the stage characters "heard" as music, such as songs and dances. Such moments would be performed musically even in a straight play, as they were in ones that Shakespeare was writing at exactly this same time in England. On the other hand, there were moments that only the audience heard as music, that were "inaudible" to the characters onstage who were represented musically as speaking. It is a dichotomy that every form of opera and every opera audience has had to come to terms with, and different types of opera can be distinguished on the basis of how they have negotiated this representational crux.

Only six scattered fragments survive from Peri's *La Dafne* in monody collections, and not surprisingly five of them are of the "heard" stage music type. The other is an example of the new operatic "unheard" dialogue music, "Qual' nova meraviglia!" ("What new marvel is this!"), in which a messenger describes Daphne's transformation from nymph to laurel tree. By later standards it is a rather tame recitative, with no expressive dissonance to speak of. We get a better sense of the *stile rappresentativo* at full strength in the same team's *Euridice*, for which all the music survives. Its recitatives show a marked advance in expressive confidence, much stronger than the general lyricism of Caccini's monodies. Whole scenes are given in recitative, and dissonance of a harshness that can still sound impressive abounds in proportion to the intensity of the dramatic situation.

We have already met Claudio Monteverdi as a great madrigalist; he was no less notable as the first great opera composer.

In this early, minimally accompanied recitative the bass line is often quite static, with entire lines declaimed over a stationary harmony; there is no thematic interplay between voice and accompaniment. Since the pattern of the verse is irregular, the harmonic changes are unpredictable. There is, in short, nothing that can be identified as a purely musical pattern, nothing that aspires to musical wholeness or memorability. Music, far from exulting in its own stylistic perfection, has been ruthlessly subordinated, a music lover might object, to the text. To which a more literary-minded listener might respond, that's just where it belongs. Both might wonder why, if the music has to be so minimal, have it at all, to which one answer would be that the musicalization accomplishes definitively what the actor accomplishes only haphazardly, depending on his gifts—namely, the surefire transmission of the affective content of the words to the listener. The composer, then, functions like a supreme actor or stage director, able by the use of harmony and dissonance to magnify the rhetorical effects of the singer's vocal inflection and delivery.

Anthology Vol 1-66
Full CD II, 8

The gravest of the recitatives in *Euridice* comes in the second scene, when Orpheus, a role that was sung by Peri himself, gets news of Eurydice's death from Daphnis, a role sung by a boy at the first performance. The declamation is entirely syllabic. Peri avoids Caccini's melismas, opting instead for a setting in which both rhythm and melody strive to imitate speech, complete with dramatic pauses and melodic leaps. While some passages therefore closely follow the affect of the words, Peri rigorously avoids illustrating the text's imagery, jam-packed though it is with opportunities for word painting—flowing water, murmuring water, light, dark, singing, and dancing. None of this is painted in tones. Instead, the focus is on feeling. When, for example, Daphnis describes the cold sweat on Eurydice's face and hair during the death throes, the music is concerned with the emotion of the describer, conveyed in a shocking clash between the voice and the bass.

The actual moment of Eurydice's death is described with even greater, colder horror: The words "i bei sembianti" ("her beautiful features") are set with hideous irony, using the ugliest harmonies the composer could devise. Orpheus's following lament is cast with great subtlety, further conveyed by musical "modulations" to match the modulations of his mood as he goes from numb shock ("Non piango e non sospiro"/"I cry not and I sigh not") through a sudden outpouring of grief ("O mio core, o mio speme"/"O my heart! O my hope") to firm resolve ("Tosto vedrai"/"Soon you will see").

Monteverdi: From Court to Commerce

Even if various dramatic works can legitimately claim to be the "first opera," the traditional telling of music history has tended to simplify such a story, crystallize varied achievements, and enthrone a solitary genius as the protagonist. It is time now to look at the man who "made" opera. A historian of Italian music once proposed that the origins of opera could be said to proceed from "Monteverdi to Monteverdi."[11] What was meant as a joke, however, contains an important insight and provides an excellent frame for discussing some issues of major consequence that take us from the court musical tales we have been examining thus far to commercial public opera. We have already met Claudio Monteverdi (1567–1643) as a great madrigalist; he was no less notable as the first great opera composer.

Monteverdi's contributions to the early repertoire of music for the stage came at different stages of his long and varied career. His first *favola in musica* dates from 1607, his last opera from shortly before his death, thirty-six years later. The first premiered when he was not quite forty and the last when he was seventy-five. The first was performed, in line with what we have already seen from Peri and others, before an invited assembly of nobles in Mantua and had a mythological theme. The last was performed before a paying public in Venice and had a theme drawn from history. Stylistically as well as socially and thematically, the two works were worlds, not just a generation, apart.

The first is *L'Orfeo*, a *favola in musica* on the same myth previously set by Peri and Caccini and very much in the same tradition (Fig. 7-7). The other, *L'incoronazione di Poppea* (The Coronation of Poppea), was designated an *opera regia* (regal work), "work" being the literal meaning of the word "opera" and the term that has stuck to the genre. Both pieces still hold a place in today's repertory, although both disappeared for centuries in between. They are the earliest and, for contemporary audiences, the exemplary representatives of the noble musical play and the public music drama, of the early court and commercial operas. Comparing them will be an instructive study in contrasts.

We need first to look at Monteverdi's life and his prominent position in the musical politics of the day. Because he was so widely recognized by his contemporaries as the most gifted and interesting composer in Italy, Monteverdi became the spokesman and the scapegoat of the emerging new musical style, what he called the ***seconda pratica***, or "second practice," that would eventually consign the ***prima pratica***, or "first practice," namely, the *ars perfecta*, to the status of a *stile antico*, or "old style." It was criticism from detractors like Giovanni Maria Artusi, mentioned in the previous chapter, that made it necessary for Monteverdi to engage in defensive propaganda. This allows us to compare his preaching with his practice, his professed intentions with his actual achievement.

***Monteverdi became the spokesman and the scapegoat of the emerging new musical style, the* seconda pratica *that would eventually consign the* prima pratica*, namely, the* ars perfecta*, to the status of a* stile antico.**

By the time he wrote *L'Orfeo* in 1607, Monteverdi had been an active composer for a quarter of a century. His first publication, a book of three-voice motets, came out in 1582, when he was a fifteen-year-old pupil of Marc'Antonio Ingegneri, an important Counter-Reformation composer who was the *maestro di cappella* at the cathedral of Cremona, his birthplace. By the late sixteenth century, Cremona, a city southeast of Milan, was already recognized as a manufacturing center for string instruments. The Amati family had established there the workshop where the design of the modern violin family began to be standardized in the earlier part of the century. Antonio Stradivari (ca. 1644/49–37), who apprenticed with Niccolo Amati and who is still thought of as the greatest of all violin makers, inherited the Cremonese art and brought it to its peak. In view of his city's traditions, it is perhaps not surprising that Monteverdi's first official appointment should have been as a string player in

L' ORFEO
FAVOLA
IN MVSICA
DA CLAVDIO MONTEVERDE
MAESTRO DI CAPELLA
DELLA SERENISS. REPVBLICA.
RAPPRESENTATA IN MANTOVA
L'Anno 1607. Et nouamente Ristampata.
IN VENETIA MDCXV.
Appresso Ricciardo Amadino.

Figure 7-7 Frontispiece to the 1615 Venice edition of Monteverdi's *L'Orfeo*.

the virtuoso chamber ensemble maintained by Vincenzo Gonzaga, the Duke of Mantua.

Monteverdi was engaged around 1590 at the Mantuan court (Fig. 7-8), where he remained for more than twenty years, the last eleven as *maestro della musica*. Artusi's attack on the harmonic liberties he took in his madrigals first came in 1600. The controversy enhanced Monteverdi's general reputation, especially when he joined in himself, sketchily at first in the preface to his Fifth Book of Madrigals (1605). That book made him by common consent and by virtue of the debates that surrounded his work the leading composer of madrigals during the final chapter of the genre's history.

Two years later—in 1607, the year of *L'Orfeo*—Monteverdi responded to his critics in what has been ever since among the most quoted documents in music history. The refutation appeared in a new book of convivial little compositions published as *Scherzi musicali a tre voci di Claudio Monteverde, raccolti da Giulio Cesare Monteverde suo fratello, con la dichiaratione di una lettera che si ritrova stampata nel quinto libro de suoi madrigali* (Musical Jests in Three Voices by Claudio Monteverdi, Collected by his Brother Giulio Cesare Monteverdi, with a Declaration Based on a Letter That Is Found Printed in His Fifth Book of Madrigals). With a statement from his younger brother, also a composer, Monteverdi issued what amounted to a manifesto of the *seconda pratica*. The term became standard, as did the famous slogan—Make the "words the mistress of the harmony [= music] and not the servant," which managed to sum up in a single sound bite the whole rhetorical program of the humanists.

The discussion of the first and second practices is itself a masterpiece of rhetoric. The chief appeal of Artusi and other upholders of the polyphonic tradition had always been to the authority of established practice. The *ars perfecta* was supreme because it was the hard-won culmination of a long history, not the lazy whim of a few trendy egotists. Giulio Cesare Monteverdi's statement initially appears to honor that glorious pedigree. The first practice, defined as "that style which is chiefly concerned with the perfection of the harmony," is traced back to "the first [composers] to write down music for more than one voice, later followed and improved upon by Ockeghem, Josquin des Prez, Pierre de la Rue, Jean Mouton, Crequillon, Clemens non Papa, Gombert, and others of those times." Finally, granting flattering recognition to Artusi's own chief authorities, Giulio Cesare concludes that the first practice "reached its ultimate perfection with Messer Adriano [Willaert] in composition itself, and with the extremely well-thought-out rules of the excellent Zarlino." All this is just what Artusi himself might have said.

But this recognition of the *ars perfecta*'s pedigree was only a rhetorical foil. In the very next breath the Monteverdi brothers claimed a much older and more distinguished pedigree. "It is my brother's aim," wrote Giulio Cesare, "to follow the principles taught by Plato and practiced by the divine Cipriano [de Rore] and those who have followed him in modern times," namely, Monteverdi's teacher, Ingegneri, plus Marenzio, Giaches de Wert, Luzzasco Luzzaschi, Peri, Caccini, "and finally by yet more exalted spirits who understand even better what true art is."[12] Plato, the Monteverdian argument implies, beats Ockeghem any day. In the age of humanism, who would dare disagree?

Figure 7-8 The family and the court of Gonzaga: Ludovico III Gonzaga, Barbara di Brandeburgo, Vittorino da Feltre, Gianfrancesco Rodolfo and Ludovico, 1474. Fresco by Andrea Mantegna (1431–1506). Palazzo Ducale in Mantua, House of Spouses (Camera degli Sposi), Italy.

Monteverdi's *L'Orfeo*: The Quintessential Princely Spectacle

L'Orfeo was officially mounted not by the Mantuan court itself but by an academy—the Accademia degli Invaghiti (Academy of those Captivated [by the Arts]). The work was first performed during the carnival season of 1607 under the guidance of Francesco Gonzaga, the hereditary prince of Mantua. The words were written by the prince's secretary, Alessandro Striggio (ca. 1573–1630), and the whole occasion seemed designed to heap praise on the prince. If much of art over the centuries has involved some manner of flattering its sponsors, the *intermedii* and *favole in musica* were certainly among the most obsequious in this regard.

The orchestra for *L'Orfeo* surpassed that of most *intermedii* in its range of colors, although only part of the full assembly of instruments plays at any one time. This means that relatively few musicians were required as long as their ranks included "doublers" who could take different, nonoverlapping parts. The score published in 1609 calls for a large continuo contingent of keyboard instruments (harpsichords and organs), plucked instruments (including harps), and bass viols. The string ensemble played mainly ritornellos between the stanzas of the strophic numbers. Finally, there was an assortment of wind and brass. The brass colors are flaunted in an opening toccata, a quasi-military fanfare that was to be played three times from various places around the hall to silence the audience and invest the proceedings with appropriate pomp.

After this purely instrumental opening, the personification of music itself, the figure of "La Musica," sings a five-stanza introductory aria interspersed with an instrumental ritornello that reappears later in the work, thus carrying an association with the power of music. Although in five acts, the work was most likely performed straight through without pauses. The first act celebrates the marriage day of Orpheus and Eurydice and consists largely of lighter choral and dance numbers. The festivities continue at the start of Act II and then turn darker when Orpheus learns

Anthology Vol 1-67a-h
Full CD II, 9–16
Concise CD I, 69–76

of his beloved's death. We will consider this act because it offers a chance to compare Monteverdi's with Peri's earlier setting and to witness how Monteverdi and Striggio contrived a determined clash between "heard" and "unheard" operatic music.

To start, Orpheus, surrounded by his friends the shepherds, rejoices in his love for Eurydice. They celebrate in a kind of concert consisting, after an invocation by the title character, of four strophic arias with lavishly scored instrumental ritornellos that were in all likelihood danced as well as sung. The first three arias are sung, respectively, by a shepherd, by two shepherds, and by the full chorus. Then comes "Vi ricorda, o bosch' ombrosi" ("Do you remember, oh shady woods"), in which Orpheus expresses his joy, using an elegant hemiola meter alternating $\frac{6}{8}$ and $\frac{3}{4}$. Repeated references in the libretto to Orpheus's lyre leave no doubt that he is playing along to accompany the singing and that the songs and dances are literally that—actual songs and dances performed onstage— "heard" music, heard by all involved.

After Orpheus has finished this catchy four-stanza number, one of the shepherds asks him to sing another song, but before he can comply, a sorrowful "Messenger," the nymph Sylvia, bursts in with the horrible news of Eurydice's death and stops the "heard" stage music for good. As the older style of song and dance music is silenced, the new music of the *stile rappresentativo* emerges in full force. From here until Orpheus and Sylvia depart, the only instruments that play are those of the basso continuo, whose music goes symbolically "unheard" onstage.

The crux of the act is the exchange between Orpheus and Sylvia, which is clearly modeled on, but just as clearly surpasses, the analogous scene in Peri's and Caccini's settings. Monteverdi actually pays Peri homage in his deployment of jarring tonalities; but where Peri had contrasted harmonies in large sections corresponding to the main divisions of Orpheus's soliloquy, Monteverdi uses the contrast at very close range to underscore the poignancy of the dialogue psychologically. The harmonic disparity between Orpheus's lines and Sylvia's symbolizes his resistance to the terrible news she has brought him. He breaks in on her narrative with G minor—"Oimè che odo?" ("Alas, what do I hear?")—as soon as she has mentioned the name of Eurydice (on an E-major harmony), as if to deflect her from the bitter message she is about to deliver, but she comes right back with E major and resolves the chord cadentially to A on the word *morta* (dead). When Orpheus responds with another "Oimè," this time he takes up the same harmony where she left it and confirms it with D, the next harmony along the circle of fifths: The message has sunk in, and he must accept it (Ex. 7-2). The simplicity here is enormously moving—the history of later opera, particularly the nineteenth-century Italian opera best known to audiences today, is filled with moments when revelatory news is conveyed. Later works tend to respond with the full arsenal of vocal and instrumental sound and fury, the opposite of Orpheus's nobly restrained response.

As in Peri's *Euridice*, the horrific events are recounted rather than portrayed. This is because the composer's primary interest is in portraying not events but emotions, those of the messenger Sylvia herself and those of Orpheus. His central soliloquy builds from stony shock to resolution, but it does so with a fullness of gradation that mirrors much more faithfully than Peri's the process of emotional transmutation. The secret lies in the bass, which begins statically but starts to move both more rhythmically and with a more directed harmonic progression, approaching some middle ground between recitative and full-blown song. After Orpheus's lament and departure, the five-voice chorus strikes up a formal dirge by turning Sylvia's opening lines ("Ahi caso acerbo"/"Ah harsh event") into a ritornello, her notes forming the bass, against which a pair of shepherds sing lamenting strophes that recall the previous rejoicing with bitter irony. In this most affecting act of *L'Orfeo*, then, the dramatic strategy has been to frame dramatic recitative with decorative arias, dances, and madrigal-like choruses. The later commercial opera would eventually reverse this perspective.

Example 7-2 Claudio Monteverdi, *Orfeo*, Orpheus gets the horrifying news from the messenger Sylvia

The next two acts take place in the Underworld. The longest aria in *L'Orfeo* comes smack in the middle of the work—"Possente spirto" ("Powerful spirit"), in which Orpheus attempts to convince Charon, the fearful ferryman who transports

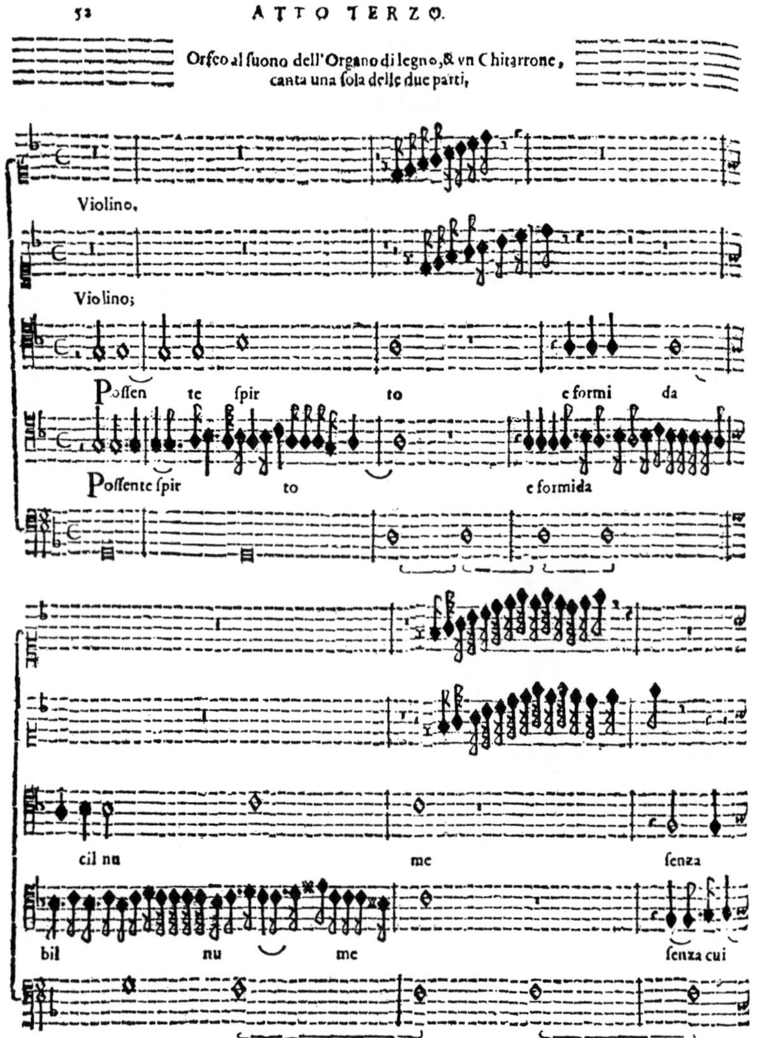

Figure 7-9 The aria "Possente spirto" from Act III of Monteverdi's *Orfeo,* with two versions of the vocal line (ornamented and unornamented).

souls to the Underworld, to give him passage. Until the final stanza, Orpheus sings increasingly elaborate music in his effort to persuade. The aria is particularly noteworthy because Monteverdi supplied two versions of the vocal line, one simply cast for the singer to ornament and the other elaborately ornamented by the composer himself—an invaluable example of the largely lost art of unnotated embellishment (Fig. 7-9).

As in Peri's *Euridice,* the librettist revised the mythological plot to avoid a tragic ending. In Ovid, after losing Eurydice a second time, Orpheus turns against all women, for which reason a rioting chorus of raving furies literally tears him to pieces. In the original printings of the *L'Orfeo* libretto in 1607, the ending runs along these lines, but a different finale appears in the score that was published two years later. The conclusion became less menacing and more spectacular, with Orpheus's father, Apollo, the divine musician, bringing him into the heavenly constellation that bears his name and thereby substituting serene apotheosis for bloody cataclysm.

Monteverdi in Venice

Monteverdi composed his next drama, *L'Arianna,* to another Rinuccini libretto, in celebration of Francesco Gonzaga's marriage in 1608. The complete work is lost, as are many other theatrical works by the composer, although in this case a famous lament survives. Within a few years Monteverdi, who had been rather notoriously mistreated by his patrons in Mantua, was casting about for a more satisfactory position. After Vincenzo Gonzaga's death in 1612, he was summarily fired in a notable show of ingratitude by Francesco, now duke, in whose honor both *L'Orfeo* and *L'Arianna* had originally been performed. Several of Monteverdi's letters testify to his resentment of the high-handed way in which the Gonzagas dealt with their servant despite his eminent standing in his profession. Like the oft-repeated anecdotes concerning Josquin, they testify to what we might call artistic self-consciousness. But where the Josquin anecdotes are almost certainly questionable, the Monteverdi letters are hard documents, the earliest we have of artistic "alienation." His hair-raisingly sarcastic reply to an invitation to return to Mantua in 1620 still makes impressive reading, and while it probably marked him as nothing more than a crank so far as the Gonzagas were concerned, it marks him for what we now might call an artistic genius and a temperamental one at that.[13]

Monteverdi spent the final stage of his career in Venice, where he moved in 1613, serving as *maestro di cappella* at St. Mark's. His tenure there did not overlap with that of Giovanni Gabrieli, who had died the year before; there is no evidence that the two greatest Venetian church composers ever met. The position suited Monteverdi magnificently, in part because Venice was its own republic, where the chief cathedral musician enjoyed a higher social prestige than could ever be attained in a court situation. He stayed on the job for three decades, until his death; after about 1630, however, he occupied the post only nominally, living chiefly on a pension in semiretirement. This, as we shall see, freed him for other kinds of work in the last years of his very long life.

Once in Venice, Monteverdi composed only in the concerted style, that is, for voices and instruments. He did not publish the service music he wrote in his actual job capacity until his retirement, but continued to issue madrigals with some regularity, publishing the Sixth Book in 1614 and the Seventh in 1619, which actually bore the title *Concerto*. Monteverdi's Eighth Book (1638), his last and the most lavish in its instrumentation, was called *Madrigali guerrieri et amorosi* (Madrigals of Love and War) and included a few extended works specially designated as being in the *rappresentativo* style. Two particularly noteworthy pieces are *Il combattimento di Tancredi e Clorinda* (The Battle of Tancredi and Clorinda), drawn from the epic poem *Gerusalemme liberata* (Jerusalem Delivered) by Torquato Tasso, and Rinuccini's *Lamento della ninfa* (The Nymph's Lament).

Combattimento relates a ferocious hand-to-hand combat that the warrior Tancredi has with a soldier whom he finally kills but who in dying reveals herself to be his former lover, Clorinda. To give adequate expression to this exceptionally violent text, Monteverdi invented a new style of writing, which he called the ***stile concitato*** (agitated style), that consisted of repeated notes articulated with virtuosic rapidity. Most of the *concitato* effects were assigned to the basso continuo and to the concertato string instruments; it was the origin of the string *tremolo* that has been a dependable resource ever since for imitating agitation both physical and emotional and linking them (Ex. 7-3).

To give adequate expression to exceptionally violent texts, Monteverdi invented a new style of writing, which he called the* stile concitato *(agitated style), that consisted of repeated notes articulated with virtuosic rapidity.

In *Lamento della ninfa* Monteverdi again turned a narrative into a dramatic scene by framing the complaint of a rejected lover, sung as a solo aria with commentary by a trio of male singers. The underlying and repeating bass line—a so-called ground bass—is a four-note segment (tetrachord) of the minor scale, descending slowly by degrees from tonic to dominant—a figure that Monteverdi, through his affecting use of it, helped establish as a sign of lament that would remain standard for the rest of the century and well beyond (Ex. 7-4).[14] This was a new sort of representational convention: a musical idea independent of any specific image in the poem, associated with the literary work not through direct imitation but by mere agreement among composers and listeners. This, of course, is the way most words acquire their meaning. The new technique could be called *lexical* signification, as opposed to *mimetic*.

Example 7-3 Claudio Monteverdi, *Il combattimento di Tancredi e Clorinda*, opening of fifth stanza of Tasso's poem

Outrage spurs them on to vengeful fury

Example 7-4 Claudio Monteverdi, Madrigals, Book VIII, *Lamento della ninfa*, mm. 1–8

Love, she said, gazing at the sky . . .

Given the nature of his job at St. Mark's, Monteverdi wrote a considerable amount of church music, much of it released in 1641 in a huge retrospective collection titled *Selva morale e spirituale* (A Righteous and Spiritual Forest). Most of the contents resemble those of an earlier assemblage from 1610: *Vespro della Beata Vergine* (Vespers of the Blessed Virgin), continuo madrigals on sacred or liturgical texts and grand concertos in the Gabrieli style. So Monteverdi's Venetian music, while written chiefly for church or as vocal chamber music, was increasingly couched in theatrical terms. Venice initially offered Monteverdi little opportunity to write actual theatrical music, and what he did compose in this vein during his tenure at St. Mark's was produced on commission from Italian court cities. He apparently wrote at least seven theatrical works between 1616 and 1630, but for the most part the music has not survived.

Opera and Its Politics

The situation in Venice changed drastically when the Teatro San Cassiano opened its doors during the carnival season of 1637 (Fig. 7-10). This was the Western world's first public music theater—the world's first opera house—and in retrospect it seems inevitable that it should have been brought forth in Venice, Europe's great meeting place and commercial center. Its founding was more of a novelty than we can easily appreciate today, after centuries of public music making for paying audiences. It made a decisive difference to the nature of the art created, to its relationship with audiences, and to the politics of art.

The new situation requires us to think not only about Monteverdi, the creator, but also of the receivers, his audience. Ever since classical antiquity much of the telling of the history of art has focused on biography, the story of great men and great deeds. We have already gotten a taste of this with Josquin des Prez and Palestrina. Ever since the nineteenth century, the era of Napoleon and Beethoven, and of a triumphant class of "self-made men," the great men celebrated by historians have typically been great neither because of high birth or hereditary power nor because of their election by God but, rather, by virtue of their individual talents and their ability to realize their destinies, especially in the face of obstacles. Beethoven, as we will forcefully see later, became the very model for such biographies in music. Monteverdi, like Josquin before him, has been given similar celebrity treatment by historians.

Figure 7-10 Carnival festivities on the Piazza San Marco, Venice.

One consequence of the focus on creative "genius" is the assumption that knowing the maker's intention is all the information we need to grasp the meaning of a work. There was considerable resistance to this model of art historiography in the twentieth century and some revision of it. This book tries to participate in that revision to a certain extent. In the previous chapter, for example, attention was paid to larger religious, social, and economic forces. Rather than just thinking about what a creator intended while creating, artworks can also be considered as reflecting the viewpoint and the expectations of their sponsors and audience. This is particularly important to take into account when it comes to dramatic music, which is often intimately bound up with politics. In order to understand the differences between Monteverdi's *L'Orfeo* of 1607 and his *L'incoronazione di Poppea* of 1643, that bond has to be explored.

All the earliest* favole in musica *were fashioned to adorn central Italian court festivities, flattering the assemblages of "renowned heroes, blood royal of kings" who were privileged to hear them.

As we have seen, all the earliest *favole in musica* were fashioned to adorn the same kind of central Italian court festivities, flattering the assemblages of "renowned heroes, blood royal of kings" who were privileged to hear them, potentates "of whom Fame tells glorious deeds, though falling short of truth," as the personification of "Musica" herself puts it in the prologue to *L'Orfeo*. Thus the revived musical drama—the invention, after all, of a group of Florentine nobles—reflected the recovered grandeur and glory of classical antiquity on the princes who were its patrons. Like most music that has left remains for historians to discuss, it was the product and the expression of an elite culture, the topmost echelons of contemporary society. To put it that way is uncontroversial. But what if it were said that the early musical plays were the product and the expression of an aristocratic class—a product and an expression that were only made possible by the despotic exploitation of other classes? That would direct perhaps unwelcome attention at the social costs of artistic greatness. Such awareness follows inescapably from an emphasis on the patronage and politics of art, and perhaps reveals an additional reason why scholarly investigation tends to focus instead on the safer matter of the creator's intentions and purely artistic accomplishments.

The Italian court spectacles glorified political power in various ways. The most obvious and impressive was the fusion of all the arts in the common enterprise of princely praise as exemplified in the earliest Medici wedding-shows, in which the monster assemblages of singers and instrumentalists were exceeded only by the elaborate stage sets and theatrical machinery. Moreover, the plots, involving mythological or ancient historical heroes, were transparent allegories of the sponsoring rulers. Should anyone miss the point, the rulers were often addressed directly in the obligatory prologues that linked the story of the opera to events of their reign.

More subtly, we can sense some unease with the virtuosity of the vocal soloists, whose singing feats might upstage the event, the story, the music, and even the patrons. Giulio Caccini railed against virtuosity in the preface to his *Nuove musiche*, where the matter is couched outwardly in terms of fastidious taste, but the social snobbery lurking within is not hard to discern. Virtuosity is common, a sort of athletic stunt that easily impresses. Those who indulge it or encourage it with their applause are to be despised as vulgar and low class. Not surprisingly, virtuosity found a natural home in the commercial music theater. This is one of the reasons for regarding the Venetian Teatro San Cassiano and the year 1637, more than the Florentine carnival and marriage presentations of *La Dafne* and *Euridice* some four decades earlier, as the true time and place of the birth of opera as we know it now. Where the earlier court spectacles are dependably celebrated in history books like this one but have disappeared from the repertoire (with the exception of Monteverdi's *L'Orfeo*), the early commercial opera bequeathed to us the conventions by which opera has lived, in glory and in infamy, into our own time.

Modern operagoers can still recognize in seventeenth-century Venetian works conventions that remain in force to this day. Ever since opera opened its doors to a paying public—a public that had to be lured to pay and attend—it has been a star-studded circus with a lively transgender sideshow, associated from the very beginning with the carnival season preceding Lent with its parties, parades, and masked dancing. Uncanny, virtuoso, nature-defying vocalism easily compensated for the missing courtly features that the early commercial opera theaters could not afford. (Hence much smaller orchestras were used as well.) Never mind the noble union of all the arts: Great singing has been the real bait for public audiences from the start.

The greatest singers of all and the most completely educated were the ***castrati***, castrated men, opera's first international stars, whose singing possessed astounding sonority and florid vocal style. Although the castrato was earlier associated with churches in sixteenth-century Italy, where females could not perform but a full range of singing voices was desired, the burgeoning commercial opera stage, with its virtuosic exhibitionism and its heroics, gave these unearthly singers their true arena for some two centuries. In an age that valued finely honed symbolic artifice, these magnificent singing objects—artists made, not born—were the gods, the generals, the athletes, and the lovers. Seventeenth- and eighteenth-century serious opera is unthinkable without them, which is a major reason why few of these works are successfully revived in opera houses today.

Here, too, there are great social costs to consider, for if it was to be musically effective, castration had to be performed on talented musical boys before they reached the age of consent. The operation was therefore officially illegal. Charles Burney, the great eighteenth-century music historian, went in search of information on the practice, only to be given a royal runaround: "I was told at Milan that it was at Venice; at Venice, that it was at Bologna; but at Bologna the fact was denied, and I was referred to Florence; from Florence to Rome, and from Rome I was sent to Naples." Greedy parents were often responsible; a prospective castrato was supposed to be brought to a conservatory to be tested "as to the probability of voice," as Burney put it, but "it is my opinion that the cruel operation is but too frequently performed without trial, or at least without sufficient proof of an improvable voice; otherwise such numbers could never be found in every great town throughout Italy, without any voice at all, or at least without one sufficient to compensate such a loss."[15]

In an age that valued finely honed symbolic artifice, castrati—artists made, not born—were the gods, the generals, the athletes, and the lovers.

By the end of the seventeenth century, serious subjects—the noble and the heroic—were just one of the available operatic modes. Commercial opera was from the first a mixed genre, in which crowd-pleasing comic characters and burlesque scenes compromised lofty themes, in violation of traditional Aristotelian dramatic rules. It is a formula familiar to us from Shakespeare's plays, which so often mix high tragedy and low comedy. Opera was later segregated into discrete categories of serious (*opera seria*) and comic (*opera buffa*). And this led to another great difference between court music spectacles and commercial opera: The latter, at first under cover of comedy, introduced oppositional politics into the genre. Commercial opera, originally instituted as a carnival entertainment, stood authority on its head.

It was already considered provocative to display operatic divas (women singers, literally "goddesses") to the public gaze. A notorious Jesuit critic, Giovan Domenico Ottonelli, denounced the theaters of the "money-grubbing musicians" as indulgent and corrupting, in contrast to the edifying spectacles mounted "at the palaces of great princes."[16] But the most significant licenses were as much political as moral. Public opera, as we will see, became a world where satyrs romped and Eros reigned, where servant girls outwitted and chastised their masters, where philandering counts were humiliated, and where—later and more earnestly—rabbles were roused and revolutions were abetted. It is hardly surprising that opera would become the most stringently watched and censored of all forms of art until the twentieth century, when that grim distinction passed to movies. Examples of opera's disruptive and destabilizing possibilities can be drawn from any phase in its history, beginning with the earliest, as we can see by comparing the courtly *L'Orfeo* with the commercial *L'incoronazione di Poppea*.

The Carnival Show: *L'incoronazione di Poppea*

In an extraordinary feat of self-rejuvenation, Monteverdi came out of retirement in his seventies and composed a final trio of operas for the Teatro SS. Giovanni e Paolo, one of several competitors that quickly sprang up to challenge San Cassiano, the original Venetian opera house. The first was *Il ritorno d'Ulisse in patria* (Ulysses's Return to His Homeland, 1640), based on Homer's *Odyssey*. The second, now lost, concerned another mythological subject, the wedding of Aeneas, drawn from Virgil's *Aeneid*. The last was *L'incoronazione di Poppea,* not a mythological story but a historical fantasy based on the writings of Tacitus and other Roman historians. The librettist was Giovanni Francesco Busenello (1598–1659), a famous poet who was active in the Accademia degli Incogniti (Academy of the Disguised), a society of libertines and skeptics who dominated the early Venetian commercial theater.

Anthology Vol 1-68a-e
Full CD II, 17–21
Concise CD I, 77

Busenello's libretto celebrates neither the reward of virtue nor the chastisement of vice. It is, rather, a celebration of virtue mocked and vice triumphant. The opera celebrates erotic love as well as the intrigue and betrayal it can entail. Yet the moral swamp Busenello narrated may also have had a moralizing goal. The Accademia degli Incogniti were patriotic Venetians, proud of the Republic that allowed them a modicum of free thought: To show Imperial Rome in the worst light, all the while enjoying the show, was to damn it with garish praise. Whatever Busenello intended, he made no secret of his having made a hash of history. He published the plot synopsis in his collected works:

> Nero, in love with Poppaea, who was the wife of Otho, sent him on the pretext of embassy to Portugal, in order to enjoy for himself his dear beloved one; thus Tacitus presented it. But here the facts are presented differently. Otho, desperate at seeing himself deprived of Poppaea, gives himself over to delirium and exclamations. Octavia, Nero's wife, orders Otho to kill Poppaea. Otho promises to do it, but not having sufficient courage to take the life of his adored Poppaea, disguises himself in the clothes of Drusilla, who is in love with him. Thus disguised he enters Poppaea's garden. Love [i.e., the god Cupid] interrupts and impedes that death. Nero repudiates Octavia, despite [the philosopher] Seneca's advice, and takes Poppaea as his wife. Seneca dies, and Octavia is exiled from Rome.

Monteverdi's setting of this most unedifying entertainment has the skimpiest of orchestras, just a little ritornello band notated in three or four staves for unspecified instruments, most likely strings. Even if budgetary constraints limited instrumentation and spectacle, this was more than compensated for by flamboyant voice types: two superbly developed prima-donna roles (the more virtuosic of them the fork-tongued, string-pulling title character, the more poignantly monodic one the wronged and rejected wife), two male parts for castrato singers (the higher of them the manipulated Emperor Nero, the other the stoical wronged husband), and a quartet of low-born comic characters. As often in Shakespeare, Monteverdi's shorter-lived contemporary, comic scenes are paired with the most serious ones.

The mixture can be seen in Act I, Scene 6, the action of which Busenello summarized as: "Seneca advises Octavia to be steadfast. Octavia's page, for the empress's entertainment, makes fun of Seneca, to whom Octavia entrusts herself; she goes to offer prayers in the temple." The philosopher's opening address is in a somber and freely rhymed recitative, but when he calls on her to embrace suffering so as to build character and denounces physical beauty for its impermanence, the music turns to devices associated with the aria—a regular triple meter, melismas, sequences, repeated words, and madrigalisms. Only at the end of his monologue, when Seneca returns to praise "la virtù costante" ("steadfast virtue"), does recitative return. Octavia briefly replies in an austere recitative. The bulk of the scene, however, belongs to her page. Here the opera's "lowest" character directly mocks Seneca, its most exalted one, in a lively patter marked by comic exaggeration throughout, including sounds of sneezing, yawning, and laughter.

Throughout the opera, Monteverdi alternated declamatory and lyrical styles as well as serious and comic with a frequency and fluidity unlike any other of the time. The approach he chose at any given time depended on the libretto at that point, and his choices thus provide clues to characterization. Lyric effusions and exaggerated madrigalisms serve an even more clear-cut purpose later in the act with a love scene that Busenello summarized as: "Poppaea and Nero speak of their past contentments, Nero remaining prey to Poppaea's beauties, promising that he wants to make her empress." The relationship between Nero and Poppaea is frankly represented as lustful, and that lust is given graphic musical representation. She flaunts her lips, her breasts, and her arms, and the composer, taking on the role of stage director, seems to prescribe not only her lines and their delivery but her lewd gestures as well. Nero, in response, makes explicit reference to their sexual encounters, even to "that inflamed spirit which in kissing you, oh dear one, I diffused in you."

Opera would become the most stringently watched and censored of all forms of art until the twentieth century, when that grim distinction passed to movies.

The final three scenes in the opera offer further contrasts. The tragic scene of Octavia's farewell to Rome as she boards the ship that is to take her into exile is immediately followed by a farcical one in which Poppaea's old nurse and counselor, Arnalta, rejoices over her mistress's impending elevation and thus of her own as well. The famous culminating scene of the opera is an arching, bristlingly sensual lust duet between Nero and Poppaea, which uses a passacaglia, a slow dance over a mesmerizing ground bass. The music, in its writhing, coiling movements, the increased agitation of the middle section, and the dissonant friction between the singers' parts, leaves no doubt that the lovers are enacting their passion before the audience, whether or not the stage director dares show them in the act (Ex. 7-5). Where *L'Orfeo*, the court pageant, celebrated established order and authority and the cool moderation that its hero tragically violates, *Poppea*, the carnival show, brings it all down: Passion wins out over reason, woman over man, guile over truth, impulse over wisdom, license over law, and artifice over nature. The work was exceptional in its own time—the plots of Venetian operas, although often racy, typically ended with everything set right.

The brilliant conclusion of Monteverdi's *L'incoronazione di Poppea* raises some fascinating authorial and performance issues as well. The order of the scenes depicting Octavia's departure and Arnalta's glee has been discussed here as in the original libretto, but the first published seventeenth-century scores reverse them. In fact there are many inconsistencies, reorderings, additions, and deletions among the various surviving sources. Most perplexing is that the great final duet does not appear at all in Busenello's synopsis or the original libretto but, rather, only in scores published after Monteverdi's death.

Example 7-5 Claudio Monteverdi, "Pur ti miro" from *L'incoronazione di Poppea* (ending)

Example 7-5 (continued)

I gaze on you, I enjoy you.
I hug you, I entwine you.
No more pain, no more death.
O my life, O my treasure,
I am yours. I am yours,
my joy, say you love me too.
You are truly my idol.
Yes, my love, yes my heart, my life, yes.

Many scholars think that the final duet "Pur ti miro" ("Yet I look at you"), once believed to be the aged Monteverdi's sublime swan song, was not written by him at all but, rather, by a younger composer (possibly Francesco Cavalli, Monteverdi's pupil and collaborator with Busenello, or Benedetto Ferrari, or Francesco Sacrati). Meant for a revival in the early 1650s, after Monteverdi's death, only this version has survived. That is another important difference between the court spectacles and the earliest operas. Although *L'Orfeo* is an exception, the court operas were usually performed just once and were then printed up as souvenirs of the festivities. These scores could become the basis of later productions, as happened with *L'Orfeo*, although that was not their primary purpose. Commercial operas, by contrast, were rarely published. Like today's Broadway musicals, they survived during their runs and revivals in a ceaseless whirl of negotiation and revision, existing in a multitude of versions—for this theater, for that theater, for the road, for this star, and so on. They were not fixed texts per se but performances, embodying much that was unwritten and unwritable, directed outward at their audience, not at posterity, history, or the classroom.

Ever since 1637, then, the world of opera has been a divided world, its two political strains—the edifying and the profitable, the authoritarian and the anarchic, the affirmational and the oppositional—coexisting uneasily, the tension between them conditioning everything about the genre: its forms, its styles, its meanings, its performance practices, its followings, its critical traditions. The same political tension lies behind the various press skirmishes, reforms, and disputes that dot operatic history—and that we shall be tracing in due course. It informs intermission disputes to this day. This tension helps to explain opera's continued cultural significance and the durability of this oldest of living secular musical traditions in the West.

Summary

The decades leading up to 1600 saw profound changes in musical style, culminating in the period often called the "Baroque." The prominence of solo singing over a basso continuo has its roots in oral performance and in genres like the frottola (see Chapter 6). Other stylistic changes, however, were brought about by humanism, turning to ancient Greece for inspiration. In 1573, the scholar Girolamo Mei completed an extensive treatise on Greek music and concluded that Greek drama was always sung monophonically, contrasting in every way with the complex counterpoint of the *ars perfecta*. He rejected the wordplay of the madrigalists, arguing that music should instead be founded on the imitation of natural speech.

The resulting *stile rappresentativo*, or representational style, was based on a single voice accompanied by a lute—called *monody*—and a melody that imitated natural speech inflections, called *stile recitativo*. Some of the earliest productions featuring music in the new style included the *intermedii* for the spoken comedy *La pellegrina* (1589). Mei's ideas particularly influenced Giulio Caccini (1551–1618) and Jacopo Peri (1561–1633). Both composers were associated with the Florentine Camerata, a group of humanists who met at the home of Count Giovanni de' Bardi. In 1601, each composer wrote a setting of *Euridice*. Because these works were based on the ancient Orpheus myth, they feature a "singer" as protagonist and, like Monteverdi's later *L'Orfeo*, invite us to contrast operatic selections that are "heard" as music by the characters on stage (songs, dances, etc.) with passages that represent in musical form what the characters presumably hear as speech. Another important work was *Rappresentatione di Anima, et di Corpo* (The Representation of the Soul and Body, 1600), by Emilio de Cavalieri (ca. 1550–1602), which features the first printed figured bass.

The printing industry was central in spreading the new style. Caccini's collection *Le nuove musiche* (The New Music, 1602) included two types of solo vocal works: strophic ones called arias and through-composed ones called madrigals. His madrigal *Amarilli mia bella* has a moderate tempo and range that mimics natural speech, what Caccini called *stile recitativo*. In the new style, the most emotionally heightened moments were captured not with word painting but by imitating the kinds of speech associated with particular emotions.

The most important figure in the "birth" of opera is Claudio Monteverdi (1567–1643). In response to critics such as Giovanni Maria Artusi (see Chapter 6), he issued a vigorous defense. In a 1607 publication, he recognized the *ars perfecta* style as a venerable tradition called the *prima pratica* (first practice) but exalted the new style, the *seconda pratica* (second practice), claiming, "the words are the master of the music." His first *favola in musica* ("Fable in music") was *L'Orfeo* (1607), a parable about the power of music that frames dramatic recitative with decorative arias, dances, madrigal-like choruses, and instrumental ritornellos for a wide range of instruments. In his setting of the scene in which the messenger relates Euridice's death (Act II), Monteverdi employs jarring tonal contrasts to symbolize Orpheus's resistance to the news. Orpheus's aria "Possente spirto" is unusual in that Monteverdi wrote out its embellishments, giving one of the few clues to the pervasive practice of extemporized ornamentation.

These earliest "musical tales" were performed in courts, as private entertainment. The opening of the first public opera house, Teatro San Cassiano, in Venice in 1637 marked a turning point in the history of opera, giving rise to many conventions of modern opera. Monteverdi had moved to Venice in 1613 to become music director at St. Mark's, where he composed church music and continued to issue books of madrigals. His *L'incoronazione di Poppea* (The Coronation of Poppea, 1643) reflects many traits of the new, commercial opera. The plot is a historical fantasy rather than myth, and it celebrates vice rather than virtue. Monteverdi freely alternates between declamatory and lyrical styles and between low and high character types in ways that often turned traditional morals or courtly authority on their heads. In keeping with the need to draw a paying audience, commercial operas compensated for their economical staging and instrumentation with virtuoso vocalists, most notably the castrati.

Study Questions

1. What cultural trends characterize the Baroque period?
2. Describe the tenets articulated in Girolamo Mei's treatise on ancient Greek music. What did he believe about ancient Greek drama, and how did these beliefs influence the composers associated with the Florentine Camerata?
3. What are the central musical features of the *stile recitativo*, as exemplified in Guilo Caccini's "Amarilli mia bella" or Claudio Monteverdi's *L'Orfeo*?
4. Why do you think the Orpheus myth was so important to the early history of opera?
5. Compare and contrast the approaches to text expression in the *stile rappresentativo* and in the polyphonic madrigals of the late 1500s (discussed in Chapter 6). How do they reflect different aesthetic goals and values?
6. What is the difference between "heard" and "unheard" music in opera? How does Monteverdi use this distinction for dramatic purposes in *L'Orfeo?* What musical techniques does he use to underscore the drama in the scene between Sylvia and Orpheus?
7. Describe Monteverdi's concepts of *prima pratica* and *seconda pratica*. What rhetorical strategy did he employ in defending the new style?
8. Compare and contrast the early court operas with the public operas produced after 1637. Describe how they differ in terms of story lines, dramatic features, and musical traits. How are these differences reflected in *L'Orfeo* and *L'incoronazione di Poppea*?
9. In what ways does commercial opera challenge the notion that artwork reflects solely the will of its creator?

Key Terms

Baroque
Camerata
castrato (pl. castrati)
favola in musica
figured bass
***intermedio* (pl. *intermedii*)**
monody
opera
prima pratica
recitative
seconda pratica
stile concitato
stile rappresentativo
stile recitativo

8

Music Travels: Trends in Italy, Germany, France, and England

"Words, words, words." So Shakespeare's Hamlet famously responds when asked "What do you read, my lord?" His questioner, pompous Polonius, would like to know what book the melancholy prince is reading, but the reply suggests that words are meaningless. Words certainly have played a crucial role in the history of music we have traced thus far in this book. Indeed, we have dealt almost exclusively with music connected with words, music that arose from words, that projected, accompanied, and illuminated words, and, in the most recent chapters, music that expressly sought to express words. The seventeenth century saw the dramatic rise of purely instrumental music in publications and also the ascendance of eminent composers dedicated to the writing of such music, music that carried new prestige.

Giovanni Gabrieli and William Byrd are two celebrated composers we have already met who wrote significant instrumental pieces, although not as significant as the pieces they wrote for and with voices. This chapter and the next introduce composers of music for keyboard and instrumental ensembles while continuing to examine the leading vocal genres of the seventeenth and early eighteenth centuries, especially the cantata, the oratorio, and opera. We will consider these compositional activities according to their geographical centers. The international style of the *ars perfecta*—or what by this point was called the *stile antico* or *prima pratica*—gradually gave way not only to new musical approaches but also to increasingly differentiated geographical styles. Whereas in the fifteenth and sixteenth centuries we saw the migration of northern talent to the south, the new Italian dominance in music led to Italian musicians and Italian musical trends being exported north. Germany continued to absorb new styles from Italy and France. The German lands were devastated by the Thirty Years War (1618–48), but by the mid-eighteenth century native-born composers were preeminent, notably Georg Philipp Telemann, George Frideric Handel, and Johann Sebastian Bach, followed by Bach's sons and later by Franz Joseph Haydn, Wolfgang Amadè Mozart, and Ludwig van Beethoven.

The differing political circumstances and artistic traditions in Italy, France, Germany, and England are reflected in the music each country produced and consumed. England, for example, with its strong theatrical tradition, represented by Shakespeare, displayed far less interest in opera than did Italy, where the genre had been born. In this age of political absolutism, no one was more absolute than France's King Louis XIV. France enjoyed unusual power and prosperity following its triumphs in the Thirty Years War, and there the king's individual tastes and special affinity for dance meant that his country cultivated its own distinct brand of dramatic music.

France and England were the only countries in seventeenth-century Europe whose borders remained fairly close to what they are today, with the exception of Portugal (itself absorbed by Spain between 1580 and 1640; Fig. 8-1). These were

Figure 8-1 The Holy Roman Empire in 1648.

also, and not by coincidence, the only two nations in Europe that were ethnically and linguistically more or less coextensive with their territory. The other European nations were either empires—multiethnic, multilingual dynastic states—or small hereditary or republican enclaves whose political boundaries had little to do with language or ethnicity. The much-weakened Holy Roman Empire, Charlemagne's tattered legacy, was the main representative of "supra-ethnicity." Its principal rival and avid foe was the Ottoman (Turkish) Empire, which in the fifteenth and sixteenth centuries expanded aggressively into southeastern Europe from Asia Minor and as late as 1683 laid waste to Vienna, the Austrian capital.

Recognition of the musical differences among various countries is reflected, for example, in the writings of Charles Burney, the English historian mentioned in the preceding chapter who produced one of the first histories of Western music, published in four handsome volumes between 1776 and 1789. The very titles of some of Burney's preparatory books for his enormous undertaking are representative; like many eighteenth-century writings on music, from modest pamphlets to weighty tomes, they compare activities in European countries. After Burney became frustrated with the limited information he could obtain in English libraries, he decided to travel and gather data firsthand. The titles of two resulting books indicate the lands he visited: *The Present State of Music in France and Italy, or the Journal of a Tour through those Countries, undertaken to collect Materials for a General History of Music* (1771) and *The Present State of Music in Germany, the Netherlands, and the United Provinces, or the Journal of a Tour through those Countries, undertaken to collect Materials for a General History of Music* (1773). This chapter and the next offer a somewhat similar musical travelogue.

TIMELINE

ca. 1614 Collected English keyboard pieces, known as the *Fitzwilliam Virginal Book*

1614–18 Michael Praetorius, *Syntagma musicum*

1617 James I appoints Ben Jonson first British poet laureate

1618 Beginning of Thirty Years War

1620 Pilgrims arrive at Plymouth, Massachusetts

1624 Samuel Scheidt, *Tabulatura nova* (with *Christ lag in Todesbanden*)

1625 Francesca Caccini, *La liberazione di Ruggiero dall'isola d'Alcina*

1625–49 Reign of Charles I in England

1629 Heinrich Schütz, *Sacrae symphoniae* (Part 1, with *O quam tu pulchra es*)

1637 Girolamo Frescobaldi, *Cento partite sopra passacagli*

1637 René Descartes, *Discourse on Method*

1642 Rembrandt van Rijn, *The Night Watch*

1642–49 English Civil War

1643–1715 Reign of Louis XIV in France

1648 Peace of Westphalia (end of Thirty Years War)

1649–60 English Commonwealth under Oliver Cromwell

1648 Giacomo Carissimi, *Jephte*

1659 Publication of Barbara Strozzi, *Lagrime mie*

1666 The Great Fire of London

1667 John Milton, *Paradise Lost*

1669 Founding of the Académie Royale de Musique in Paris

1670 Jean-Baptiste Molière, *Le bourgeois gentilhomme*

1672 Jean-Baptiste Lully secures a royal patent on French opera

1676 Lully, *Atys*

Master Organists: Frescobaldi, Sweelinck, and Others

In the seventeenth century, vastly expandable formal plans, such as the ground bass duet that ends Monteverdi's *L'incoronazione di Poppea*, enabled musical compositions to achieve a grand size. New musical forms grew directly out of an oral or improvisatory practice that continued to flourish alongside its written specimens. The written examples, especially those meant for solo virtuosos to perform, represented the cream of the oral practice—particularly effective improvisations, "keepers," retained in memory for repeated performance and refinement and eventual commitment to paper, print, and posterity.

That certainly seems to be the case with much of the music of Girolamo Frescobaldi (1583–1643; Fig. 8-2), organist at St. Peter's Basilica in Rome (Fig. 8-3) from 1608 to his death (with a brief stint in Florence); his mature works were among the most distinctive embodiments of practices arising in the wake of the Counter-Reformation. Frescobaldi was at once the most flamboyantly impressive keyboard composer of his time and the most characteristic, because it was characteristic of early-seventeenth-century music to be flamboyantly impressive. The theatricalized quality that virtually all professional music making strove to project was as avidly cultivated by instrumentalists as by vocalists. The status of purely instrumental pieces rose to the point where a major composer could be concerned primarily writing such nonvocal music, itself an important new development.

Many of Frescobaldi's compositions circulated during his lifetime only in manuscript, although the composer personally oversaw the publication of sixteen volumes between 1608 and 1637. Just four of them contain vocal compositions—motets, madrigals, and arias—with the remaining twelve devoted to instrumental works. Four of those volumes feature keyboard compositions that are among Frescobaldi's most novel, most theatrical, and most elaborately "open-ended" compositions; in that sense they reflected his vividly over-the-top (i.e., "Baroque") side. These compositions came in two main types: the formally capricious, unpredictable ***toccata*** and the ***partita***, which are variations over a ground bass.

1678 John Bunyan, *The Pilgrim's Progress*

1682 Peter the Great becomes Tsar of Russia

1683 John Blow, *Venus and Adonis*

1687 Isaac Newton's *Principia mathematica* proposes theory of gravity to explain planetary motion

1689 First known performance of Henry Purcell, *Dido and Aeneas*

1692 Purcell, *The Fairy Queen*

1737 Jean-Philippe Rameau, *Castor et Pollux*

The toccata has always been associated with pieces open in form, deriving their continuity from discontinuity, to put it paradoxically. To sustain interest they rely not on the continuous development of motives, but on contrast—in texture, meter, tempo, and tonality—between short, striking sections. Striking meant virtuosic as well; toccatas, like some earlier kinds of improvisations, were often festive display pieces that turned the very act of playing—or "touching" the keys (*toccare* = "to touch")—into a form of theater. About his own toccatas, Frescobaldi wrote that he had "taken care not only that they be abundantly provided with different passages and affections but also that each one of the said passages can be played separately; the performer is thus under no obligation to finish them all but can end wherever he thinks best."[1]

Anthology Vol 1-69
Full CD II, 22

Frescobaldi's *Cento partite sopra passacagli* (A Hundred Variations on Passacagli), the last of his keyboard publications and released in 1637, is a celebrated example of variations over a ground bass. It represents the concentrated residue of years of improvising and offers astonishing variety, with frequent and surprising forays into contrasting rhythms and tempi and startling harmonic effects. Its title is mischievously misleading, for the piece does not contain 100 variations, nor are they all examples of a ***passacaglia***. That is the Italian term for *passacalles*, a Spanish genre consisting of variations on cadential patterns that apparently grew out of the habits of guitarists who accompanied courtly singers. Among various dance forms, Frescobaldi's piece also contains the related *ciaccona*, a fast dance in syncopated triple meter also built over repetitive chord progressions. (The ciaccona, owing to its many adaptations on the French stage, has become falsely but firmly identified with France and is now most widely known as the ***chaconne***.)

The Dutch organist Jan Pieterszoon Sweelinck (1562–1621), Frescobaldi's older contemporary, succeeded his father as chief organist at Amsterdam's Oude Kerk (Old Church) while still in his teens, and he held the position until his death. Sweelinck was not a church organist in the full sense of the word. The Dutch Reformed Church, Calvinist in outlook, forbade the use of polyphonic or instrumental music during services. He was employed not by the church, but by the city of Amsterdam as a civil servant to perform what amounted to daily organ recitals following the morning and evening services. Like Frescobaldi and every other keyboard virtuoso of the day, Sweelinck was best known for his improvisations, and the works he wrote down represented the best of this daily exercise.

Figure 8-2 Girolamo Frescobaldi.

For publication Sweelinck composed a great deal of polyphonic vocal music in the main genres and styles of the late sixteenth century, most of it secular and none of it meant for actual service use. Intended for the international music trade, it was therefore composed to texts in international languages: French (chansons and metrical psalms), Latin (motets), and Italian (madrigals). His dual preoccupation with old-fashioned vocal music and up-to-date keyboard compositions

Figure 8-3 Interior of St. Peter's Basilica in Rome, where Frescobaldi played the organ.

puts Sweelinck in a position comparable to no other Netherlander but, rather, to William Byrd, his older English contemporary.

Although he never met Byrd, Sweelinck was well acquainted with several other English composers who had settled in the Catholic part of the Netherlands that is now Belgium, among them Peter Philips (ca. 1560/61–1628) and John Bull (ca. 1562/63–1628). Philips and Bull were the agents through which the advanced art of the Elizabethan keyboard composers established a Continental base. These composers wrote not just for organ but also for harpsichord (invented around the end of the fourteenth century) and the smaller **virginal** (Fig. 8-4) and clavichord. Once Sweelinck had absorbed the English styles and genres, his work began circulating in England along with native wares. Several of his pieces are found in what was known as the Fitzwilliam Virginal Book, a mammoth collection of English keyboard music and the chief source for much of Philips and Bull.

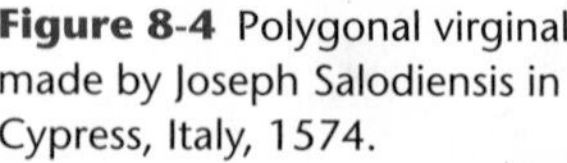

Figure 8-4 Polygonal virginal made by Joseph Salodiensis in Cypress, Italy, 1574.

Lutheran Adaptations: The Chorale Partita and Chorale Concerto

Sweelinck's historical importance also derives from his extensive and much sought-after teaching activity. His best pupils were German. For a time the three principal organ posts in Hamburg, the largest north German city, were held by his former students. Most of Sweelinck's own organ compositions are found in a huge manuscript that probably dates from the early 1630s and is otherwise devoted to chorale variations by a dozen or so of his German pupils, some in the form of collaborative sets, with individual variations contributed by both master and disciples.

In these chorale variations the basic technique is the same. The variations correspond to the stanzas of the chorale. In each of them the traditional melody is treated strictly—that is, with little or no embellishment—as a cantus firmus in a single voice. Whereas secular variation sets of the time kept the tune consistently in the uppermost register, the chorale variations not only allow the lower instrumental lines to be tune bearers in the old cantus firmus manner but also allow the hymn tune to migrate through the texture as stanza succeeds stanza. Sometimes the other lines incorporate aspects of the chorale tune, thus integrating it into the polyphony; sometimes they contrast with it as countersubjects. This, too, was a technique that Sweelinck had picked up from the English and passed along to his pupils. Sweelinck engaged as well in some friendly rivalry, recalling the emulation games of the early Netherlanders, with his prize pupil, Samuel Scheidt (1587–1654).

Do we get more aesthetic gratification from the standpoint that sees* Christ lag in Todesbanden *as "deviant" or from the one that sees it groping, so to speak, toward a more modern conception of tonality?

The end result was the Lutheran **chorale partita**, as practiced early on by Scheidt, most spectacularly later by J. S. Bach, as well as by countless Lutheran organist-composers to this day. Scheidt's partita on *Christ lag in Todesbanden* (Christ Lay in Death's Bonds), published in 1624, comes from the second volume of *Tabulatura nova* (New Tablature), printed 100 years after the earliest polyphonic vocal settings of the chorale had appeared. Once again we see "newness" as a selling point; in this instance it seems to refer both to its notation and to the musical style.

Anthology Vol 1-70
Full CD II, 23

Scheidt's piece is in five stanzas and begins with two connected settings of the chorale melody in the highest part: The first is an integrated motetlike setting, with some old-fashioned imitative foreshadowing of the cantus firmus in the accompanying voices (Ex. 8-1); in the second the successive lines of the chorale are set in relief against a series of ever-more rhythmically active countersubjects, each treated in imitation. The central third stanza is a "free" variation, the longest but most modestly scored, while the fourth variation returns to a stricter cantus firmus style. The last variation is harmonized in a very unusual fashion that could be considered either tonally wayward (to adopt the viewpoint and expectations of an observer contemporary with Scheidt) or tonally progressive (to adopt the viewpoint and expectations of an observer today). It is a fascinating case to consider, for the difference between the two historical and aesthetic vantage points is rarely so clear-cut. Do we get more aesthetic gratification from the standpoint that sees the piece as intriguingly capricious or "deviant" or from the one that sees it groping, so to speak, toward a more modern (familiar? higher? more integrated?) conception of tonality? Can we somehow view it from both standpoints at once?

The Lutheran chorale partita had its vocal counterpart as well, in which sacred genres that had developed elsewhere were adapted to specifically Lutheran use. The result was the so-called **chorale concerto**, a mixed vocal-instrumental genre that in its more modest specimens seemed a direct outgrowth of Lodovico Viadana's pioneering *Cento concerti ecclesiastici* of 1602 (pirated by a German publisher seven years later) and that in its more lavish ones could vie with the most extravagant outpourings of the Venetians. Its two main exponents, besides Scheidt, were Michael

Praetorius (1571–1621), organist to the Duke of Brunswick (Braunschweig), and Johann Hermann Schein (1586–1630), the cantor of St. Thomas's School in Leipzig, where J. S. Bach would occupy the same position a hundred years later.

Example 8-1 **Samuel Scheidt, *Christ lag in Todesbanden*: first versus, mm. 1–7**

Schein (like Sweelinck before him and Bach after him) was a contracted civil servant who reported to a town council, not a church employee or a court composer who served at the pleasure of a patron. He published a great deal of secular music as well as sacred, including the *Banchetto musicale* (Musical Banquet, 1617), an early book of dances for listening organized into standardized sequences, or **suites** (though Schein does not use the word). Played by ensembles of viols and violins, they probably served originally as dinner music (*Tafelmusik*, literally "table music") at the noble houses where he briefly worked. What so distinguished Schein's suites was his application to them of the keyboard variation technique pioneered by the virginalists and Sweelinck. The components of each suite, as Schein put it, were integrated both in mode and in "invention," meaning that they were fashioned out of a common fund of melodic ideas so that they became in effect not only a suite but a set of variations as well.

Schein's chorale concerto on *Christ lag in Todesbanden* appeared in his *Opella nova* (A New Collection of Works, 1618), which consisted, according to its title page, of "sacred concertos composed on the Italian plan." The title again attests to the fascination with the new styles and practices being developed in Italy. The piece is scored for two sopranos (boys) and a tenor over a lively basso continuo. For instructions in realizing his continuo parts, Schein actually referred the user of his book to the preface of Viadana's *Cento concerti*.

The incredibly industrious Michael Praetorius, who is said to have died pen in hand on his fiftieth birthday, produced in his relatively brief career well over a thousand compositions, most of which were issued in twenty-five printed collections published between 1605 and his death in 1621. He is also the author of five treatises, including the *Syntagma musicum* (1614–18), a three-volume musical encyclopedia. Most of his works are psalm motets and chorale concertos. His most grandiose compositions were reached in what turned out to be his culminating publication, a three-volume monster issued between 1619 and 1621 and named, significantly, after the ancient muse of oratory and sacred poetry: *Polyhymnia caduceatrix et panegyrica* (Polyhymnia, Bringer of Peace and Singer of Praise). The concertos in this collection, some scored for as many as twenty-one mixed vocal and instrumental parts, were written after Praetorius had visited the court of Dresden, where the musical establishment was the envy of all Germany.

Ruin: Germany, the Thirty Years War, and Heinrich Schütz

This Italianate splendor in Germany was fated not to last. The second quarter of the seventeenth century was a horrendous period for the German-speaking lands, marked by an unremitting series of territorial, dynastic, and religious conflicts collectively known as the Thirty Years War. What had started in 1618 as an abortive revolt of the Protestant nobility in Bohemia against the dominion of the Holy Roman Empire spread across Germany, leading to one blood-soaked battlefield after another. A peace was declared in 1635 that gave the Empire the advantage. This antagonized France, the other great centralized European power, resulting in what in effect became a general European war. Although peace negotiations were pursued in the 1640s, hostilities continued sporadically until 1648.

The result was a vastly weakened Austrian Empire, a vastly strengthened France, and a much weakened Germany. Powerful repercussions of this virtual world war were immediately felt in the arts. The military successes that made France the richest and most prosperous land in Europe laid the foundations for what the French still call their *grand siècle*, their Great Century; we will shortly see some of the musical consequences of that flowering. The impoverishing effects of the war on the arts of the German-speaking lands, on the other hand, can scarcely be imagined. The courtly arts there managed to hang on through tough times, although not without crucial adaptive change. In music, that process of adaptation may be viewed with exceptional clarity thanks to the presence of Heinrich Schütz (1585–1672; Fig. 8-5), a composer of irrepressible genius, whose long career mirrors in an intense creative microcosm the general fate and progress of his art. Despite the conditions in which he was forced to work, Schütz became the first internationally celebrated German master.

Despite the conditions in which he was forced to work, Heinrich Schütz became the first internationally celebrated German master.

Born to a family of innkeepers in the Saxon (east German) town of Köstritz near Gera, a musical instrument center, Schütz displayed his gifts early. His singing voice was noticed by a music-loving nobleman, the Landgrave Moritz of Hessen, who, over the objections of the boy's parents, had him brought to his residence in Kassel for instruction and training "in all the good arts and commendable virtues." After his voice changed, Schütz ostensibly gave up music for university studies in law, also underwritten by Landgrave Moritz, who had become a surrogate father to him.

But then one day in 1609, when his protégé was twenty-four, the Landgrave came to visit him at school with a proposition. Near the end of this life, Schütz recounted what happened: "Since at that time a very famous if elderly musician and composer was still alive in Italy, I was not to miss the opportunity of hearing him and gaining some knowledge from him."[2] The proposal was backed up with a generous cash stipend, and Schütz headed gratefully off to Italy, against his parents' wishes. The famous old musician was

Figure 8-5 Heinrich Schütz. Portrait by Christoph Spetner (ca. 1650).

Giovanni Gabrieli. Schütz spent three years in Venice under his tutelage, right up until the master's death in 1612, by which time he had become his prize pupil. "On his deathbed," Schütz recalled, "he had arranged out of special affection that I should receive one of the rings he left behind as a remembrance of him."[3] The benedictory gift not only signaled the passing of the Venetian musical heritage to a new generation but also symbolized its becoming, through Schütz, an international standard.

Schütz had recently composed a book of Italian madrigals that Gabrieli thought worthy of publication. It was issued in Venice in 1611 with an attribution to *Henrico Sagittario Allemanno*—"Henry Archer (i.e., Schütz) the German"—but its contents are completely indistinguishable in style from the native Italian product. Schütz wanted nothing else. He went back to Germany in 1613 with the intention of fulfilling his promise to his patron by adapting the glorious Venetian style to the needs of the Lutheran church, just as Praetorius and others were also doing, but with the added benefit of authenticity arising out of his actual training at the source. For the rest of his life Schütz saw himself primarily as the bringer of Italianate "light to Germany" (as his tombstone reads) and saw the composition of grand concerted motets and magnificent court spectacles as his true vocation. Given that ambition, his career was dogged by cruel frustration resulting from the long war. His contributions, not only to the musical life of his time but to the historical legacy of German music, did not match his intentions. But his musical imagination was so great and his powers of adaptation so keen that what he did accomplish was arguably a greater fulfillment of his gifts than what he set out to achieve.

On returning to Germany with his sterling credentials, Schütz went back to work for Landgrave Moritz. The next year, however, the Elector of Saxony, a personage far superior in rank to the Landgrave, called Schütz to his legendarily appointed court at Dresden, the very court that inspired Praetorius's splendid *Polyhymnia* motets. Schütz spent his entire subsequent career at Dresden, serving faithfully through thick and thin for almost sixty years (Fig. 8-6).

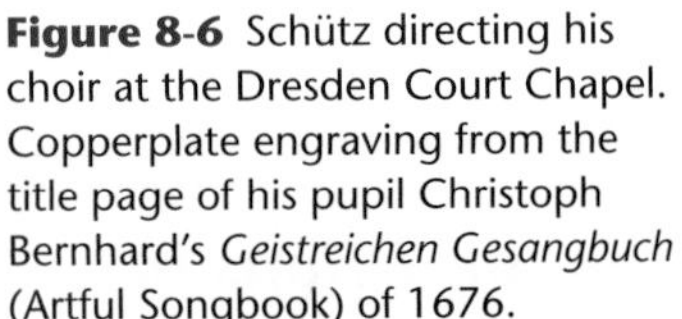

Figure 8-6 Schütz directing his choir at the Dresden Court Chapel. Copperplate engraving from the title page of his pupil Christoph Bernhard's *Geistreichen Gesangbuch* (Artful Songbook) of 1676.

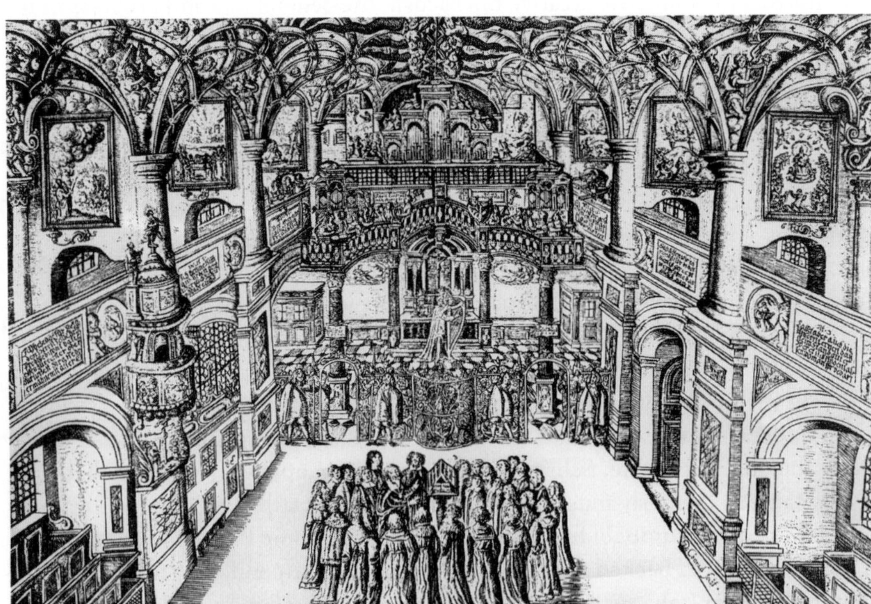

At first the times were thick, indeed downright opulent, and thus well suited to Schütz's Italianate ambitions. His first German publication, issued in 1619, was *Psalmen Davids* (Psalms of David), a book of twenty-six sumptuous concerted motets for up to four antiphonal choruses with continuo and parts for strings and brass used as available. He also composed an opera, *Daphne*, the first ever to set a German text, on the time-honored subject of Apollo and Daphne. The libretto was in fact an adaptation of Rinuccini's libretto for Peri's *La Dafne*. Except for the early book of madrigals, however, Schütz's secular output, comprising as well an Orpheus opera and a whole series of court ballets, has perished, with only the most negligible exceptions. The remaining 500 or so works by which he is known to us are virtually all sacred.

From his Latin-texted *Cantiones sacrae* of 1625 to his German-texted *Geistliche Chor-Music* (Sacred Choral Music), of 1648, Schütz's output reflects to varying degrees the austerity of wartime conditions, when court establishments were decimated by conscription and arts budgets were ruthlessly slashed. Schütz was forced to renounce the polychoral style in favor of simpler choral textures and even sparser forces. Faced with increasingly difficult conditions in Dresden, he petitioned to wait out the war in Venice. He departed in August 1628 and stayed for about a year. During this time it appears he became acquainted with Monteverdi, now the *maestro di cappella* at St. Mark's; Schütz experimented on the scene with the new declamatory styles that Monteverdi had pioneered.

The "Luxuriant Style"

Anthology Vol 1-71
Full CD II, 24
Concise CD I, 78

While in Italy Schütz published a book of fifteen comparatively modest sacred concertos with Latin texts, which he called *Symphoniae sacrae* (Part I, 1629), in tribute to Gabrieli. One of its best-known items is *O quam tu pulchra es*, which sets words from the Bible's Song of Songs that had already served countless composers going back as far as Dunstable. The title alone indicates that Schütz adapted the text, making it even more vivid by adding an opening exclamation and personalizing pronoun to the original *Quam pulchra es, amica mea! quam pulchra es!* ("How beautiful art thou, my love! how beautiful art thou!"), which becomes ***O*** *quam* ***tu*** *pulchra es*. The reason the biblical source was so popular among composers surely lies in the spectacularly erotic text, which includes a catalogue of the beloved's anatomy. This furnished Schütz with both a wonderful opportunity to display the attractions of a new luxuriant style and a pretext for pushing the style to new heights of allure.

The term "luxuriant style" (*stylus luxurians*), meaning a style brimming with exuberant detail, in contrast with the old "plain style" (*stylus gravis*), was coined by Schütz's pupil Christoph Bernhard (1628–92) in a treatise that was presumed to transmit Schütz's teachings. What mainly abounded in the luxuriant style was dissonance, which makes it the rough equivalent of Monteverdi's *seconda pratica*. Like Monteverdi, Bernhard stipulated that freely handled dissonances arose out of, and were justified by, the imagery and emotional content of a text. [4] The luxuriant style was anything but a passive response to the words; it was, rather, an aspect of rhetoric through ornamenting musical speech. *O quam tu pulchra es* shows this especially well, for Schütz actively shaped the text to his musical purposes even as he shaped the music to conform to the text's specifications. It was a process of mutual enhancement and intensification that bore an offspring more powerfully expressive than either words or music alone could be.

One of the most remarkable aspects of *O quam tu pulchra es* is the refrain, among the most ancient of all musical and poetical devices. The way Schütz employs it here, however, it acts in a double role—or, rather, it combines two roles. It is a structural unifier, necessary in a composition that otherwise sets so many contrasting textual images to contrasting musical ideas. At the same time it is the bearer of the central affective message, saturating the whole with desire by constantly reiterating and intensifying the dissonant diminished fourth. As both a structural integrator and an expressive one, the refrain blurs the line between the expressive and the structural. From now on, musical ideas would tend increasingly to function on this dual plane; ultimately that is what one means by a musical "theme."

Back to Germany at War

Schütz returned from his second Italian sojourn to find conditions in Germany greatly worsened, with the war economy interfering ever more directly with musical opportunities. Most of Schütz's singers were drafted into the army; by 1633, the Dresden musical establishment, once the envy of Germany, was to all intents and purposes disabled. The extravagant Gabrielian side of Schütz's Venetian heritage thus was deprived of an outlet. "I am of less than no use," the unhappy composer complained in a letter from the time.[5] During these bleak years Schütz's leaner side came into its own, as if by default. In 1636 and in 1639 he published collections of what he called *Kleine geistliche Concerte* (Little Sacred Concertos), radically scaled-down compositions for up to five solo voices with organ continuo. These ascetic compositions were characterized not only by drastically curtailed performing forces but also by a mournfully subjective mood.

In Schütz's new-found techniques of poignant text expression, we may observe the beginnings of a tendency that would reach a remarkable climax in music of the next century: the deliberate cultivation of unpleasant sounds, sometimes downright ugly, in the name of God's truth, as a means toward an authentic musical asceticism. It is often thought to be a specifically German aesthetic, evidence of a special Germanic or Protestant perceptiveness of scripture, as distinct from Italianate or Catholic pomp and sensuality. And yet the musical means by which it was accomplished, as Schütz's career clearly demonstrates, were nevertheless rooted in Catholic Italy. Schütz was only the father of modern German music to the extent that he served as a conveyor of those Italianate concerns.

Schütz was the father of modern German music to the extent that he served as a conveyor of those Italianate concerns.

Rebuilding the impoverished German courts and their cultural establishments could only begin after the signing of the Peace of Westphalia in October 1648, which essentially terminated the Holy Roman Empire as an effective political institution, although it would not be formally dissolved until 1806. The German Protestant states, which included Saxony, were recognized as sovereign entities. Schütz's patron, the Elector Johann Georg, emerged from the war as one of the most powerful Protestant princes of Germany. Schütz's last publications reflected these improved fortunes. In 1647 he issued a second book of *Symphoniae sacrae*, modestly scored like the first, but this time with texts in German. The next year saw the publication of his *Geistliche Chor-Music*, beautifully crafted polyphonic motets specifically intended for performance by the full chorus rather than soloists.

Finally, in 1650, at age sixty-five, he issued what is now thought of as his testamentary work, the third book of *Symphoniae sacrae,* also in German and now scored for forces of a size he had not had at his disposal for decades. The music, though, was still characterized by the terseness and sharpness of expression he had cultivated during the lean years. Schütz's extravagant and spare sides had met at last in a German synthesis.

Anthology Vol 1-72
Full CD II, 25
Concise CD I, 79

One of the crowning masterworks in this final collection is *Saul, Saul, was verfolgst du mich?* (Saul, Saul, why do you persecute me?), scored for six vocal soloists, two choruses, and a small instrumental contingent. The text consists of two lines from the Acts of the Apostles (26: 14) containing Christ's words to the Jewish priest Saul on the road toward Damascus. According to the biblical account, Saul later reported the circumstances of his conversion:

> I myself once thought it my duty to work actively against the name of Jesus of Nazareth; and I did so in Jerusalem. . . . In all the synagogues I tried by repeated punishment to make them renounce their faith; indeed my fury rose to such a pitch that I extended my persecution to foreign cities.
>
> On one such occasion I was travelling to Damascus with authority and commission from the chief priests; . . . in the middle of the day I saw a light from the sky, more brilliant than the sun, shining all around me and my travelling companions. We all fell to the ground, and then I heard a voice saying to me in the Jewish language, *"Saul, Saul, why do you persecute me? It is hard for you, this kicking against the goad."* I said, "Tell me, Lord, who you are"; and the Lord replied, "I am Jesus, whom you are persecuting. But now, rise to your feet and stand upright. I have appeared to you for a purpose: to appoint you my servant and witness, to testify both to what you have seen and to what you shall yet see of me." (Translation from *The New English Bible.*)

Thus did Saul become the Apostle Paul. The italicized words are the ones that Schütz set, with the surrounding narration of Paul's miraculous conversion conveyed by means of dramatic symbolism. The words echo one another, portrayed in the music not only by repetition but also by the use of explicitly indicated dynamics, something that was pioneered in Venice by Schütz's teacher, Gabrieli. Schütz in effect imports the musical legacy of the Counter-Reformation into the land of the Reformation, reappropriating for Protestant use the musical techniques that had been originally forged as a weapon against the spread of Protestantism.

Schütz's largest surviving works are **oratorios**, or, as he called them, *Historien*—biblical "narratives," in which narration, sung by an "Evangelist" or Gospel reciter, alternates with dialogue. Oratorios were most traditionally assigned to Easter week, when the Gospel narratives of Christ's Passion and Resurrection were recited at length. Four of Schütz's five were Easter pieces: a Resurrection oratorio composed early in his career and three late settings of the Passion according to the Apostles Matthew, Luke, and John. These last, in keeping with Dresden liturgical requirements for Good Friday, are austerely old-fashioned *a cappella* works in which the chorus sings the words of the crowd (*turba*) and the solo parts (the Evangelist, Jesus, and every other character whose words are directly quoted) are written in a kind of imitation plainchant for unaccompanied solo voices. The remaining "Christmas" oratorio, performed in Dresden in 1660, is by contrast a thoroughly Italianized, effervescent outpouring of Christmas cheer.

Giacomo Carissimi: Oratorio and Cantata

The chief Italian composer of oratorios in the time of Schütz was Giacomo Carissimi (1605–74), a priest who served as organist and maestro di cappella at the Jesuit German and Hungarian College in Rome from 1629 until his death. Not surprisingly, most of the music in Rome was religious, and although there were some secular operas performed, such as *La morte d'Orfeo* (The Death of Orpheus, 1619) by Stefano Landi (1587–1639), sacred Christian themes were common. Oratorios offered a more modest format than opera to tell religious stories. Carissimi's eleven surviving works in the genre probably represent only a fraction of the biblical narratives he composed, beginning in the 1640s. They were performed during Lent at the College and at other Roman institutions, notably the Oratorio del Santissimo Crocifisso (Oratory of the Most Holy Crucifix), which lent its name to the genre. His many foreign pupils at the College included Christoph Bernhard, who had already trained with Schütz, and the French composer Marc-Antoine Charpentier (1643–1704), who brought the practice of setting dramatic narratives from the Latin Bible back with him to his native country.

Anthology Vol 1-73
Full CD II, 26

Carissimi's most famous oratorio, *Jephte,* composed no later than 1648, takes its story from the Book of Judges. The Israelite commander Jephte vows that if God grants him victory over the Ammonites, he will sacrifice the first person who greets him on his return home. That turns out to be his beloved daughter, a virgin, who is duly slaughtered after spending two months on the mountaintop with her companions, lamenting her fate. The last part of Carissimi's setting, consisting of two laments, the daughter's and then the community's, is introduced by a portion of narrative text. In Carissimi's setting, the function of narrator is a rotating one, distributed among various solo voices and even the chorus. The daughter's lament makes use of echo effects that suggest the reverberations of her keening off the rocky face of the surrounding mountains. Carissimi's music thus not only expresses her feelings but also sets the scene. The double and even triple suspensions (on *lamentamini,* "lament ye!") in the concluding six-part chorus are a remarkable application of "madrigalism" to what is in most other ways a typically Roman exercise in *stile antico* polyphony.

Carissimi's other major service appointment was as *maestro di cappella del concerto di camera* (director of chamber concerts) for Queen Christina of Sweden (1626–89), patroness of the philosopher René Descartes. She lived in Rome following her notorious abdication in 1654 and subsequent conversion to Catholicism. For her as well as for other noble salons, Carissimi turned out well over 100 settings of Italian love poetry in a new style known generically as ***cantata***, a "sung," or vocal, piece, as opposed to *sonata*, a "played," or instrumental, one. Carissimi wrote so many cantatas that he is sometimes credited with inventing the genre, which was, however, already well established in Rome.

Like monody, the cantata was a solo successor to the madrigal. It eventually came to denote a relatively ambitious setting that mixed several forms in a quasi-dramatic sequence—strophic or ground-bass arias, little dancelike songs (an *arietta*), recitatives, and so forth. The more or less regular alternation of narrative and lyric items—recitatives that set the scene and arias that poured out feeling—first became standardized in the Roman cantata. It soon characterized all dramatic genres, especially opera. Most of the conventional aria types that later provided the core of Italian opera were tried out in the cantata as well. The genre could thus be viewed as a kind of musico-dramatic laboratory, and some cantatas can be thought of as much-reduced operatic scenes.

Barbara Strozzi: Performer and Composer

Anthology Vol 1-74

From Rome, the cantata radiated out to more northerly Italian cities, chiefly Bologna and Venice, the latter still the great center of music publishing. *Lagrime mie* ("My tears") is an especially rich example by the Venetian singer and composer Barbara Strozzi (1619–77; Fig. 8-7), a pupil of Francesco Cavalli (1602–76), the foremost Venetian opera composer at midcentury. She was the adopted (perhaps illegitimate) daughter of Giulio Strozzi, a famous poet-librettist whose words were set by almost every Venetian composer from Monteverdi on down. That Barbara Strozzi published eight books of madrigals, cantatas, and arias and did so at a time when prejudice against the creative abilities of women ran high bears impressive witness to her excellence as a composer in the eyes of her contemporaries. *Lagrime mie* comes from her seventh book, titled *Diporti di Euterpe* (Recreations of Euterpe), after the muse of lyric poetry and music. This collection appeared in 1659, when the composer was forty years old and finished with her singing career.

The text, following convention, is composed from the male perspective. A lover laments the loss of his beloved, locked away in her father's castle. The vocal range is soprano, however, and might as well have been taken by a female singer such as Strozzi herself as by a castrato. The setting of the opening line, which will return later as a refrain, is identified by harsh and unconventionally resolved dissonances and by a somewhat decorated scalar descent in the bass from tonic to dominant as a lament (Ex. 8-2). Expressive dissonance in the manner of the *seconda pratica* arrives as a palpable twinge on the word *dolore* (sadness), giving concrete auditory representation to the lover's pain. The second stanza is divided quasi-operatically into narrative and lyric segments. The culminating aria ("E voi, lumi dolente, non piangete?"/"And you, sad eyes, do not cry?") is cast in a stately triple meter. The final stanza is the most obvious harbinger of the recitative/aria pairing that would soon become standard operating procedure. The first couplet is set in a free, unpredictable style that follows the rhythm of speech in good *seconda pratica* fashion; the second returns to the flowing triple meter. The last line of the cantata provides a lyric capstone, ascending to its highest note and signaling the end by means of a full harmonic closure.

Figure 8-7 Barbara Strozzi. Portrait with bass viol by Bernardo Strozzi (ca. 1640).

Strozzi is the first woman composer we have discussed at any length since the Benedictine abbess Hildegard of Bingen and the trobairitz Comtessa de Dia in the late twelfth century. As we saw then, it was access to power, coming either from social position as a noblewoman or as the leader of a religious order, that provided the circumstances in which women could create music, have it performed, and find the means for it ultimately to be preserved through notation. In the late sixteenth and seventeenth centuries, careers began opening up to women as performers with the advent of professionalized court singing, particularly at the music-loving court of Ferrara in northern Italy, which maintained a famous *concerto delle donne,* a "consort" of virtuoso women singers for whom were written flamboyantly ornate madrigals. With the advent of public opera in Italy beginning in the 1630s, women performers reached new heights of accomplishment and renown. And yet their musical accomplishments brought women performers not enhanced social status but, rather, the opposite. Women who sang or danced in public still bore a stigma in early modern Europe, where such activities were traditionally associated with prostitutes (or courtesans, as they were known in more elevated social circles). Thus one modern study of the *concerto delle donne* and other professional court singers of the time bears the title "Courtesans, Muses or Musicians?" and confirms the fact that, unless married to a nobleman, a professional woman singer was thought of as "a remarkable renegade to be looked at, applauded, but not included in polite society."[6]

Example 8-2 Barbara Strozzi, Cantata: *Lagrime mie,* mm. 1–13

La - - - - - gri-me mi - e,
à che vi_____ trat-te - ne - - te, Per -
- che non i - sfo-ga - te il fier, il fier do - lo - - - re.

Tears of mine, why do you hold back, why don't you wash away the pain

Strozzi was nevertheless able to function as a professional composer as well as a performer, a new development. Many of the women performers at Ferrara and other north Italian courts were known to have composed a significant part of their own repertoires, but with only a single notable exception—Maddalena Casulana, who issued three books of madrigals in Venice between 1568 and 1583—they did not publish their work and are lost as composers to history. Strozzi, by contrast, was considered an important composer in her day, as was her older contemporary Francesca Caccini (1587–ca. 1641), who published a book of monodies in 1618 and composed the opera *La liberazione di Ruggiero dall'isola d'Alcina* (Ruggiero's Deliverance from the Island of Alcina) for the Medici court in Florence in 1625.

Just to name these two composers, however, is to explain their exceptional status and to realize that they are only exceptions that, as the saying goes, "prove the rule." Both of them were daughters of famous fathers who commanded great prestige in musical circles. On their fathers' coattails they could find an outlet for their talents while other gifted women, perhaps equally great, could find none. Strozzi, in an effort to mitigate the audacity of her career objectives, paid tribute to the prejudice against women composers even as she overcame it, writing in the preface to her first publication that "as a woman, I publish [it] all too anxiously," and in her second, dedicated to the Emperor of Austria, that "the lowly mine of a woman's poor imagination cannot produce metal to forge those richest golden crowns worthy of august rulers."[7]

Francesca Caccini left the service of the Medici on the death of her husband in 1626. She married again a year later, to a wealthy nobleman, and continued to compose music for entertainments at her new home, but she now did so anonymously, as appropriate for her newly elevated social rank.[8] Thus, ironically, access to a private fortune through marriage—a marriage probably contracted precisely because of her musical talents—actually took away from Caccini the outlet she had formerly possessed, by virtue of her father's fame, to the public profession of music and the dissemination of her works. Indeed, she now outranked her father socially. After her second husband's death, she returned to the Medici court, but as a lady-in-waiting rather than as a designated musician. She did, however, sing in chapel services and also taught music in a convent school. In a final touch of irony, she refused permission to have her daughter sing in a dramatic spectacle such as she had participated in during her own previous stint in service, lest it damage the girl's prospects for a good marriage or admission to a convent.

The French Taste: Sense and Sensuousness

The musical style cultivated in France during the seventeenth century was quite distinct from that developed in Italy; indeed, the two countries in some respects came to represent contrasting poles. The story is told that a courtier fond of the grandeur of Italian music once brought before the French King Louis XIV (1638–1715) a young violinist who had studied under the finest Italian masters and bade him play the most dazzling piece he knew. When the young musician was finished, the king sent for one of his own violinists and asked him to play a simple air from *Cadmus et Hermione*, an opera by his court composer, Jean-Baptiste Lully (1632–87; Fig. 8-8). The violinist was mediocre, the air was plain, and *Cadmus* was not by any means one of Lully's most impressive works. But when the air was finished, the king turned to the courtier and said, "All I can say, sir, is that that is my taste."[9]

Invoking taste, something that is proverbially beyond dispute, is always a fine way of ending an argument, especially when invoked by one to whom nobody may talk back. But while a king's taste may not be disputed, it may still be worth investigating. Nor can we say we really understand such a story unless we know who is telling it and why. This particular anecdote comes from a pamphlet, *Comparaison de la musique italienne et de la musique française* (A Comparison of French and Italian Music), issued in 1704 by a French aristocrat, Jean Laurent Le Cerf de la Viéville, in answer to a like-named pamphlet, *Parallèle des Italiens et des Français* (Differentiating the Italians from the French), released two years earlier by another French aristocrat, Abbé François Raguenet. It was the opening salvo of a press war that would last in France throughout the century—that is, until the French Revolution of 1789 rendered all the old aristocratic controversies *passé*.

Figure 8-8 Jean-Baptiste Lully.

The reason it enters our story a little ahead of schedule, and why it was so very typical of France, is that the musician it defended had been dead for almost twenty years at the time of writing, and *Cadmus*, his second opera, had had its first performance more than thirty years before. Nowhere else in Europe had operas become classics in this way; nor had any other composer of operas been exalted into a symbol not only of royal taste but of royal authority as well. Authority is what French music was all about.

Lurking behind the story, as behind most discussions of opera in France, was a political debate. It was touched off by Raguenet's admiring description of castrato singing, which he said resembled "that of the nightingale." His delight in the purely sensuous pleasure of singing not only went against the grain of Le Cerf de la Viéville's argument, which ends with strenuous exhortations to "yield to reason," but also went against the whole history of operatic reception in France. Opera had had a difficult time getting started there, in part because it had to succeed as politics before having any chance of succeeding as art. Like their English counterparts, who also possessed a glorious tradition of spoken theater (as the Italians did not), the French aristocrats saw only a child's babble in what the Italians called *dramma per musica* (play for music). To their minds, the art of music and the art of drama simply would not mix. Music in the theater, for the thinking French as for the thinking English, was at best an elegant bauble, more likely a nuisance and a threat to reason.

Tragédie Lyrique: The Politics of Patronage

The irrational, though, can have its rational uses, and nobody knew that better than Cardinal Jules Mazarin, the most artful seventeenth-century politician in France. Born Giulio Mazarini in Italy in 1602, he took the first steps, in the earliest years of the boy-king Louis XIV's reign, to establish opera in his adopted country. He recruited the services of Luigi Rossi (ca. 1597–1653), the leading composer of Rome, to write one expressly for the French court. Fittingly, one of the first officially sponsored French operas, performed at the Palais Royal on 2 March 1647, was another *Orfeo*, another demonstrative setting of the myth of music's primeval power to move the soul. For this spectacular and successful production Rossi enlisted a troupe of Roman singers and instrumentalists, a little colony of Italians in the French capital who were personally loyal to Mazarin and who, in the time-honored fashion of traveling virtuosos, could serve him as secret agents and spies in his diplomatic maneuvers with the papal court. All of this was a lesson to Mazarin's apprentice, the young king. The foundations were laid for the French *grand siècle*, and opera was destined to be one of its grandest manifestations.

The French court opera was wholly centralized and meant to glorify the state and its "Sun King," Louis XIV, who allegedly proclaimed: "L'État, c'est moi" ("I am the State").

Yet it was a very special sort of opera that would reign in France, one tailored to accommodate national tastes, court traditions, and royal prerogatives. The French autocracy was the largest ethnically integrated political entity in Europe. Its royal court was the exemplary aristocratic establishment of the day, and its musical displays would classically embody the politics of dynastic affirmation. Like every other aspect of French administrative culture, the French court opera

Figure 8-9 Promenade of Louis XIV in the gardens of Versailles, ca. 1688, by Etienne Allegrain (1644–1736).

was wholly centralized and meant to glorify the state and its "Sun King," Louis XIV (Figs. 8-9 and 8-10), who famously, at least according to legend, proclaimed: "*L'État, c'est moi*" ("I am the State").

No operatic spectacle could be publicly shown anywhere in France that had not been previewed at court. At the same time, however, French opera generally aimed far higher than the "musical tales" of the Italians, which were essentially modest pastoral plays. The French form aspired to the status of a full-fledged *tragédie en musique*, later called ***tragédie lyrique***, which meant that the treasured values of spoken drama were to be preserved as far as possible in the new medium, despite the presence of music.

To reconcile the claims of court pageantry with those of dramatic gravity was no mean trick. Only a very special genius could bring it off. At the time of Rossi's momentous sojourn in France, another far less distinguished Italian musician—just an apprentice, really—was already living there: Giovanni Battista Lulli, a Florentine boy who had been brought to Paris in 1646, at age thirteen, to serve an aristocratic Parisian who wanted to practice her Italian. She supported his training in courtly dancing and violin playing. When his patroness was exiled in 1652, Lulli found work as a servant to Louis XIV's cousin Anne-Marie-Louise d'Orleans. As a dancer and mime at the royal court, he danced alongside, and made friends with, the teenage king. The next year Lulli assumed the position as court composer of ballroom music.

His rise to supreme power was steady and unstoppable, for Lulli was a veritable musical Mazarin, an Italian-born French political manipulator of genius. Like Mazarin, he was naturalized and adopted a French version of his name: Jean-Baptiste Lully. Shortly after the founding in 1669 of the Académie Royale de Musique, Louis XIV's opera establishment, he managed to finagle the rights to manage

Figure 8-10 Ballet costume worn by Louis XIV as Apollo/the sun in a court ballet.

it from the originally designated patent holder. From then on he was a musical Sun King, the absolute autocrat of French music, which he recreated in his own image.

Lully had a crown-supported monopoly over his domain, from which he could exclude any rival who threatened his preeminence. He squeezed out his older, native-born contemporary Robert Cambert (ca. 1628–77), who withdrew, embittered, to London. Marc-Antoine Charpentier, a brilliant younger competitor, although trained in Italy and employed by the king's cousin and later by the *dauphin* (the future Louis XV), had to wait until the age of fifty before he could get his opera *Medée* produced at court, several years after Lully's long-awaited death in 1687. (The old monopolist had died of gangrene, following a celebrated self-inflicted mishap while conducting when he struck his foot with a time-beating cane.) By then Lully had produced thirteen *tragédies lyriques*, averaging one every fifteen months. His works would dominate the French repertory for half a century after his death, not in response to market forces or to public demand but, rather, by royal decree, giving Lully a vicarious reign comparable in number of years to his patron's and extending through most of the reign of Louis XV as well. His style did not merely define an art form, it defined a national identity. *La musique*, he might well have said, *c'est moi*.

Drama as Court Ritual

The ultimate theatrical representation of power, the Lullian *tragédie lyrique*, was from first to last a sumptuously outfitted metaphor for the grandeur and authority of the court that it adorned. The monumental mythological and heroic-historical plots, some chosen by the king himself, celebrated the implacable universal order and the supremacy of divine or divinely appointed rulers. Sacrificial themes predominated, as in Lully's *Alceste* (1674), his second *tragédie lyrique* and one of his most successful. It was based on the myth about a queen who gives up her life so that her husband's life-threatening malady may be cured, adapted from Euripides's Greek tragedy by Philippe Quinault (1635–88), a court poet and member of the Académie Française who became Lully's principal librettist.

The regal grandeur of French opera typically begins with an *ouverture* whose slow dotted rhythms in the opening section (which is repeated) lead to a fast imitative section in a different meter, which is also repeated. (Many overtures then return to the slow, dotted-rhythm opening.) The distinctive rhythms became a universal code for pomp. The so-called **French overture** style, which, we will see, many composers from many countries later adopted, was actually Cambert's invention. He first used it in his pastorale *Pomone* (1671), performed a year before Lully managed to secure the royal patent and ruin his rival. Lully took over his stylistic innovations and expanded them into their classic form, as we can hear in the overture to his opera *Atys*, of 1676. What the overture served to introduce was an obligatory prologue celebrating the royalty and lasting a full act, thus vastly outstripping its Italian courtly prototype. Here, mythological beings were summoned to extol the king's magnificent person and his deeds at war and peace. This is all

Anthology Vol 1-75
Full CD II, 27
Concise CD I, 80

done with choral pageantry and with suites of dances modeled on the actual ***ballet de cour*** or court ballet. An elaborate ritual in which the king himself took part (he was a very fine dancer), it symbolized the divinely instituted social hierarchy.

The ceremonial movements were accompanied by *Les Vingt-Quatre Violons du Roi* (The Twenty-Four Violins of the King), the grandest and most disciplined orchestra in Europe. The ensemble consisted of an entire string orchestra, typically scored in five parts: violins, three kinds of violas, and cellos (6 + 4 + 4 + 4 + 6), and often supplemented by a dozen wind instruments. The violins project a prominent high melodic line supported by a strong bass; the violas fill in the harmony in the middle. Throughout Lully's theatrical spectacles dancing furnished a lavish symbolic counterpoint to the words, sometimes enlarging directly on the dramatic action, sometimes contrasting with it. Everything reached culmination in a monumental *chaconne* or *passacaille*, a stately choral dance over a ground bass. It often went on for hundreds of measures, enlisting all the characters for the purpose of announcing an explicit moral. To drive it home the players wore "modern dress," adapted from contemporary court regalia, just as the dances they performed were familiar from their own ballroom: sarabandes, gavottes, and passepieds. Thus the theatrical pageant was no mere reminiscence of a social dance; it *was* a social dance enacted by professional stand-ins.

The theatrical pageant was no mere reminiscence of a social dance; it* was *a social dance enacted by professional stand-ins.

Along with this feast of symbolic movement and rich sonority went a strong prejudice against virtuosic singing, which was rejected largely for reasons having to do with the theatrical traditions of France, most importantly fidelity to articulate language, the first thing to go in flashy "operatic" singing. The lead performers in French court opera remained nominally actors, and the voice of the castrato went unheard in the land—even when, in Lully's *Atys*, the plot actually hinged on castration.

Lully's *Atys*, the King's Opera

Of course the brave castrato voice never referred to its own circumstances. The one thing its powerful timbre never symbolized was actual eunuchhood. And so the last character a castrato might have effectively represented was Atys, or Attis, the hero of Lully's ultimate courtly sacrifice-spectacle, known in its time as "the king's opera." Attis was a god of pre-Hellenic religion, later taken over as a minor deity by the Greeks. Like Adonis, he was a beautiful youth over whom goddesses fought jealous battles. Cybèle, the earth goddess, fell in love with the unwitting Attis and, so that none other shall ever know his love, caused him to castrate himself in a sudden frenzy.

In Quinault's libretto, Cybèle's rival for the love of Attis is the nymph Sangaride, to whom Attis has actually declared his affections. At the end of the opera, Cybèle causes Attis to kill Sangaride in his frenzy and then to stab himself fatally. Before he can die, Cybèle transforms him into a pine tree whose life is renewed yearly so that she will be able to love it forever. There has long been speculation, based on gossipy letters that turned out to be forgeries, that Lully's *Atys* was a symbolic representation of a love triangle that was actually being played out at the time in Louis XIV's own household, involving the king, his queen, and the woman who would later become his second wife. No wonder *Atys* became known as "the king's opera."

Anthology Vol 1-75
Full CD II, 28–34
Concise CD I, 81

The third act of *Atys* is a perfect model of courtly opera at the peak of its prestige. It begins with a short soliloquy for the title character in which he laments the loss of Sangaride to her betrothed, King Celenus of Phrygia. This little number epitomizes Lully's deliberate avoidance of vocal display in the interests of dramatic realism. It makes use of the characteristic meter and rhythm of the sarabande, thus showing that even the vocal solos reflect the underlying basis of dance in the French court opera. The setting of the text is entirely syllabic and responsive to the contours, stresses, and lengths of the spoken language, reflecting the other underlying basis of the court opera, namely, high-style theatrical declamation.

The prevailing element of various dances continues. The most famous scene, which became a standard feature of the *tragédie lyrique* for later composers, comes in the middle of the act. Cybèle has put Atys in an enchanted slumber so that she can apprise him of her love without having to confess it (which would be degrading for a goddess). This subtly erotic *sommeil,* literally the "sleep scene," or "dream symphony," begins with a prelude in which soft, sweet-toned recorders are spotlighted in a somewhat concerto-like dialogue with the string band. The rocking rhythms cradle the entranced title character and serve as the prologue to a charmed vision of Sleep himself (Fig. 8-11), who sings a hypnotic refrain in alternation with his three sons. A short recitative, in which Atys is informed that he has the honor of being loved by the exalted Cybèle, introduces a typical process of alternating recitatives and accompanied airs with refrains.

Exhortations give way to a ballet of sweet dreams (*les songes agréables*), in which the minuet danced by the corps de ballet forms a refrain to alternate with the refrains of Sleep's sons. The sweet dreams are suddenly disrupted by nightmares (*les songes funestes*). This dance is heralded by a bass who warns against offending a divine love, to the strains of an allemande in a pompous style, its regal dotted rhythms reflecting the high station of the goddess at whose behest the nightmares have appeared. The rapid-fire "patter" chorus of evil dreams that follows is in one of Lully's specialty styles. The nightmare sequence ends when the startled Atys is awakened. Cybèle arrives to comfort him but is distressed to learn that although he properly reveres her, he does not return her love. This ultimately leads to the goddess's delivering an impassioned yet dignified lament, the most extended solo turn in the opera. Despite its passionate intensity, however, it is far from what we would expect in a contemporary Italian opera at such a point. Rather, it harks back directly to such masterworks of the early, courtly Italian style as Monteverdi's famous lament for Ariadne—Lully surely knew it—in the otherwise-lost opera *Arianna* of 1608.

Figure 8-11 Costume design by Jean Berain for the *sommeil* ("sleep scene") in Lully's *Atys* (1676).

As we can see from the third act of *Atys*, French singing actors were rarely if ever called on to contend with the full orchestra. Their scenes and confrontations were played against the bare figured bass in a stately, richly nuanced recitative whose supple rhythms in mixed meters caught the lofty cadence of French theatrical declamation. Lully, for whom French was a second language, was said to have modeled this style directly on the closely observed delivery—the contours, tempos, rhythms, and inflections—of La Champmeslé (Marie Desmares, 1642–98), the leading tragedienne of the spoken drama, who created most of the leading roles in the works of the great dramatist Jean Racine (1639–99). Racine personally coached her and thus indirectly coached Lully, whose *tragédies en musique* were exactly contemporaneous with his stage tragedies. Cybèle's concluding lament in Act III of *Atys* was an obvious instance of such musicalized tragic declamation (Ex. 8-3).

Example 8-3 **Jean-Baptiste Lully, *Atys*, Act III, Cybèle's lament (sarabande), mm. 1–14**

Hope so dear and so sweet, Ah! why do you deceive me?

Elaborate ornamentation and cadenzas would only have marred this lofty style, but Lully's singers employed, as if in compensation, a rich repertoire of "graces," or ***agréments***: tiny conventional embellishments—shakes, slides, and swells—that worked in tandem with the bass harmony to punctuate the lines and to enhance their rhetorical projection. Vocal melody was far from the first ingredient or the most potent one, and the singers were held forcibly in check. Vocal virtuosity was admitted only in a decorative capacity, on a par with orchestral color and stage machinery, not as a metaphor for emotion run amok.

Jean-Philippe Rameau

Sacrificial themes served not just Lully. His greatest successor, Jean-Philippe Rameau (1683–1764; Fig. 8–12), honored Louis XV with *Castor et Pollux* (1737), which concerns the mythological twins, immortalized in the constellation Gemini, who were each tested and found willing to sacrifice his life for the sake of the other. As Rameau's opera shows, mythological characters could at times be teased a little. Louis XV's successful mediation in a recent European conflict (the War of Polish

Figure 8-12 Jean-Philippe Rameau in about 1725, portrait by Jacques Aved.

Succession) is symbolized textually by the amorous concord of Venus and Mars, the gods of love and war, and musically by a delightfully incongruous love duet of flute and trumpet. Such levity was tolerable in a prologue, for by showing the foibles of the gods it only enhanced the exaltation of the king above his mythological admirers.

There were also some rare occasions for virtuosic singing, just so long as it came from the lips of anonymous soloists from the general ensemble, representing members of the crowd, shadows, athletes, even planets—whatever the dramatic or allegorical circumstances required. There is a singing planet in *Castor et Pollux* who has a brilliant *ariette* ("Brillez, brillez, astres nouveaux"/"Shine, shine, new stars!") to greet a new heavenly constellation, part of a celebration decreed by Jupiter. The little aria embodies a kind of singing otherwise uncalled for in the opera—one that, while eminently theatrical, is essentially foreign to the dramatic purposes of the *tragédie lyrique* and therefore suitable only for an undramatic ornamental moment in a kind of interlude.

Anthology Vol 1-76
Full CD II, 35

Rameau's planetary *ariette* shows the influence of a later Italian style than Lully could have known. (We will more fully consider that style when we turn to the operas of Alessandro Scarlatti and George Frideric Handel.) What was initially perceived as crucial differences between Lully and Rameau led to another chapter in the press wars that featured so prominently in France's lively intellectual life, in this case pitting the "Lullistes" against the "Ramistes." But although Rameau is obviously later than Lully and novel enough to have inspired resistance, he is really not essentially different. The eighteenth-century philosopher Denis Diderot had it right when he called Lully Monsieur Ut–mi–ut–sol (C–E–C–G)—roughly, "Mr. Music"—but called Rameau Monsieur Utremifasollasiututut (CDEFGABCCC), for the Rameau style was the Lully style advanced—not so much challenged as intensified: richer in harmony, more sumptuous in sonority, more laden in texture, more heroic in rhythm and rhetoric, more impressively masterminded than ever.

When French composer André Campra (1660–1744) said of the fifty-year-old Rameau's first opera that it contained enough music for ten operas, he did not mean it as a compliment. That same opera, *Hippolite et Aricie* (1733), was apparently the first musical work to which the adjective "Baroque" was attached, and that was no compliment either. Rameau's prodigality of invention and complexity of style were taken by some as showing off, a representation of personal power and therefore an affront to the sovereign. Indeed, if one compares Lully's sweet *Atys* of 1676 with Rameau's pungent, even violent *Castor et Pollux* of 1737, one can experience a bit of a shock at the differences, until one remembers they were written more than sixty years apart. Then the shock of the new gives way to amazement at the hold of tradition, a hold that testifies most of all to the potency of administrative centralism and absolute political authority.

Despite the initial press war opposing them, Rameau came to assume Lully's mantle, upholding the great French tradition that would soon be threatened by the Italians. That challenge, to look ahead briefly, came about fifteen years later, with the so-called *Querelle des Bouffons* (Dispute of the Comic Actors, also known as the War of the Buffoons), a two-year press debate that followed the first performances of Italian commercial opera in Paris in 1752, when the French court opera received, according to philosopher Jean-Jacques Rousseau (1712–78), "a blow from which it never recovered."[10] Rousseau was a dilettante composer in addition to being an eminent writer, and he had a personal interest in seeing the grand machinery of the official French style, with which he could never hope to compete, replaced with the sketchy "natural" spontaneity of the Italians.

But of course Rousseau was much more than a musician, and his intense interest in *Querelle des Bouffons* suggests that much more than music was really at stake. Historians now agree that what seems a ludicrously inflated press scuffle about opera was in fact a coded episode, and an important one, in the ongoing battle between political absolutism and the emerging Enlightenment movement that raged throughout much of the eighteenth century. As always, Italian commercial opera—epitomized this time by a farce (we'll take a look at it later) in which a plucky maidservant dominates her master, subverting the social hierarchy it was the business of the French opera to affirm—exemplified and stimulated the politics of opposition.

Jacobean England: Masques and Consort Music

The English shared French resistance to Italian opera, again preferring their theater spoken. Whether courtly or commercial, opera simply did not take hold there for most of the seventeenth century. "Spoken drama with musical decorations" was about as far as the English were prepared to go. Shakespeare's plays frequently called for a bit of incidental music, not only in occasional song texts but also in the stage directions, which ask for trumpets, woodwinds, and so on to interject signals, flourishes, and fanfares. The English likewise shared the French distaste for virtuosic vocal fireworks and castrated superstars.

When last we looked to England it was during the late Elizabethan period in connection with the madrigalistic praises of the long-lived virgin queen in *The Triumphes of Oriana*. Elizabeth was succeeded by her nephew James I (reigned 1603–25), the Scottish king whose ascent to the throne of England created what is now officially known as the "United Kingdom" and who commissioned the translation of the Bible known as the King James Version. During the "Jacobean" period, music found its chief theatrical outlet in dance entertainments called ***masques***, which lay somewhere between a costume ball and the prologue to an early Italian or French court opera. The name of the genre recalls its link with masked ceremonial and carnival dancing. By the time of James I such entertainments were organized around mythological or allegorical plots in praise of the ruler or some aristocratic patron. One early masque took as its theme "The Virtues of Tobacco," recently imported to England from the New World colonies and thought to have medicinal properties.

Historians now agree that what seems a press scuffle about opera was in fact a coded episode in the ongoing battle between political absolutism and the emerging Enlightenment movement.

James I chose playwright Ben Jonson (1572–1637) as his "Master of the Revels" before elevating him in 1617 to become the first British poet laureate. The few individual songs and dances that survive from Jonson's masques were mainly the work of James's stable of court composers, including Robert Johnson (ca. 1583–1633), Thomas Campion (1567–1620), and Alfonso Ferrabosco II (ca. 1575–1628), the illegitimate son of the composer we met in Chapter 5. Some masque music survives in manuscripts that contain dances for lute or for viol "consorts," a small ensemble of similar instruments. The profusion of Jacobean instrumental music, compared with the relative paucity of vocal or theatrical music, seems a reliable guide to the musical tastes of the period. Jacobean England may well have been the earliest European society to value instrumental music more highly than vocal music. The preference was as much a social as an aesthetic indicator. Jacobean **consort music** was among the earliest instrumental chamber music, with its forerunners being the instrumental chanson arrangements Petrucci had published. Here, audience and performers are ideally one, making it a wholly secular and largely domestic art. Chamber music was an art addressed to amateurs and connoisseurs, implying privacy, leisure, and ultimately affluence.

The broader historical and political conditions to which musicians of the mid-seventeenth century had to respond are reflected directly in *A Sad Pavan for These Distracted Times*, originally for keyboard but transcribed for strings as well, by Thomas Tomkins (1572–1656). The phrase "these distracted times" was a standard contemporary euphemism for the greatest political upheaval in British history: the Civil War of the 1640s, which culminated in the trial of King Charles I for treason and his beheading on 30 January 1649. There now arose a republican form of government, called the Commonwealth, instituted under the nominal rule of Parliament but in actuality under the personal dictatorship of Oliver Cromwell, the leader of the Puritan party. Tomkins's *Sad Pavan* bears the date 16 February 1649, just weeks after the regicide, and its tone bears witness to his loyalty and his sorrow at his former patron's fate.

The fortunes of music in England and of theatrical music in particular took a decisive turn with what is known as the Stuart Restoration, the reestablishment of the British monarchy less than a dozen years after its abolition. Charles II, the thirty-year-old son of the deposed king, was summoned back from exile in France and crowned in 1660. A shrewd diplomat and skillful politician, he reigned relatively peacefully until 1685, the last three years as an absolute monarch without a parliament, but—in marked contrast with this father—a very popular despot. One of the sources of his popularity was the cosmopolitan, libertine character of his court, a most welcome contrast with the puritanical times that had gone before. Having spent his late adolescence and early adulthood in France, Charles naturally modeled his idea of kingship not on that of his executed father but on his distant cousin Louis XIV, for whom song, dance, and theater were both a political symbol and a personal passion. Charles fathered many illegitimate children, including two sons by the actress Nell Gwynn, the leading lady of the London stage and the most celebrated of his many mistresses.

Hedonism, tinged as it was with licentiousness, meant a resurgence of aristocratic tastes, values, and privileges.

The arts were increasingly viewed and cultivated as an aspect of luxurious living, on a par with other sensual delights. That hedonism, tinged as it was with licentiousness, in the context of seventeenth-century England meant a resurgence of aristocratic tastes, values, and privileges. Thus we have another example of the effect of absolutist politics—an ugly politics, most would agree today—on the growth of the fine arts; and questions are raised again about whether the elite arts that we treasure can truly flourish in a liberal political climate.

The Restoration period saw the brilliant rebirth of English art, literature, and music on a new footing. The theater that Charles II revived was, to an extent previously unimaginable in England, a musicalized theater. While opera was still generally shunned, with a few equivocal exceptions, most plays featured music, often the work of teams of composers. We would now call this incidental music, and it typically consisted of a French overture, dances, songs, and instrumental curtain music for the end of each act. The Restoration brought English music more up to date vis-à-vis the continent.

The new Restoration masques were much more elaborate than their Elizabethan or Jacobean predecessors. They were extended song-and-dance interludes within plays—sometimes with spoken dialogue, sometimes with recitatives, often only tenuously related or even unrelated to the main plot but, unlike the Renaissance *intermedii* in Italy, with well-defined dramatic plots of their own. At their extreme they could amount to virtual one-act operas or opera-ballets. An especially resonant example was the masque from 1673 on the time-honored theme of Orpheus and Eurydice by Matthew Locke (ca. 1622–77). Equally adept at dance compositions in the French manner and recitatives in the Italian, Locke was the virtual inventor of a peculiarly English mixed genre called the "**dramatick opera**."

These **semi-operas**, in effect, were *comédies-ballets* (a spoken play interspersed with music and dance) or tragédies lyriques adapted to the tastes of the English theatergoing public. To the decorative songs and dances and instrumental tunes of the earlier masque, now more present than ever, was added the spectacular stage machinery for which the French court opera was particularly renowned. The major compromise was the insistence that principal characters never sing, which followed the old pre-Lullian prejudice that sung words are poorly understood. The result was a peculiar split between protagonists who never sang and incidental characters who only sang, making the new genre quite literally a semi-sung play. Some of the most celebrated semi-operas were adaptations of Shakespeare—or, rather, readaptations of lightweight Shakespeare adaptations, some by poet laureate John Dryden (1631–1700). The first major success was *The Tempest* (1674), for which the music was supplied by a committee of five, headed by Locke. Perhaps the most ambitious "dramatick opera" was *The Fairy Queen*, based on an anonymous adaptation of Shakespeare's *A Midsummer Night's Dream*, produced in 1692 with music by a former pupil of Locke named Henry Purcell (1659–95).

Purcell's *Dido and Aeneas* and the Question of "English Opera"

Chiefly employed as an organist, first at Westminster Abbey and later at the Chapel Royal, Purcell was as close to an all-round musical genius as England has ever produced (Fig. 8-13). Within the practices and institutions of his day, he excelled in every genre, from the royal and religious ones for which he was officially employed to instrumental chamber music and harpsichord pieces. For the London stage he produced songs and instrumental pieces for more than forty plays between 1680, his twenty-first year, and 1695, the year of his much-mourned death at age thirty-six.

Purcell's *Dido and Aeneas* is his single stage work that, while still technically a masque, was meant to be sung straight through from beginning to end. It was not the first such work to do so. If by "English

Figure 8-13 Henry Purcell by John Closterman (1695).

opera" we mean a continuous musical setting of a dramatic text in English in more than a single act, then the earliest surviving one is *Venus and Adonis* (ca. 1683) by John Blow (1649–1708), another of Purcell's teachers. The one documented performance of Purcell's little opera took place in 1689 at a London girls' school ("Mr. Josias Priest's Boarding-School at Chelsey," as the libretto's title page says), but historians now generally agree that it was probably performed elsewhere earlier.

The plot of *Dido and Aeneas* was adapted by a minor poet named Nahum Tate from the famous fourth book of the *Aeneid*, Virgil's great Latin epic that tells of the hero Aeneas's return from the Trojan War. On the way he stops at Carthage, in North Africa, where he meets the Queen, Dido. She provides hospitality and they promptly fall deeply in love. But the gods send Mercury to bid the hero continue on his journey, the goal of which is to found Rome. At least that is the way the plot unfolds in Virgil; in Tate's libretto it is a false Mercury sent by scheming witches, "wayward sisters" straight out of Shakespeare's *Macbeth*, that order Aeneas to depart, leaving Dido bereft. Bidding farewell to her confidante, Belinda, Dido kills herself out of grief and shame, dying with her final lament "When I am laid in earth."

Anthology Vol 1-77
Full CD II, 36–39
Concise CD I, 82

The difficulty of setting the English language to music is said to consist in its unusual accentuation patterns, in which stressed syllables and long syllables do not necessarily coincide, the way they do in Italian. Purcell's vocal works display his extraordinary care with English prosody, following paths forged by his teachers, Locke and Blow. In many ways Purcell's setting in *Dido and Aeneas* follows the conventions of Italian recitative as we have observed them as far back as Peri and Monteverdi. For the most part, however, the "Englishness" of the work consists of an original synthesis of French and Italian ingredients that is more attributable to Purcell's individuality and exceptional receptivity to foreign trends than to his nationality as such. In his case, an apparently insular style was really cosmopolitanism in disguise. It is easy enough to catalogue the imported ingredients. Group activities—choruses, dances, and orchestral numbers—are governed by French conventions, beginning with the French overture that introduces the work. Solo singing proceeds in the Italian manner, including the sensitive recitatives and residual madrigalisms.

And yet the French and Italian strains were not wholly discrete in the seventeenth century. Both made conspicuous use of ground basses, for which Purcell also had an uncanny gift. There are three in *Dido and Aeneas*, the most famous in the second scene of Act III, the opera's denouement. After a dramatic recitative in which the weak-willed Aeneas takes leave of the lovesick queen, there is a sympathetic comment from the chorus, followed by Dido's suicide aria, to which a final chorus of lamentation is appended. Dido's aria is usually called her lament, because it is written in the style of a Venetian lament, a form we have traced from its Monteverdian origins. By the end of the seventeenth century it had become a virtual cliché. Purcell was true to the established convention in his choice of a descending tetrachord, in this case chromatic, as ground bass (Ex. 8-4).

Altogether unconventional, however, is the interpolation of an additional cadential measure into the stereotyped ground bass, increasing its length from a routine four measures to a haunting five, against which the vocal line, with its despondent refrain ("Remember me!"—the cry of Hamlet's father), is deployed with marked asymmetry. That, plus Purcell's distinctively dissonant, suspension-saturated harmony, enhanced by additional chromatic descents during the final ritornello and by many deceptive cadences, makes the little aria an unforgettably poignant embodiment of heartache.

Example 8-4 Henry Purcell, *Dido and Aeneas*, Act III, Scene 2, Dido's lament, opening

Though unforgettable, it was nonetheless temporarily forgotten. Within a few years of Purcell's death, *Dido and Aeneas* was ruthlessly cannibalized as a masque within a performance of Shakespeare's *Measure for Measure* and then laid aside. It was not the time or place for musical "classics." The opera was rediscovered during the nineteenth century—a great age for classics—and published in 1841. The first modern staged revival took place in 1895, the bicentennial of Purcell's death. Like the first documented performance, it was a student production. Yet George Bernard Shaw, not yet a famous dramatist but London's leading music critic, traveled out of his way to cover it and informed his readers that the 200-year-old "first English opera" was "not a bit the worse for wear."[11] Its popularity has grown ever since.

So it was that this very late, atypical, and geographically peripheral seventeenth-century opera, from a country where opera was practically unknown, managed to become a twentieth-century classic of the genre. That is how Dido's immensely moving yet stylistically rather offbeat lament has become the main representative of the ever-present seventeenth-century ground bass in modern repertory. The most familiar historical representatives are often not really representative of what was most common in the past but, rather, remain (or are revivable) exactly because they achieve something greater.

Summary

This chapter has surveyed some musical trends in Italian, German, French, and English music during the seventeenth century. Instrumental music became increasingly important. Italian styles were brought north and influenced German sacred music; nonoperatic vocal music flourished in Italy; and French and English composers created forms of opera suited to their respective languages and cultures.

The most important composers of instrumental music were initially organists, and their works were rooted in improvisatory practice. Girolamo Frescobaldi (1583–1643) was one of the leading composers of keyboard music, especially the toccata and the partita. The toccata was a free, improvisatory work organized in sections of contrasting texture, meter, and tempo. The partita was a set of variations on a chord pattern. In the north, keyboard composers included Jan Pieterszoon Sweelinck (1562–1621) and Samuel Scheidt (1587–1654). They produced variations on Lutheran chorale tunes known as chorale partitas, which treat the chorale tune as a cantus firmus. Other chorale-based works included the chorale concerto, a work for mixed instruments and voices.

The greatest German composer of the seventeenth century was Heinrich Schütz (1585–1672), who is widely credited with bringing Italian styles to Germany. After training in Italy, Schütz spent most of his career at the Dresden court. Early on, he produced large-scale concerted motets in the style of his teacher, Giovanni Gabrieli. After 1625, however, the availability of musicians was greatly limited by the Thirty Years War (1618–48), which ravaged Germany, and Schütz's works were conceived on a smaller scale. His sacred concerto *O quam tu pulchra es* ("O how beautiful thou art") is notable for its rhetorical text expression. The polychoral *Saul, Saul* reflects the larger forces possible when the court was rebuilt after the war ended.

In Italy, the oratorio and the cantata were the principal nonoperatic vocal genres cultivated during the middle decades of the seventeenth century. An oratorio was a dramatic work based on a religious, usually biblical, topic, typically unstaged and performed in a church. Giacomo Carissimi (1605–74), an eminent composer of oratorios, worked as an organist and choirmaster in Rome. His *Jephte* is notable for its expressive text setting. The cantata was a multisectional vocal work, incorporating recitatives, different styles of arias, and sometimes choruses. *Lagrime mie* ("My tears"), by the leading Venetian cantata composer, Barbara Strozzi (1619–77), sets each couplet of the poem in a different style, with *seconda pratica* dissonance treatment. As successful women composers in the seventeenth century, Strozzi and Francesca Caccini (1587 to ca. 1641) were exceptional.

In France, opera was dominated by Jean-Baptiste Lully (1632–87), who received a monopoly from King Louis XIV to produce what came to be called *tragédie lyrique* (lyric tragedy). In contrast to its Italian counterpart, French opera remained a court genre, created to reflect the absolute power of the king. *Tragédie lyrique* aspired to the elevated status of spoken drama; the preferred topics were Greek tragedy and mythology. The conventions established by Lully would dominate French opera well into the next century. The typical French overture consisted of a slow section with dotted rhythms, followed by a fast imitative section. The prologue of an opera incorporated an elaborate court ballet and was devoted to celebrating royalty. In terms of musical style, French opera shunned elaborate ornamentation and cadenzas in favor of small embellishments called *agréments*. These characteristics, reflected in Lully's *Atys* (1676), were largely continued by his successor, Jean-Philippe Rameau (1683–1764).

In the early seventeenth century, the English resisted opera in favor of an entertainment called the masque in which dance often played an important role. During the Restoration of the English monarchy that began in 1660, the masque was transformed into a more elaborate mixture of opera and spoken drama. Called a "dramatick opera" or "semi-opera," it was performed between acts of a spoken drama. Although it often included songs, dance, and elaborate stage machinery, the major characters did not sing. Among the most elaborate of these was *The Fairy Queen* by Henry Purcell (1659–95). Purcell's *Dido and Aeneas* is his only stage work sung from beginning to end. Culminating in Dido's famous lament over a ground bass, it has remained in the operatic repertory every since its revival in the late nineteenth century.

Study Questions

1. Describe the salient musical features of the following types of keyboard works: (a) toccata, (b) partita, (c) passacaglia, (d) ciaccona.
2. Describe the work and career of Heinrich Schütz. What types of works did he compose? In what ways was his career and output affected by the Thirty Years War?
3. What characterizes the oratorio?
4. How were the careers of Barbara Strozzi and Francesca Caccini unusual for their time? What societal challenges did they face?
5. What are the typical musical and dramatic characteristics of the *tragédie lyrique* created by Jean-Baptiste Lully and Philippe Quinault? How does its music differ stylistically from Italian Baroque music? How do the dramatic features differ from those of commercial Italian operas such as Monteverdi's *L'incoronazione di Poppea*?
6. Which aspects of Lully's *tragédie lyrique* help to define it as specific to its time and place, the French royal court? How did *tragédie lyrique* represent royal power?
7. Why did Lully's operas continue to be performed frequently so long after his death? What political and social factors contributed to their longevity?
8. Describe the English masque and "dramatick opera." How are these genres similar to opera, and how do they differ from it?

9. In what respects is Henry Purcell's *Dido and Aeneas* an unusual work? In what ways does it blend French and Italian influences?

Key Terms

agréments
ballet de cour
cantata
chaconne
chorale concerto
chorale partita
consort music
French overture
masque
oratorio
partita
passacaglia
semi-opera or dramatick opera
suite
toccata
tragédie lyrique
virginal

9

The Height of Italian Dominance: Opera Seria and the Italian Concerto Style

After our tour of musical trends in Germany, France, and England, we must return to Italy, where opera had been born and where developments in instrumental music would now prove decisive. The formal layout and harmonic strategies of the Italian concerto in particular, most significantly the standardization of tonality, are crucial to our unfolding story. The international status of Italian music at this time is reflected to this day in classical musicians' vocabulary, which remains an international dialect based largely on the terminology the Italians brought with them wherever they went.

As we return to Italy to witness a new flowering of Italian dominance in music, it is worth considering the peninsula's geographical layout. In addition to the exporting of Italian music across Europe, there was a good amount of internal importation among the different regions of the long boot of Italy, with significant new activity in the south. The north continued to be dominated by the Republic of Venice, along with Genoa to the west and Florence to the south. Extending like a stripe through the middle was the Papal State, the temporal domain of the Catholic Church, with its center at the Vatican in Rome. The south of Italy was occupied by the kingdoms of Naples and Sicily, both of which in the seventeenth century belonged to the Spanish crown. This period of subjugation, which lasted for some 200 years, was an economic disaster for southern Italy, the repercussions of which continue to this day. The city of Naples swelled with an influx of dispossessed peasants, making it by the end of the seventeenth century one of the largest but also most squalid metropolises in Europe (Fig. 9-1).

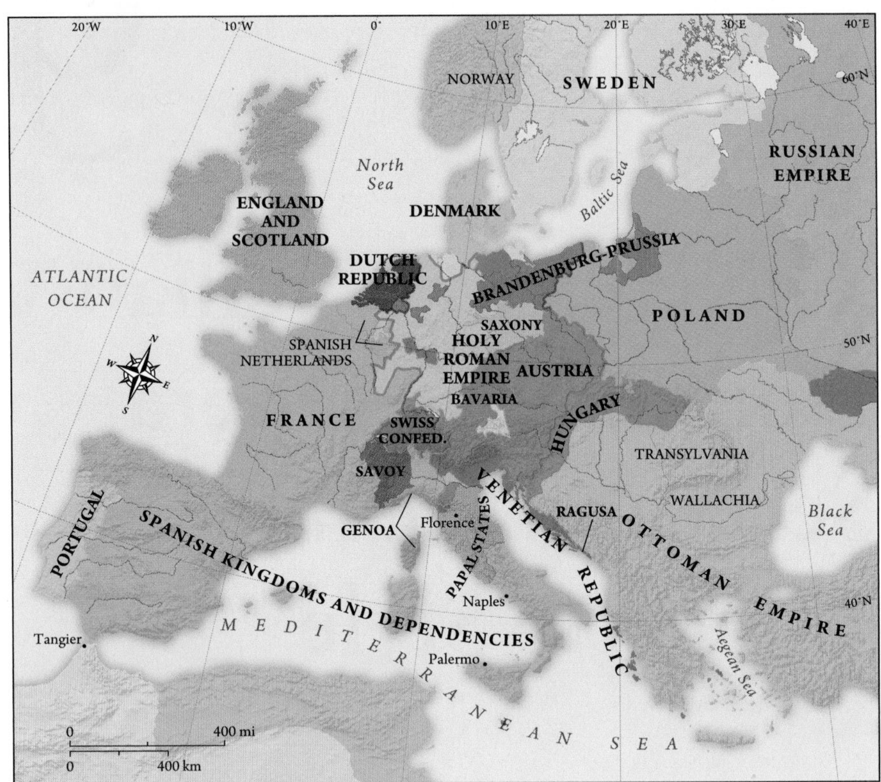

Figure 9-1 Europe ca. 1680.

TIMELINE

1650s Rise of "conservatories," or "music schools," in Naples

1683–1702 Alessandro Scarlatti's first residency in Naples

1689 Arcangelo Corelli, Church Sonata, Op. 3, No.11

1690 Founding of Arcadian Academy in Rome

1690 John Locke, *On Civil Government*

1703–40 Antonio Vivaldi's tenure at Pio Ospedale della Pietà

1707 Naples passes from Spanish to Austrian control

1709–21 Scarlatti's second residency in Naples

1711 Charles VI of Austria crowned Holy Roman Emperor

1711 Vivaldi, *L'estro armonico*

1712 Scarlatti, *Andate, o miei sospiri*

1713 Death of Corelli

1720–37 Public career of castrato singer Farinelli

1725 Death of Scarlatti; Vivaldi, *The Four Seasons*

1726 Jonathan Swift, *Gulliver's Travels*

1730 Metastasio succeeds Apostolo Zeno as Austrian court poet

1782 Death of Metastasio

These same conditions, however, helped create a musical golden age in Naples. One consequence of urban poverty was the establishment of orphanages and foundling homes. These houses where homeless boys were harbored were called a *conservatorio*, from which we get the word "conservatory," a self-maintaining organization in which costs were recouped by putting the youths to work. An obvious way to employ orphans was to make them choirboys; their training became a major preoccupation of the Naples conservatories. As the need arose, the training eventually expanded to include secular and instrumental music. The need was greatly stimulated by the importing of opera—"Venice-style music," as it was called at first by the Neapolitans—beginning around 1650. The first opera house in Naples, the renovated Teatro di San Bartolomeo, opened in 1654 and became one of the best endowed in Europe. Its repertoire began shifting around the 1680s from transplanted Venetian fare to a local Neapolitan one that quickly emerged as a major international force.

Opera Seria and Its Makers

The guiding figure behind the Neapolitan ascendency was a Palermo-born composer named Alessandro Scarlatti (1660–1725; Fig. 9-2), who dominated the Neapolitan musical scene from 1683 to 1702 and again, after Naples had passed from Spanish to Austrian rule, from 1709 to 1721. He also had important periods of service in Rome, Florence, and elsewhere. But the bulk of his voluminous output of operas (114 by his own count) and cantatas (more than 800 by modern scholarly estimate) was written for Naples. The inheritor and transformer of the Venetian tradition, Scarlatti could be looked on as the culminating figure of opera's first century. By reshaping and standardizing the legacy he inherited, he laid the foundation for the next century of operatic development, especially as regards what came to be known as ***opera seria***, or serious opera.

Figure 9-2 Alessandro Scarlatti.

Scarlatti served his apprenticeship in Rome, where he was a favorite of the aging Swedish Queen Christina, who had moved there after her abdication. When the Spanish ambassador to the papal court was named viceroy of Naples, he brought Scarlatti along with him as music director. The twenty-three-year-old musician's duties were staggering. He was under contract to compose, rehearse, and perform an average of four operas a year and also to provide sacred music for the viceroy's chapel. He also furnished on commission for noble salons an enormous number of cantatas and miniature operas, known as *serenatas*. No wonder, then, that he tended to standardize his working methods, which themselves became widely emulated by his contemporaries and immediate successors, who were just as overworked as he was.

Because much of Scarlatti's work remains unpublished or available only in scholarly editions and because, as a whole, opera or even a single act would tax our available space, the best way of observing Scarlatti's standard operating procedure is within the more modest confines of a cantata. In many respects cantata arias and their operatic counterparts were very similar. The main difference is in the chamber music scoring of the former. The basic ensemble for a cantata is voice plus basso continuo—that is, sustaining bass, usually a string instrument, and chordal "realizer," usually keyboard.

Anthology Vol 1-78

The cantata *Andate, o miei sospiri* ("Go, O my sighs") was written in 1712, during Scarlatti's second round as chief composer in Naples. It was, for Scarlatti, an especially labored-over composition, since he wrote it in friendly competition with his younger contemporary Francesco Gasparini (1661–1727), a leading Venetian composer of the day. Each composer had to write two settings of the same text, as different from one another as possible. The one we will sample here was Scarlatti's second setting, composed, as he put it on the title page, "in a devilish style, but within the rules of chromatic writing; not for your average practitioner." The harmonic extravagances to which he refers—and which start at the very beginning with two successive tritones on the repeated opening word—are not really all that unusual. Rather, they place the work within the old tradition of the "mannered" madrigal that helped give birth to the cantata. They are quite comparable to the expressive harmonic effects we saw in Barbara Strozzi's cantata *Lagrime mie*, composed half a century earlier. The most extreme moment comes in a later recitative at the parenthetical line "ma s'infinge/quel suo barbaro cor," which means "while her cruel heart pretends otherwise." The sudden, radical harmonic excursion is indeed a perfect analogue to a parenthetical thought, especially one that is not only parenthetical but also antithetical to the main sense of the words.

Completely new, however, and completely unlike Strozzi's cantata, is the thoroughgoing formal regularity of Scarlatti's setting. It is cast in four discrete sections that form two recitative-aria pairs. The poetry is designed for this division. The recitative sections are cast as "free verses" that lend themselves to the flexible declamation of recitative. The arias are cast in shorter lines with a regular meter and a simpler rhyme scheme.

The second aria in *Andate, o miei sospiri* belongs to a type that was particularly characteristic of Scarlatti and of Neapolitan music in general. Identifiable by compound meter ($\frac{6}{8}$ or, more commonly, $\frac{12}{8}$), leisurely tempo, lilting rhythms (with much use of the figure ♩. ♪ ♩) and (usually) by an eighth-note pickup, such an aria was called a ***siciliana*** and is often assumed, although without any real evidence, to stem from a jiglike Sicilian folk or popular dance. The main tune is sung by the soloist on entering (after a little introduction for the accompanists); a second section follows, whose end is marked *da capo* (from the top). This names an important structure—known informally as the **da capo aria**—that we will see in other eighteenth-century cantatas, oratorios, and operas. Indeed, many operas consisted of almost nothing but arias in this format.

The text is cast in two sections, each consisting of a single sentence. These sentences are given discrete musical settings. The first (A) is by far the longer, thanks to a continuo introduction and many repetitions of words and phrases; it cadences on the **tonic**. The second (B) is not only shorter but also tonally distinguished from the first, beginning and cadencing on a different scale degree (in effect, in a different key). Obviously the aria cannot end with this tonally subsidiary second section. The words *da capo*, written at its conclusion, direct the performers to repeat the first section, in its entirety or up to the word *fine* ("end"). (To be scrupulously precise, in this instance the marking is *dal segno*—"from the sign"—since the opening pickup is already included in the final measure of the B section.) The whole aria therefore has a tonally stable form that could be designated ABA, a tripartite structure that remained standard for the rest of the eighteenth century. Its advantage for the composer was obvious: He had to write only two parts out of three, amounting to perhaps three-fifths of the total duration. The rest was taken care of by the unwritten repeat. Its advantage for the performer consisted in the opportunities the unwritten repeat offered for spontaneous embellishment. The da capo aria became the virtuoso display piece par excellence, ensuring the kind of spectacular performance on which public opera has always thrived.

Another important operatic convention that Scarlatti did not invent but, rather, standardized was a new type of ***sinfonia***, that is, overture, consisting of a brilliant opening in fanfare style, a central slow episode, and a concluding dance. This last section, as was by then standard for dance movements, was cast in two repeated strains, the first cadencing on the **dominant** or some remoter harmony and the second cadencing on the tonic. Like the da capo aria, then, the binary-form movement embodied a "closed" tonal motion—away from the tonic and back. The resulting effect of harmonic contrast and closure, and its standard employment as the chief articulator of musical form, was perhaps the most powerful new idea that can be associated with late-seventeenth-century Italian music. It was certainly the most influential one, conditioning the development of European art music in all sorts of ways for centuries to come. Alessandro Scarlatti's stature in music history derives from his important role, by virtue of his prolific output and its high visibility, in establishing these new harmonic and formal norms.

Opera and Its Many Reforms: Neoclassicism

In 1706, while living in Rome between his two stints in Naples, Scarlatti was honored by election to a very prestigious association of musical and literary connoisseurs known as the Arcadian Academy, founded in 1690. At its head was Pietro Cardinal

Ottoboni, grandnephew of the reigning pope. For more than fifty years Cardinal Ottoboni was far and away the most lavish patron of opera in Rome. He was also an amateur librettist, whose texts, whatever their shortcomings, were eagerly set by composers, including Scarlatti, in hopes of an extravagant production and an outstanding performance.

It has been remarked that the history of opera is the history of its reforms, and the early operatic reformers around 1700 sought to recover the politics of affirmation that had attended the original invention of opera at the Italian courts a hundred years before. The Arcadians preached, and to a considerable extent practiced, lofty aesthetic ideals. Following Aristotle, as they would have claimed, but also responding to the criticism of French dramatists who heaped scorn on theatrical music, they wanted to restore opera to its original purity. This meant cleansing it of the old Venetian comic and bawdy scenes, with their conniving servants and the like, which had catered to the tastes of paying audiences, and returning opera to chaste pastoral or heroic historical spheres.

The da capo aria became the virtuoso display piece par excellence, ensuring the kind of spectacular performance on which public opera has always thrived.

Thus librettos became vehicles for noble sentiment—noble in both the literal and the figurative senses of the word. Real tragedy, which according to Aristotle required a flawed hero and a terrifying denouement, was now deemed unsuitable for moral instruction. Therein lay one crucial difference between the actual classical drama and the neoclassical drama of the European courts. A happy ending (*lieto fine* in Italian) was usually mandatory in an opera libretto, even if it contradicted historical fact. Along with this convention came others, including a schematic, idealized cast of character types presenting a social world that boiled down to the depiction of three social levels—rulers, confidants, and servants—each represented by a loving couple (or a would-be loving couple). The dramatic intrigue, played out in three acts, involved the interplay among this set of characters, augmented by one or two others (villains, jealous or rejected lovers, and false friends), until the inevitable happy ending, usually brought about by some act of largesse on the part of a wise ruler.

The ruler, in short, functioned in an ideal opera libretto the way a benevolently intervening deity—the proverbial *deus ex machine*, or "god from out of a machine"—descended, like Apollo in Monteverdi's *Orfeo*, in ancient plays and the earliest courtly operas. Intervention in the newly idealized opera could not be supernatural; it had to be human. But the human intervener, like the ruler in an absolutist state, was taken as the earthly representative of the divine. The neoclassical drama thus celebrated the "divine right of kings."

The Arcadian reformers claimed as a precursor the Venetian scholar and librettist Apostolo Zeno (1668–1750), who had founded his own academy for the restoration of taste and tradition and whose librettos were set many times over by many composers. Along with the purification and elevation of subject matter went the standardization of form and the regularization of verse. Zeno began to cast all the scenes in the same basic shape—recitative followed by a single da capo aria, after which the singer exits amid applause—and made every aria the bearer of a single vivid and consistent emotional message, cast in a simple and distinctive meter to facilitate its setting by the composer. Thus Zeno and the Arcadians sought to match at the textual level of the libretto Scarlatti's musical achievement in standardizing forms and procedures. Scarlatti, in fact, was himself admitted to the Arcadians and set several librettos by Zeno, including *Griselda* (1721).

Metastasio

Ultimate neoclassical perfection was reached by the Roman poet who wrote under the pen name Metastasio. He was born Pietro Antonio Trapassi (1698–1782), a godson of Cardinal Ottoboni himself, and was raised virtually in the bosom of the Arcadian Academy, eventually replacing Zeno as Austrian court poet in 1730. Metastasio is a figure well worth taking some time to consider. It is no easy task nowadays, even for a historian, to demote the composer from the top of the musical hierarchy, but eighteenth-century values were much different than those that arose later. At the time, the highest arbiter of taste and practice was the ruler or patron; next in order of clout came the audience; next the singer; next the librettist. The composer was there to serve them all. Now we ordinarily think just the opposite: that librettist and performer are there to serve the composer; even the audience must strive to adapt itself to the demands that composers make. The operatic food chain has been turned upside down.

Metastasio was the premier Italian librettist of the eighteenth century. Between 1720 and 1771 he wrote some sixty librettos, of which about half belonged to the genre of opera seria, the term now used for what Metastasio, following tradition, had called *dramma per musica* (play for music). His texts were set more than 800 times by more than 300 composers. At the hands of several generations of musicians, the music that clothed his words underwent considerable stylistic change.

The Metastasian libretto was a supreme balancing act, reconciling the theoretical ideals of the Arcadian reformers with the practical considerations of the stage. To meet and balance all demands, the older reform libretto was adjusted to feature six main roles, deployed in two pairs and a "remainder." At the top was the first couple: the *primo uomo,* or first man, usually sung by a castrato, and the *prima donna,* or first lady, sung by a soprano where women were allowed on the public stage or by another castrato where they were not. As the figurative meaning of "prima donna," which still survives in colloquial English, emphatically suggests, these favored singers, whatever their actual sex, had many prerogatives and insisted on them. Between the two of them, the first couple sang about half the arias in the show, amounting to as many as half a dozen arias apiece. Only they could sing a duet.

Between 1720 and 1771 Metastasio wrote some sixty librettos, of which about half belonged to the genre of opera seria, the term now used for what Metastasio, following tradition, had called* dramma per musica *(play for music).

The second couple, also noble, claimed three or four arias apiece. After them came the confidants, villains, servants, whatever. They were given no more than two arias, which had to be positioned less conspicuously than those of the higher-ranking roles. One of these characters, for example, usually sang the first aria in Act II, because in many theaters that was when refreshments were served to the audience and nobody was listening. Such arias actually came to be known as the *aria di sorbetto* (sherbet aria), and the hapless singer to whom it was assigned could expect to be drowned out by the clinking of spoons. In addition, the arias each character sang had to belong to different standard types that showed off different aspects of their vocal prowess. These included the *aria di bravura,* or virtuoso aria, full of elaborately difficult passages (known as **coloratura**); the *aria d'affetto,* or tender aria, full of long-held, swelling notes; the *aria cantabile,* or lyrical aria, in which the singer's ability to sustain long phrases was displayed; and so on.

Metastasio claimed that arias, which functioned as reflective monologues at the conclusion of every scene, were comparable not with soliloquies but with the chorus—the eternal commentator—in ancient Greek drama. In contrast with recitatives that work within the realm of the stage world, the arias, like the Greek choruses, are addressed to the audience; they are emotional weather reports, so to speak, delivered in a sort of stopped time, or a "time out." As traditionally staged, the arias were actually sung stage front, facing the spectators, accompanied by appropriate stylized poses. The artificiality of this scheme is often mocked today. And yet no matter how much opera may have changed after Metastasio, no matter how vehemently later composers, librettists, or theorists may have rejected his stylizations, this most fundamental stylization has remained: the distinction between "recitative time" (public time, clock time, time for action) and "aria time" (internal time, psychological time, time for reflection). The formalization of this distinction was the great stroke of genius that gave opera a special dramatic dimension that spoken drama could not match.

Figure 9-3 Scene from Metastasio's *Didone abbandonata.* Illustration by P. A. Martini, 1775.

Metastasio began his career in Naples, Scarlatti's old haunt, with *Didone abbandonata* (Dido Abandoned; Fig. 9-3), based on the same story from Virgil's *Aeneid* as Purcell's famous little opera of 1689. Even though it was an early work and somewhat atypical (lacking a happy ending, for one thing), it was one of Metastasio's most popular librettos, set more than sixty times by composers celebrated and obscure over the century from 1724 to 1824.

The libretto he himself regarded as his masterpiece was *Attilio Regolo,* which perhaps more than any other highlighted the theme of noble self-sacrifice, in this case of the title character, Marcus Attilius Regulus, "a Roman hero of consummate virtue" in Metastasio's description. The first composer to set the text was Johann Adolf Hasse (1699–1783), who had already written some forty serious operas, more than a dozen of them to Metastasio librettos. Even so, Metastasio sent Hasse a long letter in which he detailed his wishes as to how his words should be handled. In particular, he told the composer to set certain key passages—mainly the title character's occasional soliloquies of impassioned self-doubt—in **accompanied recitative** (*recitativo accompagnato*). This style was reserved for special effects, in which the entire orchestra, not just the continuo instruments, accompanied the singer. With the insight of the trained musician that he was, Metastasio presumed to instruct the composer how to let the music not merely represent, still less duplicate, but actually supplement the meanings of the words. Metastasio's letter was dated 20 October 1749. The premiere of Hasse's lengthy opera took place on 12 January 1750, a mere eighty-four days later.

Metastasio's Musicians

A fairly late and demanding text, *Attilio Regolo* was not often set to music. By contrast, Metastasio's most popular libretto, the most frequently reused operatic libretto of all time, was *Artaserse*, a tale about the Prince of Persia and the intrigues, murder, and love interests around his accession to the throne after the assassination of his father, King Xerxes. The text was set first for performance in Rome in 1730 by Leonardo Vinci (ca. 1696–1730), Scarlatti's successor in Naples and a composer Metastasio adored (see Fig. 9-4). He has long been thought a fountain of the Classical style that began to emerge near the end of his life. Two very famous later composers of opera, Christoph Willibald Ritter von Gluck (1714–87) and Johann Christian Bach (1735–82), made their debuts with compositions of *Artaserse*, in 1741 and 1760, respectively.

In all, there are over ninety known settings over the next century, the last being *The Regicide* in London at the incredibly late date of 1840. Among the many other composers who set *Artaserse* were Giuseppe Scarlatti, a relative of Alessandro (1747); Baldassare Galuppi, who set it for Vienna, and Niccolò Jommelli, who did so for Rome, both in 1749; Giuseppe Sarti, for the Royal Theater of Copenhagen in 1760; Thomas Arne, for London in 1762; Niccolò Piccinni, for Rome in 1762; Giovanni Paisiello, for Modena in 1771; Josef Mysliveček, for Naples in 1774; Domenico Cimarosa, for Turin in 1784; and Nicolas Isouard, for Livorno in 1794. Hasse, Metastasio's favorite composer, set *Artaserse* three times: for Venice in 1730; for Dresden in 1740; and for Naples in 1760. This long list of names and dates is worth recounting because, excepting Alessandro Scarlatti and Handel, it is a pretty complete list of the leading eighteenth-century composers of opera seria before Mozart (who also set a number of Metastasio librettos).

What is even more noteworthy, however, is that almost every one of these settings was performed in Italian, wherever it was staged, whatever the composer's

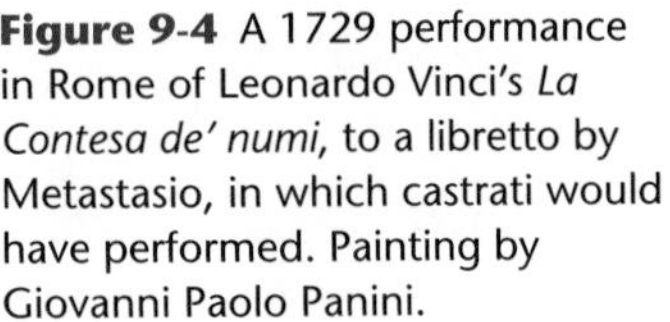

Figure 9-4 A 1729 performance in Rome of Leonardo Vinci's *La Contesa de' numi*, to a libretto by Metastasio, in which castrati would have performed. Painting by Giovanni Paolo Panini.

nationality, and whether or not the language in which it was sung was understood by the audience, which it usually was not. And that is because wherever opera seria was sung, the singers were mainly Italian virtuosos who enjoyed international careers. Just how much the singers controlled the show, generally taking the lead over the librettist and the composer, is evident in the ways they felt free to change what they performed. These changes were not limited to substituting a word or melodically embellishing a musical phrase—there were also wholesale substitutions. Most great singers carried around a "portfolio aria" that could be inserted, relevance be damned, wherever they sang.

The greatest of the eighteenth-century singers was Carlo Broschi (1705–82), a castrato known as Farinelli. Although he was the undisputed champion of his time and lived a long life, Farinelli had a short public career as a singer, beginning in Naples in 1720 and ending in London in 1737. Afterwards he joined the household of King Philip V of Spain, whom he served not only as court singer but as a trusted and powerful counselor as well. The development of Farinelli's career was mirrored in the music his talent inspired: many florid arias, indeed the fanciest, most embellished vocal music in the entire European operatic tradition. His ultimate signature tune was the famous shipwreck aria "Son qual nave ch'agitata" ("I am like a storm-tossed boat at sea"), first heard in an adaptation in London of Hasse's *Artaserse* in 1734, a mixed-bag affair featuring music by various composers. The aria was written by Farinelli's older brother, Ricardo Broschi (1698–1756), a minor Neapolitan composer who rode his sibling's coattails into the history books.

The virtuoso arias Farinelli sang included ample opportunities for free-form display, especially at the **cadenza** (short for *cadenza fiorita*, "ornamented cadence") that typically precedes and thus delays an important cadence. Cadenzas are display vehicles abounding in what their singers called *passaggii*, from which we get our English term "passage" or "passagework." In theory cadenzas were improvised by the singer on the spot, but in practice they were often worked out in advance and memorized. We have the word of many witnesses that singers considered all of the main cadences in an aria fair game for embellishment.

As often happens, it was chiefly those who disapproved of the practice who took the trouble to write about it. P. F. Tosi, himself a singer, complained in 1723 that the ends of all three sections in da capo arias were becoming overgrown with cadenzas: During the first cadenza, "the orchestra waits"; during the second, "the dose is increased, and the orchestra grows tired." But during the last cadenza, complains Tosi, "the throat is set going like a weathercock in a whirlwind, and the orchestra yawns."[1] There was a touch of envy here, perhaps, in Tosi's catalogue of abuses; we do not find much indication of audience complaint.

Operatic Culture and Politics

One might think that Metastasio would have objected to the practice of interpolating cadenzas as well as to adding ornamentation by the bushel during the da capo repeat, but that does not seem to be the case. Quite the contrary, as we see in a group portrait by the Italian painter Jacopo Amigoni, Metastasio and Farinelli were friends (Fig. 9-5). They met in 1720, when the singer, then a teenager, made his Neapolitan debut on the very occasion at which the poet's verses for music were first sung in public, and they remained on intimate terms until the end of their lives,

Figure 9-5 Jacopo Amigoni, portrait of Farinelli (center), surrounded by (left to right) Metastasio, Teresa Castellini, the artist, and the artist's page, holding his palette.

more than sixty years later. The great librettist recognized the great singer as a major influence on the development of opera seria and its supremely ornate musical style. The two of them, Metastasio and Farinelli, were likewise universally regarded during the eighteenth century as being far more important to the art of opera than any composer, and so a historian must regard them as well.

The fundamental values of eighteenth-century serious opera are therefore remote from today's values. Apparent contradictions abound. There is the clash between, on the one hand, the high-minded reformist mission, the return to classical ideals, that demanded the removal of comic scenes from librettos, and, on the other, the spectacular antics of performers, often crowd-pleasing to the point of clownishness. Some accounts from the time describe a circus atmosphere or something like what we might associate today with large sporting events or with so-called reality TV shows, for the audience, too, took part.

The audiences for eighteenth-century opera, a mixture of aristocracy and urban middle class, were famed throughout Europe for their sublime inattention. They talked, ate, and played games during the performance.

That audience, a mixture of aristocracy and urban middle class, was famed throughout Europe for its sublime inattention. They talked, ate, and played games during the performance, which was in any case more a social than an artistic event. Curtains could often be drawn in boxes to allow privacy. Even if we avoid judging such manners by contemporary standards of decorum, we are easily left bewildered. Never mind questions of mere etiquette. How is all of this evident anarchy to be reconciled with the nature of the dramas themselves, which exalt a perfectly ordained, God-given, and rigidly hierarchical social order? The explanation for these apparent contradictions lies partly in the social mixture alluded to earlier. Opera seria had a dual inheritance. Its subject matter descended from the courtly opera of old and shared its affirmative politics. The theaters were maintained in most cases by royalty, and the performances were embedded in the forms and hierarchies of absolutism. Even the theatrical schedule reflected this: Performances, particularly galas, were held on royal birthdays and name days as well as church holidays.

The librettos were metaphorical embodiments of these occasions. This was, so to speak, Metastasio's heritage.

Farinelli's heritage, on the other hand, was that of the commercial opera theater. The art of such a singer only began with the written notes. Many virtuosos did not read music well, if at all, and learned their arias by rote in order to use them as a basis for personalized embellishment. Recitatives were often improvised outright, based on the harmonies the singers could overhear from the pit orchestra and the words that they overheard from the prompter's box. However inattentive during recitatives or sherbet arias, the audience began to focus when the principal singers held forth, egging them on with applause and spontaneous shouts of encouragement at each vocal feat during the music. The singers, striking their attitudes front and center, had to work to capture their hearers' attention. They had, quite literally, to seduce the noble boxholders, drawing them out from the socializing going on in the backs of their boxes.

The only occasions when the audiences did have to behave and pay attention were those evenings when the king himself was present, enacting his role of surrogate father.

In those days, nobles and urban professionals tended to live their social lives outside of their houses, especially in the evenings. A box at the opera, rented for the season, was a virtual living space, and occupying it was a social ritual in which the musical performance was not necessarily the most important component, especially because the season consisted of only a few works, each of which had a run of many performances. The audience therefore knew the operas well and even more so Metastasio's ubiquitous librettos, for they were endlessly recycled by different composers. The only occasions when the audiences did have to behave and pay attention were those evenings when the king himself, the latent subject of the opera, was present, enacting his role of surrogate father. What could better attest to the nature of patriarchy, the social system that opera seria preeminently reflected?

For all their boisterous behavior, the opera seria audience demonstrated their comfort with the patriarchal social structure the genre embodied. It is about the crispest example the history of European music can furnish of an art invested with, and affirming, a social and political system, an oppressive system with which few of us today would sympathize. So once again the questions nag: How do we relate to the artistic products that bolstered an ugly patriarchal, absolutist politics in their time? Can they be detached from it? Can we vote for the art and reject the politics? It is the job of a book like this one to raise these questions, not answer them. In any case, though, the social use to which opera is put has changed, and changed radically, since the days of Scarlatti and Metastasio. It would make little sense to expect its content or its manner of execution to have remained the same—or to think that opera seria could be revived today, in today's opera houses, for today's audiences. For one thing, the return of the castrato voice would be about as likely as the return of public hangings. Sometimes, though, it is just those aspects of bygone art that are most bygone from which we can learn the most about ourselves and our present world and the place of art within it.

Arcangelo Corelli and New Tonal Practices

As far as we know, Arcangelo Corelli (1653–1713; Fig. 9-6) never set a word of text to music. A virtuoso violinist, he was the first European composer to enjoy international recognition as a "great" exclusively on the strength of his finely wrought instrumental ensemble works. They circulated widely in print both during his lifetime and for almost a century after his death, providing countless other musicians with models for imitation. In his chosen domain of chamber and orchestral music for strings, he was the original classic, playing a major role in standardizing genres and practices and setting instrumental music on an epoch-making path of ascendancy. The historical significance of his sonatas and concertos is tremendous, affecting European music of every sort at a time when genres, forms, and tonal practices were becoming ever more standardized.

With Corelli and his generation we encounter a truly momentous juncture in the history of music: the birth of harmonic controlled and elaborated form. We may witness, in their earliest phase, the tonal relations we have long been taught to take for granted in the Italian instrumental music of a rough quarter-century around the year 1700. And yet from the very beginning this avant-garde style of harmony was eagerly assimilated, both by composers and by listeners. For composers it made the planning and control of ever-larger formal structures much easier. For listeners it granted an unprecedentedly exciting sense of high-powered, directed momentum and promised under certain conditions a practically visceral emotional payoff. The tonal system at once gave composers the means for administering an altogether new kind of pleasurable shock to their audiences. Corelli will serve as our model to see how this all came about.

After Corelli's apprenticeship in Bologna, his career was based almost exclusively in Rome, outwardly paralleling Alessandro Scarlatti's: service to Queen Christina and Cardinal Ottoboni, membership in the Arcadian Society, and so on. His main activities were leading orchestras, sometimes numbering a hundred musicians or more, in the richly endowed churches and cathedrals of the city and appearing as soloist at aristocratic house concerts. For sacred venues Corelli perfected an existing Roman genre known as ***sonata da chiesa*** (church sonata). Such pieces were variously scored: for solo violin and continuo, for two violins, cello, and continuo (hence the name "**trio sonata**," albeit normally played by four instrumentalists), or amplified by a backup band known as the ***concerto grosso*** (large ensemble), which

Figure 9-6 Arcangelo Corelli depicted by an anonymous engraver on the title page of an Amsterdam edition of one of his trio sonatas.

unconstrained in its spontaneous unfolding. One group favors repetition, the other favors diversity. The full ensemble is dramatically subordinate but structurally dominant, while the soloist is dramatically dominant but structurally subordinate. Their effect together is one of complementation, of disparate parts fitting harmoniously into a satisfying, functionally differentiated whole, all of it grounded by the constant auxiliary presence of the basso continuo, everyone's companion and aide.

This may suggest a social paradigm or metaphor of some kind. Indeed, the concerto form has always been viewed, in one way or another, as a sort of microcosm, a model of social interaction, of coordinated or competitive activity. That is one of the things that has invested its seemingly abstract patterns with meaning and fascination for listeners. And that fascination, along with the fascination of tonal relations with their strong metaphorically forward drive to completion, is what allowed large-scale instrumental forms to emerge and to assume a place of central importance in European musical culture.

Vivaldi was able in his concertos to shock, startle, and manipulate the responses of his audience.

The remaining movements of a typical concerto amplify the sense of kinship with opera seria. A slow second movement is most often scored for soloist and continuo alone and projects the feeling of a "florid" song (*coloratura*) over a static bass. The piece is now chamber music. The final movement is usually another ritornello-style composition that brings back the full band. Typically shorter and less serious than the first movement, it provides a framing conclusion to the total three-part whole. The concerto thus reproduces in its texture the effect of a typical da capo aria: Outer sections with ritornellos frame a contrasting middle section in which the soloist is accompanied by the continuo instruments only.

Vivaldi was able in his concertos to shock, startle, and manipulate the responses of his audience, which may lead us to wonder how they expressed their reactions. One of the most striking things we found earlier in this chapter concerning the customs surrounding opera seria was the spontaneity and the uninhibitedness of the audience response, so unlike the behavior of classical audiences today but still common in popular music. Likewise, to appreciate the place of a Vivaldi concerto in its own time, it is probably not enough to listen to even the most impassioned performance. One must imagine an active audience as well—a house full of shouting, clapping, stamping listeners and the effect their demonstrations of approval may have had on the performers, as it does today with much popular music.

Music Imitating Nature: Vivaldi's *The Four Seasons*

Vivaldi's earliest concerto collection was called *L'estro armonico* (Harmonic Inspiration), Op. 3, issued in Amsterdam in 1711 and printed like most ensemble publications of the time as partbooks without score. The set of twelve concertos, scored for one, two, or four soloists, traveled far and wide, spreading Vivaldi's fame and making his music a model to many a far-flung imitator. One of the pieces, the Concerto in B Minor for Four Violins, was a particularly prized work, showing Vivaldi not at his most typical but at his most extravagant, that is, "Baroque." J. S. Bach later concocted a boisterous arrangement of the piece for four harpsichords and also arranged five other concertos from this initial collection.

L'estro armonico was followed by several other partbook collections bearing fanciful promotional titles, another big seller being called *Il cimento dell'armonia e dell'inventione* (something like "The Trial of Musical Skill and Contrivance"), Op. 8, a book of twelve concertos released in 1725. The real sensation came from the first four concertos in this volume arranged in a set called *Le quattro stagioni* (The Four Seasons), which were accompanied by explanatory sonnets. The poems spelled out the imagery of the concertos, giving inventively detailed evocations and imitations of nature as manifested in spring, summer, autumn, and winter as well as of the sensory and emotional responses the seasons inspired. The delight audiences took from the very beginning in the composer's powers of musical description is reflected in the popularity *The Four Seasons* already enjoyed in the eighteenth century, a popularity that crossed national boundaries. Today, thanks to countless recordings, the set is practically synonymous with the composer's name.

Anthology Vol 1-80
Full CD II, 44–46
Concise CD I, 83

In France, where descriptive music had an especially strong tradition and where one of the earliest important public concert series, the Concert Spirituel, got under way exactly in the year of the *Seasons'* publication, these concertos, particularly *La primavera* (Spring), became the very cornerstone of the emerging "standard repertory." (In 1775 none other than Jean-Jacques Rousseau arranged this concerto for solo flute!) As a look at the first movement of *La primavera* will show, the concerto form, with its constant and fluid components, proved easy to adapt to illustrative and narrative purposes. Here are the first and second quatrains of the accompanying sonnet, corresponding to the movement in question:

A	*Giunt'è la Primavera e festosetti*	Spring has come,
B	*La salutan gl'Augei con lieto canto,*	and merrily the birds salute it with their happy song.
C	*E i fonti allo spirar de' Zeffiretti*	And the streams, at the breath of little Zephyrs,
	Con dolce mormorio scorrono intanto.	run along murmuring sweetly.
D	*Vengon coprendo l'aer di nero amanto*	Then, covering the air with a black cloak,
	E Lampi, e tuoni ad annuntiarla eletti	come thunder and lightning,
E	*Indi, tacendo questi, gl'Augelletti*	as if chosen to proclaim her; and when these have subsided, the little birds
	Tornan di nuovo al lor canoro incanto.	return once more to their melodious incantation.

The letters running down the left margin are Vivaldi's original. They mark the exact spots in the score to which the words refer—or, rather, the exact spots where the music is designed to mimic the words in question. There is no question, then, as to the composer's exact intentions. The imitations are obvious and hardly need pointing out; and yet it will be worth our while to consider the precise relationship at various points between the musical and verbal imagery.

Letter **A** here corresponds to the ritornello, one that, as befits its mimetic character, is rather unusual. Instead of the usual thematic complex, there is a simple bouncy tune in **binary form**—an imitation folk song, as it were. Its periodic returns continually reinforce the overall mood of rejoicing at spring's arrival (Ex. 9-3a). The remaining images, **B** through **E**, correspond exactly to the four episodes that come between the ritornellos. Letter **B**, the singing of the birds, is rendered in the most straightforward way that music, the art of combining sounds, has at its disposal:

onomatopoeia, direct sound-alike imitation. Birdsong had indeed long been a violinistic stock-in-trade (Ex. 9-3b).

Example 9-3 Antonio Vivaldi, *La primavera* (Op. 8, No. 1), I: (a) mm. 1–3; (b) mm. 15–18

Letter **C**—the episode of the brook and breezes that leads to the sudden storm in Letter **D**—juxtaposes low *tremolandi* for the full ensemble, mimicking thunder, with high scales that depict lightning. Thunder, like birdsong, is onomatopoeia—a natural for music that many composers have imitated. The birds' return at Letter **E** is the masterstroke: The way the solo violins steal in diffidently on chromatic-scale fragments, as if checking out the weather before resuming their song, adds a "psychological" dimension to the realism. This is the work of an expert musical dramatist. And that is the other obvious resonance that lies behind Vivaldi's mimetic practices: the opera house, where winds and storms, birds, rustic song, and all the rest were regularly evoked and compared—in the ritornellos of "simile arias"—with dramatic situations and the emotions to which they gave rise.

The rendering of so many of these effects, such as water by the use of wavelike motion, had already long before become a stock device for composers, the kind of thing we now call a "madrigalism." And madrigalism would not be a bad term to use to characterize Vivaldi's imitative devices as well, despite the transfer from the vocal to the instrumental medium. Using it would signal the easily overlooked, somewhat ironic fact that to incorporate imitation into an instrumental concerto was actually to fall back on an old practice, one that the new Italian instrumental genres were widely perceived as threatening. (Recall old Fontenelle's plea, "Sonata, what do you want from me?") Vivaldi was aware of this. He himself once used the term *concerto madrigalesco* to denote a piece in somewhat archaic style that displayed the kind of purely expressive chromatic harmonies the old madrigalists had formerly used to paint emotively laden words.

New styles and genres do not actually replace or supplant the old in the real world; this happens only in history books.

What all this shows once again, and it is something never to forget, is that new styles and genres do not actually replace or supplant the old in the real world; this happens only in history books. In the real world the new takes its place alongside the old, and, during the period of their coexistence, the two are always fair game for cross-fertilization and hybridization.

Summary

In the late seventeenth century, Italian opera and instrumental music underwent profound changes. In opera, important changes were brought about by the literary and musical society known as the Arcadian Academy in Rome. This movement sought to restore noble sensibilities to opera and to eliminate comic elements. The most influential figure associated with this movement is the librettist Pietro Antonio Trapassi (1698–1782), who wrote under the pen name Metastasio. He and his followers established conventions that would dominate serious opera, called *opera seria*, for decades. A typical Metastasian libretto had six main roles, including the leading man (always a castrato role), the leading woman, and another noble couple; the other characters were confidants, villains, or servants. A typical scene consisted of a recitative that moved the action forward, an aria that reflected on the action, and the exit of the characters. The musical centerpiece was the *da capo* aria in ABA form. The aria had two written-out sections. The first began and ended in the same key; the second, in a contrasting key, was followed by a repeat of the first. Opera seria was a singer-dominated art, and the return of the A section was the chance for the singer to embellish. Alessandro Scarlatti (1660–1725) was an important composer of both opera seria and cantatas. His cantata *Andate, o miei sospiri* ("Go, O my sighs,"), cast as two recitative–aria pairs, is a good illustration of the style of both opera seria and cantata.

Instrumental music of the late seventeenth century was also dominated by Italians. Arcangelo Corelli (1652–1713) spent most of his career in Rome in the service of Queen Christina of Sweden, composing trio sonatas for two violins and continuo, solo violin sonatas, and concerti grossi. His sonatas were of two types. The *sonata da chiesa,* church sonata, consisted of four movements, slow-fast-slow-fast, and was often performed during Mass. The *sonata da camera,* or chamber sonata, was a suite of dance movements performed in aristocratic homes. It is in Corelli's works that we begin to see the clearest examples of tonal harmony as the driving force of a musical work. His sonatas derive their sense of forward motion from circle-of-fifths progressions, which are enhanced by melodic sequences and chains of suspensions.

Corelli's concertos, for an ensemble of string instruments and orchestra, are similar in style to his sonatas, but with expanded forces. In northern Italy, however, a different type of concerto emerged, consisting of three movements, fast-slow-fast. Its best-known composer is Antonio Vivaldi (1678–1741). Although Vivaldi composed many operas and cantatas, he is best known today for the some 500 concertos he wrote for students at the Pio Ospedale della Pietà, the renowned orphanage for girls where he worked from 1703 to 1740. The central feature of Vivaldi's concertos is the alternation between ritornello sections played by the orchestra, which functioned as a stable harmonic and melodic frame, and modulating solo episodes, full of endless invention and harmonic modulation. The interplay between solo and ritornello section unfolds differently in each concerto. Vivaldi's slow and lyrical middle movements betray the concerto's connection to opera seria.

Beginning in 1711 with the earliest published set, *L'estro armonico* (Harmonic Inspiration), Vivaldi's concertos traveled far and wide, finding many imitators. His *Le quattro stagioni* (The Four Seasons) were accompanied by explanatory sonnets. In the first movement of *La primavera* (Spring), Vivaldi coordinated particular passages of the sonnet with music that depicts winds, storms, and birds. This descriptive instrumental writing has its ultimate roots in vocal genres like the Italian madrigal.

Study Questions

1. Describe the defining characteristics of a typical Metastatian opera seria libretto.
2. Describe the da capo aria as exemplified by the second aria in Alessandro Scarlatti's cantata *Andate, o miei sospiri.*
3. How was opera culture in the seventeenth and eighteenth centuries different from that of today? Compare and contrast the attitudes and behaviors of the performers and audience, the relative status of librettist and composer, and the experience of attending a performance.
4. Discuss Arcangelo Corelli's importance as a solidifier of tonal harmony, as exemplified in the second movement of Sonata Op. 3, No.11.
5. Describe the roles of the ritornello and solo episode in Antonio Vivaldi's concertos and the interaction between them. In what respects do they represent a kind of social interaction?
6. How does the first movement of Vivaldi's concerto *La primavera* reflect the sonnet that accompanies it? How do these musical depictions of the sonnet work within the concerto form?

Key Terms

accompanied recitative
binary form
cadenza
circle of fifths
coloratura
concerto
concerto grosso
***da capo* aria**
dominant
episode
opera seria
ripieno
siciliana
sinfonia
sonata da camera
sonata da chiesa
tonic
trio sonata

10

Class of 1685 (I): The Instrumental Music of Bach and Handel

The year 1685 is luminous in the history of European music because it witnessed the birth of three of the composers whose works long formed the bedrock of the standard performing repertoire: Johann Sebastian Bach (1685–1750), George Frideric Handel (1685–1759), and Domenico Scarlatti (1685–1757). For this reason the date 1685 took on the aspect of a marker, separating the music of common listening experience from a repertoire called "early music," known and of concern mainly to specialists.

"Pre-Bach music," as it was also once actually called, is now much more available and familiar. Concert life has been enriched by many performers and ensembles who concentrate on music composed earlier than that of the class of 1685, as well as by those who perform Bach, Handel, and Scarlatti on resurrected instruments of their time, not the modern instruments usually used today. These musicians have studied the conventions that governed the performance practices of the early eighteenth century and are keen to emphasize the differences between those conventions and those to which listeners have since become accustomed.

The elevation of Bach, Handel, and Scarlatti began happening in the nineteenth century, for the reasons we will consider when dealing with the history of that time. And yet there were good reasons why the music of the class of 1685 became the foundation stone of the standard repertory and why even today their works, plus a few special cases like Vivaldi's *The Four Seasons*, remain the earliest music that non-specialist performers and performing organizations routinely play. Theirs is also the earliest music that today's concertgoers and listeners are normally expected to "understand" without special instruction, in part because general music pedagogy is still largely based on exactly this foundation. No child learns to play the piano without encountering Bach and, if one gets serious, Scarlatti. As soon as one is old enough to participate in community singing, one is sure to meet Handel.

TIMELINE

1683 Defeat of Ottoman Turks outside of Vienna

1685 **Birth of Johann Sebastian Bach, George Frideric Handel, and Domenico Scarlatti**

1700 **Bartolomeo Cristofori invents the fortepiano in Florence**

1702 **Georg Philipp Telemann establishes the Collegium Musicum in Leipzig**

1706–10 **Handel in Italy**

1707 England and Scotland unify as Great Britain

1708–17 **Bach in Weimar**

1713 Treaty of Utrecht

1713–40 Reign of Frederick William I in Prussia

1714–27 Reign of George I in England

1714 **Handel moves to London**

ca. 1715 **Bach, *Orgelbüchlein***

1717 ***Handel's Celebrated Water Music* performed for King George I on the River Thames**

1717–23 **Bach in Cöthen**

These composers were among the earliest to inherit from the Italian string players of the seventeenth century, explored in the previous chapter, a fully developed tonal idiom and to enlarge on it magnificently. From the same Italian virtuosos, Bach and Handel also inherited a highly developed instrumental medium—the *ripieno* string orchestra, to which wind and percussion instruments could be added as the occasion demanded. The new harmonic idiom and the new instrumentation together fostered the growth of musical forms of greater size, complexity, and lasting influence.

Unsurprisingly, the works of the class of 1685 that loom largest today will be those that coincide with or can be adapted to our now standard performing forces and aesthetic purposes. Yet these familiar works represent only a portion of their outputs, and not necessarily those portions considered most important or most characteristic by the composers themselves or by their contemporaries. Opera seria, the reigning genre for most of the eighteenth century, long dropped out of the repertoire, and only late in the twentieth century did it begin to enjoy some revival. Much of the music that both Handel and Scarlatti rightly regarded as their most significant has also perished from active use, while a lot of music that they regarded as quite secondary, such as Scarlatti's keyboard music and Handel's suites for orchestra, is standard fare today. Bach, who never even wrote an opera, was a marginal figure in his own time. Seeing him as a pillar of the standard performing repertory means seeing him not as his contemporaries did but, rather, in the way that later generations would. Relatively unimportant in life, Bach gradually became a musical god in death. Georg Philipp Telemann (1681–1767), a phenomenally prolific composer of over 3,000 works whom we will consider only in passing, enjoyed greater fame at the time than Handel or Bach, both of whom he knew personally.

We will consider these figures in their own historical context and examine the relationship between their living fame and their posthumous fame. The most surprising aspect of the comparison will be the realization that Bach and Handel, whom we regard from our contemporary vantage point as a beginning, were seen more as enders in their own day: outstanding late practitioners of styles and genres that were rapidly dying in their time. Scarlatti, viewed as a secondary figure today, was arguably more "cutting edge," exploring new trends that came to be associated with the Enlightenment. Ironically, it was the very conservatism of Bach and Handel that later made them so well established. The styles that supplanted theirs were destined to be fleeting. Meanwhile, Handel's conservative idiom appealed to conservative members of his contemporary audience—and these members constituted the particular social group that inaugurated the very idea of a standard repertory.

With Bach the situation was more complicated. His music came back into circulation and achieved a posthumous status it never enjoyed during his lifetime because the conservative aspects of his style—in particular, his very dense contrapuntal textures and his technique of spinning out melodic phrases of extraordinary length—made his music seem weighty and profound at a time when the qualities of weightiness and profundity were returning to fashion, in the early nineteenth century. His elevation eventually served political, nationalistic, and musical purposes. A mythology grew up around Bach according to which his music had a unique quality that lifted it above and beyond the historical flux and made it a timeless standard. It has been considered the greatest music ever written and, with still greater ideological significance, the greatest music that ever would or could be written. It was another instance of musical perfection, but in this case applied to a brilliant individual composer rather than to an ingenious style shared by many composers that marked an older era, the *ars perfecta*.

Bach's later sanctification in turn gave birth to a myth of music history itself. As we leave what is traditionally considered the Baroque era with the class of 1685, we see the beginning of the end of Italian dominance in music. Germany, which for various reasons had seemed so often to lag behind, became the site of synthesis, of the mixing together of genres and styles originally associated with Italy, France, England, and even Poland and places farther afield. German historians would later mold the story of Germany's place in history in the most consequential ways. The *history* of any art is the concern—and the creation—of its receivers, not of its producers.

1721 **Compilation of Bach's Brandenburg Concertos**

1722 **Bach, *Well-Tempered Keyboard*, Book I**

1722 **François Couperin, *Le Rossignol en-amour***

1723–50 **Bach in Leipzig**

1727–60 Reign of George II in England

1734 Voltaire, *Philosophical Letters*

1738–42 ***Well-Tempered Keyboard*, Book II**

1740 Frederick the Great crowned King of Prussia

1740 Maria Theresa crowned Holy Roman Empress

1749 **Handel, *The Music for the Royal Fireworks***

1749 Henry Fielding, *The History of Tom Jones, a Foundling*

1750 **Death of Bach**

1751 **Bach, *The Art of Fugue*, published by C.P.E. Bach**

1752 Jean-Jacques Rousseau, *Discourse on the Origin of Inequality*

1757 **Death of Scarlatti**

1759 **Death of Handel**

Careers and Lifestyles: Handel First

Bach and Handel were born within a month of one another, in adjoining eastern German provinces about 100 miles apart (Fig. 10-1). Handel, whose baptismal name was Georg Friederich Händel, was born on 23 February, in Halle. Bach's birth on 21 March was a little to the south and west, in the town of Eisenach in Thuringia, a province of Saxony. Because of their nearly coinciding origins and their commanding historical stature, Bach and Handel are often thought of as a pair. They never met, however, and in most ways their lives and careers are a study in contrasts.

Handel (Fig. 10-2) spent only the first eighteen years of his life in his native city, where he studied with the local church organist and attended the university. In 1703 he moved to Hamburg, which had a thriving opera house, where he played violin and harpsichord in the orchestra and composed two operas for the company. Having found his calling in musical theater, he naturally gravitated to Italy, the operatic capital of the world. He spent his true formative years—from 1706 to 1710—in Florence and Rome, where he worked for noble and ecclesiastical patrons and met Alessandro Scarlatti, Corelli, and other luminaries of the day. He was known affectionately as *il Sassone*, "the Saxon," meaning really "the Saxon turned Italian," in the musical sense. In 1710 he became the music director at the court of George Louis, the Elector of Hanover, one of the richest German rulers. There Handel had to assimilate the French style that all the German nobles affected in every aspect of court life, including language and music.

Bach and Handel were born within a month of one another, in adjoining eastern German provinces about 100 miles apart, yet they never met.

The great turning point in Handel's life came in 1714, when his employer, without giving up the electoral throne in Hanover, became King George I of England, although he never learned to speak English and was personally unpopular in England. Handel had actually made his English debut as an opera composer before George's accession to the throne. With the king a virtual absentee ruler—George continued to spend most of his time in Hanover—Handel was left remarkably free of official duties and gained the right to act as a free agent, an independent operatic entrepreneur on the lively London stage. He lived in England for the rest of his life. Over the rough quarter century between 1711 and 1738, Handel presented some three dozen operas at the King's Theatre in the London Haymarket, with a

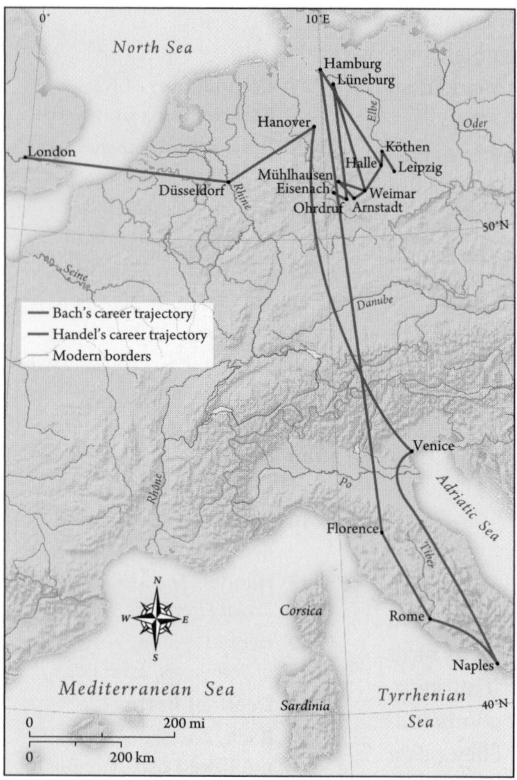

Figure 10-1 J. S. Bach's and G. F. Handel's career trajectories.

few, toward the end, at Covent Garden. Acting at once as composer, conductor, producer, and, eventually, his own promotional agent, he made a legendary fortune, the first such fortune earned by musical enterprise alone in the history of the art. (Palestrina also died a very rich man, but his fortune came from his wife's first husband's fur business.)

Beginning in the 1730s, a new generation of opera composers arrived in London. A rival company, the so-called Opera of the Nobility, engaged the latest Italian composers and, more importantly, the services of the great castrato Farinelli, around whom a virtual cult had formed. After a few seasons of cutthroat competition, both Handel and his competitors were near bankruptcy, and Handel was forced out of the opera business. With his keen business sense he divined a huge potential market in English oratorios: biblical operas presented without staging, along lines already familiar to us from the Lenten work of the Roman composers, such as Giacomo Carissimi. Handel's adaptation of this old-fashioned genre—he produced nearly two dozen between 1732 and 1752—was something quite new: full-length works in English rather than in Italian or Latin, with many thrilling choruses.

Handel's was the exemplary cosmopolitan career of the early eighteenth century, a career epitomized by his operatic middle years, in which a German-born composer made a fortune by purveying Italian-texted operas to an English-speaking audience. Handel's style was neither German nor Italian nor English but a hybrid that blended existing national genres and idioms, mixing in the French as well. France was the one country where Handel, although an occasional visitor, never lived or worked; but French music, as the international court music, informed not only the specifically courtly music that he wrote for his kingly patron but the overtures to his operas and oratorios as well. Handel, the quintessential musical synthesizer and consummate musical entrepreneur, commanded pan-European prestige.

Bach's Career

Figure 10-2 G. F. Handel, painting by Philipp Mercier.

Johann Sebastian Bach (Fig. 10-3), on the other hand, never once left Germany. Indeed, except for his student years at Lüneburg, a town near Hamburg to the north and west, his entire career could be circumscribed by a small circle that encompassed a few east German locales, most of them quite provincial: Eisenach, his birthplace, where he was orphaned at age nine and moved to Ohrdruf to live with his older brother, Johann Christoph, an organist; Arnstadt, where he served between 1703 and 1707 as organist at the municipal Church of St. Boniface; Mühlhausen, where he served at the municipal Church of St. Blasius for a single year; Weimar, where he served the ducal court as organist and concert director from 1708 to 1717; Cöthen, where he served as music director to another ducal court from 1717 to 1723; and finally Leipzig, where he served as music director at the municipal school attached to the St. Thomas Church (Fig. 10-4) from 1723 until his death.

One of the larger German commercial cities even in Bach's day, Leipzig was nevertheless only a fraction of London's size and far from a cosmopolitan center.

Still, it was a big enough town to have sought a bigger name than Bach as its municipal cantor (the name given to music directors of German Protestant churches). He was chosen only after more famous musicians, including Telemann, had declined the town's offer. Bach, for his part, felt he had been forced to take a step down the social ladder by going from a Kapellmeister's position at Cöthen to a cantorate at Leipzig. Until age put him out of the running, he sought better employment elsewhere, including the electoral court at Dresden, the Saxon capital. Leipzig was the best he could do, however, and Bach was the best that Leipzig could do. Neither seems to have been very happy with the other.

Figure 10-3 J. S. Bach in a portrait by Elias Gottlob Haussmann (a 1748 copy of a 1746 original).

Bach's, then, was the quintessential "provincial" career—humble, unglamorous, businesslike. What he wrote at any given time was in large measure determined by who was then employing him and what his assigned duties were, whether as an organist, a court musician, or a church composer. No one needed an opera from him, and nor did the opportunity arise to write one. While most of his greatest sacred vocal works date from the later Leipzig years, Bach did not ignore instrumental music during that time. He continued, for example, to produce enjoyable and instructive pieces for family use. Bach married at age twenty-two and became a father the next year. After his first wife died in 1720, he remarried the next year and eventually fathered twenty children, twelve of whom survived childhood. A number of them went on to be celebrated composers, more famous at the time than their father. It is hardly surprising that over the years Bach wrote compositions for the private enjoyment of his family and the instruction of his children. Such works continue to help young musicians learn their craft. Some of Bach's later instrumental pieces were written for the Collegium Musicum in Leipzig, a society of professional instrumentalists and students, founded by Telemann in 1702, that gave weekly afternoon concerts at a popular local coffee garden and that Bach took over in 1729.

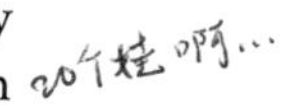

Bach's most significant instrumental works during the Leipzig years originated for more esoteric and speculative reasons. He produced a few masterworks of an old-fashioned, abstract nature in which he gave full rein to his unrivaled contrapuntal virtuosity. It may be fair to say that the sheer technical dexterity in the art of composition that Bach exhibits here has never been surpassed. In addition, he seems to have enjoyed esoteric or symbolic practices, such as spelling his name musically. The German naming of pitches is somewhat different than English practice. With the note B natural being called H, Bach could notate his name using the pitches B♭, A, C, B natural. The number 14 seems to have held some importance for him because the name *Bach,* if translated into numbers according to the positions of its constituent letters in the alphabet—a practice that goes back to Hebrew cabbalistic lore—comes out 2 + 1 + 3 + 8 = 14. Bach's numerological virtuosity has only begun to be investigated. Some scholars suspect that it may rival his musical skills; others remain skeptical.

Figure 10-4 St. Thomas Square, Leipzig, in an engraving by Johann Gottfried Krugner made in 1723, the year of Bach's arrival. The church is at right; the school, where Bach lived and worked, is at left.

Elaborate technical experimentation came increasingly into play in his late works, including the "Goldberg" Variations, a huge cycle of thirty keyboard pieces, among them a series of intricate canons, all based on a single ostinato bass line. Another exhibition of contrapuntal skill was the *Musikalisches Opfer* (Musical Offering), a miscellany of canons, complicated ricercars (old-fashioned fugues), and a trio sonata. It was all based on an unusually chromatic "royal theme" given Bach as a subject for improvisation by none other than Frederick the Great, the Prussian king, during a visit by Bach in May 1747 to the Prussian court at Potsdam, where his son Carl Philipp Emanuel Bach was employed.

Bach's ultimate speculative composition, his intended final testament, was *Die Kunst der Fuge* (The Art of Fugue), a collection of twenty-one *contrapuncti*, including canons, double fugues, triple fugues, fugues with answers by augmentation and diminution, inversion, and *cancrizans* ("crab motion," or retrograde), all based on a single D-minor subject. (We will look at some Bach fugues later in this chapter.) Bach was working on this collection at the time of his death, leaving seemingly unfinished (or perhaps the ending was later lost) the final fugue, in which the musical anagram of his name was to be worked in as a chromatic countersubject. The B–A–C–H cipher has been a potent musical emblem ever since *The Art of Fugue* was published, in 1751, in an edition supervised by Carl Philipp Emanuel, who refrained from finishing the last fugue, letting it trail off into a sketch, followed by a note explaining the reason (Exs. 10-1a and b).

Example 10-1 (a) The B-A-C-H cipher; (b) B-A-C-H cipher at the end of *The Art of Fugue*

Bach, who came from a long line of musicians, remained in the musical environment to which he had been born—the same environment that Handel had quit at his earliest opportunity. Handel had an unprecedented, self-made, entrepreneurial career that brought him unexpected glory. Bach's career, by contrast, was entirely predefined: It was completely traditional for a musician of his habitat and class. For a musician of exceptional talent, it was positively confining. We will begin by examining instrumental music by these two composers (with a few detours along the way) and turn, in the next chapter, to their vocal compositions. In both cases we will encounter traditional or conservative features as well as path-breaking new ones. And although Handel's career was so notably cosmopolitan and Bach's so thoroughly provincial, both composers were great synthesizers of different national styles. That would emerge, in fact, as the German path to musical dominance: drawing on the most successful of competing styles, the best of the rest.

The Chorale Prelude

J. S. Bach hailed from an enormous clan of Lutheran church musicians dating back to the sixteenth century. So firmly associated was the family with the profession they plied that in parts of eastern Germany the word "Bach," which means "brook" in German, was slang for musician. The *New Grove Dictionary of Music and Musicians* lists no fewer than eighty-five musical Bachs, from Veit Bach (ca. 1555–1619) down ten generations to Johann Philipp Bach (1752–1846). Fourteen members of the family were distinguished enough as composers to earn biographical articles in the dictionary, including two of Johann Sebastian Bach's uncles, three of his cousins, and four of his sons.

Most of the elder Bachs were trained as church organists and cantors. That training included a great deal of traditional theory and composition, and as church musicians they were expected to turn out vocal settings in quantity to satisfy the weekly needs of the congregations they served. The greatest composers of this type in the generations immediately preceding Bach—or at least the ones Bach sought out personally and took as role models—were three: Georg Böhm (1661–1733), who taught him during his student years at Lüneburg; the Dutch-born Johann Adam Reincken (1643–1722), a patriarchal figure who had studied with a pupil of Sweelinck; and, above all, Dieterich Buxtehude (ca. 1637–1707), a Dane who served for nearly forty years as organist of the Marienkirche in Lübeck (Fig. 10-5), one of the most important musical posts in Lutheran Germany. Within that cultural sphere Buxtehude's fame was supreme, and he received numerous visits and dedications from aspiring musicians, including both Handel, who came up from Hamburg in 1703, and Bach, who made the nearly 300-mile pilgrimage on foot in the winter of 1705–06.

> ***So firmly associated was the Bach family with the profession that in parts of eastern Germany the word "Bach," which means "brook" in German, was slang for musician.***

According to a story related by one of his pupils, the aged Reincken, having heard Bach improvise on a chorale as part of a job audition, proclaimed the younger man the torchbearer of the old north-German tradition: "I thought this art was dead," the patriarch is said to have exclaimed, "but I see that in you it lives!" The story may well be made up (as we know these kinds of benedictions often are), but it points to an important truth: Bach did found his style on the most traditional aspects of north German Lutheran musical culture. The keyboard works he composed early in his career while serving as organist at Arnstadt and Weimar show this retrospective side most dramatically.

One traditional genre that Bach inherited directly from his Lutheran organist forebears and from Buxtehude most immediately was the chorale setting. A protean genre, it could assume many forms, anywhere from a colossal set of improvised or composed variations, the type with which Bach enraptured Reincken, to a minuscule *Choralvorspiel*, or "**chorale prelude**," a single-stanza setting with which the organist might cue the congregation to sing or provide an accompaniment to silent meditation. Toward the end of his Weimar period, Bach set about collecting his chorale preludes into a liturgical cycle that would cover the whole year's services. He had only inscribed 46 items out of a projected 164 in this manuscript, called the *Orgelbüchlein* (Little Organ Book), when he got his new position in Cöthen. But in their variety, the ones entered fully justify Bach's claim on the manuscript's title page that in his little book "a beginner at the organ is given instruction in developing a chorale in many diverse ways."

Anthology Vol 1-81

We can compare Buxtehude and Bach directly by putting side by side their chorale preludes on *Durch Adams Fall ist ganz verderbt* (Through Adam's Fall we are Condemned). The first line makes reference to what for Christians was the first and greatest catastrophe in human history: Adam and Eve's eating the forbidden fruit from the tree of knowledge that led to their expulsion from the Garden of Eden and mankind's fall from grace. The ultimate subject of the chorale's text is God's mercy, by which man may be redeemed from Adam's original sin through faith in Jesus Christ. It is the stark opening line, however, that establishes the tone for the setting, since the first verse would typically have been the one directly introduced by the prelude. Both Buxtehude's prelude and Bach's, therefore, are tinged with grief. The chorale melody, unadorned by Bach, embellished slightly by Buxtehude, is surrounded by affective counterpoints. In Buxtehude's case the affect is created by chromatically ascending and descending lines that enter after a curious suppression of the bass. In Bach's setting, the most striking aspect is surely the pedal part. This in itself is no surprise: Spotlighting the pedal part was one of Bach's special predilections, and fancy footwork was one of his specialties as an organ virtuoso.

Figure 10-5 Baroque organ at Marienkirche in Berlin (1719) built by Joachim Wagner (1690–1749).

What is a powerful surprise and further evidence of Bach's unique imaginative boldness is the specific form the obbligato pedal part takes in this chorale setting: almost nothing but dissonant drops of a seventh—Adam's fall made audible! And not just the fall, but also the attendant pain and suffering are depicted, one might say evoked, since so many of those sevenths are diminished. A blatant "madrigalism," the fall, is given emotional force through sheer harmonic audacity and is then made the primary unifying motive of the composition.

Structure and signification, "form" and "content," are thus indissolubly wedded, made virtually synonymous. That was the expressive ideal at the very root of the humanism that had given rise to what Monteverdi called the *seconda pratica* a hundred years before. Monteverdi could only conceive its realization in the context of vocal music, where the text will determine the music, and never dreamed that such an art could flourish in textless instrumental music. That was what Bach, building on a century of musical changes, would achieve within an outwardly old-fashioned, even backward-looking career. Clearly, Bach's art had a Janus face, looking forward as well as back. Formally and texturally it looked back to what were even at the time archaic practices. In terms of harmony and tonally articulated form, however, it was at the cutting edge. That cutting edge still pierces the consciousness of listeners today and calls forth an intense response, while the music of every other Lutheran cantor of the time has perished from the actual repertory.

The Fugue

Bach inherited from the south German composer Johann Pachelbel (1653–1706) a process whereby the "strict" and "free" sections of a **toccata**—that is, the rigorously imitative versus the improvisatory passages—became increasingly separate from one another and increasingly regular in their alternation, with the improvisatory passages serving as introductions to the lengthy contrapuntal ones. By the early eighteenth century these sectionalized toccatas had developed into pairs of discrete pieces, the free one serving as prelude to the strict. Such a pair, although still called "toccata and fugue" or "fantasia and fugue," was by Bach's time most often simply designated "prelude and fugue." Bach was the greatest exponent of the prelude-and-fugue form, to which he contributed more than two dozen examples for organ, along with works for the instrument in even more traditional genres, such as his famous organ Passacaglia in C Minor. Most of these are early pieces, the bulk of them composed at Weimar, where he was employed primarily as an organ virtuoso.

Let's explore in some detail the elaborate contrapuntal device known as the ***fugue***, which we have already mentioned in passing a number of times. Many more fugues will be encountered in the chapters to come, as well as fugal sections within other kinds of works, ranging from choral pieces to symphonies, string quartets, and even operas. Fugues can thus be self-standing, individual pieces as well a texture or procedure found within compositions. In the description that follows, the standard modern terminology for the fugue's components and events will be employed, even though—like the word *fugue* itself—they are not strictly contemporaneous with the piece at hand.

Anthology Vol 1-82
Full CD II, 49
Concise CD I, 85

The Fugue in G Minor is one of Bach's earliest organ works, apparently written when he was in his early twenties and employed in Arnstadt, his first full-time position. While it does not have the complexity of his later fugues (one of which we will shortly explore), it is a particularly straightforward example of fugal techniques and a particularly attractive one. A fugue begins like a single colossally elaborated point of imitation from the older motet. There is a single main theme, called the ***subject***, on which the whole piece is based. In the opening section of a fugue, known as the *exposition*, the subject is introduced in every "voice." No one is singing, of course, in instrumental fugues like this one for organ, but it is still standard to refer to the different voices. A fugue must by definition have at least two voices, with three or four more common; more than that and there is the risk that one's head will burst at the complexity.

The subject in the G-Minor Fugue begins in the soprano (mm. 1–5). Next the second voice, in the alto range, comes in playing the subject "at the fifth" (meaning a fifth up or, as here, a fourth down); when played at this transposition, the theme is called the ***answer*** (mm. 6–10). The counterpoint with which the original voice accompanies the answer is called the ***countersubject***. Next to enter is the tenor (mm.

12–17), playing the subject in its original form, though down an octave, followed by another answer a fourth lower (Ex. 10-2). After this exposition of the voices, there is what is called an ***episode***, which simply means a stretch of music in free counterpoint during which the subject is withheld. The subject returns at m. 25; the entire piece alternates between fugal expositions (six in all) and five episodes. To end, Bach pulls one last contrapuntal stunt: The voices now pile in with overlapping entries on the subject and answer. This foreshortening device is called the ***stretto*** (Italian for "straitened"—tightened or made stricter) and is a common way of bringing fugues to a close.

Example 10-2 **J. S. Bach, Fugue in G Minor, BWV 578, mm. 1–19**

The *Well-Tempered Keyboard*

Anthology Vol 1-83
Full CD II, 50–51

To return to the pairing of the free **prelude** with the strict fugue, we will briefly consider a pair from Bach's most systematic statement, an enormously influential body of music, sometimes even referred to as the "Old Testament" of the keyboard, that was known to later composers such as Mozart and Beethoven at a time when little else of Bach's music was. A monumental cycle of forty-eight paired preludes and fugues, *Das wohltemperirte Clavier* is divided in two books, the first assembled in Cöthen in 1722, the second in Leipzig between 1738 and 1742. The title means "The Well-Tempered Keyboard," and its subtitle reads "Preludes and Fugues through All the Tones and Semitones." Each of the books making up Bach's famous "Forty-Eight" consists of a prelude-and-fugue pair in all the keys of the newly elaborated complete tonal system, alternating major and minor and ascending by half steps from C major to B minor (thus: C, c, C♯, c♯, D, d, and so on). To play fugues in all keys required a keyboard instrument tuned in such a way that the twelve half steps of the octave sounded equally well in tune no matter what the tonality.

Bach also greatly expanded the scope and the contrapuntal density of such preludes and fugues. Something of the range of technique and intensity of style of the WTC may be gleaned by juxtaposing the very beginning and the very end of the first book: the opening C-major prelude and the closing B-minor fugue. These are both famous pieces, although for very different reasons. The C-major prelude is a piece that every pianist encounters as a child. It is in a classic "preludizing" style that goes back to the lutenists of the sixteenth century, kept alive through the seventeenth century by the French court harpsichordists. The French called it the *style brisé*, or "broken [chord] style." Thus, descending from a literally improvisatory practice, the C-major prelude is cast in a purely harmonic, "tuneless" idiom, although with a very clearly delineated form articulated by its harmony (Ex. 10-3a).

The B-minor fugue is instead famous for its chromatic saturation and its attendant sense of pathos—a pathos achieved by harmony alone. The three-measure subject is celebrated in its own right for containing within its short span every degree of the chromatic scale, which at the same time symbolically consummates the progress "through all the tones and semitones" as announced in the subtitle of the whole cycle. What gives the subject and the entire fugue their remarkably poignant affect is not just the high level of chromaticism but also the way in which that chromaticism is coordinated with what, even on their first "unharmonized" appearance, are obviously dissonant leaps—known technically as *appoggiaturas* ("leaning notes"). The two leaps of a diminished seventh in the second measure are the most obviously dissonant: The jarring interval is clearly meant to be heard as an embellishment "leaning on" the minor sixth that is achieved when the first note in the slurred pair resolves by half step: C natural to B, D to C♯. But in fact, as the ensuing counterpoint reveals, every first note of a slurred pair is (or can be treated as) a dissonant appoggiatura (Ex. 10-3b).

It will come as no surprise to learn that these slurred descending pairs with dissonant beginnings were known as *Seufzer*—"sighs" or "groans"—and that they had originated as a kind of madrigalism. The transfer of vivid illustrative effects, even onomatopoeias, into abstract musical forms shows that those forms, at least as handled by Bach, were not abstract at all but fraught with a maximum of emotional baggage. What is most remarkable is the way Bach consistently contrives to let the illustrative idea that bears the "affective" significance serve simultaneously as the motive from which the musical stuff is spun out. Indeed, he heightened the pathos of this material by fashioning episodes—the passages in which the subject is absent—that contrast with it in the strongest way possible.

Example 10-3 **J. S. Bach, *Das wohltemperirte Clavier*, Book I: (a) Prelude No. 1 (C major), mm. 1–6; (b) Fugue No. 24 (B minor), mm. 1–16**

Bach's Imported Roots: Johann Jacob Froberger and Others

Although Bach never left Germany, in a sense musical Europe came to him in the form of manuscripts and publications. And so, despite the relative insularity of his career, Bach nevertheless mastered a great range of contemporary musical styles and idioms. In part this was simply a matter of being German. At a time when French and Italian musicians were mutually suspicious and much concerned with resisting each other's influence, German musicians tended to define themselves as universal synthesizers. Johann Joachim Quantz (1697–1773), a colleague of C. P. E. Bach's at the Prussian court, noted how the Germans were able "to select with due discrimination from the musical tastes of various peoples what is best in each," thereby producing "a mixed taste which, without overstepping the bounds of modesty, may very well be called the German taste."[1] Bach became the ultimate exponent of this "German taste."

But he had many predecessors. We know how eagerly Heinrich Schütz, born exactly a hundred years before Bach, had imported the Italian styles of his day to Germany. A younger contemporary of Schütz, the sometime Viennese court organist Johann Jacob Froberger (1616–67), a native of Stuttgart in southern Germany, traveled the length and breadth of Europe, soaking up influences everywhere. After a period studying with Frescobaldi in Rome in the late 1630s, he visited Brussels, Paris, and England and died in the service of a French-speaking German court in the German Rhineland. His most influential publication was entitled *Dix suittes de clavessin* (Ten Suites for Harpsichord), written in a style that conformed perfectly with the language of the title page. By century's end, the French style had become a veritable German fetish. Envy of the opulent French court on the part of the many petty German princelings led to the wholesale adoption of French manners by the German aristocracy. French actually became the court language of Germany, and French dancing became an obligatory social grace at the many mini-Versailleses that dotted the German landscape (Fig. 10-6).

Germans selected "with due discrimination from the musical tastes of various peoples what is best in each," producing "a mixed taste which, may very well be called the German taste."—Johann Joachim Quantz

With dancing, of course, came music. Demand for French-style dance music and for instruction in composing and playing it was so great that by the end of the seventeenth century a number of German musicians had set themselves up in business writing such pieces. One was Georg Muffat (1653–1704), an organist at the Episcopal court at Passau, who as a youth had played violin under Lully in Paris. In 1695 he published a set of dance suites in the Lullian mold, together with a treatise on how to play them in the correct Lullian "ballet style." His rules, especially those concerning unwritten conventions of rhythm and bowing, have been a goldmine for understanding the performance practices of the time.

Froberger helped to establish a standard **suite** format that provided the model for his German successors. Bach adopted a specific sequence of four dances—***allemande***, ***courante***, ***sarabande***, and ***gigue***—as the essential nucleus in all his suites, setting a precedent that governed the composition of keyboard suites from then on. Some composers, like J. C. F. Fischer (1656–1746), prefaced suites with preludes, which also became an important precedent, although not quite as universally

Figure 10-6 Dance in a Formal Garden, from a collection titled *Les menus plaisirs du roi*, French School, seventeenth century.

observed later. Bach, for example, composed suites both with and without preludes, but he always included Froberger's core dances. (Froberger's own order in his four-movement suites was allemande, gigue, courante, sarabande; his posthumous editors moved the gigues to last place.) It is worth emphasizing that these dances had, by the time Froberger adapted them, pretty much gone out of actual ballroom use. They had been sublimated into elevated courtly listening-music by the master instrumentalists of France, which meant slowing them down and cramming them full of interesting musical detail more intended for listeners than for dancers. The four dances were chosen for their contrasting tempos, meters, and moods:

1. *Allemande.* As its name suggests, this dance originated in Germany. But by the time German composers borrowed it back from the French it had changed from a quick dance to a slower, stately movement in a broad quadruple meter ($\frac{4}{4}$).
2. *Courante.* This is a grave triple-meter, notated in $\frac{3}{2}$ with many lilting hemiola effects in which $\frac{6}{4}$ patterns cut across the $\frac{3}{2}$ pulse.
3. *Sarabande.* It originated in the New World and was brought back to Europe, as the *zarabanda*, from Mexico. In its original form it was a breakneck, sexy affair, accompanied by castanets. Banned from the Spanish ballroom by decree for its alleged obscenity, it became a

majestic triple-metered dance for the ballet stage, often compared to a slow minuet, typically with an emphasis on the second beat. The most common rhythmic pattern is a half note followed by a dotted half and quarter.

4. *Gigue*. Imported to Europe from England and Ireland, the jig was a fast dance, usually in $\frac{6}{8}$ meter. In its idealized form, the gigue usually began with a point of imitation.

A "binary" form (AABB), supported by a there-and-back harmonic plan, was a universal feature of stylized dances, particularly as adopted by Germans. That shape will henceforth serve as paradigm for a fully "tonal" binary form. The new elements include the care with which the tonic is established and the determined movement to some harmonic "far-out point" in the second half of the piece before redirecting the harmonic motion home with renewed force. In the hands of Bach and his contemporaries, the binary dance became another important site for developing the kind of tonally articulated form that conditioned new habits of listening and formed the bedrock of the standard performing repertory.

Bach's Suites

As we know, Bach never went to France, but through musical publications that circulated widely in Germany he was exposed to French music. Bach made his most thorough assimilation of the French style when he was professionally required to do so. That was in 1717, when he left Weimar to become kapellmeister in Cöthen. There he had an entirely secular job, the only such position he ever occupied. His new employer, Prince Leopold of Anhalt-Cöthen, was a passionate musical amateur, who esteemed Bach highly and related to him practically on terms of friendship, even becoming the godfather to one of Bach's children. Leopold not only consumed music avidly but played it himself and had studied composition for a while in Rome with Johann David Heinichen (1683–1729), a notable German musician of the day. He maintained a court orchestra of about sixteen instrumentalists, including some very distinguished ones. And he was a Calvinist, which meant he had no use for elaborate composed church music or fancy organ playing. So Bach had no reason to compose or play in church and could devote his time to satisfying his patron's demands for secular musical entertainments.

The binary dance became another important site for developing the kind of tonally articulated form that conditioned new habits of listening.

Thus for six years Bach wrote mainly instrumental music. The first book of *The Well-Tempered Keyboard* dates mainly from the Cöthen period, but Bach did that on the side. The kind of entertainments demanded of him as part of his official duties would have taken the form of sonatas, concertos, and, above all, suites. Bach turned out several dozen of the latter, ranging from orchestral suites (which he called overtures), through various sets for keyboard, to astoundingly ingenious and demanding suites for unaccompanied violin and for cello, the latter unprecedented as far as we know. Most of his suites are grouped in sets of six. The earliest are six large ones for keyboard with elaborate virtuoso preludes and highly embellished sarabandes, probably composed in Weimar around 1715. They were published posthumously as "English Suites" and have been called that ever since, although no one really knows why. Also published posthumously were six "French Suites," which were close to the Froberger model.

Anthology Vol 1-84
Full CD II, 52–58
Concise CD I, 85–92

A quick look at Bach's French Suite No. 5, in G major, will highlight some crucial stylistic features that are symptomatic of a fundamental shift in taste, one that would eventually mark the eighteenth century as a kind of aesthetic battleground. The nucleus of the suite consists of the Frobergerian core of allemande, courante, sarabande, and gigue, augmented by a trio of slighter dances (a gavotte, a bourée, and a loure) inserted before the gigue. Bach himself used the term *Galanterien* (from the French *galanteries*) on the title page to classify these extra dances and distinguish them from the core, describing his suites and partitas, the term he later used for a set of six suites written in Leipzig, as consisting of "Präludien, Allemanden, Couranten, Sarabanden, Giguen, Menuetten, und anderen Galanterien." Note that the obligatory dances are listed in order after the Prelude, while the variable category of "minuets and other *galanteries*" is mentioned casually, as if an afterthought.

Even though the word *galanterie* can be translated as a "trifle," it denotes an important aesthetic category. It is derived from what the French called the *style galant*, from the old French verb *galer*, which meant "to amuse" in a tasteful, courtly sort of way, with refined wit, elegant manners, and easy grace. It was a quality of art—and life—far removed from the stern world of the traditional Lutheran church. With Bach, the ***galant***, while certainly within his range, is nevertheless the exceptional style—the sauce rather than the meat. With most of his contemporaries and later with his sons, the balance had rather decisively shifted to the opposite.

Agréments and *Doubles*: The Art of Ornamentation

Figure 10-7 François Couperin.

Thus far more typical of Bach's German affinities is the concluding gigue, with its fugal expositions in three real parts. For this dance, the most elaborate in the set, it is instructive to contrast it not with one of Bach's own concocted *galanteries* but with the work of his greatest keyboard-playing contemporary, François Couperin (1668–1733; Fig. 10-7), royal organist and chief *musicien de chambre* to Louis XIV. We will consider the piece that opens the fourteenth *ordre*, or "set," of harpsichord compositions that Couperin had published in 1722. Couperin's is a set rather than a suite because, following traditional French practice, the pieces in it, while related by key, are too numerous to be played or heard in one sitting and are not placed in performance order. Altogether he released four books of his harpsichord pieces, encompassing twenty-seven sets and totaling some 220 pieces.

Couperin's gigue is in a rocking $\frac{6}{8}$, the normal gigue meter; Bach's $\frac{12}{16}$ is a diminution, indicating a faster tempo than usual. None of the dances in Bach's suite carry any verbal marking as to their tempo. No such indications were needed—the name of the dance, the meter, and the note values conveyed the essential information (Ex. 10-4).

Example 10-4 J. S. Bach, French Suite No. 5 in G Major, Gigue, mm. 1–8

Example 10-4 (*continued*)

But the situation with Couperin's gigue, one of his most famous pieces, is just the opposite. In fact it is called not "gigue" but *Le Rossignol en-amour*, "The Nightingale in Love"! It is not really a dance at all but what would later be called a "character piece" or, to use Couperin's own word, a sort of "portrait" in tones, cast in a conventional form inherited from dance music. The subject portrayed is ostensibly a bird, and the decorative surface of the music teems with embellishments that seem delightfully to imitate the bird's singing. But since, according to the title, the bird in question is incongruously experiencing a human emotion, the musical imitation is simultaneously to be "read" as a metaphor—a portrait not just of the bird but of the emotion, too, in all its tenderness (Ex. 10-5a).

Anthology Vol 1-85
Full CD II, 59

Since the conventional tempo of a gigue contradicts tenderness, Couperin had to countermand it with a very detailed verbal indication, directing the performer to play "slowly, and very tenderly, although basically in time." At the stipulated tempo there is room for a great wealth of embellishment, all indicated with little shorthand signs that Bach also used and that are largely still familiar to keyboard students today. Couperin provided many ornaments, called "graces" in English at the time and *agréments* in French. Although such ornaments were learned "orally" (by listening to one's teacher and imitating) and deployed improvisationally, Couperin fought against both tendencies. He published tables of ornaments in his First Book of harpsichord pieces in 1713 (Fig. 10-8) and three years later published a treatise *L'art de toucher le clavecin* (The Art of Playing the Harpsichord) that indicated precisely how to execute the embellishments. More notably, in the preface to his Third Book (1722), in which *Le Rossignol en-amour* appears, he described himself "surprised" by those who disregarded his ornamentation in favor of their own: "It is unpardonable negligence, all the more so as the placement of such *agréments* is not arbitrary. I declare then that my pieces must be played as I have marked them, and that they will never make a real impression on people of true taste unless one observes exactly what I have marked, without adding or subtracting."[2]

For an even more intense expression, Couperin resorted to specifically composed embellishments, turns and runs that have no conventional shorthand notation. That is what he does in his coda, where he notes that the speed of the written-out trill is to be "increased by imperceptible degrees" for an especially spontaneous burst of feeling. And then he follows the whole piece with a fancy version called a *double*, in which the surface becomes a real flurry of notes and where it becomes the supreme mark of skillful performance to keep the distinctive features of the original melody in the foreground (Ex. 10-5b).

Miniatures that display the kind of exquisitely embellished, decorative veneer Couperin knew so well how to apply are often called ***rococo***, a word that derived from folding together the French *rocaille* and *coquille*, the "rock work" and "shell work" featured in expensively textured architectural surfaces of the period (Fig. 10-9). If the decorative surface were stripped away from Couperin's piece, the simplest of shapes would remain: Cadences come every four measures, the last one delayed, describing a bare-bones tonal trajectory of I–V/V–I. Nor is the emotion expressed one of great vehemence or intensity. Rococo art expressed the same sort of aristocratic sentiments, including the sort of amorous or melancholy ones that can be aired in polite society and identified as *galant*. The strong pathos of so much of Bach's instrumental music would have been out of place in such company.

Example 10-5 **François Couperin, *Le Rossignol en-amour* (14th Ordre, No. 1): (a) mm. 1–8; (b) "Double du Rossignol," opening**

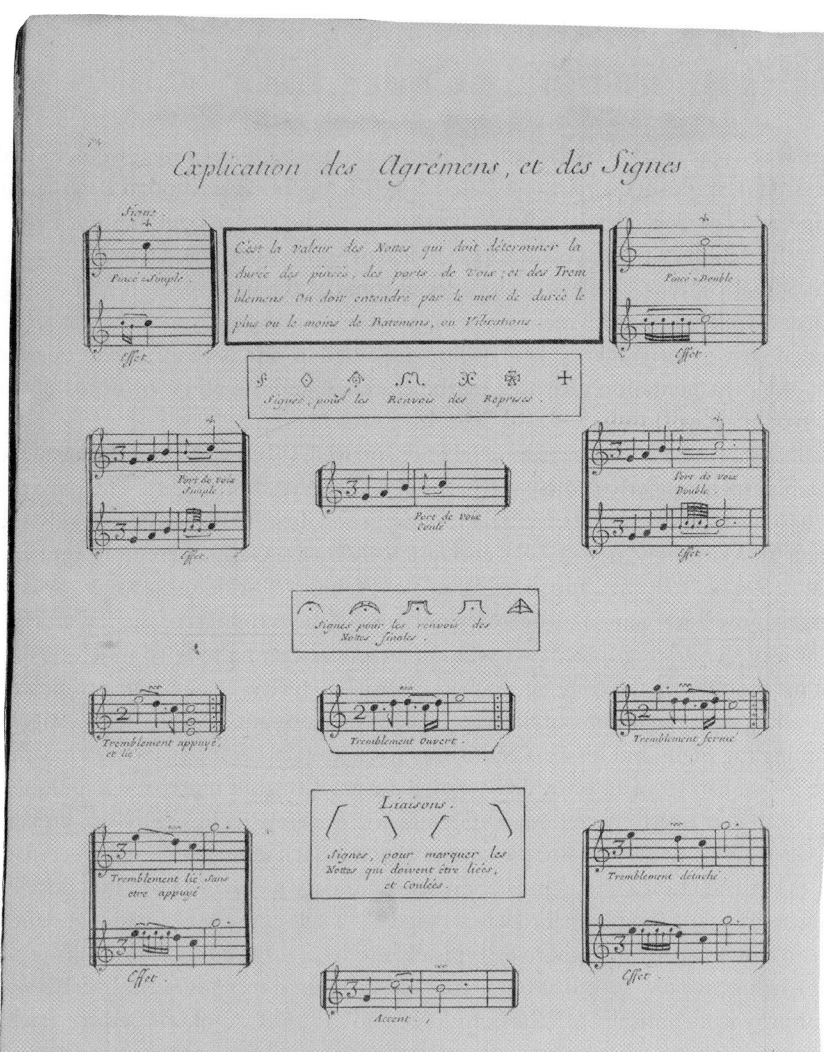

Figure 10-8 "Explication des Agrémens, et des Signes," from François Couperin's first book of *Pieces de clavecin* (Paris, 1713).

Figure 10-9 Rococo decoration. Empress Maria Theresa furnished this Rococo room of the Schönbrunn Palace in Vienna, Austria, in 1760. The walls are covered with Indo-Persian miniatures in gilded rock-work frames.

Stylistic Hybrids: Bach's Brandenburg Concertos

There was a place for such emotion, of course, and for a style of embellishment that expressed it, in the Italian art associated with the opera. Even though Bach wrote no operas, he was well acquainted with the music of his Italian contemporaries and much affected by it. By Bach's time a great deal of Italian instrumental music aspired to an operatic intensity of expression; recall some of the intense, even frightening, work of Corelli and Vivaldi mentioned in the previous chapter. And there was an associated style of instrumental embellishment, allied to, and perhaps in part derived from, the ornamentation provided by the castratos and the other virtuosos of the Italian opera stage.

Bach knew the Italian instrumental tradition well. While at Weimar, he arranged some nineteen concertos (most for harpsichord, the rest for organ). The majority was based on pieces written by Italian composers, including ones by Vivaldi and Benedetto Marcello (1686–1739), and four were by the German composer Johann Ernst (1696–1715), the short-lived Prince of Weimar. Making these arrangements is largely how Bach gained his mastery not only of the trappings of the Italian style but also of the driving Italianate harmonic practices that he took so much further than his models. By the time he reached creative maturity, he had thus assimilated the leading national idioms of his day. Like many Germans he made a specialty of commingling them; but his amalgamations were singular, even eccentric. They disclosed what can seem an unrivaled creative imagination, but one that was uniquely complicated, masterfully crafted, even at times disturbing. By fusing Italian, French, and German elements into unique configurations, Bach uncovered unsuspected affinities between forms and genres of diverse parentage and customary function. By doing so he made the familiar newly strange. As a self-conscious artistic tendency, such an aim is usually thought to be typically modern; it sits oddly with Bach's reputation, in his own day as well as ours, as an old-fashioned composer. And yet his way of uniting within himself both the outmoded and the unheard-of was perhaps Bach's crowning synthetic achievement.

> ***Bach's way of uniting within himself both the outmoded and the unheard-of was perhaps his crowning synthetic achievement.***

This applies particularly well to Bach's most familiar body of instrumental music. In 1721, while serving at Cöthen, he gathered up six instrumental concertos composed over the past few years, wrote them out in a new presentation manuscript, and sent them off with a suitably flattering dedication page, elegantly composed in French, to Christian Ludwig, the Margrave of Brandenburg (Fig. 10-10). He did so in the hope of obtaining an appointment to the Margrave's court in Berlin. The rest of the story is well known: The hoped-for patron never acknowledged receipt of the manuscript and seems never to have had the concertos performed. The fame of the Brandenburg Concertos has hidden some of their strangeness. Perhaps the most absorbing exercise of the historical imagination, where Bach's music is concerned, is the recovery of the hidden strangeness of the challenges he continually set himself.

The works are written for unusually scored ensembles. The First Concerto, in F major, has for its *concertino*, or solo group, an assorted combination of two horns, three oboes, a bassoon, and a *violino piccolo*, a smaller, higher-pitched type of violin,

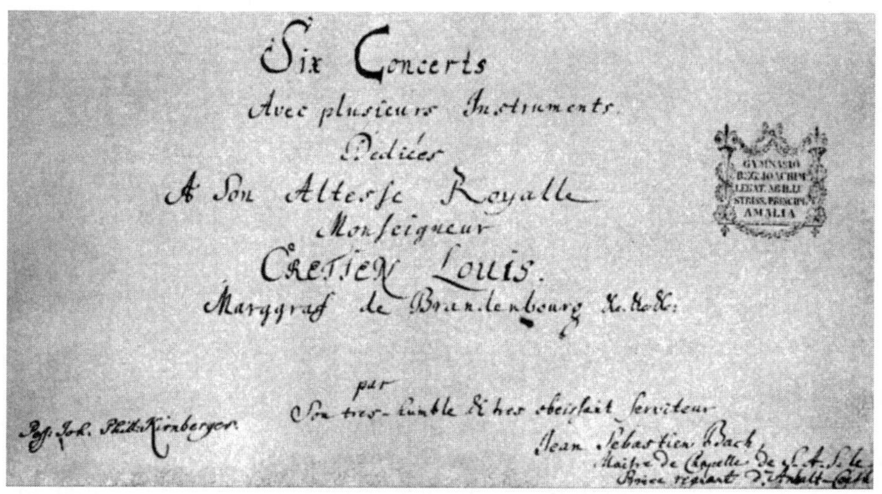
Six Concerts
Avec plusieurs Instruments.
Dediées
A Son Altesse Royalle
Monseigneur
CRETIEN Louis.
Marggraf de Brandenbourg &c. &c. &c:
par
Son tres-humble & tres obeissant serviteur
Jean Sebastien Bach,
Maitre de Chapelle de S.A.S. le Prince regnant d'Anhalt-Coethen
Poss. Joh. Phil. Kirnberger.

Figure 10-10 Bach's Brandenburg Concertos (BWV 1046). Cover of the original manuscript, with dedication in French to Margrave Christian Ludwig von Brandenburg, 1740.

then rare, now altogether obsolete. The movements are an equally strange assortment, mixing ritornello movements and courtly dances. The Second Concerto, also in F major, uses four soloists, their instruments starkly contrasting in their means of tone production and strength of volume: In order of appearance they are violin, oboe, recorder, and clarino trumpet, a piercingly high natural version of the instrument. Balancing the recorder's whisper against the trumpet's blast must have been as daunting a prospect then as it is now. The Third Concerto, in G major, has no concertino group at all; it is scored for a unique ripieno ensemble comprising nine string soloists: three violins, three violas, and three cellos, plus a continuo of bass and harpsichord. The Fourth, also in G major, uses a violin and two unusual recorders pitched on G.

The last two concertos are the most bizarrely scored of all. The Fifth, in D major, has for its concertino a violin, a transverse flute (the wooden ancestor of the modern metal flute), and—of all things!—a harpsichord in a fully written-out, soloistic capacity, not just a continuo filler. This is apparently the earliest of all keyboard concertos. To us it seems the beginning of a long line, but no one could have foreseen that when Bach had the idea. The Sixth Concerto, in B♭ major, finally does away with the otherwise ever-present solo violin. Indeed, it banishes the violin from the orchestra altogether—something for which there seems to be no precedent in the history of the concerto—and instead promotes two violas, normally the least conspicuous members of the ripieno, to soloist position. Were these bizarrely fanciful and colorful scorings the product of sheer caprice? Were they the product of immediate need or personal convenience? Or were they somehow meaningful, in a way that more normally scored instrumental music was not, and if so, to whom? These are questions to which answers can only be speculative. Such questions, to the historian, are in one sense the most frustrating kind but in another sense the most fascinating.

Recent research on the history of the orchestra shows that, from the very beginning, this most complex of all musical ensembles was often regarded as a social microcosm, a mirror of society. The orchestra, like society itself, was assumed to be an inherently hierarchical entity. This assumption was already implicitly invoked in the previous paragraph when the violas were casually described as the "least conspicuous members of the ripieno." Their inconspicuousness was the result of the kind of music they played: harmonic filler, for the most part, having neither any substantial tunes to contribute nor the harmonically defining function of the bass to fulfill. Musically, their role could fairly be described as being, while necessary, distinctly less important than those of their fellow players above and below. Even today, the violas and the second violins in an orchestra—the inner parts—are proverbially subordinate players, by implication social inferiors. Our everyday language bears this out whenever we speak of "playing second fiddle" to someone else.

Recent research on the history of the orchestra shows this most complex of all musical ensembles was often regarded as a mirror of society.

And if second fiddle implies inferiority, then first fiddle tacitly implies a superior condition. In Bach's day, before there were conductors wielding batons, the first violinist was in fact the orchestra leader. Today, when the leadership role has long since passed to the silent dictator with the stick, the first violinist is still called the "concertmaster." So when Bach banishes the violins from the ensemble, as he does in the Sixth Concerto, and puts the violas in their place, it is hard to avoid the impression that a social norm—that of hierarchy—has been upended.

The Fifth Brandenburg Concerto

Anthology Vol 1-86
Full CD II, 60–62
Concise CD I, 93

Our principal example from this collection is the extraordinary Fifth Concerto in D Major, a work of enormous scope and ambition. The first movement begins with a three-part ritornello, a fiery tutti played by every instrument in the ensemble except the flute (Ex. 10-6). For one actually watching the performance as well as listening to it, the clear implication is that the flute is to be the protagonist and that the rest of the instruments belong to the ripieno. So the fact that the violin and the obbligato harpsichord continue to play after the first tutti cadence is already a surprise. Throughout the movement the flute and violin imitate one another, playing duets, with one chasing or responding to the other. We might now assume this is a double concerto for flute and violin. At first it is not entirely clear that the harpsichord part in the solo episodes is a full equal to these upper melodic instruments; continuo players often improvised elaborate right-hand parts in chamber music, and Bach himself was known to be especially adept at doing so. The triplets in m. 10, unprecedented in the opening tutti but later much developed by the other soloists, can be read in retrospect as the first clue that the harpsichord will not be content with its usual service role, that it is to be no mere accompanist. The concertino group in this concerto is therefore flute, violin, and harpsichord.

By the time the first remote modulation gets made (to B minor), the harpsichord seems determined to dominate the show. It abandons the bass line and launches into a toccata-like riff in thirty-second notes that lasts for only three measures but succeeds in dazzling. And so things continue, the harpsichord exerting itself ever more as the movement goes on, far beyond the length of a typical concerto. About two-thirds of the way through, the harpsichord, as if seizing its moment, launches once again into the toccata riff it had initiated some ninety or so measures earlier, and this time it proves to be truly irrepressible. The thirty-second notes continue for fifteen measures, changing in figuration from scales to decorated slow arpeggios, to very wide and rapid arpeggios. With every new phase in the harpsichord's antics comes a corresponding loss of energy in the other instruments, now clearly their former accompanist's accompanists, until they simply drop out altogether, leaving their unruly companion alone to play.

Example 10-6 J. S. Bach, Brandenburg Concerto No. 5, I, mm. 1–12

Example 10-6 (continued)

What follows is something no eighteenth-century listener would have anticipated. The unimaginably lengthy passage for the *cembalo solo senza stromenti*, as Bach puts it ("the harpsichord alone without [the other] instruments"), is an absolutely unique event in the "High Baroque" concerto repertory. It is often called a cadenza, on a vague analogy to the kind of pyrotechnics that an opera singer like Farinelli would indulge in before the final ritornello in an opera seria aria. And perhaps Bach's listeners might eventually have made such a connection as the harpsichord's aberration wore on and the remaining instruments sat silent for an unheard-of length of time. But the actual style of the solo is more in keeping with what Bach's contemporaries would have called a *capriccio*—a willfully bizarre instrumental composition that made a show of departing from the usual norms of style. By the time it has run its course and allowed the tutti finally to repeat its opening ritornello one last time and bring the movement to a belated close, the harpsichord's cadenza/capriccio/toccata has lasted sixty-five measures, close to one-third the length of the entire movement, whose shape it has completely distorted.

The remaining movements in the Fifth Brandenburg Concerto have nothing to compare with this disruption. By now the harpsichord has made its point, and its status as a full partner to the other soloists is something the listener will take for granted, so there is no need to insist on it. A singlemindedness of affect that we saw in the first movement characterizes the next two, but in contrasting ways. Unlike later instrumental music that tends to explore contrast within a single movement, the music of this time tends to favor contrast between movements. In this case, the first one was fast, loud, and in a major key, scored for the full band. The middle movement, explicitly marked *affettuoso*, is slow and in the relative minor key. It is actual chamber music, scored for the soloists alone, in essence a trio sonata. Although played by three instruments, it is really a quartet, since the left and right hands of the keyboard have differing roles. The left hand, as always, is the continuo part, sometimes joined in this function by the right hand, where figures are marked, to accompany the other soloists at the imitative beginnings of sections. Elsewhere, the right hand takes part on an equal footing with the flute and violin, sometimes participating in imitative textures along with them, at other times alternating with them in a kind of antiphony.

The mood changes again for the third and final movement, which is another excellent example of fused genres. It seems to have a hard time deciding whether it is a fugue, a gigue, or a concerto. But of course it is all of those things at once. We have already seen in Bach's French Suite No. 5 how the two sections of a gigue often begin with little fugal expositions. In the Fifth Brandenburg Concerto, the opening is extended into quite an elaborate affair—in four parts, two of them assigned to the harpsichord—that lasts twenty-eight measures before the ripieno joins in to second it with another extended exposition of fifty measures' length, the whole seventy-eight-measure complex in effect making up one huge ritornello. This returns after a longer middle section, making the overall form a strict ABA.

Here, too, there is significant role reversal: Rather than an opening orchestral ritornello, the soloists begin alone and the ripieno follows. Once again a breach of traditional social hierarchies is suggested, although nothing on the scale of the colossal trespass or transgression committed by the harpsichord in the first movement. What do all these reversals, mixtures, and transgressions signify? For a long time they were thought to signify only the fertility of Bach's composerly imagination. And yet, without wishing to slight that imagination in any way, interpreting them so may not do their strangeness justice. Historians have lately begun to wonder whether, given the frequency with which the orchestra was compared with a social organism and described in terms of social or military hierarchy, Bach's musical transgressions might not resonate with ideas of social transgression or perhaps with some more personal kind of self-assertion. Little is known of the genesis of the Brandenburg Fifth Concerto or of its early performance history, but it does not seem entirely fanciful to identify Bach himself, a brilliant keyboard player, with the dominating harpsichordist. Its (his?) gradual emergence from the crowd and eventual show-stopping triumph in the first-movement cadenza may carry some larger meaning and significance.[3]

Handel's Instrumental Music

If we return briefly to Handel by way of comparison with Bach, we are faced with something of a paradox. Handel, of Bach's German leading contemporaries perhaps the most secular in inspiration and expression, was a worldly spirit and a consummate man of the theater. It is thus odd that he is most characteristically represented in today's repertory by his vocal music on sacred subjects, above all by his oratorio *Messiah*, while Bach, the quintessential religious spirit, is largely represented by secular instrumental works. And yet this may be less a paradox than a testimonial to the thoroughly secular, theatrical atmosphere in which all music is now patronized and consumed and the essentially secular, theatrical spirit that informs even Handel's ostensibly sacred work—a spirit that modern audiences instinctively recognize and easily respond to. The modern audience, in short, recognizes and claims its own from both composers; and in this the modern audience behaves the way audiences have always behaved. Handel, not Bach, was present at the creation of "the modern audience." His oratorios helped create it.

Nonetheless, Handel's secular instrumental output was by no means inconsiderable or obscure. He wrote two dozen concertos grosso, works that, simply because they were published, were far better known in their day than were the Brandenburg Concertos or any other instrumental ensemble work of Bach. Handel also composed a number of solo organ concertos for himself to perform between the acts of his popular sacred oratorios. In their origins they were thus theatrical works, but they too were published and became every organist's property. In addition, more than three dozen solo and trio sonatas by Handel survive, of which many also circulated widely in print during his lifetime.

Handel's largest instrumental compositions, like Bach's, were orchestral suites that arose directly out of his employment by the Hanoverian kings of England. One was a kind of super-suite, an enormous medley of instrumental pieces of every description, but mostly dances, composed for performance on a barge that kept abreast of George I's pleasure boat during a royal outing on the River Thames on 17 July 1717, later published as *Handel's Celebrated Water Music*. A whole day's musical entertainment, it furnished enough pieces for three separate sequences (suites in F, D, and G) as arranged by the publisher. The other big orchestral suite was composed for an enormous wind band of twenty-four oboes, twelve bassoons, nine trumpets, nine horns, and timpani, to which strings parts were added on publication. Later published as *The Music for the Royal Fireworks*, it was first performed on 27 April 1749 as part of the festivities surrounding the Peace of Aix-la-Chapelle that ended the War of the Austrian Succession, a great diplomatic triumph for King George II.

Handel, most secular in inspiration and expression, was a worldly spirit and a consummate man of the theater.

In later arrangements for modern symphony orchestra, Handel's *Water Music* and *Royal Fireworks* were for a while staples of the concert repertoire—especially in England, where they served as a reminder of imperial glory. They are the only Handelian instrumental compositions ever to have gained modern repertory status comparable to that enjoyed by Bach's "Brandenburgs." Handel's instrumental music was always a sideline, for Handel was first and last a composer for the theater, the one domain where Bach never set foot.

Summary

This chapter has explored the careers and instrumental music of the first composers whose works are included in the modern standard repertory: Johann Sebastian Bach (1685–1750), George Frideric Handel (1685–1759), and Domenico Scarlatti (1685–1757).

Bach and Handel, the primary focus of this chapter, took utterly different career paths. Handel was widely traveled, living and working in Germany, Italy, and London. Following in a family tradition of church organists and cantors, Bach spent his career in a few eastern German towns, never traveling outside Germany. Their modern reputations are quite different from what they were in their own day. Handel was best known for his operas and oratorios, which enjoyed an enormous public success, whereas Bach was known primarily as an organist; most of his works were intended for church services rather than for public consumption.

Much of Bach's work was written to fulfill the requirements of his jobs. Except for his six years in Cöthen (1717–23), he was employed as a Lutheran church musician. Many of his organ pieces are thus chorale-based works, which could take the form of a fugue, variations, or the single-verse setting called a chorale prelude. *Durch Adams Fall ist ganz verderbt* (Through Adam's Fall We Are Condemned) is from *Orgelbüchlein*, a collection of chorale preludes for the liturgical year. In the Baroque tradition of madrigalism, Bach depicts Adam's fall into sin with descending diminished sevenths. A comparison to a setting of the same chorale by the earlier composer Dietrich Buxtehude (1637–1707) shows Bach to be solidly rooted in longstanding German Protestant tradition. Bach particularly excelled at the contrapuntal procedure known as the fugue, which was often paired with a prelude or toccata. His "Little" Fugue in G Minor, BWV 578, illustrates how the fugal process unfolds through a series of imitative entries on a point of imitation in the tonic (called the *subject*) and on the dominant (called the *answer*). The forty-eight preludes and fugues in the two volumes of *Das wohltemperirte Clavier* (The Well-Tempered Keyboard, 1722 and 1738–42) were written in each major and minor key, beginning with C and proceeding through the keys by half step.

German composers in Bach's day thought of themselves as cosmopolitan musicians, absorbing the styles and genres of French and Italian music. The popularity of French musical styles reflected the German aristocracy's wish to adopt French culture and manners. Johann Jacob Froberger (1616–67) composed many keyboard suites modeled on French dance types, which later came to be arranged in the standard order allemande, courante, sarabande, and gigue. The allemande was a slow dance in quadruple meter, the courante in $\substack{3\\2}$ meter with hemiola, the sarabande a slow triple-meter movement, and the gigue a fast movement, usually in $\substack{6\\8}$, often featuring imitation. Bach's knowledge of Froberger's work is evident in the keyboard suites he composed while at Cöthen. The French Suite No. 5 shows his engagement with the *galant* style associated with elegant manners and grace. The fugal gigue, however, provides a contrast to that of François Couperin's *Le Rossignol en-amour* (The Nightingale in Love), with its highly ornamented surface texture.

Many of Bach's concertos reflect his familiarity with Italian music, which grew during his time in Weimar (1708–17). As his Brandenburg Concertos show, Bach fused French, Italian, and German elements and put his own twist on these styles. Compiled in 1721 from works he had written earlier, the Brandenburg Concertos are particularly strange in their instrumentation. In the first movement of the Fifth, for example, the harpsichord, normally a continuo instrument, emerges as the main soloist, with a long cadenza. In the final movement of the Fifth, Bach eloquently fuses elements of the gigue, Italian concerto, and fugue.

Handel's instrumental works, though less well known today than Bach's, include organ concertos (the earliest known for that instrument), *concerti grossi*, and solo and trio sonatas. His largest and most popular instrumental works were two orchestral suites written for civic occasions, today known as *Water Music* and *The Music for the Royal Fireworks*.

Study Questions

1. Compare and contrast the biographies and careers of J. S. Bach and G. F. Handel. What influences did their career paths have on the types of works they composed?
2. Compare and contrast the reputations that Bach and Handel had among their contemporaries and their reputations in modern times. What aspects of the music by the "class of 1685" still seem familiar or "modern" today?
3. Using Bach's and Dietrich Buxtehude's settings of *Durch Adams Fall ist ganz verderbt,* discuss the chorale prelude. How does Bach depict Adam's fall into sin, and how is this related to Baroque conventions of madrigalism?
4. Describe the contrapuntal procedure known as the fugue, including definitions of the following terms: subject, answer, countersubject, episode, stretto.
5. Describe the tempo and metrical characteristics of the following dances, as reflected in Johann Jacob Froberger's suites: (a) allemande, (b) courante, (c) sarabande, (d) gigue. In what ways was Bach influenced by Froberger's suites? How do Bach's French-style works differ from those of François Couperin?
6. In what ways are Bach's Brandenburg Concertos a fusion of Italian, French, and German elements?
7. Describe some examples of unusual instrumentation and uses of instruments in Bach's Brandenburg Concertos. How might these unusual uses of instruments be interpreted? What do these concertos suggest about the eighteenth-century relationships between the individual and society, the soloist(s) and the ensemble?

Key Terms

allemande
answer
chorale prelude
countersubject
courante
episode
fugue
galant
gigue
prelude
rococo
sarabande
stretto
subject
suite

II

Class of 1685 (II): The Vocal Music of Handel and Bach

In so much of Handel's music, instrumental and vocal, secular and sacred, we perceive his theatrical sensibility. He wrote more than three dozen operas on themes both serious and comic, encompassing a wide range of historical, romantic, and literary plots. That astounding output in a relatively short period of time was possible partly because operas in the first half of the seventeenth century were generally much more formulaic than they had been before or would become later. After the expected French overture to start, operas typically consisted of a string of recitatives and arias, usually in da capo form, with an occasional duet or chorus, usually sung by the soloists, that was included not so much to lend variety as to help articulate the structure at the beginning or close of an act.

The visual component of the opera was secondary. Sets tended to be modest and were changed in front of the audience; the curtain stayed up until the conclusion of the show. An opera seria role was the sum of the emotions and attitudes struck in reaction to the complicated but conventionalized unfolding of a moralizing plot in a language that was often neither the composer's nor the audience's. The great opera composer was the one who could give the cut-and-dried, obligatory attitudes a freshly vivid embodiment and who could convey them essentially without words.

For our present purpose it will have to suffice to boil Handel's entire quarter-century's production for the King's Theatre on the London Strand down to a single consummate example, a virtuoso aria giving vent to an overpowering emotional seizure, for arias were what this genre was all about. Few works could demonstrate this better than *Giulio Cesare in Egitto* (Julius Caesar in Egypt). It was first performed on 20 February 1724, right in the brilliant middle of his operatic career, and revived several times thereafter. Today it is far and away the most often performed of all of Handel's operas.

The libretto was by one of his chief collaborators, Nicola Francesco Haym, an expatriate Italian Jew who also acted as theater manager, stage director, and continuo cellist. He adapted it from an earlier opera libretto, produced in Venice in the 1670s, whose story was based on accounts of the life of the great Roman leader Julius Caesar. The plot concerns Caesar's campaign in Egypt (48–47 BCE) and his legendary love affair there with the beautiful Queen Cleopatra. We will focus on "Empio, dirò, tu sei" ("Evil, you are, I say"), an aria that comes near the beginning of the opera. Caesar has been in pursuit of his enemy Pompey, whose wife and son come to Caesar to plea for peace. While in their presence, Caesar receives the Egyptian general Achillas, who brings greetings from King Ptolemy, Cleopatra's brother. Actually, he brings more than just greetings—as a friendly offering Achillas presents Caesar with Pompey's severed head, much to the horror of the wife, son, and assembled Romans. It is this barbaric act that prompts Caesar's aria of unbridled rage:

Anthology Vol 1-87
Full CD II, 63
Concise CD II, 1

A	*Empio, dirò, tu sei,*	Evil you are, I say:
	Togliti a gli occhi miei	Get out of my sight,
	Sei tutto crudeltà.	You are nothing but cruelty.
B	*Non è da Rè quel cor*	The heart that is given to harshness,
	Che donasi al rigor	That has not mercy in its breast,
	Che in sen non ha pietà.	Is not that of a king.

"Empio, dirò, tu sei" is a perfectly thrilling specimen of aria as "concerto for voice and orchestra." Handel uses the first ritornello (Ex. 11-1a) to represent the aria's affect—here, indignation and rage—and does so in a variety of ways: minor mode, rapid tempo, and, in the violins, downward rushing scales followed by a near-continuous stream of sixteenth notes. The most spectacular representation of rage, however, is reserved for the singer. The first solo begins with the voice taking the ritornello's descending scale, but then Handel does something rather unconventional by using a series of quick modulations that signal the derangement that can come with extreme anger. The progressively fierce and florid coloratura is calculated to coincide on every occurrence with the word *crudeltà* (cruelty).

The B section of da capo arias, conventionally shorter in duration, sometimes gives a chance for contrast—a different affect that can then be rejected or questioned so as to lead back to a repeat of the opening A. In this aria, however, the affect and the musical material of the brief B section are closely related to, indeed, mainly derived from, the A section. So all-encompassing is Caesar's rage that the same indicators of fury continue unrelenting. The virtuoso melismas now fall on the word *pietà*, the quality of "pity" that Ptolemy lacks (Ex. 11-1b). The return of the A section offers one final thrill, and that is the surprise at just how the singer would ornament the already astoundingly difficult part. Handel wrote this aria for the celebrated alto castrato Francesco Bernardi (ca. 1680–1759), better known by his stage name, Senesino (Fig. 11-1), and audiences in eighteenth-century London were sure to have been astonished by his embellishments. This aria, in short, is a triumph of dramatically structured music—or of musically structured drama. The "purely musical" or structural aspects of the piece and the representational or expressive ones are utterly enmeshed. There is no way of describing the one without invoking the other, which enables the singer-actor to reach a pitch that is both literally and figuratively beyond the range of spoken delivery.

TIMELINE

1683 Defeat of Ottoman Turks outside of Vienna

1685 **Birth of Johann Sebastian Bach, George Frideric Handel, and Domenico Scarlatti**

1702 **Georg Philipp Telemann establishes the Collegium Musicum in Leipzig**

1706–10 **Handel in Italy**

1707 England and Scotland unify as Great Britain

1707 **Bach, *Christ lag in Todesbanden* (later revised)**

1708–17 **Bach in Weimar**

1713–40 Reign of Frederick William I in Prussia

1714–27 Reign of George I in England

1714 **Handel moves to London**

1719 Daniel Defoe, *Robinson Crusoe*

Example 11-1 **George Frideric Handel, "Empio, dirò, tu sei" from *Giulio Cesare in Egitto*, Act I: (a) opening, mm. 1–17; (b) "B" section, mm. 43–58.**

1723 **Bach arrives in Leipzig**

1724 **Bach, *Ein' feste Burg* and St. John Passion (later revised)**

1724 **Handel, *Giulio Cesare in Egitto***

1727 **Bach, St. Matthew Passion**

1727–60 Reign of George II in England

1728 **John Gay, *The Beggar's Opera***

1734 Voltaire, *Philosophical Letters*

1739 **Handel, *Saul***

1742 **Handel, *Messiah***

1740 Maria Theresa crowned Holy Roman Empress

1740–48 War of Austrian Succession

1750 **Death of Bach**

1752 Jean-Jacques Rousseau, *Discourse on the Origin of Inequality*

1757 **Death of Scarlatti**

1759 **Death of Handel**

Figure 11-1 Caricature of the alto castrato Senesino, the natural soprano Francesca Cuzzoni, and the alto castrato Gaetano Berenstadt in a performance of Handel's opera *Flavio* at the King's Theatre, London, in 1723.

Comparing Handel's aria with the opera seria arias mentioned in Chapter 9—mostly by actual Italian composers writing for actual Italian audiences—points up the puzzling relationship of this great outsider to the tradition on which he fed. It is Handel who displays the genre at its best for audiences today. Handel's operas are indeed more craftsmanly and structurally complex than that of his Italian contemporaries, who were concerned with streamlining and simplifying those very aspects of motivic structure and harmony that Handel reveled in. His work, in short, was stylistically more conservative and denser, which may have made it more interesting to an audience foreign to the language of the libretto. In his active counterpoint Handel affirms his German organist's heritage; and by making his music more interesting in its own right than that of his Italian contemporaries, he gave performers correspondingly less room to maneuver and dominate the show.

In this way, for all that Handel seems to dominate modern memory of the opera seria, and despite his unquestioned dominance of the London scene, at least for a while, he was never a truly typical opera composer. As time went on, his work became outmoded. Unlike the actual Italian product, his operas did not travel well but remained a local and somewhat anomalous English phenomenon, admired by foreign visitors but nevertheless regarded as strange. A crisis was reached when the castrato Farinelli refused to sing for Handel and in fact joined a rival company in 1734 to perform Johann Adolf Hasse's *Artaserse*.

Handel's grip on the London public had already been challenged somewhat earlier in the 1720s by a series of easy, tuneful operas by Giovanni Bononcini (1670–1747) imported to London together with their composer. Another blow was the huge success in 1728 of *The Beggar's Opera* (Fig. 11-2), a so-called "**ballad opera**"

Figure 11-2 A scene from John Gay and Johann Pepusch's *The Beggar's Opera* as painted in 1729 by William Hogarth. The wife and the lover of Macheath the highwayman plead with their respective fathers to spare his life.

written in English by John Gay (1685–1732), in which spoken dialogue replaced recitative of opera seria; the score consisted entirely of popular songs arranged by a German expatriate composer named Johann Pepusch (1667–1752). While fifteen performances for a Handel opera was considered successful, this cynical slap in the face of "noble" entertainments had an unprecedented run of over sixty performances during its first season and was revived nearly every season for the rest of the eighteenth century and beyond.

On all levels, from its plot (set among thieves and other London lowlifes), to its "moral" (that morals are sheer hypocrisy), to its musical and dramatic allusions (full of swipes at operatic conventions), *The Beggar's Opera* was subversive. But it also played into a prejudice that was the very opposite of frivolous—namely, a peculiarly English version of the old prejudice against certain kinds of music as corrupting forces that were contrary to the public welfare. The success of *The Beggar's Opera* was a foreshadowing that opera seria, even Handel's, could no longer count on the English audience to take it seriously. And indeed, within a decade of its production, both Handel's own opera company and the rival Opera of the Nobility had gone bankrupt.

Lofty Entertainments

Meanwhile, if Handel was to continue to have a public career in England, he knew it would have to be on a new footing. Whenever opera had encountered obstacles on its Italian home turf—for example, those pesky ecclesiastical strictures against operating theaters during Lent—its creative energies had found an outlet in oratorio. This was especially so in Rome, where Handel had served his apprenticeship decades earlier. He had even composed two Italian oratorios, *Il trionfa del Tempo e del Disinganno* (The Triumph of Time and Disillusion, 1707) and *La resurrezione* (The Resurrection, 1708). He had also already written some minor dramatic works on English texts, including a masque called *Haman and Mordecai* on an Old Testament subject. A pastiche revival of it, expanded and refurbished by someone else and now retitled *Esther*, was performed in 1732 in the explicit guise of "an oratorio or sacred drama." *Esther* attracted so much interest that Handel himself conducted a lucrative performance on the stage of the King's Theatre, where business that season was otherwise slow.

The next year he decided to write a couple of English oratorios himself (*Deborah, Athalia*). As operatic bankruptcy loomed, these experiences gave Handel an idea that the English public might welcome a new style of oratorio tailored to its tastes and interests and sung in its own language (Fig. 11-3). The result was *Saul* (1739), a musical theater piece of a wholly novel kind that differed in significant ways from previous oratorio styles. As a genre born directly out of the vicissitudes of the British entertainment market, the Handelian oratorio was a unique product of its time and place.

How was it new? The traditional Italian **oratorio** was simply an opera seria on a biblical subject, by the early eighteenth century sometimes even performed on stage with action. In England, the acting out of a sacred drama was

Figure 11-3 Handel directing a rehearsal of an oratorio, possibly at the residence of the Prince of Wales.

prohibited, so there were no sets or costumes. But *Saul* was still more or less an opera in the sense that its unstaged action proceeded through the same musical structures, its dramatic confrontations being carried out through the customary recitatives and arias. This made it easy for audience members to supply the implied stage action in their own imaginations. The imaginary action was also opened out, so to speak, in mass scenes unthinkable in opera, with opulent choruses representing the "people of Israel." Among the further advertised attractions was an especially lavish orchestra featuring a trombone choir, evocative carillons (bells), and virtuoso instrumental solos, as if to compensate for the diminished visual component. All the same, *Saul*—like *Esther* and *Deborah* before it and *Samson, Judas Maccabeus, Solomon,* and *Joshua* after it—remained centered in its plot on dramatized human relations, the traditional stuff of opera.

The Old Testament oratorios just mentioned are all tales of civic heroism and national triumph. Esther, Deborah, Samson, Judah Maccabee, and Joshua were saviors of their people, the Chosen People. Here is where Handel showed his skill in catering to his public, for the English audience—an insular, industrious, and prosperous people—identified strongly with the Old Testament Israelites and regarded the tales Handel set before them as gratifying allegories of themselves. In this respect Handel's oratorios can be viewed as the first great monuments in the history of European music to nationalism, then emerging as a new force in the world.

Israel in Egypt, his next oratorio after *Saul,* transformed the genre further away from opera. It almost completely abandons the dramatic format—that is, the representation of human conflicts and confrontations through recitatives and arias—in favor of impersonal biblical narration, much of it carried out directly by the chorus (i.e., the Nation), often split into two antiphonal choirs as in the old Venetian choral concertos. Because such choral and orchestral monumentality was a bit of a hard sell at its premiere in 1739, Italian arias were added for the next performance, which was billed as "shortned and Intermix'd with Songs."

The specifically Handelian conception of the oratorio as an essentially choral genre—a pageant rather than a drama—completely transformed the very idea of such a piece. While operas presented a string of da capo arias, the choral parts were the glory of his oratorios. So thoroughly did Handel Handelize the oratorio for posterity that it comes now as a surprise to read contemporary descriptions of his work that emphasize its novelty, indeed its failure to conform to audience expectations. One contemporary listener wrote with perplexity about Handel's next biblical oratorio—namely, *Messiah,* now the most famous oratorio in the world and the one to which all others are compared—that "although called an *Oratorio,* yet it is not dramatic but properly a Collection of *Hymns* or *Anthems* drawn from the sacred Scriptures."[1] That is precisely what the word "oratorio" has connoted since Handel's day. Now it is the dramatic oratorio that can seem unusual.

Anthology Vol 1-88
Full CD II, 64–69

Israel in Egypt, the prototype of the **"anthem oratorio,"** recounts the story of the Israelites' bondage in Egypt and their ultimate escape under the leadership of Moses. The text was most likely produced by Charles Jennens, a wealthy dilettante who paid Handel for the privilege of collaborating with him and who had already provided the libretto for *Saul* and later would for *Messiah* as well. The libretto was in any case no original creation but, rather, a sort of scriptural anthology that mixed narrative from the Book of Exodus with verses from the Book of Psalms. Six of the oratorio's vocal numbers collectively narrate the story of the Ten Plagues of Egypt inflicted by God, forcing the Pharaoh to let the oppressed Israelites leave. In musico-dramatic technique these five choruses and an aria embody a virtual textbook on the early-eighteenth-century state of musical depiction and word painting, an art of which Handel was master.

The first of the plagues—the bloody river—is cast as a choral fugue in which we encounter some time-honored devices, starting with a melodic dissonance (a diminished seventh) in the subject to portray loathing and also including fancy "madrigalisms" like long melismas on the word "water." The next number ("Their land brought forth frogs") is set not as a chorus but as what initially seems to be a truncated da capo aria. It in fact recounts three plagues—the second (frogs), fifth (pestilence), and sixth (boils) of the original biblical account. The end does not return to the sung opening—the expected da capo—but, rather, "leapfrogs" over to a purely instrumental ritornello for two violins.

Handel's oratorios can be viewed as the first great monuments in the history of European music to nationalism, then emerging as a new force in the world.

We have seen the purely instrumental imitation of nature in Vivaldi's *The Four Seasons*, but perhaps no other composer had previously taken instrumental imitations to such lengths as Handel resorted to in *Israel in Egypt*. This was epoch-making in the art of orchestration, serving expressive and poetic purposes that required an extended instrumental palette complementing the words. His imaginative approach is spectacularly apparent in "He Spake the Word." The word here, of course, is the word of God, and so the burnished sound of the trombone choir, associated with regal and spectacular church music since the time of the Gabrielis in Venice, was the inevitable choice to echo the choral announcement that God had spoken. The chorus recounts three plagues of insects, the biblical fourth (flies), third (lice), and eighth (locusts). The buzzing flies and lice are imitated by string instruments in two sizes and speeds (violin thirty-second notes and viola sixteenth notes).

The gathering storm leading to the representation of the "hailstones for rain" calls into play a large assortment of new woodwind and timpani colors. "He sent a thick darkness" introduces high bassoons doubling low violins, but later descending to their normal range and trilling, as well as softly sustained but very dissonant chromatic harmonies to represent the covering gloom. The huge tutti chords slashing on the strong beats ("He smote all the first-born of Egypt") make almost palpable the grisliest calamity of all.

Yet no matter how lofty or how grisly the theme, Handel's representation of the plagues remains an entertainment, filled with marvelous musical illustrations. Like all "madrigalisms," they largely depend on mechanisms of humor: puns (plays on similarities of sound), wit (apt conjunctions of incongruous things), caricature (deliberate exaggerations that underscore a similarity). And, as Handel knew very well, audiences react to such effects, despite the awfulness of the theme, as they do to comedy. We appreciate it when we "get" the representation of the leaping frogs and the buzzing flies and when the latter gives way to the thundering locusts.

But what of the killing of all those Egyptian boys? Are we amused by that, too? We are—or, at least, so the music directs us—just as we have been by the crop failures and bloody rivers. The withholding of empathy for the Egyptians is an essential part of Exodus, and the scorn of the biblical Israelites for the ancient oppressor is what enables the success of Handel's strategy. This separation of self and other plays also into an emerging ideology of nationalism, in which a nation's cultural and political interests are mutually reinforcing; a great deal of any nation's national pride depends on a perception of separateness from other nations and superiority to them.

Of all of Handel's oratorios, it is perhaps easiest to see in *Israel in Egypt* how the manifest religious content coexists with, enables, and is ultimately subordinate to the nationalistic subtext. Hence the essential secularism of its impulse and its enduring appeal.

Handel's *Messiah*

This applies even to *Messiah* (1742), an oratorio that was occasionally performed during the composer's lifetime in consecrated buildings and could count, therefore, as a religious observance. The work is still regularly heard in churches, but it is much more often performed in concert halls by secular choral societies or in mass audience "singalongs," perhaps better designated "get-lost-alongs" because many of the choruses are extremely difficult to sing. *Messiah* also exhibits Handel's theatrical affinities. Like most of his operas and oratorios, it opens with a French overture and has recitatives and arias. Handel's audience came to hear their favorite opera singers, castratos included, perform in his oratorios as well. Indeed, one of the most vocally elaborate and dazzling moments in *Messiah*—the fast section of "But who shall abide the day of his coming"—was revised from its original bass voice version for the famous alto castrato Gaetano Guadagni (1728–92) and made into a real showstopper.

Unusually among Handel's English oratorios, *Messiah* has a New Testament subject, the text once again compiled by Jennens. The first of its three parts is concerned with prophesies of the coming of a Messiah, thus using Old Testament scripture as well, and then with Christ's Nativity. The second part deals with Christ's suffering and death. The concluding part offers an affirmation of Christian faith and glimpses of Revelation, which brings the work into line with the most traditional ecclesiastical oratorios and with the even older tradition of narrative Passion settings. While Handel's earlier oratorios usually had characters and a clear narrative, *Messiah*, like *Israel in Egypt*, does not. Soloists are still used, but not to represent specific individuals.

Handel composed* Messiah *with his usual legendary speed—allegedly in twenty-four days—and it was first performed at the New Music Hall in Dublin on 13 April 1742.

Handel composed *Messiah* with his usual legendary speed—allegedly in twenty-four days, from 22 August to 14 September 1741—and finished the orchestral score on 29 October; the first performance was presented at the New Music Hall in Dublin on 13 April 1742. This premiere is an especially important date in the history of European music because Handel's atypical New Testament oratorio is the very oldest work to have remained steadily in the active repertory ever since its first performance. Unlike any other music so far mentioned in this book, with the single equivocal exception of Gregorian chant (which lost its canonical status at the Second Vatican Council in 1963), *Messiah* has never had to be rediscovered. The continuous performing tradition of European art music—which we can now, and for this very reason, call classical music—can therefore be said to begin with *Messiah*, the first classic in our contemporary repertoire, and Handel is therefore the earliest of all perpetually-in-repertory, classical composers.

After the Dublin premiere, Handel offered *Messiah* the next year at the Theatre Royal, Covent Garden, where it was not well received, in part because of objections to presenting a sacred work in that most profane of buildings—a theater. (Handel

Figure 11-4 Chapel at the Foundling Hospital, London, where *Messiah* was performed annually.

had advertised the oratorio as a "musical entertainment.") It was only in 1750, when he began presenting annual performances for a London charity at the local Foundling Hospital (Fig. 11-4), that the public truly embraced the work. Over the years Handel revised *Messiah* to accommodate new surroundings, performing forces, and audiences. By the time of his death on 14 April 1759, eight days after supervising his last Foundling Hospital *Messiah*, the British institution of imposing choral festivals had been established. The adaptations Handel himself began have continued ever since: Mozart reorchestrated the work in 1789 to bring it up to the dimensions of a larger orchestra, and some extraordinarily large arrangements emerged in the nineteenth and twentieth centuries. Many of these subsequent adaptations helped to make *Messiah* a unique national institution in England and viable for the great national singing orgies, particularly the Three Choirs Festival, which have continued into our own day.

"Borrowing"

In order to compose at the kind of speed required by the conditions under which they often worked, seventeenth- and eighteenth-century composers frequently recycled older compositions in newer ones. Every church and theater composer indulged in the practice. There was really no choice. The only question involved the nature of the sources plundered and the specific means employed. Was this just a process of "cannibalization"—eating one's own young by adapting one's own earlier works—or did it involve taking material from other composers, what we would today regard as plagiarism? And if the latter, did the practice carry the ethical stigma now attached to plagiarism—or, for that matter, any stigma at all? Handel was a champion borrower, adapting both his own works and those of other composers in unprecedented numbers for both instrumental and vocal pieces. It has been a matter of inescapable concern on the part of the composer's admirers, and a whole literature on the subject has sprouted up—two literatures, in fact: one in prosecution of the case, the other in Handel's defense.[2]

The prosecutors have built an astonishing record. Several of Handel's works consist largely, sometimes almost entirely, of systematic "borrowings," as they are euphemistically called. *Israel in Egypt* is among them. Close to half of the choruses were based on pieces by other composers, some of them practically gobbled up whole. The plague choruses "He spake the word" and "He gave them hailstones," both remarkable for their epoch-making orchestration, were based on a secular serenata for two voices and strings by Alessandro Stradella (1639–82), a Roman composer whose music Handel encountered during his early years in Italy. For the first and last of the plagues ("They loathed to drink of the river" and "He smote all the first-born of Egypt"), Handel called on some of his own keyboard works, the Fugue in A Minor (HWV 609) and Fugue in G Minor (HWV 605).

Noticing how many of Handel's "borrowings" involved works from the 1730s and particularly the exceptionally busy years 1737–39, some historians have tried to connect his reliance on the music of other composers with a stroke suffered in the spring of 1737, brought on by overwork, that temporarily paralyzed Handel's right hand and kept him from his normal labors. The stroke has been offered as an extenuating circumstance by some who have sought to defend Handel from the charge of plagiarism.

Stronger defenders have argued that the whole issue is anachronistic. To accuse Handel or any his contemporaries of plagiarism, they argue, is to invoke later Romantic ideas of originality for a time when borrowings of all sorts were standard operating procedure. Most composers did it. Moreover, few would deny that Handel gave added value to what he touched. No one comparing Stradella's model can fail to notice that everything that makes Handel's *Israel in Egypt* choruses noteworthy—the lofty trombone chords, the insect imitations, the storm music—came from Handel, not his victim. Comparing Handel's dazzling reworkings with their sometimes rather undistinguished originals may even cause us to wonder where true "originality" resides.

Yet it seems clear that some of Handel's contemporaries were troubled at the time with how much he borrowed. Even his librettist, Jennens, wrote to a friend that he had just received a shipment of music from Italy and that "Handel has borrow'd a dozen of the Pieces & I dare say I shall catch him stealing from them; as I have formerly, both from Scarlatti & Vinci."[3] Moreover, it appears that Handel was careful at various times to cover his tracks, which suggests that he perceived something to feel guilty about.

In the case of *Messiah*, Handel's known borrowings were of the cannibalistic sort, the kind that even now entails little disrepute because self-borrowings do not raise any question of ownership. They are generally regarded as a legitimate way for a busy professional to economize on time and labor. From our point of view there are interesting musical, aesthetic, even theological consequences to these recyclings in *Messiah*. Several of the most famous choruses require a kind of fast and florid, almost athletic singing that is quite unusual because it is so demanding. Their virtuosity is generally unlike what we find in the actual sacred choral music of the day—that is, music meant for performance in church. They are, however, utterly in the spirit of latter-day "madrigalian" genres—genres based on Italian love poetry—such as the chamber cantata pioneered by Giacomo Carissimi and Alessandro Scarlatti.

A typical text for such a piece might address Eros (Cupid) himself, the fickle god of amorous desire:

No, di voi non vo' fidarmi,	No, I do not wish to trust you,
cieco Amor, crudel beltà!	blind Cupid, cruel Beauty!
Troppo siete menzognere,	You are too wily,
lusinghiere Deità!	O flattering deities!
Altra volta incatenarmi	Another time you did manage
già poteste il fido cor;	to net my trustful heart;
So per prova i vostri inganni:	so from having experienced your tricks
due tiranni siete ognor.	I know you both for tyrants.

These are, in fact, the words of a duet composed by Handel himself in the summer of 1741, shortly before he began *Messiah*. Should it surprise or dismay us to discover that this erotic duet became the basis for not one but two choruses in the oratorio? Handel reworked the opening section into "For unto us a Child is born" and the closing section into "All we like sheep have gone astray." Identifying the origins of these choruses at least helps to explain some of their formidable musical difficulty—the elaborate melismas in "For unto us" we now learn were meant to be negotiated not by large choral groups, but rather by individual virtuoso soloists. This explains as well some of the awkward patterns of setting the text, such as the seemingly inept emphasis on the word "For" (originally "No") that begins the chorus (Ex. 11-2).

Anthology Vol 1-89a-b
Full CD II, 70–71
Concise CD II, 2

Example 11-2 **George Frideric Handel "For unto us a child is born" from *Messiah*, compared with the duet *No, di voi non vo' fidarmi***

The use of such secular material as the basis for an oratorio on the life of Christ has tended to bemuse those for whom the sacred and the secular are mutually exclusive spheres. Generations of musicians and audiences have praised how exquisitely Handel conveys the biblical text from the book of Isaiah, oblivious to the fact that when the composer first thought of the music the words were completely, scandalously different. But reusing a secular piece like *No, di voi non vo' fidarmi* only seems incongruous if we regard *Messiah* as being church music, which it was not. Despite its embodying the most sacred of themes, it was a self-proclaimed "entertainment," and its music was designed to amuse a public in search of diversion, however edifying.

The musical qualities of the original Italian duets, being delightful in themselves, could retain their allure in the new context and adorn the new text—and even, thanks to Handel's "madrigalistic" genius, appear to illuminate its meaning.

But what chiefly mattered was Handel's success. Again the old theatrical entrepreneur had seized the main chance. His adaptable nature, his uncanny ability continually to remake himself and his works in response to the conditions and the opportunities that confronted him—that was Handel's great distinguishing trait. It marks him as perhaps the first modern composer, the prototype of the consumer-conscious artist, a great freelancer in the age of patronage, who managed to succeed—where, two generations later, Mozart would still fail—in living off his pen and living well.

Bach's Cantatas

Returning now to Bach and to his very different world, we are ready to assess the music his contemporaries regarded as his major contribution. That music is his sacred vocal music, composed to a large extent in forms familiar to us from Handel's operas and oratorios but serving an entirely different audience and purpose. With only minor exceptions, Bach's vocal music is actual church music. And yet by the time of his Leipzig tenure beginning in 1723, even the music of the Lutheran Church had made an accommodation with the music of the popular theater, and this new style of theatricalized music became Bach's medium too. Bach disdained what he called "the pretty little Dresden tunes," Dresden being the nearest city with an opera theater, which he occasionally visited. And despite not writing operas himself, he nevertheless became a master of operatic devices even as he managed—utterly, profoundly, and hair-raisingly—to subvert them.

The forms of opera came to Lutheran music in part through the work of Bach's older contemporary Erdmann Neumeister (1671–1756), a German poet and theologian, who expanded the form and style of Lutheran sacred texts for music. Traditionally, Lutheran church music, even at its most elaborate, had been based on chorales. In the late seventeenth century a style had been developed in which chorales alternated with biblical verses and a new ingredient: little poems that reflected emotionally on the verses the way arias reflected on the action in an opera seria. This "oratorio" style was used especially for Passion music around Easter. Bach would write Passion cycles of this kind as well, quite elaborate ones.

Handel's uncanny ability continually to remake himself and his works in response to the conditions that confronted him was his great distinguishing trait.

Around the turn of the century, Neumeister began publishing his little oratorio texts, for which he borrowed the name of the Italian genre that had inspired him. Consisting of vividly picturesque, "madrigalesque" verses, and explicitly divided into recitatives and arias, they were dubbed "cantatas" by their author. They provided the prototype for hundreds of church compositions by Bach, although for the most part he continued to call such pieces with mixed voices and instruments "concertos," retaining the term in use since the time of Gabrieli and Schütz. Neumeister's cantata texts were published in a series of comprehensive cycles covering all the Sundays and feasts of the church calendar, and they were expressly meant for setting by Lutheran cantors like Bach, whose job it was to compose yearly cycles of concerted vocal works according to the same liturgical schedule. Bach may have written as many as five cantata cycles during his early years in Leipzig (Fig. 11-5), of which almost three survive complete.

Bach composed both secular and sacred cantatas, beginning early in his career, although most date from his tenure in Leipzig. Only a handful of his some 200 surviving cantatas were composed to actual Neumeister texts, but the vast majority of them adhere nevertheless to the format of mixing opera-like recitatives and da capo arias with the chorale verses. Bach thus became a sort of opera composer. Cantatas, however, were reflective, not dramatic works. The singers of the arias were not characters but, rather, disembodied personas who voiced the idealized thoughts of the congregation in response to the occasion that had brought them together. Indeed, the Lutheran cantata could be viewed as a sort of musical sermon, and its placement in the service confirms this analogy.

Until some sixty years ago it was assumed that Bach was able to write so many cantatas because he must have spread their composition over the course of his nearly three decades in Leipzig (1723–50). Then it was discovered that he actually wrote most of them during his very first years there, rarely producing them later unless called on to do so for a special occasion or to accommodate a particular scriptural setting. Dating his cantatas has been one of the knottiest problems in musicology; the conventional numbering system used for them has nothing to do with their order of composition.

Figure 11-5 Johann Sebastian Bach making music with students in his Collegium Musicum in Leipzig.

Death Set to Music

Anthology Vol 1-90
Full CD II, 72–79
Concise CD II, 3–5

Christ lag in Todesbanden (Christ Lay in the Bonds of Death, BWV 4) is one of Bach's earliest surviving cantatas and also one of the best known. It seems to have first been performed in 1707 at Mühlhausen, possibly on Easter Sunday (24 April) as part of Bach's application for the organist's post there. Bach revised the piece nearly two decades later when he was working in Leipzig. It consists of a set of variations on the venerable Lutheran chorale *Christ lag in Todesbanden*, which had been adapted from the Gregorian Easter sequence *Victimae paschali laudes* and which we have seen used earlier as the basis for pieces by Samuel Scheidt and Johann Schein. The text of Cantata No. 4 is exactly that of the chorale, its seven sections corresponding to the seven stanzas of the hymn. The first stanza is preceded by a brief *sinfonia* that is cleverly constructed out of materials from the chorale melody.

The elaborate first stanza, by far the longest in the cantata, is an old-fashioned cantus firmus composition in "motet style," in which the successive lines of the unadorned chorale tune in the soprano are pitted against points of imitation (some of them pre-echoes of the next line) in the accompanying voices. Although adapted here to a more modern harmonic idiom and further complicated by the intensely motivic instrumental figuration, the procedure dates back in its essentials to the sixteenth century. For the final "Hallelujah!," Bach livens things up by doubling the tempo and has the soprano part move at the same speed as the rest of the choir.

For stanza 2 the lightly ornamented chorale melody in the soprano is shadowed by a somewhat freer alto counterpart, while the two sung parts are set over a ground bass. The style of stanza 3, with its neatly layered counterpoint, is like that of an organ chorale prelude: The tenor sings the cantus firmus in what would be the organist's "left hand," and the massed violins play something like a ritornello in the "right hand"; the frequently cadencing continuo supplies the "pedal." The austere stanza 4, in the center of the cantata, is another cantus firmus setting, with the chorale tune in the alto this time, against motetlike imitations. The continuo follows in somewhat simplified form the lowest sung voice, whichever it may be, and never asserts an independent melodic function of its own.

Stanza 5 shows how the chorale may be recast as an operatic lament. Bach relinquishes the neutral "common time" signature and employs a triple meter that has inescapable dance associations. When, toward the end, the textual imagery becomes really morbid (blood, death, murderer, etc.), Bach seems literally to torture the vocal part, forcing it unexpectedly to leap downward a twelfth to a grotesquely sustained low E♯ on "death" and to leap up almost two octaves to an equally unexpected, even lengthier high D on "murderer," while the violins suddenly break into a rash of unprecedented sixteenth notes (Ex. 11-3). This sort of text painting, especially with words connected with death, occurs throughout the cantata. Comparing such tormented imagery with the jolly imagery we encountered in Handel's *Israel in Egypt* (although at times equally grisly and violent in its subject matter), we may perhaps begin to note a widening gulf between the two masters of the High Baroque.

Example 11-3 J. S. Bach, *Christ lag in Todesbanden*, BWV 4: Stanza V, mm. 64–74

In stanza 6, Bach expands the scope of his imagery to incorporate the regal rhythms characteristic of the French overture as a way of reflecting the meaning of "So feiern wir" ("So mark we now the occasion"), which connotes an air of great solemnity and ceremony that is later taken up when the singers joyously break into triplets. The final stanza (most likely composed later for Leipzig) is a hymnbook setting, the kind of simple "Bach chorale" harmonization we find in books meant for congregational singing. Bach ended many cantatas with such settings (enough so that his son Carl Philipp Emanuel could publish a famous posthumous collection of 371 of them), and it is possible that the congregation was invited to join in.

What Music Is For

One of Bach's most splendid cantatas is *Ein' feste Burg* (A Mighty Fortress, BWV 80), which he wrote in Leipzig for performance on the Feast of the Reformation, 31 October 1724. (Several of its movements were based on an earlier cantata written at Weimar.) The *Reformationsfest*, as it is called in German, is the anniversary of the famous Ninety-five Theses, or articles of protest, which Luther posted on the door of the Castle Church in Wittenberg in 1517. It is thus the most important feast day specific to the German Protestant church and is always given a lavish celebration.

Ein' feste Burg was fittingly Luther's most famous chorale, with a tradition of polyphonic settings going back to the early sixteenth century. Bach's cantata takes its musical shape from an alternation of choral movements based on chorale verses with recitatives and arias drawn from *Evangelisches Andachts-Opffer* (Evangelical Devotional Offering, 1715), a book of devotional verse à la Neumeister by Salomo Franck, the Weimar court poet. At some later time, Bach's eldest son, Wilhelm Friedemann, made the piece even more splendid by adding a *Stadtpfeifer* (town piper) contingent of three trumpets and timpani to the scoring.

From all we know of the conditions under which Bach worked, he never had at his disposal the musical forces that could do anything approaching justice to his cantata Ein' feste Burg.

The wonder is that, from all we know of the conditions under which Bach worked, he never had at his disposal the musical forces that could do anything approaching justice to this mighty fortress of a cantata. Documents survive that inform us about the puny resources he actually had access to; they tell us as well about those he wished he had at his disposal. A memorandum Bach submitted to the Leipzig Town Council on 23 August 1730, a couple of months before the celebrations at which Cantata No. 80 may have been performed in his son's "big band" arrangement, already tells the story: "A Short but Most Necessary Draft for a Well-Appointed Church Music; Together with Certain Modest Reflections on the Decline of Same."[4] Bach's main concern was the choir, which consisted in large part of the boys he trained himself as head of the church music school. He wrote:

> Every musical choir should contain at least 3 sopranos, 3 altos, 3 tenors, and as many basses, so that even if one happens to fall ill (as very often happens, particularly at this time of year, as the prescriptions written by the school physician for the apothecary must show) at least a double chorus motet may be sung. (And note that it would be still better if the classes were such that one could have 4 singers on each part and thus could perform every chorus with 16 persons.)

Next Bach lists the minimum stable of instrumentalists who should be at the disposal of any self-respecting music director. It hardly seems a coincidence that (with the exception of the bassoons, which were probably assumed to be doublers of the continuo line) the ensemble he describes is exactly that called for in Cantata No. 80. Indeed, Bach immediately provides a supplementary list of instruments—flutes, recorders, etc.—that are also needed from time to time. But this is the minimum:

2 or even 3 for the	*Violino* 1
2 or 3 for the	*Violino* 2
2 for the	*Viola* 1
2 for the	*Viola* 2
2 for the	*Violoncello*
1 for the	*Violone*
2, or, if the piece requires, 3, for the	*Hautbois* (oboe)
1, or even 2, for the	*Bassoon*
3 for the	*Trumpets*
1 for the	*Kettledrums*
Total 18 persons at least, for the instrumental music	

By Bach's own admission, then, he considered thirty-four persons (plus himself and another keyboard player) to be the bare minimum required for a performance of a grand, festive piece like *Ein' feste Burg*—and that number would have been thought puny indeed at any royal court. (Just recall Handel's *Music for the Royal Fireworks,* with its band of fifty-five wind players.) Except for avowed attempts to re-create the conditions of Bach's time (as in the so-called historically authentic performances that have been popular since the 1970s), the number would be considered stingy for a professional performance today. Yet Bach declares himself content with it.

However, the same memorandum reveals that in reality Bach could count on only eight regular instrumentalists (relying on local students or his own choristers to substitute when possible) and the choristers at the school, whose services were required not just at Bach's own church, St. Thomas's, but at other Leipzig churches (and who also had to fill in as instrumentalists, as noted). He considered only seventeen to be "usable" for music of "artistry" and "taste." It has been suggested that Bach's church music was normally performed by no more than one singer or player to a part, if that.[5] We often daydream about what the music heard today sounded like when first performed. It would seem that in the case of Bach, it might be better not to know.

Or perhaps not. We might actually learn a good deal about music and its purposes if we could hear a Bach cantata at its first performance—but only if we are prepared for a lesson that challenges our most basic assumptions about the nature and purpose of music. Those assumptions were given a classic articulation by historian Charles Burney, who knew Handel in his youth and played occasionally in his orchestras. "Music is an innocent luxury, unnecessary, indeed, to our existence, but a great improvement and gratification of the sense of hearing," wrote Dr. Burney, who went on to define it more precisely as "the art of pleasing by the succession and combination of agreeable sounds."[6] These words were published in the front matter of his *General History of Music,* which began appearing in 1776. They are still paraphrased in most English dictionaries, and few readers of this book will find them surprising.

Burney's definition of music reflects the intellectual history of the eighteenth century, when a complex of rationalistic (that is, antimystical, antimetaphysical) ideas now referred to as the Enlightenment rose to prominence and eventual dominance in Europe. They will receive a more extended discussion in the next few chapters, when their musical manifestations, which we now call "Classicism," come into view. We have already had a glimpse with Handel, who seems to have regarded his music, even the most exalted and profound, as a distinguished entertainment.

"Music is an innocent luxury, unnecessary, indeed, to our existence, but a great improvement and gratification of the sense of hearing." —Charles Burney

Bach's church music, on the other hand, is perhaps better viewed as embodying a pre-Enlightened—and, when push came to shove, a violently anti-Enlightened—temper. Such music was considered a medium of truth, not beauty, and the truth it served—Luther's truth—was often bitter. Some of Bach's most striking works were written to persuade us—no, to *reveal* to us—that the world is filth and horror, that humans are helpless, that life is pain, and that reason is useless. Even in his most exuberant works, Bach's purpose in church was never just to please, and the sounds he combined there were sometimes anything but agreeable. When his music was pleasing, it was usually in order to persuade or entice. But at times Bach aimed to torture the ear. When the world of man rather than that of God was his subject, he could write music of shocking, deliberate ugliness. The daring it took to write such passages is testimony to Bach's genius. They would have ruined Handel. But Bach's pious congregation would have understood his purpose in a way that we can manage only by dint of great imaginative effort.

We can find many examples in Bach's cantatas, and the text, of course, is the key to finding them. The cantata *Nimm von uns, Herr, du treuer Gott* (BWV 101), composed in Leipzig for performance on 13 August 1724, opens with a chorale fantasy that pits the melody of the Lutheran Lord's Prayer ("Vater unser im Himmelreich") as cantus firmus against a choral counterpoint that carries the text of a sixteenth-century hymn:

Nimm von uns, Herr, du treuer Gott	Take from us, O Lord, thou faithful God
Die schwere Straf und große Not,	The heavy punishment and great distress
Die wir mit Sünden ohne Zahl	That we with our numberless sins
Verdienet haben allzumal.	Have only too well deserved.
Behüt für Krieg und teurer Zeit,	Preserve us against war and famine,
Für Seuchen, Feur und großem Leid.	Plague, fire and devastation.

Example 11-4 is a piano reduction of Bach's setting of the second line so that the scarcely credible dissonances with which he evoked punishment, distress, war, famine, plague, fire, and devastation can be most compactly represented and easily observed. Almost all of them, semitonal clashes, false relations and all, arise out of a deployment of "nonharmonic tones" that take place in turn out of expressive "sigh" motives or their inversions, equipped with pickups that render the first notes under the slurs maximally discordant both harmonically and melodically. This music will never bring a smile, the way Handel's famine, plague, fire, and devastation can in *Israel in Egypt*. And that is only partly because of the extremity of the musical means, which go so far beyond the boundaries of what Handel or Burney or their audiences would have identified as good taste. It is also because the sufferers depicted are not "them" but "us."

Example 11-4 **J. S. Bach, *Nimm von uns, Herr, du treuer Gott,* BWV 101, opening chorus, mm. 64–74**

Example 11-4 (continued)

Even more unsettling are the choruses and arias where Bach expressed traditional Lutheran views that went against those of emerging "Enlightened" thinkers, who despised his "altogether contemptible German church texts" and the "earnest polemic of the Reformation,"[7] The words are those of Carl Friedrich Zelter (1758–1832), a composer and choral conductor who later played a major role in Bach's nineteenth-century rediscovery. Indeed, many of Bach's texts express ideas that most listeners, not only in Zelter's day but in our own, would find abhorrent, for most modern ideas of social justice, reasoned discourse, and personal integrity are derived from the ideas of the Enlightenment.

> ***Many of Bach's texts express ideas that listeners today would find abhorrent, for most modern ideas of social justice, reasoned discourse, and personal integrity are derived from the ideas of the Enlightenment.***

There is no evidence that Bach believed in them. On the contrary, we have every reason to assume that he believed not in freedom, equality, and human institutions of justice as saving forces in the world but in faith and God's grace—as may be heard in a harrowing tenor aria, "Schweig nur, taumelnde Vernunft!" ("Shut up, stumbling reason!") from the cantata *Wo Gott der Herr nicht bei uns hält* (BWV 178), composed in Leipzig in the summer of 1724. The text is a paraphrase of a stanza from a sixteenth-century hymn. Past the first line the message of the text is one of comfort, but Bach is fixated on that fierce and derisive opening line—indeed, on just the opening word. Out of it he builds practically the whole first section of his da capo aria, crowding all the rest into a cursory and soon-superseded middle section. Over and over the tenor shrieks, "Schweig nur, schweig!," leaping now a sixth, now a seventh, now an octave (Ex. 11-5). Meanwhile, the accompanying orchestra, Reason's surrogate, reels and lurches violently. The effect is nothing short of terrifying.

Example 11-5 J. S. Bach, Cantata: *Wo Gott der Herr nicht bei uns hält,* BWV 178, tenor aria, "Schweig nur, taumelnde Vernunft!," mm. 11–17

Vln. I
Vln. II
Vla.
Tenor
B.c.

Schweig, schweig, schweig nur, schweig, schweig nur, schweig,

schweig, schweig, schweig, schweig nur, tau - - - - meln- de Ver- nunft, schweig,

Even when Bach is not expressing actively anti-Enlightenment sentiments such as these in his cantatas, his settings are pervaded with a general contempt for human weakness. Take, for example, Bach's apparent lack of concern for practical performance considerations. At times he seems deliberately to engineer a bad-sounding performance by putting the apparent demands of the music beyond the reach of his performers and their equipment. Unlike Handel's music, Bach's church music serves the purposes of the church—that is, ministering to the soul's salvation—and presents modern secular performers with a dilemma: Either adapt the performance to the tastes of the modern secular audience (by modernizing the performing forces, for example) and risk losing the full force of the expressive message encoded in the music, or perform the music in an appropriate manner and risk perplexing, fatiguing, or even insulting the audience.

That is one reason why only a handful of Bach's cantatas can be said to have really joined the modern performance repertory, and a thoroughly unrepresentative handful at that. Besides a couple of amusing secular items like the so-called "Coffee Cantata" (about a young girl's passion for coffee—then a novelty—and the headaches it causes her father), composed for Bach's Collegium Musicum (which actually performed in a coffee shop; Fig. 11-6), the "popular" cantatas include No. 51, *Jauchzet Gott in allen Landen* (Rejoice in God in Every Land), a brilliant display piece for soprano and the only church cantata Bach ever composed for a woman's voice (and one of the few

Figure 11-6 A 1746 drawing of the coffee shop near Leipzig where Bach's Collegium Musicum would meet in the summer.

pieces he himself actually called a cantata); and No. 140, *Wachet auf, ruft uns die Stimme* (Awake, the [Watchman's] Voice Is Calling), in which Bach set a couple of love duets between Christ and the Christian soul in the style of "the pretty little Dresden tunes."

Bach's "Testaments"

Bach's best-known religious pieces are the ones most comparable to Handel's oratorios and to later Catholic religious music. These were the works through which Bach was eventually rediscovered and reclaimed for the performing repertoire in the nineteenth century. They include two **Passion** settings, one based on the Gospel of Matthew and the other on the Gospel of John. There is also the imposing Mass in B Minor, a grandiose concerted setting for chorus in as many as eight parts and an exceptionally mixed assortment of instruments, setting the Latin Mass, a text for which there was no liturgical use at all in the Lutheran Church. Bach, ever the compiler, assembled that Mass out of pieces that had accumulated over a period of more than two decades, including many cantata choruses. The work is therefore cast in a mixture of styles that reflects its miscellaneous origins. Performances began only when Bach had been assimilated to the secular concert repertory in the nineteenth century. Hence the curiously secular name by which it is generally known: "Mass in B Minor," after the key of the opening Kyrie, although most of the music is actually in D major.

Bach's two surviving Passion oratorios were written for church use on Good Friday, the most solemn day in the Christian year. The one based on St. John was initially performed in Leipzig in 1724, during Bach's first year there, and revived several times thereafter. The St. Matthew Passion (Fig. 11-7) was conceived on an enormous scale both as to duration and as to performing forces, featuring two antiphonal choirs, each with its own supporting orchestra. Bach composed it in relative tranquility after the maelstrom of cantata production had subsided, and it was probably first performed in 1727. In both Passions, following the post-Neumeister conventions of the genre, the text operates on three levels, which interact to produce a sort of biblical opera-with-commentary. The original Gospel text is set as semidramatic recitative. There is a narrator, called the Evangelist, but all direct discourse, the lines spoken directly by the actors in the story, is assigned to other solo voices, and lines spoken collectively by the "people," following the *turba* (crowd) convention that goes back to the sixteenth century, were sung by the chorus.

The recitatives are interrupted at strategic moments, just as they are in opera, by the second textual level: reflective arias. The arias, usually in da capo form, are not sung by characters but by "voice personas" who represent and give utterance

Figure 11-7 Bach's handwritten score for the St. Matthew Passion.

to the poet's own meditations on the events of the biblical narration and instruct the congregation on their Christian significance. In the St. Matthew Passion, all the arias as well as the reflective choruses that open and close each part are adapted from a single long Passion poem in *Erbauliche Gedancken* (Edifying Thoughts), a cycle of texts for music by a friend of Bach's, a Leipzig lawyer and playwright named Christian Friedrich Henrici (1700–64), who wrote under the name Picander and who also provided the texts for many of Bach's cantatas. The third textual element in Bach's Passions consisted of hymnbook-style chorales, which are frequently inserted to provide an additional level of commentary.

The two Bach Passion settings are quite distinct in character. The shorter and faster-moving St. John Passion is as close to a full opera as Bach ever wrote. The crowd scenes before Pontius Pilate, in particular, show the Roman viceroy, the crowd, and the Evangelist interacting with great dispatch. In the excerpt given in Example 11-6, Pontius Pilate offers Jesus back to the crowd, which rejects him and calls for his crucifixion. The sharp long-short rhythms in the orchestra recall the cry of "Crucify!" from the previous chorus. The St. Matthew Passion places more emphasis on contemplation than on action. Its emblematic sections are not the crowd choruses but the monumental framing ones on words by Picander, such as the one that opens the work, "Kommt, ihr Töchter, helft mir klagen" ("Come, O daughters, help me in my lamentation"), a conception of unparalleled breadth. A panoramic scene is conjured up by the use of antiphonal choruses (and orchestras) asking and exclaiming about Christ's crucifixion at Golgotha.

Anthology Vol 1-91
Full CD II, 80

Example 11-6 J. S. Bach, *St. John Passion,* No. 23c-23d, mm. 40–46

Example 11-6 (continued)

Bach was well aware of the special place the St. Matthew Passion occupied within his vast output. He regarded it, too, as a particular triumph among his many works. He prepared a lavish calligraphic score, resplendent with inks of different colors, to preserve it at a time when most music, including his, was composed for specific occasions, to be used and thereafter discarded. That fair copy passed into Carl Friedrich Zelter's possession and provided the vehicle for Bach's rediscovery and canonization as a musical founding father when the twenty-year-old composer Felix Mendelssohn (1809–47), a pupil of Zelter's, conducted a performance at the Berlin Singakademie on 11 March 1829. This event, a little over a century after its first performance in Leipzig, was one of immense cultural significance. The rediscovery placed Bach in a new context, one in which the very aspects of his style that had led to his temporary eclipse could now be prized: its complexity, its conservatism, its uncompromising religiosity, its sharpness. These features that had caused his music to be dismissed by some critics even during his lifetime as showing an "excess of art" and a "turgid and confused style" could now be held up as a model for emulation.[8] The conditions that brought about this change in Bach's status had a great deal to do with the burgeoning of Romanticism, to which we will return in a later chapter.

Cursed Questions

There was another aspect to the reassessment of Bach, however, that needs our attention. Bach's vocal music, little known in his time and forgotten soon after his death, was called back to active cultural duty by a nineteenth-century cultural program unrelated and perhaps alien to it. Does that matter? And does it matter that the music is now admired for reasons that may have little to do with what originally motivated it? Many lovers of Bach's music will have no trouble answering these questions. Indeed, the Bach revival can seem a miraculous salvage operation, hardly in need of defense or excuse. But the "universalization" of music originally created within a narrowly specific cultural context does entail some difficulties and cannot help raising some problems, especially if the original context was a religious one.

Bach's vocal music, little known in his time and forgotten soon after his death, was called back to active cultural duty by a nineteenth-century cultural program.

Look again at Example 11-6 and consider it from a different perspective. No mention was made the first time around that the *turba* in the St. John Passion, following the Book of John itself, is identified not as "*das Volk*," or "the people" (as it is in the Matthew Passion), but as "*die Juden*," or "the Jews." The text to the excerpt is:

> Evangelist: And it was about the sixth hour of preparation of the Passover, and he said to the Jews:
> Pilate: See ye, your King stands before you!
> Evangelist: They cried out however:
> Chorus: Away with Him, away with Him, crucify Him, crucify Him!

An accusation is being made, one that is no longer supported by responsible historical or theological scholarship, that the Jews rather than the Romans were responsible for Christ's death. That accusation has had a bearing on a history of bloody persecutions, culminating in the Holocaust, perhaps the most horrible page in the history of the twentieth century.

Obviously, Bach had no part of that. Nor was he, as far as anyone today can guess, personally anti-Semitic as the term is understood today, except insofar as he probably subscribed to Luther's doctrine that the Jews should submit to conversion on pain of punishment. In all likelihood he rarely, possibly never, met any Jews and thought little about them. The St. John Passion was intended for performance before a congregation of Christian believers for whom the Gospel text was . . . well, Gospel. The insult it contains to Jews was wholly incidental to its purpose. But today it serves other purposes and is performed before other audiences. Bach is long dead, but the St. John Passion lives on. Jews not only hear it nowadays but often participate in performances of it and are sometimes shocked to learn what it is they are singing. Are they wrong? Does Bach's music redeem the text? Would it impair Bach's work from the standpoint of its present social use if the text were emended? And if people disagree about the answers to these difficult questions, on what basis can they be decided?

The problem of the anti-Semitic message in the St. John Passion, from which some people today may actually "learn" the "fact" that the Jews killed Christ, would never have become a problem had Bach never been revived. What was merely a latent message in Bach's time, stating an accepted truth to which no one would have paid much attention per se, has become a potentially explicit message in our time and a potentially mischievous one. The problem comes in deciding just what it is in the treasured legacy of the past that should be regarded as timelessly relevant.

Domenico Scarlatti, at Last

Bach lived his life in defiance of the Enlightenment and was later revived in reaction to it. The remaining member of the class of 1685, Domenico Scarlatti (Fig. 11-8), in some respects exemplified the aesthetic of Enlightenment. The son of Alessandro Scarlatti, one of the giants of opera seria, Domenico was at first groomed for a career in his father's footsteps, for which he showed a precocious aptitude. His first opera, *L'Ottavia restituita al trono* (Octavia Restored to the Throne), was produced in Naples in 1703, when Domenico was only seventeen years old. His last, the archetypical *Berenice, regina d'Egitto, ovvero Le gare di amore e di politica* (Bernice, Queen of Egypt, or, the Contest of Love and Politics), was produced for the Roman carnival fifteen years later, at which point Scarlatti retired from the opera stage, at the age of thirty-two, with almost forty years of life still ahead of him.

In 1719 he took a position as *maestro di cappella* at the cathedral of Lisbon, in Portugal, where he produced several oratorios and other sacred vocal works and also supervised the musical education of the Infanta Maria Barbara, a gifted keyboard player. On the princess's marriage to Fernando, the crown prince of Spain, in 1728, he followed her to Madrid, where he was known as Domingo Escarlatti and served as courtier until his death in 1757, the last twenty years alongside the great castrato Farinelli, who had also retired there.

Scarlatti spent his years at Madrid as a pampered retainer, later a knight, and was free to compose whatever he wanted. What he wanted to compose was virtuosic harpsichord music for himself and, we presume, his royal pupil to perform. Unconstrained by any set requirements yet prompted by a tremendous musical curiosity and imagination, he invented what amounted to a new style of composition, which he called "ingenious jesting with art."[9] The phrase jibes with Dr. Burney's comments on the nature and value of music and reveals a wholehearted commitment to the ideal of delighting—rather than edifying, instructing, awing, or stirring—the listener. Nothing could be farther away from the monumental world of Bach.

> ***Scarlatti's style reveals a wholehearted commitment to the ideal of delighting—rather than edifying, instructing, or stirring—the listener.***

Accordingly, Scarlatti became the great miniaturist of his age, spending the last thirty to forty years of his life turning out upwards of 555 short, freestanding compositions for the harpsichord. These pieces were individually called *sonatas*, but they were in only a single movement and were often published under different names (such as *essercizi*, "studies") or even as *pièces* grouped in suites. None survives in the composer's own handwritten manuscript, which makes it impossible to know exactly what he called them or how he may have grouped them.

They are uniformly in binary form—far more uniformly than Couperin's, which are often *rondeaux* (with recurrent refrains) or *passacailles* (variations over a ground). Scarlatti himself never gathered them into suites. Early copyists and editors liked to group them in pairs, similar in key but contrasting in tempo. Scarlatti evidently preferred to provide delight in single short doses. Unlike Couperin, who also deserves credit for establishing the single characteristic piece, although published in sets, Scarlatti liked to make brash statements as well as tender ones. Like any jester, he had an exhibitionistic streak. He could never have said, with Couperin (in the preface to his first book of *Pieces de clavecin*, 1713), "I would rather be moved than astonished." Scarlatti's sonatas, though occasionally tender and lyrical, are astonishing in various ways.

Figure 11-8 Domenico Scarlatti. Portrait by Domingo Antonio de Velasco.

One way they astonish is in the outstanding instrumental virtuosity they require and display, particularly in the use of special effects like crossed hands and even glissandos. Another is their harmonic extravagance, manifested in terms of both boldly handled dissonance and an often-flamboyant yet exquisitely graded use of modulatory chromaticism. Still another is the fantastic variety with which their single basic shape is treated. Finally, there are in some sonatas the strong imprint of the local color of Spain—one that to listeners in countries where the international music trade flourished seemed "exotic." The Scarlatti sonatas are a very early instance of exotic local color being sought and valued for its "pure" musical allure, without any symbolically nationalistic overlay.

The most remarkable aspect of Scarlatti's sonatas, in fact, may be the absence in them of anything symbolic at all. At a time when music, like the other arts, was valued mainly for its imitative properties, Scarlatti sought to convey what Thomas Twining, a friend of Dr. Burney's, called "a simple original pleasure, . . . no more imitative than the smell of a rose, or the flavor of a pineapple."[10] In this, Scarlatti was true to the spirit, not of his father, but of the Italian string composers of his father's generation. His sonatas, unlike Couperin's character pieces, were works at which old French academicians like Bernard le Bovier le Fontenelle might have railed: What did such music want of the listener?

Anthology Vol 1-92
Full CD II, 81–82
Concise CD II, 6

Let us sample two from the hundreds. The Sonata in G, K. 105, has an overall shape that can be regarded as typical for Scarlatti: the usual swing from tonic to dominant in the first half, followed by a return in the second half by way of a "**far out point**." As is also typical for Scarlatti, the endings of each binary half match up with their counterparts more closely than the beginnings so that a drive to completion is achieved. What makes the sonata unforgettable, though, is not its general contours but the specific harmonic content, which is also typically Scarlattian, but in an unusually, almost uniquely concentrated fashion. Beginning halfway through the first half and even more pervasively in the second half, the harmony is rife with dissonant seconds, few of which can be considered "chord tones" and even fewer of which resolve in normally prescribed fashion to consonances. The second half offers an example of exotic local color as Scarlatti unmistakably conjures up the sound of "Flamenco" guitars, the Andalusian gypsy style that has become pervasive in Spanish popular music and that must have already been a conspicuous part of the sonic landscape in his day.

The form of the Sonata in F Minor, K. 481, a plaintive *andante è cantabile*, is rather more idiosyncratic. Both sections close with the same material, first in the dominant minor, C, and then in the tonic, yet it is the opening of the second section that astonishes. Instead of restating the first measures in the new key, it starts with a new version of mm. 9–12 and a deceptive move toward the tonic, leading to a particularly bizarre far out point (mm. 43–44). But there is something else to notice. In this sonata, the return of the original tonic happens to coincide with a return of the opening thematic material (m. 52). This dramatic "**double return**" (original key arriving together with the original theme) was something else that would become practically de rigueur by the last quarter of the eighteenth century and a defining attribute of the "Classical" sonata form. The double return is often thought typical of Scarlatti, because the most famous Scarlatti sonata of all—C Major, K. 159, a favorite of piano teachers everywhere—happens to have one. But the double return is actually a rarity in his output.

Scarlatti's sonatas, while well-liked by connoisseurs, were admired as "original and happy freaks," the offbeat products of an imaginative but isolated and pampered genius.

To Scarlatti's contemporaries, his sonatas, while much well-liked by connoisseurs, were admired as "original and happy freaks,"[11] to quote Dr. Burney—the offbeat products of an imaginative but isolated and pampered genius. Surely one of the latest bloomers among the major names in music history, Scarlatti only came into his own as a composer in 1738, with the publication of his first book, *Essercizi per gravicembalo* (Exercises for Harpsichord). By then the members of the class of 1685 were all age fifty-three, and Bach's and Handel's careers were largely behind them. Scarlatti was just beginning to be "Scarlatti," and thus his effective starting point coincided with Bach's and Handel's decline. As a composer, then, Scarlatti might better be regarded not as a contemporary of J. S. Bach but, rather, as an elder member of the generation of Bach's sons, to which we shall turn in the next chapter.

Summary

This chapter has examined the vocal music of J. S. Bach and G. F. Handel. Handel's primary contributions were to opera and the English oratorio, a genre he had a central role in developing. Bach's vocal works, by contrast, are nearly all sacred and focused on expressing the theological content of the text.

Although Handel's operas are cast largely in the same mold as earlier opera seria (see Chapter 9), they are more complex and stylistically conservative than their Italian counterparts. The aria "Empio, dirò, tu sei" ("Evil, you are, I say") from *Giulio Cesare in Egitto* (Julius Caesar in Egypt, 1724) illustrates the ways in which Handel makes the da capo aria form serve his own dramatic ends perfectly. As is typical of Handel's arias, the opening ritornello captures the central emotion of the aria, rage. The B section, typically shorter than the A section, is often in a contrasting mood and key. In this aria, however, most of its material is derived from the A section, underscoring Caesar's implacable anger.

After a quarter-century of producing very successful operas in London, Handel experienced a decline in the public appetite for opera seria in the face of increased competition. For example, John Gay's enormously successful ballad opera called *The Beggar's Opera*, produced in 1728, mocked many opera seria conventions in short songs that set new texts to popular, borrowed tunes. Handel saw a new opportunity for public success in the English oratorio. Despite their sacred subject matter, earlier Italian oratorios were very much like opera seria, with the musical focus on a series of arias. In his transformation of the genre, Handel minimized the narrative and dramatic elements and gave a new prominence to the chorus. These "anthem oratorios," such as *Israel in Egypt* (1739) and *Messiah* (1742), were more like collections of sacred vocal numbers than dramatic works. Handel's oratorios were first and foremost a form of entertainment. Madrigalism features prominently, for example, in the choruses of *Israel in Egypt*, with literal depictions of frogs, flies, and hail. In addition to raising sentiments about national identity (English audiences often identified with the Old Testament Israelites as a "chosen people"), Handel's oratorios and other works contain many "borrowings" from other composers, a trait that some have felt a need to justify.

In contrast to Handel's public oratorios, Bach's sacred vocal music was created for the services in the churches he served. Most of his cantatas were written during his first five years in Leipzig (1723–28). Introduced by the poet and theologian Erdmann Neumeister (1671–1756), Lutheran cantata texts were created from a combination of biblical passages, chorale texts, and new poetry. Bach's cantatas incorporate a wide variety of musical styles and forms, ranging from the chorale motet, with origins in the sixteenth century, to the recitatives and da capo arias associated with contemporary opera. Despite their use of operatic forms, however, cantatas are not dramatic works. The speaker in the arias is not a character but an abstract voice reflecting the thoughts of the Christian believer. *Christ lag in Todesbanden* (Christ Lay in the Bonds of Death) illustrates the variety of Bach's approaches to setting a chorale. Bach's attitude about the purpose of sacred music differed from Handel's in fundamental ways. In contrast to the madrigalisms in Handel's oratorios, which are calibrated to entertain an audience, those of Bach's cantatas are focused on expressing key theological points.

Bach's larger vocal works include his Mass in B Minor, a late compilation of movements largely adapted from earlier works, and his two surviving passion oratorios, the St. John Passion and St. Matthew Passion. In the passion oratorios, the story from the gospel is set as a recitative, with parts for a narrator (the Evangelist) and various characters. The crowd is represented by a chorus, and Christian believers' reactions to the events are expressed in arias. The St. Matthew Passion was revived in 1829 for the first time after Bach's death. That performance, led by Felix Mendelssohn (1809–47), helped spur the Bach revival.

Although he composed many cantatas and operas, Domenico Scarlatti (1685–1757) is best remembered today for his keyboard sonatas. He spent most of his career in Portugal and Spain. His single-movement sonatas are known for their virtuosity, bold harmonic progressions, chromaticism, dissonance, and "local color" associated with Spanish popular music. Although his sonatas are in binary form, a few of them have the "double return" of the tonic key and opening theme, which later became associated with "sonata form."

Study Questions

1. Describe the ways in which G. F. Handel's "Empio, dirò, tu sei" ("Evil, you are, I say") manipulates the conventional da capo aria form in the service of the drama.
2. How do G. F. Handel's oratorios differ from those of his Italian predecessors? What features account for their popularity, both now and in his own time? Describe Handel's literal depictions of the text in *Israel in Egypt*.

3. Summarize the various viewpoints modern scholars have taken toward Handel's extensive "borrowing," from his own works and those of other composers. What are your own views on this topic?
4. Describe some central textual and musical features of the cantata in Bach's time. How do J. S. Bach's cantatas challenge the idea that music is "the art of pleasing by the succession and combination of agreeable sounds"?
5. Describe the discrepancies between Bach's ideal performing forces and the forces he actually had at his disposal.
6. Why was the reception of Bach's music so different in the early-nineteenth-century "Bach revival" than it was in his own time?
7. Describe some salient stylistic and formal characteristics of Domenico Scarlatti's sonatas, illustrating your points with reference to Sonata in G, K. 105, and Sonata in F minor, K. 481.

Key Terms

anthem oratorio
ballad opera
double return
far out point
oratorio
Passion

12

Mid-Eighteenth-Century Stylistic Changes: From Bach's Sons to the Comic Style

"Bach is the father, we are the kids."[1] These words are attributed to Wolfgang Amadè Mozart (1756–91), but he was not referring to J. S. Bach. "Old Sebastian," as Mozart called him, was just a dimly remembered grandfather until Mozart reached the end of his short career, at which time he first got to know some of J. S. Bach's works as well as some of Handel's. The Bach whom Mozart regarded as a musical parent was Sebastian's second son, Carl Philipp Emanuel (1714–88), who was indeed old enough to be Mozart's father (or even his grandfather) and who, along with his much younger half-brother, Johann Christian (1735–82), was regarded by the musicians of the late eighteenth century as a founding father (Fig. 12-1).

The eminence of Bach's celebrated children has much diminished on account of the historical valorization of the Classical repertory, beginning with the works of Mozart himself and his contemporaries, most notably Franz Joseph Haydn (1732–1809). When the music of J. S. Bach was revived in the nineteenth century, he was retrospectively appended to an already-established repertory of works and, together with Handel (whose *Messiah* had never faded), proclaimed its founding father. The music of the Bach sons was not later revived, even though it had enjoyed greater fame in the sons' own time and had exerted a formative influence on Mozart and other composers.

TIMELINE

1733 **Giovanni Battista Pergolesi, *La serva padrona***

1740 Samuel Richardson, *Pamela, or Virtue Rewarded*

1740 Frederick the Great crowned King of Prussia

1740 Maria Theresa crowned Holy Roman Empress

1740–48 War of Austrian Succession

1740s **Carl Philipp Emanuel Bach's earliest works in the *empfindsamer Stil***

1745 **Wilhelm Friedemann Bach, Sonata in F**

1749 Henry Fielding *The History of Tom Jones, a Foundling*

1750 **Death of Johann Sebastian Bach**

1751–72 Denis Diderot, *Encyclopédie*

1752 ***La serva padrona* performed in Paris, helping to spark the *Querelle des Bouffons***

1752 **Jean-Jacques Rousseau, *Le devin du village***

The false genealogy that all this implied, in which the generation of J. S. Bach and Handel was cast in a direct line that led straight to the generations of Haydn and Mozart, has been responsible for many false historical assumptions. The attention of historians was diverted away from the music and the musical life of the mid-eighteenth century, when the younger Bachs, along with the most successful composers of opera seria, were at the height of their activity and prestige. The result was something of a historiographical black hole that scholars tried to plug by searching for a "missing link" between the Bach/Handel and Haydn/Mozart poles.

The death of Bach in 1750, which so neatly splits the eighteenth century into its early and late phases, separates what much later came to be labeled the Baroque and Classical periods. The date came to represent another all-too-convenient dividing point, and one that was not regarded as any kind of break at the time. During the Romantic nineteenth century the music of Bach and Handel was enshrined as the most important of the first half of the eighteenth century. In recent decades scholars have paid more attention to repertories that had faded from view, such as the so-called Mannheim School of symphonists, Italian keyboard sonatas, and the Viennese orchestral style. No period has been in greater need of fundamental research than that from the 1730s to the 1760s, what was long commonly known as Preclassic (and thus relegated by its very name to a status of relative insignificance) or labeled as Rococo, *style galant*, and *empfindsamer Stil* (sensibility style). A particularly fruitful explanation looks to influential currents in Italian comic opera. This may at first seem a humble link, but it is one that helps us get from "Old Sebastian" to the remarkable Mozart.[2]

The Younger Bachs

One way of pointing out the problem, suggesting solutions to it, and beginning to identify the new stylistic elements that emerged would be to look at the work of Bach's illustrious sons, starting with the eldest, Wilhelm Friedemann (1710–84, henceforth "WF"). He followed a career in his father's footsteps as a Lutheran organist and cantor, although he proved far less successful in terms of steady employment. WF's most prominent job, and the one he held longest, was at the Liebfrauenkirche in Halle, Handel's birthplace.

Anthology Vol 2-1
Full CD III, 1
Concise CD II, 7

It would be reasonable to expect his music to resemble his father's, and some of it, notably his church cantatas, does. And yet, as his Harpsichord Sonata in F (Falck 6a) suggests, much more of it does not. Although composed around 1735–40, that is to say, still within his father's lifetime, the work occupies a different stylistic universe from anything the elder Bach composed. In WF's sonata all three movements are in binary form, and the texture either is two-part or else makes free use of harmonic figuration. The stylistic and rhetorical gulf is the real mind boggler, and it widens with each movement. The most basic differences between WF and his father lie in the interpenetrating dimensions of melodic design and **harmonic rhythm**, the rate at which the chords change.

WF's melodic design, far removed from his father's powerful contrapuntally spinning engine, is based on the dual principle of short-range contrast and balance. The contrast comes in the continual appearance of new motives with surface variety and decorative dazzle set against a deliberate and structurally symmetrical tonal plan. Like any binary movement, this opening one follows a there-and-back harmonic course, moving from tonic to dominant in the first half of the movement and from dominant to tonic, by way of an extraordinary "far out point," in the second half.

In this style, what distinguishes one piece from another like it is not the foreordained basic plan they share but, rather, the specific means of its implementation. While some pieces rush headlong from one harmonic area to another, this one takes its time to smell the daisies (and, given the unpredictably varied motives, takes care to provide a lot of flowers to smell). This is all part of what it meant to be *galant*, with its connotations of lightweight, courtly, and "Frenchy." A stroll around the flower garden, then, reveals a very meticulous layout. Taking in the first half at a glance, we count sixteen measures, which is no accident. This portion, exactly half of the piece's total span, will be balanced by the rest (Ex. 12-1). Harmonic and melodic symmetries hold true at every level: 16 = 8 + 8 = 4 + 4 + 4 + 4, and so on making for **periodic phrasing**.

1753 **C. P. E. Bach's treatise *Essay on the True Art of Playing Keyboard Instruments* (volume 1 of 2)**

1759 **Death of George Frideric Handel**

1759 Voltaire (1694–1778), *Candide, ou l'optimisme*

1760 **Johann Christian Bach, *Artaserse***

1760 **Niccolò Piccinni, *La buona figliuola***

1762 Catherine the Great becomes empress of Russia

1762 **Christoph Willibald Gluck, *Orfeo ed Euridice***

1762 Rousseau, *Of The Social Contract, or Principles of Political Right*

1765 Joseph II becomes Holy Roman Emperor

1764–81 **J. C. Bach's public concerts in London**

1768 **C. P. E. Bach moves to Hamburg**

Example 12-1 W. F. Bach, Sonata in F (Falck catalogue No. 6a), I, mm. 1–16

Figure 12-1 Carl Philipp Emanuel Bach, Johann Sebastian Bach's second son, master of the *empfindsamer Stil* and author of *An Essay on the True Art of Playing Keyboard Instruments*.

Example 12-1 (continued)

Balance and symmetry are key to this movement. The second half, a complementary sixteen measures, beginning in the dominant but then becoming shockingly unstable harmonically, leads to the far out point and then back to the dominant before restoring the stable opening tonality and reprising the opening melodic material as well. This is the "**double return**"—original key and original theme simultaneously reachieved with mutually reinforcing effect—that we first encountered, but only as an anomaly, in Domenico Scarlatti. In the music of W. F. Bach and his contemporaries, the double return—that is, the large-scale melodic return simultaneous with the large-scale harmonic one—became standard. Indeed, it would not be much of an exaggeration to dub the whole later eighteenth century the Age of the Double Return, so definitive did the gesture become.

Empfindsamkeit: C. P. E. Bach

The distinctive features of WF's style—its melodic extravagance, its reliance on the contrast and balance of short ideas, its frequent cadences, its self-dramatizing form, its synergistic harnessing of melodic and harmonic events, even its characteristic melodic and harmonic rhythms—were antithetical to his father's style and to Handel's as well. The new melodic and harmonic techniques created not just a stylistic contrast with the old, but also an aesthetic and psychological one. A composition by J. S. Bach or one of his contemporaries was nothing if not musically unified. There was usually one main musical idea that projected a single dominant affect or feeling state. (Depending on the genre, we call it "subject," "ritornello," or some other name.) A piece might be considered sad or joyous, angry or relaxed, but whatever "affection" it conveyed tended to be consistent throughout, with no waffling between affects.

The distinctive features of W. F. Bach's style were antithetical to his father's style and to Handel's as well.

The surface of WF's sonata, as we have seen, presents not a unified but a highly nuanced, variegated, even fragmented exterior. In contrast to the inexorable consistency of JS's "spinning-out," the only predictable aspect of WF's melodic unfolding is its unpredictability. In place of a single affect, there is consciousness of subjective caprice, of impressionability, of quick, spontaneous responsiveness or changeability of mood—in a word, of "sensibility," as the term was used by eighteenth-century writers, such as the celebrated English novelist Jane Austen (1775–1817).

The German equivalent of sensibility, in this sense, was *Empfindung* (sensation) or ***Empfindsamkeit***, meaning "susceptibility to sensations." It was a new aesthetic, which aimed not at a more objective depiction of a character's sensations, as in an opera seria, but, rather, at the expression and transmission of varying human sensations. Composers of operas and large-scale religious works tended to isolate, magnify, and objectify the fixed mental states of gods, heroes, or contemplative Christian souls at superhuman intensity. They used that magnification as the basis for creating monumental musical structures that would impress large audiences in theaters and churches. Composers of the ***empfindsamer Stil***, composing on a much smaller scale for intimate surroundings such as the home, sought to capture the sentiments of real people. They tried to create an impression of self-portraiture in which the player of and listener to their music would recognize a corresponding self-portrait. In line with currents in the philosophical thought of the time, they recognized the fluidity and changeability of subjective feeling. "The rapidity with which the emotions change is common knowledge, for they are nothing but motion and restlessness," wrote the Berlin critic and theorist Friedrich Wilhelm Marpurg in 1749.[3]

The origins of artistic sensibility are to be found in literature. One of its first great exponents was the poet Friedrich Gottlieb Klopstock (1724–1803), who established the style in the 1740s with his odes and love poems. Beginning in 1770 he lived in Hamburg, home as well to WF's younger brother, Carl Philipp Emanuel Bach (henceforth "CPE"). In 1768 CPE assumed responsibility for five churches in the city after nearly thirty years of service at the court of Frederick II, the King of Prussia (Fig. 12-2). He set Klopstock's odes to music and carried on a lively correspondence with him about the relationship between music and poetry. In effect, he became a sort of musical Klopstock and the chief representative in his own medium of artistic *Empfindsamkeit.* That term is now firmly, if retrospectively, associated with CPE and with some of his keyboard music in particular. He took to an extreme the kind of musical expression without recourse to words that we have already noted in the work of his elder brother.

CPE did this all quite consciously and even wrote about it (although without actually using the word *Empfindsamkeit*) in his treatise *Versuch über die wahre Art das Clavier zu spielen* (An Essay on the True Art of Playing Keyboard Instruments, 2 vols., 1753 and 1762), the book to which Mozart was supposedly paying tribute in the comment quoted at the beginning of this chapter. CPE's *Essay* is of course full of technical information—about ornamentation, for example, and continuo realization—that is of great value to the historian of performance practice. But it also deals in less tangible matters. "Play from the soul," CPE exhorted his readers, "not like a trained bird!"[4] And then, lending his novel idea some authority by casting it as a paraphrase of the Roman poet Horace, he argued:

"Play from the soul," C. P. E. Bach exhorted his readers, "not like a trained bird!"

> Since a musician cannot move others unless he himself is moved, he must of necessity feel all of the affects that he hopes to arouse in his listeners. He communicates his own feelings to them and thus most effectively moves them to sympathy. In languishing, sad passages, the performer must languish and grow sad. . . . Similarly, in lively, joyous passages, the executant must again put himself into the appropriate mood. And so, constantly varying the passions he will barely quiet one before he rouses another.[5]

Figure 12-2 Frederick the Great of Prussia performing as flute soloist (probably in his own concerto) at a soirée in Sans Souci, his pleasure palace at Potsdam. His music master, Johann Joachim Quantz, watches from the left foreground. C. P. E. Bach is at the keyboard; leading the violins is Franticek Benda, a member of a large family of distinguished Bohemian musicians active in Germany, who spent fifty-three years in Frederick's service. This painting by Adolph von Menzel dates from 1852.

Anthology Vol 2-2
Full CD III, 2

We can see an illuminating example of musical *Empfindsamkeit* in CPE's Fantasia in C Minor, which he published as a *Probestück*, a "try-out piece," to illustrate the *Essay* in 1753. Its style is utterly different from WF's sonata, and there is nothing like it in the works of his recently deceased father.

The Fantasia opens with something that at first seems a contradiction in terms: an instrumental recitative, "sung" here as if by a superhuman singer with a multi-octave range (Ex. 12-2). (In an earlier keyboard work, the *Andante* of the second of his six so-called Prussian Sonatas, CPE had explicitly marked a similar passage "recitative.") This recourse to a patently operatic style—and the style associated in opera with "speaking," at that—suggests that the *empfindsamer Stil* communicates, as it were, an unspoken text. An operatic recitative is traditionally a formless style of music that follows the intonation of the words. Without an actual text to set in such a fantasy, the music comes, as CPE writes in his treatise, directly "from the soul" and communicates a sensibility that transcends the limiting medium of words. Such an **instrumental recitative** implies a direct address from the composer to the listener, who is taken, as it were, into the composer's confidence. The impression created is that of an individual intimately addressing a peer. It is therefore little surprise that CPE's favorite instrument for conveying this impression was the **clavichord**, an instrument capable of dynamic gradations unavailable on the harpsichord, but much softer, more in the nature of a private conversation.

Although the opening of the Fantasia in C Minor sports a purely conventional signature denoting "common time," there are no bar lines and hence no measures to count, signaling a restlessly fluctuating tempo. Approximately halfway through the piece, however, a time signature of $\frac{3}{4}$ supersedes the original one, measured out so that the new tempo (*Largo*) is strictly maintained, and what amounts to an "arioso" temporarily follows the recitative. Here the power of dynamics to delineate quick emotional changes comes into its own; rapid-fire alternations of *fortissimo* and *piano*, with the *fortissimos* on the offbeats, amount to virtual palpitations.

Example 12-2 C. P. E. Bach, Fantasia in C Minor

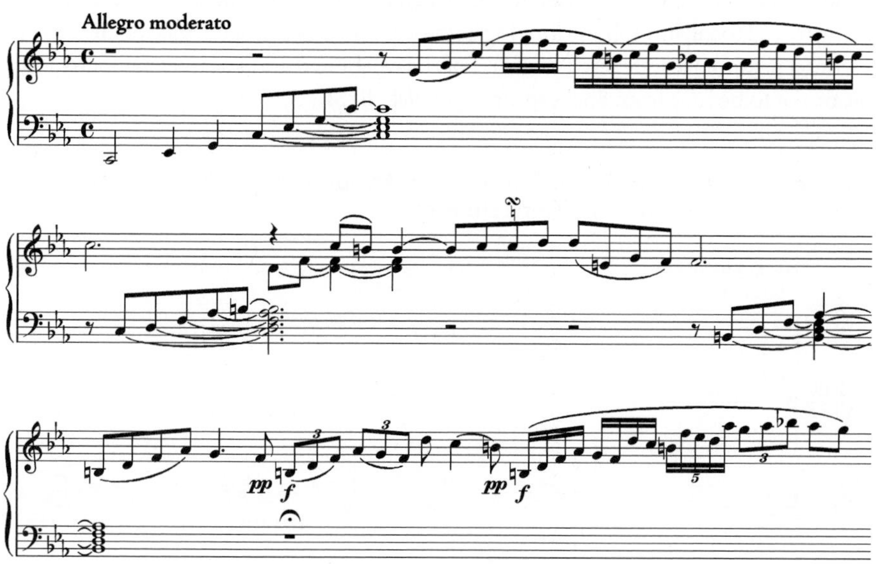

The fantasia style that opens the piece, with its rhythmic indefiniteness and increasing harmonic waywardness, is something more often improvised than actually composed, as CPE Bach informs us in his *Essay*. This is a helpful reminder that the written music on which we base our telling of history was still—is always—just the tip of the iceberg. Indeed, the vogue for *Empfindsamkeit* lent improvisation a new prestige, with CPE strongly implying that the ability to improvise is the foundation of true musical talent: "It is quite possible for a person to have studied composition with good success and to have turned his pen to fine ends without his having any gift for improvisation. But, on the other hand, a good future in composition can be assuredly predicted for anyone who can improvise, provided that he writes profusely and does not start too late."[6] A **fantasia**, then, might be characterized as a transcribed improvisation. J. S. Bach, a master improviser, wrote down only a few. For him a fantasia was usually the equivalent of a prelude—not a fully viable piece in its own right but, rather, an introduction to a strict composition. CPE wrote down many more and was inclined, in the spirit of *Empfindsamkeit*, to regard them as freestanding, complete compositions.

Transcending Words—And Putting Them Back

By casting the Fantasia in C Minor in the recognizable vocal form of a recitative and arioso and by employing an idiom that apes the nuances of passionate singing, CPE suggests an imaginary text of which the music is the intensified expression, faithfully tracking every fugitive shade of meaning and feeling. So clearly does such instrumental music aspire to the condition of speech-song in its immediacy, and so convincingly does this fantasia conjure up an imaginary, internal theater, that in 1767 the poet Heinrich Wilhelm von Gerstenberg (1727–1823), a close friend of Klopstock and an acquaintance of CPE, was moved to furnish this exact instrumental fantasia with two new vocal lines. They mainly double what was singable in the right-hand figuration. The first is fitted to a German translation of Socrates's speech before being forced to kill himself by drinking hemlock in Plato's dialogue *Phaedo*; the second carries a paraphrase in fevered doggerel of the celebrated equivocating soliloquy ("To be, or not to be . . .") from Shakespeare's *Hamlet* (Ex. 12-3).

Example 12-3 **C. P. E. Bach, Fantasia in C Minor, with Shakespeare text overlaid by Gerstenberg**

Invoking Shakespeare was a particularly pointed commentary on the *empfindsamer Stil*. Gerstenberg was a leader in the so-called *Sturm und Drang* (Storm and Stress) movement, a loose literary association that sought to exalt spontaneous subjectivity and unrestrained genius over accepted rules of art. Shakespeare was their hero. Discovered by the Germans exactly around this time in translations by the poet Christoph Martin Wieland, the great English playwright was emulated for his mixture of prose and poetry, tragedy and comedy, elevated and lowly characters and diction. In comparison with the neoclassical style of the French theater or the high style of Italian opera seria at the time, Shakespeare seemed to subvert all restraints in the name of unmediated passionate expression.

The means by which the new instrumental music would transcend the vocal were nevertheless borrowed from the vocal.

Gerstenberg believed that a style combining the declamatory freedom of recitative and the semantic specificity of words would synthesize, and hence surpass, all previous achievements in drama and music. In an important and quite obvious sense, however, Gerstenberg and those who thought like him had missed the point. CPE's intention in creating his *empfindsamer Stil* was not to express texts, however finely. For doing that, needless to say, there were plenty of precedents. Rather, his aim was to transcend texts—that is, to achieve a level of pure musical expressivity, which language, bound as it was to specific meanings, could never reach. Instrumental music could do so, moreover, with a virtuosity in the range of notes, high and low registers, and capacity for fancy runs, all of which would be impossible for any human voice to achieve. This expressive music of which CPE was the fully self-conscious harbinger was later called "absolute music" in heated nineteenth-century debates. This is the first time we have seen instrumental music that was deemed to have decisively surpassed vocal music in spiritual content and to be consequently more valuable as art.

And yet, to compound the paradox, the means by which the new instrumental music would transcend the vocal were nevertheless borrowed from the vocal. To Gerstenberg himself, CPE once wrote that "the human voice remains preeminent"[7] as an expressive medium, and in his *Essay* he advises keyboard players to "miss no opportunity of hearing capable singers," for "from this one learns to think in terms of song."[8] Only in this way can one translate one's ever-fleeting, ever-changing feelings into tones. Here at last we begin to get an inkling of the source of the tremendous metamorphosis in musical style and aesthetics that took place over the course of the eighteenth century, decisively transforming the music of Bach's sons, along with everyone else's, and inevitably opening up a striking generation gap. The ferment was caused by opera and other vocal genres, the sources from which CPE got his models for the instrumental recitative that Gerstenberg turned back into vocal music. The new style emphasized the most unstable aspects of opera, particularly recitative—musical speech—and therefore seems a throwback to the earliest days of opera, around 1600.

The London Bach: Johann Christian

To see another side of opera's stylistic impact on instrumental music, we will consider the work of a composer who wrote both operas and sonatas. And that means examining the work of yet another Bach son—the youngest one, Johann Christian (1735–82, henceforth "JC"; Fig. 12-3).

Figure 12-3 J. C. Bach. Portrait by Thomas Gainsborough.

The half-brother of WF and CPE, Johann Christian Bach became the most famous member of the family. Unlike his elder brothers, JC followed a career completely at variance with his father's. In some ways, in fact, it resembled Handel's—in its restlessness, its worldliness, and even its geographical trajectory. His main teacher was CPE, with whom he went to live in Berlin after their father's death. In 1755, at age nineteen, he made a fateful trip to Italy, where he took some additional instruction from educator "Padre" Giovanni Battista Martini (1706–84). By 1760 he was an organist at Milan Cathedral, having first converted to Catholicism in order to qualify for the job. During the same year he wrote his first opera seria, *Artaserse*, to Metastasio's libretto. From there he was summoned to Naples, opera's very nerve center, and in 1762 he received an invitation to compose for the King's Theatre in London, Handel's old haunt.

Just as in Handel's day, music in London was to a larger extent than anywhere else a public, commercial affair. JC's career followed the ups and downs of the market, with his most lucrative prospects for printed music being keyboard and chamber pieces for domestic use ("such as ladies can execute with little trouble," to quote music historian Charles Burney, an admiring friend of the composer).[9] Together with Carl Friedrich Abel (1723–87), a composer and string virtuoso, JC founded the British capital's most successful concert series, the Bach-Abel Concerts. At the same time, he maintained his ties with the opera stage—ties as much personal as professional, since he married a leading Italian soprano, Cecilia Grassi. His fame brought operatic commissions from the continent—notably from the famously musical court at Mannheim, in the German Rhineland, and even from Paris, where he set some old librettos that had previously served Lully. All in all, JC was the most versatile—and, for a while, the most fashionable—composer of his generation, turning out music in every contemporary medium and for every possible outlet. Like Handel, he could boast of being a self-made man. Unlike Handel, however, he did not die wealthy, but was so deeply in debt that it took the queen's intervention to get him decently buried and to enable his widow to return home to Italy.

Anthology Vol 2-3
Full CD III, 3

JC's first set of six keyboard sonatas was his Opus 5 ("for the Piano Forte or Harpsichord" as the title page stipulates) dates from 1766. The second item in the set is in D major, a brilliant key associated with orchestral music in which strings and brass alike are at their most naturally resonant. The sonata catches a bit of that brilliance. It sounds like a transcribed orchestral piece—more specifically, like a transcribed operatic overture of the kind JC had already composed in quantity. It was literally child's play a few years later for the sixteen-year-old Mozart, already an experienced composer, to give the sonata full orchestral dress in the guise of a Piano Concerto in D Major, K. 107, after he met JC in London during one of his youthful concert tours.

Music in London was to a larger extent than anywhere else a public, commercial affair.

The style of the sonata is the purest galant idiom, witty and ingratiating. The balanced phrases and short-range contrasts that we have observed in WF's sonatas have become so pronounced that they came to be regarded as his personal signature. "[JC] Bach seems to have been the first composer who observed the law of *contrast* as a *principle*," wrote Dr. Burney in his *General History of Music*, exaggerating only slightly. "Before his time, contrast there frequently was, in the works of others, but it seems to have been merely accidental," he went on (exaggerating a bit more, perhaps, in his enthusiasm), whereas Bach "seldom failed, after a rapid and noisy passage, to introduce one that was slow and soothing."[10]

Burney might have had in mind the opening of JC's first movement: two measures of loud chordal fanfare followed immediately by two measures of soft, continuous music, followed next by a balancing repetition of the whole four-measure complex (Ex. 12-4). Contrast and balance operate in other dimensions as well: The loud measures describe an octave's descent, for example, while the soft ones describe an octave's ascent; the former are confined to the tonic harmony, while the latter intermix tonic and dominant. Meanwhile, the texture is the work of a composer who seems, despite his surname, never to have heard of counterpoint, consisting of a well-defined melody against an equally well-defined accompaniment.

Example 12-4 J. C. Bach, Sonata in D, Op. 5, No. 2, I, mm. 1-8

The hallmarks of what would much later come to be called the **Classical style** are fully evident—short, well-defined phrases in the upper register are set above unassuming accompaniments, often with formulaic bass patterns. The most common of such patterns, three-note chords broken low-high-middle-high, has been known ever since the eighteenth century as the ***Alberti bass***, after Domenico Alberti (ca. 1710–46), an Italian composer who famously abused it (Ex. 12-5). The periodic phrases tend to be evenly balanced. Those ending on the dominant, requiring continuation, are "antecedents"; their balancing "consequents" often begin like repetitions, creating "parallel periods."

Example 12-5 J. C. Bach, Sonata in D, Op. 5, No. 2

Sociability in Music

Although it is notoriously easy to overdraw such matters, comparing CPE's Fantasy in C Minor with JC's Sonata in D Major shows up the two complementary sides of what might be called the domestic music of the mid-eighteenth century.

CPE's is solitary, introspective, inner-directed music; JC's is sociable, outgoing. CPE explores personal, private, even unexpressed feelings; we easily imagine this music performed for an audience of one (or even none but the player, seated alone at the clavichord), late at night, in a mood of emotional self-absorption, pondering, perhaps, whether "to be, or not to be." JC offers party music, implying many candles, company, a surrounding hubbub of conversation. That about sums up the difference between *Empfindung* and *galanterie*, and it is no accident that the one word is German and the other French.

It was the convivial spirit of galanterie *that gave rise to what we now call chamber music.*

It was the convivial spirit of *galanterie* that gave rise to what we now call chamber music in its modern sense. The first pieces of this kind, in fact, grew directly out of the keyboard sonata and happened initially in France. The earliest composers to attempt the transformation of keyboard sonatas into sociable ensembles were a couple of forgotten Parisian violinists: Jean-Joseph Cassanéa de Mondonville (1711–72) and Louis-Gabriel Guillemain (1705–70). As early as 1734 Mondonville published, as his Opus 3, a set of *Pièces de clavecin en sonates avec accompagnement de violon*, "harpsichord pieces grouped into sonatas, accompanied by a violin." What he offered merely as a colorful novelty quickly took root as a new musical genre, which turned into a craze.

The **accompanied keyboard sonata** initiated by Mondonville was (in theory, at least) a fully composed, self-sufficient keyboard sonata to which a violin or flute part could be added *ad libitum*, "at the pleasure of the performer." By the 1760s, accompanied keyboard sonatas were being written everywhere, and J. C. Bach and his London colleague Abel had become preeminent in this typically galant genre. In fact, JC published nearly twice as many accompanied keyboard sonatas as unaccompanied ones, which gives an idea of the genre's quick ascendancy, a rise that testifies above all to its social utility. Even CPE was moved to try his hand at this profitable genre, if only half-heartedly. According to a famous quip of JC's (like all such reported comments, possibly of questionable authenticity), "my brother lives to compose and I compose to live."[11] It would be hard to come up with a better encapsulation of *Empfindsamkeit* in relation to *galanterie*!

Intermission Plays

The music we have been examining in this chapter thus far is part of an emerging cult of the "natural," as opposed to the "artificial." Where did this natural preference come from? And where did the new style we have been tracking originate? For yet another clue we could briefly mention the instrumental music of the Venetian opera composer Baldassare Galuppi (1706–85), who in addition to his stage works left more than 100 eminently galant keyboard sonatas. The evident model for these sonatas was graceful singing, for what else would one expect from a composer who worked mainly for the stage?

Beginning in the late 1740s, Galuppi was the first major international protagonist of a new operatic genre, one that he and his main librettist, Carlo Goldoni (1707–93), called ***dramma giocoso*** (humorous drama) and that took Europe by storm as ***opera buffa*** (from *buffo*, Italian for buffoon or clown). If opera seria was a form of nobly sublimated musical tragedy, opera buffa was musical comedy—the earliest form of full-fledged comic opera. It is with comic opera that we find the great stylistic transformer of European music, the spark that ignited the musical revolution that somehow managed to take place behind the backs of Bach the Father and Handel the Cosmopolitan. In comic opera lies the common source for all the musical styles we have been tracking thus far, even the *empfindsamer Stil* exemplified by CPE. And as we shall see, by the time of Mozart's mature operas in the 1780s, opera buffa would decisively replace (or, more precisely, displace) the seria as the most vital—and even the most serious! —form of musical theater. To appreciate the role of "humorous drama" as a hotbed of stylistic transformation we must look first at its own antecedents.

During opera's first century, especially at the public theaters of Venice, it was often considered desirable and profitable to mix serious and comic scenes and characters, producing a kind of heterogeneous Shakespearean experience that gave audiences varied entertainment. Then the reformers got to work to steer things back to high-mindedness. In their efforts to restore the dignity of the earliest courtly operas and to justify the genre in light of Classical poetic theory, comic scenes were viewed as breaches of taste and banished.

But what is kicked out the front door often climbs back in through the window. The public, especially in Venice, was unwilling to give up favorite operatic treats, both the comedies themselves and the singers who performed them. Thus arose in the first decade of the eighteenth century a curious compromise: The newly standardized opera seria remained free of any taint of comedy, but little comic plays with music were shown during the intermissions. These, naturally enough, were called ***intermezzos***, or intermission plays. Usually in two short acts, they featured two bickering characters, a soprano and a bass, and were presented in between acts of a typical three-act opera seria.

The first big international hit, *Il marito giocatore e la moglie bacchettona* (The Gambler Husband and the Bigoted Wife) by Giuseppe Maria Orlandini (1676–1760), premiered in 1715 and was performed all over Italy and beyond. In keeping with the strictest Aristotelian principles, according to which tragedy portrayed "people better than ourselves" and comedy "people worse than ourselves," Orlandini's arias provide "low" music at an extreme.[12] Everything is impoverished, with textures reduced to unisons, vocal lines that are barely articulate cries of rage, and structures that are a patchwork of little sniffles, snorts, and wheezes. It might all seem a parody, and yet it came, particularly to foreign audiences, as an absolute revelation.

If opera seria was a form of nobly sublimated musical tragedy, opera buffa was musical comedy.

One of the most precious testimonials to that revelation can be found with Denis Diderot (1713–84; Fig. 12-4), the famous French encyclopedist, in his satire *Le neveu de Rameau* (Rameau's Nephew), written early in the 1760s, while the elder Rameau was still alive. From the mouth of his fictional character Diderot voiced the widespread amazement of French artists and thinkers at the art of the *buffi*: "What realism! What expression!" he exclaims. And to those who might scoff—"Expression of what?!"—he spells it out with ardor bordering on anger: "It is the animal cry of passion that should dictate the melodic line, and these moments should tumble out quickly one after the other, phrases must be short and the meaning self-contained."[13]

What Diderot describes fits perfectly with the revolutionary new style of musical discourse heard in the music of Bach's sons: melodies differing from one

Figure 12-4 "Instrument making" (*Lutherie*) from Denis Diderot's *Encyclopédie*.

another over an unassuming accompaniment and short phrases that are musically and expressively self-contained. In this they are balanced and contrasted, and they can therefore express emotions the way they naturally present themselves in the real physical—or "animal"—world. This protean changeability was the very quality we have already isolated as the essential, inexplicable newness of midcentury instrumental music. Its freshness and elemental simplicity gave the lowly comic music of the intermezzos an air of perfect naturalness that made it tremendously influential. In an age that still regarded the purpose of art as imitation of nature, this could be viewed as an improved art.

An aria of exasperated comic rage in an opera buffa contrasts remarkably with Handel's high style, as we encountered, for example, in the rage aria "Empio, dirò, tu sei" from *Giulio Cesare in Egitto*. We have already seen one comic, naturalizing response to Handel in Gay's *The Beggar's Opera*, where the use of the audience's native language, English, further drew in the listener. So, too, in the new Italian intermezzos, grand Handelian rhetoric stood revealed as the product of labored, contrived, unnatural artifice. The art of tragedy was the high rhetorical style, while the simple, low art of comedy was born of nature. It was "true." The musical agent of change in the eighteenth century was the music of comedy.

The "War of the Buffoons"—Giovanni Battista Pergolesi

Anthology Vol 2-4
Full CD III, 4–5
Concise CD II, 8

The great masterwork of the intermezzo genre was *La serva padrona* (The Maid as Mistress) by the precocious Giovanni Battista Pergolesi (1710–36), a Neapolitan composer who died of tuberculosis at the age of twenty-six and who became, partly for that reason, a figure of enduring fame (Fig. 12-5). In his short life Pergolesi managed to compose ten works for the stage, including four serious operas (two to texts by Metastasio) and three two-part intermezzos.

La serva padrona, written expressly to be played between the acts of one of Pergolesi's own serious operas, was first performed in Naples on 5 September 1733. While the evening's main event, *Il prigioniero superbo* (The Proud Prisoner), was forgotten, the intermezzo soon became extraordinarily famous, thanks to performances by traveling troupes of *buffi* who within ten years took it all around Italy and as far away as Munich, Dresden, and Hamburg. By the end of the 1740s it had been heard in Paris, and within another decade it had conquered London, Madrid, and St. Petersburg. *La serva padrona* is still occasionally performed, the earliest comic opera in the standard repertory.

Figure 12-5 Late-eighteenth-century portrait of Giovanni Battista Pergolesi, done after his early death had made him a figure of Romantic legend.

Its plot and cast of characters are of the usual kind, a contest between squabbling soprano and buffo bass. There are two sung roles, the maid Serpina and her master and guardian, Uberto, plus a mute role (Vespone, another servant) who gets to laugh once. The importance of conventions to this genre is epitomized by the heroine's name. Serpina (from *serpe,* snake) is the sharp-tongued female, a stock figure ultimately derived from the old *commedia dell'arte,* the traditional theater of masks and clowns. She delivers a great deal of the fast-paced patter that made the comic style so irresistible.

Both parts of the intermezzo contain short arias for each of the characters and a culminating duet. In the first part, the master stews over the maid's insolent behavior, finally telling Vespone to go out and find him a wife. Serpina orders Uberto to marry her; he won't hear of it; she locks the doors to prevent Vespone from leaving, and the two of them erupt in sarcastic bickering. In the second part, Serpina disguises Vespone as "Capitan Tempesta" (Captain Storm), her threatening bully of a fiancé, who is demanding from Uberto an impossible dowry. The only way out of a fight with the captain, she insinuates, is for him to agree to marry her himself. After a lot of coaxing and some agonized reflection, he gives in; Vespone removes his disguise; Uberto's been had, but he's happy. The newly engaged couple sings a duet of reconciliation. Opera of this kind demands comic contrasts. Gone was the "unity of affect" in which the opera seria had found its version of truth, and in its stead we encounter the psychological, dramatic, and representational roots of the contrast-and-balance technique that became fundamental even to instrumental music by century's end.

La serva padrona was brought to Paris, along with Orlandini's *Giocatore* and a dozen other intermezzos and comic operas, by an opera buffa troupe for a twenty-month run of more than 150 performances beginning in August 1752 (Fig. 12-6). The furor the company created led to heated debates concerning Italian versus French opera, the funny naturalist comedies versus the artificial *tragédies lyriques.* The controversy had extraordinary repercussions in the French capital and in its cultural satellites both in France and abroad. The so-called ***Querelle des Bouffons*** (Dispute of the Comic Actors or War of the Buffoons), with its stellar cast of characters, foreshadowed not only musical change, but also social and political change.

The musical agent of change in the eighteenth century was the music of comedy.

Such debates, with the opposing factions publishing open letters, pamphlets, and newspaper articles, had long been a feature of France's lively intellectual and musical life, as we have seen earlier in the conflict between the proponents of Lully and of Rameau. Moreover, in the context of an absolute monarchy, political, religious, and social issues could not be debated openly; they instead had to go underground, into highly suggestive and implied cultural

LA SERVA PADRONA
INTERMEZZO.
Del Sig.r Giõ. Batta. Pergolese.
Rappresentato in Pariggi nell' Autunno 1752.
A PARIS
Aux Adresses Ordinaires
Et chez l'Editeur rue Grenelle S.t Honoré a l'Hotel de Languedoc
Prix. 9tt Avec Privilége du Roi.

Figure 12-6 Title page of a French edition of *La serva padrona* by Giovanni Battista Pergolesi, 1752.

criticism. The debates about music, therefore, worked on various levels, and the stakes were more than aesthetic.

The writings of Jean-Jacques Rousseau (1712–78; Fig. 12-7), one of the leading figures of the Enlightenment, vividly show the political stakes. In his scathing "Letter on French Music" (November 1753), he ridiculed the high-minded *tragédies lyriques* performed by the royal musical establishment as stilted, devoid of naturalness, ugly in harmony, and ungainly in text-setting. Rousseau's participation in the debates was unusual because he did more than just argue. An enthusiastic if rudimentarily trained amateur composer, he had geared up for his attack with a one-act "intermède" of his own, *Le devin du village* (The Village Soothsayer, 1752), composed in obvious emulation of Italian intermezzos. Although written to his own French text and in a simple style that recalled French folk songs more than anything Italian, this was nevertheless "comic" music, intended as an object lesson to his musical countrymen.

Figure 12-7 Jean-Jacques Rousseau. Portrait by Maurice Quentin de La Tour.

Rousseau's appeals to natural virtue, and his attacks on the traditional musical repertoire of the royal court were linked: Both were veiled expressions of his philosophical and political hostility to the monarchical order. Diderot also expressed subversive ideas through his fictionalized "nephew of Rameau," who wished to cast his detestable uncle's work into oblivion while reveling in "the modern style" of the Italians. For "modern style" here, we can read "modern philosophy" between the lines. Among those who shared Rousseau's and Diderot's views, the *Querelle des Bouffons* was a covert forum for spreading the complex of ideas now collectively referred to as "enlightened." Rousseau came close to making all of this explicit in his *Confessions* (1782), where he stated that Italian intermezzos "struck a blow from which French opera never recovered."[14] It could be claimed with equal, imperfect, but pointed justice that the *Querelle des Bouffons*, a long generation before the French Revolution of 1789, struck the beginnings of a blow from which not only the *tragédie lyrique* but also the absolutist monarchy itself never fully recovered.

Novels Sung on Stage—Niccolò Piccinni

Throughout the eighteenth century, opera and its many "reforms" continued to reflect the social history of the age. That is why opera criticism so often makes exciting reading, even when the composers, operas, and performers discussed have been long forgotten. Both by design and by its nature, critical debate can mean far more than it says and carry weighty "subtexts," the stuff you read between the lines. If we fast-forward from the *Querelle des Bouffons* to the next opera controversy, some two decades later, we again see the interaction of the musical and the political.

Although the operas of Niccolò Piccinni (1728–1800) soon enough disappeared from the repertory, he was a prominent and controversial figure in his own day. He became the focal point of a "cause" and, in his rivalry with the somewhat older and much better-remembered Christoph Willibald Ritter von Gluck (1714–87), the object of another *querelle*, another Parisian pamphlet dispute. The issues Piccinni's career raised for contemporary audiences, critics, and composers continued to reverberate long after his death and once again had social as well as musical import. His most famous opera, *La buona figliuola* (The Virtuous Maiden), was one of the earliest to be based on a novel, then a new literary genre, with distinct social implications of its own. The opera's success was virtually unprecedented: Between its Roman premiere in 1760 and the end of the century, it enjoyed more than seventy productions across Europe in various languages.

Anthology Vol 2-5
Full CD III, 6

Figure 12-8 Pamela and Mr. B. in the Summerhouse, from the novel *Pamela, or Virtue Rewarded* by Samuel Richardson, published 1740. Painting ca. 1744 by Joseph Highmore.

Its plot came by way of Samuel Richardson's *Pamela, or Virtue Rewarded* (1740), an English novel that the title page announces is "in a series of Familiar Letters from a Beautiful Young Damsel to her Parents. Published in order to cultivate the principles of virtue and religion in the minds of the youth of both sexes." It tells the story of a chaste maidservant who so resourcefully resists the crass advances of her employer's son that the young man finally falls seriously in love with her and marries her with his family's blessing (Fig. 12-8). *Pamela* achieved phenomenal popularity with a new class of bourgeois readers, the same readership that made the novel the paramount literary genre for centuries to come. Like readers today, this audience was especially susceptible to Richardson's idealistic moral: that virtues and emotions can be practiced by all and can break down artificial barriers of class and rank. Maid and aristocrat find happiness together, much as we saw with *La serva padrona*. For aristocrats, then, the moral "love conquers all" was socially ominous. The eighteenth-century English novel was, among other things, a celebration—and, potentially, a breeding ground—of social mobility. Ever since, the *Pamela* motif has been a stock-in-trade of bourgeois fiction, in which a humble girl finds her prince, count, or millionaire.

The shape of a comic libretto depended on a plot that at first is hopelessly tangled and then is sorted out.

Translated into Italian, the novel attracted the attention of Goldoni, the leading Italian dramatist of the century as well as an active librettist. His main mission in life, as he saw it, was replacing the improvised *commedia dell'arte* with literary comedies that had fully worked-out scripts and contemporary realistic situations, worthy of comparison with celebrated playwrights like Molière and William Congreve, the mainstays of the French and English stage. Goldoni found in *Pamela* the makings of a hit, but he realized that Italian audiences would not consider the plot sufficiently believable and knew that censors policed the theater far more than they did novels. Some funny things happened, therefore, to Richardson's story on its way to the stage. The sticking point was the happy ending—or, rather, what made it happy. The elevation of a poor commoner through marriage was not possible according to Italian law; such a marriage would bring about not the elevation of the commoner but the disgrace of the noble. Hence Goldoni was forced to use another plot device, which he found in a case of mistaken identity: Pamela's father turns out to be not a poor schoolteacher but a German baron, and so she can marry her noble lover with impunity.

We may now think this turn of events lame, but at the time it made the story more convincing, not less. We know the device of mistaken identity the only way we can know it now—through a screen of cynical nineteenth-century satires (as in the English operettas of Gilbert and Sullivan) that returned it to the realm of farce. Originally it was just as thrilling a concept as the intervention of a *deus ex machina* had been in an earlier age: It was the device through which the genre's approved values—true love and artless virtue—found their just reward.

Operas eventually divided into those in which people die (tragic) and those in which they marry (comic)—but both, increasingly, do so for love, not duty. That change was the great sentimental innovation and hallmark of middle-class taste. It flew directly in the face of the aristocratic opera seria, at first its chief competitor, which celebrated noble renunciation. It marked the point at which comic opera could begin to go beyond the farce situations of the intermezzos and carry a serious or uplifting message of its own. That serious message was nothing less than a competing set of class values—the aspirations of those whose power had begun to threaten that of hereditary privilege. In Italian the new genre was eventually christened *opera semiseria*; in French, more revealingly, it was called *comédie larmoyante* (tearful comedy). In both, the happy ending was reached by way of tears and therefore carried ethical weight. But instead of the weight of traditional social obligation, it was the weight of an implied demand to be artlessly true to one's feelings.

Figure 12-9 Christoph Willibald Gluck. Portrait by Joseph Siffred Duplessis (1775).

One aspect of comic opera, noticeable already in Pergolesi, received a boost from Piccinni. The shape of a comic libretto depended on a plot that at first is hopelessly tangled and then is sorted out. Both the tangle (*imbroglio*) and the sorting were symbolized in complex ensemble finales in which all the characters participated. In an intermezzo like *La serva padrona*, these were mere duets. In full-length opera buffa, they could be scenes of great length and complexity, in which the changing dramatic situation was registered by numbers following on one another without any recitative, all to be played at a whirlwind pace that challenged any composer's imaginative and technical resources. The first two acts of *La buona figliuola* end with quintets, the third and last with nothing less than an octet, representing the full cast of characters. This innovation of complex comic finales would have a long run: Mozart and Gioachino Rossini brought it to delicious heights, and in the second half of the nineteenth century the two principal opera composers, Richard Wagner and Giuseppe Verdi, would construct ingenious finales for their comic masterpieces, *Die Meistersinger von Nürnberg* and *Falstaff*, respectively.

Noble Simplicity—Christoph Willibald Gluck

On the other side of the midcentury debate about opera were the "reforms" of Gluck (Fig. 12-9). Although mostly opposed to the style and attitudes of Piccinni's masterpiece of sentimental comedy, Gluck's **reform operas** embodied a similar infusion of sensibility. He too wanted his operas to be natural and true to real life. Famous for declaring that when composing he tried to forget that he was a musician, he strove to avoid the sort of decorative musicality that called attention to itself—and away from the drama. The implicit target of Gluck's reform was the Metastasian opera seria with all its dazzling artifices.

But where Piccinni in his comic operas sought to replace those artifices with the new sensibilities of the sentimental novel, Gluck sought to replace them by returning to the most ancient ways, as then understood. His was a self-consciously neoclassical art, stripped down and, compared with opera seria, virtually denuded. The preface to *Alceste* (1767), his second "reform" opera, based on a tragedy by Euripides, declared that in writing the music Gluck had consciously aimed "to divest it entirely of all those abuses, introduced either by the mistaken vanity of singers or by the too great complaisance of composers, which have so long disfigured Italian opera and made the most splendid and most beautiful of spectacles the most ridiculous and wearisome," just as his librettist, Ranieri Calzabigi (1714–95), had sought to eliminate "the florid descriptions, unnatural paragons and sententious, cold morality" of the unnamed but obviously targeted Metastasio.[15]

Gluck's reform was partly a process of elimination.

Gluck's first reform opera, appropriately, was *Orfeo ed Euridice*, which premiered in Vienna in 1762 and was yet another retelling of the legend that had midwifed the very birth of opera more than a century and a half earlier with Peri, Caccini, and Monteverdi. In place of the elaborate hierarchy of paired roles that Metastasio employed, Gluck's *Orfeo* has only three characters—the title duo plus Cupid, the hero's ally in his quest. The music they sing, despite the loftiness of the theme, for the most part avoids the artificial, ritualized rhetoric of high passion—namely, the heroic coloratura demanding the sort of virtuoso singing that had brought opera seria its popular acclaim as well as in some quarters its critical disrepute. With such musical eloquence now attacked as decadent and luxurious, Gluck's reform was partly a process of elimination. His ideals and rhetoric derived from what in his day was called "the true style" by its partisans.

The legitimate connection between this attitude and Greek antiquity came about as a result of contemporary achievements in archaeology, most spectacularly the unearthing of the ancient Roman cities of Herculaneum and Pompeii between 1738 and 1748 and the theories to which they gave rise. The main theorizer was the German archaeologist and art historian Johann Joachim Winckelmann (1717–68), whose first important work in aesthetics was *Gedanken über die Nachahmung der griechischen Werke in der Malerei und Bildhauerkunst* (Thoughts on the Imitation of Greek Works in Painting and Sculpture, 1755). The phrase he used to summarize the qualities in Greek art that he wanted to see imitated—"a noble simplicity and a calm grandeur"—became a watchword of the age, echoed and re-echoed in the writings of his contemporaries, including Gluck.

The heritage of the older opera seria nevertheless survives in Gluck's *Orfeo ed Euridice* as well—most obviously in the language of the libretto, but also in the use of an alto castrato for the male title role and in the high ethical tone that continues, newly purified and restored, to reign over the telling of the tale. Where Monteverdi's Orpheus had looked back on Eurydice and lost her again out of sheer weakness, the inability to resist a spontaneous impulse, Gluck's hero does so out of stoic resolution and strength of character. In response to Eurydice's bewildered pleas, Orpheus turns and looks to reassure her of his love, even though it means he must lose her. His act, in other words, has been turned into one of noble self-sacrifice: the classic seria culmination.

In other ways, Gluck's opera follows the conventions of the French *tragédie lyrique*, the majestic spectacle of the "ancient" and "divine" Lully, lately declared a classical model for imitation by French artists eager to relive the glorious achievements of the Great Age of Louis XIV. Gluck's unique mixture of what were normally considered adverse ingredients was typical of him; he was a true cosmopolitan, who had grown up in Austrian Bohemia. According to his protégé Antonio Salieri (1750–1825), his native language was Czech; "he expressed himself in German only with effort, and still more so in French and Italian. . . .

Figure 12-10 Christoph Willibald Gluck's *Il Parnasso Confuso* as performed at the Schönbrunn Palace, Vienna, in 1765.

Usually he mixed several languages together during a conversation."[16] He did the same in his music (Fig. 12-10).

The *tragédie lyrique*, the type of French musical theater Gluck chose to emulate in *Orfeo*, was, as we know, the courtliest of all court operas, and it might seem that Gluck's reform was aimed in the opposite direction from Piccinni's innovations. It was to be a reassertion of the aristocratic values that the recent seria had diluted with singerly excess, the values that opera buffa owed its very existence to deriding. Here the main impetus came from Gluck's librettist, Calzabigi, an Italian-born poet then resident in Vienna, who had boldly set himself up as a rival to the lordly court poet Metastasio.

Anthology Vol 2-6a
Full CD III, 7
Concise CD II, 9

Thus the first scene in the Gluck-Calzabigi *Orfeo ed Euridice* is a formal choral elegy, sung by Orpheus's entourage of nymphs and shepherds, which corresponds roughly with the one at the end of the second act of Monteverdi's *L'Orfeo*. Eurydice is already dead. The horrifying news of her demise and Orpheus's reaction to it, so central to Monteverdi's confrontational drama, is not shown. This will be an opera of reflection, of moods savored and considered, not instantaneously experienced. The aim of austerity—of striking powerfully and deep with the starkest simplicity of means—is epitomized by Orpheus in this first scene. His whole part amounts to nothing more than three stony exclamations of Eurydice's name—twelve notes in all, using only four pitches. It would be hard to conceive of anything more elemental. Gluck once advised a singer to cry the name out in the tone of voice he'd use if his leg were being sawn off—Diderot's "animal cry of passion" in the most literal terms.

Orpheus then sends his mourning friends away in a grave recitative, whereupon they take their ceremonious leave of him through another round of eloquent song and dance in the French manner. Orpheus's recitative is accompanied by the orchestral strings with all parts written out, not just a figured bass. "Accompanied recitative" or "orchestrated recitative" (*recitativo accompagnato*) had formerly been reserved for just the emotional high points of the earlier opera seria. This was in order to set these especially fraught moments off from the libretto's ordinary dialogue, for which would have sufficed "simple recitative" (*recitativo semplice*), later known as "dry recitative" (*recitativo secco*). In Gluck's opera, there was to be no "ordinary" dialogue, only dialogue heavily weighted with sentiment, hence no *recitativo semplice*, only *accompagnato*. It became the first opera that can be performed without the use of continuo-realizing instruments like the harpsichord.

In Gluck's opera, there was to be no "ordinary" dialogue, only dialogue heavily weighted with sentiment.

Considering that basso continuo undergirding simple recitative had been central to the invention of opera around 1600, there could hardly be any greater reform of the medium than this. Paradoxically, the elimination of the continuo had the same purpose as its invention: to adapt an existing (but constantly changing) medium to ever-greater, and ever-more naturalistic, expressive heights. The same combination of high pathos and avoidance of conventional histrionics characterizes Orpheus's arias. In "Che farò senza Euridice?" ("What am I to do without Euridice?") from the third act, Orpheus sings of his grief—but in a noble, dignified manner that is in keeping with the nobility of his deed (Ex. 12-6). That nobility and resignation constitute the aria's dominant affect, expressed through a "beautiful simplicity" (*bella simplicità*) of musical means, as Gluck put it (with Calzabigi's help) in the preface to *Alceste*.

Anthology Vol 2-6b
Full CD III, 8

Piccinni's rustic sentiment and Gluck's classical simplicity were really two sides of the same naturalistic coin. Both were equally, though differently, a sign of the

Example 12-6 Christoph Willibald Gluck, "Che farò senza Euridice" from *Orfeo ed Euridice*, Act III, Scene 1

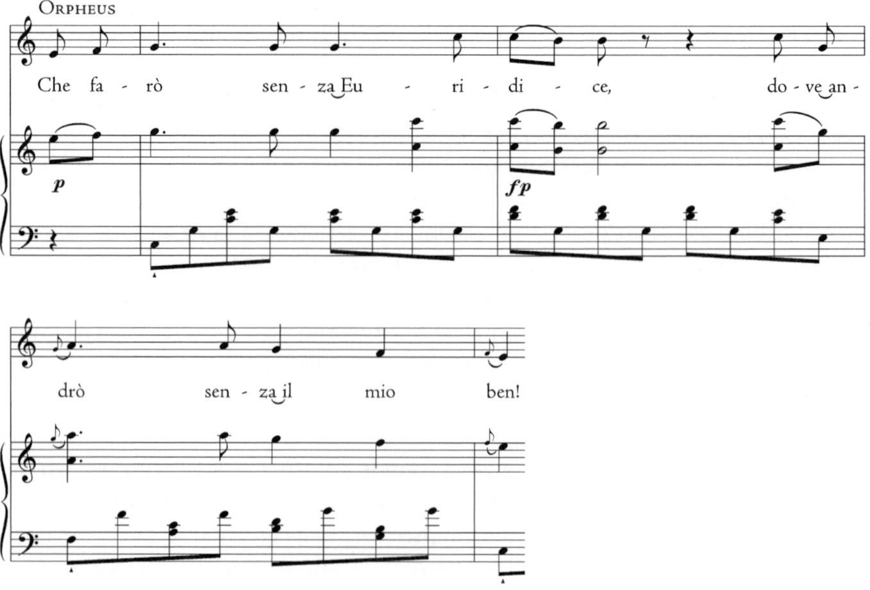

What am I to do without Eurydice? Where will I go without my love?

intellectual, philosophical, and social changes that were taking place over the course of the eighteenth century. Although the two composers could have had no inkling of it in the 1760s, when they first became international celebrities, they were on a collision course.

Gluck naturally gravitated toward Paris, the half-forgotten point of origin for many of his reforms. Having Frenchified the opera seria, he would now try his hand at the real thing—actual *tragédies lyriques*, some of them to librettos originally prepared as much as ninety years earlier for Lully. He arrived in the French capital in 1773 and under the protection of his former singing pupil, Princess Marie-Antoinette, enjoyed fantastic success. He even got old Rousseau to recant some of the brash claims he had made some twenty years before, in the heat of buffoon-battle. After seeing *Iphigénie en Aulide*, Gluck's first *tragédie lyrique*, based on a much-softened libretto after Euripides's bloody tragedy of sacrifice (adapted by Jean Racine), Rousseau confessed to Gluck that "you have realized what I held to be impossible to this very day"—namely, a viable opera on a French text.[17]

The irony was that the same stylistic mixture that had led to a French reform of Italian opera in Gluck's Vienna was now read by the French as a revitalizing Italianization of their own heritage. Perhaps only a Bohemian—a complete outsider to both proud traditions—could have pulled it off. The best symbol of this hybridization of idioms was *Orphée et Eurydice* (1774), a new Parisian version of Gluck's original reform opera. Besides translating the libretto from Italian into French, the male title role was recast so that a high tenor could sing it instead of a castrato. Gluck also added colorfully orchestrated dances and instrumental interludes.

The advocates of Gluck and Piccinni tried hard to fan controversy between the two composers and worked equally hard to cast them: Gluck as the apostle of "dramatic" values, Piccinni of "musical" ones. Compared with the *Querelle des Bouffons*, however, the *Querelle des Gluckistes et Piccinistes* was a pretty tame affair. The stakes, for one thing, were much lower. The main battle—the "noble simplification" and sentimentalization of an encrusted court art—was won before this later quarrel even started, and the two composers, privately on friendly terms, were more nearly allies than rivals.

So perhaps it is from the operatic masterpieces of the age that we can best learn an important lesson: It is a considerable distortion of the way things were to describe the so-called Enlightenment exclusively as an "Age of Reason"—especially if we persist in assuming (as the Romantics would later insist) that thinking and feeling, "mind" and "heart," are in some sense opposites. Gluck and Piccinni show us how far from true this commonly accepted dichotomy really is. The impulse that had led them and their artistic contemporaries to question traditional artifice and attempt the direct portrayal of "universal" human nature was equally the product of free intellect and sympathy—community in feeling. This last was based on introspection, on "looking within." The community it fostered was one that in principle embraced the whole of humanity. The objective of "Enlightened" artists became, in the words of a present-day musicologist, "to move an audience through representations of its own humanity."[18] And not only move but also instruct and inspire goodness: Free intellect and introspective sympathy went hand in hand as ministers to virtue.

The advocates of Gluck and Piccinni tried hard to fan controversy between the two composers.

What Was the Enlightenment?

"Man is born free; and everywhere he is in chains," wrote Rousseau at the beginning of his *The Social Contract* (1762), perhaps the most important political work of the eighteenth century. The chains to which he referred were not only the literal ones of enforced bondage, of slavery, but also the intellectual chains that people seem voluntarily to assume: religious superstition, submission to time-honored authority, acquiescence to unjust social hierarchies for the sake of social order or security. The remedy was knowledge, which empowered an individual to act in accord with rational self-interest and with the "general will" (*sensus communis*) of similarly enlightened individuals. The American revolutionary Thomas Paine, clearly influenced by Rousseau's thinking, cast this as "Common Sense" in the title of his celebrated tract of 1776.

Dissemination of knowledge—and, with it, of freedom and individual empowerment—became the great mission of the times. The most concrete manifestation of that mission was the *Encyclopédie* (1751–72), the mammoth French encyclopedia edited by Denis Diderot and the mathematician Jean d'Alembert (1717–83) with help from a staff of self-styled *philosophes*, or "lovers of knowledge." Among them was Rousseau, who wrote the music articles. By the time the final supplements were issued in 1776 the project had been driven underground, chiefly by the Jesuits, who were enraged at its religious skepticism and persuaded the government of Louis XV to revoke the official license to print. These embattled circumstances only enhanced the prestige of the *Encyclopédie*, giving it a heroic aura as a new forbidden "Tree of Knowledge" and contributing to its enormous cultural and political influence.

That influence can be gauged by a comparison with the famous essay "Beantwortung der Frage: Was ist Aufklärung?" (Answering the Question: What is Enlightenment?) by the German philosopher Immanuel Kant (1724–1804), published in 1784. The answer to the question took the form of a popular Latin motto, originally from Horace: *Sapere aude!* (Dare to know!). "Enlightenment," Kant declared, "is mankind's exit from its self-incurred immaturity," defined as "the inability to make use of one's own understanding without the guidance of another."[19]

Enlightened ideas quickly spread from France to England as well, where free public discussion of social and religious issues was especially far advanced. From England, of course, they spread to the American colonies, as already suggested by comparing Rousseau and Paine. Whether or not (as often claimed in equal measure by its proponents and its detractors) the Enlightenment led directly to the French Revolution of 1789, with its ensuing periods of mob rule, political terror, and civil instability, there can be no doubt that it provided the intellectual justification for the American Revolution of 1776—a revolution led by prosperous, enterprising men of property and education, acting in their own rational and economic self-interest. The Declaration of Independence (1776) and the United States Constitution (1787) can both be counted as documents of the Enlightenment. As mediated through two centuries of amendment and interpretation, moreover, the Constitution with its Bill of Rights, as a legal instrument that is still in force, represents the continuing influence of the Enlightenment in the politics and social philosophy of our own time.

It would be wrong to think, however, of the eighteenth-century Enlightenment within its own time as nothing but a vehicle of civic unrest or rebellion. The *philosophes* themselves believed in strong state power and saw the best realistic hope of freedom in the education of "enlightened despots" who would rule rationally, with enlightened sympathy for the interests of their subjects. A number of European sovereigns were indeed sympathetic to the aims of the Encyclopedists. Frederick the Great of Prussia—C. P. E. Bach's employer, a musician, and a great patron of the arts and sciences, many of which he practiced himself—corresponded with the celebrated French philosopher and writer Voltaire (1694–1778) and entertained d'Alembert at Sans-Souci, his palace in Potsdam. Catherine II ("the Great"), the German-born Empress of Russia and a protégée of Frederick's, corresponded enthusiastically with Diderot. But liberality of an autocrat had its limits. Kant was a bit cynical about Frederick's: "Our ruler," he wrote, "says, '*Argue* as much as you want and about whatever you want, but *obey*!'"[20] And after the French Revolution, which Frederick did not live to see, Catherine turned quite reactionary and imprisoned many Russian followers of her former correspondents.

The prototype of the enlightened despots of eighteenth-century Europe was the Austrian monarch Joseph II (reigned 1765–90; Fig. 12-11). Beginning in 1780, when he came to full power on the death of his mother, Maria Theresa, Joseph instituted liberal reforms on a scale that seemed to many observers positively revolutionary in their extent and speed. He wielded the powers of absolutism, just as the *philosophes* had envisioned, with informed sympathy for the populace of his lands. As he once declared to his brother and successor, Leopold II: "I have weakened deep-rooted traditions by the introduction of enlightened principles."[21]

Joseph annulled hereditary privileges, appropriated church properties and extended freedom of worship, made marriage a civil contract, eliminated torture and the death penalty, instituted a meritocracy within the empire's civil service, reformed the health and educational systems, and relaxed censorship. Yet within several years, given a war with Turkey and financial instability, he was forced to retreat, and few of his reforms outlived him, largely because his successor, Leopold II (reigned 1790–92), was impelled into a reactionary stance by the revolutionary events in France and because Leopold's successor, Francis II (reigned 1792–1835), created what amounted to the first modern police state under the control of the powerful Prince Metternich (1773–1859). This anxious response to the French Revolution on the part of formerly enlightened autocrats is one of many reasons for regarding the political legacy of the great historical watershed of the Enlightenment as ambiguous at best.

> ***Dissemination of knowledge—and, with it, of freedom and individual empowerment—became the great mission of the Enlightenment.***

The unfolding of Enlightenment thought in the second half of the eighteenth century provides the political context, the ideas and ideals, in which worked the three preeminent composers of what much later was dubbed Viennese Classicism. With their births spanning midcentury—Haydn in 1732, Mozart in 1756, and Beethoven in 1770—we can chart changes in career opportunities and choices, aesthetic and musical values, as well as audience expectations and reactions that coincided with Enlightenment politics.

Haydn worked most of his career for an aristocratic family. Mozart sought independence as a "freelance" composer, while Beethoven felt his genius entitled him to the support of wealthy patrons, publishers, and institutions. Mozart, whose decade living in Vienna (1781–91) coincided almost exactly with Joseph II's reign, has been called the model child of the Enlightenment. Beethoven's first large-scale composition, written at the age of nineteen, was an impressive cantata commemorating Joseph's death. His exploration of Enlightenment ideals extended over the course of his

Figure 12-11 Emperor Joseph II (1741–90) of Austria and his brother, Leopold II (1747–92). Painting by Giovanni Panealbo.

career, from that cantata, through his opera *Fidelio*, to the late vision expounded in his Ninth Symphony, in which the last movement sets Friedrich Schiller's *An die Freude* (Ode to Joy).

Summary

This chapter examines some steps in the transition between the late Baroque style of Bach and Handel and the Classical style of Haydn and Mozart. Composers who helped shape the new style included three of J. S. Bach's sons, Wilhelm Friedemann (1710–84), Carl Philipp Emanuel (1714–88), and Johann Christian (1735–82), as well as opera composers such as Giovanni Battista Pergolesi (1710–36), Niccolò Piccinni (1728–1800), and Christoph Willibald Gluck (1714–87). It is a time that sees the rise of chamber music in its modern sense.

While a typical late-Baroque composition has a single affect and is often "spun out" from a small amount of melodic material, the new style is built on contrasting motives with an emphasis on variety and balance. The harmonic rhythm is much slower, and the phrasing is symmetrically structured. Reflecting this emphasis on balance, binary form takes on a new importance.

The words *galant* and *empfindsamer Stil* describe two different styles of music that emerged during this time. *Galant* implies a style that is lightweight and courtly, without overly strong emotions. Works in this style are melody-dominated, with clear cadences, and a slow-moving, straightforward harmony. W. F. Bach's Sonata in F and J. C. Bach's Sonata in D are good examples of *galant* style. Works in the *empfindsamer Stil*, or "sensitivity style," by contrast, sought to depict the rapid changes of human emotions in a more realistic way, with sudden harmonic turns, free rhythm, and a speechlike melody reminiscent of operatic recitative. The *empfindsamer Stil* is especially associated with certain keyboard works of C. P. E Bach, such as his Fantasia in C Minor.

Many characteristics of these new styles first appeared in comic opera. Often interspersed between acts of serious opera were short comic interludes called *intermezzos*, which soon became great attractions in their own right. The most famous intermezzo was Pergolesi's *La serva padrona* (The Maid as Mistress). Its first performance in Paris sparked a debate over the relative merits of French and Italian music, called the *Querelle des Bouffons* (War of the Buffoons). Comic operas featured everyday characters instead of the historical or mythological figures of opera seria, often with cases of mistaken identity and other plot complications that upset rather than reinforce the social order. One of comic opera's leading librettists, Carlo Goldoni, introduced sentimental and moralizing elements into the genre, as reflected in Piccinni's *La buona figliuola* (The Virtuous Maiden), based on a novel by Samuel Richardson. The finale of Act II exemplifies the complex ensemble finale that became typical of comic opera.

Another important trend in opera of this period is the reform movement promoted by Christoph Willibald Gluck. The preface to his opera *Alceste* (1767) assailed the "abuses" that had entered into opera seria and declared that in opera, the purpose of the music was to serve the drama. *Orfeo ed Euridice* was Gluck's first reform opera. He strove for a more "natural" kind of expression in which the words were clearly declaimed. In comparison to opera seria, the reform operas have fewer characters and less virtuosic singing. The chorus, moreover, has a more important role than it does in opera seria. For the same reasons, Gluck abandoned the formulaic da capo aria.

Though quite different in nature, both Gluck's reform opera and Piccinni's sentimental opera reflect the spirit of the Enlightenment, which valued secular reason and naturalness above artifice. Enlightenment ideals, which helped inspire both the American and French revolutions, also shaped the reputations and music of the key figures of the "Classical" era: Haydn, Mozart, and Beethoven.

Study Questions

1. Describe the most important changes in musical style that took place between 1730 and 1760. How are these reflected in W. F. Bach's Sonata in F examined in this chapter?
2. What are the salient features of the *empfindsamer Stil*? What was its relationship to trends in other arts, and how was it inspired by vocal music?
3. Compare and contrast C. P. E Bach's Fantasia in C Minor and J. C. Bach's Sonata in D. How do these represent the *empfindsamer Stil* and the *galant* style?

4. What social aspects of musical life contributed to the rise of chamber music in the eighteenth century?
5. Describe some ways in which music criticism and debates reflected larger social and political issues in the eighteenth century, focusing in particular on the *Querelle des Bouffons* in France. How do these tie into the movement known as the Enlightenment?
6. How did the comic intermission plays of the early eighteenth century differ from opera seria, in plot and in musical style?
7. How do Christoph Willibald Gluck's reform operas contrast with opera seria, and how are these reforms reflected in his *Orfeo ed Euridice?* Why were his Parisian operas a contrast to Niccolò Piccinni's *La buona figliuola?*

Key Terms

accompanied keyboard sonata
Alberti bass
Classical style
clavichord
double return
dramma giocoso
empfindsamer Stil
Empfindsamkeit
fantasia
harmonic rhythm
instrumental recitative
intermezzo
opera buffa
periodic phrasing
Querelle des Bouffons
reform opera

13

Concert Life Lifts Off: Haydn

Posterity has bestowed the title "Father of the Symphony" on Franz Joseph Haydn (1732–1809), an honor that has some poetic justice, given the quantity, quality, range, and influence of his more than 100 surviving symphonies, even if the accolade sidelines achievements by earlier composers. Opera once again played a generative role in the development of instrumental music, making its influence felt in the symphony as the genre quickly moved from a form primarily of aristocratic private entertainment to one of public consumption that helped usher in modern concert life.

In one or another linguistic variant, the term **symphony** (*symphonia, sinfonia*) has been in the European musical vocabulary since the ninth century. By the beginning of the eighteenth, it had become attached to the Italian opera, designating what the French called the *ouverture*, or opener, the orchestral curtain raiser. The Italian *sinfonia avanti l'opera* as employed by the theater composers of Alessandro Scarlatti's generation was usually a short three-movement work (fast, slow, fast) akin to what the string players of that generation might have called a *concerto da camera*, but with more substantial instrumentation, as befitted the larger space of a theater rather than an aristocratic salon. The term, and the associated genre, did not stay put. By the end of the eighteenth century, at least 16,558 symphonies had been written. (No doubt there were many more, this number originates simply from a sum total of items listed in a mid-twentieth century catalogue.) Symphonies were beginning to live a life of their own, as freestanding three- or four-movement orchestral compositions, and were being produced in unprecedented quantities, many times more than the number of operas.

Immense production implies immense consumption. A new pattern of consumption implies a new demand; and a new demand implies a change of taste. Such changes have social as well as artistic causes, and these will be important to understanding what the symphony gradually came to mean during the eighteenth century. Sometimes opera overtures were detached from their operas and performed as symphonies. Sometimes symphonies got attached to operas and were performed as overtures. Sometimes symphonies that never had any operas attached were called overtures out of habit or because they opened concert programs.

While today we may rely on textbook or dictionary definitions for our understanding of genres, eighteenth-century musicians and listeners identified them by their contexts and social uses. A symphony was any multimovement orchestral piece performed at certain kinds of nonoperatic occasions. A crucial hint to the nature of the social occasions at which those thousands of symphonies were performed comes by way of some other early synonyms for the term in its new usage, including "**divertimento**," "scherzando," "serenata," "notturno," and "cassation." *Divertimento* comes from the Italian verb *divertire* and means entertainment music. *Scherzando* comes from *scherzare*, to have fun. *Serenata* comes from *sera*, evening; *notturno* from *notte*, night. *Cassation*, though disguised as an Italian word, actually comes from the German noun *Gasse*, meaning street, hence outdoor music.

Thus the freestanding orchestral symphony, produced in great numbers all over Europe beginning in the 1720s and '30s, was originally a genre of entertainment music, usually performed in the evenings and sometimes outdoors (Fig. 13-1). These pieces served as aristocratic party music, which over the century, responding to forces of urbanization and the economic empowerment of the bourgeoisie, became more and more available to a wider public. In the course of its becoming public it gradually became the pretext for the occasions at which it was performed, rather than their mere accompaniment, no longer background music but the main event. The growth of the symphony thus paralleled the growth of the concert as we know it today. This in turn paralleled a vastly expanding taste for aesthetically beguiling or emotionally stirring instrumental music, sought out for the sake of its sheer sensuous and imaginative appeal and listened to, increasingly, in silent absorption. Such

TIMELINE

1725 **The first Concert Spirituel in Paris**

1730s **Giovanni Battista Sammartini's earliest symphonies**

1750 **Death of Johann Sebastian Bach**

Late 1750s **Franz Joseph Haydn's earliest symphonies**

1756–63 Seven Years' War

1760–1820 Reign of George III in England

1761 **Haydn moves to the Esterházy court**

1764–81 **J. C. Bach's public concerts in London**

1765 Joseph II becomes Holy Roman Emperor

1772 **Haydn, Symphony No. 45 ("Farewell")**

1775 **J.C. Bach's Symphony in B♭ premieres in Mannheim**

1776 American Declaration of Independence

1782 **Haydn, Op. 33 string quartets**

1785–86 **Haydn's "Paris" symphonies**

1788 Edward Gibbon completes *The Decline and Fall of the Roman Empire*

1789 William Blake, *Songs of Innocence and Experience*

1789 Beginning of the French Revolution

1790 **Death of Haydn's employer, Prince Nikolaus Esterházy**

1791–95 **Haydn's "London" symphonies**

1798 **Haydn, *The Creation***

1809 **Death of Haydn**

Figure 13-1 Public concert at London's Vauxhall Gardens, ca. 1784. Watercolor by Thomas Rowlandson.

a momentous aesthetic change was something of a revolution in music history. Its beginnings, however, were modest and artistically unpretentious.

Modern Concert Life Is Born

Originally, the word "concert" was merely the French form of the word "concerto." And it was in France—in 1725—that the word was first used in its modern sense. It was then and there, in the cradle of the Enlightenment, that the vogue for public instrumental music was born. The earliest significant European concert series was the **Concert Spirituel** (literally, "sacred concert"), organized in Paris by the minor court composer Anne Danican Philidor (1681–1728). He created the Concert Spirituel as an excuse for musical entertainments on religious holidays, especially during the Lenten season, when opera houses were closed. The main ingredients of the event, held in a palace in the Tuileries gardens, were pious cantatas with Latin texts and concerted (vocal-instrumental) *grands motets* in keeping with the "spiritual" nature. Since it was a substitute for opera, it began with an overture—that is, a *sinfonia* or *symphonie*—which thus retained its traditional position as festive curtain raiser. At the very first Concert Spirituel, 18 March 1725, Corelli's famous "Christmas Concerto" served this purpose, illustrating the prevailing fluidity of genres and terms. Specially composed symphonies after the Italian operatic model quickly became standard; indeed, it was the existence of the concert series that stimulated their production. Sacred vocal works were likewise interspersed with virtuoso instrumental solos, often composed and performed by the great Italian-trained violinist Jean-Marie Leclair (1697–1764), known as the "French Vivaldi."

Concerts were typically variety shows mixing vocal music with instrumental and often sacred with secular.

The Concert Spirituel, which lasted until 1790, set the tone for concert programs throughout the eighteenth century. Almost always and almost everywhere, concerts were variety shows mixing vocal music with instrumental and often sacred with secular. A typical concert program from Vienna, dated 16 April 1791, printed in both German and Italian, begins with a "grand symphony" by Mozart as curtain raiser, followed by some opera arias by Mozart and Paisiello; a cello concerto by Ignace Joseph Pleyel (1757–1831), a former apprentice of Haydn; a choral Alleluja by the Viennese court composer Johann Georg Albrechtsberger (1736–1809), a prominent music educator who was briefly Beethoven's teacher; and, to close, a *harmonie*, or wind-band partita, "first performed in honor of the coronation of his Imperial Majesty" Leopold II, by Georg Druschetzky (1745–1819), a noted regimental musician.

Except for outdoor band concerts consisting entirely of partitas like Druschetzky's, concerts of only instrumental works were rare before the nineteenth century. The idea of what we now call a "symphony concert," with the audience listening in rapt attention to one orchestral work after another, was unheard of; a symphony was just one of the ingredients, typically the opener, and sometimes its movements were spread out over the course of the concert. The Viennese concert mentioned earlier was actually called an *Akademie*—a term that goes back to sixteenth-century Italy, where it already designated aristocratic house concerts. And northern Italy was, after France, the next great venue for public concerts in the eighteenth century. A particular center was Milan, where Lenten concerts were a fixture beginning in the 1730s. Their director, Giovanni Battista Sammartini (ca. 1701–75), was both the *maestro di cappella* at the Milan Cathedral and a leading composer of operas for the ducal theater (Fig. 13-2). At first he adapted his operatic symphonies for use at concerts, but later he wrote them in great quantities, especially for concert use. Nearly seventy such works by Sammartini survive, making his the first big name in the history of the genre.

Anthology Vol 2-7
Full CD III, 9–12

Symphony No. 13 in G Major by Sammartini probably dates from the 1730s and is one of the earliest freestanding concert symphonies now in existence, one that likely served its festive purpose both in its city of origin and later in Paris. The symphony, scored for strings with basso continuo, is in four movements, of which all but the tiny second one (a six-measure snatch of chordal connective tissue) are cast in the expected binary form. The third and fourth movements, respectively a gigue and a minuet, are traditional dance-suite items. Their harmonically defined form offers the usual pendular swing from tonic to dominant and back (the return trip by way of a far out point).

The style of the movements, however, has been modified by their Italian operatic background. The telltale traits include their relatively homophonic texture and their relatively slow and regular harmonic rhythm, which by no means precluded an interesting phrase structure. It is the first movement that differs most strikingly from anything J. S. Bach, at the time still very much alive and working in Leipzig, could ever have written and reminds us most of his sons' work—or, rather, the work his sons would later produce under the influence of music like Sammartini's. As in the compositions of Bach's sons (and also of Domenico Scarlatti), the structural reprise in the second part of the movement marks a return "home," meaning not only a returning key but a returning theme as well. The double return, which we saw at work with Bach's sons, was already fully established in Sammartini's style as the normal procedure for rounding off the opening movement of a symphony. The expanded binary form with dramatized key contrasts and double returns is a **"symphonic binary" form**, now more commonly known as **"sonata form."**

The symphony emerged as the predominant genre of instrumental music for the late eighteenth and nineteenth centuries, and its spread was facilitated by a number of social and political factors. During the eighteenth century Sammartini's city of Milan was under Austrian rule, along with the rest of northern Italy. Musical developments from there spread rapidly to Vienna, the Habsburg capital, and then outward to other cities and courts. Musical academies with their brilliant orchestral adornments became sites of conspicuous aristocratic, later public, musical consumption throughout the empire. Although practiced and supported elsewhere, including other musical centers, notably Paris, the concert symphony became the exemplary Austrian genre and the virtuoso orchestra became an Austrian specialty.

Figure 13-2 Giovanni Battista Sammartini. Portrait copied in 1778 by Domenico Riccardi from a lost painting.

The Mannheim Orchestra: "An Army of Generals"

As northern Italy (later known as the Kingdom of Lombardy-Venetia) marked the Austrian Empire's southern frontier, the so-called Rhineland Palatinate, now part of Bavaria in southern Germany, marked its most westerly extension, bordering France (Fig. 13-3). In the early eighteenth century, the seat of this substantial court was unexpectedly moved from Heidelberg to Mannheim, a small town on the right bank of

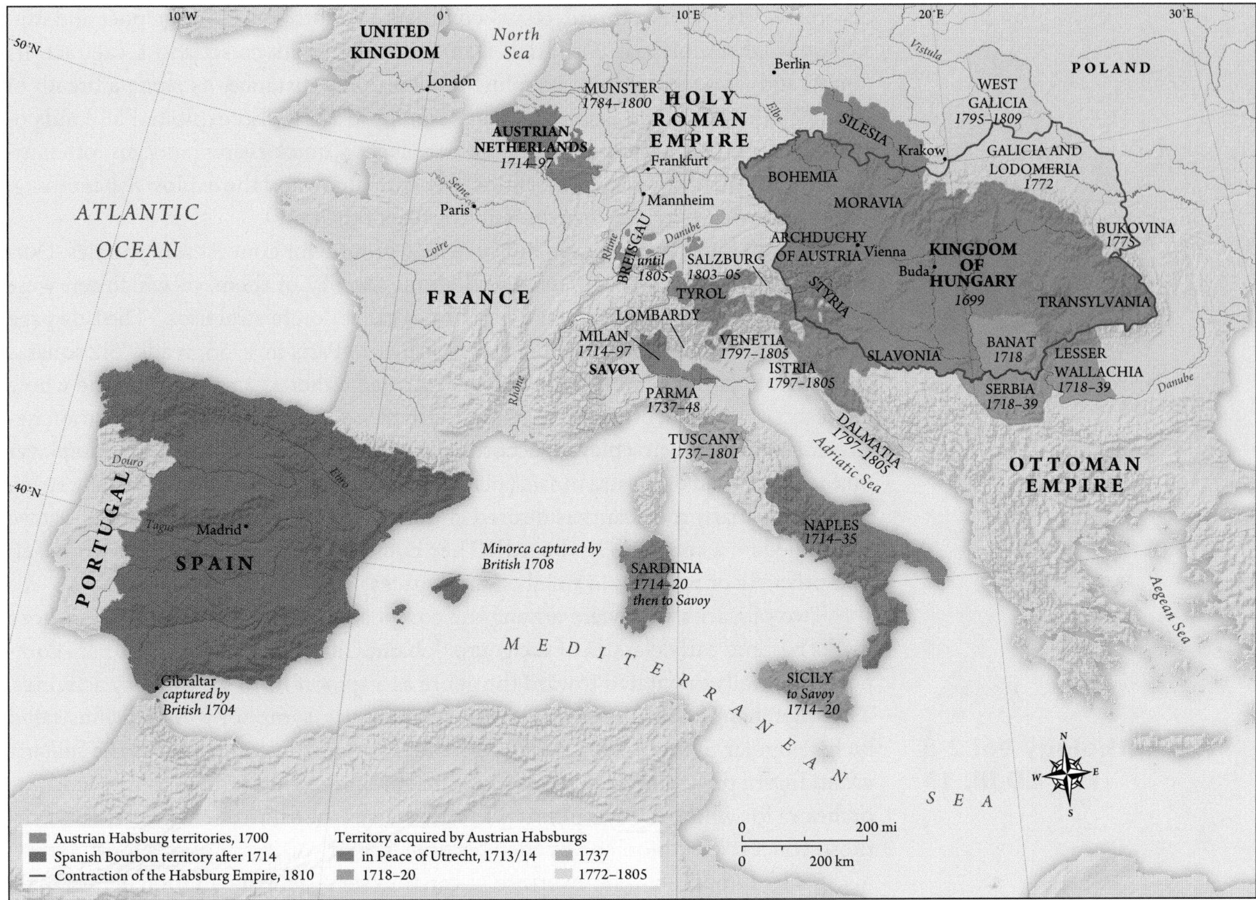

Figure 13-3 Changes in Europe in the eighteenth century.

the Rhine. A new capital had to be established, which meant building a large palace equipped with attributes of majesty. The town had no opera house, and so court instrumental music—semiweekly musical concerts—suddenly became one of the chief vehicles for rulers to display wealth and power.

When twenty-one-year-old Mozart visited Mannheim in 1777, he described the place in an enthusiastic letter to his father, telling of the ninety musicians employed there, of whom no fewer than sixty, many of them noted virtuosos, played in the orchestra—now the largest, most famous, and by all accounts most accomplished in Europe. Historian Charles Burney wrote in 1772 that "there are more solo players and good composers in this than perhaps in any other orchestra; it is an army of generals, equally fit to plan a battle as to fight it."[1] Some of these musical generals, particularly the wind players, had been brought in from the easterly portion of the empire, which bordered on or overlapped with Bohemia, the part of central Europe now in the Czech Republic. The leader was a Bohemian violinist and composer named Jan Václav Stamic (1717–57), more frequently called by his German name, Johann Wenzel Anton Stamitz.

The symphony emerged as the predominant genre of instrumental music for the late eighteenth and nineteenth centuries.

Under Stamitz and his successor, Christian Cannabich (1731–98), whose leadership Mozart admired, the Mannheim orchestra won fame for its quasi-military discipline. "Its *forte* is a thunderclap," commented another visitor, the poet and musical journalist Christian Friedrich Daniel Schubart, "its crescendo a cataract, its diminuendo a crystal stream babbling away into the distance, its *piano* a breath of spring."[2] The ensemble inspired virtuoso orchestrators who exploited all kinds of special effects that acquired nicknames: "rockets" (quick rising passages, often arpeggiated), "steamrollers" (crescendos over ostinatos), and the explosive beginning, known as the *premier coup d'archet* (first stroke of the bow).

Mannheim emerged as a major spawning ground for concert symphonies. During his short career, Stamitz produced about seventy of them, of which ten were written in three-part score and are sometimes called "orchestral trios." The title page of his Op. 1, a collection of six pieces published in Paris in 1755, reads "Six sonatas in three solo parts that are made to be performed either as a trio or with the whole orchestra." In their scoring alternatives, these pieces occupied a middle position between chamber music (played, according to the modern definition, by one player on each part) and orchestra music (played with "doubling" of parts, especially string parts, by as many musicians as desired and with the bass line doubled at the octave and joined by a continuo keyboard). They could be performed, in other words, either privately or publicly, in small or large spaces.

Two of Bach's sons were among the composers of concert symphonies whose works became early classics of the genre. Johann Christian, as a prolific opera composer, naturally gravitated toward the genre as a spinoff from his primary activities. The interchangeability of opera overture and early symphony is well illustrated by his popular Symphony in B♭, Op. 18, No. 2, originally composed as the *sinfonia avanti l'opera* preceding his *Lucio Silla*, which premiered in Mannheim in 1775. The orchestra for which the symphony was written was the same one whose feats of virtuoso concert execution had by then become legend.

Anthology Vol 2-8
Full CD III, 13

Bach's symphony—or "overture"—can thus serve as an illustration of the fabled Mannheim style. The scoring is rich, with wind parts including clarinets, a Mannheim specialty and the latest instrument to join the standard orchestral complement. The first sound heard, a loud *tutti* on the tonic triad rhythmically repeated four times, is the famous *premier coup d'archet*. It is immediately, and typically, contrasted with a quiet passage for the three upper string parts, after which the two violins reapproach the fanfare through a quick rising passage marked with a crescendo—in other words, a "rocket" (Ex. 13-1). J. C. Bach's entertaining symphonies, like those of his London business partner, Carl Friedrich Abel, uphold the ideal of high-class social music, transferred to a public occasion.

The symphonies of his older half-brother, Carl Philipp Emanuel Bach, were different. Like his father, C. P. E. Bach never wrote an opera and thus never wrote a *sinfonia avanti l'opera*. He nevertheless contributed some twenty symphonies to the burgeoning orchestral repertoire, mostly rather late in his career. Many of them exhibit the stern and stormy, harmonically restless and unpredictable idiom of the *empfindsamer Stil*, the "sentimental" or "pathetic" style—a style reserved, as C. P. E. Bach put it himself, "for connoisseurs and amateurs" of the art (*für Kenner und Liebhaber*).

In addition to the influential symphonies coming from Mannheim and from the Bach brothers, there were composers working in and around Vienna, such as Matthias Georg Monn (1717–50), Johann Baptist Vanhal (1739–1813), and Georg Christoph Wagenseil (1715–77), the last a court composer who wrote over 100 widely circulated symphonies in mid-century, many of them well known to the young Haydn and later to Mozart.

Example 13-1 J. C. Bach, Sinfonia, Op. 18, No. 2, mm. 1–7

Figure 13-4 Franz Joseph Haydn at the height of his fame. Engraving by Thomas Bush Hardy.

Haydn: The Perfect Career

By far the most influential—and in that sense the most important—composer of symphonies in the mid- to late-eighteenth century was Franz Joseph Haydn, who in two momentous ways established the genre for posterity (Fig. 13-4). First, by creating an unusually large and impressive body of works that became the object of widespread emulation, Haydn did more by his example than any other composer to standardize the symphony. And second, by finally taking the genre out of the aristocratic salon and into the public sphere, Haydn considerably enlarged both its dimensions and its cultural significance and laid the foundation for the modern concert repertory, in which at least a dozen of his symphonies are still staples.

Haydn did not do these things singlehandedly, by sheer force of will, or even intentionally, as the word is usually understood, but in miraculous symbiosis with his times. The word "miraculous" seems appropriate because his great success came both from talent—for music, to be sure, but also for seizing opportunities—and from luck. The luck would not have done a less gifted and avid man any comparable good, but without it talent and productivity alone night not have sufficed. Haydn's great good fortune has become ours, for we have inherited its results.

Haydn was, like Handel, what we would now call a self-made man. Unlike Bach, Mozart, and Beethoven, Haydn was not born into an established musical family. His father was a village wheelwright in southeast Austria and, although a master craftsman, neither highly educated nor well-to-do. There was no way in the world that his son's future career could have been predicted. Later in his life Haydn was acutely aware of the distance his talent and good fortune had taken him. According to one of his several contemporary biographers, he offered himself as an inspiration to the young, "who may see from my example that something may indeed come from nothing."[3]

The immediate result of Haydn's first sign of talent was his removal from his family. At the age of six he was sent to live with a cousin, a schoolmaster and church choirmaster in a neighboring town. There he had his only formal schooling—reading, writing, and religious studies, besides the rudiments of music. By the age of eight he was earning his own keep as a musician, first as a choirboy at St. Stephen's Cathedral (Fig. 13-5), Vienna's main church, where he had been brought by a passing nobleman who had happened to hear him sing: his first stroke of luck. His solo singing also brought Haydn to the attention of the Empress Maria Theresa. When his voice broke (not until the age of seventeen, as was usual in those days owing to a diet that would now be thought of as malnourishing), Haydn lost his place as soloist in the choir to his own younger brother, Johann Michael (1737–1806), who also made a distinguished career as a composer, though nothing like Joseph's.

Haydn did more by his example than any other composer to standardize the symphony.

A difficult time followed—years of near-starvation in Vienna, where Haydn studied voraciously, gave lessons to children, and took any musical odd job that came his way, like playing violin for a pittance in street-music entertainments. Among the books he studied was Johann Joseph Fux's *Gradus ad Parnassum* (1725), considered the bible of strict counterpoint. In addition to recent pieces by contemporaries like Wagenseil, he knew C. P. E. Bach's "Prussian" sonatas, which had a decided influence on his style. He also apprenticed himself for a while to Nicola Porpora (1686–1768), an Italian opera composer and singing teacher, accompanying his pupils at their lessons. Haydn's earliest compositions date from this trying period, and all of them, a few church pieces excepted, were merry entertainments composed for ready market consumption. They included *Singspiels*, comic operas in German with spoken dialogue, of the most plebeian sort, roughly on the order of Punch-and-Judy skits (or Hanswurst shows, as they were known in Vienna). The music for these carnival frolics is apparently lost, but it earned Haydn his first local celebrity.

Another early success came in the form of instrumental works that straddled the ambiguous line between chamber and orchestral music. At various times Haydn called such a piece a *cassation*, at other times a *notturno*, at still others *divertimento*. Six were published with a title page announcing "Sinfonies ou Quatuors" (symphonies or quartets). Haydn began writing them in the late 1750s, and they are now classified as his earliest **string quartets** (Opp. 1 and 2), because their four parts are earmarked for two violins, viola, and "basso," which could mean cello. There is no reason why they could not be performed, like Stamitz's orchestral trios, with doubled parts, however; and the designation basso could certainly be read as implying the participation of a continuo. Nor is the addition of other instruments out of the question: Manuscript sources of uncertain origin equip some of them with supplemental wind parts. These works, along with a few others that are scored in three and five parts, stand at the beginning of Haydn's production of instrumental concert music, the field that he would decisively transform and standardize, in the process finally distinguishing between chamber and orchestral genres as we know them today.

Figure 13-5 St. Stephen's Cathedral, Vienna, in 1792.

Haydn's Op. 1 and Op. 2 must have been highly adaptable to varying combinations of instruments, because they were best sellers, circulating far and wide in Europe and also in North America. Their symmetrical sequence of five movements—fast in sonata form/minuet-&-trio/slow/minuet-&-trio/fast finale—was typical of Viennese street music, but when performed by four solo strings the works were ideally suitable for home recreation as well. Haydn was again showing an understanding of the emergent music market, a business sense that would have marked him for a successful independent career if that had been his fate.

But that was not his fate. On the strength of these early successes, Haydn found a permanent position working for a noble family. Such families, housed in palaces and summer estates, often had their own orchestras and even opera ensembles. The title of *Kapellmeister* originally meant "chapel master," but in secular courts and homes it meant director of musical entertainments. The position was essentially that of a highly regarded domestic servant, which may appear demeaning to us, with our Romantic notion of what an "artist" is. It was, however, the best fate to which a professional musician in mid-eighteenth-century Vienna could aspire, unless, like Mozart, he was a performing virtuoso, which Haydn was not. In addition to a relatively high salary, a musician who landed such a post was given free food and lodging. It was, especially in contrast to Haydn's former plight, a bountiful existence.

This stroke of good fortune came when Haydn was hired by one Count Morzin to work for his family, which probably happened in 1757. The post of Kapellmeister put him in charge of an orchestra, and it was for this ensemble that he wrote or adapted his first real symphonies. There are about fifteen such pieces dating from the Morzin period, including the initial five in the standard list of Haydn's 106 symphonies (the numbered ones—104 of them—were catalogued in 1907 and were supplemented by two later discoveries). With a couple of exceptions, Haydn's earliest symphonies are three-movement works on the old *sinfonia avanti l'opera* model: a fast sonata-form movement, a slow movement, and a dancelike finale, usually a gigue or, less often, a minuet. Of the two four-movement symphonies, one (No. 3 in G Major) is cast in the format that Haydn would later establish as the norm: (1) fast sonata form, (2) slow, (3) minuet & trio, (4) fast finale. The other (No. 5 in A Major) seems to be descended from the old church sonata. Its first movement is an *Adagio ma non troppo*, followed by an *Allegro*, both in binary form; then comes a minuet and trio; last a *Presto* finale in duple meter and binary form. Movement sequence was clearly still a fluid affair.

Haydn's Years with the Esterházy Family

Haydn's next and biggest break came at age twenty-eight, when he was provided the resources through which he was able to develop his gifts to the fullest. On 1 May 1761, he signed a contract as "Vice-Kapellmeister in the service of his Serene Highness Paul Anton, Prince of the Holy Roman Empire, of Esterházy and Galantha, etc. etc." The benevolent patronage Haydn secured would last nearly five decades, until his death. Three of the five decades were spent in active, and incredibly productive, Kapellmeister duty, the remaining two as a pensioned, international celebrity, still tirelessly productive until a few years before he died in 1809.

The Esterházy family was the foremost princely house of Hungary. With that standing went a correspondingly lavish standard of living, entailing a household and a court second only to the imperial family itself. At the time of Haydn's employment the prince had two main residences, the Palais Esterházy in Vienna and the ancestral estate at Eisenstadt some twenty-five miles southeast (Fig. 13-6). The Esterházy musical establishment was huge, and almost immediately after Haydn's employment it grew considerably, not simply because of the composer's presence on the payroll but because Prince Paul Anton was succeeded in 1762 by his brother, Nikolaus Joseph, a passionate music lover and amateur musician himself. By 1766, just as Haydn acceded to the post of chief Kapellmeister for the Esterházy court on the death of his predecessor, the prince had begun to build the gorgeous summer palace, Eszterháza, a further twenty-five miles southeast of Eisenstadt in what is now Hungary. It amounted to a sort of mini-Versailles, surrounded by parks, fountains, pleasure pavilions, and servant houses.

Figure 13-6 The summer palace at Eszterháza (now Fertöd, Hungary).

The Eszterháza compound contained two theaters, one for opera and the other for marionette plays and Singspiels. In addition there were two concert rooms in the palace itself, a large hall that could accommodate an orchestra and a smaller one for chamber music. Haydn's duties included the supervision of a regular round of performances of his own music and those of contemporaries—typically one opera and two concerts a week, with additional major performances for important guests like Empress Maria Theresa, and daily chamber music at the prince's pleasure. In addition to these supervisory duties, he also had to compose, so it is little wonder that his output, like Bach's, proved to be enormous.

For the princely theaters Haydn wrote some twenty Italian operas, at first mostly comic, now mostly long forgotten, and for the puppet house five Singspiels. For the weekly concerts he composed at least seventy-five of his existing symphonies and dozens of divertimentos, mostly published as quartets. But the fairest measure of the pace Haydn had to keep would be the music that was ordered à la carte, so to speak, "at the Prince's pleasure," for Prince Nikolaus was an enthusiast of the baryton (or *viola paradon*), an unusual stringed instrument that was something of a cross between a bass viol and a guitar (Fig. 13-7). The contraption had no literature to speak of, so Haydn had to create one from scratch. Between 1765 and 1776, he furnished Prince Nikolaus, who played the instrument himself, with upwards of 200 works for baryton. Most were trios discreetly accompanied by viola and cello. He also composed duets for two barytons, which he himself played with the prince (having learned the instrument on demand), and larger chamber works, such as octets with easy baryton parts for the honoree to play.

Figure 13-7 Prince Nikolaus Esterházy's baryton.

Not only a ravenous consumer of music, the prince was a true connoisseur who appreciated the specialness of Haydn's gifts. In what has become one of the most famous of the many reminiscences his biographers have recorded, Haydn reflected on the uniquely auspicious combination of circumstances that enabled his gifts, particularly those as a symphonist, to flourish in relative isolation. "My Prince was content with all my works," Haydn told Georg August Griesinger, a diplomat who helped arrange publication of his music and wrote an early biography of the composer: "I received approval for anything I did. As head of an orchestra, I could make experiments, observe what enhanced an effect, and what weakened it, thus improving, adding to it, taking away from it, and running risks. I was cut off from the world, there was nobody in my vicinity to make me unsure of myself or interfere with me in my course, and so I was forced to become original."[4]

This testimony is an important document of the era of aristocratic patronage because it attests to the symbiosis between talent and calling, between supply and demand, that could take effect when patronage operated to best advantage. The composer met the employer's needs, whether measured in idealized terms of artistic satisfaction or in crasser ones of aristocratic exhibitionism. At the same time the employee/composer was liberated by his very exploitation, as it were, to develop his skills freely, knowing that the products of their free exercise would translate, from the employer's standpoint, into uniquely distinguished and valuable possessions.

Haydn's delight with his new working conditions is apparent in the first symphonies he wrote for the Esterházy family in 1761: a trilogy (Nos. 6–8) bearing the French subtitles *Le matin*, *Le midi*, and *Le soir* (Morning, Noon, and Night) and overflowing with special instrumental effects that exploited the virtuoso soloists in his orchestra, first among them the violinist Alois Luigi Tomasini. This provides a telling example, therefore, of symphonies carrying over aspects of the earlier concerto grosso. Haydn began experimenting with augmented orchestras, particularly with a complement of four horns that shows up in several Esterházy symphonies but that did not become standard in orchestras until well into the nineteenth century.

Expectations and Deviations: Creating Musical Meaning

Anthology Vol 2-9
Full CD III, 14
Concise CD II, 10

We will consider two of Haydn's symphonies, beginning with one written during his most experimental years of employment by the Esterházy family. This work, his Symphony No. 45, will give us further insight into that special relationship between Kapellmeister and patron. The piece was first performed, under unusual circumstances, at Prince Nikolaus's summer palace in November 1772. November is obviously not a summer month. That is what was unusual about the circumstances—and, as a result, about the piece. Its key alone—F♯ minor—makes it unique among Haydn's symphonies and practically unique among the music of its time (Fig. 13-8).

Haydn's symphonies from this period were boldly experimental. Some are related to the stage works he was writing at the time, variously recycling parts of his operas and incidental music; they frequently display dramatic and emotional qualities associated with a similarly frenzied tendency beginning to appear in German drama and literature. The literary movement known as ***Sturm und Drang*** (Storm and Stress) was named after the subtitle of a sensational play—*Die Wirrwarr* (The Confusion, 1776)—by Friedrich Maximilian von Klinger, a friend of the great German poet Johann Wolfgang von Goethe, whom he influenced with this work. With its glorification of the "state of nature," its emphasis on subjective, often violent moods, and its portrayals of social alienation, *Sturm und Drang* had obvious affinities with the *Empfindsamkeit* (sentimentality) of earlier German poetry that was directly reflected in the music of C. P. E. Bach, who had a formative influence on Haydn's style. The *Sturm und Drang* movement also led, or fed, into the Romantic movements that would soon engulf Europe, and for the first time put German artists at the forefront of European culture.

Haydn's symphonies around 1770 were boldly experimental.

The enigmatic character and form of the first movement of Haydn's Symphony No. 45 are worlds away from the festive party mood that typified the early concert symphony, and the concluding movement is so outlandish that without knowledge of the circumstances of its composition it would be altogether baffling. Midway through this finale the music suddenly fizzles out on the dominant and is replaced, seemingly for no good reason, by a graceful minuet that enters in the key of the relative major, richly scored (four pairs of violins, each with its own part). It then goes on, through a resumption of the dominant, to conclude in the distant key of the parallel major. Most puzzling is the way in which this concluding dance proceeds with the instruments of the orchestra dropping out one by one. Only the strings remain and then they too depart: first the double bass (after an extravagant and unusual solo turn) and the two "extra" violins, then

Figure 13-8 Concert hall at Eszterháza, where many of Haydn's works were first performed.

the cello, eventually everybody. As a further surprise, the "extra" violins return to finish the movement, having donned their mutes. Their softly beatific murmurings finally fade out into silence.

What can this strange ending mean? It turns out it was a response to circumstances that have been recounted, after Haydn's own recollections, by all of his biographers. Griesinger's version, first published in 1810, relates:

> Among Prince Esterházy's orchestra there were several vigorous young married men who in summer, when the Prince stayed at Eszterháza, were obliged to leave their wives behind in Eisenstadt. Contrary to his custom, the Prince once extended his sojourn in Eszterháza by several weeks: The loving husbands, thoroughly dismayed over this news, went to Haydn and asked for his advice.
>
> Haydn had the inspiration of writing a symphony (which is now known under the title of "Farewell" Symphony), in which one instrument after another is silent. This Symphony was performed as soon as possible in front of the Prince, and each of the musicians was instructed, as soon as his part was finished, to blow out his candle and to leave with his instrument under his arm.
>
> The Prince now rose and said, "If they all leave, we must leave, too." The musicians had meanwhile collected in the *antechamber*, where the Prince found them, and smiling said: "I understand, Haydn; tomorrow the men may all leave," whereupon he gave the necessary order to have the princely horses and carriages made ready for the trip.[5]

This story lent the name "Farewell" to Symphony No. 45 and probably accounts for its survival in the active repertory long after most of Haydn's Esterházy symphonies had been eclipsed by his later ones. Its fame is well deserved. It casts an appealing light on Haydn's relationship with his patron. Haydn commanded the personal respect of the nobility on account of his achievements. But there is nothing subversive about such a message; it is just as much a flattering reflection on the liberality of the prince.

Moreover, Prince Esterházy got Haydn's message from instrumental music; no words were necessary. Instrumental music was just beginning to displace vocal as the medium of greatest cultural prestige, developing what was previously an unthinkably precise and powerful expressive potential. That potential was newly realized via harmonically governed forms that were articulated through the ingenious manipulation of thematic material using techniques now collectively described in German by the term *thematische Arbeit* (**thematic work**).

Instrumental music was just beginning to displace vocal as the medium of greatest cultural prestige.

The conventions through which motives derived from themes functioned dynamically in conjunction with the tonal trajectory opened up new possibilities for musical references, giving instrumental music in effect a double sign system. On the one hand there were the old conventions, inherited from earlier styles and repertoires, whereby music could represent the sights and sounds of the natural world (such as birds, storms, and rivers) and the moods and feelings of the human world—onomatopoeia, iconicity, metaphor, and metonymy. All these conventions can be subsumed under the general heading of signs that point outward. This also included the sounds of other music—hunting horns, military fanfares, courtly dances, quotations of famous pieces, etc.—and their built-in associations. On the other hand, there was also now the newly important domain of signs that pointed inward—a sign system made up of sounds that referred to other sounds or musical events within the work itself. Some of these purely musical relationships are thematic; others relate to the conventions of form and harmony, such as the expectation of a modulation away from the tonic in the first half of a movement and a modulation back through a "far out point" in the second half.

The "Farewell" Symphony conveyed its meaning to Prince Nikolaus through a unique interaction of signs pointing both inward and outward, in this case some of them visual as well as musical. When the meaning of the work is explained today, it is apt to be the simplest outward signals that receive the emphasis: the musicians dropping out one by one from the last movement and, as we know from the story, blowing out their reading candles and physically leaving the performing space as they did so. These seem to be gestures of farewell to the prince himself and to Eszterháza.

The "Farewell" Symphony conveyed its meaning through a unique interaction of signs pointing both inward and outward.

But that does not tell the whole story. The entire symphony participates in the unfolding of the message, beginning with a strangely shaped first movement in the unusual key of F♯.[6] Its thematic and harmonic features require a well-attuned perceiver; that is why they are not usually included in the story as adapted for general audiences. Haydn's modern biographer, H. C. Robbins Landon, observed: "Prince Esterházy was a trained and performing musician: He will have heard the very odd sound of this [opening] movement; and he will have noted that the subsidiary subject [or "second theme"] appears only once, in D major, in the development section," and so on.[7] In other words, he will have noticed the many deviations from established norms that Haydn deliberately planted in the work to raise questions in a sophisticated listener's mind. The prince would have wondered why his musical expectations were constantly being frustrated.

The surprises are not just in the first movement. When the long minuet-like coda intrudes on the finale, there is a sense of tonal disruption and remoteness, matching perhaps the physical remoteness of the Eszterháza summer palace from "civilization" back in Vienna. There is a sense of an alternative reality, into which the members of the orchestra now disappear one by one. As they blow out their candles as if retiring for the night amid this ambience of unreal, longed-for bliss, the suggestion of conjugal bliss becomes palpable.

We are dealing, then, with a mode of instrumental discourse capable of very subtle shades of allusion and irony. Haydn did not normally draw as extensively on its representational resources as he does in the "Farewell" Symphony; nor did he often write a multimovement work in which the different movements are so firmly and obviously linked. The piece is a special tour de force within his output. But the resources on which he drew so extravagantly in this one case remained available for the rest of his music—and, through their widespread emulation, for all European instrumental music.

Finally, thematic and harmonic play became for Haydn a site for the virtuoso exercise of wit. His mature instrumental music is forever commenting ironically and amusingly on its own unfolding, making his art an unprecedentedly self-conscious one and one that seems uncommonly given to complimenting the discernment of its listeners. These are all aspects of politeness, refined behavior. The music of this lower-Austrian wheelwright's son thus represents an epitome of upper-class art. Haydn flatters his listeners by assuming they will understand what he is doing.

String Quartets and Concertos

After a hiatus of nearly a decade following his Op. 20 string quartets, Haydn resumed composing in the genre in the early 1780s; thereafter he gave it considerable attention, creating in the process what he saw fit to describe as "a new and special manner." The phrase has been much debated. It has been suggested that Haydn was just trying to drum up commercial interest in his latest work at a time when his patron, in view of Haydn's great and unanticipated celebrity, had at last released him from the exclusivity clause in his contract, freeing him to negotiate subsidiary deals. He was freed from writing pieces for baryton and now had an eye toward what would sell all across Europe. Unlike his symphonies, the string quartets carry opus numbers. This directly reflects his new circumstances: They were written for publication—that is, for profit—and bore dedications to important aristocrats besides Prince Esterházy, for which additional income could be expected. The landmark set of six quartets issued as Op. 33 in 1782 was dedicated to the Grand Duke (later Tsar) Paul of Russia. They were the first ones by Haydn that were not alternatively billed as divertimentos. Like the concert symphony, the quartet genre had solidified by then, in large part thanks to Haydn.

The symphony and the quartet could be regarded by the 1780s, then, as two solid precipitates, one "public," the other "private," from the earlier all-purpose instrumental blend. The great distinguishing feature of Op. 33, and possibly one aspect of Haydn's "new and special" manner, was a newly differentiated texture, no longer nearly so much dominated by the first violin as in Haydn's own earlier quartets, not to mention those by other contemporaries who also cultivated the genre, such as Franz Xaver Richter (1709–89), Johann Baptist Vanhal (1739–1813), and Luigi Boccherini (1743–1805).

This greater textural equality had been anticipated in the Op. 20 quartets, published in 1774, but there the liberation of the subordinate voices had come about largely as the by-product of an experimental, somewhat flashy revival of archaic contrapuntal textures like double and triple fugues. In his new Op. 33 quartets, the heightened contrapuntal interest was fully integrated into the taut motivic elaboration. In effect, there were henceforth two musical dimensions: horizontal, or structural, and vertical, or textural. This indeed led to "a new and special manner," which was taken up by all the other practitioners of what would be retrospectively and admiringly (if also misleadingly) dubbed Viennese Classicism.

Anthology Vol 2-10
Full CD III, 15–18
Concise CD II, 11

Haydn's "new and special manner" and its implications are apparent in the Quartet in E♭ Major, Op. 33, No. 2, which in English sports the nickname "The Joke." The first movement is inexhaustibly rife with little jolts of wit, which Webster's Dictionary defines as "the keen perception and cleverly apt expression of those connections between ideas which awaken pleasure and especially amusement." The exploration of motivic relationships, and their shrewd recombination, has always been a feature of thematic work. Only now we will find such things happening not just in the expected later parts of a movement but, rather, right from the start, and pervading the whole texture besides. Haydn followed up on Op. 33 with no fewer than five more quartet sets, each containing six pieces, although some were published in two sets of three, and also four odd items, one released as Op. 42, two as Op. 77, and a last unfinished quartet in two movements published as Op. 103 in 1806.

Haydn's lifetime total of sixty-eight quartets far exceeds the quantity and quality of his concertos, of which a few remain in the concert repertory: a keyboard concerto in D major and a concerto in E♭ for high "clarino" trumpet. Two surviving cello concertos are played, welcomed by today's virtuoso cellists, who otherwise have hardly any concertos from the period in their repertory. Few students play Haydn's four violin concertos anymore, and it is no surprise that his two concertos for Prince Nikolaus Esterházy's beloved baryton are now forgotten. As the baryton items suggest, Haydn's concertos were written to order as the sometimes unpredictable occasion arose and had little or nothing to do with the composer's personal preferences. Nor was he, unlike Bach, Mozart, or Beethoven, an instrumental virtuoso who could himself shine as a soloist. Instead, Haydn made his impact in the realm of the symphony. During his last decade of active creative life, from 1793, that was his primary interest.

During Haydn's last decade of active creative life, symphonies were his primary interest.

The Symphony Composer

Haydn remained in active service to the Esterházys and in full-time residence on their estates until Prince Nikolaus's sudden death on 28 September 1790. The latter's son and successor, Prince Anton, uninterested in music, disbanded his father's orchestra and opera establishment. This was no disaster for the fifty-eight-year-old Haydn but yet another stroke of good fortune. He remained, according to the terms of Prince Nikolaus's will, on full salary and drew a pension on top of it, but he was no longer under obligation to his patron except later to compose annual Masses. Haydn was able to settle in Vienna and pursue a fully subsidized life as a freelance artist. His new status allowed him to accept an attractive offer that unexpectedly came his way, and he embarked on what amounted to another career, as an international celebrity under newly viable economic and social conditions.

When Prince Nikolaus died, a German-born violinist and minor composer named Johann Peter Salomon (1745–1815), who had moved to England and set himself up as a concert entrepreneur, happened to be in Cologne recruiting talent for his upcoming London season. After learning the news, he went to Vienna and offered Haydn a handsome contract for an opera, six symphonies, and various miscellaneous pieces, all to be performed under Haydn's personal direction at a series of London subscription concerts. They would be given at Salomon's financial risk in a public concert hall on Hanover Square (Figs. 13-9 and 13-10) with a seating capacity of around 800, more with standees.

Salomon and Haydn crossed the English Channel together on New Year's Day 1791, for what would prove to be for Haydn the first of two extended, acclaimed, and highly lucrative stays in the British capital between 1791 and 1795. His first concert took place on 11 March, and the series continued on Friday evenings thereafter until 3 June. The initial program was typical and, as always, a miscellany. Although Haydn "presided at the harpsichord," as his contract stipulated, most of the music performed was actually by other composers.

The centerpiece of the concert was Haydn's "New Grand Overture," as the program put it. The work was actually his Symphony No. 92 in G Major, composed in 1789, not one of the new symphonies Salomon had commissioned but at least new to London. It is now nicknamed the "Oxford" Symphony because it was performed again at the University of Oxford, where Haydn had been invited to receive an honorary doctor of music degree. For the subscription series the next year, 1792,

Figure 13-9 Hanover Square. Haydn's music was performed here when he was in London; impresario Johann Peter Salomon organized concerts.

he composed several major works on English soil, and his concerts contained premieres of enduringly famous compositions.

At the time of his London visit, Haydn already had some experience composing public symphonies of more formidable scale than those he produced for Prince Esterházy. He had been writing subscription symphonies since the mid-1780s, when he received a commission from Paris for a set of six to be performed at a new concert series set up in competition with the venerable Concert Spirituel, where Haydn's works had become popular. The orchestra there was huge; when playing at full strength it could draw on forty violins and ten double basses. (The practice today of performing Haydn and Mozart symphonies with scaled-back orchestras in an attempt to be "historically correct" is therefore not always historically correct. Both composers used large ensembles when available and where appropriate for a particular performance venue.) Under the circumstances, it is hardly surprising that Haydn's "Paris" Symphonies—Nos. 82–87 in the standard numbering—have a notably expanded format. Haydn's new, much grander style would henceforth be his normal symphonic practice, since a composer of his celebrity could now count on "subscription" performances for all orchestral works.

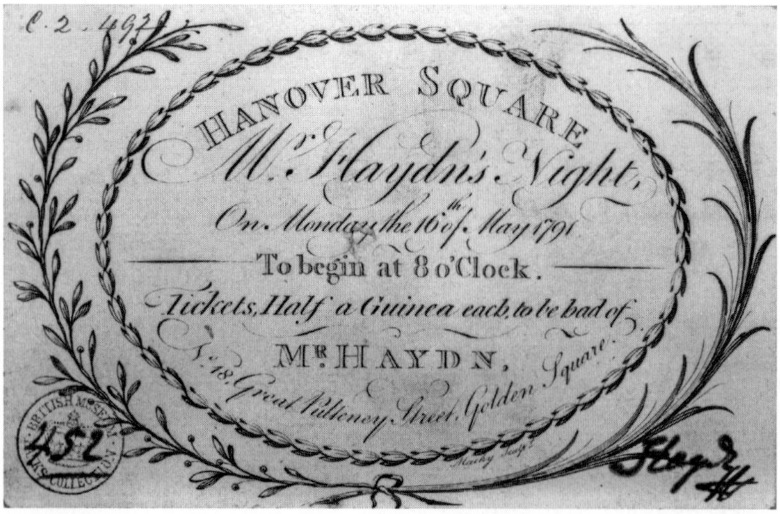

Figure 13-10 Ticket to "Mr. Haydn's Night" in Hanover Square, 16 May 1791.

Sonata Form

It was not so much the performers nor even, in a way, Haydn, who triumphed in London as it was the genre of the symphony itself. With some ninety to his name by this point, he had mastered it to such an extent that he standardized the genre into the four-movement sequence most common ever since: a fast first movement, a slow second, a dancelike third, and a brief, fast finale. This is the layout we will see in Haydn's final Symphony, No. 104 in D Major, nicknamed the "London" (Fig. 13-11).

Anthology Vol 2-11
Full CD III, 19–22
Concise CD II, 12–13

Let us begin with a wide-angle view of a first movement, discussed according to what became akin to a recipe. Opening movements of Haydn's late symphonies usually begin, as here, with a somewhat haunting slow introduction, familiar to us already from the French overture style and likewise serving a practical as well as an aesthetic purpose: The dimming of lights in concert halls was something that electricity would not make possible for another hundred years or so; the audience needed a signal to sit down (although in fact not everyone in the audience sat), quiet down, and pay attention. Haydn's introductions were occasionally soft and mysterious but more often were in the manner of a fanfare.

What is remarkably consistent in Haydn's symphonies is his personal manner of inflecting the symphonic binary or what is most commonly known today as sonata form. In terms of its thematic or melodic content, Haydn's version of the sonata form is articulated in three distinct parts, the opening one coinciding with the first harmonic section of the binary form (I→V), and the second and third Haydnesque parts together comprising the second binary section (V→I). The movement's closing section, beginning with the double return, closely parallels or recapitulates the whole opening section to the first double bar theme by theme, with such truncations and adjustments as are necessary to keep the whole closing section in the tonic key rather than modulating again to the dominant.

The first and the last parts, being similar in thematic content and layout, were later called the "**exposition**" and the "**recapitulation**." The middle part, containing the redeployment of motives originally exposed in the first part, is called the

Figure 13-11 Handwritten score of Haydn's "London" Symphony (No. 104 in D Major). London 1795; first page of the first movement.

"**development**" section in English. The development section, extending from the first double bar to the double return, embodies the most radical tonal trajectory in the movement (from dominant to far out point to retransition to the tonic) and is based on motives drawn from material heard in the exposition. The development was the site for the rigorous and ingenious display of thematic work.

This three-part structure—exposition, development, and recapitulation—possesses a psychologically satisfying trajectory. The double return "home" at the recapitulation suggests the metaphor of a journey completed. The opening exposition section does not venture very far, usually just as far as the dominant for a movement in a major key or to the relative major for one in a minor key. The middle (development) section thus provides a stark harmonic contrast, a feeling of instability and distance, including travel to a far out point. In Haydn symphonies and in other contemporary works, this contrasting middle part tends to be fairly short. In the nineteenth century the development became much longer as composers became ever more interested in the journey, the adventure in between the safe haven of the home sections. Indeed, the stabilizing return home is particularly satisfying after all the thematic work and distant harmonic points and doubly so because it is both tonal and thematic. Once the journey is over, the tonality stays put, with no need to venture even the short distance to the dominant, as happened in the exposition. That was the theory at least; we will see in practice that composers found this limiting and often indulged in brief harmonic excursions.

What this overall form amounts to is a sort of flexible "ternary" overlay coexisting with and reinforcing the binary harmonic structure. The relationship between the two elements—the three-part thematic structure and the two-part harmonic structure—could be endlessly varied. Its combination of flexibility and solidity, or of complexity and clarity, made the resulting "sonata form" or "sonata-allegro form" or "first-movement form" (three terms now in common use to denote it) one of the most adaptable, durable, and potentially eloquent formal procedures ever devised for instrumental music of all kinds, from solo sonata to orchestral overture and symphony. It was largely thanks to this happy synthesis—and to Haydn, the synthesizer-in-chief—that instrumental music would enjoy a triumphant, and unforeseen, career over the next two centuries that in a curiously fitting way paralleled the course of Haydn's own life. Like Haydn himself, instrumental music went from poor relation to leading force. It too had a sort of success story.

For Haydn and his eighteenth-century audience, form was made intelligible through a tonal, not a thematic, contrast.

The "London" Symphony No. 104

The first movement of Haydn's "London" Symphony shows some ways in which the generic recipe for something like sonata form oversimplifies how individual composers actually worked. For example, instead of contrasting exposition themes in the tonic and dominant that were typical of most symphonies, in Symphony No. 104 the theme in the second key area (the dominant) is the same as the first theme (Table 13-1). This nearly single-themed symphonic movement looks like a deviation from the norm only if a two-themed exposition is taken as the normal symphonic procedure. In fact in many Haydn symphonies the "second theme" is some kind of variant of the first one, even if not identical as in the "London." The more familiar recipe for symphonic first movements, which became

Table 13-1 Franz Joseph Haydn, Symphony in D, No. 104 ("London"), movement 1

MEASURE NOS.	FORMAL DESIGNATION	SECTION	KEYS	COMMENTS
1–17	**Slow introduction**	*Adagio*	d, F, d	Tonal trajectory of binary form
1–107	**Exposition**	*Allegro*		
1–16		Primary theme	D	8 + 8 (aa′)
16–48		Bridge	Ends on V/V	New theme, *forte*, related to primary theme
49–83		Secondary theme area	A	Same material as primary theme
84–107		Closing section	A	
108–76	**Development**			Motivic work
108–29		From mm. 3–4 of primary theme	b, e, c♯	
130–42		From beginning of primary theme	c♯, g♯, f♯, E, e	
143–76		From mm. 3–4 of primary theme	E, b, ends on V/D	Ends with dominant pedal
177–278	**Recapitulation**			
177–92		Primary theme	D	Ends with counterpoint
192–231		Bridge		Bridge theme
231–50		Secondary theme area	D	Fragments of theme come first, section truncated
251–78		Closing section		

common later, by the time of Beethoven, was for the first section to present two (or more) contrasting themes. In some instances, for example, the first theme was loud, dynamic, and "masculine," the second, soft, lyrical, and "feminine." Such gendered characterizations date from nineteenth-century commentaries, as found, for example, in the writings of the influential theorist Adolf Bernhard Marx (1795–1866).

The expectation that themes would contrast was thus primarily a later phenomenon. So, too, were descriptions of the overall shape of the movement (exposition, development, and recapitulation) as ternary form. In fact the two-themed (bithematic) ternary model, still taught in most textbooks today, originated in textbooks written in the 1830s for use in conservatory courses at Paris and Berlin. And that is why the first movement of Haydn's "London" Symphony is indispensable to any properly historical understanding of the composer and his musical accomplishments. The discrepancy between Haydn's own last symphony and the later academic description of "sonata form" is an integral part of the history of nineteenth-century music and music education. For Haydn and his eighteenth-century audience, the form was made intelligible through a tonal, not a thematic, contrast. The thematic requirement was not contrast, as it would later become, but rather its working out.

It is important to understand why Haydn's thematic efficiency came to command such authority. Haydn himself gave the reason for valuing it when he wrote of another composer's work in his diary that it flitted from idea to idea, made nothing of the themes, and so one was left "with nothing in one's heart."[8] The economy and logic of thematic development for which Haydn became famous were valued not as a demonstration of technical virtuosity but as an intensifier, and a deepener, of sentiment. With this stipulation in mind, we may indeed find Haydn's technical virtuosity as astounding as did his contemporaries, to say nothing of the generations of composers who have avidly studied and emulated his work. He created musical events and processes that left one with something in one's heart.

In contrast to the variable number and arrangement of movements of some of his earlier symphonies, the ones Haydn wrote for Paris and London are all in four movements. The inner movements grew significantly in dimensions. The second, in a slow or moderate tempo, could be in a binary, ternary, variation, or some other form. The *Andante* in the Symphony No. 104 is a ternary form—ABA′—with the contrasting middle section, tonally unstable, developing material from the A. The return of the opening A begins in the home key of G major, but this concluding section is expanded and developed, adding another thirty-five measures to the original.

The third movement of the Classical symphony was almost always a ***minuet and trio*** (actually another minuet), with a da capo repeat of the minuet creating a literal ABA form. The movement was a vestige of older Baroque suites, both in the idea of using a dance and in the scaled-back instrumentation of the middle section. The "trio" was no longer played by just three instruments, but it did usually contrast with the minuet that enclosed it with respect to tempo, lighter and more soloistic scoring and often in mode or harmonic idiom. All this can be heard in the "London" Symphony, with its regal framing minuet sections and smoothly sophisticated trio featuring elegant woodwind passages. Finally, the concluding movements of Classical symphonies were apt to be cast in a fast $\frac{2}{4}$ meter, also derived from dance, thus creating a dance pair with the minuet that actually reflected the ballroom repertoire of the time. The simplest and most common form was a ***rondo*** in which a lively opening theme alternates with "episodes." In some instances Haydn expanded this by putting "developmental sections," full of harmonic adventure and motivic ingenuity, in place of the neutral episodes of the simpler rondo form. Since this procedure shares features with sonatas, it is sometimes dubbed "sonata-rondo," and it became a favorite form for Mozart, Beethoven, and others.

For Haydn and his eighteenth-century audience, the form was made intelligible through a tonal, not a thematic, contrast.

The finale of Symphony No. 104 is not a rondo or sonata-rondo, however, but, rather, another sonata form. Its main theme is a simple eight-bar tune that may have been adapted from some popular source; a folk song and a London street cry have been proposed. Its rustic character comes from the sustained D that imitates the sound of a bagpipe. One of the most notable features of the movement is its extended coda, which itself contains developmental thematic work. This aspect of Haydn's last symphony points to the future, when the concluding movements took on ever-greater length and weight.

To the end, Haydn was expanding the horizons of his signature genre in response to the new importance of the subscription public to his art. The radical economy of thematic content together with the generous expansion of the tonal trajectory combined to enlarge the music's meaningfulness. Haydn's apparent thematic miserliness makes internal connections pervasive; that is its true purpose and achievement. In such a situation practically every phrase relates thematically to music previously heard and forecasts the music to come. The more consistent and rigorous the thematic process and the more adventurous the tonal range (Fig. 13-12).

And this was clearly a reason for Haydn's symphonic success with the public. Haydn's diary following a concert on 4 May 1795 contains this entry about his new "London" Symphony: "The whole company was thoroughly pleased and so was I. I made four thousand Gulden on this evening. Such a thing is only possible in England."[9] The newspaper reviews were equally enthusiastic in their praise of the work. One reviewer noted that "A Gentleman, eminent for his musical knowledge, taste, and sound criticism, declared this to be his opinion, That, for fifty years to come Musical Composers would be little better than imitators of Haydn; and would do little more than pour water on his leaves. We hope the prophecy may prove false; but probability seems to confirm the prediction."[10] In some ways the prediction was indeed borne out, because Haydn's late symphonies have never left the repertory, and his quartets and symphonies, like Handel's oratorios and Mozart's operas, became the first canonical works of their kind.

Figure 13-12 Haydn at the piano. Portrait by Johann Zitterer (ca. 1790).

The Culminating Work: *The Creation*

When Haydn first took up the genre of symphony it was just a distinguished sort of party music. He left it a monumental genre that formed the cornerstone of a *canon,* a publicly recognized body of works deemed by lovers of art to have universal or defining value within their culture—a value, be it noted, no longer associated exclusively with a single social class. In their public eloquence, Haydn's late symphonies thus symbolized a gradual democratization of high art. In this way the former employee to a princely house became one of the emblematic figures of the Enlightenment.

This is not to say that Haydn consciously thought of himself as a philosopher or an Enlightened thinker, still less that he harbored the sort of subversive or anti-aristocratic sentiments we now tend to associate with the era in which he lived. Nowhere, for example, does he make any reference to the French Revolution, the most cataclysmic political event of the century. Indeed, his very late works give us reason to believe that he deplored at least some of the Revolution's consequences. In a pair of monumental Masses— *In tempore belli* (In Time of War, 1796) and *In angustiis* (In Distress, 1798)—Haydn appeared as a kind of Austrian composer laureate, giving voice to his Empire's determined opposition to Napoleon. In between, in 1797, he was commissioned to write a patriotic song, "Gott, erhalte Franz den Kaiser" ("God Preserve Franz the Emperor"), which became the Austrian national anthem and eventually the German one as well. In the same year Haydn used the melody for a set of variations in his String Quartet in C Major, Op. 76, No. 3.

Even the London public to which Haydn's later symphonies made their appeal, while broader than any audience he had previously addressed with his music, remained a largely elite society; the advertisements for Salomon's concerts were pitched to "the Nobility and Gentry," the latter term referring to property owners, noble or not. Haydn was privileged to move at the highest levels of British society. He found his access to the aristocracy most agreeable and took seriously King George III's invitation to settle permanently as a free artist in England under royal patronage.

This invitation was issued during Haydn's second stay in the British capital (1794–95), which was even more successful than the first and for which he wrote six more symphonies (Nos. 99–104). Haydn was received by the royal family on 1 February 1795, after which he wrote in his diary that "the King, who hitherto could or would only hear Handel's music, was attentive to mine."[11] Indeed, the king's evident intention in trying to secure Haydn's permanent attachment to his court was to make another Handel of him and to establish Haydn's concerts as a national institution in perpetuity, like the Handel oratorio festivals given at Westminster Abbey every year.

More works were still to come from Haydn at the turn of century, after his English adventures were over. The many operas he wrote over the course of his career did not enter the repertory, but his Masses and sacred works were another story. While in England in 1791 he had attended the great Handel Festival, which he found dazzlingly impressive. He immediately perceived something we have earlier observed—that Handel's sacred oratorios, rendered in monumental performances, were for the British a symbol of nationhood, the first truly nationalistic musical genre in our modern sense of the word. Haydn wanted to offer something similar to the Austrian nation: an oratorio with text not in Latin but in the language of the people, for performance not in a Catholic worship service but under secular auspices, to reinforce the Austrian nation in its loyalty not only to a dynastic crown but also to a common soil.

Anthology Vol 2-12
Full CD III, 23–24
Concise CD II, 14

Haydn therefore leaped at the chance to write *The Creation*. The libretto is based on the Bible and parts of John Milton's *Paradise Lost*. Haydn took the libretto home with him to Vienna and had it translated (as *Die Schöpfung*) by Baron Gottfried van Swieten, an aristocrat who actively cultivated older music in Vienna. (Van Swieten commissioned Mozart to update the orchestration of Handel's *Messiah*, among other works.) *The Creation*, begun in 1796, was very much in the Handelian tradition, including da capo arias and old-fashioned contrapuntal choruses. Its popularity in Austria following its 1798 premiere fulfilled Haydn's ambition for the work and sparked the composition of a sequel, an oratorio called *The Seasons* (*Die Jahreszeiten*). First performed in Vienna in April 1801, it was Haydn's last major work, followed only by two Masses, one of them drawing on the music for *The Creation* (Fig. 13-13).

The Creation, *begun in 1796, was very much in the Handelian tradition.*

The opening of *The Creation*, however, had no Handelian counterpart and was anything but old-fashioned in conception. The Introduction, subtitled "The Representation of Chaos," was an unprecedented attempt to depict in music the disorder that preceded the biblical Beginning. "Here is your infinite empty space!" the English critic Donald Francis Tovey (1875–1940) later declared, referring to the sublimely hollow opening sonority, a gaping orchestral unison on the note C that discloses neither mode nor key (Ex. 13-2). It was an inspired interpretation, for it identified the crucial representational device: the functional degree relationships of tonality or, rather, their withholding and gradual reassertion. A cadence identifying the tonic and dominant, normally given at the outset of a composition to set up the structural norms that will govern it, is deliberately suppressed. The expected thing is normally so routinely supplied by the opening material as to be taken for granted, hardly noticed as such. Its suppression, repeatedly and teasingly replayed, is bizarre, making Haydn's

Figure 13-13 Haydn's last public appearance, 1809. Too weak to walk, he was carried to the performance of his *Creation* in Vienna's Old University in an armchair.

Example 13-2 **Franz Joseph Haydn, *Creation*, Introduction ("The Representation of Chaos") in piano reduction, mm. 1–10**

representation singularly memorable. "Tonality," as Tovey brilliantly observed, "is Haydn's musical Cosmos."[12]

Yet while Haydn's illustrative endeavor as such may have been unprecedented, the musical means by which it was accomplished had a precedent, and that precedent was the keyboard fantasia, for example, the Fantasia in C Minor (K. 475) by his friend Mozart, his junior by twenty-four years. Haydn, who wrote *The Creation* a few years after his colleague's death at age thirty-five, was both of an older generation and a continuing bridge to a later one beyond Mozart, for he was also Beethoven's teacher. We shall now turn to these two other dominant musical figures respectively in the late eighteenth and early nineteenth centuries.

Summary

This chapter addressed the rise of the public concert, the origins of the symphony, and a composer closely associated with both developments, Franz Josef Haydn (1732–1809). The symphony began as a kind of entertainment music, performed on a variety of social occasions. Its origins are closely connected with opera overtures, which were sometimes performed separately at concerts. The earliest public concerts began in 1725 with the Concert Spirituel in Paris, which were given on religious holidays and during the Lenten season, when opera houses were closed. Following this model, the eighteenth-century concert consisted of a variety of solo vocal, choral, and instrumental music, mixing sacred and secular works. The symphony was typically the concert opener.

The earliest symphonies intended for concert performance were written in the 1730s. One example, Sammartini's Sinfonia in G, is in four movements, all showing the traits of the new *galant* style, examined in Chapter 12. The first movement is in a binary form with "double return," that is, a simultaneous return of the home key and the opening theme. The last two movements are dances (a gigue and a minuet). Also influential on the development of the symphony was the orchestra of the Mannheim court, known for its virtuosic playing and special dynamic effects. Other early composers of symphonies included Johann Stamitz (leader of the Mannheim orchestra), J. C. Bach, and C. P. E. Bach.

In 1761 Haydn moved to a position at the Esterházy court, where he would spend the next three decades writing operas (little known today) and symphonies that exerted a transforming influence on the genre, making it a permanent part of the public concert and producing works that were widely emulated by other composers. Most of his 106 symphonies have four movements. The first is a fast movement in symphonic binary form, more commonly known today as "sonata form." This form grew out of binary form, but it eventually developed three distinct parts. The first part moves from I to V. The second part is modulatory, moving to the most remote tonal area, a "far out point." The beginning of the third part is signaled by a "double return" to the tonic key and the thematic content of part 1. These three sections later came to be called "exposition," "development," and "recapitulation." Haydn's expositions, however, often lack the thematic contrast that was later defined as the textbook standard for the second theme group. While Haydn makes the expected modulation to V, he often marks the arrival on the dominant with a transposition or modification of the opening theme. The second movement of a typical Haydn symphony is a slow movement, the third is a minuet and trio, and the fourth is fast, usually in symphonic binary or rondo form.

In the 1770s Haydn wrote some boldly experimental, emotionally intense works in minor keys, often associated with the German literary movement known as *Sturm und Drang* (Storm and Stress), which depicted violent moods and social alienation. Haydn's Symphony No. 45 ("Farewell") is a work in this style. Its unusual key and some other departures from convention served to signal to his employer, Prince Esterházy, that the musicians had been at his summer estate for too long and wished to return home to their families in Vienna. In the 1780s Haydn produced subscription symphonies for a concert series in Paris. Because of the exceptionally large orchestra there, these "Paris" symphonies (Nos. 82–87) were larger in scope than those he wrote for the Esterházy family. This trend was continued in the 1790s, when Haydn made two extended visits to London and produced his "London" symphonies (Nos. 93–104).

Haydn also made important contributions to chamber music. Especially important are the six string quartets that comprise his Op. 33, notable for their heightened contrapuntal activity and relative equality of voices. In choral music, his crowning achievement was the oratorio *The Creation*, which opens with a pictorial depiction of the chaos that preceded the biblical creation.

Study Questions

1. What types of music were typically performed at an eighteenth-century concert? In what ways did an eighteenth-century concert differ from a modern one?
2. How did the symphony originate? Who were some of its earliest composers, and where were their symphonies performed? What was the role of the Mannheim orchestra?
3. Describe some stylistic and formal features of an early symphony, such as Giovanni Battista Sammartini's Sinfonia in G.
4. Describe the various types of musical symbolism Haydn used in his Symphony No. 45 ("Farewell") to express his musicians' wish to go home.
5. Describe the main sections of a typical Haydn work in symphonic binary form. How does Haydn's use of this form differ from the form that was later defined as textbook "sonata form"?
6. Compare and contrast Haydn's Symphony No. 104 with Sammartini's Sinfonia in G. What stylistic and formal innovations stand out most clearly?
7. Discuss Haydn's contributions to chamber music. Why did he describe his Op. 33 string quartets as being written in "a new and special manner"?
8. What circumstances led Haydn to write the oratorio *The Creation?* How does Haydn represent chaos at the beginning of this work?

Key Terms

Concert Spirituel
development
divertimento
exposition
minuet and trio
recapitulation
rondo
sonata form
string quartet
Sturm und Drang
symphony (*sinfonia*)
symphonic binary form
thematic work

14

The Composer's Voice: Mozart

An astonished Haydn exclaimed to Leopold Mozart, "Before God and as an honest man I tell you that your son is the greatest composer known to me in person or by name. He has taste, and, what is more, the most profound knowledge of composition."[1] This pronouncement is another in the long line of famous benedictions from one generation of composers to the next, some of which we have already seen. Accounts of such blessings, even if entirely fictional, nonetheless serve a crucial role in helping to construct and perpetuate a lineage of master composers. As Haydn blessed Mozart, so Mozart does Beethoven, and Beethoven Schubert, and so forth through time.

Posterity has turned Mozart (Fig. 14-1) into an "icon"—the "image of music," tinged with an aura of holiness—for many reasons. One is his phenomenal precociousness and productivity; another is his heartbreakingly premature death at age thirty-five; yet another is his musical universality and the staggering range of his gifts, both as performer and as composer. His earliest surviving composition, a small harpsichord keyboard piece written in the notebook of his sister Maria Anna ("Nannerl"), was apparently composed just after his fifth birthday. His last was a Requiem Mass, on which he was working at the time of his death. During his brief life Mozart managed to compose such a vast quantity of music that it takes a book of a thousand pages, Ludwig von Köchel's frequently revised chronological catalogue first published in 1862, just to list it adequately and to provide the "K. numbers" used to identify his works. The quantity of music is of such a quality that the best of it has long served as a standard of musical perfection within the Western tradition.

Figure 14-1 Wolfgang Amadè Mozart.

The composer was baptized Joannes Chrysostomus Wolfgangus Theophilus Mozart on 28 January 1756. Theophilus in Greek means "love of God," as do the other language alternatives that Mozart occasionally used: Gottlieb, Amadeus, and Amadeo. Beginning in his early twenties he most often signed his name Wolfgang Amadè Mozart. He was born in Salzburg, where his formidable father, Leopold Mozart (1719–87), served as deputy music director in the court of the Prince-Archbishop, who ruled this important city-state near the Bavarian border. By 1762, when the prodigy was six years old, his father relinquished most of his duties and gave up his own composing career so that he could see properly to his son's musical education. He also began to display Mozart's amazing gifts to the courts and musical centers of Europe on a grand tour that lasted more than three years. Mozart's formative years were thus spent abroad, providing him less with a conventional formal education than with an experiential one. Mozart would later emphasize the importance of "seeing the world," especially as it allowed him to leave his native Salzburg, a city he came to detest. In his early twenties he wrote to his father: "I assure you that people who do not travel (I mean those who cultivate the arts and learning) are indeed miserable creatures."[2]

By the age of ten the boy (Fig. 14-2) was famous, having performed at courts throughout the German Catholic territories, the Netherlands, and Paris. He stayed for more than a year in London, where he was fêted at the court of King George III, became friendly with Johann Christian Bach, and underwent a series of scientific tests at the Royal Society, a prestigious scientific association, to prove that he truly was an extraordinary, gifted child and not a musically accomplished dwarf.

Leopold, a devout Catholic with little sympathy for some aspects of the Enlightenment "Age of Reason," remarked in a letter to a family friend that people were astounded by his son: "I owe this act to Almighty God, otherwise I should be the most thankless creature. *And if it is ever to be my duty to convince the world of this miracle, it is so now, when people are ridiculing whatever is called a miracle and denying all miracles.* Therefore they must be convinced. And was it not a great joy and a tremendous victory for me to hear a Voltairian say to me in amazement: '*Now for once in my life I have seen a miracle; and this is the first!*'"[3] It is largely because of his uncanny gifts and his famously complicated relations with his father that Mozart has been such a frequent subject of fiction, dramatization, psychobiography, and sheer rumor, including the persistent tall tale of his death by poisoning at the hand of Antonio Salieri (1750–1825), who held the coveted official position of Court Kapellmeister at the Habsburg Court in Vienna.

Mozart's iconic status is also due to his singular skill in moving audiences. His success at evoking emotional sympathy kindled interest in his own personality to an extent that was unprecedented at that time in the history of European music.

TIMELINE

1756 **Birth of Wolfgang Amadè Mozart**
1762 **Mozart begins a European tour as a musical prodigy**
1769 **Mozart's first opera, *La finta semplice***
1776 American Declaration of Independence
1779–80 **Mozart, Sinfonia Concertante for Violin and Viola, K. 364**
1781 **Mozart, *Idomeneo***
1781 **Mozart moves to Vienna**
1781 Immanuel Kant, *Critique of Pure Reason*
1782 **Death of Metastasio**
1782 **Joseph II appoints Lorenzo Da Ponte as poet to the court theater**

His compositions, in practically every genre he cultivated (and he cultivated all of them), have been maintained in an unbroken performing tradition from his time to ours. His works are the foundation of the current classical music repertoire in both the concert hall and the opera house and have been so ever since there has been such a repertoire, that is, since the period immediately following his death. Except for Handel's oratorios, nothing earlier has lasted in this way. Haydn, Mozart's greatest contemporary, has survived only in part. Bach, as we know, returned to full active duty only after a long time underground.

Mozart's broad and lengthy travels with his father and Nannerl, a talented musician and sometimes composer herself, extended beyond France and England to Italy, Germany (where he heard the famed orchestra in Mannheim), and elsewhere. An important consequence of these years of wandering was his acquisition of new languages, both linguistic and musical. Mozart's abundant letters are revealing, delightful, often playful and sometimes lewd (toilet humor being favored, especially in flirtatious exchanges with his pretty young cousin and later with his wife). A passage he wrote in his sister's diary offers a veritable Babel of languages—Italian, German, French, and Latin—all freely mixed together from one word to the next: "post prandium la sig'ra Catherine chés uns. wir habemus joués colle carte di Tarock. À sept heur siamo andati spatzieren in den horto aulico. faceva la plus pulchra tempestas von der Welt." (This might be translated as: "After lunch Mrs. Catherine came to our house. We played with the tarot cards. At seven o'clock we went for a walk in the garden. We saw the most beautiful storm in the world.")[4] Mozart did something comparable in his music, not only by writing operas in Latin, German, and Italian (as well as other vocal works in French and English) but also by adopting and adapting the musical styles he encountered in England, France, Italy, and Germany. By his own admission he could "more or less adopt or imitate any kind and any style of composition."[5]

Figure 14-2 Mozart as a boy, in Salzburg court uniform.

Perhaps most remarkable was Mozart's ability to create masterpieces in every genre of music current in his time, writing modest to supremely complex works, sacred and secular, instrumental and vocal, intimate and extravagant, pieces intended for the home, court, concert hall, church, and opera house. No composer before or after him has been so widely successful in the domains both of dramatic and instrumental music. Rossini, Verdi, Wagner, Puccini—a whole list of great opera composers we will meet in later chapters—wrote little besides opera, while composers such as Bach, Beethoven, Mendelssohn, Chopin, Schumann, Brahms, and Mahler either shunned music for the theater entirely or produced very little.

Mozart's successes in the dramatic and instrumental realms were mutually reinforcing. He learned from his own music. Part of the richness of Mozart operas comes from his writing symphonies, concertos, and chamber and religious music. The orchestration of his operas can be unusually elaborate, which sometimes led to the charge that instruments were distracting attention away from the voices. Mozart also used formal procedures, such as sonata form, in his operas. At the same time, the vocal, lyric, and dramatic elements associated with his operas fundamentally informed his instrumental music. We shall begin our consideration of Mozart with his operas before turning to the other genres with which they so fruitfully interacted.

The Early Operas

Mozart's operas have not only survived where Haydn's have perished, but a half dozen of them, roughly a third of his output in the genre, now form the bedrock of the standard repertory and are the earliest operas familiar today to general theatergoers. They sum up and synthesize all the varieties of musical drama current in the eighteenth century, and they have served as a model to opera composers ever since.

At age eleven Mozart wrote his first dramatic work, an intermezzo called *Apollo et Hyacinthus,* to a libretto in Latin for performance at Salzburg University. (He used a melody from it in the second movement of a symphony composed a few months later.) Within a couple of years he was equipped to turn out works of fully professional caliber in the principal theatrical genres then current. In 1769, the thirteen-year-old's first opera buffa, called *La finta semplice* (The Pretended Simpleton), set to a libretto by Carlo Goldoni, was performed in Salzburg. It was followed in late 1770 by his first opera seria, called *Mitridate, rè di Ponto* (Mithridates, King of Pontus), to a libretto based on a tragedy by Racine. In between came another early success, *Bastien und Bastienne,* a **Singspiel**, namely a German comic opera with spoken dialogue replacing the recitatives. These three genres—Italian opera both tragic and comic and German vernacular comedy—were the ones Mozart would cultivate for the rest of his career. What the early triumphs demonstrated above all was his absolute command of the conventions associated with all three, a mastery that enabled him eventually to achieve an unprecedented directness of communication that still moves audiences long after the conventions themselves became outmoded.

Mozart's first operatic masterpiece was *Idomeneo, rè di Creta* (Idomeneus, King of Crete), an opera seria written in 1780, premiered in Munich in 1781, and revised five years later for performance in Vienna. Setting an Italian translation of an old French libretto, Mozart cast it in the severe style of Gluck's neoclassical reform dramas, two of which, based on the myth of Iphigenia, had also treated the painful subject of a father sworn to sacrifice his child. By modeling his opera on Gluck's, Mozart completed his assimilation of all the theatrical idioms to which he was heir. At this time mastery was more highly prized than originality, which would only become an overriding concern in the nineteenth century. The successful appropriation of Gluck's ideals and methods, in a manner that vividly illustrates the eighteenth century's outlook on artistic creativity, transcended his predecessor's achievement and at the same time also went a long way toward transforming the reformer's innovations into conventions.

In the summer of 1781, having quarreled with the archbishop of Salzburg and having requested and ungraciously received release from his position ("with a kick in the ass," he wrote to his horrified father on 9 June), the twenty-five-year-old Mozart moved to Vienna to set up shop as a freelance musician. Serious mythological dramas like *Idomeneo* were becoming unfashionable in Vienna. While sociopolitical reforms were Emperor Joseph II's principal interest, he also paid attention to what was being performed on the court stages. He had an aversion to serious opera, ostensibly because of its costliness. Music historians have tended to despise him a bit, mainly because of his failure to give proper recognition to Mozart. In late 1787

1782 **Mozart, *Die Entführung aus dem Serail,* Symphony No. 35 ("Haffner")**
1782 Jean-Jacques Rousseau, *Les Confessions*
1783 **Mozart, Symphony No. 36 ("Linz")**
1784 **Mozart, Piano Concerto in G Major, K. 453**
1785 **Mozart, Symphony No. 38 ("Prague")**
1786 **Mozart, *The Marriage of Figaro***
1787 **Mozart, *Don Giovanni***
1788 **Mozart, Symphonies No. 39, No. 40, and No. 41 ("Jupiter")**
1788 Constitution of the United States
1789 Beginning of the French Revolution
1791 **Mozart, *La clemenza di Tito, The Magic Flute,* and Requiem**
1791 **Death of Mozart**

Joseph appointed him Court *Kammermusicus* (chamber musician) at a salary about which Mozart supposedly remarked: "too much for what I do, too little for what I could do."[6]

The 1780s—the decade of Joseph II's reign that overlapped with Mozart's time in Vienna—saw the composer's great run of comic opera, a genre he utterly transformed. First to appear was a Singspiel, composed in response to Joseph's patronage of vernacular comedies, for which the emperor had established a special German troupe at the Vienna Burgtheater (Court Theater, Fig. 14-3). It was there that *Die Entführung aus dem Serail* (The Abduction from the Harem) premiered on 16 July 1782, and it was in connection with this production that Joseph allegedly told Mozart: "Too beautiful for our ears, my dear Mozart, and vastly too many notes."[7] To which Mozart is famously said to have responded: "Just as many as are necessary, your Majesty."

Although written in German and performed in the court theater, the opera has an exotic rather than a national subject. There had long been a great Viennese vogue for "Oriental," specifically "Turkish," subject matter in the wake of the unsuccessful siege of the city by the Ottoman Turks in 1683. Making fun of the former enemy was a kind of national sport, and the Turkish military (or "**Janissary**") percussion instruments that had once struck fear in the hearts of European soldiers were now appropriated by orchestras. The raucous jangling of the Janissary band (also imitated in the Piano Sonata in A Major, K. 331, with its famous rondo "Alla Turca") is a special effect in the merry overture to *Die Entführung*, whose orchestra includes timpani, bass drum, cymbals, and triangle.

While at work in Vienna on *Die Entführung*, Mozart kept up a lively correspondence with his father back home in Salzburg. One of his letters, dated 26 September

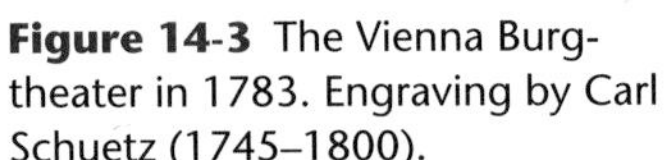

Figure 14-3 The Vienna Burgtheater in 1783. Engraving by Carl Schuetz (1745–1800).

1781, offers a revealing description of the arias he was writing. About the frenzied finale of one for the bass role of Osmin, the ridiculous guardian of the harem, he wrote:

> Just when the aria seems to be over, there comes the *allegro assai*, which is in a totally different meter and in a different key; this is bound to be very effective. For just as a man in such a towering rage oversteps all the bounds of order, moderation and propriety, and completely forgets himself, so must the music too forget itself. But as passions, whether violent or not, must never be expressed in such a way as to excite disgust, and as music, even in the most terrible situations, must never offend the ear, but must please the listener, or in other words must never cease to be *music*, I have gone from F (the key in which the aria is written), not into a remote key, but into a related one, not, however, into its nearest relative D minor, but into the more remote A minor.[8]

This sentiment has been justly taken as a sort of emblem of "Enlightened" attitudes about art and its relationship to its audience. Bach, operating before the Enlightenment, would have heartily disagreed; but so too would many composers after it. (On occasion, even Mozart himself would cross the line—in this letter he may have been telling his father what he thought he wanted to hear.) Mozart continues with a description of an aria for the hero, Belmonte, who seeks to rescue his beloved Constanze:

> Let me now turn to Belmonte's aria in A major, "O wie ängstlich, o wie feurig" [O how anxiously, O how ardently]. Would you like to know how I have expressed it—and even indicated his throbbing heart? By the two violins playing octaves. This is the favorite aria of all those who have heard it, and it is mine also . . . You see the trembling—the faltering—you see how his throbbing breast begins to swell; this I have expressed by a *crescendo*. You hear the whispering and the sighing—which I have indicated by the first violins with mutes and a flute playing in unison.[9]

While not exactly a new technique, Mozart's mastery of musical portraiture set a benchmark in subtle expressivity as well as in refinement of orchestration, a skill he had learned in part from his experiences writing instrumental pieces. Mozart's arias offered a new area in which to explore emotions and what it meant to be human. This is one reason for the unprecedented human interest in Mozart as a person. His musical portraits of certain characters have been read, persistently, though of course unverifiably, as self-portraits.

While not exactly a new technique, Mozart's mastery of musical portraiture set a benchmark in subtle expressivity.

Biographical interpretations have been advanced, for example, to explain Mozart's composing, in swift succession, exemplary works in two such contrasting genres as serious opera (*Idomeneo*) and Singspiel (*Die Entführung*). With another composer, adept powers of assimilation and command of convention might suffice to explain it. With Mozart, mere mastery of convention does not seem sufficient to account for such immediacy and versatility of expression. And so the grim *Idomeneo* may be associated with Mozart's unhappy courtship of the soprano Aloysia Weber. The jovial *Entführung*, on the other hand, may be associated with Mozart's marriage, a couple of weeks after its premiere, to Aloysia's younger sister (Fig. 14-4), whose name happened to coincide with that of the leading feminine role in the opera, Constanze.

Are such explanations necessary? Perhaps not, and they can very often be misleading, but they are certainly understandable. Mozart's uncanny human portraits in sound seem to resonate with the reality of a concrete personality. They also inspire

Figure 14-4 Constanze Mozart, wife of Wolfgang Amadè Mozart.

empathy—and this was his other breakthrough. One might respond to a work by Mozart not only by thinking "it's about him" but also by thinking that, somehow, "it's about me." The bond of kinship thus established between the composer's subjectivity and the listener's—a human bond of empathy seemingly capable of transcending differences in age, class, gender, nation, time, or indeed any other barrier—is supremely in the optimistic spirit of the Enlightenment. When the feat is duplicated in the wordless realm of instrumental music, as we shall soon see, instrumental music becomes invested with a sense of importance—indeed, of virtual holiness—it had rarely known before. We can begin to understand why Mozart could be worshiped, particularly in the nineteenth century, as a kind of musical god who worked a beneficent, miraculous influence in the world.

The "Da Ponte" Operas

After *Die Entführung*, Mozart did not complete another opera for four years. Part of the reason for the gap had to do with his growing career in Vienna as a freelancer, which meant giving a lot of concerts, which in turn meant writing a lot of instrumental music, particularly piano concertos. But it was also due to Joseph II's unexpected disbanding of the national Singspiel company and its replacement by an Italian opera buffa troupe whose regular composers, Giovanni Paisiello (1740–1816), Vicente Martín y Soler (1754–1806), and Antonio Salieri—Italians all (Martín being a naturalized Spaniard)—had a proprietary interest in freezing out a German rival, especially one as formidable as Mozart.

Mozart's letters testify to his additional frustration in searching for appropriate stories to set. At one point, in May 1783, he tells his father, "I have looked through at least a hundred librettos and more, but I have not found a single one with which I am satisfied."[10] He goes on to relate his difficulty in gaining access to Lorenzo Da Ponte (1749–1838), the newly appointed poet to the court theater (Fig. 14-5). Given Joseph II's preferences it is not surprising that he chose Da Ponte, a specialist in opera buffa, to replace the aged Metastasio, the paragon of the opera seria, who died in 1782 at the age of eighty-four.

"These Italian gentlemen are very civil to your face," Mozart complained to his father in 1783. "Enough—we know them! If he [Da Ponte] is in league with Salieri, I shall never get anything out of him."[11] It was such letters, and the intrigues that they exposed, that led to all the gossip about Salieri's nefarious role in causing Mozart's early death, and all the dubious fiction that gossip later inspired. Beethoven discussed the rumors in the 1820s. In 1830 the celebrated Russian writer Aleksandr Pushkin wrote a verse drama called *Mozart and Salieri*, which Nikolai Rimsky-Korsakov turned into an opera in 1897. The battle between the two was subsequently adapted for Broadway in Peter Shaffer's play *Amadeus* (1979), which was later adapted for Milos Forman's Academy Award-winning film (1984). Most accounts from the time, however, portray Salieri, who was the teacher of Beethoven, Schubert, Liszt, and many other composers, as a generous man and a talented musician. There were rivalries, to be sure, but fortunately no murders.

Mozart's wish to compete directly with "these Italian gentlemen" is revealed in another passage from the same letter to his father. He describes the kind of two-act realistic comedy he wanted to write, and it was precisely the kind of libretto that Da Ponte, a converted Venetian Jew, had adapted from the traditions he had learned during his early years in Italy and brought to perfection. In this he was continuing the buffa tradition of Goldoni, which sported a highly differentiated cast of characters and lengthy but speedy action finales at the conclusion of each act. Mozart was especially firm that the "whole story should be really *comic*, and, if possible, should include *two equally good female parts*, one of them *seria*, the other *mezzo carattere*, but both parts equal *in importance and excellence*. The third female *character*, however, may be entirely buffa, and so may all the male ones."[12] This mixture ensured great variety in musical style: A seria role for a woman implied all the old formulas (coloratura, extended forms, and accompanied recitatives); buffa implied rapid patter and secco (dry) recitatives; "medium character" implied lyricism. Da Ponte's special gift was that of assembling this virtual smorgasbord of idioms into a vivid dramatic shape.

Figure 14-5 Lorenzo Da Ponte. Engraving by Michele Pekenino after a painting by Nathaniel Rogers.

Mozart finally managed to collaborate with Da Ponte in the fall of 1785. The project was all but surefire: an Italian adaptation of the French play *La folle journée, ou le mariage de Figaro* (The Madcap Day; or, The Marriage of Figaro), one of the most popular comedies of the day, but a play banned at the time in Vienna. It was the second part of a trilogy by the great French playwright Pierre-Augustin Caron de Beaumarchais (1732–99). The first installment, *Le barbier de Séville* (The Barber of Seville), had already been turned into a hugely successful opera by Paisiello and premiered in St. Petersburg in 1782. These plays were the epitome of that old standby, the servant-outsmarts-master routine, familiar on every operatic stage since the earliest intermezzos, preeminently Pergolesi's *La serva padrona*. In the spirit of the late eighteenth century, the old joke became much more pointed and bolder than before as well as more overtly political: Issues of class structure, gender relations, sexual politics, and marriage are explored in depth. Both master and servant are now portrayed as rounded and basically likeable human beings rather than caricatures; they are ultimately united in "enlightened" sympathy.

In *Le nozze di Figaro* (The Marriage of Figaro), acting on behalf of the Countess Almaviva, the valet Figaro (formerly a barber), together with his fiancée, Susanna, outwits and humiliates the Count Almaviva. The Count attempts to cheat on his wife with Susanna according to the old "*droit du seigneur*," a legal right with dubious historical legitimacy (although with provocative fictional potential) that guaranteed noblemen sexual access to any virgin in their household. All three—Figaro, Susanna, and the Countess—are vindicated at the Count's expense. But the Count, in his discomfiture and apology, is rendered human and redeemed, a moment made unforgettable by Mozart's music. The gesture of mercy, central to most of Mozart's operas, thus concludes this great comedy as well. On the way to that denouement there is a wealth of hilarious moments with some memorable minor characters, including the adolescent pageboy Cherubino, played by a mezzo-soprano *en travesti* ("in trousers"), who desires the Countess (and every other woman in sight, young or old), and an elderly pair of stock comic types, a ludicrous doctor and his housekeeper, who turn out to be Figaro's long-lost parents.

Mozart reflects on the equality among characters in various musical ways, on occasion giving accompanied recitatives, for example, to servants and at one point literally exchanging the vocal parts for the original singers who created the roles of the Countess and Susanna. He thus creates a musical democracy of sorts. In contrast to earlier operas, the action is propelled forward not just through recitative but through brilliant ensembles. The work begins, unusually, with two duets for the same two characters, Figaro and Susanna. Mozart's own favorite moment in the opera was the third-act sextet, in which Figaro learns the surprising identity of his parents. Perhaps most remarkable is the second-act finale, which begins as a duet and systematically adds characters to become a septet by the end. This finale happens over an expanse of more than twenty minutes of uninterrupted, carefully structured music, a timeframe more characteristic of instrumental music and thus yet another instance of Mozart's learning from his experience composing other kinds of pieces.

Mozart and Da Ponte had such a success with *The Marriage of Figaro* that their names are now inseparably linked in the history of opera. This led to two more collaborations. *Don Giovanni* is a retelling of an old story, long a staple of popular legend, theatrical farce, plays, ballets, and operas, about the fabled Spanish seducer Don Juan, his exploits, and his downfall. The opera's first performance took place on 29 October 1787 in Prague, the capital of the Austrian province of Bohemia (now the Czech Republic), where Mozart was especially popular and where *Figaro* had been especially well received (Fig. 14-6). After *Don Giovanni* played in Vienna the next year, its success was gradual, but by the time he came to write his memoirs in the 1820s, Da Ponte (who died in New York, where he worked as a teacher of Italian literature, eventually at Columbia University) could boast that it was recognized as "the best opera in the world."[13]

Anthology 2-13
Full CD III, 25–31
Concise CD II, 15–16

Mozart's mixture in *Don Giovanni* of gravity and comedy, of terror and jest, is evident from the very opening of the work. Unlike most previous opera overtures, which had little or no musical relationship to the dramatic work they preceded, the first shattering sounds set a demonic mood and anticipate the spine-tingling finale of the opera. The dire prognosis having been given at the very start, the key shifts over to the parallel major for a typically effervescent comic *allegro* that blends seamlessly, without a final cadence, into the opening scene of the action proper. The first vocal number initially belongs to the title character's grumpy manservant, Leporello, a stock comic type always sung by a bass, who complains of his lot in life: being overworked and underpaid. The music suddenly turns dark and serious as Don Giovanni rushes on stage pursued by the enraged Donna Anna, a lady whom he has been trying to seduce—or perhaps rape: The libretto is open to interpretation by singers, stage directors, subtitle translators, and audiences alike. The Commendatore, her father, appears and challenges Don Giovanni to a duel during which the older man is mortally wounded. Thus we encounter, within only six minutes, action through ensemble, careful tonal and structural planning of a scene, and a masterful mixture of excitement and class-conscious comedy with intense drama and seriousness.

Mozart and Da Ponte had such a success with The Marriage of Figaro *that their names are now inseparably linked in the history of opera.*

Another moment in the opera is worth special mention because of its combination of ambitious musical ingenuity with penetrating social commentary. Taking his cue from the three dances (minuet, follia, and allemande) named in what is known as Don Giovanni's "Champagne Aria," Mozart in the first-act finale superimposes them. The dances are played by three suborchestras at various positions on the stage and represent the three social classes invited to a masked ball Don Giovanni has concocted. At his signal, a small stage orchestra strikes up a noble minuet, in a stately triple meter. Superimposed with it is a rustic **contredanse**, or "country dance," which is wittily introduced by some suitable tuning-up noises from the second orchestra. Its duple meter contradicts that of the dance already in progress, three measures of contredanse equaling two of minuet. Finally, the third group of musicians strikes up a boisterous German peasant dance. One of its fast triple measures equals a single beat of the concurrent minuet and contredanse. The simultaneous orchestras playing three varieties of dances present a compositional tour de force as well as a symbolic representation of a stratified society divided into upper, middle, and lower classes but working harmoniously together.

The third Mozart–Da Ponte collaboration was *Così fan tutte* (Women All Act the Same; 1790), Mozart's last opera buffa. The plot concerns a wager between a jaded "old philosopher" and two young officers. The old man bets that, if they disguised themselves, each officer could woo and win the other's betrothed, so fickle are women. The officers' easy success, much to their own and their lovers' consternation, has made the opera controversial throughout its history. The tensions within it—at all levels, whether of plot, dramaturgy, musical content, or implication—between the seductions of beauty and cruel reality are so deeply embedded as to make *Così fan tutte,* in its teasing ambiguity, one of the most philosophical of operas and an emblematic art work of the Enlightenment.

Nächstkommenden Sonntag, den 1sten Junii, wird zum Erstenmale gegeben: Il Dissoluto punito, o sia: Il D. Giovanni. Der gestrafte Ausschweifende, oder: D. Jean. Ein großes mit Chören ausgeziertes Singspiel in zween Aufzügen. Die Poesie ist vom Abt da Ponte, und die Musik hat der berühmte Kapellmeister, Hr. Mozart, ausdrücklich dazu komponirt.

Mit gnädigster Erlaubniß
wird heute, Sonntags den 15. Junii 1788.
von der Guardasonischen Gesellschaft
Italiänischer Opervirtuosen
auf dem Theater am Rannstädter Thore
aufgeführt:
IL DISSOLUTO PUNITO,
o sia:
IL D. GIOVANNI.
Der gestrafte Ausschweifende,
Oder:
D. Jean.
Ein großes Singspiel, mit Chören, vielen Decorationen und doppeltem Orchester, in zween Aufzügen.
Die Poesie ist vom Abt da Ponte, und die Musik hat der berühmte Kapellmeister, Hr. Mozart, ausdrücklich dazu komponirt.

Personen:

D. Giovanni, .	Herr Kosta.	D. Elvira, .	Dem. Miceli, die jüngere.
D. Anna, .	Mad. Prosperi Krespi.	Leporello, .	Herr Ponziani.
D. Ottavio, .	Herr Baglioni.	Zerlina, .	Dem. Miceli, die ältere.
Commendatore,	Herr Lolli.	Masetto, .	Herr Lolli.

Die Opernbücher, in Italiänischer Sprache allein, sind am Eingange für 6 Gr. gedruckt zu haben.

Die Musik ist beym Herrn Guardasoni, auf dem neuen Kirchhofe, in Landschreiber Tipners Hause, im ersten Stock zu bekommen.

Wegen Wiederholung der Arien wird ein geneigtes Publikum um gütige Verschonung gebeten.

Auch wird ein geneigtes Publikum um seines eigenen Vergnügens willen gehorsamst ersucht, sich ohne Unterschied die unentbehrliche Einrichtung wegen Verschonung des Theaters gütigst gefallen zu lassen.

Die Preiße sind folgende:

Logen des ersten Ranges.	Logen des zweyten Ranges.	Logen des dritten Ranges.
Jede Loge zu 6 Personen gerechnet, 4 Thlr.	No. 20. Große Mittel-Loge, die Person 16 Gr. Die übrigen geschlossenen Seiten-Logen, jede zu 6 Personen gerechnet, . 3 Thlr.	No. 26. Große Seiten-Loge, die Person 8 Gr. No 27. Große Mittel-Loge, die Person 12 Gr. Die übrigen geschlossenen Seiten-Logen, jede zu 6 Personen gerechnet, 2 Thlr.

Im Parterre 6 Gr. Auf der Gallerie 4 Gr.

Die Billets sind am Tage der Vorstellung im Theater zu bekommen von früh 9 bis 12 Uhr, des Nachmittags von 3 Uhr bis zu Eröfnung des Theaters: sind aber nicht weiter als denselben Tag gültig.

Der Anfang ist präcise halb 6 Uhr. Das Ende um 8 Uhr.

Figure 14-6 Poster announcing the first performance of Mozart's *Don Giovanni* in Vienna, 1788.

Mozart's Two Last Operas

Mozart's last two operas, *La clemenza di Tito* (The Clemency of Titus) and *Die Zauberflöte* (The Magic Flute), were both first performed in September 1791, less than three months before the composer's untimely death. In them Mozart reverted to the two genres, opera seria and Singspiel, in which he had excelled before his collaboration with Da Ponte. He had not quite finished *The Magic Flute* when he accepted a commission to write *La clemenza di Tito,* a setting of one of Metastasio's most frequently used librettos. The precipitating occasion was the coronation of Joseph II's younger brother, Leopold II, as King of Bohemia. *La clemenza di Tito* was fated to be the last masterpiece of the venerable genre of eighteenth-century opera seria.

The Magic Flute could not be more different. The Singspiel was commissioned by an old friend, Emanuel Schikaneder, who ran the Theater auf der Wieden, one of Vienna's suburban playhouses that catered to a far less elite audience than attended the official court theaters in the inner city. Mozart had worked with his troupe before and knew what they could do. Schikaneder wrote the libretto, probably with some assistance from others, and also played the part of the bird-catcher Papageno, the work's principal lower-class comic character (Fig. 14-7).

Along with its at-times folksy manner and its riotously colorful goings-on that reflect the vogue at the time for fairy-tale operas with magical themes, *The Magic*

Figure 14-7 Emanuel Schikaneder in the role of Papageno in *The Magic Flute.*

Flute interweaves more serious themes emblematic of Enlightenment thought. There are also various allusions to Freemasonry, a secret fraternal organization that counted Mozart and Schikaneder among its members. The plot concerns the efforts of Tamino, a Javanese prince, and Pamina, his beloved, to gain admission to the temple of Isis (the earth-goddess of ancient Egypt), presided over by Sarastro, the priest of the sun (Fig. 14-8). Tamino is accompanied by his sidekick, Papageno, who in his cowardice and ignorance cannot gain admittance to the mysteries of the temple but is rewarded nonetheless for his simple-hearted goodness with an appealing wife. The chief opposition to the deep and slow music of Sarastro comes from the fast and furious singing of Pamina's mother, the Queen of the Night, and from Monostatos, a dark-skinned guardian of the temple. The opera affirms an enlightened belief in equality of class (as represented by Tamino and Papageno) and gender (as represented by Tamino and Pamina) within reason's domain. Even Monostatos's humanity is partially recognized, suggesting at least a tentative belief in the equality of races. On seeing him, Papageno reflects, after an initial fright, that if there can be black birds, why not black men?

The range of styles encompassed by the music in *The Magic Flute* is enormous—wider than Mozart had ever attempted elsewhere—and reflects oppositions found in the story between light and dark, day and night, sound and silence, master and servant, masculine and feminine, and elevated and popular. The juxtaposition of high and low musical styles begins with the overture. Mozart opens with intensely solemn music, three chords in E$\flat$ major that will return later in the overture as well as at crucial moments in the opera. The presence of trombones further adds to the initial seriousness. But this mood does not last long. An *allegro*, which brilliantly commences as a fugue, carries the music into a jubilant realm. The stylistic diversity continues throughout the opera. At one extreme is the folk song idiom of Papageno, the child of nature always in pursuit of pleasure. At the other are the musical manifestations of the two opposing supernatural beings—the forces, respectively, of darkness (the Queen of the Night) and light (Sarastro)—both represented by opera seria idioms, altogether outlandish in a Singspiel. In Act II, the queen, seeing her efforts to thwart the noble pair coming to naught, gets to sing the rage aria to end all rage arias: "Der Hölle Rache" ("The vengeance of Hell"). Its repeated ascents to high F are a legendary test for coloratura sopranos to this day.

The Magic Flute marked Mozart's final synthesis and reconciliation of various musical, aesthetic, and intellectual threads that emerged in different ways over the course of his career. One of its ultimate themes, as in the Orpheus settings that gave birth to opera 200 years earlier, is the power of music. Pamina and Tamino (magic

Figure 14-8 Sarastro arrives on his chariot in Act I of Mozart's *The Magic Flute*. Engraving published in an illustrated monthly in 1795 in Brünn (Brno, Czech Republic).

flute in hand) state when they begin their trials: "Trust in the power of Music to lead us safely through this dark night of death."

Art for Art's Sake?—Mozart's Symphonies

Opera was not the only genre Mozart cultivated consistently throughout his career. He wrote his Symphony No. 1 in E♭ Major, K. 16, for example, at the age of eight. If he had been asked at the end of his life just how many symphonies he actually had written, the answer might well have been far off the mark—as with Haydn, the numbers by which they are identified today were given long after his death. The standard Köchel catalogue lists forty-one symphonies, yet Mozart did not actually compose seven of the ones included in that count. Other symphonies have surfaced since the tally was made, and twenty additional pieces probably should also have been counted but were not because they adapted earlier works, most often overtures. By some reckonings, therefore, either forty-eight or sixty-eight symphonies survive.

None of Mozart's symphonies except for his last ones established themselves in the standard repertoire until the twentieth century. The earliest to achieve regular performances was the Symphony in G Minor, K. 183, now known as Symphony No. 25, completed in Salzburg in October 1773. Mozart had recently returned from more than two months in Vienna, where he had gotten to know Haydn's most recent efforts, which included some symphonies in minor keys. (Mozart composed only one other in a minor key, No. 40 in G Minor, K. 550.) A further influence, similarly connected with the young composer's travels, was his third and final sojourn in Italy earlier that year. In Milan he had enjoyed a successful run of his opera *Lucio Silla,* and something of the drama of that opera seria permeates the youthful G Minor Symphony.

Another notable early symphony was connected with performances in Paris in June 1778, a trip Mozart made this time with his mother, who died while they were in the French capital. After the premiere of the Symphony No. 31 in D Major, K. 297, before the most sophisticated paying public in Europe, Mozart wrote home exultantly:

> Just in the middle of the first *Allegro* there was a passage I was sure would please. All the listeners went into raptures over it—and there was a tremendous burst of applause. But as I knew, when I wrote it, what effect it would surely produce, I had introduced the passage again toward the end—when there were shouts of "da capo." . . . I had heard that final Allegros, here, must begin in the same way as the first ones, all the instruments playing together, mostly in unison. I began mine with only the first and second violins playing softly for the first eight bars—then there is a sudden *forte*. The audience, as I anticipated, went "Sh!" in the soft beginning, and when they heard the sudden forte, began at once to clap their hands.[14]

Such behavior would be inconceivable today at a concert where Mozart's music is played. And yet in his time it was considered normal, as this letter confirms. He expected the audience's spontaneous response and predicted it—or, rather, knowing that it would be the sign of his success, he angled for it. It is mainly pop performers who do that now. Such reactions and such angling in classical music are today now regarded as uncouth. The story of how that change came about is one of the most important stories in the history of nineteenth-century music, and it will be told in the following chapters.

Mozart's instrumental style underwent an appreciable deepening after his move to Vienna in 1781 to start a risky new life as a freelance artist. In the years following his unceremonious boot from Salzburg, he lived what was by comparison with Haydn or even with his own father a much more precarious existence, enjoying a love–hate relationship with a fickle public and its novel institutions of collective patronage. For his livelihood he relied primarily on something Haydn did not have: extraordinary performance skills.

Until the mid-1780s, the symphony remained for Mozart primarily a light entertainment genre. One of his best known, Symphony No. 35 in D Major, K. 385, subtitled "Haffner," was initially composed as a serenade to entertain a party celebrating the ennoblement of a family friend, and it became a concert symphony by losing its introductory march and its second minuet. The identification of his next ones continued to be connected with travels: for Linz in 1783 (No. 36 in C Major, K. 425) and for Prague three years later (No. 38 in D Major, K. 504). (No. 37 is one of the symphonies Mozart did not write, or, rather was written primarily by Michael Haydn; Mozart contributed only the slow introduction to its opening movement.)

In the summer of 1788, Mozart composed the three symphonies that turned out to be his last, greatest, and most often performed.

Then, in the summer of 1788, he composed the three symphonies that turned out to be his last, greatest, and most often performed: No. 39 in E♭ Major, K. 543 (finished 26 June); No. 40 in G Minor, K. 550 (finished 25 July); No. 41 in C Major, K. 551 (finished 10 August). They are not known to have been commissioned for any occasion, although Mozart surely hoped to make money from them, either by programming them himself on subscription concerts or by selling them to a publisher. This independent initiative was not typical for composers at the time and points to the emerging idea of writing "art for art's sake" that would bloom in the nineteenth century.

We can hear this new seriousness in the virtually operatic first movement of the Symphony No. 40 in G Minor, with its atmosphere of pathos, so unlike the traditional affect of what was still regarded in Vienna as festive music. That operatic atmosphere is conjured up by two highly contrasted, lyrical themes, a wealth of melting chromaticism, and a high level of rhythmic agitation. In contrast to Haydn's extraordinary concision, Mozart's lyrical profusion is perhaps his most conspicuous feature. And yet it would be a pity to overlook the high technical craft with which a motive derived from the first three notes of the first theme is made to pervade the whole musical fabric, turning up in all kinds of shrewd variations and contrapuntal combinations. It is the balance between ingenious calculation and seemingly ingenuous spontaneity and the way in which the former serves to engineer the latter that can so astonish listeners to Mozart's instrumental music (Ex. 14-1).

Anthology 2-14
Full CD III, 32

Example 14-1 W. A. Mozart, Symphony No. 40 in G Minor, K. 550, I, mm. 1–9

Mozart was keenly aware of the relationship in his work between calculation and spontaneity of effect and the special knack he had for pleasing the connoisseurs without diminishing the emotional impact of his music on the crowd. His letters to his father are full of comments to the effect that (to quote one from 1782): "there are passages here and there from which only the connoisseur [*Kenner*] can derive satisfaction; but these passages are written in such a way that the less learned [*Nicht-Kenner*] cannot fail to be pleased, though without knowing why."[15] Leopold, for his part, constantly worried that Mozart liked to show off too much, thereby challenging, and in the process sometimes losing, his listeners. ("Too many notes, my dear Mozart," as Emperor Joseph II had supposedly complained.)

A prominent music encyclopedia from 1790 stated of Mozart that the "great master had from his early acquaintance with harmony become so deeply and inwardly intimate with it, that it is hard for an unskilled ear to follow his works. Even the skilled must hear his things several times."[16] This is a telling observation, and one we will encounter with ever-greater frequency in the nineteenth century—the idea that works can only be truly appreciated over time and with proper study. Entertainment and the beautiful gave way to subjective expression and the sublime.

Anthology 2-15
Full CD III, 33
Concise CD II, 17

Perhaps Mozart's most astounding technical achievement is the last movement of his last symphony, No. 41 in C Major, which is surely the most contrapuntally complex music written since J. S. Bach. The movement builds on five brief musical motives. In contrast to the lyrical profusion typical of Mozart, here he uses short, unremarkable musical tags, some formulaic. The first, which appears in the violins in the opening measures, seems to derive from an old chant that Mozart had already used in a good many works, dating as far back as the second movement of his Symphony No. 1 (K. 16). The movement unfolds in sonata form, with an impressive five-voice fugal passage in the middle of the exposition.

Mozart extensively exploits the diverse motivic material—he inverts the motives (plays them upside down), plays a theme backwards (mm. 222–30), and systematically explores a wide range of keys, both major and minor. This all builds to an astounding conclusion. After a few moments of relaxation as the strings play sustained whole notes in canon, another fugal passage begins that leads to a passage when all five themes are heard simultaneously in a five-layer cake of towering contrapuntal virtuosity (Ex. 14-2). Mozart may indeed be showing off, but he does so, as usual, in a way that never loses sight of musical expression as the ultimate goal. The difficulty of Mozart's instrumental style in the dazzling fugal finale to his final symphony creates the same sort of awe that godly or ghostly apparitions created in opera, which is why the symphony was nicknamed "Jupiter" in the English-speaking world. Such masterful displays from the thirty-two-year-old composer understandably earned the praise of Haydn, who stated in a letter soon after his young friend's death that "posterity will not again see such talent for a hundred years."[17]

"Posterity will not again see such talent for a hundred years."
—Franz Joseph Haydn

Mozart's own contemporaries recognized that his instrumental music was unusually rich in "inner portraiture." It was Mozart above all who prompted Wilhelm Heinrich Wackenroder (1773–98), an early theorist of Romanticism, to formulate the influential idea that "music reveals all the thousandfold transitional motions of our soul," and that symphonies, in particular, "present dramas such as no playwright can make," because they deal with the inner impulses that we can subjectively experience but that we cannot paraphrase in words.[18] It was because of this new art of subjective expression that symphonies achieved an aesthetic status far beyond anything they had formerly known. The instrumental medium could now rival and even surpass the vocal medium as an embodiment of human feeling.

Example 14-2 **W. A. Mozart, Symphony No. 41 in C Major, K. 551, IV, mm. 383–87; the five themes (labeled a, b, c, d, e) contrapuntally combined in the coda**

It is tempting to speculate that the novel perception of enhanced subjectivity in Mozart's instrumental music had something to do with his own novel, relatively uncertain, and stressful personal situation and that he registered aspects of this in his music. Such an artist is inclined to create "art for art's sake," as Mozart may have done in the case of his last three symphonies. And yet, of course, it was a change in the social and economic structures mediating the production and dissemination of art that gave artists such an idea of themselves. Mozart was the first great musician to have tried to make a career within these new market structures. We shall see their effects most clearly by turning now to the works he composed for himself to perform, particularly his concertos.

The "Symphonic" Concerto Is Born

Despite Haydn's unprecedented achievements with instrumental music, his catalogue contains a notable gap: The output of concertos is relatively insignificant. Mozart's concertos, on the other hand, were more numerous and proved central both to the unfolding of his career and to the power of his legacy. His standing as a concerto composer is comparable to Haydn's in the realm of the symphony: He completely transformed the genre and provided the model on which all future concerto writing depended. And that is largely because Mozart, as celebrated a performing virtuoso as he was a creative artist, was his own intended soloist—for most of more than twenty piano concertos as well as for his half-dozen violin concertos.

Mozart composed his earliest concertos in Salzburg for use as display pieces in his preteen tours. They are not entirely original works but, rather, arrangements for harpsichord and small orchestra (oboes, horns, and strings) of sonata movements by several established composers, including C. P. E. Bach. A few years later, when he was sixteen, Mozart made similar arrangements of three sonatas by J. C. Bach, whom he had met in London in 1765. He wrote his first entirely original piano concerto (now known as No. 5, K. 175) back home in Salzburg in December 1773, shortly before his eighteenth birthday.

For the next two years, however, Mozart concentrated on the violin. "You yourself do not know how well you play the violin; if you will only *do yourself credit and play with energy, with your whole heart and mind, yes, just as if you were the first violinist in all Europe*."[19] This counsel came from a leading expert on the instrument, author of *Versuch einer gründlichen Violinschule* (Treatise on the Fundamentals of Violin Playing, 1756), an authoritative and influential guide. Its author happened to be Mozart's father, the estimable Leopold. Mozart was already astounding contemporaries with his fiddling skills at age seven, and by thirteen he was the concertmaster of the court orchestra in Salzburg. He frequently performed violin concertos, both those by others and his own; while on tour he always knew he could substitute a violin concerto if the available keyboard instrument proved unsatisfactory.

In his violin concertos Mozart combined the older ritornello form inherited from the concerto grosso with the highly contrasted thematic dramaturgy of the contemporary symphony, itself heavily indebted for its variety to comic opera. Out of this eclectic mixture came the concerto style that Mozart made his trademark. Most of his early concertos are light and witty works in the serenade or divertimento mold. The Violin Concerto No. 5 in A Major, K. 219, carries the comic opera effect to an extreme. The outer sections of its finale embody a gracious dancelike refrain in $\frac{3}{4}$ time marked *Tempo di menuetto*, while the middle of the movement consists of a riotous march in the parallel minor, cast unexpectedly in the Turkish style we have already encountered in *Die Entführung aus dem Serail*.

Mozart composed all his violin concertos before his twenty-first birthday and subsequently concentrated on writing ones for piano or for various wind instruments (flute, bassoon, oboe, horn, and clarinet). His only other string concerto is the Sinfonia Concertante for Violin and Viola in E♭ Major, K. 364. The title indicates the intent: to combine elements of the symphony and concerto. Part symphony, part concerto (more the latter), a **sinfonia concertante** usually features two, three, four, or more soloists who interact more with one another than with the larger ensemble. The prominence and interdependence of the soloists are important. Mozart attempted several of these hybrids, not all of them completed, but the most prominent is the one for violin and viola, probably written in the latter half of 1779.

Mozart in the Marketplace: The Piano Concertos

By adding an element of overarching tonal drama to the form, Mozart's concertos dramatize the relationship between the soloist and the ensemble. This is best seen in the seventeen piano concertos he wrote during his last decade, when he was living in Vienna and trying to succeed as a freelancer. The professional conditions in the capital that had so favored Haydn's development and nurtured his gifts were drying up, forcing Mozart to find other means to support himself and his growing family.[20] He relied on a mixture of teaching, publications, patronage, and performances. He took on a limited number of elite female students and planned his teaching strategy carefully, charging for multiple lessons in advance so that he would be sure to be paid even if one had to be cancelled. In May 1781 he informed his father: "I could have as many [students] as I want, but I do not choose to take many. I intend to be better paid than others."[21] Some months later he told his father of other ways to make money: "I can write, it is true, at least one opera a year, give a concert annually and have things engraved and published by subscription. There are other concerts too where one can make money, particularly if one has been living in a place for a long time and has a good reputation."[22]

Piano concertos were Mozart's primary performing vehicles at concerts and aristocratic soirées. Those he composed in the Vienna years began with three in 1782–83 (now known as Nos. 11–13, K. 413, 414, 415) and extend to Concerto No. 27 in B♭ Major, K. 595, completed on 5 January 1791. Yet his concertos were not evenly spread out over time, and their chronology, in fact, is something of an index of Mozart's fortunes in the musical marketplace. At first, as a novel presence in Vienna, he was considered fashionable and was much sought after. Between 1782 and 1786 he was allowed to rent the court theater every year for a gala concert; he gave frequent, well-attended subscription concerts; and he often received invitations to perform at aristocratic salons. He lived well during this period, in an ample apartment, and had various trappings of status, including a horse, a carriage, and servants (Fig. 14-9).

At the pinnacle of his early success he proudly sent his father a list of his engagements during the Lenten season of 1784. Lent, when theaters were banned by law from presenting operas and plays, was always the busiest time of year for concerts, and Mozart had some twenty engagements over five weeks, most of them aristocratic soirées. These occasions included concerto performances, and so Mozart completed no fewer than six concertos during that golden year of 1784, with three following in 1785 and another three in 1786. But then, for a variety of reasons, including inflation, Austria's war with the Ottoman Turks, and perhaps overexposure, his fortunes declined. By 1789 he could no longer present concerts that were profitable. "I circulated a subscription list for fourteen days," he complained in a letter to a

Figure 14-9 A Mozart family portrait, ca. 1780, by Johann Nepomuk della Croce. Mozart and his sister Maria Anna ("Nannerl") are at the keyboard; their father Leopold holds a violin; the portrait on the wall shows the composer's mother, who had died in 1778 in Paris while accompanying him on tour.

friend, "and so far the only name on it is that of the Baron van Swieten!"[23] He had to move to a smaller apartment, lost his status possessions, and went into debt, so when he died his widow inherited liabilities that were only somewhat offset by the value of his clothing. This decline is also reflected in Mozart's concerto output, with only two (K. 537 and 595) completed between late 1786 and his death in 1791.

The Piano Concerto in G Major, K. 453

Heinrich Christoph Koch (1749–1816), the most encyclopedic music theorist and critic of the late eighteenth century, described the contemporary concerto in terms of its relationship to the symphony and noted that if one considers "Mozart's masterpieces in this category of art works, one has an exact description of the characteristics of a good concerto."[24] According to the pianist and composer Carl Czerny, a pupil of Beethoven, Mozart established the form of the solo concerto expressly as a vehicle for representing the same kind of intense subjective feeling we have already observed in his operas and symphonies.[25] Like all the other genres of the late eighteenth century, the concerto was formally transformed in order to serve new social purposes and meet new expressive demands.

Anthology 2-16
Full CD III, 34–36
Concise CD II, 18

Although it is no easier to select a single representative Mozart concerto than it would be to select a single representative Haydn symphony, the Piano Concerto No. 17 in G Major, K. 453, is a plausible candidate for the role. It was completed on 12 April 1784, immediately after the fabulous Lenten season mentioned earlier, during Mozart's most productive concerto year. He wrote it ostensibly not to perform himself but, rather, for his pupil Barbara Ployer, and for this reason it has an unusually complete score. The notated score of a typical Mozart concerto, however, is by no means a reliable guide to its realization in performance. When he played the G-Major Concerto himself, which he often did, he surely embellished the rather modest solo part. As we know from accounts of actual performances, the soloist also participated in an unobtrusive supporting role in all the tuttis, although that is rarely notated in the score.

Like most solo concertos, still reflecting the Vivaldian legacy, the work is cast in three movements, of which the first is a "symphonicized" or "sonatafied" ritornello form. Although pioneered by C. P. E. Bach and J. C. Bach, the technique was used so consistently and varied so imaginatively by Mozart that ever since the end of the eighteenth century it has been thought of as the foundation of the Mozartean concerto style. In addition to formal innovations, Mozart contributed his extraordinary sensitivity to orchestration, so apparent in his operas and symphonies, especially his penchant for giving greater prominence to woodwind instruments. Far from distracting attention from the soloist, this offered greater opportunities for dialogue and interaction.

In the first movement of a Mozartean concerto the exposition is deployed rather differently than in a symphony, in which the entire section is usually meant to be repeated. As in the older ritornello form, in a concerto exposition the orchestra plays throughout the first time without any solo contribution from the pianist and without making the intensifying modulation to the dominant required in a proper symphonic form. The pianist enters for what is a kind of second exposition based on the same thematic material but this time eventually modulating to the dominant. With the soloist now on board, the themes are often supplemented by passages and, occasionally, by entirely new themes reserved for the solo part.

In the G-Major Concerto, after the orchestra initially presents two principal themes, both in the tonic, the piano enters with a little written-out *Eingang* (entrance), a lead-in preceding the first theme. It appears that the soloist takes over all the early thematic material this second time around—or, rather, the piano replaces the strings in dialogue with the wind instruments. When the crucial modulation to the dominant finally takes place, the piano in the G-Major Concerto gets to announce the new key with an unaccompanied solo that contains a theme that was not part of the first orchestral ritornello. When the second theme, characteristically Mozartean in its operatic lyricism, eventually arrives in the dominant, the pianist again replaces the strings in dialogue with the winds. The exposition (and later the entire movement) ends with the orchestral ritornello.

For Mozart the acts of composing and performing were not nearly as separate as they have since become.

The Eingang, or lead-in, is just one element of a typical Mozart piano concerto that points to its performance-centered origins. Another is the ***cadenza***, a direct inheritance from the da capo aria, literally an embellishment of the soloist's final cadence, or trill, preceding the last ritornello. At the hands of successive generations of virtuosos it kept on growing until Koch, writing in 1793, had forgotten the etymological link that defined the cadenza's initially rather modest cadential function. Calling the traditional term a misconception, he defined the cadenza instead as being in reality "either a free fantasy or a capriccio"—that is, a fairly lengthy piece within a piece to be improvised by the soloist on the spot.[26] According to the terms by which Koch designated it, the cadenza in his day was a piece in which the usual forms and rules of composition were in abeyance (as suggested by *capriccio*, "caprice") and in which the soloist could concentrate entirely on pursuing an unrestricted train of individual musical thought (*fantasia*, "free imagination," as we may remember from the *empfindsamer Stil* compositions of C. P. E. Bach, the genre's pioneer).

It is hard to tell just what these descriptions had to do with what Mozart himself might have played at the point marked "cadenza" in his concerto scores, since like all true virtuosos in his day he was an expert improviser and played on the spot with the same mastery as when he played prepared compositions. He was famous for his ability to improvise free fantasias and even sonatas and fugues. "Indeed," wrote an awestruck member of one of the largest audiences Mozart ever played to (in Prague, on 19 January 1787),

> we did not know what to admire the more—the extraordinary composition, or the extraordinary playing; both together made a total impression on our souls that could only be compared to sweet enchantment! But at the end of the concert, when Mozart extemporized alone for more than half an hour at the fortepiano, raising our delight to the highest degree, our enchantment dissolved into loud, overwhelming applause. And indeed, this extemporization exceeded anything normally understood by fortepiano playing, as the highest excellence in the art of composition was combined with the most perfect accomplishment in execution.[27]

From accounts like this, we may conclude that for Mozart the acts of composing and performing were not nearly as separate as they have since become in classical music. They are more reminiscent of the relationship that the two phases of musical creation have in the realms of jazz and pop music today. So is the brisk interaction Mozart enjoyed with his audiences.

Performing fully notated works and improvising, in any case, were not completely separate. When playing a previously composed piece from memory, Mozart felt free to re-embroider or even rewrite it on the spot. When he composed concertos for others to perform, as in the G-Major Concerto, he wrote out the solo part in full, but otherwise many of the existing manuscripts contain sections of sketchy notations that served as a blueprint for extemporaneous realization. Nowadays such passages are usually rendered literally by pianists who have been trained to play only what is laid out in front of them in the sacred score. At a premiere Mozart might improvise the whole piano part from blank staves or from just a bass line, playing it, that is, half spontaneously, half from memory. This can be seen, for example, in the second movement of his Piano Concerto No. 26 in D Major (K. 537), for which Mozart only sketched out the solo piano part at the beginning (Figs. 14-10 and 14-11).

When writing concertos for others to perform, Mozart did occasionally provide music in advance, especially for Nannerl. In a letter to his father he requested that lead-ins and cadenzas be sent "to my dear sister at the first opportunity. I have not yet altered the lead-ins in the rondo, for whenever I play this concerto, I always play whatever occurs to me at the moment."[28] With the G-Major Concerto, composed for Ployer but also sent to Nannerl, he wrote two different cadenzas for the first movement and, rather unusually, for the second movement as well. Such written cadenzas usually took the form of short fantasias based more or less consistently on themes from the exposition. For many of his concertos, however, no cadenzas were written, and therefore later performers and composers, including Beethoven and Brahms, supplied them. (The potential stylistic gulf that can result when a composer living much later than Mozart writes a cadenza for one of his concertos raises interesting compositional issues.)

The lengthy second movement of K. 453 begins with delicate strings leading to a woodwind passage. Thus Mozart provides a leisurely introduction, just as he did to various solemn arias in his operas, before the soloist enters. Second movements

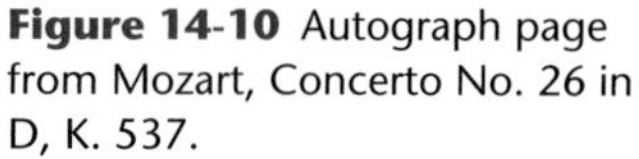

Figure 14-10 Autograph page from Mozart, Concerto No. 26 in D, K. 537.

Figure 14-11 The same passage from Mozart, Concerto No. 26 in D, K. 537, that was shown in Fig. 14-10, as posthumously edited and printed.

of concertos are usually slow, as this one is, but here the form is unusual in being a true sonata-form shape that is complemented by a striking ritornello idea. Even more than in the first movement, in this *Andante* the tensions between soloist and orchestra create emotional engagement.

The finale of the Concerto in G Major, like most of Mozart's concerto finales, is cast in the joyous, conciliatory spirit of an opera buffa finale. For his theme, he was evidently inspired by his pet bird. "That was lovely!" he wrote in his expense book on 27 May 1784, after notating a tune his starling sang. That catchy melody bears some resemblance to the music Mozart would later write for the character of the bird catcher Papageno in *The Magic Flute* (Ex. 14-3). While the rondo form remained the most popular framework for concerto finales, a significant minority, including this one, used the theme-and-variation technique. In either case, the object was the same: to put a fetchingly contrasted cast of characters on stage and finally submerge their differences in good cheer. Mozart's stock of variational characters is replete, on the happy end, with jig rhythms for the piano and gossipy contrapuntal conversation for the winds; and, on the gloomy end, with mysterious syncopations in the parallel minor, all awaiting reconciliation in the coda.

Example 14-3 W. A. Mozart, Concerto No. 17 in G Major, K. 453, III, mm. 1–8

That coda, when it comes, is even more buffa-like than most, thanks to its length and headlong momentum. With its bristling new *presto* tempo, it is similar to the ever-faster ending of an operatic act, which Da Ponte said, "always closes in an uproar," with every character cavorting on stage. Here all is given up to fanfares and madcap arpeggios (as Da Ponte would put it, "noise, noise, noise!"), the texture teeming with rapid antiphonal exchanges and with muttered comic asides like the strange minor-mode string ostinato in whole notes that frames the frenetic last statement of the theme. As we have already seen with Mozart's mature symphonies, his Vienna piano concertos likewise offer a kind of emotional diary in sound, this time enhanced by the interpretative possibilities suggested when pitting a soloist (or individual) against an ensemble (or society at large).

Public and Private Genres

Our discussion of Mozart thus far has focused on the public dramatic and instrumental genres in which he excelled and that exerted the most immediate and lasting influence on later composers. His engagement with more intimate genres, including solo keyboard music, chamber works, and songs, shows yet other sides of the composer. Meeting Haydn and playing quartets with him—Haydn on violin, Mozart on viola—was one of the catalysts for his composing especially ambitious chamber works some years before the final symphonies.

Mozart wrote a set of six quartets—"the fruits of long and laborious endeavor," as he referred to them—in direct response to Haydn's Op. 33 (then his latest work). The set was published in 1785 with a title page announcing that it was *Dedicati al Signor Giuseppe Haydn, Maestro di Cappella di S. A. il Principe d'Esterhazy &c &c, Dal Suo Amico W. A. Mozart, Opera X* (Dedicated to Mr. Joseph Haydn, Music Director to His Highness the Prince of Esterhazy, etc. etc., by his friend W. A. Mozart, Op. 10). The features of texture and motivic saturation that so distinguished Haydn's quartets were a powerful stimulus to Mozart's imagination in these quartets, the pieces in fact that elicited Haydn's benediction of Mozart that opened this chapter.

The difficulty of such chamber music, however, could lead to marketing problems because such pieces were almost exclusively designed to be played at home by nonprofessionals. The composer and publisher Franz Anton Hoffmeister apparently requested a series of piano quartets and in 1785 released the first, the G Minor, K. 478. Mozart, busy writing *Figaro*, did not get around to the second quartet until somewhat later, by which time the publisher was less interested. A contemporary review tells of how poorly the G Minor Quartet fared in the hands of amateurs and what a revelation it was to hear the piece performed by professionals. Mozart nonetheless continued to write demanding pieces, among them four mature string quintets (with added viola, his favorite string instrument). The impetus to compose could also come from a performer. The appearance on Vienna's musical scene of clarinetist Anton Stadler (1753–1812) inspired Mozart's great late works for the instrument, including the Clarinet Quintet in A Major, K. 581, and the Clarinet Concerto, K. 622, the last important composition he completed.

Much of Mozart's solo keyboard music was also meant for domestic use. Some of it was clearly connected with teaching, such as his Piano Sonata in C Major, K. 545, which he designated "for beginners" in his personal catalogue of works. These sonatas tend to exhibit clearly balanced phrasing and Alberti bass or other simple accompanimental figures. Expanding the performing forces by one are his thirty-two violin sonatas. In the eighteenth century a duo chamber piece with a fully notated piano part was generally deemed to be amplified or "accompanied" piano sonata. What we call a violin sonata, for example, would have been called a piano sonata with violin.

Another area of Mozart's lifelong engagement, one that returns us to the public sphere, is his religious music. Especially during his early Salzburg years, Mozart was required to produce a good amount of it, including more than a dozen complete Mass settings, litanies, motets, office settings, cantatas and oratorios, and various shorter works. Many moments in these pieces once again display Mozart's dramatic inclinations. After moving to Vienna he wrote little sacred music. What are generally considered his two greatest sacred works remained unfinished: the Mass in C Minor, K. 427, and the Requiem, K. 626. The Mass, which also exists in an Italian oratorio adaptation called *Davidde penitente*, K. 469, provides a vivid instance of how religious music, even the mighty Mass, was moving from the church to the concert hall. A throwback to Bach's Mass in B Minor, it is an assemblage of varied parts and styles, some quite operatic in character.

Much of Mozart's solo keyboard music was also meant for domestic use.

In the last summer of his life, while writing *The Magic Flute*, Mozart received a mysterious commission, stemming, it later turned out, from one Count Franz von Walsegg, who wanted a Requiem setting to honor his wife, who had died some months earlier at age twenty. Mozart was inundated with work at this time, for he was completing the prestigious commission to write *La clemenza di Tito* for the coronation of Leopold II in Prague. He resumed composition of the Requiem that fall, after the premiere of his last two operas, and was still working on it during his final days.

Legend has it that Mozart came to believe he was writing his own Requiem (and also that he was being poisoned). Though these legends are suspect, he did not live to complete the piece, which was finished by others, principally his student Franz Xaver Süssmayr (1766–1803). Count Walsegg copied the Requiem in his own hand and had it performed under his own name on 14 December 1793. The surviving sources and information concerning Mozart's final composition have led to some confusion about which sections Mozart wrote entirely himself, which parts he drafted, and which are entirely Süssmayr's own invention. The mysterious circumstances surrounding the Requiem, with its unusual genesis, composition, and public unveiling, seem fitting as a final reflection on a life and body of works so human that posterity remains fascinated.

Summary

Wolfgang Amadè Mozart (1756–91) is known as the most influential composer of the Classical style, contributing to all the principal genres of his time. In his short life, he produced over 600 works, starting at the age of five.

Mozart achieved perhaps his greatest supremacy in opera. His earliest efforts were devoted to mastering the common operatic traditions: opera seria, opera buffa, and Singspiel, a comic opera in German with spoken dialogue. The serious and comic were beautifully fused in many of his mature operas, including the three based on librettos by Lorenzo Da Ponte, *The Marriage of Figaro, Così fan tutte,* and *Don Giovanni,* as well as the Singspiel *Die Zauberflöte.* Although these are comic operas, they explore serious issues such as marriage, good and evil, and the relationship between social classes. While Mozart often represents upper- and lower-class characters with the traditional contrasts in musical style, he also mixes the two styles to suggest moral equality among individuals of different classes. Much of the action in Mozart's operas is advanced through ensembles, and the plot is untangled in ensemble finales that were typical of opera buffa. Mozart's mixture of serious and comic is especially evident in the opening of *Don Giovanni.*

Of Mozart's roughly fifty symphonies, the best known were written after the mid-1780s, including No. 35 ("Haffner"), No. 36 ("Linz"), and No. 38 ("Prague"). His last three symphonies, Nos. 39, 40, and 41 ("Jupiter"), are especially important contributions to the genre. The symphony in the eighteenth century was often treated as light entertainment (see Chapter 13), and these works, following Haydn's example, bring a new seriousness to the genre. The first movement of Symphony No. 40, for example, has an atmosphere of pathos that is unusual for the symphonies of the time, and the last movement of No. 41 treats five different themes in intricate counterpoint, demonstrating Mozart's compositional mastery and his familiarity with older, Baroque music, especially works by J. S. Bach, which he encountered at the home of Viennese diplomat and amateur musician Baron Gottfried van Swieten.

Mozart's contributions to the concerto were fundamental. The seventeen piano concertos he wrote in Vienna are closely linked to his career as a virtuoso performer. Like many of their Baroque predecessors, Mozart's concertos are usually in three movements. His first movements fuse the traditional ritornello form of the Baroque concerto with sonata form: The exposition is played once by the orchestra without modulation and then again by the soloist, who modulates to the dominant (see the first movement of the Piano Concerto in G Major, K. 453). The second movement is slow, and the third is fast, in rondo form, sonata form, or, less commonly, theme-and-variation form. In the eighteenth century, concerto performances involved a great deal of soloistic improvisation. Mozart rarely followed the score note for note in his own performances. We can see vestiges of this improvisatory tradition in his cadenzas and in the *Eingang*, the "lead-in" that marks the entrance of the soloist.

Mozart's chamber and solo piano works were intended for private, domestic performance. A particularly important collection is the set of six quartets modeled on Haydn's Op. 33 (1785). His best-known sacred works are the Mass in C Minor, K. 427, and Requiem, K. 626.

Study Questions

1. Describe Mozart's contributions to the following genres: (a) opera seria, (b) opera buffa, (c) Singspiel.
2. Discuss the ways in which Mozart's operas combine comic and serious elements. How do they reflect and comment on the social class structure of his time?
3. Describe the important features of Mozart's last three symphonies. Why do you think he wrote them?
4. How did Mozart support himself at different points in his career? How did he aim to address different audiences?
5. Describe the contrapuntal techniques in the last movement of Mozart's Symphony No. 41 in C.
6. Describe the first movement of a Mozart piano concerto, such as Concerto No. 17 in G Major. How does Mozart handle form? What relationships are suggested between the individual soloist and the larger ensemble?
7. How did a concerto performance in Mozart's day differ from a modern performance?
8. Briefly describe Mozart's contributions to chamber music and sacred music.
9. Why do you think Mozart is regarded with such veneration in Western musical culture?

Key Terms

cadenza
contredanse
Janissary
sinfonia concertante
Singspiel

15

The Emergence of Romanticism

Thus far we have referred many times to "Romantic" ways of thinking about music. The prospect has been raised that much of the way we today view music, musicians, and music making largely came about during the nineteenth century. What does this mean? What are the values involved, the manner in which music was understood—and re-understood—that so fundamentally changed the practices of musicians and the expectations of listeners? Why have these ways of thinking about music been so resilient that they continue to exert such enormous power? These are issues of considerable importance, and this chapter begins to address questions that will be discussed throughout remainder of the book.

Romanticism was, and still is, no single idea but, rather, a whole heap of ideas, some of them quite irreconcilable. Yet if it has a kernel, that kernel is exemplified in the opening paragraphs of a remarkable book that appeared in Paris in 1782 under the title *Confessions*—the crowning work of the Enlightenment thinker Jean-Jacques Rousseau. "I am commencing an undertaking," he wrote,

> hitherto without precedent, and which will never find an imitator. I desire to set before my fellows the likeness of a man in all the truth of nature, and that man myself.
>
> Myself alone! I know the feelings of my heart, and I know men. I am not made like any of those I have seen; I venture to believe that I am not made like any of those who are in existence. If I am not better, at least I am different. Whether Nature has acted rightly or wrongly in destroying the mould in which she cast me, can only be decided after I have been read.[1]

To be Romantic meant seeking one's uniqueness. It meant a life devoted to self-exploration. It meant believing that the purpose of art was the expression of one's unique self, one's "original genius," a reality that only exists within. The purpose of such intense subjectivity and self-expression is the calling forth of a sympathetic response; but it has to be done "disinterestedly," for its own sake, out of an inner urge to communicate. The impetus for artistic creation in the nineteenth century became less often a commission from church, state, or patron and more often a matter of inner necessity. At least that is the Romantic cliché about Romanticism—it was essential to express oneself authentically in art, to suffer for (and in) art. It was that, and that alone, that could provide a truly "**aesthetic**" experience (as defined by the philosopher Alexander Gottlieb Baumgarten, who used the term in his treatise *Aesthetica* of 1750), as distinct from an intellectual, ethical, or purely practical one. Of course, it is easy to romanticize the ideas of Romanticism. Artists still had to make a living—and we will consider the ways, some of them new, in which they did so.

The musical works we have encountered thus far that best satisfy the emergent Romantic aesthetics would probably be the last three symphonies of Mozart. And, not surprisingly, Mozart became for critics at the time the first and quintessential Romantic artist, all the more so because music became widely regarded as the most essentially Romantic of all the arts. What made it so, according to E. T. A. Hoffmann (1776–1822; Fig. 15-1), a leading music critic of the early nineteenth century, a German fiction writer, and himself a composer of minor stature, was not merely the power of music to engage the emotions but, rather, the idea that "its sole subject is the infinite." Precisely because music, unlike painting or poetry, does not represent a concrete model in nature, it "discloses to man an unknown realm, a world that has nothing in common with the external sensual world that surrounds him, a world in which he leaves behind him all definite feelings to surrender himself to an inexpressible longing." In opposition to "the external sensual world," music provides access to a transcendent realm beyond the material.[2]

For many Romantics, Germans particularly, instrumental music was therefore an altogether more exalted art than vocal music. This was a new idea. In contrast with Rousseau, who found a taste for instrumental music "unnatural," or even with the German philosopher Immanuel Kant, who thought it at once the pleasantest art and the least "cultured," for Hoffmann, words were the inferior element—by nature representational, hence merely "external." They pointed outside themselves, while music pointed within. The whole history of music, as Hoffmann viewed it, was one of progressive emancipation of music from the bonds that compromised the autonomy and absoluteness of purely musical expression. All of this was contrary to earlier notions of musical expression, which were founded on the ancient doctrine, stated most comprehensively by Aristotle, that art imitates nature.

The Beautiful and the Sublime

The geniuses to whom music owed its emancipation, Hoffmann declared, were Mozart and Haydn, whom he considered the first true Romantics, rather than Classicists, as they are traditionally viewed today. As "the creators of our present instrumental music," they were "the first to show us the art in its full glory." But whereas Haydn "grasps Romantically what is human in human life," Mozart reveals "the wondrous element that abides in inner being." Haydn is therefore more easily understood by

Figure 15-1 E. T. A. Hoffmann, self-portrait (ca. 1822).

TIMELINE

1757 Edmund Burke, *A Philosophical Enquiry into the Origin of Our Ideas of the Sublime and the Beautiful*

1776 American Declaration of Independence

1782 Jean-Jacques Rousseau, *Les Confessions*

1789 Beginning of the French Revolution

1793 The Louvre Museum opens in Paris

1795 **Founding of the Conservatoire de Paris**

1798 **Founding of the music journal *Allgemeine musikalische Zeitung* in Leipzig**

1804 Napoleon Bonaparte crowns himself Emperor

1808 Goethe, *Faust*, Part 1

1813 **E. T. A. Hoffmann, "Beethoven's Instrumental Music"**

1814–15 Congress of Vienna

1815 Napoleon defeated at Waterloo

1820 John Keats, *Ode on a Grecian Urn*

ordinary people, "more comprehensible for the majority." His art is in the spirit of Enlightenment. Mozart, by contrast, expresses for Hoffmann something essential, divine, unique. His music "leads us into the heart of the spirit realm"—for those of "us," anyway, who are equipped to make such a spiritual journey. For all these reasons Mozart's music, unlike Haydn's, gives rise not only to bliss but to fear and trembling, and to melancholy as well. To sum it all up in a single pair of opposing words, it was Mozart, according to Hoffmann and his contemporaries, who made the crucial Romantic breakthrough—from the (merely) *beautiful* to the *sublime*.

The words "beautiful" and "sublime" are now often used interchangeably in our everyday language. To say "Haydn's music is beautiful" may not seem to us to be much different from saying "Mozart's music is sublime." But to a Romantic, it was a radical distinction. The **sublime** touched on realms of the great and incomprehensible, even the painful and terrifying. For the English philosopher and statesman Edmund Burke (1729–97), writing in 1757 under the influence of Kant (whom he influenced in turn), the sublime and the beautiful presented "a remarkable contrast," which he detailed as follows:

> Sublime objects are vast in their dimensions, beautiful ones comparatively small: beauty should be smooth and polished; the great is rugged and negligent; . . . beauty should not be obscure; the great ought to be dark and even gloomy: beauty should be light and delicate; the great ought to be solid and even massive. They are indeed ideas of a very different nature, one being founded on pain, the other on pleasure.[3]

An emerging idea of art founded on unflinching subjectivity implied an enormous change in the artist's attitude toward the audience; and this, too, is a crucial component in any adequate definition of Romanticism. The history of music in the nineteenth century—at any rate, of a very significant portion of it—could be

Figure 15-2 *Moonrise over the Sea* by Caspar David Friedrich, 1821. Expresses a mood of sublime intensity comparable to what E. T. A. Hoffmann described as "infinite longing."

written (and, in this book, will be written) in terms of the encroachment of the sublime upon the domain of the beautiful, of the "great" upon the pleasant and entertaining (Fig. 15-2). It meant being concerned less with pleasing the audience than with being true to the eternal demands of art and of historical progress. This process of the sublime outstripping the beautiful was eventually cast backwards, that is, retrospectively (and Romantically) applied to earlier composers like Bach and Mozart so as to make them accord to current aesthetics. Later, in the twentieth century, which was still Romantic in so much of its thinking, the reassessment was cast even further back, to Josquin, Monteverdi, and other early "revolutionary" geniuses.

It was Mozart, according to E. T. A. Hoffmann and his contemporaries, who made the crucial Romantic breakthrough—from the (merely) beautiful _to the_ sublime.

Examples of painful, even terrifying music were already common enough in opera, as, for example, in the second-act finale of Mozart's *Don Giovanni*, when the title character is dragged down to hell. But such a scene was not what Hoffmann meant in calling Mozart Romantic. Not even Haydn's overwhelming "Representation of Chaos" in *The Creation*, culminating in the famous burst of divine illumination, qualified for that honor. There was a crucial difference between the sublime as cast in that instance by Haydn and the sublime as prized by Romantics. Haydn's representation was based on words, which made it an example of "imitation" rather than expression, and therefore, to Romantics, not fully Romantic. One reason why Mozart was thought of as a Romantically sublime composer had to do with the discomfort of sensory overload. "Too many notes, my dear Mozart" we recall Emperor Joseph II complaining in the famous story, and in so doing reacting to what Kant called the "mathematical sublime," the awe that comes from contemplating what is countless, like the stars above. Indeed, one of Beethoven's rare philosophical remarks in his writings reads: "'The moral law in us, and the starry heaven above us' Kant!!!"[4]

The Coming of Museum Culture

When Mozart allegedly remarked that C. P. E. Bach was the "father" and his own generation the "kids," he was acknowledging a conception of musical lineage that would in turn make him an extraordinarily important father figure. Mozart's and Haydn's own progeny, far more than any previous generation of musicians, thought of themselves as just that—progeny. A sense of heirship, of tradition, of obligation to illustrious forebears and their great works, becomes in the nineteenth century a stronger force in the history of musical composition than ever before. The reasons are many, but one of the most important is the growing sense of ***canon***, of an accumulating body of permanent masterworks that never go out of style and form the bedrock of an everlasting repertory. Few leading musicians in the wake of Haydn and Mozart could plead ignorance of *The Creation* or *Don Giovanni* or of either composers' late symphonies.

The reasons for the emergence of this canon over the course of the nineteenth century had much to do with the new economic conditions in which Mozart and Haydn worked at the ends of their lives. For instrumental music, the prime venue of musical performance eventually became the public subscription or benefit concert rather than the private court. Musical values increasingly came to be defined not by church, king, or aristocratic patron but, rather, by the communal judgment

of a broader public, in part as arbitrated by musicians as well as by a new class of public critics. What musicians themselves most admired and wanted to perform, write about, and emulate proved crucial in determining what lasted.

Musical values were defined in accordance with a new concept of the artistic masterwork—an almost "sacred" musical text that transmitted the permanently valuable achievements of a master creator. Thanks to this new concept, the art of music possessed artifacts of permanent worth, like the writer's published novel or the painter's colored canvas. The early nineteenth century saw the rise of the public museum. Napoleon expanded the Louvre in Paris at the turn of the century, and the great museums in Amsterdam (Rijksmuseum, 1800), Madrid, (Prado, 1819), Berlin (Das Alte Museum, 1830), and London (National Gallery, 1824) were established. And like paintings stored in these museums, musical masterworks came to be worshiped in public temples of art—that is, in newly built concert halls, which more and more also took on the aspect of museums. Mozart and Haydn (with Handel an exceptional earlier figure) were the first inhabitants. The operatic world continued to focus on the new, although canonic works—operas by Mozart, Gioachino Rossini, Carl Maria von Weber, and others—were added to an emerging "permanent" repertory.

The **museum culture** of Classical music was already under way by the turn of the nineteenth century, much promoted by the advent of a powerful catalyst: Beethoven. Clearly, this new culture would have prevailed in the long run even without him, since it was impelled by social and economic forces much more powerful than any individual artist's efforts. It is equally clear that Beethoven would have become a greatly influential figure even without the culture's support. Yet neither the authority of the one nor the greatness of the other would have attained such a speedy elevation without their interaction. The museum culture helped create Beethoven, and he helped create it. That momentous story now lies directly in our path, as we leave the eighteenth century and enter the nineteenth, the age of Romanticism.

Once again we will see that the divisions between conventionally designated historical periods, here between the so-called Classical and Romantic, are complex and untidy, especially when viewed by first-hand witnesses rather than by those who later tried neatly to categorize and explain. For example, today it is usual to call Mozart and Haydn Classical composers rather than Romantic ones, as Hoffmann did. This is due, in part, to a changed perspective from which we now tend to look back on Mozart and Haydn as the cornerstone of the permanent performing repertory, and "**classic**" is another way of saying permanent. But there was more to it than that. Historical hindsight eventually led to a new periodization of music history that came into common use around 1840, dividing the most recent phase into a Classical period and a Romantic one, with the break occurring around 1800, thus once again around a convenient chronological marker.

The museum culture helped create Beethoven, and he helped create it.

Like many distinctions that try to pass themselves off as purely artistic, the Classical/Romantic dichotomy has a crucial political subtext. Classical was the age of settled aristocratic authority; Romantic was the age of the restless burgeoning bourgeoisie, gaining force after the French Revolution in 1789. Yet even without looking beyond the boundaries of music, no one in the nineteenth century could evade the sense that a watershed had intervened between the

age of Mozart and Haydn and the present. So it was for Hoffmann when he compared the work of Mozart and Haydn, "the creators of our present instrumental music," with that of "the man who then looked on it with all his love and penetrated its innermost being—Beethoven!"

Beethoven versus "Beethoven"

This enthusiastic comparison comes from Hoffmann's essay, "Beethoven's Instrumental Music" (1813). Even as he praised Mozart's Romanticism and Haydn's, Hoffmann did so in the belief that they had been surpassed in all that made them great. Hoffmann's various writings about Beethoven reflect (and helped to create) assumptions about art and artists that have persisted ever since—ideas to which readers of this book will have been exposed and to many of which they may have subscribed, even those who have never read a single word about Beethoven. Because Beethoven and Beethovenian values have become synonymous with the culture of concert music, one can pretty much chart the checkered course of musical aesthetics since his time simply by examining reactions to him.

Ideas received in this way—informally, unconsciously, and without knowledge of their history—are likely to be accepted as "truths held to be self-evident," as "second nature." In this way, the mythic "Beethoven" stands for a great deal more than just Beethoven the man. "Beethoven" stands for a historic turning point that produced the modern musical world in which we now live. To learn about it will be in large part to learn about ourselves. Therefore before we can adequately understand Beethoven—the composer whom we will examine in the next chapter and whose legacy will haunt much of the rest of this book—we will need to know more about "Beethoven," that mythic, godlike figure of music (Fig. 15-3).

Figure 15-3 Marble statue of Beethoven by Max Klinger, 1902.

To begin with, Hoffmann's "Beethoven" represented the idea of the Romantic (or Kantian) sublime multiplied to the *n*th power. "Beethoven's music," Hoffmann raved,

> opens up to us the realm of the monstrous and the immeasurable. Burning flashes of light shoot through the deep night of this realm, and we become aware of giant shadows that surge back and forth, driving us into narrower and narrower confines until they destroy *us*—but not the pain of that infinite longing in which each joy that has climbed aloft in jubilant song sinks back and is swallowed up, and it is only in this pain, which consumes love, hope, and happiness but does not destroy them, which seeks to burst our breasts with a many-voiced consonance of all the

> passions, that we live on, enchanted beholders of the supernatural! . . . Beethoven's music sets in motion the lever of fear, of awe, of horror, of suffering, and wakens just that "infinite longing" that is the essence of Romanticism.

The cult of the creative genius, of special individuals who have special access to this realm and could communicate about it, blossomed at this time. If one ponders the most threadbare clichés about great artists, one quickly sees that most of them intimately relate to posterity's image of Beethoven: isolated, poor, suffering, eccentric, rebellious, and so forth. Beethoven stands in opposition to conventional respectability. Where previously the power of patronage, be it from church, king, or lord, had largely determined what composers wrote, the lone genius now sought to express personal emotions. Beethoven's compositions, in turn, powerfully shaped how music came to be heard and the standards by which it was judged. Many of the core musical values that are still highly prized—"original," "heroic," "organic," "transcendent," "uncompromising," and "expressive"—have been associated with Beethoven ever since his own day.

The Sacralization of Music

The Romantic view was in essence a religious, sacralizing view that portrays Beethoven as the quintessential lonely artist-hero whose suffering produced works of awe-inspiring greatness. His compositions gave listeners access to an otherwise-unavailable experience transcending all worldly concerns. It was an article of faith to many Romantics that theirs was a religious idea of art, intent on eternal values and a higher, more spiritual experience. Beauty, in the name of the new art-religion, gave way before greatness. From now on music expressive of the new world-transcending values would be called not beautiful music but great music. It is a term that is still preeminently used to describe, or at least to market, classical music, and mighty Beethoven is still its standard-bearer.

While earlier Enlightenment thought had questioned long-held religious beliefs and elevated reason, Romanticism newly enthroned art, which gradually took on many of the trappings formerly associated with religious practices and institutions. The arts, among which music held the most elevated position, could reach where reason could not and make people and society better, aesthetically, ethically, and also politically: As repressive regimes and increasing censorship closed off public expression in Germany, Austria, and elsewhere after 1815, the arts assumed greater urgency as a space for private expression. In such a political context the arts became a realm of freedom, and no art more so than music, whose exact meaning could not be pinpointed and therefore censored. This faith in art would later be shattered by the wars and terrors of the first half of the twentieth century, but during what is often referred to as the "long nineteenth century," that is, between the French Revolution and the outbreak of the First World War in 1914, the redemptive power of art, and of music in particular, offered something in which many people could believe.

"Beethoven's music sets in motion the lever of fear, of awe, of horror, of suffering." —E. T. A. Hoffmann

The newly sacralized view of art had immense repercussions on daily musical life over the course of the nineteenth century and beyond. The concert hall, like the church, became a place where people went not so much to be entertained as to be uplifted (Fig. 15-4). The masterworks heard in concert halls were treated with a reverence previously reserved for Holy Scripture. Indeed, the scores produced by Beethoven came to be viewed by the most reverential performers and audiences as if they were sacred texts, and the function of presenting them took on an aspect of evangelism undertaken by specially gifted interpreters—"great performers."

Where previously the written text of a musical composition was "a mere recipe for a performance," as the German musicologist Carl Dahlhaus once memorably put it, now the Beethovenian score became an inviolable authority object "whose meaning is to be deciphered with exegetical interpretations."[5] By invoking the concept of exegesis—scriptural commentary—Dahlhaus drew attention to the parallel between the new concept of art and that of religion. Because of its abstract character, instrumental music required the most exegesis. Where previously the work served the performer, now the performer and the critic too were to serve the work. This had enormous importance for the history of literate music as the score, the written object, came to assume dominance and authority. Recipes can be followed with relative ease, given sufficient technical skill, but texts exegetically interpreted require study and thought. As the function of composer and performer, creator and interpreter, split, those who performed music became its priests, intermediaries between the composer and the listener.

The discovery and rediscovery of past composers, their election to a pantheon of towering immortals, meant that their music came to be treated with a reverence often in conflict with the way these same works had been treated when they were new. Mozart did not think twice about altering his pieces in performance in order to please his audience with spontaneous shows of virtuosity. Performers of concertos and arias in his time and earlier improvised their passagework and cadenzas, and they were considered remiss or incompetent if they did not. For them, scores were indeed "mere recipes," blueprints for flights of fancy, pretexts for display. Beginning in the nineteenth century, however, spontaneous performance

Figure 15-4 Paris Conservatoire orchestral concert, 1843.

skills began to lose their prestige in favor of reverent curatorship, criticism, and interpretation.

These trends were aided by educational approaches in which performers were increasingly trained to reproduce the letter of the text with a perfection to which no one had ever previously aspired, and improvisation became neglected if not scorned outright. By the late nineteenth century, most instrumentalists played written cadenzas to canonical concertos from memory. Cadenzas were now just as canonical as the rest of the piece; composers wrote them down in their scores, expecting performers to reproduce them scrupulously. We can see this happen with Beethoven himself over the course of his career. He improvised cadenzas for his early piano concertos, not bothering to commit them to paper for many years, but those for his final Piano Concerto in E♭ were written down from the beginning. (Literally so in this case: The first movement of the concerto actually begins with an unexpected, written out cadenza.) Nowadays, only the most exceptional pianists have the ability to improvise a cadenza, and those who do it are as likely to be censured for their impertinence as praised for their ability.

The arts, among which music held the most elevated position, could reach where reason could not.

Improvisation skills have not died out by any means, but they have been excluded almost entirely from the literate practice of classical music. They continue to thrive in nonliterate or semiliterate repertories such as jazz and what is now called pop music, a concept that barely existed until classical music was sacralized in the nineteenth century. The **sacralization of music** over the course of the nineteenth century inhibited spontaneous behavior in performers, and the constraints gradually extended to audiences, who were now expected (as they are to this day) to behave in concert halls the way they usually did in church.

We might recall Mozart's own description of the audience that greeted his "Paris" Symphony with spontaneous applause wherever the music pleased them, as audiences still do at ballet performances or when listening to pop performers. There are accounts of listeners clapping in unrestrained delight during the scherzo of Beethoven's Ninth Symphony when the timpani offered boisterous interjections. If clapping during the music sometimes occurred, clapping between movements was expected: It was the way audiences could indicate not only approval but also that they wanted to hear the movement repeated, which often happened.

It is hard to avoid a sense of irony when contemplating the reverent passivity with which any audience today will receive the same symphonies, clapping only at the conclusion. Some concert programs now even contain guides to "concert etiquette" in which new communicants at the shrine can receive instruction in the faith. (One that appeared in New York concert program books during the 1980s even affected a parody of biblical language, giving a list of "Thou Shalt Nots.") But all this is only the latest version of a kind of agenda that began with critics like Hoffmann around 1810. As musicians and music lovers, we still live under the rule of Romanticism.

The Music Century

Owing in large measure to the enormous force of Beethoven's example, the nineteenth century was preeminently the music century. It was the century in which music embodied visionary philosophy, provided its audience with a medium in which they could live vicarious emotional lives, and became the object of emulation for other arts. It was the century in which composers could become cultural heroes and political activists, could become champions of whole nations, and could even help to define nationhood in powerful ways. This happened because the audience for classical music greatly increased as the educated and financially secure middle class grew. Music publishing ballooned into a big business; many of the most prestigious firms, some of which exist to this day, were founded in the latter half of the eighteenth century and grew during the nineteenth. Concert-hall construction rose to the challenge of accommodating much larger audiences. The manufacture of musical instruments also advanced; affordable parlor pianos became standard middle-class furniture and were mass-produced to meet public demand. The nineteenth century was the first great century of musical commerce and publicity.

New audiences required a whole new class of public educators and spokesmen. Thus new institutions of standardized professional instruction in music flourished, thanks to the newly powerful conservatory system that had originated in revolutionary France and had been exported as a by-product of Napoleon's conquests. The music conservatory found fertile soil in France, Italy, and Germany, whence it spread to outlying regions like Russia and the United States. Many important composers—Luigi Cherubini in France, Felix Mendelssohn in Germany, Anton Rubinstein in Russia—became conservatory directors and professors, training their pupils in an increasingly rigorous and standard academic discipline of composition. (What we now call sonata form, for example, was described as such by Anton Reicha, a transplanted Bohemian composer, in an influential textbook devised for the Paris Conservatoire and published in the mid-1820s.)

Many important composers became music critics, including Robert Schumann in Germany, Hector Berlioz in France, and the lesser known Alexander Serov and César Cui in Russia. There were also some very influential noncomposing critics, including Eduard Hanslick in Vienna and George Bernard Shaw in London later in the century. While theoretical and educational writings about music had long existed, they addressed an audience of professionals and amateur practitioners. It was a new musical market—new patterns of consumption by a broad nonprofessional public—that required the mediation of public spokesman and public advisers. This is one reason why many reviews read like "consumer reports," informing readers of how difficult pieces were to play, what the covers of publications looked like, how clearly and accurately the music was printed, and so forth.

The audience for classical music greatly increased as the educated and financially secure middle class grew.

The birth of modern musical criticism is usually traced to the founding at Leipzig, in 1798, of the *Allgemeine musikalische Zeitung*, a "musical newspaper for the general public," to give its name the proper nuance. Friedrich Rochlitz (1769–1842), its first editor, was an amateur musician, trained as a theologian, who had worked as a professional journalist and translator before specializing in music criticism. Rochlitz kept his post at the helm for two decades and became the most influential musical tastemaker in Germany. The momentous early articles on Beethoven by E. T. A. Hoffmann that we have been sampling were published in the *Allgemeine musikalische Zeitung* during Rochlitz's tenure. The journal itself lasted until 1848.

In seeming paradox, the nineteenth century, the century of growing commerce, technology, industry, journalism, and mass education, was also the century in which some composers chose to cultivate introspection to the point of near incomprehensibility. They rejected their predecessors, asserted the claim that they were more important than their patrons and audiences, and, in a pair of closely related, characteristically Romantic terms, purported to emancipate themselves and their art and to render both their art and themselves free or autonomous. It was thus the great century of artistic individualism. This paradox, however, was only on the surface, for individualism and self-expression were also prime middle-class ideals. In seeming to oppose their public, musicians were actually imitating it, for emancipation—political, social, economic—was their common goal. Both the composers and their listeners idealized the "self-made man."

Nationalism: I, We, and They

The subjectivity celebrated in Romanticism involves not only the individual but also his or her relationship to self-defining groups and to others—what we might call the "I," "We," and "They." One of the great questions reexamined by Romanticism was the question of where truth lay. Older concepts of truth had depended primarily on revelation, as in religion, or on the power of enforcement, as in social hierarchies. The Enlightenment depended for its notion of truth on the assumption of an inherent endowment, holding truth to be external but universal, deducible through the exercise of reason. Whether revealed, enforced, innate, or rationally deduced, these earlier concepts of truth had one thing in common: They could be formulated as "the" truth.

Romanticism provided an alternative to these notions by removing the definite article. Truth, not "the" truth, is found in individual consciousness, not decreed by public power (Fig. 15-5). Romantics prized the particular and the unique, as we recall from the preamble to Rousseau's *Confessions* that opened this chapter. In its purest or most radical form, Romantic individualism turned inward from public life, espousing a pessimistic social and civic passivity. This attitude found eloquent expression in English poet John Keats's declaration: "Beauty is truth, truth, beauty." We may call this view Romantic "aestheticism," and it is the source of the still-potent belief that art and politics are mutually indifferent if not mutually hostile terrains.

Nationalism emerges in the nineteenth century as an overwhelming personal and political force.

Far from politically passive, however, was another strain of Romanticism—one that substituted collective consciousness for individual consciousness as the arbiter of truth claims. The human collectivity most commonly invoked for this purpose was the "nation"—a new, changeable, and slippery concept. An individual's self-definition no longer came from saying something like "I am a Christian" or "I am a farmer" but, rather, "I am a German" or "I am a Czech." Nationalism emerges in the nineteenth century as an overwhelming personal and political force. A nation, unlike a state, was not necessarily a political entity. It was not primarily defined by dynasties or by territorial boundaries. Rather, a nation was defined by a collective culture, a complex combination of language, customs, religion, and historical experience. The main point is what it means to say a piece of music is typically "Russian" or "Czech," questions frequently asked; or typically "French," "Italian," or "German," questions far less often asked. The latter countries formed the "center" of Romantic musical life, represented by composers such as Beethoven

Figure 15-5 Caspar David Friedrich, *The Wanderer above the Sea of Fog*, 1818.

and Rossini, and were widely viewed as "universal," unlike composers working in countries seemingly outside of the mainstream.

The nineteenth-century concept of nation—and its corollaries like "national character," "national spirit," and "national pride"—gained maximum acceptance where nations were most obviously distinct from states, whether because many small states divided peoples who had a language in common (like the principalities and dukedoms then occupying the territory of modern Germany and Italy) or because a large state comprised regional populations that differed in these same regards (like the Holy Roman Empire). And, not surprisingly, the various ideal or hypothetical components of national character did not necessarily work together in reality: German speakers were divided by religion, Italian coreligionists by language. (What we now call "Italian" was spoken in the early nineteenth century by only a small fraction of the population of the Italian peninsula.) Nor could anyone say for sure what constituted a shared history or precisely what that had to do with nationhood, since the linguistically and religiously diverse subjects of the Holy Roman emperor or the Russian tsar certainly had a history in common. There were also the related but distinguishable concepts of ethnicity (shared "blood" or biological endowment) and of race, which played roles of varying significance and volatility in conceptualizing nationhood in various parts of Europe.

Problems of this kind are a great stimulus to theorizing, and there have been countless theories of nationhood. So-called "modernization" theories emphasize the importance of literacy to the spread of "imagined communities" over areas larger than individual cities and identify the middle class, in its struggle for political equality with the hereditary aristocracy, as the primary historical agent of national consciousness, rather than the peasantry or the still-small urban working class.[6] Whatever the definition, the politically active phase of national consciousness arose when issues of worldly power made it seem desirable to redraw the map so as to make nations ("blood") and states ("soil") coincide. That wish and the actions to which it gave rise are commonly denoted by the word "**nationalism**." Preoccupation with "I" and "We" all too easily turned into preoccupation with "Us" and "Them"—self and other, often with dire consequences for the latter. The ugliness, though, came later. In its early phases, Romantic individualism (idealizing the "I") and Romantic nationalism (idealizing the "We") had cultural effects that transformed the arts.

German Musical Values as Universal Values

Beethoven became the authoritative—at times, even, the authoritarian—symbol of the age, the one who, in the words of one self-appointed disciple, Richard Wagner, had shown "the only possible way" for music to develop further.[7] Many composers from many countries, writing in different styles, sought legitimacy by claiming to be Beethoven's true heir. His dominance can also be seen in the way some composers resisted. And here we come to the too-often-overlooked story of the new factors we have just been tracing—the musical sublime, museum culture, sacralization, the music century, nationalism, Beethoven and "Beethoven." They marked the victory of German musical art, at least as its history was written from the standpoint of the victors. The diverse origins of the style and attitude exemplified by Beethoven were suppressed and displaced to a more mythological lineage—that of Bach, Haydn, and Mozart, the earliest "canonized" composers. The German style was represented as an "unmarked," or transparent, one that was said, in language drawn from the discourse of the Enlightenment, to represent "universal" and therefore timeless human values. "There are universal values," one historian has recently observed, "and they happen to be mine."[8] This cynical definition is not of genuine universality, of course, but of ethnocentrism—a single and therefore partial viewpoint, asserted on behalf of a powerful nation that seeks dominance by representing itself as universal and impartial. The values associated with German music increasingly became those by which the music of other nations was also judged and often found wanting.

It is easy to see now why Beethoven has always been "the one to beat." One can sympathize with those who have resisted his authority, which can be done without any loss of belief in his greatness. The very fact that after two centuries Beethoven is still the standard-bearer of the universalizing claims of classical music and still receives the fury of some musicians is exactly the evidence we need of his centrality to the musical culture that we have inherited and that is now ours to modify as we see fit.

Summary

This chapter explored some fundamental changes in attitudes about music and the other arts that took place in the late eighteenth and early nineteenth centuries. This period saw a new focus on subjectivity, individual expression, and "original genius," giving birth to the movement known as Romanticism. From the Romantic point of view, the purpose of music was not so much to entertain or give pleasure as to express intense and sometimes-painful emotions or longings. Romantics such as the writer and critic E. T. A. Hoffmann valued the "sublime" or "great" in music. "Sublime" music is not pleasurable or even beautiful in the traditional sense. Its spiritual purpose is to transcend the everyday world. Contrary to earlier views, many Romantics valued instrumental music over vocal music. Because instrumental music did not refer to anything outside itself, it best expressed the Romantic ideal of inwardness.

These attitudes created certain changes in the culture of art music that resonate to this day. The public concert, rather than the private salon, became the primary venue for musical performance. Romantic attitudes gave birth to the musical canon, a set of musical "masterpieces" that would form a lasting concert repertory. Many of the criteria that allowed a work's entry into the canon were drawn from German music. Many Romantics came to view German music as expressing the "universal" in art and as a yardstick by which other music should be measured. Beethoven in particular gained status as a mythic figure. Writing about Beethoven and the sublime in music took on religious overtones. These attitudes were central in the formation of the musical canon and its "museum culture." Concert halls became like museums, preserving a permanent body of musical works.

With the new museum culture came several related developments: the discovery of composers from the past, a closer adherence to the musical score in performance, the creation of conservatories, and the emergence of music journalism. Also important to Romanticism is the idea of nationhood. The belief that nations were bound by a shared history and shared values gave rise to nationalism in music. Other related aspects of Romanticism we will discuss in the following chapters include an engagement with nature, the imaginary, and the supernatural, things far removed from everyday life, death, and common people.

Study Questions

1. Describe some changing attitudes about music in the Romantic era. What did it mean to Romantics to say that music was "sublime"? What was the difference between the "sublime" and the "beautiful"?
2. How did the attitudes about the musical score in the Romantic period differ from those in Mozart's and Haydn's time, and how were these differences reflected in performance?

3. Describe the parallels between Romantic attitudes toward art and attitudes toward religion.
4. How did Romantic ideas about music influence the public culture of art music? What aspects of the Romantic ideas about music are still with us today?
5. How do E. T. A. Hoffmann's writings on Beethoven express the new views toward music and the composer?
6. Why was German music particularly important for Romanticism? What does it mean to say that German musical values were considered "universal"?
7. Describe the new ideas about nation and nationhood that emerged in the Romantic period.

Key Terms

aesthetic
canon
classic
museum culture
nationalism
Romanticism
sacralization of music
sublime

16

Beethoven

Fateful pronouncements, prophesies, and benedictions surrounded the young Beethoven, as they had Mozart—indeed, comparisons were often made between the two composers so as to enhance a dynasty of prestige. Beethoven published his first composition, a set of piano variations, in 1782 at age eleven. The next year his teacher, Christian Gottlob Neefe, declared in a music journal that the boy "would surely become a second Wolfgang Amadeus Mozart were he to continue as he has begun."[1] Efforts were made to ensure exactly that.

At age sixteen the budding musician left his native Bonn, a smallish city on the Rhine River, and made the nearly 550-mile journey to Vienna in the hopes of studying with Mozart. According to legend, the two met and Mozart asked him to play something. Beethoven performed a flashy showpiece, to which Mozart responded tepidly. Sensing this, Beethoven requested a theme on which he could improvise and which he dispatched impressively. Mozart's anecdotal sound bite, endlessly repeated ever since, goes like this: "Keep your eyes on him, someday he will give the world something to talk about."[2]

Although Beethoven is said to have taken a few lessons with Mozart, there is only the sketchiest information about the true extent of their contact. In any event, within a couple of weeks he was called back home to Bonn to tend his gravely ill mother, who died not long after in July 1787. Five years passed before Beethoven was presented with another chance to go to Vienna. By this time, however, Mozart was dead, and Haydn would be his teacher. One of his sponsors, Count Ferdinand Waldstein, declared: "With the help of assiduous labor you shall receive *Mozart's spirit from Haydn's hands*" (the last words were heavily underscored; Fig. 16-1).[3] And so Beethoven set off to study with Haydn, arriving in Vienna as he was just about to turn twenty-two. He never saw Bonn again.

Figure 16-1 Count Waldstein's entry in Beethoven's album on the composer's departure for Vienna.

TIMELINE

1770 Birth of Ludwig van Beethoven
1790 Beethoven, *Cantata on the Death of Emperor Joseph II*
1792 Beethoven moves to Vienna
1793 Louis XVI and Marie Antoinette executed in Paris
1795 Beethoven performs his Piano Concerto No. 2 in B♭
1798–1800 Beethoven's first set of string quartets, Op. 18
1799 Beethoven, Septet for Winds and Strings, Op. 20
1799–1800 Beethoven, Symphony No. 1
1802 Beethoven's Heiligenstadt Testament
1803 Beethoven, Symphony No. 3, *Eroica*
1805 Beethoven, *Fidelio*
1807–08 Beethoven, Symphony No. 5
1808 Beethoven, Symphony No. 6, *Pastoral*
1812 United States declares war on Britain
1813 Beethoven, *Wellington's Victory*
1814–15 Congress of Vienna
1815 Napoleon defeated at Waterloo
1819–23 Beethoven, *Missa solemnis*
1822–24 Beethoven, Symphony No. 9
1824–26 Beethoven's late string quartets
1827 Death of Beethoven

Life and Works, Periods and Styles

As we examine Beethoven's life and work, we need to be aware that the connections between them, between the man and the music, take on a different importance than for any composer we have looked at thus far. The widely held view that Mozart's music expresses deep human emotions becomes with Beethoven the perception that much of his music expresses his own life, that it is deeply autobiographical. As Beethoven's life changed, so too did his music. That hardly seems remarkable or exceptional. Did not Monteverdi's music change over the course of his long career, from that written for the Mantuan court to his later Venetian compositions? Bach composed very differently for his secular position in Cöthen than he did for his later, primarily sacred one in Leipzig. Haydn's music from his Esterházy years stands in contrast to the public commissions he fulfilled for London. What is so different in Beethoven's case is that while his external circumstances did not change much—his mature career was spent entirely in Vienna and was largely subsidized by wealthy patrons and from publications—his inner life changed profoundly as he gradually lost his hearing and withdrew from society. His struggles, suffering, isolation, and inwardness all seem very Romantic, especially so when they found expression in his art.

The course of Beethoven's career and the changing styles of his music have therefore assumed unusual weight in music history. During his lifetime, critics were already mapping out early, middle, and late periods, and the scheme became ever more deeply entrenched as the century progressed. Historians, of course, have long been partial to tripartite partitions (beginning, middle, end; past, present, future; thesis, antithesis, synthesis). To biographers, such divisions are naturally useful because they correlate to youth, maturity, and old age.[4] The stages of Beethoven's career may even be seen from a later perspective as reflecting three larger ages of music history: the polite young Classicist became the fiery Romantic and ultimately a kind of challenging Modernist. The division of Beethoven's career into early, middle, and late periods has proved particularly resilient because the apparent and sometimes self-declared changes in his musical style seem to relate to crucial experiences in his life.

Figure 16-2 Portrait of Ludwig van Beethoven by Willibrord Joseph Mähler, ca. 1804.

Early Beethoven

Although he was not the miraculous prodigy Mozart had been, Beethoven's early promise was nonetheless extraordinary. He was baptized on 17 December 1770 (probably born the day before, so his birthday is conventionally given as 16 December) into a transplanted Flemish family of court musicians, like the Bachs in Germany, although far less prestigious. Beethoven was originally groomed for a career in the family mold. He gave his first known public performance as a pianist at age seven, amazed people with his playing of preludes and fugues from Bach's *Well-Tempered Keyboard*, and published Nine Variations on a March by Dressler (an obscure composer of the time). Such accomplishments must have seemed all the more astounding as his actual age was often understated by a year or two. The title page of the variations proclaimed it to be the work of a composer *âgé de dix ans*—age ten, when he was in fact eleven.

By age ten Beethoven was appointed assistant to the electoral court organist in Bonn and published three early piano sonatas. At eighteen he took over some of his father's duties as a court singer and instrumentalist. His first important compositions date from 1790, when he was nineteen: a cantata on the death of his employer's elder brother, Emperor Joseph II, was followed by another celebrating the coronation of his successor, Leopold II. The first of these cantatas gives an early indication of Beethoven's Enlightenment sentiments; he reused musical material from one of its movements years later in his opera *Fidelio*. Although there is no evidence that either of the cantatas was performed at the time, they were apparently shown to Haydn, who passed through Bonn on his way to England, and received his approval. Arrangements were made for Beethoven to go in late 1792 to study with him in Vienna.

The lessons, confined primarily to basic training in counterpoint, did not last long. Haydn was summoned back to England, and in his absence Beethoven took instruction from some other local musicians, including Johann Georg Albrechtsberger, the Kapellmeister of St. Stephen's Cathedral, and later with Antonio Salieri, the imperial court Kapellmeister who had been Mozart's uneasy colleague and alleged rival. First making a name for himself as a pianist, Beethoven became the darling of the aristocratic music lovers of the capital, and he seemed to be duplicating or even surpassing Mozart's early success as virtuoso performer and improviser. Even though the extent of his brief personal relationship with Mozart remains uncertain, his compositional debt was clearly enormous. Beethoven repeatedly asked publishers to send him copies of Mozart's music, which he diligently studied and performed. In the margins of a sketch for one of his early compositions he wrote "stolen from Mozart" (Fig. 16-2).[5]

Beethoven became the darling of the aristocratic music lovers in Vienna during the 1790s.

By the time Haydn returned from England in August 1795, Beethoven had already become a household name in Viennese musical circles. In March he had enjoyed his first big concert success, performing his Piano Concerto in B♭ Major (eventually released as his Second Concerto, Op. 19), and earlier that summer he published his official Opus 1, a set of three trios for piano, violin, and cello. He dedicated them to one of his patrons, Prince Karl von Lichnowsky, in whose palace he lived for some years in the mid-1790s. In such a close relationship, as in his more general dealings with other aristocrats, we encounter a form of patronage different from that known to Bach, Haydn, or Mozart. Beethoven dined with the nobility, and even if he may not always have known which fork to use according to proper etiquette, he was not considered one of the servants. Beginning in 1796 he made immensely successful concert tours. The Czech composer Václav Tomášek, who encountered him in Prague in 1798, wrote in his memoirs that Beethoven was the greatest pianist he had ever heard.

The genre of the symphony offered Beethoven rich opportunities.

The piano was thus the vehicle of Beethoven's initial fame and allowed him to display his multiple gifts as a performer, improviser, and composer. The piano sonata, of which thirty-six span most of his career (thirty-two are mature works), was the genre of his early masterpieces and offered more room for experimentation than did piano concertos. This can be heard in the Sonata No. 8, Op. 13, published in 1799 as *Grande sonate pathétique*. The French title, meant to convey its emotional intensity, no doubt helped promote sales and the work quickly became one of the composer's most popular. The powerful first movement in particular shows Beethoven boldly challenging expectations. It is in the key of C minor, which Beethoven would later employ for some of his most potent statements, including the Fifth Symphony. The sonata opens with a forceful introduction marked *Grave* (slow and solemn) that leads to a spirited *Allegro di molto e con brio* (very fast and with brilliance) in sonata form. Most unexpected is the abbreviated recall of the *Grave* in the middle of the movement and then again at the beginning of the coda, forceful interjections that seem to suggest some dramatic purpose.

Anthology Vol 2-17
Full CD III, 37
Concise CD II, 19

Despite all his many triumphs it seems that around the turn of the century, as he was entering his thirties, Beethoven contemplated suicide, for reasons we will consider shortly. What had he accomplished by this point in his career? He was better known as a performer than as a composer, and while he had written a good many works, it was nowhere near what Mozart and later Franz Schubert, Felix Mendelssohn, and other amazingly gifted composers accomplished by the age of thirty. Beethoven's supremacy among musicians of his generation nonetheless became established around this time, especially after a concert he organized for his own benefit on 2 April 1800. He set up prestigious comparisons with his own music—the concert opened with a Mozart symphony and the only other composer featured was Haydn. Along with a new piano concerto and, as always, an improvisation, Beethoven presented two new compositions, both nonkeyboard works: the Septet for Winds and Strings, Op. 20, and Symphony No. 1 in C Major, Op. 21. This was a crucial step, because with his symphonic debut Beethoven was now competing not only with virtuoso performer/composers but directly with Haydn on the master's own turf. The next year he published a set of six string quartets, Op. 18, which challenged Haydn in the other genre of his recognized preeminence.

The genre of the symphony offered Beethoven rich opportunities. Mozart had written some 50 and Haydn 106. Beethoven's nine would redefine the genre and its importance as a vehicle for grand musical statements—few significant composers in his wake got beyond writing nine, a number that began to assume a sort of mythical significance. Beethoven had first ventured to write a symphony during his teenage years in Bonn but did not get very far. A later attempt in Vienna likewise proved unsuccessful. By 1800, when his contemporaries encountered the twenty-nine-year-old composer's debut *Grande simphonie,* they listened to the work with fresh ears, knowing their Haydn and Mozart, but happily oblivious to how Beethoven would transform the genre within just a few years. Critics used the word "masterpiece" repeatedly and praised the work's "originality," a watchword for the Romantics. One declared it "a masterpiece that does equal honor to his inventiveness and his musical knowledge. Being just as beautiful and distinguished in its design as its execution, there prevails in it such a clear and lucid order, such a flow of the most pleasant melodies, and such a rich, but at the same time never wearisome, instrumentation that this symphony can justly be placed next to Mozart's and Haydn's."[6]

From the beginning there were surprises and eccentricities that later came to seem typically Beethovenian. A word contemporary German critics often used to describe his music was "bizarre."[7] He begins the First Symphony, for example, in what sounds like the "wrong" key. A critic remarked: "No one will censure an ingenious artist like Beethoven for such liberties and peculiarities, but such a beginning is not suitable for the opening of a grand concert in a spacious opera house."[8] Beethoven's early works challenged contemporaries while representing him building on the achievements of his illustrious predecessors. Many of these pieces from the later 1790s remained extremely popular during his lifetime, especially his song *Adelaide,* Op. 46, and the Septet.

Anthology Vol 2-18
Full CD III, 38–39

The Septet is scored for three wind instruments (clarinet, bassoon, and horn) and four strings (violin, viola, cello, and double bass), a combination associated with light outdoor music such as the divertimento and the serenade. The work harkens back to the Classical tradition, and it was the last piece of his student's that Haydn admired without reservation. Its six movements include traditional forms, with two slow movements (an *adagio* and a theme and variations) and two dance movements (minuet and scherzo); more unusual are the slow introductions to the opening and closing movements and a virtuoso violin cadenza in the finale. The phenomenal success of this piece during Beethoven's lifetime did not give the composer complete joy; he grew sick of the attention it received in contrast to works he considered much more substantial.

Disaster

"That jealous demon, my wretched health, has put a nasty spoke in my wheel."
—Beethoven

And then disaster, the reason why, despite mounting professional success, Beethoven apparently contemplated ending his life. In the summer of 1801 he confessed for the first time (at least for the first time that we know of) that he was losing his hearing (Fig. 16-3). He explained the situation in a passionate letter to his childhood friend Franz Wegeler: "that jealous demon, my wretched health, has put a nasty spoke in my wheel; and it amounts to this, that for the past three years my hearing has become weaker and weaker." Because Wegeler was a physician, still living in the composer's native Bonn, Beethoven provided a detailed account of his symptoms and lamented the constraints being placed on his personal life ("I have ceased to attend any social functions just because I find it impossible to say to people: I am deaf") and professional situation ("if my enemies, of whom I have a fair number, were to hear about it, what would they say?").[9]

The next summer Beethoven moved to the suburb of Heiligenstadt to escape the heat and hassles of Vienna's inner city. It was there, in October 1802, that he penned a famous letter to his brothers in which he expressed utter despair:

> O you men who think or say that I am hostile, peevish, or misanthropic, how greatly you wrong me. You do not know the secret cause that makes me seem so to you. From childhood on, my heart and soul were full of tender feeling of goodwill, and I was always inclined to accomplish great deeds. But just think, for six years now I have had an incurable condition, made worse by incompetent doctors, from year to year deceived with hopes of getting better, finally forced to face the prospect of a lasting infirmity (whose cure will perhaps take years or even be impossible).

Composing remained his consolation. The realization that he still had music in him and that he had an obligation to share it with the world calmed his thoughts of suicide: "A little more and I would have ended my life. Only my art held me back. It seemed to me impossible to leave the world until I had produced all that I felt was within me."[10]

This extraordinary letter, which Beethoven never sent, was discovered among his papers within days of his death, twenty-five years later. Its poignant mixture of despondency and resolution, and its depiction of a man facing unimaginable obstacles over which he was by then known to have triumphed have made the Heiligenstadt Testament, as it has come to be called, perhaps the most famous personal utterance of any composer (Fig. 16-4). It became widely known very early on because it was published a few months after Beethoven's death in the leading music journal of the time, the Leipzig *Allgemeine musikalische Zeitung,* and then soon translated in English and French journals. Most biographies of the composer present the lengthy letter in full. It is important to appreciate how fast and far these words spread, for they became crucial to the ways in which Beethoven's music was interpreted. Never before had so much personal information about a composer so quickly captured the public imagination.

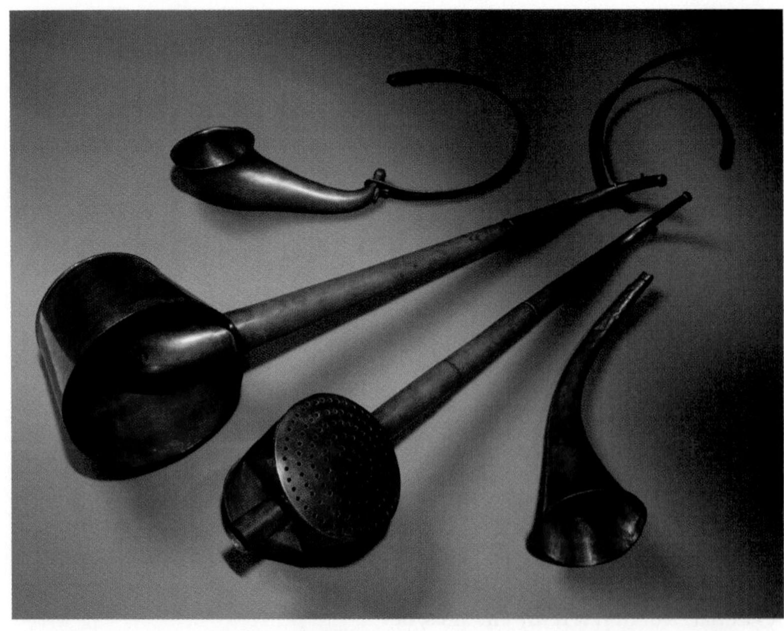

Figure 16-3 Beethoven's hearing aids.

The Heiligenstadt Testament has done more than any other single document to make Beethoven an object of inexhaustible human interest, the subject of novels, whole galleries of idealized portraiture, and movies. None of these books, images, or films would have been made were it not for the remarkable musical output that followed, for not only did the composer's deafness become central to the Beethoven mystique, it also served as one of the chief avenues by which his personal fate, as related in the press and in biographies, became the most commanding influence on the whole field of musical activity from his time to ours.

A successful deaf composer is a virtually superhuman idea. It connotes superhuman suffering and superhuman victory, playing directly into the emerging quasi-

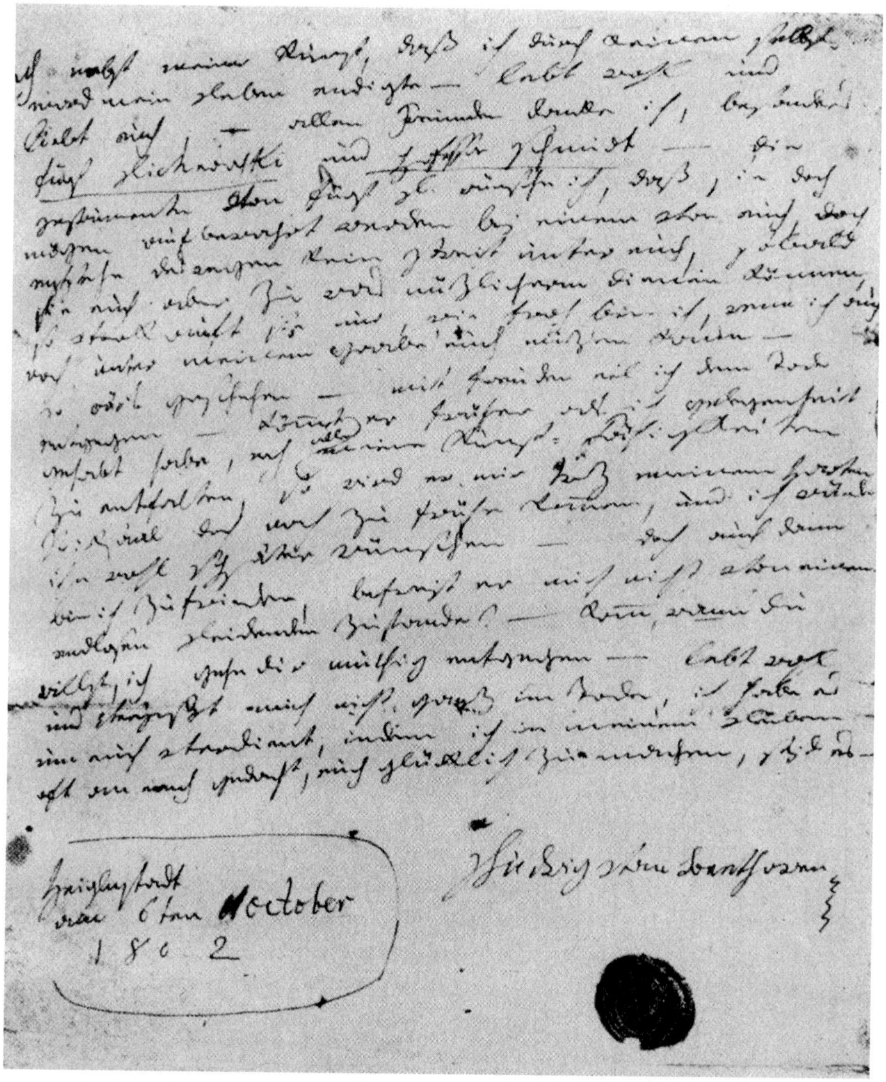

Figure 16-4 Final page of the Heiligenstadt Testament, signed by Beethoven, 1802. Unsent letter to his brothers expressing his despair over his loss of hearing.

religious Romantic notion of the great artist as humanity's redeemer. That scenario—of tremendous suffering and terrific victory—became the context in which Beethoven's music has been received. And, as we shall shortly see, that very scenario was consciously encoded by the composer in some of his most celebrated works, in which "struggles" against "fate" end in "heroic triumph."

Almost immediately after Beethoven's confession of progressive deafness and social alienation, his music underwent a momentous transformation in style; whether it is fair to infer a causal relationship will forever remain a matter for debate. He was aware of striking out in a different direction, telling the publisher Gottfried Härtel that his Variations for Piano, Opp. 34 and 35, were written in a "completely new manner." Of course composers often say such things to publishers—it is part of the sales pitch—but his student, Carl Czerny (1791–1857), also relates that Beethoven expressed some dissatisfaction with his early works and wanted to pursue a "new path."

The piece most often pointed to as ushering in Beethoven's middle period and heralding his new "heroic style" is the Symphony No. 3 in E♭ Major, Op. 55, which was written soon after the Heiligenstadt Testament. The symphony, which Beethoven titled *Eroica*, seems to express in music the struggles that Beethoven, never a fluent writer, had tried somewhat awkwardly to articulate in prose. This at least was the common view posterity embraced. But let us complicate that story a bit. Although he had begun sketching his Symphony No. 2 in D Major, Op. 36, as early as 1800, most of its composition took place during the summer and early fall of 1802—exactly at the time of the crisis confronted in the Heiligenstadt Testament. Yet its boundless humor and vitality—French composer Hector Berlioz later remarked that "this symphony is smiling throughout"[11]—challenge the simplistic connections often made between the immediate events at a given time in Beethoven's life and the music he created. Beethoven may have sought refuge in musical "comedy" at times of personal "tragedy."

Beethoven may have sought refuge in musical "comedy" at times of personal "tragedy."

The *Eroica*

Anthology Vol 2-19
Full CD III, 40

The "novel and striking effects" that one critic at the time noted in the Second Symphony were even more apparent in the Third.[12] Beethoven conceived of the work on an unprecedented scale in every dimension: size of orchestra, duration, technical demands made on the players, tonal drama, rhetorical vehemence, and a sense of overriding dynamic purpose uniting the four movements. Its uncompromising aesthetic stance seemed to aim beyond entertainment, forcing Beethoven's contemporaries to rethink what a symphony should be and do. The monumentally sublime or heroic style thus achieved became the mark of his greatness and, for his Romantic admirers, a benchmark of musical attainment.

Beethoven began sketching the symphony around the time of the Heiligenstadt Testament and did his most concentrated work beginning in May 1803, some seven months later. In contrast to his earlier symphonies, he now gave public indications of an extra-musical background connected to the piece, although what he chose to divulge shifted over time. Originally he planned to dedicate the symphony to the French general and political leader Napoleon Bonaparte (1769–1821) and entitle it *Bonaparte* (Figs. 16-5 and 16-6). Then he became disillusioned. Ferdinand Ries, a student and early biographer, related the scene:

> I was the first to bring him the news that Bonaparte had proclaimed himself emperor [in 1804], whereupon he flew into a rage and cried out: "Is he too, then, nothing more than an ordinary human being? Now he, too, will trample on the rights of man, and indulge only his ambition!" Beethoven went to the table, took hold of the title page by the top, tore it in two, and threw it on the floor. The first page was rewritten and only then did the symphony receive the title *Sinfonia Eroica* [Heroic Symphony].[13]

Ries's story is partly confirmed by the surviving manuscript, in which the title is so vigorously scratched out that Beethoven tore through the paper, although in a letter to a publisher written not much later he admitted "the title of the symphony really is '*Bonaparte*'."[14] The work was published in 1806 with the title "*Sinfonia Eroica* . . . composed to celebrate the memory of a great man." It was first tried out in several private performances, beginning in August 1804, in the palace of his patron, Prince Joseph Franz Maximilian von Lobkowitz (1772–1816), a prominent member of an old Bohemian family famous for its arts patronage. Beethoven dedicated

Figure 16-5 Beethoven's Symphony No.3, Op 55 (*Eroica*), title page, 1803, showing original dedication to Napoleon crossed out.

this and many other works to him as well, including the Op. 18 String Quartets and the Fifth and Sixth symphonies.

The public premiere of the *Eroica* occurred on 7 April 1805. Those who wrote about the symphony during the initial ten years or so of its existence did not talk about the issues most discussed today: its relation to Napoleon or to Beethoven's life. It was viewed as an "original" but "bizarre" composition, more sublime than beautiful. The early reviews show critics wanting to praise the composer and work but often confused by what Beethoven was now trying to do. As the public broadened to include more people, fissures emerged. A critic commented that general opinion was sharply divided:

> One group, Beethoven's very special friends, maintains that precisely this symphony is a masterpiece, that it is in exactly the true style for more elevated music, and that if it does not please at present, it is because the public is not sufficiently educated in art to be able to grasp all of these elevated beauties. After a few thousand years, however, they will not fail to have their effect. The other group utterly denies this work any artistic value and feels that it manifests a completely unbounded striving for distinction and oddity, which, however, has produced neither beauty nor true sublimity and power.

The critic went on to discuss a group in between, those who admire the many excellent qualities of the *Eroica* but are dismayed at the disjointed surroundings and at the "endless duration of this longest and perhaps most difficult of all symphonies, which exhausts even connoisseurs and becomes unbearable for the mere amateur."[15]

Within just a few years, however, the critical tone had changed, in consequence partly of repeated exposure. A Leipzig critic remarked, "One must not always wish only to be entertained," a sentiment echoed by another, "The connoisseur will only enjoy it as a complete work (and a repeated hearing doubles his spiritual enjoyment)

The Eroica *was viewed as an "original" but "bizarre" composition, more sublime than beautiful.*

Figure 16-6 Painting by Jean-Baptiste Isabey of Napoleon Bonaparte as First Consul (1804). Napoleon was the intended dedicatee of Beethoven's Third Symphony.

the deeper he penetrates into the technical and aesthetic content of the original work." Apparently performers agreed. Concerning a Leipzig performance in 1807, we learn from a review that "the orchestra had voluntarily gathered for extra rehearsals without recompense, except for the honor and special enjoyment of the work itself." A few years later a critic remarks that the symphony "was performed by the orchestra with unmistakable enjoyment and love."[16]

A quick overview of the *Eroica* will at once reveal the astonishing earmarks of Beethoven's heroic style, which we will consider in more detail later when examining the Fifth Symphony. Two striking tonic chords open the first movement, followed by a lyrical cello melody that is soon derailed by an unexpected note—C sharp—outside of the tonic key that already signals the conflict that will unfold over the course of the movement. The motivic, metric, and harmonic surprises continue throughout a movement of great length, unprecedented for its time.

The second movement is designated *Marcia funebre*, or funeral march, and it became one of the most influential pieces Beethoven ever composed. The C-minor opening presents a somber theme, over a drumlike bass, in the violins that is taken up by the oboe. The tone brightens later, notably in sections in major keys, but becomes even more austere during an extraordinarily intense fugal passage. The opening theme returns at the end, deconstructed so that only fragments remain.

Rather than the traditional minuet and trio associated with Haydn and Mozart symphonies and that Beethoven had used in his own First Symphony, the third movement is an energetic **scherzo**, which means "joke." The mood thus changes considerably, which confused some commentators—why such mirth after a funeral? Beethoven also plays with metric ambiguities, casting doubt on whether the movement is in duple or triple time, and gives the French horns a chance to shine in the middle trio section.

Beethoven casts the finale as an enormous set of variations, an unusual form to use for a closing movement. The theme takes some time to emerge, with initially only its harmonic skeleton given in the bass. For the theme proper, Beethoven returned to a melody he had already used in three previous pieces: in a dance set, in his ballet *The Creatures of Prometheus,* and as the theme for the piano Variations in E♭ Major, Op. 35. It seems natural that Beethoven would be attracted to, and perhaps even identify with, the mythic figure of Prometheus, the rebellious Greek Titan who incurred the wrath of the gods of Mount Olympus by stealing their sacred fire. Prometheus resisted, took risks, and suffered in order to help humanity.

In the ten years or so following the Heiligenstadt Testament and *Eroica* Beethoven's heroic style was evident in many genres, not limited to his symphonies. Other celebrated works of the period include some of his best-known piano sonatas, such as Op. 53 in C Major ("Waldstein") and Op. 57 in F Minor ("Appassionata"); the Violin Concerto in D Major, Op. 61, and the Fifth Piano Concerto in E♭ Major, Op. 73. The heroic style is even found in an oratorio, *Christus am Oelberge* (Christ on the Mount of Olives), Op. 85, a work that was very popular during his lifetime. While some critics initially took offense at Beethoven's having Christ appear as a vocal soloist, the heroic quality of his suffering and acceptance of his fate leading to the crucifixion might have again evoked some personal identification.

Fidelio

Beethoven indicated some stage directions in *Christ on the Mount of Olives,* which were omitted when the work was published in 1811. In fact, for all the "drama" found in so much of Beethoven's music, opera proved the only genre in which he failed to produce a canon of major works. The biggest project of his middle period, indeed the longest work he ever composed, was the opera *Fidelio,* initially a flop and then revised so often and so extensively that three distinct versions and no fewer than four overtures for it were written.

The premiere on 20 November 1805 was unsuccessful, for various reasons, some artistic and some political. For one thing, Napoleon's troops had just invaded Vienna, and they accounted for much of the audience, scaring off the typical Viennese patrons, some of whom left the city entirely. Beethoven revised *Fidelio* the next year, shortening its three acts to two, but still without much success. As if recognizing that his talent suffered a limitation where the theater was concerned, he concentrated thereafter on composing "incidental music" for dramatic plays, most notably for Goethe's historical tragedy *Egmont* in 1810. In 1814, when Beethoven was at the height of his popular success, he revised *Fidelio* yet again, this time with better luck, but the lone opera by the mighty Beethoven, for all its wonders, resides somewhat uneasily in the history of the genre.

The piece started out as *Leonore, oder Der Triumph der ehelichen Liebe* (Leonora, or The Triumph of Marital Love), on words by the court theater secretary Joseph Sonnleithner, assisted by a veritable committee of Beethoven's friends. Their libretto was adapted from a famous French one by Jean-Nicolas Bouilly, dating from 1798, that exemplified a kind of opera that had become something of a craze after the French Revolution. Such composers as André-Ernest-Modeste Grétry (1741–1813), Étienne-Nicolas Mehul (1763–1817), Rodolphe Kreutzer (1766–1831), Luigi Cherubini (1760–1842), and Ferdinando Paer (1771–1839), the last of whom set Bouilly's libretto before Beethoven, wrote what modern scholars have christened "**rescue operas**," a loose, anachronistic term that covers many situations. In general, though, French ***opéras comiques*** (operas with spoken dialogue and happy endings) in the decades surrounding the Revolution symbolized the theme of social emancipation in stories that portrayed an unjust abduction or imprisonment, usually at the hands of a tyrant, and a liberation, usually as the result of sacrifice—by lover, spouse, or servant, but in any case by a common person whose virtue is contrasted with the depravity of the tyrant.

Opera proved the only genre in which Beethoven failed to produce a canon of major works.

In Beethoven's opera the heroine Leonore, disguising herself as a man going by the name Fidelio, apprentices to the jailer Rocco in the hope that she will be able to free her husband, Florestan, an unjustly condemned political prisoner. Although not even sure he is still alive, she risks her life to save his. On orders from the evil Don Pizarro, she and Rocco descend to the dungeon to dig a grave for Florestan, but to the amazement of everyone she reveals her true identity just as he is about to be killed by Pizarro. At this moment a trumpet sounds in the distance, indicating the arrival of enlightened minister Don

Fernando. The scene changes from the depths of the prison to the brilliant light of day. The opera concludes with a jubilant choral finale in praise of Leonore's steadfastness, embodying the basic dark-to-light scenario we have already seen in Haydn's *The Creation* and that would be replayed repeatedly in Beethoven's instrumental works, most famously in the Fifth Symphony.

The Fifth Symphony and Fate

Anthology Vol 2-20
Full CD III, 41–44
Concise CD II, 20–21

Beethoven wrote his Symphony No. 5 in C Minor, Op. 67, sporadically over some four years, during the most productive period of his career: "I live only in my notes, and with one work barely finished, the other is already started; the way I write now I often find myself working on three, four things at the same time."[17] Although his hearing problem was initially denied, hidden, and fought, by 1806 he could write in a sketch of one his string quartets, "Let your deafness no longer be a secret—even in art."[18] *Fidelio* and other projects interrupted progress on the symphony, written primarily in 1807 and early 1808.

The Fifth did not immediately become the world's (or even the composer's) most famous symphony. During Beethoven's lifetime the *Eroica* was played more frequently in Vienna; even more popular was the second movement of the Seventh Symphony (movements were often performed separately). But the Fifth gradually came to epitomize both Beethoven's life and his musical style, hence the epitome of concert music outright. Unlike the *Eroica*, it does not carry a title, nor does it have an extra-musical connection, such as the Prometheus myth, to provide a background story. Beethoven allegedly said that the opening represents "Fate" when it "knocks at the door," but this information was only revealed much later and from a notoriously unreliable source, his assistant Anton Schindler.[19]

Despite the absence of any explanation from Beethoven himself as to the meaning of the Fifth Symphony, his life itself essentially offers a story that listeners have long projected onto the work. In another letter to Dr. Wegeler concerning his hearing, for instance, Beethoven stated that he would "seize Fate by the throat; it shall not bend or crush me completely."[20] It has proved understandably attractive to relate such statements directly to his heroic works. For Berlioz, the Fifth, more than the previous four symphonies, "appears to us to emanate directly and solely from the genius of Beethoven. It is his own intimate thought which is there developed; and his secret sorrows, his pent-up rage, his dreams so full of melancholy oppression, his nocturnal visions and his bursts of enthusiasm furnish its entire subject."[21]

"Let your deafness no longer be a secret—even in art."
—Beethoven

Beethoven's symphony offers another example of the trajectory from darkness to light. The many inflections he gave the basic opposition prompted just as many metaphorical interpretations. The music critic Adolf Bernhard Marx (1795–1866) drew out its implications with great insight when he wrote of the Fifth Symphony that its overall theme was "Durch Nacht zum Licht! Durch Kampf zum Sieg!" (Through night to light! Through struggle to victory!), sounding a keynote for Beethoven interpretation that has resonated over the centuries on many levels, from the psychological and biographical to the political and nationalistic.[22]

The Fifth Symphony distills essential features of Beethoven's music, one of the most prominent of which is its "**organicism**," the notion that all four movements seem to grow from seeds sown in the opening measures. Like the words "sublime" and "original," "organic" is another central idea in Romanticism. Behind it stood an influential concept enunciated by, among others, Beethoven's great contemporary Johann Wolfgang von Goethe (1749–1832)—poet, playwright, philosopher, and natural scientist all in one. Goethe believed that artistic form should imitate the forms of nature, first among which was the *Urpflanze*, the "primal plant," nature's microcosm, all of whose parts were symbiotic.[23] Romantics latched onto this idea, as is eloquently expressed in the English poet William Blake's "Auguries of Innocence" (1803): "To see a world in a grain of sand/ And a heaven in a wild flower." In many of Beethoven's compositions this translated into new concepts of form founded as much on thematic relationships as they are on tonal ones, and nowhere more so than in the famous Fifth. No work by Beethoven (or by any other composer) so flaunts the derivation of the whole from a single germinal seed, the four notes proclaimed at the very outset of the symphony in gruff unison (Fig. 16-7).

All four movements of the Fifth Symphony seem to grow from seeds sown in the opening measures.

Beethoven used the distinctive rhythmic figure of three shorts and a long to unify the entire symphony, which means that formal considerations are functioning not just on the level of an individual movement but, rather, over the whole work. Much as it would have horrified Haydn to mix and match four movements drawn from among his hundred symphonies to make a composite favorite, one can imagine (assuming the key sequence worked) such a thing happening without most listeners ever noticing; overt thematic and narrative connections between and among movements were rare before Beethoven. In the Fifth Symphony, however, listeners sensed the large-scale narrative arc, from darkness to light, from struggle to victory, as well as the more local connections along the way, generated primarily

Figure 16-7 Opening bars of the Fifth Symphony, written in Beethoven's hand.

from the initial motive. This has profound implications for a listener's sense of time and expectations. The weight of earlier Classical symphonies tended to be on the first movement. With Beethoven there was often a sense of moving forward, of trying to reach some goal.

After that most familiar of openings (Ex. 16-1a), the music modulates to the relative major key and the horns herald the second theme with a fanfare using the germinal rhythm. The softer, lyrical second theme, first presented by the violins, is inconspicuously accompanied in the lower strings by the same rhythm, which gradually becomes louder and more intense. The movement features Beethoven's characteristic building of intensity and suspense as well as various surprises along the way. Why, for example, does the oboe have a brief unaccompanied solo cadenza, marked *Adagio*, just after the start of the recapitulation (m. 268). Beethoven's innovation here is not simply that this short passage may "mean" something but that listeners are prompted in the first place to ask themselves what it may mean. There seems to be a new self-conscious subjectivity at work. We may interpret Beethoven's meanings in endless ways, depending on our insights and our interests. This is purely instrumental music that, without recourse to words, titles, or other extramusical features, seems to tell a story, project an internal musical logic, and make a point.

The second movement is a rather unusual variation form in which two themes alternate, the first sweet and lyrical, the second more forceful. The germinal motive appears here as well, ticking like a time bomb in the second violins and violas at mm. 76–77 (Ex. 16-1b) and again in the cellos at mm. 88–96.

Beethoven interlinks the third and fourth movements, which are played without pause. As in the *Eroica*, he replaces the polite minuet and trio with a more vigorous scherzo and trio. It begins with a soft ascending arpeggiated string theme that contrasts with an assertive horn motive, prominently featuring the germinal rhythm (Ex. 16-1c). The trio section features extraordinarily difficult string writing, partly in fugal style, that apparently often defeated musicians in some early performances—this may indeed have been a joke on Beethoven's part. At one point there are two false starts before he allows the players to "get it right." There follows another innovation: Instead of an exact "da capo" return of the opening section, as expected after the trio in a minuet or a scherzo, Beethoven recasts the opening thematic material in a completely new orchestration and *pianissimo* dynamic.

The joining of the last two movements furnishes the means for not merely the juxtaposition of C minor and C major, but the direct transformation of the one into the other, through which the symphony's overarching single gesture is finally consummated. The point is made with suitable drama—a lengthy dominant pedal to gather and focus tension, by way of a great crescendo and tremolos, not to mention the contrast between the chattering, muttering dissolve with which the scherzo comes to its inconclusive end, *pianissimo*, and the dazzling brassy blast that launches the finale on its triumphant course. For early audiences, that blast was magnified far beyond its power to shock us today by the unexpected sound of three trombones. (Up to now we have encountered the instrument only in church and in the opera pit, where they were employed for their religious associations—or, as in Gluck's *Orfeo ed Euridice* and Mozart's *Don Giovanni*, for their infernal and supernatural ones.) In the finale of the Fifth, trombones are accompanied by the contrabassoon and piccolo, until then most associated with military bands.

Beethoven patiently held all these instruments in reserve so that their entrance in the finale could make a greater impact.

That is not the full extent of the interrelationship of scherzo and finale. There is also a reprise of part of the scherzo within the fourth movement, at a point that could not be more disruptive: during the retransition, right before the recapitulation, where it seems to reintroduce C minor, most unwelcomely, just as the dominant is about to resolve for the last time to the tonic major. In a larger sense, of course, the scherzo reprise serves a strategic purpose, prolonging the suspense of "dominant tension" and enabling a replay of the transitional passage so as to launch the recapitulation with a blast comparable to the one that had launched the finale's exposition. Triumph, it could be argued, is not compromised but actually enhanced by the overcoming of one last setback.

Example 16-1a Ludwig van Beethoven, Symphony No. 5 in C Minor, Op. 67, mm. 1–10

Example 16-1b Ludwig van Beethoven, Symphony No. 5 in C Minor, Op. 67, II, mm. 76–77

Example 16-1c Ludwig van Beethoven, Symphony No. 5 in C Minor, Op. 67, III, mm. 19–26

Example 16-1d Ludwig van Beethoven, Symphony No. 5 in C Minor, Op. 67, IV, mm. 45–48, first violins

The finale, like the first movement, is in sonata form and of course draws as well on the germinal seed-rhythm, which is firmly embedded in the jubilant main theme and actually leads the theme to its highest point. More obviously, the germinal rhythm, now expressed in triplets, informs the second theme as well (Ex. 16-1d). Even the codetta is implicitly informed by it, as evidenced by the threefold pitch repetitions on the upbeats. The coda to the symphony may strike listeners today as almost too triumphantly affirmative as the music gets faster, louder, and ever more insistent. This is an unfortunate consequence of the symphony's enormous fame and overexposure. It may be difficult to recapture the novelty, the loudness, and the dramatic power that the first audiences experienced in 1808.

To this day one still listens to a symphony like the Fifth with a degree of mental and emotional engagement few previous pieces of music had demanded, and one is left afterward with a sense of satisfaction that only strenuous exertions, successfully consummated, can guarantee. Beethoven's singular ability to summon that engagement and grant that satisfaction is what invested his "heroic" music with its irresistible sense of high purpose and power. It is not the devices themselves that so enthrall the listener but, rather, the singleness of design that they conspire to create, the scale on which they enable Beethoven to work, and the metaphors to which these stimuli give rise in the mind of the listener. That purely musical tension and release is what produces such a total immersion in what E. T. A. Hoffmann called "the spirit world of the infinite."[24]

"More Expression of Feeling Than Tone Painting": The *Pastoral* Symphony

The bold heroism of the Third and Fifth symphonies and of many other works written during the "middle period" does not completely represent Beethoven's aspirations or accomplishment at the time. He did not cast every piece as dynamic affirmation; some do not conform to the heroic model but instead are reserved and lyrical. Beethoven often wrote works simultaneously, and his Fifth Symphony may be considered a fraternal twin of the Sixth. Their genesis overlapped, they share the same dedicatees, they were premiered on the same concert, and they were published within weeks of one another. Although musically the symphonies are different in many respects, there are some notable similarities, such as innovations in instrumentation (the delayed and dramatic introduction of instruments) and the binding together of movements.

The Symphony No. 6 in F Major, Op. 68, is worth our particular attention because of its programmatic aspects and the influence these had on later composers. Many titles now attached to Beethoven's compositions were placed there by someone else. Piano sonata nicknames like "Moonlight," "Tempest," and "Appassionata" were bestowed by critics, publishers, and others. The title for the "Emperor" Concerto dates from after the composer's death and is only used in English-speaking countries. Except for the *Eroica*, the Sixth Symphony, which Beethoven called the *Pastoral*, stands apart from his other symphonies, and indeed from most of Beethoven's instrumental and keyboard music, in its intentional, publicly declared, and often quite easily heard programmatic content.

The *Pastoral*, however, is not yet entirely committed to the aesthetic of so-called **program music**—pieces with elaborate background stories or extramusical influences—that would become so important during the nineteenth century with Berlioz, Franz Liszt, and other composers. Beethoven labeled the piece *Pastoral Symphony, or Recollections of Country Life* and famously stated that it contained "more an expression of feeling than tone painting."[25] The work belongs to a tradition of "characteristic" symphonies going back to the previous century. Indeed the titles he used for the individual movements closely resemble those of *Le Portrait musical de la nature*, written nearly twenty-five years earlier by the German composer Justin Heinrich Knecht (1752–1817).

One still listens to a symphony like the Fifth with a degree of mental and emotional engagement few previous pieces of music had demanded.

The music of the *Pastoral* nonetheless offers more than just subjective impressions. Notes in Beethoven's sketches are revealing: "the hearers should be allowed to discover the situations / Sinfonia caracteristica—or recollection of country life / All tone-painting in instrumental music is lost if it is pushed too far / Sinfonia pastorella. Anyone who has an idea of country life can make out for himself the intentions of the composer without many titles / Also without titles the whole will be recognized as a matter more of feeling than of painting in sounds."[26] He titled the first movement "Awakening of Cheerful

Feelings upon Arriving in the Country." The second movement he called "Scene by the Brook," and it includes distinctive birdcalls: a flute for the nightingale, oboe for the quail, and two clarinets for the cuckoo. The final three movements are played without pause. The third presents a "Merry Gathering of Villagers," which is interrupted by a "Thunderstorm; Tempest." The "Shepherd's Song: Happy and Thankful Feelings after the Storm" brings the symphony to its joyous close.

Concert Life in Beethoven's Vienna

The *Pastoral* shows Beethoven's deeply felt relationship to nature—another favorite subject for Romantic composers. A few months after its premiere, Napoleon's troops staged their second siege of Vienna. The loud mortar fire continued through the summer and caused Beethoven particular distress because it aggravated his hearing problems. In July 1809 he wrote to his publisher: "Let me tell you that since May 4th I have produced very little coherent work, at most a fragment here and there. The whole course of events has in my case affected both body and soul. I cannot yet give myself up to the enjoyment of the country life which is so indispensable for me. . . . What a destructive, disorderly life I see and hear around me, nothing but drums, cannons, and human misery in every form."[27]

On 22 December 1808 the Fifth and Sixth symphonies had been premiered on the same concert, probably the most famous of Beethoven's career and one that gives some idea of Viennese concert life at the time. The Vienna Philharmonic did not yet exist, nor was there a formal concert hall in the city. Most concerts were presented either by a charity organization or by musicians who themselves assumed responsibility for their organization and execution. Without a standing orchestra or proper performing space and with an added burden of having to get official approval to hold such a public event, the number of concerts in Vienna was limited. They were often held in ballrooms, at the university, or even in restaurants. Their number increased during certain times of the year, such as Lent and Advent, when opera performances were prohibited for religious reasons and when theaters therefore became available, as did the orchestras connected with them.

Performances of Beethoven's long and difficult new works were under-rehearsed and probably very poorly executed by today's standards.

Beethoven took advantage of Advent in 1808 to present a large selection of his most recent work. The legendary concert was long in the planning and, as it turned out, very long in the execution as well. After many appeals and delays Beethoven had successfully negotiated the use of the Theater an der Wien (Fig. 16-8), opened seven years earlier and still functioning to this day. (He lived in the building for a time in 1803; *Fidelio* premiered there two years later.) A newspaper advertised the event by noting that "all the pieces are of his composition, entirely new, and not yet heard in public."[28] The program was a typical mixture of different kinds of pieces—orchestral, vocal, choral, and keyboard—but the spotlight on a single composer was unusual. In an account of the event, the composer Johann Friedrich Reichardt (1752–1814), who was visiting Vienna at the time, recalled attending as a guest of Beethoven's patron, Prince Lobkowitz. They sat in his box "in the bitterest cold from 6:30 to 10:30 and experienced the truth that one can easily have too much of a good thing—and still more of a loud."[29] (The last remark is testimony to the shocking volume of these symphonies, the finale of the Fifth as well as the storm in the Sixth.)

Figure 16-8 Interior of the Theater an der Wien, site of the first performance of Beethoven's only opera, *Fidelio,* in 1804. Watercolor, 1825.

The all-Beethoven program opened with what was billed at this occasion as the "Fifth Symphony" but that was in fact the *Pastoral,* soon to be published and known ever since as Symphony No. 6. There followed a concert aria sung by a very young and very nervous soprano named Josefine Killitschgy. Next on the program was a single movement from a large choral work, the Gloria from the recently finished Mass in C Major, Op. 86. The first half of the concert ended with Beethoven playing the public premiere of his Piano Concerto No. 4 in G Major, Op. 58. This marked his last performance in a concerto, as he realized that the deterioration in his hearing had reached a point where he could no longer be a soloist.

The second half began with the premiere of the Fifth Symphony (labeled as the Sixth that night), followed by another movement from the Mass in C. After Beethoven presented his obligatory improvisation, he concluded with a new work written especially for the occasion, the Choral Fantasy, Op. 80. The newspaper advertisement had promised a "fantasy that ends with the gradual entrance of the entire orchestra and the introduction of choruses as a finale."[30] In certain ways the work was a trial run for the grand choral finale of the Ninth Symphony, written some fifteen years later.

While posterity may enviously fantasize about what it must have been like to hear premieres of Beethoven's music, the reality is that the actual performances of these long and difficult new works were under-rehearsed and probably very poorly executed by today's standards. In this instance the critic for the Leipzig *Allgemeine musikalische Zeitung* remarked that "it is all but impossible to pronounce judgment upon all of these works after a single first hearing, particularly as we are dealing with works of Beethoven, so many of which were being performed one after another, and which were mostly so grand and long. . . . In regard to the performances at this concert, however, the concert must be called unsatisfactory in every respect."[31] Things literally fell apart during the Choral Fantasy; Beethoven had to stop the performance and start again.

Struggle and Victory

Many of Beethoven's works in the first decade of the nineteenth century display his heroic style. Their monumental dynamism met with approval from an ever-widening bourgeois public who read in that dynamism a portrayal of their own social and cultural triumph. For these listeners, as E. T. A. Hoffmann put it most explicitly, Beethoven finally realized the universal mission of music, just as they felt that in their own lives they were realizing the universal aspiration of mankind to political and economic autonomy. This same aspiration was defined as the superhuman realization of the "World Spirit" by Georg Wilhelm Friedrich Hegel (1770–1831), the great Romantic philosopher and Beethoven's exact contemporary.

Hearing Beethoven's music as a metaphor of personal triumph of victory for the World Spirit helps explain its extraordinary appeal for more than two centuries and also its use in such a broad spectrum of political and cultural contexts. The Fifth and Ninth symphonies in particular have long histories of political appropriation during the nineteenth century and later, during the First and Second World Wars, after the fall of the Berlin Wall, and more recently in the wake of the terrorist attacks on 11 September 2001.

There is a troublesome side, however, to the seductive notion of "universal" appeal, and that is the tendency it encourages to cast cherished Beethovenian values as "universal" values, good and therefore binding for everyone. To see music that does not conform to the heroic model as deficient means discriminating against other possible musical values, aims, uses, and styles. We will encounter composers who chose not to abide by Beethoven's precedents, who espoused other musical values, or who wanted to tell different kinds of stories. In many cases they were criticized for doing so, either implicitly or explicitly, and usually without Beethoven's name even being mentioned.

To the extent, for example, that the Beethovenian ideal was identified with virility or expressed "manly" ideals of strength, it reinforced prejudice against what were perceived as feminine values, which in music included lyricism. To the extent that it sanctioned challenging rather than entertaining the audience, it could serve to underwrite gratuitous obscurity, difficulty, and aloofness, a monumental change that many have perceived in modern art to this day. To the extent that it exalted the representation of violence, whether of *Kampf* (struggle) or *Sieg* (victory), it could be used to justify aggression. To the extent that it was identified with German national aspirations or with a concept of German "national character," it could encourage chauvinism. These are some of undesirable side effects that have at times emerged from the Beethoven myth and are matters of ongoing debate.

Beethoven was accepted in his own time both by the expanding new public and by the old aristocratic elite, which continued to support him financially, although collectively rather than by direct employment. He was thus able to evade the prospect of steady work as Kapellmeister at the court of Westphalia in Kassel, where Napoleon had installed his youngest brother, Jerome, as king. A consortium of Viennese noblemen undertook in 1809 to guarantee Beethoven a lifetime allowance that more than matched the salary he was offered there, and that allowed him to devote his full time to composing as he wished, provided only that he remain in Vienna. Beethoven stayed, although the benefits of the arrangement did not last long, for a devaluation of currency drastically reduced the annuity's value. The group of patrons included Prince Lobkowitz and Prince Ferdinand Johann Nepomuk Kinsky

(1781–1812) and the Archduke Rudolph (1788–1831), the emperor's younger brother, who studied composition with Beethoven.

Rising Fame and Decreasing Productivity

Beethoven's grand concert in December 1808 might be viewed as the culmination of his heroic period. Commentators often extend it some years further, but clearly both the situation of the composer and the style of his compositions were changing. After years of immense productivity, Beethoven began to cut back and abandoned certain genres altogether, or at least for years to come. He lapsed, probably as a result of deepening deafness and personal frustrations, into a period of depression.

Goethe remarked in a letter to the composer Carl Friedrich Zelter that Beethoven "was not altogether wrong in holding the world to be detestable, but surely does not make it any the more enjoyable either for himself or for others by his attitude," adding that his deafness "perhaps mars the musical part of his nature less than the social."[32] Beethoven's admiration for the great poet, his senior by twenty-one years, was lifelong and deeply felt. Goethe's understanding of music was somewhat limited, and yet he recognized Beethoven's genius. They met only a few times, during the summer of 1812, in Teplitz, the site of a fashionable Bohemian spa. In the same letter to Zelter Goethe noted that Beethoven's talent "amazed" him, but described the man as "an utterly untamed personality."[33] For his part, Beethoven felt Goethe bowed too much to power and privilege. As he wrote to a publisher, "Goethe delights far too much in the court atmosphere, far more than is becoming in a poet."[34]

Now in his early forties, the composer suffered repeated setbacks in his personal life. Increasingly desperate advances to unwilling or unavailable prospective brides culminated in a love letter to an unnamed "Immortal Beloved," written in the summer of 1812 and discovered unsent, like the Heiligenstadt Testament, among his posthumous effects, together with a portrait of a (or is it *the*?) mysterious woman. Because Beethoven is an object of great human interest, biographers, novelists, and movie producers have devoted enormous energy to the problem of uncovering his mysterious love. Musicologist Maynard Solomon's identification of Antonie Brentano, a married woman, is now the most widely accepted solution in the English-speaking world, although reasonable (as well as unreasonable) arguments continue to be put forth supporting other candidates, including an earlier object of his desire, Josephine Deym-Brunsvik.[35]

Beethoven's desperate advances to unwilling or unavailable prospective brides culminated in a love letter to an unnamed "Immortal Beloved."

Another painful emotional drain on Beethoven was an attempt to gain custody of his nephew Karl (1806–58) following the death of his brother, Caspar Anton Carl, in November 1815. The composer's possessive behavior, culminating in a temporarily successful legal battle with the boy's mother, testified to his deep longings for a stable family life but hurt the welfare of everyone involved. The suits dragged on for years, and eventually he was dealt the dual blows of being required to transfer custody to another party and of seeing the case moved to the commoners' court. Ludwig *van*—three letters that derived from his Dutch heritage—was not Ludwig *von*, mark of the ennobled. Eventually, in the summer of 1826, Karl attempted suicide, an emotionally shattering experience for his jealous uncle.

Beethoven wrote fewer works of lasting significance in the five years after 1812. Of the pieces he did write, some (inconveniently for his mythmakers) were calculated to win popular appeal, including a noisy "Battle Symphony" known as *Wellington's Victory, or the Battle of Vittoria,* Op. 91, celebrating Napoleon's defeat by combined British, Spanish, and Portuguese forces in June 1813. The tremendous success of the piece at its premiere later that year is hardly surprising, given the political turmoil most members of the audience had been through during the preceding decade. The concert, which also saw the first performance of the Seventh Symphony, benefited wounded soldiers. *Wellington's Victory* quickly became one of Beethoven's most popular pieces, despite complaints about its artistic quality.

Nor was this Beethoven's only such work at the time. He wrote *Der glorreiche Augenblick* (The Glorious Moment), an inflated political cantata for performance before assembled dignitaries from across Europe gathered for the Congress of Vienna, which met in the wake of Napoleon's defeat to determine the political boundaries of Europe (Fig. 16-9). These pieces cast Beethoven in a rather unheroic light, as a sort of musical market speculator. That was, however, no less typical or progressive a role for a musician in economically unsettled times. He frankly acknowledged the kind of works these were in a letter to a publisher: "I have been compelled to make a considerable number of *potboilers* (as unfortunately I must call them)."[36]

Otherwise, Beethoven's output dwindled even as his compositional ambition grew. The most important compositions written between 1813 and 1818 are three piano sonatas, culminating in the huge sonata in B♭, Op. 106 (nicknamed "Hammerklavier" after the German word for piano); two cello sonatas, Op. 102; and a group of continuous songs with the poignant title *An die ferne Geliebte* (To the Distant Beloved) that must have had manifold personal resonances. The year 1817 went by without a single work of any consequence completed. Also indicative of the composer's state of mind during this period was that he worked on a number of sizeable projects—a piano concerto, a trio, a string quintet—that he finally abandoned.

Figure 16-9 John-Baptiste Isabey, the Congress of Vienna, 1814. Beethoven composed his *Der glorreiche Augenblich* to be performed for this meeting.

Beethoven was increasingly isolated personally. The exact course and extent of his deafness is not entirely clear. Although letters from around 1801 indicate that his hearing loss began when he was in his late twenties, Beethoven nonetheless continued to be active as a performer and in society for many more years. In 1818, as he was approaching the age of fifty, a new piece of the puzzle emerges, fascinating documents known as the "conversation books." He had reached the point where it was necessary for people to write out questions and comments in small notebooks that he would read and respond to orally. It is remarkable that Beethoven preserved most of these one-way transcripts—139 notebooks survive, beginning in February 1818 and lasting until a few weeks before his death in March 1827. They provide an extraordinary window into his life and activities, although they are also frustrating because we rarely know Beethoven's own side of the conversation (sometimes it can be inferred, and occasionally Beethoven wrote down his response).

Beethoven had reached the point where it was necessary for people to write out questions and comments in small notebooks.

Beethoven's deafness largely removed him, so far as the musical world was concerned, from "real time," the time frame in which daily business was conducted. His creative activities appeared now to take place in a transcendent space to which only he had access. The copious sketches he made for his compositions beginning in the late 1790s (he kept these famous sketchbooks throughout his life) have precisely for this reason exercised an enormous fascination as a lofty record of aesthetic achievement, a document of his struggle and victory.

Yet there is a danger of distorting—Romantically—his isolation. Beethoven was a shrewd businessman throughout his career (if not always a completely honest one); he continued to communicate with many in the musical world, kept up with the press, and was even sometimes involved with rehearsals. As a competent string player himself, for example, he could follow the movements of the bows of the instruments in a string quartet and get some idea of what was happening, even if he could not hear it.

Despite the decline in his productivity, the years around the Congress of Vienna marked the height of Beethoven's popularity in Vienna and saw the greatest number of performances of his work—partly due to the appeal of *Wellington's Victory* and the Symphony No. 7 in A Major, Op. 92. The third version of *Fidelio* was finally successful. But after 1815 it seemed to some that Beethoven's own glorious moment had passed. The *Allgemeine musikalische Zeitung* remarked: "Beethoven now busies himself, as Papa Haydn once did, with arrangements of Scottish folk songs; he is apparently quite incapable of greater accomplishments."[37] In fact he had already entered a new stage that would last the final decade of his life. When Beethoven heard about the magazine's remark he said: "Wait awhile, you'll soon learn differently."[38]

Late Beethoven

Beethoven began to shake off his creative lull toward the end of 1817, possibly spurred on by a flattering invitation from the Philharmonic Society of London to compose two symphonies for the coming concert season and present them in person. He never composed either and never duplicated Haydn's triumphant late-career success with a trip to London. He was sufficiently energized, however, to embark on the "Hammerklavier" Sonata, which took him almost a year to finish. Successful completion of his first large project in some years set a working pattern for the rest of his life: sustained sketching and the realization of ambitious projects that emerged with care over a protracted period of time. Aside from a handful of songs, some small piano works, and a few other pieces, large and imposing compositions, predominated during his final decade: three intense piano sonatas (Opp. 109, 110, 111), a mammoth set of keyboard variations (the "Diabelli" Variations, Op. 120), a large Mass (the *Missa solemnis*), the Ninth Symphony, and five string quartets (Opp. 127, 130, 131, 132, 135), plus a separate movement called the *Grosse Fuge* (Great Fugue), Op. 133.

Large and imposing compositions predominated during Beethoven's final decade.

Over the course of the nineteenth century many musicians came to view Beethoven's late works as his greatest, but that took quite some time—many of his contemporaries were initially baffled. Those who had followed his artistic development often found themselves presented with real challenges. Beethoven's estimable stature continued to earn him all due respect, but some listeners considered his late pieces "incomprehensible." Critics accounted for the difficulties they now faced by attributing the strange new style to a sad decline in Beethoven's health. A critic for the Frankfurt *Allgemeine Musikzeitung* noted that "some say one cannot find anything more beautiful and magnificent than this quartet [Op. 127], and that it is as good as anything musical art has to offer; others say, however: No, it is completely vague, entirely chaotic; there are no clear thoughts to be extracted, in every measure there are sins against the generally accepted rules; the composer—deaf in any case—must have been crazy when he brought this work to life."[39] Beethoven's late works seemed to come from a madman, a visionary, or a bit of both. The unusual length, structural fragmentation, exploration of counterpoint, and new deployment of instruments pointed in compositional directions that took musicians generations to assimilate.

And that seems to have been fine with Beethoven. As the most famous living composer, although isolated and often misunderstood, he composed with the knowledge that his works would be published and performed. The demands of court and church that had for so long prescribed what composers could and should write were replaced by more personal imperatives. Beethoven's late string quartets were not written to please or entertain in the way most previous music had, and this stance would have profound consequences on music history and on the relationships among composers, performers, and audiences.

The creative and performing functions were in Beethoven gradually but irrevocably severed, leaving only the first. And that sole survivor, the creative function, was now invested with an import that Romantically cast the split in ethical, quasi-religious terms. Never again would the performing virtuoso composer, on the Mozartean model, be considered the ideal. The composer—the creator—became the truly Olympian being, removed from the passing transactions of everyday musical life—improvisations, cadenzas, performances in general—and yet still a public figure, whose pronouncements were regarded as public events.

The pronouncements now were not just intended for an immediate, local, contemporary audience but, rather, for a much larger and longer one—for posterity—and with thoughts of immortality. Such an attitude about art remains in force today, and we will see its many consequences in the chapters to follow. We have already noted that Beethoven's critical reception during his lifetime emphasized that his works were intensely "original" but also often "bizarre" and that they needed time, study, and repeated hearings to be understood fully. Responding to a complaint concerning the difficulty of one of his "Razumovsky" string quartets, Op. 59, Beethoven allegedly replied, "Oh, they are not for you, but for a later age!"[40] He was charged with writing for the future rather than for the audiences of his own time. After the successful *Fidelio* revival in 1814, Beethoven placed an unusual notice in a Vienna newspaper—"A Word to His Admirers"—in which he said: "How often, in your chagrin that his depth was not sufficiently appreciated, have you said that van Beethoven composes only for posterity!"[41]

The Ninth Symphony

Beethoven's two largest late projects are another pair of fraternal twins: the Mass in D Major (*Missa solemnis*), Op. 123, and the Symphony No. 9 in D Minor, Op. 125. He undertook to compose the Mass upon hearing that Archduke Rudolph was to be elevated to the rank of cardinal and installed as archbishop of Olomouc, an important ecclesiastical seat in the Czech lands. He had meant to have it ready for the installation ceremony in March 1820, but the music expanded irrepressibly under his hand, and the whole vast design was not completed until the early months of 1823. Beethoven had missed the deadline by three years, and he ended up with a work whose stupendous length precluded its forming part of an actual church service. The first performance took place under secular auspices in St. Petersburg on 7 April 1824, on the initiative of Prince Nikolai Borisovich Golitsyn, a Russian nobleman and chamber music enthusiast who became one of the outstanding patrons of Beethoven's last years.

The Ninth was his first symphony in more than a decade and another work that broke generic precedents—lasting about an hour, having an unusual ordering of movements, and encompassing a vast finale that was a virtual oratorio for soloists, chorus, and orchestra on the text of Friedrich Schiller's famous poem "An die Freude" ("Ode to Joy"). Feeling that his music was no longer fashionable in Vienna, where audiences had become infatuated with Italian opera, notably works by Gioachino Rossini, Beethoven made inquiries with an eye toward having the new symphony premiere in Berlin. On hearing this, a group of admirers—among them his pupil Czerny, Count Moritz Lichnowsky, and the publisher Anton Diabelli—sent an affecting open letter imploring that he not leave his "second native city."[42]

Moved by the tribute, Beethoven agreed to a public concert at the Kärntnertor Theater in Vienna (Fig. 16-10), his first big concert in nearly a decade. The composer, by then stone deaf, stood before the assembled orchestra and chorus and waved his arms, but according to the later recollection of the pianist Sigismond Thalberg, who as a twelve-year-old prodigy attended the concert, the court conductor Michael Umlauf, listed as general overseer, "had told the choir and orchestra to pay no attention whatever to Beethoven's beating of the time but all to watch him."[43] The most famous story of this great event, corroborated by various witnesses and participants, relates how "after the Scherzo of the Ninth Symphony Beethoven stood turning over the leaves of his score utterly deaf to the immense applause, and [the contralto soloist Karoline] Unger pulled him by the sleeve, and then pointed to the audience, whereupon he turned and bowed."[44]

The Ninth may have challenged contemporary expectations even more than had any of his previous symphonies, and it certainly exerted an enormous impact

Figure 16-10 Kärntnertor Theater, Vienna, site of the first performance of Beethoven's Ninth Symphony, 1824.

on later composers. Again and again it prompts performers and listeners to ask what it all means. That influence begins with the mysterious D minor opening, which grows out of a void. Against the murmurings of the low strings, falling fifths emerge in the violins that build to a loud and imposing first theme. No symphony before had sounded anything like it, and it has long been likened to the creation of the world, as growth from nothingness to fulfillment. Beethoven switched the expected order of movements by placing the scherzo next, another practice later composers would sometimes imitate. A favorite with audiences from the beginning, especially for the prominent role given to the timpani, this movement projects both humor and power. The lyrical slow movement explores more personal, even spiritual realms.

The Ninth may have challenged contemporary expectations even more than had any of Beethoven's previous symphonies.

The finale opens with what Richard Wagner would later call the "terror fanfare," a highly dissonant and frantic passage that leads to an instrumental "recitative" (so marked in the score) for the cellos and basses. Fragments from the three previous movements pass in review—a few measures of the opening theme of each—only to be rejected by the string recitative. These gestures in effect cancel the message of the first three movements in order to seek a new one in the last. Following the strange, extended, and disjointed instrumental recitative comes an instrumental song played softly in the lower strings: the famous "Ode to Joy" melody. After about seven minutes the movement starts over again—the "terror fanfare" returns even more dissonant, but this time is followed by a vocal recitative with the bass soloist singing "O friends, not these tones! But rather, let us strike up more pleasant and more joyful ones." (These opening words were Beethoven's own addition, not found in Schiller's original poem.) The chorus and four vocal soloists take up the "joy" theme, which undergoes a continuing series of variations, including a march section in the "Turkish" manner. The music reaches a climax with a new theme: "Be embraced, ye millions, . . . above the starry canopy there must dwell a loving Father," which is later combined in counterpoint with the "joy" theme and eventually builds to a frenzied coda.

Of all Beethoven's works, the Ninth Symphony cast the longest shadow over the rest of the nineteenth century and over the music of the twentieth century as well. Immediately notorious, it has been both strenuously resisted and enthusiastically embraced. The resistance and submission are eloquent testimonials to the work itself as well as to the cultural attitudes that it quickened and polarized. One of the most telling contemporary comments was that of violinist and composer Louis Spohr (1784–1859). It was the reaction of one who had known and played under Beethoven in his youth, but who could not accept the new turn the master's art was taking. For Spohr the Ninth was a monstrosity that could only be explained in terms of its creator's deafness:

> His constant endeavor to be original and to open new paths, could no longer as formerly, be preserved from error by the guidance of the ear. Was it then to be wondered at that his works became more and more eccentric, unconnected, and incomprehensible? Yes! I must even reckon the much admired Ninth Symphony among them, the three first movements of which, in spite of some solitary flashes of genius, are to me worse than all of the eight previous symphonies, the fourth movement of which is in my opinion so monstrous and tasteless, and in its grasp of Schiller's Ode so trivial, that I cannot even now understand how a genius like Beethoven's could have written it. I find in it another proof of what I already remarked in Vienna, that Beethoven was wanting in aesthetical feeling and in a sense of the beautiful.[45]

This makes us recall Edmund Burke's elaborate set of contrasts between the beautiful and the sublime discussed in the previous chapter. If to be beautiful meant to be pleasing, then Beethoven's music did indeed often lack a sense of beauty. Or, rather, the composer rejected the assumption on which Spohr and many others based his judgment, that to be beautiful, that is, to please, was the only proper aim of art. Beethoven in the Ninth did at times deliberately assault the ear, most extravagantly with the "terror fanfares" that sounded a level of dissonance that would not be reached again until the very end of the century. By composing it, Beethoven tells us that he doesn't care what we think of it (or of him), that it is bigger than we are. It was, to many, an insulting message, a sort of declaration of composerly independence, an arrogant emancipation proclamation. Many decades would have to pass before the symphony would become the ultimate "feel good" piece that it is in our time.

Inwardness: The Late String Quartets

Beethoven lived less than three years after the premiere of the Ninth Symphony, finally succumbing to the effects of liver disease (made worse by heavy drinking) on 26 March 1827. During this last phase he returned to the string quartet, another genre he had not touched in more than a decade, and devoted himself to it almost exclusively (Fig. 16-11). The immediate stimulus came from Prince Golitsyn, the Russian nobleman who arranged the first performance of the *Missa solemnis*. In the fall of 1822 he had invited Beethoven to compose anywhere from one to three quartets for him and to name his price.

Figure 16-11 1823 portrait of Beethoven by Ferdinand Georg Waldmüller.

In the end Beethoven completed six late works for string quartet, including three dedicated to Golitsyn (in E♭ Major, Op. 127, the five-movement Quartet in A Minor, Op. 132, and the six-movement Quartet in B♭ Major, Op. 130) and two more full-scale works (the seven-movement Quartet in C♯ Minor, Op. 131, and the final Quartet in F Major, Op. 135). The remaining piece was the *Grosse Fuge* that was originally planned as the finale of Op. 130 but that proved simply too much for the publisher, Mathias Artaria, who pointed out that at six movements the quartet was long, even without the mammoth finale, and that the fugue was not only huge but exceedingly difficult to play. Beethoven acceded (rather unusually) to the request for a more listener-friendly conclusion and agreed to detach the fugue for separate publication (as Op. 133). The work may be Beethoven's most starkly "modern" in sound. One critic at the time said it was "incomprehensible, like Chinese."[46]

The steadfastness of Beethoven's late interest in the quartet medium can be partially accounted for by the devotion of violinist Ignaz Schuppanzigh (1776–1830). Beethoven had relied on his counsel from the beginning of his career as a quartet composer. Earlier in the century Schuppanzigh formed his own quartet and began giving the first regular public chamber music concerts in Vienna. It was at these concerts that Beethoven's middle-period quartets were first performed, notably the "Razumovsky" series, Op. 59, commissioned by the Russian ambassador in Vienna. From 1816 until 1823, probably owing to his connection with Razumovsky, Schuppanzigh relocated in St. Petersburg, the Russian capital, where he was active in promoting Beethoven's works, and not only quartets. It was he who put Prince Golitsyn in touch with Beethoven, thus serving as the late quartets' catalyst. Schuppanzigh's own professional ensemble, reconstituted in Vienna in 1823 and again offering regular subscription concerts, gave the first performances of much of Beethoven's late chamber music. His series of subscription concerts between 1823 and 1829, most of which featured one quartet each by Haydn, Mozart, and Beethoven, inaugurated a new era in the history of the public concert and the establishment of a classical canon.

There came a point, however, where Beethoven's burgeoning Romantic idealism and his writing for posterity doomed any true symbiosis with performers and audiences. When a member of Schuppanzigh's quartet saw that the seven movements of Op. 131 were to be played continuously, he asked Beethoven in a conversation book: "Does it have to be played through without stopping? But then we won't be able to repeat anything! When are we supposed to tune?"[47] Beethoven was constantly challenging performers and audiences, going against their expectations. Told that the "quartet which Schuppanzigh played yesterday did not please," Beethoven is said to have replied, "It will please them some day."[48] This is one reason his music remains so contemporary: his aesthetic attitude is often not so different from that which characterized the twentieth century. In this respect Beethoven might be seen as sharing more with the Modernist German composer Arnold Schoenberg (1874–1951) a hundred years later than he does with his own teacher, Haydn.

Beethoven's burgeoning Romantic idealism and his writing for posterity doomed any true symbiosis with performers and audiences.

Another much-repeated story recounts Beethoven's contemptuous retort when Schuppanzigh complained that a certain passage in one of the late quartets was too difficult to play effectively: "Do you fancy I am thinking of your puking little fiddle when the muse confides in me?" he supposedly replied. In fact, in Beethoven's choice of the verb "confide" we may encounter another reason for Beethoven's late preoccupation with the quartet medium: its privateness, or, as the German Romantics characteristically put it, its "inwardness."

The intimacy of chamber music offered the composer the possibility of a heightened subjectivity, a medium where he could speak his inmost, private thoughts and confide his deepest private moods as if to a musical diary. There are pages in the late quartets that can seem almost embarrassing to hear in public, as if hearing were overhearing—eavesdropping on the composer's afflicted personal existence, invading his privacy. One of these is the fifth movement of the Quartet in B♭ Major, Op. 130. Its tempo is *Adagio molto espressivo*; the parts are marked *sotto voce* ("in an undertone"); and it is subtitled "Cavatina," which to Beethoven meant a short, slow operatic aria of particular poignancy. The impression is that Beethoven is pouring out his private grief; and in case anyone should mistake it, the composer makes it even more explicit near the end, where the dynamic level becomes even more hushed (*sempre pp*), the harmony slips unexpectedly and mysteriously into the flat submediant region, and the first violin, in a passage marked *beklemmt* (constricted or stifled, "all choked up"), effectively loses its voice, its line being continually interrupted by rests as if racked by sobs.

Anthology Vol 2-21
Full CD IV, 1

In his last years Beethoven took an interest in eighteenth-century music, Handel especially, which is partly reflected in the fugues often encountered in his late works and in the evocations of the modes of religious vocal polyphony. This seems to have had a highly personal meaning for the composer, vividly embodied in the slow movement of the Quartet in A Minor, Op. 132, written in 1825. Beethoven had spent the month of April and part of May gravely sick in bed, and the movement, composed later that spring, bears the heading *Heiliger Dankgesang eines Genesenen an die Gottheit, in der lydischen Tonart* (Sacred Hymn of Thanksgiving from a Convalescent to the Deity, in the Lydian Mode). It is in effect an instrumental hymn with variations, on a theme reminiscent of an old chorale, interspersed with a contrasting exultant dance in D major, marked "neue Kraft fühlend" (feeling new strength), that also returns in varied form.[49] The Lydian mode is used to project an overwhelming intensity of feeling at which Beethoven hints verbally in the last and rhythmically most complex variation. Here he writes that the instruments are to be played *mit innigster Empfindung* (with the most inward expression), pointing to the "inwardness" that would become for all German composers the very motto of Romanticism.

With Beethoven's health deteriorating, it became increasingly clear that his time was limited, and by late 1826 people suspected the end was near. The summer had proved especially trying with the shock of his nephew's botched suicide attempt. In late September, a few days after Karl's release from the hospital, the two traveled to some fifty miles from Vienna to be with the composer's brother Johann. Their nine-week stay was sometimes tense, although not unproductive, as Beethoven worked on his last completed works, the String Quartet in F Major, Op. 135, and the new finale that would replace the *Grosse Fuge* in Op. 130.

At the head of the final movement of Op. 135 Beethoven wrote the epitaph *Der schwergefaßte Entschluß* (The Difficult Decision) and inserted a musical crypt that is not played and that has mystified musicians ever since: "Muß es sein?" (Must it be?), answered by a twofold "Es muß sein!" (It must be!) (Ex. 16-2). Both the title and the musical mottos were included in the program for the premiere of the quartet, on 23 March 1828, at a concert given by cellist Joseph Linke. The movement opens with the slow chromatic three-note motif ("Muß es sein?"), which is soon answered by a quick diatonic inversion ("Es muß sein! Es muß sein!"). This portentous question and response, stated at the outset of the very last movement of Beethoven's very last work, inevitably took on great significance for subsequent composers—his provocations and enigmas seemed to extend to the end. And yet in this case the original intention was in jest. Two years earlier a rich music lover and amateur cellist, Ignaz Dembscher, had not paid money he owed for tickets to Schuppanzigh's subscription quartet concerts. When he was told him to pay up, Dembscher asked: "Must it be?" Beethoven was amused by the story and wrote a humorous canon with the words: "Es muß sein, ja, es muß sein! Heraus mit dem Beutel!" (It must be, yes it must! Out with your wallet!). What had begun as a joke in the end became the basis for Beethoven's last quartet.

Example 16-2 Ludwig van Beethoven, String Quartet in F Major, Op. 135, IV, opening

Despite all the privacy and inwardness of his late works, Beethoven at the time of his death was far more a public figure than any composer had ever been before. The streets of Vienna were thronged with thousands on the day of his funeral, 29 March 1827 (Fig. 16-12). At the entrance to the cemetery, an oration written by the eminent Austrian writer Franz Grillparzer (1791–1872) was declaimed in high tragic tones by a prominent actor. Grillparzer's eulogy emphasized

Figure 16-12 Beethoven's funeral procession, by Franz Stoeber.

nationality, comparing Beethoven with Goethe (the "hero of verse in German speech and tongue") and tracing for him a historically false but heavily symbolic musical genealogy from Handel and Bach. "We who stand here at the grave of the deceased," Grillparzer's speech began,

> are in a manner the representatives of an entire nation, the whole German people . . . The last master of resounding song, the gracious mouth by which music spoke, the man who inherited and increased the immortal fame of Handel and Bach, of Haydn and Mozart, has ceased to be; and we stand weeping over the broken strings of an instrument now stilled.[50]

For almost a century it would be an article of faith for composers that Beethoven's stature could not be equaled, that with Beethoven the age of heroes had ended. But history, of course, continues, and standing among the mourners as a torchbearer on that cool afternoon was the thirty-year-old Franz Schubert, another celebrated composer in the German line and one to whom Beethoven allegedly gave his blessing by saying "Truly, in Schubert there dwells a divine spark!"[51]

Summary

Perhaps more than any other composer, Ludwig van Beethoven has come to epitomize Western art music and the Romantic conception of the artist. He helped to shape modern attitudes toward art music, the role of the composer, and the relationship between composer, patron, and audience. For Romantic writers and critics, Beethoven's music epitomized the ideals of Romanticism explored in Chapter 15.

Beethoven's career coincides with the ascendancy of instrumental music, and his central contributions were to instrumental genres: thirty-two piano sonatas, sixteen string quartets, five piano concertos, and nine symphonies. He struggled in the realm of opera, with his lone effort, *Fidelio*, going through multiple revisions.

In a trend that began in Beethoven's lifetime, scholars often divide his works into three periods, corresponding to changes in musical style and events in his life. While these periods were created by historians—real life seldom proceeds so neatly—they do form a convenient entry point into Beethoven's world. In the first period, lasting through about 1802, Beethoven mastered the Classical style of his predecessors, began to develop a distinctive voice, and gained fame as a performer in Viennese musical circles. The middle period, lasting through about 1814, is marked by increasing deafness and the resulting social isolation painfully expressed in his Heiligenstadt Testament, an unsent letter Beethoven wrote in 1802 to his brothers in which he revealed his hearing loss. During these years, Beethoven created his best-known works in the "heroic style," including the *Eroica* Symphony, the Fifth Symphony, the "Waldstein" and "Appassionata" piano sonatas, and the "Emperor" Piano Concerto. He also produced more lyrical and reserved works during this time, such as the Sixth Symphony. Works of this period show an unexpected contrast and experimentation with traditional forms. Boundaries between formal sections or even between the movements of a symphony may be blurred, and codas are expanded, often taking on the dimensions of a second development section.

In the third period, beginning about 1815, Beethoven's works take on a more inward quality, epitomizing the Romantic ideal of "inwardness" discussed in Chapter 15.

He developed a new interest in musical forms of the past, such as fugal writing, took an innovative approach to variation form, and explored new sonorities and remote tonal areas. Unlike so many earlier compositions, Beethoven's late works were not written to please an audience or patrons. Instead, he looked inward for inspiration and to posterity for an audience. In this way, he helped shape a new conception of art music.

Study Questions

1. How has Beethoven helped to shape modern attitudes toward art music, the role of the composer, and the relationship between composer, patron, and audience? Why does the composer's biography take on such importance for understanding his work?
2. Describe Beethoven's early years, his successes and important influences.
3. Explain the relevance of the Heiligenstadt Testament and its influence on the ways that Beethoven's music was heard and interpreted.
4. What makes Beethoven's middle period "heroic"? How do you hear these traits exemplified in his *Eroica* Symphony and Fifth Symphony?
5. What is meant by "organicism" in music? Explain how the movements of the Fifth Symphony grow from a single "seed."
6. Describe some stylistic and formal contrasts between the Fifth and Sixth symphonies. In what ways are they "unidentical twins"?
7. What kinds of works would be performed at a typical public concert in Beethoven's time? How did these concerts differ from those of today?
8. What are the salient features of Beethoven's late works? How are these reflected in the *Missa solemnis*, the Ninth Symphony, and the late string quartets?

Key Terms

opéra comique
organicism
program music
rescue opera
scherzo

17

Opera in the Age of Rossini, Bellini, Donizetti, and Weber

We saw in the last chapter that Beethoven's popularity peaked around 1814–15 and that soon thereafter his productivity declined dramatically, his public visibility waned, and his creative energies entered their late phase. These were the crucial years of the Congress of Vienna, when dignitaries from far and wide gathered in the city and concerts prominently featured Beethoven's music, including some pieces he wrote especially for the occasion. While these very public events were taking place, a native Viennese teenager, Franz Schubert, was writing his first masterpieces: the songs *Gretchen am Spinnrade* and *Erlkönig*, settings of poems by Goethe, the leading literary figure of the age. At the same time the slightly older Italian Gioachino Rossini (1792–1868) was winning wide acclaim with operas such as *Tancredi* (1813), *L'Italiana in Algeri* (The Italian Girl in Algiers, 1813), and *Il barbiere di Siviglia* (The Barber of Seville, 1816). In just a few years his operas had conquered Italy, Austria, Germany, France, Russia, and beyond.

Beethoven, Schubert, and Rossini came to represent different genres and different musical values. Beethoven, widely recognized since the death in 1809 of his teacher, Haydn, as the towering musical genius of the age, reigned supreme in instrumental music. Rossini, preeminent in the sphere of opera, emerged as Europe's most popular and widely performed composer. It took much more time for Schubert, the budding Romantic known primarily for smaller domestic pieces, to gain recognition, but his achievement and legacy were profound, as we shall see in the next chapter. The careers of all three basically ended at the same time. Schubert died at the age of thirty-one in 1828, just twenty months after Beethoven. Rossini's last opera, *Guillaume Tell* (William Tell), premiered the following year, after which the composer in essence retired, enjoying the height of his fame, at age thirty-seven. He lived a rich and famous man for nearly forty more years but composed little.

TIMELINE

1786 Birth of Carl Maria von Weber
1792 Birth of Gioachino Rossini
1797 Birth of Gaetano Donizetti
1810 Birth of Vincenzo Bellini
1813 Rossini, *L'Italiana in Algeri* and *Tancredi*
1814–15 Congress of Vienna
1816 Rossini, *The Barber of Seville*
1818 Mary Shelley, *Frankenstein*
1819 Sir Walter Scott, *The Bride of Lammermoor*
1821 Weber, *Der Freischütz*
1824 Stendhal, *Life of Rossini*
1826 Death of Weber
1829 Rossini, *Guillaume Tell*
1831 Bellini, *Norma*
1835 Donizetti, *Lucia di Lammermoor*
1835 Death of Bellini
1848 Death of Donizetti

Yet studying the achievements of these figures and of other contemporary composers principally by the genres of their most famous works obscures the connections and influences among them. Once a composition as influential as Beethoven's Ninth Symphony, Rossini's *Il barbiere di Siviglia*, or Schubert's *Erlkönig* entered the standard repertoire, the musical landscape changed forever, with wide-ranging consequences. In earlier centuries the impact of what are now viewed as key works was rarely as immediate or as pervasive. A motet by Machaut or a cantata by Bach usually did not disseminate widely, nor did such works typically matter much a few years after their creation. With the rise of a standard repertory, a musical canon, celebrated works like a Beethoven symphony, a Rossini opera, and a Schubert song enjoyed broad fame as well as lasting influence. We must be aware, therefore, of the stature of such works within their time in order to understand the music that followed.

The Popularity of Rossini

Despite Count Waldstein's prophesy, mentioned in the last chapter, about Beethoven's promising future, there is one sense in which the composer did not come anywhere near "receiving Mozart's spirit" when he went to Vienna to study with Haydn: mastery and success in the realm of opera. *Fidelio*, with its multiple overtures and substantial revisions, was a problematic project in Beethoven's career. Rossini (Fig. 17-1) was in fact the one who inherited the Mozartean operatic legacy, although not "from Haydn's hands." The Italian composer was immediately cast—and in terms that resonated far beyond the confines of the opera house—as Beethoven's rival, or, to use the language of German philosophy at the time, his dialectical opposite. The contemporary recognition of him as a counterweight to Beethoven is an acknowledgment of opera's continuing importance at a time when instrumental music was on the rise.

With the rise of a standard repertory, a musical canon, celebrated works like a Beethoven symphony, a Rossini opera, and a Schubert song enjoyed broad fame as well as lasting influence.

Rossini's fame indeed surpassed that of any previous composer, and so, for a long time, did the astonishing popularity of his works. Audiences took to his music as if to an intoxicating drug—or, to put it decorously, to champagne, with which Rossini's bubbly music was forever being compared. We have already had an inkling of his astonishing vogue in the previous chapter, when, as mentioned, it almost drove the 1824 premiere of Beethoven's Ninth Symphony out of Vienna, a city Rossini had recently conquered. More evidence of Rossini's widespread importance came from far-off St. Petersburg, the capital of Imperial Russia, where between 1828 and 1831 eighteen of his operas were performed, eleven in 1829 alone. A further indication of his popularity is the extent to which his music was arranged and performed. The allure of his melodies was not confined to the opera house but could be heard in almost every conceivable setting, from intimate domestic gatherings, cafés, and restaurants to large orchestral concerts.

Rossini was born on 29 February 1792 in the central Italian town of Pesaro on the Adriatic. His father was a professional horn player in local bands, his mother a soprano. By the age of thirteen he was already appearing as a boy singer in operatic performances and was sent the next year to Bologna for as traditionally well-rounded a musical education as could then be had anywhere in the world. He wrote his first opera the year after that. A lucky break in 1810 landed the eighteen-year-old a contract with the Teatro San Moisè in Venice, and during the next eighteen years he would compose under contract some three dozen operas for houses all over Italy and eventually abroad. His career average was better than two a year, although the pace declined as he grew more successful. Many of the early operas were written in a month or less, including his most famous work, *Il barbiere di Siviglia*, first performed on 20 February 1816 (Fig. 17-2).

Figure 17-1 Portrait of Gioachino Rossini ca. 1816 by Vincenzo Camuccini.

The conditions under which Rossini worked involved a flurry of commissions, revivals, revisions, triumphs, fiascos, and compilations. He participated as part of a team with a theater impresario, a librettist, and a performing cast. His product, like any commercial product, was subject to considerable modification once it left his hands, such that productions would freely add and subtract elements to suit the needs of presenters and in attempts to heighten audience appeal. Rossini reused a single duet from his first opera in no less than five subsequent works. The now-beloved overture to the comic *Il barbiere* was borrowed wholesale from a previous serious opera that had flopped. (One is reminded of the quip that Beethoven wrote four overtures to one opera, while Rossini wrote four operas to one overture.) It was all a kind of factory system, the economy in which Rossini flourished—music's industrial revolution.

This theatrical system centered not on scores but on performances, with the composer and librettist essentially in service roles. Their primary aim was to please everyone—the **impresario**, the singers, and the paying public. Often enough the composer did not get to choose the subject for the opera, and only rarely did he choose his librettist. Up to the very raising of the curtain on opening night he was busy with last-minute alterations at the request of prickly performers, and thereafter he would be compelled to make endless revisions, at top speed, if the opera's reception fell short of a triumph. Vocal parts had to be written in such a way as to accommodate the leading singers' personalized ornaments. Mozart would have understood this life, these activities, aims, and accommodations (as would, more recently, a composer of Broadway musicals or Hollywood films).

Rossini's musical life and activities stand in marked contrast to Beethoven's. By the end of his life the reclusive German, for reasons both within his control and very much outside of it, had largely become estranged from the practical world of music. There was also the contrast between Rossini's apparently effortless tossing off of brilliant music and Beethoven's mighty laboring, as evidenced in his countless sketches. It is Beethoven's way that is now regarded as "great composer behavior," with his many sketchbooks, a vivid record of the agonizing labor, providing the yardstick by which the working process tends to be measured. The score produced by such exacting toil is now regarded, even venerated, as a definitive text embodying the "work," of which performances can only be imperfect representations. Rossini represented a completely different value system in music, an older and more practical one. He did not leave a single sketch behind (which of course does not mean that he never made them), and he allegedly once boasted that, composing in bed, he started a new overture rather than get out from under the blankets to retrieve one that the wind had blown away. What the score represented to a composer like Rossini, as to the impresario and the cast, was simply one part of the material that made an opera performance possible.

Productions of Rossini operas would freely add and subtract elements to suit the needs of presenters and in attempts to heighten audience appeal.

Figure 17-2 Costume designs for Rossini's comic opera *Il barbiere di Siviglia* (The Barber of Seville).

Within this theatrical world Rossini was recognized as a very great figure indeed. During his lifetime he achieved a prestige and authority that rivaled Beethoven's in parts of Europe, and he certainly enjoyed much greater popular appeal. His influence on later composers, not just Italian and not just of opera, was large. His first international successes came in 1813, when he was twenty-one: *Tancredi*, a serious opera, and *L'Italiana in Algeri*, the frothiest of farces. To write in direct and rapid succession two masterpieces at opposite ends of the stylistic spectrum was in itself a remarkable feat. The next great triumph came with his appointment in 1815, at age twenty-three, as director of all the opera theaters in Naples. Although he answered to the impresario, he had earned a rare power to influence the hiring of librettists and the casting of roles. During the seven years of his prestigious Neapolitan reign, Rossini composed nine operas for the theaters under his jurisdiction and another nine for cities ranging as far afield as Lisbon. All but one of the Neapolitan operas were large tragic works, contradicting Rossini's posthumous reputation as a jester, the master of comedy.

After 1823, Rossini, already an international celebrity, worked mainly abroad. He wrote his last five operas for theaters in Paris, the wealthiest in Europe. For one season (1824–25) he served as director of the Théâtre Italien, where operas were given in Italian. He produced a single new opera, *Il viaggio a Reims* (The Journey to Reims, 1825), to celebrate the coronation of King Charles X, and later recycled some of its music for an opéra comique called *Le comte Ory* (Count Ory, 1828). Rossini ultimately transferred his allegiance to the main Paris opera house, the Académie Royale de Musique, where he adapted two works from his earlier Neapolitan period to French librettos, and to the lavish production values of what the French called *grand opéra*. *Le siège de Corinthe* (The Siege of Corinth, 1826) and *Moïse et Pharaon* (Moses and Pharaoh, 1827) certainly lived up to that billing, but they were cast into the shade by Rossini's vast historical epic *Guillaume Tell* (1829) of which the remarkable overture remains a concert staple (Fig. 17-3).

Figure 17-3 The oath of the three cantons from Rossini's last opera, *Guillaume Tell* (William Tell).

Guillaume Tell, after a German play by Friedrich Schiller, was of unprecedented scale. The arias were of a newly expansive scope, composed according to a formula that Rossini had perfected earlier. And yet the musical texture is dominated by the ensembles, many of which include the chorus for a truly huge fresco-like effect. There are also two ballet episodes and several grand processions of a kind the French had been using for some time, making the opera an eclectic summary, a kind of operatic "state of the art." Rossini retired from the stage after its premiere in August 1829. He lived luxuriously until November 1868, when he died at the age of seventy-six. And yet his productive years show a downright Mozartean precocity, intensity, and brevity. Rossini apparently regarded composing, even at the peak of inspiration and innovation, primarily as a job; having made his fortune—from the fruits of his pen as well as from investments, one of them in a gambling casino—he could reward himself with a life of leisure. While it would not be fair to repeat without qualification the old joke that Rossini gave up composing for eating (for all that he was indeed a famous amateur chef and gourmet), his early retirement does suggest the essentially commercial nature of his career, one increasingly out of joint with the new Romantic temper—possibly another reason for his decision to quit.

And, in fact, Rossini did not give up composing altogether during the last forty years of his life. Rather, he did it primarily as a sort of hobby—to amuse himself and the friends who attended his exclusive salon in the Paris suburb of Passy. The most characteristic works of this last period were 150 or so little songs and piano pieces, composed between 1857 and 1868 but not published during his lifetime, to which he gave the title *Péchés de vieillesse* (Sins of Old Age), a takeoff on the cliché *péchés de jeunesse* (sins of youth). The only large-scale works Rossini attempted during his retirement were religious: an oratorio-like setting of the thirteenth-century hymn *Stabat mater* for soloists, chorus, and orchestra, composed at a snail's pace between 1831 and 1841, and a thoroughly distinctive *Petite messe solennelle* (Little Solemn Mass, 1864) for soloists, chorus, two pianos, and harmonium, composed a few years before his death.

Rossinian Conventions: The Overture

Another difference between the Romantic sensibility, as represented by Beethoven, and the pre-Romantic one, as exemplified by Rossini, lay in their respective attitudes toward forms and genres. From the start Beethoven was strongly inclined to transgress generic and stylistic boundaries, to push the envelope so to speak. One of the ways he did this was by recombining elements (symphonic and chamber styles, for example, or sonata and fugue) formerly regarded as disparate or even opposing. The familiarity of the recombined elements ensures a degree of intelligibility, but the constant modification reflects the Romantic emphasis on individuality and originality.

Rossini, by contrast, was for the most part very respectful of genres, as a composer whose works were largely assembled out of interchangeable parts had to be, to say nothing of a composer who staked his livelihood on pleasing an audience that, like most entertainment audiences, was conservative; his audience generally knew what it liked and liked what it knew. Rossini's idea was not to experiment radically with form in every piece but, rather, to hit on a winning formula, ideally one that he could turn out better than any competitor. Having created a demand for his product, he would stay with it. So successful was Rossini in standardizing and perfecting his wares in accordance with public taste that his formulas eventually became everybody's formulas.

So successful was Rossini in standardizing and perfecting his wares in accordance with public taste that his formulas eventually became everybody's formulas.

To see the Rossinian conventions in action we will consider three of the typical operatic components: overture, ensemble, and aria. All of them were based on models inherited from past practice. Mozart was Rossini's chosen role model, "the admiration of my youth, the desperation of my maturity, and the consolation of my old age," as he once famously put it.[1] Other models included Giovanni Paisiello (1740–1816), Rossini's predecessor as opera czar in Naples, and Domenico Cimarosa (1749–1801), another Neapolitan whose career, like Paisiello's, also included a lucrative stint in St. Petersburg. There is little in Rossini that does not derive ultimately from the work of these three; but there is also little that does not have "New and Improved!" stamped all over it.

Anthology Vol 2-22
Full CD IV, 2
Concise CD II, 22

Let us consider the overture. The Italian opera *sinfonia* by the end of the eighteenth century was essentially a short symphonic "first movement." Rossini's overture to *Il barbiere di Siviglia* unfolds according to the composer's usual formula: a three-part, slow introduction, followed by a bithematic exposition in which the second theme is a woodwind solo. Next comes a bubbling crescendo codetta marking the end of the exposition; his overtures all have the same truncated recapitulation. The "Rossini crescendo" in particular was the moment people waited for: a series of ostinatos over a regular tonic-dominant seesaw in the harmony, sustaining a gradual, inexorable, magnificently orchestrated crescendo to a blazing fanfare for full orchestra in which the bass instruments carry the melodic ball. Its implied emphasis on sensuous values—volume, color, texture—and the repetition of this rollicking crescendo create a mood of festivity.

The festive mood is a generic one, unrelated to the content of the particular opera that follows. "Opera," not *this* opera, is what is being marked as festive, and the same kind of festive overtures prefaced Rossini's tragic operas as well. Indeed, the overture to *Il barbiere* was initially written for a serious opera, the forgotten *Aureliano in Palmira* (1813), the lone flop in the otherwise-golden year that produced *Tancredi* and *L'Italiana in Algeri*. Even though Rossini had salvaged an old overture and tacked it on to the new opera, it now seems a perfect encapsulation of *Il barbiere*. That shows just how interchangeable Rossinian parts could be.

From this it follows that the generic description of one Rossini overture, such as that to *Il barbiere*, can serve as generic description of them all. Does this mean that "when you've heard one you've heard them all"? By no means! What differs inexhaustibly are the absolutely marvelous details. Rossini's orchestration, for one thing, is more varied, more minutely crafted, and more richly sonorous at the climaxes than that of any other composer we have met thus far. The great nineteenth-century flowering of virtuoso orchestration starts with Rossini. His woodwind writing, above all, was epoch-making, as was his use of percussion instruments. The virtuoso solos found in some of his overtures simulate with instruments the extravagant trappings of a vocal scene. On top of this, Rossini's melodic invention was exceptionally fertile. Those lyrical themes in his introductions and those full-blown woodwind solos in the expositions may be interchangeable in function, but that function was to be catchy. Each retains a distinct profile in the aural memory. The combination of generic uniformity with distinction in particulars was Rossini's unmatched genius.

Imbroglio: The Comic Finale

If the overture provided the initial instrumental delight, the comic ensembles, especially those that concluded acts, offered occasions for extraordinary vocal fun as well as for more thrilling crescendos. As we recall from earlier comic operas going back to Piccinni, finales were the site where composers began to experiment with ways of combining fully composed music with real dramatic action, the more frenetic the better. Rossini surpassed all his predecessors in the new level of zany virtuosity, hiding his sophisticated craftsmanship behind a smokescreen of ludicrous situations and effects. He loaded his operas with more ensemble pieces than ever, meanwhile extending the finales in both length and brilliance. This required fantastic virtuosity from all concerned, resourceful composer, conductor, and rapidly enunciating singers alike.

The buffa style can only be exhibited at fullest strength in a finale; and there is no buffa finale in all of Rossini—which is to say, in all of opera—that can equal the Act I finale from *L'Italiana in Algeri* (Fig. 17-4). Here we can see what made Rossini the great counterweight to Beethoven. As the French novelist Stendhal (1783–1842) wrote in his *Life of Rossini* (1824) concerning a production in Venice: "the audience, by the end, were struggling and gasping for breath, and wiping the tears from their eyes."[2] Running through almost a hundred pages of vocal score in record time, it is much too long to include except for the libretto in our accompanying anthology.

Anthology Vol 2-23
Full CD IV, 3–8

A first-act finale, we remember, portrays the height of **imbroglio**—the moment of greatest, seemingly hopeless, tangle in the story. The whole idea, as is usual at this point in a Rossini comic opera, is that a very complicated (and ridiculous) situation has arisen, leaving everyone very confused. Here, in brief, is what has happened: Mustafà, who rules Algiers, has grown tired of his wife Elvira and decides to marry her off to his Italian slave, Lindoro. He sends his pirate commander out to find him an Italian girl. The pirates sink a ship, on which Isabella, the Italian girl of the title, is cruising in search of her fiancé (Lindoro, of course). They bring the survivors to Mustafà's court as captives. Mustafà tells Lindoro he can go home if he takes Elvira with him.

Rossini's orchestration is more varied, more minutely crafted, and more richly sonorous at the climaxes than that of any other composer we have met thus far.

That is the setup. Things come to a head as the captive Isabella catches sight of Lindoro, and the finale begins with a slow recognition section and then builds to the point when the quick-witted Isabella confronts Mustafà in a fast tempo that will only get faster. She berates him for his barbarian transgressions against universal human norms. How can he expect her to love a man who treats his wife so cruelly? How can he simply order Lindoro to marry a woman he does not love? Then, immediately contradicting herself, she insists that Lindoro, a fellow Italian, be made her retainer at once. A hopeless impasse

Figure 17-4 Title page of the vocal score of *L'Italiana in Algeri* (The Italian Girl in Algiers).

has been reached: As the assembled singers declare, "My little head is topsy-turvy, dumbfounded at such entanglements!"

It is time for metaphors in which dramatic sense is ultimately conveyed not through the meaning of the words but, rather, through their sheer sounds. The first metaphor, expressed *allegro vivace,* is the shipwreck. Then, in a concluding section called a *stretta,* this one marked *più mosso,* everybody goes into an onomatopoetical tizzy. The ladies compare their mental agitation to a little bell a-ringing ("din din"); Lindoro compares his to a little clock a-ticking ("tic tic"); Taddeo, Isabella's chaperone, compares his to a little crow a-cawing ("cra cra"); the pirate commander Ali compares his to a hammer pounding ("tac tac"); and Mustafà compares his to a cannon firing ("bum bum"). For twenty or so pages of vocal score they continue shouting and gesticulating in this vein, the chorus finally joining in to raise the hubbub to an even higher pitch of furious futility. And then the masterstroke: Contrary to all reasonable expectation, the whole thing, *din-din, bum-bum,* and all, is replayed *ancora più mosso*—yet faster! In a good performance the audience will not believe its ears. (In case anyone is worrying, the opera ends with Isabella and Lindoro in each other's arms and Mustafà and Elvira reconciled.)

Heart Throbs: The Serious Aria

Opera buffa reached its pinnacle with Rossini, and, with a few exceptional operas that followed, this was the end of the line. Not so with opera seria. Under the impact of Romanticism, serious opera flowered anew, and again Rossini was at the forefront, although this aspect of his historical contribution is less evident today. It may be argued, in fact, that the most fertile aspects of Rossini's conventions were those that pertained to the serious aria, or, more precisely, to the *scena ed aria*, the scene and aria, that replaced the recitative-plus-aria unit of old.

The Rossinian serious aria had two main sections in contrasting tempos: the ***cantabile***, or lyric effusion, and the ***cabaletta***, or brilliant conclusion. The latter usually consisted of a short stanza repeated either in whole or in part, with an orchestral ritornello in between the repetitions and a dazzling coda, all of which amounted to an eager invitation to the singer to embroider away. The double-aria conception allowed the virtuoso to show off everything from beauty of tone and breath control in the cantabile to euphoric fireworks in the cabaletta. Its structure served new dramaturgical purposes by allowing, through the emphasis on contrast, for more action to be accommodated within what had formerly been static aria time. When preceded by an orchestral introduction and an accompanied recitative, when fitted out with a turn of plot between the cantabile and the cabaletta to motivate the latter's change of mood (this "middle movement" is known as a ***tempo di mezzo***), or when enhanced by brief interventions by other characters in dialogue with the soloist, the aria could be built up into a whole ***scena***, or dramatic scene, with a self-contained dramatic trajectory.

Anthology Vol 2-24
Full CD IV, 9

The item that put this new style of aria permanently on the map was "Di tanti palpiti" ("So many heart throbs"), the hero's entrance aria (known as a ***cavatina***) from *Tancredi*. The most famous aria Rossini ever wrote, it was named after its cabaletta, the most memorable part. *Tancredi*, a "heroic musical drama," is in its externals a quasi-historical opera of the old school, even down to the casting of the title role, a valiant knight-crusader, for a so-called *musico*—a woman contralto playing a male character. In other ways, the libretto substantiates the frequent claim that Romantic opera amounts in essence to a constant rehash of the story of *Romeo and Juliet*: "star-cross'd lovers." The title character, the exiled heir to the throne of Syracuse, and his beloved Amenaide are the children of warring clans. In Voltaire's drama of 1760, on which the libretto was based, mutual suspicion prevents their union, and the drama ends with the hero's death on the battlefield. In the first version of the opera Rossini wrote a happy ending instead, which he retrofitted with a tragic finale closer to Voltaire's original for a Ferrara production a month after the Venetian premiere.

Tancredi's aria comes as he has just returned to Syracuse in disguise, torn between his love for Amenaide and his duty to his father, whose rule is threatened by Amenaide's father. The orchestral *andante* that opens the scene is one of Rossini's characteristic tone paintings, full of nature sounds that conjure up the beautiful landscape to which Tancredi addresses his first words of accompanied recitative: "O sweet, ungrateful native land, at last I return to you!" The accompaniment is rich in orchestral and harmonic color, both of which change subtly to register the hero's shifting moods, at first painful, then sweet, finally resolute. The cantabile section, "Tu che accendi questo core" ("You who set this heart of mine afire"), ends with multiple cues for embellishment and a cadenza. If the notes on the page are recognizable at this point, the singer is not doing her job. The same goes double, of course, for the repeated strains in the cabaletta. Surprising harmonic turns and vocal virtuosity work in tandem here with the meaning of the words: The whole aria is about returning, and the very words that launch a harmonic digression are "mi rivedrai, ti rivedrò" ("you will see me again, and I will see you"). The flashy coloratura at the end of the aria was, as always, only a springboard for improvised delirium (Ex. 17-1). This aria has a powerful sensuous immediacy, a sense that the music is playing directly on the nerves and calling up the listener's own memories of the emotions portrayed. As Stendhal put it in his *Life of Rossini*: "without the experience, or the memory of the experience, of the madness of love, as love is known in the happy countries of the South, it is quite impossible to interpret the phrase *mi rivedrai, ti rivedrò*."[3]

Example 17-1 **Gioachino Rossini, "Tu che accendi/Di tanti palpiti" from *Tancredi*, Act II**

Stendhal's *Life of Rossini* is far more than a biography. (As a biography in fact it is quite useless, being full of errors and fabrications.) It is a great work of music criticism, as crucial in its way and within its Franco-Italian milieu as E. T. A. Hoffmann's writings on Beethoven for an understanding of what the music of the early nineteenth century meant to its hearers. Stendhal used Rossini (just as Hoffmann used Beethoven) as a springboard for national stereotyping. What Rossini's contagious heart throbs meant to him, or stimulated in him, was a great liberating impetuosity of the Southern soul utterly in contrast with what he saw as the pompous and vapid spirituality touted in the Protestant North, where manners were restrained and souls unmusical. In Stendhal's view: "Light, lively, amusing, never wearisome, but seldom exalted—Rossini would appear to have been brought into this world for the express purpose of conjuring up visions of ecstatic delight in the commonplace soul of the Average Man."[4]

Ever-sharper distinctions were made between the "spirituality" of German Romanticism and the "sensuality" of Italian opera.

Pitting Stendhal against Hoffmann gives one indication of the increasingly split world of music in the Romantic era, with its nation-based aesthetics and its hardened antagonisms. We will see more of this throughout the century as ever-sharper distinctions were made between the "spirituality" of German Romanticism and the "sensuality" of Italian opera, contrasts between the instrumental music of the Protestant North and the vocal music of the Catholic South.

Vincenzo Bellini and Bel Canto

Figure 17-5 Vincenzo Bellini, anonymous portrait.

In the nineteenth century, serious opera reconciled dramatic and musical values. This move enabled a more evenly unfolding action with operatic events more nearly resembling real time. Another change was the gradual abandonment of women singing men's roles. Men now played men and women played women. The soprano lead was often given a confidante sung by a lower-voiced woman—a contralto or a mezzo-soprano—so that audiences could continue to enjoy virtuoso duet singing in the high registers, the brilliant cadenzas in thirds now representing devoted friendship rather than erotic love.

To see the new opera seria in its fullest flower, we must turn to Rossini's immediate successors: Vincenzo Bellini (1801–35; Fig. 17-5), who was to the early 1830s what Rossini had been to the 1820s; then to the somewhat late-blooming Gaetano Donizetti (1797–1848), who enjoyed a similar preeminence in the decade 1835–45; and ultimately to Giuseppe Verdi (1813–1901), whose operas dominated the second half of the century.

Of his more than two dozen operas, Verdi wrote only two comedies, an early flop and his final masterpiece, *Falstaff*. Seriousness and tragedy dominated the future for Italian opera. In the works of these composers we see the coming of a truly Romantic temper to the opera seria. More specifically, we can see how the cantabile/cabaletta format was continually expanded until it could encompass long scenes packed with highly diversified action. The achievements of Verdi later in the century will be considered in a subsequent chapter, but those of Bellini and Donizetti need our immediate attention, not only because they were Rossini's great direct successors but also because the style of singing that Bellini mastered carried over into the instrumental music of the time.

Bellini, the son and grandson of composers, received intensive musical instruction from the Mozartean age of four, but he did not write his first opera until he was twenty-five. He made up rapidly for lost time, however, and by the time of his death at age thirty-three (more shades of Mozart), he had completed ten operas. At least four—*I Capuleti e i Montecchi* (The Capulets and Montagues, 1830), *La sonnambula* (The Maiden Sleepwalker, 1831), *Norma* (1831), and *I puritani* (The Puritans, 1835)—remain international repertory standards. He wrote most of his operas in collaboration with the prolific Felice Romani (1788–1865), the leading librettist of the period; their close working relationship resembles some of the earlier great partnerships between composer and librettist, on par with Lully/Quinault, Gluck/Calzabigi, and Mozart/Da Ponte.

Like those earlier collaborations, they defined a phase of operatic history, one rather vaguely called ***bel canto***, or "fine singing," and the term has been applied to many things, starting as far back as the Venetian opera of the 1630s. The label has always been retrospective, however; bel canto represents something that has been lost—a golden age. As applied to the operas of Bellini's time, the usage that has remained current in common parlance, the bel canto label was applied by none other than the sixty-five-year-old Rossini, in a conversation that supposedly took place after dinner at his Paris residence one evening in 1858: "Alas for us, we have lost our native bel canto." In his view, singers no longer internalized performing traditions: "Today there is no such school, there are neither models nor interpreters, for which reason not a single voice of the new generation is capable of rendering in bel canto the aria 'Casta diva.'"[5]

Rossini inevitably named Bellini's most famous aria, Norma's cavatina in the opera that bears her name. And what was most telling was the fact that he referred to it not by the opening words of the cabaletta but by those of the cantabile, for that was precisely the difference between the opera seria of Rossini's day and that of Bellini's a decade or two later. The great music now was the slow music, a music elevated into fantastic "long, long, long melodies," as an admiring Verdi called them.[6] Bellini had an unparalleled gift for this type of melodic writing. The Bellinian cantabile was music that, like Romantic music elsewhere, sought to plumb subjective depths and scale transcendent heights.

Anthology Vol 2-25
Full CD IV, 10

As for the story line, long, long ago and far, far away remained the preferred operatic setting. In the case of *Norma* (Fig. 17-6). the place was ancient Gaul, the Celtic provinces of northwestern France, and the time was that of the Druids (ca. 50 BCE) as described by Julius Caesar in his history of the Gallic campaigns. The premise was forbidden love: Norma, the Druid high priestess (Fig. 17-7), is torn between her public duties and her guilty love for Pollione, the Roman proconsul, against whose occupying forces the Druids are planning to revolt. Her love has lately been aggravated by jealousy, for, although she has borne Pollione two children in violation of her oath of chastity, he has forsaken her in favor of Adalgisa, a temple virgin. In the end, Norma and Pollione, his love for her rekindled, perish on a sacrificial pyre in the Druid temple in voluntary atonement for their sins.

Figure 17-6 Poster for a revival of Bellini's *Norma* at the Teatro alla Scala, Milan, starring Maria Malibran (1808–36).

"Casta diva" provides the framework for a scene of grandiose proportions, also involving the participation of another soloist, Norma's father Oroveso, the Archdruid (bass), and the full chorus, with the orchestra supplemented by what was known as the *banda*, an instrumental ensemble played onstage by musicians in costume. Most of the scene's components have their counterparts in scenes like the one from Rossini's *Tancredi* that culminates in "Di tanti palpiti." But quite new are the growth in dimensions, the infusion of spectacle, and especially the enormous influx of stage action into what had formerly been an exclusively reflective domain.

The scene depicts a ritual: a sacrifice to the moon goddess offered in the hope of learning whether the time is ripe for revolt. First, in an accompanied recitative, Norma haughtily addresses the populace, advising patience. Her father objects, supported by the chorus, but she silences one and all by claiming divine inspiration. In a sort of speech-song known as ***parlante***, Norma assures them that Rome will perish—but through decadence, not military defeat. She then leads the assembled congregation in prayer. This is her famous cantabile, in which the priestess, apparently entranced, cuts the sacred mistletoe from the holy oak and, responsively with the chorus, begs the goddess to calm the hearts of her compatriots.

The extremely long melody is heard three times in all, first as a flute solo. A new key is prefigured by a sudden modulation as if graphically to portray the advent of Norma's altered state of consciousness. The first two phrases of the ecstatically embellished melody, balanced four-bar periods, are played complete, but the third phrase is cut off after three measures and followed by a fermata—a favorite device for heightening expectation before a big lyric moment: Norma singing the first stanza complete. Despite its inordinate length, the miraculous coherence of the melody is achieved by a deliberately irregular phrase structure and carefully planned melodic dissonances between voice and accompaniment that are smoothly approached and resolved. One is conscious only of peaceful lyricism, but one's ear is kept perpetually on edge by an insistent undercurrent of harmonic tension in which practically every beat, crying out softly for resolution, maintains an understated but powerful undertow. When this great wave, this surge of melodic and harmonic electricity, has at last subsided, one feels that one has been transported and deposited in a different place. One's own consciousness has been altered. That is Romanticism.

Figure 17-7 Giuditta Pasta (1797–1865) in the title role of Bellini's *Norma*.

The two stanzas of the cantabile are separated by a choral response, to which the enraptured Norma adds the kind of roulades that Rossini, in 1858, already said no one could sing properly anymore. On repetition, the cantabile is enhanced by the continued participation of the chorus and by a short coda plus cadenza. To provide a transition to the cabaletta, which requires a change of mood, something must snap Norma out of her trance. This the banda does quite handily, signaling the completion of the ritual service.

In the cabaletta ("Ah! bello a me ritorna"/"Ah, come back to me, my beloved"), Norma renews her promise that when the goddess commands, she will be ready to lead the attack. Oroveso and the chorus demand that Pollione be the first to die, and this of course sets Norma's heart afire. She promises to punish him, but the inner voice of her conscience confesses her inability to harm the man she loves. The whole cabaletta is cast in a very regular form and sung as an extended agitated aside, an expression of unspoken thoughts, set to a military march rhythm that emphasizes the war that rages within Norma's breast. Despite its rigidly conventional structure, however, it is the most personal music Norma gets to sing. "Heard" only by the audience, she addresses private words of love to Pollione, at complete variance with her public stance. This time the choral interjections between her phrases, in which the people wish ardently for a day that Norma hopes will never come, underscore not their community in prayer but their secret, irreconcilable opposition. Between them the cantabile and the cabaletta encapsulate the heroine's fatal dilemma. Such extended scenes, previously associated with ensemble finales, could now focus on one character.

Gaetano Donizetti

Living a good deal longer than Bellini and working throughout his quarter-century career at a Rossinian pace, Gaetano Donizetti (Fig. 17-8) amassed a lifetime total of some sixty-six operas, most of which were quickly forgotten. Like Rossini, he excelled in both tragic and comic works. At least three of his comic ones—*L'elisir d'amore* (The Elixir of Love, 1832), *La fille du régiment* (The Daughter of the Regiment; 1840), and *Don Pasquale* (1843)—remain repertory standards. His real hit, however, was *Lucia di Lammermoor* (Lucy of Lammermoor, 1835), setting a libretto by Salvadore Cammarano (1801–52), a staff poet and stage director at the royal

Figure 17-8 Gaetano Donizetti, in a portrait by Giuseppe Rillosi.

theaters of Naples. Their influential opera was in fact one of a handful from the time based on the best-selling novel *The Bride of Lammermoor* (1819) by Sir Walter Scott, then the most popular writer in all of Europe, whose novels and poems were the source for more than fifty operas.

The Bride of Lammermoor was one of Scott's so-called "Waverley novels," mixing Scottish local color with horrific plots, a combination that Romantic artists and audiences found irresistible. Anything set in Scotland, the mistiest locale within the British Isles, was surefire Romantic fare, and the novel was also tinged with elements of what was known as Gothic Romance: mysterious occurrences suggesting the influence of the supernatural, set against the background of stormy landscapes, graveyards, dark ruins, and dilapidated castles.

Although there are considerable plot differences between Scott's novel and Cammarano's libretto, the opera retains the central ingredient—love thwarted by family feuds yet again, à la Romeo and Juliet. Lucia of the Lammermoor family (Fig. 17-9) loves Edgardo of the Ravenswood clan. Learning of Lucia's attraction to Edgardo, her elder brother, Enrico, coldly dismisses him as an unsuitable mate and sets about breaking his sister's spirit so that she will assent to the marriage that has been arranged for her to Lord Arturo Bucklaw. Enrico contrives a forged letter in which Edgardo declares love to another woman. After reading it, Lucia can no longer resist her brother's pressure, and she agrees to sign the marriage contract. Only then does Edgardo manage to break in on the betrothal ceremony and expose the hoax. He directs his rage at Lucia, whom he believes has abandoned him. In a dramatic confrontation, Edgardo tears the ring he had given her off her hand and curses her. This, the height of the plot imbroglio, is the end of Act II, a sextet that became one of the most famous ensembles in all of opera.

Anthology Vol 2-26
Full CD IV, 11

Lucia brought to a new scale and standard the incorporation of ensemble writing within the opera seria, and it provided the prototype for what would become a distinct subgenre of operatic tragedy: the "mad scene." Like Rossini before him, Donizetti did not invent either of these contributions out of whole cloth but, rather, crystallized them in practice by providing seemingly unsurpassable models and stimulating later composers. The central scene of the third act is devoted to the wedding and its grisly aftermath, in which the raving-mad Lucia, having murdered her unwanted husband, appears among the guests. Disoriented, the heroine emerges, bloody dagger in hand, believing that she is about to marry Edgardo. She goes through an imaginary ceremony with him, calls on him to meet her in heaven, and convinces everyone that her end is near. To conclude the drama Scott's original ending is given a typically operatic twist: Having learned of Lucia's death, Edgardo echoes her promise to meet in heaven, draws his dagger, and stabs himself, thus completing the parallel with *Romeo and Juliet.*

Donizetti's* Lucia di Lammermoor *provided the prototype for what would become a distinct subgenre of operatic tragedy: the "mad scene."

Lucia's famous mad scene is portrayed in far greater detail in the libretto than in the original novel. It uses the cantabile/cabaletta format, modified to produce an appropriate dramatic climax. The flexibility with which the basic matrix could respond to new dramatic situations shows it to be as malleable as sonata form was for instrumental music. The scene begins with a sort of parlante for Lucia, introduced by horrified interjections by other characters: from her tutor, Raimondo Bide-the-Bent, and the chorus. Lucia sings against an extended flute obbligato. What the flute plays is in itself significant, since it is a distorted reprise of her first aria in Act I ("Regnava nel silenzio"/"Silence

Figure 17-9 Fanny Tecchiardi-Persiani (1812–67) as the title character in the first London production of Donizetti's *Lucia di Lammermoor* (lithograph by Edward Morton, 1839).

reigned"), in which she had described a ghostly visitation of a long-slain Lammermoor lass haunting the castle. The flute thus adds a multileveled commentary to the action, establishing itself as Lucia's demented inner voice and linking her cursed future to a cursed past. It is not the only reminiscence motif. When Lucia sees the ghost again, standing between her and Edgardo, the flute (now doubled by the clarinet) recalls the cabaletta of their clandestine love duet in Act I ("Verranno a te sull'aure"/"Born by gentle breezes"), again somewhat deformed. The last reminiscence in this heartrending parlante is a poignantly elegant embellished reprise of the C-minor music that accompanied Lucia's entrance in the Act II finale, now mauled chromatically in a way that at once boosts pathos and intensifies the portrayal of her derangement.

The cantabile aria ("Il dolce suono"/"The sweet sound") is cast as a slow waltz in an aa′ ba″ format marked *larghetto* and beginning in the flute (Lucia's alter ego) rather than the voice. Donizetti smudges the boundaries between sections as another way of representing Lucia's disordered mind. Her lyric entry ("Alfin son tua,"/"At last I'm yours") comes on the "b" section, accompanied by her horrified onlookers, whose interjections continue the main tune while Lucia, oblivious of the others, soars above them in her own private realm. Not until the closing phrase ("Del ciel clemente"/"From peaceful heaven") does the prima donna sing the main tune at last, accompanied by the flute obbligato. But by now the tune is virtually buried in coloratura and crowned by a duet cadenza that Donizetti never notated, relying instead on his performers' taste and training in the art of improvisation—to write it down would have been an insult. Ironically enough (considering that Donizetti did not compose it), this interpolated cadenza is probably the most famous spot in the opera, one fastened on by earnest emulators and parodists alike.

After the cantabile there follows a tempo di mezzo in a different tempo. Here it is a lengthy parlante for several soloists and chorus, touched off by Enrico's arrival on the scene. He witnesses Lucia's delirium in which, unaware of his presence, she curses his cruelty in what seems at first like the start of the cabaletta ("Ah! vittima fui d'un crudel fratello"/"Ah, I was the victim of a cruel brother"). But the passage reaches a quick ensemble climax and then subsides, paving the way for the true cabaletta, in a quicker waltz time, accompanied as before by the flute ("Spargi d'amaro pianto"/"Shed bitter tears"). Each of its two stanzas is followed by a response from all present, the second of them including Lucia herself, who now imagines herself in heaven awaiting Edgardo's arrival, her voice alone occupying a stratospheric space almost an octave above the choral sopranos.

The mad scene from *Lucia* is an exemplary operatic number, inexhaustibly instructive to anyone who wants to understand what makes the genre tick; in addition it crystallizes certain aspects and paradoxes of Romanticism with extraordinary clarity. The magnificent irony whereby Lucia's madness, an unmitigated catastrophe to its observers, offers solace to her, is graphically realized in the contrast between the musical style of everything that represents the outer world and its inhabitants and the perfect harmony and beauty of Lucia's own contributions, especially as regards her duetting with the flute, which—as the audience instantly apprehends—only she can "hear." That is already a mark of opera's special power: its ability to let us in through music on the unexpressed thoughts and emotions of its characters. The beautiful harmony of voice and flute, conjuring up a better place than the one occupied by the sane characters (or, for that matter, the audience), is a perfect metaphor for Romanticism's aspirations.

German Romantic Opera: Carl Maria von Weber's *Der Freischütz*

Rossini's operas and the later bel canto repertory triumphed in Italy and France, and they also had great influence in German-speaking Europe, Russia, and America. Their success presented a challenge to any composer who wanted to write operas in languages other than Italian or French. Mozart's efforts to create a viable opera tradition in German had been cut short by his early death, and his theatrical achievement was in any case dominated, as was Handel's before him, by his own Italian operas. Vernacular comic operas in German, known as Singspiels, "plays with singing," were endlessly produced in the late eighteenth century, but only Mozart's *The Magic Flute* won a permanent place in the repertoire. Even Beethoven's *Fidelio* was unable to establish German opera. The one who ultimately succeeded in this regard was Carl Maria von Weber (1786–1826; Fig. 17-10). With his *Der Freischütz* (The Free Marksman), which premiered in 1821, we encounter a new kind of musical Romanticism, a new kind of orchestral sound, and a new kind of national opera, an opera drawn from the people.

Weber, a cousin of Mozart's wife, Constanze, had already composed in a wide variety of instrumental and vocal genres by the time he wrote *Der Freischütz*. Clarinetists in particular are grateful for his friendship with Heinrich Bärmann, a virtuoso of the instrument for whom he wrote two concertos and other pieces. Weber was born into a distinguished family of musicians, and in addition to his composing he emerged as a formidable conductor and pianist as well as a critic and even an aspiring novelist. His parents ran a traveling Singspiel theater, so he grew up intimately familiar with the existing repertory of popular music-plays in German. Only when the family's tours were interrupted did they stay in one place long enough for him to get regular schooling.

Figure 17-10 Carl Maria von Weber, in a portrait by Caroline Bardua.

One of his early teachers was Michael Haydn, Franz Joseph's brother, under whose supervision the precocious composer at age sixteen produced his first successful Singspiel, *Peter Schmoll und seine Nachbarn* (Peter Schmoll and his Neighbors), which premiered in March 1803. Later that year he journeyed to Vienna to study with the aging Joseph Haydn, but the latter, increasingly enfeebled, declined to take on a new pupil. Instead, Weber spent a year as apprentice to Georg Joseph Vogler (1749–1814), known as Abbé Vogler because he was once court chaplain at Mannheim. Vogler was a rather eccentric composer but a remarkable teacher whose theories of distant modulation and interest in all kinds of exotic musics stimulated Weber's imagination.

Vogler's influence may be seen in his pupil's incidental music to *Turandot, Prinzessin von China* (Turandot, the Princess of China, 1809), in which all seven numbers are based on a purportedly authentic *air chinois* (Chinese song) that Weber found in Rousseau's *Dictionnaire de musique* (1768). Weber's own predilections led him in many directions where settings and local colors were concerned. In 1810–11 he composed a one-act Singspiel called *Abu Hassan* (on a subject drawn from *The Arabian Nights*), with a conventionally "Eastern" coloration similar to that in Mozart's *Abduction from the Harem*. He later began *Die drei Pintos* (The Three Pintos), an opera with a Spanish setting that he never finished; next came *Euryanthe* (1823), set in France in the age of chivalry; and finally *Oberon* (1826), set partly in "fairyland" as well as in Africa and Medieval France. As with Bellini, these settings can be called typically Romantic, since Romanticism was much drawn to the long ago, the far away, and the never-never.

Weber's* Der Freischütz *was the first opera to achieve the status of national emblem.

Der Freischütz, literally translated, means "The Free Marksman." Its literary source came from a best-selling collection of ghost stories by Johann August Apel and Friedrich Laun, and it was adapted as an opera libretto by Friedrich Kind, a Dresden lawyer and writer who suggested the project to Weber. The composer was probably originally attracted to the tale more for its ghostliness than for its local color, for horror stories were very much in vogue at the time. It was the age, after all, of Mary Shelley's novel *Frankenstein* (1818). Louis Spohr's *Faust* (1813) and E. T. A. Hoffmann's *Undine* (1816) were operas with supernatural elements that served as models for *Der Freischütz*. A few years later, Heinrich August Marschner (1795–1861), a younger contemporary widely regarded as Weber's heir, scored a big hit with the opera *Der Vampyr* (1828), a title that needs no translation.

Despite its generic features, *Der Freischütz* was the first opera to achieve the status of national emblem. The premiere in 1821 marked the inaugural musical offering at a new national theater in Berlin, the Prussian capital, at a time when Germans were yearning for symbols of their unity and singularity as a people. By 1824, an English writer touring Germany was struck by the way its "beautiful national melodies" were "sung in every part of Germany, by all classes, down to the peasant, the hunter, and the laborer."[7] He concluded from this that Weber, lacking the ability to invent his own tunes, had filled his opera with folk songs. In fact Weber borrowed nothing, not even a bridal chorus expressly subtitled "Volkslied" (folk song). Yet in its mere three years of existence, according to the English writer's testimony, this tune, and many others from the opera, had entered the popular oral tradition. Sung by actual hunters and peasants who did not know the opera, it had gained acceptance not just as a song in folk style but as an actual folk song.

Der Freischütz made, and has largely sustained, Weber's fame. A crucial element of its appeal and innovativeness is its representation of the German people, *das Volk*. Up to now peasants had appeared on the operatic stage only as accessories. They represented their class, not their country. The elevation of *Volkstümlichkeit* (folklikeness) to the status of a Romantic ideal changed that. Weber assembled whole casts from the peasant class—not just sidekicks (like Papageno in *The Magic Flute*) and comic relief figures, but heroes and heroines, villains, and the rest. Once peasants, people of the soil, were more than an element of contrast, they could begin to represent the soil itself, from which the nation drew its sustenance. Their music, too, could provide something more than decorative trappings. The idealization of the peasantry in Romantic opera was an idealization of a nation's mythic origins, not the peasants as they actually were or the conditions in which they actually lived, which were rarely matters to celebrate.

Like many legends from many countries, the plot of *Der Freischütz* is a basic yarn of good and evil involving a Faust-like pact with the devil. The title character's real name is Max, a role sung by a tenor. A hunter and forest ranger, he is goaded by Caspar, another forester, sung by a sinister bass, into going with him to the evil Samiel, the "Black Huntsman," to secure his diabolical aid. Samiel's abode is the Wolf's Glen, in the very depths of the forest. They seek his help because the next day Max, who has been suffering a slump, must face a test of marksmanship on which his whole future depends. If he wins a shooting match he will succeed Cuno, the chief ranger to the local prince, and marry Cuno's daughter, Agathe, whom he loves and who, of course, loves him. In the Wolf's Glen, Caspar is coached by Samiel on how to forge seven magic infallible bullets to use in the contest. What Caspar does not tell Max is that the seventh bullet goes not where the marksman directs it but wherever Samiel may wish. When the Prince lets fly a white dove and Max aims the seventh bullet at it, Agathe, who has had a prophetic dream, cries out that she is the dove. Too late: The gun is fired, and she falls—but only in a faint. It is Caspar, the evil tempter, whom Samiel has killed with the seventh bullet. Max confesses his misdeed, is forgiven, is granted the position he sought, and wins Agathe's hand.

Anthology Vol 2-27a
Full CD IV, 12

Alongside its conventional elements, the opera contains real novelties. One is the overture, which has quite deservedly enjoyed a life separate from the opera as a concert staple. With a single conspicuous exception, all of its themes are taken from vocal numbers in the opera. Weber made this overture an instrumental summary of the whole drama to follow. This had already been done by some French composers, and by the second half of the nineteenth century the procedure would become standard.

The *Freischütz* overture is a study in contrasts, between evocations of the natural and the supernatural, between dark and light, slow and fast, major and minor. It begins with a slow introduction that is initially mysterious and then suggests a natural scene with hunting horns before turning to Samiel's darker realm of the Wolf's Glen, associated throughout the opera with the sound of a diminished seventh chord punctuated with funeral drum strokes. The following *molto vivace* draws on two of the main arias in the work, one in which Max exclaims the "powers of darkness are weaving around me!" and the other from the end of Agathe's scene in Act II, where she proclaims: "All my pulses are beating, and my heart beats wildly, full of sweet enchantment at [Max's] approach!" The rousing major-key coda anticipates the final moments of the opera with its imposing choral conclusion: "Whoever is pure of heart and guiltless in life may, childlike, trust in the gentleness of the Father!"

Weber made the overture to* Der Freischütz *an instrumental summary of the whole drama to follow.

The lone part of the overture not connected to what follows is in the slow introduction, prominently scored for four soloistic French horns (in German, *Waldhörner*—forest horns), or, to be more precise, for two pairs of horns, one in C, the other in F, that alternately call to one another and sound together over a bed of murmuring strings. This seems a normal enough way to set the scene for an opera about hunters, but as sheer tone color it was an unprecedented and electrifying effect that forever changed the nature of orchestral horn writing. What made Weber's horns sound particularly "German" was the close harmony, equivalent in range and voicing to the style of part songs, such as his teacher Michael Haydn wrote, and of the men's chorus idiom practiced by singing groups.

Orchestration, as already seen with Rossini, became ever more significant for Romantic composers. The most famous section of the opera has the most innovative orchestral effects: the Act II finale, which offers the midnight forging of the bullets in the Wolf's Glen (Fig. 17-11). The scene offers a series of ghastly apparitions created by use of a light projector that produced theatrical effects such as were then popular in mass entertainment. To achieve the musical equivalent of a light show implies a musical analogy with visual imagery, which Weber achieved through effects of "chromatic" harmony (from *chroma,* color in Greek) and timbre, or tone color. The Wolf's Glen scene abounds in such effects and links them in a way already used in the overture, where the eerie chromatic harmony of the diminished seventh chord is projected through the rare timbre of unmeasured string tremolo and pizzicato. The remarkable music in this scene, coloristic to an unprecedented degree, continued to reverberate in the work of opera composers and eventually symphony composers as well for the rest of the century.

Anthology Vol 2-27b
Full CD IV, 13

Weber's orchestral effects are enhanced by his vocal writing, which mediates between song and "**melodrama**," a term that has a different technical meaning from its common use today and refers to accompanied speech, actual speaking (rather than singing) over an orchestral background. The voice of Samiel—the Satanic figure—is never set to music; it remains an unintegrated alien presence throughout the scene. When the bullet-casting begins, each of the seven are counted off by Caspar and eerily echoed by an offstage voice, accompanied, exactly as in a light show, by a fleeting hallucination. The orchestra assumes the role of magic lantern, projecting bizarre orchestral colors in dazzlingly quick succession to parallel the flashing stage lights.

Figure 17-11 Set for the Wolf's Glen scene in Weber's *Der Freischütz* (The Free Marksman) as performed at Weimar in 1822.

Weber's Wolf's Glen scene looms in retrospect as a watershed of musical Romanticism. Yet some German artists at the time were suspicious of it because the imaginative, supernatural contents were given a visually explicit representation. The composer Carl Friedrich Zelter wrote to Goethe after the premiere, praising Weber's music but mocking the staging of the Wolf's Glen scene, replete with "clouds of dust and smoke," and added that "children and women are crazy about it."[8] The debt to popular light shows—fairground entertainments, not high art—evoked criticism born of social snobbery. It was only after the opera's canonization as mystical embodiment of German nationhood that such criticism fell silent. It took precisely a "lowering" of taste to give the work such an elevated status. Thanks to it, peasantry, as figurative stand-in for the nation, was not merely represented in the work but actually incorporated into it. Whether described as a debasement of aristocracy or as an elevation of peasantry, a truly national art, like the idea of nation itself, gave differing social classes a common ground and a common bond.

The significance of *Der Freischütz* for German nationalists of a later time rested on its prior acceptance by the nation at large. The preeminent German opera composer of the second half of the century, Richard Wagner, was living in Paris in 1841 when he saw *Der Freischütz* performed in a French version put together by Hector Berlioz in which newly composed recitatives replaced the original spoken dialogue. He took the opportunity to send a chauvinistic dispatch to a newspaper back home, in which Weber's name is not even mentioned, as if the opera were issued collectively by the German *Volk*:

> O my magnificent German fatherland, how must I love thee, how must I gush over thee, if for no other reason than that *Der Freischütz* rose from thy soil! How must I love the German folk that loves *Der Freischütz*, that even now believes in the wonders of artless legend, that even now, in manhood, feels the same sweet mysterious thrills that made its heart beat fast in youth! . . . How happy he who understands thee, who can believe, feel, dream, delight with thee! How happy I am to be a German![9]

Summary

Gioachino Rossini (1792–1868) stands in stark contrast to many of the Romantic ideals explored in the last two chapters. In many respects, he was Beethoven's opposite. Rather than Beethoven's focus on instrumental music, Rossini excelled in the tradition of Italian opera. Unlike Beethoven, who epitomized the "sublime" for Romantic critics, Rossini strove to write works that were popular and pleasing. In contrast to the Romantic aesthetic, where the individual composer reigned supreme, the composer and librettist still took a secondary role in an opera production. Rossini's operas were often subject to last-minute additions and subtractions by the producers. Rather than pushing the boundaries of genres, Rossini stayed within the expected norms, hitting on a winning formula.

Rossini's most famous operas today are the ones in the comic buffa style. These follow many of the conventions established earlier in the eighteenth century (see Chapter 12), with tangled plots that are worked out in ensemble finales. (See the Act I Finale from *L'Italiana in Algeri*.) In his time, however, Rossini was just as well known for his serious operas. A typical scene in one of Rossini's serious operas begins with a recitative accompanied by the orchestra, followed by an aria or duet with two main sections: a slow section called a *cantabile* and a fast one called a *cabaletta*. (See "Di tanti palpiti" from *Tancredi.*) Sometimes the two parts of the aria are joined by a middle section called *tempo di mezzo*. Rossini's overtures typically have a slow introduction, an exposition with a second theme played by a woodwind solo, and the famous "Rossini crescendo." (See the overture to *Il barbiere di Siviglia.*)

After Rossini, serious opera became the preferred genre, furthered by two of his immediate successors, Vincenzo Bellini (1810–35) and Gaetano Donizetti (1797–1848). This style of opera is often called *bel canto*, "beautiful singing," because of its fondness for long, lyrical melodic lines. The aria "Casta diva" from Bellini's *Norma* demonstrates this style, with its long, expressive, and unpredictable melody. The plots of *bel canto* opera were usually mythological or epic. In true romantic fashion they were far removed from the everyday world. The "mad scene" from Donizetti's *Lucia di Lammermoor* shows the influence of Romanticism. The calmness of Lucia's music, which contrasts with the horror of the onlookers, allows the audience to see into Lucia's mind. The recurrence of themes from earlier in the opera (often called "reminiscence motives") plays an important role in the drama and became a common device.

In Germany, Romanticism in opera took a different turn. Weber's *Der Freischütz* was considered the consummate German Romantic opera. *Der Freischütz* was innovative for its orchestration and its emphasis on *das Volk* (the folk), evident both in the plot and in the music. Another key feature of German Romantic opera is the centrality of the supernatural, which is depicted by chromatic harmony and innovative orchestral timbres.

Study Questions

1. Describe the contrasts between Gioachino Rossini and Beethoven. How do they represent different musical values?
2. How do the following elements of a Rossini opera unfold? (a) the overture, (b) the comic finale, (c) cantabile/cabaletta
3. Discuss Rossini's "Di tanti palpiti" as an example of a cantabile/cabaletta. How does it compare and contrast with arias discussed in previous chapters?
4. Describe the changes that took place in serious opera in the 1830s and '40s with Vincenzo Bellini and Gaetano Donizetti. How does Bellini's "Casta diva" illustrate bel canto style?
5. How does *Lucia di Lammermoor* (particularly the "mad scene") tie into larger trends of Romanticism?
6. Discuss Carl Maria von Weber's *Der Freischütz* as an example of German Romantic opera. What features of its plot, drama, and music distinguish it from Italian opera? Which aspects were especially important for later German composers and audiences?

Key Terms

bel canto
cabaletta
cantabile
cavatina
imbroglio
impresario
melodrama
parlante
scena
tempo di mezzo

18

Private Art: Schubert and Inwardness

The previous two chapters focused on symphonies and operas, the most widely honored genres of public music in the nineteenth century. We saw that Beethoven and Rossini, the leading composers of their time, in many respects represented dialectical opposites, the former associated with German instrumental music, suffering and transcendence, and the latter with Italian vocal music, lyricism, pleasure, and sensuality. This opposition sets up themes that resonate in chapters to come between the German north and the Italian south, between "brains" and "beauty," and, more covertly (and condescendingly), between serious art and popular entertainment. As much as these oppositions had considerable force in nineteenth-century musical politics, there were also other significant genres, countries, musical values, and styles that we must explore. This chapter concentrates on a more private sphere of music and music making, for which Franz Peter Schubert (1797–1828) will serve as our prime example. His career gives us the chance to explore musical activities somewhat removed from the luminous public sphere in which Beethoven's symphonies and Rossini's operas cast their spells.

No matter where they were written or by whom, symphonies and operas were public pieces that were long and large and that required many musicians to perform. Some of the genres gaining new prominence early in the nineteenth century, however, were meant primarily for consumption at home. They were short and small and required just one or two players. Most prominent among these domestic genres were two that were German in origin: the ***Lied*** (plural *Lieder*), the setting of a lyric poem for voice accompanied (usually) by piano; and the *Charakterstück* (**character piece**) for solo piano. Genres such as these reflected and encouraged more intimate kinds of music making and more personal kinds of musical expression. It was through his songs and keyboard music that Schubert emerged as the early Romantic composer whose works now loom as the most decisive, transformative crossing over into the contemplation of "inwardness" (from the German *Innigkeit* or *Innerlichkeit*). Particularly private were the character pieces, purely instrumental equivalents of lyric poems that some other composers actually called *Lieder ohne Worte* (Songs Without Words).

Romanticism in general fostered a great surge of private art. The representation of private lives in biographies, autobiographies, and diaries reflected the aspirations of the middle class, who were the primary consumers of the new art. Inexpensive editions of books for home reading, addressed to a much enlarged urban and newly literate public, and of music for home singing and playing created opportunities for authors and composers. In literature this encouraged a new emphasis on lyric poetry, little poems that vividly evoked moods and that stimulated psychological withdrawal from the world. Such poems in turn inspired new generations of Romantic composers to wrap them in music.

The Lied Grows Up

Songs, of course, date back to the Middle Ages, and we have already encountered many examples of different kinds over the centuries. The Romantic Lied was brought about by a complex mixture of social, artistic, and musical factors, among them the rise in domestic music making, innovations in piano construction, and the remarkable flowering of German lyric poetry, most prominently associated with Goethe. The new Lied originated in Berlin, and once again that curious figure C. P. E. Bach, who wrote some 200 of them, played an important role in its proto-Romantic development.

From the very beginning the German Lied was associated not only with the idea of *Empfindsamkeit*, or personal expressivity, but also with the *Volkstümlichkeit*, or folklikeness, that we saw proved so important to the reception of Weber's *Der Freischütz*. The two ideals may appear incongruous, since the simplicities of communal folk song may not seem the likeliest channel for the intense expression of a unique personal psychology. In Lieder the Romantic "I" bonded musically with the Romantic "We." Accordingly, the earliest Lieder were in effect imitation folk songs with simple melodies and easy accompaniments that could be sung by nonprofessionals at home. A Berlin lawyer named Christian Gottfried Krause (1719–70) described the simple Lied ideal in *Von der musikalischen Poesie* (On Poetry for Music), published in 1752, and then got several of his friends, including C. P. E. Bach, to furnish examples.

> ***The German Lied was associated not only with the idea of* Empfindsamkeit*, or personal expressivity, but also with the* Volkstümlichkeit*, or folklikeness.***

Until the end of the eighteenth century and even for some decades to follow, the Lied was considered a lowly genre, the province of specialist composers like Johann Friedrich Reichardt (1752–1814) and Carl Friedrich Zelter (1758–1832). Reichardt was the first major figure in the history of the Lied, with more than 1,500 to his credit, while Zelter was Goethe's personal favorite, with whom he carried on a lively correspondence. What Goethe liked about Zelter's Lieder was their modesty. What he disliked in the settings by others, allegedly including Schubert, was the oversensitive,

TIMELINE

1782 Johann Wolfgang von Goethe, "Der Erlkönig"

1778 Johann Gottfried von Herder, *Stimmen der Völker in Liedern*

1797 Birth of Franz Peter Schubert

1803–15 Napoleonic Wars

1805–08 Publication of *Des Knaben Wunderhorn*

1812 Founding of the Gesellschaft der Musikfreunde (Society of Friends of Music) in Vienna

1815 Schubert, *Heidenröslein* and *Erlkönig*

1816 Ludwig van Beethoven, *An die ferne Geliebte*

1819 Arthur Schopenhauer, *The World as Will and Representation*

1822 Schubert, Symphony No. 8 in B Minor, "Unfinished"

1823 Schubert, Fantasy in C Major for piano, "Wanderer"

1823 Schubert, *Die schöne Müllerin*

1823–28 Schubert, *Moments musicaux*

1826–28 Schubert, Symphony No. 9 in C Major, "Great"

1827 Schubert, Piano Trio in E♭ Major, Op. 100

1827 Heinrich Heine, *Buch der Lieder*

1827 Schubert, *Winterreise*

1828 Death of Schubert

overcomplicated response to each successive line in a poem that smothered the words in musical artistry. This fear reveals how easily distracted (or, to put it positively, how strongly attracted) Goethe was by music. In 1809 he wrote to Zelter that however wary he may have felt, as a poet, toward music carelessly applied, no lyric poem was complete without it. Only when set and sung, he wrote, is a poem's inspiration released into "the free and beautiful element of sensory experience." He concluded that, when listening to beautiful words beautifully put to music, "we think and feel at once, and are enraptured."[1]

But the Lied nevertheless remained a relatively low-prestige affair, which is why it was cultivated so little by Schubert's great Viennese forebears, whose careers were oriented toward the aristocracy for support and toward large public musical genres for acclaim. Between 1781 and 1803, Haydn composed no more than three dozen Lieder. One of his most folklike songs became exceedingly famous: *Gott, erhalte Franz den Kaiser*! (God Save the Emperor Franz!), better known as the *Kaiserhymne* (Emperor's Hymn). With various words and at various times in history this melody has seen duty as the national anthem for three countries, and it remains one for Germany today. Mozart also left some three dozen songs with keyboard accompaniment, in three languages (French, Italian, and, mostly, German). One, at least, is a masterpiece—or so Goethe thought: *Das Veilchen* (The Little Violet).

Beethoven's involvement with the genre ran deeper; he composed about a hundred Lieder, mostly early in his career, a few of which became quite popular. Their styles, complexity, and artistic importance vary greatly, ranging from drivel and humorous parodies to songs that set the elevated words of Goethe and Schiller. At the urging of British publishers who had earlier tempted Haydn, Beethoven produced 168 commercial arrangements, principally of Irish, Welsh, and Scottish folk songs. His Lied output contains one major work: *An die ferne Geliebte* (To the Distant Beloved), Op. 98, completed in 1816. Rather than a single song, it is a set of six, bound together by composed transitions and closing with a song that incorporates a thematic recollection of the first. Appropriately enough this work bears the subtitle *Liederkreis*, literally a "circle of songs." In English the term is "**song cycle**." Beethoven's, though not quite the first, is the earliest to survive in the active repertory.

Herder, Language, and the Nation

The German Lied affords us as well an excellent opportunity to consider further the ever-mounting importance of nation and language in nineteenth-century culture and to consider the impossibility of a particular "I" without a particular "We." This idea was in large part the brainchild of the philosopher Johann Gottfried von Herder (1744–1803), who provided the main intellectual bridge between the *Sturm und Drang* movement of the 1770s and the later German Romanticism. We will return frequently to his ideas in the coming chapters. The most basic of them may seem all too obvious to us, heirs as we are to more than two centuries of Romantic thinking. Very simply, Herder contended that there was no universal human nature and no universal human truth. He rejected the "sensus communis," or common sense, posited by his one-time mentor Immanuel Kant. Rather, he argued, each human society, each epoch of human history, each and every human collectivity was a unique entity—and uniquely valuable. Human difference was worthy of study and respect and could be as morally instructive as human similarity.

Herder did not invent this notion all by himself; parts of it were derived from the writings of Jean-Jacques Rousseau and the French *philosophes*, who were among the most ardent upholders of Enlightenment and its gospel of universality. But Herder's specific emphases and his conclusions mark his thinking as particularly Romantic and particularly German. Through him, paradoxically enough, aspects of distinctively German thinking became universal, thus providing a philosophical foundation for nineteenth- and twentieth-century nationalist thought. It seems only natural and right that human particularity and diversity should have appeared natural and right to a German thinker. The German-speaking lands were then, and to some extent remain even now, a political and religious crazy quilt (Fig. 18-1). The idea of valuing particularity and diversity arose in reaction to the universalist, Enlightened assumption that progress lay in political consolidation and uniformity. From a French perspective, the politically fragmented German scene looked not only backward but weak; shortly after Herder's death Napoleon would prove the point by force of arms. Herder's particularism and the German

Herder contended that there was no universal human nature and no universal human truth.

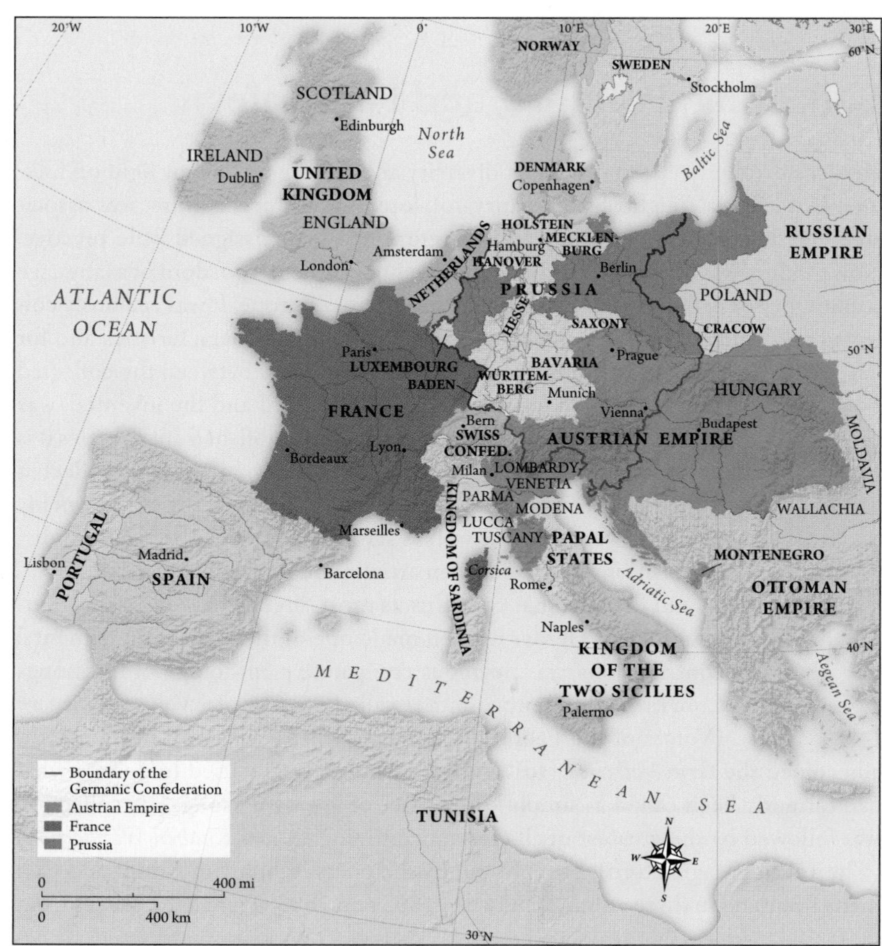

Figure 18-1 Europe before the revolutions of 1848.

nationalism that grew out of it were in part an expression of resentment against French condescension, to say nothing of the French military threat.

Herder fastened on language as fundamental to humans and the natural definer of societies. In his influential tract *Über den Ursprung der Sprache* (On the Origin of Language, 1772), he argued that because language could only be learned socially, in a community, human individuality had its limits. Since there could be no thought without language, it followed that human thought, too, was a social or community product—neither wholly individual nor wholly universal. Herder insisted that each language manifested unique values and ideas that constituted each language community's specific contribution to the treasury of world culture. Moreover—and here lay the most subversive part of all—since there is no predetermined scale against which particular languages can be measured, no language, no language community, can be held to be superior or inferior to any other. This remarkably open-minded view of the merits of cultural difference, uniqueness, and equality would not last long because certain cultures, political entities, and races began to insist on their superiority. Alongside other aspects of learned behavior and expressive culture—customs, dress, and art—language seemed to signal a precious collective spirit or personality. In such thinking the concept was born of "authenticity," faithfulness to one's essential spirit. It became an explicit goal of the arts to express the specific truth of the community they served.

Folk Song, Folklore, and Folk Tales

Herder's brotherly vision of human diversity and culture cast a new light on folklore. Until the late eighteenth century, folklore, or local oral culture, was associated chiefly with the peasantry and therefore had been assigned little prestige. Now folklore was seen as embodying the essential authentic wisdom of a language community or nation. Its cultural stock soared across Europe. It was zealously collected and studied, both for the sake of defining national characteristics and for the sake of comparing them. The boundary between the collected and the created, or between the discovered and the invented, was at first a soft one, easily blurred. In some published anthologies it is not always possible to distinguish between what was truly collected from the folk and what was newly contributed by the editors, many of whom were poets as well as scholars and who often did not distinguish rigorously between artistic and scholarly practice.

Folklore was seen as embodying the essential authentic wisdom of a language community or nation.

In the area that concerns us most directly here regarding German Lieder, Herder himself made one of the earliest fundamental contributions, an enormous comparative anthology of folk songs from many different countries called *Stimmen der Völker in Liedern* (Voices of the Peoples in Songs, 2 vols., 1778–79). In it he actually coined the term *Volkslied* (**folk song**), now universally used to denote what had formerly been called a "simple" or "rustic" or "peasant" song. His collection was followed by the greatest of all German anthologies, *Des Knaben Wunderhorn* (The Youth's Magic Horn), brought out by the poets Achim von Arnim and Clemens Brentano in three volumes between 1805 and 1808 (Fig. 18-2). Verses from this book were set by many of the leading German composers throughout the century.

Another influential literary undertaking derived from Herder came from the brothers Jacob and Wilhelm Grimm, who compiled epoch-making collections of folk tales (*Kinder- und Hausmärchen*, or Children's and Household Tales, 2 vols., 1812–15) and of German folk myths and legends (*Deutsche Sagen*, or German Sagas, 2 vols., 1816–18). By the middle of the nineteenth century, similar projects had been realized in almost every European country. The rediscovery of the folk and the consequent fever of collecting had an enormous impact on German poetry as well as on the music to which it was set.

Figure 18-2 Title page of *Des Knaben Wunderhorn* (The Youth's Magic Horn), 1808.

Lyric and Ballad

Among the arts the Romantic Lied became one of the principal vehicles of national identity, and its mission to unite the "I" and the "We" took on a newly clarified sense of purpose. The simulated folk poetry of German Romanticism came in two main formal types: lyric and ballad. The lyrics were often cast as dance songs that resemble the stanza-and-refrain forms used in Medieval poetry. Goethe's most famous song-with-refrain, owing to the large number of musical settings it attracted, was "Heidenröslein" ("Heath Rose"), a lyric poem published in 1773. He revised it in 1794 for a book of *Lyrische Gedichte* (Lyric Poems) set by Reichardt (Ex. 18-1). The text, a sustained metaphor for the deflowering of a maiden, unfolds in three apparently simple verses:

Sah' ein Knab' ein Röslein stehn,	A boy saw a rose growing,
Röslein auf der Heiden,	a rose upon the heath.
War so jung und morgenschön,	It was so young and morning-fresh,
Lief er schnell, es nah zu sehn,	he quickly ran to look at it up close.
Sah's mit vielen Freuden.	He looked at it with much joy.
Röslein, Röslein, Röslein rot,	Rose, rose, red rose,
Röslein auf der Heiden.	Rose upon the heath.
Knabe sprach: Ich breche dich,	The boy said, I'll pluck you,
Röslein auf der Heiden!	Rose upon the heath!
Röslein sprach: Ich steche dich,	The rose said, I'll prick you
Daß du ewig denkst an mich,	so that you'll always think of me,
Und ich will's nicht leiden.	for I won't suffer it.
Röslein, etc.	Rose, etc.
Und der wilde Knabe brach's	And the savage boy picked
Röslein auf der Heiden;	the rose upon the heath;
Röslein wehrte sich und stach,	the rose, defending itself, pricked away,
Half ihm doch kein Weh und Ach,	but its aches and pains availed it not;
Mußt' es eben leiden.	it had to suffer all the same.
Röslein, etc.	Rose, etc.

Example 18-1 J. F. Reichardt, *Heidenröslein*

Goethe wanted such a poem to be set in a **strophic** manner, using a single repeated musical stanza just as naturally as in a folk song. He believed the strophic approach also worked for the main narrative genre of Romantic folk poetry, which was called the ***ballad***. This is another term with long roots that now came to designate a sung narrative poem, often one that included dramatic dialogue between humans and supernatural beings and that typically ended in disaster. As a true folk genre the ballad flourished mainly in the British Isles and Scandinavia, lands of mist and mystery. The earliest German Romantic ballads were translations from English and Scandinavian originals—or, rather, imitations of the translations Herder published in his collections.

Goethe thought that in a strophic setting the singer could convey changes of mood and circumstance that happen in the poem through subtle vocal shading in delivery, even though the written music did not change from verse to verse. But many composers found this limiting. They wanted to compose music that continuously followed the poem's unfolding meaning rather than its repeating form, each word inspiring its own musical counterpart. No good single term covers this kind of setting, since as a type it is defined basically by what it does *not* do, namely, follow the text strophically. Rather than call it "nonstrophic," which would be as good (or bad) as any term, what has become standard is the equally clumsy "**through-composed**," a direct translation of the German word *durchkomponiert*. Some songs combined elements of the two, so-called modified strophic settings, in which the stanzas are varied to a degree but are still recognizably related by recurring music.

Far and away the most famous German ballad was Goethe's "Der Erlkönig" ("The Erlking"; Fig. 18-3), written in 1781 and first published as part of a Singspiel libretto called *Die Fischerin* (The Fisherman's Wife). Although very effectively disguised with specifically Romantic surface features, Goethe's ballad belongs to an ancient mythological prototype with origins going back at least as far as the Greeks: the siren song or song of fatal seduction, seduction usually addressed by supernatural women to natural men, and most often given a maritime setting, as in Homer's *Odyssey*. Goethe's immediate model was Herder's translation of a Danish folk ballad in which a knight named Sir Oluf, riding at night to summon guests to his wedding, encounters one of the Elfking's daughters, who tries to lure him into a lethal dance and mortally curses him. Herder mistranslated the original Danish *Ellerkonge* (King of the Elves, or Elfking) as *Erlkönig* (King of the Alder Trees, or Erlking), a mistake then perpetuated by Goethe and by the more than 100 composers who set his famous text to music.

Like most ballads, the eight-stanza text of "Der Erlkönig" unfolds as a story; in this case it is almost a miniature opera with four different characters. A grimly deadpan narrator sets the scene in the first stanza and tells the outcome in the last. An increasingly distraught child and his increasingly concerned father ride through the night as the sinisterly beguiling title character tries to seduce the boy. Goethe's poem ostensibly removes the element of sexual allure found in Herder's original ballad (but perhaps only succeeds in displacing it), while surrounding the horse and rider with an array of

Figure 18-3 Moritz von Schwind, *Erlkönig* (ca. 1830).

Germanic nature mythology, according to which the forest harbors a nocturnal spirit world, invisible to the civilized father, but terrifyingly apparent to his innocent son. The rationalistic father thinks he "sees perfectly" and is in control of things:

Wer reitet so spät durch Nacht und Wind? *Es ist der Vater mit seinem Kind:* *Er hat den Knaben wohl in dem Arm,* *Er faßt ihn sicher, er hält ihn warm.*	Who rides so late through night and wind? It is the father with his child. He holds the boy in his arms, he clasps him firmly, he keeps him warm.
—Mein Sohn, was birgst du so bang dein Gesicht? *—Siehst, Vater, du den Erlkönig nicht?* *Den Erlenkönig mit Kron' und Schweif?* *—Mein Sohn, es ist ein Nebelstreif.*	"My son, why do you hide your face so fearfully?" "Father, don't you see the Elf King? The Elf King with his crown and train?" "My son, it is a patch of mist."
"Du liebes Kind, komm, geh mit mir! *Gar schöne Spiele spiel ich mit dir;* *manch bunte Blumen sind an dem Strand;* *Meine Mutter hat manch' gülden Gewand."*	"Come dear child, go with me! I will play beautiful games with you; many are the bright flowers on the shore, my mother has many robes of gold."
—Mein Vater, mein Vater, und hörest du nicht, *Was Erlenkönig mir leise verspricht?* *—Sei ruhig, bleibe ruhig, mein Kind:* *in dürren Blättern säuselt der Wind.*	"My father, my father, and do you not hear what the Elf King softly promises me?" "Be calm, keep calm, my child: in dry leaves the wind is rustling."
"Willst, feiner Knabe, du mit mir gehn? *Meine Töchter sollen dich warten schön;* *Meine Töchter führen den nächtlichen Reihn* *Und wiegen und tanzen und singen dich ein."*	"Will you go with me, brave boy? My daughters shall tend you nicely. My daughters will lead the dancing each night and will lull and dance and sing for you."
—Mein Vater, mein Vater, und siehst du nicht dort *Erlkönigs Töchter am düstern Ort?* *—Mein Sohn, mein Sohn, ich seh es genau:* *Es scheinen die alten Weiden so grau.*	"My father, my father, don't you see over there the Elf King's daughters in that deserted spot?" "My son, my son, I see it perfectly, the old willows look so gray."
"Ich liebe dich, mich reizt deine schöne Gestalt; *Und bist du nicht willig, so brauch ich Gewalt."* *—Mein Vater, mein Vater, jetzt faßt er mich an!* *Erlkönig hat mir ein Leids getan!*	"I love you, I am charmed by your good looks, and if you are not willing, I shall have to use force." "My father, my father, he's clutching me now! The Elf King has hurt me!"
Dem Vater grauset's, er reitet geschwind, *Er hält in den Armen das ächzende Kind,* *Erreicht den Hof mit Mühe und Not:* *In seinen Armen das Kind war tot.*	The father shudders, he rides apace; in his arms he holds the groaning child. Sweating and straining he reaches the courtyard; in his arms the child lay dead.

The first musical setting of "Der Erlkönig" was a simple strophic version written in 1782 by Corona Schröter (1751–1802), the actress who created the title role in *Die Fischerin* (Ex. 18-2). The play opens with the title character singing the ballad as she cooks supper and waits for her husband to return. In this context it was meant as a folk song that anyone might sing to kill time. Many important Lied composers as well as countless lesser ones set the poem before Schubert did in 1815. Reichardt wrote one in 1794, and even Beethoven sketched a version he never completed. Carl Loewe (1796–1869), who was highly regarded for his ballads, wrote one that was published as his Op. 1 in 1824. Schubert's setting eclipsed all of these in fame, musical power, and profound psychological insight.

Example 18-2 **Corona Schröter, *Der Erlkönig* (first two stanzas)**

Schubert and Goethe

Schubert was the first major composer for whom the Lied was a major genre, and hence he was the composer through whom the Lied became important in the history of European music. Although he won his initial fame through small-scale works intended primarily for private consumption, this tireless and ambitious composer also wrote in the great public genres, including many symphonies, operas, and Masses and an oratorio. In the some 630 Lieder he composed beginning at age fourteen, Schubert set nearly 100 different poets, with texts ranging from classical antiquity to Shakespeare to the great poets of his own day as well as words from lesser figures and some personal friends. Goethe, whom Schubert never met, was the poet who inspired his first masterpieces and was the one whose poems he set most often (Figs. 18-4 and 18-5). In 1815, at age eighteen, he composed music both for the folklike lyric "Heidenröslein" and the ballad "Der Erlkönig."

In the some 630 Lieder he composed beginning at age fourteen, Schubert set nearly 100 different poets.

Anthology Vol 2-28
Full CD IV, 14
Concise CD II, 23

While it is customary to say that the strophic form is "natural" and the through-composed is "artistic," there is no reason why strophic settings could not be artistic in the highest degree. Schubert's *Heidenröslein* seems as natural—as much like a folk song—as could be desired, distinguished above all by the memorable perkiness of its thrice-repeated strain. The accompaniment is quite unassuming and easy to play, not so different from Reichardt and other early Lied composers.

Anthology Vol 2-29
Full CD IV, 15
Concise CD II, 24

Erlkönig, by comparison with any song that preceded it, seems to come from another world. There has rarely been as stark an example in the history of music of a work that shatters expectations and changes the course of a genre. Its novelty is immediately apparent in the almost orchestral sounding fifteen-measure piano introduction, music of terrifying intensity, dramatic force, and technical difficulty. Schubert was already a seasoned composer of dramatic ballads when he wrote it. His earlier settings had relied a great deal on operatic devices, particularly the use of recitative for lines of narration. In *Erlkönig*, recitative has shrunk down to just a single line: the horrifying final one in which the boy's death is revealed. Elsewhere the momentum is maintained at considerable cost to the poor pianist's right arm, to which the horse's incessant hoof beats are assigned. The final recitative thus silences what had seemed like unstoppable musical energy.

Schubert distinguishes the narrator and three characters in various ways, most obviously by contrasting registers—the boy sings in a high one, the father low. (There is an anecdote of Schubert's playing though the song with friends in which each one took a different role—a four-minute opera indeed!) When the Erlking sings, the pianist gets a bit of relief. The sweet crooning of the seducer—sweet, that is, until he loses patience at the end of his third speech—so occupies the attention of the terrified but fascinated child that the hoof beats fade into the background, only to return with redoubled force at each panicked outcry from child to father. That insidious ironic sweetness—experienced only from the threatened child's perspective—is scarier than the conventional spookiness found in other composers' settings of Goethe's classic text.

What keeps the dramatic pressure so high is the relentless rhythm in concert with a tonal scheme that is not content to stay put. The Erlking sings in major keys, in contrast with the minor-key horror music surrounding his interventions. Also striking is the level of dissonance at the boy's outcries, "Mein Vater! Mein Vater!" each time exclaimed a half-step higher to build tension. Consciousness of the surroundings (storm and horse's hoof beats), elements that Schubert depicted more directly than any previous setting, recedes as the subjective vision grows more vivid. The representation of the boy's inwardness interacts with and triumphs over the perception of external reality. This is the true Romantic dimension here, the source of the music's uncanny power. Objective representations of storms, battles, horses, and so forth were long familiar; the subjective manipulation is the startling new effect, prompted in Schubert's imagination by those inward aspects of the poem to which he was uniquely attentive. The objective elements are used to reveal subjective psychological states: a forceful ride for a terrified child, a storm for

Figure 18-4 *Goethe in the Roman Campagna* (1787) by Johann Heinrich Wilhelm Tischbein.

impassioned outbursts. The enormously successful *Erlkönig* not only proved central to the elevation of the Lied as a genre worthy of serious attention but also won Schubert fame far beyond Vienna. It was published in numerous official and pirated editions, translated into different languages, and arranged for instruments other than the original voice and piano. Franz Liszt and Hector Berlioz, for example, were later to orchestrate the song so that it could be sung at symphonic concerts.

Figure 18-5 Portrait of Franz Schubert by Wilhelm August Rieder, 1825.

Salon Culture and Schubertiades

Except for a few brief trips within a hundred or so miles of Vienna, Schubert spent his entire life of thirty-one years in the imperial city. Here the musical landscape resounded with the legacies of Haydn and Mozart and celebrated the living presence of Beethoven; the public was swept by wild enthusiasm for Rossini's operas and for Weber's *Der Freischütz*, which scored a great success in 1821. Schubert surely met Beethoven, although all the evidence about any encounters is anecdotal and some of it contradictory. There is no indication that Schubert met Rossini when the Italian visited the city in 1822 (and did briefly meet Beethoven). Schubert enjoyed friendly relations with Weber, which soured after he expressed disappointment with Weber's opera *Euryanthe*, which premiered in Vienna in 1823.

While these leading composers made their careers through public music, changes in politics and patronage at the time in Vienna as well as personal inclinations encouraged the younger Schubert initially to chart a different course for his own career. He was not employed by the church, the court, a rich patron, or any other institution. His music was often performed at concerts given by the Gesellschaft der Musikfreunde (Society of Friends of Music), a group founded in 1812 that remains to this day at the forefront of concert life in the city. The society endowed the first Viennese conservatory in 1817, amassed an enormous library, and erected Vienna's first formal concert hall.

By the time he was in his early twenties, Vienna was governed by a politically repressive regime under the control of the powerful Prince Clemens von Metternich (1773–1859). Politics in Austria had come a long way—a bad way—from the liberal reforms that Mozart enjoyed under Emperor Joseph II. Composers, writers, and artists now had to contend with oppressive censorship. Concerts and various other social activities required official approval in order to take place, which is one reason that so much of musical life centered around the home. In Schubert's case the private sphere of music making even spawned its own name: **Schubertiades**.

The enormously successful* Erlkönig *not only proved central to the elevation of the Lied as a genre worthy of serious attention but also won Schubert fame far beyond Vienna.

Schubertiades were a somewhat idiosyncratic Viennese example of what was emerging as an important new aspect of musical life all over Europe: the ***salon*** (Fig. 18-6). The word is French, the language of high society, and literally means "a big room," the kind found in large town houses of aristocrats or *nouveaux riches* ("the newly rich," that is, those who had earned their money in trade), where invited guests assembled. In English it was called the drawing room, short for "withdrawing room," the room to which the company withdrew after dinner for conversation and entertainment. Customarily a salon was centered around a patron. In Paris, famous ones were given by Princess Christina Belgiojoso. In Berlin, some were promoted by

Figure 18-6 A "Schubertiade" at the home of Joseph von Spaun. Drawing by Moritz von Schwind, 1868.

prominent Jewish families. In further-off St. Petersburg, Maria Agata Szymanowska, a Polish noblewoman who had enjoyed an international career as a pianist, maintained a brilliant salon beginning in the 1820s. Schubertiades catered to a somewhat less affluent, more bohemian group of civil servants, and they were unusual in that they focused on the music of a single composer. Schubert's works seemed to flourish best within an intimate group of friends.

Salons encouraged a form of music making that had high prestige but addressed small invited audiences—addressing them, moreover, and in true Romantic fashion, as individuals. The salon became a new vehicle for the channeling of art patronage, based on a newly negotiated symbiosis between social and artistic elites. Music heard at salons, much of it written to be played there, was marked by its milieu as socially elite. Reciprocally, its presence there, especially when performed by its creator, marked the occasion and the assembled company as culturally elite. Each elite helped define and support the other. There were material benefits, too, for pianist-composers were often given social contacts that led to pupils, mainly the daughters of those in attendance. That was how many composers, including Schubert for a brief time, earned a living.

Schubert's works seemed to flourish best within an intimate group of friends.

Schubert: A Life in Art

Schubert lived his short life in relative obscurity, and his enormous influence was almost entirely posthumous. In a way this is unsurprising, even fitting, since his music reflected, in its exploration of the inner "I," one of the most outwardly uneventful, essentially private lives any composer of major standing was destined to live. We have seen many composers who were born into musical families, with figures such as Bach, Mozart, and Beethoven in essence sustaining the family business. Although family music making played an important role in Schubert's childhood, it was as a pastime rather than as preparation for a musical career. His father ran a successful school, and that was the family business the Schubert sons were expected to enter.

Like Haydn, talent and some luck won Schubert a place as a choirboy in the Imperial Court Chapel and with it the chance to attend an elite school in the center of Vienna. His years there provided him with a fine education, exposure to the arts in general, and the refinement of his musical gifts. This led to extra studies with Antonio Salieri, the famous Kapellmeister, who proved to be a favorite teacher. It was at school, populated for the most part with boys from wealthier families, that Schubert met friends (and, in time, friends of friends) who would fundamentally affect his art.

Schubert's friends played an important role in his biography, not least because many of them helped to mold the story of the composer's life after his early death. An obituary stated that Schubert "lived solely for art and for a small circle of friends."[2] Aside from some scattered diary entries, several poems, and an allegorical tale known as "My Dream," Schubert himself wrote no memoirs, criticism, or essays. Fewer than a hundred of his letters survive, most of them fairly inconsequential, a fact that much encouraged myth making. Given this verbal void, Schubert's music, from a Romantic perspective, seems to provide the most tangible chronicle of his artistic and emotional existence. Listeners have long wondered what sort of man would create such pieces as he did—beautiful, sad, convivial, dark, and so on through a lengthy list of apparently contradictory qualities—and, again in Romantic fashion, they have constructed an image of the composer based on their own personal responses, themselves identifying with the composer's inwardness.

Schubert's friends cultivated an intellectual, literary, and artistic environment that greatly influenced the young composer (Fig. 18-7). Among the group there was wide interest in music, and most played an instrument, including in school and community orchestras of which Schubert was a member and for which he composed some of his early symphonies. His closest friends, however, were not professional musicians but, rather, budding poets, dramatists, painters, and civil servants. They were the ones who exposed him to great poetry, such as Goethe's. The date 19 October 1814 is sometimes called the "Birthday of the Lied" because that was the day when the seventeen-year-old Schubert composed *Gretchen am Spinnrade* ("Gretchen at the Spinning Wheel") to a poem in Goethe's *Faust.* *Erlkönig* followed the next year.

After graduating in 1816, Schubert worked briefly at his father's school, but by the end of the year, as he was about to turn twenty and encouraged by friends who helped him financially, he had renounced steady employment and opted for full-time composition. He had already written a handful of dramatic works (mainly Singspiels), four symphonies, more than a dozen string quartets (composed for family recreation), dozens of keyboard dances, and hundreds of Lieder.

During the years leading up to 1820, at a time when Beethoven's productivity was at a low ebb, Rossini's music conquered Vienna, and Schubert, like everyone else, was enchanted. "You cannot deny that he has extraordinary genius," he allegedly told a friend: "The orchestration is highly original at times, and the vocal writing too."[3] Schubert's two delightful overtures "in the Italian style" (a title given them later by his older brother) and Sixth Symphony in C Major, all

Figure 18-7 Leopold Kupelwieser's painting "The Fall of Man" (1821). Schubert (seated at the piano) and friends are playing a game of charades; Franz von Schober is the serpent, Kupelwieser the Tree of Knowledge, and Johann Baptist Jenner is Adam.

completed between October 1817 and February 1818, incorporated a vein of Italianate melody that was no longer customary in such works. The long tunes loosened up the structure and began to impart to Schubert's large-scale compositions the discursiveness that so enraptured the later Romantics. One of these overtures was performed in 1818, becoming the first secular work by Schubert to be given at a public concert. It received warm critical praise: "The second half of the concert began with a wondrously lovely overture by a young composer, Mr. Franz Schubert, a pupil of our much venerated Salieri, who has learned already how to touch and stir all hearts. Although the theme was surprisingly simple, a wealth of the most astonishing and agreeable ideas developed from it, worked out with vigor and skill."[4]

By this point Schubert had found his first important public champion in the singer Johann Michael Vogl (1768–1840), who was at the end of a distinguished opera career. (Vogl had sung the role of the villain Don Pizarro in the 1814 version of Beethoven's *Fidelio.*) In 1820 the baritone starred in a Schubert Singspiel called *Die Zwillingsbrüder* (The Twin Brothers), which ran for five performances at the same Vienna theater where *Fidelio* had premiered, and Schubert was engaged to write some incidental music for other shows. A breakthrough occurred in 1821, when, thanks to the initiative of some of his friends, a number of songs (including *Erlkönig* and *Gretchen am Spinnrade*) were published by Anton Diabelli in Vienna. The sales of Lieder earned Schubert an income that, however meager at first, at least came from his creative work rather than from teaching. He scraped together a living from publications, giving piano lessons, and relying on the kindness of friends and limited patronage. He was, although in a small way, a commercial success and a bit of an economic pioneer.

The acclaim that greeted Weber's *Der Freischütz* in November 1821 must have encouraged Schubert; alongside pervasive Rossinimania perhaps it was possible after all to succeed with an opera written in German. He started to devote much of his energy to dramatic music, producing a three-act opera, *Alfonso und Estrella* (1821–22), a Singspiel, *Die Verschworenen* (The Conspirators, 1823), and another three-act opera, called *Fierabras* (1823). Word of his activities got around, and a Dresden paper reported in July 1821 that "the excellent songwriter Schubert is said to be occupied at present with the composition of a grand Romantic opera."[5] At age twenty-four he was finally getting publicity, performances, and publications. The future must have seemed bright.

Disaster

And then disaster struck: In late 1822 Schubert became gravely ill, almost certainly due to contracting syphilis, and had to spend some time in the Vienna General Hospital. While hospitalized he is said to have composed part of his song cycle *Die schöne Müllerin* (The Beautiful Miller Maid), a kind of novel-in-lyrics comprising twenty songs and ending with the suicide of the hopeless lover beguiled by the beautiful maiden. The course of Schubert's disease meant that after an initial incapacitation he gradually got better and within a couple of years had seemingly recovered. In reality he lived under a cloud that new symptoms would emerge that might lead to madness or death. As he wrote to a friend: "I am fairly well. Whether I shall ever be completely healthy again I am inclined to doubt."[6]

The key verbal document in Schubert's life—his Heiligenstadt Testament, so to speak—is a letter he wrote at the end of March 1824, after being ill for more than a year, to Leopold Kupelwieser, a close friend and talented artist who was in Italy at the time. Schubert embraced the opportunity to:

> once again fully pour out my soul to someone. For you are so good and honest, you will be sure to forgive many things which others might take in very bad part from me.
>
> In a word, I feel myself the most unhappy and wretched creature in the world. Imagine a man whose health will never be right again, and who in sheer despair over this ever makes things worse and worse, instead of better; imagine a man, I say, whose most brilliant hopes have perished, to whom the happiness of love and friendship has nothing to offer but pain, at best, whose enthusiasm (at least of the stimulating kind) for all things beautiful threatens to disappear, and I ask you, is he not a miserable, unhappy being?[7]

Schubert then quotes the opening line from Goethe's poem "Gretchen am Spinnrade," the text he had set in his first masterpiece ten years earlier:

> "*My peace is gone, my heart is sore, I shall find it never and nevermore,*" I may well sing again every day, and each morning but recalls yesterday's grief. Thus, joyless and friendless, I should pass my days, were it not that Schwind visits me now and again and shines on me a ray of those sweet days of the past.

He goes on to lament that things socially were no longer as they used to be in Vienna because their group of friends had largely dispersed; professional matters were not going well either. He had had no luck getting either *Die Verschworenen* or *Fierabras* produced and therefore seemed "once again to have composed two operas for nothing." (Actually three; *Alfonso und Estrella* did not make it to the stage until Franz Liszt presented it thirty years later in Weimar.) As for his other compositional projects, Schubert reports: "Of songs I have not written many new ones, but I have tried my hand at several instrumental works, for I wrote two string quartets and an octet, and I want to write another quartet; in fact, I intend to pave the way toward a grand symphony in that manner."

In other words, having tried to succeed with opera, the public world dominated by Rossini, Schubert was now turning his attention to instrumental music, to the public world dominated by Beethoven. The two string quartets he mentions are in A Minor and D Minor, and his plan to write another one would result in a set comparable to Beethoven's trilogy of "Razumovsky" Quartets, Op. 59. The mentioned six-movement Octet in F Major for winds and strings is one of Schubert's most Beethovenian compositions, clearly modeled on the Septet, Op. 20. The comment that these pieces could "pave the way toward a grand symphony" may seem odd, given that Schubert by this point had already completed six symphonies. Yet he evidently considered them all to be student pieces and not representative of what he could write—a truly Beethovenian "grand symphony."

And indeed, as if by some process of "free association," the next sentence in his letter to Kupelwieser mentions the looming, living master: "The latest in Vienna is that Beethoven is to give a concert at which he is to produce his new symphony, three movements from the new Mass, and a new Overture." Schubert evidently had "inside information," perhaps from the violinist Ignaz Schuppanzigh, about the planned premiere of the Ninth Symphony that would take place in May. By way of conclusion, he adds: "God willing, I too am thinking of giving a similar concert next year."

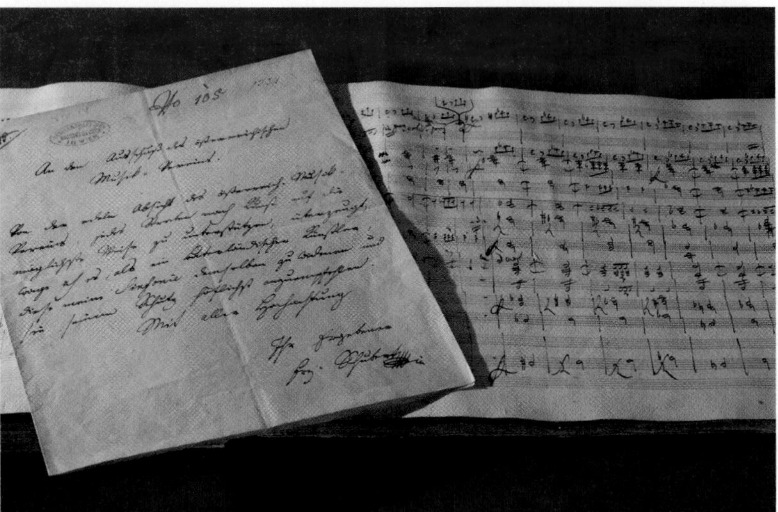

Figure 18-8 Schubert's "Great" C Major Symphony, together with his letter dedicating it to the Gesellschaft der Musikfreunde, Vienna.

Schubert's letter to Kupelwieser is revealing and remarkable: revealing in that Schubert summarizes the state of his health, social life, professional activities, and ambitions; remarkable in the way various parts of the letter might be said to perform or enact Schubertian musical characteristics. The brief quotation from Goethe provides a lyrical moment comparable to Schubert's repeated practice of inserting melodies from his songs into his instrumental works. Moreover, the tone of the letter shifts from a despairing "minor" key to an optimistic "major" one, another typically Schubertian musical trait. Finally, the letter gives some indication of the importance of Beethoven as a model, not just with respect to compositional matters, but also as a professional and artistic ideal. Schubert would continue to write some songs, including some of his greatest ones. He also pursued other paths that might bring income and attention (among them virtuoso show pieces and religious music). Yet his few remaining years were dedicated primarily to "strivings after the highest in art," as he once put it in a letter to a publisher, rather than writing "wretched fashionable stuff" that flooded the market.[8] The "highest" meant large chamber music works, piano sonatas, the hoped-for symphony (the "Great" C Major Symphony of 1825; Fig. 18-8), two Masses, and even another shot at an opera, which he never completed.

Despite his precarious health, Schubert's life was an existence devoted almost entirely to creative work. To recount it is basically to offer a chronicle of his compositions, as one of his friends, the painter Moritz von Schwind (1804–71), already hinted in mock-exasperation in 1824: "If you go to see him during the day, he says, 'Hello, how are you?—Good' and goes on writing."[9] It was seemingly a life lived almost entirely inside the heart and head—and what could be more Romantic than that? The inner life was the only life, according to Romantic doctrine; and Schubert's music seemed to grant access to it, making the composer, despite the apparent absence of outward personal drama, the subject of intense human interest and vicarious personal identification.

What Contemporaries Knew of Schubert's Music

Whether measured by quantity or by quality, Schubert's total output strains belief. His earliest-known compositions are dated 1810, when he was thirteen, so his whole career as a composer lasted no more than eighteen years. During this time—by the calculations of the preeminent Schubert scholar Otto Erich Deutsch (1883–1967), whose thematic catalogue of Schubert's works was modeled on Köchel's Mozart catalogue—he amassed a total of 998 works. This figure, however, is rather misleading, and not just for the usual reason that such reckonings invariably include lost or inauthentic pieces. Out of this near-thousand "Deutsch numbers" many represent groups of songs or dances, so the total of individual compositions is much larger. Contradicting the image of Schubert as neglected during his lifetime, a large number of his works were published in the 1820s. A chronological look at the kinds of pieces that were released can give us a good idea of how he was known to his contemporaries, of where his career was heading at the time of his early death, and of a musical culture that catered to domestic consumption.

Schubert's first eight published opus numbers (as well as Opp. 12–14) were Lieder, accounting for a total of thirty-two individual songs published in 1821–22 alone. Some, like *Erlkönig*, Op. 1, were released singly, while others appeared in sets of two to five songs, although these were not narrative song cycles like the twenty that make up *Die schöne Müllerin* or the twenty-four that make up his other cycle, *Winterreise* (Winter's Journey). Altogether during Schubert's lifetime nearly 190 individual songs were issued, an enormous number in a very short time.

Schubert's Op. 9 (1821) is a set of thirty-six brief dances, the second of which, called the *Trauerwalzer* (Mourning Waltz), became so famous that it was often attributed to Beethoven. His dances typically originated at Schubertiades as improvisations that Schubert would then write down from memory the next day. Nearly 170 were published, including *Ländler* (a slower version of the waltz), *Deutsche Tänze* (German dances, a souped-up minuet on the way to a waltz), and gallops (fast dances in duple time). Although not as historically important as his Lieder, Schubert nonetheless experimented harmonically in many of them. His dances had an enormous influence on later composers, such as Robert Schumann, Liszt, Johannes Brahms, Anton Bruckner, and Gustav Mahler.

Eight Variations on a French Song, Op. 10 (1818), was Schubert's first large keyboard work to be published. Two things are worth noting about this now-forgotten piece: He dedicated it to Beethoven, from "his worshiper and admirer" its title page reads, and he may even have delivered it to the master in person. (One memoir says Beethoven was not at home, another that he liked the work but pointed out a small error in the harmony, which mortified the young composer.) Also notable is that it is written as a **piano duet**, that is, for two people—four hands—playing at one keyboard. A new instrumental format for us, Schubert is the one who made it matter. Piano duets perfectly encapsulate domestic music making in all its practicalities and social aspects, including rites of courtship. Played at home with family and friends rather than performed in concert halls, four-hand compositions were, by the end of the century, fated to decline along with intimate music making in general. The other main purpose of four-hand music was to make opera and orchestra music available for home enjoyment. Chances to hear big public works were rare, and four-hand arrangements served some of the function that recordings do in our own time.

Schubert's few remaining years were dedicated primarily to "strivings after the highest in art," as he once put it in a letter to a publisher, rather than writing "wretched fashionable stuff."

Schubert's attraction to piano duets was lifelong—D.1, the first work in Deutsch's catalogue, is a Fantasy in G Minor that he wrote at age thirteen. He also composed dances and marches, sets of variations, fantasies, divertissements, and two big sonatas; many of these pieces were published during his lifetime. Not only do they account for some of the greatest music ever written for piano duet, but some of these compositions are also among Schubert's most innovative, which may explain why his interest in the format remained strong even late in his career, when his energies increasingly shifted to other kinds of large-scale instrumental works. Indeed, the audacious structural adventures of his finest piano duets may have helped point the way to orchestral projects that Schubert did not live to realize. His late Fantasy in F Minor (D. 940) in particular exquisitely merges his lyrical gifts with some of his most daring formal structures.

Schubert's next published opus, No. 11, are three part songs. A Schubertian part song is typically a piece designed for four solo voices (in this case for two tenors and two basses), although it could also be sung by chorus. **Part songs** were another extremely popular nineteenth-century genre geared toward domestic music making. A kind of vocal chamber music, they found a ready market. (Barbershop harmony and college singing groups in some respects continue the tradition.) Singing societies, especially all-male groups, spread across German-speaking countries, although in Vienna such gatherings could sometimes arouse the suspicion of Metternich's repressive police. Schubert modeled his part songs on those by his teacher, Salieri, and by Michael Haydn. Many are *a cappella*; in others Schubert supplied a simple piano or guitar accompaniment (Fig. 18-9).

The piano Fantasy in C Major, known as the "Wanderer" and published in 1823 as Op. 15, was Schubert's first substantial instrumental work to appear in print. Its nickname (not used by him) derives from one of his most famous songs, *Der Wanderer*. The Fantasy is a technically demanding piece and, as with the fearsome accompaniment of *Erlkönig*, was evidently beyond Schubert's own capacity to play. On a structural level, four movements are merged into one, and the overall key sequence is organized by a cycle of major thirds rather than fifths. The movements, all played *attacca* (without any intervening pause), end respectively in C major, E major, A♭ major, and C major. (It is the second movement that begins with the quotation from *Der Wanderer*.)

Figure 18-9 Schubert making music with friends (sketch by Ferdinand Georg Waldmüller).

Schubert's early published works point to the emergence of the piano as the Romantic instrument par excellence. As its construction improved and its price fell, the piano became a centerpiece of the middle-class home. Almost all of Schubert's compositions published in his time include the piano; only one string quartet, some part songs, and a few religious pieces do not. In addition to the Fantasy in C, he published three sonatas and various smaller piano works, including six *Moments musicaux*, Op. 94, and two impromptus.

These examples of primarily domestic vocal and instrumental music suggest the nature of the music business in Schubert's time and his willingness to work within market requirements, which contradicts the picture of him as a withdrawn loner. He also published five liturgical settings in Latin, including one complete Mass and a *Deutsches Requiem*, or *Trauermesse* (a setting of the funeral rite in German); none of his full orchestral Masses were printed during his lifetime. His two biggest published works were chamber music: the String Quartet in A Minor, Op. 29, No. 1 (1824), dedicated to Schuppanzigh, and the Piano Trio in E♭ Major, Op. 100 (1827). At the time of his death, then, Schubert was no famished genius but a composer of solid, if largely local, reputation. Within his seemingly unpretentious limits he was regarded as a *beliebter Tonsetzer*, a "favorite composer," by an appreciative public, although a public largely unaware that behind closed doors he was vying with Beethoven as a composer of quartets and symphonies and, less successfully, with Rossini and Weber as a composer of full-scale operas.

Crossing the Edge

The audacious structural adventures of Schubert's finest piano duets may have helped point the way to orchestral projects that he did not live to realize.

Schubert's publishing career, as just outlined, suggests that we should examine some more music released during his lifetime before branching out into terrain that was mostly unknown to his contemporaries. In this way we will have proceeded from the intimate domestic genres in which his unique construction of musical subjectivity was formed, into larger genres that he also instilled with the aesthetic of intimacy.

Besides the Lied, the piano character piece (*Charakterstück* in German or *Pièce caractéristique* in French) was the other intimate genre that assumed great importance for Romantic composers. The newly evocative Romantic genre went by various names. Beethoven wrote some short piano pieces that he called *bagatelles*, or "trifles," giving some indication of their relative weight in his mind. The Irish pianist John Field (1782–1837) became most influential through his *nocturnes*, evocative Romantic "night pieces." Around the same time emerged a trio of Czechs. First was C. P. E. Bach's pupil Jan Ladislav Dussek (1760–1812), then Václav Jan Tomášek (1774–1850), and then Tomášek's student Jan Václáv Voříšek (1791–1825), whom Schubert knew personally. Tomášek's main genre was the *eclogue*, a pastoral piece, and Voříšek was apparently the first to compose impetuous character pieces to which he gave the name ***impromptu*** (French for "offhand" or "on the spur of the moment"), which were supposed to give the effect of sudden, untamed inspiration. His impromptus were usually cast in a simple "ternary," or ABA, form, and Schubert gave the name to eight similarly structured pieces, all written in 1827.

Schubert's character pieces became another arena for extraordinary harmonic maneuvers. One Schubertian trademark, already used to varying degrees by earlier keyboard composers, was modulation to the flat submediant, which became a convention associated with the boundary between inner and outer experience. This can be quite explicit in Schubert songs, where the poetic text also indicates such a boundary. The sounding of the flat submediant came to indicate the crossing of that edge into *Innigkeit*, endowing the music on the other side with an uncanny aura. Schubert's handling of this maneuver was often especially bold because he combined it with other tonally destabilizing techniques, such as "**modal mixture**," the infiltration within a major key of harmonies drawn from its parallel minor (or sometimes the other way round). In his Impromptu in E♭, Op. 90, No. 2, an expected modulation at m. 83 to the flat submediant goes in m. 100 to the Neapolitan of the dominant of the original flat submediant (Ex. 18-3). This is a harmonic mouthful that may sound like a cataloguing equivalent of "third cousin on the mother's side twice removed," and the relationship can indeed be traced logically if one is patient. But it is the impression of distance, not the sense of harmonic logic, that registers.

Example 18-3 Franz Schubert, Impromptu in E♭, Op. 90, No. 2, mm. 77–94

Yet another way of putting it, one that suggests the full innovative potential of Schubert's harmonic and tonal freedom, is to say that the concept of home key now encompasses both major and minor modes, with the constituent harmonies of both available for arbitrary, "impromptu" substitutions. And what goes for the tonic goes for the secondary tonalities as well. The whole array of major- and minor-degree functions is freely available for use. Any key can now be thought of as encompassing, and controlling, a double mode, and a new range of related keys is available for "**tonicization**"—for setting up as alternate harmonic goals—including several that had not formerly figured among normal diatonic relations. The harmonic vocabulary of Romantic introspection is one in which a much wider range of chords can move persuasively from one to another. Never had so many routes of harmonic navigation been open to composers, so many ways of making connections, so many methods of creating and controlling fluctuations of harmonic tension. And to the extent that these fluctuations were understood as metaphors or analogues to nuances of feeling, never had purely instrumental music been so articulately expressive of the verbally inexpressible.

Anthology Vol 2-30
Full CD IV, 16
Concise CD II, 25

In these techniques and more, Schubert was the chief pioneer, precisely because his art was nurtured in the intimacy of domestic genres. For a rich, radical, and suggestive taste of all this we can sample one of the *Moments musicaux* (initially published with the incorrect French title *Momens musicals*). The six pieces that make up the set, each vaguely ternary in format, were not conceived as a unit. The sixth, in A♭ major, was given the picturesque name "Plaintes d'un Troubadour" (The Laments of a Troubadour) by the publisher when it appeared in 1825. Schubert here explores the idea of a musical "moment" (in German, *Augenblick*—"the twinkling of an eye"), a word that had a special meaning for Romantics. A piece of instrumental music called an *Augenblick* was a wordless piece in "aria time," or time-out-of-time, a subjective reverie. A piece that stops time's forward march is a piece that represents or induces the music trance (call it the composer's, the performer's, our own as we wish; distinctions become blurred with the quickening of subjectivity). And indeed, one can actually hear time stop and then resume in this music, when the harmony slips out of the circle of fifths into uncannily prolonged submediant regions that interrupt and suspend its customary progressions—and then slips back again.

The marvelous effects of the sixth of the *Moments musicaux* are projected against the old ternary form, as in a minuet and trio. It is like passing into another world, another quality of time, another state of consciousness, crossing the edge of inwardness. The transformation of chords like the flat submediant and the Neapolitan that had formerly implied dynamic process and motion into stable, static harmonies gives music that exploits the new technique the quality of timelessness and trance. The implication of propulsion is suspended, and since (to paraphrase the Greek philosopher Zeno) time is the measure of motion and motion the measure of time, the suspension of implied motion indicates the suspension of time. That is what makes "aria time" available to instrumental music, and no one exploited it more fully than Schubert. Yet these qualities in his music, especially when spread out over one of his large instrumental compositions, would cause some critics to charge that he lingered too long, that he had abandoned the Beethovenian imperative for propulsive motion.

Never had purely instrumental music been so articulately expressive of the verbally inexpressible.

Schubert's "Unfinished" Symphony

Schubert increasingly concentrated on larger forms during his last years. Even some friends were surprised to learn after his death how much he had written in the sphere of public genres, notably symphonies, chamber music, and dramatic works. For the most part these pieces only became available slowly over the course of the nineteenth century, long after the composer's death. A look at the two-movement "Unfinished" Symphony in B Minor (1822) will reveal how influential Schubert's early mastery of intimate private genres was on his most public utterances. This influence, felt by many later nineteenth-century composers, is what led to the ultimate "Romanticization" of the large-scale instrumental forms.

Anthology Vol 2-31
Full CD IV, 17

Schubert's First Symphony dates from 1813, when he was sixteen, and the next five followed at the rate of about one a year. During his lifetime no public concerts presented them. This might seem quite discouraging for a young composer except that these works served exactly the purpose for which Schubert wrote them: to learn and experiment. Although the public did not hear them, Schubert, his friends, and his colleagues did—by playing them. Their modest scoring points not to the concert hall but to what we today might call a student or community orchestra.

After these early efforts Schubert undertook a much more ambitious symphony. He wrote a neat, fully orchestrated score of the first two movements, which is dated "Vienna, 30 October 1822." These movements, marked *Allegro moderato* and *Andante con moto*, herald a new Romantic sound in their use of the orchestra, provide an excellent example of the composer's lyrical writing, display his harmonic daring, and project an extraordinary range of emotions. The orchestral manuscript breaks off after two pages of a third-movement scherzo. A more complete piano sketch showing the whole scherzo and a melodic outline of the trio have enabled several scholars to "finish the Unfinished," opportunistically tacking on, by way of a finale, the B-minor entr'acte from Schubert's incidental music to *Rosamunde* (a play performed in 1823).[10] There is no evidence that this was the composer's intention.

The incomplete torso of his original, consisting of two pathos-filled movements and ending with a slow movement in the "wrong key" appealed powerfully to Romantic sensibilities. This enhanced the symphony's popularity and made it one of the works that most haunted the memories and imaginations of later musicians. Although it did not have a "program," the nickname "Unfinished" seemed perfectly to capture Schubert's "unfinished" life and career.

Schubert in fact wrote many unfinished works, including other unfinished symphonies.

Why did Schubert not complete the symphony? Answers range from fictitious ones given in novels, operettas, movies, and the like (for instance, that he died while writing it, although he in fact lived for six more years) to more sensible speculations (that once he lost the thread of inspiration he could not readily reclaim it). Since the scherzo as it stands seems rather ordinary, it has been suggested that Schubert grew displeased with it, feeling that it could not match the two innovative movements that would precede it. Schubert in fact wrote many unfinished works, including other unfinished symphonies before and after. It may simply be that the work held painful associations for him; it was near the time of composing the B Minor Symphony that Schubert contracted the venereal disease that changed the course of his life.

The "Unfinished" Symphony was not performed during Schubert's lifetime. He gave the score to a friend in the city of Graz in gratitude for its local music society's bestowing honorary membership on him. In the mid-1860s, the prominent Viennese conductor Johann Herbeck learned of its existence and secured the work for performance. The belated premiere of the symphony in 1865, nearly forty years after Schubert's death, astonished and delighted audiences. Eduard Hanslick (1825–1904), Vienna's leading critic, described how, after hearing only a few measures, "every child recognized the composer, and a muffled 'Schubert' was whispered in the audience . . . every heart rejoiced, as if, after a long separation, the composer himself were among us in person. The whole movement is a melodic stream so crystal clear, despite its force and genius, that one can see every pebble on the bottom. And everywhere the same warmth, the same bright, life-giving sunshine."[11]

For an idea of how in this piece the mood of lyric introspection, or intimacy, transforms the public genre of the symphony, one need only consider the exposition of the first movement. Schubert's mature sonatas and symphonies rarely strike a heroic, "Beethovenian" attitude. Notwithstanding the presence of occasional dramatic outbursts, his pieces tend to be meandering, ruminative, and luminous, sooner inducing reverie than excitement. The work begins with an unusual solo theme softly played in unison by the cellos and basses. It is initially unclear whether the opening measures are a slow introduction or the first theme of the movement proper. A tremulous accompaniment figure starts up in m. 9 that sounds something like a keyboard accompaniment: a rapidly moving "right-hand" figuration in the first and second violins with pizzicato punctuation beneath in the lower strings, intoning the famous germinal rhythm of Beethoven Fifth Symphony (Ex. 18-4). Once this accompaniment is established, the oboe and clarinet enter with a lyrical theme. It is not just the lyricism of this melody therefore that is related to Schubert's mastery of the Lied, but that the whole procedure of the opening accompaniment's introducing a lyric voice is a typical song procedure. The opening of the symphony is indeed very similar to one of Schubert's songs written around the same time: *Der Zwerg* (The Dwarf; Ex. 18-5).

Example 18-4 Franz Schubert, "Unfinished" Symphony, I, mm. 1–15 (piano reduction)

Example 18-5 Franz Schubert, *Der Zwerg,* mm. 1–9

The transition—or rather lack of one—from the lyrical first theme to the second is also unusual. In a symphony by Haydn, Mozart, or Beethoven a first theme often does not make a full cadence in the tonic, as does Schubert so demonstratively in m. 38. The harmonic realm, the whole point of sonata form as practiced by its pre-Schubertian masters, was to connect that cadence into a modulatory bridge and not to allow a full cadence in the tonic until the very end of the movement. Schubert not only allows the first theme to finish but follows it with a very brief four-measure linkup (mm. 38–41) to an equally stable second theme, as if in a sense to advertise a lack of interest in "transitions." The four-measure link, played by the horns and bassoons, is a "composed fermata," or time-out-of-time, and its purpose, like that of all fermatas, is to interrupt the rhythmic momentum. It neutralizes the thrust, replacing suspense (which quickens consciousness) with relaxation, deepening the music trance. Once again an accompaniment figure starts before the actual second theme, and that theme is cast not in the expected key (the relative major) but in the Romantically charged submediant.

The development section is based throughout on the preface theme, the one theme that had been presented originally in a harmonically open-ended form requiring closure on the tonic. In fact, the first movement of the "Unfinished" Symphony itself is a virtual textbook of submediant relations and the ways in which they can be used to create both mood and form. In this way the symphony becomes a study of how the intimate and domestic forms ("lower" forms in the conventional social hierarchy of genres) could affect the "higher" forms and infuse them with inwardness.

After Beethoven

Recall that in 1824 Schubert had concluded his anguished letter to Kupelwieser with news that Beethoven was about to premiere his Ninth Symphony, adding that he hoped to give his own concert the following year. This project was not realized then or the next year or the one after that, but such a concert did finally take place on 26 March 1828. The date is significant because it marked the first anniversary of Beethoven's death.

The concert was held in a room owned by the Gesellschaft der Musikfreunde and consisted of chamber and vocal works, all by Schubert: a string quartet movement, a new piano trio, Lieder, and part songs. One of Schubert's good friends noted in his journal, "Enormous applause, good receipts,"[12] and other reports were equally enthusiastic, although the first appearance in Vienna later the same week by the great Italian violin virtuoso Niccolò Paganini diverted the attention of the local press. The prestigious *Allgemeine musikalische Zeitung* of Leipzig mentioned the concert, however, comparing it favorably with an all-Beethoven concert given just a few days earlier at which his final string quartet, Op. 135, was premiered: "If all these works, performed to perfection, afforded an indescribable aural treat, the same must be said with hardly less emphasis in praise of that *soirée musicale* which the excellent Schubert held in the very same place on the 26th."[13]

Schubert had been a torchbearer at Beethoven's funeral, where he heard Franz Grillparzer's famous oration, which posed the question "He was an artist . . . Who shall stand beside him?" The ambitious concert provided a partial answer. Before a discerning audience, Schubert presented some of his most recent compositions as performed by some of Beethoven's own favored musicians. We have seen that Schubert had been steadily moving into Beethovenian terrain by concentrating his compositional activities on piano sonatas, chamber music, and symphonies. He had begun to contact the leading German music publishers outside Vienna in the hope of increasing his fame. His big concert was another part of this strategy.

Anthology Vol 2-32
Full CD IV, 18
Concise CD II, 26

The Piano Trio in E♭, Op. 100, formed the centerpiece of the concert and would soon be Schubert's first major piece published outside Vienna. The work honors Beethoven, both by emulating elements of his style and form, and by encoding a hidden farewell in its second and fourth movements through subtle allusions to a Swedish song, as well as to pieces by Beethoven. Schubert had already made use of some of his own songs as the basis for variation movements in instrumental compositions. His Piano Quintet in A Major, for example, is known as the "Trout" Quintet because its fourth movement is based on his beloved song of the same name (*Die Forelle*). In other instances Schubert's quotations from his songs are fleeting and seem more to carry personal associations than public meanings. In the E♭ Trio Schubert alludes not to one of his own songs but rather to a Swedish one called *Se solen sjunker* (See, the Sun is Setting), the text of which in translation is:

> See the sun is setting behind the high mountain peaks,
> You take flight before the dim shadows of the night, oh fair hope
> Farewell, farewell, alas the friend forgets
> His true sweet bride, his true sweet bride, his true sweet bride.

Schubert took three melodic fragments from the song, as well as some material from the accompaniment, and used them in the haunting duet for cello and piano that opens the second movement (Exs. 18-6 and 18-7). Especially prominent is a falling octave motive attached to the words "Farewell! Farewell!"; this motive also closes the movement.[14]

The significance of the Swedish song, particularly of the "farewell" motive, emerges when other clues are considered beyond the significant anniversary date of the concert and the participation of Beethoven's musicians: The trio is partly modeled on, and the second movement specifically quotes the funeral march of, Beethoven's *Eroica* Symphony; another work written specifically for the concert, *Auf dem Strom* (On the River; 1828), likewise alludes to the funeral march of the *Eroica*. Sketches for the second movement of the trio show that Schubert originally included a quotation of the opening of Beethoven's Fifth Symphony. This homage was too obvious and Schubert cut it. Echoing the cyclic procedures Beethoven had used in his Fifth and Ninth symphonies as well as in other pieces, Schubert brings back the elegiac second-movement theme in the final movement. Although he did not publicly dedicate the work to Beethoven's memory (Schubert informed his publisher, "the work is to be dedicated to nobody, save those who find pleasure in it"), the E♭ Trio nonetheless stands as a powerful declaration of his reverence for Beethoven and as an assertion of his readiness to assume the deceased master's mantle.

> ***Schubert's* Piano Trio in E♭ *honors Beethoven, both by emulating elements of his style and form, and by encoding a hidden farewell in its second and fourth movements.***

Example 18-6 Franz Schubert, Piano Trio in E♭, Op. 100, II, 1–20

Example 18-7 Swedish song, *Se solen sjunker*

Schubert's Last Two Songs

Schubert's concert shows the thirty-year-old composer assuming a new place in Viennese musical life. He was excited by the prospects and told one publisher that the event was "crammed full . . . I received extraordinary accolades."[15] At the time he was plagued by his "usual headaches," perhaps an indication of a late stage of syphilis. Eight months later he was dead, and an anticipated repetition of the event became a memorial concert designed to raise funds for his gravestone.

In the twenty months between Beethoven's death and his own, Schubert produced some of his greatest works, including the song cycle *Winterreise*, the String Quintet in C, the Violin Fantasy in C, the Mass in E♭, an unfinished opera, three piano duets, eight impromptus, three piano sonatas, as well as various brief sacred works, dances, songs, and, at the very end, some remarkable sketches for a new symphony. Many of these works were unknown for decades, which led Hanslick to observe: "If Schubert's contemporaries rightly gazed astonished at his creative power, what shall we, who come after him, say, as we incessantly discover new works of his? For thirty years the master has been dead, and in spite of this it seems as if he goes on working invisibly—it is impossible to follow him."[16]

Schubert's final songs, written mostly in August 1828, were published posthumously as a collection titled *Schwanengesang* (Swan Song; Fig. 18-10). The Viennese publisher Tobias Haslinger had already released some of his music, and he acquired these pieces from the composer's older brother, Ferdinand. Haslinger's grouping of Schubert's last songs does not create a true song cycle like *Die schöne Müllerin* or *Winterreise*. There is no obvious narrative cohesion in *Schwanengesang*; seven of the poems are by Ludwig Rellstab (1799–1860) and six by Heinrich Heine (1797–1856). The publisher added a fourteenth song, *Die Taubenpost* (The Pigeon Carrier), set to a poem by a young Viennese writer named Johann Gabriel Seidl (1804–75), perhaps because thirteen songs would have been too unlucky a number for this memorial collection or more simply because the song appears to have been Schubert's last completed composition.

Anthology Vol 2-33
Full CD IV, 19

The two last songs could not be more different. *Der Doppelgänger* (The Double) looks directly into the abyss, while *Die Taubenpost* soars upward. *Der Doppelgänger* is one of the few songs in which Schubert tackled the burgeoning Romantic theme of mental disintegration, exploited by poets of a post-Goethe generation. The reality of psychological disturbance is confronted head-on. Heine's poems often depicted extreme or neurotic mental states triggered by thwarted desire. *Der Doppelgänger* portrays the protagonist at the scene of an unhappy love; here he encounters a stranger who turns out to be himself, endlessly replaying the futile exertions of the past. An obsession lies at the heart of the poem, which Schubert sets in an old-fashioned ground-bass form. (The ostinato theme looks back to Bach's C♯ Minor Fugue from the first book of the *Well-Tempered Keyboard*; Schubert had already used the idea in the Agnus Dei of his Mass in E♭.) Here it functions not only as formal unifier but as metaphor. The four notes outlined by the outer voices in the chords played before the voice enters contain a very unstable interval, the diminished fourth A♯-D, that unvaryingly forces an obligatory resolution of the D to C♯. The motive, turned into an ostinato that continually forces the same resolution, complements the compulsively repetitive behavior the poem describes (Ex. 18-8).

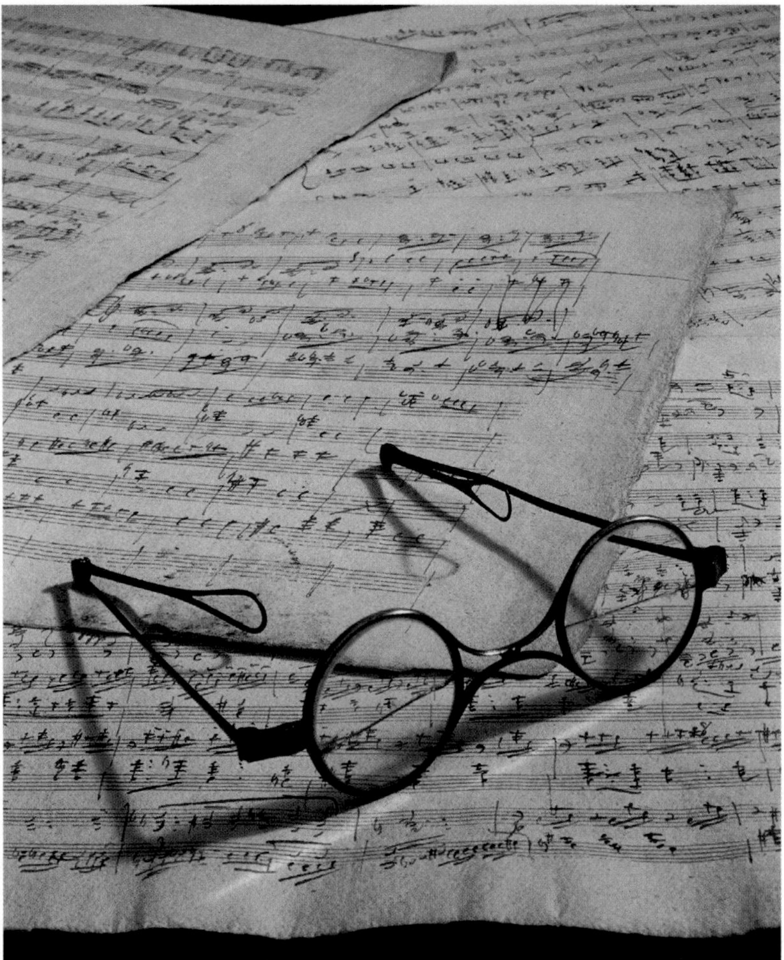

Figure 18-10 In the apartment in Kettenbrückengasse, Vienna, where Franz Schubert died in 1828, his reading glasses lie on the manuscript of *Die Taubenpost* (The Pigeon Carrier), his final song.

Die Taubenpost seems almost trivial by comparison, a relatively insignificant poem set in a lighthearted manner. In a modified strophic form, the seven verses of the poem are presented in three pairs plus a coda, and the piano once again is full partner in the song's unfolding. It is a piece filled with joy, utterly different from the despair of *Der Doppelgänger*. By all indications it is the last piece Schubert finished before he suddenly became sick in November 1828 and died less than two weeks later. A Schubertiade was held just over a month after his death, at which, according to one participant, "Vogl sang Schubert's final, not yet known compositions from the months September and October, including the last song composed before his death, 'Die Brieftaube' [*Die Taubenpost*], one of the most delightful of his songs, and another, *Der Doppelgänger*, that is one of the blackest night-pieces among his songs."[17]

Schubert supposedly requested of his brother that he be buried near to Beethoven, as indeed he was, just a few feet away. The epitaph on the grave, written by his friend Grillparzer, suggests that even those who had known Schubert well were at the time unaware of the full extent of his accomplishment: THE ART OF MUSIC HERE ENTOMBED A RICH TREASURE BUT EVEN FAR FAIRER HOPES.

Example 18-8 Franz Schubert, *Der Doppelgänger,* mm. 1–14

The night is quiet; the streets are still; in this house lived my beloved.

Summary

Alongside the very public worlds of opera and symphony, a tradition of more private and intimate music making emerged in the nineteenth century, represented by the art song, or Lied, piano pieces, and chamber music. These works were performed in intimate settings such as homes, salons, and private concerts. The composer who best represents this trend is Franz Schubert (1797–1828). Although Schubert produced larger works, including operas and symphonies, many of his most important works were written for a small group of friends.

The origins of the Lied are closely tied two trends in Romantic thought: personal expression and the discovery of the "folk." Under the influence of the philosopher Johann Gottfried von Herder (1744–1803), folklore came to be seen as a way to express both national identity and authenticity. Herder published a collection of folk songs from different countries, and leading German literary figures such as Johann Wolfgang von Goethe (1749–1832) wrote poems imitating the folk style. The earliest Lieder were imitations of folk songs in strophic form (meaning that each stanza has the same music).

Schubert is credited with establishing the Lied as a central genre in Western art music, bringing it to a new level of expressivity in works such as *Erlkönig. Erlkönig,* like most of Schubert's Lieder, reaches far beyond the folklike songs of earlier composers in its dramatic text setting. Each character in the ballad is depicted with a different vocal range, the galloping of the horse is represented in the right hand of the piano, and shifting harmonies give a sense of unrest. Schubert also wrote two major song cycles (sets of songs grouped together by the composer and unified by a common theme):

Die schöne Müllerin (1823) and *Winterreise* (1827). His last songs were published together under the title *Schwanengesang* (Swan Song).

In his lifetime Schubert was best known for smaller works, including Lieder, piano character pieces (single-movement works for piano with a descriptive title), and genres that are less well known today, such as variations, part songs, and piano duets. His piano duets are among his most innovative works. Schubert's most important large compositions for piano include the "Wanderer" Fantasy and final piano sonatas. During his last years he concentrated on large-scale works, producing his two best-known symphonies, No. 8 ("Unfinished") and No. 9, as well as longer chamber works, such as the Piano Trio in E♭ Major, Op. 100.

One of Schubert's main innovations is an expanded harmonic vocabulary that included the mixing of major and minor harmonies and modulations to distant key areas, such as the Neapolitan (the lowered second scale degree–the key of D♭ for a piece in C major) and flat submediant (A♭ for a piece in C major). In earlier music these keys were commonly used as preparations for the dominant, whereas in Schubert's works they become destinations in their own right. Modulations to remote keys came to express the idea of inwardness.

Study Questions

1. How was the early Lied influenced by trends in German literature? Describe some aspects of Johann Gottfried von Herder's thought and how it influenced Romanticism in music.
2. What is inwardness, and how is it related to the ideals and culture of Romanticism? What innovations in harmonic language does Schubert use to express the idea of "inwardness"?
3. What types of works was Schubert best known for in his time?
4. Describe the various ways in which Schubert's *Erlkönig* reflects its poetry. What musical techniques does Schubert use to depict the different voices of the poem, the movement of the horse, and the anxious mood?
5. What were Schubertiades, and how do they reflect cultural trends in Schubert's time?
6. Discuss the innovative features in Schubert's "Unfinished" Symphony. How did Schubert bring the introspective mood associated with his smaller works to this symphony? Compare and contrast this symphony with Beethoven's symphonies in the heroic style, such as the *Eroica* and the Fifth.
7. What musical techniques does Schubert use to express the contrasting moods of his two late songs, *Der Doppelgänger* and *Die Taubenpost*?

Key Terms

ballad
character piece
folk song
impromptu
Lied
modal mixture
part song
piano duet
salon
Schubertiade
song cycle
strophic
through-composed
tonicization

19

Romantic Spectacles: From Virtuosos to Grand Opera

The gradual enlargement of the public for music in response to new economic, demographic, and technological conditions brought about momentous changes in nineteenth-century concert life. One of the most profound, if sometimes indirect, influences on all performing and composing activity is often called "the democratization of taste." Attitudes toward it vary with attitudes toward democracy itself. From an elite artistic standpoint, the democratization of taste meant the debasement of taste. From the standpoint of populists it signaled the enlivening, the enrichment, and above all the enhanced accessibility and social relevance of art.

In both the concert hall and the opera house this democratization spurred a new competitiveness, as older aristocratic patronage gave way to the collective patronage of a ticket-buying public. Public performance in the nineteenth century heralded an age of spectacle, most notably in the multimedia extravaganzas Parisian opera houses mounted. Spectacle played a newly important role for solo instrumentalists as well. The surest road to success no longer lay in reaching high—toward a secure position at the most exclusive social plane—but in reaching wide by attracting large audiences. The ability to astonish became paramount; what had once been the domain principally of vocal stars now drove star instrumental performers as well. In short, the age of the globe-trotting virtuoso was born. We are still living in it.

The Devil's Violinist: Niccolò Paganini

The celebrated line of itinerant nineteenth-century virtuosos begins with the Italian violinist Niccolò Paganini (1782–1840; Fig. 19-1), who made a career of unprecedented brilliance and notoriety, arousing an unprecedented degree of zealous

TIMELINE

1803–15 Napoleonic Wars

ca. 1805 **Niccolò Paganini, *24 Caprices***

1811 **Birth of Franz Liszt**

1822 **Liszt debuts as prodigy in Vienna**

1828 **Paganini's first concert in Vienna**

1828 **Daniel-François-Esprit Auber, *La muette de Portici***

1830 July Revolution in France

1830 First locomotive-driven passenger railway opens

1831 **Giacomo Meyerbeer, *Robert le diable***

1831 Victor Hugo, *The Hunchback of Notre Dame*

1831 Eugène Delacroix, *Portrait of Paganini*

1832 **Liszt hears Paganini for the first time**

1835 Alexis de Tocqueville, *Democracy in America*

1836 **Meyerbeer, *Les Huguenots***

1837 Victoria becomes Queen of Great Britain

1838–40 **Liszt, *Grandes etudes d'après Paganini***

1840 **Death of Paganini**

1841 **Liszt, *Réminiscences de Don Juan***

1848 Revolutions in France, Prussia, Austria-Hungary, and Italian states

1848–59 **Liszt in Weimar**

emulation that went far beyond the confines of his instrument. Virtuosos in his wake aspired to achieve a comparable stature. As virtuosity assumed new importance for performers and audiences, so too did it open new compositional paths.

Paganini came not only from the land of singing but also from the land that had the longest, most illustrious tradition of string virtuosity, going back to Corelli and Vivaldi. A particularly formative influence for Paganini came when he encountered *L'arte del violino* (The Art of the Violin, 1733), a set of twelve concertos by Pietro Locatelli (1695–1764), each sporting a pair of enormous unaccompanied cadenzas called *capricci ad libitum*. Paganini modeled his first published composition, *24 Caprices* for unaccompanied violin, directly on Locatelli's pieces, and he even incorporated a theme from one of them into the first of his own set, as if flaunting his trumped predecessor as a trophy. The technical standard Paganini set with this publication was as much on the cutting edge of virtuosity as Locatelli's had been seventy years before, incorporating a whole array of dazzling tricks. Paganini's *Caprices* remain a benchmark of consummate virtuosity to this day.

Until he was in his mid-forties Paganini confined his career to Italy. He often performed his own works, which combined brilliant technique and emotional lyricism with a theatrical quality associated particularly with comic opera. In 1828 he decided it was high time to conquer northern Europe, with Vienna as his first stop. Over the course of some four months he gave fourteen concerts there—an extraordinary number—and charged unusually high prices for tickets. His performances challenged critics to come up with sufficient superlatives, with one writing: "Never has an artist caused such a terrific sensation within our walls as this god of the violin. Never has the public so gladly carried its shekels to a concert, and never in my memory has the fame of a virtuoso so spread to the lowest classes of the population."[1]

Schubert, after the successful concert he had given on the first anniversary of Beethoven's death, told a friend: "I have stacks of money now—so come on. We'll never hear [Paganini's] like again!"[2] and following the concert allegedly commented: "I have heard an angel sing."[3] Angels were not the image that usually came to mind for listeners when confronting Paganini. More often invoked was the devil, who by long-standing tradition was particularly associated with the violin. A famous piece, *Il trillo del Diavolo* (The Devil's Trill), was written in the mid-eighteenth century by Giuseppe Tartini (1692–1770), who reported that the composition appeared to him in a dream that featured the devil as violinist. It was rumored that one of the strings on Paganini's instrument came from the entrails of his murdered mistress and that he had honed his technical wizardry while languishing in prison serving a long sentence for the crime. Stendhal, among others, repeated this story in his biography of Rossini, stating that in the dungeon Paganini "learned the secret of translating his soul into sounds."[4] Even the virtuoso's name—which translates as "little pagan"—seemed to point to the darker realms.

After performances in Prague, Paganini went on to Germany. He appeared before Goethe in Weimar (the poet's response: "I have heard something meteoric"); in Hamburg before Heinrich Heine (who left a fictional memoir of the occasion); before Robert Schumann in Frankfurt; and before Russian Tsar Nikolai I when he was crowned King of Poland. Having had all his teeth extracted on account of jaw disease, Paganini now had a face that took on an even more frightfully sunken aspect. Those who heard him often commented on his appearance. Critic François-Joseph Fétis

(1784–1871), wrote: "The extraordinary expression of his face, his vivid paleness, his dark and penetrating eye, together with the sardonic smile which occasionally played upon his lips, appeared to the vulgar, and to certain diseased minds, unmistakable evidence of a Satanic origin."[5]

Figure 19-1 Portrait of the Italian violinist and composer Niccolò Paganini playing in his first performance in London at the King's Theatre in 1831; with violinist Nicolas Mori, cellist Richard Lindley, and double bass player Domenico Dragonetti.

Finally, on 9 March 1831, Paganini began a series of concerts at the new opera house in Paris with the cultural glitterati in attendance. His most fateful—indeed prophetic—encounter in the French capital, although Paganini was not aware of it, was with Franz Liszt (1811–86). The twenty-year-old sat unnoticed and incredulous in the Paris Opéra in April 1832. He heard the great virtuoso perform and vowed that he would achieve as a pianist the same level of technical virtuosity and charismatic performing style as Paganini did as a violinist. Liszt sought to become the "Paganini of the Piano," which is exactly what many critics were soon calling him.

Then, in 1834, Paganini's whirlwind was over. Continued ill health forced him, now a wealthy man, back into semiretirement in Italy. On his deathbed Paganini refused the ministrations of a priest, for which reason the church denied him a religious burial. A month after his death, his rotting body was moved to a discarded olive oil vat in a cellar in Nice until a patron intervened to have him interred. His remains still did not rest in peace but, rather, were exhumed, reburied, and moved, finally reaching Parma nearly half a century later and only then properly buried with the church's permission. His dark exploits thus continued even after his death.

Needless to say, Paganini was a legend in his lifetime. His effective international career lasted a mere six years, but the long-term historical impact of this burst of musical activity proved enormous. It went far beyond the matter of his instrumental technique, peerless and influential though it was. With his gaunt and gangling appearance and his demonic temperament, Paganini almost single-handedly forged the Romantic mystique of virtuosity as a superhuman endowment. He was Faust come to life—a role model for countless geniuses, frauds, entertainers, and adolescents ever since. Glibly put, Paganini was the instrumental world's first rock star, an idolized performer who forged a fabulous career on dazzling talent, carefully cultivated image, widespread travels, and engaging rumors and scandals, usually tied to money, sex, and death.

For an idea—probably only a dim idea—of what the shouting was all about, we can turn to Paganini's compositional legacy. There we will see marvelous technical innovations, and, more important, we will see this allied to a new poetic idea of virtuosity and its role in musical expression. That poetic idea comes across best not in Paganini's five flashy concertos but in his shorter works, particularly the caprices and the variation sets, in which he turned virtuosity into something new and frightening. His twenty-four caprices are thought to have been completed by 1805 but were published as his Opus 1 only in 1820, carrying a half-deferential, half-challenging dedication *Alli artisti*, "to the artists," that is, his rivals. The collection was met, probably just as Paganini hoped, with scorn and disbelief and was widely pronounced unplayable.

Anthology Vol 2-34
Full CD IV, 20–21
Concise CD II, 27

Two of them may serve to represent the set. Caprice No. 17 shows that Paganini had learned from the style of comic opera while also offering a combination of weirdly striking ideas: diatonic and later chromatic runs often involving complicated "downshifting" on a single string juxtaposed with ascending double stops (playing two notes simultaneously). The middle section is entirely in octaves, another Paganini specialty. Caprice No. 24, the most famous of them all, combines the genres of technical study and bravura variations. Successive variations on the brief and businesslike binary theme (Ex. 19-1a) feature in turn the "thrown" (*jeté*) bow stroke, legato string-crossings, octaves, downshifting, broken octaves, parallel thirds and tenths, and so on. Variation 9 was the shocker (Ex. 19-1b). It introduced a technique of which Paganini was the first to make extensive use, the so-called left-hand pizzicato, in which (at the spots marked +) the fingers of the left hand are drawn sharply off the strings they stop, thus plucking the pitch prepared by the next lower finger.

Example 19-1a Niccolò Paganini, Caprice, Op. 1, No. 24, Tema

Example 19-1b Niccolò Paganini, Caprice, Op. 1, No. 24, Variation 9

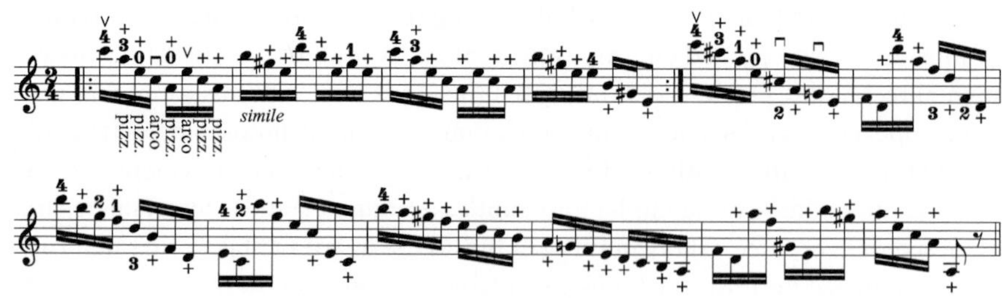

While Paganini's brilliance and demeanor in performance influenced those lucky enough to hear him, the compositions themselves also cast a spell on generations of composers long after he had left the stage. The number of major figures who wrote their own sets of bravura variations on the theme of Caprice No. 24 alone includes not only Liszt but also Robert Schumann, Johannes Brahms, Sergey Rachmaninoff, Witold Lutosławski, Alfred Schnittke, and George Rochberg.

"The Paganini of the Piano": Franz Liszt

Figure 19-2 Portrait of Franz Liszt by Henri Lehmann.

By the time the young Liszt (Fig. 19-2) heard Paganini in Paris he had been a concert artist himself for almost ten years, as well as a composer for most of that time. Liszt was born in 1811 in the village of Raiding, in the vicinity of the old Hungarian town of Sopron (then called Ödenburg), near the Austrian border, just some fifty miles from Vienna. As the alternate naming of the localities suggests, the region had a mixed Hungarian and German culture. The composer's family name is German but spelled in Hungarian fashion. His father was an overseer at the court of Prince Nikolaus Esterházy, the nephew and namesake of Haydn's patron. His mother hailed from a town in lower Austria. Liszt grew up speaking German, not Hungarian, although he showed an early interest in the music of Gypsy bands and later in life drew on his experiences to construct an exotically Hungarian "persona" for himself with which to fascinate audiences.

In the spring of 1822, the ten-year-old boy and his family moved to Vienna so that he could develop his precocious gifts. He studied piano with Carl Czerny, pupil of the still-living Beethoven, and composition with Antonio Salieri, who at age seventy remained the nominal Imperial Kapellmeister. Czerny lost no time presenting Liszt as a prodigy. His first Vienna concert took place in December 1822. After some fourteen months, Liszt moved to Paris, giving concerts in a string of south German towns along the way. In the French capital he studied composition with Ferdinando Paër (1771–1839) and with Antonín Reicha (1770–1836), the leading theory professor at the Paris Conservatoire.

After a sensational Paris debut in May 1824, Liszt conquered London. He played virtuoso fare in the blithesome *style brillant* purveyed by the popular performers of the day, and so Liszt's own early compositions were in a similar vein, as their very titles proclaim: *Variations brillantes sur un thème de G. Rossini* or *Impromptu brillant sur des thèmes de Rossini et Spontini*. His first noteworthy original composition, called *Étude en douze exercices*, consisted of twelve Czernyesque "concert studies."

And then came Liszt's Paganini epiphany in 1832. As he gushed in a letter to a friend: "What a man, what a violin, what an artist! O God, what pain and suffering, what torment in those four strings!"[6] The ambitious prodigy had grasped that in order to equal the Italian's achievement and join him at the pinnacle of instrumental mastery he would have to submit to a tremendous test of endurance. Liszt went into seclusion, one he described enthusiastically in a letter dated 2 May 1832. He was reinventing his technique from the bottom up, spending four to five hours a day on "trills, sixths, octaves, tremolos, double notes and cadenzas,"[7] but also reinventing the expressive purposes his technique would serve, for which reason he spent an equal amount of time devouring Bach, Mozart, Beethoven, and Weber.

The first creative fruit of Liszt's seclusion was a series of Paganini transcriptions in which the pianist sought equivalents on his instrument to the violinist's sublime devilries. Before the year was out he had composed a *Grande fantaisie de bravoure sur La Clochette de Paganini* (Grand Bravura Fantasy on Paganini's "Campanella"), based on one of the pieces he had actually heard Paganini perform, the finale of the Second Violin Concerto. By the end of the decade he would write a new set of concert studies (**études**), *Études d'exécution transcendante d'après Paganini* (Etudes for Transcendental Technique after Paganini), which makes use of six of the caprices.

Anthology Vol 2-35
Full CD IV, 22

While in seclusion Liszt immersed himself in literary classics that he never read in school (because he didn't go to any): Homer, the Bible, Plato, and Locke. He also explored the latest Romantic fare, including Lord Byron, Victor Hugo, and notably *Harmonies poétiques et religieuses* of the French poet Alphonse de Lamartine, which he tried at various times to "translate" into music. "If I don't go mad," he promised, at the end of the ordeal "you will find in me an artist! Yes, an artist such as is required today."[8] Liszt also dabbled in revolutionary politics. In the circles he frequented—notably the utopian religious socialists who called themselves "Saint-Simonians" (after Claude-Henri de Rouvroy, Comte de Saint-Simon, a philosopher who wished to marry traditional religion with modern science)—"an artist such as is required today" meant an artist willing to "seek out the PEOPLE and GOD, go from one to the other; improve, moralize, console man, bless and glorify God" so that "*all classes of society*, finally, will merge in a common religious sentiment, grand and sublime."[9]

Liszt believed that the artist should serve society, that what had once been the domain of the aristocracy was now that of the genius.

These quotes, capitals, italics, and all are from an essay by Liszt that appeared in a Paris music journal in 1835, which, as one of his few published writings that actually exists in his own handwriting, was probably penned without the assistance of the ghostwriting female companions he later enlisted. Art, as he wished to practice it, would be an instrument of social transformation. The virtuoso would become a sublime, rousing public orator on behalf of social progress. While it cannot be said that Liszt often played such a role in life, despite the many charity concerts he gave and other acts of personal generosity, his imagining it is already powerful testimony to the new status and concept of musical virtuosity. The magnetic, socially engaged performer-virtuoso (which in those days implied a composer, too) was the public face of musical Romanticism, as the Schubertian ideal of withdrawn subjectivity was the private face. Such power of performance continues to this day, as popular musicians are able to galvanize world attention on behalf of social causes.

Despite having profited from Paganini's inspiring example, Liszt eventually harbored reservations about his great predecessor's career. When Paganini died in 1840, he wrote a memorial article for the *Revue et Gazette musicale* in which he praised the virtuoso's unique skill but lamented his egotism. Liszt believed that the artist should serve society, that what had once been the domain of the aristocracy was now that of the genius. He concluded with words that would become something of his own professional motto:

> From this moment on, may the future artist, with his whole heart, renounce every egotistical and vain role, of which, we believe, Paganini was a last and famous example. May he set his purpose not in himself but beyond himself; may virtuosity be for him a means, not an ultimate goal; may he call to mind that *nobility obliges*, as an old proverb expresses it, just as we are able to say today with as much, nay more, justification, *genius obliges*![10]

"Génie oblige" was the Romantic artist's variant of the older aristocratic "Noblesse oblige." It is a revealing recasting, illustrating as much about Romanticism as about Liszt's own personal mission.

And Liszt was a man with a mission, or rather various missions pursued over a long and fascinating career. Unlike Paganini, he did not remain exclusively an itinerate virtuoso. In 1848, at age thirty-six, he abandoned that nomadic life and settled down in Weimar, a German backwater that still enjoyed some lingering glow from its earlier associations with the literary giants Goethe and Schiller. For the next dozen years or so Liszt concentrated on composition, performing, writing, and teaching. He had done all these activities before, of course, but now his compositions were mainly for orchestra rather than keyboard, his performing was less often as a pianist but more as a conductor of symphonic and operatic repertoire, his writing more extensive and detailed, and his teaching geared not to amateurs but to serious pianists who came from all over Europe (and beyond) to work with him. By the mid-1860s Liszt, who had been deeply religious since his youth, was reinventing himself again, now taking minor orders in the Catholic Church, becoming Abbé Liszt, and dividing his time for his last two decades nearly equally among Weimar, Rome, and Budapest.

Figure 19-3 Marie d'Agoult. Portrait by Henri Lehmann (1839).

Throughout this eventful life Liszt pursued complicated relationships with adoring women, including Marie d'Agoult (Fig. 19-3), a married countess with whom he had three children (one of whom eventually married Richard Wagner), and Carolyne von Sayn-Wittgenstein, a Polish princess. These formidable women, socially far more elevated and better educated than he, were deeply involved with his career, particularly as the co- (or ghost) writers of many of the reviews, essays, and books published under his name.

Liszt's professional relationships were also extraordinary over his long career, making him a musical ambassador of sorts between and among generations. He probably had contact with more prominent musicians than any other figure discussed in this book. As a boy he met Beethoven and by the end of his life the young French composer Claude Debussy (1862–1918). In between he encountered nearly every significant composer and performer of his century, some of whom were his students or disciples. The most important reflection of these varied relationships was his generous advocacy of composers from all countries, some of whom held vastly different aesthetic and musical positions than his own (Fig. 19-4).

Figure 19-4 *Liszt at the Piano*, by the Austrian painter Josef Danhauser (1805–45), is a fantasized scene that renders a fictional salon populated by an international cast of four writers and four composers. Seated far left is the French poet Alfred de Musset (1810–57) and next to him Amandine Aurore Lucie Dupin (1804–76), who wrote under the pseudonym George Sand. Behind them is French writer Victor Hugo (1802–85) and to his right composers Hector Berlioz and Gioachino Rossini. Nestled to the right of Liszt is the Countess Marie d'Agoult (1805–76), a minor French writer (under the pseudonym Daniel Stern) who had three children with Liszt. Presiding over it all is the imposing bust of Beethoven, who by a skillful trick of perspective has become a floating presence, a true divinity.

Transforming Music Through Arrangements

It was not only through performing, teaching, and writing that Liszt became such an influential advocate of other composers, but also through his musical transformations of others' compositions, past and present, famous and obscure. This part of his legacy, moreover, has left the most concrete evidence; his arrangements of other composers' music remain objects to play and study, while aspects of his performing and teaching have primarily been passed down as oral tradition. Since Liszt probably taught more pianists than any other leading figure in the century, musicians to this day like to play the "*x* degrees of separation" game. How many generations back from your piano teacher does one have to go before one arrives at Liszt (who, of course, studied with Czerny, who studied with Beethoven, who may have had some lessons with Mozart, and so on)?

Arrangements, especially for piano, were an essential part of musical culture before the advent of commercial recording in the early twentieth century. Limited access to live performances, particularly to orchestral and dramatic works, meant that a wide variety of transformations disseminated music and facilitated domestic music making. The larger part of Liszt's oeuvre was devoted to arrangements. They range from faithful "**transcriptions**" (reworkings that usually retain the tonality and structure of the original piece) to much freer adaptations, variously called by names like "**fantasy**" and "paraphrase," that inventively recast the original musical materials into new compositions. Liszt's most popular free-form fantasies were operatic fantasies based on works by most of the leading opera composers of his time. Some of his particularly influential arrangements were of music by friends, including Berlioz and Wagner, and his tireless efforts significantly helped to spread their fame. He also transformed the music of previous generations, including some of the most potent models for his own original compositions. He began transcribing Beethoven's symphonies in the 1830s and completed all nine by the mid-1860s. Many other virtuosos, not to mention a host of commercial hacks, also transcribed Beethoven's symphonies for eager publishers, who released competing versions just as record companies do today.

While Liszt's arrangements of Mozart and Beethoven did the older masters an interpretive service, his efforts were hardly needed to further their fame. But with a lesser-known figure like Schubert, dead just a half-dozen years when Liszt composed his first piano arrangements of songs by him in the mid-1830s, the advocacy could be tremendously beneficial. Liszt considered Schubert "the most poetic musician who ever lived,"[11] and as pianist, conductor, editor, essayist, as well as arranger, he was so engaged with Schubert's music that he eventually became the central figure in the mid-nineteenth-century reception of the composer. For most audience members in places like Dublin and St. Petersburg, the first time they encountered the name Schubert was when Liszt performed his music, usually an arrangement of a song or dance. Liszt's most popular work on tour was a dazzling solo piano transcription of *Erlkönig*.

Anthology Vol 2-36
Full CD IV, 23

One of Liszt's greatest musical transformations is his *Réminiscences de Don Juan* (1841), known informally as the "Don Juan Fantasy," which, while ostensibly a potpourri on melodies from Mozart's *Don Giovanni*, is quite obviously more than that: It offers a glimpse of an innovative performer and composer considering an earlier master. Liszt interprets Mozart's opera and in the process not only updates it but also turns it into something of a self-portrait. (Given his own reputation as a Don Juan, Liszt certainly had good reason to identify with the title character.) Indeed, Liszt's Fantasy makes an astonishing comment on the opera and on how Romantic audiences interpreted it. By juxtaposing the Don's seduction of Zerlina, evoked through a set of variations on their duet, "Là ci darem la mano" ("There, give me your hand"), and the music that accompanied the Statue's seizure of the Don—which, as Liszt brilliantly reminds us by suddenly citing it, happens on an almost identical line ("Dammi la mano in pegno!" or "Give me your hand in pledge!")—he casts Mozart's hero as predator and prey alike, at once stalker and stalked. Even more pointed is the irony when Don Giovanni's "Champagne Aria" appears near the end. Rather than providing the ultimate in "sparkling" virtuosity, it is darkly framed by the Statue's chromatically tortured line "Ah, tempo più non v'è" ("You're out of time"). The Fantasy may be viewed as a sort of musical music criticism. While surely "readable" in conventional moralizing terms, as a divine judgment on the Don's lascivious conduct, Liszt's juxtapositions impose a new layer of Romantic interpretation on Mozart's opera.

Liszt "has caused a stir as Vienna has never known. He is truly an artist whom one must see and hear for oneself." —Robert Schumann

The Lisztian Concert

Liszt's cultivation of dark forces in performance came most clearly to the fore, just as it had with Paganini, when he undertook a decade-long tour in 1838. And, like Paganini, he began his conquest in Vienna. The brilliant eighteen-year-old pianist Clara Wieck, who had been giving a series of hugely successful concerts there for some weeks already when he arrived, wrote to her future husband, Robert Schumann, that Liszt "has caused a stir as Vienna has never known. He is truly an artist whom one must see and hear for oneself."[12]

Liszt's performances were novel both musically and with regard to his demeanor. A Vienna newspaper reported on the phenomenon:

> People do anything to get tickets, and on a hot summer's day sit in the hall for a full hour before the start of the concert. The orchestra is removed so that the elite of the ladies of fashionable society may have seats near the virtuoso. Liszt remains the same, but new merits are daily discovered in him. People exchange anecdotes about his life, wait for him in the street, try to catch a word or two from him, order his portrait, buy his handwriting—in short, he becomes the vogue. Any pretext is used to make his acquaintance; he is regularly besieged with dinners, suppers, and parties. The honor of inviting him and receiving him graciously is coveted by even the great and mighty. And this is where his Parisian upbringing stood him in excellent stead. With amiable ease of manner, cheerful, chatty, and courteous, he moved in the world to which he had long been accustomed.[13]

Wieck noted in her diary that while Liszt "is playing in his concerts, he speaks with the ladies sitting around him, always stays with the orchestra, drinks black coffee, and behaves as if he were at home. That pleases everyone now, and he creates a furor."[14] This was the sort of behavior that led to what the poet Heinrich Heine dubbed "Lisztomania" (Fig. 19-5). It took Europe by storm as the handsome

Figure 19-5 "Franz Liszt Exerts His Spell on the Ladies in the Audience," caricature from the periodical *Berlin, wie es ist . . . und trinkt* (mid-1840s). The name of the journal, "Berlin, as it is . . . and drinks," is a rather clumsy pun (*ist* means "ist"; *isst* means "eats").

virtuoso crisscrossed the continent in a cyclone of concert-giving that revolutionized musical life. It was not just the level of his playing that was unprecedented. Liszt was the first virtuoso to dare appear solo for an entire evening, thus inventing the instrumental "recital" as we know it today. Indeed the very word was first used as we now do in connection with appearances he made in London in 1840.

Critics repeatedly commented on the orchestral nature of his playing (one reason he often had multiple pianos on stage was because he broke so many strings). Nearly everyone reported on his commanding physical presence and on the spectacle of his concerts: You simply had to see him. He was the first traveling virtuoso to retain the services of a personal impresario, or what we would now call a manager, an advance man who handled his professional correspondence, booked his halls, advertised his appearances, negotiated and collected his fees, and took care of his personal needs on the road. The powerful modern concert booking agencies and artist managements that run (and sometimes ruin) the lives of performers today are the descendants of Gaetano Belloni ("Liszt's poodle," as Heine dubbed him),[15] who served Liszt in this capacity during the 1840s.

The novelty of his solo recitals and the nature of his touring repertoire are fascinatingly revealed in a memoir by Vladimir Stasov (1824–1906), a prolific Russian writer on the arts, who attended Liszt's St. Petersburg debut in April 1842. There were two pianos set up on the stage, and Liszt alternated between them, "facing first one, then the other half of the hall," as Stasov recollected.[16] In addition to playing his own arrangements of Beethoven and Schubert songs, the program included arrangements of Rossini's *William Tell* Overture, the sextet from Donizetti's *Lucia di Lammermoor*, and his "Don Juan Fantasy." The only item that was not an arrangement was the grand finale, Liszt's own show-stopping *Galop chromatique*, a tour de force of velocity but something of a throwback to the old *style brillant*. Stasov summarizes:

> Everything about this concert was unusual. First of all, Liszt appeared alone on the stage throughout the entire concert: There were no other performers—no orchestra, singers or any other instrumental soloists whatsoever. This was something unheard of, utterly novel, even somewhat brazen. What conceit! What vanity! As if to say, "All you need is me. Listen only to me—you don't need anyone else." Then, this idea of having a small stage erected in the very center of the hall like an islet in the middle of an ocean, a throne high above the heads of the crowd, from which to pour forth his mighty torrents of sound. And then, what music he chose for his programs: not just piano pieces, his own, his true métier—no, this could not satisfy his boundless conceit—he had to be both an orchestra and human voices. He took Beethoven's "Adelaide," Schubert's songs—and dared to replace male and

> female voices, to play them on the piano alone! He took large orchestral works, overtures, symphonies—and played them too, all alone, in place of a whole orchestra, without any assistance, without the sound of a single violin, French horn, kettledrum! And in such an immense hall! What a strange fellow![17]

At his second St. Petersburg concert, the program included his transcription of the last three movements from Beethoven's *Pastoral* Symphony. Only at the third concert, which included Beethoven's "Moonlight" Sonata, did Liszt present the sort of repertoire that is now considered standard recital fare, although he probably omitted the middle movement, as he usually did when playing this particular sonata in public.

Many of Liszt's concerts featured improvisation, usually on familiar themes, again often drawing on opera melodies. For his "farewell" concert in Vienna in April 1823, before he moved to Paris at age twelve, Liszt had sought a theme from Beethoven, whom he met at the time. Twenty-three years later in Vienna he made an unexpected appearance at a benefit concert during which he accompanied a singer in Schubert's *Erlkönig* and in an aria from Handel's *Acis and Galatea*. After that, according to a review, he improvised on the themes from them

> and transported the audience through this extraordinarily brilliant performance to such excitement that they did not stop clapping and screaming. . . . Liszt had certainly not thought about such an improvisation before this and precisely because it was on the spur of the moment that it was so remarkably successful; he gave himself over entirely to the artistic enthusiasm of the moment and to his genius. He began with the Handelian allegro movement and then came the main motive of *Erlkönig* and these motives all interweaved with one another so artfully and effectively, sounding the one, now the other, now again fusing the two themes together at the same time that it was a true joy to follow such an inspired improvisation and one only regretted that there is no musical stenography that could record it for everyone. The effect was extraordinary.[18]

The final comment about a "musical stenography" that might "record" an event is fascinating, but this would remain a dream for more than half a century longer until the invention of the phonograph. Not only did Liszt regularly improvise long pieces, but on occasion he let flights of fancy enter while performing standard repertoire, taking liberties that had been commonplace earlier but were increasingly viewed with alarm. The idea that musical scores are sacred texts and that improvisation is a debased form of musical art affected even Liszt. By midcentury not even spontaneity could be merely spontaneous. Pianists trained in conservatories spent all their time, as the young Liszt had earlier done in Paris, on "trills, sixths, octaves, tremolos, double notes"—but not on inventing their own cadenzas. Improvisation was no longer part of the typical music conservatory curriculum, and by the end of the century, for most artists in the European literate tradition (organists being a notable exception), it had become a lost art—which is to say, the literate tradition had become more truly and exclusively literate. There are today probably hundreds, if not thousands, of conservatory-trained pianists in the world whose techniques at trills, octaves, and double notes are comparable to Liszt's, but hardly a one who can end a concert with an improvised fantasia.

Many of Liszt's concerts featured improvisation, usually on familiar themes, often drawing on opera melodies.

Spectacle on the Parisian Stage

The virtuoso represented one kind of spectacle—a dazzling solitary one. At the opposite performative extreme stood opera, which assumed unprecedented grandeur in the nineteenth century, especially in Paris, the cultural capital of Europe. For more than two decades beginning around 1830, the venerable Académie Royale de Musique—the Paris Opéra—boasted the hugest theatrical spectacles ever attempted anywhere.

The Parisian preference for such monsters was a direct reflection of France's self-image as the great political monolith of Western Europe. At a time when the maps of Germany and Italy were crazy quilts of little principalities and city-states and the multinational Habsburg ("Holy Roman") Empire was slowly crumbling, France was the same large centralized entity it had been since the fifteenth century, the only continental European country that looked on an early-nineteenth-century political map pretty much the way it looks today (see Fig. 18-1). Its territorial integrity was stable, and its military was mighty. It took the massed armies of every other major European country, even Russia, to beat back its armies during the Napoleonic Wars (1803–15). Even when subdued, France remained a giant, "the one to beat." Its arts establishment continued to reflect that traditional self-image, including a large new opera house in the heart of Paris.

For the French, visual splendor in opera was really nothing new, especially when we remember the integral role that ballet played as far back as Lully's operas in the late seventeenth century. Gluck had also been forced to accommodate local custom by adding dance numbers to the French adaptations of his Italian operas in the 1760s. These operas, with their increased use of chorus and more unified dramatic unfolding, were part of a lineage that eventually led in the late 1820s to a new and epoch-making kind of extravaganza called *grand opéra*. Along the way, works by Luigi Cherubini (1760–1842), Etienne-Nicolas Méhul (1763–1817), and Gaspare Spontini (1774–1851), among others, provided more recent models, and there were ever-increasing opportunities for composers in the wake of the French Revolution, when many new theaters opened in Paris. By the 1820s one could see imposing five-act *tragédies lyriques* at the Opéra, lighter fare at the Opéra-Comique, Italian opera (notably Rossini) at the Théâtre Italien, older repertory at the Théâtre de l'Odéon, as well as productions at other opera houses and theaters.

> ***For more than two decades beginning around 1830, the venerable Académie Royale de Musique boasted the hugest theatrical spectacles ever attempted anywhere.***

The work generally credited with combining the French tradition with a renewed state-supported grandiosity in production was *La muette de Portici* (The Mute Girl of Portici, 1828). Its composer, Daniel-François-Esprit Auber (1782–1871), is remembered less now than is one of its librettists, Eugène Scribe (1791–1861). Some said that Scribe was the greatest librettist of the nineteenth century, some that he was the worst. What all must agree is that he was a musically sensitive writer who became the century's most influential musical dramatist, the Metastasio of the nineteenth century. In the mid-1820s Scribe began his long collaboration with Auber, with whom he worked on more than two dozen projects and maintained a lively correspondence. He also collaborated with Rossini and Cherubini and then with a host of composers, including Jacques Fromental Halévy (1799–1862) and Giacomo Meyerbeer (1791–1864), who masterminded the new genre of grand opera. Near the end of his long career Scribe provided texts for Giuseppe Verdi and Charles Gounod.

Even his admirers admit that Scribe's librettos are full of hackneyed language and theatrical clichés. What he was uniquely gifted in doing, however, was what librettists are paid to do: exploit resources and create opportunities. In the words of Louis Véron (1798–1867), his nominal boss as director of the Paris Opéra in its glory days, "dramatic action . . . ought to be able to be comprehended by the eye like the action of a ballet." In order for this to happen:

> It is necessary that the chorus play an impassioned role in it and be, so to speak, one of the interesting characters of the play. Each act ought to offer contrasts in settings, costumes, and above all in ably prepared situations. The librettos of M. Scribe offer this abundance of ideas, these dramatic situations, and fulfill all the conditions for variety of setting [*mise-en-scène*] that the construction of an opera in five acts demands. When one has at one's disposal the most enormous theater, an orchestra of more than eighty musicians, nearly eighty chorus members male and female, eighty supernumeraries ["spear-carriers," or "extras," walk-ons who do not speak or sing but augment the spectacle], not counting children, a company of sixty *machinistes* [stagehands] for moving sets, the public listens and expects great things from you.[19]

The emphasis on spectacle in opera now required innovative kinds of direction, mechanical stage craft, lighting, costumes, and scenery.

The new Paris opera house on the Rue Peletier had a seating capacity of nearly 2,000 and was superbly equipped to make the magic happen (Fig. 19-6). It was the first opera house to use gas lighting instead of candles (from 1822), the first to use limelight (from around 1830), and the first to use electricity (from 1849). Its stage machinery was comparably advanced.

Why was all this important? Because the emphasis on spectacle now required innovative kinds of direction, mechanical stage craft, lighting, costumes, and scenery.

Figure 19-6 Interior of the Paris opera house on Rue Peletier during a performance of Meyerbeer's *Robert le diable* (1840s).

A new official in the history of opera also became necessary: the *metteur-en-scène*, or stage director. In this capacity Charles Duponchel (1794–1868) and Pierre Cicéri (1782–1868) worked with a staging committee of specialists. The emphasis on the visual reflected a deliberate modernization and popularization of opera. In fact, the design and mechanical innovations on which the Paris Opéra now prided itself had long been standard equipment for the melodramas, peepshows, and vaudeville comedies displayed at the boulevard theaters visited by the bourgeoisie, the growing mass audience also attracted to virtuosos. (Paganini's Paris debut in 1831 as well as the concert the next year that so inspired Liszt were given at the Paris Opéra.)

For the crowd scenes, an enormous chorus was employed that was called up to act, gesture, and fully participate in the unfolding drama.

Daniel-François-Esprit Auber's *La muette de Portici*

Véron hired Scribe to expand the libretto of *La muette de Portici*, originally a three-act text by Germain Delavigne, Scribe's frequent collaborator. He fashioned what would become the standard five acts with fully accompanied recitative, ballet and, as with most **grand opera**, a story that was historical, heroic, and tragic. The large cast of characters included ones of low birth who joined in the heroism. Antiquity, the Bible, and mythology no longer furnished the plots for grand opera but, rather, "modern" history, which in this repertory included the Middle Ages. Audiences saw history staged, creating vast tableaux of memorable visual appeal. For the crowd scenes, an enormous chorus was employed that was called up to act, gesture, and fully participate in the unfolding drama, to be, as Véron said, one of the "interesting characters." Because pantomime and the creation of striking visual poses were crucial for all involved, the choreographic element was in a sense not limited to the sections with dance.

A pair of historical events provided the plot for *La muette de Portici*: the 1647 revolutionary insurrection in Naples against Spanish rule led by a fisherman named Tommaso Aniello (called Masaniello in the opera), and the eruption of Mount Vesuvius in 1631. To history Scribe had to add romance: an ill-fated love intrigue. Fenella, the "mute girl" of the title character, does not sing a word—she was cast from among the ballet dancers and mimed to the music (Fig. 19-7). At the end, as Vesuvius erupts—an obvious excuse for spectacular stagecraft—Fenella throws herself into the burning lava after learning of her lover's death. Along with the historical plot, the spectacle, the dance, the use of chorus, the five-act structure, and so forth, *La muette de Portici* already exhibits many of the musical features that would become standard for grand opera.

Most remarkable are its large stretches of breakneck dramatic tempo, a matter not of clock time or of musical tempo as normally defined but, rather, of structure, that is, an unbroken flow of music such as we first saw in the finales of Mozart's operas. Before Scribe there was no precedent for a whole act that was in effect a continuous finale, which is to say, a fluid dramatic continuity uninterrupted by individual numbers, such as arias, duets, and ensembles. As Wagner later wrote in admiration, spectators perceived *La muette de Portici* as "something completely novel," because "one was always kept in suspense and transported by a complete act in its entirety."[20]

This development will be important to remember when considering the various operatic reforms later in the century, most of which, particularly Wagner's own, were attempts to achieve precisely such a numberless continuity. Remembering this is all the more pertinent in view of the fact that idealistic reformers of opera of a later day were inclined to look back derisively on the French grand opera, giving it in retrospect a reputation for opportunistic, exploitative commercial cynicism. Although the charge was not without some justice, two of the principal tenets of late-century reformist opera—the emphasis on closely aligning different media (poetry, music, setting, and spectacle) in a mutually reinforcing collaboration, and the achievement of dramatic or musical continuity—were powerfully anticipated by grand opera, not in opposition to public taste but in the very act of courting it.

Figure 19-7 Lise Noblet as Fenella in Auber's *La muette de Portici* (1828).

Opera and Revolution

Anthology Vol 2-37
Full CD IV, 24

Although *La muette de Portici* has long since disappeared from the standard repertory, it has lived on in history books less because of its music than because of its extraordinary reception. The opera was planned during the period of the so-called Bourbon Restoration (1814–30), toward the end of the stormy and reactionary reign of French King Charles X. By 1827 the political atmosphere was tense and theatrical censorship severe. In such circumstances an opera about a revolution might seem the very last thing France's official musical stage would consider offering for public view. *La muette de Portici* had royal backing, however, bestowed in the hope of swaying liberal opinion away from renewed revolutionary action, for the revolution depicted in the opera is disastrous for all concerned.

Yet bourgeois audiences identified so completely, against official expectation, with the powerfully portrayed peasant revolutionaries and with the imposing chorus of the people as to turn the opera into a virtual "accessory before the fact" to the revolution of 1830, the so-called July Revolution, in which political power was decisively snatched by the bourgeoisie from the aristocracy. We can see this best in the hit tune from *La muette de Portici,* "Amour sacré de la patrie" ("Sacred love of fatherland"), a patriotic duet for tenor and baritone in Act II. It became customary for audiences to applaud the revolutionary duet with special show-stopping fervor, making the occasion a virtual antigovernment demonstration. The exhilarating number became so famous that it was heard everywhere, not just in the opera house (Ex. 19-2). It was encoded in barrel organ cylinders, played in the streets and in cafés. It was issued in sheet music and enjoyed independent sales for home use. This runaway bestseller taught government and governed alike that works of art could be freely appropriated, in an age of mass dissemination, for use as political weapons. What the nineteenth century learned from grand opera was that works of art could be dangerous. In an age of emergent mass politics, music became a potential rabble-rouser—as rock 'n' roll would later become in the 1960s during the Vietnam War. Music, in this case opera, could not only mirror but also actually make the history of nations. In extreme cases it could even help make the nation.

Auber's **La muette de Portici** *taught government and governed alike that works of art could be freely appropriated, in an age of mass dissemination, for use as political weapons.*

Just how literally this was the case was driven home when *La muette de Portici* was exported to Belgium. The political situation there was much closer than the situation in France to the circumstances portrayed in the opera. Like the hero Masaniello's Neapolitans, the Belgians had been living under foreign domination. The Dutch had ruled Belgium since 1815. The July Revolution in France had emboldened Belgian patriots to seek independence. They demanded a performance of the banned *La muette de Portici* as the price of their participation in the birthday celebrations for the Dutch king, William of Orange, scheduled for 24 August 1830. *La muette,* heavily cut, opened the very next day in Brussels. The authorities, however, had cut the wrong numbers. Although the scenes of mob violence were gone, "Amour sacré de la patrie" remained. Having circulated for two years in street and sheet music, almost everyone knew the marchlike duet by heart. By the end of the number, the whole audience seemed to be on its feet, singing along. The chief of police sent a scout outside to assess the mood of the mob that had collected on the theater square. The scout returned and reported that the chief was to be assassinated in his box at the end of the performance. Riots broke out that evening, and over the next few days the revolt spread to other cities (Fig. 19-8). Unable to contain the crowds, the occupying Dutch forces withdrew. By the next year, Prince Leopold of Saxe-Coburg-Gotha had been elected King of the Belgians. His descendants reign to this day.

Example 19-2 Daniel-François-Esprit Auber, "Amour sacrée de la patrie" from *La muette de Portici,* mm. 48–52

Historians debate the spontaneity of the Belgian uprising and its precise relationship to the operatic performance that seemed to spark it. Was the demonstration an unpremeditated reaction to the patriotic duet, or was the duet the prearranged

Figure 19-8 The Belgian uprising of 1830 against the Netherlands. Painting by Egide Charles Gustave Wappers (1834).

signal to begin the demonstration? In any case it is clear that the effect of the performance on Belgian history had nothing at all to do with the intentions of its creators. Once music enters the world it can be interpreted and reinterpreted in endless ways and can serve competing political agendas.

Bourgeois Kings

The Belgian insurrection of August 1830 differed significantly from its French counterpart of the previous month, the July Revolution, to which it is often likened. The Belgian uprising was a revolt of patriots against an imposed foreign regime, the French a revolt by an aristocracy of wealth against an aristocracy of birth. The July Revolution put an end to the Bourbon dynasty once and for all, but, remembering the post-Revolutionary Reign of Terror and fearful of the proletariat, that is, the industrialized and newly populous urban working class, the victors held back from declaring republican rule anew. Instead, the newly empowered legislative Chamber of Deputies, a stronghold of bourgeois interests, declared a liberal constitutional monarchy, respectful of individual and property rights.

At France's head stood Louis Philippe (1773–1850), the gray-suited, umbrella-toting "Citizen King," whose charge was to protect bourgeois interests against aristocrat and proletarian alike. The France his reign represented—the July Monarchy—became a bastion of "conservative liberalism," a strong secular state committed to economic growth. It was thus at once a beacon of religious and civil tolerance and a bulwark of political stability. It was a brief European preview of "Americanism," the sort of capitalistic economic liberalism that only became a world force later with the emergence of the United States as a world power.

Figure 19-9 Giacomo Meyerbeer, photographed in 1855 by Félix Nadar.

Its art pointed to a later American phenomenon as well. It is hard nowadays to overlook the many parallels between the luxuriance and the implied values of the July Monarchy's most exalted art product—grand opera—and those of the Hollywood movie industry: the same basis in popular spectacle, the same emphasis on high-tech production values and special effects, the same preoccupation with richly decorated, semifantastic historical settings, and the same enthusiastic, anachronistic reinforcement of contemporary middle-class values by means of epic dramaturgy. And there was also the same social tolerance in the name of economic expansion, exemplified in the hospitality shown to enterprising Jewish talent. Halévy and Meyerbeer, grand opera's leading lights, were Jews, and Meyerbeer was a foreigner, to boot (Fig. 19-9). Indeed, Halévy's most successful opera, *La Juive* (The Jewess, 1835), to a libretto by Scribe, is an impassioned indictment of religious bigotry, although that is not what packed in the audiences. They came instead to see the staging by Duponchel and Cicéri, which bowled everyone over with its conspicuous consumption, striking realism, and enormous cast.

The gold standard for opulence, however, was set in 1836 with Meyerbeer's *Les Huguenots*, which also clothed a liberal bourgeois plea for religious tolerance in unbelievable splendor. The composer of *Les Huguenots* was born Jakob Liebmann Meyer Beer to a wealthy Berlin family, comparable to the Mendelssohns but if anything richer and more acculturated. While Meyerbeer was a totally assimilated and cosmopolitan citizen of Europe and although not religiously observant, he honored a pledge he had made to his mother, never converted, and was eventually brought back to Berlin for burial, amid huge publicity, in the city's Jewish cemetery. Trained first as a piano virtuoso, he was able to perform the D minor Piano Concerto by his beloved Mozart at the age of ten in 1801. Two years later he enrolled in the Berlin Singakademie, where he studied with Carl Friedrich Zelter, Goethe's friend and Mendelssohn's future teacher. In 1810, having embarked on a professional career and contracted his last two names into "Meyerbeer," he began two years of lessons, alongside his good friend Carl Maria von Weber, with Abbé Vogler.

Meyerbeer landed a court Kapellmeister's post in 1813, the same year that his second German Singspiel was produced, to an indifferent response. Wishing to devote himself to theatrical composition, he took the advice of Antonio Salieri, quit his job, and went to Italy to learn the tricks of the opera trade. Actually, this was not much of a gamble, since his family's fortune allowed Meyerbeer to be financially independent throughout his life. In any case, he spent eight miraculously successful years (1816–24) in Italy, much as Handel had done a century before, Italianizing not only his style but even his first name, to Giacomo, in grateful recognition of the country's long tradition.

> ***The gold standard for grand opera opulence was set in 1836 with Meyerbeer's* Les Huguenots.**

By the time of his last Italian opera, *Il crociato in Egitto* (The Crusader in Egypt, 1824), a heroic opera on the Rossini model (and the last important opera, by the way, to feature a major role for a castrato), Meyerbeer was recognized as Rossini's most viable competition. Rossini, who briefly directed the Théâtre Italien in Paris, produced *Il crociato* in September 1825, and another of Meyerbeer's operas was given at the Théâtre de l'Odéon. Meyerbeer was now favored with an actual Paris commission. It came not from the Académie Royale but from the Opéra-Comique. For that house one was expected to write three-act operas with spoken dialogue between numbers and happy endings; by then it was an established principle that a tragic opera ended with at least one death and a comic opera with at least one marriage.

Figure 19-10 Edgar Degas, *The Ballet from* Robert le diable (1872).

As originally conceived for the Opéra-Comique, *Robert le diable* (Robert the Devil), vaguely based on an old Norman legend, would have been similar to Weber's *Der Freischütz,* already popular in France since a somewhat mangled production at the Odéon under the title *Robin des bois* (Robin Hood) had appeared in 1824. When the planned production of *Robert* fell through, Meyerbeer decided to expand the scope of the project and write a five-act opera, with a libretto by Scribe and Delavigne, for the Paris Opéra, where it finally premiered in 1831. The work was hailed for combining national traditions—the German sphere of Beethovenian instrumental music and the Italian one of Rossinian vocal art. The obligatory third-act ballet is a counterpart to Weber's Wolf's Glen scene, a fiery "Valse infernale" representing a demonic orgy in a deserted cave; most spectacularly, as well as most obviously indebted to the phantasmagoria shows, it includes a swirling dance for a whole convent-cemetery's worth of risen nuns' corpses. With its dancing dead nuns this was clearly just as much an opera to see as to hear; it has been argued that the real hero behind *Robert le diable* was Cicéri, the designer (Fig. 19-10). The work nonetheless made Meyerbeer the toast of Paris. He maintained his preeminence with three more grand opera scores, each with a lengthy gestation period and a huge production, spaced out over the next thirty years.

While maintaining *Robert le diable*'s colossal scale and reliance on awe-inspiring spectacle, the operas that followed differed significantly with respect to dramatic seriousness. This was not an artistic difference alone, but one that matched the changes in the political climate. Meyerbeer's later works employed a dazzling theatrical rhetoric to produce uniformly horrifying dénouements, investing them, however artificially, with a gripping moral urgency. In these tragedies human, not supernatural, forces are at work, crushing even the good guys. The moral is the same: "Don't let things get out of control! Resolve your differences!" Grand opera shows us time and again that naked conflict, stubbornness, and prejudice lead inevitably to destruction.

In *Les Huguenots* these political morals are drawn with particular clarity, thanks to the trusty Romeo-and-Juliet formula. Raoul (Protestant) and Valentine (Catholic), a pair of star-crossed lovers, are caught in the Reformation's web. They meet their doom in the course of the infamous St. Bartholomew's Day massacre of 1572, in which many thousands of Huguenots (French Calvinists) were shot dead in the streets of Paris at the behest of Catherine de' Medici, the Italian-born, Catholic queen mother. The fifth act of the opera was given over to a reenactment of the horrible event, at the end of which the auditorium famously reeked of gunpowder and buckshot, adding yet another sensory element to the media saturation for which grand opera was famous. Like Halévy's *La Juive* the previous year, *Les Huguenots* is an indictment of religious fanaticism.

Meyerbeer's last two operas also explore historical and religious themes. In *Le Prophète* (The Prophet, 1849), the setting is sixteenth-century Holland and Germany, where another zealous movement, that of the Anabaptists ("Rebaptizers" who reject infant baptism), held sway. In *L'Africaine* (The African Girl), the last Scribe–Meyerbeer collaboration, premiered posthumously in 1865, there is an exotic geographical setting ("an island in the Indian Ocean") in which religious fanaticism, this time the Iberian inquisition, is cast as a destructive force.

It is often said that grand opera killed bel canto, just as bourgeois pretension and so-called conspicuous consumption killed aristocratic grace. One reason is the demotion of solo numbers. Arias, the dramatic as well as the musical focal points in Italian operas, became more occasional and decorative. And while every grand opera score contained its share of detachable numbers, they are often throwaways, used for the purpose of narrative exposition rather than emotional outpouring. This does not mean, however, that vocal virtuosity was banished. With seven roles challenging singers of the absolute first rank, performances of *Les Huguenots* were billed as "the nights of seven stars," and ticket prices were raised. But it was a new kind of virtuoso singing that Meyerbeer required in dramatic roles, as opposed to decorative ones: a forceful rather than graceful virtuosity that demanded an extension of the full (or "chest") voice almost to the top of the range, with a lessened dependence on refined falsetto ("head-voice") singing. This is the heroic singing style we know today as "operatic."

To sample *Les Huguenots* we can consider its celebrated fourth act, which contains three scenes. First there is a hectic recitative number in which the heroine Valentine, now married and unavailable, hides her illicit Protestant lover, Raoul, from her fanatical father, St. Bris, the mastermind of the St. Bartholomew's Day plot. After the first performances, Meyerbeer added a brief romance for Valentine alone so as to give her a lyrical moment to balance Raoul's little air at the beginning of Act V. This is the only span of time in the entire four-hour show when the stage is occupied by a single soliloquizing character expressing strong emotion. This was indeed a new kind of opera!

Anthology Vol 2-38
Full CD IV, 25–27

What follows is one of Scribe's most powerful dramatic spectacles, to which Meyerbeer composed his most famous ensemble piece: the "Blessing of the Swords," during which the massacre is plotted. St. Bris leads his men in an oath-taking with a big rabble-rousing tune ("Pour cette cause sainte"/"For this holy cause"), whose resemblance to the French anthem *La Marseillaise*, whether calculated or not, is potent (Ex. 19-3). Treated at first as if it were the beginning of an aria, its second half is immediately taken up by St. Bris and Nevers, Valentine's husband and the one truly admirable character in the opera. Nevers, realizing that it is not a battle but a craven massacre of innocents that is being planned, angrily withdraws. After he has stalked off the stage and Valentine has been shooed away by her father, the actual plot is hatched, following which three monks enter, bearing baskets full of white scarves that will serve as identification badges for Catholics during the bloodbath. The preparation for the blessing of the daggers is characterized musically by the slow dotted rhythms of the old French overture. After an oath taken to spare no one, neither women, children, nor the elderly, the stage erupts in a fast section that functions as a sort of choral cabaletta. Meyerbeer's virtuosity in the scoring of this sonorous explosion of the bloodthirsty masses was widely admired, but what seems an almost greater achievement is the way in which the composer managed to scale the sonority down by degrees to pianissimo as the conspirators disperse.

Example 19-3 Giacomo Meyerbeer, "Pour cette cause sainte" from *Les Huguenots*, compared with *La Marseillaise*

At this point Scribe thought the act was over. It was Adolphe Nourrit (1802–39), the leading tenor of the Opéra, playing Raoul, who supposedly demanded that he and his leading lady—Cornélie Falcon (1812–97), his protégée and mistress, in the role of Valentine—be given a proper love scene. It was not an easy thing to rationalize, and Scribe refused to supply it. Meyerbeer turned to a friend, Émile Deschamps, for the necessary text. Raoul emerges from hiding and immediately makes for the door so that he can warn his fellow Huguenots of the impending catastrophe. The desperate Valentine, losing her head and trying to detain him, blurts out that she loves him. Thunderstruck ("Tu l'as dit!"/"You said it!"), Raoul asks to hear her say it again, over and over (Ex. 19-4). This provides the slow portion of the duet, set in the strikingly "remote" key of G♭ major and marked *andante amoroso*. But finally, hearing the local church bells give out the fatal signal, he tears himself away and runs to his coreligionists' aid, thus providing the pretext for a race-to-the-finish conclusion (Fig. 19-11).

Example 19-4 Giacomo Meyerbeer, *Les Huguenots*, Act IV, "Tu l'as dit"

"You said it: yes, you love me! In my night [what star shines]?"

Figure 19-11 Scene from Meyerbeer's *The Huguenots* (1836).

What seemed to Scribe a contrived situation, improbable to the point of absurdity, became irresistible theater when realized. The freezing of the action into "aria time" at this terribly fraught juncture—just long enough for the two doomed characters to catch a moment's "inward" bliss before being predictably crushed by the inexorable march of external events in the brief final act—brought audiences to a frenzy of empathy. It was instantly the most successful number in the opera and much imitated by later composers, including Berlioz, Verdi, and Wagner.

Vagaries of Reception

Robert le diable logged a hundred performances at the Paris Opéra within three years of its premiere and was soon staged in nearly eighty different opera houses across nearly a dozen countries. *Les Huguenots* was also phenomenally successful and became the first grand opera to reach a thousand documented performances in Paris by the end of the century.

Yet few composers as popular, performed, and influential as Meyerbeer have so faded from recognition and from presentation. In large part this is due to the general eclipse of costly grand opera, but also to the fierce attacks on Meyerbeer in particular. The most vehement assaults came from Wagner, who was personally in Meyerbeer's debt for financial support and who owed him a musical debt as well, evidenced in his own early operas. In a notorious essay concerning Jews and music, Wagner steered clear of naming Meyerbeer, but nobody had much trouble guessing the identity of "a far-famed Jewish composer of our day" whose success is "proof of the ineptitude of the present musical epoch."[21] He claimed it was not a change in the legal and social status of affluent Jews, their so-called emancipation, that made possible their participation in the arts but, rather, the degeneration of the arts themselves, which had degraded them to a level susceptible to Jewish infiltration.

This diatribe did not go unanswered. One response, appearing in the same journal as the original rant, by Eduard Bernsdorf, argued that Wagner's diagnosis of the state of contemporary art and society was accurate, but that it was merely witless scapegoating to attribute it all to Jewish influence. "What he says about Meyerbeer is in many respects true," Bernsdorf allowed, "but not because Meyerbeer is a Jew but because Meyerbeer is a man of the nineteenth century."[22] A "modern man," in the eyes of nineteenth-century contemporaries, meant a beneficiary of progress in urban growth, transportation, commerce, and technology. The success of Meyerbeer epitomized these benefits. Nineteenth-century improvements in transport and communications, such as the railroad and telegraph, shrank distances dramatically and enabled a truer cosmopolitanism than ever before. A great deal of Romantic ideology—especially where it involved the purity of nations and ethnicities—was a direct reaction to this new cosmopolitanism. In many ways, then, Romanticism had become antimodern and reactionary. This was the kind of late Romanticism Wagner's tract espoused.

To such Romantics, the Jew—who had emerged as a force in gentile society concurrently with, and partly as a result of, the urbanization and commercial modernization of Europe—became the symbol of everything they found threatening in modern life. Defenders of German *Kultur* began to see Jews not only as tainted by commerce and as spreaders of "Modernity" but also as the henchmen of the hated French, with their cosmopolitan mores and their enlightened "civilization." What better focal point for such a phobia, then, than "a far-famed Jewish composer" who "writes operas for Paris, and sends them touring round the world"? These ancient debates would hardly merit airing in a book like this if they were merely ancient debates. Sadly, however, aspects of Wagner's anti-Semitic diatribe continue to surface, sometimes unwittingly, in present-day discussions of Meyerbeer.

Yet Wagner is not the only one to blame for Meyerbeer's eclipse. Both the instrumental virtuosity epitomized by Paganini and Liszt and the grand operas of which Meyerbeer was the most successful creator enjoyed an appeal that earned enormous revenues but also met with a considerable amount of critical scorn. While the styles, forms, venues, and personalities of this popular music would in time shift to new kinds of music, the influence of the earlier virtuosos and operatic spectacles remained. No subsequent violinist or pianist could ignore Paganini and Liszt. Likewise, the enduring repertoire of operas in the second half of the nineteenth century—above all those of Wagner and Verdi (falsely supposed to be opposites)—is fundamentally indebted, both musically and dramatically, to grand opera and is historically incomprehensible without knowledge of it.

Nineteenth-century improvements in transport and communications, such as the railroad and telegraph, shrank distances dramatically and enabled a truer cosmopolitanism than ever before.

Summary

The first half of the nineteenth century saw the rise of the traveling concert virtuoso with mass, rock-star appeal. The first artist in this new mold was the violinist Niccolò Paganini (1782–1840), who astonished audiences with his virtuosity and helped shape the Romantic image of the artist. His most important compositions are shorter works, including variations and caprices. Caprice means "according to the fancy of the performer," and the term was used to designate a piece with sudden contrasts and unexpected effects. In Paganini's caprices these contrasts were achieved with the virtuoso techniques he developed himself: octaves, unusual double stops, and left-hand pizzicato, to name just a few. After Paganini's retirement, these pieces continued to be popularized by other composers, who wrote their own sets of variations on them.

Inspired by Paganini's example, Franz Liszt (1811–86) made unprecedented breakthroughs in piano technique and brought many innovations to the concert that persist to this day. He was the first to perform an entire concert alone, thus inventing the instrumental recital. His own compositional output for the piano included hundreds of works in a great variety of styles and genres: concert études, character pieces (often arranged into larger collections), and works in a self-consciously Hungarian style. As an avid promoter of other composers, he produced hundreds of arrangements of symphonies, operas, and songs, ranging from literal transcriptions to free reinterpretations (see his *Grandes études d'après Paganini,* No. 6). His *Réminiscences de Don Juan* offers a particularly Lisztian reinterpretation of Mozart's *Don Giovanni.* In 1848 Liszt retreated to Weimar, became conductor of the court orchestra, and produced a series of larger, avant-garde works, including symphonic poems (discussed in Chapter 22).

A new concern with popular appeal was also reflected in the tradition of serious opera in France, which became known as *grand opéra* because of its dazzling sense of spectacle. Grand opera had its heyday between the 1830s and the 1860s. Its chief librettist, Eugène Scribe, created ample opportunities for crowd scenes with large choruses, elaborate stage machinery, and dance. The librettos gravitated toward historical topics with political or religious themes. In the political themes, audiences often saw analogies to political events of their own time. Daniel-François-Esprit Auber's *La muette de Portici,* set to a Scribe libretto, was a particularly potent force in French and Belgian politics, helping to facilitate the July Revolution (1830) in France and a similar uprising in Brussels one month later.

Although Giacomo Meyerbeer (1791–1864) and Jacques Fromental Halévy (1799–1862) stand out as grand opera's principal composers, contributions to the genre were also made by Rossini (*Guillaume Tell;* see Chapter 17), Verdi (*Les vêpres siciliennes* and *Don Carlos;* see Chapter 23), Wagner (*Rienzi;* see Chapter 23), and Berlioz (*Les Troyens;* see Chapter 20). Grand opera is distinguished from *opéra comique* by its use of recitative rather than spoken dialogue. To complement the dramatic forces, composers often employed a large, colorful orchestra. Although arias and choruses sometimes form extractable "numbers," they often flow together in a seamless depiction of the action.

Study Questions

1. What is the meant by the "democratization of taste" in the nineteenth century? Compare and contrast this trend with other Romantic tendencies discussed in previous chapters.
2. How did Niccolò Paganini help to shape the Romantic conception of the virtuoso artist?
3. Describe a typical Lisztian concert. What innovations did Franz Liszt make to the concert format and to piano technique?
4. Discuss Liszt's role in promoting and reinterpreting the works of other composers.
5. What were Liszt's views on the relationship between art and society?
6. What are the defining dramatic and musical characteristics of French grand opera? Compare and contrast these characteristics with the Italian operas of Vincenzo Bellini and Gaetano Donizetti (Chapter 17).
7. Describe the influence of librettists such as Eugène Scribe on grand opera.
8. Describe the relationship between grand opera and politics, focusing in particular on Auber's *La muette de Portici* and Meyerbeer's *Les Huguenots.* Why did these operas become political symbols?
9. Many composers of grand opera, including Giacomo Meyerbeer, are less well known today than they were in their own time. Why might this be?

10. Offer your own evaluation of "spectacular" productions such as grand opera or Hollywood films. What are the strengths and weaknesses of these genres?

Key Terms

caprice
étude
fantasy
grand opera
transcription

20

Literary Musicians

It seems appropriate, in a book that traces the literate tradition in music, to pause for a moment and consider the general explosion of literacy during the nineteenth century. The century witnessed a striking increase in the number of people who could read. Educational opportunities reached a far higher percentage of the population, and literature assumed ever-greater importance in cultural life. A growing urban middle class was more likely to read newspapers, poetry, and novels, all of which had become much less expensive to produce and to purchase. Similar trends emerged in the musical sphere: More people could now read musical notation, the quantity of music published and consumed multiplied, and musical instruments became more standardized and less expensive to buy. These developments enormously influenced what music composers wrote and for whom they wrote it.

We do not have much detailed information about the reading habits of most composers working before the nineteenth century. Although Bach's personal copy of the Bible survives with some of his own annotations, there is no indication that he read extensively in literature or philosophy. The estate inventories for Mozart and Beethoven give an idea of some of the books they owned, but comments about literature in their own writings and letters are relatively rare—music was their consuming interest. With the rise of Romanticism, however, many composers' literary engagement broadened and deepened. We have already seen that Schubert and his friends participated in an active reading culture. Liszt tried to educate himself through intensive study. The importance of literature for the featured three composers in this chapter—Hector Berlioz (1803–69), Felix Mendelssohn (1809–47), and Robert Schumann (1810–56)—would be hard to overestimate.

Earlier composers tended to look to other composers, past and contemporary, as the source for their art. In the nineteenth century, composers emerged who credited poets, novelists, and philosophers with providing their principal inspiration. This was partly a function of background and experience: Bach, Mozart, and Beethoven were raised by musicians to be musicians; many Romantic composers hailed from nonmusical families and benefited from much broader humanistic educations. Along with a new literary sensibility among musicians came the fact that many of them wrote extensively about music. They also wrote about themselves—musical memoirs and autobiographies came of age in the nineteenth century. Nor is it uncommon to encounter autobiography in their music. Some of the important works of Berlioz, Mendelssohn, and Schumann discussed in this chapter are connected in fascinating ways to their lives.

Many Romantic composers hailed from nonmusical families and benefited from broad humanistic educations.

The impetus for composers to write music criticism was usually financial, as in the case of both Berlioz and Schumann. Throughout history musicians have had to find ways to support themselves, by the employment or support of church, state, court, or patrons, through publications and performances, from teaching and other activities. Criticism became a newly viable option in the nineteenth century as a newly prominent figure emerged: the music critic, someone who evaluated music and musicians professionally, largely for the benefit of nonprofessionals.

Schumann began his career as a critic in 1831 writing for the Leipzig *Allgemeine musikalische Zeitung*. He soon came to feel that the journal had grown too conservative, hostile to the music he wished to champion, and so he helped found a competing magazine in the same city. The first issue of the *Neue Leipziger Zeitschrift für Musik* (New Leipzig Music Journal—Leipzig was soon dropped from the title) appeared in April 1834, with Schumann as editor, and he served as principal critic for its first decade. Although criticism helped pay the rent, Schumann also saw it as a creative outlet. He experimented with the style and form of his prose in ways that point not only to the aesthetic mission he wished to promote but also to an artistic sensibility he wanted to express both verbally and musically. His closest French counterpart was Hector Berlioz, who for some thirty years worked regularly as a reviewer and essayist, primarily for the *Journal des débats*, the leading Paris newspaper. He turned to criticism, reluctantly he said, because composing did not earn him enough money. It was at the start of that career, however, when Berlioz made his biggest splash as a revolutionary composer in revolutionary times.

Figure 20-1 Hector Berlioz. Portrait by Émile Signol (1832).

Berlioz's Literary Trinity

Three years after the death of Beethoven, two after that of Schubert, and one after Rossini's "retirement," Berlioz (Fig. 20-1), at age twenty-six, wrote what is perhaps the most startling, imaginative, and influential first symphony in the Western musical tradition. His *Symphonie fantastique* (1830) combines a novel "program" with an unprecedented orchestral sensibility to create a new kind of symphony, a truly Romantic one. Because it calls for an enormous orchestra, many contemporaries first got to know the work not in all its original Technicolor glory but, rather, in a brilliant piano transcription by Liszt, who met Berlioz on the day of the premiere

Anthology Vol 2-39
Full CD IV, 28
Concise CD II, 28

TIMELINE

1782 Friedrich Schiller, *The Robbers*
1804–05 Jean Paul, *Flegeljahre* (Years of Indiscretion)
1808 Johann Wolfgang von Goethe, *Faust* (*Part 1*)
1809 **Birth of Felix Mendelssohn**
1810 **Birth of Robert Schumann**
1822 Thomas De Quincey, *Confessions of an English Opium-Eater*
1825 **Mendelssohn, Octet in E♭ Major, Op. 20**
1826 **Mendelssohn, Overture to *A Midsummer Night's Dream***
1829 **Mendelssohn conducts J. S. Bach's *St. Matthew Passion* in Berlin**
1830 **Hector Berlioz, *Symphonie fantastique***
1830 Louis Philippe I becomes King of France after July Revolution
1834 **Schumann issues journal, *Neue Leipziger Zeitschrift für Musik***
1836 **Mendelssohn, *Paulus***
1836 **Schumann, *Fantasie* for piano, Op. 17**
1840 **Schumann, *Dichterliebe***
1841 **Clara Schumann, *Er ist gekommen in Sturm und Regen***
1842 **Founding of New York Philharmonic**
1843 **Berlioz publishes textbook on orchestration**
1843 **Mendelssohn appointed director of newly founded Leipzig Conservatory**
1844 Samuel Morse opens first official telegraph line in Washington, D.C.
1847 **Death of Mendelssohn**
1848 Revolutions in France, Prussia, Austria-Hungary, and Italian states
1850 **Richard Wagner, "Judaism in Music"**

performance in December 1830. Liszt's transcription in turn attracted Schumann's attention as a critic. Although Schumann did not experience the work orchestrally until Berlioz visited Leipzig in 1843, Liszt's piano transcription prompted him in 1835 to write a detailed review of the piece and the aesthetic issues it raised, which we will consider later. Thus two of the leading Romantic composers, Liszt and Schumann, were deeply engaged early in their careers with Berlioz's extraordinary symphony.

Although composed under the influence of Beethoven (Berlioz wrote a detailed study of Beethoven's symphonies), the *Fantastique* reveals aesthetic fault lines that would play out over the nineteenth century (and beyond) concerning what instrumental music could and should do. One of the crucial issues concerned so-called extramusical content. An increasing number of composers now drew on stories, poems, and plays, as well as themes from philosophy, religion, history, and nature and from their own lives as the "programmatic" basis for their compositions. We have seen this some before, in Vivaldi's *The Four Seasons* and in Beethoven's *Pastoral* Symphony. The contrasting merits of "**program music**" versus what came to be known as "**absolute music**" were very much debated during the nineteenth century, and as composer and critic Berlioz was very much in the fray.

Berlioz's father, who wanted him to be a doctor, could hardly have predicted this. Berlioz gave an account of his relatively privileged childhood in his *Mémoires*, a wonderfully engaging book that is testimony to both his literary gifts as a writer and his literary sensitivity as a reader. The composer tells us that he awakened to the world of art through reading. The study of Latin, particularly encountering the *Aeneid*, touched him deeply as a young boy: "It was Virgil who first found the way to my heart and fired my nascent imagination."[1] Shakespeare would emerge somewhat later as an even more powerful force, with Goethe rounding out the composer's literary trinity. Berlioz's entrance into music likewise encompassed literature: Once arrived in Paris, he went frequently to see operas, the most dramatic and novelistic of musical genres.

Berlioz's literary passions are evident in the choices he made when writing his orchestral music, choral works, and operas. (He wrote little else—some songs, no keyboard or chamber music.) He composed various pieces on Shakespearean subjects, including a concert overture, *Le roi Lear* (King Lear, 1831); a "dramatic symphony," *Roméo et Juliette* (1839); and a comic opera, *Béatrice et Bénédict* (1862), based on *Much Ado About Nothing.* Goethe provided the basis for his "dramatic legend" *La damnation de Faust* (1846; Fig. 20-2). His largest work, the opera *Les Troyens* (The Trojans, 1856–58), drew from the *Aeneid*, and with it, he proclaimed, he attempted to combine influences: "Virgil Shakespearized."

Berlioz's Fantastic First Symphony

But before all this came his seminal symphony, one based on literature more generally as well as on his own life. The work is officially titled *Épisode de la vie d'un artiste, Symphonie fantastique en cinq parties* (Episode in the Life of an Artist: Fantastic Symphony in Five Movements). The word *fantastique* had for Berlioz and his contemporaries a wealth of resonances, denoting something strange, grotesque, uncanny, unearthly—in short, Romantic. He chose not any old story for his artist's life but one with self-proclaimed autobiographical elements. We have already seen an ever-increasing subjectivity in music, from Mozart and Beethoven through the newly intimate inwardness of Schubert. With Berlioz and later Romantics autobiography becomes a more identifiable impulse, although some composers, Berlioz at times included, tried to cover their tracks.

The hero of the five-movement symphony is an artist—a musician, in fact. At the outset he is desperately in love with an idealized woman, and whenever he thinks of her, he hears a melody, thus causing a double obsession, or ***idée fixe***. Next he goes to a lively ball and from there to the repose of the country. Finally admitting to himself that his love is unrequited, Berlioz's protagonist takes an overdose of opium, too weak to kill him but strong enough to induce a bad trip. He fantasizes that he has murdered his beloved, been sentenced to death, and then reunited with her in hell, in a wild witches' Sabbath.

Program of *Symphonie Fantastique*

1. *Reveries—Passions.* The author imagines that a young musician, afflicted with that moral disease that a well-known writer [Chateaubriand] calls the *vague des passions* ["surge of indefinite passion," roughly, readiness for a big emotional experience], sees for the first time a woman who embodies all the charms of the ideal being he has imagined in his dreams, and he falls desperately in love with her. Through an odd whim, whenever the beloved image appears before the mind's eye of the artist it is linked with a musical thought whose character, passionate but at the same time noble and shy, he finds similar to the one he attributes to his beloved.

   This melodic image and the model it reflects pursue him incessantly like a double *idée fixe* [obsession]. That is the reason for the constant appearance, in every movement of the symphony, of the melody that begins the first *Allegro*. The passage from this state of melancholy reverie, interrupted by a few fits of groundless joy, to one of frenzied passion, with its stirrings of fury, of jealousy, its return of tenderness, its tears, its religious consolations—this is the subject of the first movement.
2. *A ball.* The artist finds himself in the most varied situations—in the midst of *the tumult of a party*, in the peaceful contemplation of the beauties of nature; but everywhere, in town, in the country, the beloved image appears before him and disturbs his peace of mind.
3. *Scene in the country.* Finding himself one evening in the country, he hears in the distance two shepherds piping a *ranz des vaches* [Swiss cow call] in dialogue. This pastoral duet, the scenery, the quiet rustling of the trees gently brushed by the wind, the hopes he has recently found some reason to entertain—all concur in affording his heart an unaccustomed calm and in giving a more cheerful tint to his ideas. He reflects on his isolation; he hopes that his loneliness will soon be over.—But what if she were deceiving him!—This mingling of hope and fear, these ideas of happiness disturbed by black presentiments, form the subject of the *Adagio*. At the end one of the shepherds again takes

Figure 20-2 Cover for the score of *The Damnation of Faust* by Hector Berlioz (1846).

up the *ranz des vaches*; the other no longer replies.—Distant sound of thunder—loneliness—silence.

4. *March to the scaffold.* Convinced that his love is unappreciated, the artist poisons himself with opium. The dose of the narcotic, too weak to kill him, plunges him into a sleep accompanied by the most horrible visions. He dreams that he has killed his beloved, that he is condemned and led to the scaffold, and that he is witnessing *his own execution*. The procession moves forward to the sounds of a march that is now somber and fierce, now brilliant and solemn, in which the muffled noise of heavy steps gives way without transition to the noisiest clamor. At the end of the march the first four measures of the *idée fixe* reappear, like a last thought of love interrupted by the fatal blow.
5. *Dream of a Witches' Sabbath.* He sees himself at the Sabbath, in the midst of a frightful troop of ghosts, sorcerers, monsters of every kind, come together for his funeral. Strange noises, groans, bursts of laughter, distant cries that other cries seem to answer. The beloved melody appears again, but it has lost its character of nobility and diffidence; it is no more than a dance tune, mean, trivial, and grotesque: It is she, coming to join the Sabbath.—A roar of joy at her arrival.—She takes part in the devilish orgy.—Funeral knell, burlesque parody of the *Dies irae* (the hymn sung in the funeral rites of the Catholic Church). *Sabbath round dance*. The Sabbath round and the *Dies irae* combined.[2]

As happened earlier with Beethoven, commentators and listeners have linked Berlioz's life and work so consistently that it is nearly impossible to hear their pieces "innocently." Nineteenth-century audiences increasingly wanted background information about purely instrumental works. As Schumann noted in his review, the *Symphonie fantastique* would "arouse interest because of the personality of the composer who lived through the events of the symphony himself."[3]

But not all of them. The extent to which this program was truly autobiographical is of course unknowable. Berlioz, to begin with, is not known to have used drugs, even though his father, a doctor, experimented with opium and wrote on the topic. Berlioz, moreover, was fascinated with Thomas De Quincey's pseudo-autobiographical *Confessions of an English Opium-Eater* (1822), a book featuring dream visions every bit as bizarre and spectacular as the one the composer describes. Literary sources, in fact, seem to resonate with much of the symphony's program, beginning with its reference to the "well-known writer" Chateaubriand. Berlioz's allusions to fashionable balls, pastoral scenes, and weird rituals are also to be found in books by Victor Hugo, Honoré de Balzac, Stendhal, Goethe, and other prominent writers from the time.

Nineteenth-century audiences increasingly wanted background information about purely instrumental works.

So what is from real life? In 1827 the twenty-three-year-old Berlioz conceived an all-consuming passion for what then seemed an unattainable object, his ideal and idealized woman. In September he attended performances at the Théâtre de l'Odéon of *Hamlet, Romeo and Juliet* and *Othello* presented by an English company that was in residence in Paris at the time. Although he knew almost no English at the time, he was smitten both by Shakespeare and by the Irish actress Harriet Smithson (Fig. 20-3). "By the third act, scarcely able to breathe," he wrote of Smithson's portrayal of Juliet, "it was as though an iron hand had gripped me by the heart—I knew that I was lost."[4] (As earlier crushes had already suggested, Berlioz was in love with being in love, a disposition that would find frequent expression in his music.)

Miss Smithson, however, was oblivious to her young admirer. Berlioz spent the next two years in hopeless pursuit, never even meeting her before she left Paris in 1829. He wanted to begin writing a "grand symphony" in which he could depict his "infernal passion," but he was too distracted. Then he heard some false gossip about her that also left traces in the *Symphonie fantastique*: Harriet was allegedly having an affair with her manager, and this seems to have spurred the composition.

Berlioz wrote the whole symphony rapidly in early 1830 and then cast about to get it performed in the spring. These were volatile times—the revolution that installed Louis-Philippe as the citizen king rocked Paris at the end of July. The composer was thrilled with this turn of events and was prepared to take to the streets himself. He wrote to his sister that the revolution was "made for the liberation of the arts" and said he believed his career would now "succeed ten times sooner."[5] The composer's attentions were occupied at that very time with a new amorous infatuation and with writing a cantata that would finally win him the prestigious Prix de Rome, a stipend given by the French government to support promising musicians for a five-year period the first two years of which were to be spent in Italy. Following sundry delays and postponements, the *Fantastique* was premiered at the Paris Conservatoire on the afternoon of 5 December 1830, conducted by François-Antoine Habeneck (1781–1849). The concert also included, among other pieces, Berlioz's prize-winning cantata *Sardanapale*. The audience responded enthusiastically to parts of the symphony, particularly the fourth movement execution march.

Berlioz now set off to fulfill the terms of his prize in Rome, where he revised some of the symphony and wrote a sequel: *Lélio, or the Return to Life*, which he intended to be performed together with the *Fantastique*. This addition necessitated some changes in the original program, most notably the casting of the entire symphony as an opium-induced hallucination. After returning to Paris in late 1832, he arranged a new concert at the Conservatoire to present both works. At this point he learned that Harriet had also returned to Paris, and tickets were provided for her to attend his concert. Although she remained unaware that the two works being performed were actually about her, people in the know knew, and her presence at the concert caused quite a stir. Among those attending were the writers Hugo, Heine, and George Sand and musicians such as Liszt, Paganini, and Frédéric Chopin. Berlioz finally met Smithson the next day, and they were married within the year. (It seems a pity to spoil this incredible love story, but theirs was not a happy union; the celebrity couple broke up some ten years later.)

The symphony's motivating scenario was published in advance of the premiere in various French newspapers and then actually distributed at the concert. At the time audiences were rarely given any pieces of paper when they entered a concert hall—there were no such things as program notes, artist biographies, or advertisements for what horse and carriage to buy or where to eat after the concert. At most a single-page sheet might be distributed giving the titles of the works being performed. It was therefore extraordinary that Berlioz provided the lengthy prose description of his symphony; he explained why he did so in an introductory note:

> The composer's intention has been to develop, insofar as they contain musical possibilities, various situations in the life of an artist. The outline of the instrumental

Figure 20-3 Harriet Smithson, Irish actress and first wife of Hector Berlioz.

> drama, which lacks the help of words, needs to be explained in advance. The following program should thus be considered as the spoken text of an opera, serving to introduce the musical movements, whose character and expression it motivates.[6]

To this he added a footnote: "The distribution of this program to the audience, at concerts where this symphony is to be performed, is indispensable for a complete understanding of the dramatic outline of the work." Berlioz would later have some qualms about the program, adjusting it in ways large and small more than a dozen times, and occasionally deciding not to have it handed out at all. He eventually published the best-known version in the first edition of the score in 1845.

The five-movement format is often traced back to Beethoven's *Pastoral* Symphony, also programmatic, although not nearly with such a level of detail. That symphony, which as we saw Beethoven described as "more an expression of feeling than tone painting," presents a series of moods in the tradition of the eighteenth-century characteristic, or descriptive, symphony. There was no musical precedent for a real storytelling symphony such as Berlioz was offering, and so it may be more appropriate, as he suggests in his note, to seek its precedent in the contemporary theater. The new *grand opéra,* as noted in the previous chapter, was also a five-act affair, and it seems right to regard the *Symphonie fantastique* as a sort of opera—or "instrumental drama," as Berlioz himself calls it—for orchestra.

And what an orchestra! Whether in terms of sheer size or diversity of timbres, this was at the time the biggest band ever assembled outside an opera house (Fig. 20-4). Berlioz expanded the wind and brass sections to include new instruments, such as the ophicleide. (It has long since disappeared, and the modern bass tuba that is usually used in performances today does not quite produce the same strong booming bass effect.) A special trumpetlike brass instrument called a *cornet à pistons* appears in some of the movements. Bassoons, four of them, are given a prominence never encountered in a symphony before. Berlioz specifies four types of clarinets: the standard one in B♭ but also ones in A, C, and E♭, all of which have slightly different tone colors and can therefore be called on at the appropriate moments to provide the desired atmosphere. The score specifies at least four harps, an instrument associated at the time with the salon or opera house, as well as five percussionists to play different kinds of drums, cymbals, and cloches (church bells). At the first performance, Berlioz had hoped for about 220 performers but settled for 130.

Figure 20-4 Caricature of Berlioz conducting an orchestra, by Andreas Geiger (1864).

And it is not just *who* plays but also *how* they play: The musicians are asked to produce special effects with mutes, slides, and bowing techniques. Also unusual is the so-called voicing of chords. Even a chord as common as the C-major triad can sound quite different depending on which instruments are playing which pitches in which register. Certainly many of Berlioz's innovations came from the opera house, from military bands, and from listening to Rossini, Weber, and other imaginative earlier orchestrators. Yet his voicings, like the distinctive brush strokes we associate with particular painters, are immediately identifiable.

While we cannot know for sure, some of Berlioz's strange sound world perhaps stemmed from his unusual instrumental background. He was almost alone among major composers in having virtually no keyboard skills; he played the flute and the guitar, the latter of which may help explain the peculiar chord voicings. Far more than pianist-composers, Berlioz had to think directly in terms of orchestral colors, for which he developed an unparalleled ear. In 1843 he published a textbook on orchestration, the first to give a full description of all contemporary instruments and their possibilities, many of them pioneered in his own work.

Also theatrical is the way in which Berlioz adapted the specifically operatic device of the "reminiscence motif" to organize Symphonie fantastique _in both its narrative and formal dimensions._

Following the *Idée Fixe*

The programmatic elements and orchestration, both connected conceptually more with theatrical than with traditional symphonic music, are not the only innovations in the *Fantastique*. Also theatrical is the way in which Berlioz adapted the specifically operatic device of the "reminiscence motif" to organize the work in both its narrative and formal dimensions. As he states in the program, the image of the beloved haunts the symphony from start to finish in the guise of the obsessively recurring melody, the *idée fixe* (Ex. 20-1). Beethoven had found ways of unifying large, multimovement works by recycling motives. This "cyclicism" had a profound impact on Romantic composers, who took the concept even further. Thus the *idée fixe* in the *Fantastique* appears at least once in each of the five movements.

Example 20-1 Hector Berlioz, *Symphonie fantastique*, I, the *idée fixe* in Franz Liszt's piano transcription

The best entrée into the symphony is to trace the wanderings of this musical theme throughout the work, much as one might trace a character's appearances in a novel or drama. Thanks to Berlioz's orchestral skills, our first experience of the *idée fixe* is almost physically palpable, a graphic piece of body portraiture. The body portrayed, however, is not "hers" but "his," that is, the smitten artist's. It is the physiological reaction—the irregular heart palpitations in the accompaniment—more than the melody itself that is the real tour de force of imitation here. Or, rather, we have here a fairly complicated interplay between an abstract and arbitrary symbol (the *idée fixe* melody) and the realistic imitation of nature (the palpitating accompaniment).

The "beloved" melody is given a very distinctive, arching, asymmetrical profile, rising up in quick fitful leaps and then making slow, smooth, syncopated descents. Each of the principal appearances of the *idée fixe* in the first movement (mm. 72ff, 240ff, 412ff) is differently orchestrated, and a final fragment, flattened out into undifferentiated quarter notes, appears at the end when it comes time to wind things down for "religious consolation" (mm. 453ff).

One function of the *idée fixe* is to make a familiar environment seem suddenly strange, transformed by the injection of strong emotion. The second movement—we might even say "second act"—is the ball scene, such as was commonly featured in French novels of the time. The festive atmosphere is evoked in the most direct way possible, via the use of actual ballroom music, in this case a waltz. The movement opens with harps warming up, an invitation to dance. The *idée fixe* occurs twice, with strikingly different dramatic effects. It appears first when the beloved is spotted dancing from afar (mm. 120ff) and then again near the end (mm. 302ff), when the artist and his beloved come suddenly face to face, and the surrounding music suddenly disappears. It is a classic "moment out of time" of a type rarely encountered in instrumental music but long familiar in opera, where juxtapositions of "real time" and stopped "aria time" had been essential since the genre began.

From the urban ball the scene shifts to the solitude of the country. The opening employs yet another theatrical device that would increasingly be exported to the orchestral literature: the exploration of space. Berlioz begins with a dialogue between two shepherds, the first playing an English horn, to which responds the second playing an oboe offstage. This physical separation of instrumental forces offered new possibilities, which Berlioz further exploits at the close of the movement when a storm is depicted by timpani. The thunder, we are given to understand, has gone "within" the mind of the artist. The equation of inner and outer turmoil through the use of tremolo reintroduces a note of forlorn disquiet when the solo English horn resumes the shepherd's tune and is answered not by the oboe, its former partner, but by the distant thunder of the four timpani before a fade-out. In between we hear the *idée fixe* (mm. 90ff) as well as a realistic imitation of bird calls (mm. 67ff) modeled on the same musicianly creatures Beethoven had used in the second movement of the *Pastoral.*

The fourth movement, the "March to the Scaffold," enjoyed a separate popularity during the nineteenth century as an orchestral showpiece in its own right. The movement began life as an operatic excerpt: Berlioz lifted it from an abandoned score for his earlier historical opera *Les francs-juges* (The Judges of the Secret Court). In order to adapt it to its new purpose he changed the ending, which now contains the movement's single fleeting reference to the *idée fixe* played by the clarinet in C. What follows is perhaps the most strikingly illustrative music in the entire symphony: the short sharp shock of the guillotine blade (m. 169); the head rolling into the basket (pizzicati in the same measure); and the hats-in-the-air fanfare to conclude, reminding us that public executions were once a form of popular entertainment. This moment in the symphony is inevitably one of high comedy despite the grisliness of the subject and the ostensible seriousness of the program. When wearing his critic's rather than his composer's hat, Berlioz was known to rail at such literal depictions as lapses in style or taste, but in this instance he apparently felt it served a legitimate purpose.

If the program music of the *Fantastique* was allegedly written to convey a specific story, then it might seem like cheating on Berlioz's part to recycle an execution march that he had originally written for a completely different purpose. It is only fair now to mention that in fact the core melody of the entire piece, the *idée fixe*, was also adapted from an older, discarded vocal composition: *Herminie*, a cantata Berlioz had composed in 1828 in one of his unsuccessful bids to win the Prix de Rome. The initial emotional association of the melody, however, was similar. In its earlier context the tune that symbolizes an idealized Harriet Smithson had expressed the hopeless love of the cantata's title character for a Christian knight.

The fifth and last movement, in which the artist imagines his own bizarre funeral, was at first notorious for the deliberately ugly music it contains. One can hardly hear the opening bars, with their interminably sustained diminished-seventh chords, without thinking of Weber's Wolf's Glen scene in *Der Freischütz*, an opera Berlioz revered. (He was later commissioned to write recitatives, replacing Weber's original spoken dialogue, so that the piece could be performed at the Paris Opéra rather than at the Opéra Comique.) But Berlioz's instrumental symphony, unlike Weber's opera, had to do the work of the whole dramatic production, without the help of sung words and justifying action. It is little wonder that the first part of the "Dream of the Witches' Sabbath" is the part of the *Symphonie fantastique* with the most detailed program, unmistakably represented in the music. The program justified the most outrageous, fantastic musical effects.

The whole slow introduction (*Larghetto*), with its divided strings at the start, can be related to the "unearthly sounds, groans, shrieks of laughter" listed in the program, but the "unearthly cries, to which others seem to respond" have a more specific referent in the woodwind writing, answered by the muted valve horn, a very recent invention. The "unearthliness" was due to the literally unheard-of timbre and to the octave glissandos. The transformation of the *idée fixe* into "an ignoble dance tune, trivial and grotesque," previewed at m. 21 and played in full at m. 41, was another device borrowed straight from the opera, but one destined for a long career in orchestral music. Once again timbre plays a crucial role in characterization: To depict his now-detested woman, Berlioz used another instrument new to the symphony orchestra, the small, shrill-sounding E♭ clarinet, mainly employed previously in military bands.

Berlioz's instrumental symphony, unlike Weber's opera* Der Freischütz*, had to do the work of the whole dramatic production, without the help of sung words and justifying action.

Berlioz next appropriates the stern *Dies irae* melody, the well-known Medieval chant, to symbolize the sacred. As the cellos and basses descend to their lowest note at m. 86, we are plunged into a midnight graveyard where the church bells begin to sound just before the *Dies irae* tune enters, played by four bassoons and two ophicleides (Ex. 20-2). The chant variations proceed in a curiously academic, even pedantic manner, by strict diminution. But that is only the first of Berlioz's ironic borrowings from conservatory routine. The *Ronde du sabbat* (Witches' Round Dance) itself is introduced through an ungainly but altogether "correct" fugal exposition and leads to a climactic section in which the round dance and the *Dies irae* are combined in a two-layer contrapuntal tour de force of supreme irony.

Example 20-2 Hector Berlioz, *Symphonie fantastique*, V, mm. 121–146

These devices work together, combining the sacred and the profane, to make the latter part of the symphony's finale a piece of mock church music in the academic manner—just the sort of thing a well-trained musician might imagine under the influence of opium. The orchestration reaches a peak of wildness with the *col legno* (mm. 444ff), where the violinists and violists are asked to "strike the string with the wood of the bow"; it is an incredible effect that when pulled off well in performance can sound like maggots merrily eating away on a corpse. The incongruity between the garish program and the learned, somewhat archaic compositional devices is a source of humor to those in the know, and by the end one is almost convinced that the sophisticated composer's tongue is firmly in his cheek.

Whether or not it was intended, Berlioz's fellow composers appreciated the joke, and they appropriated it. Burlesques of the *Dies irae*—in which the Catholic Church's most terrifying musical artifact, describing the Last Judgment in appalling detail, was defaced, distorted, covered with composerly graffiti of every kind—became something of a blasphemous sport in the wake of the *Symphonie fantastique.* Most directly inspired by it was Liszt's *Totentanz* (Dance of Death), a one-movement piano concerto subtitled "Paraphrase on *Dies irae* in Variation Form." Funniest of all was the *Danse macabre* (1874), an orchestral showpiece by Camille Saint-Saëns; completely serious is its use in Gustav Mahler's Second Symphony (1888–94). A later contribution to this odd little tradition was the *Rhapsody on a Theme by Paganini* (1934) by the Russian pianist-composer Sergey Rachmaninoff, a one-movement concerto consisting for the most part of variations on the theme of Paganini's twenty-fourth Caprice, with the *Dies irae* chant thrown in as a reminder of Paganini's "diabolical" persona. Since then, popular culture, from television commercials to movies, has repeatedly employed the tune Berlioz fixed in the popular imagination as the common musical emblem of death.

Discriminating Romanticisms

Now, what would fellow composer/critic Robert Schumann have made of all this? We don't have to guess, because Schumann devoted the lengthiest article of his critical career to the *Symphonie fantastique,* issued in the *Neue Zeitschrift für Musik* in six installments between 3 July and 14 August 1835. Its length was due in part to its being not just a review but a defense against the opinions of others, notably the prominent critic François-Joseph Fétis, whose review Schumann printed in translation in his journal. Schumann's review was so detailed and diligent that he later successfully submitted it and other materials for a doctoral degree. This was one of the most brilliant explications that the *Symphonie fantastique* ever received, and that is why it is so revealing to us of the contrasting attitudes we may otherwise be inclined to lump together under the general topic of Romanticism.

Only after spending five installments praising the symphony and minutely describing it for his readers both as sound and as expression, providing in the process no fewer than twelve notated examples to refute Fétis's charge that Berlioz was technically incompetent, does Schumann even mention the program. He gives it, grudgingly and with many omissions, as an afterthought, and brings the whole six-part series to a close with an amazing sermon:

> Thus the program. All Germany is happy to let him keep it: such signposts always have something unworthy and charlatan-like about them! In any event the five titles [of the movements] would have been enough; word of mouth would have served to hand down the more circumstantial account, which would certainly arouse interest because of the personality of the composer who lived through the events of the symphony himself. In a word, the German, with his delicacy

of feeling and his aversion to personal revelation, dislikes having his thoughts so rudely directed; he was already offended that Beethoven should not trust him to divine the sense of the *Pastoral* Symphony without assistance. Men experience a certain timidity before the genius's workshop: They prefer to know nothing about the origins, tools, and secrets of creation, just as Nature herself reveals a certain sensitivity when she covers over her roots with earth. So let the artist lock himself up with his woes; we should experience too many horrors if we could witness the birth of every work of art!

But Berlioz was writing primarily for his French compatriots, who are not greatly impressed by refinements of modesty. I can imagine them, leaflet in hand, reading and applauding their countryman who has depicted it all so well; the music by itself does not interest them.

Whether a listener unfamiliar with the composer's intent would find that the music suggested pictures similar to those he wished to draw, I cannot tell, since I read the program before hearing the music. Once the eye has been led to a given point, the ear no longer judges independently. But if you ask whether music can really do what Berlioz demands of it in his symphony [as Fétis had tried emphatically to deny], then try to associate with it different or contrasting images.

At first the program spoiled my own enjoyment, my freedom of imagination. But as it receded more and more into the background and my own fancy began to work, I found not only that it was all indeed there, but what is more, that it was almost always embodied in warm, living sound.[7]

Aside from affirming national stereotypes between superficial France and profound Germany, at issue here is freedom of imagination, as Schumann finally gets around to saying in the last paragraph. Music, he insists, that leaves too little to the listener's own thinking, which excludes the listener from the co-creative process, leaves the listener (out in the) cold. The alternative, for Schumann, is certainly not music without expressive content but, rather, a music that by leaving such content undefined to a certain degree allows and even forces the listener to participate in its creation. It is the music that requires this involvement on the part of the listener that affords the experience of "absolute music"—a music absolutely, rather than merely particularly, expressive.

And even Berlioz might not have disagreed. In addition to refraining at various times from distributing the program of the *Symphonie fantastique* and *Lélio*, he never wrote another detailed program to accompany his subsequent instrumental compositions, even though they all had literary associations. Exasperated at the obstacles he still encountered at the end of his life in getting his works produced in his own country, he appreciated the recognition he received abroad and called himself "three-quarters German" as a musician.[8] Minus the spirit that motivated it, this declaration was an affirmation of faith in instrumental music and its capacity to communicate its expressive content without the help of words. Such a faith became central to some composers' conception of musical Romanticisms.

We will return, therefore, to the issue of program versus absolute music many times in the following chapters, as we will also to Berlioz, who emerges, together with Liszt and Wagner, as part of a triumvirate pursuing what was cast as a musically progressive, radical, avant-garde agenda, what was actually called the "Music of the Future" (*Zukunftsmusik*), in contrast to what was criticized by partisans as a conservative style associated with composers such as Mendelssohn, Schumann, and

Johannes Brahms. As an aside, it may also be worth noting that the trio of composers who wrote the *Zukunftsmusik* was aggressively promoted as the "New German School," and yet the Frenchman Berlioz was the first to write it.

The Prodigious Mendelssohn

The bad dreams depicted in Berlioz's *Symphonie fantastique* seem quite a contrast with the sweet ones that inspired Felix Mendelssohn's early masterpiece, the overture to *A Midsummer Night's Dream*, which he wrote in 1826 at the astounding age of seventeen. Both compositions, however, are youthful, programmatic, literary, and brilliantly orchestrated. Mendelssohn's overture is based on the famous play by Shakespeare, the author who inspired so much music in the nineteenth century. Indeed, the Elizabethan playwright was adopted by the Romantics as one of their own, with the Germans in particular claiming him as an honorary citizen. Mendelssohn (Fig. 20-5), moreover, had a close personal relationship with another member of Berlioz's literary trinity, Goethe, whom he first met at age twelve. They were introduced by the poet's favorite composer, Carl Friedrich Zelter, who happened to be Mendelssohn's teacher.

Anthology Vol 2-40
Full CD IV, 29
Concise CD II, 29

Goethe took notice of the boy, as did much of musical Europe, because Mendelssohn's astonishing talent was already manifest. Schumann would later dub him "the Mozart of the nineteenth century,"[9] and indeed he was arguably the greatest composing prodigy in the history of European music. He was not, however, exploited by his parents the way Leopold Mozart exploited his children. Felix was not taken on concert tours as a child and did not develop an early, freakish fame. Nor, though coming close—with a handful of dramatic works, fourteen symphonies for strings, and one for full orchestra completed by his sixteenth birthday—did he produce the quantity of works that young Mozart did. And yet it was arguably not until Mozart was nineteen, with the violin concertos of 1775, that he began writing music in a style, and of a quality, that was entirely his own, while Mendelssohn produced works as early as the age of sixteen that have to be considered fully mature masterpieces.

The year before his Shakespeare overture he composed an Octet in E♭ Major for strings, Op. 20 (1825), which showed complete command of extended forms. He had already become infatuated with the music of Bach and Handel, nurtured by his thorough, counterpoint-saturated training with Zelter. The climactic moments in the Octet's fugal finale are crowned by exuberant quotations from Handel's *Messiah* ("And He shall reign forever and ever" from the Hallelujah Chorus), which are later subjected to a rigorous contrapuntal development. His engagement with the music of Bach would have important consequences for the rediscovery of the older composer's music and for the deployment of early-eighteenth-century compositional styles in Romantic music.

Figure 20-5 Felix Mendelssohn. Portrait by Wilhelm Hensel.

The signal event in the "Bach revival" occurred in 1829, when the twenty-year-old Mendelssohn conducted the St. Matthew Passion in Berlin. That same year the composer embarked on his "grand tour" of Europe, subsidized by his wealthy parents. For the better part of three years he traveled, spending time in England, Scotland, Italy, France, and points throughout Germany. He met cultural luminaries—Heine, Berlioz, Chopin, Schumann, among others—and recorded his impressions in music as well as in evocative letters and impressive drawings. Although an amateur, Mendelssohn was a gifted visual artist; his literary sensibility worked in fascinating alliance with his pictorial inclinations as the impetus for many compositions.

Using personal, literary, visual, and musical sources Mendelssohn cultivated a new kind of music—the **concert overture**—which became one of the leading vehicles for Romantic musical expression. We have seen earlier overtures, in their typical seventeenth- and eighteenth-century incarnations, introduce operas, oratorios, and various dramatic works. Beethoven had written overtures to plays and for ceremonial events that provided Mendelssohn with models. He expanded the conception of the overture into freestanding, poetically titled orchestral pieces, usually in something akin to sonata form. *A Midsummer Night's Dream* came first in 1826; many years later Mendelssohn added incidental music, including a famous wedding march, to accompany actual performances of the complete play. The overture opens with four magical chords suspended in the upper woodwinds that lead to quicksilver staccato writing for divided upper strings. These contrasting ideas alternate throughout the piece, perfectly capturing the elfin world of Shakespeare's imagining. Also inspired by the play are hunting horns, evocative of King Oberon's realm, the braying of the craftsman Bottom transformed into a donkey, and a love theme.

In 1828, while still in his teens, Mendelssohn composed his next overture, *Calm Sea and Prosperous Voyage*, a musical seascape inspired by two short Goethe poems, and the following year he began the *Hebrides* (also known as *Fingal's Cave*), stimulated by his experiences traveling in Scotland. Together with the somewhat-later *Fair Melusine* Overture, based on a play by Franz Grillparzer, these works display Mendelssohn's astounding ability to paint vivid musical stories and scenes from nature. Two of his five mature symphonies also incorporate souvenirs from countries to which he had traveled: No. 4 in A Major (published in 1833) ends with a finale in tarantella style and is called the "Italian," while No. 3 in A Minor (published in 1842) alludes to highland tunes and is called the "Scottish." (As the dates indicate, his symphonies were not published in their compositional order.)

Mendelssohn's extraordinary musical gifts as both performer and composer, his superb general education (private tutors instructed him and his three siblings) and time spent as a student at the University of Berlin (where he attended lectures by the philosopher Georg Wilhelm Friedrich Hegel), his extensive travels and the stimulating intellectual atmosphere cultivated by his family and circle of friends—all these proved to be factors that gradually helped position him as the preeminent figure in German musical life during the early 1840s. Although he played a highly visible part in the general discourse of Romanticism, he was hardly the clichéd suffering artist. His was the music of a confident man, embodying civic virtue in his public activities and the bliss of domesticity in his private works, particularly his albums of *Lieder ohne Worte* (Songs without Words), gently lyrical character pieces for piano that became enormously popular. Until his sadly premature death, Mendelssohn had a dream career like Haydn's, pursued under altogether different social conditions, but even more successful.

Using personal, literary, visual, and musical sources Mendelssohn cultivated a new kind of music—the concert overture.

In 1833, after his years of intermittent travel, Mendelssohn was appointed music director of the Catholic city of Düsseldorf, where he conducted orchestral music, opera, and a great deal of choral music. His tenure there culminated in 1836 with the premiere of his first oratorio, *Paulus* (St. Paul). Next he was appointed chief conductor of the Leipzig Gewandhaus (Drapers' Hall; Fig. 20-6) orchestra concerts, which under his leadership became the most prestigious concert series in Germany. He held this post with great distinction for a dozen years (1835–47), in the course of which he did more than any other musician to reinvent modern concert life in the form that we now know it. Under his directorship, subscription seasons were extended to increase the orchestra members' pay and ensure their exclusive loyalty so that standards of performance would improve. More serious programming was advanced, with symphonies given complete, uninterrupted performances, and older repertory, including Bach, maintained alongside performances of new works. An international roster of big-name soloists regularly appeared with the orchestra. Mendelssohn himself conducted a wide range of choral and orchestral works, old and new. In 1839 he gave the premiere of Schubert's "Great" C Major Symphony (1825), only recently discovered by Mendelssohn's friend Schumann.

Figure 20-6 The Leipzig Gewandhaus (Drapers' Hall) as sketched by Mendelssohn.

From 1843 Mendelssohn added to his civic duties the role of director of the newly founded Leipzig Conservatory, soon regarded as Europe's finest training school for musicians. The faculty included Schumann, violinist Ferdinand David (1810–73), and pianist Ignaz Moscheles (1794–1870). The same year he was enlisted to revitalize musical life in Berlin, becoming director of the Berlin Cathedral Choir and conductor of the symphonic subscription concerts of the Berlin Opera Orchestra. From around 1840 he was the unofficial composer and conductor laureate of England as well, where his protégé, Prince Franz Karl August Albert Emanuel of Saxe-Coburg-Gotha, a talented organist and composer, had, by marrying Queen Victoria, become the Prince Consort of the realm, known to his subjects as Prince Albert. Mendelssohn made many trips to England, and his preeminence there was cemented when his second oratorio, *Elijah*, was premiered in English at the 1846 Birmingham Festival, the grandest and most triumphal of British musical ceremonials. As obviously Handelian as *Paulus* was Bachian, *Elijah* remained, alongside Handel's *Messiah*, a favorite British choral festival item, performed as an annual national sacrament until the end of the Victorian era at the dawn of the new century. (Regarding Mendelssohn's English successes, Berlioz quipped that he was valued as "a Handel and a half.")[10]

The endless travel, multiple jobs and responsibilities, all pursued while composing, eventually seem to have taken their toll on his health. After a series of strokes in 1847, Mendelssohn died at age thirty-eight. A large statuary monument to him was erected outside the Leipzig Gewandhaus. Until its dismantling by the Nazi government in 1937, it was one of two major musical memorials in the city, the other being the monument in front of the St. Thomas Church to Bach, a monument Mendelssohn had helped fund.

Mendelssohn's *Paulus* and Civic Nationalism

For another look at Mendelssohn's extraordinary talent as well as at his activities as conductor, advocate, civic musician, and religious composer, we shall consider *Paulus,* composed between 1832 and 1836 and performed to great acclaim under the twenty-seven-year-old composer's already-experienced baton at the Lower Rhine Music Festival. The St. Matthew Passion performances seven years earlier had marked a watershed in the growth of German choral music. Hundreds of German oratorios were composed for summer choral festivals, with throngs of performers holding forth before even bigger throngs of spectators. In keeping with the nature of the venue, festival oratorios nominally followed the Handelian rather than the Bachian model: secular works on (usually) sacred themes, rather than actual service music. Just as in Handel's time, the sacred was interpreted metaphorically, as a stand-in for the national. Indeed, some of Handel's own English oratorios now returned to the German repertoire, and the composer's name returned to its German spelling, suitably re-umlauted as Händel.

An important aspect of many of the newly written oratorios, by composers including Carl Loewe and Ferdinand Hiller (1811–85), is the way they managed to crossbreed a Bachian element into the Handelian mold. Most of them incorporated the traditional German-language chorales, which may at first seem surprising, given the chorale's association with actual worship services. Although some objected to secular use of this kind, the chorale retained what Martin Luther had originally valued: the sense of community that could just as easily foster nationalism as Protestantism.

The Lutheran repertory of chorales was considered the common property of all Germans, even by composers, like Loewe, who were themselves devout Catholics. A religious repertory was in effect co-opted in the name of a nation. This was striking testimony to the ascendancy of the national—and eventually the nationalist—ideal and its transformative power in post-Napoleonic Europe. Now nation trumped even religion as a definer of human community, and the chorale became for all intents and purposes a brand of spiritual folklore—*Volkstümlichkeit* made holy.

Anthology Vol 2-41
Full CD IV, 30–31

In *Paulus* we can see the chorale in action in its new and highly fraught cultural context. We can also gain a further perspective on the relationship between religious and national culture in Germany as mediated by the oratorio, since the composer was by birth neither a Protestant nor a Catholic but a Jew. The plot of the oratorio, assembled from scripture by the composer with some assistance from others, concerned the career of the Apostle Paul of Tarsus, born a Jew, who, after an early career as a persecutor of Jewish heretics (i.e., Christians), received a divine revelation on the road to Damascus and devoted the rest of his life to preaching the Gospel of Christ. (We saw a much earlier setting of this story in Chapter 8 with Heinrich Schütz's *Saul, Saul, was verfolgst du mich?*)

Felix was the grandson of Moses Mendelssohn (1729–86), the celebrated Jewish philosopher and apostle of the Enlightenment. Yet despite descent from what might be called the German-Jewish aristocracy, the composer's father, Abraham Mendelssohn, a banker, had his children baptized in 1816 to facilitate their assimilation as "emancipated Jews"—Jews who enjoyed full civil rights—into German society. (Abraham himself and his wife converted to Protestantism in 1822, after his mother's death, and signaled the fact by adding the Christian surname Bartholdy to the family name; the composer is often called Felix Mendelssohn-Bartholdy, which is the way he usually identified himself.) Mendelssohn's oratorio could thus be viewed as an allegory not only of the composer's own career but of his family history as well.

Paulus might also be viewed as an allegory of the German nation, thanks to its chorales. This was not the first time chorales had played a symbolic role in a work by Mendelssohn. In 1829, right after his epochal performance of the St. Matthew Passion, he had accepted a commission for a symphony, now known as the "Reformation," meant to be performed the next year in commemoration of the three-hundredth anniversary of the Augsburg Confession, which marked the official beginning of German Protestantism as a genuine "-ism." Traditional Lutheran music figures in various parts of the "Reformation" Symphony, which ends with an impressive chorale fantasia on Luther's hymn "Ein' feste Burg" ("A Mighty Fortress"). By Mendelssohn's time, chorales had become increasingly common in secular instrumental pieces where they sometimes appear at a culminating moment, such as in the finale of Mendelssohn's Piano Trio in C Minor, Op. 66. As the chorale became more common in instrumental music, composers tended to use not famous existing melodies but, rather, the generic musical textures and gestures of chorale writing. One can therefore go searching a very long time for a source tune before realizing that the composer invented it. If composers could manufacture their own folk songs, why not their own chorales as well?

Nation trumped even religion as a definer of human community, and the chorale became for all intents and purposes a brand of spiritual folklore.

The chief chorale in *Paulus* is "Wachet auf, ruft uns die Stimme" ("Sleepers, awake a voice is calling"), on which J. S. Bach had based one of his most famous cantatas (BWV 140). It was a keen choice for an oratorio about receiving God's call and spreading God's truth. The presence of the tune is felt from the beginning. The overture is in effect a prelude and fugue for a traditional brass-heavy festival orchestra. The chorale melody first appears slowly and straightforwardly harmonized in the prelude and then, stripped down to its first line, as a motto-style cantus firmus sounding in counterpoint, mainly in the winds, against the working out of the fugue, mainly in the strings. The climax comes with the regaining of the prelude's major mode and the full statement of the chorale in massed winds against continuing rushing figuration in the strings.

The last chorale setting in *Paulus* is the most significant both symbolically and musically. Here Paul, having found his true calling, is addressing the Heathen, who have just mistaken him and his miracle-performing companion, Barnabas, for the gods Jupiter and Mercury. He rebukes them for their idolatry, preaching that "God does not reside in temples made by human hands." Instead, he exhorts them, "You yourselves are God's temple, and the Spirit of God dwells in you." These words are then illustrated by Mendelssohn in a remarkable exchange between St. Paul and the chorus. Paul sings, "But our God is in heaven; he creates all according to his will" to a melody that is not a chorale but, rather, a simple tune of a type that can be plausibly transferred to a crowd of heathen "folks." When they take up the refrain, however, the second sopranos sing the chorale melody "We all believe in one God," the tune to which Luther's translation of the Nicene Creed had been sung since the earliest Lutheran hymnbooks. The whole first verse of the Lutheran creed passes in review, enshrined in an oratorio given its first performance before an audience largely made up of Catholics, to consecrate an ideal of national religious union. This vividly demonstrates the link that German Romanticism had forged among language, folk, and "spirit" in the name of Nation. Through his ostensibly sacred work, Mendelssohn emerges as perhaps the nineteenth century's most important and successful civic musician.

Nationalism Takes a Racial Turn

One measure of Mendelssohn's prominent public stature was the enthusiastically approving view of him in the Leipzig press, at once the most influential and the most partisan in Germany, if not in all of Europe. Writing in the old and respectable *Allgemeine musikalische Zeitung*, Carl Ferdinand Becker declared in 1842 that Mendelssohn's works and deeds could be "only contemplated, never criticized." Yet in September 1850, less than three years after Mendelssohn's death, an article appeared in the *Neue Zeitschrift für Musik* (by then no longer edited by Schumann) that set in motion a backlash against him from which his reputation has yet to recover fully.

The article, signed K. Freigedank ("K. Free-thought"), was entitled "Das Judenthum in der Musik" (Judaism in Music) and made the claim that Jews, being not merely culturally or religiously but biologically—that is, racially—distinct from gentile Christians, could not contribute to gentile musical traditions but only dilute them. There could be no such thing as assimilation, only mutually corrupting mixture. A Jew might become a Christian by converting, as Mendelssohn had done, but never a true gentile, hence never a true German. The inclusive nationalism from which Mendelssohn benefited during his lifetime became an increasingly racialist, exclusive nationalism. A religion may be changed or shed, as a culture may be embraced or renounced. A race, however, is essential, immutable, and organic. A nationalism based on race is no longer synonymous with patriotism. It has become obsessed not with culture but with nature. Thus, for the author of "Judaism in Music," even Mendelssohn's undoubted genius could not save him from what he viewed as the pitfalls of his race. He could not "call forth in us that deep, that heart-searching effect which we await from Music," because his art has no "genuine fount of life amid the folk" and can therefore only be "reflective," never "instinctive."[11]

Through his ostensibly sacred work, Mendelssohn emerges as perhaps the nineteenth century's most important and successful civic musician.

The highest level to which Mendelssohn's Jewish spirit could aspire and achieve authentic emotional expression was the "soft and mournful resignation" found in his piano pieces, where the author of the article affected to discern a genuine and moving response to the composer's own consciousness of his racial inadequacy. He could not write an opera; oratorios—"sexless opera-embryos"—did not make the grade. Finally, the author warned, Germany's acceptance of this musician as in effect its musical president was only the most obvious sign of the "be-Jewing" (*Verjüdung*) of the nation in the name of Enlightened liberality.[12] The Jewish influence would have to be thrown off if the nation were to achieve organic greatness, its heroic destiny.

With such contents, which in our time can only be regarded with disgust, this article would hardly be worth quoting in this book but for three factors that conspired to make it a force to be reckoned with, in Mendelssohn's day and in ours. In the first place, the article is the most vivid symptom to be found in musical writings of a change in the nature of nationalism that modern historians now recognize as a major crux in the history of modern Europe. Second, it paints a picture of Mendelssohn that has remained influential even after its motives have been forgotten, owing to the radical opposition it constructs between conservatism (stemming, in this case, from Bach) and revolutionary progressivism (stemming from Beethoven) as historical forces. This dubious opposition, originating in ugly politics, has nevertheless remained a basic tenet of music historiography and a strong influence on composition ever since the middle of the nineteenth century.

Third and most immediately consequential: As readers may have guessed given the similarity to the attack on Meyerbeer discussed in the previous chapter, and as he himself revealed in 1869 when the article was reprinted under the author's true name, "K. Freigedank" turned out to be Richard Wagner, a fellow native Leipziger, just four years younger than Mendelssohn, who would shortly become one of the towering figures in music history. Wagner's words achieved an almost scriptural authority for his many followers, and he was, together with Beethoven, probably the most potent single influence on succeeding generations of European composers.

Schumann made holy battle with what he viewed as the pedestrian, commercial, unoriginal music that he thought characterized the "Philistines."

Schumann and Literature

Robert Schumann was born in 1810, a year after his friend Mendelssohn, a few months after Chopin, and just a year before Liszt (Fig. 20-7). He did not come from a musical background but, rather, a literary one: His father was a writer, translator, publisher, and book dealer. Alone among his siblings, Schumann went off to university in Leipzig, a much bigger and more important city than his native Zwickau. Initially he studied law, but that held considerably less interest for him than literature, music, and rather heavy student-life socializing.

Despite getting a late start, Schumann hoped to make his career as a pianist, and he was fortunate that Friedrich Wieck (1785–1873), one of the leading piano instructors, agreed to teach him. Wieck's star student was his own daughter, Clara Wieck (1819–96; Fig. 20-8), the prodigy already mentioned in the previous chapter in connection with Liszt's legendary 1838 concerts in Vienna and who over her long life would emerge as a powerful musical force in Europe. After years of dispute with her father, many nasty intrigues, and even legal battles, she married Schumann, nine years her senior, in September 1840, the day before her twenty-first birthday.

Schumann began as a would-be virtuoso of the new school, inspired by Paganini, some of whose caprices he arranged for piano around the same time as Liszt did. His pianistic ambitions ended soon after he turned twenty when he injured his right hand. With a performing career thwarted, he turned to composition and to writing passionate music criticism, some of it directed against the virtuoso life he had so recently been forced to abandon. In one of his early reviews in the *Neue Zeitschrift für Musik*, he warned creative artists of the "poisoned flowers"—the temptations—in their path, namely "the applause of the vulgar crowd and the fixed gaze of sentimental women."[13]

Figure 20-7 Robert Schumann. Portrait by Carl Jäger.

Schumann made holy battle with what he viewed as the pedestrian, commercial, unoriginal music that he thought characterized the "Philistines," a word that harked back to the biblical enemies of the Israelites, God's "chosen people." The term can readily be applied to the opponents of any chosen, or self-chosen, group. In the early

Figure 20-8 The young Clara Schumann, while still Clara Wieck (Vienna, 1838).

nineteenth century the name was used by artists imbued with the ideals of Romanticism to target those perceived to be their enemies, namely, the materialistic crowd, indifferent to culture and content with commonplace entertainment. Such thinking exposes a tension within Romanticism because that general public was now the primary source of support for artists. By the time, for example, that Schumann wrote a famous comparison of Meyerbeer's *Les Huguenots* and Mendelssohn's *Paulus,* he had no hesitation in condemning Meyerbeer's base motives, when the only evidence for that baseness was his success with "the masses."

It was in his almost novelistic music criticism that Schumann explicated his aesthetic views. His reviews often took the form of narratives, little stories for which he invented a fictional group called the *Davidsbund* (League of David). This gang of idealistic musicians, based on sides of his own personality, fought the Goliaths of the Philistine press and the routines of academic musical training at conservatories that fostered stylistic uniformity and conservatism. Schumann devised a cast of characters that included Florestan and Eusebius, his alter egos. The former, named after Beethoven's imprisoned freedom fighter in *Fidelio,* represented his embattled "innermost I," a concept we have associated with German Romanticism from its Beethovenian beginning. Florestan is extroverted, impulsive, and excitable. Eusebius, on the other hand, represented Schumann's kinder, gentler, more moderate and sensitive nature. A third regular character, Master Raro (the name apparently combines Schumann's own with Clara's: claRA-RObert), was associated with Friedrich Wieck. Thus we have a virtual Freudian psychoanalytic trinity: the instinctually driven, rash, and reckless Florestan (id), the milder, more sociable Eusebius (ego), and the judgmental Raro (superego). Some of Schumann's reviews consist not of a direct critique but of a reported conversation within this League of David—a public airing of private responses.

Music of Letters

Until 1841 Schumann primarily composed keyboard character pieces and songs, both private genres in which Schubert had set the standard. For most of his life Schumann kept a diary, and in 1828, at age eighteen, he noted Schubert's death with sadness.[14] He was indeed very conscious of Schubert as a forebear—exceptionally so for the time, when most German composers sought preceptors chiefly in Beethoven and, more recently, in Bach and were striving to build a national repertory in the public forms of symphony, opera, and oratorio. Schumann also venerated the great Bs, Bach and Beethoven (and helped discover another—Brahms). He later emulated them in his own large orchestral and choral works, which he wrote with increasing frequency as his career progressed.

At the outset, though, in his League of David period, Schumann was among the few who found special inspiration in Schubert, in whom he saw a sort of musical novelist. In a letter to Friedrich Wieck, Schumann compared Schubert directly to the popular Romantic novelist Johann Paul Friedrich Richter (1763–1825), who wrote under the pseudonym Jean Paul. The comparison is especially revealing because Schumann is known to have been inspired in some of his early piano pieces by works of Jean Paul, especially *Flegeljahre* (Years of Indiscretion, 1804–05), a long *Bildungsroman,* or coming-of-age novel, with which many young Romantics ardently identified. Schumann's own identification with this novel was such that he consciously modeled the personalities of his imaginary alter-ego friends, Florestan and Eusebius, on the twin brothers Walt and Vult, the novel's joint heroes.

If literary music was Schumann's ideal, he could have found no better model for it than Jean Paul's musically inspired literature. Jean Paul was a skilled amateur pianist who habitually put himself in the mood to write by improvising at the keyboard. Thus, music of a particular free-flowing style congenial to the Romantic temperament may even have helped the writer find his unusual and fascinating literary voice, with its apparently meandering, erratically digressive manner. This may have been what Schumann meant when he wrote to Wieck that "when I play Schubert, it is as though I were reading a composed novel of Jean Paul." What was most remarkable in Schubert, he went on, was his "psychological" quality: "What a diary is to others, in which they set down their momentary feelings, etc., music paper really was to Schubert, to which he entrusted his every mood, and his whole soul, musical through-and-through, wrote notes where others use words."[15]

The mutually reinforcing activities between Schumann the composer and Schumann the critic are apparent in a review he wrote of eighteen Schubert dances, Op. 33, in which he (in the guise of Florestan) invents a narrative of a masked ball that connects these otherwise-independent pieces to which Schubert had himself given no titles or program: "No. 1 in A Major. A crowd of masks, drums, trumpets, an extinguisher, a man in a wig: 'Everything seems to work out perfectly.' No. 2. A comic figure, scratching its ear, and whispering 'Pst! Pst!' Disappears. No. 3 Harlequin with his hand on his hips; exits with somersault."[16] And so forth. We encounter the same narrative inclination in one of Schumann's own earliest piano works, *Papillons*, Op. 2, composed between 1829 and 1832. This collection of twelve interconnected pieces or fragments is also largely cast as dances for a masked ball occurring in Jean Paul's *Flegeljahre*.

Schumann thus often created literary music without words. Yet even if words do not figure concurrently in his piano music, they are nonetheless often present in the form of titles, epigraphs, textual allusions, and so on. He looked not just to the content of literature but also, in fascinating ways, to the very mechanisms of the book as an object and an ideal. He often gave his pieces titles, section (or "chapter") headings, prologues, and epilogues—all of a distinctly bookish nature. One set of piano pieces carries an autobiographical title—*Davidsbündlertänze*, or Dances of the League of David—in which the individual pieces were "signed" by Florestan and Eusebius. He called another set of eight pieces "Novelettes," Op. 21, and his works were sometimes serialized, that is, released gradually over time, as was common practice with popular novels of the period.

Schumann was a "man of letters" who wrote "music of letters," beginning with his "Abegg" Variations, Op. 1, which encode by spelling out the name of a fictionalized countess named Abegg. The most famous instance of musical spelling is found in *Carnaval*, Op. 9 (1833–34), which is subtitled "scènes mignonnes sur quatre notes" (cute scenes on four notes). In fact, Schumann uses five notes (A, A♭, B, C, E♭) to spell part of his own name (SCH) and the town of Asch, where his girlfriend of the time came from. (In German practice E♭ is associated with the letter S and B natural with H.) *Carnaval*, a collection of twenty pieces, includes a large cast of characters, among them fictional ones from the *commedia dell'arte* (Arlequin, Pierrot, Coquette), as well as Schumann's critical personas Florestan and Eusebius, and some of his contemporaries, among them Clara Wieck, Paganini, and Chopin. The sixth piece, "Florestan," briefly alludes to his earlier Op. 2, at which point he marks in the score "Papillons?" Schumann's music is filled with ciphers, codes, and allusions of the most esoteric and private nature, often intended, it seems, for Clara, to whom he wanted to send secret messages.

Some of Schumann's early piano compositions are made up of fragmentary sections linked together in imaginative ways. The great German writer Friedrich von Schlegel (1772–1829) called attention to the Romantic mystique of the fragment: "Many of the works of the ancients have become fragments." He then added: "Many of the works of the moderns are fragments as soon as they are written."[17] This may sound like a complaint, but Schlegel heartily approved. His love of fragments is closely related to Schumann's obsession with unconsummated gestures, withheld information, secrets, and the rest. The notion of a fragment demands that the beholder relate it to something larger yet absent, to be supplied by an engaged imagination. The beholder, in other words, must add something. Music's hold on our imaginations comes not (or not only) from what the composer puts in but from what we ourselves are forced to contribute before we can take anything out.

"The aesthetics of one art is that of the others too; only the materials differ."
—Robert Schumann

The broad range of devices Schumann drew from literature and books should be thought of as part of his works rather than as an "extramusical" expendable or a mere concession to "unmusical" listeners. He never intended any strict conceptual segregation among the arts, and in fact he abhorred such distinctions. He was committed to the view, as he once put it, that "the aesthetics of one art is that of the others too; only the materials differ."[18]

Schumann's *Fantasie*, Op. 17

Anthology Vol 2-42
Full CD IV, 32
Concise CD II, 30

To savor the experience of literary music, we may consider Schumann's *Fantasie*, Op. 17, a major piano composition from his freshest, most idealistic period. It is a monumental three-movement work composed mainly in 1836 and dedicated to Liszt; in everything but name it is a sonata on the heroic Beethovenian scale. Between 1832 and 1838, Schumann wrote three actual piano sonatas, and indeed one of the early working titles of the *Fantasie* itself was *Grosse Sonate für das Pianoforte* (Grand Sonata for Piano).

The change in title was dictated by the concept of literary music, or rather by Schumann's sensitivity to its implications. Like his character pieces but unlike the other sonatas, this one from the outset carried a heavy cargo of literary ideas. The first movement was drafted in the early summer of 1836 as an independent composition called *Ruines: Fantasie pour le Pianoforte*. The work was temporarily renamed Sonata by late fall, when it picked up its additional two movements. In this form it was envisioned as a memorial to Beethoven, inspired by the news that a committee had been formed in Bonn to raise funds for the erection of a monument at the composer's birthplace. Schumann's rather optimistic idea was to contribute the proceeds from the sale of a hundred copies of his sonata to the project, but the monument foundered until Liszt later rescued it years later.

In December 1836, Schumann proposed the piece to a prospective publisher under the name *Grosse Sonate f. d. Pianoforte für Beethovens Denkmal* (Grand Piano Sonata for Beethoven's Monument) and listed the three movements as "Ruinen/Trophäen/Palmen" (Ruins, Trophies, Palms). The titles of the new movements were intended in their original, ancient Greek meanings, which resonated both with the antique aura of reverence suggested by the first movement and with the idea of the Beethoven monument. Trophies were memorials (war spoils displayed on pillars) erected in commemoration of victory, the most "Beethovenian" of all concepts; "palms" were the ceremonial palm branches awarded at victory celebrations.

To this Schumann now added an epigraph from Schlegel's poem, "Die Gebüsche" ("The Bushes"). It has been suggested that Schumann knew these lines not from the original poem directly but only from Schubert's setting of it, to which the music of the *Fantasie*'s final movement briefly alludes.[19] Famous both as a Romantic philosopher and as a scholar, Schlegel was the author of *Die Griechen und Römer* (The Greeks and Romans), a long-standing survey of classical civilization, and he wrote lyric poetry as well. The range of his interests and writings, in other words, ran the gamut of moods in the *Fantasie*, from the most public and monumental to the most inward, even secret. The epigraph tantalizingly invokes the latter, in a fashion reminiscent of the other unfulfilled gestures encountered in Schumann's literary music:

Durch alle Töne tönet	Through all the sounds
Im bunten Erdentraum	In the motley dream of earthly life
Ein leiser Ton gezogen	There sounds a soft, long drawn-out sound
Für den, der heimlich lauschet.	For the one who overhears in secret.

Many have guessed at the identity of this secret sound; one can never know for sure. But what made the "Ruins" fantasy an apt basis for the Beethoven tribute to begin with was the fact that it already contained a secret quotation from Beethoven, to which Schumann added others, even more veiled and less definite, when he came to write "Trophies" and "Palms." As usual, he toyed a good deal with the titles and headings. Before the work was printed he made a wholesale substitution, in which only the heading of the first movement survived: *Dichtungen: Ruinen, Siegesbogen, Sternbild* (Poems: Ruins, Triumphal Arch, Constellation). Then at the very last minute, when the music was already in proofs, Schumann suffered cold feet, changed *Dichtungen* back to *Fantasie*, and dropped the rest, even "Ruins," the original motivating image.

This is quite a stew of representation and allusion, enigma and erasure, and the more we know of the work's history the thicker the stew becomes. There are some who would claim that Schumann's right to withdraw the titles should be respected and that they should not be divulged lest they unduly influence, hence constrain, a listener's understanding. Such a view accords with Schumann's own criticism of Berlioz's program for the *Symphonie fantastique*. The chance that listeners might think of the titles as constraints was probably what dissuaded Schumann from publishing them, even though he kept Schlegel's epigraph.

But in fact Schumann did not mean to withdraw the titles entirely. His actual direction to the publisher was to replace each title with an asterism—three stars in triangular formation (thus: ⁂), a device often used in nineteenth-century typography to signal an omission, frequently the name of an anonymous author, or a dedicatee. Obviously, there is a huge difference between simply omitting a title (which may as well never have existed as far as the reader is concerned) and signaling its omission. To do the latter is to challenge the reader to guess it or to invent one. A new question is posed. Nothing is removed from the stew. Indeed, the stew only thickens with the revelation that something, presumably something private, is being concealed. The listener is invited to be involved, asked to speculate, rendered receptive and alert.

The posthumous publication of Schumann's private correspondence added a great many interpretive possibilities. In 1838 he had written to Clara Wieck, his then-distant beloved, that the original "Ruins" fantasy was conceived as "a deep lament for you," implying that it was his own life that lay in ruins because her father refused even to let them talk, let alone marry. A year later, after the whole *Fantasie* had been published, he wrote to her that in order to understand it, "you will have to transport yourself into the unhappy summer of 1836, when I renounced you." A couple of months after that, he wrote, "Aren't *you* the 'tone' in the motto? I almost think so."[20]

Autobiography may not so much definitively explain a piece as help indicate its sources of inspiration.

We should not feel that this provides a complete solution to the piece. Autobiography may not so much definitively explain a piece as help indicate its sources of inspiration. Berlioz, as we saw, was more forthcoming about divulging the connection between his music and his life, although he too was ambivalent at times. In any case, there is one spot near the end of the first movement of the *Fantasie* on which every interpretive thread in the foregoing discussion can converge, and that is the spot marked *Adagio* (m. 299ff), which turns out to be a variant of the opening/closing song in Beethoven's song cycle *An die ferne Geliebte* (To the Distant Beloved). That, of course, *was* Clara in 1836. But it was also a Beethoven "ruin," a disfigured fragment from the Beethoven composition that, perhaps more than any other, contained a poignant message for the composer of the *Fantasie.*

The passage has a poignant resonance for the music's listener, too, whether or not the listener is aware of any autobiographical resonances, for the music is contrived in such a way that the whole movement up to the point of recall seems to function as a gigantic upbeat to it. And here is the most decisive reason why the piece had to be renamed *Fantasie,* even after "Grand Sonata" and "Poems" had been tried out. "We are accustomed to judge a thing from the name it bears," Schumann had written in 1835 in the pages of the *Neue Zeitschrift für Musik.* "We make certain demands upon a fantasy, others upon a sonata."[21] As we know from other fantasies going back as far as C. P. E. Bach in the 1750s, an unstable key structure is perhaps their most conspicuous shared characteristic. What a sonata normally announces at the outset—a firmly settled, cadential establishment of the tonic—arrives only later in a fantasy and sometimes not until the end. That is what we expect in a fantasy or, as Schumann would say, what we demand from it.

The beginning of "Ruins" is marked "to be played in an extravagant and passionate manner throughout." There can be no doubt that the turbulent opening swirl, consisting of a root, fifth, seventh, and ninth, is expressing a dominant function, "longing" extravagantly and passionately for the tonic, which after many detours in fact does not happen unequivocally until the allusion to *An die ferne Geliebte* makes its tranquil, consoling C-major close. This allusion functions as the single consummation toward which the entire movement has been striving, both thematically and harmonically. Most of the main themes in the first movement are related motivically (if sometimes indirectly) to *An die ferne Geliebte.* Seeing the whole movement in this light accords even better with the motto from Schlegel, which speaks of a tone sounding "throughout," not just at the end. What is provided at the close is not a new idea but a synthesis: the simplest, most concentrated possible statement of ideas that up to that point have been presented in a diffuse and complicated manner, with varied or even contradictory implications. The quotation from Beethoven is no longer merely a quotation—that is, something brought in from outside—but the realization of impulses from within and their reconciliation.

As early as 1794, when the idea of the "aesthetic" was new and Romanticism was young, poet Friedrich Schiller commented on the need for this act of completion on the part of the beholder and the way in which it enriches the experience of art when he wrote: "The real and express content that the poet puts in his work remains always finite; the possible content that he allows us to contribute is an infinite quality."[22] By "poet," of course, Schiller meant to include all artists, and he surely meant to imply that all art forms invite the subjective contribution of the reader, viewer, or listener. Romantic artists who wished most fully to realize Schiller's idea were the ones most inclined to leave important things deliberately unsaid—to make the receiver of the art even more of a participant in the creation of meaning. Among composers it was Schumann, with his allusions, codes, and boundlessly varied unconsummated gestures, who sought this collaboration between creator and audience to the highest and most principled degree. That is what the notion of "literary music," in the profoundest sense, meant.

Schumann's "Year of Song"

Although he had written works in a variety of genres during his teens and twenties, all of Schumann's first twenty-three published opuses were piano pieces, many of which evolved from improvisations at the keyboard. Throughout his career he would become intensely preoccupied with writing in certain genres and would concentrate, sometimes for more than a year at a time, on producing little else. Piano compositions dominated until 1840, the year he married Clara, during which he devoted himself almost entirely to song. The next year turned out to be Schumann's "symphony year," when he composed two of his four mature works in the genre, as well as other orchestral music. He devoted 1842 primarily to writing chamber music, 1843 to oratorio, and 1848 mostly to dramatic music.

During 1840, the "year of song," as Schumann himself called it, he wrote nearly 150, an abundance that is somewhat surprising given that he had previously disparaged the genre. Not long before he had told a colleague: "All my life I have considered vocal composition inferior to instrumental music—I have never regarded it as great art." But his tune changed eight months later when he confessed, "I write nothing but songs now, long and short. . . . I can hardly tell you how delightful it is to write for the voice, in comparison with instrumental composition, and how agitated and excited I am when I sit down to work."[23] Or stand—as he told Clara, "I mostly compose [songs] standing or walking around, not at the piano. It is an entirely different kind of music, which does not come first through my fingers but much more directly and melodiously."[24] Indeed, Schumann began most of his Lieder by writing just the vocal melody, adding the piano accompaniment later. He also produced song cycles, which emulated Schubert's achievement so successfully that it is fair to call Schumann's the only ones that truly rival his predecessor's in stature and in frequency of performance. Five of his cycles were written in the great "song year" (Fig. 20-9).

Figure 20-9 Robert and Clara Schumann. Daguerreotype by Johann Anton Völlner (Hamburg, March 1850).

Songs offered Schumann yet another musical arena in which to engage with literature, and he set many of the greatest poets of his time. He was particularly attracted to Heinrich Heine and his *Buch der Lieder* (Book of Songs). This anthology contained a previously published collection the poet called the "Lyric Intermezzo": sixty-six brief lyrics and a prologue. Initially, Schumann probably intended to set all the poems, but after reaching number eight he became selective, although he still ended with the final poem (No. 66). He worked rapidly and in just nine days, beginning on 24 May 1840, composed twenty songs. By the time the song cycle was published, four years later, it was titled *Dichterliebe* (Poet's Love), Op. 48, and four of the original songs had been cut.

Anthology Vol 2-43
Full CD IV, 33–34
Concise CD II, 31–32

Dichterliebe is the outstanding product of 1840, Schumann's year of long-deferred marital bliss. Heine's lyrics trace the most dismal emotional trajectory imaginable, a painful saga of unrequited love. Dismal, yes, but not tragic, the way Schubert's *Die schöne Müllerin* is tragic, for the cycle ends not with suicide but (as Heine tells us) with renunciation and (as Schumann tells us) with eventual healing. Heine was a master of emotional ambivalence, and that made him the perfect partner for Schumann.

The first song, *Im wunderschönen Monat Mai* (In the lovely month of May), is an especially good candidate for supposing autobiographical implications from lived experience, since it concerns longing that is felt during the very month in which Schumann, then longing for union with Clara, is known to have composed the song. A question, though: Exactly what difference does it make to the listener to know these facts? Whatever our response—whatever the "source" of the emotion expressed in the song (whether Schumann's life, Heine's life, or that of the fictional "poet" of the title)—the task of the literary musician remains the same: to find a musical embodiment of the emotion that will complement and intensify the verbal one, thus to arouse a sympathetic vibration in the listener.

Schumann's harmonic moves in this opening song create extraordinary tension and delay resolution. In its continual refusal to settle on a clear tonality, the entire song prolongs a single unconsummated harmonic gesture—expressed most dramatically by the piano's forever-oscillating, never-cadencing ritornello—that complements the words. The final line, "my longing and desire," has the last word in a profoundly musical sense, made palpable by the very last note in the song—a B that in context functions as an unresolved seventh. After it dies away, the air tingles with the longing and desire it has created, symbolized, and embodied.

Songs offered Schumann yet another musical arena in which to engage with literature, and he set many of the greatest poets of his time.

Of course this is only the first song in a cycle of sixteen. We can hope that resolution and consummation will come in the next song. That deferral of satisfaction is not only an emotional but also an aesthetic plus: The unresolved seventh demands that the cycle continue, heightening the sense of "organic" unity that binds it into an artistic whole transcending the sum of its parts. The listener's imagination is called on again, even more urgently and explicitly, at the very end of *Dichterliebe*. The last song (No. 16)—in which the love born at the beginning of the cycle, having died, is buried—is bitter and angry, a rant. The singer mocks his own grief with a parody of a merry song and puffs it up with hyperbolic comparisons between love's coffin and the most enormous things he can think of (beer casks, bridges, and cathedrals). Only at the end does the mood begin to soften, as the voice drops out (as usual, on an unconsummated harmony) before the change of mood is consummated. It is transferred first to the music in the piano, where we are at first surprised to hear a reprise of the postlude from an earlier song in the cycle (No. 12).

But then we are more than surprised; we may even be confused to hear what sounds like another song start up, this time without the singer. This extra song is short but, unlike many of the actual songs in the cycle, melodically and harmonically complete. It does not allude to any previous song in the cycle. The texture certainly suggests words, or at least meanings, which we must supply in our imagination, influenced by the sensuous qualities of the music as well as by our own "take" on the situations conveyed by the whole cycle to this point. It is therefore not just the listener's imagination that is engaged but also the listener's subjectivity, meaning the listener's own unique combination of experience and inclination.

Schumann's Last Years

By the time Schumann was in his mid-thirties he gave up writing criticism and editing the *Neue Zeitschrift für Musik* and turned increasingly to working on large-scale compositional projects. In the 1840s he threw himself wholeheartedly into dramatic ventures that gave another kind of outlet for his love of literature, beginning with a popularly acclaimed oratorio, *Das Paradies und die Peri* (Paradise and the Peri, 1843), and *Szenen aus Goethes Faust* (Scenes from Goethe's Faust, 1844–53). Immediately after completing his lone opera, *Genoveva*, in 1848, Schumann tackled Lord Byron's semiautobiographical poem *Manfred*, which, Schumann told Liszt, "should not be advertised as an opera, Singspiel, or melodrama, but as a 'dramatic poem with music.'"[25]

As Schumann's career progressed, his activities became more public. His later large-scale compositions showed increasing mastery of technique but also a greater tendency to conform to public expectations. Earlier, as a hotheaded member of the League of David and a maverick journalist, he had summed up his attitude toward such expectations in a characteristically Romantic aphorism: "People say, 'It pleased,' or 'It did not please'; as if there were nothing higher than to please people!"[26] Later, as a civic music director and the head of a large family, however, Schumann inclined toward a more reserved "Classicism," as the term was then beginning to be understood.

The enigmatic literary qualities he had prized as a youth had come to trouble the composer, who was increasingly given to fits of nervous tension and melancholy that, as he noted in his diary, gave his life "an *idée fixe*: the fear of going mad."[27] This obsession made Schumann morbidly sensitive to symptoms of "irrationality" in his early output, and it even caused him to revise some of his most remarkable compositions to render them more conventional, hence less threatening to his own peace of mind. It was almost as if the Romantic conviction that his life and his work were esoterically connected gave Schumann the idea that altering the work might alter his fate. But his fears were eventually borne out: In February 1854 he tried to commit suicide by throwing himself into the Rhine River; he spent his last two years in an asylum.

The lives of composers are often popularly reduced to a single factor that shapes views of their entire existence. Beethoven was deaf, Schubert died so young, Schumann went crazy. But such factors can be given too much weight. Schumann's psychological struggles and sad end need not entirely define the image of this industrious and imaginative artist.

Figure 20-10 Fanny Mendelssohn Hensel. Engraving after an 1829 drawing by her husband, Wilhelm Hensel.

Genius Restrained: Fanny Mendelssohn Hensel and Clara Wieck Schumann

Felix Mendelssohn was not the only musical prodigy in his distinguished family. By the time he was born, his older sister, Fanny (1805–47; Fig. 20-10) had already shown signs of unusual gifts. She began piano studies in 1812, after the family had moved to Berlin, first with her mother and later with Ludwig Berger (1777–1839), the Prussian capital's most distinguished teacher. She also underwent the same training in theory and composition as her brother, with Zelter. Her first composition, a song in honor of her father's birthday, was written in 1819, when she was fourteen.

It was Fanny Mendelssohn who originated the genre "Songs without Words," at first called *Lieder für das Pianoforte* (Songs for Piano), and modeled on some lyrical etudes by Berger. She produced in excess of 500 compositions, including 250 songs, more than 125 piano works, a string quartet, a piano trio, and an orchestral overture. Her most extended works, like her brother's, were choral, written at a time when she was conducting an amateur choir that gave regular concerts in Berlin. They included two cantatas for soloists, chorus, and orchestra: *Hiob* (Job) and *Lobgesang* (Hymn of Praise), and the *Oratorium nach den Bildern der Bibel* (Oratorio on Biblical Scenes), completed along with the cantatas in 1831, the most active year of her composing career, when she was twenty-five.

Virtually none of Fanny Mendelssohn's music became known during her lifetime beyond the circle of her family and the friends who frequented her Sunday salons; and after her marriage to the painter Wilhelm Hensel and the birth of her son (Sebastian, named after Bach), she experienced a severe falling off of "the mood to compose," as she put it in a letter to Felix. Her artistic isolation and probably her creative blocks were the result of the discouragement she received, from her father and later from her brother, when it came to pursuing a career. Her father forbade her to publish her music or to perform in public lest she become ambitious and compromise the feminine virtues of "love, obedience, tolerance and resignation" on which the stability of family life depended, as he put it to her in a letter.[28]

Instead, six of her Lieder were published in 1827 and 1830 under her brother's name. Once only, after her father's death, did she appear as a concert pianist, performing a concerto by Felix at a charity affair in 1838. Only in 1846, a year before her death, when she was forty years old, did her thirty-seven-year-old brother give her permission to accept the invitation of two Berlin publishing houses to issue small albums of her Lieder and her Songs without Words. A few more publications, including an impressive piano trio, appeared at Felix's instigation after her death, so her catalogue includes eleven "opuses."

It was Fanny Mendelssohn who originated the genre "Songs without Words."

Goethe once ended a letter to the young Felix with "regards to your equally talented sister."[29] The life of Fanny Mendelssohn Hensel is compelling proof that women's failure to compete with men on the compositional playing field has been the result not of the "natural" deficiency that defenders of the status quo dependably allege but, rather, of social prejudice and patriarchal mores, which in the nineteenth century granted only men the right to make the decisions in bourgeois households. Encouragement is not the only factor here, but also the need for opportunities, especially with respect to large-scale forms. It hardly seems worthwhile writing symphonies or operas without prospects for performance, and in any case a composer partly learns how to write such pieces through the experiences of rehearsal, performance, and reception. The issue of encouragement and opportunity is especially poignant in the case of the Mendelssohns, who epitomized enlightened, emancipated, and assimilated Jewry, since Fanny's fate exposed the limits to emancipation and the internal resistance to it.

Fanny's frustrated and largely private career may be contrasted with that of Robert Schumann's wife, Clara Wieck, who proved a far more significant and public figure in nineteenth-century musical life, primarily as a performer. Cultivated in an almost Mozartean fashion by her ambitious father (who, like Leopold, also wrote a treatise on instrumental performance), she astounded audiences as a virtuoso pianist, already playing at the Gewandhaus in Leipzig at age nine. She was compared, rarely in a patronizing way but rather with genuine admiration, with the great touring pianists of the age, including Liszt and Sigismond Thalberg (1812–71).

Fanny Mendelssohn's frustrated and largely private career may be contrasted with that of Robert Schumann's wife, Clara Wieck.

She wrote nearly all of her compositions during the first part of her long musical career for her own use in performance. Her very earliest pieces tended toward flashy virtuoso fare, such as variation sets and a Piano Concerto, Op. 7, which she began writing at age thirteen and premiered in Leipzig with Mendelssohn conducting. In 1841 she and Robert joined forces on a collection of songs to poetry by Friedrich Rückert (1788–1866) originally published as *Zwölf Gedichte aus F. Rückerts Liebesfrühling für Gesang und Pianoforte von Robert und Clara Schumann* (Twelve Songs from F. Rückert's *Love's Springtime* for Voice and Piano by Robert and Clara Schumann). The passionate second song, *Er ist gekommen in Sturm und Regen* (He has come in storm and rain), one of three by Clara in the collection, has a dazzling piano part and sets a poem about a woman's union with the man she loves. The set of twelve was designated as Robert's Op. 37 and Clara's Op. 12 but published without identifying who had composed which of the individual songs, something that kept critics guessing. This joint venture realized a plan Robert had already devised before the two married and that he expressed to Clara in a June 1839 letter: "we will also publish a certain amount in *both of our names*; posterity should regard us as one heart and soul, and be unable to tell what is by you and what is by me."[30] But later that year, shortly before they married, Clara wrote in her diary:

Anthology Vol 2-44
Full CD IV, 35
Concise CD II, 33

> I once believed that I had creative talent, but I have given up this idea; a woman must not wish to compose—there never was one able to do it. Am I intended to be the one? I would be arrogant to believe that. That was something with which only my father tempted me in former days. But I gave up believing this. May Robert always create; that must always make me happy.[31]

The few pieces Clara wrote after her marriage were usually occasional ones, given as birthday and Christmas gifts. In the 1840s she was more famous than her husband and continued some concertizing to help support their growing family. But much of her time was taken with near-annual pregnancies—the couple had eight children—and tending to a high-strung, high-maintenance husband. She stopped composing entirely after Robert's death in 1856, when at age thirty-six she found herself a single mother of seven (one child had died). She performed extensively, taught, and tended to her husband's legacy. And, as we shall see, she became the crucial musical advisor to Johannes Brahms, one of the greatest composers of the second half of the century and the great heir to Mendelssohn and Schumann.

Summary

The nineteenth century saw an explosion of literacy among the middle class. As a result, literature began to influence music in new ways. More musical works were inspired by literature, philosophy, history, and autobiography. This chapter examined three composers who were especially influenced by these trends: Hector Berlioz (1803–69), Felix Mendelssohn (1809–47), and Robert Schumann (1810–56).

A central debate in the nineteenth century centered on the relative merits of "program music" and "absolute music," that is, music without a program. Berlioz's *Episode in the Life of an Artist: Symphonie fantastique* (1830, usually known simply as *Symphonie fantastique*) played an important role in this debate because it took program music to an unprecedented level, with five movements linked by a detailed scenario narrating the misfortunes of a lovelorn artist. The movements are musically unified by a melody Berlioz called an *idée fixe,* representing the beloved. *Symphonie fantastique* is also extremely innovative in its orchestration and its variety of orchestral colors. Berlioz wrote many other works inspired by literature, including operas, concert overtures, the dramatic symphony *Roméo et Juliette,* and a type of symphonic concerto, *Harold in Italy* (see Chapter 22).

Mendelssohn is often considered a more conservative composer, adhering to Classical genres and forms. He wrote five symphonies, oratorios, and much chamber music. His concert orchestral overtures, such as *A Midsummer Night's Dream,* were a new kind of music, inspired in part by literary models. In his role as a conductor, Mendelssohn promoted both earlier and newer music, starting the "Bach revival" with a performance of St. Matthew Passion. His own oratorios, such as *Paulus* (1836), use chorales, a symbol of German nationalism. Mendelssohn's choice of subject for *Paulus* had an autobiographical component, since he, like Paul, was a Jew converted to Christianity. The chorales in *Paulus* represent an inclusive kind of nationalism that transcended religion. The Protestant chorale, the Catholic audience, and the composer, a Jew, were joined together in this celebration of nationhood. Richard Wagner's virulent anti-Semitic attack on Mendelssohn, first published in 1850, represented a dark change in the nature of nationalism. Wagner depicted a nationalism based on race, in which he saw a characteristic that could never be changed or overcome by culture.

While Mendelssohn was inspired by Shakespeare and his travels in Scotland and Italy, Robert Schumann gravitated toward German literature by such authors as Jean Paul and Heinrich Heine. His piano works were deeply inspired by literature and autobiography. A set of fictional characters called the *Davidsbund* (Band of David), representing different sides of his own personality, appear both in his writings and in the programs and titles for certain piano compositions. Descriptive titles, programs both overt and private, and musical "spellings" of names abound in his works. Schumann was nevertheless ambivalent toward overt programs. For his *Fantasie,* Op. 17, he provided and withdrew different titles and epigraphs, ultimately asking the listener to puzzle out the score's extramusical meaning. Schumann devoted the whole of 1840 to producing songs, including the song cycle *Dichterliebe.*

He also produced four symphonies and many chamber works as well as oratorios and dramatic works.

Because of social prejudice and lack of encouragement, women did not reach their full potential as composers in the nineteenth century. Fanny Mendelssohn Hensel (1805–47), Felix's sister, was discouraged from publishing by her father and brother, although she composed hundreds of compositions, a few of which were published shortly before her death. Clara Wieck Schumann (1819–96), Robert's wife, was best known in her time as a virtuoso pianist and a promoter of music by her husband and by the young Johannes Brahms. Her compositions include virtuosic piano pieces, Lieder, a piano trio, and a piano concerto.

Study Questions

1. Describe the ways in which Hector Berlioz's *Symphonie fantastique* reflect Romanticism. How does it differ from symphonies you have studied in earlier chapters? In what ways is the *idée fixe* throughout the symphony? How do the program and the *idée fixe* influence the form of the work?
2. Discuss Felix Mendelssohn's treatment of literary and pictorial themes in his music.
3. Describe the significance of chorales in German music, especially in Mendelssohn's *Paulus.* In what respects is *Paulus* a nationalistic work? How would you characterize the kind of nationalism it expresses?
4. How did Richard Wagner's essay "Judaism in Music" represent a change in the nature of nationalism?
5. Describe the many ways in which Robert Schumann's music and critical writings were influenced by literature.
6. Describe Schumann's attitudes toward program music, as expressed in his own musical works and in his review of *Symphonie fantastique.*
7. How does Schumann's setting of *Dichterliebe* reflect a sensitivity to the poetry?
8. What are some reasons that women composers did not flourish fully in the nineteenth century?

Key Terms

absolute music	***idée fixe***
concert overture	**program music**

21

Music Imported and Exported

For many chapters we have concentrated almost exclusively on musical life in Germany, Austria, France, and Italy, with little or no mention of England, Spain, and far northern countries or of Eastern Europe, Russia, and the Americas. There was, of course, abundant music making going on in all these places, even if within the literate tradition much of the activity and training derived from the so-called Western mainstream we have been tracing. It is time to start filling in some of these gaps and to investigate the mutually influencing relations between the more familiar European musical heritage and those countries that first emerged as prominent forces during the nineteenth century, becoming even more powerful in the twentieth.

"Hats off, gentlemen, a genius!"[1] With these enthusiastic words Robert Schumann, making his critical debut three years before founding his own journal, welcomed Frédéric Chopin (1810–49; Fig. 21-1) into the ranks of published composers. One can only admire the clairvoyance with which one young twenty-one-year-old genius had recognized another of the same age. The work that caught Schumann's ear in 1831 was Chopin's brilliant set of variations for piano and orchestra on "Là ci darem la mano," the duet from Mozart's *Don Giovanni* on which Liszt would later base his mighty "Don Juan Fantasy." Chopin was a quite different breed of piano virtuoso than those we have seen to this point. In his music one encounters an amazing mixture of Beethovenian boldness, Schubertian inwardness, Bellinian lyricism, Lisztian dazzle, and a widely commented-on exotic color. He was a perceived outsider who spent almost his entire mature career on the inside, in the very heart of European musical life: the lively Paris of the 1830s and '40s.

Not everyone, however, shared Schumann's enthusiasm for this great new talent. Ludwig Rellstab (1799–1860), a much more powerful critic at the time, objected to what he considered Chopin's vandalizing of Mozart. He claimed that an arrangement of this kind displayed the "primitive origins of the Slavonic nations,"[2] calling attention to Chopin's alien origin. Despite his French surname, he was a Pole, baptized as Fryderyk Franciszek Chopin in Żelazowa Wola, a settlement near Warsaw, where he was born to the family of a French expatriate and a cultured Polish woman, who raised their children as Polish patriots.

Figure 21-1 Daguerreotype of Frédéric Chopin (1849).

While Polish patriotism burned brightly at the time, there was no such thing as Poland on the map (see Fig. 18-1). In 1795 the country had been swallowed up by its powerful neighbors: Russia, Prussia, and Austria. Although born in the Russian part and therefore legally a subject of the tsar, a Russian was the very last thing Chopin would have called himself. In a later review, Schumann noted wryly that if Tsar Nikolai I, who had put down a major Polish rebellion in 1831, "knew what a dangerous enemy threatened him in Chopin's works," simple and pretty as many of them were, "he would forbid this music. Chopin's works are guns buried in flowers." Chopin thus became the first major European composer we have seen to be actively touted abroad as a nationalist. "And because this nationalism is in deep mourning," Schumann wrote, alluding to Poland's tragic fate, "it attracts us all the more firmly to this thoughtful artist."[3]

It was mainly because the exiled Chopin's nationalism was oppressed that Schumann noticed it as nationalism in the first place. Although the Romanticism to which Schumann so ardently subscribed was itself very much the product of German nationalism, he did not consider himself a nationalist. He was accustomed to thinking of the values of his own nation, at least those to which he personally subscribed, as the general—the universal—values of humanity, thus professing an unwitting double standard (we now call it *ethnocentrism*) that actually helped perpetuate the oppression that Chopin's Poland faced. Schumann thought that in order for music to realize its highest aim it had to be "unmarked" by any defining, and therefore delimiting, national character. For him German music was unmarked. That is how one naturally tends to hear the music that surrounds one, until one is made aware of the existence of other music.

This ambivalence toward nationalism—as something only others possessed or professed and as something attractive but also limiting—shows very clearly through Schumann's critique of Chopin's composerly "nature" (a word that always needs quotation marks when applied to artists and art works):

> In his origin, in the fate of his country, we find the explanation of his great qualities and of his defects. When speaking of grace, enthusiasm, presence of mind, nobility, and warmth of feeling, who does not say Chopin? But also, when it is a question of oddity, morbid eccentricity, even wildness and hate. All of Chopin's earlier creations bear this impress of intense nationalism.

For Schumann, however, this was not enough for art of the first rank: "The minor interests of the soil on which he was born had to sacrifice themselves to the universal ones." Chopin's more recent compositions, Schumann incorrectly believed, were less demonstrably Polish and tended more toward that universal ideal. While he thought Chopin should not "completely disown his origin," Schumann wrote that "the further he departs from it, the greater will his significance in the world of art become."[4] Chopin himself may even have shared some of this ambivalence. He felt his Polish patriotism deeply and traded on his exotic origins when it came to promoting his career and his works in European society. But he also very consciously modeled

TIMELINE

1804 **Birth of Mikhail Ivanovich Glinka**
1810 **Birth of Frédéric Chopin**
1820 Aleksandr Pushkin, *Ruslan and Lyudmila*
1829 **Birth of Louis Moreau Gottschalk**
1830 Polish revolt against the Russian Empire
1831 **Chopin moves to Paris**
1834 **Chopin, Mazurkas, Op. 17**
1835 **Chopin, Ballade in G Minor, Op. 23**
1835 Nikolai Gogol, *Taras Bulba*
1836 **Glinka's *A Life for the Tsar* premieres**
1837 George Sand, *Mauprat*
1838–39 **Chopin, Preludes, Op. 8**
1844–45 **Gottschalk, *Bamboula***
1846–48 Mexican American War
1848 **Glinka, *Kamarinskaya***
1848 **Stephen Foster, *Oh! Susanna***
1849 **Death of Chopin**
1852 Harriet Beecher Stowe, *Uncle Tom's Cabin*
1857 **Death of Glinka**
1861–65 American Civil War
1865 **Gottschalk moves to South America**
1869 **Death of Gottschalk**

his art on a wide variety of non-Polish examples, not just on Mozart. He was influenced by John Field's piano music, owed a contrapuntal debt to Bach, and borrowed his florid melodic style from Italian bel canto opera, especially Bellini.

Chopin's Career: From Warsaw to Paris

Chopin's extraordinary gifts manifested themselves early in life and inevitably took him away from his Polish homeland, which at the time offered a musician little scope for a career. He published his first piece in 1817 at the age of seven and made his public debut with an orchestra the next year, playing a concerto by Adalbert Gyrowetz (1763–1850), an old-fashioned Bohemian composer whose Haydnesque works upheld an unmarked "universal" style. Only after finishing school in 1826 did Chopin enter the local conservatory for full-time music instruction. As a pianist he was already fully formed. His main interest was now composition, and the first piece to win him wide notice was the set of Mozart variations that Schumann so admired.

Chopin's foreign debut took place in 1829 in Vienna, where he made a fateful discovery: The audience reacted with greater interest not to his variations on Mozart with which he sought to flatter the Viennese by honoring their favorite son, but, rather, to Chopin's *Krakowiak*, Op. 14, a concert rondo based on a catchy syncopated Polish dance. As in the case of many other Eastern European composers, Chopin's style became more national as his career became more international. **Exoticism** sells, especially when presented as nationalism. It provides opportunities, but, as we have already seen from Schumann's ambivalent appreciation, it also limits and labels.

Chopin's success in Vienna gave him hopes of a stellar career like Paganini's. He returned to Warsaw, where he composed a pair of concertos (Op. 11 in E Minor and Op. 21 in F Minor) plus a *Fantasia on Polish Airs*, Op. 13, with orchestra. The concertos combined sparkling pianism with exotic appeal: Both their finales invoke the style of folk dances, and in the First Concerto the opening theme has the characteristically stilted gait of a regal **polonaise**, the national dance of Poland. Second themes in both pieces employ the texture and florid ornamentation of Field's dreamy **nocturnes** (night pieces), which Chopin would later develop into a major genre of his own. A little later, back in Vienna at the start of his first big tour, Chopin wrote a *Grande polonaise* for piano and orchestra that marked his most determined effort to win popular success on the scale of Paganini.

He never won it. Disappointed by his reception in Vienna, he canceled a scheduled Italian tour and made for London, "by way of Paris," as he put it in a letter home. After giving a few concerts en route in southern Germany, he was much distressed to receive the news of the sack of Warsaw by Tsar Nikolai's Russian army. Resolving not to return to Poland until it was free, Chopin arrived in the French capital in September 1831. The vibrant cosmopolitan life of Paris, then in the first flush of Louis Philippe's July Monarchy, appealed to Chopin, as it did to Rossini, Berlioz, Liszt, and so many other early Romantics, as the cultural capital of the nineteenth century. After a brilliant debut on 26 February 1832, at which he played his F Minor Concerto and his Mozart Variations, Chopin found himself a social lion amid the bourgeois elite. Patronage came his way from the Rothschilds, a prominent family of European bankers. Prestigious hostesses showered him with invitations to grace their salons, and his appearances there made him the most sought-after piano teacher in the city. Henceforth Chopin was able to renounce the concert hall. From 1838 until 1848, when forced back onstage by material need, he shunned public performance.

During this period Chopin communicated with a larger audience through publication. He became friendly with Liszt, Berlioz, Meyerbeer, and Bellini and with literary figures such as Heine, Honoré de Balzac (1799–1850), and fellow émigré Adam Mickiewicz (1798–1855), the Polish national poet. He met the painter Eugène Delacroix, who produced a famous portrait of him in 1838 that now hangs in the Louvre Museum (Fig. 21-2). In 1838 he began a ten-year liaison with the writer George Sand (her real name was Aurore Dudevant; Fig. 21-3), who made veiled references to him in her novels and with whom he wintered rather scandalously at Majorca, the Spanish island resort, in 1839. Beginning that year, Chopin spent his summers, and did most of his composing, at Sand's baronial estate at Nohant, about 180 miles south of Paris. In the city, he lived in luxurious seclusion. (A charming fictional treatment of his life with Sand, Liszt, Delacroix, and others is James Lapine's 1991 film *Impromptu*.)

Figure 21-2 Portrait of Chopin by Eugène Delacroix (1838).

Given the significance of his work in the 1830s and '40s and the aspirations it embodied, the final chapter of Chopin's life was a sad tale. His affair with Sand ended in 1847, the result of envious intrigues by her children, leaving him depressed and disinclined to work. The next year saw the outbreak of revolution throughout much of Europe and the immediate effect for Chopin was interruption of his income from teaching. He was forced to reside in England, where he again became the darling of fashionable society. He stayed there for eight months, returning in November to Paris; his longstanding tuberculosis claimed his life less than a year later. He died surrounded by fellow Poles, including his sister, who had come from Warsaw to be by his bedside. Chopin was buried in Père Lachaise Cemetery, near the graves of Cherubini and Bellini, after a funeral attended by some 3,000 mourners at which Mozart's Requiem was sung. Before burial, however, his heart was removed for his sister to take back "home" to Warsaw, and later some soil from "home" was brought to Paris to be placed on his grave. An intruder from an alien terrain, Chopin had captivated and mystified contemporaries with a strange fascination and then wasted mysteriously away, dying of the most Romantic of diseases.

The Pinnacle of Salon Music

Moving as he did in rarefied social echelons open to few musicians, Chopin cultivated an extremely refined manner that was reflected directly in the style of both his performances and his compositions. It was reported that many of Chopin's compositions began as improvisations that he later struggled to write down. Although his notation is meticulous, his music continued to evolve in performance as long as he played it, and his manuscripts abound in variants that make them an adventurous player's paradise but an editor's nightmare. Having withdrawn from public performance, Chopin had no further need of the orchestra or indeed of any playing partners. After 1831 nearly all his works would be piano solos; the only exceptions were a handful of songs to Polish texts and a cello sonata, one of his last compositions, written out of friendship with the cellist Auguste Franchomme (1808–84).

Figure 21-3 Portrait of George Sand by Eugène Delacroix (1838).

Chopin took great satisfaction that the public regarded him primarily as a creative artist rather than a virtuoso. Most impressive was the respect shown him by other great pianists of his day, many of whom featured his works on their own concerts. (Liszt and Clara Wieck both championed his music.) The ability to play Chopin "idiomatically" is still a qualifying yardstick for a concert pianist to this day. And what is idiomatic? One of the crucial performance practice matters in this regard concerns *tempo rubato*, or "stealing time." If Chopin's own description is applied, it would appear to mean a slight delay of the melody with respect to the bass, probably not to be righted until the next downbeat. Chopin was one of the first to use the word **rubato** as a performance direction, rather than relying only on traditional directions for tempo modification like *accelerando*, *ritenuto*, and so forth, or else indicating its effect with melodic ties and syncopations.

Chopin's preludes are vividly if enigmatically expressive performance pieces, although in an "improvisatory" style, a prelude to everything and nothing.

Chopin strayed furthest beyond the boundaries of what contemporaries thought normal in two mature sonatas, in B♭ Minor, Op. 35 (published in 1840), and in B Minor, Op. 58 (published in 1845). It was precisely the failure or unwillingness to reckon with the expected obligations of genre that made these sonatas hard for contemporaries to understand. Confronted with the Sonata in B♭ Minor, Schumann expressed bemusement: "The idea of calling it a sonata is a caprice, if not a jest, for he has simply bound together four of his wildest children, to smuggle them under this name into a place to which they could not else have penetrated."[5] Schumann was exaggerating. The piece is not that weird. It has a first movement that is recognizably in sonata form, a scherzo with trio, and a famous slow movement cast, like the one in Beethoven's *Eroica* Symphony, as a funeral march. The brief final presto, played *sotto voce* throughout, is indeed a wild child, unique and practically indescribable: a *moto perpetuo* all in octaves except for the last chord.

Chopin wrote only three sonatas altogether. His piano works consist overwhelmingly of character pieces: twenty-one nocturnes, twenty-seven études (literally technical studies but actually virtuoso concert works), twenty-six preludes, four ballades, four rondos, four scherzos, and four impromptus (including a "Fantaisie-impromptu"). Several one-of-a-kind items were composed late in his career: a *Fantaisie* (1841), a *Berceuse*, or lullaby (1844), and a *Barcarolle* (1846). Dances, however, account for most of his output: sixteen polonaises, twenty waltzes, and sixty-one mazurkas, written primarily after settling in Paris. In examining a tiny sample from such a rich assortment, we will concentrate on the extremes, hoping that this will suggest the amazing scope of Chopin's output and show how and why this mysterious stranger became such an emblematic figure: of genius, of Romantic suffering, of artistic perfection, of sickliness, of nationalism, of exoticism, and eventually of universality.

The Chopinesque Miniature

No composer ever exceeded Chopin's mastery of the Romantic fragment. We have encountered the prelude earlier only as the first item in a keyboard suite or as paired with a fugue. Several pianist-composers before him, including the Italian-born London-based Muzio Clementi (1752–1832), the Slovakian-born Johann Nepomuk Hummel (1778–1837), and Ignaz Moscheles (1794–1870), a Bohemian-born pianist based in London, had provided books of preludes for practical concert use. Chopin's preludes are vividly if enigmatically expressive performance pieces, although in an "improvisatory" style, a prelude to everything and nothing.

Like the preludes and fugues of Bach's *Well-Tempered Keyboard* or the instructive sets by Clementi et al., Chopin's covered every major and minor key, which is why the set, Op. 28 (1838–39) contained precisely twenty-four pieces. To mention just the initial four: The first, in C major, perfectly exemplifies the paradoxical, captivating nature of the genre, being at once fragmentary and whole, complete and yet not complete, sufficient yet insufficient. The cryptic second prelude, in A minor, is absolutely grotesque (from *grottesca,* originally referring to wall decorations in ancient excavated cave dwellings or grottos): a deliberately, fancifully ugly or absurd utterance. Fancifully ugly is the dissonant left-hand accompaniment, with its chromatic middle-voice neighbor notes that so frequently interfere with and distort the effect of the harmony tones. Fancifully absurd is the harmonic waywardness, unpredictable to the end (Ex. 21-1). There was something in this piece to bewilder everyone and something for everyone to admire. It was when both these attitudes were present and impossible to disengage from one another that Romantics were most apt to speak, as Schumann did, of genius.

Anthology Vol 2-45
Full CD IV, 36–39
Concise CD II, 34–35

Example 21-1 Frédéric Chopin, Prelude, Op. 28, No. 2

Such genius was often linked with the demonic, madness, or physical illness (and there were many in the nineteenth century who deduced from this the false converse that madness or physical infirmity were signs of genius). In one of her memoirs George Sand depicted Chopin composing the A Minor Prelude while actually coughing blood, becoming an object of "horror and fright to the population" and leading to the couple's eviction from their Majorcan retreat.[6] This image became central to the Chopin myth and to his reception. A mid-century French critic, Hippolyte Barbedette, thought the music exerted a dangerous influence: "Chopin was a sick man who enjoyed suffering, and did not want to be cured. He poured out his pain in adorable accents—his sweet melancholy language which he invented to express his sadness. . . . Chopin's music is essentially unhealthy. That is its allure and also its danger."[7] Such a one-sided but culturally significant view of Chopin is contradicted by many of his best-known pieces, including the very next prelude (No. 3), a light, outdoorsy, altogether unproblematic *Vivace* in G major, which is followed by a pianistically undemanding E minor *Largo*, No. 4.

Nationalism as a Medium

The more obvious tokens of Chopin's Polishness are to be found, not surprisingly, in his Polish dances, especially the mazurkas and polonaises, which were the works most prized by his contemporaries as characteristically "Chopinesque." The man, in other words, was identified with (reduced to?) the group from which he hailed, as is usually the case with "others." Yet here, as everywhere, Chopin forged a personal and very distinctive style out of varied, in some ways even incongruous, ingredients. The authentically national—meaning, in France, the authentically exotic—was only one of those ingredients.

The moods of these dances and the feelings they evoke vary enormously, even among the same type, for example, the **mazurka** (Fig. 21-4). As it was known abroad, largely thanks to Chopin, it was the national dance of the Mazurs, the settlers of the Mazowsze plains surrounding Warsaw. Danced by couples either in circles or in country dance sets, the mazurka came in various types—the moderate *kujawiak*, the faster *mazurek*, and the very rapid *oberek*, all of which are represented among Chopin's mazurkas. What these had in common was a strongly accented triple meter, with the strongest accents (usually on the second or third beat) marked by a tap of the heel.

Figure 21-4 Drawing of Poles dancing the mazurka, the Polish national dance.

The first mazurkas Chopin composed as an exile from Poland were a set of four published in 1834 as Op. 17. All of them feature the characteristic heel-tapping rhythm. The four are cast, like the vast majority of Chopin's mazurkas, in a ternary da capo form that could be justified in national terms but was also an accommodation to the common practice of the literate tradition, with its minuets (or scherzos) and trios. Another touch especially characteristic of the mazurkas is the use of tonic (and occasionally tonic-fifth) pedals. All four mazurkas in Op. 17 show it and thereby offer a trace of folklore, the mazurka being accompanied in its natural habitat by the *duda*, or Polish bagpipe, which could produce either a tonic or tonic-fifth drone.

Chopin's French-period mazurkas are filtered through a gauze of nostalgic memory conjured up by stinging or slithery chromatic harmony, most notably in Op. 17, No. 4, one of his most haunting fragments, in which reminiscences of the mazurka seem to hover in a kind of harmonic ether. The characteristic accompaniment pattern of the "authentic" mazurka, the steady oompah-pah against which the shifting melodic accents rebound, prominent in the first two mazurkas and only slightly lessened in the third, is now almost altogether gone, replaced by a mid-register pulsation marked *sotto voce*.

Anthology Vol 2-46
Full CD IV, 40
Concise CD II, 36

Chopin's heroic side came out most prominently in his regal or military polonaises, his chillingly macabre or ironic scherzos, a few of the nocturnes, and, above all, his ballades. The **ballade** ultimately shows Chopin at his most ambitious and proved the repository for his most serious expressions of Polish nationalism, widely understood as such by his contemporaries. We have previously encountered the Romantic ballad as a vocal genre—more specifically, settings of poems, such as Goethe's "Der Erlkönig," that emulate narrative folk songs. Poets fashioned literary ballads, often with the pretense that they were drawing on local oral tradition. That was certainly the case with Mickiewicz, the cultural hero of the Polish diaspora, who brought the ballad to Poland in his first book, *Ballady i romanse* (Ballads and Romances, 1822). It was in order to give Poland its own chivalric poetry, testifying imaginatively to a Polish knightly past, that Mickiewicz invented Polish balladry. National poetry was being used all over Eastern Europe to remodel the past as a basis for present aspirations and in hopes of a better future.

Like Chopin, Mickiewicz lived in Paris after the failed Polish rebellion against the Russians in 1831. He was at the center of an émigré community to which the composer was only peripherally attached. Chopin was nonetheless very much aware of his work and even told Schumann that his ballades (of which he had by then written two, the second dedicated to Schumann) were modeled on "certain poems of Mickiewicz."[8] This acknowledgment, plus the fact that the early German editions called the pieces *Balladen ohne Worte* (Ballads without Words), has led many Chopinists off on wild goose chases to find the individual poems by Mickiewicz whose contents were embodied in Chopin's music or even secretly set to it. But Chopin probably never meant to imply anything quite so literal. His ballads did not have an explicit program as did Berlioz's *Symphonie fantastique*. Rather, he sought to duplicate and even to surpass not the content but, rather, the effect of Mickiewicz's nationalistic narrative poetry. Chopin did this by adapting features of the traditional sonata, as dramatized by Beethoven and lyricalized by Schubert, to reflect the characteristic structure and rhetoric of the poetic ballad. It was one of the most sophisticated and successful mutual adaptations of music and literature ever achieved in a century that was largely dedicated to that achievement. No wonder it was influential.

It was inevitable that narrative content would come to be represented by means of techniques borrowed from sonata form. By its very nature the process of thematic development—in which musical events seem to be not merely juxtaposed but causally connected so that the past conditions the present and the present (both thematically and tonally) forecasts the future—has a compelling narrative aspect. And the newly radicalized contrast in thematic content—in which a lyrically expansive second subject (in a remote alternate key) had lately begun to assert equal rights to the possession of thematic development and to claim equal time—implied an equally compelling dramatic potential. There was even the possibility of a traditional narrative frame if one also deployed the traditional slow introduction and the coda.

Anthology Vol 2-47
Full CD IV, 41
Concise CD II, 37

Chopin's Ballade in G Minor, Op. 23, was completed in 1835, although it may have been sketched as early as 1831 in the immediate aftermath of the Polish revolt. There seems to be a clear similarity between its spectacularly goal-oriented overall shape and the forward-moving narrative in a ballad such as "Der Erlkönig." The whole composition is in effect a single, magnificently sustained, ten-minute, 264-measure dramatic crescendo that continually gathers momentum from an exhilarating introduction to a cabaletta-like coda. The large-scale formal ambition of the G Minor Ballade could hardly be further removed from the small aphoristic or sectional forms associated with much of Chopin's music. Because of its apparent deviations from standard operating procedure, some have been reluctant to compare Chopin's ballades with the sonatas of earlier composers or to locate the source of their rhetoric in sonata procedures. And yet the shapes and gestures that give form to the Ballade in G Minor—the bithematic exposition, the motivic reconfigurations of the first theme (mm. 36ff), the recapitulation (m. 194), the elaborate coda—all had their origins in symphonies and sonatas and derived meaning both as narrative and as drama from the listener's recognition of that fact.

Chopin had so internalized the formal layout associated with the sonata that he could deploy its elements in idiosyncratic ways. The extra recurrences of the main themes, seemingly at odds with sonata procedures, are crucial to our perception of the ballade as a ballad, which, besides being a narrative, is also a strophic song, unfolding in recurrent stanzas. By synthesizing sonata and strophic principles, Chopin brilliantly solved the problem of capturing the relationship in a ballad between the recurrent tune and the ever-evolving narrative content. Every time the first theme recurs, to pick the most obvious example, its continuation is different: The first time it gives way to the first episode, the second time to the lyrical climax, and the third time to the fiery coda (*Presto con fuoco*). Thus it is invested on each occurrence with a new narrative function, just as each repeated melodic stanza is invested in a poetic ballad with new words.

But if the ballade is a narrative, what kind of story is it telling? One scholar has recently suggested that Chopin invented the instrumental ballade as a vehicle to tell the story of Poland as Chopin and his fellow émigrés conceived it—not the story of Poland's lamentable past (although that past is surely referred to) but the story of its future, a story of impending revolution.[9] That emphasis in the G Minor Ballade is what conditioned its thrilling trajectory from a subdued beginning to a blaze of fiery, even tragic glory. And it seems that Chopin's audiences got the message. It is remarkable that the work was almost universally interpreted as Chopin's most seriously nationalistic endeavor, although, unlike the mazurkas and polonaises, its musical style is not at all marked as specifically Polish.

Nationalism in music is defined not by style alone but by a much more complex interaction between creative intentions and listener perceptions.

Chopin, in other words, pulled off the extraordinary feat of telling a national story using universal ingredients. Poland, a murdered country whose national sovereignty had been forcibly eradicated to add to the property of three European dynasties, would become the great emblem of the Revolutions of 1848 (Fig. 21-5), and Chopin, in his ballade, already displayed that emblem to all of Europe in a language everyone could understand, and respond to, as theirs. So the national question, while originally posed in terms of folklore, nevertheless quickly transcended folklore. The reception of Chopin's ballade, like that of many other national musical monuments, proved that nationalism in music is defined not by style alone but by a much more complex interaction between creative intentions and listener perceptions.

Figure 21-5 Polish troops in Paris, 1848. Engraving by Victor Adam.

America Joins In

An American composer whose career began very much like Chopin's was Louis Moreau Gottschalk (1829–69; Fig. 21-6), a native of New Orleans. He was the first composer born in America to make his mark within the European tradition of fine-art music, yet he failed to achieve Chopin's level of social prestige. America, as a young country, eagerly imported art music from Europe. Many Europeans, especially Germans, came to the "New World" to perform and teach, and over time many Americans went abroad to study in Paris, Leipzig, and other centers. Liszt had American students—although various attempts to lure him to tour the United States proved unsuccessful. Big-name composers—Pyotr Ilyich Tchaikovsky, Antonín Dvořák, Camille Saint-Saëns, Richard Strauss, and others—later visited America, beginning in the 1890s, and some popular performers came earlier, such as the singer Jenny Lind (1820–87), whom the circus impresario P. T. Barnum presented in 1850.

Gottschalk's father, London-bred and Leipzig-educated, was a prosperous merchant from a highly assimilated German-Jewish family; his mother, a skilled amateur pianist and operatic singer, was the daughter of an affluent baker of French background who had come to Louisiana as a refugee from the Haitian slave revolts of the 1790s. Gottschalk's socially ambitious parents identified wholeheartedly with European high culture and brought up their many children in an atmosphere effectively shielded from the local popular culture by

Figure 21-6 Louis Moreau Gottschalk. Wood engraving after a drawing by Henry Louis Stevens, published in *Vanity Fair*, 11 October 1862.

a well-developed European-style salon and opera-house network. As soon as their gifted son had received his basic training from the local cathedral organist, he was packed off to Paris, shortly before turning twelve, for further study.

Gottschalk was an extraordinarily precocious talent. At age fifteen he gave a recital at which he played Chopin's E Minor Concerto to an audience that included Chopin himself, who paid enthusiastic respects backstage and, at least according to Gottschalk, declared him the future "king of pianists."[10] Yet like the young Chopin, Gottschalk found he could not break through to real recognition from the European public except as an exotic—which is what turned him, against the current of his upbringing, into an American (or, more precisely, a Louisiana Creole) composer. In quick succession three sets of bravura variations were published in Paris: *Bamboula, danse des nègres*, Op. 2; *La savane, ballade créole*, Op. 3; and *Le bananier* (The Banana Tree), *chanson nègre*, Op. 4. They gave the nineteen-year-old a reputation for being, in the words of an enraptured French reviewer, a rude prodigy who composed "wild, languishing, indescribable" things that bore "no resemblance to any other European music."[11]

Of this "Louisiana trilogy," the ballade *La savane* (The Savannah) was supposedly inspired by a legend that the oak trees in the swamps surrounding New Orleans had grown up out of the skeletons of runaway slaves. The young Gottschalk heard this tale from his governess, a mulatto slave girl named Sally, who punctuated her narrative with snatches of the mournful slave song on which the variations are based. The startlingly original *Bamboula*, apparently composed in 1844–45, when the fifteen-year-old Gottschalk was recovering from an attack of typhoid fever, was issued by a Paris publisher in 1849. The title is supposedly the name, in New Orleans black patois, of an African-style drum made of bamboo, and the piece is purportedly an evocation of Saturday night social dancing at the Place Congo, a square frequented by New Orleans' free mulatto or mixed-blood population, who were largely of Caribbean descent. The tunes are not recognizably West Indian, nor was the very sheltered Gottschalk likely to have been taken as a lad to witness such goings-on first hand. But in evoking the bamboula drum, whether real or imaginary, Gottschalk devised an angular, dryly percussive style of piano playing, full of alternating exchanges between the hands. The touch, and consequently the texture, is exceptionally differentiated, the two hands (and sometimes two lines within a single hand) being radically contrasted (Ex. 21-2).

Anthology Vol 2-48
Full CD V, 1
Concise CD II, 38

This special piano touch, "wild and indescribable" to listeners used to Chopin and Liszt, in some respects foreshadowed ragtime, which emerged later in the century, especially when Gottschalk added syncopated Latin American rhythms to the mix, as he would do in his *Souvenir de Porto Rico, Marche des Gibaros* (1857). Gottschalk's brilliant exercises in Americana were composed for European audiences. He returned to America early in 1853 for what he thought would be a whirlwind tour, but his father's death that year forced him to remain and become the family breadwinner. From then on he made his career entirely within the growing American music trade. He would not be Chopin's successor as a society favorite after all. His destiny lay in the uniquely American business of popularizing high culture.

Gottschalk increased the frequency of his concert tours to unprecedented levels, causing him chronic exhaustion and periods of burnout. Thanks to the boom in American railway construction that coincided exactly with his peak concertizing period, Gottschalk covered more miles in less time than any other virtuoso of the day, playing not only in big cities but in small mill and mining towns from coast to coast and bringing European fine-art music to audiences that would never have heard it in Europe. Toward the end of his concert career he calculated that during a seven-year period he had given 1,100 recitals and logged more than 95,000 miles.

Example 21-2 Louis Moreau Gottschalk, *Bamboula,* mm. 1–24

Gottschalk's popularity led him to write pieces his European experience had taught him to disdain—parlor-piano compositions with titles like *The Last Hope* (1854), *The Maiden's Blush* (1863), and *The Dying Poet* (1863). These works, intended for home consumption, shared a commercial sentimentality found in the enormously popular songs of his compatriot Stephen Foster (1826–64), composer of "Camptown Races," "Oh! Susanna," "Beautiful Dreamer," "Old Folks at Home (Swanee River)," and others that would become classics. Yet Gottschalk's aim was not in the least nationalistic. Quite the contrary: Just as to aristocratic European audiences Gottschalk had represented untamed America, so to the "vulgar" American public, both those who came to hear him play and those who purchased the sheet music afterward to play at home, he represented European class and sophistication.

Gottschalk was forced to leave the United States in 1865 to avoid prosecution on a false charge of statutory rape. The morals charge and the attendant scandal that led to his exile reflected the social stigma and suspicion that often attached to artists in American society, where charismatic or gifted individuals could seem at odds with a social premium placed on ordinariness and conformity. European attitudes were considerably more tolerant. Both Liszt and Chopin, as we have seen, lived openly with women to whom they were not married (and who were married or had been married to others), and suffered little social stigma in consequence.

Gottschalk spent the last four years of his life in South America taking popularization to new heights in monster concerts that he organized. The pinnacle was reached in Rio de Janeiro on 24 November 1869 with the cooperation of the Brazilian Emperor Pedro II, who placed the massed bands of the National Guard, the Imperial Army and Navy, and three municipal orchestras at his disposal. "Just think of 800 performers and 80 drums to lead," Gottschalk exulted, exaggerating only slightly, in a letter to a friend.[12] The concert started with him alone on stage playing a potpourri on themes from Charles Gounod's popular opera *Faust*, followed by a new *Tarantella* for piano and orchestra. Then the curtain went up on the great mass of performers, 650 in all. After the Brazilian national anthem, played by "forty young ladies on twenty-five pianos,"[13] came the Coronation March from Meyerbeer's *Le Prophète*, a movement from Gottschalk's own "Tropical Night" Symphony, and as grand finale a new work, composed for the occasion and dedicated to the emperor: *Marcha solemne brasileira* (Solemn Brazilian March), replete with backstage cannon fire. A repetition of the entire program was scheduled for two days later, with a solo performance by Gottschalk on the evening in between.

No novelist would dare invent what happened next, for fear of losing credibility. Gottschalk collapsed during that intervening performance right in the midst of *Morte!* (She's Dead), one of his popular potboilers, and had to be carried from the stage back to his hotel room. The second "monster concert" had to be postponed and then canceled. Gottschalk never played again. He died on 18 December 1869 from the consequences of a ruptured abdominal abscess.

Art and Democracy

The American experience, which had begun with a revolution against the British Empire, was viewed in nineteenth-century Europe as an experiment in social leveling.

As an emissary from America to Europe, then from Europe to America, and finally between Americas; as a mediator between "low" culture and "high" society, and then between "high" culture and "low" society; as a shuttler between culture and commerce; and as a perpetual wanderer whose selfhood was always defined by some sort of otherness, Gottschalk led an existence on the borders. In many ways, America did too.

The United States, the exemplary late-eighteenth-century creation of Enlightened universalist politics, posed a perpetual threat to the European status quo. What it threatened was the security of traditional hierarchy. The American experience, which had begun with a revolution against the British Empire, was viewed in nineteenth-century Europe as an experiment in social leveling, hardly less ominous than the revolutionary movements that were gathering force seemingly everywhere on the European continent between 1830 and 1848. Backlash against Americanism—defined in terms of commercialism, mechanical technology, and indifference if not sheer hostility to quality in matters of culture and conduct—was already well advanced by the time the young Gottschalk sailed for Europe in 1841.The head of the piano department at the Paris Conservatoire would not even allow him to audition, despite the fact that he spoke perfect

French and had been trained by Frenchmen, because "America produces steam engines, not musicians."[14]

The democratic, nonhierarchical spirit of nineteenth-century America, was partial; the existence of slavery lasted until 1865, to pick only the most obvious contradiction. Yet its new middle-class audiences fostered a kind of golden age for popular consumption of art.[15] Gottschalk's successful career as an American public entertainer between 1853 and 1865 and his later activity as a musical impresario in Latin America are revealing of a time before the great divide between "high" and "low" culture, between "art" music and "popular" music, that became so pronounced in the twentieth century. Shakespeare plays and Rossini operas, albeit often presented in mangled forms, were considered genuinely popular entertainment enjoyed by huge numbers of Americans of all classes from across the country.

Russia: The Newcomer

So far in this chapter we have observed the tensions between the "universal" and the particularly "national" from the perspective of composers highly conscious of themselves as outsiders, presenting a sense of self that is to a large extent constructed out of a sense of difference. It is unlikely that Chopin would have written as many mazurkas as he did or Gottschalk his "Louisiana trilogy" had they stayed at home all their lives. Gottschalk's training and short career in Europe, followed by his long one in the Americas, show a fruitful interaction between the Old and New Worlds, one that is worth comparing with the interaction between Western Europe and Slavic countries, especially Russia.

Musical contacts had emerged with Russia as a result of the "Westernizing" campaign of Tsar Peter I ("Peter the Great," reigned 1682–1725), and they initially occurred mainly in Peter's new capital, St. Petersburg. For roughly a century beginning in the 1730s, Russia participated in the musical commerce of Europe, first as a consumer only, then as a producer for home consumption, and finally as a successful and influential exporter (Fig. 21-7).

Up to the time of Peter, virtually the only literate musical tradition in Russia was that of Church chant and its derivative polyphonic genres, preserved in a neumatic notation of a kind that had not been used in Western Europe since the days of the Carolingians. So alien was the secular art music of the West to native Russian music that the Russian vocabulary distinguished radically between the two. Russian chant was called *peniye* (singing). All Western art music, whether vocal or instrumental, was called *musika*. For Russia, the history of music as a continuously practiced secular fine art in the European literate tradition begins in the year 1735, ten years after Peter's death, when his niece, the Empress Anne (reigned 1730–40), decided to import a resident troupe of Italian opera singers to adorn her court with elegant entertainments. Anne's operatic project can be thought of as a continuation of Peter's legacy into a new cultural sphere.

Italian opera, though at first a wholly imported court luxury that had no contact at all with native genres (or even native musicians), eventually took root and thrived. During the long rule of Empress Catherine II ("Catherine the Great," reigned 1762–96) a very distinguished line of imported composers worked in Russia (their dates of service are given in parentheses): Vincenzo Manfredini (1762–65), Baldassare Galuppi (1765–68), Tommaso Traetta (1768–75), Giovanni Paisiello (1776–83),

Figure 21-7 *Country Festival* by Ilya Repin (1881). The collection and assimilation of Russian folklore exerted a profound influence on many composers.

Giuseppe Sarti (1784–1801, with interruptions), Domenico Cimarosa (1787–91), and Vincente Martín y Soler (1790–1804, with interruptions). These were among the biggest names in Europe. Catherine lured them to her cold, remote capital by offering them huge "hardship wages," and they definitely put St. Petersburg (which in terms of international diplomacy stood for all of Russia) on the international musical map. One of the most famous operas of the late eighteenth century, Paisiello's *Il barbiere di Siviglia* (The Barber of Seville, 1782), had its premiere there. (Rossini's more famous setting of the same Beaumarchais play came some three decades later.)

Two changes that took place under Catherine had far-reaching significance for the eventual growth of an indigenous Russian school of composition. First, comic operas (often French ones, with spoken dialogue) were performed at Catherine's court alongside the more serious Italian fare. And second, native-born composers began to receive training from the imported composers, mostly in order to furnish modest comic operas in the popular French style that the foreign celebrities felt it beneath their dignity to compose themselves.

In the late 1760s Catherine sent two young and talented Ukrainian-born composers, Maxim Berezovsky (1745–77) and Dmitri Bortnyansky (1751–1825), probably after apprenticeship with Galuppi, to study in Italy with the famous Bolognese educator Padre Martini, former teacher of J. C. Bach and Mozart. Both of them had an opera seria performed in Italy before returning to Russia. They set about modernizing (that is, Italianizing) the repertoire of the Imperial Chapel Choir, replacing traditional *peniye* with arty Italianate *musika*, and writing operas using librettos by Metastasio. By the end of the century there were dozens of Russian musical comedies by Russian composers, some of them quite elaborate and expertly composed. The initial flowering of a Westernized musical life in Russia was therefore the result of importing famous opera composers, mostly Italians, and of sending off homegrown talent to study in Italy in the hopes that they would return to create great works themselves. This strategy made eminent practical sense because there were no conservatories in the country until later in the nineteenth century.

Nor did Russia have the kinds of instrumental ensembles, orchestras, and concert series that existed in London, Paris, Leipzig, or Vienna. The cultivation of

The Russian music in the opera, on the other hand, the music the Russian characters get to sing, is highly personal and lyrical. Glinka very minimally draws on existing folk melodies. Susanin's very first sung line in Act I—"How can you think of getting married at a time like this?"—is based on a tune Glinka once heard a coachman sing; and, at the other end of the opera, the triumphant moment when Susanin reveals to the Poles that he has led them to their death in the woods instead of to the tsar, motives from the same tune are accompanied by a basso ostinato derived from one of the most famous Russian folk songs, "Downstream on Mother Volga" ("Vniz po matushke po Volge").

Glinka's objective was not to be authentic but, rather, to be recognizably Russian to an audience of urban operagoers.

Far more important than the sheer amount of folk or folklike material in the score is how Glinka uses it. This was his great breakthrough and the reason why he is justly regarded as the founding father of Russian composers. Prince Vladimir Odoyevsky, a sort of Russian E. T. A. Hoffmann, noted that Glinka "proved" in *A Life for the Tsar* that "Russian melody may be elevated to a tragic style." In so doing, Odoyevsky declared, Glinka had introduced "a new element in art."[26] What Odoyevsky meant by this was that Glinka had integrated the national material into the stuff of his heroic drama instead of relegating it, as was customary, to the decorative periphery. Before Glinka, Russian composers had never aspired to the tragic style at all. What made this integration feasible was that the main characters in Glinka's opera were all peasants, hence eligible, within the conventions of the day, to adopt a folkish idiom. The tragic style nevertheless dignifies Susanin. He is not "just" a peasant; he has become an embodiment of the nation, a veritable icon, and so had the Russian folk idiom.

While this made the opera musically progressive, it remained politically and socially reactionary, for the most advanced of Glinka's musicodramatic techniques was one that enabled him to emphasize from beginning to end the opera's overriding theme of zealous submission to divinely ordained dynastic authority. The epilogue, which portrays Mikhail Romanov's triumphant entrance into Moscow following Susanin's sacrificial death and the defeat of the Poles, is built around a choral anthem

Figure 21-9 Stage design by Andrei Roller for the first performance of *A Life for the Tsar* (St. Petersburg, 1836).

Anthology Vol 2-49
Full CD V, 2

(Glinka called it a "hymn-march") proclaimed by massed choral forces on a grand-opera scale, including two wind bands on stage, to a text by Zhukovsky that culminates in the following quatrain: "Glory, glory to thee our Russian Caesar/Our sovereign given us by God!/May thy royal line be immortal!/May the Russian people prosper through it!" (Ex. 21-3).

Example 21-3 Mikhail Ivanovich Glinka, *A Life for the Tsar,* Epilogue

Glinka's setting of these words is in a recognizable style of seventeenth- and eighteenth-century polyphonic songs that were the earliest Westernized secular genre in Russian music. In Peter the Great's time such songs, chorally sung in three or four parts, were often used for civic celebrations, in which form they were known as "Vivats." The *Slav'sya,* or "Glorification," theme is motivically related to that of Susanin's retort to the Poles on the defiant words "I'm not afraid," which was derived in turn from the opening peasant chorus in Act I and through that relationship related to the opening phrase of the overture. But that only begins to describe its unifying and "organic" role. As the composer and critic Alexander Serov (1820–71) first pointed out in an essay published in 1859, the *Slav'sya* theme, which in nineteenth-century Russia became virtually a second national anthem, is foreshadowed throughout the opera wherever the topic of dynastic legitimacy (that is, the divine right of the tsar) is broached.

Thus *A Life for the Tsar* is thematically unified in both verbal and musical dimensions by the tenets of Official Nationalism. The irony, of course, is that Glinka adapted the techniques by which he achieved this broadly developed musicodramatic plan from the French "rescue operas" of the revolutionary period and applied them to an opera where rescue is thwarted and in which the political sentiment was literally counterrevolutionary. No wonder that the opera became the mandatory season opener for the Russian Imperial Theaters.

How the Acorn Took Root

Although Glinka was primarily a man of the theater—he wrote another opera, *Ruslan and Lyudmila,* which did not enjoy the same success as his first—his influence also extended to instrumental music. He left a work, *Kamarinskaya,* that composers of the next generation took so zealously as a model that one of them, Tchaikovsky, called it "the acorn from which the whole oak of Russian symphonic music grew."[27] The work is one of three *Fantaisies pittoresques* (Picturesque Fantasies) for orchestra, composed while Glinka was visiting Warsaw in 1848 and written under the spell of Berlioz, whom he had met in Paris in 1845 and who wrote of Glinka in a review that year that he "was among the outstanding composers of his time."[28] His two other fantasies are based on Spanish themes; for Glinka, as for Berlioz, national character did not have to be native, just colorful.

Anthology Vol 2-50
Full CD V, 3

Originally called "A Wedding Song and a Dance Song," *Kamarinskaya* is based on two Russian folk themes. The title by which it is known today is that of the second melody, a well-known instrumental dance tune. It consists of a single three-measure phrase that is repeated ad infinitum as the basis for extemporized variations played by wedding bands or else by a single player on an accordion-like bayan, a concertina, or a strummed balalaika, to accompany a strenuous and often-competitive type of male dancing (performed *v prisyadku,* in a squat) well known in the West as typically Russian, thanks to its exportation by professional folk-dance ensembles, not to mention parodies of it in movies and popular culture.

Glinka's Life for the Tsar _is thematically unified in both verbal and musical dimensions by the tenets of Official Nationalism._

Glinka noticed an unexpected resemblance between the famous *Kamarinskaya* tune and the melody of a lyrical wedding song, "Izza gor, gor vïsokikh gor" ("From behind the mountains, the high mountains"), that was one of his personal favorites. The notes of the dance song are marked with asterisks in Example 21-4, most of them in strong, conspicuous rhythmic positions, and correspond with the first six notes of the wedding song. He based his brilliantly orchestrated fantasia on what thus amounts to a sort of musical pun. The two themes are first given in stark contrast, as in a conventional symphonic first movement (Introduction and *Allegro*). But then, over a thirty-one measure passage in the midst of the *Allegro*, the fast theme is magically transformed into a reprise of the slow one, by means of the progressive revelation of their kinship. Also remarkable is the way Glinka derived the fantasia's introductory and transitional passages from the melody of the wedding song by extracting motives from it (labeled *x*, *y*, and *z* in Example 21-4).

Example 21-4 Folk themes in Glinka's *Kamarinskaya*

The underlying tonal progression that lends contrast and a heightened structural unity to the dance song variations turns out to be a long-range projection of the opening motive of the wedding song. Such a thorough interpenetration of melodic and harmonic structures through the use of motives is what one is used to finding (and therefore seeking) in Beethoven; it was precisely the reason for Beethoven's preeminence among symphonists. That Glinka managed to emulate the trick using nothing but folk songs as his melodic material was an astonishing tour de force. No wonder *Kamarinskaya* was so influential. What made it so was not its folkloric content per se but, rather, the way in which it vied with Beethoven, the greatest representative of the European mainstream. The music of that mainstream was decisively exported for well more than a century to places further afield, places that in time created their own new repertories that proved so attractive that in time Europe would enthusiastically import them.

Summary

In the nineteenth century, German music and musical values became widely viewed as universal and a standard to which others should aspire (as discussed in Chapter 15). Yet the nineteenth century also saw new expressions of musical nationalism in countries outside of these areas. In Eastern European countries, Russia, and North America, these nationalisms worked against the German "norm" and thus seemed exotic. The composers that represented these other nationalisms were conscious of themselves as outsiders and came to be known largely in terms of their national identity.

The Polish patriot Frédéric Chopin (1810–49) spent most of his life in exile from Poland. After beginning his career as a virtuoso pianist, he settled in Paris and devoted himself to composition and private performances for wealthy patrons. He composed about 200 piano works, mainly character pieces of various types, ranging widely in scope and difficulty: nocturnes, études, preludes, waltzes, polonaises, mazurkas, and ballades. His preludes were inspired by Bach's *Well-Tempered Keyboard,* in all major and minor keys. Chopin's nationalism was expressed mainly in his polonaises and mazurkas, modeled on Polish dances, and in his ballades, a genre loosely inspired by the Polish narrative folk ballads of Adam Mickiewicz. Chopin's ballades did not have an explicit program; rather, he sought to evoke the effect of the narrative poetry by manipulating the narrative implications of sonata form. Chopin is also known for his contributions to performance practice, especially *tempo rubato,* or "robbed time." In Chopin's own performances, this generally meant a delay of the melody with respect to the bass.

Louis Moreau Gottschalk (1829–69) was an American nationalist composer of Creole and German-Jewish descent who had a virtuoso piano career and was widely regarded as exotic by European audiences. He found that he was best able to win recognition from European audiences by playing up exotic American elements, and so he composed works inspired by his New Orleans childhood, including *Bamboula,* Op. 2. For American audiences, by contrast, he wrote sentimental parlor music that represented European sophistication. He spent the last four years of his life in South America, producing some works inspired by Latin American music.

Russia's history of art music began in 1732, when Italian opera singers arrived at the court in St. Petersburg. Imported opera flourished particularly in the late eighteenth century under Catherine the Great, who sent Russian composers to study in Italy. In the 1790s, under the influence of Johann Gottfried von Herder (see Chapter 18), the first collections of Russian folk songs were published.

The premiere in 1836 of *A Life for the Tsar* by Mikhail Glinka (1804–57) marks a turning point in the history of Russian music. There had been many earlier operas, primarily Singspiels, in the Russian language. In Glinka's opera, however, critics saw not merely a superficial, decorative "folksiness" but, rather, a true expression of nationhood and a synthesis of Italianate lyricism, German complexity, and French spectacle. Glinka brought a new level of tragedy to Russian opera along with a new harmonic and contrapuntal complexity. One reason for the opera's success, paradoxically, was that Glinka adopted many conventions associated with mainstream Italian and French opera, reflecting his training abroad. These included accompanied recitative, virtuoso vocal numbers, and ensemble finales. Politically and socially, however, *A Life for the Tsar* was conservative, promoting submission to the divinely ordained ruler. Glinka's works were enormously influential for later Russian composers. His *Kamarinskaya* for orchestra is notable for its sophisticated use of folk songs, applying to them a motivic working-out reminiscent of Beethoven.

Study Questions

1. What is the difference between exoticism and nationalism? Why do you think Frédéric Chopin was considered a nationalist composer whereas Robert Schumann was not?
2. Which works of Chopin are overtly "Polish," and how is the Polishness expressed musically?
3. Describe the musical form of Chopin's Ballade in G Minor. How does this form express narrative content? In what respects is it a nationalistic work?
4. How did American political and cultural conditions affect the attitudes toward music and art in the United States?
5. Why was Louis Moreau Gottschalk perceived differently in Europe than in the United States? What types of works did he write for the two different audiences?
6. Why was Mikhail Glinka's *A Life for the Tsar* considered the first true Russian opera? What does it mean to say that his work was "nation-embodying"?
7. Describe the various influences on *A Life for the Tsar,* from Italian opera, French opera, and Russian folklore. In what respects was this opera politically and socially conservative?
8. What is innovative about the way Glinka uses folk songs in *Kamarinskaya?*

Key Terms

ballade
exoticism
mazurka
nocturne
polonaise
rubato

22

Musical Politics at Midcentury: Historicism and the New German School

Throughout this book we have attempted to place as much emphasis on musicians as on music, to talk about people as much as about musical works. Most of the focus, predictably, has fallen on composers, primarily as they interact with performers, teachers, students, patrons, librettists, copyists, publishers, and audiences—the vast network of individuals and institutions that create, present, and receive music. Debates about musical aesthetics in mid-nineteenth-century Germany and Austria constituted a so-called War of the Romantics that is typically cast as primarily a debate among composers. An allegedly conservative faction, represented most prominently by Mendelssohn, Schumann, and Brahms, is contrasted with a purportedly progressive group, epitomized by Berlioz, Liszt, and Wagner. Both camps to varying degrees portrayed themselves as the true and rightful heirs of Beethoven. To discover how this all came about we might broaden the context and look at some figures who appear less often in history books but who actually themselves wrote the most influential histories, criticism, and aesthetic tracts in German-speaking countries. They helped shape music history by writing music history.

Historians generally, and perhaps musicologists in particular, are seldom associated with the avant-garde. Their contemplative lifestyle and their antiquarian scholarly interests lend them an air of conservatism. But historians of a certain type—or, rather, adherents to a certain theory of history—have conspicuously allied themselves with avant-garde movements, seeing themselves not only as passive recorders of events but also as active participants in their making. This breed of activist historian

TIMELINE

1818 Lord Byron, *Childe Harold's Pilgrimage*

1834 **Hector Berlioz, *Harold en Italie***

1837 Posthumous publication of Georg Wilhelm Friedrich Hegel, *Lectures on the Philosophy of History*

1844 **Felix Mendelssohn, Violin Concerto in E Minor, Op. 64**

1845 Franz Brendel becomes editor of the *Neue Zeitschrift für Musik*

1848 **Franz Liszt settles in Weimar**

1848 Revolutions throughout Europe

1852 **Brendel, *History of Music***

1854 **Eduard Hanslick, *On the Musically Beautiful***

1854 Henry David Thoreau, *Walden*

1856 **Liszt, *Les Préludes***

1857 Gustave Flaubert, *Madame Bovary*

1859 Charles Darwin, *On the Origin of Species*

1859 **Brendel coins the term "New German School"**

Figure 22-1 Franz Brendel, music historian, editor of the *Neue Zeitschrift für Musik.*

reached a peak of prestige and authority in mid-nineteenth-century Germany, just as German music was reaching its own peak of prestige and authority and when it was widely believed that music was the highest among the various arts. The history of that country and that century, particularly of that music, cannot be fully understood without some knowledge of the history of history.

As a historical method, what is called "**historicism,**" which defines social and cultural situations by their history, has largely died out, and the name of its main musical protagonist is largely forgotten today: Franz Brendel (1811–68; Fig. 22-1). A doctor of philosophy with only a casual musical education, Brendel neither composed nor performed, but he passionately promoted the idea that "music is the sovereign art of the present."[1] His enormous impact derived from the nature of his writings and the social and political activism through which he put his beliefs into practice. His great achievement was to write his century's most widely disseminated history of music: *Geschichte der Musik in Italien, Deutschland und Frankreich von den ersten christlichen Zeiten bis auf die Gegenwart* (History of Music in Italy, Germany and France from the Earliest Christian Times to the Present). First published in 1852 and often reprinted, it aspired to say everything that was important in a way that put all facts into an overriding system that gave them meaning. The system behind his work was the one expounded by the idealist German philosopher Georg Wilhelm Friedrich Hegel (1770–1831; Fig. 22-2). It was known as the "dialectic."

Historicism and the Hegelian Dialectic

In its broadest terms, the Hegelian **dialectic** has become a cliché: Human history develops according to a process in which one concept (thesis) inevitably gives rise to its opposite (antithesis), which then interacts with the thesis to produce a resolution (synthesis) that in turn becomes the thesis to begin the process anew. Nothing is static or unalterable. The hypothetical first stage that sets history in motion stipulates that all history must be conceived as a process in a constant state of flux.

So far the theory is irrefutable: The first thing one notices in any study of history is that things change under the impact of other things. Everything that can be observed can be described either as a cause or as an effect, hence everything is both cause and effect in an endless chain. This much is not a theory of history but simply a description—rather, a tautological, or circular, definition—of how things happen. What sets the Hegelian dialectic apart from other interpretations of progress is that it purports to show not merely *that* things change or *how* things change but *why* things change. The proposition that change has purpose turns random process into law.

The law of history, as Hegel first postulated it in lectures at the University of Berlin that his pupils reconstructed from their notes and published as *Lectures on the Philosophy of History* (1837), was this: "The history of the world is none other than the progress of the consciousness of Freedom."[2] All significant historical change has contributed to this progress in the realization of human freedom, which Hegel called the progress of the "world soul." The system enabled its followers to believe, in the words of one of historicism's most implacable later foes, Karl Popper (1902–94), "that by contemplating history we may discover the secret, the essence of human destiny."[3] It seemed to offer, in sum, the authority of science and the consolations of religion. It was believed in and defended not only as history but also as prophecy.

The legacy of this thinking, most notably in the writings of Karl Marx (1818–83), has had enormous consequences for countless millions of people's lives for nearly two centuries.

Figure 22-2 Georg Wilhelm Friedrich Hegel, painting by Johann Jacob Schlesinger (1825).

In the world of the arts, the impact of historicist thinking was profound. As the first self-consciously Hegelian historian of music, Brendel cast his narrative in terms of successive emancipations, both of musicians and of the art of music itself. Before the sixteenth century all was primitive, mere "prehistory," because in Brendel's ears such music did not intelligibly express the ideas or feelings of individual creators. Musicians were slaves to the mechanical rules of counterpoint, as people generally were enslaved by the dogmas of the early Church. The first great composer, in Brendel's reckoning, was Palestrina, who, reflecting a Romantic interpretation of the Renaissance, broke through to true spiritual expressivity. What he expressed, however, was not yet a personal sensibility but, rather, the collectively held beliefs of his religious community. Freed from its sacred bonds, music could be expressed in fully human, that is, secular, terms. The rise of opera around 1600 bore witness to it. The next stage came with the emancipation of music from words in the instrumental masterpieces of the German masters. Their music, now able to realize its own essential spirit, able at last to evolve autonomously, was effectively a metaphor for the advancement of humanity toward self-realization.

The value of music could be measured best, in the Hegelian view, in terms of the degree to which it embodied its own epoch's evolutionary synthesis and pointed the way to the next. Composers were valuable to the degree that their actions advanced the tendencies inherent in the musical materials toward further autonomous evolution. It is hardly surprising that Brendel believed that the most advanced composers, hence the most valuable ones, were Germans: first Bach and Handel and then Gluck, Haydn, and Mozart.

Needless to say, Brendel resoundingly confirmed Beethoven's position as music's emancipator. He posited that every age had its perfect representatives; Bach was not invalidated by Mozart, nor Mozart by Beethoven. To bring his story up to date, Brendel looked to Wagner's operas and to Liszt's orchestral music as the summit of musical attainment. The Hegelian terms in which Brendel came to describe Liszt's achievement left no doubt that he saw his symphonic poems (discussed later in this chapter) as a new synthesis, a transcendence giving rise to a new thesis—a new dawn—for music: "It is the unity of the poetic and the musical, and the progress to a new consciousness of this unity, that deserves to be called the essential novelty in the artistic creations under discussion." With earlier composers, especially Beethoven, the poetic idea emerges over the course of a composition along with its content, while in Liszt's music "these factors constitute the point of departure, the foundation of the whole creation."[4]

> ***"The history of the world is none other than the progress of the consciousness of Freedom." —G. W. F. Hegel***

Ever since the appearance of the many editions of Brendel's book, historicism has been a force not only in the historiography of music but in its actual history as well. That is, ever since the middle of the nineteenth century, many people have believed that the history of music has a purpose and that the primary obligation of musicians is not to meet the needs of their immediate audience but, rather, to help fulfill that purpose—namely, the furthering of the evolutionary progress of the art. This means that one is morally bound to serve the impersonal aims of history, an idea that has been one of the most powerful motivating forces and one of the most demanding criteria of value in the history of music. Certainly not all composers, historians, or critics toe this line, yet many, perhaps most, do.

With this development came the related views that the future of the arts was visible to a select few and that the opinion of others did not matter. Since the middle of the nineteenth century, the world of classical music has been divided by political factions. Of this there is no end in sight, for we still live in the age of historical and theoretical self-consciousness. That self-consciousness will be something to reckon with on virtually every remaining page of this book. From here on we are truly investigating the history of the present.

The New German School

Brendel took over the editorship of the *Neue Zeitschrift für Musik* from Robert Schumann in January 1845 and remained in that powerful position until his death almost a quarter of a century later. To Schumann's eventual consternation, Brendel supported an aesthetic agenda very different from his own. His activity as spokesman for the self-proclaimed German progressives became especially evident in 1859, when, in celebration of the twenty-fifth anniversary of the founding of the journal, Brendel organized a great meeting of musicians from all parts of Germany. Out of this occasion emerged an organization called the Allgemeiner Deutscher Musikverein (General German Music Association), set up to promote the musical agenda he had promoted in his earlier writings. In his widely publicized keynote address, Brendel christened the faction of composers embodying his ideals the "**New German School**." The guest of honor at the convocation, the honorary president of the society, was Liszt, a beacon of "progress to a new consciousness" of music's historical obligation.

Brendel's elevation of Liszt may seem surprising—how could that virtuoso, that eclectic, and, in the eyes of some, that charlatan be so highly praised? He wasn't even German! But since we left him in Chapter 19, Liszt's life had undergone a remarkable change. After his decade of rock-star-like touring, he had unexpectedly retired from the concert stage in 1848 and taken up full-time residence in Weimar. Displaying the fantastic energy he had formerly devoted to his pianistic career, Liszt now became the court Kapellmeister to end all Kapellmeisters. The musical establishment in Weimar when he assumed the reins was measly: a small orchestra, chorus, and group of dancers. Liszt had little conducting experience. But by force of his personality, his high ambitions, his prestige, and the generosity of his enthusiastic patron, the Grand Duchess Maria Pawlowna of Saxe-Weimar (sister of the Russian Tsar Nikolai I), he soon turned the backward town into the command center of progressive musical trends in Germany.

Liszt used his time at Weimar to produce a remarkable series of avant-garde compositions.

Liszt greatly expanded the Weimar court orchestra. He summoned from Leipzig the already famous violin prodigy Joseph Joachim (1831–1907), a former protégé of Mendelssohn and Schumann, to preside over the orchestra as concertmaster, the leader of the first violins (Fig. 22-3). After several years of service, however, Joachim's loyalty to his mentors and their attitudes toward the Viennese classics won out over his contractual commitments to Liszt and the avant-garde. He resigned the post, later becoming one of the New

German School's most tireless public detractors, together with his close friend Johannes Brahms, another Schumann protégé. Liszt's presence brought many sincere disciples to Weimar, among the most important being the composers Joachim Raff (1822–82), Peter Cornelius (1824–74), and Hans von Bülow (1830–94), who later married Liszt's daughter, Cosima, and became one of the great pianists and conductors of the age (Fig. 22-4). These younger men, together with Liszt, formed the early nucleus of the New German School, which eventually came to be most identified with Liszt, Berlioz, and Wagner.

Figure 22-3 Joseph Joachim and Clara Schumann playing at a concert in Berlin, 20 December 1854. Pastel by Adolph von Menzel.

Taking advantage of his protected position as a court musician and conductor, Liszt placed himself at the service of the most advanced, formidable, and politically risky composers of the time, particularly Wagner, then a political exile from Germany. He gave the widely acclaimed premiere in 1850 of Wagner's opera *Lohengrin* (which is dedicated to him) as well as notable productions of operas by Schubert (*Alfonso und Estrella*), Schumann (*Genoveva*), and Berlioz (*Benvenuto Cellini*). Finally, and most importantly, Liszt used his time at Weimar to produce a remarkable series of avant-garde compositions of his own, some of which had been conceived of during his whirlwind touring years. His piano masterpiece, the Sonata in B Minor, dates from 1852–53 and is dedicated to Schumann. In general, however, Liszt wrote far less for the piano and turned to the orchestra he now led as his medium of choice. At first, since he had little training and experience as an orchestrator, he made use of assistants, but in time he became a master of orchestration in his own right.

The works Liszt produced in this fashion were the kinds Brendel extolled as "the summit of thinking," the culmination of the whole historical process toward which everything up to that time had striven. Liszt eventually called them *Symphonische Dichtungen* (**symphonic poems**), echoing the Hegelian ideal of "unity of the poetic and the musical." They are single-movement orchestra works, sometimes as long as the average symphony, sometimes only as long as a good-size first movement. They have titles and in some cases brief prose prefaces (added later and not always written by Liszt himself) to help explain the "poetic" content. Liszt composed twelve symphonic poems between 1848 and 1858 and one more, *From the Cradle to the Grave,* near the end of his life. He also wrote two programmatic symphonies—*A Faust Symphony* (1854–57), in which each movement purports to describe one of the principal characters (Faust, Gretchen, and Mephistopheles) in Goethe's celebrated play, and *A Symphony to Dante's Divine Comedy* (1855–56). In various ways Liszt's symphonic poems had plenty of precedents, in programmatic works like Berlioz's *Symphonie fantastique* as well as in the type of theatrical overture (Beethoven's *Egmont* or Weber's *Der Freischütz*) that seeks to evoke the drama it introduces. The

Figure 22-4 Franz Liszt at the piano, his daughter, Cosima, the man standing next to her is most likely the violinist Heinrich Wilhelm Ernst. Cosima's husband, Hans von Bülow, is to the right of Liszt (1865).

closest precedents, perhaps, were concert overtures by Mendelssohn and Berlioz, unconnected to any drama.

As in his Piano Sonata in B Minor, Liszt favored in his symphonic poems a compressed single-movement structure that displays features of sonata form (exposition, development, and recapitulation) but that can simultaneously be thought of as discrete movements played without pause. Liszt probably learned this from Schubert's "Wanderer" Fantasy, a piece he performed frequently and even arranged as a concerto for piano and orchestra. The four movements of Schubert's work (fast, slow, scherzo, and finale) are all linked by transitions, to be played without interruption, as we saw in Chapter 18. The "organic" continuity this creates proceeds through a complete, typically Schubertian, circle of major thirds, the four movements cadencing, respectively, in C major, E major, A♭ major, and C. Liszt became fascinated with this harmonic procedure and made it typically Lisztian, in the process disseminating it widely, thanks to his enormous prestige. He had already experimented with this formal idea in his earlier piano concertos, which while lacking any specified programmatic content were certainly not lacking in drama. All these works employ the technique of "**thematic transformation**" (*thematische Verwandlung*) on which Liszt would rely to give unconventional shape to his symphonic poems, as we will see when we examine one of them, *Les Préludes*.

Why, then, in light of apparent forerunners, did Liszt's symphonic poems seem to many contemporaries a breakthrough to a new artistic plane? The reason had to do with the nature of their poetic content, which in most cases was neither narrative nor pictorial but philosophically abstract, staking out a loftier expressive sphere than any composer except Beethoven had previously addressed, and doing so, moreover, with an explicitness that seemed to exceed even Beethoven's powers. Liszt himself implied such a claim, which, he maintained, was a contemporary musician's duty, the only way of paying Beethoven proper tribute. "There is no doubt nothing better than to respect, admire, and study the illustrious dead," Liszt wrote to an official of the Weimar court in 1855, "but why not also live with the living?"[5]

For some contemporaries Liszt's advocacy of new composers who were often misunderstood by the public seemed like avant-garde posturing, with the pretentious implication that the interests of art and of its audience had irreconcilably diverged. The audience was no longer to be entertained but, rather, to be subjected to the higher demands of history and progress, exactly as Brendel advocated. And there was more: Liszt and his spokesmen made the patently Hegelian claim that with the symphonic poem he had at last ushered in the age of music's full equality among the arts as a bearer of meaning, a necessary precondition to its "sovereignty." In an essay on Berlioz's *Harold en Italie*, a hybrid symphony/concerto that we will discuss more at the end of this chapter, Liszt came out aggressively in favor of programmatic music as "one of the various steps forward which the art has still to take." He went on the offensive against what he called "the purely musical composer," who "only values and emphasizes the formal working-out of his material" and who therefore forfeits "the capacity to derive new formulations from it or to breathe new life into it."[6] Given the Hegelian premises on which Liszt based the argument, "purely musical composers" had good reason to think their works were being declared useless and obsolete.

"The Music of the Future"

The last straw was the slogan ***Zukunftsmusik***, or Music of the Future, along with its derivatives like *Zukunftsmusiker* (Musician of the Future) for composers of the New German School and *Zukunftskonzerte* (Concerts of the Future) for performances of their works. The term may have been coined by Princess Carolyne Sayn-Wittgenstein (Fig. 22-5), the brilliantly intellectual, immensely wealthy Polish noblewoman who had already been Liszt's lover for some years since his messy breakup with Countess Marie d'Agoult. After the premiere of *Lohengrin*, when Brendel suggested that the work was beyond the capacities of present-day audiences, she allegedly replied: "Very well, we are creating the Music of the Future."[7]

The phrase began resounding in the pages of the *Neue Zeitschrift* and in Liszt's correspondence. It quickly turned counterproductive, a great source of fun for the group's antagonists. Finally, in his 1859 keynote address, Brendel called for its abandonment in favor of the label New German School, although it was immediately pointed out that New German School was a misnomer since two of its elder statesmen, Liszt and Berlioz, were not German. To this Brendel retorted that it was "common knowledge" that these two had taken "Beethoven as their point of departure and so are German as to their origins." Warming to the subject, he continued:

> The birthplace cannot be considered decisive in matters of the spirit. The two artists would never have become what they are today had they not from the first drawn nourishment from the German spirit and grown strong with it. Therefore, too, Germany must of necessity be the true homeland of their works, and it is in this sense that I suggested the denomination New German School for the entire post-Beethoven development.[8]

This remarkable pronouncement testified to a new conception of nationhood and nationalism that had arisen in the wake of Hegel, or, rather, in the wake of the political activism that Hegel had inspired among the so-called Young Hegelians. Germanness was from now on no longer to be sought in folklore, as Herder had advocated. One showed oneself a German not ethnically but spiritually, by putting oneself in humanity's vanguard. With this new nationalism Germany was now viewed as the "world-historical" nation in Hegel's sense of the word, the nation that held the key to history and served as the executor of history's grand design, the nation whose actions would lead the world to its inevitable destiny. And so it happened that, according to composer Arnold Schoenberg, a twentieth-century advocate of the concept, "German music came to decide the way things developed, as it has for 200 years."[9]

Figure 22-5 Princess Carolyne von Sayn-Wittgenstein with her daughter, Marie. Lithograph by Carl Fischer after a painting by Casanova (1844).

Absolute Music

In an era of widespread idealistic theorizing, it was considered an advantage to be ahead of one's time. The myth of the artist-prophet, which Beethoven epitomized, became pervasive. It still lives. The idea of the artist as prophet was an extension of the idea of the artist as philosopher. Added to the Romantic emphasis on greatness and the sublime was an increasing valuation of innovation and progress. With this, the purpose of music changed. Some deeply lamented the development. In 1888 the Russian composer Tchaikovsky derided the German music of his day, protesting its "detestable pretensions to profundity, strength, and power." In his view it was "all seriousness and nobility of purpose, but the chief thing—*beauty*—is missing."[10]

And indeed much of the opposition to the New German School came from outside the German-speaking lands, with many foreign musicians understandably suspecting nationalistic designs behind the universalist pretensions. The opposition's most famous single salvo, however, came from the Viennese critic and music historian Eduard Hanslick (1825–1904). In 1854 he authored a tract called *Vom musikalisch-Schönen* (On the Musically Beautiful) that went through many editions and is still in print. It is difficult today to appreciate the force of the title; but at the time, for a German critic to insist on beauty looked to some like virtual treason.

Hanslick located the beautiful in music not in its ability to convey ideas or meaning but in its sheer patterning ("arabesques") of sound, that is, in its abstract and absolute character. His position is often misunderstood. Contrary to what his critics have alleged, Hanslick did not deny the emotional effects of music, nor did he deny its power to embody and convey poetic subject matter. Instead he denied the essentially musical nature of such a task (that is, its relevance to the true aims and tasks of music as an art) and hence the ultimate musical value of those effects and that embodiment. "The Representation of Feeling," reads the title of the crucial second chapter, "Is Not the Content of Music." Needless to say, everything hinges on how the word "content" is defined and on whether it is to be distinguished from "form." Brendel had argued that beginning with Liszt "content creates its own form."[11] The New German position cast feeling and form in opposition; Hanslick's stance melded them. His very definition of musical content was *Tönend bewegte Form*—barely translatable as something like "form put in motion by sound" or "sounding form in motion."

The New German position cast feeling and form in opposition; Eduard Hanslick's stance melded them.

Although his antagonists tried to brand him a reactionary, Hanslick's ideas were in fact new. By asserting that there were timeless musical values that took precedence over both the intentions of the composer and the reception of the listener, Hanslick and his followers introduced a new faction to what was fast becoming a struggle over the right to inherit and define the elite literate tradition of European music. Hanslick would later become a great advocate for Brahms and generally proved a harsh critic of Liszt and Wagner (Fig. 22-6). Brahms, as we shall see, emerged as the model for the type of music Hanslick advocated for in his aesthetic writings. Another like-minded musician was Joachim, who was astonishingly frank with Liszt in his letter of resignation from being concertmaster in Weimar. "Your music," wrote the twenty-six-year-old Joachim to the Kapellmeister,

> is entirely antagonistic to me; it contradicts everything with which the spirits of our greats have nourished my mind from my earliest youth. If it were thinkable that I could ever be deprived of, that I should ever have to renounce, all that I

learned to love and honor in their creations, all that I feel music to be, your works would not fill one corner of the vast waste of nothingness that I would feel. How, then, can I feel myself to be united in aim with those who, under the banner of your name and in the belief that they must join forces against the artists for the justification of their contemporaries, make it their life task to propagate your works by every means in their power?[12]

Figure 22-6 Caricature of the music critic Eduard Hanslick burning incense before the image of Johannes Brahms. Engraving after a drawing by Theodor Zasche from *Figaro*, Vienna, 1890.

This could be read as a manifesto of a different sort of historicism, one that looked to the past for the timeless values Hanslick espoused rather than for justification of further progress. Mendelssohn and Schumann, Joachim and Brahms were nurtured in this faith.

In the spring of 1860, Joachim drafted a hasty response to Brendel's remarks at the conference when he had christened the New German School. Taking offence at Brendel's smug tone and his brazen snubbing of Schumann, Joachim's open letter decried the assumption that "seriously striving musicians" were in accord about the value of Liszt's music or about the worthiness of the New Germans' historicist program. On the contrary, he wrote, serious musicians "can only deplore or condemn the productions of the leaders and disciples of the so-called 'New German School' as contrary to the most fundamental essence of music."[13]

Joachim sent the manifesto to Brahms, among others, for further circulation and signatures. Unfortunately somebody "leaked" the document to an unfriendly journalist who printed it prematurely in a Berlin newspaper, with only four signatures—theirs and those of two conductors. This feeble gang of four was widely satirized, with a parody of the letter appearing in the *Neue Zeitschrift* itself. Wounded, Brahms retreated from public debate, preferring to follow the advice he received from composer Ferdinand Hiller that "the best means of struggle would be to create good music."[14]

Liszt's Symphonic Poems

Anthology Vol 2-51
Full CD V, 4
Concise CD II, 39

We can put Brendel's heady rhetoric and theorizing to the test by examining one of Liszt's symphonic poems, *Les Préludes*, by far the most prominent of those few that are still sometimes performed today. The title is that of a famous poem from *Nouvelles méditations poétiques* (New Poetic Meditations, 1823) by Alphonse de Lamartine (1790–1869), one of the loftiest, most philosophical Romantic poets. Liszt composed the piece in the early 1850s, and on its first publication, in 1856, it was actually titled *Les Préludes (d'après Lamartine)* (The Preludes, after Lamartine) and carried a prefatory note that looked like a summary of the poem:

> What else is our life but a series of preludes to that unknown Hymn, the first and solemn note of which is intoned by Death?
>
> Love is the glowing dawn of all existence; but in whose fate are the first delights of happiness not interrupted by some storm, the mortal blast of which dissipates its fine illusions; the fatal lightning of which consumes its altar; and where is the cruelly wounded soul which, on issuing from one of these tempests, does not endeavor to rest his recollection in the calm serenity of life in the countryside? Nevertheless man hardly gives himself up for long to the enjoyment of the

beneficent stillness which at first he has shared in Nature's bosom, and when "the trumpet sounds the alarm," he hastens to the dangerous post, whatever the war may be, which calls him to its ranks, in order at last to recover in combat the full consciousness of himself and the entire possession of his energy.

The program has been tailored for music. Following the sonorous invocation of the great Question (mm. 1–46) it comprises four episodes: Love (mm. 47–108), Storm (mm. 109–181), Pastoral Calm (mm. 182–344), and Battle and Victory (m. 345 to the end), including a recapitulation of the Question (m. 405). This layout basically corresponds to the movements of a conventional symphony, even if not in the most conventional order, and the whole ends very conventionally with Beethovenian triumph. It also exhibits the standard "there and back" harmonic construction that had for so long controlled musical discourse.

Liszt's **Les Préludes,** *while heavily indebted in concept to Berlioz, also self-consciously advertises its descent from Beethoven.*

Les Préludes, while heavily indebted in concept to Berlioz, also self-consciously advertises its descent from Beethoven. After a mysterious pair of pizzicato Cs that seemingly invoke the lyre of the muse whom Lamartine summons at the outset of his poem, the Question is broached in the form of a three-note figure, probably derived from the last movement of Beethoven's last string quartet (F major, Op. 135) with its "Must it be?" motto (Ex. 22-1). The treatment Liszt gave to his question about the meaning of life embodied in the three-note motif provides the basis for the major themes in the ensuing composition—every answer to it is fashioned out of the question's intervals and contour (Ex. 22-2).

Over the course of *Les Préludes* the opening motive is transformed in ingenious ways to create vastly different programmatic moods (amorous, stormy, pastoral, and military), so much so that the listener might not immediately grasp that they derive from the same motivic germ. Such "thematic transformation," as Liszt called it, is similar to Berlioz's use of the *idée fixe* in his *Symphonie fantastique,* especially as he presented it deformed in the final movement, but Liszt's range and subtlety of transformations are far greater. There is a genuinely Beethovenian element as well in the whittling down of the decisive unit of recognition from a full-fledged theme to a tiny motive. This refinement—the weaving of an entire symphonic fabric out of a motivic thread that seems to come, in turn, directly out of the poem—can be seen as a deliberate justification of Brendel's claim that Liszt's symphonic poems ushered in a new age of music in which "content creates its own form." The overall coherence in *Les Préludes* and in many of Liszt's other works from this time, brought about by thematic transformation and the streamlining of the overall form by means of transitions, creates an impression of "organic" structural unity such as Beethoven earlier achieved in his Fifth Symphony.

But What Does It *Really* Mean?

So it may come as a disquieting (or perhaps an amusing) surprise to learn that *Les Préludes* was mostly conceived of in an altogether different poetic context and thus preexisted the content that supposedly created it. What we now know as the symphonic poem *Les Préludes* was originally conceived as an overture to *Les quatre élémens* (The Four Elements), a quartet of choruses that Liszt wrote in 1844 to

Example 22-1 Ludwig van Beethoven, String Quartet in F Major, Op. 135, IV, opening

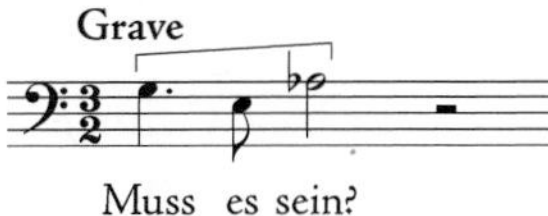

Example 22-2 Table of themes derived from the main motive in Liszt's *Les Préludes*

The Question
a. m. 3

b. m. 35

I. Love
c. m. 47

d. m. 69

II. Storm
e. m. 109

f. m. 131

g. m. 161

III. Pastoral Calm
h. m. 182

i. m. 214

IV. Battle and Victory
j. m. 346

words by a minor French poet named Joseph Autran (1813–77) and based largely on themes drawn from the choruses. Liszt, understandably, later tried to cover his tracks about the origins of *Les Préludes*—to hide the fact that the stated story was not actually what had motivated his composition.

But does the corrected record really invalidate the claims of the New Germans? The claim was never made, after all, that music explicitly paraphrased only one particular poetic idea, but, rather, that it paralleled the content and conveyed its emotional impact to the listener. In any case, who gets to decide in the end what a work of art really means? The creator? A critic, historian, or listener? Someone experiencing the work in Liszt's own time or today? The music, it seems, can accommodate a variety of readings, even those that are anachronistic. One might claim, for example, that Liszt had a science fiction movie in mind when he composed *Les Préludes*. Although that would clearly be impossible, does it necessarily mean that having such a program in mind while hearing the piece today is "wrong"?

Who gets to decide in the end what a work of art really means?

The music of *Les Préludes* by itself may impress a naive listener (that is, a listener without any preconceptions) the way an allegorical painting might strike a naive viewer. Both might be greatly pleased and moved by the sheer sonorous or visual display; yet both might also be aware that there is a dimension of meaning to which they lack complete access. In most of his symphonic poems Liszt for the most part draws on recognizable generic types, or *topoi*, kinds of music that are widely recognizable as amorous, stormy, pastoral, military, and so forth. While a listener might perhaps confuse a love passage with a religious one or a storm with a war, the listener would probably not mix up a love section with a military one. And within each of these types there is an enormous range of ideas that can be invoked—a Star Wars scenario might not really be so different from a Battle of the Huns, which was in fact the impetus behind one of Liszt's symphonic poems (*Hunnenschlacht*, after a painting from the mid-1830s by Wilhelm Kaulbach).

In *Les Préludes*, therefore, it comes down to a choice of allegories. Liszt presented one, via Lamartine, as part of a broad agenda to which he, Brendel, and the rest of the New German School attached enormous aesthetic, historical, and political importance. For this reason he insisted on only the "Lamartine" reading of the music and deliberately suppressed the original "Autran" one. Yet neither his insistence on the one program nor an insistence on the other as the true meaning of the music can be determined simply by reading the music. A third, fourth, or twentieth program might be just as convincing, hence just as "true."

This range of possibilities raises important issues about the meaning of a piece of music and whose opinions about works matter in certain times and places. In the 1850s and '60s, the contentious interpretation and evaluation of Liszt's symphonic allegories were tied to the idea that music needed to evolve in the direction that a self-selected vanguard of German composers had pointed out for it. At the same time, as we shall later see, Italian operas were being subjected to similar interpretive contests between those who read them as revolutionary allegories and those who preferred to take their plots at face value. In the twentieth century, controversies swirled around the artworks created in the great European totalitarian states—Dmitry Shostakovich's music in the Soviet Union is the most famous case—some reading them as allegories of political dissent, others as allegories of political submission, still others as uplifting artistic utterances without political association.

These clashing interpretations were (and are often still) advanced in a categorical fashion that can only be supported ideologically (that is, on the basis of belief), never tested empirically (that is, on the basis of observation). But in no case can the necessity for interpretation be seriously questioned. The basic aesthetic "fact" that the music embodied and represented some kind of "poetic" content and did so both in its thematic matter and in its form is accepted by all of the contending parties, although some felt that the music was thereby enhanced, others that it was thereby diminished. These are among the issues raised by the New German School that have never gone away and probably never will.

The Concerto Transformed

The New German agenda had implications not only for issues of meaning in music but also for the genres in which composers chose to write. Liszt, Berlioz, and Wagner composed primarily orchestral music and operas. Liszt, of course, also wrote an enormous amount of piano music, but no mature opera, whereas Wagner for the most part composed only operas. The New German School shunned chamber music, which, on the other hand, was avidly cultivated by Schumann and composers in his orbit, notably Mendelssohn and Brahms. With the exception of Schumann's *Genoveva*, the latter group for their part stayed away from writing operas.

One genre that elicited responses from both sides in midcentury was the concerto. It has been a while since we have examined one, so an update is in order before looking at its reconceptualization brought about by changing aesthetics as well as by the new concept of instrumental virtuosity that arose in Paganini's wake and that Liszt brought to even greater heights. Like many other Romantic reconceptualizations, this one can be traced back if desired to Beethoven. And of course such a tracing was desired by both the New Germans and the Schumann/Mendelssohn/Brahms axis. The one side could point to Beethovenian progressive innovations as an ideal precedent and validation, while the other side could point to the seriousness of Beethoven's concertos, transcending the mere virtuosity of the vulgar Liszt, and to his continuation of the Classical tradition. Beethoven had inherited the concerto, after all, from Mozart. The directness of that succession can be seen, for example, in his Piano Concerto No. 3 in C Minor, Op. 37 (1800), the first movement of which is obviously modeled on that of Mozart's C Minor Concerto, K. 491 (1786).

The concerto form that Beethoven inherited was the "symphonized" variant of the old ritornello form, in which a full-blown but nonmodulating orchestral exposition stands in for the first ritornello, to be recast, now featuring the expected modulation, with the participation of the solo instrument upon its entry. Mozart's concertos upheld the ideal of cooperation between soloist and ensemble—that is, "to work in concert" (as derived from the Italian word *concertare*: to plan together, to hatch a plot)—rather than emphasizing the contest or opposition that later composers came to favor. Yet the heightened caprice and dynamism that Mozart brought to the concerto genre caused a heightened awareness in the nineteenth century of its potentially symbolic or metaphorical aspect, its possible reading as a social paradigm or a venue for social commentary. Artists

The heightened caprice and dynamism that Mozart brought to the concerto genre caused a heightened awareness in the nineteenth century of its potentially symbolic or metaphorical aspect.

imbued with the individualistic spirit of Romanticism interpreted the paradigm as one of social opposition, of the One against the Many, with an outcome that could be either triumphant (if the One emerged victorious) or tragic (if the decision went the other way).

Romantic subjectivity decisively altered the balance of forces in favor of the soloist, the lonely "hero." Beethoven's Fourth and Fifth Piano Concertos, Opp. 58 and 73 (1805–06 and 1809) were widely regarded as changing the equation in the relationship between soloist and orchestra, and, unusually, they placed the soloist front and center at the very opening of the first movements. Real integration of solo and tutti in a single thematic exposition came not much later. There was a forerunner of sorts in Weber's *Konzertstück* in F Minor (1821), a single-movement "concert piece" more or less in the form of a traditional symphonic first movement with slow introduction, but with the piano and the orchestra freely sharing the thematic material from the outset.

Yet as Beethoven was symphonizing the concerto and elevating its aesthetic ambition, the new virtuosity also increased the need for performing vehicles used by traveling performers. A long list of pianists, including Johann Nepomuk Hummel, Frédéric Kalkbrenner, Ignaz Moscheles, Sigismond Thalberg, Clara Wieck, and Frédéric Chopin, produced pieces for piano and orchestra, some as variation sets or forms other than a concerto proper. Berlioz's reaction to Chopin's concertos alerts us to one concern: "All the interest is concentrated in the piano part; the orchestra in his piano concertos is nothing but a cold and almost useless accompaniment."[15] While there is some justice to such criticism of pieces in which the orchestra asserts itself principally in the tutti passages but tends to do rather little when the piano is present, it may not be appropriate to judge these works either by the standards of Beethoven's symphonic concertos or by later-nineteenth-century ones. Orchestral parts often had to be fairly simple to accommodate itinerant virtuosos who rarely knew how good the orchestra in the next town would be or how much rehearsal time would be available to prepare for a performance.

For other composers a new relationship between soloist and orchestra became standard operating procedure, requiring no compromise in the difficulty for anyone involved. We see this, for instance, in the mature concertos by Mendelssohn, Liszt, and others around the middle third of the century. The new relationship involves the sharing of thematic material between the soloist and orchestral forces as well as the nature and the role of the cadenza. In Mendelssohn's two piano concertos—in G Minor, Op. 25 (1831), and D Minor, Op. 40 (1837)—the cadenza, rather than preceding the final tutti, forms a transition that joins the first and second movements in an unbroken continuity.

Anthology Vol 2-52
Full CD V, 5

In his Violin Concerto in E Minor, Op. 64 (1844), Mendelssohn's last orchestral work, the fully written-out cadenza is cast in the role of "retransitioner," elegantly bridging the development and recapitulation. The reentry of the first theme against the soloist's continuing arpeggios is a justly celebrated moment. Equally elegant is the way in which the solo violin and the orchestra share the thematic material in the exposition and recapitulation. At the outset, it is the violin, singing in its most brilliant register, that gets to announce the soaring opening theme, thus following Beethoven's innovation of having the soloist start the show. The second theme, by contrast, is played by a wind choir over a violin pedal. In the recapitulation, the orchestra gets both themes: the first brilliantly accompanied by the violin's continuing figuration as noted, the second presented as it was in the exposition but with enriched instrumental colors. This sort of piece required both an expert soloist, here Mendelssohn's colleague Ferdinand David, and expert orchestra, Mendelssohn's own at the Gewandhaus in Leipzig.

Hand in hand with the integration of solo and tutti, the overall form was compressed by means of transitions, minimizing formal breaks and creating an impression of "organic" structural unity similar to what Liszt did in his symphonic poems. Although Romantic in its striving after organic unity, the virtuosity in Mendelssohn's concerto is nonetheless of the brilliant, ingratiating sort. The soloist and orchestra are forever deferring to one another, graciously concerned that each gets its share of the spotlight. That carefully maintained equality could even be called the perfection of the Mozartean concerto ideal. In any case it was a short-lived moment of amicable equilibrium, soon to be upended by other compositional and aesthetic agendas.

Mendelssohn may have been influenced in some of his formal ideas for the piece by Schumann's one-movement *Phantasie* in A Minor for piano and orchestra, composed in 1841, which later served as the first movement of the more conventional and much more famous three-movement Piano Concerto in A Minor, Op. 54, completed in 1845. The complete concerto wonderfully balances the performing forces, with the soloist and the orchestra cooperating in the thematic presentations as well as in the transitional, episodic, and developmental passages. All the sections of the first movement may be related to conventional sonata design, but they have different tempos, sometimes highly contrasting ones. Yet each of these highly contrasted spots has the same thematic material, or, rather (with the exception of a *tempo primo* that functions as a literal recapitulation), each section is based on a variation—to speak Lisztianly, a transformation—of the same thematic idea, in which a common opening phrase is every time given a new continuation. Viewed this way, the first movement of Schumann's concerto begins to look like a set of linked character pieces that might have been variously signed by one of his creative alter egos, Florestan or Eusebius.

Schumann's concerto anticipated some of Liszt's innovations in its structural compression and thematic transformations. Liszt had written flashy virtuoso pieces for piano and orchestra during his touring days, but it was only once he settled down in Weimar that he completed two full-fledged concertos of much greater ambition. Concerto No. 1 in E♭ Major is dedicated to Henry Litolff (1818–91), a French pianist-composer of English birth, who was experimenting with an enlarged concerto concept that he called *concerto symphonique*. This was in some respects a modernization of the old *symphonie concertante*, a symphony with important parts for a group of virtuoso soloists, from the time of Haydn and Mozart. Liszt's debt is evident in the dedication of the concerto, in its structural weight rather than its brilliance of conception, and in its colorful orchestration, which included piccolo and triangle, which Litolff had been the first to use in the context of a keyboard concerto.

Yet where Litolff's concertos were expansive four-movement affairs, Liszt opted for the structural compression and thematic unity he was using at the same time in his Piano Sonata in B Minor and in his symphonic poems, for which Schubert's "Wanderer" Fantasy again served as an inspiring model. Indeed it was concerning the E♭ Major Concerto that Liszt gave his most detailed account of "thematic transformation," found in a letter to a relative. He described it as "the *binding together* and rounding off of a whole piece at its close" and added that the idea "is somewhat my own."[16] Although Liszt's concertos lack the programs connected with his symphonic poems, their transformed themes also sometimes take on distinctive types, such as pastoral and military.

The thematic transformations in Liszt's concertos testify to his impressive organizational skills: virtuoso composing to match virtuoso playing. And yet the result, for all its tightness and control, is a unique and unpredictable form. The impression such a concerto is designed to make in its unfolding is that of a spontaneously inspired fantasy, an unfettered train of associative thought, in which the soloist, the dominant personality, enjoys an unprecedented freedom to lead the orchestra—and the audience—where he or she wants.

Genre Trouble: Berlioz Again

The genre of the concerto as it evolved over the first half of the nineteenth century was shaped by the rise of the new virtuosity and of the public concert. Romantic subjectivity, Beethovenian heroism, structural and thematic innovations, all initially developed in other genres, also began to influence their composition. A relatively early work by Berlioz, *Harold en Italie* (Harold in Italy), demonstrates how the boundaries among genres are never as clear-cut as textbook generalizations suggest.

Figure 22-7 Stradivarius viola.

In 1832 Paganini, the legendary figure who inaugurated the new virtuosity, became the proud owner of a Stradivarius viola (Fig. 22-7). Frustrated by the lack of concertos featuring the instrument, he came up with the idea of commissioning one from Berlioz, a composer he greatly admired and whose *Symphonie fantastique* he had recently heard in Paris. In his *Memoirs*, Berlioz recounts that: "To please the great man, I attempted to write a solo for the viola, but a solo combined with orchestral accompaniment in such a way as to leave the orchestra full freedom of action; for I was confident that by the incomparable power of his playing Paganini would be able to maintain the supremacy of the soloist. The concept struck me as new."[17]

Soon after Paganini approached Berlioz in mid-January 1834, the project was announced in the press: "The work will be entitled *The Last Moments of Mary Stuart*, dramatic fantasy for orchestra, chorus, and solo viola. Paganini will play the viola part at the first public performance."[18] In the end, everything changed about this planned mixing of genres. The program was altered, the chorus dropped, and Paganini gone. Berlioz finished the piece, now titled *Harold en Italie*, in the summer and showed it to the violinist, who was not pleased with a work that was more a symphony than a concerto, more a showcase for a virtuoso orchestra than for a preening soloist with a prized instrument. Berlioz reports Paganini responding, "That's no good. There's not enough for me to do here. I should be playing all the time."[19] It is to Berlioz's credit that he did not compromise his artistic vision, and it is to Paganini's credit that when he eventually heard *Harold en Italie* performed some years later by someone else he stated that he had never been "so powerfully impressed" at a concert and graciously gave Berlioz 20,000 francs. This allowed Berlioz to write his next big work, *Roméo et Juliette*, which he dedicated to Paganini.

With *Harold en Italie* Berlioz created a nonvirtuoso concerto that was really his second symphony. He stated that his idea was "to write a series of orchestral scenes in which the solo viola would be involved, to a greater or lesser extent, like an actual person, retaining the same character throughout. I decided to give it as a setting the poetic impressions recollected from my wandering in the Abruzzi [mountains northwest of Rome], introducing the viola as a sort of melancholy

Figure 22-8 J. M. W. Turner's painting of scene from *Childe Harold's Pilgrimage*, Italy (1832).

dreamer, in the style of Byron's *Childe Harold*."[20] The solitary Romantic idealist is thus represented by the soloist.

Unlike the elaborate story Berlioz had concocted a few years earlier for the *Symphonie fantastique*, the names of the individual movements are the principal programmatic clues to an atmospheric mood drawn in part from Lord Byron's poem *Childe Harold's Pilgrimage* (1818; Fig. 22-8) and from Berlioz's own time spent in Italy after winning the Prix de Rome. As the composer remarked, the piece is unified by a motto (the viola's first theme) that appears throughout but is used differently than in his earlier symphony: "Whereas the theme of the *Symphonie fantastique*, the *idée fixe*, keeps intruding like an obsessive idea on scenes that are alien to it and deflects the current of the music, the Harold theme is superimposed on the other orchestral voices so as to contrast with them in character and tempo without interrupting their development."[21]

With* Harold en Italie *Berlioz created a nonvirtuoso concerto that was really his second symphony.

The last of the four movements opens with reminiscences of the preceding ones, an idea derived from the finale of Beethoven's Ninth, another boundary-blurring work and one that Berlioz had recently heard for the first time in performance. *Harold en Italie* is literary, picturesque, programmatic, and unified thematically among its four movements. Liszt transcribed the work for viola and piano and wrote one of his most important essays about it, which was quoted earlier. Such a piece displays a richness of musical and aesthetic ideas that defeats easy categorization.

Summary

This chapter dealt with developments in German musical thought that had a profound influence on the reception of music in the nineteenth century. Certain composers, such as Mendelssohn, Schumann, and Brahms, were considered conservative; others, such as Berlioz, Liszt, and Wagner, were seen as progressive. What gave rise to these categories is an approach to history called "historicism," influenced by the philosophy of Georg Wilhelm Friedrich Hegel (1770–1831). In Hegel's "dialectical" process of history, a starting concept, called a thesis, gives rise to its opposite, called the antithesis. The two concepts interact to produce a resolution called a synthesis, which then becomes a new thesis.

Hegel believed that all history moves toward a progressive goal of human freedom. Franz Brendel (1811–68) applied Hegel's theory of history to the history of music. Brendel believed that German composers such as Bach, Mozart, and Beethoven took the most decisive steps toward historical progress. He characterized all music before the sixteenth century as "primitive," because, he thought, it expressed the beliefs of the religious community rather than those of the individual composer. The rise of instrumental music was another crucial stage in this process, because it freed music from a dependence on words.

Brendel extended this historicist view of history into his own day. He believed that the goal of music history was the perfect synthesis of the poetic and the musical, and the composer he saw as best fulfilling this ideal was Franz Liszt. Although Liszt was not German, Brendel termed this "new music" and its representatives "the New German School," claiming that Beethoven was Liszt's spiritual predecessor. During his period in Weimar (beginning in 1848), Liszt composed radically innovative works, including a new genre called the *symphonic poem,* a single-movement work intended to express a poetic idea or pictorial image. Brendel valued Liszt's thirteen symphonic poems because the source of their inspiration was often not just literary but philosophical (see *Les Préludes*). Liszt's symphonic poems have features of sonata form, but with contrasting sections that can be thought of as different movements played without break. Their "content" is developed through a technique Liszt called "thematic transformation": A theme is varied and transformed over the course of the work, reflecting the narrative journey of the program.

The ideas of the New German School were not universally accepted. In an important treatise, their chief opponent, Eduard Hanslick (1825–1904), argued that the beautiful in music lay in its sound and form. Although music can express emotions and poetic content, Hanslick believed, this was not its central aim or purpose. Rather, music should follow its own inherent laws that transcend the composer's intentions and the listener's reactions. For Hanslick, the music of Brahms best fulfilled these aesthetic views.

The mid-nineteenth century also saw changes to the genre of the concerto. The growth of virtuoso culture led to an increase in demand for new concertos. In some concertos, the soloist came to dominate, and most of the musical interest is in the solo part. Other composers, however, created concertos that were equally demanding for both the soloist and the orchestra. In Mendelssohn's Violin Concerto in E Minor, Op. 64, the orchestra and soloist share thematic material in a way that is formally innovative but almost "Classical" in its sense of balance. Other concertos were influenced by the new trends in orchestral music. Liszt's E♭ Major Piano Concerto, for example, uses thematic transformation. Berlioz's *Harold en Italie,* commissioned by Niccolò Paganini as a viola concerto, is more like a symphony in scope, with a literary program linked to the poet Lord Byron.

Study Questions

1. What is historicism, and how is it related to G. W. F. Hegel's idea of dialectic?
2. Describe Franz Brendel's view of music history and the ideals of the New German School. Why did Brendel see Liszt as the composer who best represented these ideals?
3. Describe Eduard Hanslick's philosophy of art, comparing and contrasting it with Brendel's. What do you find most compelling in each side of the debate?
4. What is a symphonic poem? How is it different from a symphony, both in underlying philosophy and in musical form?
5. Describe the program of Franz Liszt's *Les Préludes*. How is the program represented in the music?
6. To what extent can music represent a specific program? Do you agree that "a third, fourth, or twentieth program might be just as convincing, hence just as 'true'"?
7. Describe innovations in the concerto of the mid-nineteenth century, especially as reflected in Felix Mendelssohn's Violin Concerto in E Minor, Liszt's piano concertos, and Hector Berlioz's *Harold en Italie*.

Key Terms

dialectic
historicism
New German School
symphonic poem
thematic transformation
***Zukunftsmusik* (Music of the Future)**

23

Class of 1813: Wagner and Verdi

A specter has been haunting the last few chapters of this narrative: the specter of Richard Wagner (Fig. 23-1). His name and his ever-increasing authority have been invoked various times in passing, most notoriously as the author of the anti-Semitic essay "Judaism in Music," which he published (anonymously) in 1850, attacking Giacomo Meyerbeer and Felix Mendelssohn. His name will continue to resonate in coming chapters—indeed no other composer of his time or perhaps any later time has exerted such an impact on succeeding generations.

Wagner's musical imagination was so powerful, backed up by a technique so novel and so impressive, that neither the music of his own day nor that of succeeding generations is conceivable without him. His influence was greatest among German musicians but was also strong in France, England, Russia, the United States, and elsewhere. That Wagner's phenomenal impact was not limited to music but extended to other arts, cultural life, as well as politics is itself key to his unusual stature. Such an effect on philosophers, writers, artists, and filmmakers is unprecedented for a composer. To mention just literature, Wagner's works proved to be of fundamental importance for figures such as Charles Baudelaire, Marcel Proust, James Joyce, and Thomas Mann.

With Wagner, moreover, we are in an unusually strong position to investigate his aims, since he wrote so prolifically about them. He wrote the librettos for all of his operas; in addition, his extensive writings encompass reviews, fiction, drama, essays, and books as well as diaries, countless letters, and a massive autobiography, *My Life*, which covers just the first half of his career. Wagner seemingly had an opinion about everything; he expressed his views passionately on a vast range of artistic, cultural, and political issues, including music, religion, vegetarianism, and other matters. So emblematic is Wagner of his time and his country, in their most glorious as well as their most horrible aspects, that he has become a figure of furious and apparently unresolvable debate. His legacy has been one of constant controversy, quarrels, and fanaticism. Alone among nineteenth-century composers, Wagner can still provoke a riot in the concert hall, particularly in the state of Israel, where a strict if unofficial ban on the public performance of his works is occasionally broken, only to be countered with loud protests.

Wagner, in short, is an extraordinarily difficult and problematical artist who has never stopped being difficult and a problem. That in its way is a tribute to his genius: Only an artist of the greatest and most unshakable stature could have become so great and unshakable a problem.

Figure 23-1 Richard Wagner. Portrait by Franz von Lenbach (1871).

Art and Revolution: Wagner's Early Career

In view of his eventual transformative position in history, the first extraordinary fact of Wagner's biography is the ordinariness of his beginnings. No composer of comparable achievement had a slower start. He was not a Mozartean or a Mendelssohnian prodigy, nor was he a Lisztian virtuoso. His earliest artistic interest was in the theater, a profession cultivated by members of his family. Wagner developed an early passion for Greek drama. While at school in his native Leipzig he worked on translations from Homer's *Odyssey* and tried to write an epic of his own. His first completed creative effort was a pseudo-Shakespearean tragedy, dating from 1828, when he was fifteen. It was his wish to set this play to music that led him to take lessons in music theory and composition, and he later studied violin and counterpoint at the Leipzig Thomasschule, where Bach had taught a century before. In the time-honored tradition, he also learned by copying and arranging music of past masters. He tried to publish a piano transcription he made of Beethoven's Ninth Symphony in 1830–31; the effort failed, but the firm of B. Schott & Sons sent the teenager scores to Beethoven's *Missa solemnis*, two late string quartets, and other works as a sign of encouragement. Wagner's various autobiographical writings, which are notoriously unreliable, tend to minimize the extent of his formal training so as to make the emergence of his genius seem all the more spontaneous.

Wagner is an extraordinarily difficult and problematical artist who has never stopped being difficult and a problem.

By the time Wagner reached the age of thirty he had gained some experience as a conductor at a couple of provincial opera houses, but as a composer he had accomplished little worth remembering; the older Wagner rejected much of this youthful music. Among his early works were piano sonatas, songs, overtures, and even a promising Symphony in C, written in a Beethovenian style at age nineteen. His first opera was *Die Feen* (The Fairies, 1833–34), after a scenario by the eighteenth-century Venetian playwright Carlo Gozzi; it was never performed during Wagner's lifetime. There followed *Das Liebesverbot* (The Ban on Love), after Shakespeare's comedy *Measure for Measure*, which received one performance in 1836 and then disappeared from the stage until the 1920s. The music, as Wagner admitted in retrospect, was derivative of the repertory current at the time and was bizarrely eclectic, mixing Weber, Marschner, Auber, and Bellini.

TIMELINE

1813 **Birth of Richard Wagner and Giuseppe Verdi**

1830 Victor Hugo, *Hernani*

1833 **Wagner begins composing his first opera, *Die Feen***

1839 **Verdi's first opera, *Oberto*, premieres at La Scala in Milan**

1842 **Verdi, *Nabucco***

1842–49 **Wagner in Dresden**

1843 **Wagner's *The Flying Dutchman* premieres in Dresden**

1845 **Wagner's *Tannhäuser* premieres in Dresden**

1848–52 **Wagner writes librettos for *The Ring of the Nibelung***

1848 Alexandre Dumas the younger, *The Lady of the Camellias*

1848 Karl Marx, *Communist Manifesto*

While his first attempt had looked primarily to German opera and his second to Italian, Wagner had greater success with his third, *Rienzi* (1838–40), which was more French, a Meyerbeerian grand opera on a subject from Roman history. Although its rousing overture remains a familiar concert piece, the opera itself has faded from the repertoire. In 1839 Wagner went to Paris, where he hoped the not-yet-finished *Rienzi* might be staged, and remained there for two and one-half miserable years. He utterly failed to establish himself as a composer, and kept from starving only by accepting low-paying work from music publishers making piano arrangements of popular operas and by writing short stories, reviews, and other articles for publication in both France and Germany. When *Rienzi* was finally accepted for performance, it was in Dresden. The lifelong resentment with which Wagner looked back on his time in Paris had a considerable impact on the subsequent direction of his work and political views.

He did, however, receive some important musical impressions in Paris, where the quality of orchestral performances amazed him. In addition to experiencing François-Antoine Habeneck perform Beethoven symphonies, Wagner encountered Berlioz's music. In the fall of 1839 he heard the French composer conduct his new dramatic symphony *Roméo et Juliette*, a work in the symphony-oratorio tradition of Beethoven's Ninth. Although Wagner would later downplay Berlioz's formative significance in order to play up Beethoven's, in his own recollection *Roméo* opened for him "a new world of possibilities which I had not then dreamed of,"[1] both in the handling of the orchestra and in the transmutation of drama into instrumental music. A quarter of a century later, in a presentation copy of the orchestral score to one of his own operas, Wagner inscribed: "To the great and dear author of *Roméo et Juliette*, the grateful author of *Tristan und Isolde*." He also acknowledged his debt to Berlioz in a letter to Liszt dating from 1850, when he stated that "there are only three of us who belong together nowadays, because only we are our own equals, and that's you—*he* [Berlioz]—and I."[2]

> ***The title characters in all three of Wagner's Romantic operas—the Dutchman, Tannhäuser, and Lohengrin—were heroic intruders who irrevocably disrupt a corrupt or complacent social order.***

The Dresden premiere of *Rienzi* on 20 October 1842 was a huge success, followed almost immediately by an incredibly lucky break: the sudden death of the Royal Court Kapellmeister, an Italian named Francesco Morlacchi. Wagner, who until then had held an official conducting position only in Riga and nowhere for the past four years, was offered the prestigious job. He supervised a production there in February 1843 of his next opera: *Der fliegende Holländer* (The Flying Dutchman), his first on a German legendary subject and by common consent his first masterpiece. His six-year tenure at Dresden, so auspiciously inaugurated, would reach its conclusion in the spring of 1849 on the city barricades, with the opera house in flames. Wagner had gotten drawn into the revolutionary politics sweeping Europe at the time. His active agitating in speeches and articles over the previous year was viewed as one of the precipitating causes of the unrest in Dresden, and a warrant for his arrest was issued on 16 May; eight days later, with Liszt's help, he escaped to Switzerland. He would not set foot on German soil for nearly fifteen years.

After *Dutchman*, Wagner next composed two grand Romantic operas: *Tannhäuser* (premiered in Dresden, 1845) and *Lohengrin* (Weimar, 1850), which continued his series of German legends for the stage and marked him out as the hope of what would soon be called the New German School by Franz Brendel. The combination of antiquarian Romanticism in his works with revolutionary politics in his life is only a surface paradox: Both the nostalgic aesthetics and the futuristic politics were symptoms of a general utopianism that seized the European cultural avant-garde during the revolutionary decade of the 1840s. Moreover, the title characters in all three of Wagner's Romantic operas—the Dutchman, Tannhäuser, and Lohengrin—were heroic intruders who irrevocably disrupt a corrupt or complacent social order: revolutionaries, in short, figures with whom Wagner could identify intensely.

The Dutchman in Wagner's version (borrowed from writer Heinrich Heine) is a phantom sea captain condemned to eternal wandering in his phantom ship as penalty for blasphemy. He is redeemed by the sacrificial love of a pure maiden named Senta, daughter of a greedy merchant sailor who had offered her to the Dutchman for the sake of material gain. To her father's despair she is willing to die to free the stranger (Fig. 23-2). Tannhäuser, on the other hand, was a historical figure, one of the Medieval German knightly poet-musicians mentioned in Chapter 2. In the opera, the full title of which is *Tannhäuser und der Sängerkrieg auf Wartburg* (Tannhäuser and the Singers' Contest on the Wartburg), he is a knight who has been seduced by Venus, the Roman love goddess. He scandalizes his peers with lascivious songs but is ultimately redeemed by the sacrificial love of Elisabeth, another pure maiden. In this opera, Wagner brilliantly contrasts the impressive choralelike solemnity of the music associated with the religious pilgrims and the extraordinary sensuality of the music suggestive of the Venusberg, the goddess's abode. The latter music flaunts the lessons in timbre and orchestral texture that Wagner had learned from Berlioz. The Venusberg episode that opens the opera is usually performed today in a later, extended version Wagner made for a famously unsuccessful Paris revival in 1861. By this time Wagner had broken through to a harmonic idiom unforeseen in 1845.

In retrospect, however, the most Wagnerian moment in *Tannhäuser* is the title character's long narrative in the last act, known as the "Rome monologue," in which the composer sought to create a new kind of union between words and music, something similar to earlier attempts to invent or reinvent opera. As in a recitative, say, by

1849 **Wagner, *Art and Revolution***
1849 Dresden uprising; **Wagner flees to Switzerland**
1850 **Wagner's *Lohengrin* premieres in Weimar**
1851 **Verdi, *Rigoletto***
1851 **Wagner, *Oper und Drama***
1853 **Verdi, *Il trovatore* and *La traviata***
1857–59 **Wagner, *Tristan und Isolde***
1864 Ludwig II crowned King of Bavaria
1871 Italy united under King Victor Emmanuel
1871 German states united outside Austria
1871 **Verdi's *Aida* premieres in Cairo**
1876 **Wagner's *Ring* cycle premieres in Bayreuth**
1877 Thomas Edison invents phonograph
1882 **Wagner's last opera, *Parsifal*, premieres in Bayreuth**
1883 **Death of Wagner**
1887 **Verdi, *Otello***
1893 **Verdi's last opera, *Falstaff***
1901 **Death of Verdi**

Figure 23-2 *The Flying Dutchman.*

Monteverdi or by Gluck, Wagner's vocal line closely follows the contour and rhythm of the spoken language and responds, with great flexibility, to the meaning and emotional sequence of the narrative. The orchestra supports the vocal line with a supple web of expressive and illustrative "reminiscence motifs," that is, themes that have accumulated associations and meaning over the course of the opera. This section of *Tannhäuser* in particular pointed toward his goal, ever more apparent in each succeeding opera: to dispense entirely with recitatives and set numbers (like arias or duets) so as to achieve a true through-composed continuity, what he later termed *unendliche Melodie* (**endless melody**), a seamless stream in which every note is thematic and meaningful.

In *Lohengrin* the title character is a legendary knight of the Holy Grail. The libretto is Wagner's own synthesis derived from anonymous Medieval epics and from the romances of the Minnesinger Wolfram von Eschenbach (ca. 1170 to ca. 1220). One of the most noteworthy parts of this opera is the prelude (*Vorspiel*) to the first act. Instead of a conventional overture in several contrasting sections or with differing themes, Wagner's prelude aspires to complete formal unity, carried along as if on a single breath of endless melody.

The Artwork of the Future, Modeled on the Imagined Past

Wagner is the first composer we have encountered who wrote his own librettos—or, as he put it, the "poems" for his "dramas." A playwright even before he was a musician, he sought to create the supreme artwork, in which different artistic media were united. Neither the words nor the music were privileged in his conception; the drama arose out of their union. Wagner's theorizing about such matters became explicit during a momentous hiatus in his composing. After the Weimar premiere of *Lohengrin*, under Liszt's direction in 1850, no new premiere of a complete Wagner opera would take place until 1865. Except for a frustrating bout in the summer of 1850, Wagner composed hardly a note between 1848 and 1853. Not that he was inactive during this time: He reflected and wrote on the purpose and future of his art. It was a willed self-transformation, unparalleled, and yielded momentous results.

The extraordinary ambition of Wagner's career is evident in his capacity to plan ahead and then patiently realize ideas conceived decades earlier. After fleeing Germany in 1849, he spent most of his exile years living in Switzerland, where he began to produce a series of essays and books known as his Zurich writings. In *Die Kunst und die Revolution* (Art and Revolution, 1849) we encounter for the first time, in crude but highly quotable form, the theory of music drama that he would spend the rest of his life putting into practice and to which he gave further expression in an extended pamphlet called *Das Kunstwerk der Zukunft* (The Artwork of the Future, 1849) and a full-length book called *Oper und Drama* (Opera and Drama, 1850–51). Wagner's Zurich writings reflect the revolutionary ideas of prominent contemporary thinkers and activists, including the German philosopher Ludwig Feuerbach (1804–72), French socialist Pierre-Joseph Proudhon (1809–65), exiled Russian anarchist Mikhail Bakunin (1814–76), and Karl Marx (1818–83). Wagner knew Bakunin personally. Exactly when and how much he read of the others' writings is unclear, but their socially subversive thought was current among revolutionary intellectuals. Beginning in the mid-1850s he became profoundly influenced by the writings of the German philosopher Arthur Schopenhauer (1788–1860), whose pessimistic worldview is felt in his late operas.

Like most of the reformist tracts in operatic history (think again of Monteverdi or Gluck), Wagner's Zurich writings purported to revive and renew the ritual theater of ancient Greece and to recapture its fabled ethos. Unlike earlier reformers, however, but very much in the philosophical spirit of his time, Wagner conceived of that ethos in broadly social terms. Greek tragedy was in his view the mainstay of Athenian democracy. The ancient Greeks had brilliantly combined the various arts—music, poetry, dance, as well as acting, costumes, architecture, and more—but with political decline over time these components had become separated and degraded. "Hand-in-hand with the dissolution of the Athenian State marched the downfall of Tragedy," Wagner proclaimed in *Art and Revolution*. "As the spirit of community [*Gemeinschaft*] split itself along a thousand lines of egoistic cleavage, so was the great united work [*Gesamtkunstwerk*] of Tragedy disintegrated into its individual factors."[3] The disunited splinters were the proud separate arts as practiced in modern times, each with its own canons of isolated excellence, each with its own zealously guarded traditions of craft and technique. While some of the arts, notably music, had flourished as they pursued separate paths, they remained incomplete and needed to be reunited. Wagner's mission, as he saw it, was to put the pieces back together again in a synthesis of the arts, the ***Gesamtkunstwerk*** (total or united artwork), a word Wagner himself rarely used but that has come to represent his artistic project.

For Wagner, this reuniting of the arts in the new, perfect drama would also mean a regeneration of society, an intentional meeting of art and revolution. As the arts splintered and the state fell apart, people took consolation in Christianity, which Wagner considered a sign of weakness. He came close to the position of Marx, for whom religion was "the opium of the people." Not that Wagner opposed all religion. As he made clear in some of his later essays, such as "Über Staat und Religion" (On State and Religion, 1864) and "Religion und Kunst" (Religion and Art, 1880), art itself was his religion (*Kunstreligion*), as it had been the religion of the Greeks. Crucial in this regard was that the subject matter of Greek drama and of his own operas was myth, the greatest repository of fundamental truths.

From Theory into Practice: *The Ring of the Nibelung*

If Wagner's career had ended at mid-century, he would be remembered today for his three Romantic operas and as a blustery political radical in the enthusiastic but ineffectual spirit of the failed revolutions that sprang up across Europe in 1848 in the hopes of economic and political reforms. Not the theorizing but the creative work, not the intention but the deed, has won Wagner his towering stature. The intentions implicit in his Zurich writings could hardly have been embodied more explicitly than they were in his next creative project, the largest musical entity ever produced within the European literate tradition. Wagner called it a "stage festival play for three days and a preliminary evening," consisting of four separate works collectively entitled *Der Ring des Nibelungen* (The Ring of the Nibelung). It would take him twenty-five years to complete this gigantic theatrical cycle, which totals some fifteen hours of music.

The mammoth project had modest beginnings. In the fall of 1848 Wagner drafted the "poem" for a new work to be called *Siegfrieds Tod* (The Death of Siegfried). The legend of Siegfried the Dragon-Slayer looms large in the *Völsungasaga,* an Icelandic epic about the mythic origins of the Nordic peoples. The *Nibelungenlied,* a thirteenth-century German epic, also relates many of Siegfried's exploits, including his seizure for his superior Volsung race of the great gold hoard of the Nibelungs (a race of dwarfs), his capture of the Icelandic queen Brynhild (Brünnhilde in the opera), his death through her treachery, and her atonement through self-immolation (plunging herself into a fire she has started), leading to the golden age of gods and Germans.

Wagner's aim in *Siegfrieds Tod* was to link the personal tragedy of the great German folk hero Siegfried, a traditional sort of operatic subject, with the Medieval Icelandic epics known as Eddas, the history of the gods. In so doing he hoped to elevate the drama to the level of a cosmogony, the story of the origins and destiny of the world; this would provide a suitably mythic subject for his socially transforming "Art Work of the Future." Wagner planned to begin *Siegfrieds Tod* with a lengthy prologue that showed the three Norns, figures comparable to the three Fates of Greek mythology, who weave eternally the rope of destiny. He started drafting the libretto for the opera but broke off, partly because he knew there were no imminent prospects for performance, exiled as he was from his homeland. More to the artistic point, it struck him that the story started too late, that he had to provide a dramatic and musical background for Siegfried rather than just have the Norns narrate it. He felt he needed a musically realized version of the past history of the drama that would give him the means of triggering through hearing the kind of emotional response to the action, whether portrayed directly or narrated, that only music can elicit. There had to be a preexisting musical reality with which the Norns' narrative and everything else in the final drama could suggestively connect.

Figure 23-3 *Götterdämmerung.* Brünnhilde's sister, Waltraute, urges her to return the magic gold ring to the Rhinemaidens. Illustration by Arthur Rackham.

The first step was to depict Siegfried's coming of age as a hero, his killing the dragon, and his winning Brünnhilde. This was accomplished in another poem, called *Der junge Siegfried* (Young Siegfried), written in the spring of 1851. Next, to explain how the sleeping Brünnhilde had got where she was (on a rocky peak surrounded by fire) when Siegfried broke through and awakened her and to clarify Siegfried's qualifications for his heroic calling (being the incestuous—thus purebred—offspring of two Volsungs, Siegmund and Sieglinde), Wagner preceded *Der junge Siegfried* with another poem, *Die Walküre* (The Valkyrie, that is, Brünnhilde), written between November 1851 and July 1852.

In the process of creating *Die Walküre,* Wagner reconfigured the drama of the *Ring,* making it center on Wotan, the chief of the Gods and Brünnhilde's father, rather than Siegfried. Wotan's original sin, that of destroying the World Ash Tree by hacking his invincible spear from it, became the deed for which the whole history of the Ring was the atonement. It all now ended tragically, not with the redemption of the gods (as in *Siegfrieds Tod,* which had to be drastically revised and was renamed *Götterdämmerung,* or Twilight of the Gods; Fig. 23-3), but with their violent destruction. Finally, to introduce the beginning of this history, namely, the theft of magic gold from the River Rhine and the forging of an all-empowering ring out of it by the dwarf Alberich, a Nibelung, Wagner wrote one

Table 23-1 Chronology of Wagner's *Der Ring des Nibelungen*

POEMS	MUSIC
Siegfrieds Tod (1848–49; revised 1852)	*Götterdämmerung* (3 acts) (1869–74)
Der junge Siegfried (1851; rev. 1852)	*Siegfried* (3 acts) (Acts I & II 1857; Act II scored 1864–65; Act III 1869–71)
Die Walküre (1851–52)	*Die Walküre* (3 acts) (1854–56)
Das Rheingold (1852)	*Das Rheingold* (1 act) (1853–54)

last poem to serve as prologue, in the form of a single mighty, two-hour-plus act: *Das Rheingold* (The Rhine Gold), completed in November 1852. With the four poems finally ready, Wagner turned to writing the music, this time proceeding in the chronological order of the narrative, as opposed to the order in which he wrote the librettos (Table 23-1).

Wagnerian Leitmotifs

One of the great challenges Wagner understandably encountered while composing the music of the *Ring* was finding ways to unify vast works meant to be performed over the course of four days, an unprecedented time span, while maintaining the interest of the listener. He accomplished this in part through large-scale key structure and associative tonalities within the "**music dramas**" (the term commonly used in preference to "opera"). Further, in order to invest them with the attributes of epic, Wagner envisioned a sweeping structure in which a scene or even an entire act would be articulated by means of tiny musical particles in ever-changing combinations. Rather than the customary numbers of conventional opera, Wagner's building up of a great whole out of a uniformly deployed fund of tiny but intensely meaningful parts would lend "organic unity," as he called it, to the enormous enterprise. The action of the music drama would unfold in a way that evoked the timelessness of myth, taking its shape within the mind of the spectator under the influence of the particles streaming by, endlessly associated and reassociated by the events depicted or described.

While Wagner's earlier Romantic operas had used a small number of reminiscence motifs, the new music dramas employed a far larger and interrelated web of musical ideas. Wagner called these particles *Hauptthemen* (main themes) or *Grundthemen* (fundamental themes), but they are best known as *Leitmotiven* (leading motifs), a term used by some of Wagner's associates rather than by the composer himself. (In English the word is usually spelled "leitmotif.") A **leitmotif** is usually far shorter than what is typically meant by a full-fledged theme, and some are really atomic particles—a mere turn of phrase, a chord progression, even a single chord or, at their most minimal, a single interval. Earlier reminiscence motifs had served a dramatic purpose. In purely instrumental works, composers such as Berlioz and Liszt found ways of unifying pieces musically with the *idée fixe* and thematic transformations. Wagner's innovation is that his many recurring and transforming leitmotifs serve both dramatic and musical purposes. They indeed evoke a conceptual as well as a sensory response; their whole intended magic, in short, lies in their capacity to link the sensory and conceptualizing faculties. Leitmotifs are the chief vehicle through which the artistic synthesis at the heart of the Wagnerian enterprise operates in his later operas. The influence on subsequent composers, especially in operas and film scores, was extraordinary.

Wagner's innovation is that his many recurring and transforming leitmotifs serve both dramatic and musical purposes.

In the *Ring*, Wagner employs more than a hundred leitmotifs. In 1876, the year the complete cycle finally premiered, Wagner authorized Hans von Wolzogen (1848–1938), a young aristocratic disciple, to compile what he called a *Thematischer Leitfaden durch die Musik zu Richard Wagners Festspiel "Der Ring des Nibelungen"* (Thematic Guidebook Through the Music to Richard Wagner's Festival Play "The Ring of the Nibelung"), the first of countless such books in which the leitmotifs are listed and given names for ready reference. The motifs represent many different things, including characters, places, objects, emotions, and even abstract matters, such as "fate." The guides specify that one particular leitmotif represents Valhalla (the home of the gods), another one Siegfried's sword, and so forth (Exs. 23-1a & 23-1b). Leitmotifs can be sung, played by the orchestra, or both, allowing for a kind of running commentary within the drama.

Example 23-1a Richard Wagner, "Valhalla" leitmotif

Example 23-1b Richard Wagner, "Sword" leitmotif

Whether the labels that Wolzogen and later commentators have attached to Wagner's leitmotifs are all equally useful is another matter. Many scholars have deplored them as simplistic or inaccurate, though by what measure their accuracy can be gauged is hard to guess, since Wagner himself never named them, and all the labels are therefore conjectural. He evidently wished to let the meanings of the motifs emerge by a wordless process of association with the unfolding drama. The exact names others have assigned them may therefore limit meaning rather than serving as a stimulus to the listener's subjective involvement in the drama. The occurrence and recurrence of leitmotifs, borne along in what Wagner called the "sea of harmony," are what define the significant moments in his music dramas.[4]

Wagner's leitmotifs often share common features, thus forming families that create a remarkable web of interrelations. The mother of all leitmotifs is the one evidently associated with primeval nature at the very start of the cycle. The beginning of

Das Rheingold is essentially an E♭ major chord spread out over a nearly four-minute span. Here Wagner displays his mastery of what he called "the art of transition"—the seamless passing from one musical entity to another. The primal "nature" motive (Ex. 23-2a) speeded up represents the eternally rolling Rhine river itself (Ex. 23-2b) and is later transformed into the motive for Erda, the goddess of earth, by changing the meter and the mode (Ex. 23-2c); when turned upside down the motive comes to represent the Fall of the Gods (Ex. 23-2d).[5]

Example 23-2a Richard Wagner, "Nature" leitmotif

Example 23-2b Richard Wagner, "Rhine" leitmotif

Example 23-2c Richard Wagner, "Erda" leitmotif

Example 23-2d Richard Wagner, "Erda"/"The Twilight of the Gods" leitmotifs

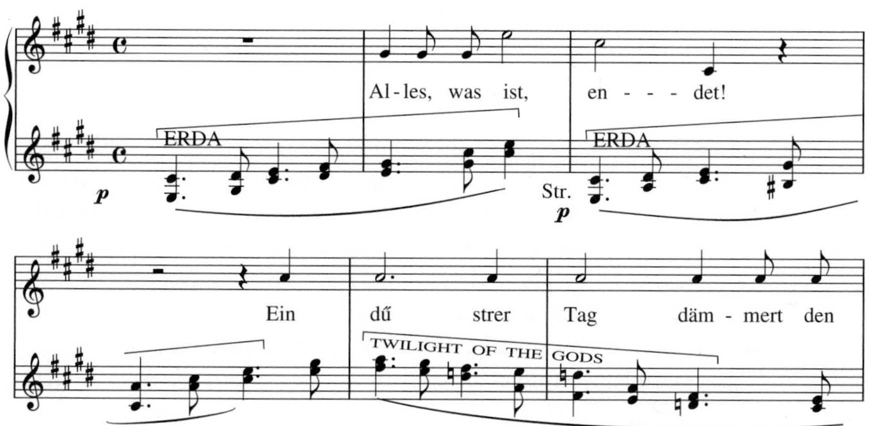

Words, Orchestra, and Theater

In addition to his conception of musical motifs, Wagner had a theory about the words to be sung, not limited to the mythic subject matter or details of plot, but extending to their actual sound. This is hardly surprising, since he wrote all the words himself, precisely because of his frustration with "*the imperfection of our modern verse,* in which I could find no perceptible trace of any natural melodic source, nor any standard of musical expression. The trouble was its *utter lack of genuine rhythm.* I could never have set my *Siegfried* if I had to rely on such verse. Thus I needed to invent a speech-melody of an altogether different kind."[6] Wagner attempted something new here by looking to the past, employing the ***Stabreim*** of old bardic poetry (short for *Buchstabenreim,* or "rhyming with letters"). From this he developed a highly rhythmic but unrhymed verbal idiom full of assonance and alliteration on heavily accented syllables, out of which arose a rhythm that animated the music in turn. Although to modern audiences the language of the librettos can seem embarrassingly artificial, Wagner viewed his texts as an equally important achievement along with his music and would assemble groups of admirers to whom he read the poems aloud long before composing the music.

Leitmotifs and word declamation are intimately connected to Wagner's conception of a "sea of harmony." Putting ourselves in the position of one who has heard no more recent music—in the position, that is, of Wagner's original audience—we will be struck, above all, by the unprecedented range and freedom of modulation and on occasion by its blinding rapidity. We will also notice long stretches of unchanging harmony. We will be struck by the extreme rarity of full authentic cadences, which occur only at the most decisive moments, and, by the reverse of that coin, the extraordinary abundance and variety of deceptive cadences. And we will observe the way these harmonic effects are closely geared to the words and dramatic action at any given moment.

The orchestra playing all these leitmotifs and conveying the vast harmonic sea is larger than the ones we have encountered in Rossini, Weber, or Meyerbeer, innovative orchestrators from whom Wagner learned. Perhaps most immediately noticeable is the greater prominence he gives to brass instruments, including several new ones introduced by him. The so-called Wagner tubas, tenor tubas in B♭ and small bass tubas in F, were meant to fill the gap between the French horns and the trombones. The singers pitted against the large Wagnerian orchestra had to possess powerful voices as well as ones that could endure the length of his operas. Special Wagner singers emerged, such as the "Heldentenors" (heroic tenors) who could project through the massed instruments and sustain such powers for hours on end.

Wagner's aesthetic theories also touched on the nature, purpose, and physical construction of the ideal opera house. He longed to have one built exclusively for his music dramas—his mature operas that is, from *The Flying Dutchman* forward. In keeping with his political views of eliminating class distinctions and inspired by the model of the ancient Greeks, Wagner envisioned not a traditional opera house with a main floor, tiered boxes, and cheap gallery sections reflecting the economic strata of society but, rather, a raked amphitheater on the Greek model. He also wanted the orchestra to be invisible, with no chance of the conductor and players distracting attention from the drama onstage. He had all this in mind over the many years of writing the *Ring*, but then it seemed just a fantastic dream.

His dream eventually came true after the completion of the *Ring* in the mid-1870s, made possible by a godsend: funding from Ludwig II (1845–86), the newly crowned king of Bavaria in southern Germany. The infatuated teenage monarch summoned Wagner to Munich, in 1864, paid off his mountainous debts, lifted bans on his travel, and commissioned the completion of the *Ring*. He even briefly made Wagner an unofficial yet powerful political adviser. At Ludwig's insistence, but without Wagner's participation, *Das Rheingold* and *Die Walküre* were staged in Munich in 1869 and 1870. Such royal munificence profoundly altered Wagner's political and social views, which took a reactionary and loyally monarchist turn. It also brought Wagner's operatic "reform" historically into line with previous ones: Like those of the Florentine Camerata or Gluck, Wagner's was now no revolutionary exploit but a project under the protection of a crown, about as socially conservative a concept as the history of music provides.

King Ludwig—often referred to as "mad" because of his penchant for building fantastical castles, his obsession with Wagner, and his erratic behavior—also gave crucial support for the realization of Wagner's ideal theater. The small town of Bayreuth, located in the eastern-central part of Germany, was chosen as the site. The foundation for the new opera house was celebrated with a performance of Beethoven's Ninth Symphony in 1872, conducted by Wagner; the building (Figs. 23-4 and 23-5) was finished for the first complete *Ring* performances in 1876. The simple structure was constructed along the lines Wagner had envisioned; when architect Gottfried Semper sent a preliminary sketch, Wagner scrawled on it "Get rid of the ornaments."[7] The amazing acoustics in the auditorium have enthralled audiences ever since, and the Bayreuth Festival remains active to this day—still run by Wagner's heirs and still performing only his mature operas each summer.

Figure 23-4 Festspielhaus at Bayreuth.

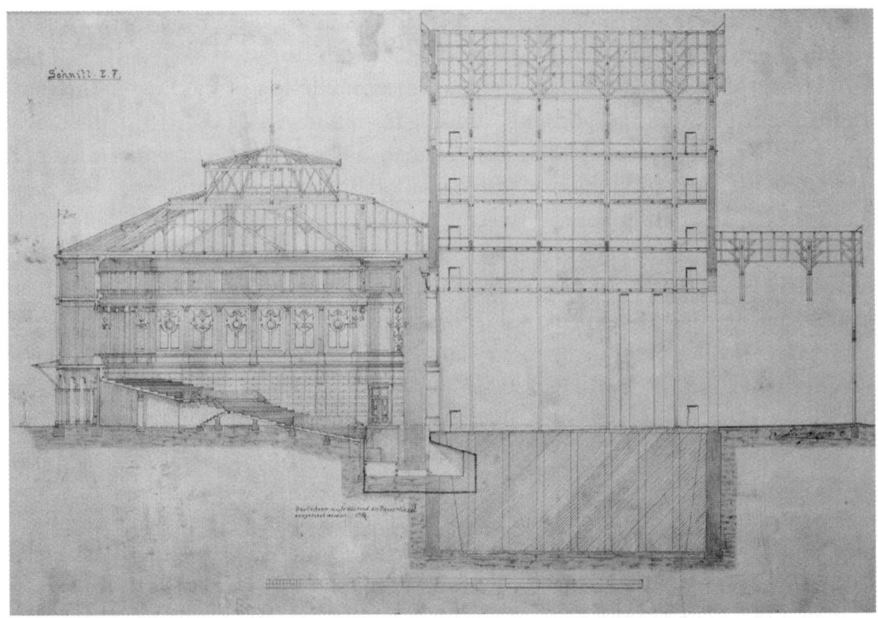

Figure 23-5 Festspielhaus in longitudinal cross section.

The Ultimate Experience: *Tristan und Isolde*

While composing the second act of *Siegfried,* in despair at the slim prospects for ever getting the *Ring* performed, Wagner stopped work and turned to writing two new dramas that he envisioned would be short and much easier to perform: *Tristan und Isolde* (completed in 1859, premiered in 1865), followed by his one mature comedy, *Die Meistersinger von Nürnberg* (The Mastersingers of Nuremberg, 1867). In the end, both operas turned out to be long and demanding; they also gave Wagner the opportunity to move in new directions.

Tristan is a love story adapted from a famous Medieval story: A man and a woman are seized with a forbidden love (Act I); they attempt to act on it but are forcibly separated, the man being mortally wounded in the process (Act II); the man dies and the bereft woman, overwhelmed at the sight of her lover's corpse, dies in sympathy (Act III). In a program note he wrote to clarify the content of the work as embodied in its prelude, Wagner reduced the story quite graphically to the feeling it symbolized. "Suddenly aflame," he wrote,

> they must confess they belong only to each other. No end, now, to the yearning, the desire, the bliss, the suffering of love: world, power, fame, splendor, honor, knighthood, loyalty, friendship—all scattered like an empty dream; one thing alone still living: yearning, yearning, unquenchable, ever-regenerated longing—languishing, thirsting; the only redemption—death, extinction, eternal sleep![8]

One of Wagner's signal achievements in *Tristan* was finding a way to express such longing and desire in music. He did this by exploiting the fundamental analogy between the harmonic language of his time and listener expectations. The music, by forecasting closure and then delaying it, calls attention to its own need for harmonic resolution. "Its" need, of course, is actually the listener's psychological need. The fluctuating musical tension is meant to evoke the fluctuating tensions—psychological, emotional, sexual—of our lives as we live them. Harmonic forecasts and delays play directly on the listener's expectation, or, to put it more strongly, on the desires that the music induces in the listener.

The opening three measures of the *Tristan* prelude constitute perhaps the most famous and surely the most commented-on single phrase of music ever written. The dissonant first harmony is so distinctive and seemingly unprecedented that it has been christened the "*Tristan*-chord." Its quality as sheer aural sensation is much enhanced by the mixture of orchestral colors in which it is clothed; and this in turn is the result of its being the point of convergence for two leitmotifs that later function independently: the rising sixth with conjunct chromatic descent in the cellos, and the rising chromatic tetrachord in the oboe (Ex. 23-3).

Anthology Vol 2-53a
Full CD V, 6
Concise CD II, 40

Example 23-3 **Richard Wagner, Prelude to *Tristan und Isolde,* mm. 1–11**

The unresolved dominant seventh in m. 3 is made even more oppressively palpable in the following sequential repetitions of the opening phrase. Each phrase of the continuation begins with cello notes drawn from the dominant harmony, previously left hanging, and proceeds through a *Tristan*-chord to a new dominant, to be similarly left ringing, unresolved and unconsummated, in the air. The effect of the third phrase is intensified and prolonged in a manner that may be fairly described as sadistic: Its harmonized portion is repeated after a fermata that extends the agony of incompletion, and after another similarly agonizing fermata the last two melody notes are repeated—and, to rub it in, repeated again at the octave—then reharmonized with the hanging dominant from m. 3, only to resolve in a deceptive cadence supporting yet another accented appoggiatura. Any listener who by now is not feeling "yearning, yearning, unquenchable, ever-regenerated longing—languishing, thirsting," et cetera, has simply never learned to respond to the syntax of tonal music.

How Far Can You Stretch a Dominant?

The Wagnerian innovation was not the *Tristan*-chord itself but, rather, the deliberate failure to resolve the dominant seventh that follows it. The prelude is a voyage on the sea of harmony that may be thought of as representing the voyage of the ship transporting Tristan and Isolde from Ireland to Cornwall, aboard which Act I takes place. The young knight Tristan (Fig. 23-6) has been sent by his uncle, King Mark, to bring back

Figure 23-6 Wagner's *Tristan und Isolde.* Painting by Wilhelm von Kaulbach.

the Irish maiden Isolde to be his queen. Isolde is intent on killing Tristan with a death potion, but her servant, Brangäne, substitutes a love potion that binds the title characters in an ecstatic embrace to end the first act.

The second act represents what Wagner called "night's wonder-world." The main event is an extended nocturnal love scene between Tristan and Isolde, arranged with the reluctant compliance of Brangäne, who stands watch over the lovers. The situation, as noted in Chapter 2, is the Medieval dawn song—*Alba,* or, in German, the *Tagelied*—in which lovers curse the arrival of dawn because it must bring to an end their night of pleasure. (We find a similar situation in Shakespeare's *Romeo and Juliet,* with the character of the nurse providing Brangäne-like warnings.) The long central action is in effect an enacted *Tagelied* cast in three big sections.

While the first section is thrillingly passionate, in the second the music settles down into a relatively stable key area (A♭ major) as the lovers lose themselves in a higher reality. Brangäne's cry of "Habet acht!" ("Beware!") acts as a refrain, to which the lovers pay no heed. The third section uses shorter note values, suggesting greater speed, and a more insistently goal-directed harmony. In a final approach to the looming, inevitable cadence, the singers' by-now-delirious sequences are accompanied by a steady chromatic descent in the bass that spans an entire octave, finally zeroing in on F♯ for what one feels sure is to be the long-awaited consummation. It almost happens, but instead we get a classic Wagnerian harmonic subversion. The process is repeated: the same melodic trade-offs in the vocal parts; the same chromatically descending bass. This time, however, another ingredient, even more insistently directed at the goal, is added, in the form of a sequence in the orchestra of a single bar's unit duration, consisting of nothing but endless reiterations of the four-note chromatic ascent first heard in the second measure of the prelude, rising from the *Tristan*-chord.

Twenty-eight times in all this motive resounds. At irregularly contracting intervals it is extended by an extra note smuggled in via a triplet to jack the sequence up by a single chromatic degree. After another classic Wagnerian move in the form of a shocking *piano subito,* the singers' parts are drawn into the irresistible soaring sequence. The bass, meanwhile, finally hits bottom on F♯ and stays there, grinding out twelve bars of dominant pedal intensified by a *molto crescendo,* at last pounding out the complete dominant seventh of B major in root position. At this point the rising sequence finally delivers Isolde's part to the leading tone. No composer had ever generated a comparable dominant-tension, for never before had a composer felt the need so to dramatize music's most basic business.

And then, disaster. Isolde's high B, the long-promised triumph of the tonic, is harmonized instead as the seventh in an excruciatingly grating dominant-ninth chord couched in the most cacophonous voicing imaginable, as King Mark comes rushing onstage with his large entourage. This is perhaps the cruelest deceptive cadence ever perpetrated; the lovers' rapture—not to mention the listeners'—is interrupted on the very point of consummation. Tristan, after first securing Isolde's promise to follow him into "the land where dark night reigns, from which my mother sent me forth," allows himself to be fatally wounded in a duel with one of King Mark's retainers.

The third and final act portrays the attainment of the rapturous fulfillment in death. Tristan dies in Isolde's arms, and she, contemplating his corpse, undergoes what Wagner calls her *Verklärung* (Transfiguration), as expressed in a last monologue that has popularly become known as the *Liebestod* (Love-Death), the term popularized by Franz Liszt's brilliant piano transcription of this ending. At the climax of her orgiastic death by love, Isolde sinks dead into Brangäne's arms as the curtain falls. Her climactic solo aria is a truncated recapitulation, in diminished note values, of the much longer final section of the Act II love duet just discussed. The first three-quarters of it is virtually identical, but then, instead of the bloodcurdling deceptive cadence that cut off the duet before its consummation, we get—finally—a cataclysmic authentic cadence, the most strongly voiced cadence in the entire opera. At this radiant moment, one may say, Isolde's soul passes irrevocably into "night's wonder-world," where it can join Tristan's, the lovers achieving in that transcendent space the union denied them on earth.

Anthology Vol 2-53b
Full CD V, 7

Wagner consolidates the sense of long-postponed consummation by attending in the last five measures of the opera to a bit of unfinished business left over from the first three measures of the prelude, heard nearly five hours earlier. He allows the original unresolved *Tristan*-chord to sound one last time, along with its attendant leitmotif, the four-note chromatic ascent. Only this time the note that finally resolves the *Tristan*-chord is given an extraordinary spotlight when Wagner clears all of the surrounding harmony away, allowing just the oboes to peep through the orchestral texture for a brief instant, immediately before the final, long-desired tonic chord.

Life and Art: Beyond Good and Evil

Such musical power and effect can raise disturbing questions, as so much of Wagner's music does. His contemporaries confronted not only Tristan's and Isolde's adulterous deeds but also Wagner's own flouting of moral conventions, among them many affairs during both of his marriages. One close relationship was with Mathilde Wesendonck, the wife of one of his benefactors in Zürich, in which the triangle of the composer and the two Wesendoncks vividly paralleled that of Tristan, Isolde, and King Mark. Later, more notoriously, he began living with Liszt's daughter, Cosima, who deserted her husband, Hans von Bülow (a devoted Wagnerian, even afterward), to become Wagner's second wife in 1870, after having already given birth to three of Wagner's children, operatically named Isolde, Eva, and Siegfried.

Wagner was perhaps the most powerful advocate for the implied proposition that a great artist's private life, however scandalous, was to be condoned out of reverence for his artistic genius—the idea that art, in Friedrich Nietzsche's famous phrase, was "beyond good and evil." In this view artists were not subject to the same moral strictures as everyone else. Wagner's art repeatedly explores the forbidden and the repressed, another factor that lends his works their special persuasive power. This begins to suggest what many in the twentieth century thought: that the most appropriate context in which to appreciate Wagner's achievement is provided by the later psychoanalytic theories of Sigmund Freud, another explorer of the unconscious desires that drive our conscious lives in directions we might be afraid to acknowledge.[9]

Nor are these the only perilous terrains toward which Wagner beckoned his listeners with his astounding persuasive skills. His project of redefining German identity led to xenophobia, expressed in bigotry—against Jews, against the "Enlightened" French, and by extension against internationalism and rationality themselves—symptomatic of a late-nineteenth-century strain of exclusionary nationalism. Wagner's appeal to the "feeling's-understanding," as he called it, implying a cerebral bypass, can look like the appeal of later German demagogues to "think with the blood" rather than with the reasoning brain.[10]

The ending of *Die Meistersinger von Nürnberg* is often cited as an example of Wagner's aggressive nationalism. The story, set in the sixteenth century, is about the proud young Walther von Stolzing, guided by the old mastersinger Hans Sachs (a real historical personage). Walther harnesses his native genius and produces the greatest song of the day, winning not only the singer's prize but also the hand of Eva, the woman he loves. But Wagner, egged on by his wife, Cosima, could not resist the urge to give the final scene a nationalistic turn, relevant to its contemporary context when the German states under Prussia's leadership were heading toward national unification and a vindictive war on France in 1870. Sachs gives a final oration that concludes with these words:

Habt Acht! Uns dräuen üble Streich': *zerfällt erst deutsches Volk und Reich,*	Beware! Evil threatens us: if the German land and folk should one day decay
in falscher welscher Majestät *kein Fürst bald mehr sein Volk versteht,*	under a false foreign rule soon no prince will understand his people any more,
und wälschen Dunst mit wälschem Tand *sie pflanzen uns in deutsches Land;* *was deutsch und echt, wüßt' keiner mehr,* *lebt's nicht in deutscher Meister Ehr'.*	and foreign mists with foreign conceits they will plant in our German land; what is German and pure no one will know if it does not live in our esteem for our German masters.
Drum sag ich Euch: *ehrt Eure deutschen Meister!* *Dann bannt Ihr gute Geister;*	Therefore I say to you: Honor your German masters! Then you will have protection of the good spirits;
und gebt Ihr ihrem Wirken Gunst, *zerging' in Dunst* *das heil'ge röm'sche Reich,* *uns bliebe gleich* *die heil'ge deutsche Kunst!*	and if you remain true to their endeavors, even if mists should dissolve the Holy Roman Empire, there would still endure our holy German art!

The Last Opera: *Parsifal*

Like most of Wagner's operas, the idea for his last one, *Parsifal*, dated back decades earlier. His interest in setting the Medieval legend came in part from reading Wolfram von Eschenbach's early-thirteenth-century epic *Parzival*. He began composition soon after the artistically triumphant but financially disastrous premiere of the

Ring at Bayreuth in 1876. Wagner suffered a mild heart attack in the spring of 1881, and he may have sensed that little time remained to him. He finished orchestrating *Parsifal*—which he called a "consecration festival play"—in January 1882, and it premiered that July in Bayreuth. *Parsifal* proved an artistic success as well as financially viable. At the last performance on 29 August Wagner took over the baton during the final act and conducted the rest of the work. It would be the last time he led one of his operas. He died of a heart attack in Venice less than six months later, at the age of sixty-nine.

Parsifal tells the story of a simple young man who through his awakened compassion heals Amfortas, the wounded king who, with his knights of Monsalvat, guards the Holy Grail, the chalice that caught Christ's blood at the Crucifixion. In the first act Parsifal meets Gurnemanz, one of the knights and later witnesses the service unveiling of the Grail, but he is uncomprehending of Amfortas's pain, which can be cured only through the compassion of a "pure fool," and is sent away. In the second act Parsifal resists the attractions of sensuous flower maidens and of the beautiful Kundry. He emerges triumphant over the evil sorcerer Klingsor, the one who initially wounded Amfortas by stabbing him with the sacred spear that pierced the side of Christ on the Cross. Upon receiving Kundry's passionate kiss, Parsifal exclaims, "Amfortas, the Wound!" and understands for the first time his destiny to end Amfortas's suffering. Klingsor throws the spear at Parsifal, but it stops, suspended in midair. Parsifal makes the sign of the cross and the sorcerer's magical world vanishes.

The third act recapitulates the first in its structure (the second had provided an exotic and erotic contrast). The aged Gurnemanz, dressed as a hermit, hears groaning and finds the repentant Kundry collapsed on the ground. Parsifal, who has wandered for years in search of Monsalvat, enters in full armor, carrying the spear he has retrieved for the knights. Welcomed by Gurnemanz, he is told he is on sacred ground, that it is Good Friday, and that he should lay down his arms. Recognizing Parsifal as the one he had dismissed so many years earlier, Gurnemanz informs him of Amfortas's ever-worsening state. Parsifal ultimately becomes the knights' new leader and presides over the unveiling of the Grail as they proclaim: "Highest holy Wonder! Our Redeemer redeemed!" (Fig. 23-7).

In *Parsifal* Wagner exploits a broad harmonic palette, associating chromaticism with the pain of Amfortas and with the magical world of Act II while more stable harmonies attend the Knights of the Grail. Some of the special sound qualities of *Parsifal* come from the fact that this was the only opera Wagner wrote specifically for Bayreuth, with its hidden orchestra pit and extraordinarily resonant acoustics. The brilliant layering of instruments, forever blending sounds, produces an unusual luminosity. In fact, each of Wagner's mature operas possesses a distinctive aural quality, and yet they all remain unmistakably Wagnerian.

Figure 23-7 Final scene of Wagner's *Parsifal*.

For Wagner's most ardent followers, *Parsifal* was a transcendent conclusion to a brilliant career that had transformed the genre of opera. Detractors variously viewed the work as mean spirited, decadent, and a mystification. In its obsession with community and purity, *Parsifal* can be seen as Wagner's most disturbing political statement. It may superficially seem to be a Christian opera, although it was heavily influenced by other sources, especially Buddhism and the thought of Schopenhauer. *Parsifal* proved the last straw for Nietzsche, Wagner's onetime friend and propagandist, who now saw Wagner "fallen sobbing at the foot of the Cross."[11] While the theological, philosophical, racial, and dramatic issues raised by *Parsifal* were hotly debated, and continue to be, its musical qualities, the nature of the instrumental writing, its distinctive sound world, its sonic beauty, furthered Wagner's powerful legacy.

No matter what they thought of Wagner or how they valued his achievement, his contemporaries, and many listeners ever since, have been forced to acknowledge the unprecedented and perhaps never equaled rhetorical force of his music. Whether they loved or hated it, most recognized that the experience of Wagner was emotionally compelling in a way that few musical experiences had ever been before.

Verdi: Upholding the Italian Tradition

Throughout this book we have encountered composer pairings, dynamic duos whose names have been linked for a variety of reasons. Some pairs reflect historical convenience (Leonin and Perotin as the first brand names in Western music), the calendar (Bach and Handel in the Class of 1685), aesthetic skirmishes (Gluck versus Piccinni), or stylistic affinity (Haydn and Mozart). We are now confronted with another accident of the calendar as well as an important aesthetic and geographical opposition, with Wagner and Giuseppe Verdi (1813–1901; Fig. 23-8), the two dominant figures in opera during the second half of the nineteenth century.

Verdi was Wagner's exact, if longer-lived, contemporary and the preeminent late-nineteenth-century representative of what was by then the oldest and most distinguished living tradition in European music: Italian opera. Wagner's enormous influence, in music and beyond, for good and for ill, may make him seem the more significant historical figure, although that does not necessarily make him the more effective dramatist or the superior composer. Wagner and his energetic supporters so dominated the musical discourse of the time that it is hardly surprising to find most composers, Verdi included, being spooked by his powers. Verdi himself highlighted the opposition between Germans as the "sons of Bach" and Italians as the "sons of Palestrina." He made the remark, echoed on other occasions, late in life to Hans von Bülow, who at some previous time had evidently made some disparaging comments about Verdi but who had recently written him a letter expressing newfound admiration. Verdi responded:

Figure 23-8 Giuseppe Verdi. Portrait by Giovanni Boldini.

> This unexpected letter of yours, written by a musician of your stature and your standing in the world of art, was a great pleasure to receive! Not because of personal vanity, but because I see that the truly superior artists judge without prejudice of school, nationality, or period.
>
> If the artists of the North and South have different tendencies, it is well they are different! They all should hold fast to the character of their own people, as Wagner very rightly says.

> You are fortunate to be still the sons of Bach. But we? We, the sons of Palestrina, once had a great school, and it was our own. Now it is a bastard growth, and ruin threatens.[12]

Verdi's concern reflects the north/south, brains/beauty oppositions we have encountered earlier. Verdi was in fact a more famous composer than Wagner for most of his career. His works formed the bedrock of the standard operatic repertory beginning in the 1850s, and they continue to form it today, when they remain much more frequently performed than Wagner's. By Verdi's time, Italians had enjoyed operatic preeminence for centuries. And thanks to the exportability of their product, Italian musicians had long come to see themselves as world conquerors, arbiters of universal taste. Since the rise of German instrumental music, with its heavy baggage of questionable (to Italians) philosophy, Italian musicians seemed happy to divide the musical world into two spheres of influence: the vocal, where their superiority was undeniable, and the instrumental, which the Germans were welcome to if they wanted it. Any German (Mozart, say, or Handel) who strove to excel in vocal music had to learn the trade from them and practice it on their terms; even when it came to language, these Germans wrote in Italian. Beethoven, with his one troubled opera, and Weber, with his glorified Singspiels, could be tolerated with condescension. They posed no threat.

But now, through Wagner, the newcomer German tradition had put the Italian on the defensive and had begun to assert universalist claims not only at home but abroad. The nature of the Wagnerian music drama implied a dual claim to dominance, incorporating both vocal and instrumental supremacy but ultimately seeking to transcend both spheres. Wagner was pioneering a new form of mass entertainment, which is one reason his work was so influential beyond the genre of opera. His dramatic project was winning converts even in Italy, where in the 1860s an increasingly vocal group of self-styled literary and musical intellectuals called *scapigliati* (disheveled ones) began agitating for new directions in the arts, including opera.

While Wagner's extensive theorizing and his genius for self-promotion had managed to get him widely accepted as the standard of musical contemporaneity, Verdi worried that the great Italian tradition was in serious decline: "Our young Italian composers are not good patriots. If the Germans, proceeding from Bach, have come to Wagner, they do so as good Germans, and all is well. But when we, the descendants of Palestrina, imitate Wagner, we are committing a musical crime and are doing a useless, nay, harmful thing."[13] Verdi's take on the future was different from that of the New Germans, even though he too desired a certain kind of purity; his motto, at least later in life, was "Let us go back to the old: It will be a step forward."[14]

"When we, the descendants of Palestrina, imitate Wagner, we are committing a musical crime and are doing a useless, nay, harmful thing."
—Giuseppe Verdi

Early Verdi: The Galley Years

Verdi spent the early part of his career as a staff composer for various major Italian opera houses, rather like those whom Hollywood movie studios would employ in the mid-twentieth century. He worked at the pleasure of different managements for some fourteen years, from 1839, when his first opera, *Oberto*, premiered at Milan's La Scala (Fig. 23-9), Italy's most prestigious venue, to 1853, when *La traviata* was

Figure 23-9 Interior view of Teatro alla Scala, Milan, ca. 1830. Painting by Ladislaus Rupp.

unveiled at La Fenice in Venice. He was in constant negotiation with theaters and casts, writing frantically on commission, with at first limited control over the subjects and librettos of the operas. Verdi looked back on this period as his "years in the galley," comparing himself to the slaves who sweated over the oars in ancient Roman ships. These were the hectic factory conditions described earlier with Rossini, conditions that made sticking to tried-and-true musical conventions a necessity.

The merciless conditions under which Italian operas were produced led to fairly standardized methods. An individual opera, however, did have a style—a ***tinta*** (color/tone), as Verdi and others called it—to make it effective and memorable. (Verdi on occasion mentioned multiple *tinte* within a single opera, associated with different characters or situations.) It was something of an intangible, this tinta. It might consist of recurrent tone colors or instrumental combinations in one opera, in another of recurrent harmonic effects. It could be the result of melodic turns or of characteristic rhythms or any combination of idiosyncrasies that provided a characteristic musical foundation apart from the level of theme or even leitmotif and also from the level of whatever local color a libretto might require.

Between the ages of twenty-three and forty, Verdi produced nineteen of his twenty-six operas (or twenty-eight, if two major revisions are counted) in collaboration with seven librettists and nine theaters. His literary tastes tended toward distinguished literature, historical dramas, and contemporary theater. The successful *Oberto* was followed the next year by *Un giorno di regno* (King for a Day, 1840), one of Verdi's few flops and his only comedy until the very end of his career. It was written to an old libretto in the Rossinian tradition during a time of great personal sorrow—Verdi's wife died while he was composing it; his two children had died not long before.

Nabucco (short for *Nabucodonosor*, or "Nebuchadnezzar," 1842), Verdi's third opera, made him a national figure. At the height of his early fame, 1844–47, he managed to turn out eight operas in less than four years, beginning with *Ernani* (1844), based on a notorious blood-and-thunder melodrama by the French writer Victor

Hugo (1802–85). None of this batch had permanent success, but *Macbeth* (1847, revised 1865) has earned a place in the standard repertory. Signs of growing international recognition begin in 1847, with commissions from London (*I masnadieri*, after Friedrich Schiller's play *Die Räuber*, or *The Robbers*) and Paris (*Jérusalem*, reworked from *I Lombardi alla prima crociata*, a historical drama set at the time of the Crusades). *Luisa Miller* (1849), which uses another Schiller play, premiered in Naples, as had *Alzira* (1845), based on the eighteenth-century French writer Voltaire.

"Viva Verdi!": Risorgimento Politics

Verdi became the most famous and frequently performed Italian opera composer during a famously turbulent period in Italian history known as the ***Risorgimento*** (Resurgence)—the name given by Count Vittorio Alfieri (1749–1803), an early nationalist poet, to Italy's struggle toward independence and national unity. As Alfieri's noble rank implied, the Risorgimento was a revolutionary movement led from above, by the aristocracy and the educated bourgeoisie, the art-consuming classes. The objective was to rid Italy of foreign rulers—Austria in the north, France in other areas, including the environs of Rome—and to unite the independent Italian states under a single authority. The factions furthest to the left backed republican rule, those furthest to the right papal rule; the ultimately successful liberal middle favored a constitutional monarchy under Victor Emmanuel II, King of Sardinia, heir of the House of Savoy, whose capital was the industrial city of Turin in northwestern Italy.

Independence and unification were achieved in stages, beginning with abortive uprisings organized in the 1820s in the wake of Napoleon's defeat and the Congress of Vienna. The proclamation of the kingdom in 1861 united most of Italy and landed Verdi the post of deputy in the new national parliament. Venice and Rome were the last places to be incorporated, the former as a diplomatic by-product of the Austro-Prussian War of 1866 (Victor Emmanuel having prudently allied himself with Prussia), and the latter as a similar by-product of the Franco-Prussian War of 1870. In 1871 the Italian state, incorporating the entire peninsula as it exists today, was established with Rome as its capital.

The 1840s, the decade of Verdi's apprenticeship, was a time when the arts, led by the example of poets and novelists such as Alessandro Manzoni (1785–1873) and Giacomo Leopardi (1798–1837), began to be significantly affected by Risorgimento ideals and to affect the movement in turn. It was, in the words of the revolutionary patriot Giuseppe Mazzini (1805–72), a time of "social poetry." The Romanticism it embodied, unlike the Romanticism of the northern countries, was largely hostile to morbid individualism. For Mazzini, a suffering Romantic hero was a thing of "wretchedness and impotence."[15] The proper role of literature, he believed, using the very word (*risorgere*) that gave the great movement its name, was not to glorify or wallow in private pain but "to soothe the suffering soul by teaching it to *rise up* toward God through Humanity."[16]

Part of the necessary political project was, simply, to teach the suffering Italian soul that it was suffering. Austrian rule was not particularly burdensome to the northern Italians, and Milan, both the

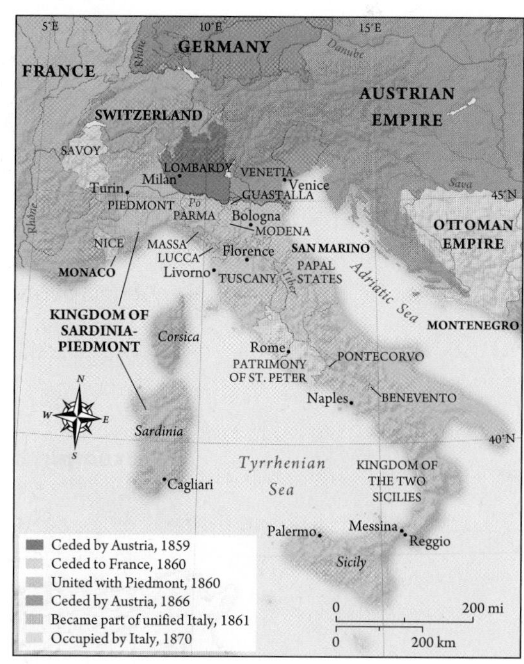

Figure 23-10 The unification of Italy (1859–70).

seat of the Austrian administration and the site of La Scala opera house, was for the most part a flourishing and contented city.[17] It became the function of art to rouse not only the rabble but also the educated classes to action, to give the latter a political conscience despite their relative well-being and the passivity to which material contentment so easily gave rise. This vividly suggests the source of the special Verdi style that guaranteed his early eminence: It aimed to make tangible cruelty, strife, force, and aggression.

The Popular Style: "Va, Pensiero"

The most striking effect in the early Verdi operas and the one most obviously allied to the mood of Risorgimento was the big choral number sung—crudely or sublimely, according to the ear of the beholder—in unison to start and containing a blazing middle section, in which the chorus suddenly opens out, rabble-rousingly, into chordal harmony, *fortissimo*. As a symbol of solidarity and of concerted action it could be read as political allegory. No matter what the actual plot of a given opera, no matter in what distant time or place it took place, audiences were able to make connections to their own situation and that of their country. The prototype was "Va, pensiero, sull'ali dorate" ("Go, my thought, on golden wings"), the chorus of Hebrew slaves in the third act of *Nabucco* (Ex. 23-4). Its text, by poet and occasional composer Temistocle Solera (1815–78), is a paraphrase of the famous 137th Psalm ("By the waters of Babylon . . ."). The chorus was an inspired interpolation into what was otherwise a love triangle plot—a prince of Jerusalem vs. two rival princesses of Babylon—set against a background of biblical warfare.

Rossini, struck by the originality of its conception, called "Va, pensiero" "a grand aria sung by sopranos, contraltos, tenors and basses."[18] Indeed the melody was as ornate as a Bellinian cantabile, the noble opening section of a bel canto aria, but with a simple four-square phrasing more characteristic of folk and street music. A chorus cast in such a popular form could all the more easily travel back to the street and into the oral tradition, helped on its way by the ever-present organ grinders and street singers who populated the thoroughfares of nineteenth-century Italian cities and disseminated theatrical hits. "Va, pensiero" was gradually translated into folklore in this way. This chorus became an emblem not only of Verdi as Italy's national composer-laureate but also of the Italian nation itself, the unofficial national anthem. It was sung in 1901 by the throngs surrounding Verdi's horse-drawn hearse on the day of his burial in Milan, led by the augmented chorus of La Scala, under the baton of Arturo Toscanini, who although a conductor rather than a composer eventually inherited Verdi's mantle as national emblem and musical ambassador to the world.

Example 23-4 Giuseppe Verdi, "Va, pensiero" from *Nabucco*

A
Chorus, tutti sotto voce
Va, pen - sie - ro, sull' a - li do - ra - te; Va, ti po - sa sui cli - vi, sui col - li

Go, my thought, on golden wings;
go, alight upon the slopes, the hills

Much of this significance was read back on the chorus from the perspective of the united Italy. Two legends in particular had sprung up around the chorus: first, that the original audience of *Nabucco* in 1842, seized by a patriotic delirium, had compelled an encore; and second, that the cries of "Viva Verdi!" (Long Live Verdi!) that filled the air on that occasion were a code for *Viva V. E. R. D. I.*—"Viva **V**ittorio **E**manuele, **Re d'I**talia" (Long Live Victor Emmanuel, King of Italy; Fig. 23-11). It turns out there was indeed an encore that night—but of another number. As to the second legend, the use of Verdi's name as an acronym for the king of united Italy started up only on the very eve of unification, when demonstrations in support of Victor Emmanuel's claim to the throne were no longer politically risky.[19] Such a display would not have been possible in 1842, when the Austrians ruled Milan. The growth of the Verdi myth thus proceeded in stages corresponding to those of the Risorgimento itself.

Figure 23-11 VIVA V.E.R.D.I.! During the war of 1859 between Sardinia and Austria over the northern Italian territories that included Milan and Venice, Verdi's name became a rallying cry as an acronym for Vittorio Emanuele, Re d'Italia, who was supported by Italian patriots like Count Camillio Cavour (and Verdi). The defeat of Austria paved the way for the first united (northern) Italian state, proclaimed in 1861, in which Verdi was an honorary senator. (It took another decade for the whole Italian peninsula to be united.)

But while less dramatic, that correspondence in myth is still evidence of a connection between the composer and the cause and points to Verdi's music as a catalyst to political militancy and eventual action, something we saw earlier with Auber's *La muette de Portici*. In any case, the success of the patriotic unison chorus in *Nabucco* stimulated Verdi himself to further action. His next two operas, *I Lombardi alla prima crociata* (The Lombards on the First Crusade, 1843) and *Ernani* (1844), also made a point of incorporating a similar choral set piece. Audiences were demanding them.

Dramatic moments in these early operas can therefore approach oratorio in their use of chorus and in their association with national politics. But there was also a new role for singers, especially for the tenor. In the old days of the opera seria the leading couple had been a soprano and a castrato—and then for a while, even more artificially, a soprano and a "musico," that is, a woman dressed as a man. Only with the generation of Bellini and Donizetti had the romantic hero become a natural-voiced man, although at a high register and with a lyric delivery. The great change in the technical training of singers was the institution of the ***tenore di forza*** (or *tenore robusto*), the "strength tenor." This new tenor maintained his full, or chest, voice over his entire range—even up to his highest notes, which assumed the vibrant, ringing tone we now associate with leading tenors. Those who have excelled at it—Enrico Caruso (1873–1921), Jussi Bjorling (1911–60), not to mention the "Three Tenors" (Placido Domingo, Luciano Pavarotti, and José Carreras), who in the 1990s became the highest-paid classical music act of all time—were the emblematic opera stars of the twentieth century.

Tragicomedy in the Shakespearean Manner

The librettist of *Ernani*, based on Hugo's politically risky liberal play *Hernani* (1830), was Francesco Maria Piave (1810–76), with whom Verdi collaborated over the next eighteen years on more than a dozen projects. Their partnership was by no means equal. The composer dominated the librettist mercilessly, reversing the traditional theatrical hierarchy and in so doing epitomizing the vastly heightened status of music in the later nineteenth-century artistic scheme of things. The mature Verdi always had precise notions of what the dramatic situation required in terms of music. By demanding of his librettists both exact versification and an extreme economy of words, Verdi controlled his mature operas almost as completely as did Wagner, who actually wrote both the words and the music.

But there the resemblance ceased. Where Wagner wanted to take opera back to its roots by impersonating Aeschylus and other ancient Greek tragedians, Verdi, one might say, wanted to become an operatic Shakespeare. What that meant was, in a word, dramatic "realism": the fusing of all existing dramatic genres into a single seamless idiom known as "tragicomedy," the true reflector of human character and experience. Fusion, which usually entailed the overthrow of formal constraints, had been Hugo's watchword, as expressed in the preface to *Hernani*. Hugo also invoked Shakespeare and the tragicomic, as did Verdi's fellow Risorgimento agitator Manzoni when he remarked that "it was not any mere violation of rules that led Shakespeare to this mixture of the grave and the burlesque, the touching and the low; he had simply observed this mixture in reality and wished to convey the strong impression it made on him."[20] The modern literary scholar George Steiner deftly summed up the difference between the epic and the tragicomic—the Wagnerian and the Verdian—by noting that

> even in the blackest hours of a Shakespearean tragedy or a Verdi opera the morning light of human laughter, the feline energies of human rebound are close at hand. . . . The masters of the absolute—Aeschylus, Sophocles, Racine, Wagner—concentrate the sum of the world to a single immensity of encounter. Shakespeare and Verdi, on the contrary, know that the instant in which Agamemnon is murdered [in Aeschylus's *Oresteia*] is also that in which a birthday party is being celebrated next door.[21]

The tragicomic vision, then, is one that projects drama in terms of foils and contrasts, including the contrast between poetry and prose. The most famous Shakespearean contrast of this sort is the farcical prose scene of the drunken porter at the gate (Act II, scene 3) that follows immediately on the horrific murder offstage of King Duncan in *Macbeth*; and the most sustained example of Shakespearean tragicomedy is the character of the jesting Fool who shadows King Lear, the most pitiable of all Shakespearean tragic victims. It is no coincidence that Verdi's tenth opera was a *Macbeth* or that the phantom haunting the composer's career was his unrealized ambition to create an operatic *King Lear*. (He ultimately ended his career with two Shakespeare operas, the tragic *Otello* and comic *Falstaff*.) True, the operatic *Macbeth* omits the scene with the porter, but the fact remains that the double-edged Shakespearean ideal of fusion and contrast was Verdi's main objective in tweaking the conventions of Italian opera into new configurations that depended to an unprecedented extent on devices of irony.

Il trovatore and *La traviata*

Between 1850 and 1853 Verdi produced a trio of masterpieces—*Rigoletto* (1851), *Il trovatore* (The Troubadour; 1853), and *La traviata* (The Fallen Woman, 1853)—that have remained the cornerstone of the Italian repertory in opera houses throughout the world. Their triumph bought Verdi's freedom from galley slavery. Before we look in some detail at the final act of *Rigoletto*, modeled on another politically liberal drama by Hugo, we should briefly examine the other two.

Il trovatore was based on a fairly recent play (*El trovador*, 1836) by the Spanish poet Antonio García Gutiérrez (1813–84), a follower of Hugo. The libretto was by Salvatore Cammarano, one of Donizetti's chief collaborators (the librettist for *Lucia di Lammermoor*) and hence a poet of the old school. It needed some doctoring to suit Verdi's more modern concerns. The composer wanted to get away from the traditional set pieces of number opera and welcomed the "new and bizarre." He commented: "If in operas there were no more cavatinas, duets, trios, choruses, finales, etc. etc., and if the entire opera were, let's say, a single piece, I would find it more reasonable and just."[22] But Cammarano stuck to his habits, and of the three "middle Verdi" masterpieces *Il trovatore* is the most formally conventional in its distinct numbers. It is also the most dramatically convoluted, ripe for such delicious parody as the Marx Brothers gave it in their film *A Night at the Opera* (1935).

La traviata, the most radically realistic opera of the three, was based on *La dame aux camélias* (The Lady of the Camellias) by Alexandre Dumas the younger (1824–95), a play that Piave adapted during the first year of its Parisian run, 1852. Using a current theatrical hit with a contemporary setting as the basis for an opera was a bold move, despite a similar attempt by Verdi in a slightly earlier opera called *Stiffelio* (1850). Even bolder was his determination to keep the time frame of the opera as contemporary as that of the drama. (Here he was overruled by the Venetian censors; the setting of the first production was pushed back to the mid-eighteenth century.) Boldest of all was the choice of a drama centering on the life and loves of Violetta, a courtesan, in other words, a high-class prostitute. But as Verdi wrote to a friend, it was "a subject of the times," and that justified all license.

That *La traviata* is Verdi's most intimate opera may be because the timely subject of the play and the opera mirrored actual events that touched deeply personal chords in both the playwright and the composer. Dumas' play was itself adapted from his own earlier novel, which was in turn largely autobiographical—he had been in love with Marie Duplessis (1824–47), the real-life Violetta. (Franz Liszt was also in love with her—just about everybody was in love with her.) As for Verdi, he was living in Paris at the time with Giuseppina Strepponi (1815–97), a former singer, and some of his family and friends did not approve of their relationship. (They would eventually marry.)

That* La traviata *is Verdi's most intimate opera may be because the timely subject of the play and the opera mirrored actual events that touched deeply personal chords.

It is no surprise, therefore, that the character of Violetta, the fallen woman of the title, was greatly idealized by Dumas and even more so by Verdi. The plot concerns the love of Violetta (Marie/Giuseppina) for Alfredo Germont (Dumas/Verdi), a young man "of good family," and its thwarting, first by her unacceptability to Alfredo's father and finally by her early death from tuberculosis. The whole story unfolds against the background of Parisian ballroom festivities, and the opera's tinta, easy to hear, is carried by its many actual, remembered, and etherealized waltz tunes, as in Violetta's cantabile ("Ah fors'è lui"/"Ah, was it he?") and cabaletta ("Sempre libera"/"Always free") at the end of Act I, which are cast as waltzes in contrasting tempos. At the other end of the opera, having been told by the doctor that death is imminent, Violetta takes leave of the world to the strains of another slow waltz-time cantabile; and when

Alfredo arrives just in time to see her die, they sing a duet that functions as the corresponding fast-waltz cabaletta. At the last minute Violetta receives the remorseful blessing of Alfredo's father and dies to the reprised strains of a waltz.

Throughout, but most conspicuously in this last scene, when Violetta expires in the arms of Alfredo, the tragic strains that accompany the sufferings of the protagonists are shadowed offstage by the happy strains of revelry, underscoring the contradiction at the heart of Violetta's existence but also providing that ironic mix of tragic and comic that, for Verdi as for Shakespeare, added up to life. As Steiner puts it, "The joy of the Parisian revelers beats against the windows of the dying Violetta in *La traviata* not in contrapuntal mockery but simply because the varied pulse of life is more constant than any particular sorrow; Shakespeare and Verdi anchor their host of characters in history, in the local color of historical epoch and circumstance, distrusting that monotone of eternity so compelling to Wagner."[23]

Rigoletto: Opera as Modern Drama

Rigoletto gives us Verdi's irony at fullest strength. It is one of his most Shakespearean works, despite its source in Hugo's play *Le roi s'amuse* (The King Amuses Himself). Verdi immediately saw in it an ideally Shakespearean subject, since the eventual libretto's title character, the hunchback Rigoletto (Triboulet in Hugo), was at once the tragic victim and a court jester by trade—Fool and Lear in one! "*Le Roi s'amuse*," Verdi wrote to Piave, "is the greatest subject and perhaps the greatest drama of modern times. Triboulet [Rigoletto] is a creation worthy of Shakespeare!! What is Ernani next to him?!! This is a subject that cannot fail."[24] Although Verdi had high hopes, Hugo's play had been a complete flop at its one and only performance in 1832, when the French censor condemned it for portraying a French king as a philanderer. (As a precaution against Italian censors, in Piave's libretto the royal rake is demoted to the level of a duke, the locale moved to Mantua, and the action set in the sixteenth century.)

The whole plot of *Rigoletto* hinges on a single wrenching irony. In the first act, Rigoletto, as the Duke's court jester, mocks the father of a girl his master has seduced and abandoned and receives a furious parental curse, which Verdi sets to a reminiscence motif that will reappear at crucial moments in the opera. In the second act Rigoletto's own daughter, Gilda, is seduced by the Duke; Rigoletto contracts Sparafucile, a professional hit man, to avenge his paternal honor by murdering the Duke. Through a series of chilling mischances, Gilda is murdered, devastating the poor jester and ultimately fulfilling the curse. The two roles Rigoletto played in life—jester and father—thus fatally collide. The contrast, embodied starkly in the two scenes of Act I, was made for music: Up until the moment of the curse, the first scene is pure comic opera; the second scene is tragedy. Act III is an unprecedented mixture throughout of the comic and the terrible.

Hugo's original play failed in part because of its Shakespearean mixture of genres. Verdi, however, realized that music could do the job that the spoken theater had failed to accomplish. He noted that "all the horrible plot vicissitudes arise from the frivolous, rakish personality of the Duke. Hence Rigoletto's fears, Gilda's passion, etc. etc., which make for many excellent dramatic moments, among others the scene of the quartet which as regards effect will remain one of the best our theater can boast."[25] The quartet to which Verdi refers here is the centerpiece of the final act. He achieved the "excellent dramatic moment" by tweaking the conventions of the genre to cast the "frivolous, rakish personality of the Duke" in maximum relief. A virile *tenore di forza* role, the Duke is the very opposite of the character type implied by his voice type. He uses his ringing tones not to affirm but to mock romantic love. This becomes clear from the outset in the Duke's heartily cynical Act I *ballata* (dance-song or ballad) "Questa o quella" ("This One or That"), in which he professes to love and value (that is, scorn and slight) all women equally. This shockingly ironic item is the opera's very first set piece.

Figure 23-12 Engraving on cover of a score for Verdi's *Rigoletto*, showing the quartet in Act III.

In the last act, the ironies and reversals are compounded and end in tragedy. The setting is a ramshackle inn. The Duke has been lured there to be murdered by Sparafucile, whose sister, Maddalena, runs the dive. The whole act is played on a split set that depicts both the interior of the inn (upstairs and downstairs) and the road outside (Fig. 23-12). The all-pervading device that will lend irony to every number is the mutual isolation of the two halves of the stage and the characters inhabiting them. On the inside are the Duke, Sparafucile, and Maddalena. On the outside are Rigoletto and Gilda.

Rigoletto has brought Gilda to this sordid place not to witness the impending murder, of which she has no inkling, but so that she can see the lewd behavior of the cad who feigns to love her. Through a crack in the wall the two outsiders observe the Duke's arrival, and they hear him sing a carousing ditty over wine as he awaits Maddalena's services as a prostitute. That song, the hypocritical "La donna è mobile" ("Woman Is Fickle"), is another of the Duke's little pop tunes (Ex. 23-5). Aware that despite its nauseating immorality (or because of it) the aria would be the opera's great hit, Verdi had gone to unusual lengths to keep it under wraps until the first performance so that the organ grinders and sheet-music pirates would not leak it prematurely to the street. He held it back from orchestral rehearsals almost to the last minute, privately coaching the tenor Raffaele Mirate, who sang the role of the Duke. Its eventual success was almost *too* great, since many who do not really know the opera ascribe to it, or even to Verdi, the song's trivial gaiety without realizing that its crude brashness was a calculated ironic foil. At first hearing, the irony is a mere matter of clash between jolly song and gloomy setting. But over the course of the act its range of reference, and consequently the range of its ironic resonance, will grow as it begins to function as a reminiscence motif, one of the most hair-raising in all of opera.

Anthology Vol 2-54
Full CD V, 8–12
Concise CD II, 41–45

After some banter between the Duke and Maddalena comes the quartet "Bella figlia dell'amore" ("Lovely Daughter of Love"), the most famous ensemble Verdi ever composed. Besides the typically popular nature of Verdi's melody, full of internal repetitions and melodic rhymes, there is, again, the underlying dramaturgical irony. This is not a traditional quartet in which four characters each reflect in lyric stopped-time on a change in the dramatic course. It is, rather, a double duet that takes place in real time, with two insider characters, the bawdy Duke and the beguiling Maddalena, and two outsiders, the indignant Rigoletto and the heartbroken Gilda. By the end of the quartet the four characters are a study in contrasts: the Duke, as ever, oblivious to all but his fleshly desires; Maddalena, as ever, mordantly detached (but aroused); Gilda crushed; and Rigoletto bent on revenge.

Example 23-5 Giuseppe Verdi, "La donna è mobile" from *Rigoletto,* Act III

A woman is fickle, like a feather in the wind, changeable of speech and of thought.

Rigoletto, not wishing for Gilda to witness the murder, now sends her off to disguise herself in male traveling attire and await him in Verona. Against a background suggestive of a tolling clock, Rigoletto gives Sparafucile the down payment on the murder contract. A storm is gathering, literally and psychologically, as Sparafucile and the Duke make conflicting demands on Maddalena (the former to help with the murder, the latter to sleep with him), putting her in an unexpected quandary. Sparafucile invites the Duke to spend the night; he dozes off with "La donna è mobile" on his lips. The clock chimes again, signaling the start of what should be the last moments of the Duke's life. Unexpectedly, however, Gilda (disguised as a boy) returns to the scene, against her father's instructions. Still infatuated by love, she is drawn back to the Duke, and from her position on the outside she overhears Sparafucile and Maddalena plotting inside the inn. We hear further reminders of the looming storm, for which Verdi makes use of a male chorus, humming closed-mouthed behind the scenes, to represent the voice of the howling wind. (Stage murders rarely take place in good weather.) The storm music gives shape to the drama's resolution and lends a gruesome mood to the final act.

As Maddalena rather fancies the Duke, she does not want to see him murdered and so convinces her brother to kill someone else instead should the chance arise. The disguised Gilda, overhearing this, immediately decides to sacrifice herself for her unworthy lover. When Rigoletto returns at the stroke of midnight, he receives the promised body in a sack. The prevailing recitative suddenly stops as a song is overheard—"La donna è mobile," jaunty and insouciant as ever, as the unsuspecting Duke starts to make his merry way homeward after his rendezvous with Maddalena. Irony compounded and recompounded! The merry song, giving evidence that the body in the sack cannot be the Duke's, now carries a horrifying double message to Rigoletto and the audience, who now must witness the terrible fulfillment of the curse in the corpse of his beloved daughter.

A Job Becomes a Calling

After the great trio of *Rigoletto*, *Trovatore*, and *Traviata*, not just Verdi, but Italian opera as a whole, no less than German, sailed out on uncharted seas. The cantabile-and-cabaletta formula began to die out as Italian opera followed the general trend toward numberless, continuous form. In becoming more realistic, Italian opera inevitably lost its special identity. What it gained was immediacy of pathos—an immediacy Verdi learned from no musical contemporary (certainly not from Wagner) but, rather, from literary models like Hugo and, in back of him, the omnipresent Shakespeare.

It is absurd to label Wagner and Verdi as "progressive" and "conservative" poles, although that is how historians writing in the tradition of the New German School have tended to present them. Just as wrong is to attribute the special qualities of Verdi's late work, beginning in the 1870s, to Wagner's influence, even though that was the decade during which Wagner began to receive staged performances in Italy. Verdi's knowledge of Wagner's work translated not into imitation but into a fascinating individual variant; nor was acquaintance with Wagner the biggest or most telling change that took place in the composer's life during the decade in question.

The main event in Verdi's life during his sixties was, quite simply, his retirement. The two decades following *La traviata* had been extremely lucrative ones for the composer. He followed the footsteps of Rossini and Donizetti to Paris for two five-act grand operas in French—*Les vêpres siciliennes* (The Sicilian Vespers, 1855), with a libretto by Eugène Scribe, and *Don Carlos* (1867), after a historical play by Schiller. In between these came a commission from the Russian tsar's own imperial Italian opera house in St. Petersburg for *La forza del destino* (The Force of Destiny, 1862), which was Verdi's last collaboration with Piave and for which he received an enormous fee. Verdi's other big foray abroad, a premiere in Cairo, proved even more exotic; *Aida* (1871) has a distinctive tinta achieved through melody, harmony, and instrumentation. But to the extent that the new opera seemed stylistically up to date or in any way different from what Verdi's audience expected, the difference was automatically attributed to Wagner's influence. Verdi obviously did not appreciate the view, telling his publisher "on top of all that I am an imitator of Wagner!!! A fine outcome after thirty-five years to wind up as an imitator!!!"[26]

Following *Aida*, Verdi called it quits. Composing for him—in keeping with his trying apprenticeship and the unsentimental attitudes of the professional theater—seems to have been a demanding job, and he may have regarded the opportunity to renounce it in favor of gentleman farming as a promotion. Rossini's death in 1868 left him the richest composer-entrepreneur in Europe, another self-made man of art. For years already he had been tempted to do as Rossini had done and to use his earnings to escape from the hectic, exhausting world of opera. He was genuinely interested in farming the land on an estate called Sant'Agata near his north Italian birthplace of Busseto, which he had purchased in 1851 and had been expanding ever since. Verdi's extensive correspondence suddenly had less artistic content (and less political content too after he resigned his honorary seat in parliament) and began filling up with discussions of crops, livestock, soil, and manure.

Verdi's knowledge of Wagner's work translated not into imitation but into a fascinating individual variant.

He did not cease all musical activity. In addition to supervising productions and revising some of his earlier operas, he wrote some new music. The only instrumental work of any significance from Verdi's pen is a string quartet dating from 1873 and written, one might imagine, with tongue-in-cheek. The piece seems to send up many of the conventions associated with the genre, German conventions after all. Far more important is the Requiem Mass composed in commemoration of the venerable Manzoni, like Verdi a symbol of the Risorgimento and an honorary senator. The work premiered on 22 May 1874, the first anniversary of Manzoni's death. Various opera revisions also loomed large. Verdi lavished a great deal of time during his "retirement" on two of his weightier historical operas: *Simon Boccanegra* (1857, revised 1879–81) and *Don Carlos,* which became virtually a new opera in 1884 and 1886 (usually performed in Italian as *Don Carlo*).

Finally, in 1884, thirteen years after *Aida*, Verdi allowed himself to be persuaded by his publisher, Guilio Ricordi (1840–1912), and by his ardent would-be literary collaborator, Arrigo Boito (1842–1918), to attempt an opera under these new, utterly unoperatic conditions of creative emancipation. Boito, who was a composer in his own right, had been one of the leading *scapigliati*—the young bohemian artists who thought the likes of Verdi outmoded—in the 1860s, and had a noble fiasco under his belt to prove it, an opera called *Mefistofele* (1868; revised 1875 and 1876) to his own very metaphysical libretto after Goethe's *Faust*. Impressed with a libretto that Boito gave him in 1879, Verdi tested him as a collaborator by having him help with the revision of *Simon Boccanegra*. Finally convinced of Boito's ability and his devoted respect, Verdi left full-time farming and took up his old job.

As anyone might have guessed, the subject that lured Verdi out of retirement came from Shakespeare—a Shakespeare treated with unprecedented fidelity and (with one huge exception, the climactic ensemble finale in Act III) an adventurous disregard of traditional libretto structure. That disregard was especially evident because the subject, *Othello* (or *Otello*, to use the Italian name), had already served Rossini some seventy years in a hugely successful, traditional opera seria that was still being performed. Verdi revered Rossini—indeed the Requiem was initially conceived as a group effort of Italian composers to honor his death—but this new project seemed to invite comparison and contest.

In *Otello* Verdi strove even more than before to achieve what opera critics since the beginning of the century had called the "continuous finale": a flexible interaction of literary and musical devices modeled on the finales of the Mozart/Da Ponte comedies, now stretched over whole acts. For the sake of continuity, both Verdi and Wagner committed wholesale violations of traditional form. For both composers, ultimately, the conscious objective became an individual fidelity to artistic ideals rather than to audience expectations.

Verdi's operas shun the supernatural, while Wagner's embrace it. Verdi's operas present action, while Wagner's revel in static tableaux.

Masterly Amusement: *Falstaff*

The tradition that Verdi inherited was essentially the comic tradition in which humankind is responsible for its own fate. The specifically operatic tradition that led to him is the one that proceeded through ever greater infusions of opera buffa styles, forms, and attitudes into opera seria. The dramatic tradition that led to Wagner is the tragic tradition, in which humans are the helpless playthings of the gods. Verdi's operas shun the supernatural, while Wagner's embrace it. Verdi's operas present action, while Wagner's revel in static tableaux.

Thus it is no surprise to find that Wagner's last opera, *Parsifal,* was an out-and-out metaphysical drama, replete with actual sacred rituals enacted onstage and ending with miraculous healings and redemptions—or that Verdi's last opera was *Falstaff* (Fig. 23-13), fashioned by Boito from Shakespeare's *Merry Wives of Windsor* (often viewed as the playwright's least successful comedy), with lines drawn from other of his plays as well. (Falstaff's Act I monologue on honor, for example, is transferred from a battle scene in *Henry IV, Part 1.*) It was Verdi's first opera buffa in fifty years and an astonishing departure for a composer approaching the age of eighty. But with benefit of hindsight one could hardly imagine a more fitting consummation to Verdi's career than his exploration of the wacky world of the lovable knight Sir John Falstaff.

Figure 23-13 *Illustrazione italiana*, cover of special issue, "Verdi and Falstaff" (1893).

While working on *Falstaff,* Verdi let it be known that "I am writing it in moments of absolute leisure, simply for my own amusement."[27] That made it respectable. And so did the assumption that underlay the composer's disinterested amusement: consciousness that his new manner of continuity and compression served the purposes of art. *Falstaff* is hardly a neglected masterpiece, but it has never enjoyed the popular fame of many of Verdi's earlier operas; there is a striking disparity between its exalted professional reputation as musicians' music and its somewhat more limited public appeal. *Falstaff* may come as close to musical perfection as any piece in the operatic literature, and it does so in the most subtle, compassionate, and humanely touching ways. Wagner aspired to "endless melody," and, without the heavy theorizing, Verdi achieved something similar with the seamless economy of *Falstaff.* It is largely a perpetual-motion scherzo from start to finish; every note is melodic and memorable, although few are presented in traditional arias or ensembles; some witty leitmotifs aside, not many tunes are repeated.

When Verdi said he was writing *Falstaff* for his own amusement he was not just offering an excuse in case of its incompletion or failure. The autumnally wise comedy looks back on his career and on the genre of opera itself. Verdi filled the work with self-quotations and with allusions to other composers, including Mozart, Rossini, and even Wagner. He mocks such longstanding operatic conventions as the love duet, the revenge aria, the exit scene, and the comic finale. The character of Ford, a jealous husband, is presented in an almost entirely serious manner, and hence the irony is supremely comic. Ford's ravings and cries for revenge revisit emotions Verdi had so often explored before. Verdi's earlier operas were big on male bonding—friendship and oath-taking duets often ring down the curtain. Ford's Act II monologue ("E sogno? o realta"/"Is it a dream, or reality?"), after which Falstaff and Ford parody conventional operatic exits by arguing about who should go first, is merely one such witty reflection on the genre.

The "Merry Wives" (plus one widow and one prospective bride) form a charming, chattering group to contrast with the male characters. Verdi also wove in two young lovers, Fenton and Nannetta, throughout the opera. (Boito wrote to Verdi, "As one sprinkles sugar on a tart, so I should like to sprinkle the whole comedy with this merry love."[28]) They sing one of the few recurring melodies in the work, not a Wagnerian instrumental leitmotif, but a typically Italian lyric moment featuring a couplet from Boccaccio's *Decameron* ("Bocca baciata non perde ventura/Anzi rinnova come fa la luna"/"The mouth that has been kissed does not lose its savor/ indeed it renews itself as does the moon"). Another recurring theme comes when a comic old woman, Mistress Quickly, sings "povera donna" ("miserable woman"), which is a literal quotation, with the same pitches and in the same key, of Violetta's lament that ends the first act of *La traviata*. Two subsidiary characters, Sir John's attendants Bardolph and Pistol, provide another self-quotation: When fat Falstaff praises his enormous belly, his lackies sing "Falstaff immense," parodying the words and music imposingly used to praise the Egyptian god Phtha in *Aida*. There are many such moments in the opera, testimony to Verdi's private amusement in this late project. After *Falstaff*, after age eighty, Verdi still composed a few pieces, modest sacred ones, that again look back to the rich Italian cultural heritage of Dante and Palestrina.

Verdi ends his last opera, and his operatic career, with a joyous final fugue, a gesture that harkens back to Mozart's finales and ironically casts him as a "son of Bach" by displaying his own contrapuntal mastery overlaid with pure Italian lyricism. Here he takes leave of his art, as did Shakespeare through the character of Prospero when the revels ended in his late play *The Tempest*. "I alone am the source of your pleasure," Falstaff says before he states the final fugal subject then taken up by the entire ensemble:

Tutto nel mondo è burla.	Everything in the world is a prank.
L'uom è nato burlone,	And man is born a joker.
nel suo cervello ciurla	His reason is always
sempre la sua ragione.	confused in his head.
Tutti gabbati! Irride	All are duped! Every man
l'un l'altro ogni mortal,	laughs at the others,
ma ride ben chi ride	but he laughs best who has
la risata final.	the last laugh.

Summary

Richard Wagner (1813–83) brought transforming developments to opera. Reflecting his view that drama was central, he created what he considered a new genre, music drama. Underlying his innovations were several related philosophical views. The first is the interrelationship between the arts—poetry, set design, staging, and music. These elements worked together toward the expression of the drama in what Wagner called the *Gesamtkunstwerk*, or total artwork. To ensure maximum control over each element, Wagner wrote his own librettos and even helped design his own theater in Bayreuth. The orchestra played a fundamental role in the drama, providing both a continuous musical fabric, often called "endless melody," and developing the opera's system of leitmotifs. A leitmotif is a bit of music, recognizable by a distinct melody, harmony, and rhythm, that is associated with a person, place, thing, emotion, or abstract concept ("fate," for example). These musical motifs and the meanings they represent are varied and transformed over the course of the opera. Complementing this rich orchestral fabric is a speechlike vocal line derived from the rhythms of his librettos. Wagner's most important earlier operas are *The Flying Dutchman* (1843), *Tannhäuser* (1845), and *Lohengrin* (1850).

Wagner was a prolific and controversial writer on art, aesthetics, and politics. During a hiatus from composing between 1848 and 1853, he produced a series of writings on the purpose and future of his art, including *Das Kunstwerk der Zukunft* (The Artwork of the Future, 1849) and *Oper und Drama* (Opera and Drama, 1851). In these writings, he espoused the idea of the unity of the arts, which was put into practice with *Der Ring des Nibelungen*, a cycle of four operas written between 1848 and 1874. The *Ring* cycle is based on the Norse mythology of a Medieval Icelandic epic, dealing with the origins and destiny of the world. Another innovation of Wagner's music is its extended chromatic harmony. In the opening of the prelude to *Tristan and Isolde* he introduced the famous "*Tristan* chord," which symbolizes the unfulfilled longing of the principal characters by remaining unresolved until the end of the opera. His final opera, *Parsifal*, deals with the knights that guard the Holy Grail, the chalice that caught Christ's blood at the Crucifixion.

The dominant figure in Italian opera in the second half of the nineteenth century was Giuseppe Verdi (1813–1901). In his early years, Verdi worked within the established traditions of Italian opera. Distinct numbers such as arias, duets, and choruses are effectively incorporated into larger periods of uninterrupted music. With their popular appeal, his early works became associated with the movement for Italian independence and unification known as the Risorgimento (resurgence). "Va, pensiero," the chorus of Hebrew slaves in his third opera *Nabucco* (1842), became something of an unofficial national anthem.

Verdi strove for dramatic realism and the mixture of comic and serious often called "tragicomedy," a great contrast to Wagner's epic and mythological topics. Although he worked with distinguished librettists, including Francesco Maria Piave and Arrigo Boito, Verdi exerted a great deal of control over his librettos. He was especially drawn to Shakespeare and Victor Hugo as sources. His best-known operas include *Rigoletto* (1851), *Il trovatore*, and *La traviata* (both from 1853). Tragicomic and ironic situations are particularly evident in the final quartet of *Rigoletto*.

Verdi's later operas, beginning in the 1870s, moved toward a numberless, continuous form. *Aida* (1871) has a distinct "exotic" flavor created by its melody, harmony, and instrumentation. After a hiatus of thirteen years and with the influence of a new librettist, he composed two works based on Shakespeare, *Otello* (1887), and the comic opera *Falstaff* (1893).

Study Questions

1. Describe Wagner's views on art, as expressed in *The Artwork of the Future* and *Opera and Drama*. How did these views inform his music?
2. What is a *Gesamtkunstwerk*, and how is it reflected in Wagner's music dramas?
3. How do Wagner's leitmotifs work to support the development of the drama? How do they affect the way one listens to his scores?

4. Describe Wagner's innovations in extended harmony, especially in *Tristan und Isolde*. How do they support the unfolding of the drama?
5. Compare and contrast Wagner and Verdi's operas in terms of their libretti and their dramatic features. What were the dramatic goals behind the works of each composer, and how were they realized in their choice of sources and in their libretti?
6. Describe the Risorgimento and its relationship to the popular style of Verdi's early operas.
7. Describe the mixture of the tragic and comic in Verdi's operas, especially in *Rigoletto*. What musical means does Verdi use to express irony in the quartet of the final act?
8. How did Verdi's *Falstaff* differ from his earlier operas?

Key Terms

endless melody
Gesamtkunstwerk
leitmotif
music drama
Risorgimento
Stabreim
tenore di forza
tinta

24

Slavic Harmony and Disharmony

The influence of the New German School did not stop at the German border. One of its most enthusiastic disciples was Bedřich Smetana (1824–84; Fig. 24-1), now generally considered the first important nationalist composer of the Czech lands. How could a Czech nationalist also be a New German? We may begin to understand the paradox by considering a letter Smetana wrote to a friend shortly after his thirty-sixth birthday:

> First of all I must ask you to excuse all my mistakes, both in spelling and grammar, of which you will certainly find plenty in this letter, for up to the present day I have not had the good fortune to be able to perfect myself in our mother tongue. Educated from my youth in German, both at school and in society, I took no care, while still a student, to learn anything but what I was forced to learn, and later divine music monopolized all my energy and my time so that to my shame, I must now confess that I cannot express myself adequately or write correctly in Czech.[1]

Indeed Smetana, the son of a prosperous brewer, was brought up to call himself Friedrich rather than Bedřich and to aspire to a cosmopolitan career like any urban, educated, middle-class child of a loyal Bohemian subject of the Austrian emperor. His place of birth (Bohemia, the part of the Czech lands that lies north of Moravia), his native language (German), and his early cultural orientation were all the same as critic Eduard Hanslick's, although his ethnicity was different (as his surname, which means "cream," suggests).

So in one important sense Smetana did not come from beyond the borders of the German lands at all, since those borders, as drawn politically, extended far beyond the German-speaking core. Smetana ultimately came to identify with his Slavic ethnicity rather than with his original language, his German cultural milieu,

TIMELINE

1825 Alexander Pushkin, *Boris Godunov*

1857 **Death of Mikhail Glinka**

1857–58 **Miliy Balakirev, *Overture on Russian Themes***

1861 Tsar Alexander II abolishes serfdom in Russia

1862 **Balakirev founds Russian Free Music School**

1862 **Anton Rubinstein founds St. Petersburg Conservatory**

1865–69 Leo Tolstoy, *War and Peace*

1866 **Balakirev, *Anthology of Russian Folk Songs***

1866 **Bedřich Smetana, *The Bartered Bride***

1869 **Modest Musorgsky, *Boris Godunov* (first version)**

or his lifelong political allegiances, and this identification vividly encapsulates the metamorphosis that the idea of nation underwent in the course of the nineteenth century. The "divine music" that Smetana said claimed his time and energy was the music of the great German tradition, not that of the Czech countryside, which like the Czech language was then regarded as the property of illiterate peasants. He never did learn to speak the language flawlessly, nor did he ever get to know much authentic Czech folk music. Instead, he eventually became quite good at producing his own authentic Czech music.

A piano prodigy, Smetana had a life-changing experience in March 1840, when at the age of sixteen he heard Liszt perform in Prague. Against the wishes of his father, Smetana renounced higher education in favor of a career as a professional musician, hoping to become "a Liszt in technique and a Mozart in composition."[2] Early in 1848, not knowing where else to turn, he impulsively sent Liszt the manuscript of his Opus 1 piano pieces: *Six morceaux caractéristiques* (Six Character Pieces). He also made three requests: first, for permission to dedicate the works to Liszt; second, for Liszt's assistance in getting them published; and third, for a loan to help set up his own music school.[3] Liszt ignored the last request, but he praised the music lavishly and sent it to his own publisher, winning Smetana's eternal gratitude.

During the 1840s Smetana barely scraped by, despite succeeding in opening his school with other financial backing. The year 1848 was as politically eventful in Bohemia as elsewhere in Europe, and Smetana's early compositions reflected its turbulence. He wrote his share of patriotic marches and anthems during the Prague revolt that June, as well as two more substantial pieces: the *Jubel-Ouvertüre* (Festive Overture, 1848–49) and the *Triumf-Sinfonie mit Benützung der österreichischer Volkshymne* (Triumphal Symphony Using the Austrian People's Hymn, 1854), inspired by the marriage of the new Austrian emperor, twenty-three-year-old Franz Joseph I, who would reign for almost seventy years. Smetana greeted Franz Joseph's accession to the throne with high hopes for Czech legislative and fiscal autonomy within a federalized empire. Instead, a repressive and ultimately counterproductive policy of "Centralization and Germanization," enforced by a ruthless secret police, created a stifling political atmosphere and did more to stimulate the growth of Czech cultural nationalism than liberalization could possibly have achieved.

Figure 24-1 Bedřich Smetana. Anonymous portrait, ca. 1865.

A Czech Abroad

Despite efforts to stamp it out, the use of the Czech language among the educated classes grew. The capital, Prague, was transformed over the second half of the nineteenth century from a German- to a Czech-speaking city. No matter what language dominated there, the musical establishment did not initially embrace Smetana's music, notably his Piano Trio in G Minor, which Liszt praised highly while visiting the city in 1856. "Prague did not wish to acknowledge me, so I left it,"[4] Smetana informed his parents at the end of the year as he emigrated to Göteborg, Sweden's main seaport and second-largest city.

He was an instant success there. During his first year he opened another music school, was named the director of the city's leading choral society, and inaugurated a prestigious series of chamber music concerts. Perhaps most decisive of all in reshaping his career, though, was further contact with Liszt, whom he visited at Weimar in the summer of 1857. Smetana became so committed a disciple that Liszt invited him to attend the great 1859 convocation of musicians in Leipzig and to join the Allgemeiner Deutscher Musikverein. He became in effect an exemplary New German, in some ways the most advanced of them all. He wrote to Liszt that he now better understood "the *necessity* of the progress of art, as taught by you in so great, so true a manner, and made it my credo. Please regard me as one of the most zealous disciples of our artistic school of thought, one who will champion its sacred truth in word and deed."[5]

1869–76 **Alexander Borodin, Second Symphony**

1872–75 **Smetana, *Má vlast* (*My Fatherland*), including *Vltava* (*The Moldau*)**

1876 Alexander Graham Bell invents the telephone

1877–78 **Pyotr Ilyich Tchaikovsky, Fourth Symphony**

1879 **Tchaikovsky, *Eugene Onegin***

1879 Fyodor Dostoyevsky, *The Brothers Karamazov*

1881 **Death of Musorgksy**

1881 Tsar Alexander II assassinated

1893 **Tchaikovsky, Sixth Symphony (*Pathétique*)**

1893 **Death of Tchaikovsky**

The initial fruit of Smetana's conversion was, no surprise, a series of symphonic poems, among the earliest to follow Liszt's example. First came *Richard III* (1858), after Shakespeare, which had its counterpart in Liszt's *Hamlet*; next followed *Wallensteins Lager* (Wallenstein's Camp, 1859), after Schiller, a "battle piece" that had its counterpart in Liszt's *Hunnenschlacht* (Battle of the Huns). Smetana further advanced the aims of the New German School in *Macbeth* (1859), later retitled *Sketch to the Scene Macbeth and the Witches*—a symphonic poem in every sense except medium, for it was composed for solo piano. By this point Smetana could fairly be described as one of Europe's most progressive musicians, and so he remained to virtually the end of his career, when he wrote a programmatic—indeed autobiographical—string quartet (*Z mého života*, or *From My Life*, 1876) that culminates with fine contempt for beauty in a ghastly high violin harmonic mimicking the onset of the deafness at age fifty that heralded the composer's eventual deterioration from syphilis. Despite these credentials and accomplishments, Smetana is for the most part remembered differently, slotted into conventional music histories as a leading nationalist and not as a leading progressive of his time; the explanation for this comes not so much from his music but, rather, from the ways music history is typically written.

Fed up with provincial Göteborg, Smetana returned to Prague in June 1862. What lured him home was a career opportunity: the announcement of a competition for a Czech opera to open a new national theater in Prague (Fig. 24-2). Five years later Smetana would become its principal conductor; eventually he became artistic director. Ever since Weber's *Der Freischütz* and especially since Glinka's triumph with *A Life for the Tsar*, it was assumed that the founding of a truly national musical life could best be achieved through an inspiring representation of the nation on the operatic stage, a purpose that required an opera with big numbers and recitatives, not a folksy Singspiel. In Poland Stanisław Moniuszko (1819–72) did this with *Halka* (1848), and Ferenc Erkel (1810–93) did so in Hungary with several historical operas, beginning with *Hunyadi László* (1844).

Smetana was adamant that a true national opera need not and should not rely on folk songs.

Smetana was determined to play that decisive role in the Czech lands, where to that point the only vernacular operas were Singspiels about peasants. He did so in seven works that covered all genres and established Czech opera as part of an international repertoire. His maiden effort was called *Braniboři v Čechách* (The Brandenburgers in Bohemia, 1862–63), which concerned a Medieval war of liberation and that won Smetana the opera competition he entered. Although he paid close attention to the peculiar accentual pattern of the Czech language in this work, there is not the slightest hint of folk music in it. Indeed, he was adamant that a true national opera need not and should not rely on folk songs, even in the case of comic operas, where they were traditionally used. He believed that "imitating the melodic curves and rhythms of our folk songs will not create a national style, let alone any dramatic truth—at the most only a pale imitation of the songs themselves."[6] There is an echo of New German ideology in his rejection

Figure 24-2 Prague Provisional Theater, built in 1862. Antonín Dvořák was a member of the Provisional Theater Orchestra between 1862 and 1873, where he played under Bedřich Smetana.

of *Volkstümlichkeit* (folklikeness), and also echoes of Robert Schumann's admonition that national character is decoration rather than substance and can act only as a brake on musical progress. There is also an echo of the object lesson implicit in Glinka's achievement, to the effect that national musics had to be internationally respectable and competitive if they were to become a dependable source of national pride and prestige.

What makes all this seem strange is the insistence of Czech musicians and music lovers, from Smetana's day to ours, that his style is intensely and inherently national in character, instantly recognizable as such by any native listener. What is the source of this *českost*, or "Czechness"? Is Smetana's music Czech because he intentionally made it so, because listeners heard it as such, or for some more complex mixture involving both creation and reception? According to Michael Beckerman, the leading American expert today on Czech music, *českost* (or Russianness, or Germanness, or any-ness at all) arises not directly out of style, whether a personal style or a collective vernacular, but rather out of "musical symbols rich in associative possibilities." For their actualization, a compact or bargain is required between producer and consumer. "*Českost* comes about," Beckerman writes, "when, in the minds of composers and audiences, the Czech nation, in its many manifestations, becomes a subtextual program for musical works, and as such, it is that which animates the musical style, allowing us to make connections between the narrow confines of a given piece and a larger, dynamic context."[7]

Má vlast

Although Smetana first sought to realize "Czechness" in the realm of opera, we can also observe it within the Lisztian genre of the symphonic poem, which he brought to extraordinary heights even after his sudden deafness in 1874. Beginning in the mid-1870s he created a monument of *českost* that many have regarded as his masterpiece: a cycle of six symphonic poems to which he gave the collective title *Má vlast* (My Fatherland). It is actually a rather heterogeneous collection of pieces, all of which premiered separately; it was not until the first four had been composed that the idea of performing them as a cycle even occurred to Smetana. Three of the symphonic poems—including the first two, *Vyšehrad* (The Castle on High, 1872–74) and *Vltava* (The Vltava River, 1874; Fig. 24-3)—are descriptive of places or of nature. (The remaining nature piece is No. 4, *From Bohemian Fields and Groves*, 1875.) The third (*Šárka*, 1875) is drawn from pre-Christian Slavic mythology. The last and longest two (*Tábor*, 1878; *Blaník*, 1879) deal with episodes in the fifteenth-century religious wars led by Jan Hus (ca. 1369–1415), the pre-Reformation Protestant

Anthology Vol 2-55
Full CD V, 13
Concise CD II, 46

whose achievements the Austrian authorities were in Smetana's time bent on eradicating through a policy of "re-Catholicization."

These symphonic poems are interconnected by the use of recurring musico-poetic emblems. *Tábor* and *Blaník* are both shot through with a fifteenth-century Hussite hymn, *Ktož jste Boží bojovníci* (Ye Who are God's Warriors), which all Czechs know by heart (Ex. 24-1):

Example 24-1 Hussite hymn: *Ktož jste Boží bojovníci* ("Ye Who Are God's Warriors")

Ye who are God's Warriors and of his law,
Pray to God for help and have faith in him,
That finally with him you may be victorious.

Smetana also devised frames for the entire cycle along the lines of a Berliozian idée fixe or an operatic reminiscence motif, but with more specific national resonances. The motif is first heard as a harp solo at the very beginning of *Vyšehrad*, where its evocative timbre gives the impression of a bardic storyteller relating an invented past (Ex. 24-2). In Smetana's preface to the score he explains that "the poet's memory is carried back to the remote past by the sound of the harp of the bard Lumír. There rises the vision of the castle on high [Vyšehrad] in its ancient splendor, its gleaming golden crown that was the proud dwelling place of the Premysl kings and princes, the ancient dynasty of Bohemia."

This opening motive given by the harp returns not only in the first piece of the cycle but also later, for example, at the end of *Vltava*, the symphonic poem that has most strongly established itself as a repertory item independent of the others. Reasons for its separate popularity, especially with non-Czech audiences, are not difficult to surmise. It makes virtuosic use of some very traditional, widely accepted representational devices. Its program, or sequence of events, is represented in the music in an unusually straightforward, descriptive fashion, beginning with the murmurings of the distant rural tributaries of the great Vltava River, which flows past hunters, past a wedding party with dancing, and past a moonlit night before reaching the urban splendor of Prague. The style of the music, while never

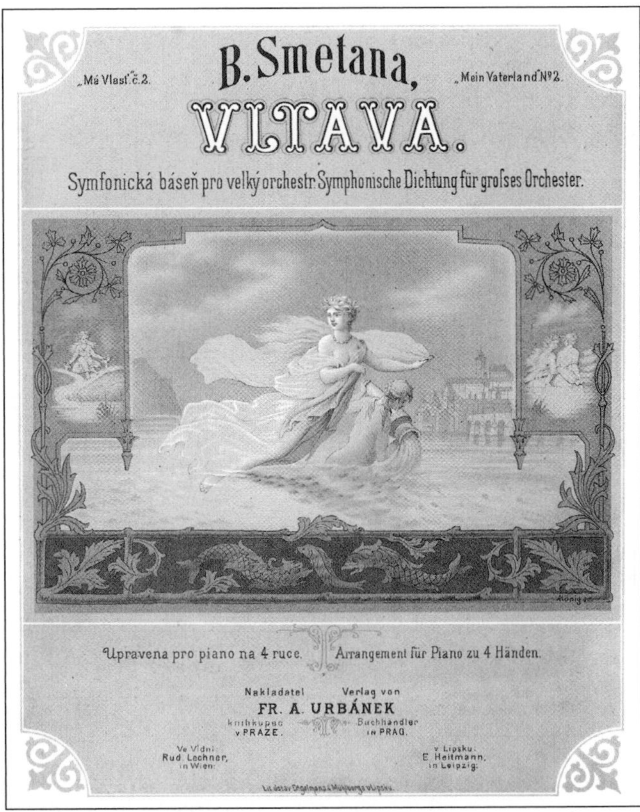

Figure 24-3 Illustrated title page from *Vltava* (The Moldau), 1874, the second symphonic poem in Smetana's *Má vlast* cycle.

actually quoting a Czech folk song, is of a marked popular character that appeals to foreign audiences by virtue of its exotic coloring and brilliant orchestration.

Example 24-2 Harp solo at the outset of Bedřich Smetana's *Vyšehrad*

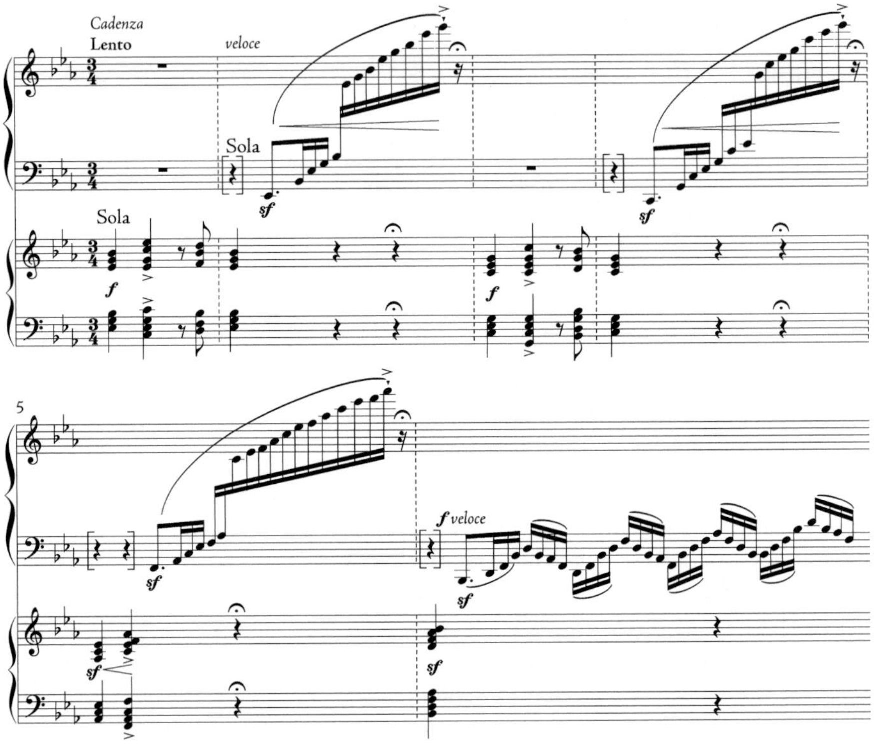

By adding a few enumerations and indictors of key to Smetana's program, one arrives at a serviceable list of its musical sections:

1. (E minor) The Vltava River springs from its two sources, splashing gaily over the rocks and glistening in the sunshine.
2. (E minor) As it broadens, the banks re-echo with the sound of:
3. (C major) hunting horns and
4. (G major) country dances.
5. (A♭ major) Moonlight—dance of the water sprites.
6. (E minor) Vltava returns.
7. (Modulatory and developmental) See now, the Rapids of St. John, on whose rocks the foaming waves are dashed in spray.
8. (E major) Again the Vltava broadens toward Prague, where it is welcomed by
9. (E major) the old and venerable Vyšehrad.

The pictorial effects here are as skillful as they are traditional. The undulating streams in section 1 partake of a convention that we have observed as early as the madrigals of Monteverdi and again in Vivaldi's *The Four Seasons.* The hunt fanfares (section 3) go back just as far conceptually, and their orchestral realization derives from Weber's *Der Freischütz*. The peasant wedding (section 4) is cast as a polka, a popular Slavic dance. The end brings the *Vltava* theme into sudden juxtaposition with the explicitly labeled "Vyšehrad Motive." The latter theme is proclaimed in a majestic rhythmic augmentation with respect to the rushing river music that continues beneath it, carrying echoes of the forest fanfares, and so the effect of climactic magnificence is inescapable, even to an audience unaware of the thematic recall. To an audience properly aware, of course, the effect is an ecstasy of *českost*.

The Fate of a Tune: From Folk Song to Anthem

Another reason why *Vltava* is so popular is because of the recurrent broad theme representing the main stream of the river (Ex. 24-3a), which became the most famous melody Smetana ever wrote. Needless to say, as the emblem of the Czech national river, hence as a beloved emblem of nationhood in its own right, the theme has been presumed, by Czechs and non-Czechs alike, to be a folk song. And it *is* a folk song, but not a Czech one. It is a Swedish tune that Smetana heard in Göteborg as part of the incidental music to a folk pageant by a playwright whose sister-in-law was a pupil in Smetana's piano institute (Ex. 24-3b).

Possibly Smetana did not remember the origins of the tune when he appropriated it as an epitome of *českost*; the fact that his memory might thus have disguised the tune as an invention is all the evidence we need to refute the notion that *českost* or any other kind of national character is an inherent property of a tune, invented or otherwise. The Swedish origin of the melody that has represented Czech nationalism to the world for more than a hundred years is an excellent reminder that art is artful rather than natural. Neither *českost* nor any other artistic character is an essence waiting to be tapped by genius. Like all the others, *českost* is a construction in which composer and listener, producer and consumer, must collaborate.

And the listener is just as free as the composer to alter the terms of the bargain. A decade after Smetana's *Vltava* had become an international repertory standard, its big tune was co-opted by an arranger named Popovici for a collection of "Moldavian" (Eastern Romanian) songs, where it was given the title *Carul cu boi* (Cart and Oxen) and where in 1888 it drew the attention of Samuel Cohen, a Bohemian-born musician then living in Palestine. Cohen fitted to it the words of *Tikvatenu* (Our Hope), verses published in Jerusalem two years earlier by the Polish-born Hebrew poet Naftali Herz Imber (Ex. 24-3c). The resulting hymn, *Hatikvah* (The Hope), was first published as such in 1895 in Breslau, a city in East Prussia (now Wrocław, Poland). Two years later it was adopted by the First Zionist Congress, meeting in Switzerland, as the official Zionist anthem and as such became the national anthem of the State of Israel on its founding in May 1948. The *Vltava* theme, in its Czech manifestation, can thus be looked on as a stage in the history of a melody as it passed from its Swedish origins to its Israeli destination. But of course even this characterization is misleading. There are no origins and no destinations in such histories, only stages.

Example 24-3a Bedřich Smetana, *Vltava* theme

Example 24-3b Swedish folk song: *Ack, Värmeland, du sköna* ("Oh Vaermland, You Beautiful")

Example 24-3c Zionist hymn, *Hatikvah* ("The Hope")

Competing Reputations at Home and Abroad

The end of *Vltava* pales beside the orgy of *českost* at the end of *Blaník*—the culmination of the whole cycle—when the Vyšehrad motive is reprised in counterpoint with the Hussite hymn. The thematic juxtaposition creates grand nationalistic pomp, symbolic of a national glory that was only a dream in 1882, when the cycle was first performed as a totality. Its dramatic counterpart is the final act of Smetana's opera *Libuše,* first performed the year before and based on the central founding myth of Bohemia. The title character, the legendary first queen of the land, has a prophetic vision in which all the heroic events of the national history (to her, the national future) pass in review, culminating in a vision of the Prague castle, magically illuminated, while the clairvoyant queen sings exultantly, "My beloved Czech nation will not perish." The populace enthusiastically responds while the orchestra pounds out the distinctive rhythm of the Hussite hymn.

Smetana's comic operas, which celebrated the peasantry in idealized harmony with the upper classes, were infused with folksy charm. His second and best-known opera, a Figaro-ish comedy of peasants and landowners called *Prodaná nevěsta* (The Bartered Bride, 1866; Fig. 24-4), has proved a highly exportable commodity, affably representing the Czech nation to other nations. In its friendly local color it may have reinforced a reputation for buffoonery that breeds condescension. Nonetheless, it quickly became popular all over Europe; and today the Czechs themselves regard this most popular Czech opera as a national treasure, a compendium of folk life and character types expressed (in a very Mozartean way) through a compendium

Figure 24-4 Stage design for Smetana's comic opera *The Bartered Bride.*

of national dance rhythms. Originally, however, it was Smetana's monumental and progressive compositions, not his folksy ones, that appealed most to Czech national sentiment. Thus for a long time Smetana was honored at home as the composer of *Libuše* and *Má vlast* and abroad as the composer of *The Bartered Bride* and *The Moldau* (to use the tellingly more familiar German name of *Vltava*).

Smetana, a loyal Austrian subject who saw his country's best chance for national revival within the structure of a liberalized empire, remained cool throughout his career toward cultural products coming from the Slavic east, which (like Chopin) he associated with Russian imperialism. A "pan-Slavic" movement had emerged at midcentury in the hopes of unifying the Slavic peoples of Russia and Eastern Europe as well as various populations from the Balkans and the Ottoman Empire. Smetana felt no special pull toward Russian music or musicians. This became abundantly clear when the prominent Russian composer Miliy Balakirev, whom we will meet in a moment, came to Prague in January 1867 to conduct the first performances of Glinka's operas outside Russia. As the newly named chief conductor of the Prague opera theater, Smetana was tangentially involved in these productions, and Balakirev blamed him for everything that went wrong, accusing him of sabotage on behalf of what he labeled the "Polonophile" party, Slavs who had taken up the Polish cause against Russia after the bloody events of 1830–31.

Payback time came four years later, when *The Bartered Bride* received its foreign premiere in St. Petersburg. Composer and critic César Cui, Balakirev's comrade-in-arms, was waiting. An excerpt from his review, published in the Russian capital's leading daily on the morning of 18 January 1871, will be enough to put to rest any notions of pan-Slavic solidarity among musical nationalists or any idea of an ecumenical nationalist movement in music. "I frankly confess to my readers," Cui began,

> that it is much more pleasant to write about the Czech composer Smetana than about Beethoven. No matter what I write about Beethoven, I will always remain beneath my subject, while no matter what I write about Smetana, I will always be above it, so empty and nonsensical is this opera of his. . . . The best thing about *The*

> *Bartered Bride* is its slight whiff of Czech music, related to ours, which gives the opera a bit of color and makes it more bearable. . . . But as to quality, the music is simply a blank. Every sort of nothingness passes in review: sentimental nothingness, and pastoral nothingness, and poetic nothingness, and plain nothingness. . . . It's not a composition, it's the improvisation of a tolerably gifted fourteen-year-old.[8]

Slavic Disharmony

We saw in Chapter 21 how Russia initially imported foreign talent, especially Italian opera composers, to create a fine-art musical culture. A second stage was reached when a Russian, Mikhail Glinka, who received training abroad to acquire both beauty and brains, created the first Russian music that proved not just popular at home but also popularly exportable, as the advocacy of Berlioz and others testifies. This exportability would increase with later Russian composers, culminating with the enormously famous Pyotr Ilyich Tchaikovsky near the end of the century and then having a decisive impact on musical modernism at the start of the twentieth.

The fact that Russia was developing a lively and internationally attractive musical culture does not at all mean it was a monolithic one. We have just encountered some Slavic disharmony between Czechs and Russians, and that discord extended to some internal struggles among Russians themselves back at home. This period of heated musical politics coincided with what was more generally a turbulent time in Russian history: the aftermath of Russian defeat in the Crimean War (1853–56) and the upheavals wrought in the 1860s by the emancipation of the serfs, Russian peasants who had been bound by feudal law to work the estates of landowners as personal property. To curb social unrest and maintain the good will of the educated classes, Russian censorship was significantly relaxed in the 1860s and '70s. This was just part of the far-reaching reforms in the early part of the reign of Tsar Alexander II (who ruled from 1855 to 1881), the successor to his father Nikolas I, the reactionary leader who had crushed Poland in 1831.

The debates and battle lines among prominent Russian musicians had many similarities with those we have seen in other parts of Europe at the time, notably the aesthetic conflicts pitting the Berlioz, Liszt, Wagner camp against the Mendelssohn, Schumann, Brahms one, or, if we think in terms of their spokesmen, between Karl Franz Brendel and Eduard Hanslick. In Russia, one prominent group centered around Miliy Alexeyevich Balakirev (1837–1910), who promoted a supposedly progressive aesthetic line against a purportedly conservative—and conservatory—opposition. The main protagonist of that other faction was Anton Rubinstein (1829–94), a tireless organizer of Russian musical life (Fig. 24-5). In 1859 he founded the Russian Musical Society, the sponsoring organization behind the country's first full-time professional symphony orchestra, and three years later he established the St. Petersburg Conservatory, the first accredited school of its kind on Russian soil. His younger brother, Nikolai Grigoryevich Rubinstein (1835–81), started the Moscow Conservatory in 1866. Both institutions enjoyed government funding and patronage.

The fact that Russia was developing a lively and internationally attractive musical culture does not at all mean it was a monolithic one.

A piano virtuoso of international fame and an incredibly prolific composer, Anton Rubinstein saw the future of Russian music in terms of its professionalization under the sponsorship of the aristocracy and the stewardship of imported master teachers. It was a measure of his colossal energy and fame that he was able to gain such sponsorship despite his Jewish birth and German training, which led to some antagonism against him. Already in 1855 Rubinstein had published an article called "Russian Composers" in a Viennese arts journal in which he outlined his Peter the Great–like program for Westernizing Russian music and also hinted that Russian musical nationalism was merely a sign of immaturity and dilettantism.

Figure 24-5 Anton Rubinstein. Painting by Ilya Repin, ca. 1880.

Even Rubinstein's worst enemies recognized that his motives were patriotic, and everyone acknowledged that he, both as lobbyist and as role model, deserved credit for creating the social and institutional means through which a professional musical life might flourish in Russia. Nevertheless, his tactless article met with a chorus of righteous indignation. It could even be said that his words touched off Russian musical nationalism as a self-conscious artistic tendency. For Rubinstein, music was inherently and essentially "a *German* art"; in his opinion "a deliberately national art cannot claim universal sympathy but awakens an ethnographical interest at best."[9] Six years later he elaborated this position in an article entitled "The State of Music in Russia," which was published in *Vek* (The Age). Its appearance this time in a Russian journal was only possible because of the liberalization under Alexander II, when, for a short period, it was permissible to criticize policies and to propose solutions. Rubinstein seized the opportunity brought by the lessening of political control, founded the Russian Musical Society, and opened the St. Petersburg Conservatory. His goal was to raise educational standards and secure civic rights for musicians comparable to the "privileges accorded to the other arts such as painting, sculpture, and the rest."[10]

The leader of the avowedly nationalistic backlash was Balakirev, Glinka's presumed heir since their meeting in late 1855. (Glinka himself had withdrawn from the Russian scene as, disillusioned, he moved to Berlin, where he died two years later.) Balakirev founded what was called the "New Russian School." The one who so named it was the circle's own spokesman, a librarian by profession, named Vladimir Stasov (1824–1906), a friend of Glinka's who proved an energetic and effective propagandist and who argued lustily against the establishment of a conservatory system in Russia. Balakirev competed directly with Rubinstein as a public musician and educator. He too founded an educational institution, the Free Music School, where no tuition was charged. He conducted concerts featuring Russian works as well as advanced compositions from the West and eventually took over Rubinstein's Russian Music Society, the organization that brought Berlioz for a second trip to Russia in the winter of 1867–68 and that made him an honorary member.

It was in the spirit of opposition to the rising German-dominated professionalization of St. Petersburg's musical life that the charismatic Balakirev gathered around him a group of talented young musical mavericks in the late 1850s and '60s. This New Russian School was a sort of real-life "Davidsbund," to borrow the Schumannesque word for it, opposing academic authority on the one hand and philistinism on the other. With the aid of Stasov's propaganda, they gradually achieved recognition under a whimsical nickname Stasov had invented for them: *moguchaya* **kuchka**, which means a "mighty little bunch" but is often rendered in English as the "**Mighty Five**" or "Mighty Handful."

Stasov coined the term inadvertently in a review of a concert in May 1867 presented by the Free Music School in connection with a Slavic Congress promoting the pan-Slavic movement. After opening with Glinka's *Kamarinskaya* (of course), which had to be repeated, the program featured compositions from different Slavic countries, including pieces by Liszt (not a Slav at all) and Moniuszko. Stasov was particularly proud of the new Russian pieces, which made a great impression on "our dear guests from the Slavic West." He ended his review "with a wish: God grant that our audience never forget today's concert; God grant that they always remember how much poetry, feeling, talent, and skill there is in the small but already *mighty little bunch* (*kuchka*) of young Russian musicians."[11] The five outstanding members of the bunch—Balakirev, César Cui (1835–1918), Alexander Borodin (1833–87), Modest Musorgsky (1839–81), and Nikolai Rimsky-Korsakov (1844–1908)—were all, except for Balakirev, gifted amateurs and autodidacts who held day jobs: Cui worked as military fortifications expert, Borodin as a celebrated chemist, Musorgsky as an army officer, and Rimsky-Korsakov as a naval cadet.

Russian composers of this generation were effectively frozen out of the country's musical establishment. Unless one went abroad for training, as Glinka and Rubinstein did, one had to content oneself with self-education. Moreover, there were next to no performance outlets for one's creative labor unless one was a performing virtuoso. For some years the Balakirev circle met daily and later on at least once a week. They studied not textbooks but scores, usually four-hand piano arrangements of European classics, as well as more recent works from Schumann, Berlioz, Liszt, and others. Cui described the early meetings of the Balakirev circle in a memoir:

> We formed a close-knit circle of young composers. And since there was nowhere to study (the conservatory didn't exist) our *self-education* began. It consisted of playing through everything that had been written by all the greatest composers, and all works were subjected to criticism and analysis in all their technical and creative aspects. We were young and our judgments were harsh. We were very disrespectful in our attitude toward Mozart and Mendelssohn; to the latter we opposed Schumann, who was then ignored by everyone. We were very enthusiastic about Liszt and Berlioz. We worshiped Chopin and Glinka. We carried on heated debates (in the course of which we would down as many as four or five glasses of tea with jam), we discussed musical form, program music, vocal music, and especially operatic form.[12]

The kuchka *was no band of narrow nationalists. Except for Glinka, all the objects of their admiration were located to the west of Russia—and how could it be otherwise?*

These were the same issues, in other words, then being debated in the rest of Europe, for the *kuchka* was no band of narrow nationalists. Except for Glinka, all the objects of their admiration were located to the west of Russia—and how could it be otherwise? Glinka was at this point, the late 1850s, the only Russian to worship. That was precisely because he alone, among Russians, was then considered on a level with the Europeans. The homegrown music of Russia, the tonal products of the soil and its peasant keepers, was not admired and not discussed. That is because Russian musicians in the European literate fine-art tradition have always measured themselves by the only terms available—that is, the terms of the tradition within which they have chosen to pursue their compositional careers. They have always construed their identities in a larger European context from a sense of relatedness to cultivated Europe, not peasant Russia.

Because of their outsider, nonprofessional status, the *kuchka* composers had little choice but to claim legitimacy primarily on the strength of their ethnicity. They promoted a myth of Russian authenticity from which the conservatory would be by definition excluded. The myth was later exported to France by Cui, who wrote reams of press propaganda on behalf of the group, including a series of articles in French that appeared in 1878–79 in the *Revue et gazette musicale,* the leading Paris music magazine, and was published in book form a year later as *La musique en Russie.* Practically the whole subsequent historiography of Russian music in the West has been based on its fairytale of the radical uprising by a heroic school of honest nationalists—the *kuchka*—fighting the good ethnic fight against an entrenched band of aristocratically supported foreigners—the Rubinsteins' conservatories.

Nineteenth-century Russian composers, more than any other comparable group, have been confined to an exotic ghetto.

The notion was later given a decisive boost in the early twentieth century through the efforts of the powerful Russian impresario Sergey Diaghilev, whom we will later see playing a crucial role in music during the first decades of the twentieth century. He exploited the French taste for exoticism in promoting his organization, the Ballets Russes (Russian Ballet), as purveyors of the authentic Russian soul. The concerts, operas, and ballets Diaghilev presented in Paris and elsewhere, brimming with folklore and exoticism, solidified the notion in the West that the authenticity of Russian music depended on its Russianness. Ever since, "How Russian is it?" has been the main critical question asked of Russian music by Western audiences and critics. It had to be answered plainly enough for non-Russian ears to hear. And as a result, nineteenth-century Russian composers, more than any other comparable group, have been confined to an exotic ghetto. Fascination has long mixed with condescension when Western Europeans looked at the Russians, alien and "Asiatic" by virtue of their long-lasting "Mongolian captivity" (vassalhood to the descendants of Genghis Khan in Medieval times), their geographical remoteness, their Eastern Orthodox religion, even their crazy alphabet.

Kuchka Music

The attempt to build a national Russian school on a foundation of folklore can be traced to Glinka, just as the New German School can be traced to Beethoven, although neither Glinka nor Beethoven ever had any conception of such a project or historical role. The earliest truly *kuchkist* composition was Balakirev's *Overture on Russian Themes,* written in 1857–58, about a decade before the group was named. It was at once a creative response to Glinka's *Kamarinskaya* and a calculated rebuttal to Anton Rubinstein's complaints about the inadequacy of native Russian music. Balakirev wrote it as if to prove that Russian instrumental music need not be immature or provincial, and he relied on published anthologies of Russian folk songs to provide his themes.

In the years immediately following the composition of this overture, Balakirev studied Russian folk songs closely, with an eye toward their creative exploitation. Dissatisfied with the quality of the existing publications he had used before, he made an expedition of his own in the summer of 1860 along the Volga River. The songs he collected in the Russian heartland were issued in 1866 as an epoch-making volume of forty arrangements: *Sbornik russkikh narodnikh pesen* (Anthology of Russian Folk Songs). Balakirev's anthology was particularly notable for its technique of harmonization. The harmonic style of his settings, which colored not only his own music but any number of other compositions that came out of the school he founded, was his personal invention. It is not a folk style; actual peasant harmonizations sound nothing like Balakirev's. But the style became instantly recognizable to connoisseurs of art music as generically Russian, thanks to its thorough assimilation into the later compositional practice of Balakirev and his circle. Rimsky-Korsakov, who himself became a great and famous teacher, passed it along in turn to his many pupils. Though it may not be an authentically peasant or folk style, it is indeed the distinctive style of the New Russian School, that is, the Mighty Five.

The air of authenticity notwithstanding, what distinguished Balakirev's overtures (especially a second *Overture on Russian Themes* from 1864, which was eventually reclassified as a symphonic poem) was the ironic fact that, unlike Glinka's *Kamarinskaya*, they are cast as orthodox symphonic allegros in sonata form with introductions; in other words, they were to that extent "German," which gave them another sort of prestige. It took both the Russian authenticity and the German formal heritage to achieve a "Russian School" that could compete successfully on the world stage.

Modest Musorgsky's Realism

History, language, and melody made Russian opera the genre that best suited impressive nationalist statements. In this project, Musorgsky's *Boris Godunov* proved to be the most celebrated achievement of the second half of the century, as Glinka's *A Life for the Tsar* had been for the first. Musorgky's extraordinary accomplishment in this opera has earned him the highest reputation among the *kuchka* composers (Fig. 24-6). He was, like Smetana, one of the most innovative composers of the nineteenth century, although his reputation in the West tends to highlight his identity as a Russian more than as a progressive. His nationalism, combined with his insecure nonprofessional status (having been trained not for a musical career but for a military one), led him to adopt an extreme outsider's attitude toward the existing traditions and institutions of musical Europe. He rejected with equal fervor what had served Glinka so well: both the standard curriculum of the German conservatory—counterpoint, mastery of form, systematic theory, any manifestation of "braininess"—and the aesthetic of Italian opera—bel canto, ornate melody, all conventional canons of musical "beauty."

Figure 24-6 Modest Musorgsky. Portrait by Ilya Repin painted in the hospital a week before the composer's death in February 1881.

What is left after renouncing both brains and beauty? Good character, obviously. That is where Musorgsky's high moral commitment to "truth" was born, a commitment he thought of as being particularly Russian, in opposition to the falsities of the German and Italian routine. In his commitment to **realism**, with its contempt for fine manners and convention, he found a mentor in composer Alexander Dargomïzhsky (1813–69), like him an aristocratic dilettante frozen out by the professional establishment, and a model in Dargomïzhsky's unfinished opera *Kamennïy gost'* (The Stone Guest). The literary source for the work was a dramatic poem by the great Russian writer Alexander Pushkin (1799–1837) inspired by the walking, talking statue from Hell in Mozart's *Don Giovanni*. Dargomïzhsky had attempted to solve the problem of operatic form by dispensing with the libretto altogether, basing his work directly on Pushkin's text, which made him for Musorgsky "the great teacher of musical truth."[13]

Musorgsky decided he could go even further. Rather than use verse, he proclaimed that the ultimate in musical truth could be achieved only if composers set librettos in conversational prose, with the music faithfully mirroring the tempo and contour of actual conversational speech. This was a particularly strict application to music of *mimesis*, or "imitation of nature," which was based on the idea that art derives its power from the mirroring of reality. It was the same idea that we saw had inspired the invention of opera in the humanist academies of Florence almost three centuries earlier. Musorgsky believed that what should be imitated was the natural speech one observed in real life. Never before had a composer envisioned the renunciation of verse, however terse, as the basis of musical setting. Outside the realm of church liturgies in oral tradition (for example, Gregorian chant), no one had ever seriously questioned the status of regular poetic meter as a basic musical ingredient.

Musorgsky did not shrink from questioning assumptions about "the nature of music" in his quest for the ultimate musical embodiment of nature. He gloried in an extraordinarily radical posture because it turned all of his liabilities into advantages. Far from handicapped by a lack of formal musical training, he was privileged by his maverick, self-taught status to think the unthinkable. His conservatory would be the conservatory of life. He wrote in a letter that "whatever speech I hear, whoever is speaking (or, the main thing, no matter what he is saying), my brain is already churning out the musical embodiment of such speech."[14] He said this in the summer of 1868, when making his first attempt to realize these ideals in practice—or, to put it in the scientific terms he preferred, to carry out his first "experiment in dramatic music in prose."

Musorgsky started with an exercise similar in concept to Dargomïzhsky's *The Stone Guest*: a verbatim setting of a preexisting comic play by Nikolai Gogol (1809–52) called *Zhenit'ba* (Marriage). In his writing of naturalistic prose recitative Musorgsky had an advantage over composers working in other languages because the actual pattern of spoken Russian imposes a sort of beat on most utterances that can be represented fairly accurately in regular musical notation. Musorgsky developed an acute ear for the tempo of Russian speech. The harmonic language in *Marriage* is also daring. He kept the tonal motion purposely static and ambiguous for long stretches. With no key signature to be found anywhere, tonal ambiguity is maintained by means of an unprecedented reliance on augmented and diminished intervals in the melody, supported by chords of corresponding intervallic content in the accompaniment. These, of course, are the "unvocal" intervals shunned in lyrical melodies, hence all the more desirable if lyricism is to be renounced and the illusion of ordinary speech sustained despite the use of sung pitches. Musorgsky in the end never finished this dramatic musical experiment, but the lessons learned from *Marriage* found full expression in *Boris Godunov*.

Art and Autocracy

Operas on historical themes were popular everywhere in the nineteenth century; the Parisian grand opera, as we know, consisted of virtually nothing but. Representations of history in all artistic media had a special importance in Russia, however, because by the latter half of the nineteenth century Russia was the only remaining autocratic state in Europe. Everywhere else monarchies had been at least to some degree constitutionalized, promoting varying degrees of democracy. In Russia, however, the tsar's authority was absolute, neither restricted by law nor shared with a parliament. Censorship of public speech and public press was uniquely stringent, and open debate about public policy was uniquely circumscribed by law. Nowhere else was the content of art subjected to such scrutiny, both by official censors on the lookout for subversion and by subversive thinkers on the lookout for ammunition. Nowhere was there less interest in art that would be merely decorative.

Under these circumstances, discussion of political and social issues had to go underground, and liberal opinion usually had to be camouflaged in a sort of coded language. Discussion of sensitive matters often had to take place in the guise of art or scholarship, on the understanding that sophisticated readers would interpret such writings, objects, and performances metaphorically, alive to its potential contemporary relevance. It was difficult, if not impossible, to say whether or not the subtexts and the values being read into artworks were the artist's own. Interpretation is always a two-way street. In Russia it became a teeming thoroughfare.

Interpretation is always a two-way street. In Russia it became a teeming thoroughfare.

Art in Russia sought to be engaged with civic and social issues. Russian aesthetics tended toward the ethical, and art was valued to the extent that it was seen to do good. This set of values greatly magnified the general drift away from Romanticism toward realism, which regarded beauty with skepticism. It gave outsider artists like Musorgsky, already predisposed toward a countercultural, avant-garde posture, a greatly empowering sense of mission. His artistic and aesthetic coming-of-age, moreover, coincided with the welcome social reforms and easing of censorship during the reign of Tsar Alexander II. (These social reforms were not to Musorgsky's personal benefit: His family was one of the many petty aristocratic clans ruined by the emancipation of the serfs.)

Musorgsky evolved his radical new style for the sake of subtly addressing political issues, proclaiming "the past in the present—there's my task!"[15] He found the ideal subject on which to exercise his skills in *Boris Godunov*, a fairly old (1825) and little-known play by Pushkin, composed in deliberate imitation of Shakespeare's histories, particularly the *Henry IV* plays. Like Shakespeare's King Henry, with his famous soliloquy, "Uneasy lies the head that wears the crown," Boris Godunov was a troubled ruler. According to widely accepted (but now refuted) tradition, Boris had ascended to the Russian throne in 1598 by having murdered the legitimate heir, the nine-year-old Tsarevich Dmitry (youngest son of Ivan the Terrible). Tormented both by his conscience and by a pretender to the throne who claimed to be the resurrected Dmitry, Boris undergoes a steady decline throughout the opera, leading to an early death, as chaos tragically envelops Russia in a "time of troubles."

Pushkin's play quickly became a covert treatise on kingship and legitimacy, dangerous subjects to raise within the borders of an absolute monarchy. If it was still little known in 1868, that was because it had languished under the censor's ban until just two years earlier and had never been performed. The play otherwise seemed to have everything Musorgsky needed: the Shakespearean mixture of poetry and prose, tragedy and comedy; a wide range of character types from beggar to noble, to be characterized by distinctively musicalized speech; a large role for the crowd, which could be treated as naturalistically as the soloists. The composer evidently did not care, at first, that there were hardly any female characters or that Pushkin had treated the one character who might have been suitable for a prima donna role in sketchy fashion and never provided her with a proper love scene.

But he did come to care about the length of the text. Musorgsky intended to set Pushkin's play verbatim, as he had *Marriage*, but *Boris Godunov* was a full-evening's spectacle. If set to music as it stood, it would have rivaled Wagner's *Ring*. It had to be radically scaled down, and in fact only two scenes remained just as Pushkin had written them. For the rest, Musorgsky simply threw out every scene in which the title character failed to appear and then regrouped and mixed in what remained. Almost every line of the opera's text came from Pushkin, but less than half of Pushkin was used: It was the truth and pretty much nothing but the truth, so to speak, but not the whole truth.

The Coronation Scene in *Boris Godunov*

Anthology Vol 2-56
Full CD V, 14
Concise CD II, 47

The most famous part of Musorgsky's *Boris Godunov* comes in the prologue, in the so-called Coronation Scene (Fig. 24-7). Its principal text consists of a single speech for the title character, set off by one of Musorgsky's few additions to Pushkin's script: a choral procession, sung to the tune of an old Russian folk song (Ex. 24-4). The song is there, of course, to lend an authentic period flavor to the depiction of a public ritual. The tune was indeed famous—not least, ironically enough, because Beethoven had used it in his String Quartet in E Minor, Op. 59, No. 2, dedicated to Count Razumovsky, the Russian ambassador in Vienna. Musorgsky also used most of the words to the song—"As to thee, God in heaven, there is glory, let there be glory to the Tsar," which clearly recommended themselves as Coronation fodder, although they in fact were not connected to coronations.

Example 24-4 ***Slava,*** **original folk melody (from Nikolai Lvov and Johann Pratsch,** ***Russkiye narodnïye pesni,*** **1790)**

Just as there is Glory to thee O God on high! Glory!

In contrast to the radical realism he strove for in *Marriage*, here a less stark declamatory realism informs Boris's central monologue, when amid the celebratory joy of the crowd he expresses guilty gloom. The vocal range has been much widened; upbeats are sometimes lengthened to full-beat quarter notes, and the use of consonant melodic leaps lyricalize the utterances. These departures from the conversational norm are admitted in order to elevate Boris's diction to the level of tragic eloquence; he assumes, as it were, the emotionally exalted tone that Russians actually adopt, even in casual or domestic surroundings, when they recite poetry. César Cui christened this style "melodic recitative."[16] It may still be classified as recitative because of its strict one-note-per-syllable declamation, its abundance of short repeated notes, its faithful mirroring of the intonational contour of the spoken language, and (beyond the two opening phrases) its absence of melodic repetitions, so its shape is wholly dependent on that of the text. The poetry is the mistress, as Monteverdi would have said, the music the handmaiden. But each melodic phrase in Boris's case has "song potential"—one can easily imagine its development into an arioso.

The realism of the Coronation Scene is not limited to speech and the voice but extends to instrumentation and harmony. The most radically realistic harmonic effect is

Figure 24-7 Stage design for second scene of the Prologue ("Coronation Scene") in the first performance of Musorgsky's *Boris Godunov*, St. Petersburg, 1874.

specified by the opening stage direction: a "solemn peal of bells." The lengthy orchestral prelude depicts this tolling with just two chords, both of them describable in common-practice terms as dominant-sevenths with their roots on A♭ and D, respectively (Ex. 24-5). The common-practice description is quite misleading, however, since neither of them ever resolves to its implied tonic. Musorgsky's progression produces a stasis. He shapes the passage in which it occurs by rhythmic rather than harmonic means: at first by surface diminutions, then by doubling the harmonic rhythm, both of these devices copied from actual bell-ringing techniques. After the whole section is repeated with the position of the two chords reversed, all Musorgsky can do to bring it to an end is drown it out with the heavy percussion. There is no possible functional cadence, which makes it far more subversive of tonal practice than Wagner's *Tristan und Isolde*. However ingenious and sophisticated Wagner's usage (and there is no denying that Wagner gave his innovative idea far more resourceful and sophisticated treatment than Musorgsky could hope to do), it remained within the system of functional relations. Musorgsky's was at the limits of the system and perhaps moved beyond it.

Example 24-5 Modest Musorgsky, coronation bells in *Boris Godunov* (Prologue, Scene 2)

Revising *Boris Godunov*

After completing *Boris Godunov* in December 1869 Musorgsky tried to get it performed, but the opera was roundly rejected by the review committee of the Russian imperial theaters because it lacked a prima donna role. That was easily supplied, since Pushkin had included some scenes showing Dmitry the pretender's progress in Poland, where the Princess Marina Mniszek seduced him. Musorgsky expanded their encounter into the required love duet and even added a scene in Marina's dressing room to give her a solo aria. All this made the opera more conventional, less realist.

The legend arose that Musorgsky had to revise the opera against his will in order to make it palatable to musical and political authorities. In fact, he seems to have made many changes on his own initiative. It turns out that he had played the original version through for a select group of friends and was disconcerted at the response: "As regards the peasants in *Boris*, some found them to be *bouffe* (!), while others saw tragedy."[17] He thus found that in the ears of his sympathetic audience prose recitative immediately meant "comedy," however tragic the actual content of the drama. Musorgsky's first impulse to revise the opera came not from the demands of the imperial theaters but from his own private experience of communications failure. It led him to reconsider his whole operatic technique, indeed his entire aesthetic stance, with an eye toward clarifying the genre of the opera—that is, toward making decisive the contrast between what was comic and what was not and generally toward elevating the tone of the opera to the level of tragedy, Shakespearean or otherwise. The lesson we may draw from his experience is that realism undercuts tragedy and aligns itself with comedy, which entails a lowering of tone. All this, of course, is saying no more than what common sense already knows—that tragedy, like all beautiful or uplifting ("high") art, is a lie. Fully to disenchant art in the name of literal truth risks destroying its power.

In addition to Musorgsky's own two versions of *Boris* (1869 and 1874) there are other ones as well, assembled posthumously by later composers, editors, and stage directors. Indeed, one rarely hears Musorgsky's compositions exactly as he wrote them. Because he had difficulty completing projects, particularly large-scale dramatic ones, and because of his unconventional style, supportive contemporaries and later admirers felt the need to lend a helping hand. They completed unfinished works or recast them in formats considered more publically palatable. The most famous case is *Pictures at an Exhibition* (1874), a suite Musorgsky originally composed for solo piano but which is best known in Maurice Ravel's masterful orchestration from 1922. More than a dozen other arrangements of this work have been made, including one by the rock group Emerson, Lake, & Palmer.

Realism undercuts tragedy and aligns itself with comedy, which entails a lowering of tone.

Rimsky-Korsakov lavishly reorchestrated *Boris Godunov* in 1896 (revised 1908) and played an even greater role in creating a performable version of *Khovanshchina* (The Khovansky Affair), Musorgksy's second historical opera, which was unfinished when Musorgsky died from alcoholism in 1881. Rimsky provided similar rescue operations for further pieces of Musorgsky and other composers (he was the one to finish and orchestrate Dargomïzhsky's *The Stone Guest*). He also wrote noteworthy operas of his own. With *Mlada* (1892), a mythological opera composed under the impact of the first complete performances of Wagner's *Ring* in Russia, Rimsky found his true métier in fantasy and was increasingly preoccupied in later life with post-Lisztian harmonic explorations, often involving the "tone-semitone" scale, commonly known today as octatonic, which alternates half steps and whole steps.

Figure 24-8 Pyotr Ilyich Tchaikovsky in 1893, the last year of his life. Portrait by Nikolay Kuznetzov.

Pyotr Ilyich Tchaikovsky

While we should not exaggerate the divisions between the Russian camps of "progressive" *kuchkists* and "conservative" conservatory composers—there was some amiable contact, shared performances, and so forth—it is true that Anton Rubinstein and his heirs generally held different musical values and goals, largely based on their different musical experiences and training. Rubinstein spent his formative teenage years in Paris and Vienna and even studied in Berlin for a while with Siegfried Dehn, Glinka's teacher. One of Rubinstein's earliest pupils, in turn, was Pyotr Ilyich Tchaikovsky (1840–93; Fig. 24-8), an alumnus of the St. Petersburg Conservatory's first graduating class (1866) and later a professor at the Moscow Conservatory. Tchaikovsky's international fame, achieved by the age of forty, is apparent from an invitation to participate in the 1891 inaugural concerts at New York's Carnegie Hall as well as from an honorary degree Cambridge University bestowed on him two years later. His works were championed by leading German performers, such as conductors Hans von Bülow and Hans Richter. He was Russia's first great international musical celebrity.

As with Mozart, the composer he most revered, Tchaikovsky was equally drawn to the operatic and instrumental domains and made equally significant contributions to both. In addition, he elevated a genre that we have paid no attention to since the Baroque era: ballet. Dance had long held a special place in French culture, going back to Lully under Louis XIV. Although Gluck, Mozart, Beethoven, and other composers in German-speaking countries wrote ballets, the explosion of full-length major scores came only in Paris during the nineteenth century. Some of the perennial favorites were written by French composers who are now otherwise generally forgotten, but it was Tchaikovsky who brought the genre to its late-century summit with *Swan Lake* (1875–76), *The Sleeping Beauty* (1889), and *The Nutcracker* (1892).

From the composer's large output we will sample an opera and a symphony written during the same fraught period in his life. In *Eugene Onegin* (1879), an opera based, like *Boris*, on a work by Pushkin, he created the other great monument of Russian realism in music. Since the literary model in this case was not a Shakespearean historical drama but a novel of relatively contemporary Russian society and mores, "monument" is not quite the right word. The scale of the opera is small. Originally intended for performance by the Moscow Conservatory's opera workshop, the work makes rather modest technical demands. Its remarkable emotional potency comes from its manipulation of symbols that interrelate genres of popular art with their associated social milieus.

If Tchaikovsky was the "great poet of everyday life" and "a genius of emotion," to quote the kind of critical comments that have stuck to him, it was not because he alone found poetry in everyday life (every novelist does that) or because he was a genius at having emotions (we're all geniuses at that). It was because he knew how to channel life and emotion with great power and precision through coded conventional forms. Like Pushkin, Tchaikovsky represented people primarily in social contexts. He delighted in showing to what extent the emotions we subjectively view as our own unique spontaneous experience are in fact mediated by social codes, class positions, and standards of group behavior.

Pushkin's *Eugene Onegin*, the most beloved work of Russian fiction, is famously short on plot. The title character, an aristocratic dandy from the city, meets Tatyana, a simple and openhearted country girl; she is smitten, he brushes her off; six years later he is smitten, she is married. There is also a subplot about Onegin's friend, a country squire who dabbles in poetry and fancies himself a uniquely sensitive soul, and Tatyana's sister, Olga, a shallow beauty with whom the dabbler poet is in love. Onegin and the friend fight a pointless duel over Olga and the friend is killed. Tchaikovsky concentrated less on the overtly dramatic aspects of this unassuming story and more on its reflections of character and daily life. He did this by abstracting its musical idiom from the melodic and harmonic turns that identified the music of its time and place, the most conspicuous of which is the use of melodic sixths in shaping melodies, either as direct leaps or as filled-in contours. The interval abounded in the so-called *bïtovoy romans*, or "household romances," of the 1830s and '40s, songs composed not for the professional recital stage but for sale as sheet music the amateur could enjoy playing at home.

> ***Tchaikovsky delighted in showing to what extent the emotions we subjectively view as our own unique spontaneous experience are in fact mediated by social codes, class positions, and standards of group behavior.***

The first vocal music in *Eugene Onegin* is one such romance, sung offstage by Tatyana and Olga to an early lyric poem by Pushkin. At the end of the verse it incorporates a reference to a tune already heard at the beginning of the opera's prelude, which will function throughout the drama as Tatyana's leitmotif and which also outlines a descending melodic sixth (Ex. 24-6). The full meaning of these sixths is revealed when Tatyana has her most private and personal moment onstage, known as the Letter Scene, in which she recklessly pours out her heart on paper to Onegin. One of the most extended arias in all of Russian opera, it is actually a string of four romances in different tempos and keys, linked by recitatives. The use of the romance idiom sets limits on scale—both the formal scale of the aria and the emotional scale of the character. However touching her portrait, Tatyana remains, like all the characters in the opera, the denizen of a realistic novel, not of a historical spectacle. One of Tchaikovsky's great achievements was that his music can perform exactly those revealingly intimate functions for which Pushkin's narrative voice was prized. The result is a masterpiece of stylized operatic realism.

Anthology Vol 2-57
Full CD V, 15

Example 24-6 **Pyotr Ilyich Tchaikovsky, *Eugene Onegin,* Tatyana's leitmotif**

Russian Symphonies

Russian symphonies in the nineteenth century came under two brand names. One was provided by the composers in the Balakirev Circle and the other by those associated with the Rubinstein brothers' conservatories in St. Petersburg and in

Moscow. Each group produced one outstanding symphonist in the 1870s. From the *kuchka* it was Borodin, the remarkable chemist-composer. The national colorings of his Second Symphony (1869–76, revised 1878) made it an instant international hit. The work arose alongside the earliest sketches for his epic opera *Prince Igor*. When he temporarily abandoned that grand work in the early 1870s, he transferred to the symphony music originally conceived to illustrate scenes of Russian heroic antiquity, on the one hand, and exotic voluptuousness, on the other. Rather than segregate these images by movements, as the opera would have segregated them by scenes and acts, Borodin mixed them according to a traditional symphonic recipe. He reserved the warrior material for the assertive first themes in the outer movements and the main body of the scherzo and used the yielding, serpentine, feminine tunes for the second themes in the outer movements as well as in the scherzo, for a trio section replete with belly dancer's percussion (the triangle standing in for her finger cymbals).

Tchaikovsky was the leading symphonist on the conservatory side, producing six of them between 1866 and 1893 as well as the *Manfred* Symphony (1885), essentially his Symphony No. 4½, based on a poem of the same name by Lord Byron. Despite his resolutely European orientation and his conservatory training, Tchaikovsky was just as acutely aware as the *kuchkists* were of the condescension with which Western Europeans regarded Russians. "You can read it in their eyes," he remarked in a letter,

> "You're just a Russian, but I am so kind and indulgent that I favor you with my attention." The hell with them! Last year [1876] I found myself against my will at Liszt's. He was nauseatingly deferential, but a smile that never left his lips spoke the sentence I underlined above with perfect clarity.[18]

Tchaikovsky made this remark to Nadezhda von Meck, a wealthy and rather eccentric widow, who in 1876 began a remarkable correspondence with the composer that would last for some fourteen years. During this time she offered him friendship, emotional support, and considerable financial assistance. One of the odd things about their relationship is that she stipulated that they were never to meet in person—and they never did.

Anthology Vol 2-58
Full CD V, 16

Tchaikovsky complained about Liszt while composing his Fourth Symphony (secretly dedicated to her as "my best friend"), a work that seemed to break with the symphonic tradition as it was viewed in the nineteenth century. Like Schubert's "Unfinished" Symphony, it embodies values other than Beethovenian ones. It lacks almost completely the highly atomized motivic texture that we will later see Johannes Brahms had developed out of Beethoven or the thematic transformations Lisztian symphonists employed. Accepting the conventional four-movement framework, Tchaikovsky instead created something approaching a suite of giant character pieces: a symphonic waltz for a first movement, explicitly marked *in movimento di valse* (in waltz tempo); an *Andantino*, marked *in modo di canzone* (in the manner of a ballad), with a very Italianate middle section, appropriate for a symphony partly composed during a stay in Venice; an orchestral tour de force of a scherzo, marked *pizzicato ostinato*; and a finale consisting of variations on a famous Russian folk song.

While somewhat unusual for a symphony, these features were not unprecedented. What did seem new was Tchaikovsky's use of expansive melodies in place of tight motivic designs and the constant conspicuous reference to song and dance. (These were Schubertian traits, although Tchaikovsky probably knew little of the Viennese composer's music.) In the Fourth Symphony, the first movement's main waltz theme, for example, is twenty-five broad $\frac{9}{8}$ measures in length, consisting of a regular eight-bar phrase to a dominant half-cadence and an expertly extended answering phrase that leads back to a full cadence on the tonic. Tchaikovsky was beholden to a Franco-Italianate lineage rather to the Germanic symphonic tradition. One begins to suspect the existence of a parallel tradition of the symphony, ignoring Beethoven, that passed from Mozart to Rossini and from him to French composers Charles Gounod and Georges Bizet. These were the composers whom Tchaikovsky admired, particularly his French contemporaries, and especially the opera and ballet composer Léo Delibes (1836–91), who is no longer thought of as an important figure but whom Tchaikovsky venerated as the Mozart of his day.

As a result of their unusual features, the German-dominated literatures of music history and music appreciation textbooks have tended to treat Tchaikovsky's symphonies as demeaned specimens, greatly appealing to audiences but nevertheless revealing some innate limitation in the composer. Tchaikovsky, of course, chose his methods quite deliberately, with full knowledge of what he was rejecting. What he was rejecting, in a word, was his great contemporary, Brahms, whose music, as he put it to Madame von Meck, was "made up of little fragments of something or other, artfully glued together," with the result that he "never expresses anything, or if he does, he fails to do it fully."[19] Tchaikovsky was acutely aware of a deficiency, as he saw it, in Brahms, one that came about in direct consequence of what is now generally considered the German composer's greatest strength. For him, Brahms's virtuosity in constructing large musical entities out of atomic particles represented no dialectical triumph but merely an unresolved, and therefore fatal, contradiction. "Aren't his pretensions to profundity, strength, and power detestable," Tchaikovsky wrote to another correspondent, "when the content he pours into those Beethovenian forms of his is so pitiful and insignificant?" These comments strongly suggest that Tchaikovsky's deviations from the Beethovenian, or at least the Brahmsian, straight-and-narrow were conditioned less by a lack of symphonic aptitude than by the wish to "express something fully."[20]

But what? And how? The first movement of the Fourth Symphony contains two impressive clues. The first is its sheer stridency and violence, quite contradicting, or, at the very least, investing with heavy irony, the implications of its waltz tempo. The stridency is proclaimed before the waltz even makes an appearance, in the ear-splitting brass fanfares with which the symphony begins and out of which the whole slow introduction is fashioned (Ex. 24-7). The violence intrudes almost as early, in the peremptory diminished seventh chord that cuts the fanfares off. That is operatic behavior; and the dramatic impression is confirmed when the fanfares begin acting like a Berliozian idée fixe. The peak of violence, a real catastrophe, occurs in the development section, when the fanfares suddenly return and make three collisions with the waltz theme, each more terrifying than the last. (They also return in the fourth movement to disrupt the folksy festivities.) This is not merely structure but dramaturgy. As with Beethoven, we are prompted to ask what it all means. The music suggests an encoding of events, a narrative—in short, a program. This is precisely what Madame von Meck assumed, and she wrote to Tchaikovsky to inquire about it.

Example 24-7 Pyotr Ilyich Tchaikovsky, Symphony No. 4, I, opening

His long letter in response is now often taken as the symphony's actual, explicit, or official program by those who have forgotten that Tchaikovsky never published it or publicly alluded to it during his lifetime; who have not noticed its obvious borrowings from the famous implied program of Beethoven's Fifth and explicit program of Berlioz's *Symphonie fantastique*; and who have not weighed into the balance that the composer furnished the information at the specific request of the patron who paid his bills. But even if we regard the program as a hasty verbal paraphrase of ideas best wordlessly expressed in music, its affinity with the shape of the musical argument is obvious. Here is, as Tchaikovsky put it, "roughly the program of the first movement":

> The Introduction is the *kernel* of the whole symphony, without question its main idea: [here the fanfares are quoted]. This is *Fate*, the force of destiny, which ever prevents our pursuit of happiness from reaching its goal, which jealously stands watch lest our peace and well-being be full and cloudless, which hangs like the sword of Damocles over our heads and constantly, ceaselessly poisons our souls. It is invincible, inescapable. One can only resign oneself and lament fruitlessly: [Here the waltz theme is quoted].
>
> This disconsolate and despairing feeling grows ever stronger and more intense. Would it not be better to turn away from reality and immerse oneself in dreams? [Here the second theme is quoted.] O joy! A sweet tender dream has appeared. A bright, beneficent human form flits by and beckons us on: [Here the end of the exposition passage is quoted]. How wonderful! How distant now is the sound of the implacable introductory theme! Dreams little by little have taken over the soul. All that is dark and bleak is forgotten. There it is, there it is—happiness!
>
> But no! These are only dreams, and *Fate* awakens us from them: [Here the fanfares are quoted again as they appear at the beginning of the development section]. And thus, all life is the ceaseless alternation of bitter reality with evanescent visions and dreams of happiness. There is no refuge. We are buffeted about by this sea until it seizes us and pulls us down to the bottom.[21]

Tchaikovsky goes on at great length about all four movements of the symphony and concludes by saying that before sending the letter he reread it and was "horrified at the obscurity and inadequacy of the program. For the first time in my life I have had to put into words and phrases musical thoughts and musical images." Those thoughts and images, of course, are familiar from earlier composers, especially in relation to the topic of "Fate." In the realm of the symphony, it extended back at least as far as Beethoven's Fifth. Perhaps even more common are fate themes in operas, as found in Verdi's *La forza del destino*, Wagner's *Ring*, Bizet's *Carmen*, and elsewhere. In such orchestral and dramatic works "Fate" provides not only an element in the plot but also something to be represented musically.

Although we can never know for sure whether Tchaikovsky really had this all in mind while he was writing the work or whether he made it up afterward to please his patron, he did express similar comments to an esteemed colleague. The composer Sergey Ivanovich Taneyev (1856–1915), who had studied with Tchaikovsky and who eventually wrote a piano reduction of the symphony, criticized the "disproportionate length" of the first movement, which he felt was more like a symphonic poem. He also noted the striking opening brass fanfare that returns at crucial moments in the first and last movements and the frequent changes in tempo, all of which as with Madame von Meck made him think there must be an underlying program. Tchaikovsky responded:

> Of course my symphony is program music, but it would be impossible to give the program in words; it would be ludicrous and only raise a smile. . . . I must tell you that in my simplicity I imagined my plan for the symphony to be so obvious that everyone would understand its meaning, or at least its leading ideas, without any definite program. . . . In reality my work is a reflection of Beethoven's Fifth Symphony; I have not copied his musical contents, only borrowed the central idea. . . . Let me add that there is not a single measure in this Fourth Symphony of mine that I have not truly felt and which is not an echo of my most intimate spiritual life.[22]

Autobiography in Music?

Is it fair or relevant to our experience of the music to note that Tchaikovsky wrote the deeply pessimistic program he provided to Madame von Meck at what was arguably the low point of his personal life and in the immediate aftermath of what was surely the most dramatic episode in his biography? Despite his homosexuality (or rather because of it and his fear of exposure), Tchaikovsky had in the summer of 1877 impulsively accepted a proposal of marriage from Antonina Milyukova, a former pupil of his at the Moscow Conservatory, who had developed a crush on her harmony professor. What followed was a great fiasco of anguish, revulsion, flight, separation, and extended convalescence abroad (which is how he happened to be working on the Fourth Symphony in Venice). Was the symphony, as Tchaikovsky described his music in general, a "cleansing of the soul, which boils over with an accumulation that naturally seeks its outlet in tones, just as a lyric poet will express himself in verse"?[23] Should that matter to us? Does regarding the music as confessional enhance understanding of it? Must we know an artist's biography in order fully to appreciate the artist's output? Or is the meaning of the symphony sufficiently conveyed by the wordless sounds alone?

The alternatives suggested by these questions are neither exhaustive nor necessarily incompatible, but the existence of the famous letter to Madame von Meck has led to the reading of not just the Fourth Symphony but a great deal of Tchaikovsky's music as autobiographical—and reading it, inevitably, in light of the marriage debacle and the conditions that precipitated it. We are again confronted with the issue of what background information we know when we listen to a piece of music, be it knowledge of Beethoven's Heiligenstadt Testament, Schubert's epistolary outpouring to his friend Kupelwieser, or Berlioz's explicit program for the *Symphonie fantastique*.

As soon as we are dealing with expression in any artistic medium, we are necessarily dealing with conventions of representation. Representation necessarily relies on similarities and associations; music must largely work through mediating codes. We already know that one of the codes on which Tchaikovsky relied in the Fourth Symphony was that of dance genres, since he expressly labeled one of his themes as a waltz. Recalling that a great deal of eighteenth-century music, particularly Mozart's, also relied on dance genres and their associations as mediators of musical representation, and knowing that of all composers Tchaikovsky loved Mozart best, we are equipped with some clues to interpret Tchaikovsky's expressive strategies. In particular we can track his deliberate deviation from the structural principles that otherwise reigned in the world of the late-nineteenth-century symphony.

Although not explicitly marked, the fanfares that Tchaikovsky interpreted as the Fate theme in his letter to Madame von Meck are cast just as recognizably in a dance meter as the expressly designated waltz theme. They are in the meter of a polonaise, the majestic dance we have already seen Chopin and Glinka use to such different ends. It had its origin in Polish court processionals and remained the most socially elevated of all the ballroom dances of the nineteenth century. By extension, the polonaise was often associated with military parades, that is, with martial rhythms and brass bands. The stylistic giveaway is the triplet on the second half of the second beat (cf. Ex. 24-7), also found at the beginning of the polonaise that opens the third act of *Eugene Onegin*—composed, as it happens, concurrently with the Fourth Symphony.

Just as in the Fourth Symphony, the polonaise in *Eugene Onegin* is paired conceptually with a waltz that occupies the analogous position at the beginning of Act II (Fig. 24-9). Between the two of them they define a social trajectory. The waltz is played at a party for Tatyana, the country girl who has rashly declared her love for the title character and to whom he feels disdainfully superior. The polonaise is played at a high-society ball in St. Petersburg, where Onegin reencounters Tatyana six years later, and is smitten in his turn; she, however, now socially outranks him and turns him down. The moral: A polonaise will always trump a waltz!

Must we know an artist's biography in order fully to appreciate the artist's output? Or is the meaning sufficiently conveyed by the wordless sounds alone?

And so it is in the Fourth Symphony. It is easy to see how the attributes of a polonaise could have attached themselves to Tchaikovsky's Fate theme. There are the military associations, connoting hostility and implacability as well as the idea of grandiosity and invincible power. In addition, perhaps, is the idea of impersonality, dwarfing individual concerns, as the unwritten laws of society frustrated Onegin's amorous designs, or as the idea of Fate frustrates the subject-persona of the Fourth Symphony, symbolized by the waltz theme, in pursuit of happiness. The submission of waltz to polonaise—of subject to Fate—is denoted in the symphony's coda, when the waltz is reprised for the last time in triple augmentation, that is, at the speed of the polonaise, each beat of the waltz theme now stretched out to the length of one full measure, and therefore no longer a waltz at all. A moment like this fully expresses a sublime dramatic terror that was altogether alien to a composer like Mendelssohn or Brahms, although Berlioz would surely have sympathized.

Figure 24-9 Stage set for a 1910 performance of Tchaikovsky's opera *Eugene Onegin* (first performed in Moscow, 1879).

And so might have Mozart. Tchaikovsky revered him not only for the beauty of his music but also for his ability to express human emotions, which many listeners assumed reflected his own feelings. Were the emotions Tchaikovsky portrayed also his own? In the case of the Fourth Symphony, his biography tends to confirm the idea. But beware: Once the idea is accepted as a general rule, biographical fallacies are bound to follow. Consider the case of Tchaikovsky's last symphony, the Sixth in B Minor, Op. 74, subtitled *Pathétique* (A Symphony of Suffering; Fig. 24-10). The subtitle and its implications are due mainly to the last movement, which is extremely unusual in form and character. Tchaikovsky's *Pathétique* was the first nineteenth-century symphony ever to put the slow movement last. Not only that, but the movement, suggestively marked *Adagio lamentoso*, ends with a long, drawn-out decrescendo. The symphony ends, in other words, as if in polemical defiance of the Beethovenian prescription that symphonies enact and perpetually reenact narratives of triumph and transcendence. For the audience who heard Tchaikovsky conduct it at its St. Petersburg premiere in October 1893, it was indeed a puzzle. The symphony was "not disliked," Tchaikovsky wrote to his publisher, "but it has caused some bewilderment."[24]

Nine days later, Tchaikovsky died suddenly of cholera, most unexpectedly. The symphony was played again, *in memoriam*, subtitle now in place, as it had not been at the premiere. This time the audience was an audience of mourners, listening hard for portents. And that is how the symphony became a suicide note. Depression was the first diagnosis, "homosexual tragedy" came later. Even those who realize that the work was composed too early to have been the direct expression of Tchaikovsky's "final tragedy" cite it as evidence of his generally miserable state of mind. Yet documentary evidence suggests that Tchaikovsky's mood near the end of his life contradicts the "evidence" of the music. By the time in question, with the help of loving family and friends, he had come to terms with his sexuality, found an acceptable way of living within the moral constraints of his society, and seems to have been a reasonably happy man. Indeed, the act of producing the Sixth

Figure 24-10 Manuscript page from Tchaikovsky's Symphony *Pathétique* (Sixth Symphony).

Symphony brightened his last summer. "I have never felt such self-satisfaction, such pride, such happiness," he wrote to his publisher, "as in the consciousness that I am really the creator of this beautiful work."[25]

The despairing finale of Tchaikovsky's Sixth Symphony, like the cheerful finale of Beethoven's Second, should stand as a warning, rather than an encouragement, to those who under the influence of "pop psychology" would assume that art is by nature autobiographical. The cases are complementary: Beethoven's Second, which we may remember Berlioz said "smiles throughout," was composed concurrently with the composer's desperate realization, attended by thoughts of suicide and expressed in his heart-rending Heiligenstadt Testament, that his deafness was irrevocable. The agonizing, heart-rending finale of Tchaikovsky's Sixth Symphony, by contrast, was composed during as happy a period as the composer ever knew.

What does all of this prove? Only that art is . . . well, artful. There is no art of which this is truer than the Romantic art of confession, of which Tchaikovsky's mature symphonies are outstanding examples. "Always be sincere," the comedy team of

Flanders and Swann used to say, "whether you mean it or not." That might have been Tchaikovsky's motto. His matchless ability to "do" sincerity with utter conviction brought the Romantic tradition in music—a thing of artifice, illusion, and manipulated codes—to its very climax.

Summary

This chapter addressed musical trends in Eastern Europe and Russia. The first nationalist composer from Czech lands was Bedřich Smetana (1824–84), an enthusiastic supporter of the New German School. He was known for his symphonic poems and for his eight operas in the Czech language, including *Libuše* and *The Bartered Bride*, the first opera in Czech to be widely successful internationally. His *Má vlast* (My Fatherland) is a cycle of six symphonic poems based on Czech history, legends, and landscape, the most famous of which is *Vltava* (The Moldau). Smetana's life and career turn on several apparent contradictions. Although his focus on program music established him as a New German, he is known today mainly as a Czech nationalist. He approached Czech culture, moreover, as something of an outsider. The Czech language and folk music were associated primarily with a peasant culture that was far removed from Smetana's background and his cosmopolitan, German-language education. Although the central tune in *Vltava* came to be seen as a quintessential expression of Czech nationhood, it is actually not a Czech folk song at all but a Swedish one, and it has since become the national anthem of the state of Israel.

In Russia, there were two distinct musical movements, sometimes in conflict with one another. One branch promoted a professionalized music culture along Western European lines. A central figure in this movement, the composer and pianist Anton Rubinstein (1829–94), founded the St. Petersburg Conservatory in 1862. The other movement sought to create a distinctively Russian, nationalistic music. The leading representatives of this movement were the composers known as the "Mighty Five": Miliy Balakirev (1837–1910), Alexander Borodin (1833–87), César Cui (1835–1918), Modest Musorgsky (1839–81), and Nikolai Rimsky-Korsakov (1844–1908). Outsiders in Russia's musical establishment, they had careers in other fields and met as a group to study the works of Schumann, Liszt, and Berlioz. They also studied and used actual folk songs (Balakirev published an anthology of tunes he had collected in 1866). They created a distinctive harmonic language that came to be associated with Russian nationalism.

Russian opera was shaped by a set of unique circumstances, particularly the absolute power of the tsar and extreme censorship that came hand in hand with autocracy. Commentary on political and social issues had to be camouflaged, and the arts became an important vehicle for this discourse. There was a drift away from Romanticism and toward realism. In the opera *Boris Godunov*, Musorgsky demonstrated a commitment to realism by dispensing with verse in favor of conversational prose. In the coronation scene, Tsar Boris's monologue is set in a declamatory vocal style, with short, repeated notes and a melodic shape derived from the text. This scene also illustrates a distinctive harmonic practice associated with the "Mighty Five," prolonging and alternating chords (in this case two dominant seventh chords) that do not resolve in terms of traditional tonal harmony.

As a graduate of the St. Petersburg Conservatory, Pyotr Ilyich Tchaikovsky (1840–93) shaped his career along different lines. His best-known works include the opera *Eugene Onegin*; symphonies Nos. 4, 5, and No. 6 (*Pathétique*); and ballets such as *Swan Lake* and *The Nutcracker*. *Eugene Onegin*, based on a play by Alexander Pushkin, is another expression of the Russian tendency toward realism, drawing much of its musical idiom from domestic songs that had been popular in the 1830s and '40s, when the story is set. His symphonies depart from the Germanic models and tight motivic designs of Beethoven and Brahms. Tchaikovsky opted instead for lyrical, expansive melodies. His orchestral music abounds with references to song and dance, reflecting in part the influence of Mozart.

Study Questions

1. How were nationalistic composers in Eastern Europe and Russia influenced by the New German School described in Chapter 22?
2. In what sense is Bedřich Smetana both a New Germanist and a Czech nationalist? How and why were his works received differently in Bohemia and outside Bohemia?
3. What factors make people hear Smetana's *Vltava* as a nationalist work?
4. Who were the "Mighty Five"? What were their goals? Which composers did they admire the most, and why?
5. Describe Modest Musorgsky's realism in *Boris Godunov*. How is it reflected in the text setting and orchestral writing of the Coronation Scene?
6. Discuss the importance of traditional song and dance for Pyotr Illyich Tchaikovsky's music, especially in the Fourth Symphony and in *Eugene Onegin*.
7. Compare and contrast Tchaikovsky's Fourth Symphony with the symphonies you have studied by Beethoven. In what respect did Tchaikovsky's symphonies break from this tradition?
8. What is at stake when Tchaikovsky's symphonies are understood as being autobiographical? What makes autobiographical interpretation persuasive or unpersuasive?

Key Terms

***Kuchka* or Mighty Five**

realism

25

The Musical Museum and the Return of the Symphony

The symphony—or rather the traditional, nonprogrammatic, multimovement symphony—fell on hard times after Beethoven's Ninth. Schubert wrote his "Great" C Major Symphony in 1825, the year after Beethoven's, although it was not premiered until 1839; the unveiling of his "Unfinished" Symphony took even longer, until 1865, more than forty years after its composition. Mendelssohn's five mature symphonies and Schumann's four, although more or less standard repertory items today, were not considered the two composers' most significant (that is to say, their most "innovative") statements. That these symphonies tend to get little attention in history books shows the ease with which the historian's attention is captured by novelty.

If the symphony did not thrive in the 1830s and '40s, when fewer and fewer were premiered or published, things got decidedly worse after 1850. The genre was no longer considered a site of real creative energy; rather, it was seen as illustriously outmoded. Its meteoric career had carried it in the course of little more than a century from aristocratic party music to momentous public oration, but its place had apparently been preempted by the programmatic works pioneered by Berlioz and Liszt. Wagner went further, boldly declaring in *The Artwork of the Future* that Beethoven's Ninth had made all purely instrumental music obsolete.[1]

Not a single symphony composed in the 1850s or '60s has survived triumphant in the repertoire.[2] The genre became one cultivated largely by conservatory professors. One of the most prolific symphonists of the period was Anton Rubinstein, the fire-breathing piano virtuoso but conservative composer we met in the previous chapter who founded the St. Petersburg Conservatory. Among his counterparts in Germany and Austria were Julius Rietz (1812–77), Carl Reinecke (1824–1910), Max Bruch (1832–1920), and the Danish-born Niels Gade (1817–90) in Leipzig; Joachim Raff (1822–82) in Frankfurt; and Robert Volkmann (1815–83) in Vienna and Budapest. These largely forgotten figures maintained the genre through its fallow period but did not make any lasting contribution to it. In France, no composer could graduate from the Paris Conservatory without a Classical-style symphony under his belt to demonstrate formal mastery. This is how charming student efforts by the sixteen-year-old Camille Saint-Saëns (1835–1921) and the seventeen-year-old Georges Bizet (1838–75) got written in the mid-1850s. Two symphonies by Charles Gounod (1818–93) from the same time were the by-product of his meeting with Felix Mendelssohn and hearing him conduct the orchestra at the Leipzig Gewandhaus.

The most popular music history text of the 1880s, the *Illustrierte Musikgeschichte* (Illustrated History of Music) by Emil Naumann, seemed uncertain of the symphony's future: "Reflecting now on the achievements of the past, we observe in the tonal art an organic whole. It is complete and finished. What is to come one cannot divine."[3] There seemed to be nothing left to do. But Naumann had missed an important development: A symphonic revival was already under way; we have just seen one example with Tchaikovsky. What resuscitated the genre's prestige, renewed its prospects, and attracted talented composers was a volatile compound of historical and social factors that transformed concert life, cementing the powerful notion of a classical tradition in music that is still with us today.

TIMELINE

- **1824 Birth of Anton Bruckner**
- **1830** U.S. President Andrew Jackson signs Indian Removal Act
- **1833 Birth of Johannes Brahms**
- **1841 Birth of Antonín Dvořák**
- **1855** Henry Wadsworth Longfellow, *Song of Hiawatha*
- **1860s First African American spirituals published**
- **1861 Brahms, Piano Quartet in G Minor, Op. 25**
- **1868 Brahms, *A German Requiem***
- **1870 Musikverein concert hall opens in Vienna**
- **1870–71** Franco-Prussian War
- **1873 Brahms, Haydn Variations for orchestra**
- **1876 Brahms, First Symphony**
- **1879** Electric light invented by Thomas Edison
- **1884 Bruckner's Symphony No. 7 premieres in Leipzig**
- **1886 Camille Saint-Saëns, Symphony No. 3 in C Minor, ("Organ")**
- **1887 Dvořák, Piano Quintet in A Major, Op. 81**
- **1888 César Franck, Symphony in D Minor**
- **1888** George Eastman perfects Kodak camera
- **1891 Carnegie Hall opens in New York**
- **1892–95 Dvořák in New York**
- **1894 Dvořák, Symphony in E Minor ("From the New World")**
- **1896 Edward MacDowell, Second "Indian" Suite**
- **1896 Amy Beach, Symphony in E Minor ("Gaelic")**

New Halls and New Orchestras

Along with the growth of cities in the wake of industrialization came a broadening of the musical audience into what could be truly thought of as a public: a cross section of society—or, at least, of affluent society, people with money to spend. The concert hall began to rival the opera house as a potential source for profit making, and venues of a size comparable to opera theaters but specifically designed for orchestral concerts—the kind of concert hall familiar today—began to proliferate. As concert halls got bigger, less expensive seats became more available, thus broadening the potential audience.

The Leipzig Gewandhaus, built in 1781, enjoyed a particularly distinguished history, most associated in the nineteenth century with Mendelssohn's glorious reign at the helm of its orchestra. After a century of use, a new hall was constructed in 1884; with some 1,600 seats it had more than triple the original capacity in order to accommodate the large audiences that were by then flocking to symphony concerts. Vienna had no concert hall at all until 1831, when the Gesellschaft der Musikfreunde built one, which was replaced in 1870 by the Musikverein (Music Society). Its main hall, familiarly known as the "Golden Hall" because of its lavish appointments and superb acoustics, accommodates some 1,750 (Fig. 25-1) and remains the principal concert venue in the city. The same year Dresden opened its Gewerbehaussaal (Chamber of Commerce Hall), which was about the same size as the Musikverein.

With new halls came new, permanent professional orchestras, while prominent existing orchestras prompted the construction of new halls. The Vienna Philharmonic (founded in 1842) and the Dresden Hofkapelle began offering full-season subscriptions like those of the precocious Gewandhaus. Shorter orchestral subscriptions had been a fixture of Parisian music life since 1828, when the Société des Concerts du Conservatoire was founded by François-Antoine Habeneck, who introduced Beethoven symphonies to France and conducted the premiere of Berlioz's

Figure 25-1 Interior of Vienna's "Golden Hall" of the Musikverein (Music Society), designed by Theophil Hansen in 1870.

Symphonie fantastique. In 1853, a rival concert organization, the Société des Jeunes Artistes du Conservatoire, started giving concerts under Jules-Étienne Pasdeloup (1819–87), and other concert organizations emerged in the decades that followed. Before the end of the eighteenth century, London, like Leipzig, boasted a full-fledged concert hall (the Hanover Square Rooms, where Haydn appeared), and in the nineteenth century new spaces were inaugurated, notably the immense Royal Albert Hall, which opened in 1871.

Russia's first professional orchestra was founded at St. Petersburg in 1859 by the aristocratic Russian Musical Society, the same organization that sponsored Anton Rubinstein's conservatory. Its concerts were given in what was formerly known as the Assembly Hall of the Nobility, a relatively small space built in the 1830s for fashionable balls. Large halls like those in Western Europe came much later. Somewhat paradoxically, a burgeoning public concert life in Russia on the bourgeois model had to await the Communist (that is, antibourgeois) Revolution of 1917.

The most prestigious nineteenth-century concert hall in America was New York's Music Hall (now known as Carnegie Hall, after Andrew Carnegie, the steel magnate who financed it), having a seating capacity of 2,784. It opened its doors in 1891 with Tchaikovsky appearing as the guest star at the inaugural gala. It was the home for what is now called the New York Philharmonic, founded in 1842, just as Boston's Symphony Hall (capacity 2,645) was built in 1900 for the Boston Symphony Orchestra, founded in 1881.

The size of the audience for symphony concerts reached a new level in the second half of the nineteenth century and just seemed to keep growing.

The Triumph of Museum Culture

The size of the audience for symphony concerts reached a new level in the second half of the nineteenth century and just seemed to keep growing. But here we face a potentially grim irony: Symphonic music began reaching its new plateau of popularity and prestige exactly as its production was falling off. What pieces were all those excellent new professional orchestras playing in their wonderful new concert halls?

The answer becomes apparent by looking at nineteenth-century concert programs, which vividly indicate the growth of a music "museum culture" that we first explored in Chapter 15. The repertoire of most orchestras as well as of chamber music societies consisted largely of the "Viennese Classics"—Haydn, Mozart, and Beethoven—plus selected works by Schubert, Mendelssohn, Schumann, and a few others, with those of living composers generally admitted insofar as they were composed in traditional forms. The symphonic repertoire to a certain extent became frozen at the century's midpoint. According to one study, about 80 percent of all the music performed in Vienna, Leipzig, Paris, and London around 1800 was the work of living composers, while after 1850, and especially by 1870, the ratio of living to dead composers performed was almost exactly reversed.[4] The concert hall had thus effectively become a museum over the course of the century, and so it has remained to the present day. The newly professionalized, newly democratized, and newly profitable concert world of the late nineteenth century stuck to the tried and true.

Along with the expansion of concert life came the attending mechanisms of ever more music journalism, program notes and concert guides that helped listeners navigate these events, and popular sheet music arrangements, particularly for piano, through which the public could learn a piece by playing it. As had already long been the case with theater and opera, concert life assumed broader social functions, becoming a place to meet people, to see and to be seen. The very nature of a public concert as a social gathering furthered the rigidity of the repertoire, with a smaller and smaller number of favorite pieces endlessly recycled. The music of the enshrined masters became a kind of liturgy and concert attendance a kind of secular religion.

As the orchestral repertoire was conceived as "complete and finished" (to recall Naumann's assessment), the objectives of composers and performers began to diverge. Composers obviously wished to add to the repertoire, but their additions were welcomed by performers and audiences mainly insofar as they seemed compatible with the existing collection of the museum of musical works, which is to say, rarely. The symphonies of Raff or Rietz or Reinecke or Rubinstein might be played occasionally, especially locally, but there seemed no pressing need to add them to the permanent collection. And thus we have at last defined classical music as the term is used today and pinpointed its origin: Classical music is the music in the permanent collection as it became defined during the nineteenth and early twentieth centuries.

Classical music is the music in the permanent collection as it became defined during the nineteenth and early twentieth centuries.

Composers were now really in a bind. They had in essence to create instant classics—compositions that in their high-minded seriousness could somehow simultaneously project both enticing novelty and enduring value. It may sound like something that could not be done, but someone did it: Johannes Brahms (1833–97; Fig. 25-2). In the process, as musicologist J. Peter Burkholder observes, he provided "the model for future generations of what a composer is, what a composer does, why a composer does it, what is of value in music, and how a composer is to succeed."[5] In this formulation, of course, "a composer" here stands for modern composers, namely, "composers obsessed with the musical past and with their place in music history."[6] The definition encapsulates yet another paradox: Modernity in music was importantly defined by a relationship to the past, not just a relationship to the present and future.

New Paths: Johannes Brahms

Figure 25-2 Johannes Brahms. Portrait by Carl von Jagemann.

Brahms was the first leading German composer who grew up within our modern conception of classical music. Born in the north German city of Hamburg in 1833, he moved in his late twenties to Vienna. Formerly one of the most musical of cities, Vienna (like the symphony itself) had not seen much significant composerly action in more than three decades, since the deaths of Beethoven and Schubert in the late 1820s. Brahms was just old enough to have had a personal link to early Romanticism. It could not have been a more distinguished connection, in fact, since from the age of twenty he had been identified as a protégé of Robert Schumann.

The initial meeting between Brahms and Schumann, on 30 September 1853, was arranged by the brilliant violinist and composer Joseph Joachim (1831–1907; Fig. 25-3), whom we met earlier as concertmaster of Liszt's orchestra at Weimar, the command center for the New German School. Born in Hungary, Joachim had received his early training in Vienna before studying in Leipzig with Mendelssohn, who knew from personal experience what it meant to be a prodigy. The following year the two went together to London, where Joachim played the Beethoven Violin Concerto, a work that he more or less introduced into the standard repertoire and for which he wrote a cadenza that is still often used today. Joachim was devastated by Mendelssohn's early death, and he next took the Weimar position under Liszt, to whom he dedicated his own first Violin Concerto. It did not take long for Joachim to realize, however, that Liszt's musical agenda, let alone his actual music, represented the opposite of his own aesthetic ideals.

After resigning from the Weimar job in his early twenties, Joachim met Robert and Clara Schumann and soon thereafter introduced them to Brahms, with whom he had recently been concertizing. By then Robert's mental health was declining, and early in 1854 he made his famous suicide attempt by throwing himself in the Rhine River. But prior to these sad events, the Schumanns took the young Brahms into their home and hearts. Robert was already seeing himself as an embattled Classicist in opposition to the emergent New German School. In view of his earlier distinction as the quintessential Romanticist of the keyboard and the Lied and his former championship, as critic, of Berlioz and Liszt, this all seemed an ironic outcome. He found himself pitted against the historicist party, whose official organ, in added irony, was the *Neue Zeitschrift für Musik*, the journal he had himself founded, now edited by Franz Brendel.

As a courtesy to his predecessor, Brendel gave Schumann space in the magazine for what turned out to be his very last article: "Neue Bahnen" (New Paths), a brief piece in praise of the practically unknown Brahms. On the front page in the issue of 28 October 1853 Schumann hailed the twenty-year-old as the musical messiah the artistic world had been awaiting since Beethoven's death. He wrote:

> it has seemed to me that there would and must suddenly appear some day one man who would be singled out to make articulate in an ideal way the highest expression of our time, one man who would bring us mastery, not as the result of a gradual development, but as Minerva,

Figure 25-3 Johannes Brahms (left) and Joseph Joachim.

> springing fully armed from the head of Cronus. And he is come, a young creature over whose cradle graces and heroes stood guard. His name is *Johannes Brahms,* and he comes from Hamburg, where he has been working in silent obscurity, trained in the most difficult theses of his art by an excellent teacher who sends me enthusiastic reports of him, recommended to me recently by a well-known and respected master [Joachim].[7]

Here we encounter yet another benediction legitimating a gloried musical tradition. It was a dream review—a great critic/composer welcoming a new genius and proclaiming him music's savior. But Schumann's article also created extraordinary expectations, which put severe pressure on the young Brahms. Schumann had based his lavish praise on just a few works. Three early piano sonatas he found were "like disguised symphonies," which gave hope for greater things to come. An actual Brahms symphony, Schumann predicted, would mark the rebirth of Romanticism at its best, uncontaminated by the programmaticism associated with the likes of Berlioz and Liszt.

Symphonic Attempts

The very sense of heritage and obligation that Schumann had thrust on Brahms seems to have held him back from writing a symphony. The same hesitation afflicted an increasing number of composers obsessed with the past and with their place in history. Whereas the first symphonies of many earlier figures had served as learning exercises, Brahms felt obligated to produce a masterpiece, a work for the permanent collection, on his very first try. After some abortive attempts, exasperated by a sense of failure, he gave up for years to come. He declared to one of his friends that he would never compose a symphony, adding, "You don't know what it is like to walk in the footsteps of a giant."[8]

The giant, of course, was Beethoven. But in fact all the musical past was stalking Brahms, and the problem was compounded by the rise of the musical museum, the dominating presence of earlier masters. Composing a traditional symphony rather than a Lisztian programmatic work, which could be measured by other aesthetic criteria, became nearly impossible. So while Brahms's early piano, vocal, and chamber music earned admiration from musicians, critics, and audiences, people wondered when he would turn to what really mattered: symphonies and operas.

Brahms felt obligated to produce a masterpiece, a symphony for the permanent collection, on his very first try.

On 27 February 1854, four months after having written "New Paths," Schumann attempted suicide, which led to his confinement in a sanatorium for the remaining two years of his life. Brahms visited him fairly often, which Clara was forbidden to do, and actually took his place at the head of the Schumann household, helping raise their children. Brahms remained on intimate terms with Clara to the end of her long life, less than a year before his own death. (Yes, of course people gossiped about the relationship between the bachelor composer and the widowed pianist, fourteen years his senior.) His intense personal experiences with the Schumanns and the loyalty it bred bound Brahms ever more tightly to their position in German musical politics. He would become the standard bearer of the Mendelssohn/Schumann heritage in what is now sometimes called the War of the Romantics, which pitted the more classically minded Romantics against the self-proclaimed "Music of the Future" coming from the New Germans. But this conservative/

progressive rhetoric reflected the views of spokesmen for the respective camps, figures like Eduard Hanslick and Franz Brendel, more than it did the actual music. Brahms, as we shall see, was also writing music of and for the future, partly built on innovative uses of the past.

With everyone expecting a symphony, Brahms had in fact begun to sketch one while Schumann was still alive, initially as a Sonata in D Minor for Piano Duet, which he played through with Clara. By the end of July 1854 three movements were drafted, the first of them orchestrated as well. He sent the score to Joachim, who later told one of Brahms's biographers that it began with a covert (that is, unannounced as a "program") visualization of Schumann's anguished leap into the Rhine. Typically Brahmsian are various allusions to other pieces, most notably two other symphonies in D minor: Beethoven's Ninth and Schumann's Fourth. Brahms never finished this symphony, but the first movement later went into his Piano Concerto No. 1 in D Minor, Op. 15 (published 1861), and the third movement, even more radically transformed, later found a home in a choral work, *Ein deutsches Requiem* (A German Requiem, 1868).

The first big job Brahms got after receiving Schumann's rave review allowed him to spend three months a year, from 1857 to 1859, in quite old-fashioned conditions, working as teacher, pianist, and choral conductor in the minor princely court of Detmold, a small city in north-central Germany. Brahms was thus one of the last composers to enjoy, however briefly and part-time, the security of aristocratic patronage. He composed little during these years, but with a small orchestra available to him he turned out two serenades written in a frankly retrospective style. The very name, of course, was a throwback to outdoor party music. The Serenade No. 1 in D Major, Op. 11, for a time even bore the title "Symphony-Serenade," although it was originally written as a chamber work for wind and string instruments in the tradition of similar instrumental combinations by Beethoven, Schubert, Hummel, and others. Brahms expanded this four-movement chamber work (now lost) to a six-movement piece for orchestra. The two added movements were a pair of old-fashioned minuets and a second scherzo in which Brahms cleverly juxtaposed allusions to Haydn's Symphony No. 104 and Beethoven's Symphony No. 2.

At this time Brahms evidently did not much care about being perceived as cutting-edge. The D Major Serenade would hardly have been thought an effective protest against the militancy of the New German School. Reliance on Classical models could only have looked weak compared with Liszt's bold forays in his recently published symphonic poems, which is precisely why Brahms could not offer it as a symphony. As he put it himself to a friend who inquired about the change of title, "if one wants to write symphonies after Beethoven, then they will have to look very different!"[9]

Brahms's Chamber Music and "Developing Variation"

So Brahms kept putting off composing a symphony and concentrated on other genres, continuing to write piano music, Lieder, and choral works. Except for the First Piano Concerto, which made some use of the aborted symphony, most of his orchestral music dates from later in his career. He would first become a major force with his chamber music, twenty-four works in all, produced over the entire length of his career: three string quartets, five piano trios (including one with horn in place of cello and one with clarinet in place of violin), three piano quartets, one piano quintet, two string quintets, two string sextets, a quintet for clarinet and strings, three sonatas for violin and piano, two sonatas for cello and piano, and two sonatas for clarinet (or viola) and piano.

Chamber music, dormant like the symphony at mid-century and shunned by the New Germans, would become an important site for progressive experimentation in the early twentieth century.

In the middle years of the century, chamber music, like the symphony, received less attention from composers. The New German attitude toward chamber music was frankly disdainful; they generally did not write it—there is none by Berlioz or Wagner and only a few minor pieces by Liszt, mostly arrangements of his own piano compositions. Chamber music in its Brahmsian incarnation marked a change no less decisive than the one he would eventually make in the symphonic sphere.

The growth of orchestras geared toward a broad public seems to have inspired something of a backlash among some musical connoisseurs who placed a heightened premium on chamber music. Rather than the old noble aristocracy of birth and breeding, musical life was increasingly governed by a middle-class aristocracy of *Bildung*, or education, of taste and culture—breeding of another sort. One of Brahms's closest friends, a famous surgeon and amateur violist named Theodor Billroth, once gave a superb illustration of this educational breeding in a letter congratulating the composer after a performance of one of his symphonies. Its music, he implied, was possibly too good for the genre:

> I wished I could hear it all by myself, in the dark. . . . All the silly, everyday people who surround you in the concert hall and of whom in the best case maybe fifty have enough intellect and artistic feeling to grasp the essence of such a work at the first hearing—not to speak of understanding; all that upsets me in advance. I hope, however, that the musical masses here have enough musical instinct to understand that something great is happening there in the orchestra.[10]

The aristocracy of *Bildung* differed from the aristocracy of birth in its appreciation of, to quote Friedrich Nietzsche, "music that sweats." We might well wonder as Billroth did how many of the details—especially the extraordinarily fine-grained motivic structure of this formidable "musicians' music"—were heard, that is, noticed and actively followed by regular audience members. As we shall see in chapters to come, however, the fascination Brahms's chamber music exercised on later composers would be a powerful stimulus to stylistic innovation in the twentieth century. The ultimate paradox is that chamber music, dormant like the symphony at mid-century and shunned by the New Germans, would become an important site for progressive experimentation in the early twentieth century.

We will consider a relatively early example of Brahms's chamber music, which dates from 1861, just before he moved to Vienna. After the elevation of the string quartet by Haydn, Mozart, and Beethoven, composers in the latter half of the nineteenth century focused more on writing chamber music with piano. The innovations in piano construction masterfully exploited in solo works by Liszt, Chopin, and others allowed for new orchestral sonorities. Brahms's Piano Quartet in G Minor, Op. 25, looks back to Vienna's illustrious past as well as forward to its Modernist future, in particular to thematic techniques that Arnold Schoenberg would later hail in a famous lecture called "Brahms the Progressive." Brahms cast the quartet in four movements: an expansive opening one, an introspective intermezzo, an *Andante con moto,* and a breathless *Rondo alla Zingarese,* that is, a rondo finale in "the Hungarian style." Clara Schumann premiered the work on 16 November 1861 in Hamburg, and on the same day one year later Brahms himself presented it in Vienna, performing as pianist with the Hellmesberger String Quartet. Hanslick praised Brahms as "possibly the most interesting among our contemporary composers," but he found the themes of the quartet "insignificant . . . dry and prosaic."[11]

Anthology Vol 2-59
Full CD V, 17
Concise CD II, 48

Indeed, the work generally did not have long lyrical melodies as we have found in Schubert or Tchaikovsky. The sophisticated motivic elaborations and transformations, moreover, were no longer limited to the development section but were now present from the outset, for the most part determining how the music would proceed from moment to moment. Larger and larger musical entities became constructed out of smaller and smaller particles. That may seem rather like what we identified as the signal achievement of Wagner's *Ring,* with its kaleidoscopic texture of leitmotifs. Brahms, like Wagner, did his thematic thinking primarily in terms of motifs rather than full-blown melodies. Whether one was writing opera or chamber music or symphonies, it became a crucial composerly problem during the latter part of the century to resolve the fundamental tension between "the brevity of the musical ideas and the monumentality of the formal designs," in the words of musicologist Carl Dahlhaus.[12]

The intricate motivic work of the G Minor Quartet begins with its opening measures. Dahlhaus remarked on the theme's brevity and, echoing Hanslick, on the insignificance of the material but pointed to the thematic implications and elaborations; he notes that "compositional economy, the building of music out of minimal capital, was taken to extremes by Brahms."[13] The first measure is transposed in m. 5, freely inverted in mm. 2–3 and 6–8, and presented harmonically in m. 4 (Ex. 25-1). Schoenberg called this Brahms's technique of "**developing variation**."[14] The concentration on minute motivic relations requires active engagement and response from the listener, the kind of attention Billroth was getting at in his letter to Brahms.

Example 25-1 **Johannes Brahms, Piano Quartet in G Minor, Op. 25, I, mm. 1–14**

Example 25-1 (*continued*)

Choral Fame

It is one of the ironies surrounding his career that Brahms, who never wrote an opera and who was later hailed for his role in reviving the symphony, should have gained his first real fame as a composer of choral music. It was, however, a time-honored road to success for German composers, given the country's many singing societies and summer festivals. For a while it was the field in which Brahms specialized, beginning with the amateur chorus he led in Detmold, followed by an amateur women's chorus in Hamburg. His first major appointment in Vienna was in 1863 as director of the Singakademie, one of the city's main choral societies. Much of Brahms's repertory with the group concentrated on *a cappella* and continuo-accompanied literature, and in the process he discovered a wealth of sixteenth- to eighteenth-century music, particularly Heinrich Schütz and other early German masters up to J. S. Bach, whose choral works were then only then beginning to be published.

Brahms's activities as a choral conductor were decisive because of the impact of "early music" on his composing. He became an enthusiast, sought out leading musical scholars of his generation—Gustav Nottebohm, Friedrich Chrysander, and Philipp Spitta—as friends, and actually engaged in some musicological work of his own, making many arrangements of early German choral music and participating in the preparation of editions of music by Couperin, Handel, C. P. E. Bach, Mozart, Schubert, Schumann, and others.

His choral masterpiece, *A German Requiem* (Fig. 25-4), is not a liturgical work but, rather, a deeply personal setting, inspired in part by the death of his mother, of selected passages from Martin Luther's translation of the Bible that deal with consolation, acceptance of fate, and transcendence of suffering through love. As a piece composed by a Protestant but meant for performance throughout the German-speaking lands, including Catholic Austria and Bavaria, it continued the ecumenical Mendelssohnian tradition of using music as a liberal uniter of the religiously divided German-speaking peoples. Fugal writing abounds in it, and there are many passages that bear traces of older music.

Allusion to earlier music also made a significant contribution to the Requiem's companion piece, the *Triumphlied* (Song of Victory, 1871), a three-movement cantata, likewise on a biblical text, for antiphonal mixed choirs accompanied by the largest

Figure 25-4 Manuscript page in Brahms's handwriting from *A German Requiem*.

orchestra Brahms ever employed. It was composed in the aftermath of the Franco-Prussian War, in expectation of the proclamation of Prussian King Wilhelm I as emperor of a united Germany, in which Austria was not included. The *Triumphlied* was extremely popular during Brahms's lifetime, and the reasons for its near-total neglect today seem to have more to do with its political association than its musical qualities. It is a vivid expression of the German nationalism of its day that renders adoration to country and ruler in explicitly religious terms. Despite his move to Vienna, Brahms remained a proud German who particularly admired Wilhelm I's prime minister, Otto von Bismarck, the Prussian "Iron Chancellor" responsible for engineering the long-awaited unification (Fig. 25-5).

Figure 25-5 Brahms's music room in Vienna; the portrait of Otto von Bismarck (with ribbon attached) is located between a reproduction of Raphael's *Sistine Madonna* and the huge bust of Beethoven at the upper right.

Inventing Tradition

The first purely orchestral work with which Brahms enjoyed real success was the Variations for Orchestra on a Theme by Joseph Haydn, originally composed for two pianos in the summer of 1873 and based on a theme that may not have been Haydn's. (Brahms's source was labeled "Chorale St. Antoni," or "St. Anthony's Hymn," and was probably a religious folk song for which Haydn merely provided a harmonization.) The Haydn Variations was one of his many instrumental works with conspicuous ties to the Classical and pre-Classical repertoire. As a fortieth birthday present, the pioneer music historian Philipp Spitta gave Brahms the first volume of his landmark biography of J. S. Bach, then hot off the press. It included a long preliminary study of German keyboard and choral music in the century leading up to Bach's birth, in which Brahms found the discussion of ground-bass forms (chaconne, passacaglia, etc.) particularly interesting—and inspiring. He corresponded with Spitta about them, asked for more examples, and finished off the Haydn Variations with a giant set of ostinato variations.

By making Haydn shake hands with Bach, Brahms consciously sought a synthesis that connected the German present to a longstanding German past, a feat that made him the preeminent living German master in the view of many musicians and critics. It was a partial solution to the problem of the "giant's footsteps," that is, the looming Beethoven problem. Looking to the music of Bach and other early masters as well as to Schubert offered fruitful alternatives to Beethoven's dominating stature. Mendelssohn and Schumann had likewise found some liberation with this strategy. This was another kind of historicism, different from the New German kind that looked toward a better future. What might be called the Brahms Project, born of Mendelssohn and Schumann, looked to the past, not just to Beethoven, as a source for musical renewal. We have seen the bestowing of benedictions that perpetuate tradition by anointing a composer of the next generation—Brahms, we might say, cast his benediction backward, to Bach and Handel, Mozart and Haydn, Beethoven and Schubert.

By making Haydn shake hands with Bach, Brahms consciously sought a synthesis that connected the German present to a longstanding German past.

Over the five-year period between the premieres of *A German Requiem* and the Haydn Variations, Brahms achieved real celebrity, not to mention a secure income from publishing royalties from a wide variety of music. Now financially independent, he was able to help support family, friends, and struggling young artists. Both his fame and his finances were boosted by popular works meant for consumption at home. This included a set of sentimental waltzes, published in 1869 under the title *Liebeslieder* (Love Songs), for piano duet and vocal quartet singing words translated from Eastern European folk texts by a fashionable poet, Georg Friedrich Daumer. Its success led to another set in 1875. Like his eighteenth-century predecessors, Brahms was trying for a broad social reach, writing both serious works for the concert hall, the new Temple of Art, and popular works for domestic music making. Brahms genuinely loved much of the popular music of his time, especially that of Johann Strauss, Jr., Vienna's "Waltz King."

As we know from the furious Hungarian finale of the G Minor Piano Quartet, he was also deeply attracted to Hungarian music and had been ever since his teens, when Hungarian refugees from the revolutions of 1848 passed through his native

Hamburg. His first professional tours had been with the Hungarian violinist Eduard Remenyi (1828–94) and then with Joachim. By the time Brahms composed the piano quartet he had already written his Variations on a Hungarian Song, Op. 21, No. 2, and the earliest of his very popular Hungarian Dances for piano duet. He would return to the Hungarian style many times, not only in songs, dances, and piano variations, but also more ambitiously in other chamber compositions and in his concertos. Joachim, who had written a "Hungarian" Violin Concerto himself, dedicated to Brahms, wrote of the piano quartet's finale: "You have outstripped me on my own territory by a considerable track."[15] Joachim was Hungarian; Brahms, of course, was not, which is yet another warning to avoid essentialist arguments when thinking about what constitutes national music.

By the time of his fortieth birthday, Brahms was a highly acclaimed figure with a following that bridged all the strata of the music-loving and music-buying public, from amateurs to scholars. His success roundly contradicted the beliefs of the New Germans, refuting their claims much more effectively than the open letter of 1860 written with Joachim to protest Brendel's claims about the Music of the Future. Wagner came to regard Brahms—young enough, after all, to be his son and someone who genuinely admired his operas—as a threat. From the Wagnerian point of view, opera, or, rather, "music drama," was the uncontested and incontestable peak of musical achievement. As we know, Wagner felt that he was Beethoven's true heir. His one-time friend Nietzsche jotted down this note: "The tyrant who suppresses all individuality other than his own and his followers'. This is Wagner's great danger: to refuse to accept Brahms, etc.; or the Jews."[16]

Brahms posed a real challenge when he finally came forth with his First Symphony in 1876. The year is significant: It was also when Wagner's *Der Ring des Nibelungen* finally had its Bayreuth premiere. The symphony had certainly taken Brahms a long time. After his unsuccessful attempt to write one in the mid-1850s, the project had languished. In the summer of 1862 he had tried again and had been able to show friends his first full-fledged symphonic movement; after some further revisions and the later addition of a slow introduction, it became the first movement of the First Symphony. Clara Schumann wrote with delight to Joachim, quoting its "rather audacious" opening phrase and commenting: "The movement is full of wonderful beauties, with a mastery in the treatment of the motives that is indeed becoming more and more characteristic of him. Everything is so interestingly interwoven, yet as spirited as the first outburst; one is thrilled by it to the full, without being reminded of the craft."[17]

Yet once again Brahms set the symphony project aside. Encouraged by the response to the Haydn Variations, he returned to it in the summer of 1874, resuming work not with the next movement in order of performance but, rather, with the finale. It was only when the outer movements were in place that he saw the work's trajectory as a whole and could quickly fill in the middle movements, an *Andante sostenuto* in an A-B-A form, with an agitated middle section, and an *Un poco allegretto e grazioso*, which, like most of Brahms's third movements, functions as a brief interlude. The harmonic layout owes a debt to Schubert, whose music Brahms knew particularly well; he edited Schubert's symphonies and various waltzes, orchestrated some songs, and performed his music extensively. The four movements of the First Symphony follow Schubert's tonal trajectory in the "Wanderer" Fantasy along a circle of major thirds; and within movements as well, Schubertian harmonies and tonal progressions rule.

"The symphony is long and difficult," Brahms wrote to a friend. "My symphony is long and not exactly charming," he wrote to another. Finally, and most revealingly, he wrote to a third: "My symphony is long and in C minor."[18] *In C minor*. To anyone conversant with the symphonic tradition into which Brahms was trying, against the odds, to break, the words were enough to make the blood run cold. It meant he was taking on the model of models: Beethoven's Fifth. Vying with that masterpiece meant incurring a host of obligations far beyond achieving a tight motivic construction. There was also the obligation to reenact (yet without merely repeating) Beethoven's archetypal trajectory, embodied in the rhetoric of "Struggle and Victory."

As with the aborted symphony Brahms had attempted more than twenty years earlier, the First Symphony includes allusions to earlier music. There are references to Schumann's *Manfred*, Wagner's *Tristan und Isolde*, and, most obviously, to Beethoven's Fifth and Ninth Symphonies. Such a high level of allusion was a regular fixture in Brahms. Despite the lack of public programmatic content, his music was often anything but abstract in conception; the subtle allusions were typically ones intended for insiders to hear, not meant for the general listener. His music was as laden with symbolism as Beethoven's Ninth itself, probably even more so, but unlike the works of the New Germans it contained no built-in decoder key, no public aids to interpretation, and hence no single certifiable message.

The intricate web of motivic relationships in Brahms's First Symphony, which Clara immediately noticed, is similar to what we saw in the G Minor Piano Quartet. In place of the traditional thematic content of symphonic discourse, Brahms had substituted a mosaic of motifs in an ever-shifting contrapuntal design. The imposing *Un poco sostenuto* introduction to the opening movement sets the serious tone for the symphony and is followed by an *Allegro* rich in thematic material and motivic unfolding. Brahms's orchestration is also worth noting, for it is unusually dark and dense. It did not take long for critical debates to arise about whether his symphonies were truly orchestral or rather more like blown-up chamber music, which was the Wagnerian view espoused in attempts to diminish Brahms's accomplishment.

Victory Through Critique

In his First Symphony Brahms was contending not just with the Giant's Fifth in C Minor. One of the most contentious points at issue between the New Germans and their opponents in particular was the historical status of the Ninth Symphony. Wagner had notoriously cast it, in suitably religious terms, as the "redemption of Music from out of her own peculiar element into the realm of *universal art*," and "the human evangel of the art of the future."[19] In other words, Beethoven's union of music and text, of vocal and symphonic media in the last movement, closed the door on the further development of abstract instrumental music, making Lisztian programmatics and Wagnerian synthesis, the *Gesamtkunstwerk*, the inevitable future for music.

Anthology Vol 2-60
Full CD V, 18
Concise CD III, 1

Brahms's response was to revisit the finale of the Ninth and cast it as a nonprogrammatic and purely instrumental work. The First Symphony is goal oriented; that is, its destination is the fourth movement, which opens with a slow, minor-key introduction. This *Adagio* has a solemn opening phrase that turns out to be a foreshadowing of the main theme of the movement played in ultra-slow motion and at a very high register. The music accelerates and grows increasingly turbulent; it is not quite clear where all this is heading until a dramatic timpani roll is sounded and the tonality shifts from minor to major. Commentators have evoked many metaphors for the moment when a majestic alphorn theme sounds forth, like the sun breaking through the clouds (Ex. 25-2a). This pastoral theme first appeared years earlier in the form of a birthday greeting Brahms sent to Clara from Switzerland and that may have carried some personal meaning between them (another hidden allusion?). The theme has archaic rhythms (a "Lombard" snap in the second measure, a "double dot" in the fourth), a rustic "raised" fourth degree (the F♯ in m. 6), and, in the original birthday greeting, words that parody old German folk songs: "High in the mountains, deep in the valley, I greet you a thousandfold!"[20] The alphorn theme is followed by another kind of emblem, this time a religious one, when a choir of trombones, horns, and bassoons intones a choralelike theme (Ex. 25-2b).

Example 25-2a Johannes Brahms, Symphony No. 1, IV, alphorn theme

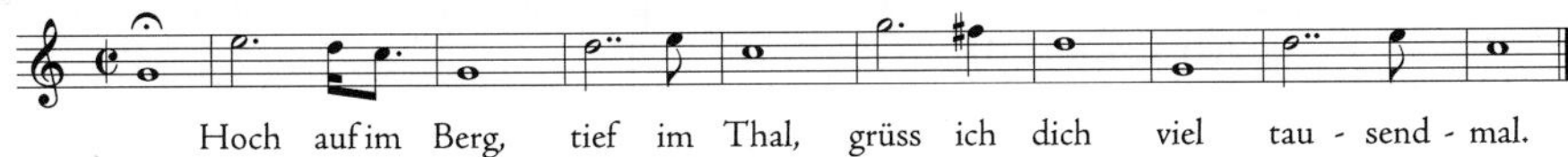
Hoch auf im Berg, tief im Thal, grüss ich dich viel tau - send - mal.

Example 25-2b Johannes Brahms, Symphony No. 1, IV, chorale theme

After all this introductory material—and at about the same point as in the last movement of Beethoven's Ninth—the tempo changes to *Allegro non troppo, ma con brio* and we hear what appears to be the movement's main theme. As in the Ninth, it takes the form of a great wordless hymn played by the strings. The resemblance to Beethoven's choral theme, the "Ode to Joy," is so pronounced and was so widely noted as to have become a standing joke, the best-known version of which had Brahms answering someone who had pointed it out to him by saying, "Yes indeed, and what is really remarkable is that every jackass notices it at once."[21] Sometimes this testy response is interpreted to mean that Brahms found the suggestion that he lacked originality irritating. More likely, if he actually said it, he meant that the mere resemblance is uninteresting. The implications were what counted. There can hardly be any doubt that he intended his hymn theme as a paraphrase of Beethoven's. If the two are written out in the same key, they even have a measure in common, and Brahms, by developing the phrase in which that measure occurs, all but insists that we notice it (Exs. 25-3a and 25-3b). Far less immediately noticeable is the strong resemblance of the opening phrase of the melody to a C-minor ground bass from the chorus "Ach, Herr! Lehre uns bedenken" in Bach's Cantata No. 106 (Exs. 25-4a and 25-4b). But Bach's work was nearly completely unknown at the time, and so, jackasses or not, nobody noticed it.[22]

Example 25-3a Johannes Brahms, Symphony No. 1, IV, main theme

Example 25-3b Ludwig van Beethoven, Symphony No. 9, IV, choral theme (transposed)

Example 25-4a J. S. Bach, ground bass from Cantata No. 106, "Gottes Zeit ist die allerbeste Zeit"

Example 25-4b Johannes Brahms, Symphony No. I, IV, opening of main final theme

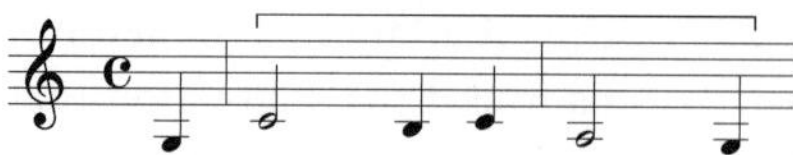

The fact that Brahms chose to make so obvious a reference to Beethoven's "Ode to Joy" theme takes on increasing significance as the movement progresses. The most significant aspect of the reference was the simple fact that it was entirely—and pointedly—instrumental. By alluding to Beethoven's joy theme but omitting the voices and words, Brahms seemed to be correcting what he felt was the wrong turn Beethoven had taken half a century before. What Wagner had interpreted one way, Brahms took completely differently. Brahms's friend, the musicologist Chrysander, quickly got the point and publicized it. Far from being the "weak and impotent imitation" the New Germans were calling it, Brahms had created "a counterpart to the last sections of the Ninth Symphony that achieves the same effect in nature and intensity without calling on the assistance of song."[23] This alone was enough to show that Brahms's attitude toward tradition was not merely reverential or unimaginatively derivative but active, participatory, and anything but uncritical. In Chrysander's words, he had "led the way back from the symphony that mixes playing and singing to the purely instrumental symphony," ending the eclipse of the latter genre and restoring its historical validity. As we shall see, the subsequent history of the genre confirmed his success.

But there was even more than that to Brahms's critique of "Wagner's Beethoven." Like the finale of the Ninth, Brahms's last movement is in a hybrid form, the identity of which has long been debated. Rather than trying to decide whether it is a sonata, a rondo, a set of variations, a rondo-sonata, or whatever, it would be better, as in the case of Beethoven, to take stock at the outset of its disparate ingredients and then trace their interaction. Prominent among them are the pastoral and religious emblems from the introduction, namely, the alphorn theme and the brass chorale. The difficulty critics and analysts have arises from the unexpected behavior—or, perhaps, the unexpected fate—of what immediately follows: the main hymn theme. The manner in which it is introduced, establishing a new and faster tempo after a slow introduction that had ended on the dominant, identifies it as the first theme in a sonata-form exposition. This sets up the expectation that it will be followed by a contrasting second theme, experience motivic development in distant keys, and finally achieve a decisive restatement in the tonic to signal the movement's impending closure.

Up to a point that is just what happens. After its initial statement by the strings, the hymn theme is repeated by the winds, as if replaying the strategy whereby Beethoven's choral theme had spread its brotherly contagion. A third repetition gives way to a preliminary motivic development of the Bach-derived phrase, opening onto a modulatory bridge that leads to the expected second theme (or, rather, group of themes) stated in the dominant, beginning in m. 118. The exposition continues to satisfy expectations with a rousing closing theme, its move into exuberant triplets multiplying the Beethovenian resonances by alluding to the analogous moment in the finale of Beethoven's Fifth. The development, too, arrives right on time, although it begins with a ploy that would long remain a Brahmsian trademark: an apparent premature recapitulation of the main hymn theme in the tonic key, which then unexpectedly modulates to a distant one before it is through. Yet the expected "real" recapitulation never comes. The hymn theme never again recurs as a whole, but only in its various motifs that gradually recede into the music's general motivic play. Instead of its expected return in the tonic, we get the introduction's alphorn theme, also in C major, to stand in for it, followed on schedule by the second theme in the tonic and then with a closing theme in tow. So there is recapitulation after all; it is just that the main hymn theme has been deliberately excluded from it (Table 25-1).

The movement eventually builds to a fanfarelike coda (*Più allegro*) that begins with one last motivic allusion to the alphorn theme (pared down by now to its first three notes). The final climax comes not with a glorification of the hymn theme, which is again preempted, but, rather, with the religious chorale, unheard since the slow introduction, now at full volume. That music, too, evokes a vocal collectivity, but an older one than Beethoven's. Beethoven is not dethroned, merely subsumed into a larger view of a German musical tradition that begins with Bach or perhaps even earlier, with Luther. And so the newness of the renewed symphony, as proclaimed by Brahms, was confirmed by reference to an unsuspected synthesis with what was recognizably old.

Table 25-1 Johannes Brahms, Symphony No. 1, movement 4

MEASURE NOS.	FORMAL DESIGNATION	SECTION	KEYS	COMMENTS
1–61	**Slow introduction**	*Adagio*	c	
1–29				Fragments of primary theme, mm. 2–3 and 13–14
30–46		Alphorn theme	C	
47–51		Chorale theme		
52–61		Alphorn theme		
62–185	**Exposition**	*Allegro non troppo, ma con brio*		
62–93		Primary theme		Cf. Beethoven's "Ode to Joy" (Ninth Symphony)
94–117		Bridge		From primary theme
118–47		Secondary theme	G	A set of tiny variations over a four-note descending tetrachord ground bass
148–85		Closing group		
186–284	**"development"**			In some respects like recapitulation
186–219		Primary theme	C, E♭, B	
220–84		Bridge	Begins in C	
285–367	**"recapitulation"**			
285–301		Alphorn theme	C	
302–31		Secondary theme	C	
332–67		Closing theme	E♭	
367–end	**Coda**			Faster and with developmental features
367–406		Begins with fragments of primary theme	E♭, e, C	
407–16		Chorale theme		
417 to end		Coda continues		

Reconciliation and Backlash

Not surprisingly, Eduard Hanslick embraced the work:

> Seldom, if ever, has the entire musical world awaited a composer's first symphony with such tense anticipation—testimony that the unusual was expected of Brahms in this supreme and ultimately difficult form. . . . If I say that no composer has come so close to the style of late Beethoven as Brahms has in this finale, I don't mean it as a paradoxical pronouncement, but rather as a simple statement of indisputable fact.[24]

Indeed, not many critics disputed the fact—the majority did comment on the connection to Beethoven—but not all welcomed the work as warmly as had Brahms's critical champion.

The signal moment in the work's early history was its ecstatic acceptance by the pianist and conductor Hans von Bülow, likened by some to a religious conversion. Bülow, we may remember, was a charter member of the New German School. A pupil and personal disciple of Liszt at Weimar and a close associate of Wagner, he had married the former's daughter and lost her to the latter, although not until he had conducted the premieres of both *Tristan und Isolde* and *Die Meistersinger*. Bülow made a specialty of Beethoven's Ninth, which he once conducted twice on the same concert with the Berlin Philharmonic so as to demonstrate his faith in its peerlessness, that is, the unworthiness of any other work to share billing with it. After hearing Brahms's First, played to him in advance of publication by the composer at a summer resort in 1877, Bülow rushed into print with an article hailing it as "the Tenth Symphony." He ended with an avowal—"Bach, Beethoven, and Brahms do not alliterate with one another by chance"[25]—that has lived on ever since in the catchphrase "the three B's," proclaiming a new holy trinity of classical music.

"Seldom, if ever, has the entire musical world awaited a composer's first symphony with such tense anticipation—testimony that the unusual was expected of Brahms in this supreme and ultimately difficult form." —Eduard Hanslick

This was all too much for Wagner. After Brahms was awarded an honorary doctorate in 1879 by the University of Breslau, with a diploma proclaiming him "the leader in the art of serious music in Germany today," the master of music drama struck back. In "On Poetry and Composition," an essay composed in fury amid the publicity surrounding Brahms's degree, Wagner let his pen run wild. "I know of some famous composers," he wrote, "who in their concert masquerades don the disguise of a street singer one day, the hallelujah periwig of Handel the next, the dress of a Jewish Csardas-fiddler another time, and then again the guise of a highly respectable symphony dressed up as Number Ten."[26] What brought on this insulting verbal caricature was Wagner's evident realization that the New German School could no longer assert exclusive rights to the interpretation of German musical history. Wagner's claim to Beethoven's mantle, implicit in his works and explicit in his writings, was now irrevocably in dispute with the emergence of Brahms. There would henceforth be two interpretations of the great tradition: the radical historicist one of Liszt and Wagner, which cast it as a kind of permanent revolution, and Brahms's liberal evolutionist one, which cast it as an incremental and consensual growth, building on a gloried past.

At the very least, Brahms was crucial in making the traditional symphony a viable option once again, a genre that could now be pursued without the stigma of being considered unoriginal and unimaginative. The chances of inclusion in the musical museum's permanent collection may have been about as slim as ever, but at least the effort to gain entry was newly respectable and attractive. Brahms himself, once he had broken the logjam, followed up with three more symphonies in less than a decade. His Second (1877) had no protracted birth pangs; its labor was quick and easy. Brahms may have felt liberated to some degree from the burden of expectations set up by Schumann so long before and turned to writing quite a different kind of symphony, an often-pastoral work in a bright D major. The First and Second present an intriguing juxtaposition of gravity and cheer, which some have interpreted as a glimpse of the two sides of Brahms's personality.

After the Third (1883), the final Fourth Symphony (1884–85) ends with a monumental chaconne over a ground bass adapted directly from Bach's early cantata

Figure 25-6 Anton Bruckner. Portrait by Ferry Beraton (1889).

Nach dich, Herr, verlanget mich (Lord, I long for thee; BWV 150). To base the latest link in the tradition on so early a model was a token of the timelessness of German musical values and yet another rebuttal to the Music of the Future.

The Symphony as Sacrament

Brahms's main Viennese rival as a symphonist was Anton Bruckner (1824–96), a decade-older composer who was also a latecomer to the symphony (Fig. 25-6). His work was often compared invidiously with Brahms's, especially by Hanslick, and the two composers regarded each another with suspicion. They spoke disparagingly of each other, with Brahms referring to his rival as "that bumpkin" who wrote "symphonic boa constrictors"[27] and Bruckner declaring for his part that he would rather hear a Strauss waltz than a Brahms symphony any day.[28]

Bruckner was trained as an organist and church choirmaster, and he quietly plied that trade at St. Florian's, a monastery near the Austrian city of Linz. He led an unassuming existence devoted principally to God and music, dual passions that he merged in some of his most magnificent compositions. He devoted most of the first half of his life to learning his craft, for a long time thinking that he needed to acquire ever more skills. In the 1850s, already in his thirties, he studied counterpoint with the noted Viennese theorist Simon Sechter, who insisted he study rather than write original compositions. For some six years Bruckner ceased his own creative work and honed his contrapuntal technique. In 1868, at age forty-four, he moved to Vienna, where he lived for the rest of his life. He taught at the Conservatory and the University of Vienna as well as privately and played the organ at the Imperial Court Chapel. Bruckner never shed his upper-Austrian roots, retaining its regional dialect and dress. Although he rarely traveled, trips to France and England, in 1869 and 1871, respectively, convinced some who heard him that he was the greatest organist and improviser of the day.

Bruckner's compositional achievement took longer to be recognized than did Brahms's. This was due in part to contemporary musical politics in Vienna and to the perception among some musicians that Bruckner was moving the art in the wrong direction. Hanslick opposed what he viewed as a Wagnerian agenda in Bruckner's symphonies. Of the premiere of the Eighth Symphony in 1892, he wrote:

> I found this newest one, as I have found the other Bruckner symphonies, interesting in detail, but strange as a whole, indeed repellent. The peculiarity of this work consists, to put it briefly, of importing Wagner's dramatic style into the symphony.... It is not impossible that the future belongs to this nightmarish hangover style—a future we therefore do not envy![29]

Of course, these were exactly the qualities that others applauded, such as the young composer Hugo Wolf, most remembered for his brilliant and challenging Lieder. There is something of a paradox in the fact that the provincial, unfashionable, devoutly Catholic Bruckner, supported by politically reactionary groups, was at the time perceived as a more musically progressive figure than Brahms, who was more cosmopolitan, intellectually cultivated, an anticlerical Protestant, and politically liberal.

Bruckner's compositional legacy consists primarily of Masses and symphonies, although he also wrote a variety of smaller works, both sacred and secular, including an ambitious string quintet. His three Masses (in D minor, E minor, and F minor) came relatively early, but the spiritual nature of his early religious compositions left its mark when he turned to symphonies. A flowing cello line in a Bruckner slow movement may seem as if it set words from the Benedictus of a Mass, for example, and indeed on several occasions he did import his sacred music directly into his symphonies.

That Bruckner was a master organist also profoundly influenced his orchestral style. His symphonies bear unmistakable traces of organ improvisation: extremely slow, sustained adagios and a heavy reliance on sequences and rhythmic ostinatos in the allegros—traits that led to the longest symphonies ever written up to that point. The orchestration of his mature symphonies tends to be slightly larger than Brahms's, more like a compact version of Wagner's in the *Ring*, without piccolo, English horn, or bass clarinet but including "Wagner tubas," plus contrabass tuba to furnish the burnished Wagnerian sonority. The orchestra, however, is deployed in a manner strikingly different from Wagner's. Bruckner often presents the instrumental sections (strings, winds, brass) as antiphonal choirs. This is another procedure transferred from his organ technique, in which a "registration" is set so that the different keyboards will activate contrasting ranks of pipes that can be played off one against another or combined for tuttis. His frequent homorhythmic textures evoke choirs of actual voices in the manner of chorales or of antiphonal psalmody.

Bruckner's move from church to concert hall came in the wake of his belated exposure to Wagner's music. It was, above all, Wagner's musical style, with its luxuriant orchestra, its harmonic daring, and its complex motivic textures, that captivated Bruckner, who had no inclination at all for dramatic composition and who paid no attention to Wagner's theories. For all the Wagnerian influence, Bruckner's symphonies have a resolutely traditional design in four movements and are not overtly programmatic. The Beethovenian number nine looms for Bruckner; he symbolically "rewrote" Beethoven's Ninth, not once but repeatedly. As one scholar has pointed out, Beethoven's last symphony provided Bruckner with "his four main movement types—the far-ranging first movement, the big adagio built from the varied alternation of two themes, the sonata-form scherzo, and the huge cumulative finale—as well as the tendency to begin a symphony with a faint background sound, emerging almost imperceptibly out of silence."[30]

For all the Wagnerian influence, Bruckner's symphonies have a resolutely traditional design in four movements and are not overtly programmatic.

Bruckner began writing his official First Symphony (1865–66) at age forty-one, although it was preceded by a "study" Symphony in F Minor (1863) and followed by an unnumbered Symphony in D Minor (1869). He dedicated his Third Symphony (1872–73, revised 1876–77, 1887–89) to Wagner, whom he first met at the premiere of *Tristan und Isolde* in Munich in 1865. While the Fourth (1874, revised 1878–80, 1888) eventually became one of his most performed, the Seventh (1881–83) marked the turning point of his career at its triumphant premiere in Leipzig on 30 December 1884. The Eighth Symphony (1887, revised 1890) caused the composer considerable pains. Self-doubt hounded Bruckner and led him to devote a considerable amount of energy to revising his symphonies, one of the reasons he never finished his final Ninth Symphony (1887–96). In an effort to secure easier access to performance, some of his pupils even began making simplified versions of his works and publishing them with their teacher's reluctant approval, further adding to a confusion of versions through which performers today still have to chart their course.

Most of Bruckner's symphonies begin with the same musical gesture of a theme gradually emerging against tremolo strings, thus reenacting a kind of creation myth derived from Beethoven's Ninth. The lengthy slow movements of his later symphonies constitute the works' center of gravity and develop an aspect of the Beethoven legacy to which most other nineteenth-century composers did not respond. In form, they derive from the slow movement of Beethoven's Ninth, with its alternation of two sections: ABABA, with the As growing progressively more ornate (or, in Bruckner's case, more heavily laden with counterpoint and further extended through modulations and motivic development) and the Bs having the character of serene interludes, moving at a more measured pace and a slightly faster tempo. In his Eighth and Ninth symphonies Bruckner placed the slow movement after the scherzo, thus following the ordering of Beethoven's last symphony.

Some of Bruckner's symphonies end by using a triumphantly unifying device in a grand coda: The opening theme of the first movement is superimposed on the main theme of the finale. This points to a procedure called "**cyclicism**" that goes back most prominently to Beethoven, Schubert, and Mendelssohn and that became more common over the course of the century. Beethoven's Fifth and Ninth Symphonies (as well as his song cycle *An die ferne Geliebte*, Piano Sonata in A Major, Op. 101, and various other works) had prominently reused themes or passages from earlier movements in later ones, a type of recall that was obvious to any listener. Schubert did similarly in the finale of his Piano Trio in E♭ Major, Op. 100, which recycles the opening theme of the second movement to great effect. Berlioz's deployment of the *idée fixe* in the *Symphonie fantastique* is another influential example of cyclicism. Mendelssohn used cyclicism in his early Octet as well as in his Third Symphony and other works. Robert Schumann's Second Symphony is a particularly notable example; in it an opening brass motto recurs in each of the movements. Brahms's Third Symphony also uses cyclical procedures, although more subtly. Tchaikovsky was much more overt when deploying the fateful themes in his Fourth and Fifth Symphonies. The return of musical material from earlier movements not only helped unify large works but also allowed for a certain kind of dramaturgy within purely orchestral compositions. Few did this more spectacularly than Bruckner when he capped a monumental symphony with a contrapuntal wedding of themes spanning the entire work.

Antonín Dvořák

Reviewing Brahms's Fourth Symphony at its Vienna premiere in 1886, Hanslick marveled that the city had witnessed nineteen symphonic premieres by as many composers over the previous twelve-month period. "It looks as though Brahms's successes have stimulated production, following the long silence which set in after Mendelssohn and Schumann," he concluded. Hanslick exaggerated his friend's personal responsibility for the phenomenon, but he was certainly right to marvel.[31] By the 1880s new symphonists were emerging. Most impressive was the geographical reach of this revival, as the symphony came to flourish in France, Russia, Scandinavia, Bohemia, and the United States. One could even point to some Italian symphonists (since the eighteenth century, truly a contradiction in terms)—for example, Giovanni Sgambati (1841–1914) and Giuseppe Martucci (1856–1909), whom a later

Italian composer gratefully dubbed "the starting point of the renaissance of nonoperatic Italian music."[32]

We will start by looking at some of these developments not far from Vienna, with Antonín Dvořák (1841–1904; Fig. 25-7), the leading Czech composer after Smetana and one who was justly regarded as a Brahms protégé. After studies in Prague Dvořák began to play viola in an orchestra conducted by Smetana, and by the mid-1870s he was serving as organist at a parish church in the city. He enjoyed a particular streak of early recognition, beginning in 1875, when he won an Austrian State Stipendium, intended to help poor young artists. The jury, based in Vienna, consisted of such influential figures as Hanslick and conductors Johann Herbeck and Otto Dessoff. The next year Brahms became a juror, and Dvořák succeeded again, as he would in future years as well.

Figure 25-7 Antonín Dvořák conducting at the 1893 World's Fair in Chicago. Painting by V. E. Nadherny.

Brahms was in fact so impressed that he did more than offer a benediction and award—he contacted his own publisher, Fritz Simrock, in Berlin: "Dvořák has written all manner of things: operas (Czech), symphonies, quartets, piano pieces. In any case, he is a very talented man. Moreover, he is poor! I ask you to think about it! The [Moravian] duets will show you what I mean."[33] Dvořák gratefully responded to the "Highly honored Master" with "deeply felt thanks for everything" and informed him of a commission from Simrock "to write some Slavonic dances. Since, however, I did not know how to begin properly, I have taken the trouble to procure your famous 'Hungarian Dances,' and I shall take the liberty of using these as an exemplary model."[34] Like Brahms's enormously popular dances, Dvořák's dances were originally written for piano duet and later orchestrated. (Indeed, Dvořák orchestrated seven of Brahms's Hungarian Dances in 1880.)

Dvořák's first publications were thus of popular national fare, the exotic route still being the easiest way for a young composer from the non-German provinces to promote himself. It is, however, a fair measure of the double standard that informs a lot of musical historiography to note that his Slavonic Dances as well as two books of Moravian Duets for mixed voices and piano typecast him as a nationalist in a way that Brahms's almost exactly analogous publications—the Hungarian Dances and *Liebeslieder-Walzer*—did not. Moreover, while no one ever thought of Brahms's Hungarian Dances as the expression of the composer's essential personality (because he was not a Hungarian), the opposite assumption was made in the case of Dvořák. This happened despite the fact that, as scholars have demonstrated many times over, he did not use authentic melodies even when he could have, and the "Czech" style he presented to the world at large was unlike the Czech style that Czechs then recognized as Czech. Dvořák nevertheless at times found himself trapped in a sort of national ghetto. The categorization of him as a Czech composer inevitably led to biased expectations and, in some cases, to poor reviews when he failed to conform to German (or French or American) listeners' ideas of properly "Czech" behavior.

Meanwhile, despite his location in Prague (not exactly a small town, but provincial in Viennese eyes), Dvořák was a musician of wide and eclectic background. As a teenager he had played in the Prague Conservatory orchestra when it needed to be augmented for big works like Wagner's *Tannhäuser* and *Lohengrin*, and he began his musical career a fervent Wagnerian. (In 1863 he played when Wagner conducted in Prague.) He already had written two operas of his own by the age of thirty: *Alfred* was a grand historical opera in German, and *The King and the Charcoal Burner* was a comedy in Czech. His output eventually included eight more operas, of which one, *Rusalka* (1900), became an international repertory item.

Alongside this steady production of operas Dvořák produced an equally steady stream of orchestral and chamber works. Here his indebtedness to Brahms as a model is as apparent as is his indebtedness to Wagner in the realm of opera, except that he was more prolific than Brahms. His series of fourteen string quartets, composed between 1862 and 1895, was the most impressive achievement since Beethoven, and he cultivated the other main chamber genres of his time too: five piano trios, two piano quintets, a piano quartet, two string quintets, a string sextet, and more.

Anthology Vol 2-61
Full CD V, 19

His Piano Quintet in A Major, Op. 81, may be viewed within the larger nineteenth-century Germanic chamber music tradition, particularly the increased prominence of pieces for piano and strings such as we mentioned already with regard to Brahms. Dvořák knew Schumann's Piano Quintet in E♭ Major (1842) and Brahms's in F Minor (1862). In his early thirties he had written his own in A Major, Op. 5, which was performed but never published. His considerable fame by the 1880s prompted Simrock to request early works that he might be the first to publish. Dvořák went back and started to revise the quintet but soon decided to write a new one entirely, also in the key of A major. The new A Major Piano Quintet makes use of a Slavic *dumka*, which is a Ukrainian lament, in the second movement, and a *furiant*, a fast dance, in the following scherzo. Despite such Czech moments, the piece largely follows an international style similar to Brahms.

Dvořák also produced a wide range of orchestral music. His Piano Concerto (1876) and Violin Concerto (1879; written for Joachim but never performed by him) are overshadowed by his Cello Concerto, Op. 104 (1894–95), composed near the end of his life, a work many now consider the supreme concerto in the cello repertory. Lisztian in both title and content are his three Slavonic Rhapsodies (1878). He also cultivated concert overtures on the Mendelssohnian model (*My Home* from 1882, *Carnival* from 1891, and *Othello* from 1892) and turned out a set of *Symphonic Variations* (1877), a genre for which Brahms's Haydn Variations provided practically the only model.

Both in his nine symphonies and in his concertos Dvořák occasionally recycled themes from movement to movement to a degree that lent his works a tinge of cyclic "programmaticism." Nor did he have any qualms about composing symphonic poems. In fact, they constituted his last orchestral works, written in 1896–97. Four of them (*The Water Sprite, The Noonday Witch, The Golden Spinning Wheel*, and *The Wood Dove*) were based on the ballads of Karel Jaromír Erben (1811–70), famous as a folklore collector, "the Czech Grimm." Dvořák was inspired not only by Erben's stories but also by the actual rhythms and melodic flow of his words. Some of Dvořák's rhythms and melodies fit precisely the contour of lines from Erben's poems, and so, although the words familiar to Czechs are not heard, they nonetheless left traces.

> ***Dvořák occasionally recycled themes from movement to movement to a degree that lent his works a tinge of cyclic "programmaticism."***

Dvořák's decision to take up program music associated with the New Germans did not at all please his early supporter Hanslick. The critic commented on the composer's new direction, stating that "a little friendly warning perhaps does not come amiss":

> I am afraid that with this detailed programmatic music Dvořák has stepped onto a slippery slope which, in the end, leads to—Richard Strauss. . . . I just cannot accept that I must now put Dvořák . . . on a level with Richard Strauss; he is a true musician who has proved a hundred times that he needs no program and no description to enchant us through the medium of pure, absolute music.[35]

We will meet the German composer Richard Strauss soon enough—suffice it to say for now that he was taking the Lisztian symphonic poem to a maximal extreme in the late nineteenth century. Over the course of his career Dvořák thus pursued genres, forms, and styles associated with both Wagner and Brahms. This was a sign of things to come, as later composers attempted to combine what had previously been considered opposing aesthetics.

Dvořák in the New World

Dvořák spent the years 1892–95 in the United States, invited by the American philanthropist Jeannette M. Thurber to serve as director of the National Conservatory of Music in New York City. The job called for no folksy exotic but, rather, for a world-class master of European music in the broadest sense. Thurber was endowing the institution much in the same spirit that had motivated Anton Rubinstein in Russia thirty years before. The aim was to encourage the spread and cultivation of European art music to new shores, to further the musical colonization of the New World by the Old.

Dvořák's Symphony in E Minor, his ninth and last, was composed during his stay in America. Subtitled *Z nového světa* (From the New World), it received its first performance in Carnegie Hall on 16 December 1893 under the baton of the Hungarian-born Anton Seidl (1850–98), an eminent Wagnerian conductor who was then at the helm of the New York Philharmonic. While immediately successful and an enduring repertoire item ever since, the symphony initially occasioned much debate. Its subtitle could be read in various ways. Did it simply mean a symphony written in the New World—"Impressions and Greetings," as the composer once put it, to those back home?[36] Or did it imply that the thematic content—or perhaps even the "poetic" content—was in some sense inherently American?

Anthology Vol 2-62
Full CD V, 20
Concise CD III, 2

To get some idea of the work, we will consider its second movement, the famous *Largo*. Compared with its counterparts in Brahms's symphonies, it is a curiously sectional, episodic piece and seems to hark back to Schubert, a composer whom Dvořák also revered. The movement begins with a sort of prefatory chromatic woodwind and brass chorale that alternates with the main theme, given out as an English horn solo, always an "exotic" timbre. The next section, in the parallel minor and at a slightly faster tempo, also consists of an alternation of rounded tunes (more obviously contrasting this time) in a format that can be summarized as ABABA. The "B" section has a walking bass that seems to evoke a procession. After a shift back to major, a much faster tune, notated in short note values and presented ostinato fashion, serves as the medium of a crescendo to a surging climax, after which a return is made to the opening music, presented haltingly, with fermatas that interrupt the "singing" in a manner that recalls the muted end of the second-movement funeral march of Beethoven's *Eroica* Symphony.

The "New World" Symphony, like an increasing number of late-nineteenth-century symphonies, is complex in its cyclic structures, with each later movement recalling sections from earlier ones. In the coda to the last movement, motifs from all four movements, motifs that have already been sounding at various points throughout the finale, come together in new and striking configurations. Even without a program, these thematic reminiscences, especially at such a level of concentration and climactic display, together with its general funereal mood of the *Largo*, strongly suggest what the New Germans called "poetic content." But what might its program be?

Figure 25-8 *Hiawatha's Departure*, after a poem by Henry Wadsworth Longfellow. Published by Currier and Ives, c. 1868.

A possible answer to this question can be deduced from a comment Dvořák made to a New York reporter on the day of the symphony's premiere. He pointed out that the second movement was unusual in content and structure: "it is in reality a study or a sketch for a longer work, whether a cantata or an opera which I propose writing, and which will be based upon Longfellow's *Hiawatha*"[37] (Fig. 25-8). He made similar comments in his correspondence with Mrs. Thurber. One of her original wishes in hiring Dvořák to head the National Conservatory was that he write an American national opera in order to provide an example for native-born composers. She even suggested Henry Wadsworth Longfellow's poem *The Song of Hiawatha* (published in 1855) as the basis for the libretto.

It was an almost inevitable choice. Operas on national myths had played an important role in establishing many national schools, and in some countries—Germany with Weber's *Der Freischütz,* Russia with Glinka's *A Life for the Tsar,* and his own country with Smetana's *Libuše*—such operas had served not only as musical cornerstones but also as cornerstones of the nation's sense of nationhood. Longfellow's poem had long been on the verge of serving this purpose, providing the United States with a sort of national epic despite the actual hostility of the government to its Indian population, a policy that in its late-nineteenth-century excesses approached genocide. Nonetheless the Iroquois League, a mutual-defense confederation of five Indian nations, and the figure of its legendary founder, Mohawk or Onondaga chief Haionhwat'ha, could play the role of mythical national hero. The musicalization of that mythology is what Mrs. Thurber had asked of Dvořák. He never completed the opera, but the music he sketched for it can be heard in at least two of the movements of the "New World" Symphony and probably in all four. The middle section of the *Largo,* with all its funereal imagery, most likely corresponds with the death and burial of Hiawatha's bride, Minnehaha ("Laughing Water").

The remaining question, especially relevant in the case of a composer who often gave his music some other national tinge, is whether the themes and motifs conceived originally in connection with a vocal *Hiawatha* or instrumental "New World" Symphony were intended to be heard as "American"; if so, then on what musical basis? Dvořák's gave this deliberate teaser: "the influence of America can be felt by anyone who has a 'nose.'"[38] He is known to have been very much drawn to **African American spirituals** and their professional arrangements called "plantation songs."[39] In an article published in *Harper's New Monthly Magazine* (February 1895), Dvořák called them "the most striking and appealing melodies that have yet been found on this side of the water." One of the students at the National Conservatory was Harry T. Burleigh (1866–1949), an African American singer and choral conductor, who over the course of his career made almost 200 arrangements of spirituals for chorus and who recalled singing dozens of them to Dvořák during the period of the "New World" Symphony's gestation. There are numerous pentatonic melodies in the symphony that seem to resonate stylistically with spirituals, among them the *Largo*'s English horn theme. Another, the second theme from the first movement, can be heard as incorporating a brief quotation from the spiritual "Swing Low, Sweet Chariot."

Dvořák did not hesitate to give fatherly advice to American composers to do as the Czechs had done and submit the indigenous musics of their country, namely, Indian melodies and African American spirituals, "to beautiful treatment in the higher forms of art."[40] There is every reason to suppose that in his *Hiawatha* opera and in the symphony that had spun off from it, he intended to provide them with an object lesson. Whether or not this can be proved, the fact remains that his melodies were taken as "American"—particularly the English horn theme. Although not a spiritual to begin with, this tune was eventually published as one, under the title "Goin' Home," with words by William Arms Fisher. One may wonder what "plantation songs" are doing in a work that sought America's mythic past in Indian lore. The use of them implies that for Dvořák, coming as he did from the outside, Native American and African American folklore were interchangeably American in connotation, which was hardly the view taken by American composers.

An American Response

Dvořák's advice to American composers was not universally embraced. In fact, it was resented by some native-born composers, chiefly white Anglo-Saxons from affluent families, who had received their professional training in the conservatories of Europe and shared Dvořák's basic loyalty to the unmarked, "universal" Germanic style. And indeed Edward MacDowell (1860–1908), a New York–born composer who had studied in Germany and who was living in Boston during Dvořák's time in New York, had already composed an "Indian Suite," Op. 48, based on published field transcriptions, more than a year before the "New World" Symphony.

MacDowell's temporary residence in Boston made him the most eminent representative for a while of the first self-styled and recognized "school" of American composers in the European art-music tradition. Besides being the first American composer since Louis Moreau Gottschalk to establish a strong European reputation (partly through the generous efforts of Liszt), MacDowell was, like Gottschalk, a virtuoso pianist who toured Europe with his own concertos and concert transcriptions. He produced four monumental sonatas in the Lisztian mold: "Tragica," Op. 45 (1892), "Eroica," Op. 50 (1895), "Norse," Op. 57 (1899), and "Keltic," Op. 59 (1900). Although his Piano Concerto No. 2 in D Minor, Op. 23, remains a Lisztian repertoire item, he is best known for his many character pieces for piano, issued in sets with evocative titles like *Sea Pieces, Fireside Tales, New England Idyls,* and *Woodland Sketches,* which contains the famous "To a Wild Rose."

MacDowell had actually been Mrs. Thurber's choice to lead the National Conservatory of Music, a job that she felt by rights should go to a native-born composer, but he shunned the required administrative duties; at the time there was no other American who matched his prestige. Yet shortly after Dvořák's departure from New York in 1896, MacDowell took his place as a leading cultural figure in that city when he accepted appointment as head of the newly founded Music Department at Columbia University. Just as he had feared, the heavy pressures of his job took a severe toll on his creative energies and his mental health.

Perhaps he should have stayed in Boston, whose great museums and nearby universities made it a cultivated center that defined itself in opposition to New York, the commercial capital of the nation and the center with the most prominent performing institutions. Boston, however, took the lead for quite some time when it

Figure 25-9 Amy Marcy Cheney Beach.

came to the production and cultivation of composers, most of whom had studied in Europe. John Knowles Paine (1839–1906) was the first professor of music at Harvard, which made him the first professor of music at any American university. His training came from three years (1858–61) at the Berlin Conservatory; he spent the rest of his life imparting the German tradition at Harvard. Other major figures in a "Boston School" (sometimes called the Second New England School) also studied in Europe, including George Whitefield Chadwick (1854–1931), who taught at Boston's New England Conservatory of Music, and Horatio Parker (1863–1919), who taught at Yale. The School's subsequent generations consisted of pupils of Paine, Chadwick, and Parker, among them Arthur William Foote (1853–1937), Frederick Shepherd Converse (1871–1940), Edward Burlingame Hill (1872–1960), Daniel Gregory Mason (1873–1953), Charles Ives (1874–1954), and John Alden Carpenter (1876–1951). Like their teachers, they were all New Englanders by birth or education, were uniformly of Anglo-Saxon stock, and (with the exception of Ives and Carpenter, who went into business) earned their living as academics or organists.

The group had another important member, however, who studied neither in Europe nor with any of the founders but whose achievements realized the Boston School's aspirations in a particularly distinguished way: Amy Marcy Beach (née Cheney, 1867–1944; Fig. 25-9), perhaps the era's most successful woman composer of large-scale pieces. In line with a pattern we have seen earlier, her gender kept her from the pursuit of a professional career, despite evidence of highly advanced talent. Her wealthy parents thought it unsuitable for a well-bred girl to study at a European conservatory and instead engaged private teachers for her, mainly in piano playing, a proper social grace that she took to virtuoso extremes. Her training in composition was confined to some informal study of scores with the Austrian conductor Wilhelm Gericke, then head of the Boston Symphony Orchestra, and a single year of harmony and counterpoint with a local instructor. She taught herself fugue and orchestration by working through the Paris Conservatoire textbooks in those subjects and by attending the rehearsals of the Boston Symphony.

As a pianist, meanwhile, she flourished, making her first appearance with orchestra at the age of sixteen and a formal, highly successful, Boston Symphony debut in 1885 with Chopin's F Minor Piano Concerto. Later that year she married Henry Harris Aubrey Beach, a socially prominent Boston surgeon. Marriage precluded any more concertizing, and it appeared that her compositional talent would go the way of Clara Wieck's and Fanny Mendelssohn's—that is, wither on the vine. But the childless union between the eighteen-year-old musical prodigy and the forty-two-year-old society doctor turned out to be fortunate for her work. Her husband's wealth gave her unlimited leisure, indeed forced it on her, and he encouraged her composing. She was free to write in the larger forms, and she had a ready and admiring public in Boston society. Indulged at first as a local favorite, "Mrs. H. H. A. Beach" (as, in accordance with domestic custom, she signed her work) eventually acquired a national reputation, with a special champion in Anton Seidl, the celebrated conductor who had premiered Dvořák's "New World" Symphony. Many of her works were published and her reputation spread to Europe, where she returned to concertize for three years, once again under the name Amy Beach, after her husband's death in 1910.

Beach embarked on her first and only symphony in 1894, almost immediately after hearing the Boston premiere of Dvořák's "New World," also in E Minor, on which it was obviously modeled. While her piece does not employ cyclic returns to anything like the extent that Bruckner's and Dvořák's do, its complex and broadly constructed outer movements were developed out of a single fund of motifs, in this case drawn from one of her many art songs, *Dark Is the Night*, Op. 11, No.1 (published in 1890). The middle movements (and the closing theme in the first) were based on the melodies of what she called "Irish-Gaelic" folk songs, for which reason the piece bears the title "Gaelic."

Beach's symphony, which the Boston Symphony premiered with great success in October 1896, was an ambitious work in its proportions and craftsmanship. It was impressive enough to earn an accolade from Chadwick, who wrote the composer that her work was "full of fine things, melodically, harmonically, and orchestrally, and mighty well built besides," and that from now on she was, as far as he was concerned, "one of the boys."[41] Beach's "Gaelic" Symphony sought to engage directly in the aesthetic debates of the day as they intersected with social ones. Her use of Irish folklore was a response to Dvořák, comparable to Brahms's response to Beethoven in his First Symphony. It was both a declaration of affiliation and a corrective. Like Dvořák, she sought a melodic content that advertised a specific national origin. But that national origin was "American" in a sense that only Boston, perhaps, would have fully understood or endorsed. "We of the north," Beach wrote in a letter to the *Boston Herald* in which she took explicit issue with Dvořák's prescriptions, "should be far more likely to be influenced by old English, Scotch or Irish songs, inherited with our literature from our ancestors."[42]

Like the composers of Europe, then, Beach defined the national not merely in terms of soil (as Dvořák had urged Americans to do) but in terms of blood as well. She identified herself musically with the country from which she descended ethnically, assuming that that "Celtic" blood descent identified her as an American aristocrat. Behind the notion of the "Boston American" lay that of the "Mayflower American" or, in Beach's case, the notion of nationality upheld by the Daughters of the American Revolution, to recall by name a politically conservative and often a socially intolerant organization of which she was a leader.

War Brings Symphonies to France

For composers of the Boston School, another influential symphonic model besides Dvořák's "New World" was the Symphony in D Minor by César Franck (1822–90; Fig. 25-10), which preached less a national than a spiritual sensibility. Despite his Germanic surname, Franck was a French-speaking Belgian composer who plied his trade in Paris and whose career mirrored Bruckner's in various ways. He hailed from the cultural provinces, born in Liège, a medium-sized Belgian town, and received his early education there before coming to Paris with his family. For the greater part of his career he earned his living as a church organist and wrote substantial music for the instrument. His most important compositions and teaching came during the last two decades of his life. In 1872 he secured a post at the Paris Conservatoire, not in composition but, rather, in organ playing. His class nonetheless quickly became an unofficial composition seminar that attracted a circle of composers who admired him despite (or perhaps in part because of) his maverick status.

Figure 25-10 César Franck at the organ. Portrait by Jeanne Rongier (1885).

Franck's importance as a teacher sets him apart from most previous composers. Mozart, Beethoven, Schubert, and many others reluctantly gave piano lessons to earn money. Wagner, Verdi, and Brahms avoided teaching entirely, even though they exerted great influence on younger composers. Liszt (who Franck knew and much admired) may come closest to him in having disciples, some very distinguished, which was less true of such teacher/composers as Bruckner, Tchaikovsky, Dvořák, and Paine.

The most noteworthy aspect of Franck's status as beloved teacher and role model remains the simple fact that he made his mark primarily as a composer of instrumental music. This was virtually unprecedented in a French composer, for Berlioz made his name with orchestral as well as dramatic music. Opera, and to a lesser degree ballet, had long dominated the French national scene. Franck's wide circle of pupils and disciples, who remained prominent and active well into the new century, promoted him as the spiritual guide of a resurgent French spirit in music, which they summed up in the slogan *Ars gallica*. All the Latin phrase means is "French art," but when applied to a certain school of composers, it meant a French art that arose in nationalistic response to losing the Franco-Prussian War of 1870–71.

On 25 February 1871, shortly after French defeat by the Germans, a group of youngish French musicians headed by Camille Saint-Saëns founded an organization they called the **Société Nationale de Musique** (National Musical Society), with *Ars gallica* as its motto. This concert-sponsoring association sought to promote exclusively the work of living French composers and to assert through music the unique spirit of France in a manner that would elevate and educate public taste. The preamble to the group's bylaws stated that "The proposed purpose of the Society is to aid the production and popularization of all serious works, whether published or not, by French composers."[43] Despite these avowedly nationalistic aims, the Société Nationale, through its declared emphasis on "serious" music of "lofty artistic aspiration" and its practical emphasis on substantive instrumental forms, became in effect the vehicle for the unprecedented Germanization of French music. In retrospect it is clear that a sense of national shame brought about by military defeat also helped motivate the Society's dual objective of repudiation and emulation: first, to restore a high purpose to art; and second, to surpass the achievements of German instrumental music.

From its founding Franck served on the board of directors of the Society, and his works provided an inspiring model, among them the Piano Quintet in F Minor (1879), a neo-Bachian *Prelude, Aria, and Finale* for piano (1887), and an even more neo-Bachian *Prelude, Chorale, and Fugue* (1884). In his last years he composed a set of *Symphonic Variations* for piano and orchestra (1885), a Violin Sonata (1886), and a String Quartet (1889). His four symphonic poems (including one, *Psyché*, with chorus) and vocal works (operas and oratorios) were less successful than the essays in absolute music. He composed his lone symphony, one of his final pieces, in 1886–88, when he was already in his middle sixties. It features his characteristic cyclicism, frequent modulation, Wagnerian chromaticism, and a marked spiritual dimension. The symphony announces its allegiance to Germanic rather than French tradition not only in its general aesthetic and stylistic orientation but also in specific details. To write a symphony in D minor was in itself such an announcement; it is yet another piece haunted by Beethoven's Ninth. The premiere of the symphony, in February 1889 by the Paris Conservatoire orchestra, had an equivocal success, greatly exceeded by its first American performance by the Boston Symphony less than two months later.

Franck's invocation of Beethoven's spiritual domain went beyond the Ninth to encompass the most emblematic and aura-surrounded works of all, the late quartets.

The symphony's thematic kernel was none other than the opening "Must it be?" motif from the last movement of the F Major String Quartet, Op. 135. Taken ultraseriously, as everything in late Beethoven was eventually taken, the phrase had haunted the whole nineteenth century. Among its offspring we have already seen are the generative phrase in Liszt's *Les Préludes* and the "Fate" leitmotif that haunts Wagner's *Ring*. In Franck's symphony the motif not only furnishes the first movement with its thematic springboard, but it is also incorporated into the main themes of the succeeding movements and returns in the coda to the finale. Franck's pupil and biographer Vincent d'Indy (1851–1931) officially dubbed this process of multimovement motivic unification "cyclic form."[44] No one ever claimed that Franck was its inventor—we have already seen many precedents—but the insistence on its spiritual necessity was distinctive of the Franck school. A decade after his mentor's death, in 1890, d'Indy continued Franck's legacy by founding the Schola Cantorum, which provided an alternative to the Paris Conservatoire.

Besides the high-minded symphonies of Franck and his pupils—they include five by d'Indy and one by the short-lived Ernest Chausson (1855–99)—there are five by Saint-Saëns, the first four (two unnumbered) dating from the 1850s, very early in his career. Most famous is his last one, the flamboyantly virtuosic Symphony No. 3 in C Minor (1886), which is popularly known as the "Organ" Symphony. Despite his role as the original architect of the Société Nationale, placing Saint-Saëns within the various opposing musical camps of his time is not always easy, in part because what he declared verbally often seems at odds with what his compositions demonstrated musically. Distinguishing between his conservative and progressive tendencies is further complicated by an unusually long career and propensity to write pieces that combine religiosity, advanced harmonic language, flashy virtuoso technique, and salon charm. If not quite a man of mystery, Saint-Saëns was certainly a man of contradictions and shifting affiliations.

In the "Organ" Symphony he followed Liszt's model of transforming themes and in fact dedicated the symphony to him, partly in gratitude for earlier help promoting his career. Not only were thematic transformations and cyclic elements of the work Lisztian, but so was the idea of incorporating the organ into an orchestral piece, something Liszt had done in his symphonic poem *Hunnenschlacht*. After a short *adagio* introduction (music that breathes the same air as Wagner's *Tristan*) comes the principal theme that unifies all four sections of the work and that is recast and transformed in ingenious ways. The initial presentation of the theme by the violins recalls the opening of Schubert's "Unfinished" Symphony, but the contour of the melody itself is the old Gregorian chant *Dies irae*, that musical emblem of death often invoked by composers, including Berlioz and Liszt. The organ first appears in the connected slow movement that follows. The second half of the two-part symphony begins with a C minor scherzo that in the middle contains a fast and brilliant C major trio featuring sparkling keyboard writing. The organ makes its boldest appearance at the start of the finale, which leads to a chorale and then an energetic fugue, before a majestic coda in C major.

German critics liked to point to the eclecticism in Saint-Saëns's symphony as evidence that, despite everything, the French were *au fond* (at bottom) irredeemable (or, as the familiar joke would have it, that deep down they were superficial). The reputed culinary specialty of the French, chefs to the world, stood for mindless—or, worse, soulless—sensual gratification. In the twentieth century, especially after the French had their chance to avenge themselves on the Germans in battle, this ordering of aesthetic priorities was for a while decisively reversed, as we shall soon see.

Summary

During the 1850s and '60s, successful new symphonies were few and far between. While these decades saw the rise of the concert hall as an institution, the majority of works performed were those of the "Viennese Classics"—Haydn, Mozart, and Beethoven. The later decades of the nineteenth century, however, saw a reinvigoration of the form, led by Johannes Brahms (1833–97). Although Beethoven's symphonies were the dominating influence in this reinvigoration, each composer took different things from Beethoven's example.

Brahms is widely considered the counterweight to the aesthetic views espoused by the New German School (see Chapter 22). He was deeply steeped in music of the past, especially German music. As his four symphonies, two piano concertos, and many important chamber works show, he excelled in genres that were neglected by the representatives of the New German School. In many works, he looked to pre-Classical models such as Bach and Handel. His early reputation as a composer was forged on his choral music, of which his masterpiece is *A German Requiem.*

Because the symphony had assumed such an important role in the "museum culture" of the concert hall, Brahms felt that his First Symphony had to be a masterpiece. After a very long gestation period, he completed it in 1876. As in many Beethoven symphonies, the fourth movement is the weighty goal of the first three movements. Its main theme is a clear allusion to the "Ode to Joy" theme of Beethoven's Ninth Symphony. Many of Brahms's works are generated from a process often called "developing variation": Small motivic fragments are constantly varied, developed, and "worked out," not only in the development sections but throughout, as in the Piano Quartet in G Minor, Op. 25.

Anton Bruckner (1824–96) was primarily a composer of symphonies (nine numbered ones) and Masses. Although he composed no operas, his symphonies were influenced by Wagner in their harmonic language, dense textures, large orchestra, and great length. He combined instruments, however, in a way quite different from Wagner, influenced by his work as a church organist. In France, César Franck (1822–90) composed instrumental music along lines established by German composers. He was a founding member of the Société National de Musique, a group established to promote works by French composers. With its emphasis on larger instrumental forms, however, the Société National actually became a vehicle for the composition of a French music modeled on that of German composers. Franck's Symphony in D Minor was an especially influential work for American composers after its successful performance in Boston in 1889.

Another important contributor to the symphony was the Czech composer Antonín Dvořák (1841–1904). Influenced both by Brahms and the New German School, he excelled in the symphony (he wrote nine in all), chamber music, opera, and the symphonic poem; he also composed popular national pieces, such as his Slavonic Dances. Dvořák sometimes alludes in his music to folk songs and dances; his Piano Quintet in A Major, Op. 81, though very much in the Germanic chamber music tradition, includes some Slavic elements. During a visit to the United States

(1892–95), he composed his Symphony in E Minor ("From the New World"), which is often heard as evoking African American music and which was probably based in part on his sketches for an opera on Henry Wadsworth Longfellow's poem *The Song of Hiawatha*.

Dvořák urged American composers to create their own nationalist music by turning to Native American and African American sources. Instead, many Americans turned to their own ethnic heritages. One such composer was Amy Beach (1876–1944). Beach's "Gaelic" Symphony is modeled on Dvořák's "New World," but uses Irish folks songs as the basis for some of its melodic material.

Study Questions

1. Describe the trend toward new concert halls and orchestras in the nineteenth century. What repertory was performed in these concert halls? In what sense was the concert hall a "museum culture"?
2. What is meant by developing variation, and how is it reflected in Johannes Brahms's Piano Quartet in G Minor, Op 25?
3. In what ways is Brahms's First Symphony modeled on Beethoven's symphonies, particularly the Ninth?
4. Describe the various influences on Anton Bruckner's symphonies, including those of Beethoven, Wagner, and his experience as a church organist.
5. How do you interpret Antonín Dvořák's subtitle "From the New World"? Do you consider his "New World" Symphony an "American" work? Why or why not?
6. How did American composers go about creating a distinctive American music? What approach to American music is reflected in Amy Beach's "Gaelic" Symphony?
7. Describe César Franck's role as a composer of instrumental music in France.
8. Drawing together the material in this chapter with that of Chapters 22 and 23, compare the ways in which the following composers responded to Beethoven, either in their music or in their rhetoric: Wagner, Liszt, Brahms, and Bruckner.

Key Terms

African American spiritual
cyclicism
developing variation
Société National de Musique

26

Dramatic Alternatives: Exoticism, Operetta, and *Verismo*

During the second half of the nineteenth century various operatic alternatives arose to French extravaganzas, to music drama in its Wagnerian and Verdian incarnations, and to the emerging nationalist fare. One popular approach was not entirely new or entirely unknown to French grand opera, music dramas, or the nationalists: pursuit of the exotic, looking for subject matters in distant times and places. A dominant trend, however, was to cut things down in size, sometimes through parody or by trying to create a more human scale on the stage. The real, in both comic and tragic operas, came to overshadow the fantastic.

The representation of a distant community as exotic constituted a sort of inverse nationalism. The purpose of this kind of exoticism is the bolstering of one's own sense of community by contrast. It is thus hardly an act of world fellowship in the spirit of Johann Gottfried von Herder but, rather, often an act of patronizing distinction and ultimately of exclusion. The oldest and most widespread exoticism in the European musical tradition is that of "**Orientalism**," the musical representation of non-European (generally Asian) peoples.[1] We have glimpsed it as far back as Mozart's Singspiel *Die Entführung aus dem Serail* (The Abduction from the Seraglio) of 1782, but by that time it already had a long history. "Turkish" operas—operas making fun of Turks or other Muslims—were a Viennese specialty. Earlier, in France, Lully's incidental music to Molière's play *Le bourgeois gentilhomme* (1670) had lampooned the Turks, Europe's most formidable antagonists since the time of the Crusades; isolated examples go back even further.

Stereotyping the Other: "Orientalism"

One reason the European musical representation of the Orient enjoyed an enormously renewed vogue during the nineteenth century involves the historical and economic turnabout whereby the Europeans, rather than the Asians, had become expansionist aggressors. Manifestations of musical as well as artistic, literary, and scholarly Orientalism were a direct outgrowth of the movements of colonial and imperialist armies, beginning with Napoleon's Egyptian campaigns of 1798–99. The subsequent publication of the twenty-four-volume *Description of Egypt* by Edme François Jomard, a geographer and antiquarian who traveled with Napoleon's army between 1809 and 1813, aroused great interest, as did the lavishly illustrated album *Journey in Lower and Upper Egypt* by Baron Dominique Denon, another member of Napoleon's entourage. These works touched off a French craze for all things "Near Eastern." The distinguished writer and diplomat François-René Chateaubriand published a best-selling travel book, the semi-imaginary *Itinerary from Paris to Jerusalem*, in 1811; Victor Hugo's wholly imaginary *The Orientals*, a book of exotic poems, appeared in 1829. France, therefore, is the first place to look for signs of the new Romantic wave in musical Orientalism.

The wave reached an early crest in compositions by Félicien David (1810–76), who made a pilgrimage to Egypt in the mid-1830s by way of the Turkish cities of Constantinople (Istanbul) and Smyrna (Izmir) and summed up his impressions in a monumental "Ode-Symphony" called *Le Désert* (The Desert; Fig. 26-1). This symphony with voices, in the manner of Beethoven's Ninth, had a deliriously successful premiere in December 1844 and remained a concert staple for several decades thereafter, although, like its author, it is virtually forgotten today.

The main thrust of musical Orientalism quickly turned toward opera and attracted the most prominent French composers in the second half of the century. By David himself there was *Lalla-Roukh* (1862), based on a story about the love life of an Indian princess. By Meyerbeer there was his last opera *L'Africaine* (1865), which—the title notwithstanding—also concerns the love of an Indian princess, in this case for Vasco da Gama, the Portuguese explorer. By Léo Delibes (1836–91) there was *Lakmé* (1883), yet another tale about the love of an Indian princess (and priest's daughter), this time for an English officer. By Jules Massenet (1842–1912) there was *Le roi de Lahore* (The King of Lahore, 1877), in which the title character dies, spends an act in Hindu heaven, and returns to life in the guise of a beggar to claim a virgin priestess for his bride. By Georges Bizet (1838–75) there were *Les pêcheurs de perles* (The Pearl Fishers, 1863), a love triangle—yes, there is a virgin priestess—set in Ceylon (Sri Lanka), and *Djamileh* (1872), about a slave girl who wins the heart of an Egyptian ruler. By Ambroise Thomas (1811–96) there was *Le Caïd* (The Khayyid, 1849), about the amorous misadventures of a North African chieftain. Finally, of all these operas, the one that retains the securest place in repertory today is Camille Saint-Saëns's *Samson et Dalila* (1877), based on the famous biblical story.

Figure 26-1 Title page of first edition of Félicien David's *Le Désert* (Paris, 1845).

Whether comic or tragic, all of these operas are love stories given an unusually frank and sensual treatment that would have been considered morally offensive at the time if they had been set in the

TIMELINE

1851 Henri Murger, *Scènes de la vie de bohème*

1858 Jacques Offenbach, *Orpheus in the Underworld*

1859 Charles Gounod, *Faust*

1868 Johann Strauss Jr., *On the Beautiful Blue Danube*

1874 Johann Strauss Jr., *Die Fledermaus*

1875 Georges Bizet, *Carmen*

1877 Camille Saint-Saëns, *Samson et Dalila*

"Occident"—the West. The idea of the Orient as a sexual playground gave license for the enjoyment of carnal fantasies, their immorality diminished by the non-Christian setting. The portrayal of women as exotic sex symbols or sex toys was only one of the stereotypes for which the Orientalist manner made allowance; others included acts of despotic violence, depraved luxury, picturesque or orgiastic rites and sacrifices, and so on. An otherwise-inadmissible voyeurism could be indulged by censoriously presenting exotic primitives far away in space and time. Audiences loved it.

Along with these strange stories arose what came to be recognized as Oriental musical devices that helped conjure up qualities associated with the alien plots and characters. A certain kind of music could signify sexiness, another violence, a third barbarous ritual. For this technique to work, accuracy had to be sacrificed to stereotype, with the music often lacking any authentic counterpart in reality. But that is precisely the point: The very expression "the Orient" is already an example of such stereotyping, since the East is "the East" only to "the West." The act of naming is what brings the thing into being. And that thing is a thing of metaphor, of imaginary geography and historical fiction. It creates a reduced, totalized, and omnisciently known "other" against which a no less reduced and totalized sense of oneself can be constructed. The phenomenon is well worth our attention: What can seem quaint and harmless in the arts has often proved despicable and deadly in history.

Anthology Vol 2-63
Full CD V, 21

A famous example of operatic Orientalism is the Act III ballet sequence from *Samson et Dalila*, the Bacchanale, a feast in honor of the god of wine. The Philistines, an ancient people who have left no actual musical traces, are seen carousing before the idol of their god, Dagon, right before the hero, Samson, brings the temple down to end the opera. Saint-Saëns created a fancifully exotic mode containing not one (as do some Arabian modes) but two augmented seconds (B–A♭, F♯–E♭), intervals that in various contexts had a tradition of evoking Arabs or Jews or gypsies or symbolizing their supposed attributes (here, orgiastic excess). At the same time a drumbeat accompaniment below divides the eighth notes in every pair of $\frac{2}{4}$ measures into groups following the asymmetrical pattern 3 + 3 + 2, a rhythmic cycle found in many kinds of non-European music, including Arabian as well as black Caribbean ("Afro-Cuban") and Latin American (Ex. 26-1). The net result is an imaginary, all-purpose Orientalist music that nevertheless communicates a specific image to properly attuned European listeners. It all works by the successful use of stereotypes, catering to contemporary prejudice, as memorably encapsulated in Chateaubriand's *Itinerary* when he wrote of the Turks that they spend their time "ravaging the world or else sleeping on carpets, amidst women and perfumes."[2]

Example 26-1 Camille Saint-Saëns, Bacchanale from *Samson et Dalila*, Act III

Bizet's *Carmen*

1880 Giovanni Verga, *Cavalleria Rusticana*

1887 **W. S. Gilbert and Arthur Sullivan, *Ruddigore***

1889 World's Fair in Paris showcases the Eiffel Tower

1892 **Ruggero Leoncavallo, *Pagliacci***

1892 Ellis Island opens in New York City

1896 **Giacomo Puccini, *La bohème***

1898 Spanish-American War

1898 John Luther Long, "Madame Butterfly"

1900 **Puccini, *Tosca***

1903 Wilbur and Orville Wright take first powered flight

1904–06 **Puccini, *Madama Butterfly***

Orientalist stereotypes came to pervade the representation of both masculine barbarity and feminine sensuality in the latter half of the nineteenth century. An Orientalist musical style could now connote barbarity or sensuality in any context, even when the music was far removed from the operatic stage. The view of Oriental difference as something sinister and its transference to ethnic characters of all kinds, especially sexy women, was a significant artistic symptom of late-nineteenth-century cultural politics. The most familiar bearer of Orientalist musical features in the standard operatic repertoire, the title character of Bizet's *Carmen* (1875; Fig. 26-2) is not even an Oriental by the usual definition. As a Spanish gypsy, however, she is a member of an ethnic minority (one with origins that can be traced to South Asia, however). Bizet composed *Carmen,* originally with spoken dialogue, based on a luridly naturalistic novella of seduction and murder by Prosper Mérimée (1803–70). It was premiered at the Théâtre National de l'Opéra Comique, a "family theater" whose codirector resigned rather than present an opera that culminated in a brutal crime of passion in which the tenor stabs the soprano in full view of the audience. Some comedy! There were also objections to the music because the popular genres on which it was based were not those of good French homes but, rather, of vagabonds, gypsies, and others thought socially undesirable.

Carmen's exotic heritage made her an outsider to French society and a threat to its values. Bizet highlighted this by casting each of her solo numbers in an explicitly designated Spanish or Latin American dance form, including a habanera and seguidilla. The interpretation of ethnic difference as alluring peril is also embodied in the plot, in which a good soldier, Don José, is brought to ruin by Carmen's irresistible charms. The story of the clash of cultures became an archetype in later nineteenth- and early-twentieth-century opera. One scholar has wryly summarized the situation as one in which a "young, tolerant, brave, possibly naive, white-European tenor-hero," in pursuit of love or sex, comes into contact with a "mysterious dark-skinned, colonised territory" and is punished for it, usually along with the sex object that lured him into disaster.[3]

Anthology Vol 2-64
Full CD V, 22
Concise CD III, 3

What some found offensive, others found powerfully alluring. Carmen's famous "Habanera" (literally, "Havana song") was a Cuban import. Bizet used a song called "El arreglito" by Sebastián Yradier (1809–65), a Spanish composer who claimed to have collected it on location, leading Bizet to believe it was a folk song. Its descending chromatic scale was a badge worn by Oriental femmes fatales all over Europe. One could hardly spell things out more plainly than Carmen does in her refrain: "If I say I love you, watch out!" As the "Habanera" evokes Carmen's forthright sex appeal musically, so the opera as a whole gawks at what from the audience's perspective were essentially alien and forbidden beings: gypsy girls who worked in a cigarette factory, an only slightly camouflaged "house of ill repute" (Ex. 26-2).

In the end, of course, traditional morality wins out. The opera, for all its brutality and sexuality, has become a family favorite after all. The seductress is killed by her prey, exacting society's revenge. The music powerfully endorses Don José's act, even as it had formerly intensified Carmen's dangerous appeal. Nowadays it is as easy to question the justice of the plot's horrific resolution as it is difficult to resist the music's seductions. As in Verdi's *La traviata,* a woman whose allure has led a man astray pays with her life. The difference lies in the unflinching portrayal of allure and vengeance alike. Unlike Violetta, Carmen has no "heart of gold," and she meets a violent death.

Figure 26-2 Céléstine Galli-Marie (1837–1905) in the title role at the Paris premiere of Georges Bizet's *Carmen* at the Opéra Comique, 3 March 1875. Chalk lithograph by Antonin-Marie Chatinière.

Example 26-2 Georges Bizet, "Habanera" from *Carmen*, Act I, mm. 1–10

Love is a wild bird whom nothing can restrain.
And it is quite in vain to call it . . .

Russian Orientalism

Orientalist fashion was hardly limited to France. We have already mentioned Verdi's *Aida*; Oriental themes and exotic evocations appear in other of his operas as well. His Italian contemporaries and successors also embraced it, most notably Giacomo Puccini, whom we will consider later in this chapter. The phenomenon was less common in German opera, dominated as it was at the time by Wagner; Peter Cornelius's opera *Der Barbier von Bagdad* (The Barber of Baghdad, 1858) is principally a curiosity, as is Karl Goldmark's *Die Königin von Saba* (The Queen of Sheba, 1875). It would emerge more forcefully after the turn of the century with Richard Strauss's *Salome* (1905).

Orientalism found particular favor in Russia. Composers there were, if anything, even more obsessed with the development of Orientalist styles than in

France, in part because of Russia's engagement throughout the nineteenth century in imperialistic expansion into neighboring Islamic territories. Through this process the Russian empire came to occupy an enormous landmass. Its various peoples intermingled and intermarried to a much greater degree than in the Western European empires. Exotic Orientalism became a distinguishing feature of much Russian music, a way of asserting a particular identity as musical creators independent of Europe at a time when Russia was just joining the European fine-art tradition. In a famous essay written in 1882 the critic Vladimir Stasov looked back at "Twenty-Five Years of Russian Art"; he listed "the Oriental element" as one of the four major characteristics that justified its assertion of equal rights. (The others were its skepticism of European tradition, which made it independent; its striving for a unique national character, which made it authentic; and its "extreme inclination toward program music," which made it progressive.)[4]

Exotic Orientalism became a distinguishing feature of much Russian music, a way of asserting a particular identity as musical creators.

Orientalist interest on the part of Russian composers goes back to Glinka's second opera, *Ruslan and Lyudmila* (1842), drawn from a mock epic by Pushkin that is set partly in fictitious eastern lands. All the members of the "Mighty Five" made conspicuous contributions to the Orientalist wave: Miliy Balakirev in an orchestral work called *Tamara* (1882), based on a poem by Mikhail Lermontov; César Cui in an opera, *A Prisoner in the Caucasus* (1857; revised 1882), based on a poem by Pushkin; Alexander Borodin in his opera *Prince Igor* (posthumously produced in 1890) and in a "musical picture" for orchestra called *In Central Asia* (1880); Modest Musorgsky in an unfinished opera based on Gustave Flaubert's novel *Salammbô*; and Nikolai Rimsky-Korsakov in many works, including two symphonic suites: *Antar* (1868) and the very popular *Scheherazade* (1888), based on the *Arabian Nights.* The conservatory camp in Russia for the most part shunned Orientalism. Anton Rubinstein, who wrote nearly twenty operas, shied away from exotic themes, and Tchaikovsky was likewise not inclined to emphasize his otherness from Western European culture. Apart from a single character in a single opera (*Iolanta,* his last) and two brief "Arabian" and "Chinese" dances in a single ballet (*The Nutcracker,* his last and most popular), he did not engage in musical portrayals of "the East."

It was Borodin who brought Russian Orientalist engagement to its peak of development, in *Prince Igor,* which was far from finished at the time of his death in 1887, although he had been working on it for eighteen years. (As mentioned in Chapter 24, he used some musical material from the opera in his Second Symphony.) Based on *The Song of Igor's Campaign,* a twelfth-century epic and Russia's first literary masterpiece, Borodin's opera was truly a monument to Russian Orientalism, composed at a time when its plot—a tale of ill-fated hostilities between a Russian prince and Turkic nomads called Polovtsy—was being played out in real life in the Russian empire's wars of aggression in Central Asia. The most famous music in the opera are the "Polovtsian Dances" in the second act, which display a whole cluster of Orientalist signs: melodic undulations tied over the beat, a chromatic pass from the sixth scale degree to the fifth, a throbbing drumbeat in the bass, plus, in its orchestral garb, the sound of the English horn, the closest orchestral counterpart to the "snake-charmer's" pipe and another clear Orientalist marker (Ex. 26-3).

Anthology Vol 2-65
Full CD V, 23

Example 26-3 Alexander Borodin, Polovtsian Dance from *Prince Igor*

Gounod's *Opéra Lyrique*

Alongside the interest in exoticism, there were other operatic trends beginning in mid-century in which France also played a leading role. A new genre—sometimes called ***opéra lyrique*** (or *drame lyrique*), after its principal venue, the Paris Théâtre Lyrique (opened 1851)—emerged in more or less conscious opposition to the bloated *grand opéra*. The Théâtre Lyrique's principal showpieces were two operas by the prolific Charles Gounod (1818–93): *Faust* (1859; Fig. 26-3), after Goethe's play, and *Roméo et Juliette* (1867), after Shakespeare's play. As exemplified by Gounod, the genre could be described as a hybrid that retained the accompanied recitatives of grand opera (although more tuneful ones) but that cut the musical forms and the characters down to comic-opera size. The musical emphasis is on characterization through attractive melodies reminiscent of domestic songs and ballroom dances rather than on impressive structures.

Figure 26-3 Poster for a production of Charles Gounod's *Faust* at the Théâtre Lyrique in Paris (ca. 1875).

Gounod made little attempt to embody Goethe's metaphysical content in his Faust opera; he accented not an intellectual message but, rather, the emotional lives of the leading man and leading lady. In *Faust*, the very unsatanic Méphistophélès is for the most part reduced to a merry puppet master who sings in an appropriately swaggering *opera buffa* style: His strophic "Le veau d'or" ("Calf of gold") aria in jig time, one of the opera's most popular numbers, is a drinking song in everything but name. The comic transformation, or lowering of the role, is entirely calculated, a well-aimed slap at German pretension. Gounod's opera became one of the most performed works of the century, and not just in France, where the opera surpassed even Meyerbeer's *Les Huguenots* in number of performances. On 22 October 1883, the opera (sung in Italian) inaugurated the first season of New York's Metropolitan Opera, where it played so often that some snidely referred to the building as the *Faustspielhaus,* punning on Wagner's *Festspielhaus* in Bayreuth. Its extraordinary popularity in New York is captured in the opening chapter of Edith Wharton's novel *The Age of Innocence* (1920).

Gounod was nonetheless denounced by some, including Wagner, for popularizing (which to critics meant trivializing) great literature. Similar charges were lodged against his slightly older contemporary Ambroise Thomas, whose most successful operas were *Mignon* (1866), after Goethe's novel *Wilhelm Meisters Lehrjahre* (Wilhelm Meister's Apprenticeship), and *Hamlet* (1868), written in collaboration with the same team of librettists as Gounod's *Faust* (Michel Carré and Jules Barbier). Thomas's *Hamlet* ends not with the title character's death, as in Shakespeare, but with his victory and coronation. Gounod's and Thomas's heir in the next generation was Jules Massenet, who combined the techniques of *opéra lyrique* with more contemporary and realistic subject matter. He, too, paid his respects to Goethe (*Werther,* 1892), but his most enduring contribution is *Manon* (1884), after an eighteenth-century novel by a French writer known as Abbé Prévost, about rapturous but ultimately disastrous illicit love. Under cover of a period setting, the opera treats its subject with a frankness that surpassed that of Verdi's *La traviata,* similar to the naturalism of what was called *verismo,* an artistic movement that soon radiated from Italy throughout the world of opera and that we will examine later in this chapter.

Jacques Offenbach and Opera About Opera

Under Wagner's influence, as German opera became ever more apocalyptic, on the way to *Götterdämmerung,* and as grand opera became ever grander, on the way to Verdi's *Don Carlos* and *Aida,* a contrarian strain began to appear: works that shunned extravagant operatic behavior in pursuit of human or personal truth. One inevitable by-product was a newly satiric breed of comic opera in which the symbolic butt of humor was the genre of opera itself. In a way this was a throwback to the very origins of comic opera in the early eighteenth century, the intermezzos between the acts of courtly extravaganzas. The new genre consisted of full-scale works pitched at the same bourgeois public that attended the opera. Verdi himself, as we saw, also poked fun at operatic conventions in his final opera, *Falstaff.*

> ***In mid-century there emerged a newly satiric breed of comic opera in which the symbolic butt of humor was the genre of opera itself.***

The man who crystallized the trend was Jacques Offenbach (1819–80), a German-born Jew whose father, a synagogue cantor, had brought him to Paris at the age of fourteen to perfect his technique as a virtuoso cellist; he later performed with such luminaries as Liszt, Mendelssohn, Anton Rubinstein, and Joseph Joachim. After some years spent conducting at various Paris theaters, Offenbach began producing one-act farces, which he first called by the ordinary name ***opéras comiques,*** used for pieces that mixed spoken dialogue with musical numbers. In the mid-1850s he started dubbing them *opérettes,* a term that seems to have been coined by Louis August Joseph Florimond Ronger (1825–92), called Hervé, an organist and singer who in the early 1840s began producing one-act *vaudevilles-opérettes* and *parodies-opérettes* in little boulevard theaters. **Operetta** simply means "little opera," but it stuck to the Hervé-Offenbach genre and came to designate its special brand of frivolous buffoonery. The tunes were sometimes familiar, taken as they were from well-known operas, and Offenbach excelled in the silliness that Rossini had earlier indulged in by exploiting nonsense sounds and animal noises. His favored librettist was Ludovic Halévy (1834–1908), nephew of the composer of *La Juive*. Their operettas frequently relied on familiar operatic plots and situations but twisted them in the retelling.

Offenbach himself reserved the term *opérette* for his one-act farces. When he began writing full-evening works he called them *opéra bouffe*. As the genre spread, particularly captivating Vienna and England, however, the word *operetta* served to designate longer works as well. What they all had in common was the compulsion to parody opera. Although operetta never took hold in Russia as a homegrown thing, the tsarist autocracy permitted performances of French works, deeming them a useful public diversion at a time of mounting civil strife. During the 1870s, two private establishments were set up to provide St. Petersburgers with the latest amusements from Paris.

Out of the nearly 100 dramatic works that Offenbach churned out in the course of his thirty-three-year career, one stands out as emblematic: *Orphée aux enfers* (Orpheus in the Underworld; Fig. 26-4), his first two-act show, produced in 1858 at Offenbach's own Théâtre des Bouffes-Parisiens, and in 1874 expanded into a four-act extravaganza. Together with *La belle Hélène* (Fair Helen of Troy, 1864), *La vie parisienne* (Parisian Life, 1866), and *La Périchole* (1868), it was his wildest success, and not just in Paris. In 1876, for the American Centennial, Offenbach came to the United States, presenting two operettas and concerts in Philadelphia and New York. At the tail end of his shortish life he worked feverishly on a full-fledged opera in five acts called *Les contes d'Hoffmann* (The Tales of Hoffmann), an ambitious work based on the fantasy stories of E. T. A. Hoffmann, the German Romantic writer whom we know best as a music critic, especially for his writings on Beethoven.

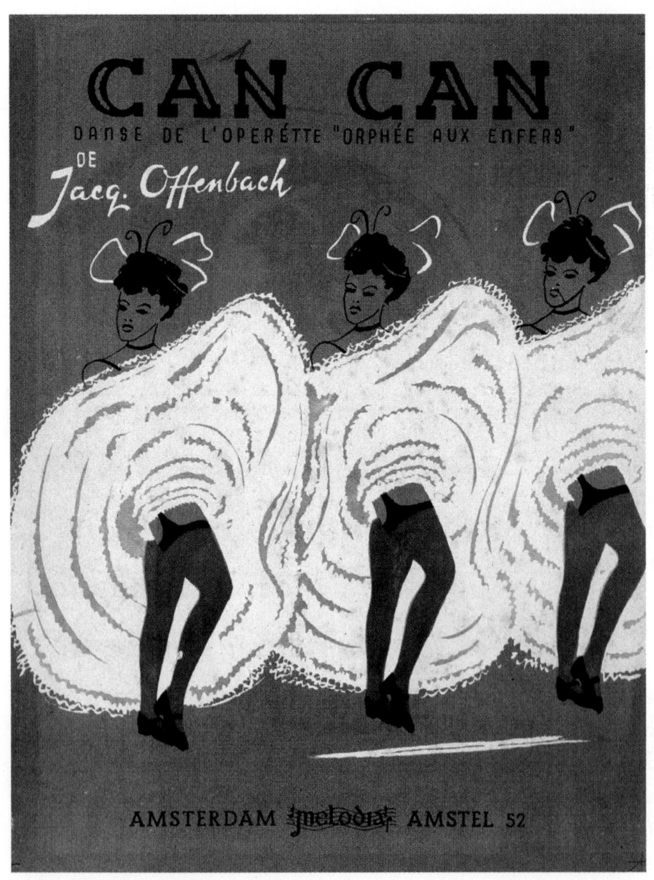

Figure 26-4 Poster for the operetta *Orpheus in the Underworld* by Jacques Offenbach featuring cancan dancers.

Orpheus was present, we will recall, at the very creation of opera around 1600. The Orpheus myth was founded on music's ethical power, the supreme article of faith for all serious musicians. Since the time of Monteverdi's *Orfeo* the story had been revived, most famously by Gluck, whenever the need was seen to reassert high musical ideals against trivial entertainment values. So there could scarcely have been a more calculated slap at sanctimony (or a more deliberate middle-class slap at aristocratic taste) than an Orpheus opera that was all frivolous excess. In Offenbach's version, Orpheus is a hack violinist whose bored wife, Eurydice, cannot stand either his music or his dreary personality. She prefers a neighbor, the farmer Aristaeus. To remove his rival from the scene, Orpheus plants snakes in the farmer's field, but, of course, it is his wife who gets bitten. Aristaeus reveals himself to be Pluto, the king of the underworld, in disguise. He takes Eurydice, now delighted to be dying, down with him to reign over the underworld. Good riddance, thinks Orpheus, until a character called Public Opinion (standing in for the Greek chorus) comes onstage to persuade him that for the sake of appearances he'd better try to rescue his wife.

The fourth act contains the broadest musical satire. It opens on a Bacchanale in the midst of which Orpheus comes to claim Eurydice. Pluto, now himself only too happy to be rid of her, lets her go, with the standard proviso that Orpheus not look around at her until they have reached the opposite shore of the River Styx. When it looks as though Orpheus will succeed, Jupiter hurls a thunderbolt at Orpheus's rear end, causing him involuntarily to turn around. Eurydice is lost to him—and to Pluto as well, for Jupiter transforms her into a Bacchante, a priestess of Bacchus, the wine god.

The end of *Orpheus in the Underworld* contains Offenbach's most famous music. At the height of the Bacchanale, Jupiter calls for "a dainty minuet, as in the days of the Sun King." After a couple of minutes' minuetting, though, the ballroom explodes spontaneously into what the assembled gods call a *galop infernale* but which the audience could not help recognizing as a cancan. The fastest of all polka- or quadrille-type ballroom dances, it had come to France from North Africa in the 1830s and had by the 1850s migrated from the ballroom to the dance hall, where lines of girls entertained men with their high kicking and splits, both of them excuses for the titillating display of frilly bloomers and bare legs. The curtain, as almost always in an operetta, falls on a general dance. It is that final dance frenzy, the predestined victory of mindless celebration, that validates operetta's claim as the ultimate escapist entertainment of its day. Not since the high days of Rossini's comic operas was so much fun presented on the musical stage.

Johann Strauss II—The Waltz King and Viennese Operetta

Vienna proved to be the next great arena for operetta. In keeping with the city's strong association with social dance, it was fitting that the main protagonist there should have been Johann Strauss II (1825–99), the so-called "Waltz King," who eventually became, like his father before him and his brother after him, the "k. k. Hofballmusikdirektor" (Imperial and Royal Music Director of the Court Balls). For decades he led the city's foremost dance orchestra; he made prominent appearances in cities abroad, including Paris, London, Berlin, Boston, and New York.

Just as Offenbach had a forerunner in Hervé, Strauss had one in Franz von Suppé (1819–95). Born in the polyglot Austro-Hungarian Empire (in what is now Croatia), Suppé had a Belgian father and a Czech-Polish mother and grew up speaking Italian. In the 1850s he began imitating Offenbach's one-act shows, working up to true Viennese operettas in which the words were not adapted from French. But the Waltz King put von Suppé in the shade. Strauss's *Die Fledermaus* (The Bat, 1874), composed when he was almost fifty, established him as Offenbach's only viable rival. Its libretto was adapted from a play by the very team—Halévy and Henri Meilhac—who were responsible for Offenbach's *Belle Hélène* as well as Bizet's *Carmen*.

Die Fledermaus is a domestic farce about a rich husband and wife who each try to deceive the other and who find each other out at the end. Minor hypocrisies and lighthearted marital infidelities, it is assumed, are simply the way of the world, and the only thing to do is wink. What Strauss lampoons mainly is not morals, however, but music. The wife's lover, a tenor, is mistaken for the husband and arrested on an old misdemeanor charge. At the beginning of Act III, before all the characters converge on the jail where the plot's tangles are to be sorted out, the tenor's real misdemeanors are committed, when his voice is heard from offstage warbling snatches of his favorite arias (all in Italian, including one by Wagner, whom Strauss greatly admired). The drunken jailer, overhearing, garbles them all, including Verdi's "La donna è mobile."

Dance is prominent, especially in Act II, which is set at a ball given by the Russian Prince Orlofsky. More operatic spoofing comes from casting the prince, a young rake hopelessly jaded by wealth, as a contralto in trousers, an in-joke for operagoers, the oldest of whom could remember, in 1874, the heroic "musico" roles in Rossini. The act reaches its climax in the dizzying dance without which no operetta was complete. It is a waltz, which screamed "Vienna!" as loudly as the cancan yelled "Paris!" (Fig. 26-5). Strauss's operetta waltzes resemble his famous dance hits, such as *An der schönen, blauen Donau* (On the Beautiful Blue Danube), Op. 314 (1867), and *Geschichten aus dem Wienerwald* (Tales from the Vienna Woods), Op. 325 (1868), to name two of the most famous of his nearly 500 opus numbers.

Anthology Vol 2-66
Full CD V, 24

A Strauss waltz was actually a string or medley of waltzes, frequently equipped with an evocative slower introduction. One of their most notable stylistic idiosyncrasies left traces on the more general idiom of European music, and that is the freedom with which the sixth degree of the scale is harmonized, appearing as a functional consonance both within the dominant (where it adds a ninth to the chord) and against the tonic (where it is usually described simply as an "added sixth"). The familiar opening strain of the "Blue Danube" waltz supplies perhaps the classic illustration (Ex. 26-4). The popularity of the Viennese waltz, which can be traced back to Schubert's time, was also perpetuated by Brahms, who when once asked for his autograph wrote out the opening of his friend's "Blue Danube" with the words "unfortunately not by Johannes Brahms."

Figure 26-5 Court Ball in Vienna. Watercolor by Wilhelm Gause (ca. 1900).

Example 26-4 Johann Strauss II, opening strain of the "Blue Danube" Waltz

England's Gilbert and Sullivan

In 1875, a London theater manager named Richard D'Oyly Carte commissioned a one-act work to make up a double bill with Offenbach's *La Périchole.* He approached Arthur Sullivan (1842–1900), a graduate of the Leipzig Conservatory who was then serving as principal of a newly opened music academy called the National Training School, what later became the Royal College of Music. The libretto for *Trial by Jury* was by William S. Gilbert (1836–1911), who specialized in skits that burlesqued standard operas of the day. Combining mockery of passing fads with underlying conformism, Gilbert and Sullivan's one-acter can seem a classic expression of Victorian England, that is, the state of the nation during Queen Victoria's long reign from 1837 to 1901.

Gilbert and Sullivan had already collaborated several years earlier, quite unmemorably, on an Offenbach-style comedy called *Thespis* and had given no thought to future collaborations. *Trial by Jury* marked the beginning of the most successful operetta team in the history of the genre. With *The Sorcerer* (1877) the pair hit their stride, producing the first of twelve operettas with spoken dialogue. With *HMS Pinafore; or, The Lass That Loved a Sailor* (1878) they achieved an unprecedented hit for an English operetta—indeed for an English work of any kind since Handel's day. Other shows include *Patience* (1881), *Iolanthe* (1882), *Princess Ida* (1884), *The Yeoman of the Guard* (1888), and *Gondoliers* (1889). So successful were these pieces that D'Oyly Carte built a special theater, the Savoy, to keep the whole "G & S" canon in circulation. Its patent on the operettas lasted until 1961, canonizing not only the works themselves but also traditions of performance in a fashion that Gilbert and Sullivan would no doubt have taken delight in spoofing had they lived to see it.

Both *Sorcerer* and *Pinafore* aim pointed barbs at specific operatic (but not only operatic) targets. The most conspicuous object of parody in the former was Weber's *Der Freischütz.* In the latter, Gilbert and Sullivan borrowed the basic premise—mistaken identity due to an exchange of babies by a befuddled nanny—from the much-ridiculed libretto of Verdi's *Il trovatore.* In *Ruddigore* (1887), the mad scene from Donizetti's *Lucia di Lammermoor* is parodied by a character named Mad Margaret. *The Mikado* (1885), the most popular of their works outside English-speaking countries, takes on Orientalism.

The Pirates of Penzance (1879; Fig. 26-6) contains one of their most glorious operatic spoofs, in the form of a double chorus. Pitting one sex (in this case policemen) against the opposite sex (in this case a group of single young women), it ends with a marvelous contrapuntal montage. The policemen confess their reluctance to expose themselves to danger; the maidens vainly seek to raise their morale with a

Figure 26-6 Poster for *The Pirates of Penzance* by Gilbert and Sullivan.

promise of posthumous fame. The ensuing impasse produces a common operatic situation: the "extended exit," in which the action about which all are singing is impeded by the singing itself. The maidens sing, "Go!" The police sing, "We go!" The comic character of Major-General Stanley, standing outside the music and observing its contradiction to the action, sings, "Yes, but you don't go!"

Gilbert and Sullivan eventually began burlesquing not only the foibles of standard opera and the upper classes but even their own mannerisms as endearingly absurd institutions. One such operatic convention is the "**patter song**," in which a character has to enunciate at rapid-fire speed. It is usually sung in Savoy operas by the "comic baritone," a stereotyped role typically marked by pompous ineptitude and/or lechery. In *Pirates* that role is filled by the Major-General, whose patter song "I Am the Very Model of a Modern Major-General," with its list of all the superfluous intellectual baggage he carries around in place of military expertise, is the archetype of the genre. Patter songs were in themselves parodies of a standard opera buffa technique that went all the way back to Pergolesi and his contemporaries, and that technique was itself a parody, translating the virtuosity of opera seria coloratura into the virtuosity of speedy enunciation, chiefly for bumbling basses at the opposite end of the spectrum, both in range and in moral character, from the male and female sopranos singing the heroic leads. (Rossini would have appreciated the parodies by G & S, since he wrote similar ones brilliantly himself.)

Anthology Vol 2-67
Full CD V, 25

So when, in *Ruddigore*, Gilbert and Sullivan parodied their own patter songs in a patter ensemble, it was a parody of a parody of a parody. It takes the form of a trio in which the male lead, Robin Oakapple, is encouraged by the comic baritone (Sir Despard Murgatroyd) and his sister, the contralto Mad Margaret, to solve the dilemma on which the plot turns—and which we need not go into here, for reasons expressed by Sir Despard at the end of the trio: "This particularly rapid unintelligible patter isn't generally heard, and if it is it doesn't matter." Rossini couldn't have said it better.

Italian *Verismo*

Another kind of operatic reinvention came from Italy. Here the tendency was also to cut things down in size, not comically but, rather, by making opera more immediate and related to the audience's experience. The Italian name for the new trend was ***verismo***, or "truthism." Verismo called, at least theoretically, for the rejection of traditional vocal virtuosity in the name of forceful emotional simplicity. It was under cover of this rigorously naturalistic idiom that Italian opera crossed into the twentieth century.

Verismo was originally a literary movement, led by Giovanni Verga (1840–1922), a writer and dramatist most famous for his short stories of life and strife among the peasants and lower classes of rural Sicily. Verga perfected a narrative style of blunt plainness and objectivity, seemingly without the intrusion of any authorial point of view. But that impression of letting the facts speak for themselves was actually a highly manipulative procedure, since of course the author gets to choose the facts. An impression of realism was created by the innovative use of local dialect and by a pessimistic mood. People fail in Verga's stories because they are overmatched by implacable natural and social conditions.

In some ways verismo opera was to Romantic opera as short stories were to novels. There was the same radical reduction in scale, the same lowering of tone and simplification of technique through which intensity took the place of grandeur. All of these features are well displayed by the two most successful specimens of the genre: *Cavalleria rusticana* (Rustic Chivalry, 1890) by Pietro Mascagni (1863–1945) and *Pagliacci* (Clowns, 1892; Fig. 26-7) by Ruggero Leoncavallo (1857–1919), both of them one-act operas that are now often performed together on a double bill affectionately known by operagoers as "Cav. and Pag." (To be accurate, *Pagliacci* is nominally a two-act opera in which the acts are connected by an intermezzo and played without an intermission.) *Cavalleria* was based on a famous story by Verga himself, selected for musical setting in a competition by a canny publisher, Edoardo Sonzogno, who wanted to capitalize on the new literary vogue. In an unusually direct way, therefore, operatic verismo derived from its literary prototype.

Figure 26-7 The world-famous Italian tenor Enrico Caruso as Canio in Ruggero Leoncavallo's *Pagliacci*.

Both operas culminate in brutal crimes of passion—murders committed by jealous husbands. The bloody deeds are portrayed with an eye primarily to sensationalism and shock value. It is of little importance whose side the audience is on; it is manipulated in *Cavalleria* to sympathize with the lover and in *Pagliacci* to sympathize with the husband. The main objective in these shabby little shockers of verismo is the same: titillation, the administering of thrills to a comfortable and complacent bourgeois audience, rather than the exposure of social problems and their corrections, let alone a call to political action such as Verdi's Risorgimento operas had sought to inspire. By the 1890s the political goals of a unified Italy had pretty much been achieved; popular culture could now revert to a more traditional, entertaining role.

Verismo was widely viewed as a catalyst to voyeurism, comparable in some ways to the appeal of Orientalism. Because of verismo's preoccupation with the mores of the southern lower classes and their naturalistic depiction, often in dialect, it led to a new variety of Orientalism in tune with the new concept of nationhood that arose in united Italy. In the theaters of affluent northern Italy these rustic scenes of life among the poor southern people were picturesquely exotic and thus nurtured assumptions of cultural as well as economic superiority. This, too, was regressive titillation of a sort, and one that reopened cultural divisions within the nation that the Risorgimento had tried to heal or at least to mask.

In both *Cavalleria* and *Pagliacci*, the lyric high points are brief ariosos for the *tenore di forza* (the lover in one, the husband in the other) in the voice's highest register. These powerful explosions of melody emerge out of ongoing dramatic continuities. The more famous of the two is "Vesti la giubba" ("Put on your costume"), which ends the nominal first act of Leoncavallo's opera. It is possibly the most parodied aria in all of opera, but the mockery it has attracted is testimony to its power. It is sung not by the victim of the crime but by the clown Tonio, the enraged husband, who has just found out about his wife's affair but who has to put on his makeup and costume and go out to perform anyway, to make 'em laugh. It is introduced by a recitative, famous for the naturalistic transformation of the tenor's high A into a bout of crazed laughter. The arioso contains no melodic repetitions at all. That absence of preconceived form was a high realist cause. And yet the arioso does not sound at all formless because its phrase structure and modulatory scheme take sly advantage of many conventions that render it fully comprehensible within the ordinary operagoer's experience. That is a sure-fire recipe, handled with mastery and aplomb, seemingly free and innovative but in fact giving listeners everything they are led to desire.

Anthology Vol 2-68
Full CD V, 26

Some found this a transparently manipulative exercise. From the traditional Romantic perspective such an opera could seem both trivially sensational and reprehensibly safe. Gabriele D'Annunzio (1863–1938), an Italian writer famous for his lofty transcendentalism who detested verismo, published a practically libelous review of *Cavalleria* in which he dismissed Mascagni as an insignificant bandmaster and a "breakneck melodrama manufacturer" whose success was due solely to his publisher's genius for publicity.[5] One who came quickly, if somewhat unexpectedly, to Mascagni's defense was Tchaikovsky. The Russian composer perhaps took a certain pleasure in shocking an interviewer, a St. Petersburg reporter who probably expected a conventional recoil at the mention of the twenty-nine-year-old Italian upstart. Instead, he elicited a ringing endorsement, couched as an almost explicit refutation of D'Annunzio's charges:

> People are wrong to think that this young man's colossal, fabulous success is the result of clever publicity. . . . Mascagni, it's clear, is not only very gifted but also very smart. He realizes that nowadays the spirit of realism, the harmonization of art and the true-to-life, is everywhere in the air, that [Wagner's] Wotans, Brünnhildes, and Fafners do not in fact excite any real sympathy on the part of the listener, that human beings with their passions and woes are more intelligible and tangible to us than the gods and demigods of Valhalla.[6]

Playing the Wagner card may have been unnecessary, but Russian composers were even more sensitive than Italians to German claims of universality. Tchaikovsky goes on to state that Mascagni "operates *not by force of instinct* but *by force of an astute perception of the needs of the contemporary listener*" (the italics are his). Tchaikovsky meant this as praise, although others at the time thought Mascagni's success was pure pandering, a cynical bid for popular success.

Innovation and Popularity—"Canon" versus "Repertory"

What really divided the musical world near the end of the nineteenth century, at the dusk of Romanticism and the dawn of Modernism, was exactly that relationship between the artist and "the contemporary listener." We will return to the issue time and again in the remaining chapters. More than any other, it defined the terms within which the history of "art music" would unfold in the twentieth century, the first century that had need of such a category. Because we are about to enter our exploration of music in the new century, this distinction will become all the more relevant. A few preliminary questions: What could be the reason for defining from the outset some—but only some—musical genres as "art"? What is excluded from the definition? What should the excluded portion be called? "Popular"? Does that mean music that people actually want to play and to hear? Will the remainder of this book be the history of "unpopular" music?

What really divided the musical world near the end of the nineteenth century, at the dusk of Romanticism and the dawn of Modernism, was the relationship between the artist and "the contemporary listener."

An early focal point of the twentieth-century controversy about art vs. commerce was the last great figure in the gloried Italian operatic line: Giacomo Puccini (1858–1924), whose works remain central to the core repertory at every opera house in the world. From the very beginning of his career there were some who called him Verdi's legitimate heir and others who refused to take him seriously. Despite Puccini's long-since settled place in the active repertoire and in the hearts of opera lovers, it is remarkable that the dispute lingers even as the centennial of his death approaches. Just as odd is the fact that he often gets only brief mention in general histories of classical music, even though his commanding stature within the world of opera has been a historical fact for more than 100 years and would seem therefore to constitute a robust claim to the composer's historical significance.

Since there is no chance of Puccini's being dislodged from his place in the operatic repertoire, no matter how much critical scorn is heaped on him from some quarters, it is clear that something else is at stake. The critical invective identifies him as one of the twentieth century's emblematic figures. The phrase "shabby little shocker," applied a couple pages earlier to the masterpieces of verismo, was borrowed from an appraisal of Puccini's *Tosca* (1900) made by the distinguished American musicologist Joseph Kerman in the course of a tirade against the composer in his *Opera as Drama* (1956; new edition 1988, with all the abuse in place). *Tosca* is, of course, one of the most popular works in the repertoire, thought by many operagoers to be a masterpiece, on a par with Verdi and far above the level of Mascagni or Leoncavallo.

Puccini's treatment at the hands of some historians is symptomatic of a general trend that merits study in its own right. That trend is the gradual divergence, over the course of the twentieth century, between the concert "repertory," the musical works actually performed for and consumed by audiences, and what is often called the "canon," the body of works and the pantheon of composers that are considered worthy of critical respect and academic study. That divergence, in which the history of music becomes not the history of music performed but the history of, well, something else, is largely the result of historicism, the intellectual trend first described in Chapter 22, according to which history is conceived in terms not only of events but also of goals. In the case of music these goals have chiefly pertained to the "disinterested" advancement of style, a concept that depends on German aesthetic philosophy (for the Kantian notion of "disinterestedness") and also on the narrative techniques of history itself (for the notion of "advancement"). It becomes a vicious circle in which recognition in history books is accorded to those composers whose music supposedly makes stylistic progress.

Accordingly, the historiography of music in the twentieth century has been fundamentally skewed, on the one hand, by the failure of actual events to conform to the purposes historicists have envisioned and, on the other, by the loyalty not only of many historians but also of many greatly talented composers to historicist principles. A large quantity of the music composed since the late nineteenth century, much of it the music deemed most interesting and significant by historians, has been written not for the concert repertory but for the canon. If one looks beyond the standard operas to orchestral programming, the symphonies and concertos by Sergey Rachmaninoff, Jean Sibelius, Edward Elgar, and other contemporaries of Puccini are among the most performed and popular. Their repertory works, however, are much less studied than many rarely heard canonic pieces.

Puccini wrote for the concert repertoire (for "the needs of the contemporary listener," in Tchaikovsky's words), as did most of the century's materially successful—that is, popular—composers. So despite his fame and his high historical profile, he has been slighted in the circularly conceived history of the historicist canon. And even though the present account is taking time out to discuss this state of affairs, which we will see has great relevance for developments in the twentieth century, there is no chance that we will solve it. A narrative history concentrates by nature on change, hence on innovation, and it has been one of the hallmarks of repertory music, at least since the advent of historicism, that it tends to be less innovative, stylistically, than canon music, which is written with the needs of the narrative in mind. That does not lessen its value to the audiences it serves, but it does lessen the news value of repertory music to historians of style. A description of Puccini's style or technique will not add enormously to what we already know about the style and technique of Italian opera at the end of the nineteenth century. But that is a poor criterion of selection; it plays into the historicist purposes that more recent historiography, including this book, has sought to challenge.

Giacomo Puccini's Ascent

In his student years Puccini exposed himself to a wide range of operatic styles: Verdi, of course, but also the younger *scapigliati* mentioned in Chapter 23, Wagner, and the recent French trends associated with Gounod, Massenet, and Bizet. He came of age during the ascendance of verismo and made a significant contribution to it. Like Mascagni's later *Cavalleria rusticana*, Puccini's brief first opera, *Le villi* (1883), was composed for the publisher Sonzogno's competition. After struggling through an initial version of an opera called *Edgar* (1889), he scored his first big hit, in 1893, with *Manon Lescaut*, on the same realistic subject that had already attracted Massenet. Like Verdi's great trio of *Rigoletto*, *Trovatore*, and *Traviata*, Puccini wrote a famous trio at the midpoint of his career. All were done with librettists who collaborated with Puccini as a team: Luigi Illica (1857–1919) and Giuseppe Giacosa (1847–1906), both well-known playwrights.

They based *La bohème* (1896) on *Scènes de la vie de bohème* (Scenes of Bohemian Life), a best-selling sentimental novel by the French writer Henri Murger that romanticized and considerably prettified the dire circumstances of a group of struggling young writers and artists ("bohemians") inhabiting the garrets of Paris. The central plot line concerns the romance of Rodolfo, a starving poet, and Mimi, a consumptive seamstress: In Act I they meet by chance; in Act II they are happily in love; in Act III they quarrel and are reconciled; in Act IV she dies. Their simple love story is set in relief by a busy backdrop of picturesque Parisian street and café life. Act II, with its café waltzes and songs, subsidiary flirtations, and anecdotal hubbub, is almost entirely given over to the backdrop. There is no denying the theatrical effectiveness of the recipe. Yet objections are often raised against the opportunistic manipulativeness of the situation, particularly the device of inescapable doom contributed by Mimi's disease, a factor present from the outset of the opera.

Tosca (1900) was based on a popular play by the French dramatist Victorien Sardou that was created as a star vehicle for the great actress Sarah Bernhardt; the title character is also a great actress, a fictional diva living at the time of the French Revolution. The play, first staged in 1887, was still in current repertory when Puccini set it. That became his standard procedure: Of the seven operas that followed *Tosca*, four were derived from recent plays the composer happened to see in the theater, sometimes in languages he did not understand. (Half in jest, Puccini once said that his being able to follow a play despite ignorance of its language testified to its operatic potential.) Both the play and the opera are cast in the brutally naturalistic mode then fashionable, replete with an onstage murder, an offstage (but audible) scene of torture, an execution, and a concluding suicide. More than in any other Puccini score, the musical texture of *Tosca* is suffused with reminiscence motifs, sometimes treated in an abstract manner that justifies the use of the Wagnerian term leitmotif. That Puccini, unlike Verdi, rarely suffered accusations of "Wagnerism" testifies to the increasing internationalism of procedures and techniques in turn-of-the-century opera.

Madama Butterfly, billed as a "Japanese Tragedy," went through four distinct versions between 1904 and 1906 (Fig. 26-8). Its source was an acclaimed dramatization by the American theatrical producer David Belasco, which Puccini saw in London while attending the English premiere of *Tosca*. The play, based on a tale supposedly drawn from real life by the American writer John Luther Long, is a sob story about a Japanese geisha nicknamed Chô-San (Cio-Cio-San in the opera), or Butterfly. She is seduced, "temporarily wedded" (according to Japanese law at the time, which cruelly discriminated against the rights of women), and then abandoned when pregnant, by a nonchalant American naval officer named Pinkerton. The tragic sequence of events ultimately leads to Butterfly's suicide.

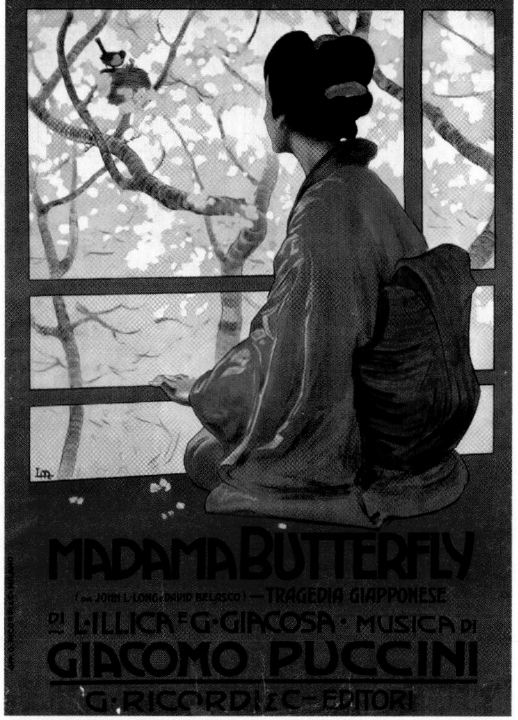

Figure 26-8 Cover of the vocal score for Giacomo Puccini's *Madama Butterfly* (1906).

Madama Butterfly relies a great deal on local color, as we have already seen operas with exotic settings, especially Oriental ones, were prone to do. Puccini incorporated the characteristically pentatonic tunes of at least ten Japanese folk songs into the score, mostly in the first act, which depicts Butterfly's wedding to Lieutenant Pinkerton, who is also identified by a bit of local color: the opening phrases of "The Star-Spangled Banner." It is, after all, only in the presence (that is, through the eyes and ears) of the American Pinkerton that the Japanese milieu is exotic. Japanisme is largely dispensed with in the vastly longer second act, which takes place three years later, played for the most part in Pinkerton's absence and concerned mainly with Butterfly's worsening fate.

Butterfly displays her steadfast faith in her husband's return both by turning down an advantageous match with a rich suitor and by singing what may be the most famous aria in all of Puccini: "Un

Anthology Vol 2-69
Full CD V, 27
Concise CD III, 4

bel dí" ("One fine day"), in which she chides her protective servant Suzuki for doubting that Pinkerton will come back and imagines the joyful scene that awaits her. In Act II's second part, Pinkerton does return—but with his American bride, Kate, and only to reclaim his son from Butterfly, who gives him up and then kills herself. Like the arias and ariosos in late Verdi and verismo operas, "Un bel dí" is terse. Its form could be described as da capo, since it begins and ends with a distinctive eight-bar melody that only has to be sung once to be memorable (Ex. 26-5). In between the two statements comes a disproportionately long middle section that begins with a balancing sequential idea but then devolves into what sounds like recitative, sung in "conversational" note values with long strings of repeated pitches. Even though this is an aria, we are thus informed that it is being enacted in real time as Butterfly narrates to Suzuki her fantasy of reconciliation.

Example 26-5 Giacomo Puccini, "Un bel dí" from *Madama Butterfly*, mm. 1–8

The reprise of the opening phrase carries more emotional punch than the usual da capo return because it is sung triumphantly, at the opposite end of the dynamic scale from the gently wistful opening, casting the whole aria in retrospect as a single gathering crescendo to a climax. Once past the first phrase, moreover, the voice part again devolves into a recitative-like style, dividing the notes of the melody into short repeated notes, while it continues to sound forth, intact, in the orchestra. Looking back at the beginning now, we notice that even there the singer followed the melody somewhat selectively. The tune as such, it turns out, belongs more to the orchestra than to the voice. Butterfly's climactic statement of the main theme is immediately followed and trumped by a coda in which, after six measures' headlong ascent to a brilliant high B♭, she falls silent, and the theme passes entirely into the orchestra for its conclusion, as if achieving a transcendent emotional pitch that can only be represented wordlessly.

Within the very confines of the aria, in other words, the theme is already being treated as a reminiscence motif, producing at short range the emotional rush that the device of reminiscence had previously held in reserve. The aria's brevity, its climax-driven structure, and its pumped-up wordless coda conspire to deliver a sort of accelerated catharsis, an instant emotional gratification for the audience, who get to share Butterfly's fantasy. From this point until the end of the act, the reminiscence theme from "Un bel dí" will serve as the emblem of Butterfly's false belief in Pinkerton's return, the belief that sustains her and that, by her own avowal, gives her the only reason to live. Like its Verdian antecedents it has been invested with an ironic double meaning; its every return not only confirms her faith but also forecasts her doom. For the rest of the opera this reminiscence motif plays its part in heightening the spectators' awareness of the impending catastrophe, and (let's face it) their (no, *our*) enjoyment of it. It can be argued, and of course it has been, that all tragedy is voyeurism, that by definition it contains or implies the enjoyment of another's misfortune, and that the noble concept of catharsis—tragedy's soul-cleansing function as defined by Aristotle—is an idealizing mask for sentiments far less noble.

The particular tragic formula repeatedly employed by Puccini, in which the emblematic character is neither a robust *tenore di forza* nor an evil bass-baritone but, rather, a tender young woman who is victimized by an inescapable situation (grinding poverty, fatal disease, the patriarchal order, imperialism) and slowly tortured to death, brings the hidden sadism of dramatic representation dangerously near the surface of consciousness. It can be argued that watching a strong hero—Oedipus, Orpheus, Othello—brought low by fate in consequence of a moral flaw is edifying. It is harder to make such an argument in the case of a defenseless woman like Mimi or Butterfly.

Puccini's success raises a whole series of related questions: Has his enduring popularity been due to his skill in administering sadistic gratification? If so, then shall we place the blame on Puccini or on the ones who have made him popular, namely, a large public? Is an art that caters to "bad" instinct bad art? Does such catering promote social evil or (by giving our evil fantasies an acceptable outlet) social good? Is the fact that the art of the *fin de siècle*, the "end of the century," was so full of sadistic representations the result of "decadence," as some have charged, or the result of greater candor in dealing relatively openly with matters that had formerly been more heavily cloaked in hypocritical metaphor? Two more questions: Was the habit of representing women in art as sacrificial victims an early reaction to the burgeoning social emancipation of women? Did Puccini's success at rendering "great sorrows in little souls" (as he put it himself) magnify the souls or mock the sorrows?[7] These are some of the heady issues that Puccini's operas raise, issues that go beyond his musical style to address key dramatic aims and social conditions.

Puccini's pace slowed after *Butterfly*, in part due to the death of his collaborator, Giacosa, in 1906. His next opera, based on another Belasco play, explored very different exotic locale: the American Wild West. *La fanciulla del West* (The Girl of the Golden West), set in the Sierra Nevada mountains of California during the mid-nineteenth-century gold rush, premiered in 1910 at the Metropolitan Opera in New York, with Enrico Caruso singing and Arturo Toscanini conducting. *La rondine* (The Swallow, 1917), Puccini's undervalued attempt at an operetta, was followed the next year by three one-act operas also written for the Met: *Il tabarro* (The Coat), *Suor Angelica* (Sister Angelica), and *Gianni Schicchi*. Puccini's final opera, *Turandot* (Fig. 26-9), another foray into Orientalism after a dramatized fairy tale by Carlo Gozzi, was

Figure 26-9 Cover of the first edition of the libretto to Puccini's *Turandot* (Milan: Ricordi, 1924).

first performed posthumously in 1926, with its closing duet completed by a younger composer named Franco Alfano (1875–1954). Another cruel Orientalist fantasy of feminine humiliation, it offered up two victims to the audience: The slave girl Liu, who fills the tender maiden slot, is driven by torture to suicide; the title character, the haughty princess of China, is brought low by love, which compels her reluctant submission to her wooer, Calaf, the *tenore di forza.* His aria "Nessun dorma" ("None shall sleep") emerged in the late twentieth century as competition for "Un bel dí" in popularity.

Turandot was the very last Italian opera to enter the permanent international repertoire. As we shall see, there have since been only a handful or two of later additions to that repertoire, and they have been the work of French, Austrian, Russian, English, and American composers, not Italians. In part, this drying up of the original fount of opera reflects the fate of the genre in general: Its status as a popular medium of spectacular entertainment was usurped in the twentieth century by the movies, especially after the advent of "talkies" only three years after Puccini's death. And yet if films are to be regarded, in effect, as the operas of the twentieth century, then Italy has not ceded its place after all. Puccini's heirs have been the great Italian film directors, especially those, like Roberto Rossellini, Vittorio De Sica, and Federico Fellini, who made up the so-called neorealist school of the 1940s and '50s, which, arguably, inherited the mantle of verismo.

Summary

This chapter surveyed some trends in opera in the last half of the nineteenth century, including "Orientalism," a tendency, seen particularly in French opera, to represent non-European peoples as exotic "others." There are examples by Giacomo Meyerbeer (1791–1864), Léo Delibes (1836–91), Jules Massenet (1842–1912), Georges Bizet (1838–75), and Camille Saint-Saëns (1835–1921). The best-known examples in today's repertory are Bizet's *Carmen* and Saint-Saëns's *Samson et Dalila.* In Act III of *Samson et Dalila,* Saint-Saëns uses augmented seconds and an asymmetrical rhythmic pattern to represent the ancient Philistines. The title character of *Carmen,* a Spanish gypsy, is represented as a danger to middle-class norms and values. Carmen's overt sexuality and ethnic difference are represented in the music with a descending chromatic scale and with tunes and rhythms derived from Afro-Cuban music, the habanera. Another mid-century trend in French opera is *opéra lyrique,* a genre with reduced dramatic forces and attractive melodies reminiscent of popular forms, such as ballroom songs and dances. Examples include *Faust* and *Roméo et Juliette* by Charles-François Gounod (1818–93). Orientalism also found favor in Russia, for the Russian empire was in the process of extending itself eastward into Islamic areas of Asia. In addition to the orchestral showpieces of Rimsky-Korsakov's *Scheherazade* and Balakirev's *Tamara,* Alexander Borodin explored these themes in his opera *Prince Igor,* especially its "Polovtsian Dances."

The later century also saw the rise in popularity of the *opérette,* or operetta, a light genre that gently poked fun at the conventions of opera. Its first successful composer was Jacques Offenbach (1819–80). Working in Paris he drew on familiar opera plots and well-known opera tunes to create satire. One work, *Orphée aux enfers* (Orpheus in the Underworld), is a comic retelling of the Orpheus story. Operetta later spread to Vienna, with hits such as Johann Strauss II's *Die Fledermaus* (The Bat). Strauss was known as the "Waltz King," and his *An der schönen, blauen Donau* (On the Beautiful Blue Danube) exemplifies the typical traits of a concert waltz. Operetta also became popular in England; Gilbert and Sullivan's many hits in the genre include *H.M.S Pinafore* (1878), *The Pirates of Penzance* (1879), and *Ruddigore* (1887).

Verismo was a trend toward extreme realism in Italian literature and opera. Its aim was to depict reality with blunt plainness and often with violence, focusing on the lower classes. *Cavalleria rusticana* by Pietro Mascagni (1863–1945) and *Pagliacci* by Ruggero Leoncavallo (1857–1919) are both short, one-act operas with continuous music and without preconceived musical set numbers, underscoring the "naturalness" of their realism; both operas end with crimes of passion.

Giacomo Puccini (1858–1924) was the most successful Italian opera composer of this period. His operas, including *La bohème* (1896) and *Tosca* (1900), exhibit the traditional Italian focus on lyrical melody, stringing together the traditional numbers, such as arias, duets, and choruses, into a continuous musical flow. He made effective use of reminiscence motifs and orchestration for local or exotic color. In *Madama Butterfly* (1904–06) Puccini incorporates pentatonic tunes reminiscent of Japanese music. Although Puccini's operas are some of the best-loved pieces in today's repertory, they have not always received much attention in histories of music, undoubtedly because of the value those histories place on "progress" and stylistic innovation rather than on pleasing a paying crowd.

Study Questions

1. What is the difference between a "repertoire" and a "canon"? How does this distinction apply to Giacomo Puccini?
2. Define "Orientalism," and describe some cultural reasons for its popularity. What musical techniques are used to represent the exotic in Georges Bizet's *Carmen* and in other operas? In which countries did "Orientalism" prove to be most attractive?
3. What is *opéra lyrique,* and how did it differ from *grand opéra* and *opéra comique?*
4. What is operetta? In what countries did it flourish, and who were its main composers? How did operettas parody serious opera?
5. What is *verismo* as a literary movement? How do *verismo* operas such as Ruggero Leoncavallo's *Pagliacci* reflect the realistic aims of the movement?
6. Discuss Puccini's effective use of local color and reminiscence motifs in *Madama Butterfly,* especially in the aria "Un bel dí."

Key Terms

opéra lyrique
operetta
Orientalism
patter song
verismo

27

Early Austro-German Modernism: Mahler, Strauss, and Schoenberg

The years we will be exploring in this and the two following chapters, encompassing roughly the last decade of the nineteenth century through the First World War (1914–18), are often called the early Modernist period in music. It was a time of enormously accelerated stylistic innovation. Music had not changed so radically in hundreds of years, nor had it proved so shocking to many contemporaneous listeners. Some today still find works from this period shocking, even after more than a century.

The term ***Modernism*** requires comment. To make an "-ism" out of being modern is on the face of it paradoxical. If *modern* simply means "of or pertaining to present and recent time," as the *American College Dictionary* defines it, then we all are modern by default, and always have been, since we cannot live at any other time than the present. To be Modernist, then, must mean something more. It is not just a condition but an attitude and a commitment. Modernism asserts the superiority of the present over the past (and, by implication, of the future over the present), with all that that implies in terms of optimism and faith in progress. It was the responsibility of Modern artists to find ways of reflecting this historical moment and momentum.

There are obvious problems with other labels now commonly used to describe music written after 1900, such as "contemporary," "new," and "avant-garde." For one thing, there is always a contemporary art, always something new, and always some artists who try or seem to be "ahead of the times." Yet the twentieth century proved different from other historical eras because of the wide variety of musical styles that proliferated, the vast broadening of countries actively engaged in a thriving international musical culture, and the unprecedented breadth of dissemination made possible through technological innovations, most notably recordings, film, radio, TV, and computers.

Not everyone, of course, shared an optimistic view of the future; many felt oppressed by the stress of industrialization and its social discontents. The cultural phase we are about to investigate was referred to in some places as the *fin de siècle* (end of the century), not only because it coincided with 1900 but also because it reflected superstitious premonitions of ultimate revelation and possible catastrophe such as attend any significant milestone in the calendar. The generation gap in musical life that began to widen between disillusioned Romantics and young Modernists can be illustrated by a story. Gustav Mahler (1860–1911; Fig. 27-1), one of this chapter's protagonists, was taking a walk with Brahms at an Austrian spa during the summer of 1896. According to Richard Specht, who wrote biographies of both composers,

Figure 27-1 Gustav Mahler photographed at the Vienna Court Opera House, 1907.

> Brahms began discoursing, as usual, on the decline and fall of music, but Mahler suddenly took his arm and, pointing down to the river they were passing with his other hand, exclaimed, "Just look, doctor, just look!" "What is it?" Brahms asked. "Don't you see, there goes the last wave!" It was a good symbol for the eternal movement in life and in art, which knows of no cessation. But I seem to remember that it was Brahms who had the last word, thus: "That is all very fine, but perhaps what matters most is whether the wave goes out to sea or into a swamp."[1]

This tension between generations suggests that although everyone is modern, not everyone is Modernist. Some live in the present with resignation, others with indifference, still others in a state of resistance to it. Modernists, on the other hand, live in the present with enthusiasm and intensity, an enthusiasm requiring audacity, self-consciousness, a heightened alertness to the surrounding world, and, above all, urbanity in every meaning of the word, from citified and sophisticated to artificial and mannered. All of this sounds like the very opposite of Romanticism as originally defined—in terms, that is, of spirituality, naturalness, spontaneity, naiveté, authenticity, and transcendence of the worldly. Modernism celebrates qualities reviled by Jean-Jacques Rousseau or Johann Gottfried von Herder. It does so, moreover, with irony (as anything so self-aware must do), so attempts to reduce Modernism to a set of core beliefs quickly turns into an exercise in chasing one's own tail.

But of course we have been observing a sophisticated interrelationship between highly self-conscious technical innovation and expanded musical resources over the course of the nineteenth century, carried out in the very name of Romanticism. The century, after all, was also the great age of industrialization and urbanization. We have already witnessed the immense changes in artistic aims and means that were brought about as by-products of underlying demographic changes, as the populations of Europe and America became increasingly concentrated in cities. Nor are we strangers by now to irony. We know how calculated the impression of Romantic spontaneity could be. And we may also be wondering what the difference therefore could possibly be between Modernism and the New German School's "Music of the Future," which was also predicated on optimism and faith in progress.

Haven't we seen it all before? Was there ever a more sophisticated composer than Richard Wagner? Was there ever a more artificial technical innovation than the *Tristan*-chord, however elemental and seemingly natural its representational power? Claude Debussy (1862–1918), the most important French composer at the turn of the century, quipped that Wagner's music "was a beautiful sunset . . . mistaken for a dawn."[2]

So now is the time to state explicitly the implicit paradox that ran through our whole discussion of Wagner and his musical agenda. The most radically innovative composer of the late nineteenth century—or at least the man so reputed—was in fact no friend of Modernity. On the contrary, the social vision that motivated his artistic reforms was one of restored premodern concord. At least by the time he finished the *Ring*, Wagner was not a forward-looking utopian but the very opposite, a nostalgic, which is to say, a reactionary, one. The nostalgic vision, widely shared in the nineteenth century in direct reaction to the social confusion caused by modernization, informed not only Wagner's spectacular artistry but also his horrid politics. On the other hand, despite Brahms's reputedly more conservative music (and however much he may have worried about whether that music might be headed for a modern swamp), this did not stop him from heartily embracing liberal politics and scientific advances. It is fitting that the first recording made by a major composer was of Brahms playing the piano.

This chapter explores the Austro-German musical context at the fin de siècle, the next one investigates the French context, and the following one surveys trends elsewhere in Europe and America. As we will see soon enough, the ends and the means were quite different in France than in Germany—first among composers such as Debussy, Erik Satie, Gabriel Fauré, and Maurice Ravel and then among foreigners attracted to Paris, such as Russian composer Igor Stravinsky and, somewhat later, a large group of young Americans, including Aaron Copland. These figures interacted with a vibrant intellectual and cultural scene. The great impresario Sergey Diaghilev, for example, brought together dancers, musicians, poets, and painters to collaborate on projects. Marcel Proust (1871–1922) labored on his immense novel *À la recherche du temps perdu* (In Search of Lost Time) while listening to Wagner's operas. Painters pursued new styles, such as Impressionism, Cubism, and Dada, that often were no longer representational but, rather, abstract, playful, and psychological.

Beyond Vienna, Paris, and other long-established musical centers, the twentieth century saw the emergence of internationally recognized composers from places that previously had not enjoyed much attention or acclaim. Music during the century increasingly became truly international as time and space shrank in consequence of new forms of rapid travel and communication and as recordings could widely spread music of diverse places and historical periods.

TIMELINE

- **1884** Joris-Karl Huysmans, *Against Nature*
- **1889** Thomas Edison has Brahms record a piano piece
- **1889 Gustav Mahler's Symphony No. 1 premieres**
- **1893** Oscar Wilde, *Salomé*
- **1895** Lumière brothers show first moving pictures to a paying audience
- **1899 Arnold Schoenberg, *Verklärke Nacht***
- **1900** Sigmund Freud, *The Interpretation of Dreams*
- **1903** Wassily Kandinsky, *The Blue Rider*
- **1904 Mahler's Symphony No. 5 premieres**
- **1905 Richard Strauss, *Salome***
- **1905** Albert Einstein publishes path-breaking papers on physics
- **1907–08** Gustav Klimt, *The Kiss*
- **1908–09 Mahler, *Das Lied von der Erde***
- **1909 Arnold Schoenberg, *Erwartung***
- **1911 Schoenberg, *Theory of Harmony***
- **1911 Schoenberg, Six Little Piano Pieces, Op. 19**
- **1911 Strauss, *Der Rosenkavalier***
- **1911 Death of Mahler**
- **1911–13 Anton Webern, Six Bagatelles for String Quartet, Op. 9**
- **1911–13 Webern, Five Pieces for Orchestra, Op. 10**
- **1912 Schoenberg, *Pierrot lunaire*, Op. 21**
- **1914–18** First World War

The Modern Condition

For a Romantic reactionary like Wagner the very incarnation of corrupted Modernity was the figure of the emancipated, assimilated, urbanized Jew. And so, inevitably it might seem, two of the paradigmatic early musical Modernists within the German sphere—two of the leaders in the radical acceleration of stylistic innovation that we will now be tracing—are Mahler and Arnold Schoenberg (1874–1951), emancipated, assimilated, and urbanized Austrian Jews (Fig. 27-2.) They both eventually converted to Christianity, although Schoenberg converted back to Judaism in 1933, soon after the Nazis came to power. Both composers worked primarily in Vienna during the first decade of the new century. (Schoenberg spent part of that time in Berlin; Mahler was based in New York during his last years.)

Vienna had long been the *Musikstadt,* the City of Music to which Gluck, Haydn, Mozart, Beethoven, Brahms, and so many other musicians had moved. But at the dawn of the twentieth century Vienna was alive with more than just music: Arts and ideas reached extraordinary heights, creating an unusually vibrant cultural scene. As the rapidly growing capital of a multilingual empire, Vienna attracted many immigrants who vitalized the city; the arts offered a field in which some of them could succeed. We have touched numerous times over the course of this book on how music relates to larger intellectual, artistic, and political circumstances. Yet most of the musicians we have treated thus far did not have much personal contact with leading philosophers, painters, poets, or politicians. The idea of fusing ideas and the different arts, what Wagner had felt he could pretty much do singlehandedly, assumed much greater urgency in the early twentieth century.

Figure 27-2 *A Hypermodern Conductor,* caricature of Gustav Mahler by Hans Schliessmann in *Fliegende Blätter,* March 1901.

In the visual arts, Vienna was home to the so-called Secession, which included figures such as Gustav Klimt (1862–1918; Fig. 27-3), united under the motto *Der Zeit ihre Kunst, der Kunst ihre Freiheit* (To the Age Its Art, To Art Its Freedom). Philosopher Ludwig Wittgenstein (1889–1951) grew up in the city, physicist Ernst Mach (1838–1916) moved there from the Czech lands, and journalist Theodor Herzl (1860–1904) came as a teenager and went on to found modern political Zionism. Adolf Hitler (1889–1945), long before he became Germany's fascist dictator, was a young Austrian art student who also moved to the city; he went regularly to hear Mahler conduct at the Vienna Court Opera and in so doing memorized Wagner's operas.

One of the most influential figures was Sigmund Freud (1856–1939), the pioneer of psychoanalysis, who like Mahler was born to a Jewish family, in what is now the Czech Republic. His explorations of the "unconscious" had a profound impact on contemporary culture, and we remain heirs in countless ways to his thinking. His writings about dreams, sexuality, repressed desires, and the constitution of the human psyche opened new ways of thinking about everyday life. Using the names of ancient Greek gods, he eventually proposed two opposing forces, *Eros* and *Thanatos,* an erotic drive and a death drive, respectively, which found expression in a great amount of Modernist art. (Wagner's *Tristan* had already offered a good example.) It is not just that some musicians knew or were treated by Dr. Freud (Mahler, for one) but that his ideas seemed both to reflect and to influence the psychological preoccupations of the time.

If Freud was the emblematic figure for a science of the psyche, the great physicist Albert Einstein (1879–1955), working not far away, in Switzerland, was changing the landscape of modern science and ultimately, like Freud, the ways people

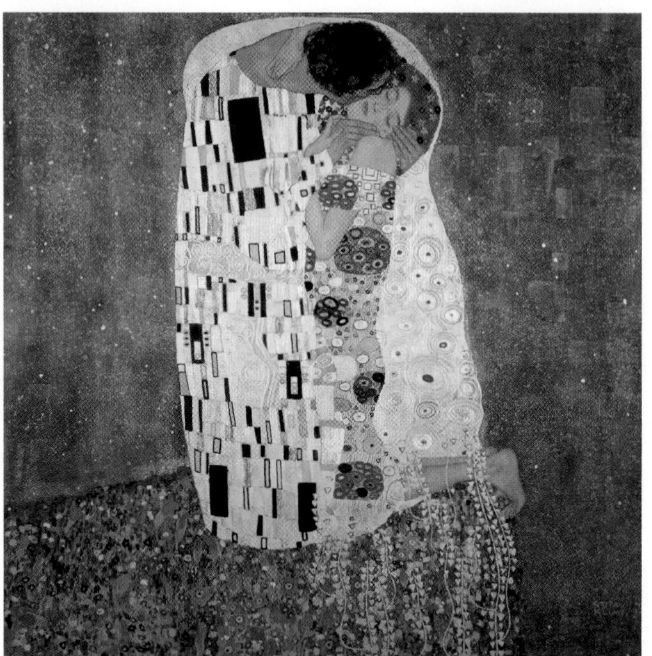

Figure 27-3 Gustav Klimt, *The Kiss*, 1907–1908.

viewed the world. In a series of path-breaking scientific papers beginning in 1905, Einstein proposed the Theory of Relativity, which had an incalculable impact on the course of the twentieth century. Einstein's innovations are emblematic of technological developments that changed daily life for most people. The earlier invention of the telegraph and the railroad, as well as developments in electrical engineering, had already fundamentally advanced communication and transportation. Such breakthroughs only accelerated in the new century, along with others in science and medicine. Despite all the technical innovations in the world surrounding them, Modernist composers at the turn of the century rarely wrote pieces about railroads or electricity, although some did. Rather, in keeping with Freud, much of the most controversial art explored psychological themes.

The new recording technologies had enormous consequences for music. In 1889 American inventor Thomas Edison (1847–1931; Fig. 27-4) sent an engineer to Europe, where he captured Brahms playing part of his Hungarian Dance No. 1 in G Minor. In 1905 Mahler made piano rolls using a device similar to a player piano in which the music is punched into rolls of paper. Schoenberg and Stravinsky lived long into the twentieth century and, to varying degrees, became involved with making recordings. Some composers began to concern themselves with the medium of film, the major new artistic medium of the century. Another long-lived early Modernist to record much of his orchestral legacy was Richard Strauss (1864–1949). At the turn of the century, he was at the forefront of German stylistic innovation.

Figure 27-4 Thomas Edison with his phonograph, invented in 1877.

Although Mahler, Strauss, and Schoenberg were radically forging new musical styles, they were by no means ignorant of tradition or necessarily hostile to it. Indeed, they identified strongly with the distinguished legacy of German music in all its aspects, the Wagnerian one emphatically included. They saw themselves as its heirs and rightful continuers. Mahler, who never taught, nonetheless served as mentor to a generation of young composers who revered him; Schoenberg emerged as one of the great teachers of the century, first in Europe and for the last twenty years of his life in America. His student's students (and their students, and so on) continue his legacy to this day.

Maximalism

Ezra Pound (1885–1972), a prominent American poet who was living in London in 1914, wrote the following weary words as the First World War commenced: "This is the whole flaw of 'emotional' music. It is like a drug: You must have more drug, and more noise each time."[3] After Wagner, Bruckner, Franck, Verdi, Brahms, and others, a young composer at the end of the nineteenth century might well have wondered what to do next—how could one top their accomplishments? Operas and symphonies had gotten longer, louder, and ever more complex; it seemed one either had to press forward or retreat. Or one could try to redefine the terms of the debate altogether.

The most prominent German and Austrian composers to a certain degree came to one conclusion, although they expressed it in rather different ways. During the period 1890–1914, Modernism manifested itself chiefly in the manner to which Pound drew attention, which is why it is perhaps best characterized by what we will call "**maximalism**": as a radical intensification of means toward traditional expressive ends. Many aspects of music could be—and were—radically intensified. What aesthetic dimensions could be maximalized? Emotional expression, the primary prerequisite of Romantic art, is clearly one. Another is a sense of awe in the presence of the sublime. At its peak, the maximalizing tendency in early Modernist music gave rise to works that dealt with metaphysical issues that had long preoccupied philosophers. Another dimension was sensuality, which proved to be a dominating Modernist concern, and not just in Freud's Vienna.

And by what intensified musical means could composers achieve newly desired maximal ends? One could expand, as Wagner had already begun doing, the two dimensions in which compositions exist: the temporal and the sonorous. Giving musical works a new awe-inspiring vastness—by extending their length, amplifying their volume, and complicating their texture—became an obsession for many composers. The vastness included ever-larger orchestras and ever-greater concern with timbre. Another way of enlarging the sense of musical space was to increase the range and maneuverability of key relationships. Wagner had also set a benchmark to be exceeded in the sheer level of tolerable dissonance and, even more important, the postponement of its resolution. The Brahmsian tradition could also be maximized. Here the benchmark was musical logic and motivic saturation, the loading of the texture with significant motifs to be kaleidoscopically recombined.

We will see as well that the intensity of allusions, autobiography, and extramusical reference could be taken to greater extremes than even the most self-involved nineteenth-century composers had practiced. While it might seem difficult to go beyond what Berlioz and Schumann had done, Mahler and Strauss found ways appropriate to a new century and reflective of the depth psychology Freud pioneered. Mahler, many think, incorporated in his scores not only the most deeply felt personal experiences from his life—the deaths of siblings and of his eldest daughter, a fraught relationship with his beautiful, much younger wife—but also the sonic experiences of everyday life, of the street, café, military field, and so forth. While some contemporaries found his juxtaposition of spiritual sublimity and banality confusing, the combination was eventually viewed as one of his most radical innovations. Strauss also explored sublime and commonplace issues, often with a great sense of irony. He was more prone to parody the Beethovenian heroic (the title of one of his works is *Ein Heldenleben*, or A Hero's Life, 1897–98) than to praise it, and examples of the everyday sounds he deployed in his works include depictions of his nagging wife and their screaming baby son in his *Symphonia domestica* (1902–03).

Giving musical works a new awe-inspiring vastness became an obsession for many composers.

Gustav Mahler: Conductor and Composer

Gustav Mahler was the quintessential Modernist representative of what has been called *Weltanschauungsmusik*—roughly, "music expressive of a world outlook" or even "philosophy-music."[4] He once professed his aim to write a symphony "so great that the whole world is actually reflected therein—so that one is, so to speak, only an instrument upon which the universe plays."[5] His nine numbered symphonies, plus part of a tenth left unfinished at his death in 1911, brought the line of Austro-German symphonic composition to a climax. After Mahler there was no Germanic symphonist of comparable prominence; the important twentieth-century schools of symphony writers have been Scandinavian, Russian, and Anglo-American.

Mahler's career was one of the great success stories in music history. He was born in a small Bohemian town into the family of a Jewish distiller and tavern keeper. Of the fourteen children only six survived into maturity, leaving him the eldest. He first showed talent as a pianist, gave an impressive public recital at the age of ten, and at sixteen was sent to the Vienna Conservatory. Although he audited a few of Bruckner's lectures at the University of Vienna, he was careful to insist that he was never formally Bruckner's pupil. Mahler did not begin to make a reputation as a composer until he was already a famous conductor, especially of opera. To scan a list of his conducting posts is to witness an astounding, truly meteoric rise to the pinnacle of his profession. He began with positions at provincial opera houses before assuming major posts in Prague, Leipzig, Budapest, and Hamburg. Finally, in 1897, he was offered the greatest plum: the directorship of the Vienna Court Opera, probably the most powerful musical position in all of Europe. To get the job he had accepted pro forma baptism in the Catholic faith. Mahler held the post for a decade, leaving it for prestigious and lucrative appointments in New York, first with the Metropolitan Opera and then with the New York Philharmonic.

As a conductor Mahler established a record of authoritarian perfectionism in which heavy demands were made not only on musicians but on audiences as well. He zealously reinstated the customary cuts in Wagner's long operas, for example, darkened the houselights at the opera to discourage socializing, and prohibited the entrance of latecomers. As a composer himself, Mahler identified with the composers whose works he conducted. Along with the other leading conductor of the day, the somewhat younger Arturo Toscanini, Mahler introduced a new standard of technically accomplished performances (Fig. 27-5).

> ***Mahler once professed his aim to write a symphony "so great that the whole world is actually reflected therein—so that one is, so to speak, only an instrument upon which the universe plays."***

Despite his long association with opera, Mahler never wrote one himself. (Early in his career he made a performing version of Carl Maria von Weber's unfinished *Die drei Pintos*, or The Three Pintos.) For his mature works Mahler concentrated exclusively on songs and symphonies, the respective Viennese legacies of Schubert and Beethoven. As a conductor, he was deeply involved with Wagnerian drama, which also influenced the music he composed. In a letter to music critic Max Marschalk, he declared that "we are now standing—I am sure of it—at the great crossroads that will soon separate forever the two diverging paths of symphonic and dramatic music." Mahler was casting his lot on the symphonic side. The statement may seem paradoxical, for, as we shall see, no composer ever used so many dramatic and otherwise vocally or textually oriented means toward symphonic

Figure 27-5 Gustav Mahler conducts a rehearsal for the premiere of his Symphony No. 8 in Munich in September 1910.

ends. Mahler himself acknowledged this apparent contradiction in the letter's very next sentence: "Wagner appropriated the means of expression of symphonic music, just as now in his turn the symphonist will be justified in helping himself to the new possibilities of expression opened to music by Wagner's efforts and in using them for his own means."[6] Bruckner had already been viewed as creating symphonies that were Wagnerian with respect to their orchestration and harmonic strategies. Mahler was the first to overlay the Beethovenian symphonic tradition with a Wagnerian dramaturgy and philosophical import. If Wagner can be said to have written symphonic dramas, Mahler was creating dramatic symphonies.

Mahler's Lieder

Mahler began confronting the symphonic challenge after writing a limited number of pieces in other genres, including chamber music, an ambitious cantata (*Das klagende Lied,* or The Song of Lamentation), and some incidental music for the theater. Otherwise, his first significant works were songs, pointing to the Schubertian side of his heritage. The Lied, especially in Vienna, had continued to flourish since the time of early Romantics. Brahms wrote many, and Mahler's classmate, Hugo Wolf (1860–1903), is remembered today almost exclusively for his extraordinary contribution to the genre.

Mahler's Lieder divide into two distinct phases. In the 1880s and '90s he concentrated on folk poetry, specifically texts drawn from *Des Knaben Wunderhorn* (The Youth's Magic Horn), the influential three-volume anthology of German folk lyrics assembled by the poets Achim von Arnim and Clemens Brentano and published between 1805 and 1808. Mahler set some two dozen *Wunderhorn* texts, most with full orchestral accompaniments, and, even more tellingly, incorporated some of the songs into three of his symphonies (Nos. 2–4). Despite using folk texts, the musical style of these settings tends to be enormously sophisticated; a supposedly simpler past is seen from a Modern, urban perspective. Celebrated composers before him had set *Wunderhorn* poems—Weber, Loewe, Mendelssohn, Schumann, and Brahms among them—but in Mahler's case the attraction to folklore was yet another symptom of the Modern condition. The heightened sense of distance from the land and from its inhabitants created the need for an authenticity that only the imagined folk could supply. Modernity's quickened sense of loss—of innocence, of goodness, of well-being and peace—demanded the undiluted restorative powers of actual folklore. This reflects the wistful irony of the thoroughly Modern, thoroughly urban spirit, conscious of its separation from the natural world and alienated by that consciousness from its own stressful environment.

Mahler's *Wunderhorn* songs thus communicate a deeply ironic double message, indicating at once the urgent need for a return to simple values and the utter impossibility, at this late date, of ever achieving simplicity. The seemingly naive sentiments wishfully manifested by his choice of texts are contradicted by the highly sophisticated music he created for them. No folk ever wrote a Mahler folk song. A nostalgic obsession ran like a thread through Mahler's work over the course of his career. Nostalgia is perhaps the most modern and complicated—or, in one word, the most Modernist—of all emotions. Mahler was unusually adept at evoking similar feelings in purely instrumental works as well. In his Sixth and Seventh symphonies (1903–04 and 1905–06), for example, he included among the percussion instruments in the orchestra cowbells, the bells placed around the necks of cattle to locate strays. He composed most of his symphonies during the summers, when he did not have conducting commitments, amid the natural beauty of the Austrian mountains; he devoted mornings to composing, afternoons to hiking in nature, and evenings to reading classic literature and philosophy.

After more than a dozen years of setting almost nothing but *Wunderhorn* texts (he used a poem by Nietzsche in his Third Symphony), Mahler turned in a completely different direction at the turn of the century as he began setting the poetry of Friedrich Rückert (1788–1866), most notably a song cycle of five texts called *Kindertotenlieder* (Songs on the Death of Children). Mahler's concentration on just two genres, song and symphony, ultimately led to synthesis in what may be considered his unnumbered next-to-last symphony, scored for voices and orchestra, called *Das Lied von der Erde* (The Song of the Earth, 1908–09), in which he turned to a third poetic source—ancient Chinese poetry.

From Symphonic Poem to First Symphony

In the nineteenth century, symphonies emerged as the proving ground of greatness, which helps explain why Brahms and Bruckner took so long to complete one. Berlioz, Liszt, Strauss, and others had tried to reinvent the genre entirely, writing not a traditional "Symphony No. 1" but, rather, symphonic poems and other kinds of large orchestral works based on extramusical programs. Mahler struggled with this imposing dual heritage. Although he wrote most of his First Symphony during the spring of 1888, when he was twenty-seven, the work went through various revealing incarnations before reaching the final state in which it is known today.

Anthology Vol 3-1
Full CD VI, 1
Concise CD III, 5

The genres of symphony and symphonic poem began to converge toward the end of the nineteenth century, so it is not surprising that Mahler initially conceived the piece as the latter. In November 1889, he premiered a "Symphonic Poem in Two Parts" in Budapest. The five-movement composition was greeted with some bewilderment and hostility, and he set about revising it, now calling it *Titan*. (The title most likely alludes to the once-famous novel by Jean Paul, Schumann's literary hero.) Still in two parts and five movements, each part and movement now had a specific title. Mahler provided some programmatic explanations, very minimal for the first and last movements, none at all for the second and third, and an extended comment about the innovative fourth one, a funeral march that had particularly puzzled the first audience:

TITAN: A Tone Poem in the Form of a Symphony

Part I. *From the Days of Youth: Flower-, Fruit-, and Thorn-pieces*

1. "Spring without End" (Introduction and *Allegro Comodo*).
   The introduction presents the awakening of nature from a long winter's sleep.

2. "Blumine" (*Andante*).

3. "Under Full Sail" (Scherzo).

Part II. *Commedia humana*

4. "Stranded!" (A Funeral March "in the manner of Callot").
   The following may serve as an explanation: The external stimulus for this piece of music came to the composer from the satirical picture, known to all Austrian children, "The Hunter's Funeral Procession," from an old book of children's fairy tales: The beasts of the forest accompany the dead hunter's coffin to the grave, with hares carrying a small banner, with a band of Bohemian musicians in front, and the procession escorted by music-making cats, toads, crows, etc., with stags, deer, foxes, and other four-legged and feathered creatures of the forest in comic postures. At this point the piece is conceived as the expression of a mood now ironically merry, now weirdly brooding, which is then suddenly followed by:

5. "Dall' Inferno" [From Hell to Paradise] (*Allegro furioso*).
   The sudden outburst of the despair of a deeply wounded heart.[7]

Mahler conducted the *Titan* twice, in Hamburg in 1893 and in Weimar the following year, but was still not satisfied with its shape. He decided to drop the second movement, a lilting *Andante* originally written as incidental music, and to call the work simply Symphony in D Major, no longer mentioning the two-part format, any of the movement titles, or the other extramusical clues devised earlier. A piece that had initially been unveiled as a Lisztian programmatic composition was now presented as a more traditional Brahmsian symphony, although one with a strong lyric element drawn from song.

Opinion was divided in 1900 when Mahler first conducted the piece with the Vienna Philharmonic. One critic reported that the work:

> was truly a bone of contention for the public as well as for the critics. This is not to say that the piece wasn't superficially a success: A large majority of the audience applauded, and Mahler was repeatedly called out. But there were also startled faces all around, and some hissing was heard. When leaving the concert hall, on the stairs and in the coatroom, one couldn't have heard more contradictory comments about the new work.

It seems that many were concerned about the suppression of all background information about the work: Mahler was "not well served by this veil of mystery . . . it was cruel of the composer to deprive his unprepared Philharmonic audience of not only the program book, but also any technical guide to this labyrinth of sound."[8]

Eduard Hanslick, still active after many years and battles, identified himself as a "sincere admirer" of Mahler the conductor. Although he did not wish to rush to judgment about this "strange symphony," he said he felt a responsibility to tell his readers that the work was for him that "kind of music that is not music." Hanslick, the great champion of absolute music, wanted to understand what was behind the work:

> Mahler's symphony would hardly have pleased us more *with* a program than without. But we cannot remain indifferent to knowing what an ingenious man like Mahler had in mind with each of these movements and how he would have explained the puzzling coherence. Thus we lack a guide to show the correct path in the darkness. What does it mean when a cataclysmic finale suddenly breaks forth, or when a funeral march on the old student canon "Frère Jacques" is interrupted by a section entitled "parody"? To be sure, the music itself would have neither gained nor lost anything with a program; still, the composer's intentions would have become clearer and the work therefore more comprehensible. Without such aid, we had to be satisfied with some witty details and stunningly brilliant orchestral technique.[9]

Like the frustrated Hanslick, many listeners were baffled by Mahler's juxtapositions of seriousness and parody, as well as by his merging of symphonic and song-like genres. One young critic, Max Graf, perceived that this was in fact the start of something fresh and believed that only a new "generation can feel the work's great emotional rapture, pleasure in intensely colored sound, and ecstasy of passion; only they can enjoy its parody and distortion of sacred emotion."[10] And indeed for this and other reasons the next generation of composers we will meet later in this chapter, those centered around Schoenberg, worshipped Mahler.

Maximalizing the Symphony

Mahler marked the mysterious introduction to the first movement of the First Symphony *Wie ein Naturlaut*—"Like a sound from nature." The very start is an astonishing pedal point of the sustained pitch A spread out over seven octaves. The music seems to grow organically from the interval of a falling fourth. As some critics remarked, this imitative sound of a cuckoo is "unnatural," since Mahler did not use the more accurate interval of the minor third as Beethoven had in his *Pastoral* Symphony. The two notes are in fact the opening of the main theme, derived from Mahler's own song *Ging heut' morgens übers Feld* (This Morning I Went out Over the Fields). It is the second in his early song cycle *Lieder eines fahrenden Gesellen* (Songs of a Wayfarer), for which Mahler wrote his own texts, though very much in the tradition of (and with some literal textual borrowings from) *Des Knaben Wunderhorn*.

Mahler used songs in the next two movements as well. One of his earliest, the dancelike *Hans und Grethe*, provides melodic material for the scherzo, which opens as a *Ländler*, an Austrian folk dance that was to become one of the composer's favorites. It is hardly surprising that Mahler felt the third movement required the most explanation. It begins with a solo double bass playing in an extremely high register yet another song. This one, however, is not one of Mahler's own but, rather, a minor-key version of the popular *Bruder Martin* (Brother Martin, better known in its French version as *Frère Jacques*; Ex. 27-1). Evoking a funeral march, it is first presented as a round, or canon, but is interrupted by what sounds like spirited dance music in a Bohemian style such as Mahler had heard played in village squares while growing up in the Czech lands. This is an early example of his mixing the serious with the popular. The movement contains another contrast when the fourth of the *Wayfarer* songs, *Die zwei blauen Augen* (The Two Blue Eyes) appears as an ethereal interlude.

Example 27-1 Mahler, Symphony No. 1, opening

The finale moves from fiery defiance to reconciliation and culmination, from Hell to Paradise, as Mahler's original title had it, beginning with a terrible dissonance harkening back to the "terror fanfare" of Beethoven's Ninth Symphony. Natalie Bauer-Lechner, a confidant of the composer, informed a Viennese critic that in the end the hero of the work becomes the master of his fate: "Only when he has triumphed over death, and when all the glorious memories of youth have returned with themes from the first movement, does he get the upper hand: and there is a great victorious chorale!"[11] We thus encounter the familiar Beethovenian trajectory yet again, with another heroic Titan emerging victorious over struggle and death.

"Down with Programs!"

Even before the premiere of the original version of his First Symphony, Mahler had begun composing another symphonic poem, which he for a time called *Totenfeier* (Funeral Rites). He later said that in this massive funeral march "it is the hero of my D Major Symphony whom I bear to the grave there, and whose life I catch up, from a higher standpoint, in a pure mirror."[12] This symphonic poem again turned into a symphony, his Second, known as the "Resurrection," a monumental piece written for the largest orchestra ever used up to that time and capped off by a magnificent chorus that is reserved until the end of the final movement, an all-out attempt to surpass the finale of Beethoven's Ninth in every dimension: length, sonorous magnitude, and philosophical depth. While the First Symphony had used unsung songs, the five-movement Second makes two references to the *Wunderhorn* collection, one unsung and one using voices. The purely instrumental third movement is based on *Des Antonius von Padua Fischpredigt* (St. Anthony of Padua's Sermon to the Fishes). Between this and the choral finale, Mahler interpolated in its entirety a *Wunderhorn* song entitled *Urlicht* (Primordial Light), a setting for alto solo that expresses a child's faith in salvation.

Mahler sometimes acknowledged programmatic components in his early symphonies, and sometimes he denied them. Sometimes he admitted that he needed a verbal or poetic hook on which to hang the music of a large-scale composition; at other times he maintained that whatever programmatic content he might agree to describe would only be an accommodation to the duller members of the audience. In a kinder vein he wrote to the critic Marschalk: "When my style still seems strange and new, the listener should get some roadmaps and milestones on the journey—or rather, a map of the stars, that he may comprehend the night sky with its glowing worlds."[13]

The letters Mahler wrote while composing his six-movement Third Symphony (1895–96), his longest work, suggest that titles and extramusical ideas could help him conceive and execute vast projects. His Fourth Symphony (1899–1900), his shortest at about fifty minutes and requiring a soprano soloist in addition to a more modest orchestra, was by Mahlerian standards a miniature that brought the series of *Wunderhorn* symphonies to a close. He was increasingly reluctant to say much about his music, perhaps to distance himself in part from the music of his friend and rival Richard Strauss. He declared in 1900: "Down with programs, which are always misinterpreted! The composer should stop giving the public his own ideas about his work; he should no longer force listeners to read during the performance and he should refrain from filling them with preconceptions."[14]

"Down with programs, which are always misinterpreted!" —Gustav Mahler

If we invoke again the convenient three styles periods most familiar to us from Beethoven, then we can say that Mahler at the turn of the century began his middle period. At the age of forty both his personal life and his compositional career entered a new stage. His next three symphonies (1901–05) did not include voice or chorus, hence no texts. They were not given overt programs, although at one performance the Sixth bore the title "Tragic." He started work on the Fifth Symphony during the summer of 1901, after a year marked by a near-death experience in February (internal hemorrhaging) and by his resignation as principal conductor of the Vienna Philharmonic. (He remained director of the Vienna Court Opera.) He moved into a newly built house at an idyllic resort in the Carinthian Mountains. Upon his return to

Anthology Vol 3-2
Full CD VI, 2

Vienna for the new season, he soon met, and a few months later married, the beautiful Alma Schindler (1879–1964; Fig. 27-6), who was half his age. By the time he could return to finish the Fifth the following summer, they were expecting their first child.

Figure 27-6 Alma Mahler (née Schindler).

It was while writing the Fifth Symphony that Mahler composed his two last *Wunderhorn* songs and moved on to setting the poetry of Rückert. Although he no longer overtly included songs in his symphonies, subtle allusions remained. The Rückert song *Ich bin der Welt abhanden gekommen* (I Am Lost to the World) projects a very similar mood through very similar musical means as the *Adagietto* movement for strings and harp in his Fifth Symphony. This haunting symphonic movement is today the most famous music Mahler ever wrote, in large part because of its evocative use later in ballets and films, most notably Luchino Visconti's 1971 cinematic adaptation of Thomas Mann's novella *Death in Venice.* A deathly atmosphere is fostered by the slow tempo in which the movement came to be performed in the later twentieth century, sometimes nearly twice as slow as Mahler himself performed it. (His performances checked in at less than eight minutes, roughly the same as his conducting protégés Willem Mengelberg and Bruno Walter).

Mahler apparently wrote the *Adagietto* not as a funereal lament but, rather, as an amorous offering to Alma. Mengelberg noted in his score: "This *Adagietto* was Gustav Mahler's declaration of love for Alma! Instead of a letter, he sent her this in manuscript form; no other words accompanied it. She understood and wrote to him: He should come!!! (both of them told me this!)."[15] The music resonates with attributes both of a love song and of a death lament, suggesting once again that the two forces are intrinsically linked. Freud, with whom Mahler would have a famous meeting in 1910 concerning his marital problems with Alma, explored the fundamental drives of love and death, which find such remarkable expression in this movement. In addition to suggesting his own Rückert song, Mahler seems to allude to Wagner's *Tristan und Isolde,* that most sensual of operas, which so effectively merges the two drives in the so-called *Liebestod,* or Love Death.

Mahler conducted the first performance of the Fifth in Cologne on 18 October 1904. Afterward Richard Strauss wrote to him: "Your Fifth Symphony again gave me great pleasure in the full rehearsal, a pleasure only slightly dimmed by the little *Adagietto.* But as this is what pleased the audience the most, you are getting what you deserve."[16] Mahler's most beloved movement has pleased audiences from the start, even if it did not engage Strauss so. Eventually it came to represent Mahler as a maximally emotional composer of fatal longing.

The Late Works

"Vorbei!" (It's over!), the painter Gustav Klimt was heard to mutter as a large group of prominent cultural figures saw Mahler and his wife off from Vienna's West Train Station in December 1907. Mahler's final years were spent in New York, although he returned to Austria to compose in the summers. He won his greatest popular success in 1910 with the premiere of the Eighth Symphony (1906), known as the "Symphony of a Thousand." The performance, in Munich's New Music Festival Hall, employed 858 singers and 171 instrumentalists, for a total of 1,029 performers (plus Mahler conducting). An oratorio in all but name, scored for a full complement of vocal soloists, plus chorus and orchestra, it contains no purely instrumental music at all. Rather, its two movements consist respectively of a setting of the Latin hymn

Veni, creator spiritus and of the mystical closing pages of the second part of Goethe's *Faust*. As Mahler told his biographer Specht:

> Its form is something altogether new. Can you imagine a symphony that is sung throughout, from beginning to end? So far I have employed words and the human voice merely to suggest, to sum up, to establish a mood. . . . Here the voice is also an instrument. The whole first movement is strictly symphonic in form yet completely sung. It is really strange that nobody has ever thought of this before; it is simplicity itself, *The True Symphony*, in which the most beautiful instrument of all is led to its calling. Yet it is used not only as sound, because the voice is the bearer of poetic thoughts.[17]

By the time the grandiose Eighth Symphony premiered, Mahler had already finished the more intimate *Das Lied von der Erde*, a six-movement work subtitled "Symphony for Tenor and Alto Voice and Orchestra." Although he decided against assigning it the haunted Beethovenian number nine, *Das Lied* is clearly symphonic while at the same time continuing the tradition of the orchestral song cycle that Mahler had cultivated earlier. For *Das Lied von der Erde* he turned to a volume of eighth-century Chinese verse paraphrased by Hans Bethge (1876–1946) into German from various earlier translations. Mahler selected poems from those collected in Bethge's *Der chinesische Flöte* (The Chinese Flute, 1907) and edited, cut, and expanded them to shape usable texts for six songs of varying lengths and moods. He was attracted by ones touching on the themes of the brevity of life, drunkenness, youth, loneliness, beauty, spiritual rebirth, and ultimately bidding farewell to the world that will go on living forever. To match the exoticism of the text selection, Mahler infused his score with a quasi-Asian flavor through the use of the pentatonic and whole-tone scales, instruments like the tam-tam, and occasionally a vocal style reminiscent of Chinese opera. It is unclear exactly how much, if any, he knew of authentic Chinese music, although he may have heard some early cylinder recordings. By this time he had also conducted Puccini's *Madama Butterfly*, which is likewise Orientalist.

Der Abschied (The Farewell), the final movement of *Das Lied*, is nearly as long as the other five combined and offers a late example of Mahler as a philosophical composer. In this movement of symphonic proportions, he shows how far he had come in combining the modest Lied and the monumental symphony, for it is neither song nor symphony but both at once. It transcends formal conventions as it explores the metaphysics of transcendence, ending with an ethereal ninefold repetition of the word *ewig* (forever).

Das Lied von der Erde, the Ninth Symphony (1909), and the unfinished Tenth Symphony are often considered a sort of final "farewell" trilogy—although Mahler turned just forty-seven when he started writing them. Death haunted Mahler's life and his music, most notably in the funeral marches found in so many of his songs and symphonies. But as one commentator has observed, while his earlier works have "images" of death, the late ones "taste" of it.[18] The Ninth Symphony is a purely instrumental work that ends with an extraordinary slow movement. The final page offers the least rousing finale of any symphony but also one of the most moving. Mahler provides one last example of unsung song and self-allusion when the first violins play a melody from the fourth song of *Kindertotenlieder*. The tune originally accompanied the words "Der Tag ist schön auf jenen Höh'n" (The day is beautiful on those heights), telling of parents' vision of their dead children at play on a distant mountain. The music becomes ever softer and stiller, almost more silence than sound, until the listener may remember a heartbeat-like rhythm that had opened the symphony but now recognize it as consciousness of one's own heartbeat. In this extraordinary way Mahler implicates his listeners into the work, which ends *ersterbend*—"dying away."

The summer of 1910 was difficult for Mahler, burdened as he was by preparations for the premiere of the Symphony No. 8, by learning of his wife's infidelity with the young architect Walter Gropius, and by a trip to Holland to consult Freud about the situation. He worked on his Tenth Symphony, a projected five-movement work of which the first was nearest completion when he died. (Other composers and scholars subsequently tried to finish the later movements based on sketches.) Soon after Mahler's death the following May at age fifty, Schoenberg dedicated his important treatise on harmony "to the memory of Gustav Mahler . . . this martyr, this saint." He later came to represent another figure as well: a prophet. Some advocates argued that Mahler's music not only prophesied his own life but also foretold important developments in music and even in twentieth-century world history.[19]

Figure 27-7 Portrait of Richard Strauss.

Richard Strauss

Hanslick's perplexed response to Mahler's First Symphony was consistent with the critic's general dislike of program music. We have earlier seen Hanslick despairing that a composer he greatly admired, Antonín Dvořák, was beginning to write symphonic poems that he thought sounded like Richard Strauss (Fig. 27-7). Strauss was indeed taking Wagner's style to its maximum and was viewed, even more than Mahler, as the radical Modernist of the time. His orchestral works broke new sonic barriers, and his operas scandalized audiences, at least where they were allowed to be performed at all.

Strauss began his long compositional career as many do: by writing relatively conventional music in the style of older masters. He was born in 1864 in Munich and raised in a musical household (not connected in any way to the Strauss dynasty of Viennese waltz wizards). His father played principal French horn in the Munich Court Orchestra, and Strauss's early compositions were Brahmsian, anchored in traditional forms according to his father's conservative tastes. Then came his "conversion," as Strauss would later recall. The musician Alexander Ritter (1833–96), thirty-one years older than Strauss and associated with both Liszt and Wagner (he was married to Wagner's niece), became his artistic mentor. Strauss turned to the Lisztian domain of the symphonic poem, which he rechristened *Tondichtung*, or tone poem. He also began to develop, as Mahler was doing at the same time, a prominent conducting career.

After writing two conventional symphonies before the age of twenty, Strauss cautiously moved in the direction of program music with a four-movement "symphonic fantasy" called *Aus Italien* (Out of Italy, 1886). His first tone poem was *Macbeth* (1888), inspired by a production of Shakespeare's play he attended. After its premiere Strauss remarked: "There were a few people present who noticed that behind the horrible dissonances there lay something more than dissonance for its own sake—namely, an idea."[20] Strauss's interest in ideas and philosophy was later reflected in *Also sprach Zarathustra* (Thus spake Zarathustra), after Nietzsche, an impressive contribution to the heady literature of *Weltanschauungsmusik*.

Like his beloved Mozart, Strauss succeeded with both instrumental and dramatic music. In addition to Lieder, which he produced abundantly throughout his career, Strauss's primary genres were the largest ones: symphonic poems and operas. Following *Macbeth* came *Don Juan* (1888–89), *Tod und Verklärung* (Death and Transfiguration, 1888–89), *Till Eulenspiegels lustige Streiche* (Till Eulenspiegel's Merry Pranks, 1894–95), *Also sprach Zarathustra* (1896), *Don Quixote* (1897), *Ein*

Heldenleben (A Hero's Life, 1897–98), and two large tone poems labeled as symphonies: *Symphonia domestica* (Domestic Symphony, 1902–03) and *Eine Alpensinfonie* (An Alpine Symphony, 1911–15).

Maximalizing Opera

After the failure of his Wagnerian first opera, *Guntram* (1892–93), and the premiere of the more successful *Feuersnot* (Fire-Famine, 1900–01), Strauss scored a tremendous success in 1905 with *Salome*. This one-act opera sets a prose play from 1893 by Oscar Wilde (1854–1900), the Irish writer who in 1895 was sentenced to two years in prison with hard labor for acts of "gross indecency" related to his homosexuality. *Salomé*, which Wilde originally wrote in French, was one of many representations of the celebrated dancing princess in various artistic media that cropped up at the fin de siècle (Fig. 27-8). The play was already a benchmark of decadence, having been banned in London but wildly successful in Berlin, where Strauss saw a performance in 1903. Strauss had already been tinkering with an adaptation but immediately recognized that with its gripping theatrical power all the play needed was to be translated into German and discretely pruned to be set to music exactly as it stood.

The basis of this supremely sensual play, ironically enough, was the Bible. Two of the Gospels contain the story of King Herod and John the Baptist, which Wilde freely adapted. In the opera the king perversely desires that Salome, his beautiful stepdaughter, dance for him. She shuns the advances of her many suitors, desperate men who are shown committing suicide as a result. She cares for no one—that is, until she spies the emaciated John the Baptist in his prison cell and finds herself strangely attracted to him. She asks for a kiss and is angrily rebuffed. As recompense for her "Dance of the Seven Veils" (that is, her striptease) before Herod, she demands the prophet's head on a silver platter. She dances orgiastically with the bloody severed head and, delirious with desire, kisses it on the mouth. Scandalized by her necrophilia, Herod has her put to death straightaway.

Figure 27-8 Aubrey Beardsley, *The Climax*, illustration for Oscar Wilde's *Salomé* (1893).

This is strong stuff, to say the least, and points once again to the Freudian connection between desire and death, a hallmark of the slippery concept of "**decadence**." In the mid-1880s the term was introduced into discussions of art and life. The interrelationship was notably explored in the novel *À rebours* (Against Nature, 1884) by the French writer Joris-Karl Huysmans (1848–1907), whose sickly aristocratic artist-hero Duc Jean Des Esseintes was the very embodiment of rarefied, artificial, esoteric, exacting taste. Fatally jaded and misanthropic, Des Esseintes is repelled by anything natural and healthy while fatally drawn to risky behavior of all kinds—substance abuse (as we would call it now); sexual encounters ("unnatural loves and perverse pleasures," in Huysmans's words); and defiance of conventional, bourgeois hygiene. Decadence was opened up, so to speak, for the tourist trade. At the same time, sex and sensuality were also being explored in the visual arts in the highly decorative approach called *Jugendstil*, or "youth style."

For Freud, sex could be "polymorphously perverse"—unrestricted to those sexual acts that straightforwardly promote procreation. If we try to extend this concept to music, we could think of chords that do not have to connect in ways that straightforwardly produce a functional cadence, so long as their succession gives pleasure. An acceptance of perversity was another component of decadence. We might approach an understanding of decadence—or at least perversity—by imagining a child at play with building blocks. For a while, if intelligent and interested, or at least well behaved, the child will follow the instruction book and connect the pieces structurally, producing normal buildings and bridges. Later, however, in order to maintain interest, the child may start connecting the pieces with one another in more creative ways, fashioning weird shapes that have no practical application but give pleasure (to the maker, at least). And so it was with harmonic connections. Where the instruction books continued to prescribe the circle of fifths, Modernist composers happily experimented with semitones and other cycles of intervals, producing progressions that evoked sensations, as Strauss proudly put it, of "iridescent silk," or as his conservative father complained, of having "your trousers full of crawling June bugs."[21]

Modernist composers happily experimented with semitones and other cycles of intervals, producing progressions that evoked sensations, as Strauss proudly put it, of "iridescent silk."

Strauss's *Salome* prompted even greater scandals than Wilde's original play, both for the obvious ways in which it intensified the challenge to conventional morality and for the novelty of its musical procedures. The uncannily effective *Salome,* like *Tristan,* was disquieting, but, unlike *Tristan,* it depicted a passion no one in the audience could admit to identifying with. Its glamour was magnified by censorship: Mahler sought permission to give the premiere in Vienna but was refused in the name of public morals. The premiere took place in Dresden on 9 December 1905 with Strauss conducting.

Anthology Vol 3-3
Full CD VI, 3

Some of the most extreme music in *Salome* comes in the last scene, in which the title character gets her man—or at any rate his head—and gets to consummate her "unnatural love" and reap "perverse pleasure" to the full. The music reaches its own maximum in musical perversity in the illicit but pleasurable connections in the last half-dozen pages of the score. This is Salome's own decadent *Liebestod.* The music consists almost entirely of material drawn from the "Dance of the Seven Veils," presented in a maximalistically distorted form, even as the Dance had itself been an Orientalist distortion of a few significant leitmotifs heard throughout the opera. The harmonic background to the oboe's "snake charmer" tune at the beginning of the dance, for example, recalls an A-minor/F-minor oscillation established earlier in the opera to be associated with thoughts of sex and death (Ex. 27-2).

Example 27-2 Richard Strauss, *Salome,* Salome's dance, opening

After Salome's final line in the opera ("I've kissed you on your mouth"), as she stands in a passion-trance with the bloody head pressed to her lips, the orchestra reaches an earsplitting dynamic peak immediately before the unmistakable resolution to C♯ major (Ex. 27-3). Strauss's mixed harmony here is a maximalized cadence that achieves the appropriate syntactical purpose—and does so with greater power than ever before. In effect it provides the opera with its orgiastic Tristanesque (or Isoldesque) concluding cadence, after which the quick killing of Salome is a tonally insignificant, though dramatically shattering, appendage. Strauss's ending does full justice to the difference between the spiritual sublimation of Isolde's sex drive and the kinky gratification of Salome's.

Example 27-3 Richard Strauss, *Salome*

Strauss continued his decadent explorations in his next opera, *Elektra* (1908), whose story had been dramatized by all three of the great ancient Greek tragedians—Aeschylus, Sophocles, and Euripides. The version that Strauss set was "rewritten for the German stage" by Hugo von Hofmannsthal (1874–1929), a distinguished poet and playwright who went on to create five more operas with the composer. This hugely cultured and aristocratic gentleman undoubtedly played a part in eventually moderating Strauss's Modernist zeal. The grisly *Elektra*, at the very beginning of their collaboration, was his maximalist extreme.

The destructive power that the strong title characters in *Salome* and *Elektra* wield over the men in their lives no doubt reflected aspects of the contemporaneous social emancipation of women. Yet these decadent operas end with the violent deaths of their title characters, deaths that in both cases were not in the originals but, rather, just in their fin-de-siècle adaptations. In the Bible we do not learn of Salome's fate. It was Wilde who has Herod turn to his wife and say, "She is a monster, that daughter of yours, a monster!" before ordering his soldiers to "Kill that woman!" In Greek mythology, the character of Electra marries and lives on. It was Hofmannsthal who killed her off. It is hard not to see these alterations as Modern male vengeance on the threatening figure of the increasingly empowered Modern woman.

By the time of Strauss's next collaboration with Hofmannsthal, *Der Rosenkavalier* (The Knight of the Rose, 1911), a comedy set in eighteenth-century Vienna, his music had become far more overtly traditional, if no less brilliant. This was the year Mahler died. Strauss's final tone poem, *An Alpine Symphony*, was conceived in part as an homage to his friend. Had Strauss died around the same time, his reputation and legacy would be viewed very differently than it is today. But he lived on, writing music that, as we shall see, did not seem to fit its time during the 1920s, '30s, and

'40s, even if it prefigured a more distant musical future near the end of the century. The radical Modernist mantle was being assumed by a new generation.

Figure 27-9 Arnold Schoenberg, self-portrait.

Arnold Schoenberg

Leading this next generation of German-Austrian composers was Arnold Schoenberg (Fig. 27-9). Perhaps no other composer, Wagner excepted, has so strongly asserted himself, his ideas, and his works into music history. Schoenberg's whole career was fraught with ironies, beginning with the fact that he who became one of the outstanding music theorists and composition teachers was himself largely self-taught. The Vienna-born composer initially had little musical instruction beyond elementary violin lessons. He later taught himself cello and played in amateur quartets and orchestras, but he never became accomplished on any instrument. He got some informal instruction in harmony from a playing partner; but when it came to composing in traditional forms, he had to look up information in an encyclopedia. In 1895, working as a bank clerk at the time, Schoenberg showed some of his early efforts to Alexander von Zemlinsky (1871–1942), a young conservatory-trained composer who was conducting an amateur orchestra in which Schoenberg played. Zemlinsky, who later became Schoenberg's brother-in-law, gave his friend a few lessons in counterpoint and some general advice. Schoenberg earned his living over the next several years by conducting amateur choruses, orchestrating operettas, and composing in his spare time.

Although he is typically viewed as one of the most disruptive composers in the history of Western music, few matched Schoenberg's intense awareness of that history or his technical mastery of its traditions. These are not unrelated issues—he knew the musical past well and came to feel that his innovations would secure the future of German music. His desire for both continuity and change places his music squarely within the gloried Viennese heritage, one that he tried to expand, challenge, and pass on to his own students, most notably Alban Berg (1885–1935) and Anton Webern (1883–1945). This trinity is sometimes referred to as the "**Second Viennese School**" by those who seek to put them in a direct line of succession from a fictional "First Viennese School" of Haydn, Mozart, and Beethoven. The term is unfortunate, partly because it positions Berg and Webern as perpetual pupils and also because it obscures competing currents in the vibrant musical life at the time. There were other kinds of German Modernism, such as found in the operas of Franz Schreker (1878–1934), as well as in the music of imaginative but more conservative figures such as Max Reger (1873–1916), Hans Pfitzner (1869–1949), and Franz Schmidt (1874–1939); Vienna was also enjoying a so-called Silver Age of operetta, represented by Franz Lehár (1870–1948), Emmerich Kálmán (1882–1953), and others.

December 1899, the date Schoenberg placed on the manuscript of his first masterpiece, *Verklärte Nacht* (Transfigured Night), Op. 4, is neatly symbolic of the end of the nineteenth century. *Verklärte Nacht* is a tone poem scored, unusually, for string sextet rather than for orchestra, as if Schoenberg were deliberately casting himself as heir to both the programmatic aesthetic associated with the New Germans and the chamber-music tradition of Brahms. Its program was inspired by Richard Dehmel (1863–1920), one of Germany's leading poets and a prominent decadent. As Schoenberg later wrote to Dehmel: "Your poems have had a decisive influence on my development as a composer. They were what first made me try to find a new tone in the lyrical mood. Or rather, I found it even without looking, simply by reflecting in music what your poems stirred up in me."[22] Dehmel's poetry is sensual and often erotic, resonant with Freud's psychoanalytic theories, which were first being articulated around this time. The narrative in *Verklärte Nacht* tells of a magnanimous man who forgives his lover for having become pregnant by someone else. In Schoenberg's musical interpretation, the man's promise to accept the child as his own transforms the anguished mood of the D-minor beginning of the piece into a radiant D major that gleams at the end.

Schoenberg courted controversy throughout his life, and even the lushly sensual, maximally Romantic *Verklärte Nacht* had a rocky Viennese premiere in March 1902. The composer, who was in Berlin at the time, later reported that the concert "ended in a riot and in actual fights."[23] The conservative Wiener Tonkünstlerverein (Vienna Musicians' Society) objected over what its jury considered to be a compositional error: a chord that might arguably be analyzed as a dominant-ninth chord in "fourth inversion" (ninth in the bass) but that is better justified as the product of voice leading by semitones in all voices in contrary motion (Ex. 27-4). That, at least, was what Schoenberg claimed, in an essay he wrote almost half a century later (from which the example, asterisk and all, is taken), was the reason the score was rejected.[24] Perhaps more disturbing was that Schoenberg appeared to be inserting programmatic inspirations into the realm of chamber music, which had for the most part retained its purity, as in Brahms's own two string sextets. On top of it all was the shocking subject matter of the poem.

Example 27-4 Offending passage from Arnold Schoenberg, *Verklärte Nacht*

Whatever the reason for it, the early experience of rejection seems to have equipped Schoenberg with the resentment and the sense of alienation that some Modernist giants needed. From then on, in a transformation that dated from the turn of the century, it became a point of pride for him and many of his followers to be pushing the envelope of stylistic and technical innovation. Some four decades later, by then famous and infamous, Schoenberg looked back in an essay called "How One Becomes Lonely":

> My *Verklärte Nacht*, written before the beginning of this century—hence a work of my first period, has made me a kind of reputation. From it I can enjoy (even among my opponents) some appreciation which the works of my later periods would not have procured for me so soon. This work has been heard, especially in its later version for [string] orchestra, a great many times. But certainly nobody has heard it as often as I have heard this complaint: "If only he had continued to compose in this style!"

To this charge Schoenberg gave a response he said surprised people: "I have not discontinued composing in the same style and in the same way as at the very beginning. The difference is only that I do it better now than before; it is more concentrated, more mature."[25] For audiences often frightened by his later music, the extravagant lyricism, broad melodies, and luxurious harmonies of *Verklärte Nacht* hardly seemed like the work of the same composer. Yet from a compositional perspective, many of Schoenberg's concerns, as we shall see, remained remarkably consistent throughout his long career.

A New Synthesis

One of the ways Schoenberg went about achieving his startling innovations was by merging what had previously been considered opposing musical ideals. When he was born, in the mid-1870s, German musicians generally allied themselves either with the Wagnerian camp or with the Brahmsian one. By the end of the century, Schoenberg, being of a younger generation, felt little need to choose. He emphasized the precedents for his stylistic departures both in Wagner's "roving harmony" and in what he called Brahms's technique of "developing variation." Of the two, the Wagner connection was the one more easily perceived by his contemporaries. But Schoenberg also prized his descent from Brahms, whose techniques of working out motives were the source of his own idea of a ***Grundgestalt***, or "basic shape": a motivic complex that could serve as a source for everything that happened in a composition. All melodic shapes, all harmonies, all contrapuntal textures were to be derived from it by the composer—and therefore, at least theoretically, their relationships could be uncovered through analysis.

In a lecture called "Brahms the Progressive," Schoenberg argued that Brahms was in fact not quite so conservative as commonly thought, especially in the way that he manipulated small groups of notes, constantly developing and varying them into new combinations (hence the name of the technique: "developing variation"). This is why Schoenberg could in good faith say he was doing much the same thing in *Verklärte Nacht* in 1899 as he was more than thirty years later: He was manipulating pitches by having them develop into something new but related. To label Brahms a progressive was nothing if not contrary, since the older composer had himself opposed the idea of musical progress that was proclaimed in his own day by the Hegelian-minded New German School. Schoenberg clearly had an ulterior motive: In his eyes, what was progressive about Brahms was the fact that he was a sort of Schoenberg-in-waiting, whose motivic webs foreshadowed his own in density.

Schoenberg's early pieces were the subject of an article Berg later wrote called "Why Is Schoenberg's Music So Difficult to Understand?" (1924), which explores the unprecedented level of motivic saturation in Schoenberg's music through an analysis of the First String Quartet, Op. 7 (1905). Berg claimed that there was "hardly any" material in the piece, even in its accompanimental figuration, that cannot be traced to its germinating motifs. Having quoted the first ten measures, Berg noted that he had in fact supplied the reader with the whole forty-five-minute quartet in a nutshell. The music was more difficult to understand than any other contemporary music because comprehending its rigorous motivic complexities required more cognitive work from the listener.[26]

Schoenberg wrote relatively little orchestral music during this early period of his career, concentrating rather on songs, chamber pieces, and keyboard pieces.

He may have been reluctant to produce works that would have to compete with those of Mahler and Strauss, although he did write a large symphonic poem *Pelleas und Melisande* (1902–03). His First Chamber Symphony, Op. 9 (1905–06), is scored for an extraordinary combination of fifteen solo instruments (five strings, eight woodwinds, and two horns). In this piece Schoenberg continued to explore a structural plan that he had already used in his First String Quartet, which overlays a continuous multimovement format onto sonata form. The Chamber Symphony thus consists of an uninterrupted series of five movements (rather than the usual four) that can be thought of as exposition, scherzo, development, slow movement, and recapitulation/finale, an idea that goes back to Schubert's "Wanderer" Fantasy and to Liszt's symphonic poems.

The largest early work is *Gurrelieder* (Songs of Gurre) for five solo voices, a speaker, three male choruses, a double (eight-part) mixed chorus, and a large orchestra. Based on poems by the Danish writer Jens Peter Jacobsen (1847–85), *Gurrelieder* was composed over the course of a single year beginning in March 1900, but not orchestrated at the time. Strauss was impressed with what he saw, and so he helped secure funding to support the younger man while he scored the colossal piece. Schoenberg returned to the project in 1910 and completed it the next year. The maximalist epic, in the tradition of Mahler's Eighth, was enormously successful when it premiered on 23 February 1913 in Vienna conducted by Franz Schreker.

Expression Becomes an "ism"

By the time *Gurrelieder* premiered, Schoenberg had long since stopped composing such large pieces in a lush Romantic idiom. A couple of years earlier he had written a letter to a close friend, the Russian painter Wassily Kandinsky (1866–1944; Fig. 27-10), that gives a sense of his new preoccupations: "One must express *oneself!* Express oneself *directly!* Not one's taste or one's upbringing, or one's intelligence, knowledge, or skill. Not all these *acquired* characteristics, but that which is *inborn, instinctive*."[27] As Schoenberg came to see it, the only things that his early works displayed were taste, upbringing, intelligence, knowledge, and skill. "**Expressionism**," a term that over the course of a decade or so became fairly common to describe contemporary German art, is now part of the standard art historian's vocabulary, and Schoenberg himself eventually accepted it.

"Art belongs to the unconscious!" Schoenberg was using, as we would now say, a "buzzword."

We can get a good idea of the shift from late Romanticism to Expressionism by looking at the sentence that immediately precedes Schoenberg's outburst to Kandinsky: "Art belongs to the *unconscious*!"[28] Schoenberg was using, as we would now say, a "buzzword." Expressionism, especially as preached and practiced in Vienna, cannot be fully understood apart from Freud's psychoanalytic movement, which sprang up at the same time and in the same place. Both movements had the same compelling if paradoxical aim: to explore the human unconscious, in the one case through scientific inquiry, in the other through art.

But how can one do that? According to Freud, the "inner occurrences" that condition human subjectivity, and that provide the most authentic subject matter for Expressionist art, are governed by emotions, drives, and wishes of which the human subject is unaware, often because they are socially unacceptable and therefore "repressed" from consciousness. As Schoenberg put it in a program note accompanying his Five Orchestral Pieces, Op. 16 (1909), "the music seeks to express all that swells in us subconsciously like a dream."[29] Even before one asks how one is to make such subject matter intelligible or communicable—and one might shudder at the thought of the nightmares such art could communicate—one has to ask how such a subject matter can even be apprehended by the artist's own conscious creative faculty. How can one express what is unknowable? The artist's task is to portray something—or, rather, the results of something—that is hidden not only from others but even from the one doing the portraying. Some access to repressed thoughts and feelings, Freud argued, was possible through dreams, through "free association" (saying the first thing that comes to mind upon prompting), through slips of the tongue ("Freudian slips"), as well as through jokes and art. Modern Viennese culture offered fascinating chances to test these theories.

Figure 27-10 Wassily Kandinsky, *Composition VI*, 1911.

The earlier Romantic puzzle of absolute music—music that describes the indescribable and expresses the inexpressible—was thus updated for the psychoanalytic age. To realize the demands of Expressionism without compromise would entail the old philosophers' riddle of a "private language," a manifest contradiction in terms. Or was it? Could one, truly recording one's "inner occurrences" and doing full justice to their uniqueness, utter anything but nonsense? Schoenberg's work posed the cursed question of intelligibility with particular urgency. Incomprehensibility was always an accusation against Modernist art; in the wake of Schoenberg it achieved the dimensions of a crisis.

"Emancipation of Dissonance"

Later in his life Schoenberg liked to say that the musical explorations that made him notorious were thrust on him against his will. Generalizing from what he perceived to be his own experience, he asserted that "Art is born of 'I must,' not 'I can'."[30] A period of severe psychological disturbance immediately preceded the radical change in Schoenberg's music style. In 1906–07 he suffered a major depression, one of several such periods that made his creative output sporadic. Schoenberg's wife deserted him and their two small children for a lover, the Expressionist painter Richard Gerstl (1883–1908), who committed suicide when she returned to her family. This turbulent episode has often been singled out as the catalyst for Schoenberg's radical new idiom. The extremity and the sheer violence of the style that emerged after these personal upheavals may well have been conditioned by the extremity and violence of the emotions for which Schoenberg now sought a creative outlet. He did so not only in music, where he was a professional, but also in painting, where he was a talented amateur (cf. Fig. 27-9).

Since Schoenberg was a teacher and theorist as well as a composer, we have an unusual opportunity to compare his theory with his practice. The most important of his theoretical writings was *Harmonielehre* (Theory of Harmony), which appeared in 1911 with a dedication to the memory of "Holy Mahler." The lengthy volume was largely a distillation of nearly a decade of teaching experience. Like any other harmony textbook, it begins with elementary instruction on major and minor scales, triads and inversions, progressions, modulations, and the like. Its last section, however, dealt with what was at the time avowedly experimental material, starting with a brief chapter, "Consonance and Dissonance," in which that most categorical harmonic distinction is boldly relativized.

Schoenberg's discussion here was actually a veiled description of his own recent music, cast artfully as a speculation on what the future may have in store. The difference between consonance and dissonance, he asserts, is only a matter of degree, not of kind. Dissonances, Schoenberg proposes, are simply "the more remote consonances." It is a first step toward liberating musical thinking from conventions of taste, upbringing, intelligence, knowledge, and skill that he had railed against to Kandinsky the same year that *Harmonielehre* was published.

Schoenberg called the logical conclusion toward which such thinking aimed the "emancipation of dissonance."[31] He came to believe that the composer was no longer obliged to resolve complex harmonies into simpler ones. When chords are no longer dependent for their understanding and use on their relationship to functional harmonies (i.e., harmonies with roots), the common practice called *tonality* that had been in place for nearly 300 years becomes moot. One of the closing chapters in *Harmonielehre*—significantly, the first in which Schoenberg cites his own works as examples—bears the title "On Fluctuating and Suspended Tonality." Fluctuating tonality involves keys that are suggested but never fully established cadentially, and therefore inherently unstable. The prime example, unsurprisingly, is the Prelude to Wagner's *Tristan und Isolde*. Suspended tonality is a situation in which no key at all is forecast. Rather, what holds such music together is the coherence of the thematic material.[32]

Atonality: "The Air of Another Planet"

These are the conditions under which music is "**atonal**," a word that became standard terminology despite Schoenberg's objections.[33] He opposed the term because its connotations were purely negative: To say what something is not is a far cry from saying what it is. He preferred to call his music "**pantonal**," suggesting a single transcendent, all-encompassing tonality, but the word failed to catch on. An unfortunate consequence has been the creation of a spurious antonym—"tonal" music—that has arisen in the wake of the polemics surrounding "atonal" music. The term never existed before because it never had any reason to exist.

The question of tonal vs. atonal often intrudes needlessly into discussions of consonance vs. dissonance or of chromatic vs. diatonic and confuses the issue. The definition of tonality rests neither on levels of consonance nor on degrees of chromaticism, but on the functional differentiation of scale degrees. If high chromaticism is taken as a sign of atonality, then the Prelude to *Tristan und Isolde* might be regarded as a harbinger of atonality, when in fact few compositions depend more crucially on the functional distinction between the dominant (in this case endlessly prolonged) and the tonic (in this case excruciatingly withheld). Similarly, if high dissonance is taken as a sign of atonality, then the "terror fanfare" that opens the last movement of Beethoven's Ninth Symphony might be seen as a precedent.

As our discussion of Schoenberg's music continues, it should become evident that in music, as in so many other arenas, insisting at the outset on black-and-white distinctions is counterproductive. It hinders observation, desensitizes the mind to nuances and ambiguities, and reduces analysis to pigeonholing. Experience teaches us that life is lived (and art is created) in infinite shades of gray. So to understand what Schoenberg meant when he spoke of his breakthrough into a pantonal idiom, one in which tonality is permanently fluctuating (or permanently suspended), we need to evaluate the relevant musical procedures, their results, and the reasons why Schoenberg felt he needed them.

Schoenberg's move toward pantonality occurred over a period of several years. It is partly seen within his Second String Quartet, Op. 10 (1907–08), the work with which his Expressionist style is often said to begin. As he had done in *Verklärte Nacht,* Schoenberg transferred to chamber music devices more often found in contemporary orchestral music. Following the example of some of Mahler's symphonies with vocal soloists, Schoenberg added a soprano in the third and fourth movements, singing poems by Stefan George (1868–1933), a leading avant-garde figure. The first movement uses a sort of sonata-form structure and sets the lyrical tone for the quartet. Schoenberg's debt to Brahms is evident in the manipulation of motives that grow out of one another. The second movement scherzo includes an example of unsung song when a popular Viennese street tune, "Ach, du lieber Augustin" (O, My Dear Augustin), bursts forth in the middle trio section. As Mahler was doing at the same time in his symphonies, Schoenberg risks an affront by including banal musical material within a work of high art. The slow movement, a theme and variations in a very chromatic but still functioning G♭ major, incorporates a setting of George's "Litanei" (Litany), a quasi-religious poem about renunciation. It ends with a prayer, "Kill my longings, close my wounds, take my love away and grant me Thy peace!" The quartet's finale could be understood as the answer to the prayer. It is a setting of longer poem called "Entrückung" (Rapture). The title and the opening line—"Ich fühle Luft von anderem Planeten"/"I feel air from another planet"—have become emblems of the musical departure Schoenberg intended his setting both to symbolize and to enact (Ex. 27-5).

Example 27-5 Arnold Schoenberg, String Quartet No. 2, IV (*Entrückung*), arranged by Alban Berg for voice and piano, mm. 21–26

The Rosé Quartet, led by Arnold Rosé, Mahler's brother-in-law, gave the premiere of the piece on 21 December 1908, with soprano Marie Gutheil-Schoder. The performance was greeted with more outrage than had *Verklärte Nacht* six years earlier. Schoenberg later recalled that the event caused

> riots which surpassed every previous and subsequent happening of this kind. After the first measure of the second movement, the greater part of the audience started

to laugh and did not cease to disturb the performance. It was very embarrassing for the Rosé Quartet and the singer. . . . But at the end of this fourth movement a remarkable thing happened. After the singer ceases, there comes a long coda played by the string quartet alone, . . . This coda was accepted without any audible disturbance. Perhaps even my enemies and adversaries might have felt something here.[34]

There are further accounts of the scandal the performance caused. A leading Viennese critic, Ludwig Karpath, arose from his seat shouting, "Stop it! Stop it! We have had enough!" His review, and others, initiated a famous debate. Schoenberg challenged Karpath to a kind of musical duel to see who was the more adept at harmony and counterpoint. The battle lines were being drawn yet again. With the Wagner/Brahms controversy now a thing of the past, new contests over the function and proper language of music began to take shape. In some respects, they continue to this day.

Erwartung

To experience Expressionism in its full power we need to delve further into Schoenberg's repulsive yet fascinating psychological terrain. The word "repulsive" here is not an aesthetic judgment but, rather, accords with the composer's own stated claims. The use of art to explore what was ugly or disturbing was another longstanding project that Expressionism brought to a head. It should come as no surprise that Schoenberg's most extreme essay in the Expressionist vein should have been a portrait of an obsessed madwoman to set alongside—and surpass—counterparts in Wagner and Strauss.

In creating *Erwartung* (Expectation), Schoenberg brought musical Expressionism to its extreme—which in effect meant bringing German Romanticism itself to its final shriek. Considering that for a century or more art had been defined as inherently Romantic and music as the most essentially Romantic of the arts, the magnitude of Schoenberg's achievement in *Erwartung*—or at least of his attempt—must be regarded as historic. His accomplishment won him devoted disciples and enormous authority; it also ensured that his name would remain a lightning rod for controversy second only to Wagner's. The difference here is that Schoenberg made few concessions to his listeners, and therefore listeners have generally shunned his music from the outset, whereas Wagner, for all his rhetoric, courted public opinion and composed for popular success.

Schoenberg's madwoman was the protagonist of a nearly half-hour "**monodrama**" (drama with a single character) that he composed in just over two weeks during the summer of 1909. *Erwartung*, Op. 17, subtitled *Angsttraum* (nightmare), depicted a prolonged foreboding of psychic horror, the kind of maximalized emotional tension without hope of relief for which only emancipated dissonance—dissonance with no expectation of resolution—seemed able to capture. Like Wagner's *Ring*, *Erwartung* had to wait many years for its premiere. When it was first heard in Prague in 1924 it enhanced Schoenberg's prophetic aura and gave the music the force of revelation to his devotees.

The libretto offers another excellent example of the culture of Freud's Vienna. It was composed at Schoenberg's request by a family friend of the Zemlinskys named Marie Pappenheim (1882–1966), a writer who had recently come to the city to study medicine (Fig. 27-11). The disjointed monologue she devised has been compared with the emotionally overwrought running babble a patient in psychoanalysis might utter from the couch. That was surely no coincidence. Marie Pappenheim's brother, the psychiatrist Martin Pappenheim, was an early follower of Freud; a relative, Bertha Pappenheim, was the notorious "Anna O.," often considered to have been the first psychoanalytic patient. A patient of Josef Breuer, Freud's early collaborator, Bertha Pappenheim underwent a celebrated but later bitterly contested cure from hysteria by means of hypnosis and "recovered memory." Whether true memories or merely fantasies produced through hypnotic suggestion, the therapeutic results of her "talking cure" were a medical and literary sensation. It was the ongoing (indeed, still-raging) controversy over the reliability of hypnotically induced results that led Freud to modify the method so as to replace hypnosis with the talk therapy known as free association.

Figure 27-11 Marie Pappenheim, painting by Arnold Schoenberg.

It was precisely the ambiguity of psychic phenomena, the impossibility of distinguishing with certainty between recalled (or even lived) experience and fantasy, that Marie Pappenheim now sought to exploit artistically in the libretto she fashioned for Schoenberg. Its dramatic situation is simplicity itself: A woman (nameless, like most characters in Expressionist dramas) finds herself at the edge of a forest, anxiously looking for her lover. At the end of the opera she stumbles on his corpse and immediately begins a jealous rant that leaves us wondering whether she has murdered him. The brief drama consists entirely of her "inner occurrences," as Schoenberg would say, a compound of immediate sensation, memory, fantasy, and hallucination. At the end, as in contemporary literary experiments with the "stream of consciousness," we are left to wonder whether what we have witnessed was real, a dream, or a psychotic symptom. Like Salome, Schoenberg's woman symbolized, in her violent loss of emotional control, the imagined consequences of the stresses to which modern civilization subjects its members. Thus, like much fin-de-siècle art, *Erwartung* expressed a crucial ambivalence, using a radically innovative approach and a vocabulary of extreme Modernity, in order to critique the Modern world.

Schoenberg's critique was much stronger than earlier ones. Previous manifestations of the madwoman theme had camouflaged her with the exotic trappings of antiquity (classical, biblical, and primitive), enhancing her voyeuristic allure and distancing her from her uncomfortable contemporary relevance. Schoenberg and Pappenheim gave the nameless madwoman a raw, unvarnished treatment that laid the social and psychological message bare. She is nothing but reflection; we are left unsure whether indeed she has an external life to match her inner turmoil. Her intense subjectivity coupled with her namelessness allows her to represent both an autonomous contemporary psyche, in all its unfathomable complexity, and an archetypal Every(wo)man. Indeed, Schoenberg made the parallels between his opera and its German antecedents inescapable. Where the woman imagines kissing her dead lover, Schoenberg reminds the listener of Strauss's necrophiliac Salome. And when she lets out the one word—"Help!"—that she unambiguously speaks (or shrieks) aloud rather than to herself, he quotes a similar frenzied moment from the part of Kundry, the madwoman in Wagner's *Parsifal* and the ancestor of a whole fin-de-siècle line.[35]

At the Opposite Extreme: Atonal Miniatures

The Expressionist intensity of *Erwartung* and the massiveness of *Gurrelieder*, of Mahler's Eighth Symphony, and of Strauss's *Alpine Symphony* suggest that Maximalism was maxing out just before the outbreak of the First World War in 1914—unless, that is, a composer chose to go in the other direction. One manifestation was the aphoristic miniature, where Schoenberg and his colleagues abandoned almost all tonal references. The next three examples give three such microscopic pieces in their entirety, written for increasingly elaborate performing media.

Anthology Vol 3-4
Full CD VI, 4
Concise CD III, 6

Example 27-6 is the last of Schoenberg's *Sechs kleine Klavierstücke* (Six Little Piano Pieces), Op. 19, a set of aphoristic piano pieces, composed in June 1911. Its brief nine measures convey something of the emotion he felt at Mahler's funeral the previous month. No single pitch emerges from the texture with sufficient frequency to suggest itself as a possible tonic; major or minor triads are not in evidence, nor are dominant-seventh chords. It would appear that the whole conventional vocabulary of music has been suppressed in favor of a private language. The intricacy of the piece was mandated by Schoenberg's famously contradictory aims, according to which a spontaneous impression had to be supported by a very deliberate, even cerebral, process of control. On the one hand, Schoenberg aimed to compose Expressionistically, as if by primitive instinct, avoiding all trace of established routine; and on the other, he felt a strong obligation to unify his composition "organically," according to the standards set by the past masters he revered. What unified compositions was no longer a theme in the traditional sense but the *Grundgestalt*, or "basic shape," the germ that generated all motivic, harmonic, and contrapuntal aspects of a work.

It would appear that the whole conventional vocabulary of music has been suppressed in favor of a private language.

Example 27-6 Arnold Schoenberg, *Sechs kleine Klavierstücke*, Op. 19, No. 6

Webern strove for even greater compression. "Every glance a poem, every sigh a novel," was how Schoenberg put it in a preface he contributed to the first edition of Webern's *Sechs Bagatellen für Streichquartet* (Six Bagatelles for String Quartet), Op. 9 (1911–13). Example 27-7 is the fifth of them and goes on for twelve measures; but as they are half the length of Schoenberg's measures, the piece is actually shorter. Finally comes the fourth of Webern's *Fünf Stücke für Orchester* (Five Pieces for Orchestra), Op. 10 (1911–13), which lasts only six measures at a faster tempo and is the

Anthology Vol 3-5
Full CD VI, 5
Concise CD III, 7

Anthology Vol 3-6
Full CD VI, 6

shortest of all (Ex. 27-8). (Webern exceeded its brevity only once, in a five-measure piece for cello and piano composed in 1914.)

The motivation for these concise works seems similar. Webern articulated it in a memoir about the writing of the Bagatelles: "I had the feeling here that when all twelve notes had gone by, the piece was over. . . . In my sketchbook I wrote out the chromatic scale and crossed off individual notes. Why? Because I had convinced myself: This note has been there already."[36] He exaggerated slightly. No piece, whether by him or by Schoenberg, was ever over after a single round through the twelve pitch classes, although the three pieces sampled here come close. We might also note the profusion of performance markings consistent with traditional Romantic expressivity. In Webern's Bagatelle every note carries detailed directions, and an extraordinary range of tone colors (pizzicato, tremolando, on the bridge, with mute) is employed, a practice Schoenberg called ***Klangfarbenmelodie*** (tone-color melody or melody of tone colors). In Webern's incredibly spare orchestral piece there are dynamic and expressive markings in almost every measure, indeed almost for every note.

Example 27-7 Anton Webern, *Sechs Bagatellen für Streichquartet,* Op. 9, No. 5

The most famous of Schoenberg's compositions from this time was *Pierrot lunaire* (Moonstruck Pierrot, 1912), a collection of twenty-one miniatures, that became the lone work of his Expressionist phase to achieve a measure of popularity (Fig. 27-12). The lengthy subtitle is worth quoting in English, for it is a succinct

Anthology Vol 3-7
Full CD VI, 7–8
Concise CD III, 8

description of this eccentric piece: "Thrice seven poems from Albert Giraud's *Pierrot lunaire* (translated by Otto Erich Hartleben), for a speaking voice, piano, flute (alternating piccolo), clarinet (alternating bass clarinet), violin (alternating viola) and cello." Schoenberg's poetic source was a collection published in 1884 of fifty little poems, all of which concern the antics of the title character, Pierrot, the proverbial clown whose persona as ever-hopeful but always-disappointed lover originated as one of the masked roles in the old commedia dell'arte. Giraud made a show of going back to a pre-Romantic source by casting his Pierrot poems as *rondels,* adapting one of the stylized late Medieval fixed forms. Each poem has thirteen lines, divided 4 + 4 + 5, of which the first and second lines come back as the seventh and eighth and the first comes back again as the last. The use of this strict archaic format as well as the focus on a masked character and his erratic doings make these poems inhabit an odd domain that crosscut the funny-peculiar and the funny–ha-ha.

Example 27-8 Anton Webern, *Fünf Stücke für Orchester,* Op. 10, No. 4

Schoenberg increased Giraud's already considerable ironic distance by resorting to a variant of the device of melodrama—dramatic recitation to musical accompaniment—rather than conventional singing for his *Pierrot* settings.

Figure 27-12 The performers of the 1912 premiere of Arnold Schoenberg's *Pierrot lunaire.*

This, too, had a long history going back centuries. We encountered at least one melodrama in the nineteenth century, in Weber's *Der Freischütz.* A more immediate model was by Wagner's disciple Engelbert Humperdinck (1854–1921), best known for his delightful opera *Hänsel und Gretel* (1893). His melodramas stood closest to Schoenberg's because he was the first to control the speaker's part by the use of a relatively full musical notation that specified both rhythm (exactly) and pitch (approximately). In his opera *Die Königskinder* (The King's Children, 1910), Humperdinck used little Xs in place of note heads, turning the notes so marked into what he called *Sprechnoten* (speaking notes) (Ex. 27-9). Schoenberg probably picked up the idea directly from Humperdinck and used it some in *Gurrelieder.* In *Pierrot lunaire* he transferred the Xs from the note heads to the stems so that the technique could extend to half notes and dotted halves (Ex. 27-10). He called the device ***Sprechstimme*** (speaking voice) or *Sprechgesang* (speech song) and used it in various works over the rest of his career.

Example 27-9 Engelbert Humperdinck, *Die Königskinder*

im Brun - nen - spie - gel sah ich mich ein

The accompanying chamber ensemble in *Pierrot lunaire* is modeled incongruously (but in fact very shrewdly) on the sound of a cabaret orchestra, such as Schoenberg had encountered—and even written for—in Berlin. It turned the whole sensation of *Pierrot lunaire* into one of a strange nightclub act at the furthest remove from the elite environment Schoenberg's advanced music otherwise inhabited. Early performances, conducted by the composer, featured Albertine Zehme, the actress who commissioned the work and to whom it is dedicated. She would declaim the poems alone onstage under a spotlight, dressed not as Pierrot but as Columbine, the beckoning female figure in the old masked comedy, and with the instrumentalists concealed behind a screen. Audiences found it titillating, and after a remarkable initial Berlin run to full houses, Schoenberg found himself with a relatively lucrative road show on his hands. He and Zehme toured the piece for more than a decade.

Example 27-10 **Arnold Schoenberg, *Pierrot lunaire,* No. 1, *Mondestrunken,* mm. 1–6**

The opening piece, *Mondestrunken* (Moondrunk), sets the scene for all the hallucinatory verses to come, showing Pierrot swilling "the wine that through the eyes is drunk," that is, the moonlight that makes him rave. In the unrhymed singing translation given next, the refrain lines are set in italics to show the standard pattern of Giraud's rondels. On each recurrence the meaning of the returning lines is somewhat altered by the context.

1 *Den Wein, den man mit Augen trinkt,*	*The wine that through the eyes is drunk,*
2 *gießt nachts der Mond in Wogen nieder,*	*at night the moon pours down in torrents,*
3 und eine Springflut überschwemmt	until a spring-flood overflows
4 den stillen Horizont.	the silent horizon.

5 Gelüste, schauerlich und süß,	Desires, shuddering and sweet,
6 durchschwimmen ohne Zahl die Fluten!	are swimming through the flood unnumbered!
7 Den Wein, den man mit Augen trinkt,	*The wine that through the eyes is drunk,*
8 gießt nachts der Mond in Wogen nieder.	*at night the moon pours down in torrents.*
9 Der Dichter, den die Andacht treibt,	The poet, whom devotion drives,
10 berauscht sich an dem heiligen Tranke,	grows tipsy on the sacred liquor,
11 gen Himmel wendet er verzückt	enraptured, he turns to heaven
12 das Haupt und taumelnd saugt und schlürft er	his head, and reeling, sucks and slurps
13 den Wein, den man mit Augen trinkt.	*the wine that through the eyes is drunk.*

The all-important intervallic shape or cell that provides the melodic and harmonic raw material is presented at the very outset in the form of an ostinato in the piano part and is derived from a single whole-tone scale (Ex. 27-10). It may be easily traced throughout the piece, sometimes literally repeated, sometimes varied through interpolations, intervallic alteration, or sequences. But the importance attached to the specific pitches A, B, and F is flatly contradicted by the *Sprechstimme* technique, especially considering that Zehme was notoriously unconcerned with the niceties of pitch. In fact Schoenberg claimed later that despite his fastidious notation, he neither expected nor wanted any great exactness from the speaker. This may be confirmed by listening to a recording Schoenberg himself made in 1940 of *Pierrot lunaire* with a different singer. Thus a seemingly important feature of the tonal organization as represented by the score turns out to be entirely chimerical when it comes to the actual sound. Schoenberg, so often meanly accused of writing mere *Papiermusik* (on-paper music) or *Augenmusik* (music for the eyes), here purposely calls attention to it in jest.

A much more thoroughgoing irony of this kind, and a funnier one, is found in *Der Mondfleck* (The Moonspot), No. 18 in the cycle:

1 Einen weißen Fleck des hellen Mondes	*A white fleck of shining moonlight*
2 auf dem Rükken seines schwarzen Rokkes,	*on the back side of his black frock coat,*
3 so spaziert Pierrot im lauen Abend,	so strolls Pierrot one balmy evening,
4 aufzusuchen Glück und Abenteuer.	in pursuit of fortune and adventure.
5 Plötzlich stört ihn was an seinem Anzug,	Suddenly something's wrong with his appearance,
6 er besieht sich rings und findet richtig—	he looks round and round and then he finds it—
7 einen weißen Fleck des hellen Mondes	*A white fleck of shining moonlight*
8 auf dem Rükken seines schwarzen Rokkes,	*on the back side of his black frock coat.*
9 Warte! denkt er: das ist so ein Gipsfleck!	Wait! thinks he: a speck of plaster!
10 Wischt und wischt, doch bringt ihn nicht herunter!	Wipes and wipes, but it won't vanish!
11 Und so geht er giftgeschwollen weiter,	On he goes, his pleasure poisoned,
12 Reibt und reibt bis an den frühen Morgen	rubs and rubs till almost morning at
13 einen weißen Fleck des hellen Mondes.	*a white fleck of shining moonlight.*

Now here is an analyst's delight. The piece begins with a strict canon at the octave between the violin and the cello, a freer canon (or perhaps a sort of fugue) at the twelfth between the clarinet and the piccolo, and in the piano part a harmonized version of the clarinet-piccolo canon, in doubled note values (that is, at half the tempo), with the parts inverted. In the middle of the tenth measure, moreover, the string and wind parts reverse direction, producing a perfect melodic and rhythmic palindrome, while the piano continues to develop its fugue. This is all extraordinarily complex, except that this canon or a fugue is written in a style that recognizes no distinction between consonance and dissonance, so, harmonically speaking, literally anything goes. The essence of counterpoint has always been its "dissonance treatment." That, and that alone, is where the skill is required and displayed. What makes Bach's *Musical Offering* or *Art of Fugue* an example of astonishing virtuoso technique of composition is not just the complexity of the texture, but the fact that the complexity is achieved within such exacting constraints. Take away the constraints and you have rendered the tour de force entirely pointless. Of course Schoenberg knew that perfectly well—much better than his humorless admirers. Look again at the text: It is all about frenzied but pointless activity.

We will hear more of Mahler, Strauss, and Schoenberg in later chapters. Mahler, who died the earliest, lived on through the enormous influence his music had on younger composers, not limited by any means to his Viennese colleagues. In part owing to the later Nazi ban on his music, the music was not particularly well known by general audiences in midcentury. A resurgence of interest in the 1960s, sparked in part by the centennial of his birth, made Mahler, by the end of the millennium, one of the most frequently performed and revered of all twentieth-century composers.

Strauss lived a long life, dying in 1949 at age eighty-five. Although Modernist composers typically viewed his later music as irrelevant after the First World War, his early scores were already considered worthy of joining the musical museum and his late works turned out to prefigure developments at end of the twentieth century. We will look at some of his later accomplishments in another chapter. Schoenberg is the figure who will remain most in our attention, through his own activities, his ongoing self-reinvention, and the music of his students and followers.

Summary

This chapter examined Modernist trends between the late 1880s and 1914. The trends we surveyed include "maximalism," an intensification of emotional expression and sensuality, enlarging of performing forces and traditional forms, and expansion of tonality.

These tendencies are evident in the nine symphonies (and an uncompleted tenth) of Gustav Mahler (1860–1911), who applied Wagnerian-style drama to the symphony and the one who brought the German symphony to its culmination. Mahler also excelled in composing songs; his early ones were based on folk poetry, specifically *Des Knaben Wunderhorn* (The Youth's Magic Horn). Although Mahler often quoted his songs in his symphonies, his ambivalence toward program music is reflected in the different versions of his Symphony No. 1. Mahler first wrote it as a symphonic program; later he dropped the program, presenting it instead as a piece of "absolute" music. Mahler often mixes seriousness with parody and "high" elements with "low." The third movement of his Symphony No. 1 (1899), for example, uses a minor-key version of the popular tune known as *Frère Jacques*. The Modernist works of Richard Strauss (1864–1949) include a series of symphonic poems and operas. Influenced by decadence, his third opera, *Salome* (1905), links death and desire in a typically fin-de-siècle retelling (based on a play by Oscar Wilde) of the biblical story of Salome, King Herod, and John the Baptist.

As a leading figure of musical Modernism, Arnold Schoenberg (1874–1951) was acutely aware of history and claimed an important role in it for himself and his students Anton Webern (1883–1945) and Alban Berg (1885–1935). After early works in late Romantic style, such as his string sextet *Verklärke Nacht* (Transfigured Night, 1899), Schoenberg turned to "atonality," a musical language in which chords and pitches lack the functional relationship accorded them in tonal music. In his *Harmonielehre* (Textbook of Harmony, 1911) Schoenberg argued that dissonance was only a more remote consonance and therefore did not need to resolve.

Some of Schoenberg's atonal works were influenced by Expressionism, the artistic movement that sought to explore the drives and desires of the unconscious. In his monodrama *Erwartung* (Expectation, 1909), an anxious woman stumbles on the corpse of her lover. It is not clear whether these are actual events; the interest lies in the character's inner, psychological world, a world that Sigmund Freud explored in his development of psychoanalysis in Vienna at the time. Schoenberg's *Pierrot lunaire* (1912) is a series of twenty-one miniatures based on poetry by the Symbolist Albert Giraud. The poetry is delivered in a kind of dramatic recitation Schoenberg called *Sprechstimme* (speaking voice), with an ensemble of five instrumentalists, modeled on the sound of a cabaret orchestra.

Study Questions

1. What is meant by "maximalism"? How is it evident in the works of Gustav Mahler and Richard Strauss?
2. Describe some of the reasons for Mahler's attraction to folk poetry. In what ways do Mahler's settings of these poems express an ironic attitude toward folk elements?
3. Describe Mahler's ambivalent attitude toward program music. How is this ambivalence reflected in the history of his symphonies?
4. Discuss the third movement of Mahler's Symphony No. 1 as an example of his mixture of the "high" and the "low" as well as of seriousness and parody.
5. How does Strauss's *Salome* exhibit decadence and Freudian psychology? What musical and dramatic techniques does Strauss use to express desire?
6. Taking *Verklärke Nacht* as an example, describe how Arnold Schoenberg's music combines principles inherited from Brahms and Wagner.
7. What is "atonality"? What did Schoenberg mean by the "emancipation of dissonance?"
8. What is Expressionism? In what respects is Schoenberg's *Erwartung* an Expressionist work?
9. What examples of irony do you find in Schoenberg's *Pierrot lunaire?*

Key Terms

atonal
decadence
Expressionism
Grundgestalt
Klangfarbenmelodie
maximalism
modernism
monodrama
pantonal
Second Viennese School
Sprechstimme

28

Modernism in France

While Mahler, Strauss, Schoenberg, and others in the Austro-German sphere were furthering the legacies of Wagner and Brahms, composers in France had musical preoccupations of their own. We may remember Ezra Pound's observation about needing greater quantity and strength of a drug to achieve ever-heightened effects. Rather than go to the maximal extremes of some Germans and Austrians, many French composers charted a radically different course. They seemed less inclined to write overtly philosophical music, seeking instead to restore decorative values and pleasure to a place of honor. Rather than a source of power, they sought in music a source of pleasure; rather than the sublime, they sought beauty. Stimulated by antagonism toward Germany, by an interest in neglected indigenous traditions, by concurrent movements in literature and painting, and by encounters with music from far away, many French musicians began to cultivate new musical styles and techniques that added further layers to the astonishing diversity of early-twentieth-century music.

Like all Modernisms, the French version was characterized by a suddenly accelerated rate of stylistic change and innovation. It was often highly self-conscious, reflective, ironic, and urbane. But while many Germans aimed at a maximalized emotional or psychological content, many French wanted to deflate the Wagnerian rhetoric and therefore placed a renewed premium on immediate physical sensation. Many French composers tried to purge art of those "human, all too human" concerns, as Nietzsche had called them, that threaten to turn it into a sweaty, warty human document of only short-lived value (since emotions are fleeting and desire can be satiated) instead of an elegant object of pleasure. "Frivolous!" comes the German retort; to which the French, unperturbed, come right back: "Pretentious!"

first encountered in Russian music (Ex. 28-3). When the professor, Ernest Guiraud, commented, "It's all very meandering," Debussy at first responded with patronizing indignation. But then he broke down and laughed at his own pretension, admitting in effect that aesthetic edicts like the ones he was issuing were as often spouted by fools as by geniuses. "I feel free because I have been through the mill," he admitted to his former teacher, "and I don't write in the fugal style because I know it."[4]

Example 28-3 "Debussy at the piano strikes these chords" (comment by Maurice Emmanuel, the stenographer)

Debussy's 1894 Sarabande shows how he was attempting to discipline his vision and subject his rule of pleasure to a bit of theoretical scrutiny. The piece does not meander. Like Satie's, it abides by the formal and tonal conventions of its genre, but it does so in the same novel fashion that Satie had pioneered, if with far greater technical finesse. From the point of view of exorcising Wagner, the first measure of Debussy's Sarabande would be hard to beat. Its very first chord, a half-diminished seventh, is aurally similar to a *Tristan*-chord, but its dissonances are not treated as something to be resolved (Ex. 28-4). Instead, the chord is moved up a minor third in strictly diatonic parallel motion to a minor-seventh chord, the dissonances of which are treated similarly. In effect, both chords have been treated as consonances, floating freely in musical space, liberated from the constraints of voice leading. There is no sense that the necessary resolution of the dissonance is being deferred, and consequently there is no provocation of desire. The harmony no longer analogizes emotion, save the emotion of delight in sheer sensuous gratification. Beauty, in short, has made a comeback.

Anthology Vol 3-10
Full CD VI, 11

Example 28-4 Claude Debussy, Sarabande from *Pour le piano*, mm. 1–8

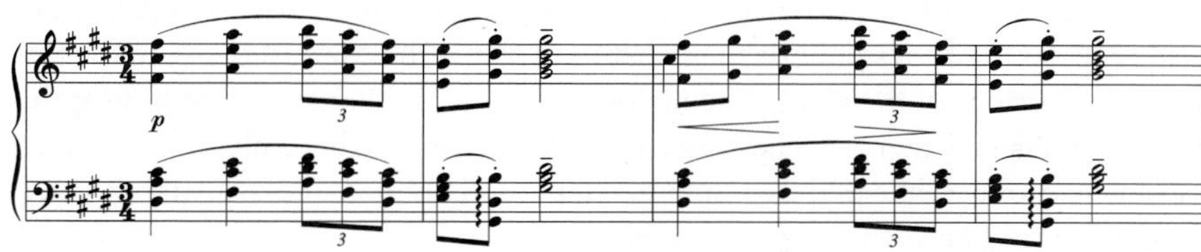

Example 28-4 (*continued*)

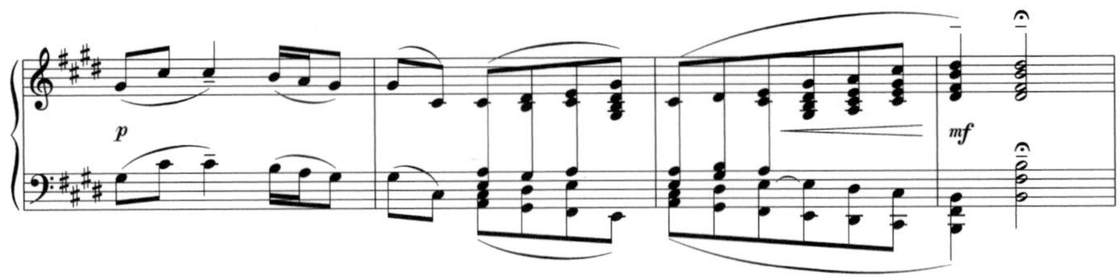

Voiles: Sails and/or Veils

Anthology Vol 3-11
Full CD VI, 12
Concise CD III, 10

For an intensified version of the harmonic idiom exemplified by Satie's and Debussy's sarabandes, a good place to look is a piano piece Debussy composed a decade and a half later: "Voiles" (1909), the second in a set of twelve *Préludes* for piano published in 1910. The idea of a collection of freestanding preludes, independent compositions for the keyboard, stems from Chopin, a composer Debussy worshipped and claimed as a forerunner. Unlike Chopin's preludes, Debussy's carry descriptive subtitles; but unlike most titles, Debussy gives his not at the heads of the pieces, but at the ends, modestly enclosed in parentheses and preceded by dots of ellipsis, as if to demote them to the rank of whispered interpretive suggestions rather than explicit prescriptions. In the case of "Voiles," the teasing is exaggerated by the ambiguity of the word. "Le voile," with masculine article, means "veil" or "mask"; "la voile," with feminine article, means "sail" or "sailboat." In the plural, the word can mean either.

Leaving the implications of the title aside for the moment, we are struck by a different sort of ambiguity. The first forty-one measures of the piece are composed almost entirely out of the notes of a **whole-tone scale**, which excludes half steps by definition and which therefore has no scale-degree functions at all (Ex. 28-5a). Heretofore whole-tone harmony had functioned in Debussy's music the way it had in Russian music, that is, in interaction with diatonic harmony, creating momentary blurs. Now it is the main point of reference. Everything coexists in relative harmoniousness and in what seems a single extended instant of time. A sense of unfolding is achieved not through harmonic variety (which is unavailable) but by an accumulation of melodic ideas in counterpoint.

Slightly past the middle of "Voiles" a radical change takes place: A key signature of five flats suddenly appears, and the whole-tone collection gives way to a pentatonic one, the scale built on the piano's black keys (Ex. 28-5b). The ear is refreshed. Like the adjacent notes in the diatonic scale, those in this pentatonic scale form intervals of two different sizes (whole steps and minor thirds), and so the harmony comes into somewhat sharper focus. When the whole-tone collection is later reasserted, a new motif is introduced that imitates the foregoing black-key glissandos and provides a sort of synthesis to mediate and soften the contrast between the two previous sections of the piece. The melodic content of the first section is recapitulated, but in a new register. The very end of "Voiles" is suitably ambiguous, and the closing harmony, while perhaps not predictable and not possible to justify as a conventional tonic, nevertheless seems right.

Example 28-5a Claude Debussy, "Voiles" (*Préludes*, Book I), mm. 1–13

Example 28-5b Claude Debussy, "Voiles" (*Préludes*, Book I), mm. 41-48

Impressionism and Symbolism

If *voiles* is taken to mean "sails," Debussy's music can seem painterly—that is, concerned in its subtly calibrated timbres (colors) and blurry harmony with depictions of outdoor scenes or, more generally, with establishing correspondences between the aural and the visual. The term "Impressionism" was applied to his music in the late 1880s, in an analogy with the famous school of French painters that had begun to flourish somewhat earlier and that took its name from a painting by Claude Monet (1840–1926) called *Impression: Sunrise*, first exhibited in 1872 (Fig. 28-3). But it was not just French painters who influenced Debussy—the English artist J. M. W. Turner (1775–1851) and American-born James Whistler (1834–1903) were also potent forces.

Like many style-identifying terms in the history of the arts, "**Impressionism**" was at first a derogatory label. The critic who coined it in response to Monet's painting did not mean it as a compliment. Misunderstanding the painter's intention, which was to capture transitory visual impressions (such as the play of light on a surface) naturalistically and with extreme precision, the critic implied that the broken colors and indistinct outlines in Monet's painting were the result of sloppy technique. Similarly, the secretary of the Académie des Beaux Arts, who first applied the term to Debussy in evaluating a suite called *Printemps* (Springtime, 1887), used it as a synonym for what he took to be the young Debussy's chief liability: "a strong feeling for color in music which, when exaggerated, causes him to forget the importance of clarity in design and form."[5]

Not surprisingly, Debussy found the label Impressionism annoying, "a convenient term of abuse,"[6] or at least, like any stereotype, a term of confinement. But creators do not get to choose the labels of movements; critics and others invent them, history then either adopts or rejects them, often revealingly so. Schoenberg did not like the designation "atonal," and we will later encounter more recent figures

Figure 28-3 Claude Monet, *Impression: Sunrise*, 1872.

who shunned designations like "jazz" and "minimalism." As in the case of the visual artists, the term "Impressionism" stuck despite resistance, and eventually it lost its disapproving connotation. Instead, it came to name a quality that seemed to link the expressive aims of the new styles in French painting and music and that strongly distinguished them from contemporaneous trends in Germany, notably Expressionism. The common ingredients of Impressionism, which critics have always found hard to specify in words, however keenly they are felt, include such things as calculated effects of spontaneity; fascination with subtle gradations in color and texture that produced an ambiguous, highly suggestive surface; and a greater interest in sensuousness than in psychology or strongly declared emotion. Naturally, all these traits could easily be described as failings by hostile critics: vagueness, confusion, and lack of expressivity.

Music, Debussy felt, was not "the expression of a feeling, it is the feeling itself."

Even the strikingly static effect of Debussy's harmony—the absence of forward drive—could be viewed as painterly, an effort to lessen the discrepancy between an art that unfolds in time and one that extends in space. His frequent use of visually oriented titles supports the parallel. The second book of *Préludes* (1911–13) includes two—"Bruyères" (Mists) and "Feuilles mortes" (Dead Leaves)—that seem to echo the titles of typical Impressionist paintings. Also striking is the absence of people, or, rather, of personalities, among Debussy's subjects. One finds representations aplenty in his music of the sea, of the wind, of gardens in the rain and balconies in the moonlight, but less often of actual individuals. His landscapes are uninhabited, even if they bear traces of former habitation, as in "Des pas sur la neige" (Footprints in the Snow). Like much of Impressionist painting, Debussy's art was not an art of empathy. Music, Debussy felt, was not "the expression of a feeling, it *is* the feeling itself."[7]

When the word *voiles* in the title of Debussy's piano prelude is taken to mean "veils," connoting mystery and concealment, Debussy's music can seem not just painterly but also literary. In its reluctance to draw explicit connections or to maintain a strongly linear narrative thrust, it seems concerned with the issues being raised in the literary domain by the poets and other writers who belonged to the Symbolist school. **Symbolism** was a somewhat older movement than Impressionism in painting, going back to Charles Baudelaire (1821–67). This poet, critic, and theorist of Modernity was strongly influenced, on the one hand, by Wagner and, on the other, by the American writer Edgar Allan Poe (1809–49). Baudelaire lived a decadent life and died penniless in drug-induced insanity.

Literary Symbolists of the late nineteenth century typically traced their movement to a specific poem of Baudelaire's, the sonnet "Correspondances," published in 1857 in a collection called *Les fleurs du mal* (Flowers of Evil, sometimes translated Poison Blossoms):

La Nature est un temple où de vivants piliers
Laissent parfois sortir de confuses paroles:
L'homme y passe à travers des forêts de symboles
Qui l'observent avec des regards familiers.

Comme de longs échos qui de loin se confondent
Dans une ténébreuse et profonde unité
Vaste comme la nuit et comme la clarté,
Les parfums, les couleurs et les sons se répondent.

Il est des parfums frais comme des chairs d'enfants,
Doux comme les hautbois, verts comme les prairies,
—Et d'autres, corrompus, riches et triomphants,

Ayant l'expansion des choses infinies,
Comme l'ambre, le musc, le benjoin et l'encens,
Qui chantent les transports de l'esprit et des sens.

[Nature is a temple where living pillars at times send out muddled words: There, man passes through forests of symbols that watch him with familiar looks. Like long echoes that blend from afar in a deep penumbral wholeness as vast as the night and the light, aromas, colors and sounds give answer. There are aromas, cool as baby flesh, sweet as oboes, green as the fields—and others, tainted, rich and thriving, having the power of infinite expansion, like amber, musk, balsam and incense—that sing of the transports of spirit and sense.]

There are two crucial ideas here: ***synesthesia***, the equivalence and interchangeability of sense experiences of hearing, taste, smell, sight, and so forth, and the *occult*, or hidden, knowledge that synesthesia imparts. To see symbols in all things is to lend them a hidden meaning and to approach the sensory as if it were the spiritual, and vice versa, as the initial comparison of nature to a temple suggests. Symbolism was partly a revival of what historians today call the "premodern" or magical worldview, an outlook that sought the hidden resemblances of all in all. With this in mind one can understand Baudelaire's great attraction to Wagner and the rich Symbolism he found in his operas.

At its most extreme, Symbolism offered through art a way of seeing past the appearances of the lived world into the higher reality of the *au-delà*, the world "beyond" the senses. Art or literature that drew connections too explicitly—that said what it meant and meant what it said—was limited and limiting in its evocative power. "By describing what is [and only what is], the poet degrades himself and is reduced to the rank of schoolmaster," wrote Baudelaire; "by telling us what is possible he remains faithful to his vocation."[8] Or as Debussy's friend Stéphane Mallarmé (1842–98), the leading Symbolist poet of the next generation, once exclaimed when an editor complimented him on the lucidity of an essay he had just submitted, "Give it back! I need to put in more shadows."

Debussy's *Pelléas et Mélisande*

Debussy's association with Symbolism was of major importance to the conception of some of his most significant works. He composed a song cycle, *Cinq poèmes de Baudelaire* (1890); and the orchestral composition that won him his first real fame, *Prélude à L'après-midi d'un faune* (Prelude to the Afternoon of a Faun, 1894), was inspired by a famous Mallarmé poem. The list of Symbolists whose work Debussy set or on which he contemplated basing orchestral and dramatic projects could be extended, including two planned operatic projects based on works by Poe, the writer who had so inspired Baudelaire. But these works were never finished, so a lone opera remains: *Pelléas et Mélisande*. Debussy drafted the five-act opera from August 1893 to August 1895 and then waited for the prospect of actual performance before revising and orchestrating the work, finally completing it in 1902 (Fig. 28-4).

Anthology Vol 3-12
Full CD VI, 13
Concise CD III, 11

Figure 28-4 Claude Debussy's *Pelléas et Mélisande*, Act IV, Scene 4, in the original production (Paris, Opéra Comique, 1902), as printed in the periodical *Le Théâtre.*

Pelléas et Mélisande was a slightly abridged and practically verbatim setting of a key Symbolist drama, the work of Maurice Maeterlinck (1862–1949), a Belgian writer who became the movement's leader after Mallarmé's death. The opera is not only a Symbolist drama, but also in many respects a drama about Symbolism. Pelléas and Mélisande, a pair of lovers who call to mind Tristan and Isolde, are not the only central characters; rather, the tragic hero is Golaud, Pelléas's brother and Mélisande's husband. In a jealous rage near the end he kills Pelléas, and Mélisande dies not long after. The parallels between this plot and that of Wagner's opera are hard to miss. Lovers in spite of themselves, Pelléas and Mélisande die, directly and indirectly, of wounds inflicted by the heroine's rightful husband. Both operas could be viewed as mythic variants of the "eternal love triangle," variants that subvert the middle-class moral according to which, if forced to choose, one must sacrifice the gratification of one's desires to the greater good of the social order.

One of the challenges Debussy faced writing the opera was the apparent aimlessness of the action, or, rather, the extreme passivity of all the characters except Golaud: "Despite its dream-like atmosphere," he wrote of Maeterlinck's play, "it contains far more humanity than those so-called 'real-life documents'" of verismo.[9] Debussy's letters show his frustration: "I've spent days trying to capture that 'nothing' that Mélisande is made of," he wrote to one friend.[10] To another he wondered whether there was anything left for a composer to do anymore but recycle operatic clichés: "Impossible to count how often since Gluck people have died to the chord of the [Neapolitan] sixth, and now, from [Massenet's] Manon to Isolde, they do it to the diminished seventh!"[11] Finally, he confided to his friend Ernest Chausson, "I was premature in crying 'success' over *Pelléas et Mélisande.* After a sleepless night (the bringer of truth) I had to admit it wouldn't do at all. It was like the duet by M. So-and-so, or nobody in particular, and worst of all the ghost of old Klingsor [the sorcerer in *Parsifal*], alias R. Wagner, kept appearing in the corner of a bar. So I've torn the whole thing up."[12]

The scene to which Debussy was referring was the first one he had composed, the climactic fourth scene of the fourth act, in which Pelléas and Mélisande exchange nocturnal confessions of love in a garden and Golaud, intruding on them, kills his brother and rival. The plot here is the closest to Wagner's *Tristan*, the score that Debussy knew by heart. He makes conspicuous references to the *Tristan*-chord, especially at places where the word *triste* (sad) appears or even the performance direction *tristement* (sadly). But his *Tristan*-chords, unlike Wagner's, are not harmonically active; they do not form part of any progression to a harmonic goal. Instead, they float free, untethered by voice leading, free of harmonic glue. In the scene as a whole, one is conscious of Debussy's effort not to impose any abstractly musical shape, although the use of leitmotifs provides some recurring material and an audible debt to Wagner.

Both tonally and dramaturgically the scene can be broken down into three parts. The agitated and swiftly paced first part culminates in the declaration of love, perhaps the most resolutely unrhetorical such declaration in all of opera. The second, which begins with the scene's first explicitly notated key signature (F♯ major), comprises its lyrical core: Pelléas's part slows down to "aria tempo" (half notes and quarters rather than quarters, eighths, and sixteenths) as he sings of his love. The vocal delivery, as so often in this opera, is chant-like, yet here is one of the few times when it approaches a more traditional aria (Ex. 28-6). Mélisande, as ever, is erratic, matter-of-fact "nothingness," and although she reciprocates Pelléas's passion verbally, her music tends to break the mood. The swift third section culminates in the lovers' desperate kiss in expectation of death and in Golaud's attack. Here even sleepy Mélisande manages a fairly long, fairly high note. Amidst the doggedly understated context it comes across as a veritable *Liebestod*.

Example 28-6 Claude Debussy, *Pelléas et Mélisande*, Act IV, Scene 4, mm. 81–87

Example 28-6 (*continued*)

PELLEAS
Don't you know why I have to go away?
You don't know that it is because . . . I love you
MELISANDE
I love you too . . .
PELLEAS
Oh! What did you say, Mélisande!
I hardly heard what you said . . .

Richard Strauss attended a performance of Debussy's opera in 1907, two years after his own scandalous *Salome*, and turned to his host after the first act asking, "Is it like this all the way through?" On being assured that it was, he protested, "But there's nothing in it. No music. It has nothing consecutive. No musical phrases, no development."[13] Modulations are always unpredictable and unanticipated. The listener is rendered as passive as the characters, borne along by the ill-defined yet incessant harmonic flux, although if one looks hard enough one can discern a tonal plan. Strauss's perplexity was a tribute to Debussy's success at getting rid of the Wagnerian glue, relinquishing the harmonic driver's seat to a much freer play than the foreordained goals guaranteed by the circle of fifths and other harmonic conventions. Debussy's restraint, responsive to a new psychological mood, proved far more subversive to traditional practice than Strauss's hyperactivity.

"Essentially French": Fauré and *Mélodie*

Figure 28-5 Gabriel Fauré.

An older contemporary of Debussy, also greatly influenced by Symbolism, was Gabriel Fauré (1845–1924; Fig. 28-5), who had studied both composition and organ with Saint-Saëns. From 1896 he was professor of composition at the Paris Conservatoire, from 1905 to 1920 its director. His many settings of decadent and Symbolist poetry helped cultivate a genre of art song that the French call ***mélodie***. (The actual use of the word originated long before, going back at least to Berlioz.) Fauré famously set texts by Paul Verlaine (1844–96), a leading Symbolist whose poetry was celebrated for its elegance and euphony—in short, its "musicality." His treatise in verse, "Art poétique" (1874), begins with a line that became a slogan: *De la musique avant toute chose*, "Music above all!" Composers naturally agreed, and Verlaine's verses quickly became the most-set poetry in the French language. Fauré wrote seventeen of his *mélodies* to poems by Verlaine;

Anthology Vol 3-13
Full CD VI, 14
Concise CD III, 12

nine of them appear in his first song cycle, *La bonne chanson* (The Good Song), Op. 61, (1892–94).

Verlaine's poetry often evoked the same pseudo-archaism that provided other French composers with a source of stylistic rejuvenation. The poems in *La bonne chanson,* a wedding offering to the poet's bride, were (despite the private and personal sentiments they expressed) of this artificial, highly crafted type. Verlaine even toyed with the idea of calling the set *Vieilles bonnes chansons,* or "Good Old Songs." The name would certainly have fit "Une Sainte en son auréole" (A saint within her halo), which Fauré chose to begin his cycle. It is a sort of mock-troubadour song modeled on 700-year-old prototypes like those discussed in Chapter 2, replete with the imagery of the distant lady ("the mistress of the castle in her tower"), direct comparisons with "the noble ladies of yore," and a final reference to her unuttered "code name." Fauré's cycle was dedicated to Emma Bardac, his married mistress, who later became Debussy's second wife. It was a situation suggestive of "courtly love," the idealized knightly worship of a married lady from afar, which had provided Medieval love songs with their subject matter.

Despite his frequent recourse to the saturated chromaticism of post-Wagnerian harmony, Fauré created a pseudo-Medieval style that gave his music the same sort of "brand-*old*" freshness at which Verlaine had aimed in his works. The piano part in "Une sainte" opens with a thrice-repeated descending pentatonic scale suggestive in some contexts of folklore, but here like troubadour lyrics—or even Gregorian chant, just then undergoing a process of zealous restoration at the Benedictine Abbey of Solesmes some 150 miles southwest of Paris (Ex. 28-7). French composers were intensely interested in this project, since they regarded the Frankish chant as the earliest French music. Of course, as we learned in Chapter 1, they were wrong: The chant was Roman, not French; but as French historian Ernest Renan famously put it right around this time, "getting its history wrong is part of being a nation."

Example 28-7 Gabriel Fauré, "Une Sainte en son auréole," mm. 1–20

Example 28-7 ***(continued)***

A Saint set in her stained-glass glow,
Milady in her castle town,
All the sweet words that, here below,
Praise grace and sing love's gentle power.

Perhaps more vividly than any other composition of the period, Fauré's exquisite Requiem, Op. 48, painstakingly composed and revised over a span of twenty-three years (1877–1900), illustrates the characteristics that French musicians then wished to propagate as essentially French, as opposed to what was accordingly to be classified as essentially German or stereotypically Italian or even what had once been considered typically French. Fauré's is a greatly truncated setting of the Requiem Mass—the work does not even contain a *Dies irae,* the terrifying section that inspired theatrically thrilling hellfire-and-damnation responses from Berlioz in 1837 and from Verdi in 1874. Instead, as the critic Émile Vuillermoz (at one time a composition pupil of Fauré's) remarked, Fauré's Requiem is "a look toward heaven and not toward hell."[14]

The final section of the Requiem pointedly confirms this attitude. It is a setting of the antiphon *In paradisum deducant te Angeli* (May the Angels lead you into Paradise), which is not even part of the Requiem Mass as such but is sung on the way to the gravesite before burial on those occasions when burial immediately follows the service. This comforting representation of angelic harping is also a representation of a state of heavenly bliss, in which nothing remains to be desired. Therefore, the musical representation of desire, from which so much German music had drawn its sustenance, is virtually suppressed. Indeed, Fauré was mythologized even before his death, at age seventy-nine, as the Frenchest of the French.

Figure 28-6 Maurice Ravel at the piano.

Maurice Ravel

Maurice Ravel (1875–1937; Fig. 28-6) was the other leading Impressionist composer and eventually became more often performed than Debussy. This was due to the extraordinary popularity of a few works, such as *Bolero* (1928), which he once described as "a piece lasting 17 minutes and consisting wholly of 'orchestral effects without music'—one long and very gradual crescendo."[15] A pupil of Fauré, Ravel wrote in a colorful and sensuous style marked by a deep affinity for Russian music. His orchestration of Musorgsky's *Pictures at an Exhibition* from 1922 is far better known than the original piano suite.

Like many artists in an age of increasing celebrity, Ravel was asked to make all kinds of pronouncements, some irrelevant, others revealing. In a 1911 interview published in *The Musical Leader*, a British journal, he said:

> The work done in France today is by far more simple than the music by Wagner, his followers, or his greatest disciple, Richard Strauss. It has not the gigantic form of Beethoven and Wagner, but it possesses a sensitiveness which other schools have not. Its great qualities are clearness and order. It is intensely rich in musical matter. There is more musical substance in Debussy's *Après-midi d'un faune* than in the wonderfully immense Ninth Symphony by Beethoven. The French composers of today work on small canvases but each stroke of the brush is of vital importance.[16]

In later interviews, including some that followed the First World War, Ravel admitted to admiring the work of his German contemporaries, although with reservations. His relative tolerance may have had something to do with his heritage. Born in the Pyrenees to a French father and a Basque mother, he thought of himself as ethnically exotic and was drawn to other manifestations of national or ethnic exoticism, including Jewish ones, which he treated with unusual sympathy in his *Deux mélodies hébraïques* (1919) and other works.

In *Rapsodie espagnole* for orchestra (1908), Ravel saturated his music with brilliant orchestral effects and with **octatonic** scales, an eight-note alternation of whole steps and half steps he had learned from Rimsky-Korsakov; in turn the work would have a great impact on Igor Stravinsky.[17] There is some irony in the fact that the most famous musical evocations of Spain were not written by Spanish composers. Among the pieces familiar to Ravel were Rimsky's *Capriccio espagnol* (1887) and Bizet's *Carmen*. But these pieces, as with "Spanish" works by Liszt, Glinka, Chabrier, Debussy, Edouard Lalo, and many others, tended to take a fairly superficial look south, adapting melodies, rhythms, and moods rather than capturing (or even trying to capture) more than surface features. We will return to Ravel's later engagement with another "exotic" musical current, namely, jazz, in a subsequent chapter.

New Possibilities for Women

Changes in the social and legal status of women in the early twentieth century helped to create an institutional climate in which women composers could compete more fairly. We have seen the American Amy Beach go it on her own and succeed. Germany, which had boasted Clara Schumann in the nineteenth century, produced no comparable figure for some time after her death, although the English composer Dame Ethel Smyth (1858–1944) enjoyed one of her great successes when her opera

The Wreckers premiered in Leipzig in 1906. Most noteworthy were the new possibilities in France, which give us the occasion to revisit the realities and some of the achievements of women composers at the start of the century.

In recent decades some feminist critics have read the history of art as driven primarily by the male ego—"machismo," as we often call it now (from the Spanish)—with harmful effects on the fate of women artists as well as on the content and quality of art itself. In an article provocatively entitled "Why Have There Been No Great Women Artists?" (1971), art historian Linda Nochlin subjected the notion of "greatness" to a cultural analysis and concluded that it rested in part on a foundation of fierce self-assertion and competition—behavior traditionally deemed unacceptable in a woman, however talented. In this way the question posed by the article's title could become self-fulfilling and circular: There are no great women artists because women are socially barred from greatness. The social costs of artistic success for a woman, amounting to virtual ostracism, were prohibitive. "The choice for women," Nochlin wrote, "seems always to be marriage *or* a career, i.e., solitude as the price of success *or* sex and companionship at the price of professional renunciation."[18] This unhappy set of alternatives is well illustrated even by the relatively happy career of Beach, who had to put her performing career "on hold" during her childless marriage and only reasserted herself as a professional after her husband's death.

Women were first allowed to compete for the Prix de Rome in 1903.

France, as it happens, was a country where the institutional means for artistic success became available to women toward the end of the nineteenth century. The ban on feminine participation in the yearly contests for the Prix de Rome was lifted, first in painting, then in music. This greater democratization of the artistic and musical academies coincided with a weakening of the academies' power to act as gatekeepers regulating access to the arts and professions. (Much later the student uprisings in Paris during 1968 put an end to the Rome Prize altogether after 165 years. Many leading French composers had won it at one time or another, often after several attempts, but some, like Ravel, never did.)

Women were first allowed to compete for the Prix de Rome in 1903. Over the next decade there were four female finalists for the prize, two of them—Nadia and Lili Boulanger—from a single family.[19] The younger of the two Boulanger sisters, the tragically short-lived Lili (1893–1918; Fig. 28-7), became the first woman to win it. In keeping with a pattern in the visual arts, the Boulanger sisters were the daughters (and granddaughters) of successful composers who had taught at the Paris Conservatoire. Their father, who was in his seventies when they were born, had won the Prix de Rome himself in 1835. This created a certain amount of good will toward Nadia (1887–1979) when she first entered the competition in 1906; but although she tried four times, and although each time a significant number of jurors judged her work to be the best, she never rose beyond the level of "second runner-up." We will see the important role she later played as one of the preeminent music educators of her day.

Figure 28-7 Lili Boulanger.

Lili Boulanger may have learned from her sister's trials; in 1913 she won the prize. Her winning cantata, set to a prescribed text drawn from Goethe's *Faust*, was something of a salad of near quotations from *Parsifal* and *Siegfried*; it shows that the default mode for young French composers was still tinged with Wagnermania. In several later works she achieved a much greater individuality, but she composed little in any case because she became chronically ill shortly after taking up residence in Rome; she died in March 1918, at the age of twenty-four. Her most characteristic compositions are choral: several psalm settings, a *Vieille prière bouddhique* (Old Buddhist Prayer), a war elegy called *Pour les funérailles d'un soldat* (For a Soldier's Funeral). At the time of her death she was working on an opera based on a play by Maeterlinck, *La princesse Maleine.*

Lili's last completed composition, *Pie Jesu* for mezzo-soprano (or choirboy), string quartet, harp, and organ, dedicated to Nadia, bears a clearly emulative relationship to Fauré's Requiem. Despite the steady atmospheric murmur of semitones in the ostinato accompaniment, the organizing principles of the music are by now familiar from our survey of the French music of the period. The vocal line is "modal" in the fashion of the restored Medieval chant. Where the key signature contains one sharp, cadences are made to E, but the leading tone is conspicuously suppressed in "Dorian" fashion. The accompaniment, moreover, is progressively purged of its Wagnerian chromaticism, achieving diatonic purity to accompany the concluding "Amen." The harmonic change reflects the triumph of faith over fear and is also a triumph of gluelessness and the essence of France (Ex. 28-8).

Anthology Vol 3-14
Full CD VI, 15
Concise CD III, 13

Example 28-8 Lili Boulanger, *Pie Jesu*, mm. 3–9

Kind Lord Jesus, Grant them rest.

Ballet: A Missing Genre

Except for a brief mention in Chapter 24 with respect to Tchaikovsky, an entire genre, with a history extending back for centuries, has been missing from our account of European art music: that of theatrical dance and the music written to accompany it—ballet. It is no accident that the word is French, given the rich historical tradition in the country, where it came to be regarded as a self-sufficient "wordless opera." ***Ballet d'action***, or plot ballet, was indeed designed to vie with opera for dominance in the realm of music theater. In such a ballet, a scenario, or planned sequence of danced numbers, took the place of the libretto in an opera. The scenarist, who might or might not be the choreographer, the designer of the actual danced steps, had a task similar to the librettist's, which was to express the content of the plot, often a well-known story, in terms of danceable situations. A method of alternating plot presentation and emotional reflection, reminiscent of the alternating recitatives and arias in opera and clearly modeled on them, became standard. The equivalent of recitative was pantomime, or gestural mimicry, in which elements of plot were acted out in a stylized way. The actual dances, like operatic arias, expressed in more general terms the characters' emotional reactions to the events of the plot.

In short, the fledgling Romantic ballet was poised in nineteenth-century France to present itself as a full-fledged alternative to opera. But how viable an alternative and how great a threat to it? For most of the century, not very. For one thing, opera remained more favored, for singing seemed able to express a greater emotional range. Opera productions, moreover, were expected to include ballet, sometimes very spectacularly staged. A further strike against ballet was its association with what, in the aftermath of the French Revolution, became identified as outmoded aristocratic taste. The relatively lowly status of the composer in its scheme of things discouraged major musical figures of the nineteenth century from becoming involved in ballet.

One of the most successful nineteenth-century French composers of ballet was Adolphe Adam (1803–56), known primarily for his comic operas, who wrote more than a dozen *ballets d'action*. His masterpiece, *Giselle* (1841), is the sole survivor still performed (Fig. 28-8). The other major figure was Léo Delibes (1836–91), a pupil of Adam's, who wrote two ballets that have remained repertory staples: *Coppélia* (1870) and *Sylvia* (1876). Yet during the latter part of the nineteenth century, as the high spiritual ideals of the Société Nationale de Musique emerged, there was increasing hostility to ballet. *Ballet d'action*, scarcely a century old, was dead.

The golden age of the Russian classical ballet came with the reign of Marius Petipa (1818–1910), widely regarded as the century's greatest choreographer.

Or so it would have been, had it not escaped to Russia. That was because in Russia, the last stronghold of absolute monarchy, theaters remained under the direct control of the crown until 1882. Ballet was fostered to an extent unheard of anywhere else on the continent. By the beginning of the nineteenth century the Russian court was already a magnet for French choreographers, exactly as it had been for Italian opera composers. The golden age of the Russian classical ballet came with the reign of Marius Petipa (1818–1910), widely regarded as the century's greatest choreographer, who from 1869 until his death headed the company at St. Petersburg's Mariyinsky Theater, later called the Kirov.

Russian composers shied away from composing the music for the imperial Russian ballet until Tchaikovsky. His first ballet, composed in 1875–76, was *Swan*

Figure 28-8 Carlotta Grisi (1819–99) in Adolphe Adam's *Giselle,* Act II (lithograph from a drawing by Jules Challamel). Note the conventions of miming: The ballerina's right arm is in the *J'écoute* ("I'm listening") position.

Lake, which was modeled in several ways on Adam's *Giselle.* His two others—*La belle au bois dormant* (The Sleeping Beauty, 1889) and *Casse-noisette* (The Nutcracker, 1892)—brought the *ballet d'action* to its zenith of development. The two works are quite different. *The Sleeping Beauty* is a *ballet à grand spectacle,* Petipa's specialty—a ballet that mixed a strong plot line with a wealth of exotic divertissement and apotheoses, spectacular climaxes that summoned huge and brilliantly costumed ensembles, the *corps de ballet.* The shorter and sparer *Nutcracker,* after a tale by the German writer E. T. A. Hoffmann, is of an equally distinctive (and equally French) type, called *ballet-féerie.* The term designates a ballet that casts fantasy creatures—fairies, genies, and the like—and that also aims lavishly for a special marvelous lightness of effect. These culminating ballets of Tchaikovsky are masterpieces of what the composer called the "tasty," or sensuously delectable. Nothing could be further removed from the weighty spiritual or expressive tasks that German composers assigned their art. Tchaikovsky thus succeeded in raising the artistic status of ballet in late-nineteenth-century Russia, eventually turning it, in a gloriously ironic and unexpected twist, into a prestigious media for early-twentieth-century Modernist music.

Ballet Finds Its Theorist

Intellectual prestige was added to the social and artistic prestige of the Russian ballet when a young student, Alexandre Benois (1870–1960), attended the premiere of *The Sleeping Beauty,* found the experience overwhelming, and began discussing it with his friends, a group of rich, young, artistically inclined intellectuals. "Tchaikovsky's music was what I seemed to be waiting for since my earliest childhood,"[20] Benois wrote in his old age, long after becoming a famous painter, theatrical designer, and art historian. It embodied "the aristocratic spirit, untouched by any democratic deviations." As he saw it, the Russian Imperial Ballet was an antiquated and isolated French entertainment preserved "in a state of mummification," which meant that it had been saved from the general decline of the art of dance throughout the rest of Europe.

But far more than that, ballet had stood aloof from the progressive trends of serious Russian art in the nineteenth century—the trends represented by great novelists like Leo Tolstoy (1828–1910) and Fyodor Dostoyevsky (1821–81) and by composers like Musorgsky or even the Tchaikovsky of the operas and symphonies. Precisely because of this—because ballet was mere play and self-indulgent diversion, because it had remained true to seemingly outdated principles of beauty and stylization—it was far less tainted than opera with the residue of realism and was uncompromised by the social concerns that weighed down Russian literature of the time. The Russian ballet, in short, was a kind of sleeping beauty in its own right, an outmoded aristocratic toy irrelevant to all serious artistic endeavor until, by a curious quirk of fate, the nature of serious artistic endeavor changed in such a fashion as to make it relevant again.

It was Benois and his friends, nurtured by an artistic movement known as *Mir iskusstva* (The World of Art), who planted the awakening kiss. While Benois remained the chief theorist, the new chief executive was Sergey Diaghilev (1872–1929; Fig. 28-9), a man of enormous energy and vision who organized *Mir iskusstva* art exhibitions, edited a superb arts journal of the same name, and became, it is no exaggeration to say, the greatest impresario the world has ever seen. His efforts sparked a resurgence of ballet and briefly made ballet one of the major sites of artistic and musical innovation. Benois, like Wagner, wanted to combine the different arts into a kind of ideal *Gesamtkunstwerk*, but he had a quite different take on what the priorities were: "Ballet is perhaps the most eloquent of all spectacles, since it permits the two most excellent conductors of thought—music and gesture—to appear in their full expanse and depth, unencumbered by words, which limit and fetter thought, bringing it down from heaven to earth."[21] Benois proposed that ballet was the final step in music theater's liberation from the tyranny of the spoken word. Ballet, he insisted, was the artistic wave of the future.

Figure 28-9 Sergey Diaghilev (1906), painted by Leon Bakst. The figure in the background is Diaghilev's childhood nanny.

And so it became, thanks to Diaghilev. Beginning in 1906, at first with heavy financial backing from the Russian crown, Diaghilev embarked on an epoch-making "export campaign," as Benois rather drily called it: a yearly Russian season in Paris, the cultural capital of the world. Diaghilev's first Parisian venture was an exhibition of Russian painting, from Medieval icons to the work of the *Mir iskusstva* circle itself. The next year, 1907, he presented a series of dazzling "historical concerts" in which all the greatest Russian musicians of the day took part: Rimsky-Korsakov, the dean of living Russian composers; Alexander Glazunov (1865–1936), Rimsky-Korsakov's star pupil; the pianist-composers Alexander Scriabin, Sergey Rachmaninoff, and others. These concerts were not only historical (that is, presenting works from the full range of Russian musical history) but also historic: They provided a conduit that brought the latest Russian music to French ears like those of Debussy and Ravel.

In 1908, Diaghilev mounted a legendary production at the Paris Opéra of Musorgsky's *Boris Godunov* (in a version arranged by Rimsky-Korsakov), which set a benchmark for luxuriance and spectacle. The next year, he offered a mixed "Russian season" of music theater, including ballet for the first time. The Russian ballets especially amazed the French, who had considered the genre to be their national property but who now saw their version of it thoroughly surpassed. The ballet spectacles, unexpectedly, proved far more successful with the public than the operas. Diaghilev decided to follow Benois's advice, which he had until then resisted, and he specialized thenceforth in presenting Russian ballets to Parisian audiences.

And yet the French critics in 1909 had complained that what Diaghilev's **Ballets Russes** (Russian Ballet) presented in its first season did not duplicate the exotic impression created by the Russian operas and that without an overlay of recognizably Russian style (which meant, for French ears, a folkloristic or Oriental style) they could not regard the Russian ballet as a truly authentic artistic product. Here indeed was an irony: The Russian ballet, originally a French import and proud of its stylistic heritage, now had to become stylistically Russian so as to justify its exportation back to France. Diaghilev's solution was to commission, expressly for presentation the next season in Paris, something without precedent in Russia: a ballet on a Russian folk subject, with music cast in a conspicuously exotic Russian style. He began to look around for a composer willing to complete so strange a task.

Stravinsky's *The Firebird* and *Petrushka*

Four composers, all pupils of Rimsky-Korsakov's, refused before Diaghilev found his man. Igor Stravinsky (1882–1971) was an ambitious member of a younger generation who had yet to make a name for himself and who therefore had everything to gain from the international exposure Diaghilev promised. As the son of a leading bass in the Russian Imperial Opera, Stravinsky's exposure to music had started young. Fyodor Stravinsky was not anxious, however, for his son to pursue a musical career and insisted that he go to law school, which Igor did without ever graduating. The musical impulse could not be silenced, however, and he set off to study with Rimsky-Korsakov, who provided private lessons free of charge. Rimsky supervised the composition of Stravinsky's Symphony in E♭ Major, Op. 1, which was followed by two brightly colored showpieces, the *Scherzo fantastique*, Op. 3, and *Fireworks*, Op. 4.

Stravinsky's first full ballet for Diaghilev was very much a team effort. The scenario was largely the work of the choreographer, Mikhail Fokine (1880–1942), a brilliant dancer who had trained under Petipa. The title, *The Firebird* (*Zhar-ptitsa*, or *L'oiseau de feu* as it was called at the Paris premiere), was symbolic: the Firebird, a Slavic mythological creature of great beauty whose feathers were treasures of incalculable value, had been adopted by the *Mir iskusstva* circle as the trademark of art-for-art's-sake (Fig. 28-10). Fokine patched together a story line from several well-known folk tales that told of how, with the aid of the Firebird, Ivan Tsarevich, the Prince Charming character, won the hand of the Princess Nenaglyadnaya-Krasa (Unearthly Beauty) by freeing her from a spell cast by the sorcerer Kashchey-Bessmertnïy (Immortal Kashchey).

Figure 28-10 Costume design by Leon Bakst, for the Firebird, danced by Tamara Karsavina, in Stravinsky's *The Firebird.* Produced by Sergey Diaghilev's Ballets Russes in 1910.

Stravinsky's music for *The Firebird* fell into two broad categories. One was the folkloric, reserved for the human characters, the Prince and the Princess. The other was the fantastic, or *féerique*, associated with the supernatural characters, the Firebird and Kashchey. This dual style had been Rimsky-Korsakov's specialty, mastered in his late fairy-tale operas, the last two of which he composed during Stravinsky's period of apprenticeship (*Legend of the Invisible City of Kitezh and the Maiden Fevroniya* and *The Golden Cockerel*). Rimsky had mined the music for the human characters from his own published collection, *One Hundred Russian Folk Songs* (1877) and the music for the supernatural ones from the resources of the octatonic scale of alternating whole steps and half steps. Encouraged by Diaghilev, Stravinsky strove to maximalize the work of his teacher, as Mahler and Strauss had been maximalizing the work of Wagner.

Stravinsky's *Firebird* soon achieved its own dual life. The premiere of the ballet in June 1910 proved a triumph for Russian music, and Stravinsky fashioned its dances into a suite that became a popular concert work. He therefore managed with this wildly successful score to appeal both to the broad theater and concert audience as well as to the composing and critical fraternity, a feat he would duplicate many times over the course of his long career. In this way he gained an eminence among twentieth-century composers and a prestige that would last to the end of his life, more than sixty years later.

Stravinsky now faced the challenge of topping his first success. The next season, 1911, Diaghilev produced a new ballet called *Petrushka,* which proved to be even more popular. Although the primary impetus this time had come from Stravinsky, the history of the project and its outcome again reveal the essentially collaborative nature of the Diaghilev enterprise. While finishing *The Firebird,* the composer had an idea for a sequel: a primitive sacrificial rite in which a virgin danced herself to death before an idol of the ancient Slavic sun god. Stravinsky decided to change course, however, and write a light and funny concert piece for piano and orchestra that would spoof the antics of a Romantic virtuoso. Casting about for a title, he noticed that some of the searing trumpet blasts he had composed were reminiscent of the kazoo-like instrument that produced the shrill voice of Petrushka (Little Pete), a fairground puppet character who was "always in an explosion of revolt." Armed with a cudgel, he would beat up anybody in sight. The skit always ended with his being dragged off to hell by a big black dog.

When Diaghilev heard the music, he talked Stravinsky into turning his new work into a ballet, the scenario of which was devised with Benois. It combined the puppet-theater and fairground ambience with a love triangle adapted from the old commedia dell'arte as revived in the nineteenth century by acrobatic mimes: Pierrot (the sad clown) loves Columbine (the ingénue), who loves Arlecchino (the happy clown). Benois recast these roles in terms of the fairground theater: Petrushka himself, a ballerina puppet, and an African puppet commonly called a "blackamoor." The two-tiered action unfolds in four scenes. The outer ones show the fairground and its revelers; the inner ones present the love triangle.

As in *The Firebird,* the plot is a wild mixture of sometimes-incongruous topics presented to the French as authentically Russian. The music further maximalizes the fantastic/realistic opposition long traditional in Russian opera and that Stravinsky had already explored in his earlier ballet. Once again the human element is represented by diatonic folklore and the nonhuman (the secret world where the puppets live) by a chromaticism á la Rimsky based on circles of major and minor thirds, that is, symmetrical divisions of the octave by three or four half steps. But this time the musical contrast, like the poetic contrast it reflects, is treated with a wily irony: The "people" in *Petrushka,* with only negligible exceptions, are represented facelessly by the corps de ballet. Only the puppets have individual personalities and emotions.

The novel treatment of harmony and tonality made the second tableau of Stravinsky's **Petrushka** ***for a while the last word in Modernism.***

Although based on musical echoes of everyday life, the outer (human) scenes in *Petrushka* are transformed into something far removed from everyday reality by Stravinsky's magic-making orchestration and musical simplicity based on the folk tradition. The puppets' secret world, in contrast, is virtually devoid of allusion to folk or popular music. This music is expressive—that is, human—with a vengeance. In its ceaseless ebb and flow, its waxing and waning, it analogizes the inner world, the world of passions and feelings, with their onsets and abatements. The novel treatment of harmony and tonality made the second tableau of *Petrushka* for a while the last word in Modernism. The point that Stravinsky passed and that Rimsky-Korsakov (and even Ravel, in the *Rapsodie espagnole*) had always skirted was the point at which octatonicism became not just a color or an exotic accessory to more conventional tonal harmony but a

Figure 28-11 Vaslav Nijinsky as the title character in the 1911 premiere of Stravinsky's *Petrushka.*

tonality in its own right. The octatonic collection is raised structurally to the level of what we ordinarily mean by a key, governing a hierarchy of pitches. It establishes not only a vocabulary of pitches but also a set of stable structural functions. Hence departures from it and returns to it—on various levels, from that of local "chromaticism" to that of "modulation"—are possible without compromising its role as stable point of reference.

The octatonic collection that serves as reference point in the second scene ("Chez Pétrouchka") is the whole-step/half-step scale that includes the C-major and F♯-major triads, which, when superimposed, produce what has become universally known among musicians as the *Petrushka*-chord (Ex. 28-9). Now, just as Wagner's *Tristan*-chord was not the first half-diminished seventh chord in history, neither was the *Petrushka*-chord unprecedented. And yet again there was a significant maximalizing difference: the F♯ is deliberately made to sound like a foreign element jostling the key (or at least the chord) of C major. Stravinsky uses the *Petrushka*-chord to accompany outbursts of painful emotion arising out of conflict among the characters. Despite the novelty of his materials, Stravinsky deploys octatonicism and the *Petrushka*-chord in ways that make long-accepted musical sense. Such a radical intensification of traditional expressive means once again is precisely what is meant by maximalism.

Petrushka was taken very seriously in part because Stravinsky maintained a proper musical "grotesquerie," in keeping with the puppet theme, and in part thanks to the superb performance in the title role of the dancer Vaslav Nijinsky (1890–1950; Fig. 28-11). Sarah Bernhardt, the great French tragedienne, said after seeing Nijinsky, "I'm very afraid: I've seen the greatest actor on earth!"[22] Dame Edith Sitwell, an English poet of the avant-garde, who caught the show in London, wrote: "Before the arrival of the Russian ballet in England, the average person had never dreamt that movement could convey a philosophy of life as complete and rounded as any world could be."[23] Diaghilev & Co. were proving as right Benois's theory that words were not necessary for great musical theater.

Example 28-9 ***Petrushka*-chord**

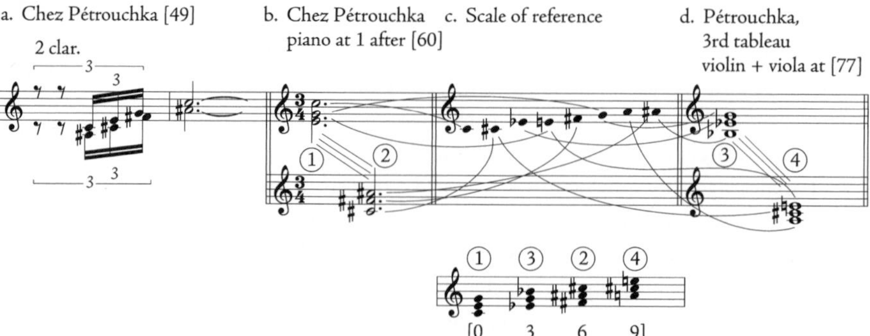

The Rite of Spring

With the rapturous reception of *Petrushka* in mind, Stravinsky returned with a new sense of urgency to "The Great Sacrifice," the Stone Age ballet he had begun sketching the year before. The idea for such a piece, resonant with "neoprimitivist" interests in the arts that sought a new style through evocations of prehistory and premodern cultures, was not particularly original. Visual artists such as Pablo Picasso (1881–1973) had been exploring similar themes for some years, and the Russian version of Symbolist poetry was rife with images of pre-Christian antiquity. Stravinsky consulted with the man who would eventually write the ballet's scenario, the painter and archeologist Nikolai Roerich (1874–1947), a connoisseur of Slavic antiquity, who had made a special study of Russian pagan festivals. They planned the first tableau of "The Great Sacrifice" around these holiday rituals, paying special attention to a passage in an eleventh-century manuscript in which a Christian monk had described the wild customs of the surrounding pagan tribes, the "Radimichi, the Vyatichi, and the Severi." The very diction (as indicated in the brackets in the following excerpt) found its way into the scenario Stravinsky and Roerich worked out, and it is now reflected in the titles of the dances:

> Living in the forests like the very beasts, there were no marriages among them, but simply games [*igrï*] in between the villages. When the people gathered for games, for dancing, and for all other devilish amusements, the men on these occasions carried off wives for themselves [*umïkakhu zhenï sebe*], and each took any woman with whom he had arrived at an understanding. In fact, they even had two or three wives apiece.[24]

The ceremony described here became the *Igra umïkaniya* (Game of Abduction) in the first tableau in *Le sacre du printemps*, known in English as *The Rite of Spring*. The ballet calls for an enormous orchestra deployed to spectacular effect. The ballet is in two tableaux—*The Adoration of the Earth* and *The Sacrifice*—each of which has an introductory section, a series of dances, and a concluding ritual. The opening minutes of the piece give an idea of Stravinsky's innovative style. A solo bassoon, playing in an unusually high register, intones a melancholy melody, harmonized with a vamping bass and an octatonic countermelody. The bassoon melody is the first of at least a dozen folk tunes that Stravinsky adapted for the piece, although he later denied having done so, except for this opening one. Having earlier mined Rimsky-Korsakov's *One Hundred Russian Folk Songs* (1877) for melodies in *Firebird* and *Petrushka*, he now turned to a recently published anthology of Lithuanian wedding songs. Stravinsky thus initially sought validation for his stylistic extravagances in ethnographic authenticity. Maximal dissonance was one of his chief means for evoking the pitiless brutality and inhumanity of primitive religion as he imagined it. By beginning with a piece of folk "reality" and applying a radical new technique to it, Stravinsky sought authenticity and modernity at once.

Anthology Vol 3-15
Full CD VI, 16–19
Concise CD III, 14–15

The most maximal dances in *The Rite of Spring* are the ritualistic ones that conclude the two respective tableaux. The "Dance of the Earth" at the end of part 1 is a montage of ostinatos, one of which is an adaptation of an instrumental dance tune, or *naigrïsh*, of the kind that, sixty-five years earlier, had furnished the point of departure for Glinka's seminal *Kamarinskaya*. Stravinsky, inevitably conscious of this legacy, was resolutely attempting to top it. In any event, the "Dance of the Earth" was a momentous achievement, for it shows how profoundly Stravinsky's musical imagination was stirred by the manipulation of elements abstracted from folk songs. It is at once one of the most radical sections of *The Rite* and the dance most rigorously based on folk-derived source melodies.

The only dance that exceeds it in intensity is the one that had to: the "Sacrificial Dance" that ends the ballet. It revels in the crashing force of a huge orchestra and a chronically elevated level of dissonance. Stravinsky employed an equally extreme dislocation of meter in order to convey the lurching, wrenching quality of the dance that will lead the "Chosen One" to her inevitable death. The technique of constantly shifting the lengths of measures occurs earlier in the ballet, but here it is taken to a new level. Stravinsky's metric and rhythmic innovations might be considered the emancipation of rhythm.

Stravinsky's metric and rhythmic innovations might be considered the emancipation of rhythm.

The rhythmic innovations in *The Rite* are of two distinct types. One is the static, unchanging ostinato, or vamp, sometimes quite literally hypnotic, as when the Elders charm the Chosen One to perform her dance of death. The other type of rhythmic innovation was a great novelty—for European art music, that is; in Russian folklore it had long been a fixture. This was the rhythm of irregularly spaced downbeats, requiring changes in the notation of meter and bar lines. The most radical form of the variable-downbeat technique is one in which the shifting meters are coordinated on the "subtactile" level—that is, by an equalized note value that is less than the duration of a felt beat, or *tactus*. (When a drill sergeant tells his squad to march in "double time," he is instructing them to march at the rate of the subtactile pulse.)

There was no precedent for this technique, even in earlier Russian art music; it was Stravinsky's discovery. In the concluding "Sacrificial Dance" it reaches its zenith, both in terms of complexity of pattern and in terms of fractionated counting value (sixteenths rather than eighths; Ex. 28-10). Particularly fascinating, innovative, and influential was the way in which Stravinsky contrived to have his two rhythmic/metric types—the static ostinato and the active shifting stress—coexist within a single texture. The extreme terror of the *Rite of Spring*, especially its savage conclusion, was something that the audience felt—and can still feel, if the orchestra today can refrain from showing off the relative ease with which, a century later, it is now possible to perform the demanding piece.

Example 28-10 **Igor Stravinsky, *The Rite of Spring* (piano four-hands arrangement), "Sacrificial dance"**

Example 28-10 ***(continued)***

Scandalized Reactions

Stravinsky's music for *The Rite of Spring,* with choreography by the twenty-three-year-old Nijinsky, seemed to insist on the power of Mother Nature rather than the beauty of human nature. The legendary premiere of the ballet on 29 May 1913 in Paris marked one of the great scandals in music history. Diaghilev's company had presented another significant premiere two weeks earlier that was in some respects just as noteworthy, if not nearly as notorious. Debussy's *Jeux* (Games) essentially disappeared from the stage and concert hall after its initial performances, only to be rediscovered in midcentury, at which time it exerted considerable influence on a new generation of composers. Debussy and Stravinsky were in close contact while they were writing their ballets, frequently discussing their projects and sharing their scores. After the two played through *The Rite of Spring* in a four-hand version, Debussy said that the work haunted him "like a beautiful nightmare!"[25]

Stravinsky had composed the *Rite* between September 1911 and March 1913, after which the work went into an unusually extensive period of rehearsals, thus dwarfing the preparation for *Jeux.* The final dress rehearsal, on 28 May, the day before the premiere, was given before a large audience, with some critics in attendance. Things apparently went smoothly. An announcement in the newspaper *Le Figaro* promised

> the strongly stylized characteristic attitudes of the Slavic race with an awareness of the beauty of the prehistoric period. The prodigious Russian dancers were the

> only ones capable of expressing these stammerings of a semi-savage humanity, of composing these frenetic human clusters wrenched incessantly by the most astonishing polyrhythm ever to come to the mind of a musician. There is truly a new thrill which will surely raise passionate discussions, but which will leave all true artists with an unforgettable impression.[26]

At the premiere of* The Rite *of Spring, as Stravinsky succinctly reported in a letter home, "things got as far as fighting."

The premiere was devised to be a big event. Ticket prices at the newly built Théâtre des Champs-Elysées were doubled, and the cultural elite of the city showed up. It was the "real thing—a big 'Paris' scandal,"[27] a critic remarked, something that could be set beside the fiasco of Wagner's *Tannhäuser* half a century before. And the reasons were similar: The audience expected one thing and got another. With Wagner, it was a short divertissement in the first act rather than an extravagant operatic ballet. With Stravinsky, it was prehistoric peasants on stage instead of fairy tale characters, stamping on the earth rather than soaring above it. The other ballets on the program that evening, danced to music by Chopin, Weber, and Borodin, were familiar and safe fare. No wonder that with the *Rite*, as Stravinsky succinctly reported in a letter home, "things got as far as fighting."[28]

There are conflicting accounts of what exactly happened with Stravinsky's ballet, the second piece on the program, and legends quickly emerged expounded by people who were not in attendance. Some present apparently considered Nijinsky's choreography to be incompetent (Fig. 28-12). We will never know exactly what Nijinsky created; despite strenuous efforts to reconstruct the original by studying photographs, memoirs, and other evidence, his contribution is now essentially lost, as are all such transitory performances in an age before easy filming and video.

From the very start of the performance there was laughter and an uproar among the audience, but whether this was principally in response to what was being heard or what was being seen is unclear. One critic observed that "past the Prelude the crowd simply stopped listening to the music so that they might better amuse themselves with the choreography."[29] Although the music was inaudible at times through the din, conductor Pierre Monteux pressed on and saw the ballet through to the end. Five more performances were given over the next two weeks, and then the Ballets Russes took the ballet on tour. Within the year the piece was triumphantly presented as a concert piece, again with Monteux conducting, and ever since the concert hall has been its principal home, just as with *Firebird* and *Petrushka*. Yet it is well worth remembering that all three extraordinary works were originally theater pieces, collaborative efforts forging the talents of Stravinsky, Diaghilev and his team, and a large ensemble of musicians and dancers.

Among those who hailed Stravinsky's music as a masterpiece, however, were some who also perceived a worrisome message in the ballet. "This is a biological ballet," declared Jacques Rivière, the editor of the *Nouvelle revue française*, Paris's most sophisticated literary and intellectual journal.[30] The adjective summons up a variant of *neoprimitivism* called *biologism*, one of the bleakest, most antihumanistic of all philosophical visions. **Primitivism**, the belief that what is least mediated by modern society—children, peasants, "savages," raw emotion, plain speech—is closest to the truth was compatible with all the noblest aspirations of Romanticism. Biologism was more pessimistic. Skeptical of all humane ideals, it held life to be no more than the sum of its physical facts and drives: birth, death, procreation, survival. Anything else was mere ornament and a lie. The sanctity of revealed religion was thus challenged, especially Christian religion, for the ballet reduced the Holy Eucharist to a cannibalistic rite no different from those practiced by any number of savage tribes. It was all too easy to draw a horrifying parallel between the culminating virgin sacrifice in *The Rite of Spring* and the sacrifice commemorated in Christianity's most solemn act of worship.

In contrast with such weighty issues, Debussy's *Jeux* could not seem more trivial. The "game" in the title is tennis, and the basic plot was printed in the Ballets Russes program book:

> The scene is a garden at dusk; a tennis ball has been lost; a boy and two girls are searching for it. The artificial light of the large electric lamps shedding fantastic rays about them suggests the idea of childish games: They play hide and seek, they try to catch one another, they quarrel, they sulk without cause. The night is warm, the sky is bathed in pale light; they embrace. But the spell is broken by another tennis ball thrown in mischievously by an unknown hand. Surprised and alarmed, the young man and the girls disappear into the nocturnal depths of the garden.[31]

THE TWITCHING, BOBBING, TURN-YOUR-TOES-IN, CUBIST DANCE.

NIJINSKY'S REVOLUTION IN CHOREOGRAPHY: THE POST-IMPRESSIONISTIC AND PREHISTORIC DANCE, "SACRE DU PRINTEMPS."

Nijinsky appears not to be content with his success in the graceful dances which have made his name so familiar to all lovers of the Russian Ballet. Dancing should, he thinks, strike a new line, just as Post-Impressionists consider that reversion to primitive forms in painting may direct the art into new channels. Therefore, it was to the most primitive form of his art that the great dancer determined to go, the result being that we were treated to one of the most astounding and nerve-shattering dances that have ever been performed. To Stravinsky's music, in itself blood-curdling from its weird dissonances and orchestral groans and shrieks, a prehistoric people regaled us with bobs and jerks, turned-in toes, Swedish-exercise-like movements, and, in one place, a simultaneous shaking like a jelly, similar to Teddy Payne's famous performance with the bombs in a former Gaiety piece. It must be confessed that the higher critics of dancing seemed to see in this reversion to the excessively primitive a movement of enthralling interest in the history of the choreographic art. Further developments will be awaited with interest. (*See Article elsewhere.*)

Figure 28-12 Les Adolescents in Stravinsky's *The Rite of Spring*. Photos of the Paris premiere from a scathing review in *The Sketch Supplement*.

There had been various versions of the scenario along the way—including one in which it is not another tennis ball that interrupts the proceedings but, rather, a crashing airplane. Nijinsky, who was Diaghilev's lover for a period, wrote in his diary that the impresario's original idea was for a ballet about "three young men making love to each other,"[32] but this was changed to a less provocative theme. We don't know exactly what Debussy made of all this—a letter to his publisher refers to the "rather *risqué* situation," but then "in ballet, immorality passes through the ballerina's legs and ends in a pirouette."[33]

The trivial, everyday aspects of the scenario were in any case just as much a taste of things to come in France as was the shocking neoprimitivism of Stravinsky's ballet. So too was the way Debussy structured musical time in the work. Many ideas go by, never to be repeated; colors and instrumentation change continually; the dynamic level rarely rises above *piano*. Each of the three dancers is associated with a meter—$\frac{3}{8}$, $\frac{3}{4}$, and $\frac{2}{4}$—and all come together for a triple embrace that forms the climax of the piece. *Jeux* was Debussy's last completed orchestral work. He composed less during the final five years of his life, before his death from cancer at age fifty-five. His last years, during the First World War, saw further militant rejection of German aesthetics and an embrace of a much older French one, notably the heritage of Rameau and Couperin. His final works were three of a projected set of six abstract sonatas for diverse instrumental combinations.

The younger Stravinsky would live for nearly sixty more productive years after the momentous premiere of *The Rite of Spring*, a piece that quickly became one of the key works in the history of Western music and established its composer as one of the key figures of musical Modernism. His blending of Russian traditions with Modernist musical innovations was also very much a sign of the times. Countries that have not previously gotten much of our attention, those at the periphery or with less prominent compositional heritages, now began to emerge in what was an increasingly international musical scene with many new musical voices and new varieties of musical Modernism.

Summary

This chapter explored developments in French music in the late nineteenth and early twentieth centuries. Valuing the decorative above the philosophical, French composers pursued different strategies than did the Germans explored in the preceding chapter. For inspiration they turned to literature and the visual arts as well as to music from Russia, Asia, and the United States. Their anti-Wagnerian sentiments were expressed in satires of Wagner and in pieces written in the older styles of Baroque composers. "Golliwogg's Cakewalk" by Claude Debussy (1862–1918) includes a parody of Wagner's *Tristan und Isolde*. *Trois sarabandes*, by Erik Satie (1866–1925), uses Baroque dance forms and treats Wagnerian chords as if they were consonances, detaching them from the idea of harmonic tension and release that Wagner had so thoroughly exploited.

In contrast to Wagner and other German composers, Debussy's harmonic vocabulary is saturated with whole-tone and pentatonic scales that minimize goal directedness, removing the "harmonic glue" that connects successive chords to one another in traditional harmony. These traits are illustrated in the piano piece *Voiles* (1909). Critics in Debussy's time associated his music with the indistinct lines and subtle gradations of color in Impressionist painting. Debussy, however, had closer connections to the literary movement known as Symbolism. Symbolist poetry focused on the equivalence of sense experiences and the hidden meanings of the sensory world, seeing them as a path to spiritual understanding. Debussy's opera *Pelléas et Mélisande* (1893–1902) is a setting of a play by the symbolist Maurice Maeterlinck (1862–1949). Although the plot of *Pelléas et Mélisande* bears some resemblance to Wagner's *Tristan und Isolde* in its suggestion of illicit love, little actually happens on stage. With its avoidance of directed harmonic progressions and its emphasis on speech-like vocal lines, the opera depicts the Symbolist drama perfectly.

Gabriel Fauré (1845–1924), Maurice Ravel (1875–1937), and Lili Boulanger (1893–1918) worked in the same milieu. Fauré is known for his quintessentially French songs, some on Symbolist texts, and for his *Requiem*. Although Ravel wrote some works in the Impressionist style associated with Debussy, he was also open to "exotic" influences, apparent in his Spanish-influenced pieces, such as *Bolero* (1928) and *Rapsodie espagnole* (1908), and in later works that borrow from American jazz. France was one of the first countries where the means for musical success were available to women, and Lili Boulanger won the coveted Prix de Rome in 1913.

Despite its long association with the French, ballet gained renewed importance as a musical genre under Russian influence. The Russian dance theorist Alexandre

Benois (1870–1960) and the impresario Sergey Diaghilev (1872–1929) sought to make ballet a site of artistic musical innovation and the ultimate synthesis of all the arts. Beginning in 1909, Diaghilev's Russian ballet season in Paris was the site for several radically innovative works, including Debussy's *Jeux* (1913) and Igor Stravinsky's *The Firebird* (1910), *Petrushka* (1911), and *The Rite of Spring* (1913). Following in the footsteps of his teacher Nikolai Rimsky-Korsakov, Stravinsky (1882–1971) combined Russian folk song with an innovative melodic and rhythmic language based on the octatonic scale (alternating half steps and whole steps), ostinatos, blocks of static harmony, and uneven downbeats. The premiere of *The Rite of Spring* in 1913 provoked outrage. Its plot was based on prehistoric sacrificial rituals, its choreography departed from the graceful gestures expected of French ballet, and its music was filled with unfamiliar melodic and rhythmic innovations. Stravinsky depicts the brutality of the rites with maximal dissonance.

Study Questions

1. Describe the various reactions to Wagner among French composers and the ways that French composers tried to exorcise his influence. How are these anti-Wagnerian traits reflected in Erik Satie's *Trois sarabandes* and in the music of Claude Debussy?
2. Describe the harmonic language created by Satie, Debussy, and Gabriel Fauré. What are its essential traits, and how does it differ from that of Wagner?
3. What is Impressionism, and why is the music of Debussy, Fauré, and Ravel often described as Impressionist?
4. What are the characteristics of Symbolist poetry? How did it influence Debussy and Fauré? In what respects is Debussy's *Pelléas et Mélisande* a Symbolist work?
5. How did ballet emerge as an important form of cultural expression in Russia? Describe the goals and achievements of Alexandre Benois and Sergey Diaghilev.
6. Describe the convergence of various stylistic influences that went into Stravinsky's musical language in his ballets *The Firebird* and *Petrushka*.
7. What rhythmic and melodic innovations lie at the heart of Stravinsky's *The Rite of Spring*?
8. Why did *The Rite of Spring* cause such a stir at its premiere in 1913?

Key Terms

ballet d'action
Ballets Russes
Impressionism
mélodie
octatonic
primitivism
Symbolism
synesthesia
whole-tone scale

29

National Monuments

The previous two chapters introduced leading figures in the Austro-German and French spheres, whose music largely dominated—or came to dominate—Modernist compositional practice and aesthetic debates during the first half of the twentieth century. In the view of many musicians and critics, the various strategies of maximalized Romanticism and burgeoning Modernism eventually boiled down to a sharp conflict between two groups of younger composers. Schoenberg headed one camp, while the other was associated with Stravinsky. During the middle third of the twentieth century these two composers represented the leading Modernist factions, with some of the controversies between them being reminiscent of battles and divides encountered in earlier centuries. Yet looking beyond Austria, Germany, and France reveals a much wider and richer variety of Modernist concerns and practices. The stylistic range of twentieth-century music became unusually diverse (even more so when one includes popular as well as literate music), especially as it played out after the cataclysmic First World War. New compositional and aesthetic concerns emerged in countries that have not previously received much of our attention because they had yet to produce composers who entered the so-called mainstream.

Most of the figures we will consider in this chapter, composers such as Jean Sibelius in Finland, Ralph Vaughan Williams in England, Manuel de Falla in Spain, Béla Bartók in Hungary, Leoš Janáček in Moravia, Alexander Scriabin in Russia, and Charles Ives in the United States, participated to varying degrees in the Modernist trends we have just been tracing, but they also sought to bring to their music something of the indigenous traditions of their own countries. We have seen this already in Stravinsky's extraordinary and very influential blending of folklore and Modernism as a Russian working in France. Such negotiations are the reason for immediately identifying where these composers came from: National interests and traditions profoundly affected their art.

National interests and traditions, of course, likewise deeply affected the art of Germans like Wagner, Strauss, and Schoenberg and French composers such as Debussy, Fauré, and Ravel, but this influence tends to be less remarked on, indeed it can seem invisible, because the traditions of those respective countries were long, strong, and deemed universal. As we have seen with figures such as Glinka, Musorgsky, and Dvořák, for nineteenth-century composers working outside of Germany and France, it was recognition abroad that helped to foster preeminence at home. And in time, the achievements of some of these composers strongly influenced composers abroad—Musorgsky's music was a revelation to various French composers, as was Stravinsky's to a later generation; Dvořák's "New World" Symphony had a huge impact on American composers, whether they liked it or not.

Composers living outside France, Germany, and Italy faced similar challenges, ones already familiar to us from their nineteenth-century counterparts: how to create or enhance an indigenous national music in relation to so-called universal legacies. This dilemma took on new force during the First World War and afterwards; since Germany had been the enemy, basking in the music of Wagner could seem downright unpatriotic. Yet for most of the composers we will now consider, studying abroad, or at least extensive travel, was the rule. As a practical matter of training and exposure, centers like Berlin, Vienna, and Paris offered superb educational and cultural opportunities that for the most part were not available at home. If a young composer early in the twentieth century was seeking out the latest in interesting new musical directions, Strauss, Mahler, and Debussy would immediately have come to mind as models. But after learning in distant places and from prominent figures, many composers looked for ways to create music connected to their own national and cultural heritage. By employing a variety of historical and local musical traditions, folk materials, mythology, language, and spiritual and political references, composers in these countries forged their own distinctive voices. Their accomplishments were in turn emulated by other composers and eventually came to represent national rather than individual styles. In one way or another, at one time or another, most of these composers expressed the same sentiment: to reflect their indigenous culture while creating music that would eventually be respected, indeed acclaimed, by international audiences.

Especially after Germany's 1918 defeat and the end of World War I, there was an increasing internationalism in European and American musical life. The International Society for Contemporary Music (ISCM), founded in 1922, promoted composers from all over the world. The Allgemeiner Deutscher Musikverein (General German Music Association), which Liszt and Franz Brendel had founded in 1861 to promote the New German School, began to embrace a far more inclusive range of composers. Even the elite Verein für musikalische Privataufführungen (Society for Private Musical Performance), a concert series that Schoenberg and Berg created in Vienna in 1918, performed an unusually eclectic array of European composers. The chances to hear and to be heard expanded.

Figure 29-1 Drawing of Jean Sibelius by Albert Edelfelt, 1904.

Jean Sibelius

One of the first composers around the turn of the century to create an internationally recognized national music was Jean Sibelius (1865–1957; Fig. 29-1). He fits the pattern we will see in this chapter time and again: training abroad, influence from established Modernists, engagement with indigenous traditions in his own country,

TIMELINE

1854 Henry David Thoreau, *Walden; or Life in the Woods*

1898 **Spanish-American War**

1898–99 **Edward Elgar, "Enigma" Variations**

1900 **Jean Sibelius, *Finlandia***

1902 **Charles Ives, *The Celestial Country***

1905 First "Nickelodeon" movie theatre opens in Pittsburgh

1905 **Manuel de Falla, *La vida breve***

1906 **Béla Bartók, *Bagatelles* for piano, Op. 6**

1906 **Bartók, *Dance Suite***

1910 **Alexander Scriabin, *Prométhée: Le poème de feu***

1910 **Ralph Vaughan Williams, *Fantasia on a Theme of Thomas Tallis***

1911 **Leoš Janáček, *On an Overgrown Path***

1912 Titanic sinks

1914–18 World War I

1914 **Ives, *Three Places in New England***

1915 **Scriabin, *Vers la flamme***

1917 Bolshevik Revolution in Russia

1917 Finland declares independence from Russia

1918 Poland and Czechoslovakia achieve independence

1920 **Ives, Second Piano Sonata, *Concord, Mass., 1840–60***

1927 **Henry Cowell founds *New Music Quarterly***

and celebrity at home eventually resulting in recognition as an exemplary figure on the international stage. In Sibelius's case the country was Finland, a small one dominated by powerful neighbors. This political situation furthered the possibility for an eminent composer to do more than just create a representative musical voice: He could actually play an important role in the construction of a national culture. Sibelius's many symphonic poems and seven symphonies gained him widespread recognition, first in Finland, then in the rest of the Nordic countries, and ultimately across Europe, the United States, and elsewhere. The domestic and international recognition are of course mutually dependent; they are what make a composer not only national but also exemplary.

His early fame was conventionally that of a nationalist in a time of considerable political fervor. Finland was a grand duchy within the Russian empire until 1917; pro-Finnish pride and anti-Russian sentiment ran high, feelings that Sibelius registered to varying degrees in many compositions. The irony was that Finland had for centuries before been dominated in culture, politics, and language by Sweden. Sibelius was himself a Swedish-speaking Finn who learned Finnish. (We may remember Smetana, the great Czech composer, struggling to learn Czech.) His musical education and models were based on Germanic Europe. After early training as a violinist, he enrolled at the Helsinki Music Institute, where Ferruccio Busoni (1866–1924), a prominent Italian pianist and composer, had recently been hired as a young professor and with whom Sibelius developed a fruitful relationship. Upon graduating at age twenty-three in 1889, Sibelius was awarded a stipend to continue his training in Berlin and, after a brief return home, he received further funding to go to Vienna to study with Karl Goldmark and Robert Fuchs. At the time he took keen interest in the music of Bruckner and got to know Wagner's operas well, even making a pilgrimage in 1894 to Bayreuth, where *Tristan* and *Parsifal* particularly enthralled him. Strauss and Debussy emerged as important Modernist influences on his early music.

Sibelius also found some models closer to home in the music of Tchaikovsky and the Norwegian composer Edvard Grieg (1843–1907). Sibelius's main national inspiration came not from music but, rather, from Finland's founding literary epic, the *Kalevala*. That enormous work had been transmitted orally for hundreds of years before the poet Elias Lönnrot published an edition in 1835. It never existed in antiquity in the imposing form in which Lönnrot released it, heavily edited and organized into a single coherent narrative. The *Kalevala* served to imbue the modern Finns—that is, the urban, educated, cosmopolitan classes of Finnish society—with a sense of kinship and national cohesion. For his music Sibelius looked not only to its mythic stories but also to the recitation patterns of the verse itself. When he visited America in 1914 and was awarded an honorary doctorate from Yale University, the commendation noted, "What Wagner did with Teutonic legend, Dr. Sibelius has done in his own impressive way with the legends of Finland as embodied in her national epic. He has translated the *Kalevala* into the universal language of music, remarkable for its breadth, large simplicity, and the infusion of a deeply poetic personality."[1]

Sibelius's earliest use of the epic was in the symphonic poem *Kullervo*, Op. 7 (1891), named after a character in the *Kalevala* whose tragic life and death are charted over the course of five movements. Scored for two vocal soloists, male chorus, and orchestra, the piece was never published in its entirety during his lifetime and was given only a few early performances. After the atmospheric tone poem *En saga* (1892), Sibelius returned to the national epic as the basis for an orchestral cycle entitled *Four Legends from the Kalevala*, Op. 22 (1893–95), parts of which were initially conceived as an opera. While the character of Kullervo was dark and tragic, Sibelius here portrayed the more sympathetic figure of Lemminkäinen, tracing his travels to an enchanted island, his sojourns to the land of the dead, and later his return home. Like Smetana's *Má vlast*, the cycle of four tone poems could be performed together or separately: *Lemminkäinen and the Maidens of the Island, The Swan of Tuonela, Lemminkäinen in Tuonela*, and *Lemminkäinen's Return. The Swan of Tuonela* is the most frequently performed of the four. As Sibelius explained, "Tuonela, the land of death, the hell of Finnish mythology, is surrounded by a large river with black waters and a rapid current, on which the Swan of Tuonela floats majestically, singing."[2] His delicate scoring casts the swan's song for the English horn, which hovers above shimmering divided strings.

Anthology Vol 3-16
Full CD VI, 20

Although Sibelius would later return to Kalevalaic stories, his most famous tone poem came at the turn of the century and was not related to the epic. *Finlandia* (1900) is a piece that aided the cause of Finnish independence from Russia and eventually become an unofficial national anthem. Originally entitled *Finland Awakens* (*Suomi Herää*), it is a noisy festivity culminating in a cantabile hymn that has been given words in various languages and joined the oral tradition. (In English one well-known version sets words by Lloyd Stone, "A Song of Peace," and was popularized in the 1960s by the folk trio Peter, Paul & Mary.) Depending on one's political allegiance, the tone poem could be read as celebratory or defiant. The Russian authorities cooperated in solidifying the patriotic status of *Finlandia* by banning it. Before 1917 it was usually performed in Finland and Russia under the neutral title *Impromptu*, but the evidently intentional similarity between Sibelius's anthem tune and an existing patriotic song by a local composer that actually bore the title "Awaken, Finland!" (*Herää, Suomi!*) conveyed the political message plainly enough to Finnish ears. The piece made Sibelius a national hero, and a state stipend helped support him for the rest of his long life.

Sibelius's first two symphonies (1899, 1902) were large, impressive compositions that owe some debt to Tchaikovsky, as does his celebrated Violin Concerto (1903–04). Over the next few years, however, his music took an unexpected ascetic turn. The symphonies beginning with the Third (1907) became increasingly compressed—shorter, highly concentrated, and motivically saturated. Although he was still capable of grand statements, as heard for example in the finale of the Fifth Symphony (1915, revised 1916, 1919), Sibelius's preferred manner became dark and at times downright anticlimactic—many compositions fade out to conclude. Sibelius met Mahler when the Austrian was visiting Helsinki in October 1907. To Mahler's enthusiastic claim that a symphony must be an all-embracing statement ("Like the world!"), he allegedly countered that, on the contrary, what mattered most in a symphony was "severity and style and the profound logic that created an inner connection between all the motifs."[3] Four years later, on completing the Fourth Symphony (1910–11), he wrote to Rosa Newmarch, an English admirer, that it "stands as a protest against present-day music, having nothing, absolutely nothing of the circus about it."[4]

Sibelius allegedly said that what mattered most in a symphony was "severity and style and the profound logic that created an inner connection between all the motifs."

Sibelius's productivity lessened considerably after the First World War, with his Sixth Symphony coming in 1923 and the final, the Seventh, the following year. In the latter Sibelius reached what was for him the limit of compression—a twenty-minute single movement of highly complex but tautly unified content whose actual form has been an enduring riddle for generations of analysts and commentators.

Sibelius lived another thirty-three years—to the age of ninety-one—an amazing span, considering his lifelong abuse of alcohol and tobacco. But there were no more surviving symphonies and, after the last of his symphonic poems, *Tapiola* (1926), no more major works.

The sphinx-like silence seemed like the outcome of an unstoppable trajectory. Sibelius now loomed not merely as a Finnish national monument but as the very embodiment of "The North"—harsh, frosty, inscrutable, and humbling. His authority, especially in the 1920s and '30s, was enormous. His birthday became a national holiday. On the occasion of his seventieth, in 1935, he was feted at a banquet to which all the past presidents of Finland had been invited, along with the prime ministers of Norway, Denmark, and Sweden. During this time there was hardly a composer of symphonies who was not profoundly—and often openly, even reverently—beholden to his example.

With Sibelius having been promoted by the Nazis during World War II as a result of his country's alliance with them (motivated by a well-grounded fear of Soviet Russia, which had fought a war of aggression with Finland in 1939–40), his reputation fell on hard times. The musical avant-garde wrote off his music as reactionary. Sometimes the anger was extreme—Schoenberg acolyte René Leibowitz wrote a pamphlet entitled *Sibelius, le plus mauvais compositeur du monde* (Sibelius, the Worst Composer in the World), but his music was enthusiastically embraced by many of the leading conductors of the century, including Arturo Toscanini, Thomas Beecham, Serge Koussevitzky, Herbert von Karajan, Colin Davis, Leonard Bernstein, and James Levine, among others. His reputation has endured vicissitudes and challenges, but the long controversy is in itself testimony to Sibelius's potency, as is the considerable influence he had on later composers.

England

The musical situation in England at the end of the nineteenth century remained surprisingly provincial, given the country's great political and economic clout. England continued its long and rich cultural tradition, particularly its hallowed literary one, and exercised enormous power as a global empire, although one that would soon begin to decline after the First World War. But as had been the case for quite some time, English musical interest when it came to composition had been largely imported. We know Handel spent most of his career there; Haydn, Weber, Mendelssohn, Wagner, Dvořák, and other prominent continental composers visited and enlivened concert life. A generation of English composers who competed with illustrious foreigners emerged in the late nineteenth century with figures such as Hubert Parry (1848–1918), Irish-born Charles Villiers Stanford (1854–1924), and, most importantly, Edward Elgar (1857–1934). As late as 1904, however, a German writer named Oscar Adolf Hermann Schmitz wrote a book about musical culture in England called *Das Land ohne Musik* (The Country without Music) that captured ongoing continental condescension.

Elgar came to prominence at the turn of the century with his orchestral *Variations on an Original Theme* (popularly known as the "Enigma" Variations). An important factor bringing him international fame and exploding the myth of England as a "country without music" was the prestige of the conductor who premiered the work. He was Hans Richter (1843–1916; Fig. 29-2), who had conducted the

Figure 29-2 Hans Richter conducts Edward Elgar's *Dream of Gerontius* at Birmingham Town Hall, 1909.

premiere of Wagner's *Ring* cycle in 1876 as well as the premieres of Brahms and Bruckner symphonies and of Tchaikovsky's Violin Concerto. Richter now became Elgar's great champion, giving many subsequent premieres, including that of *The Dream of Gerontius* (1900), Elgar's most famous oratorio, which secured his position at the very forefront of English composers. Richter propagated his music in the main European centers, giving him an international profile that dwarfed those of his fellow countrymen. Elgar's status as a viable British musical representative to the world was a necessary precondition for his country's emergence (or rather reemergence) as a significant producer, not just a significant consumer, of music.

The preeminent English composer of the next generation was Ralph Vaughan Williams (1872–1958; Fig. 29-3). Although England offered excellent educational opportunities in music—he availed himself of them at the Royal College of Music and Cambridge University, studying with both Stanford and Parry—Vaughan Williams felt a need to hone his skills on the continent. He studied briefly in Berlin with Max Bruch (1838–1920), a member of Brahms's generation, best remembered for a violin concerto and other concerted works, including a *Scottish Fantasy* for violin and orchestra. Later, Vaughan Williams studied in Paris with Maurice Ravel, who was his junior by three years.

Like most of the composers discussed in this chapter, Vaughan Williams attempted to use what he had learned internationally to help create and promote a national music. In this effort he looked to English folk songs as well as to the country's musical past more than three centuries earlier in Tudor times. In a lecture entitled "Who Wants the English Composer?" (1912), he asked: "Is it not possible that the English composer has something to say to his own countrymen that no one of any other age and any other country can say? Have we not all about us forms of musical expression which we can purify and raise to the level of great art?"[5] From across the British Isles, Vaughan Williams collected over 800 folk songs, which he called the "common stem" of English music and which became a source for some of his own compositions.

Figure 29-3 Ralph Vaughan Williams in the 1920s.

Anthology Vol 3-17
Full CD VI, 21

In an early orchestral work, *Fantasia on a Theme of Thomas Tallis* (1910), Vaughan Williams looked not to an oral folk tradition but, rather, to a melody by the sixteenth-century English composer Thomas Tallis (1505–85), a composer in Henry VIII's Chapel Royal, mentioned in Chapter 5. Vaughan Williams had encountered the tune in 1906 while editing *The English Hymnal*, a collection for which he wrote original melodies and adapted some forty folk songs (Ex. 29-1). The piece is scored for string quartet and double string orchestra, with an antiphonal deployment of the two groups of strings and their responsorial interplay with the soloists creating a sort of mystical, wordless liturgy. The magnificently rich textures that Vaughan Williams, trained as a violinist, was able to elicit from the chosen medium evokes another set of cultural memories—the abundant repertoire of English fantasias for consorts of viols that date mainly from the early seventeenth century. The *Fantasia* begins with three distinct themes that are developed in a series of variations. Tallis's Phrygian-mode tune appears only discretely at the beginning, played *pizzicato* in low strings, but it later sounds forth in Tallis's original nine-voice scoring. The work ends with a final statement of the initial three subjects.

Example 29-1 **Vaughan Williams, *Fantasia on a Theme of Thomas Tallis***

While the *Fantasia* turned to the Tudor past, the first two of Vaughan Williams's symphonies called on folk traditions and urban vernacular music. *A Sea Symphony* (1903–09, revised 1923), actually a cantata for soloists, chorus, and orchestra with words by American poet Walt Whitman, uses two folk songs in its scherzo. *A London Symphony* (1911–13, revised 1918) incorporates the famous chimes of Big Ben, the Westminster tower clock atop the houses of Parliament, sounding through the mists at the beginning of the first movement and at the end of the fourth in very Ravellian harp harmonics, which casts the composer as a British Impressionist. There are also intermittent references to local urban music: transcribed street cries ("Sweet Lavender!"), the tunes that announced the approach of a London horse-drawn cab, Salvation Army bands, Cockney concertinas (similar to an accordion), and various

opening and concluding phrases. This kind of work would show a certain analogy with Bach's treatment of chorales. Two main types can be distinguished among works of this character:

a. In one case accompaniment, introductory and concluding phrases are of secondary importance, and they only serve as an ornamental setting for the precious stone: the peasant melody.

b. It is the other way round in the second case: the melody only serves as a "motto" while that which is built around it is of real importance. In any case it is of the greatest importance that the musical qualities of the setting should be derived from the musical qualities of the melody.

2. Another method by which peasant music becomes transmuted into modern music is the following: the composer does not make use of a real peasant melody but invents his own imitation of such melodies. There is no real difference between this method and the one described first.

3. There is yet a third way in which the influence of peasant music can be traced in a composer's work. Neither peasant melodies nor imitations of peasant melodies can be found in his music, but it is pervaded by the atmosphere of peasant music. In this case we may say, he has completely absorbed the idiom of peasant music which has become his musical mother tongue. He masters it as completely as a poet masters his mother tongue.[14]

What Bartók describes as "a third way"—the most creative of them—is similar to what other composers at the time were also discovering as a fruitful strategy: Adopt from folklore not specific thematic material but, rather, style characteristics, abstractly conceived. Bartók's reference to the "mother tongue" is significant, precisely because he knew that urban composers like himself did not learn the idiom of peasant music from their mothers but had to master it through deliberate application, as an adult learns a foreign language. So the "Hungary" that this music represents, composed according to Bartók's precepts, is an idealized Hungary constructed by combining rural raw material with the most sophisticated Modernist techniques of elaboration and development: the Hungary of a utopian imagination.

Bartók's creative and scholarly encounter with folk music outpaced in geographical scope that of his contemporaries in other countries. He was not a narrow nationalist but much more a universalist recalling the philosophy of Johann Gottfried von Herder, the original Romantic nationalist. Bartók was liberal, and his musical nationalism was pluralistic. He studied, and in his creative work assimilated, the folk music of all the peoples who inhabited "greater Hungary"—Romanians, Slovaks, Croats, and Serbs—and even more ethnically remote peoples like the Turks and the Arabs of North Africa. He researched all this music on location and published treatises on it. Narrower nationalists reviled Bartók for the catholicity of his musical range. Little wonder that in 1940 he felt compelled to leave a Hungary that had allied itself politically with the German Nazis, the most dangerously narrow nationalists of all.

Bartók incorporated the melodies of peasant songs into original compositions, often alongside the Modernist stylistic methods of figures like Strauss, Debussy, and Stravinsky. His remarkable synthesis resulted from an unerring eye for musical qualities latent in the folk material that could be brought into conformity with those Modernistic concepts that attracted him. Although he was as committed a Modernist as any of the composers whose work we looked at in the previous two chapters, he felt a need unfelt by the others to justify his stylistic predilections to his social conscience. Grounding his music in folklore provided a national validation for his art. Bartók believed his assimilation of folk materials kept his music within the bounds of "nature." In an article from 1928 he stressed the following point: "Our peasant music, naturally, is invariably tonal, if not always in the sense that the inflexible major and minor system is tonal. (An 'atonal' folk music, in my opinion, is unthinkable.)"[15]

Bartók believed his assimilation of folk materials kept his music within the bounds of "nature."

For Bartók, Modern music, however ambitious, had to rest on a "natural" basis. Composers and their audiences had to speak a common language, and that language had to be determined by "nature." This belief was enormously important with respect to heated debates concerning the comprehensibility and accessibility of Modern music. The same social assumptions that motivated aspects of Bartók's professional activity set it sharply at odds, both aesthetically and ethically, with most of his contemporaries. He wrote, for example, a wealth of pedagogical piano music designed to train musicians from childhood in the idiom of contemporary music. Kodály's pedagogical work was even more extensive than Bartók's, and many regard it as his most important achievement. The idea of Schoenberg or Webern writing music to train children or incorporating folklore into their work except as an ironic invocation of innocence is almost as unthinkable as was the idea of an "atonal folk music."

Anthology Vol 3-18
Full CD VI, 22–23
Concise CD III, 16–17

The first pieces in which Bartók tried in concentrated fashion to work out his peasant-song idiom comprised a set of fourteen Bagatelles for piano, Op. 6 (1908). The set contains everything from straightforward harmonized folk song to Modernistic experiments. Simplest is Bagatelle No. 4, which is nothing more than a song Bartók himself had recorded on a phonographic cylinder from the singing of a peasant the year before (Ex. 29-2). His harmonization of the melody may reflect his interest in Debussy's music at the time. This bagatelle conforms to the method labeled "1a" in Bartók's essay. The original tune occupies the foreground, the composer's additions, however imaginative and suggestive, being merely the "ornamental setting for the precious stone." At the other extreme, the "third way" described in the essay, is Bagatelle No. 2, in which Bartók does not use any actual folk melodies, nor does he imitate one; it nonetheless relates to Hungarian folk music in various respects, such as the use of symmetrical arrangements of pitches, a characteristic of some Hungarian folk songs.

Anthology Vol 3-19
Full CD VI, 24–27
Concise CD III, 18–19

In compositions written shortly before 1910, Bartók established methods that he was to employ throughout his career, which meant his style was remarkably consistent. For another example of the "completely absorbed" presence of folk materials from diverse locations, we can consider his *Dance Suite*. Composed in 1923, it marked the fiftieth anniversary of the unification of three towns into the capital city of Budapest. The six movements, played without pause, are connected by a recurring "Ritornell" (*ritornello*). Although Bartók does not use any actual folk songs, the movements nonetheless project distinctive features of music he had studied, including Hungarian, Arabic, and Romanian. The finale brings together material from the earlier movements to suggest a multicultural round dance, a "brotherhood of nations," to use Bartók's own words for this type of finale.[16]

Example 29-2 **(a) Béla Bartók, Bagatelle, Op. 6, No. 4; (b) folk song model for this Bagatelle**

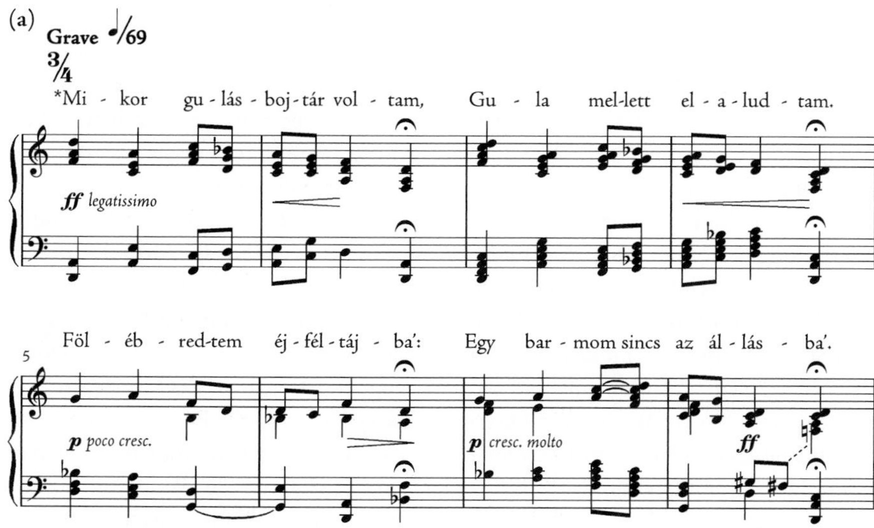

When I was a cowhand I feel asleep near the cattle. I awoke about midnight. Not one cow was left.

Such diversity and folk-synthesis style characterized many of Bartók's most important compositions. Particularly notable are his six string quartets. The genre of the string quartet had fallen on hard times after Beethoven and Schubert. Romantics like Schumann and Mendelssohn continued to write them, but chamber music with piano increasingly accounted for the more substantial works. In the early twentieth century, however, the genre enjoyed a remarkable revival with works by Debussy and Ravel, by the Second Viennese School, by Bartók, and later by the Russian composer Dmitry Shostakovich. Bartók's six quartets were composed between 1908 and 1939, a period that encompassed virtually his entire mature career in Europe; he moved to America for the last five years of his life. Bartók's intense cultivation of the genre, one of the emblems of the European art music tradition and a proving ground for craftsmanship, attests to his concern with synthesizing the particularly national with the universal as well as for conceiving the universal in terms of tradition and advancement in equal measure. We will encounter further evidence of this achievement in Chapter 32 when we consider one of his last orchestral compositions.

Karol Szymanowski and George Enescu

Modern Hungarian nationalism developed in the context of the Austro-Hungarian Empire, in which the country was neither fully independent nor entirely subjugated. The situation in Poland, Romania, the Czech lands, and elsewhere in Central and Eastern Europe was more oppressive, for these small countries were dominated by stronger outside forces. The principal early Modernist composer in Poland was Karol Szymanowski, born in 1882, the same year as Stravinsky and just a year after Bartók. Like most of the composers encountered in this chapter, he variously traveled to, and learned from, Germany and France and became deeply influenced by compositional currents in those countries. At the same time he was drawn to the musical traditions of his native land, particularly to its folk music.

Born on his family's estate in Ukraine, Szymanowski received his earliest musical training at home before moving to Warsaw in his late teens for formal study. In his mid-twenties he went to Berlin in the hope of expanding his horizons; after some time back in Poland he spent nearly two years in Vienna beginning in 1911. Wagner and Strauss were the principal models of his youth. Szymanowski also developed an interest in Asian music and, like Bartók, traveled to North Africa. His Modernist allegiances gradually turned from late German Romanticism to the French Impressionism of Debussy, to the neoprimitivism of Stravinsky, and to the Russian mysticism of Alexander Scriabin, whom we will meet later in this chapter. He eventually merged this wide range of influences with explorations of Polish folk music, especially from the region of the vast Tatra Mountains. Szymanowski's search for his own voice during the First World War produced a kind of Impressionist mysticism, exhibited in his First Violin Concerto (1916) and also in his Third Symphony (1914–16), the opera *Krol Roger* (King Roger, 1920–24), and a setting of the Stabat Mater (1925–26).

George Enescu (1881–1955), the leading Romanian composer at the time, was born the same year as Bartók and was hailed as a prodigy. At age four he took up the violin, the next year began composing, and was soon studying with the top teachers at the conservatory in Vienna, where he came to Brahms's attention. At age thirteen he went off to study in Paris, where his teachers included Fauré and Massenet; in some circles he is still better known by the French form of his name, Georges Enesco. Adding to his accomplishments as a performer and composer, he became a distinguished teacher. Multiple commitments ultimately limited the time he devoted to composition. In addition to chamber music, five symphonies, and a violin concerto, he spent many years writing an impressive opera, *Oedipe* (1936). Enescu's career shows a potential danger of indigenous appropriations: They can prove hard to escape. At age twenty he wrote two Romanian Rhapsodies, Op. 11, that merged a French style with Lisztian rhapsodizing and actual folk melodies. He later regretted the day he composed these early gems, for the Rhapsodies became so popular that they overshadowed his later, more substantial pieces.

The Oldest Modernist: Leoš Janáček

Leoš Janáček (1854–1928) was almost thirty years older than the generation of Stravinsky, Bartók, Szymanowski, and Enescu. If Bartók and Enescu were prodigies, Janáček was a late bloomer, a composer who came into his own only around the age of sixty and who produced most of his greatest scores in the years leading up to his death in 1928 at age seventy-four. Janáček therefore had a strangely shaped career, one that made him by a fairly wide margin the oldest composer who is customarily regarded as a representative twentieth-century figure, alongside contemporaries young enough to be his children or even his grandchildren. He was older than Mahler, Strauss, and Debussy, but his music is more often (and more tellingly) compared with that of Stravinsky and Bartók.

Born in Brno, the capital of Moravia in the Czech lands, Janáček was initially viewed as provincial by the standards of Prague, the Bohemian capital, a city itself viewed as provincial from the vantage point of Vienna, the focal point of musical life in Central Europe. Although his early studies took him to Prague, Vienna, and Leipzig, he returned to Brno to found a music school and for decades composed virtually unnoticed. He wrote the work that ultimately made his fame—the opera *Jenůfa*—between 1895 and 1903; it premiered to considerable acclaim in Brno in 1904. After that, however, the opera languished for years as Janáček fruitlessly tried to secure performances abroad or at least in Prague. He had to wait twelve years, until 1916, when *Jenůfa* was finally produced with great success in the capital. Performances in Vienna, in New York at the Metropolitan Opera, and elsewhere soon followed. At age sixty-two Janáček had at last arrived.

The success of *Jenůfa*, a kind of Czech verismo shocker, stimulated its formerly pent-up composer into a frenzy of creativity. In the twelve years that remained to him, Janáček wrote five more operas: *Výlet pana Broučka do XV. století* (Mr. Brouček's Excursion to the 15th Century, 1917), a patriotic comedy designed to greet the impending proclamation of independent Czechoslovakia; *Káťa Kabanová* (1921), a realistic tragedy after the classic play *The Storm* by the Russian dramatist Alexander Ostrovsky; *Příhody Lišky Bystroušky* (The Cunning Little Vixen, 1923), based on a series of whimsical captioned drawings published in a Brno newspaper; *Věc Makropulos* (The Makropoulos Affair, 1925), based on a surrealistic play by Karel Čapek; and *Z mrtvého domu* (From the House of the Dead, 1928), based on a grim novel of prison life by Fyodor Dostoyevsky.

In addition to these operas, Janáček in his later years wrote a large concert setting of the Slavonic Liturgy, *Glagolská mše* (Glagolitic Mass, 1926); a major song cycle, *Zápisník zmizelého* (The Diary of One Who Disappeared, 1919); several orchestral works, including a *Sinfonietta* (1926) composed for an outdoor national sports rally; and chamber works, most prominently two string quartets and two chamber concertos for piano. It seemed virtually a life's work crammed into a dozen years. In an unusual case like this, one may look for as many biographical explanations as possible; one that is often cited is an invigorating infatuation with a woman named Kamila Stösslová. They met in 1917, when the composer was sixty-two and she twenty-six; both were married. As his enormous correspondence with her documents, she served as muse and inspiration during these astonishing years of creativity.

Janáček insisted that his music be stylistically accessible to the population on whose natural artifacts it drew, which is the main reason he is generally classified as a folklorist. He never rejected this categorization and in his early days made the same kind of expeditions into the field that Bartók would later undertake. With an older collaborator named František Bartoš (1837–1906) he published a collection of 174 Moravian folk songs in 1890; this sold so well that an abridged volume was released with piano accompaniments. Janáček subsequently made folk song arrangements for male chorus.

Speech Tunelets

Janáček's later music did not so much grow out of folk song as out of a natural element that he valued even more as a wellspring for art. He declared in 1926 that "if I grow at all, it is only out of folk music, *and out of human speech*," the most basic expressive element of all, which Janáček passionately believed underlay all folklore as well as all cultivated art.[17] The rhythms, accents, and intonation of different languages have long been recognized as determinants in the distinctive musical sounds of individual nations. It makes sense to conclude that such aspects of composers' native tongues could affect the character of the melodic lines they write. Janáček's veneration of speech as thought and feeling made incarnate led to a music closely based on the rhythms and intonations of the Czech language. He was even more attuned to language than Musorgsky, the radical Russian "realist," who as we know had been preoccupied with speech patterns and who may, in fact, have had some influence on Janáček. Dvořák had also been keenly attentive to language in his four symphonic poems based on texts by Karel Jaromír Erben. (Janáček conducted these works and published detailed analyses.)

Janáček's veneration of speech as thought and feeling made incarnate led to a music closely based on the rhythms and intonations of the Czech language.

Janáček's special interest in the Czech language and its relation to his music went back to the late 1890s, when he began jotting down in notebooks what he called *nápěvky mluvy*—literally "speech tunelets," better known in English as "**speech melodies**." It seems significant that the beginnings of his interest in notating speech melodies coincided roughly with an end to his collecting of folk songs. For Janáček, the one effectively replaced the other as the essential bearer of musical truth. Folk song was the highly stylized and already generalized product of what, at the level of speech, was fully specific and particular. The melodic curves and rhythms of speech, though dictated to a large extent by the conventions of language, were at the same time influenced by spontaneous emotion and by a person's individual identity. They were, in Janáček's words, "windows into a person's soul."[18]

To gather potential models for his music, Janáček obsessively jotted down whatever distinctive speech he heard around him—even, notoriously, the last words of his dying daughter. This practice provided "objective" and "scientific" evidence for what most composers tried to capture vaguely and subjectively. He began carrying around stopwatches and even more exact time-measuring devices that gave readings of very short durations. His behavior gave him a local reputation for eccentricity on which caricaturists were quick to capitalize (Fig. 29-7).

Figure 29-7 Leoš Janáček with his stopwatch (caricature by Hugo Boettinger, 1928).

In a series of articles, Janáček demonstrated with notated musical examples what he thought of as his most significant discovery: the fact that speech melodies revealed subliminal thoughts and emotions unexpressed by the words alone. Native Czech speech is rhythmically distinctive in a manner that it became Janáček's goal to capture in his compositions; that is chiefly what gave his later music its edge and what made a Modernist of him. Actually, of course, it was no discovery at all, just as it was no discovery to observe that a speaker's tone of voice can contradict the uttered words. Anyone sensitive to irony (indeed, anyone who has been caught in a lie) knows that much.

The librettos of Janáček's early operas had been in verse, but the success of *Jenůfa* gave him the courage of his musical convictions. He now insisted on a concise prose style that would not interfere with the natural rhythms of the spoken language and began writing the librettos himself. Janáček's finicky care with prosody arose out of his belief that objectively rendered speech patterns were an infallible register of human subjectivity.

So profound and formative was Janáček's dependence on Czech speech rhythms that it remained evident in his music even when there were no sung words, similar to the "third way" in which folk music informed pieces by Bartók that did not use any actual folk tunes. The rhythms pervaded his instrumental music, thus informing every musical level with the dramatic significance of speech. This can be heard in a little piano piece, *Lístek odvanutý* (A Blown-Away Leaf), originally composed in 1901 for harmonium (an instrument like a small organ) and eventually published in a set called *Po zarostlém chodníčku* (On an Overgrown Path). Ostensibly a folkloristic work, it is really a study in long, unstressed "syllables." To accommodate them, the basic duple meter of the melody in the second strain is distended to $\frac{5}{8}$; the final eighth is never played, however, just "waited out" (Ex. 29-3). During his astonishingly productive final decade, Janáček would become increasingly obsessed with spareness. He even began ruling his own staves rather than using manufactured music paper for his orchestral scores, lest all those empty measures seduce him into padding his orchestration.

Anthology Vol 3-20
Full CD VI, 28

Example 29-3 Leoš Janáček, *A Blown-Away Leaf* (from *On an Overgrown Path*, No. 2), mm. 1–9

Alexander Scriabin: From Expression to Revelation

Despite Janáček's Teutonic training and proximity to Vienna (Brno, only some eighty miles away, was largely German-speaking), he harbored a strong antipathy for the Austro-Germans. This was a change from the attitudes of his Czech predecessors, Smetana (for whom German was his first language) and Dvořák (whose career had strong German connections). Janáček was a pan-Slavist who greatly admired Russia; he traveled there, learned the language, and drew from Russian sources as the basis for some of his operas and orchestral works.

The leading Russian maximalist of the early twentieth century was Alexander Scriabin (1872–1915; Fig. 29-8), who actually lived for much of his career in Western

Figure 29-8 Piano concert with Alexander Scriabin under the direction of Serge Koussevitzky. Painting by Robert Sterl, 1910.

Europe, primarily in France, Switzerland, and Italy. In 1906–07 he made an extended trip to the United States. Unlike his younger countryman Stravinsky, Scriabin showed scant interest in Russian folk music but, rather, looked for inspiration to artistic and literary currents during what is known as Russia's "Silver Age." Beginning in 1898, he was an active member of "mystical Symbolist" circles, attending the meetings of the Moscow Religious Philosophical Society, a forum for avant-garde poetry and theology. By 1905, he had discovered theosophy, an esoteric mystical doctrine that sought to reconcile Christianity with the transcendentalist religions of South Asia, particularly Hinduism and Buddhism. The common belief was seeing the purpose of life as the achievement of a transcendent enlightenment that would free the soul from the shackling temporality of human desire and allow it to join the eternal unity of the Godhead.

Theosophy was spearheaded by a society founded in New York in 1875 by Helena Petrovna Blavatsky (1831–91), a Russian aristocratic émigré. Mystic symbolists and theosophists considered art a medium of Gnostic revelation—that is, the direct imparting of divine knowledge unmediated by the imperfect and limited human intellect. Within their circles Scriabin was hailed as a prophet, because his artistic medium was the least trammeled by specific representational meaning. Scriabin modified his style consciously so as to enable his music to serve the spiritual purposes his philosophical and religious beliefs demanded.

A piano prodigy, Scriabin initially seemed destined for the career of a virtuoso-composer like Liszt or, more precisely, like Chopin, with whom he identified powerfully and on whose very distinctive style he at first attempted to fashion his own, going so far as to adopt such characteristically Chopinesque genres as the mazurka. He was drawn even more to those most poetic of Chopin's pieces, the freestanding aphoristic preludes. Between 1888 and 1896 he composed a set of twenty-four preludes, published as Op. 11, and he continued to write them throughout his career, right up to his final work, a set of Four Preludes, Op. 74, published in 1914. In addition to his many miniatures, Scriabin wrote ten piano sonatas, which became ever more compact as his career progressed. From the Fifth Sonata on they were all single-movement works, and from the Sixth Sonata on, as whole-tone and octatonic collections took over the functions formerly exercised by major and minor tonalities, he dispensed with the use of key signatures. From an art of the sensuously—at times erotically—beautiful, Scriabin's music developed by degrees into an art of mystical—at times sublime—revelation. His late preludes in particular point to a common Russian and French bond with Symbolism, although in Russia this bond achieved a maximalized religious ecstasy that was not approached musically in France until later in the century with Olivier Messiaen.

From an art of the sensuously—at times erotically—beautiful, Scriabin's music developed by degrees into an art of mystical—at times sublime—revelation.

Scriabin's largest pieces were his five symphonies in which he joined the ranks of orchestral maximalists like Mahler and Strauss. Both these composers deserve to be invoked, for despite Scriabin's designation, the last two "symphonies" were single-movement programmatic works that could just as well have been called tone poems. His First Symphony (1900) includes an oratorio-like finale that uses vocal soloists and chorus in the Beethoven Ninth tradition. He found his true symphonic calling when he put aside words and began inventing musical analogues for the new ideas about art's significance that he got from the mystical Symbolists and theosophists. This started with the Third Symphony, Op. 43, subtitled *Le poème divin* (The Divine Poem, 1902–04), and continued in his Symphony No. 4, Op. 54, subtitled *Le poème de l'extase* (The Poem of Ecstasy, 1905–08), which became his most famous composition.

His Fifth Symphony, Op. 60, subtitled *Prométhée, le poème du feu* (Prometheus, the Poem of Fire, 1908–10), opens with what an early biographer called Scriabin's "**mystic chord**" (Ex. 29-4).[19] Scriabin had his own name for the chord. At an early rehearsal of *Prométhée*, his friend and fellow pianist-composer Sergey Rachmaninoff, stunned at the sound of it, asked "What are you using here?" Scriabin answered, "The chord of the pleroma."[20] The *pleroma*, a Christian Gnostic term derived from the Greek for "plenitude," was the all-encompassing hierarchy of the divine realm, located entirely outside the physical universe, at immeasurable distance from man's terrestrial abode, totally alien and essentially "other" to the phenomenal world and whatever belongs to it. Scriabin would have encountered the word in Madame Blavatsky's compendium *The Secret Doctrine* (1888), the theosophists' bible, where it is associated with Promethean concepts like "Spiritual Fire" and "Astral Light" and with angelic androgyny (unisexism). What we know as the "mystic chord," then, was designed by the composer to reveal what was in essence beyond the mind of man to conceptualize. Its magical stillness was a mystical intimation of a hidden otherness, a world and its fullness wholly above and beyond rational or emotional cognition.

Example 29-4 Alexander Scriabin's "mystic chord"

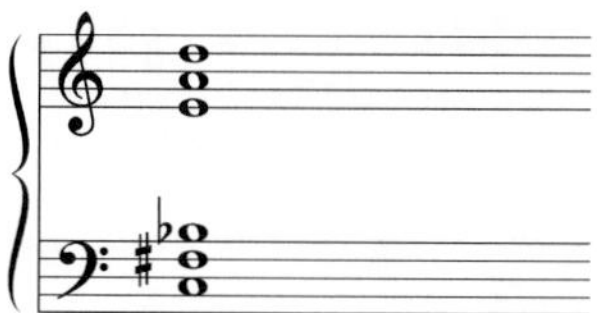

Much of Scriabin's late music inhabits a realm from which the diatonic scale, with its functionally differentiated degrees and its strong drive to resolution, has been virtually eliminated. Its presence may be felt at times behind the scenes, directing some vestigial harmonic progressions along the old circle of fifths, but for the most part we have proceeded from the lived world of human senses and desires, long and effectively represented by the functions of diatonic harmony, to the world of spiritual revelation, the world of the pleroma, represented by a unique musical idiom in which there is a strong sense of harmonic fluctuation and root movement—walking, indeed darting, around and between chords and scales—but in which any sense of harmonic direction and potential closure has been weakened to the point of virtual extinction.

Anthology Vol 3-21
Full CD VI, 29

We can get some sense of Scriabin's visionary aspirations and unerring sense of harmony from *Vers la flamme* (Toward the Flame), Op. 72 (1914), a work that incorporates the idea of direction into its very title. The piece dates from the last full year of Scriabin's composing career and represents his style and technique at their most advanced. Scriabin contrived to maintain a sense of forward momentum and eventual cadence and completion, in keeping with the implications of the title. He uses both whole-tone and octatonic scales and opens with the sort of parallelisms already familiar to us from Debussy. The general effect of the piece can be grasped by comparing the beginning, marked *pianissimo* and *sombre* (dark), with the *fortissimo* conclusion and the right hand approaching the very top of the keyboard (Ex. 29-5). These are the two aspects of the piece's starkly concentrated dynamic unfolding: from soft to loud and low to high. It has a very slow harmonic rhythm accompanying a frenetically active and varied surface. With the rate of harmonic progression so slow, every chord change registers as a large event. What gives the sense of finality to the end is not a gesture of reinforced return, which we would expect in a traditionally tonal composition, but a gesture of completing a pattern. Such pattern completion in Scriabin's mystical music emerged as an effective alternative way of creating tonal expectations and achieving tonal fulfillments. *Vers la flamme* was a benchmark in this process.

Example 29-5a Alexander Scriabin, *Vers la flamme*, Op. 72, mm. 1–5

Example 29-5b Alexander Scriabin, *Vers la flamme*, Op. 72, mm. 129 to the end

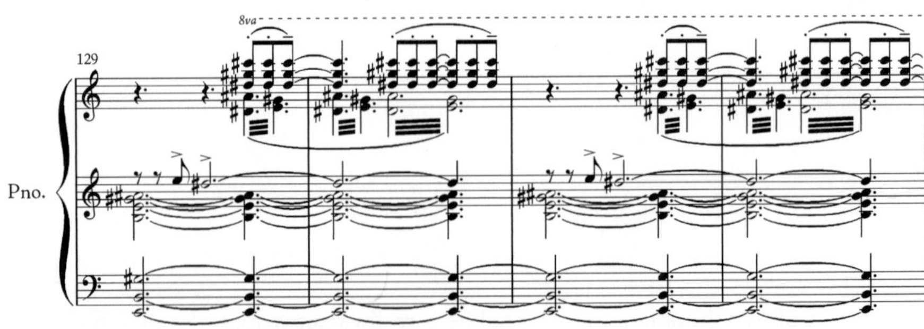

Example 29-5b ***(continued)***

Mysterium and the Ultimate Aggregate Harmonies

Scriabin's great unfinished—indeed unfinishable—project was called *Mysterium,* which he referred to as his "ultimate work" and which consumed his energies during his final years. *Mysterium,* as originally conceived, was to have been the last word in art: a communal creation, and a combination of all artistic media in a single coordinated expressive act. The composer, who had long been dabbling in Symbolist poetry, drafted a text for the piece that summarized theosophical doctrine concerning the origin and destiny of the cosmos. As he worked, he began to imagine not a mere artwork but an all-encompassing ritual enactment, lasting seven days and seven nights, in which there were to be no spectators, only participants; it would be performed once only, in a specially constructed temple in India; and it would so transform the consciousness of the participants as to give them—and with them, the entire world—access to a higher plane of consciousness transcending humanly imagined time and space. It would literally bring human history to an end.

The reader may be feeling relieved that Scriabin did not live to realize this plan: He died in 1915 of blood poisoning shortly after his forty-third birthday. But as much as two years before his death the composer had conceded that he, being only human after all, could not accomplish such a world-transforming goal. He was, despite the insinuations of his detractors, far from crazy, inasmuch as he was able to recognize his erstwhile delusions and scrap them. Instead of the *Mysterium,* he settled on a more modest project, which he called the *Acte préalable* (Preparatory Act), that would at least impart to its hearers something of the euphoric grandeur of the mystical-Symbolist ideal.

Some musical sketches exist for this work, which contain a series of **aggregate harmonies**—"ultimate" chords, each containing all twelve pitches of the chromatic scale. That is what gave the aggregate harmony its poetic significance: What better means could there be for musically representing the universal, or All-in-One, in its literal plenitude? A "twelve-note chord" is everywhere, and everything, at once (Ex. 29-6). Other composers, notably Schoenberg and Ives, were also driven to the limit—that is, to the use of twelve-tone chords or aggregate harmonies—in the period between 1911 and 1915, the years leading up to and immediately following the outbreak of World War I. These projects were also left unfinished, like Scriabin's *Mysterium,* and were never published or performed during their creators' lives. Despite their not being known publically, these unfinished works nonetheless further illustrate the maximalizing obsession of the early twentieth century.

Example 29-6 **Aggregate harmonies from Alexander Scriabin's sketches for the *Acte préalable***

The desire behind such conceptual pieces using aggregate harmonies was to have music be a medium of occult revelation. The composers' wrestled with the world beyond (hence hidden from) the senses, already associated with the Symbolists' concept of the *au-delà*, of the beyond. The grandiose torsos they created are at the end of the line that goes back to "Representation of Chaos" that opens Haydn's *Creation* and that reached successive milestones with Beethoven's Ninth, Wagner's *Ring*, and Mahler's symphonies. They were all grand visionary statements on the borderline between philosophy and religion, a region addressed by Wagner's *Götterdämmerung* and by Mahler in his grandly visionary Second Symphony, which dealt in its final movements with eschatological matters—matters of literally *ultimate* significance—rarely broached in secular art. In the early twentieth century they became an important impulse driving the engine of stylistic maximalism. What better way of exemplifying the way in which music was driven by ideas than with pieces of music that only existed, during their composers' lifetimes, as ideas?

Scriabin renounced the *Mysterium* in favor of the *Acte préalable*, and then he renounced the *Acte préalable* in favor of silence. He starkly faced the maximalist's dilemma: The fulfillment of his aims spelled the end of his—or any—art. Attention everywhere, not just in the officially atheistic Soviet Union but (as we shall see) in Western Europe and America as well, would increasingly focus on the real world and its crises, which entailed a substantial loss of faith even in ordinary Romanticism, let alone its ultimate, maximal, religiously transcendent phase.

Charles Ives

We saw in Chapter 25 that in some respects late-nineteenth-century America replicated musically what had occurred earlier in Russia. Classical music gradually evolved either by importing foreign talent or by sending Americans abroad to study. The principal difference between America and Russia was that, despite the cultivation of native talent, no nineteenth-century American composer attained an international stature comparable to that of Glinka, Musorgsky, or Tchaikovsky. This is perhaps not so surprising, given America's relative youth. Nor is it surprising that as the United States emerged as a superpower in the twentieth century, its musical life blossomed in the classical sphere and, even more influentially, in popular music. By the end of the millennium, America was exporting vast quantities of music, both classical and pop, to countries all over the world.

As America entered the twentieth century there was some resistance to Dvořák's prescription that composers create a distinctive American music by using indigenous music, such as Native American melodies and African American spirituals, as he had done in some of his own "American" works. Over time the mining of native traditions did spur musical innovations. Yet the most influential figures drew on the country's vaunted spirit of self-reliance to forge their own identities by means of experimentation and self-discovery.

The writer first to articulate some of these inspirational values was Ralph Waldo Emerson (1803–82), who founded a distinctively American strain of idealist thought known as New England **Transcendentalism**. Flourishing in and around the town of Concord, Massachusetts, between the 1830s and 1850s, the movement is often cited as the first indigenously American school of philosophy, although its roots came overwhelmingly from German thought and poetry. Transcendentalists were people who had embraced a "tendency to respect their intuitions," regardless of whether such intuitions could be supported by actual experience, observation, or rational argument. By trusting individual instincts, they could gain direct access to the all-encompassing wisdom of God. The only requirement was that instinct or intuition be truly that, rather than one's conventional schooling in disguise. This proved a very difficult requirement indeed. The call to unlearn one's learning was given its most memorable literary expression in *Walden; or Life in the Woods* (1854), the philosophical memoirs of Emerson's disciple Henry David Thoreau (1817–62).

New England Transcendentalism has entered our narrative at this late point because it inspired Charles Ives (1874–1954; Fig. 29-9) with enough vision and self-reliance to allow him to emerge as the figure whom many consider to be the first great American composer. His extravagantly idealistic principles and his social and material conditions led to an unusual "nonprofessional" musical career. In this, his trajectory somewhat resembled those of the "amateur" Russian composers of his parents' generation (the so-called Mighty Five), although he had benefited from a more rigorous formal education.

He was born in Danbury, Connecticut, into the family of George Ives, the town bandmaster. As a young teenager he began following in his father's footsteps as a town musician, serving as Sunday organist in local churches, before going off to study at Yale University in 1894, the year his father died. In later life he idealized the memory of his father both in words and in musical deeds: His compositions often nostalgically evoked the nineteenth-century band music his father performed as well as the congregational hymns he had accompanied in his youth. He was exposed to a range of vernacular music that he would mine in his own compositions for years to come. To his father, an enthusiastic musical tinkerer though an unsuccessful composer, he gave most of the credit for arousing in him an appetite for musical adventure and discovery. His father's musical profession, however, had not earned him much in the way of income or social respect, and George ended up as the black sheep of the family. That may have been one of the factors that eventually dissuaded his son, despite strong artistic inclinations and enormous talent, from pursuing a professional musical career. Instead, he became a prosperous businessman.

At Yale Ives studied with Horatio Parker (1863–1919), a leading figure in the Boston School of composers who, like most of his successful contemporaries, had studied in Europe. Ives went through a thorough training that culminated in the writing of a traditional First Symphony rather in the style of Dvořák. After college he secured the post of organist and choirmaster at New York's Central Presbyterian Church, a prominent place of worship with an affluent congregation, where he worked from 1900 to 1902. Ives proudly identified himself to journalists as Parker's

Figure 29-9 Charles Ives in Battery Park, New York City, ca. 1917.

former pupil in his first important bid for public recognition as a composer: *The Celestial Country*, a cantata for soloists, chorus, and instrumental accompaniment that he performed with his choir in April 1902. The conservative work was modeled on Parker's oratorio *Hora novissima* (1893). *The Celestial Country* was halfheartedly described by critics as "scholarly" and "earnest."[21] Like the First Symphony, also finely crafted, it pointed toward a traditional career in the Parker mold. The conventional next step for Ives would probably have been a boat ticket to Europe and a few years of study in Germany.

But instead he took the unexpected step of resigning his church post and renouncing a professional career in music. The 1902 premiere of *The Celestial Country* was the last public performance a work of his would receive for twenty years. His Second Symphony, completed around 1909, was not played until 1951. The two decades of his creative seclusion at the start of the twentieth century, moreover, were the very ones during which he composed the amazing scores on which his reputation now rests: two more symphonies and a number of other orchestral pieces, two string quartets, four violin sonatas, two piano sonatas, various keyboard works, and more than 160 songs.

For the most part Ives composed during the evenings, weekends, and holidays, because he was otherwise engaged in the insurance business. Business was the socially accepted place at the time for an American man, including many in Ives's extended family. After college he had taken a job at the Mutual Insurance Company, which he had pursued as a fallback during the years in which his sights were set on a musical career. In 1906, he and another Mutual agent started their own firm, which became for a while the most successful insurance agency in the country. His business career gave him the freedom to write music that expressed his idealistic commitments, but it came at a price. His musical life continued, although now it was conducted in almost total isolation from active engagement with performers, publishers, patrons, and the press.

Terms of Reception

In 1920 few people knew about Ives, but that time marked a turning point in his personal and professional life. He had suffered a severe heart attack in September 1918, followed by a series of strokes, which left him in precarious health for his remaining thirty-five years. Except for a few exceptional efforts his creative life effectively came to an end. At the same time, his music was finally beginning to be heard. In 1920 he privately published his Second Piano Sonata, subtitled *Concord, Mass., 1840–60*, as well as *Essays before a Sonata*, a little book to be read alongside the sonata in order to explain what he called its "substance." In 1922 he arranged the private publication of his *114 Songs*. A few other compositions appeared in the *New Music Quarterly* series edited by Henry Cowell (1897–1965), a California composer devoted to the cause of disseminating what he called "ultra-modern music." Ives gave financial support to Cowell's projects and to many other contemporary music organizations. In 1931, the conductor and writer Nicolas Slonimsky (1894–1995) performed an "Orchestral Set" called *Three Places in New England* at New York City's Town Hall; he then went on to present it in Boston, Havana, and Paris; the work was commercially published in 1935.

Performers thus gradually began discovering Ives's music and introducing it to audiences, in most cases long after it was written. This slow release was somewhat akin to Schubert's reception with the posthumous release of his greatest works, the big difference being that Ives had the satisfaction of being alive to enjoy some of the acclaim and to comment on it. He came to be honored as a (or even as *the*) founding father of American music—its first original master and the author of its Declaration of Independence from Europe (or, as the conductor and composer Leonard Bernstein put it at the time of the premiere of the Second Symphony in 1951, "our Washington, Lincoln and Jefferson of music").[22]

Another key event was the first public performance of the complete *Concord* Sonata by pianist John Kirkpatrick at a New York recital on 20 January 1939. The concert received a remarkable review in the *New York Herald Tribune* from the influential critic Lawrence Gilman, who pronounced Ives's sonata to be "exceptionally great music—it is, indeed, the greatest music composed by an American, and the most deeply and essentially American in impulse and implication."[23] Gilman's extraordinary sympathy for the work was the result of a deeper sympathy with Ives's purposes, which in the case of the *Concord* Sonata was the translation of the spiritual essence of Transcendentalist philosophy into music. He found in Ives a real American composer, not one who could be perceived as a European interloper like Dvořák. And there was more: Gilman saw the spirit of discovery in Ives's "audacious experiments in the organization of sound and the development of scales and counterpoint and rhythms which, for those who have studied their outcome in his later works, make the typical utterances of Schönberg sound like Haydn sonatas." The critic urged his readers to "bear in mind that when Ives was evolving this incredible ultra-modernism of the American nineties, Schönberg, then in his early twenties, had not yet ventured even upon the adolescent Wagnerism of his 'Verklärte Nacht'; and the youthful Stravinsky was playing marbles."[24]

As this review clearly showed, Gilman measured Ives's greatness not by the aesthetics of any expressive tendency but, rather, by those of Modernism, the historiographical legacy of the New German School, which values artists chiefly in proportion to their technical and formal innovations, to the cause of writing the music of the future. This was not the best vantage point from which to view Ives or, some might argue, any artist. And it made for some trouble later as well as for some serious devaluing of Ives's achievement. The Ives boom might easily be deflated if in fact it turned out that Ives had not been so ultra-modern so early.

The first to make such a claim, that Ives had in fact been a Great Anticipator rather than a Great Emancipator, was composer Elliott Carter (b. 1908), who as a boy had known Ives and who has recounted visiting him one day while he was preparing one of his pieces, probably *Three Places in New England*, for performance: "A new score was being derived from the older one to which he was adding and changing, turning octaves into sevenths and ninths, and adding dissonant notes. Since then, I have often wondered at exactly what date a lot of the music written early in his life received its last shot of dissonance and polyrhythm." The visit left Carter wondering "whether he was as early a precursor of 'modern' music as is sometimes made out."[25] These questions have been addressed by several scholars, including Maynard Solomon, who suggested that Ives himself had been caught up, following Gilman's celebrated review, in the Modernist tendency to "confuse the patent-office with the Pantheon, to regard the invention of a new technique as the most significant measure of creativity."[26]

The first to make such a claim, that Ives had in fact been a Great Anticipator rather than a Great Emancipator, was composer Elliott Carter.

Ives's aesthetic outlook is perhaps better understood when its connection with the European—and particularly the German—past is also acknowledged alongside his Modernism. Like the Transcendentalism to which he professed allegiance, his artistic aims and commitments may be neither quite as radical nor as indigenously American as often claimed. His radical techniques were frequently called on to celebrate the very opposite of progress: Their purpose, ironically, was to evoke nostalgically a vanished or imaginary rural America. To put Ives's fundamental expressive concerns in focus, we will consider two works: the *Concord* Sonata, the subject of Gilman's excited praise, and *Three Places in New England*, the subject of Carter's equivocal memoir.

"Manner" and "Substance": The *Concord* Sonata

Questions about dating were fundamentally un-Ivesian, since they were wholly concerned with what Ives referred to as "manner" (the way something was said) rather than "substance" (the something itself). Moreover, those composers who provided his models of substance were hardly radicals: He listed Brahms, Franck, d'Indy, and Elgar among his influences. These figures expressed orthodox spiritual values in a way that by the early twentieth century was deemed distinctly old-fashioned.[27] Their brand of spiritual uplift was among the things that would be discredited by World War I, at least as far as a younger generation of Modernists was concerned.

Franck appears to have been Ives's unlikely special favorite. If we take Franck, rather than the more obvious Liszt, as the particular model in the *Concord* Sonata, Ives's attempt at a sort of antimodernist spiritual revival turns out to have been surprisingly specific. We will remember the strong impact of Franck's Symphony in D Minor had on American composers, especially on the Boston School, of which Parker was a latter-day member. In its aspiring quality, Franck's symphony was the most Germanic of French symphonies and a standard-bearer for the supremacy of "substance" over "manner." It was filled with the lofty spirit of Beethoven's Ninth and also mined Beethoven's last quartet for a germinating motive that audibly haunted the work and carried its spiritual message from first movement to last.

Anthology Vol 3-22
Full CD VI, 30
Concise CD III, 20

Ives made a similar Beethovenian appropriation in the *Concord* Sonata: The first four notes of the Fifth Symphony, perhaps the most famous single motive in all music, pervade the work and carry its spiritual message through all four movements. Each bears the name of a Transcendentalist writer (or family of writers) associated with Concord: Emerson, Hawthorne, the Alcotts, and Thoreau. Most of the *Essays before a Sonata* (the title of which was already an evocation of Emerson) was devoted to describing the connections Ives felt between his music and the ideas of these New England thinkers. The overriding message that united them all, the essence of New England Transcendentalism, was symbolized in the Beethoven motive, to which Ives devoted a special explanation in the chapter on Emerson:

> There is an "oracle" at the beginning of the *Fifth Symphony*; in those four notes lies one of Beethoven's greatest messages. We would place its translation above the relentlessness of fate knocking at the door above the greater human message of destiny and strive to bring it towards the spiritual message of Emerson's revelations, even to the "common heart" of Concord—the soul of humanity knocking at

> the door of the divine mysteries, radiant in the faith that it *will* be opened—and the human become the divine![28]

From the opening page of "Emerson" to the quiet closing pages of "Thoreau," the Fifth Symphony motive suffuses and unifies the otherwise-sprawling *Concord* Sonata. "Emerson" abounds, especially with Beethoven's call, sometimes presented as a major third, sometimes minor. The optional flute solo at the end of "Thoreau"—an evocation of Thoreau's description of his own nocturnal flute playing on the shore of Walden Pond—places the Fifth Symphony motto in the context of a long melody that sums up many of the sonata's themes. (In the *Essays before a Sonata* Ives associates the melody with "human faith"; Ex. 29-7.) In "The Alcotts," a domestic portrait in a distinctly tamer style than the other movements, Ives makes use of different European and American pasts. The European tradition continues as the Fifth Symphony motive is presented in the context of indigenous American hymnody, a spiritual tradition. Ives merges the Beethoven motto with the openings of two well-known tunes from the Protestant hymnal—Simeon B. Marsh's *Martyn* ("Jesus, Lover of My Soul) and *The Missionary Chant* ("Ye Christian Heralds") by Charles Zeuner.

Example 29-7 Charles Ives, *Concord* Sonata, IV ("Thoreau")

Nostalgia

Some of Ives's scores seem to stand in contrast to dreamy Transcendentalism. These include wildly humorous scherzos of a hearty, heavy, unsubtle kind, also reminiscent of Beethoven. Perhaps we might call them "scherzoids," since they do not always conform to the customary Classical scherzo-and-trio form layout. The Ivesian difference was that his scherzoids were usually programmatic, and the programmatic content was almost invariably nostalgic, evoking the composer's idealized, even fictionalized, New England boyhood. These affectionate pictures offer the sense of carefree youth in a socially homogeneous and harmonious, preindustrial setting, in which all stylistic excesses were justified in the name of fun or of "realism"—presenting things "just as they [never] were." It was America's own pastoral primitivism that proclaimed the moral superiority of an unspoiled, abundant countryside over the polluted, corrupt, and disgusting modern city.

Anthology Vol 3-23
Full CD VI, 31
Concise CD III, 21

The most famous and in many ways most characteristic of Ives's scherzoids is "Putnam's Camp," the second of the *Three Places in New England*. The place in question is a historic site near the composer's birthplace, a field that served as campground to the troops under the command of Israel Putnam, the Revolutionary War general who was Connecticut's most illustrious military hero. Ives's program note sets the scene:

> Near Redding Center, Conn., is a small park preserved as a Revolutionary Memorial; for here General Israel Putnam's soldiers had their winter quarters in 1778–1779. Long rows of stone camp-fire places still remain to stir a child's imagination. The hardships which the soldiers endured and the agitation of a few hot-heads to break camp and march to the Hartford Assembly for relief, is a part of Redding history.
>
> Once upon a "4th of July," some time ago, so the story goes, a child went there on a picnic, held under the auspices of the First Church and the Village Cornet Band. Wandering away from the rest of the children past the camp ground into the woods, he hopes to catch a glimpse of some of the old soldiers. As he rests on the hillside of laurel and hickories, the tunes of the band and the songs of the children grow fainter and fainter;—when—"mirabile dictu" [wonderful to tell]—over the trees on the crest of the hill he sees a tall woman standing. She reminds him of a picture he has of the Goddess of Liberty,—but the face is sorrowful—she is pleading with the soldiers not to forget their "cause" and the great sacrifices they have made for it. But they march out of camp with fife and drum to a popular tune of the day. Suddenly a new national note is heard. Putnam is coming over the hills from the center,—the soldiers turn back and cheer. The little boy awakes, he hears the children's songs and runs down past the monument to "listen to the band" and join in the games and dances.
>
> The repertoire of national airs at that time was meager. Most of them were of English origin. It is a curious fact that a tune very popular with the American soldiers was "The British Grenadiers." A captain in one of Putnam's regiments put it to words, which were sung for the first time in 1779 at a patriotic meeting in the Congregational Church in Redding Center; the text is both ardent and interesting.[29]

To a certain extent the whole composition could be described as a takeoff on "The British Grenadiers." The tune first appears in the flute, almost complete, but being part of a dream, it is fantastically distorted and then fragmented. Wherever it pops up, however, it has plenty of company. In the outer sections it serves mainly as a countermelody accompanying the tune of an earlier Ives composition, "Country Band March." Against it, marches by John Philip Sousa (1854–1932) make occasional appearances in a very uneven pairing: The famous "Semper Fidelis" (1888) is played by the trombone and tuba while "Liberty Bell" (1893) is played by the first violas, where it hardly stands a chance of being heard. At the same time, to complete the collage, a snatch from Stephen Foster's "Massa's in de Cold, Cold Ground" (1852) sounds forth gaily in the flute (Ex. 29-8).

To attempt a full catalog of allusions in "Putnam's Camp" would be fruitless, since some of them are so brief or inexact in the telling as to be ambiguous. Others stick out, as Ives meant them to, like sore thumbs. At one point, for example, the trumpet, flute, and first violins string together the first phrase of "Yankee Doodle," each instrument entering in a different key. A joke comes at the very end of the piece, with the bass instruments starting up "The Star-Spangled Banner," only to be drowned out by the roar of the final chord, topped with a snatch of "Reveille" in the trumpet. Ives's use of hymns, folk and popular songs, military calls and marches, and so forth place him with most of the other composers treated in this chapter, although he never undertook collecting. He didn't need to—these were tunes he and most everyone knew.

Example 29-8 Charles Ives, "Putnam's Camp" (*Three Places in New England,* II), mm. 27–30

Example 29-8 (*continued*)

Ives put the material he found to imaginative use, notable for its subtlety, fragmentation, and juxtapositions. Most famous in "Putnam's Camp" is the pitting of two groups of instruments against one another at different tempos. The originating idea behind two hypothetical bands encountering one another is among the most durable of all Ivesian legends, recounted by Henry Cowell and his wife in *Charles Ives and His Music* (1955), the first book-length study of the composer. "The germ," the Cowells wrote,

> of Ives's complicated concept of polyphony seems to lie in an experience he had as a boy, when his father invited a neighboring band to parade with its team at a baseball

> game in Danbury, while at the same time the local band made its appearance in support of the Danbury team. The parade was arranged to pass along the main street as usual, but the two bands started at opposite ends of town and were assigned pieces in different meters and keys. As they approached each other the dissonances were acute, and each man played louder and louder so that his rivals would not put him off. A few players wavered, but both bands held together and got past each other successfully, the sounds of their cheerful discord fading out in the distance. Ives has reproduced this collision of musical events in several ways: From it, for example, he developed the idea of combining groups of players (sections of the orchestra) to create simultaneous masses of sound that move in different rhythms, meters, and keys.[30]

This famous anecdote is pretty obviously a tall tale, concocted for the same reason that prompted Ives to assure a sympathetic critic that his radical ways "came not only from folk music he was brought up with but to a very great extent from the life 'around and in him.'"[31] Ives's strange music would seem unacceptably esoteric and elite were it not validated by his everyday experience.

Like Scriabin and Schoenberg around the same time, Ives accumulated sketches for an ambitious orchestral work, known as the *Universe Symphony*, which he never completed and which remained only a concept (Fig. 29-10). But what a concept! According to his autobiographical *Memos*, dictated in old age, the symphony was to be literally the Story of Everything—or, in Emersonian terms, the revelation of THE ONE. There would be three orchestras, the first consisting of nothing but percussion and representing "the pulse of the universe's life beat."[32] The other two would divide the remaining instruments into high and low groups. And there would be three overlapping movements, to be played without pause or significant variation in tempo: "I. (Past) Formation of the waters and mountains. II. (Present) Earth, evolution in nature and humanity. III. (Future) Heaven, the rise of all to the spiritual."

Figure 29-10 Manuscript page from Charles Ives's *Universe Symphony*, 1911–16.

This resonates with Scriabin's *Mysterium*—and with the whole antecedent line of European symphonic transcendentalism: the line of "Weltanschauungsmusik" from Haydn to Mahler. As if in uncanny sympathy with the Russian composer's final project (of which he could have known nothing), Ives reached tonal saturation with aggregate chords of all twelve pitches. But this is not so surprising: Both Scriabin's project and Ives's were epitomes of mystical philosophies (in Ives's case Transcendental, in Scriabin's Theosophical). For both of them the aggregate harmony logically symbolized "epitome" itself.

Societal Commitments

Although the diverse group of composers discussed in this chapter hailed from a wide geographical range, they nonetheless shared some striking commonalities, musical differences and stylistic individuality notwithstanding. As young men most of them sought training abroad or traveled extensively in the hope of acquiring practical skills and having musical experiences not available in provincial locations. They then attempted to find ways of expressing aspects of their countries' indigenous culture and traditions in their compositions. Some did this by calling on what was then considered "lower" music, notably folk song and local urban music. But there were other strategies as well: Sibelius found his initial inspiration in Finland's national literary epic, Janáček in the patterns and sound of the Czech language. Vaughan Williams combined a pastoral tradition evoked by folk materials with historical inspiration from the music of England's musical past; Scriabin drew from a mystical tradition characteristic of Russia's Silver Age; Ives drew from the American Transcendental movement.

In the process these composers revitalized or constructed styles that came to represent the music of their respective countries, and they came to be viewed as national monuments. Although before the First World War they may not have looked as radical as Schoenberg or Stravinsky, they had enormous influence, both on compositional history and on culture more generally. Many of them exhibited a high level of social engagement. Sibelius and Szymanowski made efforts to help small nations oppressed by mighty neighbors. Some engaged in activities that had an educational impetus, such as writing pedagogical compositions or teaching and heading up music schools. Vaughan Williams collected folk music, edited a hymnal, and led choral societies, while Bartók displayed interest in teaching young musicians and in devising imaginative pieces with them in mind. These commitments stand out at a time when Modernist music was increasingly becoming detached from everyday society and ever more concerned with its own internal musical materials. In the process, as we shall see, the relevance of classical music for the general public greatly diminished.

Summary

This chapter examined some composers who combined the maximalist tendencies of the twentieth century with elements of nationalism, fusing their international training with the folk music, language, and culture of their own countries. Jean

Sibelius (1865–1957), for example, based many of his symphonic poems, including *The Swan of Tuonela,* on the Finnish epic *Kalevala.* Sibelius drew not only on the stories of the *Kalevala* but also on the recitation patterns of its verse. Another of his symphonic poems, *Finlandia,* became an anthem in the cause of Finnish independence from Russia. The distinctive sound of Sibelius's music lies in its use of modal melodies, ostinatos, and pedal points.

Hungarian composers Béla Bartók (1881–1945) and Zoltán Kodály (1882–1967) turned to the folk music of rural peasants. In this respect, their works contrast with the Hungarian-style pieces of Franz Liszt, based on urban popular music. Bartók traveled widely, both inside and outside of Hungary, collecting and studying folk music. He prescribed three ways to achieve folk-based composition: in his words: (1) "take over a peasant melody unchanged"; (2) "invent [an] imitation of such melodies"; or (3) absorb "the idiom of peasant music" so that the work "is pervaded by the atmosphere of peasant music." By emphasizing elements of folk music that were compatible with Modernism, Bartók marvelously synthesized the two.

Other Eastern European composers who fused Modernism and nationalism include Karol Szymanowski (1882–1937) in Poland, George Enescu (1881–1955) in Romania, and Leoš Janáček (1854–1928) in Bohemia. Janáček incorporated the speech patterns of the Czech language into his music, creating the varied texture exemplified in his *On an Overgrown Path,* No. 2. Other contributors to twentieth-century nationalism include Ralph Vaughan Williams (1872–1958) in England and Manuel de Falla (1876–1946) in Spain.

In Russia, Alexander Scriabin (1872–1915) was the leading maximalist of the early twentieth century. Scriabin's work was inspired by his involvement with theosophy, a religious movement that focused on the direct experience of divine knowledge. In his piano pieces and five symphonies, Scriabin captures this sense of the divine beyond the physical world by using harmonies such as the "mystic chord," which consists of a series of augmented, diminished, and perfect fourths. Scriabin's *Vers la flamme* achieves its effect by moving very slowly from a low pianissimo at the beginning to a high fortissimo at the end.

Considered by many as the first great American composer, Charles Ives (1874–1954) was also a successful businessman. His works are experimental in their use of dissonance, their rhythmic complexity, and their polytonality (using many keys at once). Despite these qualities, however, Ives's works are deeply rooted in American tradition, borrowing church hymns, marches, patriotic songs, and parlor songs. Ives's Second Piano Sonata, subtitled *Concord, Mass., 1840–60,* illustrates his interest in American literature and philosophy. He was especially drawn to the New England Transcendentalism associated with Ralph Waldo Emerson (1803–82) and Henry David Thoreau (1817–62). Each movement of the sonata is named after a different Transcendentalist writer associated with Concord. His "Putnam's Camp," the second of *Three Places in New England,* uses patriotic tunes in fragmentation and juxtaposition.

Study Questions

1. Describe the ways in which each of the following composers fused Modernism and nationalism, using music, literature, or philosophy from their own countries: (a) Jean Sibelius; (b) Ralph Vaughan Williams; (c) Manuel de Falla; (d) Béla Bartók; (e) Leoš Janáček; (f) Charles Ives.
2. Describe Bartók's various approaches to incorporating folk materials into his music. How are these reflected in the *Bagatelles* No. 2 and No. 4 and in the *Dance Suite*?
3. How did Bartók's attitude toward the public and the role of music contrast with those of Schoenberg and his followers (Chapter 27)?
4. In what respects was Janáček a nationalist? How and why did he incorporate speech rhythms into his works?
5. How do Scriabin's works embody the mystical ideals associated with theosophy?
6. What is New England Transcendentalism? How did it inspire Ives's music?
7. Describe the various ways in which Ives uses preexisting musical material, both in his *Concord* Sonata and in "Putnam's Camp." What ideals (about music or society) do these pieces suggest?
8. Describe the critical reception to Ives's work. Why has there been a controversy surrounding his revisions of his own works?

Key Terms

aggregate harmonics
ethnomusicology
magyar nóta
mystic chord
polytonality
speech melodies
style hongrois
Transcendentalism
verbunkos
zarzuela

30

Neoclassicism and Twelve-Tone Music

The First World War, known simply as "The Great War" until there was a second twenty-five years later, was a horrific watershed in European history. It put a dismal end to what historians in its wake have called "the long nineteenth century," which had begun with another watershed event, the French Revolution, in 1789. Optimism and faith in progress were the Great War's first and most permanent casualties. "Great" the war surely was, if greatness is measured in terms of awful numbers. It smashed four empires: the ancient Austrian, the recent German, the far-flung Ottoman Turkish, and the huge but bordering Russian, which would soon be reconstituted as the Soviet Union (Fig. 30-1). It was the first war to be fought not only on land and sea, but also in the air. It was also the first to witness the use of machine guns, tanks, aerial bombing, and poison gas. It included terrible episodes of genocide, most catastrophically of Armenians.

The military carnage was on a scale never before imaginable. Of the four most heavily engaged countries, the British lost nearly a million men (out of an adult male population of some 20 million), the Russians and French 1.7 million each, and the Germans and Austrians more than 3 million combined. The total war dead approached 9 million. Measured against the puny proximate cause of the war—Austria's avenging the assassination in June 1914 of the emperor's heir, Archduke Franz Ferdinand, by a Serbian nationalist in Sarajevo—and the benefits it secured (despite all the rhetoric, none at all), these futile losses produced a desperate and irreparable disillusionment, a tremendous loss of optimism. "This is not war," an Indian soldier conscripted to fight with the British wrote home after being wounded, "It is the ending of the world."[1]

The wave of shock and nausea produced by the Great War reverberated keenly, if not always explicitly, in the arts. The horrors of war made suspect the seriously spiritual and exalted art of the previous century, which had reached its maximal point in the late Romanticism and early Modernism we have examined in the three previous chapters. The rhetoric of hope and glory now rang false. Dignity and elegance, beauty and love, and progress to perfection now seemed a lie. For many there emerged a strong preference for the matter-of-factly said over the rhapsodically sung, for reason over feeling, for reportage over poetry. One of the principal artistic responses to the war came in the form of irony, black humor, and cynicism. Indeed, irony has been an indispensable ingredient in Western art ever since.

TIMELINE

1914–18 World War I

1917 The United States enters World War I

1917 Bolshevik Revolution in Russia

1918 Arnold Schoenberg founds the Society for Private Musical Performances

1918 Igor Stravinsky, *Histoire du Soldat*

1919 Treaty of Versailles ends the war between Germany and the Allied Powers

1920 Women gain the right to vote in the United States

1920 Stravinsky, *Symphonies d'instruments à vent* and *Pulcinella*

1921–23 Schoenberg, *Suite for Piano*, Op. 25

1923 Stravinsky, *Octet*

1923 Schoenberg, *Five Pieces for Piano*, Op. 23

1925 Alban Berg, *Chamber Concerto*

1926 Berg, *Lyric Suite*

1927 Charles Lindbergh flies solo across the Atlantic

1928 Amelia Earhart becomes the first woman to fly across Atlantic

1928 Anton Webern, Symphony, Op. 21

1928 Alexander Fleming discovers penicillin

1929 Worldwide stock market crashes; the Great Depression begins

1933 Adolf Hitler becomes the Chancellor of Germany; the Nazi regime begins

1933 Schoenberg emigrates to the United States

1951 Stravinsky, *The Rake's Progress*

Neoclassicism

Some European countries were particularly unhappy with the terms of the Treaty of Versailles (1919) after the war ended. The Austro-Hungarian and the Ottoman empires ceased to exist entirely. Germany was forced to accept sole responsibility for the conflict and to pay heavy reparations. The League of Nations was formed in the hope of keeping animosities in check, but bitterness, fear of the spread of communism, and a worsening economic situation would lead to another world war barely two decades later. The mood in America was rather different. Having entered the war late, the United States experienced relatively light losses (some 114,000), and its economy was growing. The prestige that its soldiers and its president, Woodrow Wilson, were accorded after victory allowed optimism to persist for much of the 1920s, at least until the New York stock market crash in October 1929 that ushered in the Great Depression.

This disparity between Old World pessimism and New World optimism may help to explain one young American composer's bewilderment in 1923 when he attended the premiere in Paris of a new woodwind octet, the latest work by Igor Stravinsky, the most famous and fashionable composer alive (Fig. 30-2). On that night, Aaron Copland, then a student finishing up his second year studying composition in France, happened to attend a concert at the Paris Opéra in which Stravinsky was conducting a program of his own music. For thirteen years, since the unveiling of *The Firebird* ballet, and especially since the scandalous opening night of *The Rite of Spring* in 1913, Stravinsky's name had been synonymous with Russian neoprimitivism at its most exotic, piercing, even orgiastic. It had been only four months since the premiere of his latest ballet, *Les noces* (The Wedding), featuring dancers, vocal soloists, and a chorus singing, sometimes shouting, fierce or bawdy ritual songs in Russian, accompanied by a clangorous ensemble consisting of nothing but four pianos and a monster assemblage of percussion.

Stravinsky, however, had become eager to move beyond the exotic Russianness people associated with his music. He would reinvent himself at a crucial time in world politics and in his own life. The upheavals that shook Russia in 1917—first the February Revolution that toppled the tsar, then the October coup d'état that put the new Soviet government in place—had deprived Stravinsky of his family inheritance and also of much of his income. He would not set foot in Russia for nearly fifty years. He lived in Switzerland for a while before settling in Paris in 1920, becoming a French citizen in 1934, and then moved five years later to America, where he took citizenship in 1945.

Like almost everyone attending the Stravinsky premiere that October night in 1923, Copland was in for a shock. Nearly twenty years later, in 1941, still marveling at it, he recalled his "general feeling of mystification" on hearing the Octet for winds

Figure 30-1 Europe before and after World War I.

(flute, clarinet, and pairs of bassoons, trumpets, and trombones). "Here was Stravinsky," he wrote,

> having created a neoprimitive style all his own, based on native Russian sources—a style that everyone agreed was the most original in modern music—now suddenly, without any seeming explanation, making an about-face and presenting a piece to the public that bore no conceivable resemblance to the individual style with which he had hitherto been identified. Everyone was asking why Stravinsky should have exchanged his Russian heritage for what looked very much like a mess

Figure 30-2 Drawing of Igor Stravinsky, by Pablo Picasso, 1920.

> of eighteenth-century mannerisms. The whole thing seemed like a bad joke that left an unpleasant aftereffect and gained Stravinsky the unanimous disapproval of the press.[2]

And yet, looking back, Copland could report an even bigger surprise:

> No one could possibly have foreseen, first, that Stravinsky was to persist in this new manner of his or, second, that the Octet was destined to influence composers all over the world in bringing the latent objectivity of modern music to full consciousness by frankly adopting the ideals, forms, and textures of the preromantic era.[3]

Indeed Copland, although he had not known it himself in 1923, was seeing his own future. Stravinsky's Octet helped usher in a new creative period, not only for Stravinsky but also for much of European and Euro-American concert music. The new style is commonly called **Neoclassicism**. Although this catchphrase will require a lot of qualification and amendment, it can be a useful label. Stravinsky's huge prestige made his sudden recourse to "eighteenth-century mannerisms" a more newsworthy event than anybody else's could have been at the time.

Yet Neoclassicism in music was symptomatic of a pronounced general swerve in the arts—one can perceive a similar trend in painting, for example, in the work of Stravinsky's collaborator Pablo Picasso. In this regard it might be said that the history of twentieth-century music as something really aesthetically distinct from that of the "long nineteenth century" begins not at the fin de siècle, with the maximalized Romanticism of Mahler, Strauss, Debussy, and early Stravinsky and Schoenberg but, rather, here, in the early interwar years. Copland's keen evaluation of Stravinsky's Octet identifies some of the core issues. He associates the new manner with "objectivity" and with the deliberate adoption of a "preromantic" stance, announced externally by the unexpected resurrection of eighteenth-century gestures. It was, moreover, a Tower of Babel style that looked not just to the Classicism of Haydn and Mozart but also to the earlier Baroque period as well as to jazz and various forms of popular music becoming all the rage during the so-called Roaring Twenties. Although Neoclassicism was primarily tonal, it was not always so. In the second half of this chapter we will encounter Neoclassical impulses in a new kind of atonal music cultivated by Schoenberg and his colleagues.

Stravinsky's Octet helped usher in a new creative period, not only for Stravinsky but also for much of European and Euro-American concert music.

The feature of Stravinsky's Octet that most forcibly impressed early listeners like Copland—namely, the imitation of what sounded like music from an earlier time—was actually not new, however attention-grabbing and however durable it has proved to be as a mark of Neoclassicism. The deliberate imitation of older musical styles has a long history going back many centuries. Opera was born out of one such revival. If the unofficial slogan of twentieth-century Neoclassicism was "Back to Bach," we have encountered something similar before with Mendelssohn. Brahms had an unusually acute historical consciousness that affected many of his compositions. We will remember that pieces in the "ancient style" by French composers around the turn of the nineteenth century attempted to exorcize the dominance of Wagner and that Debussy, the fiery early Modernist, ended his career during the First World War by writing a set of sonatas deeply indebted to the past.

Particularly relevant for Stravinsky were pieces by his hero, Tchaikovsky, including four orchestral suites, some of which contain "neobaroque" movements.

The Fourth Suite, Op. 61 (1887), subtitled *Mozartiana,* in turn consisted of Tchaikovsky's own orchestrations of pieces by his hero, Mozart. In fact the opening movement is based on Mozart's Gigue for piano (K. 574), which was itself a pastiche of Bach and Handel. Looking to the past was clearly nothing new. One very recent example was by another Russian, Sergey Prokofiev (1891–1953). In the summer of 1917, between the two revolutions in Russia, he retreated to a country house that had no piano. Both as a lark and as an exercise to discipline his ear, he wrote a symphony "in the style of Haydn," his Symphony No. 1 in D Major. Its "eighteenth century" was the usual imaginary one; Prokofiev's third movement, for example, was not a minuet, as in a typical Haydn symphony, but an anachronistic gavotte with quirky harmonic progressions breaking every rule of eighteenth-century voice leading. Prokofiev's "Classical" Symphony incorporated ingratiating nostalgia, composerly homage, and technical note play.

Igor Stravinsky's Neoclassical Path

Stravinsky, too, had had his own recent experiences with looking to the past. At the end of the war he composed *Histoire du soldat* (The Soldier's Tale, 1918), a theatrical work with music based on a Russian folk story, updated and translated into French. It was written, in collaboration with the Swiss author Charles-Ferdinand Ramuz, with the times in mind; in a Europe at war, many could relate to soldiers' tales. The piece is modestly scored for seven players (violin, double bass, clarinet, bassoon, cornet, trombone, and percussion), a far cry from the massive *Rite of Spring* and an ensemble that gives evidence of Stravinsky's growing awareness of jazz. The initial idea was to tour with the piece, which also featured a narrator, two actors, and two dancers; the title page says the work is to be "read, played, and danced." The tale involves a soldier's encounter with the devil, with whom he exchanges his violin for future fortune. The soldier later gets the violin back and plays it to cure a sick princess, who proceeds to dance a tango, a waltz, and a ragtime. The devil himself dances a more furious number, followed by a great chorale, similar to Luther's "Ein feste Burg," before he ultimately succeeds in dragging the soldier to hell. *Histoire du soldat* thus combines mythic situations with contemporary experiences, invoking along the way popular music of various kinds, including American popular music, as well as the Lutheran chorale.

Sergey Diaghilev had played no part in commissioning either *Les noces* or *Histoire du soldat,* but he now wanted to line up his favorite composer to help create a new sensation and provoke new public interest. Diaghilev had recently enjoyed great success when his choreographer, Leonide Massine, staged a ballet called *The Good-Humored Ladies,* based on music by Domenico Scarlatti. Stravinsky was eager to work with Massine as well as with Picasso, who had been enlisted to do the sets for the new ballet, which came to be called *Pulcinella,* with its characters drawn from the Italian commedia dell'arte (Fig. 30-3). Diaghilev proposed basing the ballet on music by early eighteenth-century composer Giovanni Battista Pergolesi, whose *La serva padrona* we know from Chapter 12. It turns out that most of the melodies Diaghilev had collected during trips to Italy were not actually written by Pergolesi, but they charmed Stravinsky nonetheless. Scored for a thirty-three-piece chamber orchestra, the resulting ballet premiered in Paris in May 1920. As Stravinsky later recalled, "*Pulcinella* was my discovery of the past, the epiphany through which the

Figure 30-3 Set design by Pablo Picasso for Sergey Diaghilev's *Pulcinella* ballet, music by Igor Stravinsky, after works of Pergolesi. First representation in Paris Théâtre de l'Opéra on 15 May 1920.

whole of my late work became possible. It was a backward look, of course—the first of many love affairs in that direction—but it was a look in the mirror, too."[4]

Histoire du Soldat and *Pulcinella* both looked to the musical past (and the former sideways as well to the popular present). They were both programmatic stage works. But Stravinsky's budding Neoclassicism soon took a purely instrumental turn with *Symphonies d'instruments à vent* (Symphonies [or Concords] of Wind Instruments), a memorial to Debussy. In 1920 a French music journal, *La Revue Musicale*, published the work's closing section (arranged for piano) in a Debussy commemorative issue, and a big stir was created by this amazingly spare music. In fact it is in connection with the *Symphonies* that the term Neoclassicism was first used to describe Modern music. This was done in a 1923 article by the critic Boris de Schloezer, who, like Stravinsky, was a Russian exile in Paris. For him, what made the *Symphonies* Neoclassical was the assumption that the score was "only a system of sounds, which follow one another and group themselves according to purely musical affinities; the thought of the artist places itself only in the musical plan without ever setting foot in the domain of psychology. Emotions, feelings, desires, aspirations—this is the terrain from which he has pushed his work."[5] This view of the *Symphonies* clearly resonates with Copland's observations about the objectivity of Stravinsky's Octet, that is, the purging of Romanticism from it. Both pieces had a scaled-down, objectified, wind-dominated instrumentation exploring the "mannerisms" of the past.

By the 1920s many artists had decided to give unambiguous preference to irony over sincerity.

In retrospect some of the same aesthetic concerns can be seen going even further back in Stravinsky's career. While everyone else was being dazzled by the riotous dissonance of *The Rite of Spring* and marveling at Stravinsky's *âme slave* (Slavic soul) and the sublime terror his music evoked, French critic Jacques Rivière, shortly after its premiere, had called it "the first masterpiece we may stack up against those of Impressionism." He continued: "The great novelty of *The Rite of Spring* is its renunciation of 'sauce.' Here is a work that is absolutely pure. Nothing is blurred, nothing is mitigated by shadows; no veils and no poetic sweeteners; not a trace of atmosphere." Despite the *Rite's* enormous orchestra and coloristic effects (Fig. 30-4), Rivière stated: "The work is whole and tough, its parts remain quite raw; they are served up without digestive aids; everything is crisp, intact, clear and crude. Never have we heard a music so magnificently limited." This is because Stravinsky had decided to use "those instruments that do not sigh, that say no more than they say, whose timbres are without expression and are like isolated words, it is because he wants to enunciate everything directly, explicitly, and concretely. His voice becomes the object's proxy, consuming it, replacing it; instead of evoking it, he utters it."[6]

Figure 30-4 Drawing by Jean Cocteau of Igor Stravinsky rehearsing *The Rite of Spring*.

Fast-forward ten years to the time of the Octet, and the idea of "renunciation of 'sauce'" became apparent to everyone. This signaled a radical change in musical aesthetics. Such a work displayed a new Modernism very much at variance with the Romantic, Expressionist, and Impressionist traditions, which valued spirituality, sincerity, naturalness, spontaneity, and a host of other qualities that cannot withstand the presence of irony. This had been a tension that early Modernist artists had to bear. Some, notably the French composers of Satie's and Debussy's generation, more willingly sacrificed Romantic values. Others, like Schoenberg, tried tenaciously to have it both ways: to be fully Modern but also fully spontaneous, spiritual, and self-expressive.

The desire to be Romantically expressive and Modernly ironic at the same time disturbed Stravinsky when he was confronted with a rare Schoenberg composition that did take an ironic stance. He had mixed feelings after attending an early performance of *Pierrot lunaire* as Schoenberg's guest. He grudgingly embraced the instrumental writing, and even imitated it a bit in his next work, three songs on Japanese poems. Despite its ironic elements, Stravinsky nonetheless found *Pierrot* aesthetically outmoded. By the 1920s many artists had decided to give unambiguous preference to irony over sincerity. This was a more significant rupture than the one created by early maximalist Modernism. However shocked audiences had been with the radical stylistic means and the harmonic and metric innovations, early Modernism had nevertheless largely remained faithful to the immediate aesthetic heritage of the nineteenth century. The ironic break meant the rejection of the immediate past, a true break with tradition. The break created divisions and dissension among artists as well as between artists and audiences.

In a 1926 book about Stravinsky, the Soviet critic Boris Asafyev viewed the legacy of Romanticism as "hypnotic, sterile, hedonistic." It encouraged passivity, whereas for Asafyev the goal of contemporary music was to bring the virtuosity formerly expended on casting hypnotic spells "out into the world of actuality," which required a style "nearer to the street than to the salon, nearer to the life of public actuality than to that of philosophical seclusion."[7] Thus Asafyev hailed Stravinsky's Neoclassical phase not as a restoration of the past but as an awakening to contemporary reality. For Asafyev a work like the Octet did not mark a return to Bach but, on the contrary, asserted "the dynamics of life." Such music "has not been able to escape the influences of contemporary city streets."[8] At the end of the Octet, for example, Bach morphs unexpectedly into what sounds like a Charleston, one of the dance rages of the Roaring Twenties.

These writings about Stravinsky by Rivière, Schloezer, and Asafyev are of considerable historical significance, primarily because they had an enormous impact on the composer himself. They influenced him decisively to develop his own brand of Neoclassicism. We are always influenced by the benedictions of those who praise us, especially when the praise is so intelligent, so exuberant, and so timely. Stravinsky did what was necessary to keep that praise coming.

The Music of Stravinsky's Octet

Anthology Vol 3-24
Full CD VI, 32–33
Concise CD III, 22

The Octet may have been Stravinsky's first fully conscious manifestation of the Neoclassical style, and he immediately became an ardent propagandist for the new aesthetic. In his autobiography, *Chronicles of My Life* (1936), he summed it up by saying that "music is, by its very nature, essentially powerless to *express* anything at all, whether a feeling, an attitude of mind, a psychological mood, a phenomenon of nature, etc."[9] It is time now to turn to the music of the Octet and see what all the fuss was about. The opening Neoclassical gesture—a cadential trill in the two bassoons—is courtly, decorous, charming (Ex. 30-1). But that characterization depends on the context: What is courtly, decorous, and charming in a work signed "Mozart" is brash and polemical in a work signed "Stravinsky" (at least on first hearing).

Example 30-1 Igor Stravinsky, Octet for Winds in Arthur Lourié's piano transcription, I, mm. 1–4

Like other of Stravinsky's Neoclassical works, the three movements of the Octet carry time-honored Italian designations (*Sinfonia, Tema con variazioni, Finale*). "He declares that he is creating a new epoch with this," wrote fellow Russian émigré Prokofiev to a friend back home, "and that this is the only way to write nowadays."[10] Prokofiev was skeptical; to him Stravinsky's Neoclassical music sounded like "Bach with smallpox,"[11] an astute observation. Stravinsky once described his pastiche procedure in works like the Octet as a revival of "the constructive principles" of eighteenth-century Classicism.[12] It would, however, be more accurate to call it a revival of certain aspects of the stylistic features of eighteenth-century music, but with constructive principles that bear the mark of Stravinsky's older neoprimitivist style, such as static ostinatos, stable dissonances, and abrupt disjunctures. The opening trills say "eighteenth century" without actually sounding like eighteenth-century music, because the harmony and voice leading in which they are embedded would have been impossible in the eighteenth century. Bach never sounded like this—the listener gets that immediately.

The kind of stuttering melody that follows the bassoon trill in the flute is also characteristically Stravinskian, but the figuration that takes over in the same instrumental part shortly afterward again says "eighteenth century" and, more particularly, "Bach." The form takes an ironic turn as well. The title of the first movement, *Sinfonia,* to a historian connotes an opera overture, the cradle of sonata form. And sonata form is the form this music takes, for the first time in Stravinsky's work since his student days nearly two decades earlier, when he wrote his conventional Symphony in E♭ under Rimsky-Korsakov's direction. This *Allegro moderato* is complete with first and second themes and a recapitulation that arrives right on schedule. The second movement theme and variations begins with a little in-joke to reward those in the know about Stravinsky's harmonic idiom and its sources in his Russian training. The classically regular eight-measure theme, played *ben cantabile* (singing nicely) at the outset by flute and clarinet at the double octave, is one of Stravinsky's longest octatonic melodies. Of course no such scale was ever used during the eighteenth century; again Stravinsky's Neoclassical style shows itself to be an ironic mixture of styles in which everything is used with equal self-consciousness and nothing can be taken stylistically for granted (Ex. 30-2).

Example 30-2 Igor Stravinsky, Octet for Winds in Arthur Lourié's piano transcription, II, mm. 1–4

The *Finale* seems at first the most candidly pastiched movement of all, sporting a walking bass, a resolutely contrapuntal manner, and later some specific references to the music by Bach that musicians knew best in the 1920s (Ex. 30-3). Yet it is also the movement that most obviously refuses the harmonic norms of eighteenth-century (i.e., tonal) music. The C-major scale in the second bassoon that marches up a tenth and down again for thirty-two measures at the outset is as inert an ostinato as anything in *The Rite of Spring*, with no modifications to accommodate its contrapuntal partners. Eventually these merge with the unmistakable syncopated rhythms of American dance music, vintage 1923. Strangely enough, this fits in perfectly with Stravinsky's Bach-like style, too, as the ending of the Octet shows. The characteristic Baroque rhythms—the walking basses, the energetic anapests—all involve eighths and sixteenths, values below the level of the *tactus*, or "felt" beat (most often represented by the quarter note). They are, therefore, subtactile pulses. Ragtime and dance-music syncopations, too, relied on a well-articulated subtactile pulse—that is, the little rhythmic subdivisions to which the accented long notes are shifted in a syncopated jazz style. Equalized subtactile pulses had earlier played an important role in Stravinsky's Russian ballets. This common rhythmic feature allowed Stravinsky to draw on a wide assortment of seemingly unrelated idioms and yet have it all come out sounding "like Stravinsky."

Example 30-3 Igor Stravinsky, Octet for Winds in Arthur Lourié's piano transcription, III, mm. 1–12

Some Ideas About the Octet

Stravinsky accompanied the appearance of the Octet with a manifesto, "Some Ideas About My Octuor" (using the French word for *octet*), which he published in a London arts magazine in January 1924. It was an early example of many such publicity pieces with which he sought to manage the reception of his work. Originally, this dry little essay must have been meant as a joke at his readers' expense, another avenue for ironic play, and his words were taken seriously, at least by those unfamiliar with the music. Eventually Stravinsky seems to have taken them seriously himself.

Serious or not, it is an excellent gloss on the whole notion of objectivity in art that carried so much weight with composers who rejected the grand emotions, expressions, and philosophical strivings of late Romanticism. Stravinsky begins with this announcement: "My Octuor is a musical object."[13] Here are a few of his key points, every sentence a paragraph unto itself, slightly abridged and edited to compensate for his (or his translator's) faulty English, and numbered for ready reference:

> **1.** My Octuor is not an "emotive" work but a musical composition based on objective elements which are sufficient in themselves.
> **2.** I have excluded from this work all sorts of nuances, which I have replaced by the play of volumes.
> **3.** I have excluded all nuances between the *forte* and the *piano*; I have left only the *forte* and the *piano*.
> **4.** The play of these volumes is one of the two active elements on which I have based the action of my musical text, the other element being the tempos [Stravinsky has "movements"] in their reciprocal connection.
> **5.** This play of tempos and volumes that puts into action the musical text constitutes the impelling force of the composition and determines its form.
> **6.** I admit the commercial exploitation of a musical composition, but I do not admit its emotive exploitation. To the author belongs the emotive exploitation of his ideas, the result of which is the composition; to the performer belongs the presentation of that composition in the way designated to him by its own form.
> **7.** Form, in my music, derives from counterpoint. I consider counterpoint as the only means through which the attention of the composer is concentrated on purely musical questions. Its elements also lend themselves perfectly to an architectural construction.
> **8.** This sort of music has no other aim than to be sufficient in itself. In general, I consider that music is only able to solve musical problems; and nothing else, neither the literary nor the picturesque, can be in music of any real interest. The play of the musical elements is the thing.[14]

Stravinsky's entire anti-Romantic platform passes here in review. Plank 1 pronounces the ban on emotion and expression. Planks 7 and 8 declare the formalist agenda: Music is architecture in time and nothing else. Plank 6 refuses to honor the Romantic insistence that art and artists be "disinterested," devoid of any ulterior motives, especially commercial ones. Stravinsky is also at pains to describe the dynamics and tempos of the composition in absolute terms, tying the performer's hands by proclaiming the sanctity of the text. Plank 3 somewhat exaggerates the case; the Octet has its share of crescendos and decrescendos, but more characteristic are markings like "*p* subito" or "sempre *p*" or "staccato e *mf* sempre." There are frequent streams of constant note values (as in a lot of Baroque music, it is true) that enforce uniformity of tempo, since there are no differences to exaggerate.

Stravinsky reached the ultimate point in the direction of inelastic uniformity in works for piano he wrote in the 1920s for his own use as performer. These pieces were among the most severe and uncompromising of his early Neoclassical works, perhaps because his piano playing was not at a level to compete with flamboyant virtuosos like fellow Russian émigrés Rachmaninoff and Prokofiev. He tried to make a virtue of nonflamboyance. The success he had with audiences—as we know because Rachmaninoff and Prokofiev grumbled about it in their letters—shows that he shrewdly calculated the allure of fashion. Whatever Stravinsky did was "chic."

Stravinsky's activities as conductor and pianist were forced on him by necessity, after the revolutionary events in Russia had greatly reduced his income. Whether he otherwise would have undertaken such work at this point in his career is anyone's guess. He had little conducting experience—the performance of the Octet that Copland attended was the first time he had undertaken a premiere and the first time he had led an entire concert himself. There certainly were practical motivations: although commissions and publications brought in a handsome income, they required a lot of time and work. A performance with an orchestra, on the other hand, took just a few days, was lucrative, and satisfied a public that favored direct encounters with celebrities.

For some three decades after the Octet, Stravinsky's music continued to renounce "sauce." The range of his Neoclassical works is large, including not only many chamber and keyboard pieces but also symphonies, concertos, choral music, ballets, and even an opera. He had written his student symphony in his mid-twenties and a quarter century later returned to the genre in conventional as well as unconventional ways. The *Symphony of Psalms* (1930), which seems more like a cantata, was followed by the Symphony in C (1938–40) and the Symphony in Three Movements (1942–45). His Violin Concerto (1931) uses old-fashioned movement designations (Toccata, Aria I and II, Capriccio); the absence of flashy cadenzas is consistent with Neoclassicism.

The culmination of this period of Stravinsky's career came in 1951 with the premiere of the opera *The Rake's Progress*, completed when he was almost seventy. The three-act work, by far the longest of his career, was inspired by a series of paintings (later engravings) by the English artist William Hogarth (1697–1764) that depicted the moral and material decline of a rich, young good-for-nothing. On the basis of Hogarth's images, the English poet W. H. Auden (1907–73) had devised a scenario in collaboration with the composer and worked it up into a libretto in collaboration with poet Chester Kallman (1921–75). The Neoclassical score sported harpsichord-accompanied recitatives, strophic songs, da capo arias, and formal ensembles, including a moralizing quintet at the end to draw explicit lessons from the foregoing action, obviously modeled on the final sextet of Mozart's *Don Giovanni*. Although composed to an English text, the work had its premiere on 11 September 1951 in Venice, before a cosmopolitan festival audience at the famous eighteenth-century Teatro La Fenice (Phoenix Theater). But this event did not mark the end of Stravinsky's composing or of the continued surprises his music offered, as we will see in Chapter 34.

The Ivory Tower

The exploration of irony, elevation of objectivity, and shunning of Romanticism were also embraced by composers elsewhere in Europe, including Germany, where it often went by the name *Neue Sachlichkeit* (New Objectivity). More about these trends of the 1920s will be taken up in the next chapter. First, however, we will look at another path back to Bach, one pursued largely for different aesthetic reasons and with results that sound completely unlike Stravinsky's, despite some fascinating elements in common.

While Stravinsky became more and more famous as well as increasingly productive during the years between *The Rite of Spring* and the Octet, the same period marked a grave creative crisis for Arnold Schoenberg. Around the time of the Great War he composed only fitfully when not entirely blocked. For four years he did not finish a single composition, although he started many. When his Five Pieces for Piano, Op. 23, was published in 1923, it was his first new composition to appear since 1914. Schoenberg's embattled, alienated posture was like that of many Modernists, who otherwise shared little in common. "The customer is always wrong" became an implicit motto for such artists, and their goal was not to reach any sort of broad-based audience. Schoenberg later went on at some length about his situation in his 1937 essay "How One Becomes Lonely": "I knew I had the duty of developing my ideas for the sake of progress in music, whether I liked it or not; but I also had to realize that the great majority of the public did not like it."[15]

Near the end of his fallow period Schoenberg spent time involved with the concert series he created, the **Society for Private Musical Performances**. It was subsidized by subscriptions, by the contributions of its members, and by occasional donations from wealthy patrons. Its offerings were not advertised in the papers, and critics were barred from attending. Subscribers were not informed of the programs in advance so as to ensure "equal attendance at every meeting," and even applause was forbidden.[16] Although the musicians who participated were mostly young and unknown (some later became famous), their performances before a small, exclusive audience, thanks to mandated insistence on adequate rehearsal, were legendary in their accuracy. Some pieces were repeated within programs or in successive programs multiple times.

The venture was short-lived. The Society's first concert took place in December 1918 and the last in December 1921. Within that short time, however, it managed to present 117 concerts at which 154 contemporary compositions by a wide variety of composers were given a total of 353 performances. Even if Schoenberg ran the Society dictatorially, he seems to have been genuinely altruistic in his motives. He did not allow any performances of his own music until the second season, and the repertory was remarkably broad, featuring not just the expected Austro-German Modernists, but also a very large quantity of Debussy, Bartók, Stravinsky, and many others. The most frequently performed composer was the recently deceased Max Reger (1873–1916), who had been deeply influenced by Bach and the Classical masters before Stravinsky's fashionable Neoclassicism began and who pursued their legacy without irony.

"I knew I had the duty of developing my ideas for the sake of progress in music, whether I liked it or not; but I also had to realize that the great majority of the public did not like it."—Arnold Schoenberg

The Society's aims and practices were an outgrowth of the neo-Hegelian aesthetics familiar to us from the New German School, according to which art is valued not with reference to its consumers but with reference to its own autonomous history. The public is at best irrelevant to this history, at worst a brake on it. Art needs protection from people. It needs the sanctuary that Schoenberg's Society provided. More recently, that sanctuary has been sought in institutions of higher learning, and partly for the same reason. The "Ivory Tower" has proven to be Schoenberg's most controversial legacy. Does the public have any legitimate claim on artists? Are artists entitled to social support without any requirement of a reciprocal social responsibility? Has society a right to expect work of social value from the artists it supports? Does protection from the public help or hinder the development of art? The dichotomy between the elitist model epitomized by Schoenberg and an array of populist models emerging at the same time, which we will consider in the next chapter, became one of the most argumentative issues in twentieth-century musical politics.

Most disquieting of all for the twentieth century, the great century of democracy and totalitarianism alike, is Schoenberg's most central precept, which he enunciated explicitly in an essay of 1946, written in America, where for ten years he had been living as a refugee from Nazi persecution: "If it is art it is not for everybody; if it is for everybody it is not art."[17] Can such a proposition be defended in a democracy? If so, is there something wrong with art? Or with democracy?

In Search of Utopia: Schoenberg and Twelve-Tone Technique

Schoenberg's long compositional silence in the late 1910s and early 1920s signaled an impasse; he needed to find a new way of composing. He later recalled that it was "the first time in my career that I lost, for a short time, my influence on youth."[18] The reason? A French journalist summed it up: "Schoenberg is a Romantic; our young composers are Classic."[19] That sense of vulnerability initially caused Schoenberg's furious rejection of Neoclassicism and led to some sniping at Stravinsky. For his part, Stravinsky liked to poke fun at those who claimed to be writing the music of the future. He claimed, instead, to be writing the true music of the present. He went around telling interviewers, tongue-in-cheek, that "modernists have ruined modern music." In January 1925 a New York reporter asked him who he had in mind: "Stravinsky smiled. 'I shan't mention any names,' said he. 'But they are the gentlemen who work with formulas instead of ideas.'"[20] It is not entirely obvious that Stravinsky had Schoenberg in mind, but Schoenberg had no doubt he did.

If Stravinsky was truly writing the music of the present (and Schoenberg was by implication a thing of the past), then why, Schoenberg wanted to know, did Stravinsky look to the even more distant past for models in his Neoclassical compositions? In Schoenberg's view Stravinsky was trying to turn back the clock on the development of music, substituting restoration for the progress it was every artist's obligation to advance. For Schoenberg, this was not just an aesthetic issue but a moral one, involving not just taste but the artist's responsibility. After reading Stravinsky's New York interviews, Schoenberg responded musically by composing a choral work to his own texts, *Three Satires*, Op. 28. The last one is called "Der neue Klassizismus" (The New Classicism) and concludes with the lines: "Classical perfection—that's the latest style!" Schoenberg, like Stravinsky, named no names, although the target was clear to everyone. In the second satire he could not resist a direct hit: "But who's that drumming away there? Why, it's little Modernsky. He's had his hair cut in an old-fashioned queue, And it looks quite nice! Like real false hair! Like a peruke [pigtail wig]! Just like (or so little Modernsky likes to think), Just like Papa Bach!"

Yet there is a great irony here, for the fact is that, despite their mutual disdain and their bombastically expressed differences, in the 1920s Schoenberg and "little Modernsky" were participants in the same postwar reaction. Both were renouncing "sauce," seeking objectivity, and looking to the past. Schoenberg's technical breakthrough of those years, the so-called twelve-tone music to which we will now turn, was as much a Neoclassicizing effort as anything done in the name of Papa Bach. For a long time, however, what Schoenberg did was considered by his followers (and his followers' followers) to be the very emblem of musical progress, yet another stage in German composers' quest to write and rule the music of the future.

After the white heat composition of *Erwartung* in 1909, Schoenberg had been largely occupied with working on a brief one-act opera called *Die glückliche Hand* (The Lucky Hand) for nearly three years between 1910 and 1913 (Fig. 30-5). He moved away from the intuitive approach and occult spirit of the earlier Expressionist opera to a much more carefully worked-out and rationalized one. His creative crisis, in both its personal and its musical dimensions, may have had something to do with his need to lessen a reliance on intuition, stigmatized at the time in Vienna as both feminine and Jewish through the influential writings of Otto Weininger (1880–1903), a philosopher who killed himself at age twenty-three in the building where Beethoven had died. Schoenberg may have also felt that composing a purely instrumental work on the scale of *Erwartung*, a long atonal composition without a structuring text, would have been impossible to do. Schoenberg and, even more so, Webern tended to write very short pieces around this time; after largely abandoning audible thematic designs and the structural hierarchies provided by the tonal system, they were evidently uncertain as to the means by which they could create extended instrumental works. This was a serious compositional challenge that needed to be addressed, and Schoenberg's answer was what came to be known as twelve-tone music.

Figure 30-5 Photograph of Arnold Schoenberg sent to Wassily Kandinsky on 12 December 1911, with the inscription: "Dear Mr. Kandinsky, I am discharging in musical tones—a commitment I have long wished to fulfill. 12/12/1911. Arnold Schoenberg."

The sources of Schoenberg's new technique of using an ordered collection of all twelve tones as the basis for a composition have been variously described and furiously disputed. Schoenberg had already experimented with "aggregate compositions" that exploited the total chromatic spectrum in various ways. His large occult project, comparable to Scriabin's *Mysterium* or Ives's Universe Symphony, was the oratorio *Die Jakobsleiter* (Jacob's Ladder), which he started to compose in 1917 but never finished. Along with Webern, he had written some tiny pieces in which a subdivision (or even an entire work) reaches its end when the last member of the twelve-tone chromatic scale appears for the first time. There were also the recent theories of Josef Matthias Hauer (1883–1959), who experimented with a novel technique that he called *Nomos*, after the ancient Greek word for "law." This consisted of a particular ordering of the twelve tones of the chromatic scale that would serve as the basis for a composition. Hauer, whose career amounted to so much less than Schoenberg's, later became embittered because he thought Schoenberg had stolen his intellectual property. Schoenberg's followers, in retaliation, have tended to minimize Hauer's contribution. At our present historical remove, it is fairly easy to take a nonpartisan view, acknowledging that Hauer probably gave Schoenberg an important idea but that Schoenberg, a far more gifted composer, did far more with it.

The controversy points to an increasingly important issue that will emerge many times during the rest of this book: a battle over priority—which composer did something first. We have already seen some of the debates concerning Ives's "rush to the patent office," his apparent need to seem ahead of the times even if it meant redating works or revising to make them seem more radical than they originally were. With Schoenberg, the notorious *Prioritätstreit* (battle over priority), as it was called as early as 1925, can strike us now only as a tempest in a teapot.[21] But at the time it mattered greatly, to Schoenberg as much as to Hauer.[22] Precisely because the matter of priority was taken so seriously, not only by the parties involved but also by onlookers, it is a revealing symptom of the lure of innovation so integral to Modernism.

Giving Music New Rules

From 1921 on, most of Schoenberg's compositions would adopt a chromatically exhaustive twelve-note series as their basis. He called this a *Tonreihe*, using a German word for "series" (*Reihe*) that has "row" as its English equivalent; hence the term "tone row" has become standard usage. At first he called the method on which he now relied *Reihenkomposition*, "composition with rows," more commonly known as serial composition or **serialism**. English usage in this case has favored Hauer's term, *Zwölftontechnik*, "**twelve-tone technique**." (Some writers label it "dodecaphony," from the Greek for "twelve.") Eventually Schoenberg called his method "composition with twelve tones related only to one another" rather, that is, than to a predefined tonic.

Schoenberg first used the technique in a waltz that was the last of five piano pieces from Op. 23, the set that marked his return to productivity. A **tone row** is not a melody but, rather, an ordering of all the twelve pitches of the chromatic scale from which both motivic and harmonic content will be derived. There is the "**prime**" form of the row, an ordering that determines other related rows in four different ways. The row can be *transposed*: A series of twelve tones that begins on the pitch "C" might be transposed to one beginning on "D" but keeping the same interval relationships between adjacent notes in the row. A row can be *inverted*: If a series begins, for instance, by ascending the interval of a fourth, its **inversion** will begin by descending a fourth, and so on. Rows can also be ordered *backwards* (**retrograde**) or *both inverted and played backwards* (retrograde inversion). As a result, a given row has forty-eight different versions through various combinations. These procedures relate, of course, to longstanding compositional techniques; we have seen some of them in the Middle Ages, in the Renaissance, in the contrapuntal art of Bach, and in the dazzling finale of Mozart's "Jupiter" Symphony.

Schoenberg called his method "composition with twelve tones related only to one another."

The internal properties of a row are crucially important for the particular piece of which it is the basis. Rows are often subdivided into three-, four-, or six-note segments (that is, into four trichords, three tetrachords, or two hexachords) that bear some special relationship to one another. The twelve-tone method allowed

Schoenberg to engineer great feats of compositional planning and motivic saturation. Various ways of dividing up a row can produce different kinds of textures, from homophonic (melody + accompaniment) to homorhythmic (chordal) to intricately contrapuntal.

The term "twelve-tone," although we are certainly stuck with it, remains something of a misnomer, for what gives a tone row its distinction is not its pitch content (every tone row has that in common with every other tone row) but, rather, its ordered interval content, which enables a row to maintain its identity when transposed. Schoenberg carefully worked out which transpositions or inversions would realize the form-defining or harmony-defining properties he wanted in a piece. His strict adherence to the ordered twelve-note series in his compositional practice elevated it to the status of a *Grundgestalt*. This "basic shape," or intervallic constellation, informs an entire composition, down to its smallest details, and gives it its "organic" motivic consistency. And that, of course, was the great breakthrough that allowed the composition of large-scale, abstract, and autonomous atonal music of constant and at-all-times-demonstrable motivic coherence despite the renunciation of predefined tonal hierarchies and recognizable melodic themes. The method also furthered Schoenberg's project of the "emancipation of dissonance," in that his music could now more easily be freed from the programmatic associations found in Expressionist compositions. Like Stravinsky's Neoclassicism, twelve-tone techniques encouraged greater abstraction and objectivity.

Anthology Vol 3-25
Full CD VI, 34–36
Concise CD III, 23–24

Schoenberg's first major work written using twelve-tone row technique throughout was a five-movement Suite for Piano, Op. 25. The pieces in it—*Präludium*, *Gavotte* and *Musette*, *Intermezzo*, *Menuett*, *Gigue*—had accumulated over an eighteen-month period between July 1921 and March 1923, about the same time as Stravinsky was writing and premiering his Octet. All the movements are based on a single twelve-tone row, its inversion, and the transposition of each by a tritone (Ex. 30-4). Inverting a row, like inverting any motive, reverses the direction but not the size of each interval. Transposition, of course, has no effect at all on intervallic sequence. So the four rows are merely four ways of representing a single intervallic succession (i.e., a single *Grundgestalt*). Even before hearing the music of Op. 25, its particular row complex gives us a foretaste of the harmonic world of the piece. The row has been deliberately constructed so as to create close relationships between exactly these four forms, thus producing an even more pervasive unity than other row forms could achieve. The character of the composition will be to a significant degree determined by the relationships that derive from the structure of the row.

The constitution of some rows allow for concrete musical relationships in which some aspect of a musical configuration changes while some other aspect remains the same. That is the essence of the "developing variation" technique that Schoenberg found to be implicit in Brahms's motivic textures. This is a principal feature of twelve-tone composition, as Schoenberg practiced it, that allowed him to claim that this method, no less than his earlier atonal style, was a natural (or even an inevitable) evolution of traditional, mainstream techniques rather than a break with them, despite its rejection of tonality. Indeed, twelve-tone techniques, by rationalizing the composition of atonal music and making it more orderly and coherent, significantly strengthened the bonds that connected atonal music with the formal methods of the classical mainstream. In this sense, it was also a "Neoclassical" move, another response to the postwar "call to order." And so too is a more playful feature: The opening tetrachord of the row's retrograde in Op. 25 spells BACH (bear in mind that in German "B" means B♭ and B-natural is "H").

Example 30-4 **Row complex from Arnold Schoenberg, Suite, Op. 25**

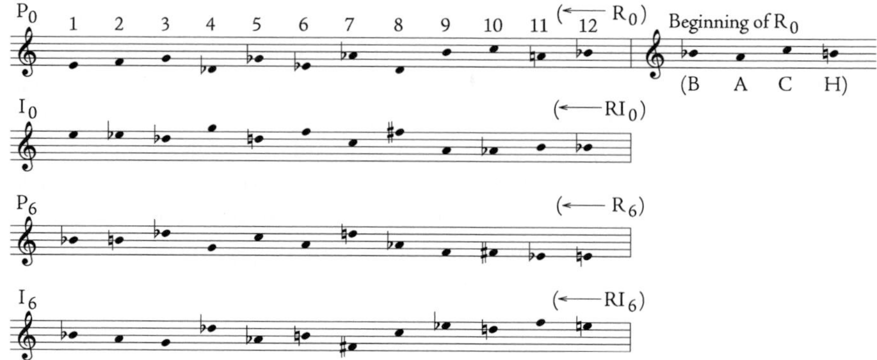

Schoenberg's affinity with aspects of the Neoclassical aesthetic, for all the scorn he poured on "little Modernsky" with his false "Papa Bach" wig, is evident in his own allotment of minuets, gavottes, and gigues. His defenders justify his recourse to eighteenth-century forms by emphasizing that the twelve-tone technique was still novel. His first published twelve-tone composition had taken the form of a waltz—not merely an old form, but a "light music" genre. Indeed Schoenberg shared with many composers an attraction to popular music, to irony and humor. Another early twelve-tone suite, for an instrumental septet (Op. 29; 1926), tentatively included a movement called "Foxtrot," before Schoenberg changed the title to the more neutral "Tanzschritte" (dance steps).

Schoenberg's career was dedicated henceforth to justifying the claims he had made for his method, elaborating and standardizing procedures so that its principles could indeed become law. In later works he placed great emphasis on whatever might enhance the status of the row as *Grundgestalt.* Principles of symmetry and of devising two hexachords that would complement one another became the basic determinants of structure, and they were taken to ever-greater extremes by some of Schoenberg's followers. His own inclination was to synthesize the new twelve-tone technique with as many aspects of traditional practice as possible.

The twelve-tone composers, who shared with Neoclassicists a preference for abstract or generic forms, went even further in shaping the contents of their work according to rational structural principles. In effect content was made equal to form. The analytical transparency of the twelve-tone technique gave it an aura of uprightness in the spirit of scientific "positivism" (verifiable empirical inquiry). This proved an important spur to its spread, just as some critics attacked the procedure for its "artificiality" and "arid intellectualism." In any case, the most arcane of compositional methods, "atonal" composition, all at once became the most lucid. It withheld few secrets from a determined analyst, although the untrained ear was still usually baffled. Like a scientific proof, a twelve-tone composition proceeded logically, by inference from an apparent premise (the row). No music better illustrated the debunking, objective, and antimetaphysical spirit of postwar disillusion than this descendant of Expressionism.

Back Again to Bach

The twelve-tone method allowed Schoenberg at once to connect with the musical past and to lay claim to the future. In his view this involved preeminently a German past and a German future. We have already mentioned the inscription of Bach's name in the row of Op. 25. In 1928 Schoenberg flaunted dozens of BACH allusions in his Variations for Orchestra, Op. 31, his first large-scale "public" twelve-tone composition and one that proclaims his line of descent from the great master of counterpoint. Webern inscribed Bach's name even more elaborately in the row for his String Quartet, Op. 28, a work that is based entirely on a row consisting of three statements of the cipher (Ex. 30-5).

Example 30-5a Tone row for Anton Webern, String Quartet, Op. 28

Example 30-5b Anton Webern, String Quartet, Op. 28, I, mm. 1–15

Example 30-5b (*continued*)

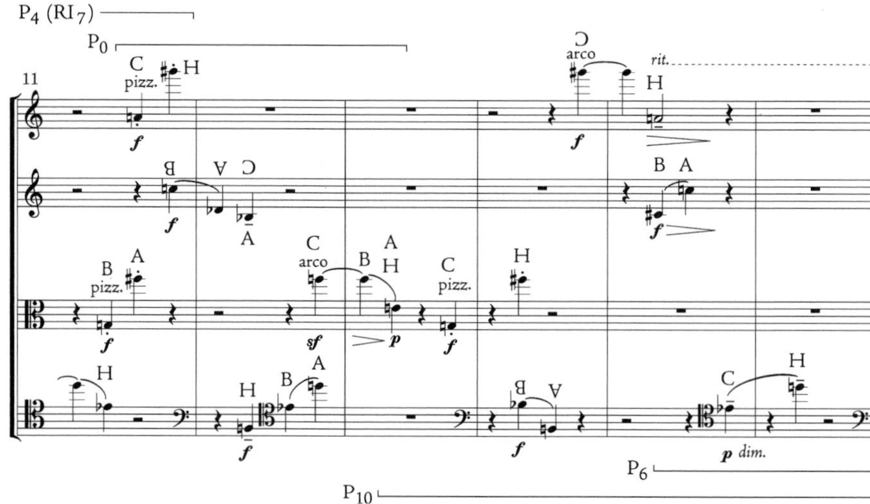

But who was Bach to Schoenberg? Certainly not the same man as Stravinsky's Bach, whose archaism represented timelessness, and whose abstract mastery represented universality. Schoenberg's Bach was not a universal figurehead but a national one. Bach, for Schoenberg, was the touchstone of German musical art. This explains the special venom with which Schoenberg derided Franco-Russian attempts like Stravinsky's to appropriate him. Schoenberg's particularly embittered nationalism reflected that of a resentful nation after its military defeat in the Great War and the humiliating terms of the ensuing treaties.

Schoenberg's writings abound in passages that underscore the connection with Bach. "It was mainly through J. S. Bach," he alleged in an essay called "National Music" (1931), "that German music came to decide the way things developed, as it has for two hundred years."[23] What guaranteed German domination, moreover, was precisely the technique that Schoenberg saw himself as having inherited from Bach and, through the twelve-tone system, was perfecting: "contrapuntal art, i.e., the art of producing every audible figure from one single one."[24] Lest anyone miss the point, Schoenberg spelled out his confrontational claims. First with respect to twelve-tone music: "If at the climax of contrapuntal art, in Bach, something quite new simultaneously begins—the art of development through motivic variation—and in our time, at the climax of art based on harmonic relationships, the art of composing with 'twelve tones related only to each other' begins, one sees that the epochs are very similar."[25] And with reference to himself: "My music, produced on German soil, without foreign influences, is a living example of an art able most effectively to oppose Latin and Slav hopes of hegemony and derived through and through from the traditions of German music"[26]—traditions that went back to Bach but traditions that in Schoenberg's view only Germans could legitimately claim.

The Variations for Orchestra and the other pieces by Schoenberg and his colleagues that invoke the German master asserted these claims musically. Schoenberg's view of the importance of twelve-tone technique informed what is now his most notorious remark, which he allegedly made in the early 1920s in a conversation with his teaching assistant, the musicologist Josef Rufer: "Today I have discovered something which will assure the supremacy of German music for the next hundred years."[27] Ever since Rufer recounted the remark in 1959, this has been one of the most disputed assertions in the history of European music.

The irony here is that the ascendance of Adolf Hitler and National Socialism in Germany shattered Schoenberg's life. As a Jew, he was forced to flee Europe and came to America in October 1933. After a hard winter teaching in New York and Boston, he spent a restorative summer in the peaceful cultural oasis of the Chautauqua Institution in western New York State. He then settled in Los Angeles, where he lived until his death in 1951. Although he still occasionally wrote tonal compositions (he on occasion told his American students that "there is still plenty of good music to be written in C major"),[28] he concentrated on twelve-tone pieces, including keyboard, chamber, and orchestral works. He never finished the magnum opus begun in Europe, an opera called *Moses und Aron*, one of the few incomplete operas that nonetheless is occasionally performed and recorded.

Alban Berg's Twelve-Tone Romanticism

The first composers after Schoenberg to adopt his twelve-tone methods were, naturally enough, his former pupils Alban Berg (Fig. 30-6) and Anton Webern, who took his example in quite different directions. Berg, born in 1885 into an affluent Viennese family, had not displayed any unusual musical talent as a youth. He began studying with Schoenberg in 1904 and, like Webern, became deeply, even obsessively, devoted to his teacher, whom he assisted in countless ways long after formal lessons ceased. Berg pursued an accelerated version of his teacher's career, writing early works that are stylistically late Romantic before turning to an atonal and Expressionistic idiom near the end of the first decade of the twentieth century. He was called to serve in the Austrian army from 1915 to 1918, accumulating experiences during that time that would inform his opera *Wozzeck*, the story of a poor soldier. (We will look at that influential masterpiece in some detail in the next chapter, when we consider trends in theater music.) Berg completed *Wozzeck* in 1922, shortly before he adopted twelve-tone methods. It premiered in Berlin in 1925 and became one of the mere handful of broadly successful operas of the century. This fact alone alerts us that with Berg we confront a figure whose music has found far greater audience acceptance than that of either his teacher Schoenberg or his colleague Webern.

Figure 30-6 Portrait of Alban Berg by Arnold Schoenberg, 1910.

Berg may have been ambivalent about his popular triumph with *Wozzeck*, which made him a celebrated composer for the final ten years of his life. The eminent philosopher Theodor W. Adorno (1903–69), his student, was with him after the opera's premiere and recounts "literally consoling him over his success." In Adorno's estimation, "Schoenberg envied Berg his successes, while Berg envied Schoenberg his failures."[29] There is good reason, however, to be skeptical about such a story, which all too easily bolsters the alienation ethic of the Modernist artist that Adorno always did his best to endorse. Berg's unusual position in twentieth-century music comes from his effective juggling of an advanced Modernist musical language with a Romantic, communicative, and deeply expressive sensibility. As devoted as he was to Schoenberg, Mahler was his great musical hero, and Berg may best be considered Mahler's greatest heir.[30]

Berg's keen dramatic sense not only informed his two operas but is also evident in many of his purely instrumental compositions. He first used twelve-tone techniques in the Chamber Concerto for violin, piano, and a wind ensemble of thirteen instruments (1925). In this fiftieth-birthday offering to Schoenberg he fashioned a row that incorporated the names Schoenberg, Berg, and Webern as pitch ciphers and used it sporadically in the piece. (Recall that E♭ is spelled as ES or S in German.) The work opens with a five-bar motto encoding their names as musical themes played respectively by the piano, the violin, and a French horn from the accompanying band (Ex. 30-6):

Example 30-6 Alban Berg, motto from the Chamber Concerto

ArnolD SCHönBErG = A–D–E♭–C–B–B♭–E–G;
Anton wEBErn = A–E–B♭–E;
AlBAn BErG = A–B♭–A–B♭–E–G

Berg was fascinated by intellectual games, puzzles, ciphers, and codes of all kinds, and his scores are packed with riddles and hidden symbols. Some of them (like numerological symbolism) reflected his personal superstitions and a widespread occult interest current in Vienna at the time. These hidden elements, as we shall see, also often had urgent autobiographical significance for him and were a spur to composition. And sometimes, to be sure, they were simply playful. The very fact that Berg took such delight in loading his music with so much hidden brainy baggage is an aspect of a jesting, ironic stance. Modernist music, increasingly, meant one thing to audiences, another to professionals. That some of Berg's twelve-tone compositions appeal to both groups has proved a rarity.

Anthology Vol 3-26
Full CD VI, 37
Concise CD III, 25

We can see the role of playful research and of precompositional work in Berg's *Lyric Suite* for string quartet (1926), a piece that mixes free atonality and strict twelve-tone technique. He uses what is called a symmetrical "all-interval" row, in which each of the hexachords contains all the intervals from half steps to perfect fourth (or, when inverted, from the perfect fifth to the major seventh), with the self-inverting tritone coming once, in the middle, as the boundary between the hexachords (Ex. 30-7). Berg uses these idiosyncratic row manipulations and permutations (as well as equally meticulous rhythmic and tempo calculations) in the service of an expressivity as intense as anything in his operas. Indeed, the *Lyric Suite* has a lot of hidden personal resonances and yet packs a dramatic force that makes it interesting even to those unaware of its secret meanings.

Example 30-7 All-interval row in Alban Berg, *Lyric Suite*

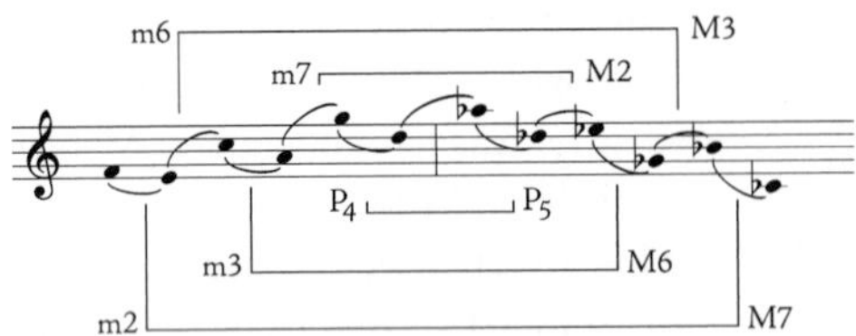

Berg dedicated the *Lyric Suite* to Alexander Zemlinsky, the former teacher and brother-in-law of Schoenberg who had also been the former teacher and frustrated lover of Alma Schindler before she married Mahler. It turns out, however, that there is a private program—and a private dedication—behind the quartet. The very titles of the six movements—*Allegretto gioviale* (jolly allegro); *Andante amoroso* (love-struck andante); *Allegro misterioso* and *Trio estatico* (mysterious allegro and ecstatic trio); *Adagio appassionato* (passionate adagio); *Presto delirando* (delirious presto); and *Largo desolato* (broken-hearted largo)—as well as the inclusion of various musical quotations in the piece, struck some early listeners and critics as windows into what Adorno called "a latent opera," a love story in six parts.[31]

Berg was fascinated by intellectual games, puzzles, ciphers, and codes of all kinds, and his scores are packed with riddles and hidden symbols.

The real dedicatee of the *Lyric Suite* turns out to have been Hanna Fuchs-Robettin, with whom Berg began an affair 1925 that ended ten years later with his death at age fifty. News of their relationship came as a surprise to many when it was finally discovered decades later because it is utterly at odds with the picture of domestic bliss painted by Berg's widow, Helene Berg. She outlived her husband by more than forty years, jealously guarding his memory and reputation; it was only after her death in 1976 that various facts emerged that offered new insights into Berg's music. Hanna was the sister of novelist Franz Werfel, Alma Mahler's third husband. When Berg had traveled to Prague in 1925 for performances of orchestral excerpts from *Wozzeck*, conducted by Zemlinsky, Alma took him to the home of the Fuchs-Robettin family, where he met Hanna and quickly fell in love with her.

In the 1970s, two sleuths, working independently, pieced together their hidden story. Musicologist Douglass Green uncovered a sketch that revealed the last movement—the *Largo desolato*—to be a secret setting of a despairing poem by Baudelaire, "De profundis clamavi" ("Out of the depths have I cried unto thee" [Psalm 130]), from the collection *Les Fleurs du mal* as translated into German by Stefan George.[32] A second discovery, this one made by composer and scholar George Perle, involved tracking down a copy of the *Lyric Suite* score owned by Hanna's daughter Dorothea, who lived in Pennsylvania. This copy, a gift from Berg to Hanna, contained annotations by the composer indicating every occurrence of the pitches B-F-A-B♭. Thus Berg for the benefit of his secret lover linked her initials to his (HF/AB = BF/AB♭ as named in German). The discovery helped to explain how some of the puzzling licenses Berg took with the order of the twelve tones were contrived to produce conjunctions of the lovers' initials (hence, symbolically, the union of their persons). Measure numbers, metronome markings, and other features in the piece are often guided by the lover's fateful numbers: Berg as 23 (based on his horoscope and used in other compositions) and Hanna as 10 (the number of letters in her name).

The score Perle discovered also revealed that the *Andante amoroso* is dedicated "to you [Hanna] and your children."[33] Berg repeatedly uses the two pitches C-C ("Do-Do" according to the solfège system), to represent the nickname of daughter Dorothea. The *Allegro misterioso* commemorates a specific date—20 May 1925—a day the lovers-to-be spent in Prague shortly after they had first met, when "everything was still a mystery—a mystery to *us*."[34] The initial "mysterious" feelings (wonderfully evoked by muted strings) are soon realized for what they are. The music "suddenly breaks out" into a *Trio estatico,* where it is not hard to imagine a first kiss. The fourth movement quotes from Zemlinsky's *Lyric Symphony* (1922), an imposing orchestral song cycle in which the words originally were: "You are my own, my own." The concluding *Largo desolato,* the movement that has the Baudelaire poem behind it, evokes the ultimate opera of impassioned love, Wagner's *Tristan und Isolde,* by quoting that work's famous opening chord.

The complexity of the *Lyric Suite* on so many musical and extramusical levels is astounding. In one of his annotations to Hanna, Berg commented, "I have written these [letters and numbers], and much that has other meanings, into this score for you (for whom, and only for whom—in spite of the official dedication on the following page—every note of this music was written). May it be a small monument to a great love."[35] Thus this compositionally advanced Modernist work is also in many respects "Romantic," in both a personal and a historical sense. We have not gone into so much detail about a composer's private life since discussing the end of Romanticism, with Mahler and early Schoenberg in the first decade of the twentieth century. Berg's Romantic Modernism goes a long way in explaining his enduring popularity when atonal and twelve-tone works continue to be typically avoided by audiences.

Berg's biography also played a large role in his final two works. His second opera, *Lulu,* based on a pair of plays by Frank Wedekind (1864–1918) about a ruthless femme fatale, was left unfinished at the time of his death in 1935. Perhaps because of unease with its highly erotic theme, Helene Berg suppressed the nearly complete third act of the opera, the partial orchestration of which was ultimately undertaken by Austrian composer Friedrich Cerha and first performed in 1979 in Paris. One reason Berg did not finish orchestrating the opera was because he had interrupted work on it to write a Violin Concerto, his last composition. It had been commissioned by American violinist Louis Krasner early in 1935 and was dedicated "to the memory of an angel." This was meant as an eloquent memorial to Manon Gropius (the daughter of Alma Mahler by her second husband, Walter Gropius, a famous architect), who died of polio in April of that year at age eighteen. Yet secrets and messages seem to lurk in this final piece as well, not only what appear to be further references to Hanna, but also what some sleuths have argued is an allusion to a much earlier romantic escapade, when Berg had fathered an illegitimate child at age seventeen with a household servant.

The traditions of the concerto foster a highly theatrical role for the violin soloist in relation to the full orchestra. As Berg had learned in composing *Lulu,* twelve-tone techniques were most effectively deployed in conjunction with more traditional approaches to melody, gesture, and form (Ex. 30-8). Perhaps most noteworthy is Berg's continuing fascination with the tenuous line between the tonal and the atonal, immediately evident with the tonal implications of the opening row, which consists mainly of an alternation of major and minor thirds, as first played by the violin during the introductory measures (Ex. 30-9a). Berg later merges this row with a chorale, *Es ist genug* ("It is enough"), adapted from a striking harmonization by Bach, the text of which, entered in the score at the appropriate point in the finale, has an appropriately funereal meaning honoring Manon (Ex. 30-9b). Berg thus invokes Bach as well, not wearing a Stravinskian wig or invoking a Schoenberg/Webern spelling game but, rather, by calling on Bach's actual music so as to exploit its deepest emotional and spiritual associations. Such a combination of the expressive, autobiographical, and dramatic lies at the core of Berg's music.

Example 30-8 Alban Berg, Violin Concerto: mm. 1–8

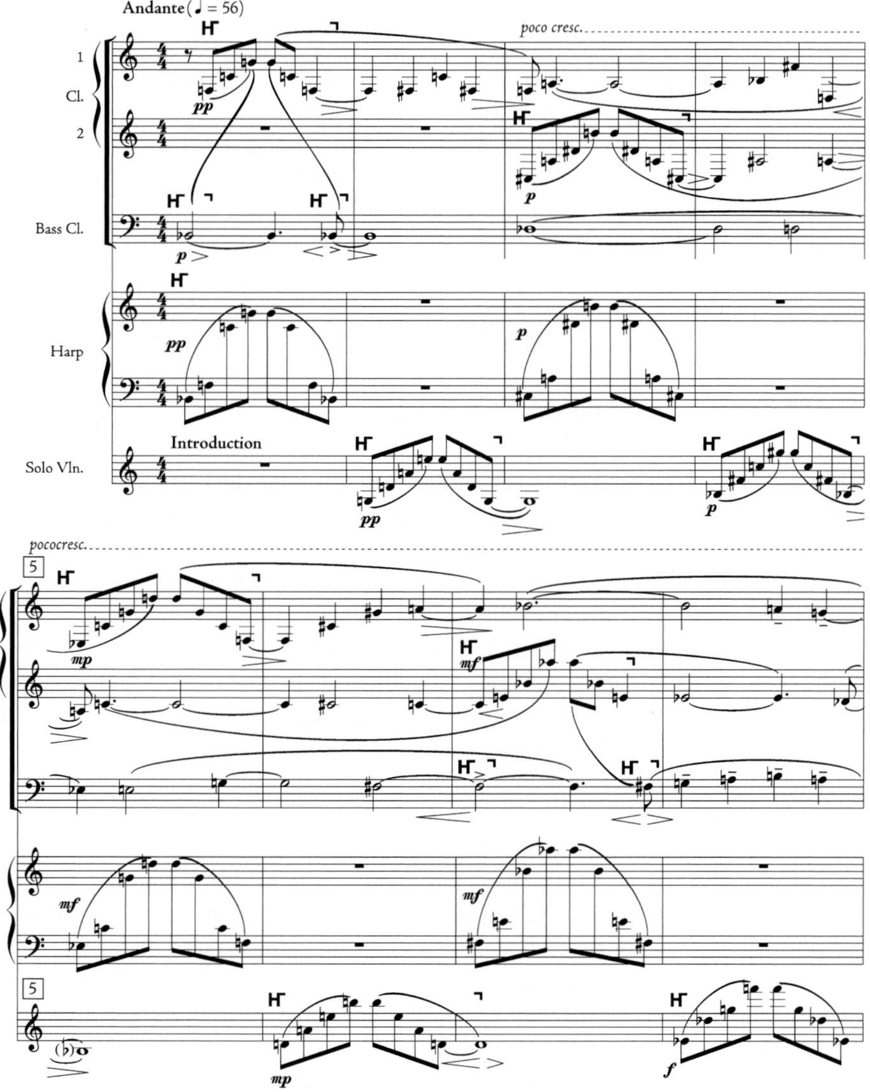

Example 30-9a Alban Berg, Violin Concerto, entrance of solo violin (mm. 15–18)

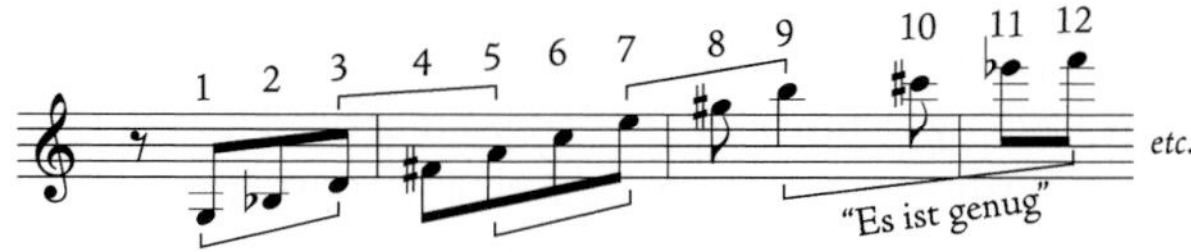

Example 30-9b J. S. Bach, harmonized chorale, "Es ist genug!"

Es ist ge - nug! Herr, wenn es Dir ge - fällt
It is enough! Whenever you please, Lord, take me . . .

Epitome: Anton Webern

Webern (Fig. 30-7) used the twelve-tone method quite differently. Drawn even more strongly than either Schoenberg or Berg to symmetrically constructed rows, he was also drawn to extremes of structural rigor and economy. This is no surprise, because it reflected inclinations we have already glimpsed in his radically compressed Expressionistic works. "Adherence to the row is strict, often burdensome," Webern wrote, "but it is *salvation*!"[36] While this new law made larger forms possible again, even Webern's larger forms were tiny. His entire mature compositional output fills just three compact discs. Movements of some pieces last less than a minute. His orchestrations can call for the large ensembles favored by Mahler and Strauss, but he uses these imposing forces sparingly, often to pointillist effect. Silence plays a crucial role in his music as well.

The number of minutes, measures, and instruments is, of course, no indication of Webern's artistic worth, historical stature, or influence, which, we will see, became extraordinary. While Schoenberg invented (or, as he preferred to say, "discovered") the twelve-tone technique, Webern provided the paramount model for its later development and utility. For a period during the 1950s and '60s Webern's small body of compositions was arguably the most influential one around. His ideas and example, even more than Schoenberg's, set the agenda for the musical trends that many Modern composers pursued after the Second World War.

Figure 30-7 Anton Webern in 1911.

One of Webern's first twelve-tone compositions was a piano minuet (1925), which again underscored the close relationship between the new technique and the general disciplinary aims of Neoclassicism. Over the course of the next twenty years Webern completed around a dozen works intended for publication: two orchestral, three choral, one for piano, four for chamber ensembles, and two sets of songs. They all used the technique his teacher had initiated.

It may have been Webern's training in musicology that predisposed him to take a more purely intervallic view of twelve-tone composition than the other members of his circle. He was aware of the many works by such Renaissance composers as Heinrich Isaac (on whom he wrote a doctoral dissertation), Jacob Obrecht, and Josquin des Prez, in which a cantus firmus was turned upside down or back to front for the sake of variety or for virtuoso compositional display. Webern liked to claim that the "Netherlanders," as they were then called, were his forebears.

To get a sense of Webern's aesthetic, sound world, and masterly manipulations of rows, we can look to his Symphony, Op. 21 (1928). Unlike any symphony we have encountered thus far, it is in two movements and lasts a total of just ten minutes. Its economical row is contrived so as to reduce the number of independent row forms and multiply the field of potential relationships among them. The primary row consists of half steps and thirds, with a tritone in the middle: A-F♯-G-A♭-E-F/B-Bb-D-C♯-C-E♭; the entire row is an intervallic palindrome: Its retrograde form is the same as the prime transposed by a tritone (Ex. 30-10). This ordering eliminates the retrograde as an independent row form, leaving only twelve possible primes and twelve possible inversions. With the row thus doing "double duty," serving as its own retrograde, and with inversion therefore the only meaningful transformation of it, the Symphony became a study in tightly controlled multidimensional symmetry (Ex. 30-11). That seems in fact to be what Webern meant by calling the work a symphony. There is little or nothing in its formal procedures to compare with those of the traditional symphony, but the texture is maximally "harmonious," or "sym-phonic" in the etymological sense, well known to a musicologist like Webern. Everything in it fits ideally with everything else. In a lecture he gave in March 1932, Webern exulted in the tightness of structure he had achieved thanks to the palindromic row: "Greater unity is impossible. Even the Netherlanders didn't manage it."[37]

Anthology Vol 3-27
Full CD VI, 38
Concise CD III, 26

While Schoenberg invented the twelve-tone technique, Webern provided the paramount model for its later development and utility.

Example 30-10 Tone row and its properties for Anton Webern's Symphony, Op. 21 (1928)

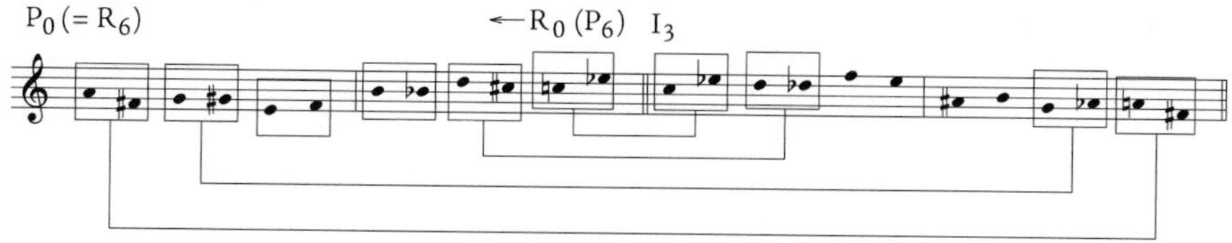

Webern's music generally epitomizes the Janus-faced aspect of early twelve-tone music, looking back to the Renaissance and forward to future musical developments that gained currency after the Second World War. He went further than any other composer of his time in the direction of tight organization, which he and his colleagues identified as "progress," that is, the inevitable fate of music foreordained by its history. Such music asserts, in every single note, its claim of lineal descent from Bach (or from the Netherlanders), from whom that history was traced. Yet it is easy to overestimate the complexity of this music. Both its highly rationalized compositional methods and the immense sum total of motivic relationships to which nearly everything else is sacrificed lend themselves to exhaustive verbal or graphic description. This, like any other kind of detail-heavy programmatic paraphrase, can all too readily turn attention away from the sound-object so described. But the sound-object as such is neither dense nor arcane. Webern's textures are famously spare and transparent, and in terms of events per unit of time, his music is far less heavily laden than Schoenberg's or Berg's.

Example 30-11 Anton Webern, Symphony, Op. 21, I, mm. 1–25

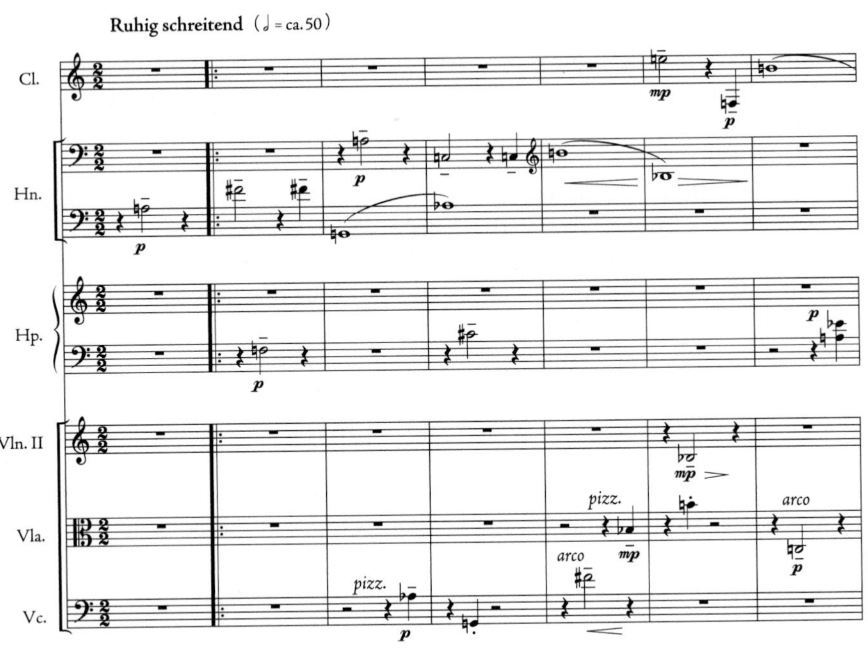

Example 30-11 (*continued*)

In the end it may be the analytic descriptions of Webern's compositions that most boggle the mind. The music lays everything bare. The descriptions can cover it up; they make analysis sound more like a math textbook than a music one. In part this has been a deliberate strategy. Surrounding Modernist art with a cult of obscurity has been a trusty protective measure, keeping the hostile crowd at bay. Webern himself tended to cast the difficulty of his art in heroic terms. "It's nonsense to advance 'social objections'" to the difficulty of the new music, Webern told a lecture audience in 1932, when most of the opposition came from the political left. "Why don't people understand that? Our push forward *had* to be made, it was a push forward such as never was before. In fact we have to break new ground with each work: Each work is something different, something new.... How do people hope to follow this? Obviously it's very difficult."[38]

But in private correspondence and in one exceptional case in an article meant for publication (but that went unpublished until 1978, more than thirty years after his death), Webern described his music with great emotion. The article, significantly enough, concerned his String Quartet, Op. 28 (1936–38), the work mentioned earlier that is totally governed by the BACH cipher (see Ex. 30-5). Webern celebrates his own skill by revealing the intimate relationship between the structure of the row and his ability to fashion an unprecedented canon in retrograde:

> You see, the second four notes of the row fashion their *intervals* from the *retrograde* of the first four, and the last four notes relate to the second four in the same way. But this means that the entire Quartet is based on nothing else than this specific *succession of four pitches*! Now it so happens that the first four notes of the "original" form of the row, transposed to B♭, yield the four letters BACH. Thus, my fugue subject presents this name three times (with the subject's three motives of four notes each making up the twelve notes of the row), but only *secretly* because, on the other hand, the original form NEVER occurs in this ostentatious transposition!!! All the same though, the *four notes* do underlie the *entire Quartet*!![39]

The specific combination of satisfaction in the achievement of structural consistency and exuberant triumph at its concealment from the uninitiated was typical of elitist Modernism and reached its peak in the literature dealing with twelve-tone music. We see once more the joy in connecting to Bach, the great German contrapuntalist. What we do not find is the thing found in Berg: the assurance that the elaborate compositional means were a conduit to a cathartic emotional payoff. Webern's aesthetic had become as objective and impersonal as Stravinsky's claimed to be. The joy he sought (and sought to convey) was the joy of wondrous intellectual contemplation.

Amid all the talk of constraint, obedience, compliance, and obligation, there is something else in Webern's exuberant description of his creative product, something that goes beyond aesthetics into the domain of ethics. In the context of the turbulent 1930s, it is hard not to relate Webern's artistic vision to the utopian cravings that dominated European social and political thought. Like Stravinsky's contemporaneous parables of submission, Webern's musical utopias, the most orderly and disciplined worlds of music ever to have been conceived and realized up to that time, seem in their tidy beauty of conception and their ruthlessly exacting realization to broach a theme that was on the mind of many artists of the time: the theme—ominous to some, inspiring to others—of art and totalitarianism. But clarity and order, in fact, were not the most prevalent musical concerns to emerge in the 1920s and early '30s. Rather, the Roaring Twenties is more broadly represented by new kinds of musical freedom and populism, to which we will now turn.

Summary

The terrible bloodshed of the First World War (1914–18) shattered the spiritual and exalted ideals that underlay Romanticism, and many composers renounced the musical styles associated with the nineteenth century. This chapter explored the different reactions to this environment, reflected in the music of Igor Stravinsky and of Arnold Schoenberg, Alban Berg, and Anton Webern.

Stravinsky responded to this anti-Romantic climate with marked changes to his musical style. In the new style, called Neoclassicism, he imitated the gestures and forms of pre-Romantic music. Stravinsky's Neoclassical works include the ballets *Histoire du soldat* (The Soldier's Tale, 1918) and *Pulcinella* (1920), instrumental works such as the *Symphonies d'instruments à vent* (1920) and the Octet (1923), and the opera *The Rake's Progress* (1951). Although these pieces are audibly linked to earlier works by composers such as Pergolesi, Bach, and Mozart, Stravinsky approaches earlier music with a certain irony, superimposing elements of Modernism on the old style. The Octet, for example, combines a walking bass and counterpoint characteristic of Baroque music, with ostinatos, dissonances, and a prominent octatonic scale (alternating half steps and whole steps). Stravinsky became a vocal defender of the objective, anti-Romantic aesthetic, famously declaring that "music is, by its very nature, essentially powerless to *express* anything at all, whether a feeling, an attitude of mind, a psychological mood, a phenomenon of nature, etc."

A different way forward after the Great War was the twelve-tone technique of Schoenberg and his colleagues, introduced in the early 1920s. In the twelve-tone method, the harmony and thematic material are generated from a series of twelve notes, with none repeated. The basic, or "prime," form of the row can generate other forms: its inversion (with the intervals between each successive note inverted), its retrograde (reverse), and the inversion of the retrograde. Each one of these forms can occur at any transposition, resulting in a total of forty-eight forms. This ordered series of intervals permeates every aspect of the composition. The rows are often divided into trichords, tetrachords, or hexachords that are intervallically related, providing for even more unity.

Although Schoenberg disparaged Stravinsky's Neoclassicism, his twelve-tone technique can be thought of as yet another expression of a similar impulse. In contrast to the maximalist excesses of his prewar works (see Chapter 27), Schoenberg sought a more rational working out of expression. He believed he was the true heir of the German tradition, following in the footsteps of Bach and guaranteeing German dominance in music history.

Schoenberg's former pupils Berg and Webern took the twelve-tone method in two different directions. Berg managed to fuse the objective and rational with the Romantic, as illustrated in his *Lyric Suite*, a twelve-tone work with a hidden, autobiographical program based on a secret love affair. Reflecting his penchant for intellectual games, Berg intertwines ciphers for the initials of his lover with his own initials. Because of its dramatic qualities, continued relation to aspects of traditional tonal procedures, and expressive gestures, Berg's music has proved more popular with audiences than either Schoenberg's or Webern's.

In contrast to Berg's twelve-tone style, Webern used the technique in the service of his fascination with economy and symmetry. Most of his works are extremely brief and sparse in orchestration. He had a natural affinity with the music of Renaissance composers, evident in his frequent use of canon. All these traits are illustrated in his Symphony, Op. 21. Webern's preoccupation with structure was to prove very influential for the next generation of serialists.

Study Questions

1. In what sense is Igor Stravinsky's Neoclassicism "ironic"? How does Stravinsky express this irony musically, especially in the Octet?
2. What views did Stravinsky express about art during his Neoclassical period? In what sense were they anti-Romantic? How did they draw on and respond to critics' reactions to his work?
3. Compare and contrast Stravinsky's views on aesthetics with those of Arnold Schoenberg. What was Schoenberg's attitude toward Stravinsky's Neoclassicism, and why did he hold that attitude?
4. What was the Society for Private Musical Performances? How did it reflect a change in the relationship between the composer and the public?
5. Describe Schoenberg's attitude toward the music of the past. Why did he believe he was carrying forward the German musical tradition and assuring Germany's central position in music history?
6. Describe how the forty-eight forms of a twelve-tone row are derived in serialism.
7. Compare and contrast the approaches to serialism in the music of Alban Berg and Anton Webern, particularly in Berg's *Lyric Suite* and Webern's Symphony, Op. 21. In what sense is Berg a twelve-tone Romanticist? How do Webern's works differ from Berg's?

Key Terms

inversion
Neoclassicism
prime
retrograde
serialism
Society for Private Musical Performances
tone row
twelve-tone technique

31

Interwar Currents: The Roaring Twenties

While some composers, after the trauma of the Great War, developed and pursued Neoclassicism and twelve-tone technique, their music ultimately reached only a very small portion of the general public. The really big musical news of the time was an explosion of popular styles and of the electronic means of disseminating music through recordings and radio. The **Roaring Twenties** is often referred to as the "Jazz Age," although by that time **jazz** had already been evolving for decades, having started in the American South and spread quickly to other parts of the country and abroad. As with other forms of popular music, an in-depth consideration of jazz is beyond the scope of this book, devoted as it is to notated music in the West. At its core, jazz is principally an improvised art, although many jazz pieces have been notated at some point, increasingly so in our time. Unlike the popular music of past centuries, which often did not survive in written form, much of the tradition of jazz is preserved because of the recording technologies that were emerging nearly simultaneously. This has meant that many great improvised jazz pieces can still be heard, reconstructed, and notated many decades later. Recordings provide an essential archive of the leading figures in jazz since the early twentieth century.

The term *jazz* was used early on to designate what had formerly been called **ragtime**, the highly syncopated African American music that was extremely popular in the 1890s and was most associated with the piano sheet music of Scott Joplin (1867?–1917; Fig. 31-1). The etymology of the word jazz and its American origins are obscure. One scholar summed up the thorny matter by writing that "the term 'jazz,' first applied around 1916 (in New Orleans) to a rough and sexy strain of African American music, soon was synonymous with any syncopated

Figure 31-1 Scott Joplin about 1911.

mass-marketed popular music."[1] Jazz enters our story now not only because of its increasing prominence in everyday musical life but also because of the considerable effect of its syncopated rhythms and exuberant instrumental display on a great many composers, especially between the two world wars.

Other expressive dimensions are to be found in "**the blues**," an African American folk genre that fed into jazz around the time of the Great War. The name seems to stem from "the blue devils," a colloquial expression for melancholy traceable back for centuries. As a musical term, blues can refer generally to a style of expressive performance as well as specifically to a musical form that was standardized around the turn of the century. As a form, the blues is a framework for poetic and melodic improvisation. The singer of a "12-bar blues" typically improvises a short poem in which the second line is a repetition of the first and the next and last line ends with a word that rhymes with the ending word of the other two. Each line coincides with a four-bar musical phrase in $\frac{4}{4}$ time. The first is supported by the tonic harmony throughout; the second moves from the subdominant (two bars) to the tonic (two bars), and the third is similarly divided between the dominant and the tonic (Fig. 31-2). The rhyming word usually coincides with the third downbeat of a phrase, the rest of the time being filled out by the instrumental accompaniment, at first most often played on guitar or banjo and later on the piano. This alternation of forces is one instance of "**call and response**" techniques commonly associated with African and African American music.

Anthology Vol 3-28
Full CD VI, 39
Concise CD III, 27

We can hear this in the opening stanza of "St. Louis Blues" (1914) by the African American composer, trumpeter, and bandleader W. C. Handy (1873–1958). This song was one of the most famous composed and published (i.e., commercial) examples of what had been a predominantly oral genre. The extraordinary popularity of "St. Louis Blues" meant it was performed by many leading jazz musicians. Among the most famous recordings are those of singer Bessie Smith (1894–1937), including collaborations with bandleader Louis Armstrong (1901–71). Indeed, as is often the case with popular forms of music, exemplary performers such as Smith and Armstrong are better remembered than Handy, the song's composer.

One of the distinctive features of the blues is the unstable third degree, conspicuous in Handy's melody both in the opening melodic "scoop" notated (very approximately) by the use of a grace note, and in the B♭s (also notated approximately) that clash with the B natural of the tonic triad as cross relations both direct (in line 1) and oblique (in lines 2 and 3). A blues singer like Smith will sing these notes sharp, so that they lie "in the crack" between the minor and the major third, and will refer to them as **blue notes**. (Also called blue notes are flattened leading tones and dominants or any note "bent" for expressive purposes.) The characteristic jazz syncopation, in which a long or accented note is made more intensely expressive by placing it ahead of the beat on which it is expected, is also present in Handy's melody, consistently placed at the end of the first measure in every line. Again the notation sets an exact place—displacement by one eighth note—for what is flexible and diverse in actual performance (Ex. 31-1).

	Bar 1	Bar 2	Bar 3	Bar 4
Phrase 1	I: / / / /	/ / / /	/ / / /	/ / / /
Phrase 2	IV: / / / /	/ / / /	I: / / / /	/ / / /
Phrase 3	V: / / / /	/ / / /	I: / / / /	/ / / /

Figure 31-2 Basic harmonic structure of twelve-bar blues.

Example 31-1 W. C. Handy, "St. Louis Blues," first stanza

(I) I hate to see— de ev-nin' sun go down,—
(IV) Hate to see— de ev-nin' sun go down— (I)
(V) 'Cause ma ba - by he done lef' this town.— (I)

European "Jazz": Parisians in America

The 1920s also became the Jazz Age in Paris and other European centers. We have already mentioned the early influence of ragtime in Debussy's "Golliwogg's Cake-walk" (1908). By the end of the war, Stravinsky, the great trendsetter of the day, put a ragtime in *Histoire du soldat* and noted on the manuscript of his *Ragtime for Eleven Instruments* that it was finished on 10 November 1918, the very day of the German surrender. That coincidence neatly symbolized one of the main attractions of American popular genres for the European allies: It seemed about as un-German as music could get.

The reach of jazz had expanded during the war and was further enhanced in its wake by earwitness contact. American popular musicians, many of them African American, brought their music to Europe and were lionized, especially in Paris. Some, like the clarinetist Sidney Bechet (1897–1959), came for frequent, lucrative tours. Others stayed, like singer Josephine Baker (1906–75; Fig. 31-3.) Having originally arrived in 1925 to star in a show called *La revue nègre* at the Théâtre des Champs-Elysées (the very hall where *The Rite of Spring* had had its scandalous premiere), Baker quickly moved on to the Folies-Bergère, the number-one Paris nightspot, became the darling of café society, opened her own nightclub, got wealthy, and in 1937 took French citizenship. Her success was an inspiration to many African Americans, and in later life she was one of the early icons of the American civil rights movement.

Some Europeans got acquainted with American jazz at its source. Ernest Ansermet (1883–1969), a distinguished conductor who worked for years with Diaghilev's Ballets Russes, wrote back to his friend Stravinsky from America, where the dance company was touring in 1916. He noted that whereas the general classical music establishment was hopelessly dominated by Germans, nevertheless "there is at the bottom of this immense country a forgotten or lost soul which has found its way into the *incredible music* you hear in cafes!!" He was particularly struck by jazz musicians' ability to "improvise splendidly and with genius."[2] Some years later, in the course of touring the United States, the French composer Darius Milhaud (1892–1974) went to Harlem in upper Manhattan, then the epicenter of jazz nightclubs and speakeasies, in which illegal alcoholic beverages were served during Prohibition (1920–33). His memoirs contain a vivid description of what he heard and how invigorating it was—a "revelation" he called it:

> Against the beat of the drums the melodic lines crisscrossed in a breathless pattern of broken and twisted rhythms. A Negress whose grating voice seemed to come

CASINO DE PARIS
JOSEPHINE BAKER
ZIG
LA JOIE DE PARIS

Figure 31-3 Josephine Baker in a poster for the Casino de Paris.

from the depths of the centuries sang in front of the various tables. With despairing pathos and dramatic feeling she sang over and over again, to the point of exhaustion, the same refrain, to which the constantly changing melodic pattern of the orchestra wove a kaleidoscopic background. This authentic music had its roots in the darkest corners of the Negro soul, the vestigial traces of Africa, no doubt. Its effect on me was so overwhelming that I could not tear myself away. From then on I frequented other Negro theaters and dance halls.[3]

TIMELINE

1899 **Scott Joplin, *Maple Leaf Rag***

1911 **Irving Berlin, "That Mysterious Rag"**

1912 Pablo Picasso, *Guitar, Sheet Music, and Wine Glass*

1914 **W.C. Handy, "St. Louis Blues"**

1917 **Erik Satie, *Parade***

1917 Guillaume Apollinaire coins the term *surrealism*

What eventually emerged from his experience was a ballet, *La création du monde* (The Creation of the World, 1923), in which Milhaud used a "jazz band" scoring similar to what he had heard in Harlem. Despite the occasional syncopated riffs, parts of the ballet are written in a sedately Bachian chorale-prelude style. In addition to its Neoclassical vogue, this provides a suitably religious frame for the action and draws parallels between an authentic African creation myth, which showed a seething mass of exotically costumed dancers representing the primal soup from which life would gradually erupt, and the Western, or biblical, one.

Anthology Vol 3-29
Full CD VI, 40

Maurice Ravel was another French composer much drawn to jazz. His most potent jazz stylizations came in generically titled classical scores such as his two piano concertos from the late 1920s and his Violin Sonata (1923–27). The middle movement of the sonata, subtitled "Blues," touches on virtually every feature of the style described for Handy's "St. Louis Blues." It has twanging pizzicato chords that cast the violin as a kind of banjo, plunking out the rhythmic framework after which the melody seems to be improvised. The chords are the expected I, IV, and V, although the standard blues pattern is merely suggested, not reproduced. To those with a score in hand, the clash occurring at the piano's entrance is implicit from the start in the bitonal superimposition of key signatures that suggests the ambiguity of a blue note. We also hear the characteristic blues **syncopation,** with small note values tied over the beat to longer ones. The last chord contains another sort of blue note, in the form of an unresolving, stable flat seventh that was the stereotypical jazz finishing chord (Ex. 31-2).

Jazz "will prove to be an effective factor in the founding of an American school of music . . . worthily deriving from, and in turn contributing to, a noble national heritage in music."—Maurice Ravel

Ravel described this blues movement to an American audience in Texas during his lone visit to the United States, a concert tour in 1928. He noted how composers in other countries, including Russia, Italy, and Germany, were also using American popular music and yet were still able to retain their own native sound: "The styles become as numerous as the composers themselves," and this is because "the individualities of these composers are stronger than the materials appropriated."[4] He told the audience that jazz "will prove to be an effective factor in the founding of an American school of music . . . worthily deriving from, and in turn contributing to, a noble national heritage in music."

In these musings of Ravel one can detect some of the Old World condescension that many had detected some thirty years earlier in Dvořák's equally well-meaning advice. Like his predecessor, Ravel skirted many questions that were of far greater weight to Americans than they were to Europeans, for whom America was an exotic and still somewhat mythical place. Leaving aside for the moment the highly fraught question of its origins, and granting that jazz was a distinctively American genre, did that entitle it to represent the diverse population of the United States? Could the music of a minority culture, and an often-despised one at that, represent the majority? And could jazz, a genre that had emerged since Dvořák's time and that had long since been commercialized, qualify as folklore? The assumption that the world's cultures and civilizations were all located on a single evolutionary timetable, with Europe on top, was of course the principle that justified Europe's colonial expansion and all its attendant cruelties. Ravel and others seemed to imply that it would be left to the white Europeans (or the Euro-Americans) to exploit the musical resources of "the Negro" fully.

1920–33 **Prohibition in the United States**
1921 **Paul Hindemith, *Kammermusik Nr. 1***
1922 James Joyce, *Ulysses*
1923 **Darius Milhaud, *La création du monde***
1924 **Alban Berg's *Wozzeck* premieres**
1924 **George Gershwin, *Rhapsody in Blue***
1925 **"St. Louis Blues" recorded by Bessie Smith with Louis Armstrong**
1925 **Aaron Copland, *Music for the Theatre***
1927 *The Jazz Singer*, first "talkie"
1927–28 **Virgil Thomson, *Four Saints in Three Acts***
1928 **Kurt Weill, *The Threepenny Opera* (lyrics by Bertolt Brecht)**
1929 Worldwide stock market crashes; Great Depression begins
1933 Adolf Hitler becomes the Chancellor of Germany; the Nazi regime begins
1933 Gertrude Stein, *The Autobiography of Alice B. Toklas*
1933 **Max Steiner, *King Kong* score**
1935 **Gershwin, *Porgy and Bess***
1943 **Duke Ellington's *Black, Brown and Beige* premieres at Carnegie Hall**

Example 31-2 Maurice Ravel, Violin Sonata, II ("Blues"), ending

In Search of the "Real" America: Americans in Paris

By the time Ravel gave his speech in 1928, such issues as these were being hotly debated among young American composers as they grappled with shaping a distinctive American style for classical music. Aaron Copland (1900–90; Fig. 31-4), present as we know for the Paris premiere of Stravinsky's Octet in 1923, had come to France to study. He found an inspiring teacher in Nadia Boulanger (1887–1979; Fig. 31-5), as would many Americans in the decades to come. It was a good time to be an American artist in Paris, since the French regarded the United States as their wartime savior and were embracing jazz and popular American culture generally.

Copland's generation formed their musical tastes in the period of anti-Germanic backlash that followed the Great War, making them susceptible to the fashionable

Figure 31-4 Aaron Copland in Paris, early 1920s.

currents dominant in the French capital. And thus a new chapter in the history of American concert music—of musical "Americanism"—was opened by composers who received their finishing in Paris during the 1920s, so often under the tutelage of Boulanger that their cohort became known as the "Boulangerie" (French for "bakery"). Copland was among the first to join. From a magazine advertisement, he learned of a school for American musicians that the French government planned to set up in Fontainebleau, a small town outside Paris. He saw in the establishment of this school "a gesture of appreciation to America for its friendship during World War I."[5] Of Boulanger herself another student said: "What endeared her most to Americans was her conviction that American music was just about to 'take off,' just as Russian music had done eighty years before."[6] She proved to be the one member of the faculty sympathetic to the Modernist music Copland and others wanted to write. So while Schoenberg propagated his aesthetic through a long teaching career in Vienna, Berlin, New York, and California, Boulanger promoted the aesthetic of Stravinsky, who rarely took on students himself. (Stravinsky apparently felt that Boulanger could more effectively transmit his legacy.)

Even before going to Europe in the summer of 1921, Copland had begun a perky little piano piece called "Jazzy" in a popular style, but had kept it hidden from his composition teacher in New York, a former Dvořák pupil named Rubin Goldmark (1872–1936). Copland's serious interest in jazz began not in America but in Vienna, during a brief visit in 1923. The foreign setting played a crucial part in awakening that new sympathy: "When I heard jazz played in Vienna, it was like hearing it for the first time," Copland wrote.[7] Even more decisive, though, was his discovery—a discovery that astonished him—that many cultured Europeans, unlike their American counterparts, regarded jazz with high respect.

In the end it was an Americanized Paris that brought the new generation of American composers their vision of America; it was a characteristic irony of the time that it should have taken a Parisian apprenticeship to create a viable American school. Boulanger's Paris apartment became a famous gathering place for prominent artistic figures. One of the musicians with whom she put Copland in contact was the Russian conductor Sergey Koussevitzky (1874–1951), whose marriage to an heiress had made him financially independent. Like Stravinsky, Prokofiev, and Rachmaninoff, he was an émigré from postrevolutionary Russia. From 1917 to 1924 his base was Paris, where he formed his own orchestra and gave concerts at which, thanks to his self-subsidizing, he could afford to program a great deal of contemporary music. In 1924 Koussevitzky was appointed music director of the Boston Symphony Orchestra, and over the next quarter century he would commission and premiere a formidable array of masterpieces with the ensemble. He wanted Boulanger, who was an accomplished organist, to perform with the orchestra during his inaugural season. She in turn arranged for Copland to compose a work for her; the result was his Symphony for Organ and Orchestra, which she premiered with the New York Symphony Orchestra in January 1925 and presented soon thereafter in Boston. The New York premiere was a major event for the virtually unknown Copland and brought him a good amount of attention. To the chagrin of Copland and his parents, the conductor, Walter Damrosch, announced from the podium that "if a gifted young man can write a symphony like this at twenty-three [actually, twenty-four], within five years he will be ready to commit murder!"[8]

Figure 31-5 Nadia Boulanger in the late 1930s/early 1940s.

Copland's music soon took a defiant turn that reflected European Modernist attitudes. With Boulanger's encouragement he started to experiment with what was then called "symphonic jazz." His suite *Music for the Theatre* (1925) features a typical theatrical (or pit) orchestra of some eighteen players, including piano. He dedicated the piece to Koussevitzky, who gave the premiere. A review in *The Boston Post* confirmed it as an act of mild aggression calculated to win a place for American music as an alternative to the traditional European repertory. It was, the critic wrote, "a tonal bombshell that left in its wake a mingling of surprise, perplexity, indignation and enthusiasm."[9] Koussevitzky next commissioned a piano concerto from Copland that premiered in January 1927; it aroused the indignation that *Music for the Theatre* had, but little of the enthusiasm. One critic wrote that "some have complained that the work had no spiritual value, only animal excitement; but what else has jazz?"[10] Such a remark was typical of an ugly racial undercurrent frequently encountered in the reception of jazz. A further twist in Copland's jazz experiments was that they evoked a racial backlash in some quarters from those who both objected to his musical sources and made innuendos about his Jewish background and (in a few cases) his homosexuality. The not-so-subtle message was that neither an African American nor a Jew could be a true American. Despite some jazzy moments that would appear in various later pieces, Copland decided to distance himself from that specific association with popular music and instead went on to develop a different kind of musical populism in the late 1930s and '40s, his most famous music, which we will consider in Chapter 33.

Copland's jazz experiments evoked a racial backlash in some quarters.

Tin Pan Alley and Musicals

It will be useful to compare the troubled reception of Copland's jazz-influenced compositions with the altogether different response around the same time to some similar works by another American composer: George Gershwin (1898–1937; Fig. 31-6), Copland's near contemporary from a very similar background. He too was born in Brooklyn to Jewish parents who had immigrated to the United States from Russia. He even studied with the same teacher, Rubin Goldmark, although at a later stage of life and more briefly than Copland. Both Copland and Gershwin pursued their musical careers beginning in their teens. After graduating from high school, Copland decided to head off to Paris, whereas Gershwin, who came from a much poorer family, dropped out of school at fourteen, the youngest age then legal, in order to earn a living.

A precocious pianist, gifted with a remarkable ear, Gershwin found work as a "song plugger" for a music publisher. His job was to play popular sheet music by request so that prospective purchasers could hear the songs the firm was selling. The position required a fluent piano technique, keen sight-reading skills, and a talent for stylish improvisatory embellishment. It was only natural that a song plugger would turn to writing popular songs himself. Such songs, with their strictly standardized format, were the stock-in-trade of **Tin Pan Alley**,

Figure 31-6 George Gershwin: Self-portrait in oils (1934).

the location and nickname for the music-publishing industry that grew up in New York in the 1890s. Tin Pan Alley was heavily populated by Jewish entrepreneurs and songwriters. Its products were used in domestic parlors as well as in the variety theaters on Broadway and in their Yiddish counterparts on the Lower East Side.

Within a couple of years, Gershwin moved to the more prestigious theater world uptown on Broadway, becoming rehearsal pianist for a show called *Miss 1917*. This plotless musical revue had as its song writers Victor Herbert (1859–1924) and Jerome Kern (1885–1945), two reigning Broadway composers. At the time American musical comedies (commonly known as **musicals**) were blossoming, putting an indigenous spin on the European tradition we saw represented by the operettas of Offenbach, Johann Strauss II, Gilbert and Sullivan, and others in the latter half of the nineteenth century. Early musicals by George M. Cohan (1878–1942), for example, yielded many popular songs, such as "Over There" (1917), the megahit of the war years. The leading Tin Pan Alley composer was the Russian-born Irving Berlin (1888–1989). "That Mysterious Rag," written with Ted Snyder in 1911, is typical of the industrial formula, a necessity for maintaining high commercial productivity. (Indeed, Tin Pan Alley resembled Italian opera of a hundred years before, another high-volume literate genre that consequently relied on similarly stereotyped formal designs.) The standard popular song form was the thirty-two-bar chorus or refrain, usually preceded by one or two introductory verses that could be omitted (Ex. 31-3).

Anthology Vol 3-30
Full CD VI, 41

Example 31-3 Irving Berlin and Ted Snyder, "That Mysterious Rag"

Example 31-3 (*continued*)

Gershwin's first runaway hit was "Swanee," a song published in 1919 that was recorded the following year by singer Al Jolson (1886–1950) and earned the composer a royalty of $10,000 in its first year, a fantastic sum in those days. More important, it made him a bankable composer for Broadway producers. Between 1920 and 1924, Gershwin wrote the scores for Broadway shows, both revues and musicals. Some seventy-two of these songs were harvested for publication as sheet music, complementing songs that he wrote for insertion into shows by other composers and some further items composed directly for sheet-music sale. Added to ones written earlier, they made a total of well over a hundred songs, many setting words by his older brother, Ira Gershwin (1896–1983), his chief songwriting collaborator.

The Gershwin brothers' musicals included *Lady Be Good* (1924), *Oh, Kay!* (1926), *Funny Face* in (1927), *Girl Crazy* (1930), and *Of Thee I Sing* (1931), which won a Pulitzer Prize. Their successful collaboration mirrored some of the other great teams of musical theater in the 1920s and beyond. Kern wrote *Showboat* in 1927 with words by Oscar Hammerstein II (1895–1960), who later was the chief wordsmith for Richard Rodgers (1902–79). Together they created *Oklahoma!* (1943), *Carousel* (1945), *South Pacific* (1949), *The King and I* (1951), *The Sound of Music* (1959), and other Broadway shows as well as films. A somewhat later duo was songwriter Frederick Loewe (1904–88) and lyricist Alan Jay Lerner (1918–86), whose musicals included *What's Up?* (1943), *Brigadoon* (1947), *Paint Your Wagon* (1951), *My Fair Lady* (1956), *Camelot* (1960), and *Gigi* (1973; adapted from the version first created as a musical film in 1958).

Gershwin's "Experiment in Modern Music"

Gershwin was unexpectedly given an opportunity to cross over into more serious terrain in 1924 when Paul Whiteman (1890–1967), a popular bandleader with a classical background, invited the young Broadway composer to compose an extended work for piano and large dance orchestra. Whiteman cannily requested a **rhapsody**, which was not so much a form as a title popularized by Liszt's *Hungarian Rhapsodies*. It connoted a Romantically free form, an opportunity for pianistic display, and a programmatically nationalistic statement of a sort that many American composers were then contemplating. The piece that Gershwin came up with, *Rhapsody in Blue*, was first performed in an orchestration by Whiteman's arranger, Ferde Grofé (1892–1972), on 12 February 1924 at Aeolian Hall in New York City.

Anthology Vol 3-31
Full CD VI, 42
Concise CD III, 28

The premiere of *Rhapsody in Blue* came near the end of a long concert called "An Experiment in Modern Music," with a note in the program book proclaiming that the "educational" purpose of the experiment was to highlight "the tremendous strides which have been made in popular music from the day of the discordant jazz, which sprang into existence about ten years ago from nowhere in particular, to the really melodious music of today which—for no good reason—is still being called jazz."[11] Striking is the phrase "From nowhere in particular . . .". The concert was in essence an attempt to sanitize contemporary popular music and elevate it in public esteem by divorcing it from its roots in African American improvised music and securing endorsements from luminaries of the classical music establishment, many of whom were in attendance that evening.

Gershwin opened *Rhapsody in Blue* with what he called an "icebreaker," a term used on Broadway for a device to grab the audience's attention: a clarinet glissando of a type that was pioneered as a special effect by African American jazz players. It was imparted to Gershwin by Ross Gorman, a player in Whiteman's orchestra. The piece then settles down into a medley of five tunes, each resembling a Tin Pan Alley chorus in one way or another and all adhering quite strictly to the obligatory AA′BA format. They are connected by cadenzas and virtuoso passages.

Rhapsody in Blue could be seen as fulfilling Dvořák's prescription for an American music that would elevate the musical utterances of the folk by means of "beautiful treatment in the higher forms of art." The ambition, we should note, was upward. Gershwin was explicitly sympathetic to his sources, commenting in 1933 that he regarded jazz "as an American folk-music; not the only one, but a very powerful one which is probably in the blood and feeling of the American people more than any other style of folk-music."[12] Gershwin later acknowledged that he "took 'blues' and put them in a larger and more serious form," adding "That was twelve years ago and the *Rhapsody in Blue* is still very much alive, whereas if I had taken the same themes and put them in songs they would have been gone years ago."[13]

Rhapsody in Blue was a huge popular success at its premiere. The critics, too, were kind. One of the most intelligent and important among them, Deems Taylor, allowed that Gershwin's composition "hinted at something new, something that had not hitherto been said in music."[14] Gershwin, he predicted, would provide "a link between the jazz camp and the intellectuals." W. J. Henderson, then the dean of New York critics, saw Whiteman's concert as a milestone, achieving "the total eclipse of the other kind of moderns—all save one, Stravinsky."[15] *Rhapsody in Blue* turned out to be perhaps the most lucrative piece of concert music ever composed, earning the composer more than a quarter of a million dollars from performance and recording royalties and rental fees during the first ten years of its existence, both in its original scoring for dance band and in its 1926 symphonic version (also the work of Grofé). It is worth noting that much of this income was earned from sales of piano rolls, recordings, and radio broadcasts, making Gershwin the first composer of classical music to benefit conspicuously from the new mechanized and electronic dissemination media of the twentieth century.

Gershwin, one critic predicted, would provide "a link between the jazz camp and the intellectuals."

In the wake of *Rhapsody in Blue* Gershwin received a commission for a traditional three-movement Piano Concerto in F, a more ambitious and in some ways more sophisticated work, which received its premiere in Carnegie Hall on 3 December 1925. The critics again were welcoming, one going so far as to remark that "of all those writing the music of today," Gershwin "alone actually expresses us."[16] Gershwin intended his jazz-inflected concert music to reflect contemporary

American urban life—that is, American Modernity. He described *Rhapsody in Blue* as "a musical kaleidoscope of America, of our vast melting pot, of our national pep, of our blues, our metropolitan madness."[17] The Concerto in F, for similar reasons, was originally to have been called *New York Concerto*.

In 1928 Gershwin traveled to Europe and was celebrated everywhere, by audiences as well as by leading Modernist composers—Prokofiev, Milhaud, Ravel, and Berg—who accepted him as a peer (or more than a peer: A famous anecdote relates that Gershwin asked Ravel for orchestration lessons; after inquiring what Gershwin had earned from his music the previous year, Ravel remarked, "Then it is I who should be taking lessons from you." This may well be a tall tale; in other accounts the envious colleague was Stravinsky).[18] No American composer ever equaled Gershwin's European conquest. This was attributable partly to its timing at the height of the Jazz Age, when everything American was singularly in vogue in Europe. The compositional product of Gershwin's European visit was a tone poem, *An American in Paris*, premiered in December 1928. The slower middle section, which according to Gershwin's program note expresses the title character's homesickness, reverts to the idiom of the *Rhapsody in Blue*. The bustling outer sections, however, in which Gershwin worked the dissonant blare of taxi horns into his orchestration, shows him calling on ideas associated more generally with European Modernism.

All through the late 1920s Gershwin continued working on Broadway; after 1930 he worked in Hollywood, where he met and befriended the exiled Arnold Schoenberg. In 1933 he signed a contract to write what turned out to be his most ambitious score, an "American folk opera" called *Porgy and Bess* (Fig. 31-7). For this work Ira Gershwin wrote a libretto in African American dialect based on a novel-turned-play by DuBose Heyward about life among the poor black residents near

Figure 31-7 George Gershwin's *Porgy and Bess*. Production of the original Broadway musical, 10 October 1935 to 25 January 1936, at the Alvin Theatre.

Charleston, South Carolina. The opera premiered in Boston in preparation for its Broadway run beginning in October 1935.

Porgy and Bess as well as Gershwin's orchestral music have joined the standard operatic and concert repertory, and not only in America. They are, moreover, the only American works of symphonic jazz to have done so; all others, including Copland's, lapsed long ago into obscurity. A publicity sound bite that was widely used to introduce Gershwin to movie and radio audiences in the 1930s described him as "the man who made an honest woman out of jazz."[19] That could never be said of Copland, who was sometimes viewed as having degraded the higher forms of music by his use of jazz. With his elite European education and his sophisticated technique, Copland's assertively Modernistic use of jazz represented a downward social dynamic. It sparked in some audiences the fear of jazz as a socially regressive force. When the Russian composer Alexander Glazunov heard *Rhapsody in Blue* he described it as "part human and part animal."[20] The remark was taken as a compliment because it was assumed that Gershwin's mission was to humanize the animal instincts of jazz. Yet the very same racist view of American popular music worked against Copland. His music threatened to animalize humanistic art.

Controversies about the origins, status, and authenticity of jazz are seen particularly poignantly in the career of another major American figure to negotiate between jazz and classical traditions: Edward Kennedy "Duke" Ellington (1899–1974; Fig. 31-8), widely considered the greatest jazz composer of the period. He approached the intersection of styles coming not from a classical background as Copland did but, rather, from a jazz one written by an African American.

Born in a middle-class black neighborhood in Washington, D.C., by his mid-twenties Ellington was living in New York, where he exploded onto the Harlem musical scene, playing in ballrooms, dives, and everything in between. He formed his own ensemble of about a dozen musicians—it kept on expanding—and was soon touring the United States and Europe. Like most jazz musicians, he began by writing short pieces for his big band that would fill the three minutes or so of a 10-inch 78-rpm record (another minute on a 12-inch disc). Ellington, however, wanted to explore extended forms, less limited by the timings of records or by the standard formulas of jazz sets as performed live at nightclubs. In the early 1930s he announced a piece that would "portray the experiences of the coloured races in America in the syncopated idiom"[21]—the phrase "syncopated idiom" was typical of Ellington's shying away from using the word *jazz*, instead referring to "Negro" or "American" music.

Figure 31-8 Duke Ellington with his orchestra, 1929.

On 23 January 1943 Ellington presented the first in a series of annual concerts he would give at Carnegie Hall over the next decade. The event featured one of his major works, *Black, Brown and Beige*, a large-scale suite lasting some forty-eight minutes (the third movement largely written by his long-time arranger and collaborator Billy Strayhorn) that related the history of African Americans as reflected in their music. The piece was intended to be "an authentic record of my race *written by a member of it*"[22]; the telling italics are the composer's own. Ellington was one of the few prominent jazz composers who produced a large body of notated music. The distinctive timbres and moods he elicited from the brilliant and idiosyncratic musicians of his big band reached their height in the 1930s and '40s, although he continued tirelessly to compose, perform, and tour until his death.

Surrealism: Satie's *Parade*

The new prominence and influence of American popular culture, including jazz, Broadway musicals, and Hollywood films, grew rapidly in the 1920s and '30s. The enormous spread of music was made possible through new modes of dissemination, most importantly electronic recordings, commercial radio stations, and sound movies, or "talkies." These developments complicated the already uneasy relationship between traditional forms of elite culture and an increasingly pervasive mass popular culture. The great divide between "high" and "low" would be an ever-present theme for the rest of the century—and for the rest of this book. Some artists found popular idioms inspiring, for some they were contemptible, and for others, just plain threatening. But more and more, popular culture was omnipresent and had to be dealt with, one way or another.

On 18 May 1917, at the very height of the Great War, Diaghilev's Ballets Russes premiered a new work at the Théâtre du Châtelet in Paris called *Parade*. There was not much Russian about this ballet, even though the choreographer was the Russian Leonid Massine. The music was by Erik Satie, the scenario by the writer and filmmaker Jean Cocteau (1889–1963), and the sets and costumes were designed by Picasso (Fig. 31-9). A *parade*, in French, means not only what in English is called a parade, but also a sideshow performed outside a vaudeville theater or music hall to lure a crowd. The new ballet featured a conjurer, a "Chinese magician," and other carnival performers, all of whom went about their everyday business in Cocteau's undramatic scenario.

Anthology Vol 3-32
Full CD VI, 43–44
Concise CD III, 29–30

For the most part the Parisian audience, whose members presumably went gladly enough to circuses and music halls to see actual conjurors, dancers, and acrobats, hated *Parade*. They objected to the inappropriate low level of taste to which it seemed to pander, insulting ballet's proud aristocratic heritage. Some no doubt considered it an affront to present such artistic frivolity in a time of bloody conflict. The audience at the premiere of *Parade* reacted much like the first audience at *The Rite of Spring*. People hissed and booed this seemingly bland, innocuous offering just as they had Stravinsky's wildly dissonant, violent ballet four years earlier. Like Stravinsky's ballet, the new ballet had touched a nerve. Cocteau suggested, indignantly, that the audience had refused to consider that art could be beautiful "without an intrigue of mysticism, of love, or of annoyance."[23]

The great divide between "high" and "low" would be an ever-present theme for the rest of the century.

Parade was Cocteau's pointed answer to Diaghilev's famous challenge, "Étonne-moi" (Astonish me). He had succeeded in astonishing Diaghilev and the audience alike, precisely by avoiding any conventional attempt to astonish or impress. And so did Satie's primitive, plainly orchestrated, emotionally aloof score. There was enough drama in ordinary life, *Parade* implied. Let art celebrate ordinariness—"normalcy," to use American President Warren Harding's war-weary word—as the precious thing it is. That was the "realism" the ballet's subtitle

Figure 31-9 Erik Satie's *Parade*: Costume design by Pablo Picasso.

advertised. But that word, too, carried ironic baggage. For one thing, thanks to technology, contemporary reality now contained a great deal of unreality. In its various allusions to silent film stars, such as Mary Pickford and the great comedian Charlie Chaplin, *Parade* was perhaps the first work of "high art" music to pay tribute to the movies, the newest of the entertainment media and the only specifically twentieth-century one. Movies were gradually becoming a part of everyday life, and yet, at the same time, they were of all media the most instantaneously transporting and manipulative, which is to say the most unreal. They offered an alternative (or what we now call a "virtual") reality through which the imagination could truly overpower the senses. More evidence of the antirealism (magic realism, dream realism) of *Parade*'s "realism" were Picasso's costumes, especially the huge Modernistic constructions that were like cubist paintings come to life (see Fig. 31-9).

Satie's music for *Parade* includes a central "Rag-time du paquebot" (Ragtime of the Passenger Steamer) that parodies Irving Berlin's "That Mysterious Rag." Satie's orchestration includes such realistic sounds of modern life as a steamboat whistle, a siren, a pistol, and a typewriter. In their balletic context, however, these realistic sounds were anything but realistic. Abstracted from life and placed in a zany world of art, their everyday quality became uncanny.

At the same time the French poet Guillaume Apollinaire (1880–1918) was experimenting in his verse with something similar: colloquial language and homely imagery in startling juxtapositions. He tried this effect in a promotional piece he wrote for Diaghilev that appeared in the newspapers in advance of the *Parade* premiere and then in the program book for the ballet. The little article became famous for the way it conveyed the enchantment that could arise out of artistic transformations of the ordinary. Since this was wartime, Apollinaire made a nationalistic appeal: He saw in *Parade* a chance to shift the center of artistic gravity from Germany to France and claimed to find in Satie's music "a clarity and simplicity in which you can see the wonderfully lucid mind of France itself."[24] The phrase "clarity and simplicity" became a kind of mantra for many French and French-influenced musicians. These words obviously relate to the Neoclassicism that was emerging at this same time, and they can be traced further back to Stravinsky's "renunciation of 'sauce'." In Apollinaire's view, moreover, Picasso and Massine's collaboration, in which some of the constructed cubist costumes looked like walking stage sets, succeeded in "consummating for the first time a union between painting and the dance—between the plastic and the mimic—which heralds the arrival of a more complete art." Such a comment might be viewed as a subtle rebuke of Wagner, whose egotism led to a one-man *Gesamtkunstwerk* rather than genuine collaborations among artists working in different media.

Apollinaire also appreciated the strange form of realism in which, for example, a girl in *Parade*, "as she cranks an imaginary car, will express the magic of everyday life," thus giving the audience a chance "to appreciate the grace of modern movement—something they had never suspected." In his opinion Cocteau had misnamed his grand collaborative enterprise a "realistic ballet." To communicate the full effect of this "new alliance" of media, Apollinaire decided, a new word was needed: *sur-*

réalisme. The word soon shed its hyphen and entered the vocabulary of Modern art around the world: **Surrealism**. It was a brilliant find: The original hyphen made it clear that *surréalisme* had been coined on an analogy with the standard French word *surnaturalisme* (supernaturalism), the very thing the new art rejected. The core concept was a collage of ordinary things, the everyday, not the supernatural.

What lent the magic was not the things but the collage itself. **Collage**, which comes from *coller*, "to paste" or "to stick together," became another watchword. Around 1912 Picasso began pasting household items into his paintings (at first a swatch of a tablecloth, later bits of newspaper, postage stamps, and so forth; Fig. 31-10). The idea related as well to "Dada," a movement from around the same time that sought to extend the concept of art to its limits—or, rather, to find out what those limits were. For instance, mundane items (most famously, a urinal) were exhibited as if they were artworks. But in Picasso's collages and in what eventually became Surrealist art, there was no "as if." The assemblage was artful by design: In collage, art was not challenged by reality; rather, reality was challenged by art. The recognizable world was subverted by decontextualization—or recontextualization in incongruous juxtapositions—and became a dream world.

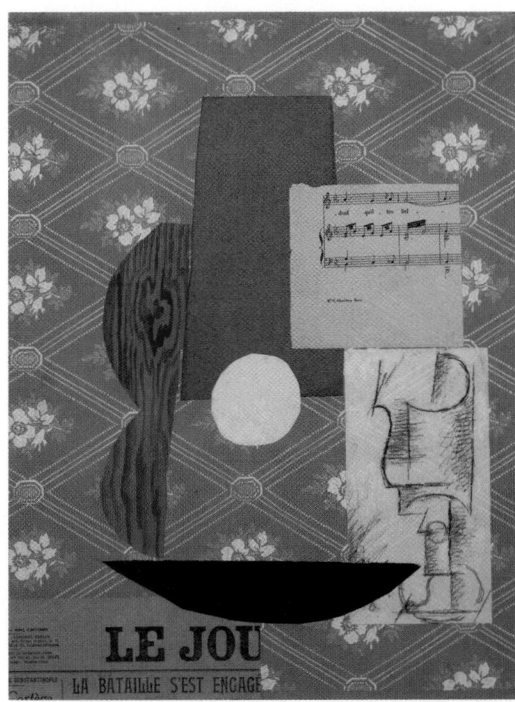

Figure 31-10 Pablo Picasso, *Guitar, Sheet Music, and Wine Glass*, 1912.

New Fashions: Les Six

A new crop of young composers, most of whom venerated Satie, were just as eager to cast off the trappings of French Impressionist mystery as they were to exorcise German Romanticism by celebrating the artistically transfigured everyday. The forever-enterprising Diaghilev enthusiastically commissioned and produced their work. Three one-act ballets that premiered in 1924 and 1925 typified the new genre: *Les biches* (The Does) by Francis Poulenc (1899–1963), Milhaud's *Le train bleu* (The Blue Train), and *Les matelots* (The Sailors) by Georges Auric (1899–1983). The plots of these ballets were purposely shallow. Cocteau said of Milhaud's offering that it "is more than a frivolous work. It is a monument to frivolity!"[25] The ballets deliberately avoided romantic love, portrayed superficial social activities associated with the Roaring Twenties, and made various references to everyday life and to popular culture.

Satie took the idea to its logical extreme when he conceived of *musique d'ameublement*, or "furniture music," described by Milhaud as "background music that would vary like the furniture of the rooms in which it was played," hence, "music that would not be listened to."[26] Satie fulfilled commissions from wealthy friends with little snippets bearing titles like *Tenture de cabinet préfectoral* (Wall hanging for the bureaucrat's office) and *Carrelage phonique* (Audible floor tiles). This was art deposed, with a vengeance, from its pedestal, as if to exact penance for the Romantic pretensions art had exhibited before the Great War and for whatever it might have contributed to the grandiose thinking that had provoked that bloodbath.

French artists and intellectuals like Satie, Cocteau, and the group of younger composers who gathered around the two absorbed American popular culture. The most prominent group was known as **Les Six** (The Six), by analogy with the Russian Five (Fig. 31-11). It included Poulenc, Milhaud, and Auric, all of whom readily incorporated

Figure 31-11 "Les Six" with Jean Cocteau. Left to right: Francis Poulenc, Germaine Tailleferre, Louis Durey, Cocteau, Darius Milhaud, and Arthur Honegger, 1931. Georges Auric, who did not attend, is shown in a drawing on the wall by Cocteau.

jazz, or, more properly, American dance-band music, as a component in their Modernist adventures. The other three members of the group, which was named by a critic on the basis of their chance appearance together on a concert program in 1920, were somewhat less drawn toward Americanism or to ironic Modernism. Arthur Honegger (1892–1955), a French-speaking Swiss who inclined, like his native country, to a blend of French and German styles, won fame on the strength of his oratorio *Le roi David* (King David, 1921), five symphonies, and the popular *Pacific 231* (1923), a "symphonic movement" depicting a locomotive. The career of Germaine Tailleferre (1892–1983) eventually failed because of unhappy marriages, financial pressures, and the traditional prejudice against women composers. She had considerable success writing film and television scores. The music of Louis Durey (1888–1979) is decidedly obscure, but his lucky charter membership in the celebrated group of Six has obliged every subsequent textbook to mention his name, as this one has now done.

The mightiest five of the Six actually collaborated on a project in 1921 when Cocteau finagled a commission from the Paris-based Ballets Suedois (Swedish Ballet) for a collectively composed ballet. Cocteau's scenario for *Les mariés de la Tour Eiffel* (The Wedding Party on the Eiffel Tower) portrays a perfectly ordinary middle-class wedding party, which has come to the lowest platform of the Eiffel Tower for a banquet and a group photo. The photographer's "Watch the birdie"—in French, "*Un oiseau va sortir*" ("A bird is about to come out [of the camera]")—is the signal for the surreal juxtapositions to begin. Among the creatures that emerge from the giant prop camera onstage are an ostrich, a lion, a dove, and a bathing beauty. Along comes a fat boy who massacres the wedding party with the unlikely ammunition of Ping-Pong balls and steals their banquet food, some of which he proceeds to feed to the Tower itself. Of course the wedding party recovers from being murdered and sells its group photo to an art dealer for a fantastic sum. The special combination of impossible (surreal) and ordinary components is cemented by a music similarly pervaded by everyday genres and "surreal" harmonies.

From Subject to Style: Surrealist "Classicism"

After Satie's death in 1925, his mantle of sophisticated naiveté fell on Poulenc and Milhaud. Apollinaire's famous definition of Surrealism came in the prologue to his play *Les mamelles de Tirésias* (The Breasts of Tirésias, 1917), the first explicitly designated *drame surréaliste*. In 1944, at the height of the next world war, Poulenc set Apollinaire's by-then-forgotten play to music as his first opera libretto. The interwar years had seen Poulenc turn unexpectedly to religious subject matter in several choral works that left his earlier fashionable Modernism behind. With his setting of *Les mamelles de Tirésias* he turned back once again, just as unexpectedly, to his earlier Surrealist roots. The new war had made Surrealism timely again.

Milhaud's version of Surrealism is associated with his theory of **polytonality**, which might be described as a technique for creating collages of keys. Inspired by some famous passages in the music of Stravinsky (the C/F♯ fanfares in *Petrushka*) and Richard Strauss (the necrophiliac kiss in *Salome* and the ending of *Also sprach Zarathustra*), Milhaud devised a systematic theory to which he gave a thorough exposition in an article, "Polytonalité et atonalité" (1923). Putting his theory in competition with Schoenberg's, Milhaud distinguished them by asserting that "between polytonality and atonality there are the same essential differences as between diatonicism and chromaticism."[27] Polytonality is diatonicism multiplied. Milhaud's polytonality made it possible to construct unheard-of harmonies by juxtaposing simple melodies and chords in novel combinations.

Milhaud's polytonality made it possible to construct unheard-of harmonies by juxtaposing simple melodies and chords in novel combinations.

Milhaud's first crop of polytonal experiments dates from around 1918, when the composer returned to France after living for some years in Brazil. These early works combined polytonality with exotic South American subject matter and include a mystical ballet, *L'homme et son désir* (The Man and his Desire, 1918) and the entertaining *Saudades do Brasil* (Memories of Brazil, 1920–21), a suite of dances for piano in which vivid recollections of urban popular music are given a Surrealistic twist. *Ipanema*, the fifth item in the suite, is a samba, an Afro-Brazilian dance, named after one of the districts of Rio de Janeiro. It could be said that the harmonies at the opening, in which E♭ minor and F major triads are reciprocally superimposed every two bars, are not polytonal in any functional sense, since neither harmony is established as a functional tonic. In the middle section, however, the superimposed chords, C and G♭, as in *Petrushka*, are each given dominants; the functional independence is eventually resolved ten measures later (Ex. 31-4). Some might argue that only the Surrealistic collage technique saves this simple samba dance from banality. But one could just as well say that only the banality of the dance tune saves the polytonal texture from unintelligibility.

Anthology Vol 3-33
Full CD VI, 45

Example 31-4 **Darius Milhaud, *Saudades do Brasil*, V (*Ipanema*), mm. 33–46**

Figure 31-12 Salvador Dali, *The Persistence of Memory,* 1931.

Milhaud's functional Surrealism depends as much on the ordinariness of the components as on the extravagance of their juxtaposition. The commonplace and the fantastic—or, if you prefer, the hackneyed and the preposterous—achieve, ideally, a state of synergy. Polytonality provides simple diatonic melodies and ordinary chords with a context that transforms their significance. This is akin to Surrealist painting, in which objects rendered with almost photographic precision are arbitrarily juxtaposed (Fig. 31-12). The commonplace, the unremarkable, the stuff of everyday life were all "rehabilitated," to use Cocteau's word, within an art that no longer sought the rare, the mystical, or the occult and no longer aspired to high eloquence, grandiosity, or Romantic aspirations to the sublime. Much French music of the postwar period was a desacralized art, an art brought down to earth, a thing made "to please"—that is, both to exist in and to adorn the lives of its users.

American Surrealism

For an example of American Surrealism we can look to another notable young American in Paris. Virgil Thomson (1896–1989), a Harvard-educated Missourian, came with the Harvard Glee Club during the summer of 1921 and decided to stay on for a year to study with Boulanger. After graduating from college and attending Juilliard, he returned to Paris in 1925 and lived there for much of the next fifteen years. On his return to the United States in 1940 he was hired as a music critic by the *New York Herald Tribune*; he became one of the composer-critics in the distinguished line going back to Berlioz and Schumann. Thomson devoted much of his time in Paris to translating French musical Surrealism, which as we have seen incorporated many faux-Americanisms, back into the authentic American vernacular.

The American expatriate community in Paris at the time included such novelists as F. Scott Fitzgerald (1896–1940) and Ernest Hemingway (1899–1961), whose major theme was postwar disillusionment. They are often said to represent the "lost generation," the epigraph to Hemingway's first published novel, *The Sun Also Rises* (1926). The name was allegedly invented by Gertrude Stein (1874–1946; Fig. 31-13), an American writer who lived in Paris from 1903 until her death and who maintained a celebrated salon at her home that emerged as the informal headquarters for American artists and intellectuals. Beginning in 1927, Thomson and Stein collaborated on two operas. The first one, *Four Saints in Three Acts*, premiered in 1934. It has to be regarded as the principal text of musical Surrealism in terms of its impact on contemporary audiences and their consciousness of Modern art. Collage remained the watchword: within the text, within the music, and in the relationship of text and music. Stein was interested in aspects of what is sometimes called "stream of consciousness." This style is governed by free association, which violates norms of semantics, syntax, and grammar while relying on phonic and rhythmic play like puns and jingles to achieve its effect.

Figure 31-13 Pablo Picasso, *Gertrude Stein*, 1905–06.

Four Saints in Three Acts actually had four acts, not three, and many more saints than four. American composer John Cage, whom we will meet in Chapter 34 as a major force in music after the Second World War, wrote a critical study of Thomson's music in which he pointed out that the best one could do by way of analyzing the score of *Four Saints in Three Acts* was to cite statistics: "There are 111 tonic-dominants, 178 scale passages, 632 sequences, 38 references to nursery tunes, and one to 'My Country, 'Tis of Thee.'"[28] The music refers openly—and ecstatically—to the idiom of American Protestant (Southern Baptist) hymns, the commonplace musical vernacular of the Kansas City–born composer's own youthful environment. This finally ensures that the idiom of the opera will strike listeners—American listeners, anyway—as genuinely *sur-realistic*. And it resonates poignantly with Thomson's typically "lost generation" recollection that "I wrote in Paris music that was always, in one way or another, about Kansas City."[29] The irony was that he had to go abroad to discover his American roots. He was not alone.

Thomson and Stein later collaborated on a second opera, *The Mother of Us All* (1947), about the American suffragette Susan B. Anthony. For a more manageable taste of their partnership than these two operas we can look at a brief song from 1926 on the subject of Susie Asado, a flamenco dancer. Stein's text begins as follows:

Anthology Vol 3-34
Full CD VI, 46

Sweet sweet sweet sweet sweet tea.
Susie Asado.
Sweet sweet sweet sweet sweet tea.
Susie Asado.
Susie Asado which is a told tray sure. A lean on the shoe this means slips slips hers.
When the ancient light grey is clean it is yellow, it is a silver seller.
This is a please this is a please there are the saids to jelly. These are the wets these say the sets to leave a crown to Incy.

Writing like this, with its alliterations and sonic associations, its controlling rhythms, its stutters, and puns (e.g., *sweet tea* = *sweetie*), is clearly borrowing a great deal from music. Thomson meticulously modeled the vocal part on the rhythms and cadences of conversational English. The minimalist approach is little more than a medium for the words, almost a kind of incantation (Ex. 31-5).

Example 31-5 Virgil Thomson, *Susie Asado*, opening

Thomson was just as interested as Stein in the interplay of sound and meaning. He later wrote "that if a text is set correctly for the sound of it, the meaning will take care of itself." Describing Stein's text in particular, he continued: "With meanings already abstracted, or absent, or so multiplied that choice among them was impossible, there was no temptation toward tonal illustration, say of birdie babbling by the brook. You could make a setting for sound and syntax only, then add, if needed, an accompaniment equally functional."[30] The accompaniment in *Susie Asado* is also a collage, a bag of basic musical elements—chords, arpeggios, and scales—and, at times, a collage of keys in the Surrealist polytonal mode most associated with Milhaud. Thomson generally avoids "tonal illustration," trying to have the music convey the meaning of the text (no flamenco rhythms!), and maintains a freedom of syntax just as daring as Stein's.

The ultimate effect of Thomson's Surrealism was that of finding oneself, the reassurance any member of a lost generation craves. And that may be the ultimate message that Surrealist collage offered the wounded psyches of postwar Europeans and Americans. In a society where so much of life had lost its meaning after a senseless war, meaning took on new meaning. In the face of technology and reason run amok, a consolation art could offer was that of irrational acceptance and faith. Thomson spelled it out when he exhorted listeners, in a note accompanying the first recording of excerpts from *Four Saints in Three Acts*, not "to construe the words of this opera literally or seek in it any abstruse symbolism." Instead, he wrote, "If by means of the poet's liberties with logic and the composer's constant use of the simplest elements in our musical vernacular, something is here evoked of the child-like gaiety and mystical strength of lives devoted in common to a nonmaterialistic end, the authors will consider their message to have been communicated."[31]

Music in the Weimar Republic

And what of defeated Germany after the Great War, trying as it was to rebuild amidst political and economic ruin? Schoenberg's response, as we have seen, was to invent a new method, composing with twelve-tone rows, that he hoped would ensure the continued greatness of the German musical tradition. Many Germans found the terms of the peace treaties following the war humiliating, for their country was being required to pay large amounts in reparations. Cunning politicians capitalized on such popular resentment, which eventually led to the rise of Adolf Hitler and National Socialism.

Yet, especially at first, some wanted to move beyond the past and sought to create a new, liberal German democracy in what came to be known as the Weimar Republic, the name given to the postwar regime because its constitution was drafted in Weimar in 1919. Many native composers were also skeptical about German transcendence and promises of immortality, permanence, and lasting value. This suspicion helped create a cult of the perishable, the short-lived, and the transient akin to what had been happening in France. Obsolescence and the rejection of "masterpiece culture" was the price of true contemporaneity in art. One movement to emerge in the early 1920s was called ***neue Sachlichkeit*** (New Objectivity), a term meant to convey concreteness, alertness, sobriety, hard reality, matter-of-factness—all opposed to the Romantic make-believe.

Just as elsewhere in Europe and America, there was great German interest in the popular, contemporarily relevant, and the broadly communicative. One result was a new kind of topical theater called ***Zeitoper***, a term that might be approximately translated as "opera of the times" or even "now-opera." A *Zeitoper* was an opera about things right now rather than enduring things. It was not necessarily about current events; indeed, some of the most conspicuous were cast as allegories. The composer who wrote a *Zeitoper* was acting as a citizen-commentator, not a priest of art, and the work was valued for its contemporary relevance, not its timeless merit. We can see this in *Jonny spielt auf* (Johnny Strikes Up, 1927), which proved to be the hit of the decade and was widely performed across Europe and beyond. *Jonny* was the work of the young composer Ernst Krenek (1900–91), a Czech-born citizen of Austria. The opera made him a celebrity at age twenty-six and secured his financial independence until the Nazi takeover of Vienna forced him to move to the United States. *Zeitoper* deserved its name. For a few years it had a prominence in the cultural life of its time matched only by the French and Italian grand operas of the nineteenth century and never equaled later; opera soon lost its status as mass entertainment.

Just as elsewhere in Europe and America, there was great German interest in the popular, contemporarily relevant, and the broadly communicative.

It makes sense that *Zeitoper* and *neue Sachlichkeit*, together with the related idea of ***Gebrauchsmusik*** ("music for use" rather than for contemplation), should have arisen after Germany's defeat. The chief standard bearer for anti-Romantic notions of the time was Paul Hindemith (1895–1963), a fabulously gifted all-round musician who was an internationally acclaimed viola soloist as well as Germany's leading young composer in the 1920s and '30s. He had begun his career as an Expressionist with a trio of short, scandalous operas, widely attacked and sometimes banned—*Mörder, Hoffnung der Frauen* (Murder, Hope of Women, 1919), which glorified rape; *Das Nusch-Nuschi* (1921), an opera about castration that showed signs of postwar irreverence by holding up to ridicule one of the most sublime moments in Wagner's *Tristan und Isolde*; and *Sancta Susanna* (Saint Susanna, 1922), about sexual hysteria in a convent. He next wrote a full-scale opera, *Cardillac* (1926) and then *Hin und Zurück* (There and Back, 1927), a very short opera that first unfolds as a tragedy and in the middle turns the plot and music in reverse so as to offer a happy ending.

At the end of the decade came Hindemith's comic *Neues vom Tage* (1929). The title, literally "News of the Day," is what newsboys shouted on German city streets; the English equivalent would be "Read all about it!" or "Extra! Extra!" Its subject involves such ideas as contemporary celebrity, sensation-mongering, publicity, and instant comment—ideas that have only grown more timely as the intrusive news media have become ever-present. A divorcing couple, Eduard and Laura, attract the attention of the press, which follows them everywhere, even into the bathroom. (Act II begins with the presumably naked Laura in an onstage bathtub, singing a satiric aria about the modern miracle of indoor plumbing.) They hire publicity managers and restage their quarrel nightly for the benefit of a gawking public. In the process they fall in love again, but the public insists on its own satisfaction and they must divorce as promised.

Anthology Vol 3-35
Full CD VI, 47

Hindemith's instrumental music also displayed timeliness and popular elements. The last movement of his Kammermusik Nr. 1 (Chamber Music No. 1, actually a sort of symphony for chamber orchestra) was titled "Finale: 1921" and quoted a foxtrot popularized that year by a German dance band. The next year's model, *Suite "1922"* for piano, is in five movements: "Marsch," "Shimmy," "Nachtstück," "Boston," and "Ragtime." Urbane Modernity of another sort was embodied in the music Hindemith wrote for himself to perform, epitomized in a further product of 1922, the Sonata for Solo Viola, Op. 25, No. 1. This was *Spielmusik* (player's music), in which the activity of performing it was its content. "I composed the first and fifth movements in a buffet car between Frankfurt and Cologne and then went straight on to the platform and played the sonata," the prolific Hindemith boasted in a footnote to his enormous catalogue of works.[32] The 1920s marked the composer's ironic and Modernist period. He later disowned the more scandalous of his earlier operas and revised the already serious *Cardillac* in the early 1950s. By the time Hindemith next makes an appearance in this book, it will be as an altogether tamer, if no less brilliant, composer whose life, like those of so many artists, was shaped by the political forces of war and exile.

Alban Berg's *Wozzeck*

The popular and timely operas of the period by Krenek, Hindemith, and most others eventually lost their appeal and generally disappeared from the international repertory. The most enduring German-language opera from the 1920s was *Wozzeck*, by Alban Berg. It combined aspects of Romanticism and of high Expressionism with postwar disillusionment, irony, political critique, archaic musical forms, and references to popular culture. Conceived in 1914 and composed between 1919 and 1922, after Berg had spent several miserable years in military service, *Wozzeck* became enormously influential; it remains a staple of the operatic repertory to this day. After the Berlin premiere in December 1925, the opera became an international hit, despite its atonal harmonic idiom and its considerable difficulty for performers. Many productions were mounted both in Germany and abroad, including an early production in Leningrad that Berg attended and that affected a generation of young Russian composers (Fig. 31-14). This all came to a halt in 1933, when performances were forbidden by the Nazi regime.

Anthology Vol 3-36
Full CD VI, 48–52
Concise CD III, 31–32

Any attempt to explain the unexpected success of this challenging composition must begin with the story. Berg based the opera on *Woyzeck*, a play by Georg Büchner (1813–37), a short-lived German writer who had been rediscovered by the Expressionists. Inspired by a notorious crime committed in 1821, the brutal play depicted the mental and moral degeneration of the title character, a miserable, oppressed soldier, who, crazed by jealousy and despair, murders his common-law wife, Marie, with whom he has had a son. One sees the passive and dull-witted soldier abused by everyone with whom he comes in contact—by his captain, who treats him as a personal servant; by a doctor who employs him as a guinea pig for mad-scientist experiments; by a conceited drum major who seduces Marie and for good measure beats him up; and by Marie herself, who taunts him over his humiliation—until he is driven to tragic action.

Unfinished when Büchner died at age twenty-three, *Woyzeck* was speculatively pieced together by an editor who misspelled the title as *Wozzeck* due to the author's notoriously difficult handwriting. The play was first published in 1879 and premiered in Munich in 1913; Berg saw it in Vienna the next year. For the opera, he excerpted fifteen of its some two dozen brief scenes and set them practically verbatim, the way Debussy had earlier set Maeterlinck's *Pelléas et Mélisande*. Over the course of the three-act, ninety-minute opera, these fifteen scenes often have a cinematic quality in their variety and cross-cutting of styles. Berg indicated in the score exactly when the curtain should fall after each scene and wrote orchestral interludes to be played while the sets were changed. The pacing of the opera is therefore quite rapid, and part of its appeal is that the plot builds relentlessly to its shattering climax. Berg's opera traded brazenly in the kind of shocking violence made popular by the operas of the Italian verismo school.

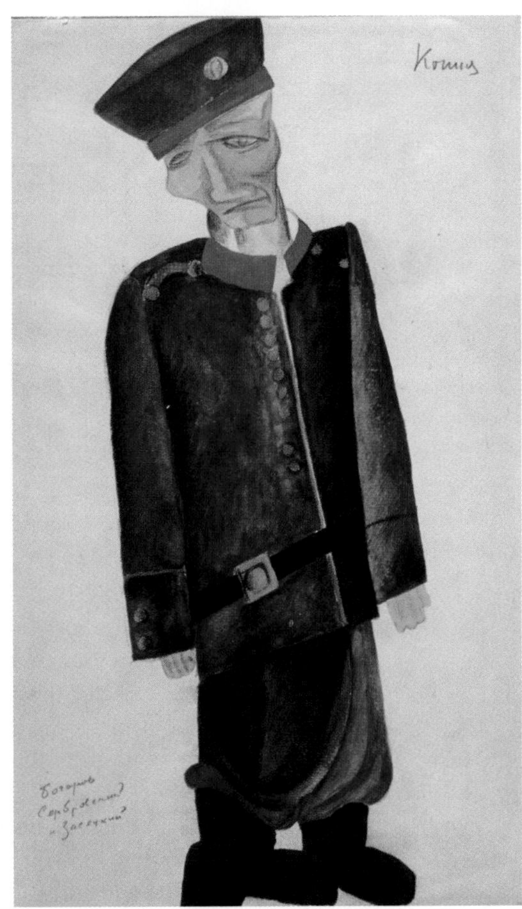

Figure 31-14 Costume design by Joseph Lewin for the title character in *Wozzeck* for the Leningrad performance of 1927.

Unlike the deadpan reportage of Büchner's original play, Berg's musical treatment was highly manipulative, operatic in the full sense of the word, replete with the interventions of the orchestral interludes that commented on the action by the use of prominent leitmotifs. Berg saw himself as exposing the social problem of poverty, specifically society's ill treatment of *wir arme Leut*, "we poor folk," as Wozzeck puts it in the first scene. This phrase reverberates thereafter as the opera's chief musical leitmotif (Ex. 31-6). Berg acted as his title character's defense attorney, as he frankly put it in an essay on the opera, justifying Wozzeck's crime by "an appeal to humanity through its representatives, the audience."[33] The opera's classic status testifies to the composer's success. What was exceedingly unusual was the way in which Berg went about making the case, for the relationship between the humanizing music and the horrific action is not at all direct. It is mediated through a huge and potentially distracting, or at least distancing, barrage of composerly virtuosity.

Example 31-6 Alban Berg, *Wozzeck*, Act I, Scene 1, "Air" ("Wir arme Leut")

We poor folk! Do you see, Captain, money, money! Somebody who has no money!

Some of that virtuosity was of a familiar kind: brilliantly colored orchestration, incorporation of many kinds of ambient music (folk songs, marches, waltzes, all reflected through an atonal distorting mirror), intricate motivic work and leitmotivic transformations. Berg had learned some of this from a highly successful opera composer of the time, Franz Schreker, for whose opera *Der ferne Klang* (The Distant Sound, 1912) he had helped prepare the piano-vocal score released by Universal Edition, the leading Viennese publisher of modern music.

In *Wozzeck* Berg invokes a whole array of musical forms and genres associated with instrumental music and seemingly alien or irrelevant to opera. Some of these are just as obsolete as the ones Stravinsky was reviving in his Neoclassical scores around this time. The first scene of the opera, for example, in which Wozzeck is shown shaving the abusive Captain, is cast in the form of a grotesque orchestral suite with sections marked "Präludium," "Pavane," "Cadenza," "Gigue," "Gavotte," "Air," and "Reprise" (which presents the Präludium in reverse). As commentators have repeatedly pointed out, so far as the listener in the opera house is concerned this information is altogether arcane and immaterial. One could go further and show that the designations often do not even accurately fit the tradition of Baroque dances and forms they supposedly represent. If these references are in-jokes for musicians to admire, then they seem quite at odds with the cathartic social tragedy that brought *Wozzeck* success in the opera house. But, as we saw earlier with Berg's *Lyric Suite,* hidden devices were central to his compositional method and often carried deep personal meaning.

The hidden devices continue in various ways throughout the opera. Each act has an elaborate compositional scheme. The five scenes of Act I present the principal characters and are themselves character studies. The second act is cast as a five-movement symphony:

Scene 1: "Sonata," in which Marie, preening herself after her night with the Drum Major, nevertheless accepts money from Wozzeck to care for their child, and experiences a fleeting moment of bad conscience;
Scene 2: "Fantasia and fugue," in which the Captain and the Doctor, taunting Wozzeck, plant the first inkling in his mind that Marie has been unfaithful;
Scene 3: "Largo," in which Wozzeck confronts Marie, who is cold and defiant;
Scene 4: "Scherzo"—the "grand opera" scene at a tavern where Wozzeck sees Marie dancing in the arms of the Drum Major;
Scene 5: "Introduction and Rondo," in which the Drum Major beats up Wozzeck later that night in the soldiers' barracks.

Having experienced this series of humiliations, the formerly passive Wozzeck is now ready for the retaliatory action that is enacted in Act III, which is structured through a series of ingenious technical studies. Each scene of this last act is designated an "Invention," concerned with some elemental musical particle, namely, a theme, a note, a rhythm, a chord, a key, and eighth-note motion. The first scene, in which Marie reads from the Bible to her son and repents of her sins, is called an "Invention on a Theme" and takes the form of a theme, six brief variations, and a concluding "fugue." Marie recites passages from the Bible about Mary Magdalene using the *Sprechstimme* technique and reverts to singing voice for her own anguished commentary. The last two variations, in which Marie reads with mounting emotion, move clearly into the key of F minor. Here and elsewhere in the opera, tonal harmonies underscore moments of particular emotional warmth.

For Scene 2 the location shifts to the side of a lake, where Wozzeck murders Marie. This "Invention on a Note" is haunted from beginning to end by the pitch B. At the climactic moment, when the moon rises blood-red and Wozzeck comes after Marie with a knife, B is simultaneously sustained by the strings as a pedal in six octaves, pervading the whole range of the orchestra; at the same time B is beaten as a rhythmic tattoo by the kettledrum, which crescendos to the moment of the lethal deed and decrescendos to the end of the scene. The same rhythmic tattoo forms the basis of the third scene, "Invention on a Rhythm," which takes place in a tavern, where people spot blood on Wozzeck's hand. Scene 4 is an "Invention on a Six-Note Chord," in which Wozzeck rushes back to the scene of the crime to retrieve the incriminating knife. He finds the murder weapon and throws it into the lake but, fearing it is too near the shore, wades out to retrieve it and drowns. The Doctor and the Captain happen by, hear ominous sounds arising from the lake, and flee.

There follows the great expressive climax in *Wozzeck*, the interlude between the final two scenes, which Berg called an "Invention on a Key" and which provides a true catharsis after Wozzeck's tragic death—or, rather, a catharsis to mark Wozzeck's death as tragic. As such it is notably at odds with Büchner's tight-lipped little play. A Mahlerian orchestral mood combines with a Wagnerian review of the opera's principal leitmotifs and reaches a searing turning point when a deafening twelve-note aggregate sonority suddenly gives way to an obsessively reiterated V–I bass progression in D minor. The interlude is, by several orders of magnitude, the biggest of the tonal moments that impinge on the atonal world of this opera, and it was based on a very early unpublished piano work that Berg had composed as a teenager. The final scene, designated "Invention on an Eighth-Note Motion," depicts Wozzeck and Marie's little son on his hobbyhorse and a group of children who sing a sort of atonal version of "Ring around the Rosie" in a $\frac{12}{8}$ meter with unrelenting eighth-note motion. The uncomprehending boy is cruelly taunted by the others over his mother's death.

The obsessive focus on one musical element in each scene of Act III reflects the psychological obsessions that drive the crazed Wozzeck. By turns we are bombarded with relentlessly repeated pitches, rhythms, and chords as the opera runs its bloody course. But the moment we notice the technical virtuosity of Berg's compositional method, we are put at some distance from the characters and situations being portrayed. Despite the vividly realistic and Expressionistic resources that Berg inherited from his immediate predecessors, at the same time there is, in ironic contradiction, a terrific self-consciousness, a tendency that marked much postwar Modernism.

Perhaps the reason audiences respond to *Wozzeck* "despite" its atonal language turns out to be the same as the reason atonal music later became popular in film soundtracks as a representational device. Audiences understand it in both contexts as a metaphor for physical or psychological abnormality; it symbolizes stress, aberration, horror. It consummately conveys the terror in Wozzeck; but to summon pity the composer ultimately returns to tonality, employing his "Invention on a Key." In his public success with the atonal idiom, still unequaled and probably never to be surpassed, Berg exposed its limitations. What *Wozzeck* seemed to be suggesting, unwelcome as the news might be even to Berg himself (to say nothing of Schoenberg), was that the "emancipation of dissonance" was meaningful mainly to highly trained musicians, not to average listeners, for whom dissonance and consonance remained, and would always remain, a meaningful antithesis.

Music for Political Action

Despite its ironic aspects, *Wozzeck* showed a serious level of political engagement that some composers believed was necessary after the war. Such composers felt that the newly detached and ironic brand of art, well suited as it was to social comment, had to justify its existence by virtue of a worthy social purpose, not just the satiric fun offered by Hindemith and Krenek, not to mention the French mirth makers. Although Krenek did not enjoy another popular success after *Jonny spielt auf*, the other leading composer of "now operas," Kurt Weill (1900–50; Fig. 31-15) was often compared to Berg. Weill, the son of a well-known synagogue cantor in Germany, was a composing prodigy and received musical training of the most elite caliber. At eighteen he enrolled in Engelbert Humperdinck's composition class at the Berlin Conservatory; two years later he began studying with Ferruccio Busoni. His early works included a symphony (1921), two string quartets (1919, 1923), a violin concerto (1924), and *Sinfonia Sacra* (1922), which sports three neo-Baroque movements. The musical style that Weill employed, however, was very far from that of the early Neoclassicists, resembling instead the pantonal idiom of Schoenberg's Expressionist phase.

Figure 31-15 Kurt Weill with his wife Lotte Lenya in 1942.

The success of Weill's creative political engagement was partly due to his chief collaborator in adapting opera to contemporary demands: Bertolt Brecht (1898–1956). Brecht was already known for theatrical reforms that went a long way toward destroying the conventional illusions of theater, which strove to convince spectators that the scripted action they were witnessing was real. Not that anybody was ever really convinced, of course; but audiences were eager to play along with conventions, whether of Romanticism or of realism, for the sake of the emotional payoff they received in return for their "willing suspension of disbelief."

One of the main conventions on which theatrical illusions of reality depended was the imaginary "fourth wall" that separated the audience from the actors, who were never allowed to see through it. All illusion of reality could be destroyed the moment the players showed any awareness of the audience's presence, let alone addressed it directly, by breaking through that invisible fourth wall between stage and auditorium. There were, of course, various precedents, the best known perhaps being in Shakespeare plays that conclude with an epilogue in which a character entreats the audience for applause; we saw something comparable in how Verdi ended *Falstaff*. The wall had likewise occasionally been broken in farce and satire, which made the least pretense to realism.

Brecht called his theatrical style "epic theater." In place of an illusion of real action, his plays incorporated narrative, montage (scenes played in counterpoint from various separately lighted areas of the stage), and direct address to the audience. Sets and lighting were deliberately nonrealistic, and he even allowed the staging process—the work of stagehands, the moving of props, the backstage assembly areas—to be seen by the audience. Breaking the fourth wall in these ways made the artificiality of the drama evident to the spectators and enabled them to retain an awareness of their actual situation rather than being beguiled by the dramatic illusion. Indeed, recognition of how artificial the theater was resulted in an effect Brecht called *Verfremdung*. The word is usually translated as "alienation" or "**defamiliarization**," but all it really means is that theater makes its action and workings as "strange" or "foreign" (*fremd*) as possible. Such strangeness gives audiences a distanced perspective that enables them to keep the play and its message distinct.

It would be no distortion of Brecht's purpose and no insult to his integrity to say that his epic theater was an instrument of political propaganda. That was its justification. According to Weill, the role of music was similar. He spoke of "service to the general public," which for both Brecht and Weill meant political education as a stimulus to revolutionary political action. To achieve this purpose, music had to change not only its style, renouncing the paralyzing emotional hypnosis that Wagner had practiced so well, but also its function within the drama. Weill declared that "music cannot further the action of a play or create its background," but instead "achieves its proper value when it interrupts the action at the right moments," in order to adopt an attitude toward the action and influence the spectator's response to it.[34] The musical interruptions in a play serve as a jolt, to puncture whatever illusion of reality remains and to reengage the full, wide-awake attention of the audience. To be memorable, music must be simple and direct. In practice, this meant imitating the form, and to some extent the style, of popular music.

Anthology Vol 3-37
Full CD VI, 53–54
Concise CD III, 33

The most famous and influential creation of the Brecht/Weill team was a play in dialogue with musical numbers called *Die Dreigroschenoper* (The Threepenny Opera, 1928). Like *Jonny spielt auf*, it was a legendary box-office sensation of the Weimar era, having over 300 performances in a single Berlin theater during the first year of its run. By 1933, the publisher had licensed a total of 133 productions worldwide. A Singspiel in the eighteenth-century sense, this work had a specific model, *The Beggar's Opera* (1728), familiar to us from Chapter 11, of which Brecht had a working translation done by Elisabeth Hauptmann. The music for that satirical "ballad opera" about London lowlife consisted of harmonized popular tunes. Weill quoted one of them for effect, but otherwise he wrote an original score, which he and Brecht cleverly subtitled *Songspiel.*

In the original production (Fig. 31-16), an antioperatic thrust was maintained by casting cabaret singers and dramatic actors who could more or less carry a tune in the singing roles, rather than opera singers. (One of the actresses was Weill's wife, Lotte Lenya, who supervised a famous New York revival in English translation, which ran on Broadway for 2,611 performances in the mid-1950s.) The original pit orchestra consisted of seven cabaret musicians playing a total of twenty-three instruments. The interruption effect of the music was enhanced by radically changing the lighting for each song, displaying its title on a screen, and keeping the instrumentalists visible to the audience at all times.

Die Dreigroschenoper makes a fascinating comparison with *Wozzeck*, since both operas had as their stated aim the exposure of a social problem, namely, society's hypocritically criminalizing mistreatment of the poor. *Die Dreigroschenoper* maintains a tone of unmitigated anger and sarcasm, challenging the audience's presumption of moral superiority and indicting its complacency. Yet Weill's music rejects the sort of advanced musical techniques Berg embraced. Where Wozzeck, though he ends a criminal, is presented as a good man more sinned against than sinning, the main character of *Die Dreigroschenoper*, Macheath (alias Mac the Knife), is the head of a gang of street robbers, in other words, a professional felon. One of Brecht's ways of breaking the fourth wall is through the use of captions. The first one reads: "A fair in Soho. The beggars are begging, the thieves thieving, the whores whoring. A ballad singer sings the 'Ballad of Mac the Knife'." This late addition to the score, which is the most famous number in the work, soon became a standard performed by many celebrated jazz musicians.

Figure 31-16 Finale from the premiere performance of Kurt Weill's *The Threepenny Opera* at Berlin on 31 August 1928. L to r: Erich Ponto, Roma Bahn, Harold Paulsen (as Mackie Messer on the gallows), and Kurt Gerron.

Macheath's marriage to Polly Peachum is condemned by her father, the ringleader of London's beggars. Peachum arranges to have him arrested and hanged, but the criminal is ultimately saved by a pardon from the King, thus providing a parody of a happy ending. In the eighteenth-century *Beggar's Opera*, Macheath's frank villainy is used as a witty foil to expose the hypocritical villainy of polite society. No better way is proposed, and the satire is of the mildest, friendliest sort. In Brecht's twentieth-century adaptation, Macheath's villainy is decried as the inevitable result of social injustice. The message of the play, which Weill's music intervenes to underscore, is that villainy must be eradicated humanely, not by zealous, self-righteous punishment but by attacking its root cause, poverty.

The Act II finale, which carries the title "Ballade über die Frage: 'Wovon lebt der Mensch?'" ("Ballad about the question 'What keeps a man alive?'") makes the comparison with *Wozzeck* particularly pointed since it deals explicitly with the plight of "poor people." It takes place just after Macheath has escaped from prison. He had been betrayed by a group of whores whom he has continued to patronize although married (to two women at once, it turns out) and who have been bribed to betray him by Peachum, not for any reason of justice but merely so that his daughter can come back home and go on working for her father without pay. The ballad, sung by Macheath together with one of the whores who has turned him in, describes the dog-eat-dog reality that poor people must confront, a world in which the idle moralizing of the well-fed has no place. It is sung in front of the curtain, directly to the audience. Not only does this breach the fourth wall, but it also amounts to a stepping out of character, as Brecht often prescribed: "The actor must not only sing," he wrote, "but show a man singing."[35] This number has no other purpose than to defy the audience's right to pass a moral judgment on the action it has observed: "For even honest folk [yes, you!] will act like sinners/ Unless they've had their customary dinners!"

Can "serious" art ever be an effective medium for political propaganda or a spur to social action?

The style of *Die Dreigroschenoper* was the result of a deliberate, radical, and controversial renunciation of operatic conventions. Yet can an art dedicated to shocking the middle-class public out of its complacency be said to have succeeded when that very public consumes it with delight? Can "serious" art ever be an effective medium for political propaganda or a spur to social action? Brecht and Weill seem to have been surprised by their success and to have harbored some qualms about it. Among the simpler products of their collaboration were what Brecht called *Lehrstücke* (didactic pieces or lessons) and *Schulopern* (school operas). These pieces were meant for amateur performance that would discipline not just the participants' performance skills but also their political attitudes. They also furnished the eventual spectators with moral and political instruction. Brecht also worked on similar projects with the communist composer Hanns Eisler (1898–1962), who had been a star pupil of Schoenberg's before he turned to more politically engaged scores.

From Vienna to Hollywood: The Death of Opera?

Operas such as *Wozzeck*, *Jonny spielt auf*, and *Die Dreigroschenoper* provoked a good amount of debate in the 1920s and early 1930s, which gives some indication of how seriously artworks were taken in Weimar Germany. Theater pieces by Krenek, Hindemith, Berg, and Weill were successful and popular in a way that almost no opera has been since that time. New pieces and progressive politics were most notably merged in the experimental productions presented by the legendary Kroll Opera in Berlin. The operatic economy in Germany during the time was the last truly thriving—that is, consumption-driven—economy in the history of opera. Composers wrote for a ready market and were in great demand. Premieres were as well attended as revivals and commanded the lively interest of both the press and the public. The place that opera occupied in those days was like that of movies in our time. The flowering of popular, timely, and engaged German operas ended, however, after the Nazis came to power.

Opera in essence ceased as a major living musical genre. There will be operas to discuss in later chapters (and even a couple of important composers who specialized in the genre), but they will be relatively few and far between; almost none of them enjoyed performance statistics to match the ones just discussed. What happened? First of all, most obviously, the Great Depression, the economic slump that began with the New York stock market crash in October 1929, quickly encompassed the globe, causing many banks to close and, in their wake, many opera houses and theaters as well. But whereas the spoken theater eventually surpassed its previous economic levels, the production of new operas effectively ended in Germany and elsewhere. What killed it? In some places commercial musicals for one, but much more potently the "talkies," which were really often "singies." Movies preempted the operatic audience and became the operas of the mid- to late twentieth century. Opera houses were thus left with a closed-off museum repertoire just like that of the concert hall, to which successful new additions have been exceedingly few, and with a more specialized audience rather than a general public hungry for entertainment.

With the advent of sound movies, opera found its preeminence as a union of the arts compromised and its standing as the grandest of all spectacles usurped. The kinds of subjects that had been opera's chief preserve—myth and epic, historical costume drama, romance, fast-paced farce—were all ideally suited for the new medium of film. Movie actors and actresses were literally, not just metaphorically, larger than life. Cinematic transport to distant times was instantaneous. Evocative atmosphere, exotic or realistic, could be even more potently conjured up on the silver screen than on the best-equipped operatic stage. Given music's unique powers to induce moods and create emotional catharsis, a movie soundtrack could be remarkably like an opera, its composers having learned valuable lessons from the older genre, particularly from Wagner's use of leitmotifs and scoring. The creative energy that had been invested in the opera business shifted in the twentieth century to the movie industry, as did considerable financial resources. Blockbuster emotional experiences that operas had once delivered were now far more dependably provided by the movies.

The transmutation of opera into film is epitomized by the career of the Viennese composer Erich Wolfgang Korngold (1897–1957), a composing prodigy on the order of Mozart and Mendelssohn. Korngold's father, Julius, Vienna's preeminent music critic after Eduard Hanslick's death, had Leopold Mozartean ambitions for his son, already foretold by his given middle name. In 1906, at age nine, Erich played his cantata *Gold* for an amazed Mahler, who suggested he study with Alexander Zemlinsky, Schoenberg's former teacher. At the age of eleven Korngold wrote a ballet that was performed to wide acclaim at the Vienna Court Opera.

Korngold became one of the most active and successful participants in the explosive operatic culture of Weimar Germany. His third opera, *Die tote Stadt* (The Dead City, 1920), spread his fame with productions far and wide (Fig. 31-17). It is a Symbolist drama, with an action that takes place in a space ambiguously located between dream and reality. The music is sophisticated both in leitmotivic structure and in sonority, the young Korngold being, among other things, a virtuoso orchestrator in command of the full array of Wagnerian and Straussian resources. In his operas, particularly the lavish *Das Wunder der Heliane* (Heliane's Miracle, 1927), he applied these hypnotic techniques to subject matter that combined bombastic religiosity and coy eroticism to produce something that might be christened "sacroporn." Dramas akin to this became very familiar to movie audiences through Hollywood's many mythical and biblical epics, such as *Quo Vadis* (1951), *The Ten Commandments* (1956), and *Ben-Hur* (1959).

Despite Korngold's enormous popularity his operatic career was abruptly cut short in 1938, when Austria was annexed by the Nazi-controlled Third Reich.

Actually, he was already in America when the *Anschluss* (annexation) took place, having earlier accepted a contract as a staff composer at the Warner Brothers studio. Between 1935 and 1946 he furnished original scores for nineteen films and won two Academy Awards. Although he completed *Die Kathrin* (1939), an opera already in progress when he went to America, Korngold never wrote another one. The Viennese opera style that he cultivated evolved into the Hollywood style of the 1930s and '40s, established by him and by other German and Central European immigrants like Max Steiner (1888–1971), Ernst Toch (1887–1964), and Franz Waxman (1906–67). It was Steiner, especially in his scores for such films as *King Kong* (1933) and *Gone with the Wind* (1939), who standardized the Wagnerian techniques of "**underscoring**," that is, putting continuous, leitmotif-laden music behind the dialogue in a talking picture. This enabled the mutation of opera into cinema in method as well as style.

Schoenberg and Stravinsky, who both lived in Hollywood, flirted unsuccessfully with the film industry. Less well-known composers made it their specialty, even if they tried to balance their Hollywood ambitions with their former classical careers. The composer of the soundtracks to the epics *Quo Vadis* and *Ben-Hur*, Hungarian-born Miklós Rózsa (1907–95), commented in his tellingly entitled memoir *A Double Life*: "My 'public' career as a composer for films ran alongside my 'private' development as a composer for myself, or at least for nonutilitarian purposes: two parallel lines, and in the interests of both my concern has been to prevent them meeting."[36] The Russian violinist Jascha Heifetz (1901–87), perhaps the greatest instrumental virtuoso of the time and yet another transplant to California, premiered both Korngold's Violin Concerto (1937, revised 1945), which made direct use of some earlier movie material, and Rózsa's Violin Concerto, Op. 24 (1956), parts of which were later used as a film score.

Figure 31-17 Maria Jeritza in *Die tote Stadt* by Erich Wolfgang Korngold.

By the early 1940s Los Angeles was home to a host of eminent composers, not just Schoenberg and Stravinsky but also Rachmaninoff, Weill, and Eisler as well as many performers, artists, and intellectuals. Other prominent Europeans had relocated elsewhere in the United States. The reasons, of course, were war, political oppression, and economic opportunity. The artistic consequences of upheaval and war were varied, thus contributing to the already diverse musical approaches we have seen in this chapter and the previous one—Neoclassicism, twelve-tone music, the ascendance of jazz, Broadway, Hollywood, and *Zeitoper*. The growing divide between elite and popular styles, between high and low, was now further widened by composers who were compelled, either by official policy or out of personal conviction, to respond directly to the political situation in which they lived.

Summary

This chapter considered some further results of the anti-Romantic sentiments that followed the First World War. American vernacular music, especially ragtime, jazz, and blues, was increasingly influential on both sides of the Atlantic. Some typical features of blues are illustrated in W. C. Handy's "St. Louis Blues" (1914). In Europe, African American popular music was especially influential for composers who worked in France, including Stravinsky, Ravel, and Darius Milhaud (1892–1974). At the same time, American composers wrestled with the question of how to create a distinctively American art music. Many went to Paris to study with the renowned Nadia Boulanger (see Chapter 28). During his study with Boulanger, Aaron Copland (1900–1990) wrote several jazz-influenced works, including *Music for the Theatre* (1925). Audiences and critics had mixed reactions to these works because of their mixing of "high" and "low" culture.

One composer who successfully straddled the boundary between popular music and art music was George Gershwin (1898–1937). Gershwin started his career on Tin Pan Alley, the nickname for New York's music-publishing industry where popular songs were produced, including Irving Berlin's "That Mysterious Rag." Gershwin was soon writing Broadway musicals. At the same time, he produced pieces intended for classical audiences, such as *Rhapsody in Blue* (1924) for piano and orchestra. In *Rhapsody,* commissioned by jazz bandleader Paul Whiteman and advertised as "an experiment in modern music," and in his opera *Porgy and Bess* (1935), Gershwin successfully presented jazz-derived styles to classical audiences, in the United States and abroad, as American art music. Working in a different context, the jazz big band, Edward Kennedy "Duke" Ellington (1899–1974) composed intricately orchestrated arrangements of his own tunes and other jazz standards; he also premiered new works like *Black, Brown and Beige* (1943), which aimed to relate the history of African Americans.

Another trend was represented by *Parade* (1917), a ballet produced by Diaghilev that celebrated a low art form, the variety sideshows performed outside of theatres to lure a crowd. *Parade* was a collaboration between the composer Erik Satie (see Chapter 28), the avant-garde poet Jean-Cocteau, who designed the scenario, Pablo Picasso, who designed the costumes, and the choreographer Leonide Massine. *Parade* can be seen as a model for anti-Germanic, French aesthetics because of its clarity and simplicity and because it celebrated the everyday and ordinary. The French poet Guillaume Apollinaire (1880–1918) coined the term "Surrealism" to describe it. The appeal of Surrealist art lay in how it created new art by assembling everyday objects into collages.

The composers known informally as "Les Six" (The Six) were influenced both by Surrealism and by American popular culture. The best-known members of Les Six were Darius Milhaud and Francis Poulenc (1899–1963). Milhaud applied the Surrealist collage aesthetic to tonality. By mixing diatonic melodies and chords into new combinations, he created what he called "polytonality." The primary representative of musical Surrealism in the United States was Virgil Thomson (1896–1989). He and American writer Gertrude Stein collaborated on several projects, including the opera *Four Saints in Three Acts* (1934). In *Susie Asado,* Stein's text emphasizes the sound rather than the meaning of words, and Thomson's musical setting avoids expressing particular images or depicting concrete actions in the drama, instead emphasizing the rhythm of the text.

Anti-Romantic trends were also evident in interwar Germany. The preoccupation with the everyday gave birth to *Zeitoper,* "opera of the times," based on themes of the present, and *Gebrauchsmusik,* music for everyday use. Paul Hindemith (1895–1963) was a leading German figure in this movement. In a different way, Alban Berg (1885–1935) fused aspects of Romanticism and Expressionism with the contemporary emphasis on the here-and-now in his opera *Wozzeck* (1924). Based on a play by Georg Büchner (1813–37), *Wozzeck* depicts the mental deterioration of the title character and society's neglect of the poor. Although the opera is atonal, Berg includes many references to everyday music (marches, waltzes, etc.) and models each scene on a traditional form or genre (suite, sonata, invention, etc.), although these structures go largely unnoticed by the listener. In contrast, Kurt Weill (1900–50) and playwright Bertolt Brecht (1898–1956) created deliberately political operas such as *Die Dreigroschenoper* (The Threepenny Opera, 1929), which rely directly on the immediate accessibility of popular song and dance music.

Study Questions

1. Name and explain at least five ways in which World War I changed musical life in Europe.
2. Describe the ambivalent attitudes toward jazz among American composers and audiences. Why do you think jazz was taken more seriously in Europe than in the United States?
3. What were George Gershwin's main contributions to classical and popular music? How did he straddle the boundary between them?
4. What was Surrealism? Describe the ways in which Erik Satie's *Parade* celebrated the "ordinary."
5. Who were Les Six? What were the various influences on their music?
6. How are Surrealistic trends evident in the collaborations between Virgil Thomson and Gertrude Stein?
7. What is *Zeitoper?* What is *Gebrauchsmusik?*
8. How does Alban Berg's *Wozzeck* make use of traditional forms and genres? In what way does this display of technique create an "ironic distance" from the subject matter?
9. What was the idea behind Bertolt Brecht's "epic theater"? How are these ideas reflected in *Die Dreigroschenoper?* In what respects is this an overtly political work?
10. How do Hollywood movies resemble operas from the twentieth century (or earlier periods)? In what ways are they different?

Key Terms

blue note
call and response
collage
defamiliarization
Gebrauchsmusik
jazz
Les Six
musicals
Neue Sachlichkeit
polytonality
ragtime
rhapsody
Roaring Twenties
Surrealism
syncopation
the blues
Tin Pan Alley
underscoring
Zeitoper

32

Music and Totalitarianism in the Soviet Union and Western Europe

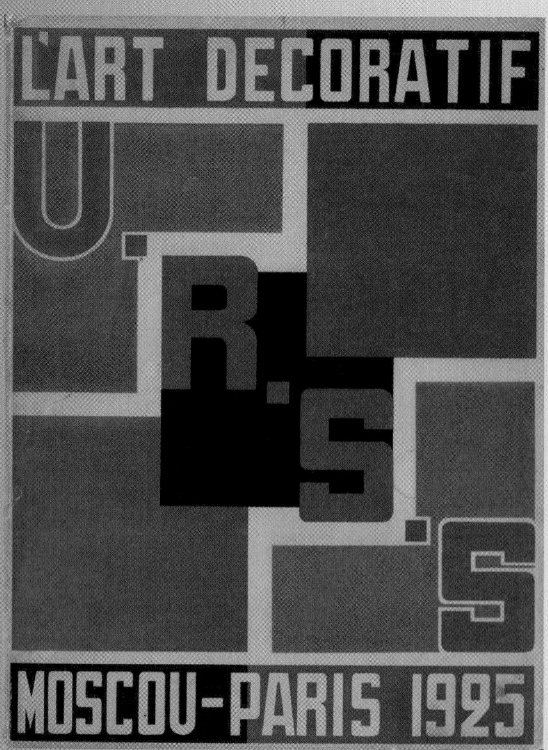

The Roaring Twenties were dealt a deadly blow with the stock market crash in October 1929, leading to the Great Depression. Hard economic times, however, were just one of the factors that now fostered a perceived need for strong leadership. The most malignant political response was the rise of totalitarian regimes that would again plunge the world into war.

Totalitarianism is the concentration of political power in the hands of a ruling elite, in the most extreme case in the hands of a single person, exercising that power in the name of an all-encompassing worldview or ideology. Government assumes a totalizing purpose: the achievement of a completely controlled social order in all areas of public and even private life; the total solution of economic problems; the total reeducation of citizens to erase any other potentially competing source of power (such as religious authority or the Enlightenment concept of inherent human rights); the total mobilization of the population in the interests of the state, enforced by coercion and, if necessary, by terror; and often the total domination of weaker neighbors. Totalitarian regimes are usually characterized by extreme censorship, repression, lack of personal freedoms and the right to travel, and, in the darkest times and places, incarceration and death.

There had been coercive governments in the past, to be sure, and many of the repressive techniques employed by the totalitarian states in the twentieth century, such as the use of terror tactics and professional informers ("secret police"), had precedents in revolutionary France and in the later post-Napoleonic reaction. The term *totalitarian*, however, is reserved for regimes that, having the use of new surveillance technology and mass media, were able to operate on a far grander, more totalizing scale than their predecessors. For artists this meant pressure to produce work in line with official demands. Some fled (or tried to), some dissented, others collaborated, some withdrew, others died.

Three great totalitarian powers arose in Europe: first the Soviet Union under Joseph Stalin (1879–1953), then Fascist Italy under Benito Mussolini (1883–1945), and finally National Socialist (Nazi) Germany under Adolf Hitler (1889–1945). Each promoted itself as the world's only truly modern state, a claim that was supported by its power to manipulate and mobilize mass psychology through **propaganda**. In September 1939 Hitler's insatiable territorial aggression led to the outbreak of the Second World War, the bloodiest military conflict in history.

The Rise of the Soviet Union

With the destruction of the great imperial states of Europe in the wake of the First World War, the predominant political question was what kind of state should replace them. The question was answered in Russia even before the end of the war, when the Bolshevik (Communist) party, led by Vladimir Ilyich Lenin (1870–1924), took power in a coup d'état engineered on 25 October 1917. What emerged called itself the government of Soviets, after the Russian word for "council," the nominal seat of power under the new regime. In 1922, following a civil war through which the Soviet government was able to control most of the territory of the former Russian Empire, the name of the country was changed to the Union of Soviet Socialist Republics (USSR). The Soviet Union lasted until 1991, when the power of the Communist Party collapsed and the union fell apart into its constituent republics. Enduring for more than seventy years, the Soviet Union had outlasted the other twentieth-century totalitarian states by decades.

Totalitarianism is the concentration of political power in the hands of a ruling elite, in the most extreme case in the hands of a single person, exercising that power in the name of an all-encompassing worldview or ideology.

The Soviet form of totalitarianism purported to be the realization of a social vision put forth in the writings of the political economist Karl Marx (1818–83). His analysis of capitalism, the entrepreneurial system through which the advanced societies of Europe and America had amassed their wealth, predicted that inescapable contradictions within capitalism would ultimately lead to a revolt from below, from the working class, or "proletariat." Such a revolution would put political and economic power in the hands of the social classes that actually produced the wealth exploited by capitalists for the sake of their own enrichment.

Marx and Friedrich Engels (1820–95), another German economic theorist, issued *The Communist Manifesto* in the great revolutionary year 1848, and their essay on **communism** concluded with a prediction that ultimate revolutionary success would come from urban workers, who thus far had lacked the organization to mobilize their collective strength. "Workers of the world, unite!" the *Manifesto* proclaimed; "You have nothing to lose but your chains." The outcome of proletarian revolution, Marx and Engels prophesied, would be a utopian "classless" society. Their doctrine assumed that the world revolution would begin in countries where capitalist development had advanced furthest, not ones that lagged behind economically. They never dreamed that the first communist revolution would be in economically backward Russia.

Totalitarianism in Russia began to take hold when Stalin assumed power. In 1922 he became general secretary of the Communist Party of the Soviet Union's Central Committee, a position he held until his death in 1953. After Lenin died in 1924, Stalin consolidated control and initiated a series of "Five-Year Plans" for economic reform, industrialization, and collectivization. A reign of terror emerged in the 1930s with the "Great Purge," in which millions were killed or sent to gulags—penal labor camps (Fig. 32-1). Stalin presided over the most oppressive of the twentieth-century totalitarian states if judged by the general regimentation of the population and intrusion into the daily lives of its inhabitants. It was impossible to dissent or even simply to withdraw from public affairs in such a society. Anyone not engaged in productive, salaried employment (and all citizens were in effect the government's employees) was judged a social parasite and prosecuted under law. The situation became increasingly miserable as the country fell apart economically. Millions died as a result of mass starvation. An era of "show trials" started in which scapegoats were subjected to orchestrated campaigns of denunciation and coerced confessions that deflected popular discontent away from the real culprits: the economic planners themselves and their enforcers.

During the first decade and a half after the Revolution, the arts in Russia were much less subject to direct state intervention than they would be once Stalin was fully in control by 1929. Modernism was not initially discouraged, since revolutionary politics was seen as a form of avant-gardism that deserved an appropriate reflection in art. As a term originally carrying military resonances, "avant-garde" implies belligerence, countercultural hostility, and an antagonism to existing institutions and traditions. "You are revolutionaries in art, we are revolutionaries in life," said writer Anatoly Lunacharsky, the first Soviet commissar of culture and education, to Sergey Prokofiev when the composer announced his intention to move to the West. "We ought to work together."[1] A new kind of society called for a new kind of art.

TIMELINE

1922 Joseph Stalin becomes head of the Communist Party in the Soviet Union

1922 Benito Mussolini and Fascists seize power in Italy

1926 Arturo Toscanini conducts the premiere of Giacomo Puccini's *Turandot*

1929 Worldwide stock market crashes; Great Depression begins

1932 Doctrine of Socialist Realism adopted in the Soviet Union

1933 Adolf Hitler becomes Chancellor of Germany; Nazi regime begins

1933 Arnold Schoenberg emigrates to the United States

1934 Dmitry Shostakovich's *Lady Macbeth of the Mtsensk District* premieres

1935–36 Sergey Prokofiev, *Romeo and Juliet*

1936 *Pravda* editorial condemns Shostakovich's *Lady Macbeth of the Mtsensk District*

1936 Prokofiev returns to the Soviet Union

1936 Paul Hindemith emigrates to Switzerland

1936 Carl Orff, *Carmina Burana*

1937 Shostakovich's Symphony No. 5 premieres

1938 Prokofiev, *Alexander Nevsky* (score for Sergey Eisenstein film)

Figure 32-1 Vorkuta Gulag, north of the Arctic Circle, built by forced laborers in 1931.

Music in the Soviet Union

1938 **Hindemith's *Mathis der Maler* premieres**

1938 Hitler-Stalin Pact

1939 Hitler invades Poland; World War II begins

1940 **Béla Bartók and Hindemith emigrate to the United States**

1941 Japanese attack Pearl Harbor; the United States enters the war

1944 **Bartók's *Concerto for Orchestra* premieres**

Spectacular instances of collaboration between art and government occurred in the visual arts and took the form of Soviet propaganda posters designed by some of the most advanced painters and photographers of the day. At the International Exhibition of Modern Decorative and Industrial Arts in 1925 the Soviet contingent made an enormous impression on viewers and critics in Paris, the very nerve center of international Modernism (Fig. 32-2). The Soviet musical scene in this period was tamer, although a Modernist work such as *The Iron Foundry* by Alexander Mosolov (1900–72), from his ballet *Steel*, written to mark the tenth anniversary of the Revolution, tried to help the hopeful cause of building a great Soviet future. There had been virtually no musical avant-garde to speak of in the immediate prerevolutionary period—Russia's Silver Age—with Scriabin prematurely dead in 1915 and both Stravinsky and Rachmaninoff already living abroad. Alexander Glazunov stuck to a decidedly Romantic musical style. Prokofiev chose not to heed Lunacharsky's suggestion and moved to America in 1918; he was to remain abroad for nearly twenty years, although he never renounced his citizenship.

In 1923, two major professional associations of Russian musicians were organized. One, the Association of Contemporary Music (called the ASM, after its Russian initials), comprised the traditional establishment. Its foremost creative figure, Nikolai Yakovlevich Myaskovsky (1881–1950), produced twenty-seven symphonies and thirteen string quartets and was Prokofiev's closest musical colleague. Two other leaders were Prokofiev's teachers: Reinhold Glière (1875–1956) and Mikhail Gnesin (1883–1957).

The opposing organization was the Russian Association of Proletarian Musicians (RAPM). Militantly countercultural, hopelessly doctrinaire, intolerant, and self-righteous, this group of radical proletarians wanted to throw out all sophisticated traditions and build the new Soviet music on the rubble. RAPM defined itself by what it opposed: It was antimodernist, anti-Western, and antijazz but also antifolklore and antinationalist in the spirit of Marxist internationalism. In place of existing classical, popular, and folk music (except revolutionary songs and a few works of Beethoven, the "voice of the French Revolution"), RAPM promoted revolutionary utilitarian music, mainly march-like "**mass songs**" for group singing, set to agitational propaganda (*agitprop*) lyrics. The ASM and RAPM contended for six years, until 1929, when the latter was given administrative control over Soviet musical institutions, including conservatories. Myaskovsky, Glière, Gnesin, and others were fired from their teaching positions. Grades and examinations were abolished, and admission was restricted to students of acceptable class background.

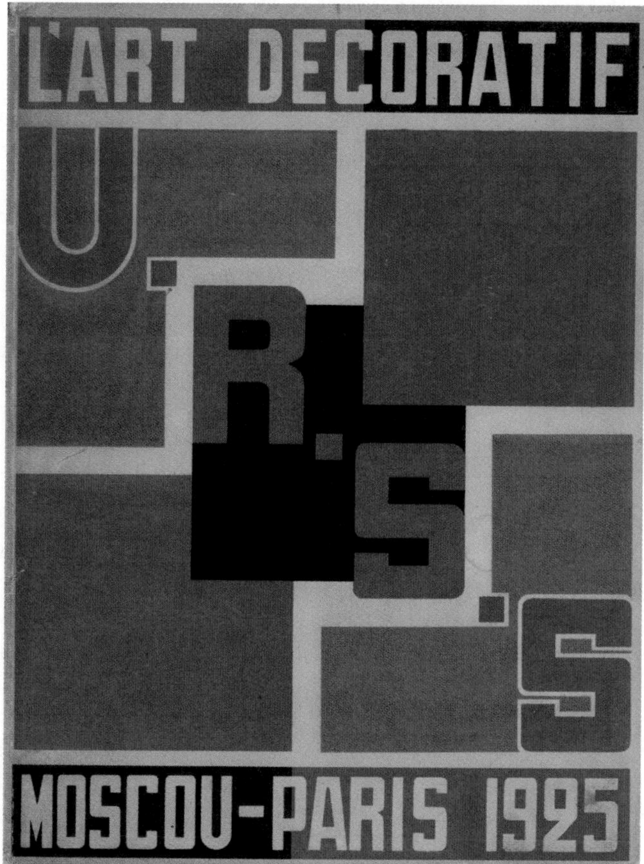

Figure 32-2 Poster by Alexander Rodchenko for the Soviet section of the International Exhibition of Modern Decorative and Industrial Arts held in Paris in 1925.

The Doctrine of Socialist Realism

Nowhere were the arts so policed and watchdogged as in the Soviet Union. The government under Stalin came up with a theory that would effectively transform the arts into a delivery system for state propaganda. In 1932 existing arts organizations were replaced by all-encompassing creative unions that allowed for effective government control. The new Union of Soviet Composers was dedicated to a professional contemporary art music that would remain accessible to workers and peasants because it would draw on familiar folk and popular idioms. Stalin himself summed up the new ideal in a phrase: "an art national in form and socialist in content."[2] In this climate the RAPMists were stripped of power and forced to make public recantations. Nominal power reverted to the old guard as the grateful old conservatory professors were given back their classrooms and installed as willing puppets in the organizational structure of the Composers' Union. But the real power, of course, lay elsewhere, and the real purpose of the organization, though not immediately apparent, was to centralize authority and enforce conformity.

The official doctrine that would guide the arts was called **Socialist Realism.** It was defined in countless Soviet encyclopedias and dictionaries as "a creative method based on the truthful, historically concrete artistic reflection of reality in its revolutionary development."[3] The wording was framed by Andrey Alexandrovich Zhdanov (1896–1948), a member of the Central Committee of the Soviet Communist Party responsible for overseeing the arts. It was enunciated in 1932, at the first Congress of the Union of Soviet Writers, by novelist Maxim Gorky (1868–1936), who had just returned from emigration and who allowed himself to be used as a figurehead.

Early discussions of Socialist Realism and the specific problems of its application to music, the least inherently realistic of the arts, were carried on in meetings, open forums, and the music journal *Sovetskaya muzïka* (Soviet Music), the Union of Composers' official organ. The nature of the doctrine is better seen in its application than in its theory. Socialist Realism turned out to have much less to do with Marxist socialism than with traditional Russian attitudes to the arts, such as those articulated decades earlier by the great writer Leo Tolstoy (1828–1910), for whom all art had to be communitarian, educational, and comprehensible to everyone. The new Soviet theory also echoed the doctrine of Official Nationalism that we saw was expounded nearly a century earlier during the reign of Tsar Nikolai I (see Chapter 21).

Joseph Stalin himself summed up the new Soviet ideal in a phrase: "an art national in form and socialist in content."

Zhdanov in fact fashioned a trio of terms to express the essence of Socialist Realism as if expressly to echo the Tsar's trio of *pravoslaviye* (Orthodoxy), *samoderzhaviye* (autocracy), and *narodnost'* (nationality). The last term remained the same. Like the Official Nationalism of previous century, Socialist Realism demanded that art be rooted in folklore or at least in styles familiar and meaningful to all without special training. The two new terms were *partiynost'* and *ideynost'*. The former means loyalty to the Communist Party and conformity with its official doctrine, which, though it claimed to be a stable point of political and moral reference, proved to be as changeable as the weather and therefore unpredictably dangerous to artists. *Ideynost'* means "being full of ideas," which in practice amounted to a requirement that works of art have a content that could be easily grasped and paraphrased. This also proved tricky, especially when it came to evaluating textless music. Instrumental genres were consequently downgraded in the Soviet scheme of musical value, and various theoretical attempts were made whereby the ideological content of instrumental music could be rendered "objectively" intelligible and hence open to censure.

Figure 32-3 Portrait of composer Dmitry Shostakovich ca. 1950.

Dmitry Shostakovich

So much for theory. The story of Stalinist totalitarianism in practice, where music was concerned, can best be told—in fact, in some ways can *only* be told—in terms of the creative biography of Dmitry Dmitriyevich Shostakovich (1906–75; Fig. 32-3), the Soviet Union's emblematic musician. Shostakovich was the one composer wholly formed there who would achieve unquestionable world eminence. His work was actively promoted by the regime as an emblem of Soviet cultural achievement and a vindication of the theory of Socialist Realism. His actual biography, containing as it did dramatic collisions and painful compromises with Soviet authority, is emblematic in another way: It symbolizes the plight of artists who are subject to direct political control. The consequences of real or perceived resistance could prove life-threatening, which meant that artists worked under conditions rarely faced by creative figures elsewhere, either before or since. The controversies that have swirled about Shostakovich's legacy since his death are emblematic in yet a third way, demonstrating the contests over the meaning of art to which conditions of censorship and political manipulation inevitably give rise.

Shostakovich became nationally famous at the age of nineteen when his First Symphony, his conservatory graduation piece, was premiered on 12 May 1926 in Leningrad (the former Russian capital, St. Petersburg, renamed in honor of Lenin). World fame followed less than two years later, when Bruno Walter performed the symphony with the Berlin Philharmonic. Other famous conductors, such as Otto Klemperer, Leopold Stokowski, and Arturo Toscanini, soon championed the work as well. This remarkably mature work, very much a sign of its times, shows Shostakovich to have been well abreast of fashionable currents in European music, notably Neoclassicism. While working full steam on the opening movements, the composer had informed a friend that "it really ought to be called a symphony-grotesque."[4] The first and second themes in the first movement, for example, are a cheeky military march and a shyly flirtatious waltz. The second movement, nominally a scherzo and trio, contrasts a maniacal gallop (in which the piano takes a leading part) with some sort of antiquated hymn. The finale, another gallop (or possibly a circus march), brazenly and explicitly mocks the pathos of the affecting slow movement—and implicitly mocks the listener who had been taken in by it. The sentiment of "We won't be fooled again!" is written all over this icily brilliant score.

The young Shostakovich had already developed a keen dramatic sense from various jobs accompanying silent films on the piano in movie theaters. His innovative first opera, *The Nose* (1928), derived from a short story by Nikolai Gogol (1809–52), proved that the twenty-two-year-old composer had enormous theatrical talent. The opera burlesques the conventions of the genre in an unsubtle yet impressively inventive manner. Shostakovich comes across as someone out to debunk the musical status quo from within. It was at the time an authentically Soviet attitude toward bourgeois traditions. Until the end of his third decade, he was regarded everywhere as the brash young musical genius of a brash young society. He was idealistic in his political hopes for communism. His Second Symphony (1927) was entitled *To October, a Symphonic Dedication* (the month commemorating the Revolution in 1917) and includes a chorus praising Lenin. The Third Symphony (1929), called "The First of May," also features a choral ode.

> ***Until the end of his third decade, Dmitry Shostakovich was regarded everywhere as the brash young musical genius of a brash young society.***

Shostakovich greeted the 1932 restructuring of the arts as a boon and embarked on another opera, also based on a famous nineteenth-century novella, but this time a serious one: *Lady Macbeth of the Mtsensk District* by Nikolai Leskov (1831–95). It is the story of Katerina Izmailova, a childless merchant's wife in the middle of the great Russian nowhere, who rebels against her patriarchal surroundings by murdering her husband, her father-in-law, and her husband's saintly nephew. She and her lover, Sergey, are discovered in the act of killing the little boy and sentenced to exile in Siberia. On the way there, Sergey takes a shine to another woman, whom Katerina duly murders by jumping with her into a freezing river in which both of them drown. It is hardly surprising that the authorities eventually attacked Shostakovich for not presenting an inspiring example of Socialist Realism. What he offered instead was stark lived Soviet realism of another kind: a world of hopelessness, of inhumanity, and of people being shipped off to oblivion.

Shostakovich and his librettist, Alexander Preys, tried to turn Leskov's story of ungovernable passion and mayhem into a Soviet morality play. The objective conditions under which Katerina is forced to live justify her acts of violence, which are presented as acts of liberation. (Still, the murder of the nephew had to be eliminated because, as Shostakovich acknowledged, "killing a child always makes a bad impression.")[5] Shostakovich's music balanced his earlier satirical manner against a more lyrical and conventionally beautiful idiom. The latter he reserved for Katerina, the former for her victims, so the dubious heroine of this very inhumane opera becomes the lone character with whom it is possible for the audience to identify musically as a human being. Katerina's is the only music that has emotional "life," as traditionally portrayed in opera. All the other characters are presented as subhuman.

Lady Macbeth of the Mtsensk District was a huge success with audiences and critics alike after its nearly simultaneous premieres in Leningrad, the composer's hometown, and in Moscow, the Soviet capital, in January 1934 (Fig. 32-4). It played to full houses for two years and was performed in the West as well, captivating audiences, as *Wozzeck* had a decade earlier, with strong doses of sex and violence. Then came Shostakovich's downfall. A festival of Soviet music was held in Moscow in 1936 for which the opera company in Leningrad sent its two most successful productions. On the evening of 17 January, Stalin attended a performance of *Quiet Flows the Don*, a corny "song opera" (a Soviet genre somewhat similar to a Broadway musical but sung throughout) by a hack composer named Ivan Dzerzhinsky. Stalin loved it and summoned the hack, the conductor, and the director to his box for praise. Nine days later, however, things went very differently when Stalin returned to the same theater to see *Lady Macbeth*, along with an entourage that this time included Zhdanov. Shostakovich grew worried as Stalin and his retinue left without comment before the final curtain.

Two days after that, what soon became known as the "Historic Document" appeared in *Pravda*, the Communist Party's official newspaper. It was an unsigned

Figure 32-4 Scene from the 1934 Moscow premiere of Shostakovich's *Lady Macbeth of the Mtsensk District* directed by Sergey Eisenstein.

editorial entitled "Muddle Instead of Music," and a historic document it was indeed. Shostakovich's opera was brutally attacked both for its libretto and its music. The main thrust of the criticism was puritanical. "The music croaks and hoots and snorts and pants in order to represent love scenes as naturally as possible," *Pravda* fumed; "and 'love,' in its most vulgar form is smeared all over the opera."[6] Such qualities, the editorial insinuated, were why the piece had enjoyed its sensational international success. It was a submission to "the depraved tastes of bourgeois audiences," whom it titillated with its "witching, clamorous, neurasthenic music." And then came the threat. In phrases intended to rein in the composer, the chief organ of Soviet power denounced him for "trifling with difficult matters" and hinted that "this game might end very badly."

No artist likes getting a bad review, but with this one Shostakovich knew he was dealing with more than mere aesthetic criticism—the words were far more menacing. The article was soon followed by another in *Pravda* attacking his ballet *The Limpid Stream* and then by yet another. The musical establishment lined up in opposition to Shostakovich. *Lady Macbeth,* until then the jewel of the Soviet operatic stage, was summarily banned, not to return until 1963, in a revised and renamed version stripped of its "pornophony," as one American critic had dubbed it.[7]

Shostakovich was probably singled out for attack not so much because his works gave particular offense but because of his preeminence among Soviet composers of his generation. If someone of his brilliance, fame, and success could be summarily slapped down, then nobody was safe. Some of Shostakovich's surviving friends later recalled that at the time of the *Pravda* editorial the composer fully expected to be arrested and imprisoned. The worst never happened, but for the rest of his life, or at least until the end of Stalin's reign, he had to live with the threat of a "bad end." That this tortured figure continued to function as an artist and a citizen has lent his career and many of his works a heroic luster that no benignly neglected Modernist composer in the West can hope to rival.

Contested Readings: The Fifth Symphony

Shostakovich faced terrifying challenges in how to proceed after the sustained government attacks, which came as he was in the process of writing his massive Fourth Symphony. The work went into rehearsals in December 1936, but at the very last moment, just before the premiere, it was withdrawn. The impressive symphony would have to wait twenty-five years for unveiling, in 1961. Shostakovich began a new symphony in April 1937. The first three movements of the nonprogrammatic Fifth were written with incredible speed; the composer later recounted that he wrote the *Largo* in just three days, although the finale slowed him down. The most conspicuous difference between the Fifth Symphony and his earlier works is the suppression of the grotesque and satirical mode, formerly a hallmark of his style. The scherzo, where one might have expected a madcap caricature of a march or gallop, was a rather heavy, traditionally Germanic triple-metered affair in an idiom seemingly derived from that of the early symphonies of Mahler, whose music Shostakovich revered.

Anthology Vol 3-38
Full CD VII, 1

The Fifth Symphony won Shostakovich his rehabilitation and return to official favor. The premiere took place on 21 November 1937 with the Leningrad Philharmonic under Yevgeniy Mravinsky, at that time a relatively unknown young conductor who would go on to a prominent career. The event came at the height of Stalin's purges, in the midst of mass arrests, disappearances, and executions. According to reliable reports, many listeners wept openly during the symphony's slow movement. Members of the audience, one by one, began to stand during the extravagant finale, and the work was cheered for fully half an hour when it was over. Yet the enormous enthusiasm from musicians and nonmusicians alike could well be viewed as a statement against the Soviet authorities' rebukes of the composer. As Shostakovich knew from past experience, artistic triumphs could spell political danger.

The Fifth Symphony was officially considered a recantation. The composer, at least outwardly, sought to further that impression. We cannot be sure exactly what he thought because no public utterance by a public figure in Stalinist Russia can be presumed actually to come from its apparent source. In the present case the utterance took the form of a newspaper article called "My Creative Answer," which was published in a Moscow newspaper on the eve of the symphony's first performance in the capital (25 January 1938).

Shostakovich (or the ghostwriter of the article) announced that in the wake of the Leningrad premiere, "among the often very substantial responses that have analyzed this work, one that particularly gratified me said that 'the Fifth Symphony is a Soviet artist's practical creative answer to just criticism.'" The author went on to state that "at the center of the work's conception I envisioned *a man* in all his suffering" and that "the Symphony's finale resolves the tense and tragic moments of the preceding movements in a joyous, optimistic fashion." That man, the symphony's hero, is explicitly identified with the composer and his recent past: "If I have really succeeded in embodying in musical images all that I have thought and felt since the critical articles in *Pravda*, if the demanding listener will detect in my music a turn toward greater clarity and simplicity, I will be satisfied."[8] In keeping with the explicit demands of Socialist Realism, a special effort was made to dissociate the symphony's "tense and tragic moments" from any hint of "pessimism," a forbidden message for art to convey since it promoted passivity and low productivity. "I think that Soviet tragedy, as a genre, has every right to exist," the author of the article published over

Shostakovich's name declared, "*but:* its content must be suffused with a *positive idea*, comparable, for example, to the life-affirming ardor of Shakespeare's tragedies."[9]

Some objected to the symphony nonetheless. A critic writing in *Sovetskaya muzïka* faulted Shostakovich for occasionally falling short of his intentions as set forth in "My Creative Answer." In the critic's view, the slow movement, which had provoked the flood of weeping in the hall, was a failure because "this numbness, this torpor is the very *negation* of the life-affirming principle."[10] That would have made the symphony unacceptable, one feels after reading the review, had not the finale saved the day—or tried to—by breaking the objectionable mood, especially with its insistently, earsplittingly yea-saying D-major coda. The critic ended his review with cautious approval but with a question on his mind: Had Shostakovich truly succeeded in dispelling the pessimism he so vividly portrayed (and possibly conveyed) in the *Largo*?

There are many people now, both in and out of Russia, who believe that Shostakovich's Fifth Symphony was an act of bearing witness, a dissident work.

With that, the critic unwittingly (or perhaps wittingly?) signaled the real story of the Fifth's reception, in which the official reading contended with a sort of folk tradition of "dissident" readings that put the symphony's supposed message in quite another light. This tradition, carried on in private (or in coded language) can be pieced together from scattered documents and reminiscences. With regard to the Fifth Symphony the tradition begins with a diary entry made by Alexander Fadeyev, the very orthodox head of the Soviet Writers' Union, after he heard the 1938 Moscow premiere. He wrote: "A work of astonishing strength. The third movement is beautiful. But the ending does not sound like a resolution (still less like a triumph or victory) but, rather, like a punishment or vengeance on someone. A terrible emotional force, but a tragic force. It arouses painful feelings."[11]

Such a view turned the official reading of radiant optimism on its head, judging most successful the very movement that the official critic had called the least convincing and leaving open the possibility that the finale "failed" on purpose. Myaskovsky, writing to Prokofiev, confessed that he was surprised that Shostakovich could have come up with a finale so "utterly flat."[12] Others made similar comments. Were these writers using code? And was even Georgiy Khubov, the "official critic," using code when he called such insistent attention to the slow movement's "torpor"? By now a whole library of late- and post-Soviet memoirs, accounts by émigrés, and secretly published dissident writings attests that "torpor" was precisely the mood that reigned among the populace during the political terror whose very peak coincided with the symphony's premiere.

There are many people now, both in and out of Russia, who believe that Shostakovich's Fifth Symphony was an act of bearing witness, a dissident work. In 1979, four years after the composer's death, a book called *Testimony* was published in New York, purporting to be memoirs of Shostakovich as transcribed from conversations with an émigré journalist named Solomon Volkov. It contains this unequivocal characterization of the symphony:

> I think it is clear to everyone what happens in the Fifth. The rejoicing is forced, created under threat, as in [the first scene of Musorgsky's opera] *Boris Godunov*. It's as if someone were beating you with a stick and saying, "Your business is rejoicing, your business is rejoicing," and you rise, shaky, and go marching off, muttering, "Our business is rejoicing, our business is rejoicing." What kind of apotheosis is that? You have to be a complete oaf not to hear that.[13]

The authenticity of this alleged memoir has been most effectively questioned,[14] but in the end it is not relevant to the point at issue here, which is the way in which the folk reading has triumphed, both in Russia and abroad, over the official one as Soviet power grew weaker and eventually collapsed. We will never know what Shostakovich intended. As is always true of instrumental music, multiple readings were available to listeners despite all attempts at government control. Those who wished to believe in the work's dissident message had a consolation that was otherwise unavailable under conditions of Soviet censorship. And that is why nowhere on earth was instrumental music ever valued more highly by multitudes of listeners than in the Soviet Union. That high social value was purchased at an exorbitant price in suffering. It illustrates more poignantly, perhaps, than any other episode in the history of music just what it is that has made music so special among the arts. It was something that the Romantics had valued in art: that the meaning of a work of art was not limited to the creator's intentions.

Nowhere on earth was instrumental music ever valued more highly by multitudes of listeners than in the Soviet Union.

The Fifth Symphony officially redeemed Shostakovich and went on to become his most popular work, an instant "classic." And although the Sixth Symphony (1939) did not fare as well, the Seventh, begun in Leningrad while the city was under siege by the Germans, was performed to great acclaim in Russia and elsewhere in 1942 (Fig. 32-5). The massive first movement contains a lengthy orchestral crescendo, lasting some eight minutes, that many likened to an "invasion."[15] Known as the "Leningrad" Symphony, it was for a while the most famous and influential piece of contemporary classical music. It secured Shostakovich's position as the leading Soviet composer in the eyes and ears of the world and landed him on the *Time* magazine cover of 20 July 1942.

In the wake of this phenomenal international success expectations ran high, but the Eighth Symphony (1943) generally disappointed. After a lightweight Symphony No. 9, a sort of anti-Beethoven's Ninth, Shostakovich did not attempt another symphony for nearly a decade, during which time things got worse for him. Together with Prokofiev, Aram Khachaturian (1903–78), and other prominent composers, he was again denounced in 1948. His most important compositional statements had to remain "in the drawer": *From Jewish Folk Poetry*, the First Violin Concerto, and the Fourth and Fifth string quartets went unperformed and were in most cases revealed only after Stalin's death in 1953.

Shostakovich was largely reduced to writing film scores and patriotic fare. All Soviet composers had to write overtly Soviet pieces, whether compelled directly to do so or moved by a genuine political commitment (or a pragmatic sense of what would be good for their careers). Many of these works featured vocal soloists and chorus. Shostakovich wrote an oratorio called *Song of the Forests* (1948), celebrating the reforestation of the country after the ravages of war and drought. His film score for *The Fall of Berlin* (1949) ends with a resounding paean to Stalin. Because anniversaries were taken very seriously in the Soviet Union, he repeatedly produced pieces to commemorate significant occasions, especially the 1917 October Revolution. In 1927, he wrote *To October, a Symphonic Dedication*, which he later called his Second Symphony. Twenty years after that he produced a brief cantata, *Poem of the Motherland* (1947); in 1957 his Eleventh Symphony; and finally, in 1967, a symphonic poem, *October*, Op. 131.

Such good behavior helped effect a second rehabilitation, as did humiliating public statements Shostakovich was forced to make, including at a conference in

New York in 1949. Despite the rollercoaster ride of favor and disfavor that marked his career, Shostakovich emerged as one of the most prolific and most often-performed composers of the century. He produced a total of fifteen symphonies and the same number of string quartets. He composed concertos for some of the preeminent Soviet instrumentalists of his day, including violinist David Oistrakh (1908–74) and cellist Mstislav Rostropovich (1927–2007). The punishing experience with *Lady Macbeth* cut short his dramatic career and deprived the musical world of what might have been great operas. Shostakovich's music not only charts his own fraught experiences as a brilliant composer living and working within a brutal system but also presents what one can view as the secret diary of life in the Soviet Union.

Figure 32-5 A Soviet soldier buying a ticket to the performance of Shostakovich's Seventh Symphony in besieged Leningrad, Russia, 1942.

Back in the USSR: Sergey Prokofiev

To many observers, particularly those abroad, the most dreadful humiliation was not Shostakovich's but Prokofiev's. Unlike any other major Soviet composer, Prokofiev (Fig. 32-6) had the experience of a former émigré. Rejecting commissar Lunacharsky's entreaty in the heady early days of the Revolution to stay in Russia and write revolutionary music, he went off in 1918 to New York; he spent the next few years in America before moving to Europe. He fully engaged with the Western trends of the time, mixing maximalism, Neoclassicism, and Russian exoticism. In addition, he enjoyed a cosmopolitan career as a pianist. His many friends and admirers in the West assumed (as Prokofiev himself must have assumed) that his international reputation would insulate him from bureaucratic meddling when he decided to move back to the Soviet Union in 1936. Beginning in 1927 he had already made periodic visits to his homeland, and a gradual wooing process was initiated that eventually led to his permanent return, along with his Spanish wife (raised in New York) and their two young sons.

The year 1936 would seem a most inopportune time for Prokofiev to return. That year saw Shostakovich bitterly denounced in *Pravda*, and the horrors of Stalin's purges were growing more evident. Many explanations have been offered that go beyond understandable homesickness. Perhaps Prokofiev was frustrated that, for audiences abroad, the role of the "great Russian composer" was already filled (by Stravinsky), as was that of the "great Russian pianist" (by Rachmaninoff). The irony is that he found a rival at home, too. His years back in the USSR were partly overshadowed by the fame and achievement of Shostakovich, whom he had initially underestimated. On a trip back in 1935 Prokofiev wrote to his friend and fellow émigré composer Vladimir Dukelsky (better known for the popular music he wrote in America under the pseudonym Vernon Duke): "They make too much of him here, by the way."[16]

Figure 32-6 Portrait of Sergey Prokofiev, by Piotr Petrovich Kontchalovski, 1934.

Prokofiev was an enormously gifted composer for the stage and screen, writing operas, incidental music, ballets, and film scores; one attraction of being back in the USSR was the chance to collaborate with formidable colleagues in other art forms.

His first great stage work from the time was already under way when he returned—the ballet *Romeo and Juliet* (1935–36), which was followed by a number of operas, including an epic setting of Tolstoy's novel *War and Peace* (1941–43). In these pieces, as well as in a wide range of concert music, among them seven symphonies and as many concertos, Prokofiev capitalized on his natural melodic gifts and the direct emotional appeal his music could generate. A retreat from his earlier Modernist style to what he called a "new simplicity" may retrospectively seem to have been politically calculated, but it nonetheless suited his talents well.[17] Like Shostakovich, he produced his share of official patriotic stuff, including a mammoth *Cantata on the 20th Anniversary of the October Revolution* (1937) and a notorious work praising Stalin, *Zdravitsa* (1939).

Anthology Vol 3-39
Full CD VII, 2–4
Concise CD III, 34

One of his most successful Soviet pieces served multiple purposes. The film score for *Alexander Nevsky* (1938) gave Prokofiev the opportunity to work with the visionary director Sergey Eisenstein (1898–1948) and to help create one of the most acclaimed movies produced in the Soviet Union (Fig. 32-7). The film and its music had a strong political component, although they proved moving targets that shifted in and out of favor. Like Prokofiev, Eisenstein had lived in the West, working in Hollywood during the early 1930s. He had already been hailed as a pioneer of the silent-film era with such works as *The Battleship Potemkin* (1925) and *October: Ten Days That Shook the World* (1927). Prokofiev had proved his own film credentials earlier with *Lieutenant Kijé* (1933) and was eager to team up with Eisenstein as he embarked on his first sound film. (He would later collaborate on the director's last work, *Ivan the Terrible*, which began filming in 1942.)

In the great Russian tradition going back to operas such as Glinka's *A Life for the Tsar* and Musorgsky's *Boris Godunov*, *Alexander Nevsky* is based on a famous historical figure. Prince Alexander of Novgorod (1220–63) initially earned renown in 1240 for defeating the Swedish army on the Neva River, hence his name "Nevsky," which means "of the Neva." He went on to put down the invading Teutonic Knights at a battle on the Peipus Lake in 1242. The Teutonic Knights, of course, were ancestors of the modern Germans, and so a work celebrating victory over them was heartily embraced by the Soviet authorities as Hitler's expansionist ambitions became ever more apparent. But soon after filming in the summer and fall of 1938, the Soviet Union signed a treaty with Germany, the so-called Hitler–Stalin Pact, and the film project was no longer politically viable. Its fortunes changed yet again in June 1941 when Hitler, disastrously for Germany as it turned out, broke the agreement and

Figure 32-7 Scene of the Battle on the Ice from *Alexander Nevsky*, film directed by Sergey Eisenstein.

invaded the Soviet Union. *Alexander Nevsky* was again a welcome, and now most useful, propaganda tool, which proved enormously successful. The relevance of the work is clear from Alexander's monologue at the end: "If disaster ever threatens again," he proclaims, "I'll call all of Russia to arms. If you stand back, you'll be severely punished. I'll punish you myself, if I'm alive. And if I die, my sons will!"

On a musical level, he noted, "that at times he was prepared to cut or add to his sequences so as not to upset the balance of a musical episode."[18] The composer thus wrote music to suit the director's needs, and the director on occasion crafted sequences to fit the music. Music plays an enormously important role in the film, and Prokofiev later adapted large portions of it as a separate cantata that has remained one of his most often-performed compositions.

For a taste of the music we can look at three consecutive short movements from the cantata: "The Crusaders of Pskov," "Arise, People of Russia," and "The Field of the Dead." These show the most important aspect of the piece, namely, the contrasting representations of the enemy and of the Russians. The Germans are associated with a kind of militarized Gregorian chant in fractured Latin (*Peregrinus expectavi*) that differs markedly with the extravagantly lyrical depictions of the Russians based on folk song. "Arise, People of Russia" was apparently so popular and so in line with Party politics that Soviet State Radio kept broadcasting it, even at times when Prokofiev's music was otherwise banned. The hauntingly beautiful "Field of the Dead" is sung by a mezzo-soprano soloist and relates a scene after the battle in which a Russian maiden, the female heroine Olga from Novgorod, walks around on the battlefield in the growing darkness, carrying a torch and searching for survivors among the fallen. Despite the propagandistic text and context, this lament movingly reflects the suffering experienced by the Russian people, whether their loved ones perished in war or in Stalin's camps.

One of Prokofiev's last public triumphs was his Fifth Symphony, a contribution to the war effort akin to Shostakovich's "Leningrad" Symphony, written three years earlier. The composer conducted the premiere on 13 January 1945, just as victory over the Germans was within reach. A month later Prokofiev fell, apparently the result of a mild stroke, and his productivity declined during his last years, although he continued to produce significant pieces to the end eight years later. He died on 5 March 1953, a notable day in Soviet history: Joseph Stalin died less than an hour later.

Italian Fascism

> ***The turmoil that followed the First World War led to significant political agitation in countries that emerged out of the defeated empires of Germany and Austro-Hungary.***

The turmoil that followed the First World War led to significant political agitation in countries that emerged out of the defeated empires of Germany and Austro-Hungary. Faced with totalitarian threats from the Soviet Union (which, following Marx, declared "World Revolution" to be its goal), racked by internal political agitation, and beset by economic chaos, the fledgling democracies were insecure and unstable. There was considerable sentiment everywhere that revolution could be resisted only by counterrevolution or by a preemptive counter-totalitarianism that would prevent the spread of communist power. The looming presence of the Soviet Union on the world stage was thus among the factors that brought other totalitarian regimes to power. The two countries that had more or less dominated the

European musical scene in the eighteenth and nineteenth centuries, Italy and Germany, became totalitarian states. It is also an obvious historical fact that Italy and Germany lost their commanding musical positions during the twentieth century. One pertinent question, then, is how and to what degree these two facts may be related; another is why significant achievements in various art forms occurred under conditions of Soviet totalitarianism.

Italy moved toward totalitarianism when a political organization called the *Partito Nazionale Fascista* (National Fascist Party), led by Benito Mussolini, seized power in a coup d'état on 29 October 1922. (The party took its name from the *fasces*, or bundles, tightly wound gatherings of wooden rods from which axe heads projected, which were carried by imperial guards to symbolize unity and power in ancient Rome.) **Fascism** upheld the role of elites in political leadership and the ideal of social hierarchy. As with Soviet Communism, Italian Fascism ultimately deteriorated in practice into an autocratic dictatorship propped up by an enormous bureaucracy. The difference was that Fascist authoritarian power did not deny the right of individual enterprise but tried instead to discipline or co-opt it. Its core constituency, in sharp contrast to Soviet power, was the bourgeoisie. Italy's arts policy was far less intrusive than the policies of the other totalitarian states. This was in keeping with the principles of the corporate state, which respected individual initiative and the autonomy of the professions and was therefore not inherently hostile to Modernism.

In fact, Mussolini, whom his followers called *Il Duce* (The Leader), took pride in his advanced artistic views and gladly had Italy play host to international festivals of contemporary music. During the first decade of its existence, Italian Fascism was widely admired from afar. "Mussolini has made the trains run on time," ran the familiar refrain. His admirers in the 1920s included some leading politicians in the democratic governments of Western Europe and America. Even Winston Churchill (1874–1965), who as prime minister of the United Kingdom was to lead his nation in war against Mussolini, had warm words for him in the 1920s. And Mussolini was downright popular among some artists, particularly some elite Modernists who felt ever more threatened by the empowerment of the uneducated working class. Stravinsky, as an exiled Russian nobleman impoverished as a consequence of the Revolution, was especially admiring. The Neoclassical Stravinsky consciously cast himself as the Mussolini of music, who wanted to do for Modern music what the Italian leader promised to do for modern Europe. Nor was Stravinsky the only composer to draw an explicit connection between the ideals of Neoclassicism and those of Fascism. Alfredo Casella (1883–1947), an Italian composer educated in France and a great enthusiast of both Mussolini and Stravinsky, thought that the political and artistic movements were "full of audacity and life" and were together bringing about a national reawakening.[19]

The most eminent Italian composer of the period and the one most lavishly promoted by the government was Ottorino Respighi (1879–1936). Although he wrote operas, what brought him international fame were his superbly scored programmatic suites for orchestra. He had enjoyed a cosmopolitan education, studying with Giuseppe Martucci in Bologna, Nikolai Rimsky-Korsakov in St. Petersburg, and Max Bruch in Berlin, before settling in Rome. Three of his most popular orchestral scores are impressions of various aspects of the city he loved: *Fontane di Roma* (Fountains of Rome, 1915–16), *Pini di Roma* (Pines of Rome, 1923–24), and *Feste romane* (Roman Festivals, 1928). Influenced by the orchestral music of Strauss, Debussy, and Rimsky, he took their differing ideals of sound and color and forged them into a personal and unabashedly extroverted instrumental style. Some of his music was nostalgic or archaic, in the Neoclassical fashion. He arranged three orchestral suites (1917, 1923, 1931) of *Antiche arie e danze per liuto* (Ancient Airs and Dances for the Lute). Other works derived thematic material from Gregorian chant, such as *Vetrate di chiesa* (Church Windows, 1925). Paintings by the Renaissance artist Sandro Botticelli inspired the *Botticelli Triptych* (1927).

A leading composer of the next generation, Luigi Dallapiccola (1904–75), although initially an admirer of Mussolini, proved to be a rare figure working under totalitarianism to express his liberal political concerns in music. He composed principally using twelve-tone techniques (Berg, whom he met in 1934, was an inspiring model), which he combined with an Italianate lyricism related to his country's operatic heritage as well as with elements of fashionable Neoclassicism. His choral work *Canti di prigionia* (Songs of Imprisonment, 1938–41) uses words by famous historical figures (Queen Mary Stuart, Boethius, and Savonarola) who were unjustly imprisoned for voicing their convictions. Soon afterward he started work on his opera *Il prigioniero* (The Prisoner), saying "it became increasingly clear to me that I must write an opera which . . . would portray the tragedy of our times and the tragedy of persecution felt and suffered by millions of individuals."[20] It is a measure of the less severe conditions in Italy that Dallapiccola could write these powerful protest pieces and survive, bearing witness in a way that would have been impossible in either the Soviet Union or Nazi Germany.

Arturo Toscanini and Music Making in the New Italy

Mussolini came to power just as Giacomo Puccini, Italy's most famous composer, was writing *Turandot*, his last opera, not quite finished when he died in 1924. The other preeminent Italian musicians at the time were not composers but performers: the great tenor Enrico Caruso (1873–1921) and conductor Arturo Toscanini (Fig. 32-8), who led the premiere of *Turandot*. (They made a celebrated trio: Puccini wrote operas for Caruso to sing and Toscanini to conduct.) Aware of the historic importance of music in framing national reputation, Mussolini heaped special scorn on the recently deceased singer: "Caruso and the like were or are the old Italy."[21] After centuries of Italian musical prestige being tied to vocal music and opera, Mussolini now favored symphony orchestras, "whose performances give an idea of collective group discipline."[22] The chief musical representative of the new Italy was Toscanini, who revolutionized orchestral performance in a way that also exemplified the ideal of streamlined performance practice identified in Chapter 30 with Neoclassicism. A Toscanini performance, to a degree previously unprecedented, was a display of "collective group discipline" that aimed above all for a scrupulous realization of the musical text.

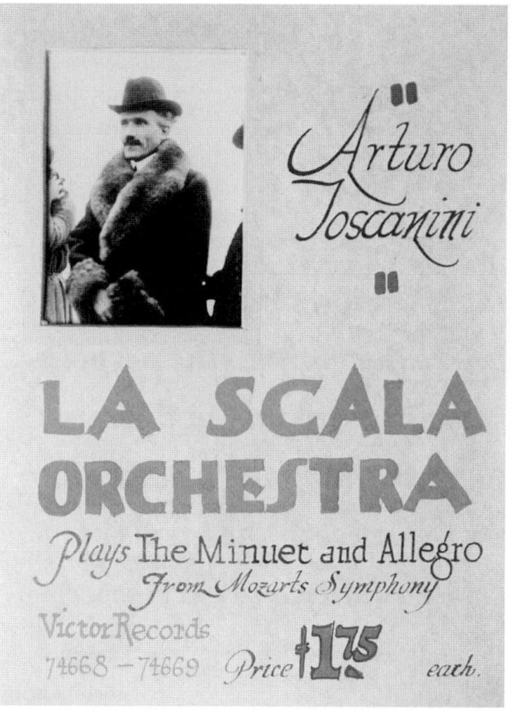

Figure 32-8 Advertisement for a 1920–21 record featuring Arturo Toscanini conducting La Scala Orchestra.

When Mussolini ascended to power, Toscanini was known primarily as the supreme opera conductor in Europe. Since 1898, with several interruptions for duties abroad (including at New York's Metropolitan Opera), he had been the artistic director of La Scala in Milan, Italy's premier performing arts institution. His range was broad, encompassing Wagner, Tchaikovsky, and Debussy in addition to the full Italian repertoire, including many world premieres. Toscanini also had a longstanding interest in the symphonic repertoire. He achieved international fame as a symphonic conductor during the 1920–21 season, when he made a tour of Europe and America with a newly constituted La Scala Orchestra (called the Orchestra Arturo Toscanini for the occasion). In some eight months they gave 133 performances before audiences totaling over a quarter of a million. These concerts were received everywhere as a revelation. The crisp attacks and cutoffs, the transparent textures, and the rhythmic precision of Toscanini's performances far exceeded contemporary standards, as may be heard on recordings he made with his orchestra at the Victor Talking Machine studios in Camden, New Jersey.

By 1926 Toscanini was dividing his time between La Scala and the New York Philharmonic. He participated in the most prestigious European summer festivals, leading legendary performances of Mozart, Verdi, and Wagner operas with the Vienna Philharmonic in Salzburg and becoming the first non-German to be invited to conduct at the annual Wagner festival in Bayreuth. He retired to Italy in 1936 at the age of sixty-nine, but the very next year he received an invitation from the head of the National Broadcasting Company to return to America to lead a handpicked orchestra that would be created for him, that would do its performing on the radio rather than in the concert hall, and that would record the standard symphonic repertoire for Victor. Toscanini conducted the NBC Symphony for seventeen years, until he re-retired, in 1954, at the age of eighty-seven. He died in New York in January 1957, two months short of his ninetieth birthday.

For the culminating phase of his career, then, Toscanini worked almost exclusively in the broadcast and recording media, achieving through technology a fame no classical musician had ever previously known. He fulfilled Mussolini's musical prediction for the New Italy, which is ironic, since Toscanini and Mussolini had fallen out in the 1920s, and the conductor became identified as a fierce anti-Fascist who lent his celebrated name and priceless services to Allied wartime efforts. He refused to conduct in Italy, Germany, or Austria. (Richard Strauss was enlisted as his replacement to conduct *Parsifal* at the 1933 Bayreuth Festival.) And yet, despite his admirable political views, the kind of performances Toscanini achieved were attributable as much to the dominating force of his personality and his dictatorial behavior as to his musical insight. Musicians who played under him were subject to summary dismissal; they experienced a reign of terror that is documented in countless anecdotes as well as in recordings that survive of rehearsals. Toscanini justified his behavior precisely the way political dictators do, by claiming that the ends justified the means. "Gentlemen, be democrats in life but aristocrats in art,"[23] he told his orchestras. Only the strictest hierarchy of command could achieve the precision for which Toscanini became famous and which the musical world has treasured ever since. Toscanini's methods and his results point to the perpetually renegotiated dilemma concerning the relationship between the competing, possibly incompatible ideals of equality and excellence.

Toscanini's methods and his results point to the perpetually renegotiated dilemma concerning the relationship between the ideals of equality and excellence.

Toscanini's importance is noteworthy for another reason as well: his commanding stature is indicative of a fundamental shift in musical prestige during the twentieth century. The museum culture of classical music made living composers less prominent while performers, leading conductors above all, became the new superstars. In the past, as we know, most composers were performers, sometimes the greatest of their day (Mozart, Mendelssohn, Liszt, and Mahler, for example). But the most famous twentieth-century performers tended not to compose, and those eminent composers who did perform, such as Stravinsky and Copland, were motivated largely by economic considerations and concentrated mainly on presenting their own compositions in concert.

Music in Nazi Germany

> ***The museum culture of classical music made living composers less prominent while performers, leading conductors above all, became the new superstars.***

The seeds of Mussolini's downfall were sown in 1939 with the military alliance Italy formed with Nazi Germany and Adolf Hitler. This "pact of steel" ultimately resulted in Italy's losing the Second World War and in Mussolini's execution in 1945. Hitler had come to power in 1933 with a platform of economic recovery, nationalist renewal, and barefaced racial intolerance. He practiced repressions and betrayals that rivaled, and in some ways even exceeded, those of the Soviet government. His quest for expansion led to war, and he eventually committed the century's most horrendous acts of politically rationalized and legalized mass murder.

A combination of factors, including hyperinflation, bitter resentment at the national humiliation of losing the First World War, and longstanding religious divisions in different parts of Germany, brought Hitler and his National Socialist Party to power. Another factor was, once again, the threat of Soviet-style subversion. The German Communist Party had become a potent force during the latter phases of the democratic Weimar Republic; this caused many to mistrust democracy as a safeguard of their interests. It was his party's strong showing in the free parliamentary elections of 1932 that led to Hitler's being appointed Germany's chancellor, the equivalent of prime minister. He quickly did away with the democratic institutions that had allowed his rise to power and began systematic persecutions, not only of political opponents but also of minority groups such as Jews, Romani, homosexuals, and the mentally and physically disabled. The Nazis directed their most extreme hatred at the Jews, who unlike the other targeted minorities had been politically active, culturally prominent, and therefore disproportionately powerful. They were easy scapegoats for the economic downturn that Hitler had promised to remedy.

The arts policies of the Nazis were motivated by the same horridly racial and ethnic biases as their political policies. Arts censorship applied Nazi race theory to art. Insofar as their aesthetics had a theory, it followed a pseudoscientific one of "degeneracy," which condemned as pathological whatever the German leadership opposed. In 1937 the government sponsored a huge exhibition in Munich of otherwise-banned Modern art under the title *Entartete Kunst* (Degenerate Art), which was followed the next year by a somewhat smaller exhibition in Düsseldorf called *Entartete Musik*. The cover of the catalogue depicted a deliberately ape-like caricature of the blackface title character from Ernst Krenek's *Jonny spielt auf*, the wildly popular Zeitoper of a decade earlier (Fig. 32-9).

The Degenerate Music exhibition contained a list of banned Jewish musicians, including a few who were either mistakenly or deliberately made honorary Jews for the occasion: Alexander Glazunov, Maurice Ravel, Erik Satie, and Camille Saint-Saëns. (Krenek was listed as Jewish by marriage.) Due to his Russian heritage,

Figure 32-9 Cover to the catalogue for the exhibition *Entartete Musik* (Degenerate Music), 1938.

Stravinsky was assumed to be a foe of the Nazis, something the composer himself vehemently denied, pointing out to his German publisher that his "ancestors were members of the Polish nobility."[24] Quite different was the reaction of Béla Bartók, who withdrew from concertizing in Germany after 1933. Because he was a citizen of Hungary, an ally of Germany, he was believed to be a friend of the regime and therefore left out of the *Entartete Musik* exhibit. He protested his exemption. As these examples show, for the Nazis the first question about a work of art was never: What does it say? It was, rather: Who is speaking, friend or foe? Such inconsistencies were common in German political life; one prominent Nazi official allegedly stated "I decide who is a Jew."

Countless Jewish musicians perished in Nazi concentration camps. None of them had reached unusual fame before their death, although some composers who had been labeled as degenerate at the time were discovered posthumously, and their works, including pieces actually written while in confinement, were published. The Czech composer Erwin Schulhoff (1894–1942), who combined avant-garde techniques with jazz, died at a concentration camp in Wülzburg. The most extensive musical activity was associated with Terezín (Theresienstadt in German). Located near Prague, it became a way station for thousands of Jews before they were deported to extermination camps such as Auschwitz.

Although there is a real danger in romanticizing a situation of tragic upheaval and confinement that usually led to death, one nonetheless marvels at the creative works produced under such circumstances. Terezín boasted a cultural and intellectual life where artists, academics, and professionals were given a certain amount of freedom in their daily lives. "Boasted" is the right word: The Nazis recognized the beneficial propaganda potential of showcasing prisoners going about a range of "normal" activities. Musical life was particularly rich and prominently featured orchestral, choral, and chamber music and even opera. Some figures, notably Viktor Ullmann (1898–1944), Pavel Haas (1899–1944), and Hans Krása (1899–1944), continued to compose. The youngest among them was Gideon Klein (1919–45), a promising musician who was sent to Terezín in December 1941, just days before his twenty-second birthday. He spent nearly the next three years there, and worked closely with Ullmann, Haas, and other musicians. Klein wrote principally vocal and chamber works both before and during his confinement. Some were experimental, exploring Schoenberg's twelve-tone techniques or microtonal procedures associated with his own teacher, Alois Hába. The pieces he wrote while imprisoned were meant for specific performances and include a piano sonata and string trio. Deported to Auschwitz in October 1944, he died soon after turning twenty-five.

Varieties of Emigration

By the mid-1930s many of the most prominent German and Austrian musicians had fled Europe. Some, like Jews or Communists, had to do so, for remaining would have been fatal, as it proved for the composers at Terezín. Schoenberg, formerly an ardent German cultural chauvinist, who defiantly reconverted to the Hebrew faith of his ancestors in Paris in 1933, went to the United States, where he spent his last seventeen years. Most of those fleeing fascism came to America, "driven into paradise," as Schoenberg put it.[25] Other forced émigré musicians included Kurt Weill, Hanns Eisler, and Erich Wolfgang Korngold; noted conductors Bruno Walter and Otto Klemperer; and the philosopher and music aesthetician T. W. Adorno. Many leading German scientists, scholars, and professors, including eminent musicologists, also ended up in the United States. American cultural and academic life was thus enormously enriched by Germany's brain drain. At the end of the war it found itself home to the greater part of the former European intellectual and artistic elite.

Most of those fleeing fascism came to America, "driven into paradise," as Schoenberg put it.

Bartók, Stravinsky, and Hindemith were also in America at war's end, but they were voluntary émigrés. Bartók was purely a principled exile, a committed anti-Fascist and outspoken opponent of the Nazi regime. He suffered hardships in America, where he was by no means a celebrity. Income from sporadic lectures and performance supplemented a stipend from Columbia University, where he pursued ethnomusicological research in folk music. His health was failing (the diagnosis of leukemia was initially concealed from him), and he composed little.

Serge Koussevitzky, the enterprising conductor of the Boston Symphony Orchestra, offered the reluctant composer a generous commission that resulted in the Concerto for Orchestra, which Bartók wrote quickly in 1943. This dazzling orchestral tour-de-force reflected that he recognized the capabilities of an ensemble like the Boston Symphony. The five movements unfold in an arch shape Bartók favored (ABCBA), with the outer movements in sonata form, scherzos in second and fourth place, all framing the elegiac central movement. He explained in a program note: "The general mood of the work represents, apart from the jesting second movement, a gradual transition from the sternness of the first movement and the lugubrious death-song of the third to the life-assertion of the last one."[26] As in so many works throughout his career, Bartók does not so much quote folk materials as he calls on the style, gestures, and sonority of a wide variety of music that stems from central Europe, including Hungary, Romania, and Slovakia. Koussevitzky premiered the Concerto for Orchestra to great acclaim in December 1944, and the piece immediately brought Bartók welcome attention and new commissions. His writer's block broken, he wrote the Sonata for Solo Violin, the Third Piano Concerto, and sketches for a viola concerto before his death in September 1945.

Anthology Vol 3-40
Full CD VII, 5
Concise CD III, 35

Stravinsky's emigration was more opportunistic than voluntary. At the beginning of the war, he was already in the United States, a guest professor at Harvard University. Although his political sympathies were equivocal to say the least, he decided to remain in America and bought a house in Hollywood, not far from where Schoenberg was living. (Nearby as well were Rachmaninoff, Adorno, Alma Mahler, and other prominent émigrés.) Stravinsky took American citizenship in 1945. The physical proximity of the two great early Modernists did not lead to any lessening of personal and aesthetic tensions between them. During the eleven years that they lived as neighbors they are said to have met only a couple times, by chance.

Before Paul Hindemith (Fig. 32-10) came to America in 1940 he endured some years of what is often called "inner emigration," largely withdrawing from public life after various failed efforts to get in good favor with the regime. Since his scandalous operas of the 1920s (*Neues vom Tage* particularly offended Hitler), he had tempered his style, but the more radical Nazi contingents nonetheless opposed him

Figure 32-10 Paul Hindemith in 1942.

and launched a press campaign to discredit him. That Hindemith had inner emigration on his mind even while still in Germany is evident from his opera *Mathis der Maler* (Matthias the Painter), composed to his own libretto, which he began writing in 1934 and which received its premiere in Switzerland in 1938. A symphony on themes from the opera, also called *Mathis der Maler,* was actually composed earlier. Ostensibly the opera deals with the life and times of Matthias Grünewald, a famous fifteenth-century German religious painter. In so doing, the work depicts an artist who retreats, spiritually wounded, from the turbulent world of contemporary politics—a world replete with class warfare and book burnings—into the timeless world of art. It offers an allegory of the composer's own inner emigration.

By October 1936 Hindemith's works were entirely banned, and he began to think of leaving Germany; he immigrated with his half-Jewish wife to Switzerland and in 1940 moved to America. He taught at Yale University and elsewhere, performed, and continued composing. He produced some influential theoretical books that complemented his lifelong activities as a distinguished teacher. His works from this time often show an interest in counterpoint and exploring abstract musical issues, an aesthetic oasis for Shostakovich and other composers around the same time. We see this in Hindemith's series of fugues and interludes that he eventually decided to call *Ludus tonalis,* subtitled "Studies in Counterpoint, Tonal Organization, and Piano Playing." The once-brash young composer, now no less brilliant musically, had mellowed.

Youth Culture

An irony in Hindemith's case is that much of his professional project, specifically, his writing music understandable to the average listener and his commitment to music education, was congruent with Nazi policy, even if he arrived at it independently. The one who filled this role to the hilt was Carl Orff (1895–1982), the only German composer to achieve international eminence during the Nazi years and the only one whose music—or at least one work—survives in the international repertory. That lone work is *Carmina Burana* (1936), a "scenic cantata" based on "Goliard" poems, that is, Latin poems by German clerics and students of the late Middle Ages that lustily celebrated the vagabond life (Fig. 32-11). Orff grouped the texts into "scenes" based on their subject matter: songs of nature, love, drinking, and so forth. The music is full of simple diatonic melodies in a vaguely antique (modal or at least "leading-toneless") style and driven by vigorous, unyielding ostinatos. The opening number ("O Fortuna"), which returns as the finale, sets the tone. Although written out in full, it is a strophic song in three stanzas (the first a bit truncated, the last somewhat embellished) to a tune that until the final melisma uses only the first five degrees of a D minor scale (Ex. 32-1). It is Orff's own melody, though it is meant to sound like an authentic Medieval tune.

Anthology Vol 3-41
Full CD VII, 6–8

Carmina Burana, scored for three soloists, three choruses, and a huge orchestra, including five percussionists, presents a streamlined populist adaptation of Stravinsky's neoprimitivist manner, which made it appealing to a wide audience. Stravinsky, whose music was by this time banned again in Nazi Germany because he was an "enemy national" living in the United States, dismissed Orff's imitations of his own youthful style, calling it "Neo-Neanderthal."[27] (More recently it has been described as "pop Gothic.") In its insistent simplicities and its hypnotic rhythmic monotony, Orff's music, which so effectively roused primitive, unreflective enthusiasm in millions, seemed to invite its listeners, to put it as Hitler did, to "think with their blood" instead of their brains.

Example 32-1 Carl Orff, *Carmina Burana*: No. 1, "O Fortuna," mm. 5–16

[O Fortune, like the moon you are changeable], ever waxing and waning;
hateful life first oppresses and then soothes [as fancy takes it]

After the premiere of *Carmina Burana* in 1937, at which a certain amount of unofficial discomfort was expressed at the frank sexual innuendoes, the popularity

Figure 32-11 Stage design for the premiere of Carl Orff's *Carmina Burana* at the Frankfurt am Main Opera House, 1937.

of the work won official approval as a display piece celebrating Nazi "youth culture." Although some dismissed *Carmina Burana* with high-Modernist snobbery, the public greeted the simple music for its infectiousness and its ability to bond an audience in the spirit of *Gemeinschaft*, or "community." Defenders of Orff could remind his critics that Nazis and totalitarians were not the only ones who had called for art to fulfill a communitarian aim and carry a social message. In Weimar Germany, Weill and Eisler, not to mention Bertolt Brecht, had made a similar appeal from the political left and might well have welcomed music like Orff's had it been set to a different sort of text.

Orff's orgiastic and paganistic cantata and subsequent works in which he attempted to recreate the success were embraced as part of the propaganda war the Nazi Party was waging, and beginning in 1940 it was performed at Party and government functions. The enduring popularity of Orff's cantata since the war, both inside and outside of Germany, raises a question: whether the origin or original context of an artwork has a decisive bearing on its interpretation or its effect, or whether a work like *Carmina Burana* can now be enjoyed "innocently," devoid of any historical context. Orff's continued fame also led to postwar debates as to whether difficult Modernist art, insofar as it is so much less easily exploited for evil political purposes, might after all be morally superior to "accessible" art. (Whatever Schoenberg may have been, he was no rabble-rouser.)

These are hard questions. One of the things that makes them so is the fact that they cannot be answered simply on the basis of the composer's intention. Nothing that has been said about Orff's work is evidence of his own political beliefs. After the war, like most Germans, he said that he had been opposed to the Hitler regime. The present discussion has not accused him of Nazism, just as the discussion of Respighi made no claims about his personal commitment to Mussolini's policies. Were it established that Orff was anti-Nazi and Respighi anti-Fascist, the information would be relevant to their biographies but not of decisive import in interpreting their works, which left their hands the moment they were performed and have in any case outlived them. The question of political meaning is much less one about intention than about reception at a given time—and over time.

But neither intention nor reception alone can be decisive. If an author's intention were the sole criterion for evaluating his work, Wagner's *Ring* would surely draw picket lines today (as it does in the state of Israel); and if reception were the sole criterion, then Bruckner symphonies would draw protests, since the Nazis claimed him, along with Wagner, as a spiritual forerunner. In any case, musical life in Nazi Germany continued to function at a high professional level, as recordings from the time attest. The performance traditions that had previously been established for the classics reached new heights under the leading German conductor of the day, Wilhelm Furtwängler (1886–1954). While Toscanini was highly praised for his precision, his German counterpart was predictably acclaimed for his spiritual depth.

The question of political meaning is much less one about intention than about reception at a given time—and over time.

Since the Second World War it has been much more difficult to claim that exposure to the greatest masterpieces of art is inherently ennobling. The Germans continued to be sincere and discriminating lovers of the finest music all through the period of Nazi atrocity. During the Third Reich a rich musical life did not inhibit the prevailing barbarism of the period in any way. In this sad observation may unexpectedly lie Orff's best defense, for if Bach and Beethoven could not prevent Nazi barbarity, it is hard to claim that the likes of Orff could have inspired it.

Shades of Gray: Hartmann, Webern, and Strauss

We have seen that emigration had its degrees and nuances. The most honorable case of inner emigration among composers who remained in Germany was that of the Munich composer Karl Amadeus Hartmann (1905–63). By the time of the Nazi takeover, he had already made a name for himself with a few piano and chamber pieces of a "new-objective" character, but from 1933 to 1945 not a note of his music was played in Germany. The financially independent composer continued to write, however, "for the drawer." He produced three of his eight symphonies during the war in a newly subjective, neo-Romantic style, all of them bitterly lamenting or protesting pieces at a time when official Nazi art, like all totalitarian art, was invincibly optimistic.

In the fall of 1942, Hartmann traveled to Vienna and took lessons from Webern, but he never adopted the twelve-tone technique. By then Schoenberg had already been living in America for nearly a decade, and Berg had been dead for seven years. Webern might himself be considered another inner emigrant, withdrawing as he did from his adverse surroundings into a purer world of art and scholarship. From the time of the German annexation of Austria in 1938 until his unlucky death, on 15 September 1945, in the aftermath of the German defeat (accidently shot by an American soldier during the course of a raid on his home due to his son-in-law's black-market activities), Webern was shut out of public musical life. He subsisted on private lessons and a small pension. He continued to compose for the drawer at his very slow, devoted pace, completing his three last compositions (Variations for Orchestra, Op. 30, and two Cantatas, Opp. 29 and 31) in the early 1940s.

The irony in Webern's case is that he expressed considerable enthusiasm for Hitler and much of the Nazi program. When Hartmann found this out in 1942 he cut short his studies with him. Webern was unable to grasp the fact that the music to which he was committed was considered "degenerate." He persisted in the belief that the historical inevitability of twelve-tone music paralleled the historical inevitability of Nazism, that both were the fruits of German greatness, and that eventually he (or someone) would be able "to convince the Hitler regime of the rightness of the twelve-tone system."[28] And, in fact, there were a few officially tolerated twelve-tone composers in the Third Reich, most notably Winfried Zillig (1905–63), a former pupil of Schoenberg's, and Paul von Klenau (1883–1946).

And then there was Richard Strauss. Yes, he was still alive, active, and writing music that has ultimately proved to be the most enduring German contribution from the 1940s if measured in terms of performances, recordings, and acclaim. Yet, at least in various stylistic respects, some of these pieces could have been written sixty years earlier, in the 1880s. We will remember that after some twenty years as a maximal Modernist, Strauss changed course around 1911, the year his friend Mahler died. He concentrated for the next three decades on writing operas, with works such as *Die Frau ohne Schatten* (The Woman without a Shadow, 1919), *Die ägyptische Helena* (The Egyptian Helen, 1928), and *Arabella* (1933). His image was tarnished by a brief term from 1933 to 1935 as president of the German *Reichsmusikkammer*, the State Music Bureau. It was largely his interest in revising royalty laws and in lengthening the term of copyright for composers that induced Strauss to accept this bureaucratic post. His collaboration offered the Nazis the most potent musical insurance they could acquire against the charge of barbarism, while Strauss hoped he would return to being the central figure in German musical life.

Strauss's daily existence became increasingly difficult in the early 1940s as he endured various indignities and distresses, some because his daughter-in-law was Jewish; she and his two grandchildren were repeatedly threatened. As he approached age eighty, Strauss grew depressed and, at the suggestion of friends and family, took comfort in composing. He wrote essentially private works, scored mostly not for the enormous orchestras of the earlier tone poems and operas but, rather, for intimate ensembles. Some of them look back nostalgically to pieces he had written at the very beginning of his career. Strauss himself affected to belittle these works as just something to do "so that the wrist does not become too stiff and the mind prematurely senile."[29] He declared them "without an iota of music-historical significance" and was utterly unconcerned with breaking new ground. He did not give them opus numbers, viewing his last opera, *Capriccio* (1941), as his official farewell. (His next piece, he quipped, would be "scored for harps.")[30] The Second Horn Concerto, two sonatinas for winds (subtitled "From an Invalid's Workshop" and "The Happy Workshop"), a Duet-Concertino for Clarinet and Bassoon with String Orchestra and Harp, an Oboe Concerto, and *Metamorphosen for 23 Strings* are the major instrumental compositions from his final years.

Metamorphosen (1944–45) is a monument to Strauss's despair at the destruction of German cultural ideals and monuments and contains references to two of Germany's giants: Beethoven and Goethe. The musical core of the work is derived from the funeral march of the *Eroica* Symphony, which Strauss quotes at the very end, writing in the score: *IN MEMORIAM!* The composer had immersed himself at this time in the complete works of Goethe, his favorite author.[31] The destruction of the poet's house and the bombing of other cultural landmarks had been particularly painful: "I am in a mood of despair," Strauss wrote to a friend on 2 March 1945. "The Goethe house, the world's greatest sanctuary, destroyed! My beautiful Dresden, Weimar, Munich—all gone!"[32] The Munich house in which Strauss was born and the opera theaters in which his operas premiered were obliterated or damaged. "My life's work is in ruins," he stated.[33]

As a great composer for voice—of songs and operas—and married to a singer, it is appropriate that Strauss ended his career with ethereal Lieder scored for soprano and orchestra, which his publisher released posthumously as *Four Last Songs*. In these works, dating from 1946–48, he turned to the Romantic poet Joseph Eichendorff for *Im Abendrot* (Evening's Glow) and to the contemporary writer Hermann Hesse for *Frühling* (Spring), and *September*, and *Beim Schlafengehen* (Going to Sleep). The longest of the set, *Im Abendrot*, opens with an orchestral introduction that recalls the composer's Romantic past. As the voice discreetly enters there is a solo violin passage that evokes a passage from *Ein Heldenleben* (1897–98) in which Strauss had painted a musical portrait of his wife, Pauline. The song—and Strauss's career—ends with a quotation from *Death and Transfiguration*, one of his symphonic poems written sixty years earlier, accompanying the words "can this then be death?"

Strauss's last works are filled with a deep and personal (some might say self-involved) nostalgia for an earlier, now-lost world in the wake of enormous devastation. How aware he was of the extent of the barbarism around him is disputed. The millions murdered in the death camps, bombed in the cities, or killed on the fields of battle did not have the luxury of such cultural nostalgia. In the wake of such stark realizations, much of art, at least much of the music we will consider in Chapter 34, moved decisively away from subjective expression or political engagement. First, however, we must look at musical developments of the 1940s in America and Allied Europe. There the political engagement was often no less prominent than what we have seen arise in totalitarian systems. The fundamental difference was that, rather than being coerced from above, this engagement arose from other kinds of convictions.

Summary

This chapter surveyed the music composed and performed under totalitarian regimes in the Soviet Union, Italy, and Germany in the 1930s and '40s. Joseph Stalin (1878–1953) came into power in the Soviet Union in 1924, following the death of the first Soviet leader Vladimir Ilyich Lenin. Beginning in 1932, the government assumed complete control over the arts, promoting the doctrine of Socialist Realism. Under this policy, the arts were supposed to be accessible to all and preferably rooted in folklore. In practice, the doctrine forced artists to work under extreme control and censorship.

The career of Dmitry Shostakovich (1906–75) illustrates the difficulty of these circumstances and their impact on music. With his two operas, fifteen symphonies, and fifteen string quartets, Shostakovich emerged on the world stage as the great Soviet composer. Despite this renown, he was haunted by problems with the authorities. His opera *Lady Macbeth of the Mtsensk District* had successful performances in Leningrad and Moscow in 1934. After Stalin came to see the opera in 1936, however, the official Soviet newspaper *Pravda* condemned it for what it considered vulgarity and degeneracy. On the eve of the Moscow premiere of his Fifth Symphony in 1937, a newspaper article claimed that Shostakovich had characterized the Fifth as a "response to just criticism." Although the Fifth was officially viewed as a recantation of the directions he took with *Lady Macbeth*, some have interpreted its last movement as a coded statement of dissent, noting that its "optimism" seems forced. Because of the repressive climate in which Shostakovich worked, we cannot know his true intentions.

Sergey Prokofiev (1891–1953) returned to the Soviet Union in 1936, having lived abroad since 1918. His seven symphonies, concertos, and stage works reflect a mixture of styles, including maximalism, Neoclassicism, and Russian exoticism. As his ballet *Romeo and Juliet* (1935–36) and several operas show, Prokofiev turned to simpler styles after returning to the Soviet Union. His music for the patriotic film *Alexander Nevsky* (1938), which recounts the victory of Prince Alexander of Novgorod (1220–63) over the Teutonic Knights, illustrates how political circumstances can determine the reception of musical works. Although it was suppressed while Germany and the Soviets were allied (1938–41), both the film and the music were eagerly promoted by the authorities as soon as Hitler invaded the Soviet Union in 1941.

In Nazi Germany, artistic censorship took on a racial component. The Nazis associated Modernist art with Jewishness and condemned it as pathological or "degenerate," even going so far as to feature both Jewish and non-Jewish composers in an exhibition of degenerate music. The Italian dictator Benito Mussolini (1883–1945) was less inclined than Stalin to impose censorship on the arts. Mussolini valued the precise, correct performances exemplified by conductor Arturo Toscanini (1867–1957), himself an opponent of the Fascist government.

European composers reacted to totalitarian forces in various ways. Many, including Arnold Schoenberg, Béla Bartók, Igor Stravinsky, and Paul Hindemith, emigrated to the United States. Others withdrew from public life, a form of "inner emigration." Hindemith's opera *Mathis der Maler*, written before he left for the United States, depicts the artistic isolation of the painter Matthias Grünewald, reflecting alienation from the political forces around him. Carl Orff (1895–1982), Anton Webern, and Richard Strauss remained in Germany during the Nazi era. Orff's *Carmina Burana* was hailed by the Nazis as a celebration of youth culture and used as propaganda. Strauss's late works were in a retrospective style, suggesting nostalgia for prewar times.

Study Questions

1. What was Socialist Realism?
2. Describe the sequence of historical events that led to the suppression of Soviet artists in the 1930s. Why are Dmitry Shostakovich's opera *Lady Macbeth of the Mtsensk District* and his Fifth Symphony such important works in the history of Soviet censorship?

3. Describe the debate over whether Shostakovich was a dissident or a collaborator. How and why do these different views influence the way you hear his Fifth Symphony?
4. What types of works did Sergey Prokofiev write after returning to the Soviet Union? Discuss his music for the film *Alexander Nevsky* as an example of the ways that political circumstances can influence the reception of a work.
5. Why was instrumental music favored over opera in Mussolini's Italy?
6. Why was Arturo Toscanini such an important figure in the history of twentieth-century music? What was his contribution to the history of performance?
7. In what ways did the Nazi government in Germany mix artistic censorship and racism? What kinds of music were promoted in Nazi Germany, and what kinds were considered "degenerate"?
8. How did totalitarian governments and the resulting war influence the lives, careers, and works of the following composers? (a) Ottorino Respighi; (b) Béla Bartók; (c) Arnold Schoenberg; (d) Paul Hindemith; (e) Carl Orff; (f) Anton Webern; (g) Richard Strauss

Key Terms

communism
fascism
mass song
propaganda
Socialist Realism
totalitarianism

33

Music and Politics in America and Allied Europe

In an increasingly interconnected world, the European political cauldron of the 1930s and early 1940s was not so distant from America, where political ferment was also rife in the wake of the Great Depression and where the prospect of communism frightened many citizens (while being attractive to others). The United States remained a source of democratic stability as totalitarian ambitions in Europe led again to war, in 1939. America was itself propelled into the conflict with the Japanese attack on Pearl Harbor in December 1941. Strong leadership and unusually centralized powers marked the presidency from 1933 to 1945 of Franklin Delano Roosevelt (1882–1945). Just as the political climate greatly affected the arts in Western Europe and the Soviet Union, so too did it fundamentally influence cultural life in America.

Before looking at the implications of these heightened politics, an update is in order concerning musical activity in America during the early interwar years, focusing on an experimental impulse through which some composers shook off many long-held European conventions. We have already touched on some currents in Chapter 31 with respect to the Jazz Age and the migration to Paris of young composers, such as Aaron Copland and Virgil Thomson. Although Charles Ives would live for more than thirty more years, it was in the 1920s that poor health led him largely to give up composing. By now a very wealthy man due to his insurance business, he actively supported new music, particularly what was viewed as experimental or what was called at the time "**ultra-modern**" styles.

We have seen how in the late nineteenth and early twentieth centuries American composers associated with the Boston School of composers, figures like John Knowles Paine, George Whitefield Chadwick, and Ives's teacher Horatio Parker had gone to Europe for training, mainly to Berlin and Leipzig, and then perpetuated that training and tradition once back home at Harvard, Yale, and elsewhere. Some younger Americans continued to go to Europe for finishing, although by the 1920s more often it was to France to study with Nadia Boulanger than to Germany. The experimental approach, however, offered a distinctive mission for those Americans less interested in perpetuating older European styles. Partly through Ives's financing and especially in connection with Henry Cowell (1897–1965) and his journal *New Music Quarterly*, a recognizable school of American ultra-moderns came into view, among them Carl Ruggles (1876–1971), Edgard Varèse (1883–1965), Wallingford Riegger (1885–1961), Dane Rudhyar (1895–1985), Ruth Crawford Seeger (1901–1953; Fig. 33-1), and Cowell himself.

Figure 33-1 Ruth Crawford in the 1920s. Photograph by Ferdinand de Gueldre.

Anthology Vol 3-42
Full CD VII, 9
Concise CD III, 36

With the exception of Varèse, these composers tended to share both a technical orientation and an expressive purpose, which like Ives's own may be jointly summed up as transcendental maximalism, employing radical means toward spiritual ends. Rudhyar and Crawford, for example, were drawn to theosophy, and they used their music to convey its occult concepts. The French-born Rudhyar was a practicing astrologer. In 1928 Cowell published a set of preludes by Crawford in *New Music Quarterly*. She composed the sixth in 1927, marking it *Andante mystico* and dedicating it "with deep love and gratitude to Djane [sic], my inspiration."[1] Ruggles wrote relatively little; his largest work is the orchestral fantasy *Sun-Treader*, published by Cowell in 1934.

As for Cowell himself, his earliest and most radical music was written for performance at the Temple of the People, a theosophical colony in Halcyon, California, which the young composer joined in 1916. In his early piano works, he employed extended piano techniques by laying palms, fists, and forearms on the keyboard. The results, called "elbow music" by detractors and "concordances of many close-lying notes" or "secundal harmonies" by their more sympathetic admirers, became celebrated as "**tone clusters**," the term Cowell devised for them in 1921 (Fig. 33-2).[2] Cowell probably discovered this device the way countless children do, and he

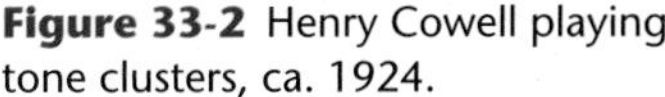

Figure 33-2 Henry Cowell playing tone clusters, ca. 1924.

notated it for the first time in *Adventures in Harmony*. This "novelette" for piano dates from around 1913, when the composer was in his midteens, and was written at the request of his piano teacher, who was a devoted member of the Halcyon temple.

Anthology Vol 3-43
Full CD VII, 10

As the precocious son of an Irish immigrant, Cowell developed an interest in Celtic myths. *The Tides of Manaunaun* (1917), also for piano, consists of a jig-like tune (hence identifiably "Irish"), accompanied by forearm clusters spanning two octaves (Ex. 33-1). This makes for a split-level effect, one hand confined to traditional modes and scales, the other to clusters. Cowell's music often displays a nonchalance with regard to stylistic discrepancy, the mixture of seemingly experimental and familiar techniques.

Example 33-1 Tone Cluster from Henry Cowell, *Tides of Manaunaun* (1917), mm. 18-23

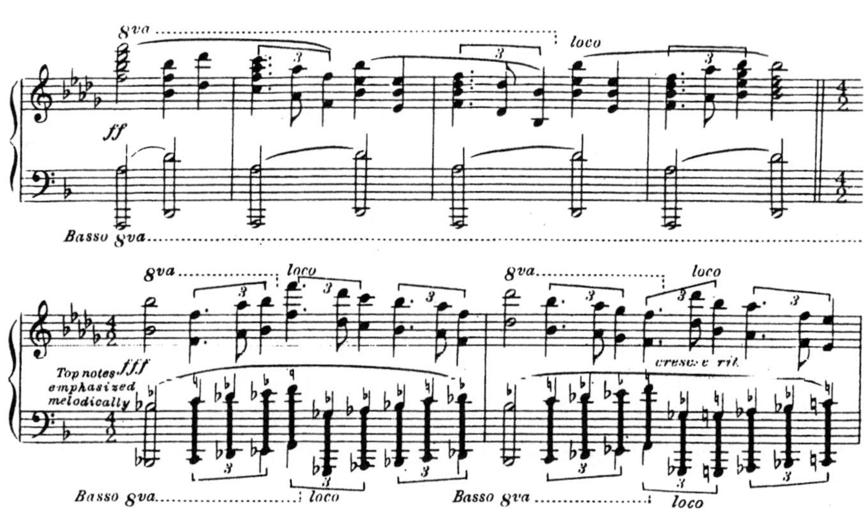

Cowell's experimental inclinations got a boost during a short trip to New York in the fall of 1916, when he met the phenomenally long-lived Leo Ornstein (1893–2002). Ornstein, a young immigrant from Russia, made music that celebrated—or at least was obsessed with—speed, aggression, and the mechanization of modern life. He gave sensational piano recitals involving modestly clustery pieces bearing titles like *Suicide in an Airplane* (1913) and *Wild Men's Dance* (1915). These pieces were at the time the most spectacular American musical responses to the call put out by the Italian Futurists—the *futuristi*—a boisterous group of Italian artists headed by the poet Filippo Tommaso Marinetti (1876–1944) and the painter Luigi Russolo (1885–1947). Their **Futurism** called for an "Art of Noises" that would replace conventional music with more appropriate sonic representations of the machine age. In this spirit (and in friendly competition with Ornstein), Cowell produced *Dynamic Motion* (1916), which at first he announced to audiences as an evocation of the New York subway.

As was also happening in Europe and the Soviet Union at the time, American composers established musical societies and concert series to showcase their music. The Franco-American Musical Society, founded in 1920, changed its name a few

TIMELINE

1917 Henry Cowell, *The Tides of Manaunaun*

1927 Ruth Crawford Seeger, Prelude No. 6

1929 Worldwide stock market crashes; Great Depression begins

1931 Edgard Varèse, *Ionisation*

1933 President Franklin Delano Roosevelt launches New Deal economic programs

1934 John and Alan Lomax, *American Ballads and Folk Songs*

1935 American Communist Party pursues policy of the Popular Front

1937 Spanish Civil War

1938 Aaron Copland, *Billy the Kid*

1939 Roy Harris's Third Symphony premieres

1939 World War II begins

1940–41 Olivier Messiaen, *Quartet for the End of Time*

years later to Pro Musica Society and was based in New York City. In 1921 Varèse helped found the International Composers' Guild, which presented only brand new compositions and became most associated with Ives, Cowell, Ruggles, and Riegger. Some of its members split off in 1923 to form the League of Composers; five years later Varèse founded the Pan American Association of Composers, which promoted new music from all over the Americas and sought to present it in Europe as well (Fig. 33-3). Not long after Copland returned from Paris, he established an innovative concert series with Roger Sessions (1896–1985). All this activity meant that classical musicians in the New World were generating and presenting new worlds of sound.

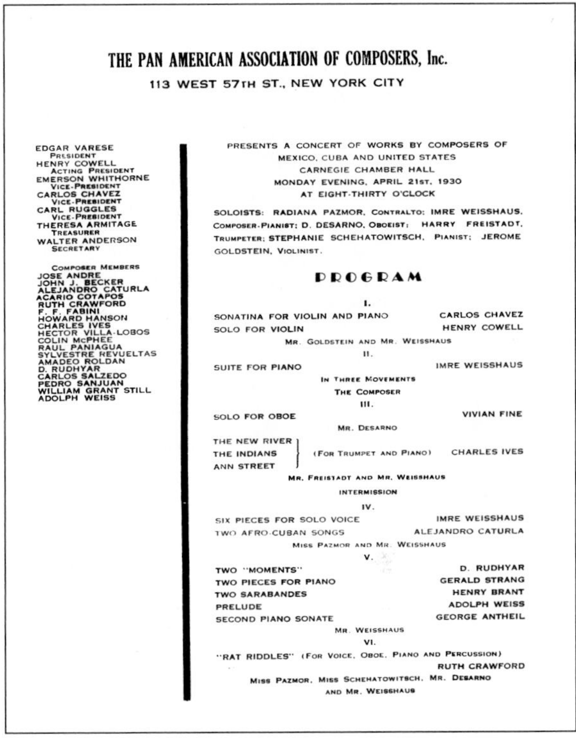
THE PAN AMERICAN ASSOCIATION OF COMPOSERS, Inc.
113 WEST 57TH ST., NEW YORK CITY

EDGAR VARESE
PRESIDENT
HENRY COWELL
ACTING PRESIDENT
EMERSON WHITHORNE
VICE-PRESIDENT
CARLOS CHAVEZ
VICE-PRESIDENT
CARL RUGGLES
VICE-PRESIDENT
THERESA ARMITAGE
TREASURER
WALTER ANDERSON
SECRETARY

COMPOSER MEMBERS
JOSE ANDRE
JOHN J. BECKER
ALEJANDRO CATURLA
ACARIO COTAPOS
RUTH CRAWFORD
F. F. FABINI
HOWARD HANSON
CHARLES IVES
HECTOR VILLA-LOBOS
COLIN McPHEE
RAUL PANIAGUA
SYLVESTRE REVUELTAS
AMADEO ROLDAN
D. RUDHYAR
CARLOS SALZEDO
PEDRO SANJUAN
WILLIAM GRANT STILL
ADOLPH WEISS

PRESENTS A CONCERT OF WORKS BY COMPOSERS OF MEXICO, CUBA AND UNITED STATES
CARNEGIE CHAMBER HALL
MONDAY EVENING, APRIL 21ST, 1930
AT EIGHT-THIRTY O'CLOCK

SOLOISTS: RADIANA PAZMOR, CONTRALTO; IMRE WEISSHAUS, COMPOSER-PIANIST; D. DESARNO, OBOEIST; HARRY FREISTADT, TRUMPETER; STEPHANIE SCHEHATOWITSCH, PIANIST; JEROME GOLDSTEIN, VIOLINIST.

PROGRAM

I.
SONATINA FOR VIOLIN AND PIANO — CARLOS CHAVEZ
SOLO FOR VIOLIN — HENRY COWELL
MR. GOLDSTEIN AND MR. WEISSHAUS

II.
SUITE FOR PIANO — IMRE WEISSHAUS
IN THREE MOVEMENTS
THE COMPOSER

III.
SOLO FOR OBOE — VIVIAN FINE
MR. DESARNO
THE NEW RIVER
THE INDIANS
ANN STREET
(FOR TRUMPET AND PIANO) — CHARLES IVES
MR. FREISTADT AND MR. WEISSHAUS

INTERMISSION

IV.
SIX PIECES FOR SOLO VOICE — IMRE WEISSHAUS
TWO AFRO-CUBAN SONGS — ALEJANDRO CATURLA
MISS PAZMOR AND MR. WEISSHAUS

V.
TWO "MOMENTS" — D. RUDHYAR
TWO PIECES FOR PIANO — GERALD STRANG
TWO SARABANDES — HENRY BRANT
PRELUDE — ADOLPH WEISS
SECOND PIANO SONATE — GEORGE ANTHEIL
MR. WEISSHAUS

VI.
"RAT RIDDLES" (FOR VOICE, OBOE, PIANO AND PERCUSSION) — RUTH CRAWFORD
MISS PAZMOR, MISS SCHEHATOWITSCH, MR. DESARNO AND MR. WEISSHAUS

Figure 33-3 Program for a concert of the Pan American Association of Composers, 21 April 1930 in New York City.

Edgard Varèse

Edgard Varèse (Fig. 33-4) was one of the most active figures in America during the 1920s; he was also one of the century's great musical experimenters. He once remarked that his goal was "the liberation of sound—to throw open the whole world of sound to music."[3] Born in Paris, his family moved to Italy when he was nine. His father made him study mathematics and engineering, but the boy's interests inclined more toward music. At age twenty Varèse returned to Paris, where he studied with Albert Roussel, Vincent d'Indy, and Charles-Marie Widor, among others. In 1907, after reading Ferruccio Busoni's recent and influential *Entwurf einer neuen Ästhetik der Tonkunst* (Sketch of a New Aesthetic of Music), he went to Berlin and sought out the author as a mentor. His upbringing and training meant that he was exposed to and much in sympathy with the Italian Futurists and with Busoni's visionary ideas for new kinds of music. Varèse moved to New York in 1915 and at first tried to make a career as a conductor. His early music has not survived because it was destroyed in a fire at a Berlin warehouse where it was being stored. Although his body of work is small—not much more than a dozen pieces altogether—Varèse eventually exerted considerable influence on certain twentieth-century composers. He wrote most of his surviving pieces in the 1920s and later stopped composing for years as he waited for technology to catch up with his ideas.

His earliest American opus, which he crafted between 1918 and 1921, was a gigantic orchestral score called *Amériques* that Leopold Stokowski premiered with the Philadelphia Orchestra in 1926. The original version called for 140 players and showed the influence of Stravinsky's *The Rite of Spring*, urbanized by the inclusion of two sirens, obviously not a conventional orchestral instrument. Varèse's music of the 1920s and '30s was out of joint with its time. He was nurturing, or trying to nurture, the complementary spirits of neoprimitivism and Futurism, seeking to keep the optimistic "Art of Noises" alive in a period when the defense of high culture favored pessimistic retrenchment. The summit of his musical Futurism was a trio of compositions written in New York that sported titles borrowed from the world of science: *Hyperprism* (1923) and *Intégrales* (1925) were scored for small

1941 The United States enters World War II

1942 **Copland, *Fanfare for the Common Man***

1942 Manhattan Project formed to create the first atomic bomb

1942 Japanese Americans interned in war relocation camps

1945 **Benjamin Britten's *Peter Grimes* premieres**

1945 World War II ends

1946 **Copland's Third Symphony premieres**

1949 **Harry Partch, *Genesis of a Music***

1950–53 Korean War

1962 **Britten, *War Requiem***

Figure 33-4 Edgard Varèse in the early twentieth century.

wind bands with outsized percussion sections; *Ionisation* (1931) was for percussion alone—thirteen players on a total of forty-one instruments.

Ionisation makes easily recognized expressive gestures that aim at a traditionally cathartic emotional effect, a far cry from both the prevalent Neoclassicism and jazz styles of the time. Beginning darkly and quietly, with siren tones of curving pitch and indeterminate flowing expanse, the piece musters increasingly definite rhythms, mounting volume, and a gradually rising range until it reaches a blazing climax that contains the first fixed musical pitches (played by piano, tubular chimes, and glockenspiel) in the piece. This moment seems as if it were the outcome of the electrochemical reaction named in the title.

Not long after writing *Ionisation*, Varèse felt he had exhausted the sources available to him, and between 1934 and 1954 he completed only three relatively insubstantial works. During the 1940s he dropped into obscurity. He was at a technological impasse, imagining a music that could not be realized in actual sound. As early as an essay from 1917, Varèse had written: "I dream of instruments obedient to my thought . . . their contribution to a whole new world of unsuspected sounds, will lend themselves to the exigencies of my inner rhythm."[4] He would resurface later, as we shall see, when technology caught up.

Microtones: Splitting the Semitone

Other composers shared Varèse's desire to experiment. Their activities began to raise questions in some listeners' minds as to whether what was being produced was music at all, an issue we will see most starkly in the next chapter with regard to the career of the leading midcentury American experimentalist, John Cage. The American experimental tradition led not only to new sounds and the use of unconventional instruments (such as sirens) but also to the invention of entirely new instruments as well as to the exploration of new and unusual tuning systems, such as those using microtones. **Microtones** are commonly defined as pitch differences smaller than a half step, the interval that has functioned in official music theory since the days of Medieval chant. Thus for centuries the half step was viewed as the inviolable musical atom, the smallest pitch discrimination treated as meaningful in ordinary musical discourse. Once the twelve-tone, equal-tempered chromatic scale had become the standard, the most common way of conceptually splitting this atom was to imagine it divided evenly by two, into **quarter tones**.

Composers and theorists had experimented with different tunings going back for centuries, and such tunings are commonly encountered in non-Western music. We have already mentioned the related phenomenon of blue notes in jazz, which similarly rely on microtonality, although in an unfixed, unnotated way. But ever since the sixteenth century, there have been musicians dedicated to "just intonation"—a natural tuning system they thought more capable of producing true emotional catharsis than the equal temperament associated with the modern piano. New composition according to just-intonation principles blossomed in the twentieth century. Busoni, in his *Sketch for a New Aesthetic of Music*, had theorized the possibility of something really new: music based on a tripartite rather than a binary division of the tone (third-tones rather than semitones). He made no move, however, toward implementing the scheme.

One of the earliest experimenters in the field was Julián Carrillo (1875–1965), a Mexican composer who in the mid-1890s began research into what he called the "sonido trece" (thirteenth sound) system, involving successive splits of the semitone into quarters, eighths, and sixteenths of a tone. Carrillo's stance with regard to microtonality was uncompromising. It required an investment in instruments, a new system of notation, and the pitiless sacrifice of common practice. Two other composers who started publishing their work in the 1920s were Alois Hába (1893–1973), a Czech, and Ivan Wyschnegradsky (1893–1979), a Russian émigré living in Paris, both of whom experimented with nontraditional tunings.

Charles Ives claimed that his father experimented with quarter tones by rigging up various microtonal contraptions—such as a box of violin strings with weights attached—to overcome the limitations of arbitrary theory. As Ives observed, we hear microtones whenever we listen to nonmusical sounds, for they exist in unlimited unordered profusion in the world of nature. A music that incorporated microtones would thus be, in the pantheistic Transcendentalist view, a more natural and universal music.

Anthology Vol 3-44
Full CD VII, 11

Ives's involvement with microtones is most obvious in his *Three Quarter-Tone Pieces* (1923–24) for two pianos tuned a quarter tone apart. The work may be viewed with equal justice as Ives's ultimate nostalgic tribute to his father and to the homespun Yankee-tinker aesthetic he loved to effect or as a rare instance in which Ives was acting as a full-fledged member of the current avant-garde, contributing to what was at the time a modest vogue. Although based to some typically indeterminable extent on old sketches, the pieces were among the last Ives wrote. His solution to the instrument problem was eminently practical, in that it did not require the invention of any new ones. The score presupposes that the first piano is tuned a quarter tone sharp. (Since no reputable piano tuner will agree to put so much extra stress on the instrument's mechanism, in practice the second piano is tuned flat.) Olin Downes, music critic of the *New York Times*, dismissed the results, saying simply "that the music sounded a good deal out of tune."[5]

The American experimental tradition led not only to new sounds and the use of unconventional instruments (such as sirens) but also to the invention of entirely new instruments as well as to the exploration of new and unusual tuning systems.

New Sounds, New Instruments, New Tunings

Another American to become interested in tuning systems was Harry Partch (1901–74; Fig. 33-5), who devised a forty-three-interval scale for which he invented a large instrumental ensemble. He once described himself rather acerbically as a "musician seduced into carpentry," and in so doing he pinpointed the gravest problem experimenters with nonstandard tunings faced before the spread of electronics: that of practical hardware, instruments that could reliably make the sounds they imagined or dreamed of.[6] Partch was as close to a total maverick or alternative figure as the history of music can provide. He not only talked the talk of a maverick; he walked the walk as well: For a while during the depths of the Great Depression in the mid-1930s he was a "hobo," homeless and wandering through America. A diary he kept during this period, published posthumously under the title *Bitter Music*, shows him translating his social alienation into an artistic program. Four pieces, gathered up into a collection called *The Wayward*, constitute a unique panorama of Depression-era life, with titles like *Barstow: Eight Hitchhiker Inscriptions from a Highway Railing at Barstow, California*

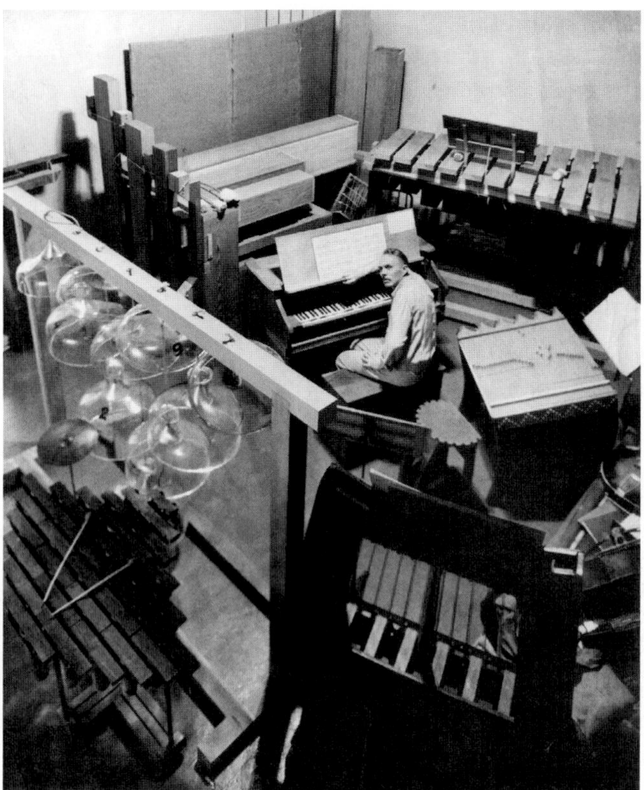

Figure 33-5 Harry Partch surrounded by his instruments, 1952.

(1941, revised 1968), *U.S. Highball: A Musical Account of a Transcontinental Hobo Trip* (1943, revised 1955), and *The Letter: A Depression Message from a Hobo Friend* (1943, revised 1972).

Inspired by his resentments, Partch turned his back on the entire tradition of Western music after the ancient Greeks—its tuning systems, its instruments, its conventional notations, its social practices, its customary concert hall venues—and sought to reinvent them all. His book *Genesis of a Music: An Account of a Creative Work, Its Roots and Its Fulfillments* (1949, enlarged 1974) contained a detailed and mathematically sophisticated treatise on his tuning system and a description, replete with photographs, of the numerous imaginatively designed, visually beautiful, and skillfully built instruments he had had to make in order to provide the unequally tempered tones that his modal theories demanded.

Other American experimentalists included the eclectic Lou Harrison (1917–2003), a student of Cowell's who likewise constructed new instruments in collaboration with his lifelong partner, William Colvig; his innovative music often used just intonation and microtonality and looked to non-Western cultures. Canadian-born Henry Brant (1913–2008) experimented with collage effects, new instruments, and the distribution of sound sources in musical space (sometimes referred to as the spatialization of sound). His *Music for a Five and Dime Store* (1932) is scored for violin, piano, and kitchen hardware. Another Canadian composer lived far from the fray: Colin McPhee (1900–64), who found his inspiration in the gamelan ensembles from the island of Bali in Indonesia, where he spent most of the 1930s. He wrote an important book on the music of Bali and composed works that, if not as extreme as those by some of the figures already mentioned, nonetheless incorporated fresh sounds and instrumentation as well as new approaches to rhythm. The preoccupation with rhythm is also apparent in the music of Conlon Nancarrow (1912–97), a committed Communist who fought in the Spanish Civil War. Disillusioned with American politics, he moved in 1940 to Mexico, where he eventually became a citizen. He produced a formidable series of more than fifty extravagantly elaborate studies for player piano; he meticulously punched holes in long piano rolls that allowed him to create intricate works unplayable by a human pianist.

In the case of some of these adventurous North Americans, beginning with Ives, their music was discovered (or rediscovered) relatively late in the composers' lives or only posthumously. As experimentalists, they tended to exist outside the traditional sphere of mainstream concert life associated with chamber music societies, symphony orchestras, and opera companies. Starting in the 1970s, recordings and a growing interest in the experimental tradition brought greater recognition of their achievements. Nancarrow was awarded a MacArthur Foundation "genius" fellowship in 1982, and celebrations marking milestone anniversaries helped some of these composers make up for former obscurity.

The experimental impulse, at first a seemingly viable American contribution to Modern music distinct from Europe, by the 1940s lost some steam for a while. Some composers worked in isolation (Nancarrow and McPhee) or generally stopped writing (Ives and Varèse). Others, like Cowell, "retreated" to a more conservative style, for which reason the works they wrote during this time are often taken less than seriously by those historians who principally value experimentation and innovation. Some of the radicals changed their ideals as the practicalities of life became more challenging in hard economic times. But there also emerged, for understandable reasons, a new desire on the part of many artists to reach and engage a larger audience. Politics—world politics, not just the specialized artistic politics of competing composers and warring musical societies—came to dominate musical life in America, as we have already seen it was doing in Western Europe and the Soviet Union.

Ferment on the American Left

The Great Depression demanded not the hustle and "metropolitan madness" (as Gershwin called it) that had characterized the Roaring Twenties or the experimentation of the ultra-moderns but, rather, a music that could sustain faith with eloquence.[7] A new national image began to take hold of the arts in America in the early 1930s, and by the end of the decade mounting fears about the war in Europe led to increased populist patriotism.

There was also the broadening international reach of communism, which came out of the Soviet Union. In an attempt to unite the left against the rise of German fascism and thereby promote the security of the Soviet Union, Communist parties throughout the world were instructed to form alliances and coalitions with more moderate, nonrevolutionary progressive groups and to shift their focus from international working-class solidarity to patriotic resistance against the fascist threat. A large number of song anthologies appeared, including two volumes of "mass songs" issued in 1934 and 1935 under the title the *Workers' Song Book*. This was part of an overall policy announced in 1935 known as the **Popular Front**. To achieve their aims, Communist parties would soft-pedal their political radicalism and international ties, especially to the USSR, and emphasize their indigenous roots. The American Communist Party had a relatively easy task implementing such directives because the Popular Front could draw directly on the revolutionary founding myth of the United States. Particularly effective were "revolutionary" quotations from the founding fathers and above all from Abraham Lincoln, who had achieved mythic status as the Great Emancipator.

A significant musical consequence was that the 1930s in the United States witnessed a renewed interest in white folklore. Folk music was adopted, and often radically adapted, as agitation and propaganda on behalf of the labor movements of farmers and workers, those who were most sorely affected by the Depression. Folk music, increasingly regarded as the product of an American "proletariat," was performed as an adjunct to progressive political action. Research was done by Charles Seeger (1886–1979), a minor composer but a distinguished musicologist; his second wife, the ultra-modernist Ruth Crawford, wrote some leftist songs and fashioned many folk song settings; and his son Pete would go on to be a celebrated folk singer.

John A. Lomax revised his classic anthology *Cowboy Songs and Other Frontier Ballads* (1910) in 1938 in collaboration with his son, Alan Lomax (1915–2002), who went on to become the century's foremost collector of such American songs. Their *American Ballads and Folk Songs* (1934) followed the example of the original Lomax publication by furnishing piano accompaniments as an aid to popularization. Also collected was Southern Baptist hymnody, or "Sacred Harp" singing, popularized by the literary historian George Pullen Jackson, who sought to minimize the African American roots of spirituals.[8] A collection based on early published sources was S. Foster Damon's *Series of Old American Songs* (1936), which presented in reproduction 100 American folk and popular songs written before the Civil War. Olin Downes and Eilie Siegmeister's *A Treasury of American Song* (1940) became the basis for a Broadway musical, *Sing Out Sweet Land!* (1944). By then, white rural folk song had become an integral part of American popular culture, no longer associated exclusively with the political left. The original radical intent behind a dustbowl song like Woody Guthrie's "This Land Is Your Land, This Land Is My Land" (1940), had morphed into a feel-good hymn for the nation.

The original radical intent behind a dustbowl song like Woody Guthrie's "This Land Is Your Land, This Land Is My Land" (1940), had morphed into a feel-good hymn for the nation.

The folk music revival of the 1930s did not immediately affect the composition of concert music. At first, composers with leftist inclinations modeled their activity on that of their German counterparts, figures such as Kurt Weill and Hanns Eisler. Marc Blitzstein (1905–64), the most notable example, studied with Nadia Boulanger in Paris and briefly with Schoenberg in Berlin, where he heard Weill and Brecht's *Die Dreigroschenoper* in its first production. (Blitzstein's translation of *The Threepenny Opera* later played in New York.) Encouraged by the exiled Brecht, whom he met in New York in 1935, Blitzstein wrote *The Cradle Will Rock* (1936–37), a "play in music" in ten scenes to his own libretto. Its combination of entertainment and political diatribe was intended to persuade middle-class audiences to join the class struggle on the side of the proletariat.[9]

Aaron Copland and Politics

Aaron Copland was among the composers most influenced by this folk music activity, which merged well with his leftist politics. After his abortive jazz experiments of the mid-1920s, he had been writing in an abstractly Modernist and decidedly urban idiom. By the mid-1930s political commitment and increasing populist inclinations began to come to the fore in his music as well as in his life. During the summer of 1934 he made an impromptu speech on behalf of Communist politicians in Minnesota, and in 1936 he supported the Communist presidential ticket. Copland composed a one-act ballet called *Hear Ye! Hear Ye!* (1934) that satirizes an obviously corrupt American courtroom. He also wrote a mass song called *Into the Streets May First*, which won a Communist-sponsored contest for the best setting of a poem for May Day, the international workers' holiday. The song shows Copland addressing the problem of how to achieve an appropriate style for proletarian art. He strove to maintain a striking modern idiom, full of unexpected modulations and pungent harmonies, while still staying within the capacities of amateur performers. He also increasingly became a spokesman for classical music by addressing general audiences. His book *What to Listen for in Music* (1939) proved to be a best seller.

By the end of the decade Copland's folklorism was reaching its peak. It exerted its maximum impact on the American musical mainstream in three ballets composed between 1938 and 1944, works that finally made him the exemplary American composer, the commonly accepted, if not quite undisputed, standard-bearer of musical Americanism. *Billy the Kid* (1938) has a scenario by impresario Lincoln Kirstein,

Anthology Vol 3-45
Full CD VII, 12–13
Concise CD III, 37

who commissioned the work and emerged as a sort of American Diaghilev. The ballet portrays the title character, a notorious New Mexico cattle rustler and murderer, in his legendary light as a Robin Hood figure and relates his violent death in 1881 at the hands of a former friend turned lawman. Copland mined the contents of several anthologies of cowboy songs Kirstein gave him for this ballet "Western." His second ballet also looked to cowboys and the Wild West: *Rodeo*, commissioned in 1942 by choreographer Agnes de Mille, complete with square dancing and familiar folk tunes that often appear recognizably in their entirety. Copland's Americanist style reached its fullest development in the third ballet, *Appalachian Spring* (1944), which won the Pulitzer Prize. He composed it for the eminent choreographer Martha Graham (1894–1991) and included a set of variations on the Shaker song "Simple Gifts," which became something of an emblem for Copland's accessible yet technically sophisticated manner (Fig. 33-6).

These ballets offered listener-friendly music and thus could be said to keep faith with the Popular Front's call for a music that resisted the complications of the Modernism with which Copland had formerly been associated. To an extent unmatched by any of his contemporaries, Copland succeeded in maintaining both stylistic individuality and a high level of interesting technical detail, two prime Modernist values, yet without compromising the naturalness and easy comprehensibility of his new style. In his hands, the new simplicity seemed an innovation, or at least a radical departure. The reasons for that freshness of effect are elusive, but some of them can perhaps be accounted for in terms of voicing (i.e., chord spacing) and orchestration, while others seem to reflect a flair for the nationalist assimilation of folklore at a very basic level of style (which, as we recall, was the secret of Stravinsky, Bartók, Falla, and others).

Copland was an Americanist in the largest sense, much drawn at first to Mexico and later to South America. Even before his three celebrated ballets, he had written *El Salón México* (1932–36), named after the most famous dance hall in Mexico City, in which he used popular tunes he had found in two published collections. Mexico's leading musician, Carlos Chávez (1899–1978), conducted the premiere in the capital in August 1937. Chávez was a kindred spirit who became a good friend. Like Copland, he was a composer, organizer, conductor, educator, and writer. The two had met in New York City a decade earlier, and Copland first visited Mexico in 1932 at his invitation. Copland was immediately attracted to the socialist aspects of Mexican politics and wrote in a letter to Chávez: "When I was in Mexico I was a little envious of the opportunity you had to serve your country in a musical way. Here in the U.S.A. we composers have no possibility of directing the musical affairs of the nation—on the contrary, since my return, I have the impression that more and more we are working in a vacuum."[10]

Figure 33-6 Martha Graham performs her signature dance, *Appalachian Spring*, 1944.

Copland's many visits to Central and South America, usually on trips sponsored by the U.S. State Department, were a source of inspiration for some of his own music, and he in turn inspired composers whom he met there. The artistic fruits that came in the aftermath of the Mexican Revolution starting in 1910 are

Figure 33-7 Frida Kahlo, *Self-Portrait on the Border Between Mexico and the United States*, 1932.

probably best known today through the art and writings of Diego Rivera, Frida Kahlo, Octavio Paz, and Rosario Castellanos (Fig. 33-7). Music also enjoyed a new flowering in works by composers such as Chávez, his teacher Manuel Ponce (1882–1948), and his colleague Silvestre Revueltas (1899–1940). Like Copland, Chávez and Revueltas were able to combine trends of European Modernism, such as Stravinskian neoprimitivism and Neoclassicism, with indigenous traditions, subject matter, and politics.

Revueltas had a tragically short career. He was born on 31 December 1899, in Mexico, and initially trained as a violinist in Mexico City, Austin, and Chicago. During the 1920s he divided his time between the United States and Mexico. He took up conducting and worked with Chávez as assistant conductor of the newly formed Orquesta Sinfónica Nacional de México. He led other ensembles as well, including the student orchestra at the National Conservatory of Music, where he taught. In 1937 he went to Spain with a group of Mexican artists to support the Republican efforts in the Civil War against the fascist leader, Francisco Franco.

In the latter half of the 1930s Revueltas composed scores for a half-dozen Mexican movies. His early death did not allow time for him to make concert suites of music drawn from the film music, but others did so later, most notably for *La noche de los Mayas* (The Night of the Mayas), based on Chano Urueta's 1939 movie of the same name. It deals with the interaction of the modern world with ancient Mayan culture in the Yucatán Peninsula. The score to *La noche de los Mayas* combines elements characteristic of traditional popular music in Mexico with trends in European modern music from the 1920s and '30s, most noticeably those associated with Stravinsky. A four-movement suite assembled from the film inevitably brings to mind a symphonic structure; indeed this is the closest piece we have to a symphony by Revueltas.

American Patriotic Works

Copland put his Americanist style to overtly patriotic use in *Lincoln Portrait*, commissioned shortly after the Japanese attack on Pearl Harbor in December 1941 that propelled the United States into the Second World War. Copland incorporated two familiar songs: Stephen Foster's "Camptown Races" (1850), which adds a period flavor, especially given that Lincoln used it as a campaign song in 1860, and "On Springfield Mountain" (or, "The Pesky Sarpent"). After the fast-paced middle section, the solemn opening returns, this time accompanied by a speaker reading quotations from Lincoln's speeches chosen for their bearing on the predicament of a nation thrust into a military conflict that would test its resolve and its democratic principles. The last of the five extracts is the conclusion of Lincoln's most famous speech, the Gettysburg Address, resolving "that this nation under God shall have a new birth of freedom and that government of the people, by the people, and for the people shall not perish from the earth." The narrator does not need to know how to read music to deliver the text—many politicians and celebrities have intoned the eloquent words.

Lincoln Portrait was a product of the Popular Front aesthetic. Celebrating Lincoln was the radical left's passport to general acceptability; and this was even more the case after 1941, when the United States and Soviet Russia unexpectedly found themselves war allies united against Nazi Germany and Imperial Japan. During the war and for a short while thereafter, friendship toward the Soviet Union became official American policy. We might even notice various similarities between Copland's *Lincoln Portrait* and the Soviet doctrine of Socialist Realism, discussed in the previous chapter, found in the sort of official pieces that Shostakovich, Prokofiev, and others composed using the words or ideas of Marx, Lenin, and Stalin. Copland's Americana grew out of personal commitment, not governmental pressure, but the grand gestures, recourse to folklore, and use of political texts were nonetheless shared by some of the most prominent American and Soviet composers around this time, as was the appeal to a new simplicity, a feature Copland admired in Shostakovich's music.[11]

Copland's other exemplary assertion of nationalism was *Fanfare for the Common Man*, also composed in 1942. The conductor of the Cincinnati Symphony Orchestra commissioned leading composers to write a series of orchestral fanfares that would serve as concert openers during wartime. Copland's contribution, which premiered in March 1943, was the only one of the eighteen programmed to survive the circumstances of its time and join the repertory. The celebratory piece lasts just four minutes and is scored for eleven brass instruments and percussion. The main theme, initially given out unharmonized by three trumpets in unison and then with four horns in two-part counterpoint, takes Copland's homespun "wide open" style to extremes. Absolutely diatonic and contoured in great soaring arches, it is projected in its solo statement over nearly two octaves and in its duet form over nearly three. The trumpet part has only four instances of stepwise motion, the horn part none. Phrases typically end in wide descents through multiple skips. The counterpoint is homorhythmic and proceeds mainly by similar motion (Ex. 33-2).

Example 33-2 Aaron Copland, *Fanfare for the Common Man*, mm. 1–21

Example 33-2 (*continued*)

These are traits—mined in equal measure from folklore and from the wide intervals and angular contours of Copland's earlier Modernistic style—that began to communicate "America" to concert audiences both at home and abroad.

Needless to say, they were quickly copied, not only by other classical composers but also by film and commercial composers who sought an instantly recognizable evocation of America. In this way they became a stereotype, and "Coplandesque" became an adjective denoting a certain range of moods—pastoral, wistful, Western, domesticated—that in turn conjured up a comforting vision of home to Depression-era and wartime America.

The novelty and the originality, rather than the literal authenticity, of Copland's folk song treatments gained them their acceptance as American musical emblems. The decisive success that a leftist homosexual Jew from Brooklyn, triply marginalized by birth and temperament from the definition of an all-American hero, finally enjoyed in defining America musically further testifies to what we have already seen many times as a musical-historical truth: In art, what is "national" is a socially negotiated discourse rather than a natural essence. Popular acceptance, as evidenced both by audience reaction and by professional emulation, determines the authenticity of musical nationalism. Yet by the same token this authenticity can always be questioned, as some did in Copland's case.

"Coplandesque" became an adjective denoting a certain range of moods—pastoral, wistful, Western, domesticated—that in turn conjured up a comforting vision of home to America.

The strong ideological component of Copland's wartime works resonated with both Communist ideals and the aims of American society at large. After the war those aims became sharply differentiated. Beginning in the early 1950s, to be identified as a Communist carried a ruinous stigma in the United States. Copland was forced to disavow his earlier political affiliations and claimed that his Americanist style was simply a way of reaching the larger audiences made available by radio, records, and movies. His music by this point was sufficiently popular and he sufficiently esteemed as a musician and public figure for the claim to be accepted. But the connection between his widely emulated Americanist idiom and the Popular Front is a historical fact.[12] Unless it is taken into account, the development of American music during the Great Depression years cannot be adequately understood. There is no reason to assume that Anglo-American folklore would have achieved its exemplary status in American concert music under other circumstances.

The Great American Symphony

The Second World War prompted an earnest optimism and loftiness of expression epitomized by the cliché image of writers aspiring to produce the "Great American Novel." For a "Great American Symphony" to emerge, greatness itself would have to stage a musical comeback: The playful, ironic, and irreverent mood that had been so basic to the aesthetic of the 1920s would somehow have to be overcome. Ultramodern experimentation, associated with technology and cities, also seemed inappropriate to the newly troubled times. A distinctive school of American symphonic writing had begun to flourish during the Depression years. It was borne aloft by a government-subsidized proliferation of orchestras administered by the Works Progress Administration (WPA), part of President Roosevelt's "**New Deal,**" a policy of fighting unemployment with government spending.

New value was placed on the traditional mythology of the American West, which emphasized open spaces, adventure, fortitude, and self-reliance, in other words, the "pioneer spirit." The first American symphonist to exploit these ideals was Roy Harris (1898–1979), "an Oklahoma Composer Who Was Born in a Log Cabin on Lincoln's Birthday," to cite just part of the long title of an unpublished promotional biography written on Harris's behalf by Nicolas Slonimsky.[13] Although his rural background was the very antithesis of Copland's New York, Harris took Copland's advice and went off to study with Nadia Boulanger in Paris. In later life he downplayed the importance of his Parisian years; his was a brand of Americanism that defined itself vehemently against the authority of Europe. To be American was to be spontaneous, wild, and free. It was no accident that Harris's first symphonic effort was hailed in the press in 1933 as a characteristically "Western" work.

Harris's greatest success as an exemplary American came in February 1939, when Serge Koussevitzky premiered his Third Symphony with the Boston Symphony Orchestra. It is a sort of programless symphonic poem, in a single movement but with relatively autonomous sections in contrasting tempos that seemed to owe a noticeable debt to Sibelius, particularly to the Finnish composer's Seventh Symphony (1924). But was it programless? A note by Harris for the first performance outlined its form with a certain amount of expressive characterization: I. Tragic, II. Lyric, III. Pastoral, IV. Fugue—dramatic, V. Dramatic-Tragic. This was enough to prompt speculation on the part of one critic that the lofty tone of the symphony spoke "of the bleak and barren expanses of Western Kansas, of the brooding prairie night."[14] Harris himself later linked the score to wartime tensions.

Another leading symphonist was Howard Hanson (1896–1981), a Nebraska-born composer of Scandinavian ancestry who, even before Harris, had accepted Sibelius as his chief symphonic model. In 1924 Hanson was appointed director of the newly established Eastman School of Music, affiliated with the University of Rochester in western New York, a post he held for forty years. (Sibelius had himself earlier turned down an offer to teach composition there.) Koussevitzky commissioned two symphonies from Hanson, the Second ("Romantic," 1930) and the Third (1938), which also exemplified the high symphonic rhetoric of the times.

Another institutional base for American composers was strengthened in 1945 when William Schuman (1910–92), a pupil of Harris's, was appointed president of the Juilliard School of Music in New York, one of America's most distinguished conservatories. Schuman had scored a big public and critical success with his own Symphony No. 3 (1941), a massively energetic work in two composite neo-Baroque movements (Passacaglia and Fugue, Chorale and Toccata). A similarly large and affirmative Third Symphony (1947) came from Walter Piston (1894–1976), a charter member of the "Boulangerie" along with Copland and Thomson. The vitality of the Americanist symphonic school can be measured by the high productivity of its members: Harris altogether produced thirteen numbered symphonies, Schuman ten, Piston eight, Hanson seven. Roger Sessions, who stood somewhat aloof from the other composers named so far thanks to a more chromatic, more internationalist dissonant style, was nevertheless an enthusiastic symphonist. He and Peter Mennin (1923–83), a younger member of the group (and Schuman's successor as president of Juilliard), each logged the mythic symphonic number nine; David Diamond (1915–2005) wrote eleven numbered symphonies.

Some other symphonists were a bit less prolific but nonetheless remembered. Virgil Thomson wrote three, of which the first, his *Symphony on a Hymn Tune* (1928), quotes indigenous material to establish an American character in the context of a purely instrumental symphony. William Grant Still (1895–1978), an Oberlin College graduate who studied with Chadwick and Varèse, wrote five, of which the *Afro-American Symphony* (1931) was the first written by an African American to be performed by a leading orchestra. Samuel Barber (1910–81), trained at the Curtis Institute of Music in Philadelphia, composed two. His Symphony in One Movement (1936) is another piece that looks to Sibelius; themes from the composer's Seventh Symphony even appear in his sketches. Barber wrote his next symphony as a serviceman during the war; what he referred to as the "Flight Symphony" was premiered by Koussevitzky in March 1944 as the "Second Symphony (Dedicated to the Army Air Forces)." Leonard Bernstein wrote the first of his three symphonies, entitled *Jeremiah* after the biblical text of Lamentation, at age twenty-three in 1942, thus further adding to the long catalogue of symphonies marked by the war.

Copland did not reach—or attempt to reach—in the first two of his three symphonies the crown of Great American Symphony. We already mentioned his Symphony for Organ and Orchestra (1924); his second, called the *Short Symphony* (1932–33), was premiered in Mexico City by Chávez, to whom it is dedicated. Copland began composing his Third Symphony on a commission from the Koussevitzky Foundation and incorporated into the piece his recent *Fanfare for the Common Man*. Written between the summer of 1944, right after the American landing in Normandy ("D-Day"), and the summer of 1946, it emerged as the grand statement that so many composers had been trying for years to achieve. With its scoring for an enormous orchestra, hymn-like sections, and fanfare-like sections, it embodied the mood of euphoria that accompanied the victorious end of the war. The introduction to the finale uses the *Fanfare for the Common Man*, although musical ideas and motives from that earlier work permeate parts of the first three movements as well. The *Fanfare* receives its grandiose finale in a coda that some commentators have compared with the climax of the "Ode to Joy" in Beethoven's Ninth. Koussevitzky conducted the premiere with the Boston Symphony on 18 October 1946, and the work was immediately hailed as a masterpiece.

But something festered beneath the praise. A few of Copland's composer friends were uncomfortable with the overly triumphant tone, or they became so as the euphoric mood of 1946 gave way to sobriety in 1947. Concern was expressed about its over-the-top exuberance. Bernstein, Copland's close friend and Koussevitzky's star conducting protégé, led the European premiere in Prague on 25 May 1947; two days later he wrote to Copland, "Sweetie, the end is a sin."[15] About a year later Bernstein wrote again, from the newborn state of Israel, to say that he now thought the work "quite magnificent" but then confessed that he had "made a sizable cut near the end and believe me it makes a whale of a difference."[16] Copland was at first as miffed by Bernstein's "nervy" deed of cutting a total of ten measures, but he went on to say, "I came to agree with Lenny and several others about the advisability of shortening the ending."[17] The symphony is in any case an effective memento of its euphoric time. The triumphant optimism of *Fanfare for the Common Man* and its sister symphony, welcome while war was being waged and won, made some uneasy once there were new political realities. Copland's Third thus bears comparison with the two most famous symphonies by Shostakovich. Its affirmative finale recalls the concerns about the ending of the Soviet composer's Fifth Symphony, while its engagement with the war links it to the Seventh, the "Leningrad," the most celebrated symphony in the world at the time.

Accessible Alternatives

The majority of the symphonies just mentioned were accepted as "Americanist" on the strength of stylistic features such as melodic breadth; a basically diatonic (though often dissonant) harmonic idiom; jazzy, syncopated, asymmetrical rhythms; and sonorous, often brassy or percussion-heavy orchestration. Nearly forty years after Schoenberg's first atonal compositions, the populist American style was predominantly tonal. And this was the case, not just for symphonies but also for many concertos, operas, and chamber music.

Anthology Vol 3-46
Full CD VII, 14
Concise CD III, 38

Samuel Barber was a leading figure when it came to concertos, with ones for violin (1939), cello (1945), and piano (1962). His best-known composition, *Adagio for Strings,* began life as the second movement of his String Quartet, Op. 11 (1936), and achieved extraordinary fame after Arturo Toscanini conducted the composer's own string orchestra arrangement with the NBC Symphony during a national broadcast in late 1938. The piece was generally well received, notably by *New York Times* critic Olin Downes, but it also sparked controversy in letters to the paper. Some complained that the work was not identifiably American, while others objected that it was not modern.[18] Toscanini performed it on tour in South America and England and recorded the work, all further enhancing its fame.

Barber later made another arrangement of the *Adagio for Strings,* a choral version to which he fitted the words of the Agnus Dei from the Roman Catholic Mass. It may not be surprising that this final reincarnation of the original quartet movement should be religious—a solemn, even chant-like character is one of its striking features from the beginning. The work opens with the first of a series of slow phrases consisting of a stepwise diatonic melody accompanied by chords from the other strings. The music builds to a powerful climax, louder, more chromatic, and in the strings' highest register, before returning to the calm opening theme. The expressivity and lyricism of the work epitomizes not only elements of Barber's style but also an elegiac quality found in the work of many of his American contemporaries. This quality has made it an attractive choice to film directors to include in movies such as *The Elephant Man* (1980), *El Norte* (1983), *Platoon* (1986), and *Amélie* (2001).

Many European composers were still writing accessible tonal music as well, in some cases for American orchestras. Sergey Rachmaninoff (Fig. 33-8), for example, enjoyed a particularly close relationship with the Philadelphia Orchestra. Although he composed less after leaving his native Russia, concentrating instead on his pianistic career, his *Rhapsody on a Theme of Paganini* (1934) for piano and orchestra is as lushly Romantic a composition as his popular early concertos from the start of the century. His great box-office popularity and excellent reputation as an interpreter of the museum repertory allowed his new but conservative music to join that exclusive repertory at a time when audiences and concert promoters were often actively resistant to new music. There were many, during the 1920s and '30s, who regarded Rachmaninoff as the greatest living composer, precisely because he was the one who seemed best capable of successfully maintaining the familiar and prestigious style of the nineteenth-century classics into the twentieth century. That he was capable of doing so, moreover, and that his style was as distinctive as any contemporary's, could be used to refute the Modernist argument that traditional styles had been exhausted.

Figure 33-8 Sergey Rachmaninoff.

Opera in Midcentury

Opera was a genre where tradition reigned. The enormous expense connected with producing opera meant that companies tended to commission, cultivate, and perform fairly conservative composers, at least in America and England. Copland's two operas are modest in scope—he wrote *The Second Hurricane* (1936) as a "play opera" intended for high-school performance; *The Tender Land* (1952–54) was originally composed for television and eventually became a frequent offering at conservatories and music schools. Carlisle Floyd (b. 1926) produced a sort of American verismo, as seen in his best-known opera, *Susannah* (1955). The most prolific figure was the Italian-born Gian Carlo Menotti (1911–2007), who worked for most of his career in the United States. Menotti's was a strangely lopsided career, with most of his compositional successes and prestigious prizes coming early; his later years were particularly devoted to the music festivals he founded, the Spoleto Festival of the Two Worlds, held in Spoleto, Italy, and in Charleston, South Carolina. Menotti, who wrote his own librettos, also wrote the text for *Vanessa* (1956–57), the first of two full-length operas by his long-time companion, Samuel Barber.

Menotti's scores are often reminiscent of Puccini, both in their melodic and harmonic idiom and in their formal procedures. After his first stage work, the comic *Amelia al ballo* (Amelia Goes to the Ball, 1936), he enjoyed success with modestly scored pieces that could be more easily performed by amateur or education ensembles or that aimed for a different kind of distribution through radio and television. A Christmas opera, *Amahl and the Night Visitors* (1951), a story of the three kings and a miraculous healing, was commissioned by NBC television and broadcast annually for a dozen years; it may well be the most widely seen opera of all time. Four operas eventually played on Broadway: *The Medium* (1945), *The Telephone* (1947), *The Consul* (1949), and *The Saint of Bleecker Street* (1954). This further blurred the lines between opera and musical theater, something we have already seen with George Gershwin's *Porgy and Bess*, Weill's *Die Dreigroschenoper*, and Blitzstein's *The Cradle Will Rock* and that later extended to works such as Bernstein's *Candide* (1956) and *West Side Story* (1957) and Stephen Sondheim's *Sweeney Todd, the Demon Barber of Fleet Street* (1979), among others.

In Europe some of the most notable operas were one-hit wonders for their composers, not sustained efforts to shape new operatic practice. Among the handful of works that became international repertory standards are Stravinsky's *The Rake's Progress* (1951) and Francis Poulenc's *Dialogues des Carmélites* (1956). Some others achieved a toehold in the repertory, notably Bohuslav Martinů's *Julietta* (1938); Hans Werner Henze's *Boulevard Solitude* (1952) and *The Bassarids* (1966); and *Die Soldaten* (The Soldiers, 1965) by Bernd Alois Zimmermann (1918–70), a grimly brilliant and Modernist extravaganza that owes a debt to *Wozzeck*.

Benjamin Britten

The major composer to specialize in opera after Richard Strauss was the Englishman Benjamin Britten (1913–76; Fig. 33-9), whose career is all the more surprising, given England's dearth of significant opera composers for two and a half centuries, since the time of Henry Purcell in the late seventeenth century. Britten's

Figure 33-9 Benjamin Britten (at the piano) and Peter Pears. Photo by Lotte Jacobi, 1939.

accomplishment made him the musical darling of his nation. He achieved unprecedented social recognition, being given the Order of Merit in 1965 and near the end of his life the noble title Lord Britten of Aldeburgh by Queen Elizabeth II. He always explicitly stated that his commitment to opera stemmed from a larger view of his calling to public service. This is also seen not only in music he wrote to educate children, most famously *The Young Person's Guide to the Orchestra: Variations and Fugue on a Theme by Henry Purcell* (1945), but also in music written for children to perform, such as *Noye's Fludde* (1958).

Between 1941 and 1973, Britten produced a total of seventeen works for the lyric stage. He established his reputation right after the war with his second opera, *Peter Grimes*, which premiered in London on 7 June 1945. In the wake of its commercial success around the world, Britten began turning out operas almost yearly. His next major hit was *Billy Budd*, after Herman Melville's shipboard story. In 1953 came *Gloriana*, a prestigious commission to celebrate the coronation of Queen Elizabeth II, although the portrayal of the queen is less than sympathetic and the work was a flop. *The Turn of the Screw* (1954), after Henry James's ghost story, was a chamber opera written for small performing forces. This meant the piece could easily tour, as it did with the English Opera Group, which Britten founded together with his lifelong partner, tenor Peter Pears (1910–86). Much of the couple's activities were an outgrowth of a strong commitment to take art to the people.

Britten's next opera, *A Midsummer Night's Dream* (1960), after Shakespeare, premiered at Aldeburgh, a coastal village where he and Pears had established a summer festival. After a series of shorter stage works, Britten ended his theater career with *Owen Wingrave* (1971), composed for television performance, and *Death in Venice* (1973), after a novella by Thomas Mann. In these works Britten experimented with different musical languages, touching at times on twelve-tone techniques and exotic sounds modeled on Asian music, but he always remained connected with his audience. While none of the later pieces matched the colossal success of *Peter Grimes*, which will be our focus, at least four—*Billy Budd, The Turn of the Screw, A Midsummer Night's Dream,* and *Death in Venice*—have joined it in the international repertoire.

A Modern Antihero: Britten's *Peter Grimes*

In 1939, as war loomed, Britten and Pears followed a wave of leftists and pacifists who emigrated from England to North America. They settled for a while in the environs of New York City, where they befriended Copland. Britten continued an earlier creative association with the English poet W. H. Auden (1907–73) to write his first opera, *Paul Bunyan* (1941) and went on to compose some important instrumental works in America, including a Violin Concerto and a *Sinfonia da Requiem*. Britten and Pears—not without apprehension at the fate that might await them as conscientious objectors—decided to return to England in 1942. While they were waiting for transit, Koussevitzky, acting on Copland's recommendation, performed the *Sinfonia da Requiem* with the Boston Symphony Orchestra, which led to a $1,000 grant from the Koussevitzky Foundation that allowed Britten to write *Peter Grimes* (Fig. 33-10).

Anthology Vol 3-47
Full CD VII, 15
Concise CD III, 39

The opera is based on a long narrative poem called *The Borough* (1810) by the English poet George Crabbe (1754–1832), best known for his grimly realistic depictions of rustic life in the coastal district of Suffolk, Britten's native region. The poem characterizes Peter Grimes as a cruel fisherman who is responsible for the death of three of his apprentices. In their reading, however, Britten and Pears found that Grimes, sadist though he was, was not a clear-cut villain. They felt he could be portrayed in a way that would help expose social hypocrisy and injustice. Grimes was thus a character to set beside the similarly prophetic Wozzeck, the delinquent yet pitiable antihero of Berg's opera, a work that had made such a strong impression on Britten that he had for a time nurtured the hope of studying with Berg. *Wozzeck* would be a model for *Peter Grimes* in ways that went far beyond the general similarity of their protagonists.

Grimes was able to indulge his cruelty thanks to the English workhouse system, which supplied him with indigent orphan boys, utterly without civil rights, whom he could exploit for his own purposes. The good people in town observe what he is doing, but they do not question him. Indeed, they would hear the cries of the boys and calmly remark that "Grimes is at his exercise." After the most recent apprentice mysteriously dies, the town decides to ostracize Grimes, who now must fish alone, and he so in waters where no one else dares go. Crabbe's original poem therefore exposes a double injustice: Grimes's cruel exploitation of his helpless apprentices, and the townspeople's hypocritical disapproval of behavior in which they are complicit.

The plight of the criminal fisherman who is banished was an attractively complex theme for modern artists like Britten and Pears, heirs as they were to a more relativistic notion of responsibility and blame, a more exacting sense of social justice, and a more compelling interest in psychological complexities than Crabbe had nearly 130 years earlier. They thoroughly recast the title role and the surrounding dramatic plot. "A central feeling for us," Britten later told an interviewer, "was that of the individual against the crowd, with ironic overtones for our own situation. As

Figure 33-10 Benjamin Britten's *Peter Grimes* in its first production, Sadler's Wells Company, London (now the English National Opera), 1945.

conscientious objectors we were out of it. We couldn't say we suffered physically, but naturally we experienced tremendous tension. I think it was partly this feeling which led us to make Grimes a character of vision and conflict, the tortured idealist he is, rather than the villain he was in Crabbe."[19]

Like Shostakovich in *Lady Macbeth of the Mtsensk District* (another opera that had impressed Britten and that he would emulate), the composer saw his task with respect to his title character as one of exoneration. He and Pears went even further than Berg or Shostakovich in softening the portrait of Grimes, making him the innocent, if blundering, victim of prejudice and unjustified persecution. For Pears, who sang the title role at the premiere, "Grimes is not a hero nor is he an operatic villain." What is he then? "He is very much of an ordinary weak person who, being at odds with the society in which he finds himself, tries to overcome it and, in doing so, offends against the conventional code, is classed by society as a criminal, and destroyed as such. There are plenty of Grimeses around still, I think!"[20]

In the opera Grimes is given two apprentices, not three. The prologue portrays an inquest into the death of the first, who had died of thirst aboard Grimes's boat. The death is attributed to "accidental circumstances," but Grimes is warned not to expect the benefit of the doubt again. To reduce the story in the opera to its barest bones: In Act I, Grimes procures another apprentice with the assistance of Ellen Orford, the village schoolteacher, whom he hopes to marry after clearing his name and gaining the town's respect by prospering. In Act II, against Ellen's passionate entreaties, Grimes forces the exhausted (and, as Ellen has discovered, roughly treated) new apprentice out to sea on a Sunday to fish. Or so he intends; pressured to hurry by Grimes (who hears an approaching posse of villagers), the boy loses his footing on a cliff side and falls to his death. In Act III, the apprentice's jersey is discovered on the beach and a manhunt is organized to bring Grimes to justice. He eludes them but turns up later, dazed and incoherent, and is discovered by Ellen and by Captain Balstrode, his only other defender, who instructs Grimes to row out to sea and sink his boat, drowning himself, rather than face the implacable if mistaken judgment of the townspeople.

But are they mistaken? Grimes, while no murderer, is indeed responsible for the second boy's death. Yet without the fanatical mob of villagers at his heels, Grimes would not have been so reckless. The theme of ambiguously shared guilt, already found in Crabbe's original poem, is starkly dramatized. The prevalence of guilt is subtly shifted to the townspeople by showing them biased against Grimes from the start and by showing him to be, as Britten put it, an idealist, full of poetic visions and wholesome aspirations, and therefore morally superior, at least by inclination, to the crowd that condemns him—just as, in the view of the opera's creators, their own status as conscientious objectors was morally superior to that of a society then engaged in bloody warfare.

Like Berg's **Wozzeck** *and Shostakovich's* **Lady Macbeth,** *Britten's* **Peter Grimes** *relies heavily on interludes.*

Like Berg's *Wozzeck* and Shostakovich's *Lady Macbeth*, Britten's opera relies heavily on interludes, not only as a way of filling the time between scenes but also as a vehicle for manipulative authorial commentary. The interludes in *Peter Grimes* alternate in function between scene setting (at the beginning of acts) and meditations on the hero's fate (in the middle of them), with the storm at the center of Act I combining both roles. Unlike the many relatively realistic storms composers had written in orchestral works—going back to Vivaldi's *Four Seasons* and Beethoven's *Pastoral* Symphony—Britten offers a more modern perspective by evoking a psychological storm.

We have also seen operatic mad scenes before, notably with Donizetti's *Lucia di Lammermoor* and Berg's *Wozzeck*. Grimes's mad scene follows the last orchestral interlude and consists of a nearly incoherent recitative, accompanied by the offstage voices of the posse calling his name and by a single tuba representing a distant foghorn. The structure is provided by a medley of melodic reminiscences—the opera's principal leitmotifs—that sum up the action Grimes obsessively recalls. Ellen arrives and offers to take him home. Finally, Balstrode approaches and, in spoken dialogue, issues the death sentence. Grimes rows out to sea in silence, and there is a reprise of the interlude that opened Act 1 showing the town awakening to a new day.

Britten's and Pears's portrayal of the title character has long caused controversy. People recognized an autobiographical component in relation to their pacifism. The Britten scholar Philip Brett went further by suggesting another allegorical dimension that entailed so touchy and unresolved a social issue in contemporary life that (as Ellen says when she finds the apprentice's jersey) it became "a clue whose meaning we avoid." That issue is homosexuality, or, more specifically, hidden, "closeted" homosexuality, "the love that dare not speak its name." That Britten and Pears were conscientious objectors and lovers was widely known (that is, widely and correctly assumed) at the time of their exile and return. Homosexual acts between consenting adults were illegal in Britain and could be vengefully prosecuted, no matter how eminent the offender. Even when unprosecuted, there could be a social stigma, as Britten and Pears well knew. Their musical achievements and the discretion with which they conducted themselves in public allowed them to become world-famous recipients of official honors. Read as part of an allegory depicting the plight of social outsiders, Grimes's implicit acceptance of his "guilt" might be explained without evoking sexuality. But in light of the stigma attached to his creators' relationship, Grimes's internalized guilt is among the opera's most compelling social themes—one that communicated itself strongly to audiences even without speaking its name.

Brett writes, "One of the things Britten's operas (as well as his other works) seem to achieve is an exploration of various issues surrounding sexuality that the composer could not discuss in any other public form," and he goes on to claim that Britten's "perseverance in this endeavor is one of the truly remarkable and even noble features of his career."[21] That the treatment of sexuality in *Peter Grimes*, though veiled in allegory, was conscious and deliberate can be seen clearly enough in retrospect if we reread Pears's characterization of Grimes ("an ordinary weak person, . . . classed by society as a criminal") in light of his and Britten's "crime." And if any doubt remains, there is a letter from Pears to Britten from 1944, soon after Britten had started sketching the music for the opera, in which he reassured the composer that "the queerness is unimportant & doesn't really exist in the music (or at any rate obtrude)."[22]

None of this means that Peter Grimes was actually envisioned or presented by Britten and Pears as homosexual or that he should be portrayed that way in performance. And yet there are other aspects of the opera that indirectly broach matters associated with the theme of homosexuality, matters that recur in other works of Britten as well. Unlike Tchaikovsky or Copland or any other composer known or thought to be homosexual, Britten did "thematize" the topic repeatedly, especially in later operas, such as *Billy Budd*, *The Turn of the Screw*, and, most especially, *Death in Venice*. His operatic dramaturgy and even his musical style depend to an unusual degree on juxtapositions of "exotic" and "normal" elements, whose latent meanings have been revealed and reevaluated over time, engaging performers, audiences, and critics in continual dialogue. That is what makes for a long cultural shelf life, the kind that characterizes "classics."

"The Composer's Duty"

As we have seen, a great deal of high Modernist art projected an alienated stance that the general public found difficult to comprehend. Britten, who was in personal ways genuinely alienated from contemporary society, had a "longing to be used" by that very society.[23] He perceived his most useful role as being someone who could, by pleasing his audience with satisfying artistic experiences, lobby for points of view that challenged, and sought to undermine, the complacency of the majority. The phrase "longing to be used" comes from a speech he delivered in the United States in 1964, entitled "On Receiving the First Aspen Award," a prize that honored "the individual anywhere in the world judged to have made the greatest contribution to the advancement of the humanities."[24]

The sizeable cash award was bestowed in particular recognition of his huge oratorio, *War Requiem*, Op. 66 (1962), in which Latin words of the traditional Requiem Mass, sung by a soprano soloist and choruses with large orchestra and organ, are juxtaposed with grim, posthumously published antiwar verses by Wilfred Owen (1893–1918), a pacifist poet killed in action a week before the armistice that ended World War I. The poems are sung by tenor and baritone soloists, personifying soldiers, accompanied by a chamber orchestra. The inclusion of Dietrich Fischer-Dieskau (b. 1925), the great German baritone, in the original performing roster at Britten's request turned the occasion into one of symbolic reconciliation between former enemies. Owen's poems, performed in juxtaposition with such texts as *Libera me, Domine* ("Deliver me, O Lord"), concluded with a meditation on war's waste of life in the form of a dialogue between a killed British soldier (sung by Pears) and a German (sung by Fischer-Dieskau) whom he had previously killed. The soprano soloist in the recording under Britten's direction was the Soviet singer Galina Vishnevskaya (b. 1926), whose participation balanced that of Fischer-Dieskau as a reminder of the former wartime alliance between England and the Soviet Union.

Britten used his moment of triumph at Aspen to deliver a sermon about the social responsibility of artists and the responsibilities of society toward its artists. "I do not write for posterity," Britten remarked. "I write music, now, in Aldeburgh, for people living there, and further afield, indeed for anyone who cares to play it or listen to it. But my music now has its roots in where I live and work."[25] This theme was Britten's mantra. Earlier in the talk he had indicated why such a seemingly amiable, unobjectionable position had nevertheless to be advanced militantly:

> There are many dangers which hedge round the unfortunate composer: pressure groups which demand true proletarian music, snobs who demand the latest *avant-garde* tricks; critics who are already trying to document today for tomorrow, to be the first to find the correct pigeonhole definition. These people are dangerous—not because they are necessarily of any importance in themselves, but because they may make the composer, above all the young composer, self-conscious, and instead of writing his own music, music which springs naturally from his gift and personality, he may be frightened into writing pretentious nonsense or deliberate obscurity.[26]

To those who saw themselves as living mainly in history, who treated their potential audience as a hindrance, and who therefore cultivated an aura of inaccessibility, Britten offered a primer on manners: "It is insulting to address anyone in a language which they do not understand."[27] But even greater dangers lurk to the left and right, he told his American audience, because with totalitarian powers "great official pressure is used to bring the artist into line and make him conform to the State's ideology." (Britten greatly admired Shostakovich, a kindred spirit in many ways with whom he had a number of warm meetings.) The danger in capitalist countries, Britten argued, was that "money and snobbishness combine to demand the latest, newest manifestations, which I am told go by the name in this country of 'Foundation Music'."[28] Britten was alluding to wealthy foundations that funded avant-garde music without thinking about audiences; he concluded that "it is the composer's duty, as a member of society, to speak to or for his fellow human beings."[29]

Britten was the leading English composer to emerge in the 1940s and remained the preeminent figure in his country for the next three decades, despite the continued activity of the older Ralph Vaughan Williams, of his nearer contemporary Michael Tippett (1905–98), who was also a significant opera composer, and of a younger generation that further enhanced England's musical stature.

Benjamin Britten perceived his most useful role as being someone who could, by pleasing his audience with satisfying artistic experiences, lobby for points of view that challenged, and sought to undermine, the complacency of the majority.

Olivier Messiaen: "The Charm of Impossibilities"

The preeminent figure in France during this time was Olivier Messiaen (1908–92; Fig. 33-11), a few years older than Britten and a fascinating contrast to his contemporaries of all nationalities. The idea of composing for society, enacted in different ways by composers such as Copland, Shostakovich, and Britten, or of composing for history ("for posterity" as Britten put it), as Schoenberg, Webern, and many others did, finds yet another alternative in Messiaen: He wrote for what he viewed as timeless truth. "Let us have a *true* music," italicizing the word himself, "that is to say, spiritual, a music which may be an act of faith; a music which may touch upon all subjects without ceasing to touch upon God; an original music, in short, whose language may open a few doors, take down some as yet distant stars."[30]

While his parents were not believers, what Messiaen called "the theological truths of the Catholic faith" were the core of his life and work.[31] His mother was the poet Cécile Sauvage, and his father Pierre, a professor of English, made a critical translation of Shakespeare. An "attraction to the marvelous," which Messiaen experienced as a boy reciting Shakespeare's plays for his brother, was "multiplied a hundredfold, a thousandfold" with his discovery of Roman Catholicism.[32] Messiaen was a rarity among leading twentieth-century composers in being an active church musician. For more than forty years, he served as organist, playing week in and week out, at the Église de la Sainte-Trinité, one of the largest churches in Paris. He wrote many of his most important works for its huge Cavaillé-Coll organ and was without question the most important organist-composer of the twentieth century. Like César Franck before him, who had also served as church organist for many years and

Figure 33-11 Olivier Messiaen and Yvonne Loriod.

who also wrote a highly spiritualized kind of music, Messiaen was also a famous and much-sought-after teacher. The intellectual and artistic freedom he sought to foster is confirmed in the tributes of his many prominent students, some of whom we will meet in coming chapters.

The words quoted earlier about Messiaen's quest for "*true* music," despite all their religious euphoria, come from the preface to his *Technique de mon langage musical* (Technique of My Musical Language, 1944), one of the most systematic expositions that any composer has ever given to the mechanisms of his art. And past the preface, the treatise is true to its title. It resolutely ignores all meaning to treat "technique and not sentiment." Messiaen breaks down his methods in extraordinarily schoolmasterly fashion into their rhythmic, melodic, and harmonic dimensions. The theorizing made him a potent force in the technique of contemporary music, even among those who had no interest in religion. He managed to transform theological dogma into musical dogma, which may be a reason he objected to being called a mystic. Rather, he was a "scholastic" in the Medieval sense of the term. Like Saint Thomas Aquinas, he sought to embody the mysteries of faith in a rational and transmissible discourse. No wonder his self-analysis was so thorough and so influential. What were spiritual means for him became musical ends for many others.

Messiaen's *Quartet for the End of Time*

Anthology Vol 3-48
Full CD VII, 16–18
Concise CD III, 40

Messiaen wrote his influential treatise during the war, following release from a German prisoner-of-war camp in Silesia, where he was sent after being captured in June 1940. It was there that he composed his most famous work, the *Quatuor pour la fin du temps* (Quartet for the End of Time, 1940–41). He wrote it for himself and three other musicians at the camp, letting their presence dictate the choice of instrumentation: violinist Jean Le Boulaire, clarinetist Henri Akoka, cellist Etienne Pasquier, and Messiaen himself at the piano. The circumstances of the premiere at the Stalag on 15 January 1941 became legend, one that Messiaen actively perpetuated (Fig. 33-12). He recounted how the musicians had played in the bitter cold, he on a miserable upright piano, Pasquier on a cello missing a string, before an entranced audience of 5,000. He exaggerated. No doubt the piano was inadequate, but the cello did have all its strings, and the hall was relatively small, not capable of holding so many. Yet there are independent reports of the extraordinary impact the piece had on those listening, and its appeal has remained potent ever since.[33]

What were spiritual means for Messiaen became musical ends for many others.

The title *Quartet for the End of Time* has multiple implications. Most directly it is a reference to the Apocalypse as described in the tenth chapter of the Book of Revelation, the last book of the New Testament. The piece is prefaced by an epigraph that describes the image of the Angel of the Apocalypse raising his right hand to God in Heaven and swearing: "There shall be no more time; when the seventh angel shall sound his trumpet, the hidden purpose of God will have been fulfilled, as he promised to his servants the prophets." This end of time was one of Messiaen's eternal subjects, not necessarily related to wartime; for those who initially heard the piece, however, the connections between war and apocalypse seemed inevitable. Messiaen further acknowledged a musical "play on words" in the title: the end of conventional notions of rhythm and meter, of "past and present," a musical concern he explored in his treatise.

Messiaen also sought the unconventional in melody and harmony. His chief innovation with respect to pitch was the use of what he called "**modes of limited transposition,**" which depend on invariance achieved by means of symmetry. For him the term meant the invariance found in two scales: the whole-tone scale, which retains its pitches when transposed by any number of whole steps (thus being, except for the untransposable chromatic scale, the mode of most stringently limited transposition); and the octatonic scale (alternating half steps and whole steps). He extended the idea of symmetry from tonality and pitch to meter and rhythm. The number of beats per measure as well as the length of the beats themselves are unpredictably variable in some of his pieces. The variable lengths can come about by adding an extra sixteenth note that lengthens one of the eighth-note pulses to a dotted eighth, a device Messiaen based in part on the musical theory of India. Also Indian in origin is the idea of "**nonretrogradable rhythm,**" which means a rhythmic palindrome: an arrangement of note values that reads the same both forward and backward.

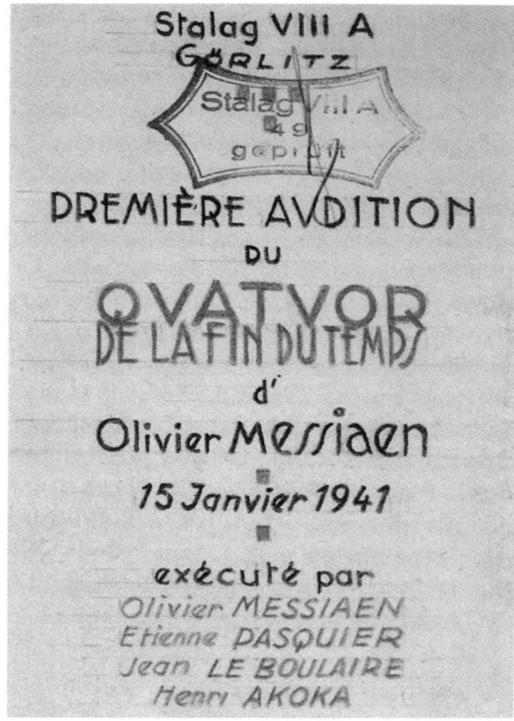

Figure 33-12 Invitation to the premiere of Messiaen's *Quartet for the End of Time*, 1941.

Putting the two axes of symmetry together—the harmonic axis represented by the modes of limited transposition and the temporal axis represented by the nonretrogradable rhythms—allows the coordination of the vertical (spatial) and horizontal (temporal) dimensions in dual representation of invariance = constancy = immutability = eternity. That is the time-transcending truth that religion reveals through music in Messiaen's aesthetic universe. And that, Messiaen explicitly informs the reader, is the source of his mysterious hold on the listener. "Let us think now of the hearer of our modal and rhythmic music," he writes:

> He will not have time at the concert to inspect the nontranspositions and the nonretrogradations, and, at that moment, these questions will not interest him further; to be charmed will be his only desire. And that is precisely what will happen; in spite of himself he will submit to the strange charm of impossibilities: a certain effect of tonal ubiquity in the nontransposition, a certain unity of movement (where beginning and end are confused because identical) in the nonretrogradation, all things which will lead him progressively to that sort of *theological rainbow* which the musical language, of which we seek edification and theory, attempts to be.[34]

As Messiaen viewed music history, the Middle Ages began with melody; centuries later harmony blossomed. With Berlioz and the Romantics timbre emerged as a principal concern, and in the twentieth century rhythm came to prominence. He explored Greek and Hindu rhythmic systems and worked for many decades on a treatise on rhythm. The mathematical complexity of his music adheres in his "note values distributed in irregular numbers, the absence of equal times, the love of prime numbers, the presence of nonretrogradable rhythms, and the action of rhythmic characters."[35] Many of the rhythmic techniques he used were common during the Ars Nova of the fourteenth century, the heyday of complex mensural notation. Equally striking was his idea of reviving, in effect, the concept of the isorhythmic motet. He did so for the same purpose the original Medieval practice had served: to represent the divine eternal harmony of the cosmos. Repeated rhythmic patterns (*talea* in Latin, *tala* in Sanskrit) were the chief Medieval means for representing cosmic harmony. Messiaen also revived the other aspect of Medieval isorhythm, namely, the abstractly conceived pitch ostinato, or *color*.

We can find most of these compositional concerns, as well as an early instance of his use of birdsong, in the first movement of the *Quartet for the End of Time*, "Liturgie de cristal," which is a prophetic evocation that Messiaen explained as follows: "The birds awaken. A solo blackbird [the clarinet] or nightingale [the violin] improvises, surrounded by dustwhirls of sound [the piano], and by a halo of harmonics lost high up in the trees [the cello]. Transpose this onto a religious plane: You have the harmonious silence of heaven."[36] The piano part is organized isorhythmically throughout, with its pitch and rhythmic contents in two independent repeating cycles. The rhythmic cycle, a pattern of seventeen durations, is indirectly taken from a thirteenth-century Sanskrit treatise. The pitch cycle consists of a series of twenty-nine chords. Above the isorhythmic piano part, the cello contributes a line, played entirely in ethereal harmonics, that takes the form of a five-note melodic ostinato organized symmetrically by being both a whole-tone scale and a rhythm that is non-retrogradable. The remaining parts, for clarinet and violin, are marked "like a bird" and imitate two distinct birds singing at dawn (Ex. 33-3).

Example 33-3 Olivier Messiaen, *Quatuor pour la fin du temps*, I ("Liturgie de cristal"), mm. 1–6

The *Quartet for the End of Time* is in eight movements that project a wide range of moods, colors, and effects; three of them (Nos. 4, 5, 8) Messiaen adapted from earlier compositions. The framing sections of the second movement, "Vocalise, pour l'Ange qui annonce la fin du Temps" (Vocalize, for the Angel Who Announces the End of Time), "evoke the power of this mighty angel, crowned with a rainbow and clothed in a cloud. . . . The middle section evokes the impalpable harmonies of heaven. In the piano: gentle cascades of blue-orange chords, encircling with their distant carillon the plainchant-like song of the violin and cello."[37] As this comment shows, Messiaen thought in terms of harmonic colors—his synesthesia meant that he actually saw colors when he heard certain chords. The third movement is scored for clarinet alone and is entitled "Abîme des oiseaux" (Abyss of the Birds). It offers another instance of Messiaen's use of hopeful birdsong: "The birds are the opposite of Time; they represent our longing for light, for stars, for rainbows, and for jubilant song!"[38] The fourth movement, "Intermède" (interlude) for violin, clarinet, and cello, is the most straightforward in the piece, a scherzo beginning in a hearty unison.

The slow fifth movement, "Louange à l'Éternité de Jésus" (Praise to the Eternity of Jesus), is for cello and piano alone. "Here, Jesus is considered the Word of God," according to Messiaen. "A long phrase in the cello, inexorably slow, glorifies, with adoration and reverence, the eternity of this mighty yet gentle Word 'of which the ages never tire.'"[39] An utter contrast is the sixth movement, a thunderous monody for all four instruments in unison called "Danse de la fureur, pour les sept trompettes" (Dance of Fury, for the Seven Trumpets). This is a sort of speculative transcription of the apocalyptic angelic call in which Messiaen said he represented "music of stone, fearful granite sonorities," displaying "the irresistible movement of steel, enormous blocks of purple fury, of icy intoxication."[40] In this breathless section Messiaen explores both added values and nonretrogradable rhythms. Example 33-4 consists of a lengthy melody in which each measure is cast as a rhythmic palindrome. The first and last measures have identical (nonretrogradable) rhythms as well, and the third and fourth measures from the end are rhythmically identical, adding extra (or, more precisely, inner) dimensions of self-reversibility to the symmetry of the whole.

Example 33-4 **Olivier Messiaen, *Technique de mon langage musical,* example 33**

The seventh movement is entitled "Fouillis d'arcs-en-ciel, pour l'Ange qui annonce la fin du Temps" (Cluster of Rainbows, for the Angel Who Announces the End of Time), while the final "Louange à l'Immortalité de Jésus" (Praise to the Immortality of Jesus), for violin and piano, returns to the mystical stasis often found in

Messiaen's music and conveys a peace that must have had special meaning for the composer, performers, and listeners in the prison camp. About a month after the extraordinary premiere of *The Quartet for the End of Time*, Messiaen and the cellist, Pasquier, were liberated from the prisoner camp and returned to Paris. The violinist, Le Boulaire, was freed the next year and clarinetist Akoka, who was Jewish, amazingly was able to escape together with his family and survived the Nazi period.

Faith, Nature, Color, and Rhythm

Like the *Quartet for the End of Time*, the majority of Messiaen's compositions have Christian titles and themes. His organ music is the most explicit in this regard, but the religious references are also found in works for the concert hall, such as the two-hour piano cycle *Vingt regards sur l'enfant Jésus* (Twenty Gazes on the Child Jesus, 1944) and *Visions de l'Amen* (Visions of Amen, 1943) for two pianos. In this religious art Messiaen seemed interested, not in sin, darkness, or evil, but, rather, in mystery, enchantment, love, and joy. In some works he connected his faith with his secular inspirations and passions, such as the story of Tristan and Isolde, his preferred symbol of human love, which served as the basis of the trilogy *Harawi* (1945), the *Turangalîla-symphonie* (1946–48), and *Cinq rechants* (1948).

The *Turangalîla-symphonie*, a ten-movement, seventy-five-minute blockbuster for an enormous orchestra, was premiered by the Boston Symphony Orchestra under Leonard Bernstein in 1949 and, despite its length and extravagant demands, became one of his most often-performed postwar symphonic works. The ensemble is not only huge but unprecedentedly varied as well. There are parts for fifteen different percussion instruments requiring eight players, and six keyboard instruments, including a piano prominent enough to require a virtuoso soloist with feature billing (for decades it was usually played by the composer's second wife, Yvonne Loriod), and an ondes martenot, one of the earliest electronic keyboard instruments. The title is a composite of two Sanskrit words: *turanga*, meaning the measurement of time by movement, and *lîla*, meaning the play of the divine will on the cosmos (and, by poetic extension, the force of love). "*Turangalîla* signifies, at one and the same time, a love song, a hymn to joy, time, movement, rhythm, life and death,"[41] the composer wrote, leaving room for almost any desired interpretation of his music.

Messiaen's use of birdsong became a major preoccupation that helped him overcome a creative block in the 1950s. Just as Bartók traveled extensively "in the field" to notate folk songs, so Messiaen circled the globe notating and recording various species of birds. This ornithological life-drawing would become an obsession that culminated in a cycle of piano compositions called *Catalogue d'oiseaux* (Catalogue of Birds, 1956–58). Works for his later years included *Des canyons aux étoiles* (From the Canyons to the Stars, 1971–74) and a monumental orchestral swansong, *Éclairs sur l'Au-delà* (Illuminations of the Beyond, 1988–92), completed not long before he died. His largest project, which took nearly a decade to compose, is an opera, *Saint François d'Assise*, which premiered at the Paris Opéra on 28 November 1983. He also continued theoretical work that resulted in the massive 4,000-page *Traité de rythme, de couleur, et d'ornithologie* (Treatise on Rhythm, Color, and Ornithology, 1949–92), which Loriod completed and published after her husband's death.

Although many of his scores are among the most technically complex and analytically challenging works ever written, compositions that amply reward the investigations of music theorists, Messiaen's music has attracted exceptionally devoted performers to present them and audiences eager to listen. Despite his impeccable academic credentials, Messiaen was honest enough to remark that "generally modern music is aggressive, intellectual, interesting, gripping, but isn't pretty. . . . I think we need to get back to charm, to sweetness, or just simply to what sounds good."[42]

Late in his life Messiaen spoke of a fourfold dilemma in his career: A believer, he preached "faith to atheists," an ornithologist, he spoke of birds to "people who live in cities," as one who sees colors listening to music, he wrote for those who "see nothing," and as a "rhythmician," he composed in an age that thinks rhythm and a steady beat are one and the same. Here Messiaen enumerates the four principal components of his self-definition: faith, love of nature, harmonic color, and rhythmic explorations.[43] What may have ultimately surprised him was that so many godless, color-blind, rhythmically challenged city dwellers found so much in his mystically joyous, naturally lyric, brilliantly colorful, and rhythmically complex music. This represents a type of accessibility—an engagement of audience members' faculties—that differed from the forced accessibility of the Soviet sphere or the democratic populism associated with Copland. Nonetheless, especially after the atrocities of the Second World War, a new generation of young composers was prompted to give up on all such ideals of communication, regardless of whether the impulse came from political pressure, populist commitments, personal testimony, or religious expression. After the horrors of another war, art had to start over again.

Summary

This chapter explored trends in the United States and its European allies in the 1930s and '40s, focusing on experimental music and the influence of the political left. Experimental trends in American music had begun earlier, with composers such as Charles Ives (1874–1954), Ruth Crawford Seeger (1901–53), Henry Cowell (1897–1965), and Edgard Varèse (1883–1965). One experimental aspect of their music was the incorporation of new sounds that began to push the boundaries of what was considered "musical." Cowell, for example, used tone clusters, produced by pressing the piano keys with forearms and having the performer strum the piano strings. In pieces such as *Ionisation* (1931) Varèse incorporated sirens and "sound masses." Harry Partch (1901–74) and others experimented with intervals smaller than a semitone, called *microtones*. Most of these composers had careers outside of the musical establishment.

The 1930s and '40s saw an increasing prominence of white American folklore, a trend that was particularly associated with the political left. In the mid-1930s the American Communist aligned itself with less radical forms of leftism, known as the Popular Front, and used indigenous American culture and history rather than Soviet imagery to promote their ideas. The collections of folk songs, hymns, and old popular songs that appeared in the 1930s and '40s under the auspices of the left profoundly influenced the music of Aaron Copland, himself sympathetic to leftist ideals. With his ballets *Billy the Kid* (1938), *Rodeo* (1942), and *Appalachian Spring* (1944), all on themes of American rural life, Copland created a sound that is still heard as iconically American, with widely spaced sonorities, open fifths and octaves, and dissonant but diatonic chords. With works such as *El Salón México* (1932–36), Copland also looked to Latin America for inspiration.

Copland and others turned to patriotic or populist themes in part because of the crises of the Great Depression and World War II. In addition, during this time period, musicians and artists were financially bolstered by the employment programs and new ensembles sponsored by Franklin Delano Roosevelt's "New Deal." During the 1930s and '40s, several composers produced distinctively American takes on the traditional genres of symphony and opera. Successful American symphonists included Roy Harris (1898–1979), Copland, William Schuman (1910–92), Walter Piston (1894–1976), and Roger Sessions (1896–1985). *Adagio for Strings* by Samuel Barber (1910–81) has become a permanent part of the standard repertory, and the opera *Susannah* by Carlisle Floyd (b. 1926) is still performed with some frequency. Gian Carlo Menotti (1911–2007) produced dramatic works that played both on Broadway and in traditional opera houses.

The operas of the British composer Benjamin Britten (1913–76) stand out as central contributions to English-language opera. The title character of his *Peter Grimes* (1945) is a fisherman in an English seaside town, responsible for the death of two apprentices. In his adaptation of the original story, Britten portrays Peter as a more sympathetic character, in part by emphasizing the hypocrisy of the townspeople who judge him. As both a pacifist during wartime and a homosexual—his lifelong partner Peter Pears sang the title role—Britten could personally identify with the plight of a social outsider. Some have interpreted the opera as an allegory for the social stigma surrounding homosexuality. Features of Britten's writing include diatonic dissonance, colorful timbres, and bitonality, which he employs to dramatic and political ends.

The leading French composer of the period was Olivier Messiaen (1908–92), who blended an intense religious focus with individualistic compositional techniques. While the title of his *Quatuor pour la fin du temps* (Quartet for the End of Time, 1940–41), composed and premiered in a German prisoner-of-war camp, derives from the Book of Revelation, it also refers to the unconventional meter and rhythm of the music. Messiaen's "nonretrogradable rhythms," the same backward and forward, were complemented by his "modes of limited transposition," which could only be transposed by a limited number of intervals without replicating the same pitch series. Messiaen's works are also saturated by various kinds of canons and isorhythm, but despite these complexities they have won a wide range of admirers.

Study Questions

1. Describe the types of experimental music composed in the United States between 1910 and 1940. Who were the leading composers, and how did they experiment with new types of sound? In what respects were these composers outside the mainstream culture of art music?
2. Explain the political background behind the increasing popularity of American folk music in the 1930s and '40s. What was the Popular Front, and why did it use folk music to achieve its aims?

3. Describe the different ways in which Aaron Copland's works represent "Americanist" style. How was Copland's music influenced by the political landscape and his own political beliefs?
4. Which American composers contributed to opera and symphony in the 1930s and '40s? Describe some of the most important American works in these genres.
5. In what ways does Benjamin Britten's depiction of Peter Grimes differ from that of George Crabbe's original poem? What does Britten do to make Peter a sympathetic character? Why has *Peter Grimes* been viewed as an allegory for the mid-twentieth-century social stigma surrounding homosexuality?
6. What were Britten's views on the social responsibility of artists, and how are these reflected in his *War Requiem*?
7. How would you describe the relationship between religious faith and musical techniques in Olivier Messiaen's music? Describe some of the techniques he used in *Quartet for the End of Time*.

Key Terms

Futurism
microtones
modes of limited transposition
New Deal
nonretrogradable rhythms
Popular Front
quarter tones
tone clusters
ultra-modern

34

Starting from Scratch: Music in the Aftermath of World War II

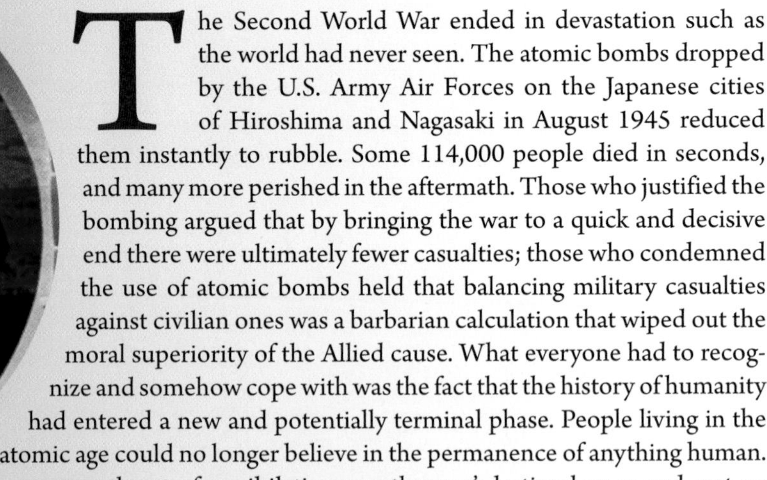

The Second World War ended in devastation such as the world had never seen. The atomic bombs dropped by the U.S. Army Air Forces on the Japanese cities of Hiroshima and Nagasaki in August 1945 reduced them instantly to rubble. Some 114,000 people died in seconds, and many more perished in the aftermath. Those who justified the bombing argued that by bringing the war to a quick and decisive end there were ultimately fewer casualties; those who condemned the use of atomic bombs held that balancing military casualties against civilian ones was a barbarian calculation that wiped out the moral superiority of the Allied cause. What everyone had to recognize and somehow cope with was the fact that the history of humanity had entered a new and potentially terminal phase. People living in the atomic age could no longer believe in the permanence of anything human.

The constant threat of annihilation was the war's lasting legacy and cast an enormous shadow over the second half of the twentieth century. It was that period's dominant fact of life (Fig. 34-1).

The conclusion of the war once again changed the political landscape of Europe and had international implications that went far beyond the embattled continent. By the end of 1946, the victors' euphoria had given way to mutual suspicion among the erstwhile Allies. The United States and the Soviet Union, united temporarily to defeat the shared German enemy, now saw their foreign policies diverge into bitter antagonism. The Soviets had sustained extraordinary losses during the war, as many as 20 million lives, and were more intent than ever on national security. Joseph Stalin insisted on a buffer of friendly states (that is, Communist-dominated governments) along the length of its European frontiers. The Soviets thus sealed off areas of the former German Reich that were occupied by the Red Army and fomented take-overs in other Eastern European countries. As early as March 1946, fewer than seven months after the war's end, former British Prime Minister Winston Churchill could speak of an "Iron Curtain" that had descended over Europe, dividing East from West. A new kind of war, the Cold War, had begun (Fig. 34-2).

To block further Soviet expansion, the North Atlantic Treaty Organization (NATO) was established in 1949, the members of which were pledged to consider an armed attack on any one of them an attack against them all. The Soviet Union countered NATO with the formation of the Warsaw Pact, a mutual defense treaty signed in 1955 by the USSR and the countries that by then formed the "Soviet Bloc" of buffer states: Albania, Bulgaria, Czechoslovakia, Hungary, Poland, Romania, and the German Democratic Republic (GDR), namely, the "East German" part that the Soviet army occupied. In retaliation "West Germany" was admitted to NATO, thus putting the border between East and West right in the middle of the old common foe. Symbolic of the times was the division of the city of Berlin into the Soviet-controlled sector of East Berlin and the American, British, and French sectors that became West Berlin. In the summer of 1961 an actual wall was constructed by the GDR.

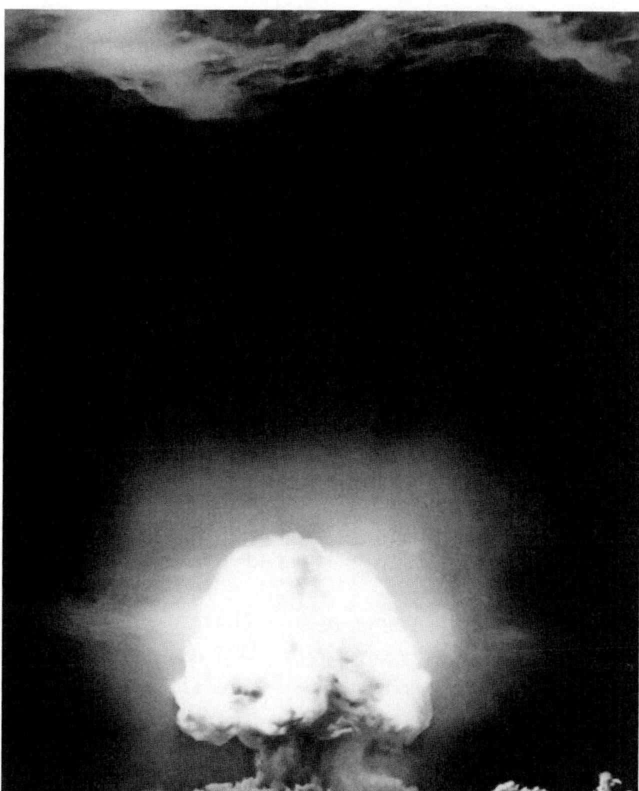

Figure 34-1 Nuclear bomb test.

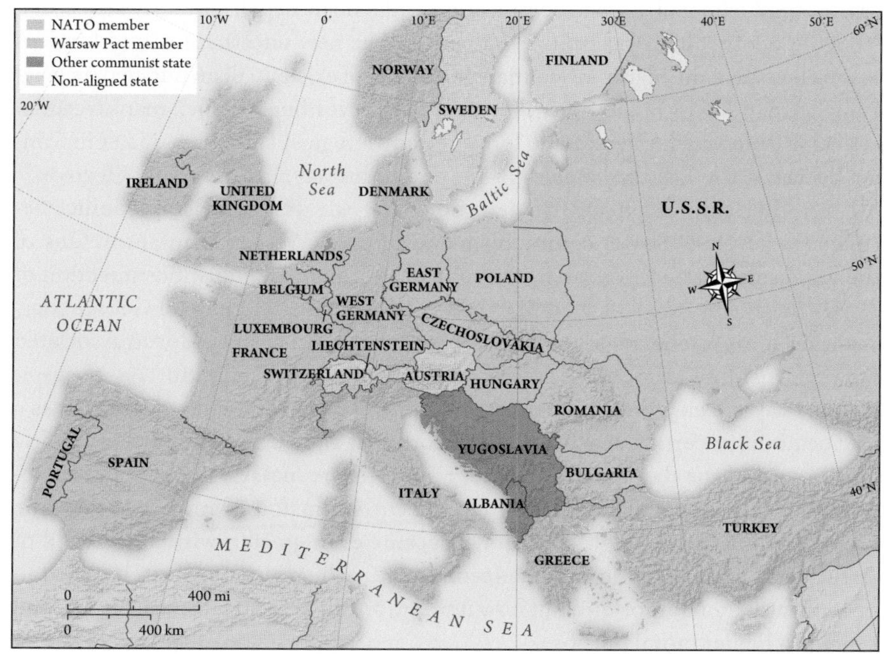

Figure 34-2 Cold War military alignments.

TIMELINE

1940 **John Cage, "The Future of Music: Credo"; *Bacchanale***

1943 Jean-Paul Sartre, *Being and Nothingness*

1945 World War II ends

1946 **International Summer Courses for New Music established in Darmstadt, Germany**

1948 Samuel Beckett, *Waiting for Godot*

1948 **Pierre Schaeffer coins the term *musique concrète***

1949 North Atlantic Treaty Organization (NATO) formed

1949 **Olivier Messiaen, *Mode de valeurs et d'intensités***

1950–51 **Elliott Carter, First String Quartet**

1950–53 Korean War

1952 **Pierre Boulez's essay "Schoenberg Is Dead" published**

1952 **Cage, *4'33"***

The Cold War was a major factor in Euro-American foreign policy and internal politics until the fall of the Berlin Wall in 1989, the subsequent "Velvet Revolution" in Czechoslovakia and other East Bloc countries, and the ultimate collapse of the Soviet Union in 1991. Thus for more than four decades there was intense political and ideological rivalry between the United States and its European allies, on the one hand, and the Soviet Union and its "satellites," on the other. After the Soviets successfully tested an atom bomb of their own in 1949, the Cold War constantly threatened to erupt into an actual military engagement with the potential to destroy civilization. In a widely used phrase of the time, the world was permanently poised on "the brink of World War III," now with the threat of "mutually assured destruction" through thermonuclear weapons. Suspicion of espionage ran high (becoming familiar in popular culture through spy novels and movies), directed not only at the potential enemy but at fellow citizens as well. No one knew whom to trust.

Zero Hour: The Impact on the Arts

The resulting crises in the arts may have been even greater than after the First World War. Added to everything else there was now much more uncertainty about the future. There was also the necessity of dealing with the previously unimagined horrors that had happened during the war and what this might mean concerning the very essence of human nature. Germany's systematic killing of millions of Jews, homosexuals, Romanies (gypsies), the mentally ill, and others perceived as undesirable revealed an inhumanity that had to be accounted for. What good was cultivating the humanities if they did not humanize, if unbelievable cruelty could come from the same people who created and cherished magnificent literature and music?

Many wondered what kind of art could now be created—or whether any art could be created at all. Theodor W. Adorno, who emerged as the high priest of Modernism (and who had studied composition with Alban Berg), famously stated that "to write poetry after Auschwitz is barbaric."[1] The new uncertainties and burdens were reflected in the highly influential philosophy of existentialism pursued by Jean-Paul Sartre (1905–80) and other French writers, according to which man's freedom is a curse from which there can no longer be any refuge in faith. A character in Samuel Beckett's play *The Unnamable* (1953) puts it this way: "I can't go on. I'll go on."

Another component of the new Cold War was the increasing conflict between the ideals of Soviet communism and those of Western capitalism. One of the ways a devastated Europe was rebuilt was through an enormous injection of American money, the so-called Marshall Plan, named after General George Marshall. Yet some intellectuals and artists, particularly leftists like Adorno associated with the Institute for Social Research at the University of Frankfurt, were suspicious of capitalism, consumerism, and commercialism. These factors served as a provocation for certain artists to create work that was "uncompromising," to use a buzzword of the day, art that did not appeal to the masses, but supposedly remained true to its own materials and to the current historical moment. Thus the great divide between "high" and "low" became even greater, with a new kind of "art for art's sake." True to the nineteenth-century historicist project, it aimed to be innovative and important, but now it was more divorced from everyday life and claimed a higher moral purpose.

German writers who looked to the future in the defeated parts of Europe saw the present as a *Stunde Null*, a **Zero Hour**, meaning a time without a past. Many felt a strong necessity to start from scratch, to reject the past as something tainted if not actually destroyed in the totalitarian horrors. Among serious composers in Western Europe and America the most noteworthy development was the unexpected resurgence and dominance of twelve-tone composition, or serialism, to use the preferred postwar term. The word "serious" is the right one in this context, for it was the word then employed. It derived from German usage, in which the distinction between classical and popular music was couched as one between *ernste Musik*, or "E-Musik"—that is, "serious music"—and *Unterhaltungsmusik*, or "U-Musik," meaning "entertainment music."

In fact there were now different kinds of serious music, and some believed that only certain styles were historically relevant to artistic progress. We can see this attitude in a few particularly influential postwar writings that continued to uphold the historicist position first asserted nearly a century earlier by the New German School about constant progress in the arts. One influential book was *Schoenberg and His School: The Contemporary Stage of the Language of Music* (1947), written in French by the composer, conductor, and teacher René Leibowitz (1913–72). He asserted that the language of music was a universal language that had undergone a single historical development, of which the most advanced contemporary stage was the only historically valid and viable one at any given time. For Leibowitz that stage was the one reached by Schoenberg and his followers; any music not at that level of historical evolution was of no historical consequence and therefore of no serious interest. Leibowitz stated that unless one has recognized the basic fact that twelve-tone serial music was "the only genuine and inevitable expression of the musical art of our time," one had no right to call oneself a composer at all.[2]

While this position became an article of faith for many, some, such as Aaron Copland, were shocked at the "dogmatic" and "fanatical" tone.[3] The authoritarian subtext was apparent. Phrases that Leibowitz used, like "master of our time," had disquieting resonances, to put it mildly, in a world just rid of Hitler and one in which Stalin's murderous terror continued. And yet the book's message was heard and widely obeyed—even by Copland, who soon thereafter, and against his own expectations, began sketching his own first twelve-tone composition.

The Nazis had banned the work of Schoenberg and his colleagues, which gave their scores not only the aura of forbidden fruit but something more as well. Twelve-tone music became a symbol of resistance and, by extension, a symbol of creative freedom. Such music was also viewed by many as a symbol of incorruptible purity, precisely because it was, to use the Soviet term, so "formalist." It seemed to deal only with "purely musical" relationships of structure rather than with "extramusical" considerations of expression, the now-discredited baggage of the long nineteenth century. Serialism seemed to be incapable of being co-opted for purposes of either political propaganda or commercial manipulation. In his influential *Philosophie der neuen Musik* (Philosophy of New Music), a book he published in 1949 shortly after returning to Germany from his wartime exile in America, Adorno argued that composers should respond to "the inherent tendency of musical material" rather than to any call from the wider world. Twelve-tone music seemed to embody a perfect artistic "autonomy."[4]

1955 The Soviet Union forms the Warsaw Pact

1957 **Milton Babbitt's essay "Who Cares If You Listen?" is published**

1958 **Columbia-Princeton Electronic Music Center founded**

1958 **Edgard Varèse, *Poème électronique***

1960 **Krzysztof Penderecki, *Threnody to the Victims of Hiroshima***

1961 Berlin wall built dividing East and West Germany

1962 **Group for Contemporary Music ensemble formed**

1963 President John F. Kennedy assassinated

1964 The Beatles make their first American tour

1964 **Babbitt, *Philomel***

1965 U.S. troops enter Vietnam

1966 **Igor Stravinsky, *Requiem Canticles***

1971 **Morton Feldman, *Rothko Chapel***

The great divide between "high" and "low" became even greater, with a new kind of "art for art's sake."

The ultimate statement of the Zero Hour position came not in these books but in a short article: "Schoenberg est mort" (Schoenberg Is Dead), a manifesto published in February 1952, seven months after Schoenberg's death, by Pierre Boulez (b. 1925), a twenty-six-year-old French composer who had studied with Olivier Messiaen and Leibowitz. His intolerant rhetoric came to this frightening climax: "Since the Viennese discoveries, any musician who has not experienced—I do not say understood, but truly experienced—the necessity of the dodecaphonic language is USELESS. For his entire work brings him up short of the needs of his time."[5]

But if the twelve-tone method was Boulez's answer, then why attack Schoenberg? It was because of the emergence of Anton Webern as the new ideal for Zero Hour serialists. During his lifetime he had remained a rather esoteric figure, and his small body of work was still in part unpublished. Webern's purity suited the dislocated, amnesiac mood of the times. If all the past had to be rejected, then Schoenberg had to be rejected too. Had he not advertised himself as an upholder of the great tradition? For Boulez, Schoenberg's big mistake had been his attempt to reconcile the new means of tonal organization with traditional "classic" forms and traditional "expressive" rhetoric.[6] Schoenberg could thus be lumped together with the other Neoclassicists of the interwar period as a practitioner of what Adorno called "moderate Modernism."[7] Webern, on the other hand, pointed the way, in a work like his *Symphony*, to actual "serial structures" based on "serial functions." Besides forgetting Schoenberg, Boulez advised, "Perhaps we might enlarge the serial domain with intervals other than the semitone: micro-intervals, irregular intervals, complex sounds. Perhaps we might generalize the serial principle to the four constituents of sound: pitch, duration, dynamics/attack, and timbre. Perhaps . . . perhaps . . ."[8]

Toward Total Serialism: Olivier Messiaen's *Mode de valeurs et d'intensités*

Anthology Vol 3-49
Full CD VII, 19
Concise CD III, 41

In other words, Boulez's proposition was to serialize elements other than just pitches, extending the process to rhythmic note values, dynamics, and timbre. Although he cast this as hypothetical, by 1952 some of this expansion had already been put into practice, both by Boulez himself and by others. The first famous work to do so was a short piano piece by his teacher, Messiaen, called *Mode de valeurs et d'intensités* (roughly, Scheme of Note Values and Dynamics), composed during the summer of 1949 and published the next year as the second in a set of four *Études de rhythme* (Rhythmic Studies). It is not a twelve-tone work but, rather, a study in "hypostatization," the total determination ("fixing") of a limited group of sonic elements or events. The idea had a direct precedent in Webern, who had experimented with the fixed assignment of particular pitches to particular registers. Messiaen extended the principle to the domains of duration, dynamics, and attack. The material out of which he assembled *Mode de valeurs* consisted of thirty-six different notes that are all systematically catalogued in a table that precedes the score (Ex. 34-1).

Messiaen later said that the four-minute piece was "prophetic and historically important, but musically it's next to nothing."[9] Its impact was nonetheless enormous. Boulez found *Mode de valeurs* particularly inspiring, not only for the way in which it seemed to integrate "the four constituents of sound" but also for the way in which the whole piece arose out of a set of axioms, rigorously predetermined rules. It promised a new utopia: "**total**" or "integral" **serialism**. What had to happen next was to introduce strict serial ordering into the four domains (pitch, duration, dynamics, attack), which is what Boulez did in *Structures* for two pianos (1951). He paid tribute to his former teacher by adopting the pitch succession from *Mode de valeurs* as a tone row, turning what had been for Messiaen a quarry of "stones" for a mosaic into a rigorously ordered pitch and intervallic sequence. Messiaen's twelve chromatically graded durations were likewise put in a definite and rigorously maintained order, derived from the pitch order but made to operate independently. Boulez expanded Messiaen's collection of seven degrees of loudness to twelve, simply by making the gradations finer; the collection of twelve attacks was taken over with only slight modifications. Once everything was set, the composer could sit back, as it were, and let the music write itself. The real labor, one might say, was "precompositional."

Anthology Vol 3-50
Full CD VII, 20

Example 34-1 Olivier Messiaen, *Mode de valeurs et d'intensités*, prefatory table

This piece uses a scheme of 36 pitches, 24 note values, 12 attacks, and 7 dynamic levels. It is written entirely according to the scheme.

Attacks: 1 2 3 4 5 6 7 8 9 10 11 (*sf* *sf*)

(with the neutral, unsigned attack, this makes 12.)

Dynamics: *ppp* *pp* *p* *mf* *f* *ff* *fff*
1 2 3 4 5 6 7

Tones: The scheme comprises 3 Divisions, or melodic groupings of 12 tones, each extending through several octaves, with overlaps. Tones of the same name differ in pitch, duration and loudness.

Division I: chromatic degrees from 1 to 12 (*etc.*)

Division II: chromatic degrees from 1 to 12 (*etc.*)

Division III: chromatic degrees from 1 to 12 (*etc.*)

24 durations in all: 1 2 3 4 5 6 7 8 9 10 11 12 13 14 15 16 17 18 19 20 21 22 23 24

Here is the scheme:

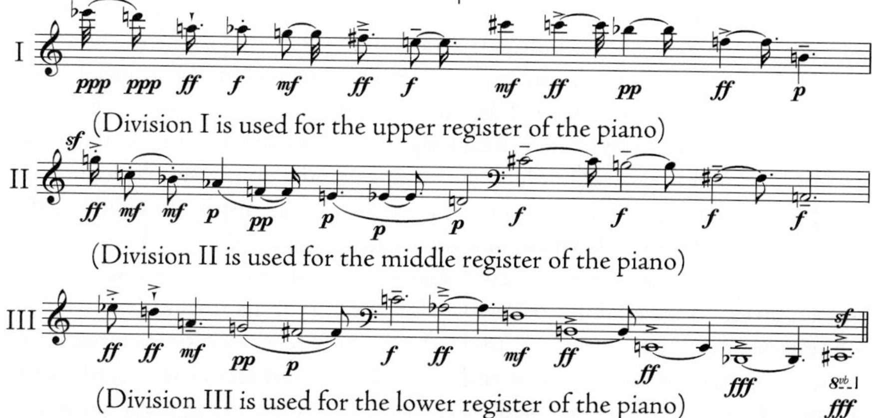

In bluntest terms, then, the paradox created by total serialism came to this: Once the algorithms—the mathematical recipe—governing a composition have been determined, it is possible to demonstrate the decisive correctness of the score more objectively than is possible for any other kind of music; but in the act of listening to the composition, one has little way of knowing this. The music yields its secrets—that is, its governing rules and procedures—not to human ears but, rather, to the mind of a determined analyst armed with the score. The value of technical analysis as a separate musical activity, not coincidentally, experienced an unprecedented boom after the war. Boulez allegedly said at the time that the age of the concert had passed; scores did not need to be played any longer, just "read"—i.e., analyzed. This helped spur the growth of a new musicological specialization, that of music analyst, loosely identified with the much older and broader calling of music theorist.

Darmstadt

The hub of activity for Zero Hour composers was a unique institution that had been set up in 1946 in Darmstadt, a small town located in central Germany, in the American-controlled zone of occupation. The *Internationale Ferienkurse für Neue Musik* (International Summer Courses for New Music) aimed to spread American political and cultural values as part of the general Allied effort, set up with American financial backing, to reeducate the German population in preparation for the establishment of democratic institutions. A more specific goal was to provide a meeting place where musicians from the former fascist areas of Europe might further their musical reeducation through exposure to styles that had long been prohibited.

The early years of Darmstadt summers were led by established older figures, such as Wolfgang Fortner (1907–87), Leibowitz, Ernst Krenek, and Edgard Varèse. In 1951–52 three young composers began to dominate: Boulez, Karlheinz Stockhausen (1928–2007), a German who had moved to Paris early in 1952 to study with Messiaen, and Bruno Maderna (1920–73), an Italian composer and conductor (Fig. 34-3). In the years to follow, many of the major figures of the European and American avant-garde joined as well: Hungarian György Ligeti (1923–2006); Italians Luciano Berio (1925–2003) and Luigi Nono (1924–90); and Iannis Xenakis (1922–2001), a Romanian-born Greek who had a thorough training in mathematics and engineering before he decided on a musical career and moved to Paris, where he also studied with Messiaen.

Boulez allegedly said that the age of the concert had passed; scores did not need to be played any longer, just "read."

German composer Hans Werner Henze (b. 1926) left a vivid recollection of the early Darmstadt scene that captures something of the new orthodoxy: "Things had become pretty absurd. Boulez, who saw himself as the supreme authority, was sitting at the piano, flanked by Maderna and myself—we must have looked like reluctant assistant judges at a trial, as young composers brought their pieces forward for opinion. He brusquely dismissed anything that wasn't Webernian: 'If it isn't written in the style of Webern it's of no interest'."[10] A famous incident occurred in a composition class that Schoenberg was supposed to have taught but could not because of his final illness. Adorno, himself an occasional composer, took on the job and evidently inquired about the development of motives in an embryonic total-serial piece that a student had submitted. Stockhausen remarked, "Professor, you are looking for a chicken in an abstract painting."[11] The sassy remark became a Darmstadt legend.

We will remember that Schoenberg had originally developed the twelve-tone technique in the 1920s partly in response to a pressing compositional problem: how to construct large atonal compositions in the absence of tonal structures. His new method in no way precluded him from continuing to write emotional, indeed expressionist music. But total serialism now offered an escape from both expression and subjectivity. For Boulez, the abstract, pure, unemotional, elegant qualities of total serialism, its rhetoric and cult of difficulty, were all to be upheld as necessary protections against those who tried to control art through either politics or commercialism.

Figure 34-3 Pierre Boulez, Bruno Maderna, and Karlheinz Stockhausen at Darmstadt, 1956.

Some critics predictably countered that there could be no greater regulation of art than that of total serialism. They resented the idea of a music that disclosed so little to an ordinary listener. Others objected to the misappropriation of scientific prestige. And some saw nihilism in all this. Yet rather than an expression of belief in nothing, total serialism demanded a kind of renunciation that might instead be seen as expressing existential despair. It was the passionately intense reaction of artists who could no longer believe in the supreme value of the individual self, the autonomous subject exalted by Romanticism, at a time when millions of selves just as individual as theirs might vanish at the push of a button. There was no point in expressing feelings when the best-laid plans seemed so futile and personal feelings so trivial in the face of such destructive power. The authoritarian manner was bravado in the face of impotence. Total serialism allowed something "realer" to emerge. And what could be realer, more pure and elegant, than numbers?

Indeterminacy: John Cage and the "New York School"

The American counterpart to the postwar musical avant-garde in Europe was a group of composers, artists, and performers gathered around the charismatic figure of John Cage (1912–92), who became for a while one of the most influential creative figures in the world. The American's methods differed so radically from those of his European contemporaries as to hide some basic affinities. Indeed, it is fair to say that what they shared went much deeper than their differences, for both groups sought "automatism," the resolute elimination of the artist's ego or personality from the artistic product. It was a traditional Modernist aim pushed to a hitherto-unimaginable extreme.

Cage and his followers went about the task with such stunning directness as to put themselves almost wholly outside what anyone could possibly think of as the musical mainstream. It was an adventurous continuation of American experimentalism harkening back in certain respects to Charles Ives, Henry Cowell, and the ultra-modernists. Cage, a confirmed maverick, was long seen as a joker—or at least a "Dadaist"—on the margins of the legitimate musical world. In the view of many average listeners he was not a composer at all and what he produced was not music. But for many of his admirers he was not only a great composer but someone who was fundamentally redefining what music is.

Like Cowell, his early mentor and teacher, Cage was born and raised in California. Besides some childhood piano lessons, he had little formal music education, never attended a conservatory, and never acquired the basic skills in ear training normally thought necessary for creative work in music. He audited some of Schoenberg's theory courses beginning in the summer of 1935 but was mainly self-taught, except for some sporadic private lessons with Adolph Weiss, who had himself studied with Schoenberg in Berlin. "The whole pitch aspect of music eludes me," Cage once cheerfully told an interviewer, no doubt exaggerating for effect.[12] It could be fairly said, nonetheless, that his career was devoted to countering the supremacy of traditional pitch organization—harmony, counterpoint, and all the rest—as the basis for making music. A few apprentice works aside, Cage's earliest original compositions were for moderate-size percussion ensembles that included pots and pans and other household items—"Living Room Music," as he titled one piece. Like some early ultra-modernists, he incorporated percussion associated with various Asian and Caribbean repertoires, such as the Indonesian gamelan and Afro-Cuban popular music. He continually experimented with new musical instruments and sound sources over the course of his career.

In 1940, at age twenty-eight, Cage boldly stated his goal in a lecture called "The Future of Music: Credo": "The present methods of writing music, principally those which employ harmony and its reference to particular steps in the field of sound, will be inadequate for the composer, who will be faced with the entire field of sound."[13] Where Schoenberg had "emancipated the dissonance" and Stravinsky had emancipated rhythm, Cage now proposed to complete the job and emancipate noise. Having envisioned a music that might include, as he put it, "a quartet for explosive motor, wind, heartbeat, and landslide," and anticipating objections from those for whom "the word 'music' is sacred and reserved for eighteenth- and nineteenth-century instruments," Cage suggested that the word be abolished and be replaced with "a more meaningful term: organized sound." The composer—the "organizer of sound"—deals "not only with the entire field of sound but also with the entire field of time."[14]

The music of the future, as Cage envisioned it, would not merely replace one type of sound with another on its sounding surface but would entail an entirely new ordering of musical elements, with duration rather than pitch as the fundamental organizing principle. Duration, he argued, was the most basic musical element, since all sounds—and silence, too—had it in common. Cage felt he could rightfully claim that he was the only contemporary musician who was dealing newly with music at its root, its core radical level. Most of his early percussion pieces, like much of the music he would write later, were based on abstract durational schemes—"empty containers," he called them, to be filled with sounds—that replaced the abstract harmonic schemes of the classical tradition.

Music for Prepared Piano

Some of Cage's new sounds came from an old instrument reincarnated. In 1940 he was asked to write music to accompany a dance performance in a venue that was too small to accommodate an ensemble. He devised a neoprimitivist dance solo

Anthology Vol 3-51
Full CD VII, 21
Concise CD III, 42

called *Bacchanale* that required just one piano, but used in a new way. Recalling Cowell's experiments in extended piano technique, such as tone clusters, Cage ingeniously turned an ordinary piano into a one-man percussion band (Fig. 34-4). He did this by inserting metal screws, pencil erasers, and other ordinary devices between the piano strings to deaden the pitch or otherwise alter the timbre. He called his invention the "**prepared piano**"; skeptics called it the "well-tampered clavier." A glance at the score of *Bacchanale* shows that Cage's neoprimitivism was of the conventional, ostinato-driven sort established by Stravinsky's *The Rite of Spring*. What cannot be gleaned at all from the score is any idea of what the piece actually sounds like in terms of pitch or timbre, since the sounds of a prepared piano no longer have any predictable relationship to the struck keys that activate the strings. The pianist plays normal notation, but the resulting sounds are magically strange and disconnected (Ex. 34-2a and 34-2b).

Between 1940 and 1954 Cage produced some two dozen works for prepared piano. The summit of his achievement was an hour-long set of *Sonatas and Interludes* (1946–48), in which the sonatas were of the Scarlattian type: single binary-form movements, with repeats. It was one of Cage's few concessions to then-fashionable Neoclassicism. A few years earlier he had written *The Perilous Night* (1944), which Cage referred to as his "autobiographical" piece.[15] He apparently associated the work with the traumas around his sexual reorientation, culminating in divorce from his wife and the beginning of a personal and professional partnership with dancer and choreographer Merce Cunningham (1919–2009) that lasted to the end of his life. Cage was understandably distressed when a critic, who could not get over the shock of the novel prepared-piano timbres, dismissed this most intimately confessional of all Cage's works with the remark that it sounded like "a woodpecker in a church belfry."[16] The wounded composer talked about this experience for the rest of his life: "I determined to give up composition unless I could find a better reason for doing it than communication."

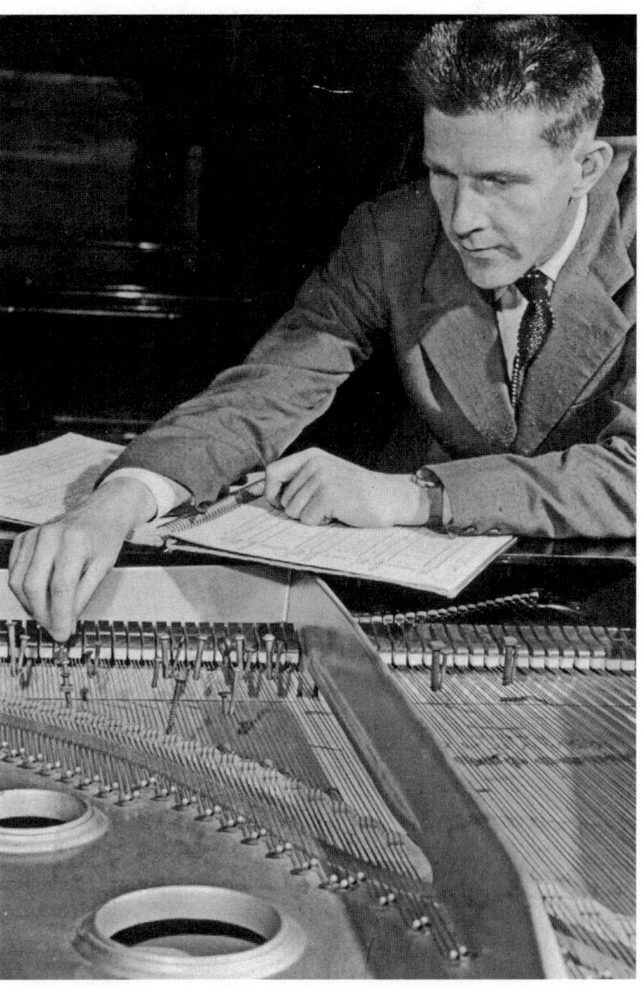

Figure 34-4 John Cage preparing a piano by placing coins and screws between the strings in Paris, France, 1949.

Cage ultimately found his answer through immersion in the quietistic philosophy of Zen Buddhism, a fashionable preoccupation among Euro-American intellectuals in the late 1940s and early 1950s. He was one of many New York artists who flocked to Columbia University, beginning in 1945, to hear lectures on the subject given by the American-educated D. T. Suzuki (1869–1966), Zen's chief ambassador abroad. Japanese for "meditation," Zen is a mental discipline that aims at sudden spiritual illumination by systematically rejecting the illusory safety of rational thought, which it regards as contrary to nature. In long sessions of ritualized contemplation, the mind is cleared of all expectation. The principle of nonexpectation relates to Cage's ideal of experimental music. In his writings and interviews he loved to express his ideas in the baffling manner of a *koan,* a deliberately paradoxical riddle or saying.

Example 34-2a John Cage, *Bacchanale,* "piano preparation" chart

Piano Preparation

Tone	Material	String (left to right)	Distance From Damper
	small bolt	2-3	circa 3"
	weather stripping*	1-2	**
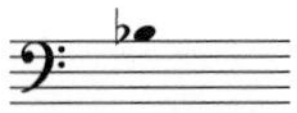	screw with nuts & weather stripping*	2-3 1-2	** **
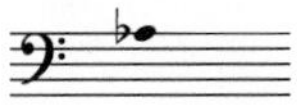	weather stripping*	1-2	**
	weather stripping*	1-2	**
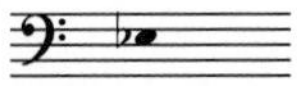	weather stripping*	1-2	**
	weather stripping*	1-2	**
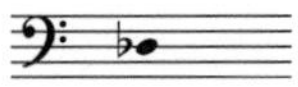	weather stripping*	1-2	**
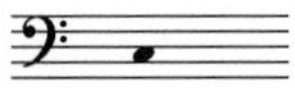	weather stripping*	1-2	**
	weather stripping*	1-2	**
	weather stripping*	1-2	**
	weather stripping*	1-2	**

*fibrous

**determine position and size of mutes by experiment

Example 34-2b John Cage, *Bacchanale,* mm. 1–5

Rather than communication, Cage adopted the purposes of research: not the kind of theoretical research in which many other composers engaged but experimental research in which the outcome of one's actions was unpredicted and, as far as possible, uninfluenced by desire or intention. Cage's abundant ingenuity would now be lavished on strategies to frustrate the planning of results so that the object he produced would be completely free of his own emotions, wishes, and preferences. Although he often described the elaborate methods he devised as involving indeterminacy or chance, they were anything but anarchic. The liberation of sound demanded the suppression, indeed even the enslavement, of all human beings concerned—composer, performer, and listener alike—for it demanded the complete suppression of the ego.

Around the same time that Cage was absorbing Zen, an aspiring young composer named Christian Wolff (b. 1934) introduced him to the *I Ching*, or "Book of Changes," an ancient Chinese manual of divination, the art of reading premonitions to gain knowledge unavailable to reason. The user of the *I Ching* would toss three coins (or six sticks) six times to determine which of sixty-four possible hexagrams (combinations of six continuous or broken lines) to consult in answer to a question about the future or some other unobservable thing. By associating the hexagrams with musical parameters (pitch, duration, loudness, attack, and so forth), Cage was able to convert the coin-tossing method into a means of eliminating his compositional habits or desires, or, as he put it, "memories, tastes, likes and dislikes."[17] Once he had decided how the coin tosses would determine the musical results, he could relinquish control of the process and compose "nonintentionally," as Zen prescribed.

Cage's mixture of Zen with the *I Ching* was a practical stroke of genius. The predetermination of the relationships between the divination charts and the musical results was precisely the sort of music-producing algorithm that Boulez, Stockhausen, and their Darmstadt colleagues had been seeking via the application of multiple serial principles. The difference was simply that whereas Boulez, having determined the broad outlines of structure, handed the specific contents of his work over to the serial operations designed to control it, Cage handed the specific contents of his work over to chance. Boulez was not unaware of the paradox inherent in a process of composition that applied the most stringent controls, only to bring forth a product that, as far as even the most educated listener was concerned, might as well have been the product of chance. Indeed, for all their differences in background and method, Cage and Boulez immediately recognized that they were kindred spirits. They met in Paris in 1949, when Boulez had just written his Second Piano Sonata, which left Cage "trembling in the face of great complexity."[18]

The *I Ching* gave Cage the means of equaling, in fact surpassing, Boulez's iconoclastic tour de force. The first work Cage composed by tossing coins was titled *Music of Changes* (1951). Like Boulez's Sonata, it was a huge, monumentally serious multimovement work for piano in an atomized, or pointillistic, style. Boulez in turn published a manifesto of his own, called "Aléa" (from the Latin for dice), in which he described the "open form" concept of his partially completed Third Piano Sonata (1955–57), carefully tracing its origin not to Cage but to the French literary avant-garde. His main contribution to the evolving theory of musical contingency was the word "**aleatoric**," now often used to describe music composed (or performed) to some degree according to chance operations or spontaneous decisions.

In 1958 Cage and pianist David Tudor (1926–96) visited Darmstadt, where they gave concerts and the charismatic Cage directed a seminar on experimental music. Some Europeans, with their sense of inherited tradition (try as they might to repudiate it), could not reconcile themselves to the randomly generated sounds with which Cage, the innocent American, was happy to fill his time containers. Cage loved to tell the story of a Dutch musician who said to him, "It must be very difficult for you in America to write music, for you are so far away from the centers of tradition." Cage naturally replied, "It must be very difficult for you in Europe to write music, for you are so close to the centers of tradition."[19]

Boulez and Cage kept up a lively correspondence for some years but eventually had a falling out. The Frenchman's serial operations established multiple relationships among the events that took place in the score and that could be analyzed. Cage's chance operations gave up all traditional artistic values. In a way, the best proof that Cage practiced what he preached, unquestioningly accepting the gifts of chance, is the presence in *Music of Changes* of occasional triadic harmonies that a serial composer would have been sure to purge from the score. Cage may have been easy for some to dismiss as a prankster, yet his schemes were just as complicated, just as exacting, just as pitiless as a total serialist's. Chance operations were anything but labor-saving. Cage's motives did not differ much from those of the serialists, and his music resembled theirs far more than either side was prepared to admit. What differed were the means, which in the eyes of many seemed to outweigh motives and ends. And that says a lot about musical Modernism in the 1950s.

Silence

In addition to experimenting with sounds from old and new instruments and exploring the possibilities of chance procedures, Cage's most important contribution to musical aesthetics dealt with new ways of thinking about music in general. Indeed, it became something of a critical cliché to say that he was not—or not just—a composer but, rather, an inventor, writer, poet, and philosopher. In any case, Cage reopened longstanding questions about the nature of a musical work—to use the language of philosophy, about its ontological status. How does "the work" as such relate to its performances? To its written score? Is a Brahms symphony, for example, the actual manuscript sheets the composer wrote, the first published edition, a modern critical edition, a performance (the first? the "best"?), a recording (which?), or something else? This problem with notated music is quite different from the visual arts, where a painting, such as the *Mona Lisa*, may be endlessly reproduced but the identity of the work is generally recognized as the physical object Leonardo da Vinci painted at the start of the sixteenth century and that hangs today in the Louvre in Paris.

Many of Cage's compositions sought to undermine the traditional definitions of a musical work. His *Imaginary Landscape No. 3* (1942) is scored for audio-frequency oscillators, two variable-speed turntables, an electric buzzer, and several other pieces of audio equipment. *Imaginary Landscape No. 4* (1951) calls for twenty-four players playing twelve radios under the direction of a conductor, with two players assigned to each radio, one controlling the volume knob, the other the tuner.

Cage's most famous piece offers the greatest challenge: *4′33″* (1952), his extreme experiment in indeterminacy. Subtitled "Tacet for any instrument or instruments," it is four minutes and thirty-three seconds of silence. Cage called it his "silent piece," though that is a misnomer. It is, rather, a piece for a silent performer or performers who enter a performance space, signal the beginnings and the ends of three movements (whose timings and internal "structural" subdivisions have been predetermined by chance operations), but make no intentional sound. If the performer is a pianist, for example, the signals may be given by noiselessly closing and raising the keyboard lid. The piece consists of whatever sounds occur within a listener's earshot, including the sounds of the listener's own body.

Cage often maintained that his aim in composing *4′33″* was to erase the boundary between art and life. But sounds are not the only thing that a composer controls, and sounds are not the only thing that constitutes a musical work. Under the social regimen of modern concert life, the composer controls people as well, and a work is defined not just by its contents but also by the behavior that it elicits from an audience. The performer usually dresses formally and engages in the expected ceremony of concert behavior. In *4′33″* the audience is invited—no, commanded—to listen to ambient or natural sounds with the same attitude of reverent contemplation they would assume if they were listening to a symphony. That is an attitude born not of nature but of Beethoven, Brahms, and the museum tradition of classical music. *4′33″* forces us to think about the conventions both of musical works and of concert life. Like most musical works, it has a published, copyrighted score. The space on its pages corresponds to the elapsing time. One of the pages is blank.

Cage reopened longstanding questions about the nature of a musical work.

"Permission": Cage's Influence

Cage had enormous influence, and not just on musicians. The painter Robert Rauschenberg (1925–2008), one of his closest friends, said Cage's example "gave me license to do anything,"[20] especially when what he wished to do defied the established Modernists of the day. The composer Morton Feldman similarly claimed that Cage gave not only him but everybody "permission."[21] Cage's joyously

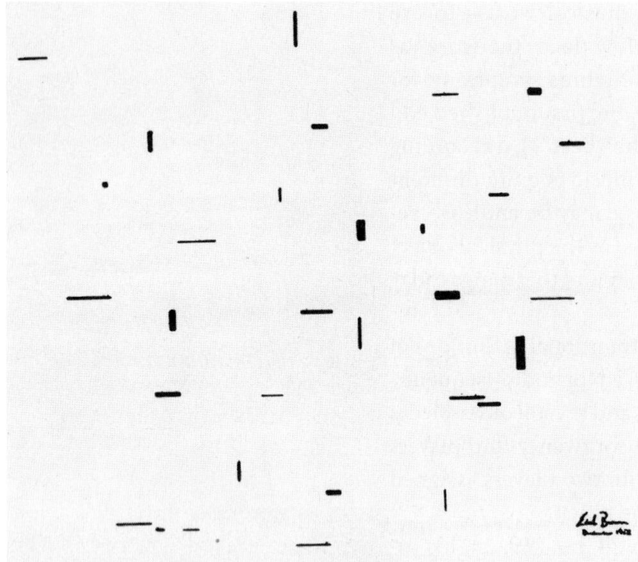

Figure 34-5 Earle Brown, *December 1952.*

accepting attitude made him a charismatic facilitator and liberator. It was a role comparable in many ways to that played by Liszt a hundred years earlier with respect to the avant-garde of the New German School, except that Cage's influence extended to a greater degree to other artistic media.

Some of the conceptual experimentation found not just musical expression but also visual and theatrical expression. Earle Brown (1926–2002) developed a "graphic notation" that eventually dispensed with conventional musical notation. In *December 1952,* he created a score consisting of nothing but lines and rectangles on a white background (Fig. 34-5). The symbols represented "elements in space"; the score was "a picture of this space at one instant." He thus freed performers from their usual constraints and made them fully "aware" participants in the making of his music. In its conceptual openness it resembled Cage's *4′33″*; but in eliciting the performer's associations Brown was letting back in all the "memories, tastes, likes and dislikes" that Cage had zealously sought to exclude. It was a sort of Rorschach test, the inkblot test named after a Swiss psychiatrist who theorized that individuals will project their unconscious attitudes onto ambiguous situations. Cage's own graphic notations, by contrast (and as might be expected), were precisely specified and tightly controlled.

Theatrical experimentation was associated with "**happenings**," or minimally planned performance events. Operating at the border between theater and music, they mixed Cage's purposeful purposelessness with the ideology of the so-called absurdist theater cultivated by playwrights like Samuel Beckett (1906–89) and Eugene Ionesco (1909–94). Their plays, most famously Beckett's *Waiting for Godot* (1948–49), expressed the bewilderment, alienation, and despair of existentialist philosophy by abandoning logical plot development, meaningful dialogue, or intelligible character delineation. Cage engineered his first happening in 1952 at Black Mountain College, a progressive educational institution in North Carolina. He programmed some overlapping sound containers (or "compartments," as he called them this time) in advance through chance operations and allowed himself and his fellow performers to choose an activity to perform during their allotted time. Cage himself, standing on a ladder, read a lecture that contained some compartments of silence; some poets climbed other ladders when their time came and read; others ran a movie, projected slides, played phonograph records, danced, or played the piano, while Rauschenberg suspended some paintings above the audience's heads.

In the late 1950s Cage taught a course at the New School for Social Research in New York City called "Composition of Experimental Music." The class in 1958 included a number of poets, painters, and composers, among them George Brecht, Allan Kaprow, Jackson Mac Low, and Dick Higgins—some of whom later participated in a loose performance association called Fluxus. The best known among them, La Monte Young (b. 1935), had a big influence on its style and aesthetic with a set of instructions called *Compositions 1960.* The seventh was one of the few such compositions to incorporate conventional musical notation; others consisted of instructions such as "push the piano to the wall; push it through the wall; keep pushing."[22] *Piano Piece for David Tudor #1* is most often cited by connoisseurs of eccentricity: "Bring a bale of hay and a bucket of water onto the stage for the piano to eat and drink. The performer may then feed the piano or leave it to eat by itself. If the former, the piece is over after the piano has been fed. If the latter, it is over after the piano eats or decides not to."

A Fluxus member named Ben Vautier (b. 1935) created a number of *Audience Pieces* that came close to psychological abuse. One involved locking the audience into the theater; the piece was over when (if) they escaped. The peak of aggression against the audience was reached by Nam June Paik (b. 1932), a Korean-born composer whose *Hommage à John Cage* consisted, according to one account, of "moving through the intermission crowd in the lobby of a theater, cutting men's neckties off with scissors, slicing coats down the back with a razor blade and squirting shaving cream on top of their heads."[23] As Merce Cunningham recalled, "the piece went on for quite a while, and then Nam June disappeared. And we all sat and waited, and some time later, he telephoned from someplace to tell us the piece was over."[24] Cunningham thought it was wonderful, but others, sitting and waiting to no apparent purpose, may have been perplexed at their strange imprisonment by the rules of concert decorum. Exposing these rules may have been Paik's very purpose. He produced a scandal in 1967 with a happening called *Opéra sextronique*, which consisted of a cellist, Charlotte Moorman, appearing on stage "topless" (i.e., bare-breasted, in the slang of the time). Alerted in advance, the police were on hand to arrest Moorman on a charge of public indecency.

An English counterpart to New York's experimental scene was centered on Cornelius Cardew (1936–81), who after a conventional elite training at the Royal Academy of Music and time working as Stockhausen's assistant in Cologne, helped form an ensemble in 1969 called the Scratch Orchestra, "a gathering," as Cardew later put it, of "musicians, artists, scholars, clerks, students, etc., willing to engage in experimental performance activities."[25] For outsiders, further definition had to await the publication of the anthology *Scratch Music* (1972), containing examples by Cardew and fifteen other members of the Orchestra. Very few "scratch" pieces employed musical notation as normally defined. Many consisted of drawings that, without oral explanation, could not readily be translated into performance. Some, however, consisted of verbal prescriptions that occasionally suggested vivid aural results. "Take a closed cylinder (empty Pepsi-Cola tin)," one began. "Bang it. Drop things through the holes the Pepsi came out of."[26]

Preserving the Sacrosanct: Morton Feldman

Figure 34-6 Morton Feldman, 1963.

Morton Feldman (1926–87; Fig. 34-6) was the Cage associate who proved to be his most zealous competitor in the pursuit of aesthetic autonomy. The two met at the intermission of a New York Philharmonic concert at Carnegie Hall in 1950 after a performance of Webern's Symphony. While most of the audience was waiting patiently for a Rachmaninoff work on the second half of the program, the two avant-gardists decided to leave with the Webern music fresh in their ears. For some years they spent hours together each day, often hanging out at the Cedar Bar in downtown New York together with visual artists of the so-called Abstract Expressionist School, including Jackson Pollock (1912–56), Willem de Kooning (1904–97), and Philip Guston (1913–80).

While Cage's music involved a meticulous and demanding methodology, Feldman's earliest pieces were more abstract. Anticipating Earle Brown by a couple of years, he developed a rudimentary graphic notation so as to avoid specifying exact pitches, which all too easily fell into predictable patterns that reflected the conditioned responses of human beings in society rather than the autonomy of an aesthetic object. Beginning in 1954, however, Feldman abruptly abandoned graphic notation because performances had convinced him that his method had an undesirable side effect. As he later put it, "I was not only allowing the sounds to be free—I was also liberating the performer."[27] As Cage had realized before him, liberating people only frees them to follow their habits and whims, which once again deprives the music of its autonomy. Feldman, too, felt it necessary to put limits on discretion, which meant reverting to conventional pitch notation. The difference in musical effect was not great; Cage wryly observed, "Feldman's conventionally notated music is himself playing his graph music."[28]

Pieces from this phase of Feldman's career are written in what is sometimes called "free-rhythm notation," in which the effect of the music depends on relative uniformity of action within a limited latitude of variation, the composer counting on his vague performance directions to activate a basically similar response in all performers. In later years Feldman demanded ever-greater reserves of passive endurance on the part of listeners. The music of his last two decades, fully notated, entered an unprecedented time scale. *For Philip Guston* (1984), a trio dedicated to his closest artist friend, wends its quiet, basically uniform, yet wholly unpredictable way for four and a half hours. The Second String Quartet (1983), Feldman's longest work, lasts more than six hours. Yet it is anything but "furniture music." Complete performances of such pieces, in which the traditional concert format and its attendant etiquette are fully maintained, are obviously infrequent. The complete Second String Quartet was not attempted during Feldman's lifetime. Its first uncut performance, by a young ensemble called the Flux Quartet, took place in October 1999 and was treated by audience and press alike as a once-in-a-lifetime event. In this way Feldman managed to preserve the specialness of the aesthetic experience. Only by dint of extreme measures could the Romantic sacralization of art continue into the age of science.

Anthology Vol 3-52
Full CD VII, 22

Rothko Chapel (1971) is a tribute to another of Feldman's visual artist friends, Mark Rothko (1903–70), who shortly before committing suicide was engaged in creating a series of paintings for a nondenominational chapel in Houston, Texas (Fig. 34-7). Feldman's piece is scored for viola, celesta, percussion, wordless chorus, and solo soprano and solo alto parts, an instrumentation influenced by the octagon shape of the chapel and by Rothko's hauntingly abstract paintings. As the composer described it in his program notes, the piece is divided into four "highly contrasting merging sections": "a longish declamatory opening"; "a more stationary 'abstract' section for chorus and chimes"; "a motivic interlude for soprano, viola and tympani"; and "a lyrical ending for viola with vibraphone accompaniment, later joined by the chorus in a collage effect."[29] The extraordinary conclusion, in which the viola begins to intone a melancholy diatonic melody that Feldman had written as a teenager, shows the influence of Hebrew chanting.

Figure 34-7 Interior of the Rothko Chapel in Houston.

Conversions

Alongside American experimentalism there also emerged in the United States an academic serial approach, akin to that of the Zero Hour Europeans. Indeed, some unlikely figures both in America and Europe began adopting the twelve-tone technique. A few, like Paul Hindemith, Francis Poulenc, and Benjamin Britten, dabbled only briefly. After Stalin's death in 1953, some young Soviet composers, such as Andrey Volkonsky and Edison Denisov, also secretly started writing twelve-tone music as an act of symbolic nonconformism; senior statesman Shostakovich did a bit of experimenting of his own in his late string quartets, last two symphonies, and other works.

Several composers, however, underwent more significant conversions to serial techniques. One was Aaron Copland, the preeminent representative of the Americanist populist style. For him the adoption of serial methods in some of his later pieces was a calculated retreat from explicit Americanism and from populism, both of which had become politically suspect in the tense early years of the Cold War. Copland's unexpected turn to the decidedly unpopular twelve-tone idiom came in the wake of his run-in with the Committee on Un-American Activities of the U.S. House of Representatives during what is known as the McCarthy Era. At this time Senator Joseph McCarthy, in pursuit of communists, led aggressive investigations that destroyed the lives of many innocent Americans. In public hearings artists and others were denounced as traitors or communist sympathizers; "blacklisting" made well-known figures unhirable, especially individuals connected with Hollywood filmmaking. (Copland himself had composed a half-dozen film scores and won an Academy Award for *The Heiress* in 1949.)

After four years of increasing suspicion, Copland's reckoning came in 1953. Although he got off easy in the end, not even called back for a second hearing, the experience seems to have left a mark on his music. His Piano Quartet (1950) already displayed a "middle of the road" approach to twelve-tone composition. With its expansive intervallic leaps and wide-open chord spacing, the music—to anyone who knows the composer's Americanist works—sounds palpably "Coplandesque." Over the roughly twenty years remaining to his creative career, Copland maintained two compositional approaches, one diatonic and the other serial. He called them his "popular" and "difficult" styles, although on occasion he referred to them as his "public" and "private" manners. His lengthiest twelve-tone composition was the *Piano Fantasy* (1957) and the largest was *Connotations* (1962), an orchestral piece written for a nationally televised gala concert by the New York Philharmonic. The event, conducted by Leonard Bernstein, inaugurated the orchestra's new home in an immense complex of performance spaces known as the Lincoln Center for the Performing Arts in New York City.

Copland maintained two compositional approaches, one diatonic and the other serial. He called them his "popular" and "difficult" styles.

The really big catch—and the really big surprise—among conversions to serialist methods was Igor Stravinsky. Asked in 1952 by a Paris newspaper about his views on the twelve-tone method, the composer had responded: "The twelve-tone system? Personally I have enough to do with seven tones. But the twelve-tone composers are the only ones who have a discipline I respect. Whatever else it may be, twelve-tone music is certainly pure music."[30] He left out, however, the most newsworthy part: that he himself had begun to adopt the system he had long opposed and that was associated with his early Modernist opposite (and Los Angeles neighbor), the recently deceased Arnold Schoenberg. The conversion of the most celebrated living composer to the cause was an enormous boost to the prestige of serial music. It seemed to support the whole deterministic view of history argued by Schoenberg and his followers: that serialism was the inevitable next step in musical progress, music's historical destiny.

As we have seen, Stravinsky's Neoclassical style, begun around 1920, culminated thirty years later with his opera *The Rake's Progress*, which premiered in Venice on 11 September 1951. Although popular with the initial high-society audience, many musicians wrote off the opera as a trifling, fashionable pastiche. And no wonder: Its archly pretty, stylistically retrospective music jarred with the bleak Zero-Hour mood that reigned in Europe. Its obsessive stylistic self-consciousness, now easily understood as consciousness of art in crisis, seems today just as much a response to its uncertain times as the work of the Darmstadt avant-garde. In 1951, though, it seemed the product of a composer blissfully out of touch with the contemporary requirements of his art. For the first time in his life, Stravinsky found himself rejected by the younger generation of European musicians. The effect on his self-esteem was traumatic.

And so Stravinsky reinvented himself yet again, this time with the crucial help of Robert Craft (b. 1923), an aspiring young conductor he had met in 1948. Craft became his assistant, remaining a member of the composer's household until Stravinsky's death in 1971 at age eighty-eight. The young musician made himself indispensable in any number of ways. He shared conducting duties on concert tours and rehearsed orchestras before recording sessions. He served as an interlocutor—essentially a ghost writer—through whom Stravinsky published five famous volumes of memoirs in dialogue form. His most important service, however, was in enabling Stravinsky to weather the post-*Rake* creative crisis by providing the seventy-year-old composer access to new modes of musical thinking and writing he had previously ignored and even scorned. When Stravinsky suddenly felt the need to catch up, Craft stood ready to assist, giving him scores and recordings of works by the Second Viennese School and the younger generation of European Modernists. In so doing he made possible the last years of Stravinsky's active creative life.

Stravinsky's assimilation of serial technique evolved in a gradual and idiosyncratic way. In effect, he became a serial composer before becoming a twelve-tone one, meaning that he gave a serial treatment to a "row" of fewer than all twelve notes, in some instances using just four or five. This can be seen in works such as the *Cantata* (1951–52), Septet (1952–53), *Three Songs from William Shakespeare* (1953), and *In Memoriam Dylan Thomas* (1954). Two large-scale works that followed—the cantata *Canticum Sacrum* (1955) and the ballet *Agon* (1957)—used twelve-tone rows, but did so as short, self-contained episodes in what are otherwise tonally centered, nonserial compositions. With *Threni* (1958), a thirty-five-minute oratorio, Stravinsky turned out a work that used twelve-tone rows of standard design throughout.

Anthology Vol 3-53
Full CD VII, 23–25

Stravinsky's serial technique can be seen at its ripest in the *Requiem Canticles* (1966), a setting of several short selections from the text of the Mass of the Dead for contralto and bass soloists, small chorus, and orchestra. Completed when the composer was eighty-four years old and failing, he expected that it would be his final work, yet its musical technique nonetheless remained faithful to the questing spirit of Modernism. Indeed, Stravinsky tried out a few novel devices for the first time and several aspects of the work initially made it an enigma for analysts, a point of pride for the composer. The last three sections sum up the three principal textures found within the piece. The Lacrimosa is an accompanied vocal solo; the Libera me is choral and chordal; the Postlude, also chordal, is an instrumental commentary.

The Libera me is especially poignant because it simulates an actual Russian Orthodox service for the dead, or *panikhida*; it not only prefigures the composer's own *panikhida* four years later but also shows him wresting from the serial method a kind of harmony he might have composed easily at an earlier phase of his career. The harmony in the Lacrimosa, too, is ingeniously retrospective. By referencing an octatonic scale, Stravinsky retained a familiar feature of his earlier music. Indeed, as with Copland, Stravinsky retains many distinctive elements of his style, such as the frozen (or "hypostatized") harmonic space, that form common bonds among his early maximalist Russian works, midperiod neo-Classical ones, and late serial compositions.

Academicism, American Style

Robert Craft conducted the premiere of the *Requiem Canticles* on a concert in October 1966 at Princeton University, whose administration had commissioned the piece. It was a fitting venue, for over the preceding two decades Princeton had become, largely through the efforts of composer and theorist Milton Babbitt (1916–2011; Fig. 34-8), the American stronghold for the theory and practice of serial music. Princetonian serialism differed critically from that of Darmstadt, with which it was inevitably compared. Darmstadt's version was the fruit of pessimism, reflecting the Zero Hour mentality of war-ravaged Europe; it thrived on the idea of the cleanest possible break with the past. Princetonian practice reflected American optimism. It rode the crest of scientific prestige and remained resolutely committed to the idea of

Figure 34-8 Milton Babbitt (right) with Peter Mauzey and Vladimir Ussachevsky in 1958 with the RCA Mark II music synthesizer.

progress. In this respect it seems entirely fitting that as serialism began to flourish at Princeton, the exemplary scientist of the age, physicist Albert Einstein, was happily ensconced a few miles away at the Institute for Advance Study.

Babbitt, trained in mathematics and formal logic as well as music, quickly saw the possibility of rationalizing the technique and theoretical foundations of twelve-tone composition on the basis of what mathematicians call "set theory," which he formulated in his 1946 Ph.D. thesis. Since there was at that time neither a qualified reader on the Princeton music faculty nor an officially instituted Ph.D. program in music theory or composition, Babbitt was not awarded a doctorate, although he had already been hired to teach by the math department. The situation spurred Babbitt to lobby for recognition of music composition as a legitimate branch of music research. Meanwhile, his unaccepted dissertation, circulating in typescript, became widely influential.

Several terms that Babbitt derived from mathematics, particularly "**pitch class**" (the class of pitches related by octave transposition and designated with a single letter name), quickly became standard parlance, even outside the domain of serial theory, for they named musical universals that had previously required cumbersome phrases to define. Another is "**aggregate**," meaning the complete set of all twelve pitch classes. His appropriation of the mathematical term "**combinatorial**" enabled him to name how constituent hexachords can combine interchangeably to produce aggregates; the term made it possible to clarify an important concept within serial music that went all the way back to Schoenberg but that had never before been adequately defined or properly understood for lack of a name.

Babbitt's early compositions put his theories into practice and in fact achieved impressive feats of logical construction a bit earlier than the first monuments of Darmstadt total serialism. Like his dissertation, however, most of these works were unpublished and unknown, which meant that a frustrated Babbitt had to stand by and see himself scooped by composers he regarded as his intellectual inferiors, a hard fate indeed for a dedicated Modernist. One exception was his *Composition for Four Instruments* (1948), which was issued in 1949 by *New Music Edition*, a shoestring periodical founded by Henry Cowell and edited by Elliott Carter. In this piece Babbitt used what he called "derived sets," twelve-tone rows that could be broken down into four trichords of identical intervallic content (Ex. 34-3). The work is scored for flute, violin, clarinet, and cello, four instruments of contrasting range and timbre. The basic row from which the entire piece is derived is stated complete—once only—at the very end. *Composition* is a model, in this regard, of a formalistically conceived work of art. It takes its shape and has its reason for being in the exhaustive working out of its own material's potential for elaboration.

Anthology Vol 3-54
Full CD VII, 26

Example 34-3 The four derived sets in Milton Babbitt, *Composition for Four Instruments*

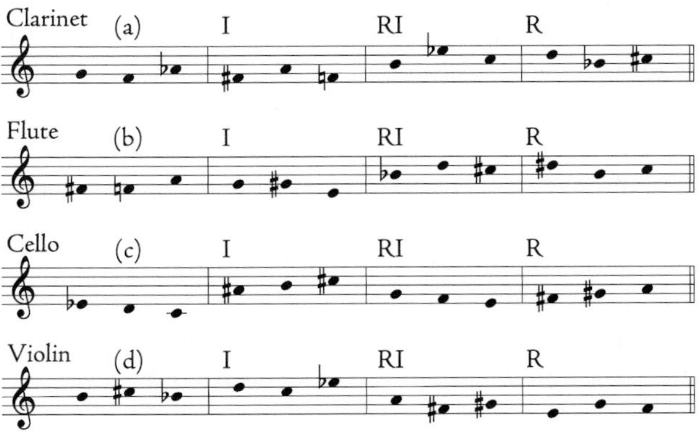

While many were happy to dismiss him as too academic, Babbitt reveled in his academicism, portraying himself in this regard as a singularly legitimate heir to Schoenberg, another great composer-teacher with a high awareness of his intellectual responsibilities and pressing historical conscience. Moreover, Babbitt was in tune with one of the dominant philosophical trends of his time, especially logical positivism, the attempt to introduce the methods and precision of math and science into the field of philosophy. Philosophy was supposed to stop being a speculative field and become an analytical one, devoted to maintaining rigorous standards of inference and proof. By loading his compositions with demonstrable relations far more intricate than what anyone would actually hear (as he was the first to admit), Babbitt musically demonstrated the limitless power of serial procedures and numbers, which he associated not merely with the power of the mind but with the power of absolute truth and with the freedom to express it. He sought liberation from the potential tyranny of taste by making truth rather than beauty the criterion of artistic achievement. The measure of good music, like good science, would be not the pleasure that it gave, the emotion it expressed, or the political tendency that it served but, rather, the truth that it contained—objective, scientifically verifiable truth.

As long as science retained its unprecedented prestige in America, Babbitt's ideas carried considerable weight, at least in academic circles. As it happened, that prestige and that weight received a powerful boost in 1957, when the Soviet Union successfully launched the first artificial space satellite, called Sputnik, in an orbit around the earth. Taken by surprise, American scientists and politicians made educational reform a Cold War priority. Government investment in scientific endeavors—"big science" as it was called—gave scientific advancement in peacetime something of the sense of urgency that wartime bomb development had earlier commanded.

The new "Ph.D. music" was spurred on by the creation of composition programs at research universities, new journals, and specialized performing groups. The first such campus "new music" ensemble was the Group for Contemporary Music, formed in 1962 at Columbia University. Two of its founders, Charles Wuorinen (b. 1938) and Harvey Sollberger (b. 1938), were graduate students there in composition. The twentieth century had already seen an increasing separation of roles between composer and performer, and the extremely difficult new music seemed to demand a new breed of specialist virtuoso, interested in performing such pieces and capable of producing unusual sounds through a variety of **extended performance techniques**: augmented ranges, novel sounds from traditional instruments, special fingerings to produce chords or "multiphonics" on woodwinds, and so on. (Berlioz would have approved.)

Milton Babbitt once half-ruefully joked, "Everyone wants to compose our music but no one wants to listen to it."

Babbitt once half-ruefully joked, "Everyone wants to compose our music but no one wants to listen to it." Composing this kind of Modernist music is a fascinating game, as can be analyzing and performing it. It is the listening process that has proved durably problematic. Viewed thus, the fate of academic serialism has been predictable. It has fared no differently from the other forms of academic music we have encountered in this book, going back to the Middle Ages.

Electronics: An Old Dream Comes True

It would seem inevitable that everything we have been exploring thus far in this chapter—total serialism, the quest for new sounds and instruments, impersonal chance procedures, Ph.D. music, logical positivism—that all this would link up with twentieth-century science through the creation of electronic music. That was what Edgard Varèse had been waiting for. Electronics would allow the precision Babbitt craved: "the notion of having complete control over one's composition, of being complete master of all you survey."[31] It was what the young John Cage had called for in "The Future of Music: Credo," where he predicted "that the use of noise to make music will continue and increase until we reach a music produced through the aid of electrical instruments which will make available for musical purposes any and all sounds that can be heard."[32]

Although they may have disagreed about most things, the warring avant-garde factions were united in welcoming new technological marvels. Electronics offered the most dramatic chance to wipe the slate clean of all existing traditions and techniques and create a truly twentieth-century music. These hopes had a considerable prehistory that might be traced back to music boxes and more elaborate mechanical contrivances even before the use of electricity. The advent of electric power spurred inventions in the early twentieth century, such as the Telharmonium (alias Dynamophone), a 200-ton apparatus for producing "scientifically perfect music." It was exhibited in New York in 1906, and, in the view of Ferruccio Busoni, it held the promise of musical emancipation. "Music was born free," Busoni declared, "and to win freedom is its destiny."[33]

Visions of freedom and naturalness had inspired experimentation with all kinds of artificial contrivances. The Italian Futurists had sought a musical application of the principles enunciated in the Futurist Manifesto of 1909. It called for the erasure of artistic memory; in practical (but not necessarily serious) terms, for the destruction of museums and concert halls; and the consecration of art celebrating twentieth-century life: warfare and conquest on an unprecedented scale and, above all, machines that would provide the means to realize these ideals. Another manifesto, four years later, came from the Futurist painter Luigi Russolo (1885–1947), who celebrated the "MUSIC OF NOISE" and who conducted some "Futurist concerts" in 1914 in Milan, Genoa, and London and some years later in Paris.

Soon enough new electric musical instruments were indeed being invented. One of the earliest was eventually called the **theremin,** invented in 1920 by a Russian physicist named Lev Sergeyevich Termen (1896–1993). His machine featured a pair of antennas that set up an electromagnetic field, into which the intrusion of any electrical conductor (such as a moving hand) would touch off a signal from a radio oscillator (Fig. 34-9). An amateur cellist, Termen amused himself by moving his hands in such a way as to make the invisible field respond with favorite tunes. The theremin became a pervasive sound effect in radio dramas (beginning with the *Green Hornet* mystery serial) as well as in science fiction and horror movies. More significant in terms of the musical repertory was the ondes musicales (musical waves), unveiled in 1928 by the French engineer Maurice Martenot (1898–1980) and now called **ondes martenot,** after him. It produces sound on the same principle as the theremin, altering the pitch along a smooth continuum, but also has a keyboard to make conventional tunings available. Messiaen was the foremost composer to write consistently for the instrument.

During the mid-1930s in Germany a device called the Magnetophon was invented for converting sound signals into magnetic impulses that could be stored indefinitely on a paper tape coated with a metallic oxide and then reconverted—"played back"—into sound. Envisioned primarily as an office dictation device, the initial sound quality was poor, but it steadily improved. The new technology offered attractive opportunities for commercial recordings of musical performances. Good "takes" of different passages could be spliced together, preserving the best playing. Performances on records could be made virtually flawless. The standard joke later became the one about the soloist, admiring a playback, being teased by the recording engineer: "Yes, don't you wish you could play like that?"

Soon it became apparent that recording technology might also serve the purposes of composition and allow some of the things that Busoni, Varèse, Cage, Babbitt, and others had long dreamed of. The cutting and splicing techniques, for example, could be used to create all kinds of sound collages. Playback speed could be varied,

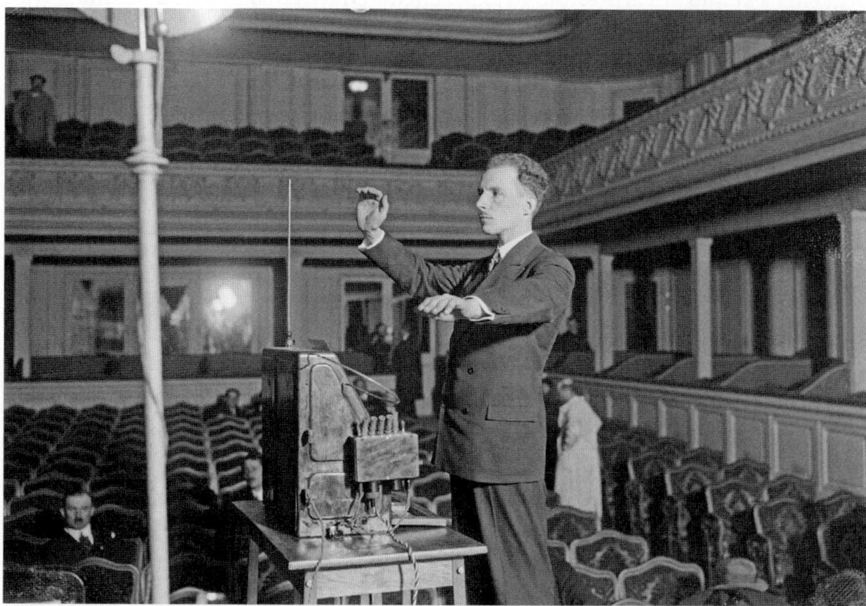

Figure 34-9 Lev Sergeyevich Termen (Leon Théremin) with his *termenvox* (theremin).

with consequent alterations to the pitch, rapidity, and timbre of recorded sounds. Tapes could be manipulated in various ways: played backward, spliced, put in a continuous loop; additional recording-studio devices such as echo chambers, sound filters, and mixers seemed to offer endless and exciting possibilities. Electronics could also create a wide variety of sounds for which no musical notation existed and to which no existing rules of composition were applicable.

Musique Concrète Versus *Elektronische Musik*

From the beginning, composers formed themselves into two main camps, one wanting to encompass the whole universe of life sounds from the real world into their music, and the other—*synthesists* we might call them—seeking to create artificially new sounds. Those using real-world sounds came first chronologically. They were the French composers of ***musique concrète***, a music that advertised itself and sought its justification on the basis of its relationship to the sound-world of "concrete" sensory reality. The term was coined in 1948 by Pierre Schaeffer (1910–95), a sound engineer employed in Paris by the French national broadcasting network. His first *concrète* compositions, made by montaging sounds from phonograph discs, included *Concert de bruits* (Concert of Noises, 1948), an *Étude aux chemins de fer* (Railroad Study), and an *Étude aux casseroles* (Saucepan Study).

Schaeffer was quick, however, to avail himself of other possibilities that tape editing allowed. Together with sound engineer Pierre Henry (b. 1927), he founded the Groupe de Recherche de Musique Concrète and began issuing fully formed compositions on tape. The masterpiece of the original *musique concrète* studio was Henry's *Orphée 53*, a ritualistic drama, existing only as sounds on tape, that enacts the death of Orpheus, torn limb from limb by the Furies. Many prominent postwar avant-gardists, including Messiaen, Boulez, Xenakis, and Stockhausen, paid visits to Schaeffer's studio at Paris Radio to experiment. Only Xenakis stayed, working with *musique concrète* in pieces like *Diamorphoses* (1957), which incorporated the sounds of jet engines, earthquakes, and automobile crashes.

The leader of electronic music in Italy was Luciano Berio, who after living in the United States on a fellowship, returned home and made contact with Bruno Maderna, the somewhat older Italian avant-gardist. Together they established the Studio di Fonologia Musicale at the state-supported radio station in Milan. Berio's *Thema* (1958), subtitled "Omaggio a Joyce" (Homage to Joyce), is widely regarded as a masterpiece of *musique concrète*. Its sound source was a reading by the composer's wife, the American singer Cathy Berberian, of the first page from the eleventh chapter ("Sirens") of James Joyce's epic novel *Ulysses* (1922).

The synthesists, on the other hand, felt the Zero Hour impulse required a different high-tech outlet. ***Elektronische Musik***, to use the original German formulation of "electronic music," referred to music based exclusively on electronically synthesized sounds—the purer, the better. Synthetic sounds carried no stigma from the world of entertainment, unlike the amusing or terrifying noises of *musique concrète* reminiscent of radio sound effects or film and cartoon soundtracks. For composers in the Germanic Modernist orbit, the neutrality of synthesized sound, its freedom from worldly associations, constituted its chief appeal.

The hub of operations was the studio at Radio Cologne, set up in 1951 with the aid of the American occupying forces under the direction of Herbert Eimert (1897–1972), an early follower of Schoenberg. Eimert saw electronic music as a source of new "parameters" that could be manipulated serially (overtones, for example, governing timbre), extending the serial reach far beyond what was controllable on conventional instruments. The symptomatic early electronic compositions from Cologne were the two serial *Studien* (1953, 1954) by Stockhausen, constructed from the purest sound of all, that of "sine waves," single frequencies without any overtones, obtainable only under laboratory conditions in the studio, never in nature, and therefore as "unconcrete" (or unreal) as one could get.

The rivalry between *musique concrète* and *elektronische Musik* quickly became the latest bout in the old contest between French *clarté* and *esprit* (clarity and wit) and German *Tiefgründigkeit* (profundity) and between the agreeable naturalness of French art and the earnest artifice of German. An official statement from the French camp in 1957 condemned the Teutonic manufacture of synthetic sounds: "*Musique concrète* makes use of real sounds, which are natural. . . . *Musique concrète* stems more from acoustics, therefore, than from electronics."[34] Yet the two positions were already being reconciled somewhat in 1956 with Stockhausen's *Gesang der Jünglinge* (Song of the Youths), an electronic fantasy inspired by a parable from the biblical Book of Daniel. The music places the sound of a boy's voice chanting the text together with electronically synthesized signals, but the two layers are kept distinct. Even the recorded voice was manipulated according to serialist principles, as were the "trajectories" by which the sound was circulated among the five groups of playback loudspeakers set up for the first performances.

Stockhausen later applied his collage techniques to real-world sounds, often prerecorded music. His *Hymnen* (1967) is based on the sounds of national anthems from around the world. Like Scriabin a half century before him, he started to advertise his music as a means for actually producing the social and historical changes that it symbolized. Like his near contemporary Cage, Stockhausen began at this point to assume the role of a spiritual guru, which may help explain why the British rock group the Beatles put him among the crowd on the cover of their album *Sgt. Pepper's Lonely Hearts Club Band* in 1967.

The New Technology Spreads

The composing process for computer-assisted music was at first incredibly cumbersome, and it would remain so for a while.

"Computer music" in America may be said to have begun in 1957 in Summit, New Jersey, when Max V. Mathews (1926–2011), an engineer at Bell Telephone Laboratories, produced computer-generated musical sounds with a "transducer," an instrument he invented that could convert audio signals into digital information to be stored or manipulated by a computer and then reconverted into audio signals. The initial purpose was to simulate and recognize speech so as to automate some tasks telephone operators usually performed.

The composing process for computer-assisted music was at first incredibly cumbersome, and it would remain so for a while. The composers who had the time and resources for such exploration were, naturally, associated with universities. Columbia and Princeton were pioneering, partly because they were located near Bell Labs, with Vladimir Ussachevsky (1911–90) and Otto Luening (1900–96)

Figure 34-10 Otto Luening and Vladimir Ussachevsky in the small teaching studio behind McMillan (now Miller) Theater at Columbia University, ca. 1960.

leading efforts at Columbia and Babbitt at Princeton (Fig. 34-10). Charles Dodge (b. 1942), who studied at both universities, wrote that "using a computer, it is realistically possible for a composer to structure all elements of his composition (e.g., tempo, timbre, rate and shape of attack and decay, register, etc.) to the same degree as pitch and rhythm."[35] In those days and in those places, "to structure," of course meant "to serialize."

Columbia opened an impressive new studio to house the RCA Mark II music **synthesizer**, a gigantic machine that occupied an entire wall. It had about 750 vacuum tubes and a mechanism that activated a multitude of binary switches by scanning punched cards. Under the terms of a generous Rockefeller Foundation grant, the new electronic music studio was to be called the Columbia-Princeton Electronic Music Center. This became the model for the electronic music studios that soon mushroomed on many American campuses where musical composition was taught, especially those that began instituting doctoral programs on the Princeton model.

Not everyone was impressed with the initial results. Decades earlier Varèse had somewhat gloomily predicted in his essay "The Liberation of Sound" (1936): "I am afraid it will not be long before some musical mortician begins embalming electronic music in rules."[36] When he came to visit the Columbia-Princeton Electronic Music Center he was dismayed at the paltry use to which the machine was being put, saying that for him "working with electronic music is composing with living sounds, paradoxical though that may appear." Although he admired Babbitt's work, he recognized that Babbitt wanted to be "above" the musical material, whereas Varèse wanted "to be *in* the material, part of the acoustical vibration, so to speak. Babbitt composes his material first and then gives it to the synthesizer, while I want to generate something directly by electronic means."[37]

Varèse began composing *Déserts,* his last big piece, in 1949, and when he completed it in 1954 it was his first finished ensemble score in more than twenty years. It features a typical Varèsian group of four woodwind players on nine instruments, ten brass instruments, a piano, and five percussionists manning forty-eight instruments. To this Varèse added three electronic interpolations of "organized sound" that commented on the music (and which the composer said could be omitted in performance). The piece premiered in December at the Théâtre des Champs-Elysées, the site, nearly four decades earlier, of the stormy premiere of *The Rite of Spring.*

Figure 34-11 The Philips Pavilion, designed by Le Corbusier for the World's Fair in Brussels, Belgium, 1958.

His piece for tape alone, *Poème électronique,* was installed with more than 400 speakers in a pavilion designed by Swiss-born French architect Le Corbusier at the Brussels World's Fair in 1958 (Fig. 34-11). Heard by nearly 2 million visitors over the six-month course of the fair and issued thereafter on commercial recordings, Varèse's eight-minute *Poème* is probably still the most widely disseminated all-electronic composition in the history of the medium. He viewed the work as the high point of his career, the single consummate realization of his musical aims. "For the first time I heard my music literally projected into space," he recalled.[38] It proved to be the last time as well. Unfortunately, that spatial projection is the one aspect of *Poème électronique* that, since the scrapping of the pavilion at the end of the fair, can no longer be experienced except as it finds pale reflection in the two channels of domestic stereo reproduction.

Although John Cage generally steered clear of academic affiliations, he too got involved with tape and electronics. *Williams Mix* (1952) was realized with the help of his friends Louis and Bebe Barron, who had set up a little electronic music studio in their apartment where they produced soundtracks for science fiction films, eventually including some famous ones like *Forbidden Planet* (1956). Cage copied an encyclopedic library of about 600 different recorded sounds and cut them up into tape snippets, which he then stored by size in about 175 envelopes inside six big boxes labeled A through F, as follows:

A city sounds
B country sounds
C electronic sounds
D manually produced sounds, including "normal" music
E wind-produced sounds, including voice
F small sounds requiring amplification to be heard

Using the *I Ching,* Cage determined what snippets would be spliced into eight tracks for simultaneous playback. Working for five months straight with Earle Brown, the two labored most of the day tossing coins and splicing away. Chance ruled: They did not even have a machine to play what they were creating. Brown recalled: "He didn't need to hear. You only need to hear when you're doing something by taste. It took so long, so bloody long, and it was boring to do all that cutting and splicing. John and I sat at opposite sides of the table and we talked about everything in the world."[39] Indeed, electronic music in its infancy was incredibly labor-intensive, even with state-of-the-art equipment. Most of the big, arduous, and expensive undertakings of the early days can now be done easily on a laptop computer. In retrospect, of course, the hard and boring work lent a heroic aspect to the legend of the tape-music pioneers and became a point of pride.

Electronics and Live Music

Tape and electronics were used not only in separation from traditional instruments. From the very beginning, the contradiction between the potentially asocial electronic medium and the eminently social conventions of the public concert was perceived as a problem to be solved. Audiences, assembled in a darkened hall, facing an empty stage, felt imprisoned at electronic concerts. Putting a pair of speakers on the stage provided a focus for the audience's gaze but made them feel silly. One solution, of course, was to integrate electronics into conventional performance media, to combine tape or computers with live musicians. The first composer to make a specialty of doing this was Mario Davidovsky (b. 1934), an Argentine who settled permanently in the United States in 1960. He became a protégé of Babbitt's, who arranged a fellowship for him at the newly founded Columbia-Princeton Electronic Music Center. His series of *Synchronisms*, as the title suggests, are counterpoints of electronic sounds and virtuoso performances on a wide variety of instruments or voices. The challenge, for composer and performer alike, is to match the virtually unlimited electronic sound spectrum by exploiting the extended playing techniques that new-music performers were then pioneering. The conception proved extremely fruitful.

A less expected form of interaction between live and prerecorded media surfaced around 1960, when a number of composers—many of them, as it happened, of East European nationality—began composing works for conventional instruments that emulated electronic sounds. The new media had opened up new ways of thinking about sound. György Ligeti received his mature training at the Franz Liszt Academy in Budapest in the late 1940s. Like Bartók before him, he developed a keen interest in folk music, which he collected and studied. But he found that in Communist Hungary he had to consign most of his less conventional compositions to the "drawer," out of sight of the authorities. He seized the chance to leave Hungary in the wake of the failed 1956 revolution, which briefly toppled the Communist regime before being itself crushed by the Soviet army. Ligeti crossed into Austria in December and was in Cologne by February 1957, where he worked in Stockhausen's studio and at the studio Eimert had set up at the state-supported radio station in that city. That year, too, he spent the first of seven summers at Darmstadt.

Ligeti began work on a tape composition that was to consist entirely of slowly shifting continuous sounds. After spending some time developing the work in the studio, however, he decided to start over and write *Atmosphères* "for large orchestra without percussion," as the eventual title page announced. The absence of percussion has been interpreted as controversial, because so many works of the 1950s avant-garde followed Varèse's example by greatly expanding the percussion section, even in chamber pieces. But percussion instruments chiefly serve articulative purposes, and the whole point of *Atmosphères* was to banish articulations from a music of constant timbral and textural flux—"a music" that Ligeti described as "without beginning or end."[40] The work was widely performed and exerted enormous influence on other composers, although Ligeti himself moved on to writing music with different stylistic profiles.

Other approaches were adopted by some Polish composers who came to prominence during the "thaw" decade that followed Stalin's death, in a movement that has been called the "Polish Renaissance," associated with Andrzej Panufnik (1914–91), Witold Lutosławski (1913–94), Krzysztof Penderecki (b. 1933), and Henryk Górecki (1933–2010).[41] The most forceful impression of recreating the sound world of electronic music in live performance was made by Penderecki in what he called "sonority pieces," full of tone clusters, extreme registers, and unusual timbres. Best known was a work for fifty-two solo strings called *Threnody to the Victims of Hiroshima* (1960). Its effect is similar to Ligeti's *Atmosphères*, but the notation is different. The same long-held, gradually changing tones that Ligeti wrote with conventional note values and very slow metronome settings are notated here simply in terms of their durations in seconds, as measured across the page from left to right (Ex. 34-4).

After the fall of the Communist regime in Poland in 1991, Penderecki let it be known that the piece published as the *Threnody to the Victims of Hiroshima* was first performed under the decidedly neutral title *8′37″* and had been rejected by the publishing house as too expensive. He said he gave it the politically fraught title after the fact so as to make it an attractive commodity for promotion by the Communist government. The story is plausible, if only because once past the opening "screams" there is nothing in the piece of a comparably suggestive character. The screams are screams, it would appear, only because they have been so labeled. Does this make the composer a cynic? A careerist? Or just someone who knew how to outsmart a formidable and often oppressive state bureaucracy and thereby win a symbolic victory over authority and oppression?

Threnody to the Victims of Hiroshima was indeed a difficult and expensive score to print. The fact that the Polish State Publishing House for Music was eventually willing to make the considerable outlay may have been a response to the similarly expensive promotions that prestigious Western publishing firms accorded avant-garde works by composers like Stockhausen and Ligeti. The goal of showcasing the avant-garde was to display a commitment to creative freedom, a propaganda benefit in the Cold War. Co-optation was a game played by on both sides of that war. Ligeti benefited from it too, in 1968, when American film director Stanley Kubrick exploited *Atmosphères* and three other Ligeti pieces for the soundtrack of his futuristic fantasy *2001: A Space Odyssey* and reaped for the composer a gold mine of publicity and name exposure such as no avant-gardist had ever imagined (Fig. 34-12). What both of these stories prove, if nothing else, is that not even the

Figure 34-12 The soundtrack for Stanley Kubrick's film *2001: A Space Odyssey* (1968) featured pieces by György Ligeti.

avant-garde, which by definition supposedly resists commercial or ideological exploitation, was able to resist it as the twentieth century, the most commercial and ideological of centuries, ran its course.

Example 34-4 **Krzysztof Penderecki,** ***Threnody to the Victims of Hiroshima,*** **opening**

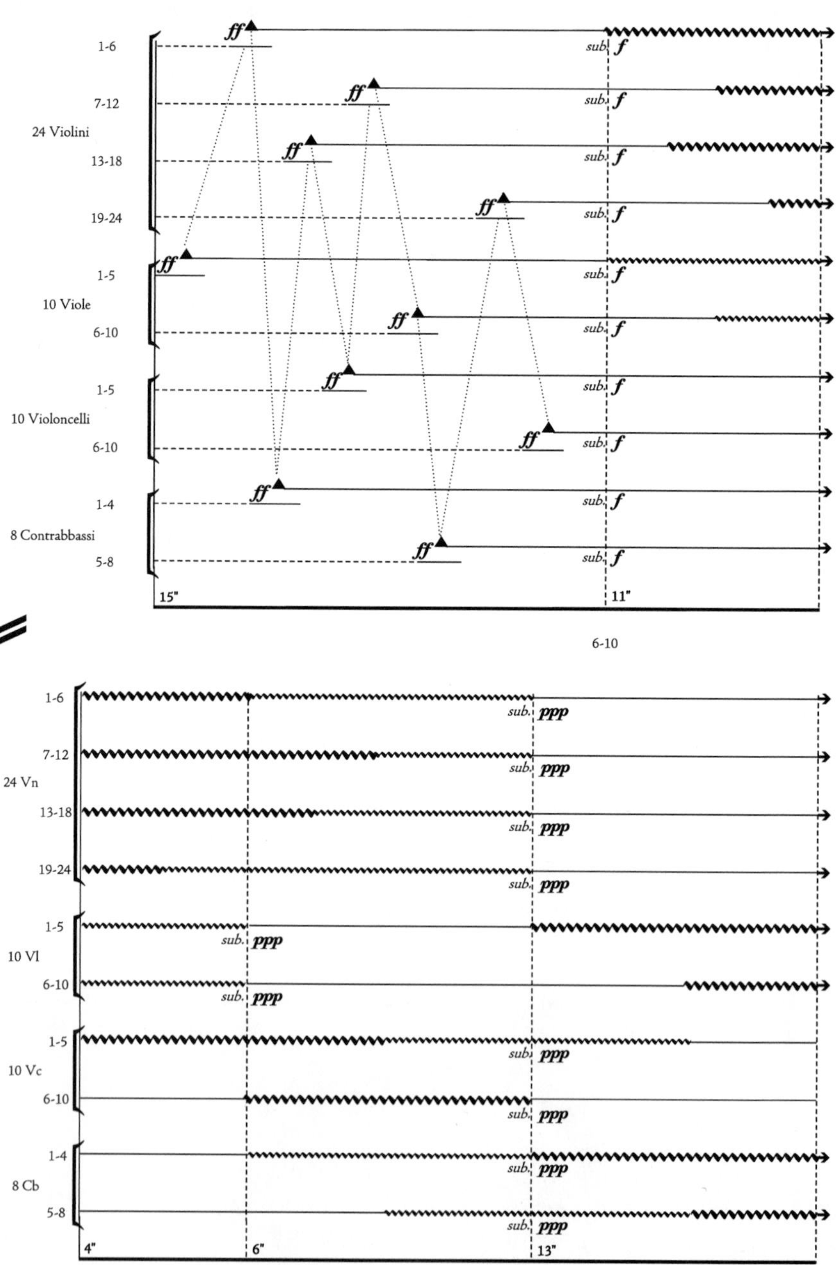

Example 34-4 (*continued*)

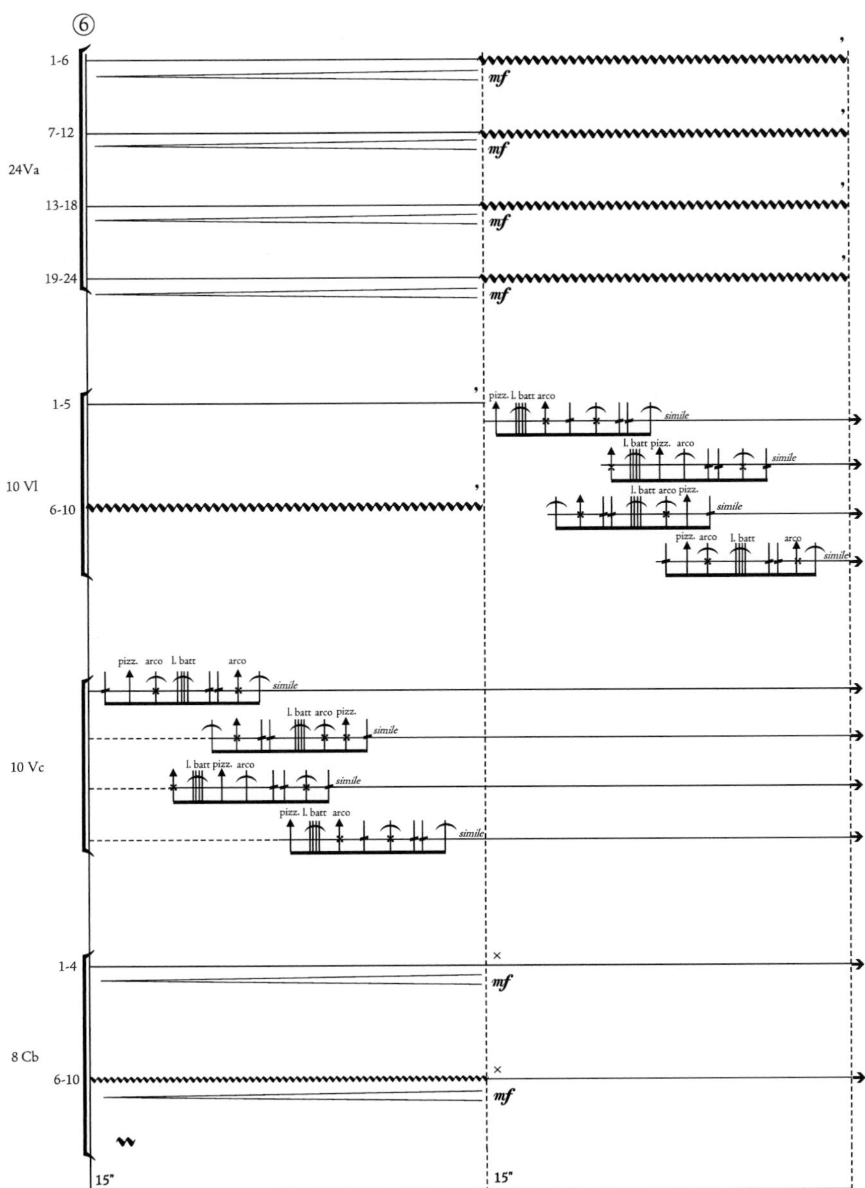

Music in History: Elliott Carter

Elliott Carter (b. 1908), the composer by the end of the century who many musicians and critics considered America's leading figure in writing elite, challenging, and extraordinarily demanding music, for the most part steered clear from universities, serialism, and electronics. His chief medium was instrumental music with abstract titles, most prominently the string quartet. Despite having had an early mentor in Charles Ives, he deliberately rejected an Americanist creative identity in favor of a "universal," that is, generically Eurocentric, one.

Carter's position of eminence evolved slowly. The son of a wealthy lace importer, he had few material concerns. After graduating from Harvard with a master's degree in 1932, he went to Paris for three years of study with Nadia Boulanger and came home a confirmed Neoclassicist. During the following decade, his music conformed to the Americanist idioms most associated with Copland; he wrote a rather Coplandesque ballet *Pocahontas* (1936) and Harrisesque symphony (1942), but that did not last long. Carter's personal connection with Ives and Henry Cowell and his familiarity with the ultra-modern American music gave him a different background from that of his French-trained American colleagues.

In the end, Carter charted another course for himself—his consuming interest became musical time. He later outlined his "philosophic conceptions" in an essay called "Music and the Time Screen" (1971), which recalled a distinction that Stravinsky had drawn in his earlier *Poetics of Music* (1947) between ontological (or objective) time, ticked off by a clock, and psychological (or subjective) time, meaning time as we humanly perceive it.[42] While Stravinsky had contrasted the pair, correlating ontological with "Classic" (good) and psychological with "Romantic" (bad) musical habits, Carter saw music as deriving its value from its capacity to mediate between the two temporal aspects. He sought ways of combining and contrasting aspects of time—of "passage" or unfolding—within a single texture. One way to do this was to superimpose different temporal schemes, as Ives had done. As for the harmonic context in which this would happen, Carter decided that an atonal harmonic language, or at least one that was dissonant and chromatic, was a contemporary necessity, but he was skeptical of serialism—especially total serialism. He was therefore faced with the necessity of finding a way, as he put it in an interview, "to regain the sensitivity to individual notes."[43]

Carter became interested in what he called the "multiple perspective" that one sometimes finds in operas, for example, in the three simultaneous dances in the Act I finale of Mozart's *Don Giovanni*. He started to experiment with ways of allowing the components of his multiple perspectives to develop independently rather than superimposing static but contrasting characters. Simultaneous *accelerandos* and *ritardandos* combined with regular beats that were almost impossible to notate exactly, which gave his music an exceedingly forbidding visual appearance. This begins to hint at some of the problems that Carter's music has created not only for listeners but even for professional analysts and to suggest why his music, like the total serialism he shunned, has acquired a reputation for intellectual abstraction and perceptual opacity.

Elliott Carter sought ways of combining and contrasting aspects of time—of "passage" or unfolding—within a single texture.

Tempo modulation, or what is usually called "**metrical modulation**," is Carter's trademark innovation, although, as he has repeatedly acknowledged, the procedure has a long history going back to fourteenth-century French music, Beethoven (specifically his last Piano Sonata, Op. 111), and more recently Stravinsky and Webern.[44] Carter has also pointed to various non-Western traditions—Indian, Arabic, Balinese, and West African—as sources of his rhythmic techniques and to the combination in some mid-century jazz of free improvisation with strict time. The sheer range of influence flaunts Carter's considerable knowledge and shows how increasing access to so many different kinds of music through recordings gave composers of all stripes inspiring new ideas.

To see Carter's theory in practice we will consider the composition in which he initially implemented the new musical resources at full strength. He wrote his First String Quartet between the fall of 1950 and the spring of 1951 while living on a Guggenheim Fellowship in the lower Sonoran Desert near Tucson, Arizona. That bare biographical fact has done much to encourage Carter's "hermetic" image—deserts, after all, are where hermits live. The "uncompromising" character is reflected in Carter's comment that the quartet was his way of "say[ing] to hell with the public and with the performers too."[45] Henceforth his responsibility would be to his art alone and to its history—both the history he had inherited and the history he would make.

Anthology Vol 3-55
Full CD VII, 27
Concise CD III, 43

The First Quartet is a monumentally engineered construction of multiple perspectives. The first movement, "Fantasia," is a study in fixed vs. fluid tempi (Ex. 34-5). A number of themes, each associated with a certain tempo (that is, an "ontological," or objective clock-measured, beat duration) are put through a series of polyrhythmic or "polytemporal" montages, each linked with the next by taking one of the tempos as a constant. Carter's rhythmic idiom could be termed a modernized and expanded mensural system, thus harkening back to fourteenth- and fifteenth-century mensural music, with all that the term implies—namely, that notated durations no longer have inherent metrical significance but denote only spans of time that can be freely manipulated and interrelated. The tempi in the quartet are so radically differentiated in beat length that one can really sense a texture made up of "multiple perspectives."

Example 34-5 Elliott Carter, First String Quartet, I, mm. 19–29

Example 34-5 ***(continued)***

The First Quartet enjoyed a remarkable *succès d'estime,* or "reputation success." The extraordinary difficulty of the piece made Carter wonder if anyone would want to play it, let alone listen. "Yet within a few years of its composition," he recalled, "it won an important prize and was played (always with a great deal of rehearsal) more than any work I had written up to that time."[46] Its success not only taught him that he had been wrong to feel it his "professional and social responsibility to write interesting, direct, easily understood music." He was emboldened to assert that any composer who followed such a mandate was wrong: "There is every reason to assume that if a composer has been well taught and has had experience (as was true of me in 1950), then his private judgment of comprehensibility and quality is what he must rely on if he is to communicate importantly."[47]

The last word is of course the key, for it is the one that carries implications about value. Carter had indeed communicated "importantly," as the reception his work confirmed. Although it took a while, the First Quartet was premiered in 1953 at Columbia University by the Walden Quartet, the resident quartet at the University of Illinois. The academic affiliation of the performing group, the academic venue, and the subsidized occasion were all indicative of the kind of marginal public existence an advanced composition could count on. The piece also helped to establish Carter's international reputation, for it won the *Concours international de quatuor* (International Quartet Competition) in Belgium. The quartet was performed in Rome at a festival sponsored by the Congress for Cultural Freedom, a group that was part of a Cold War campaign, with financial backing secretly provided by the U.S. Central Intelligence Agency, to showcase cultural masterpieces. This meant sponsorship of various kinds of music, including the avant-garde, the type most obviously uncongenial to totalitarian taste. That such supported music was also uncongenial to "free world" public taste was no obstacle to its promotion. This made it possible for artists such as Carter to have outstandingly successful public careers in the virtual absence of an audience.

Carter's Later Career

Carter's prestige kept on growing with his Variations for Orchestra (1953–55) and Second String Quartet (1959), which won the Pulitzer Prize, as did his Third Quartet in 1971. In that last work, the polyrhythms became so complex that the publisher prepared a "click track" to guide the players (wearing earphones) through their individual parts. Carter remained for the rest of the century the chief standard bearer of autonomous musical art and a bulwark against the Postmodern tendencies that began to emerge in the 1960s and that threatened the Modernist faith. Whether he wanted it or not, Carter had become the representative figure for the traditional Modernist view of art and its autonomous history at the very moment when that view, for reasons that will emerge in the final two chapters, quickly lost ground.

Critics chose precisely the most utopian aspects of Carter's music on which to lavish their praise, and they began describing his stature and his achievement in extravagant terms. Stravinsky, for example, hailed his Double Concerto for Harpsichord and Piano with Two Chamber Orchestras (1961). Example 34-6 shows a representative page (far from the most complicated) from the concerto's score, chosen because Stravinsky happened to single it out for praise. The first thing that leaps out upon examination is how difficult the music must be to perform, offering the kind of challenges that spurred the creation of specialist performing ensembles. The extreme fluidity of both rhythm and tempo are its most conspicuous features, closely followed by the enormous variety of detail. Carter provided listeners little assistance when he wrote a long but rather uninformative program note, which amounted to a blow-by-blow description in an entirely formalist manner. (Only later did he divulge a program with some literary elements.)

Stravinsky, for his part, cheerfully confessed himself unable to understand the detail-heavy music except in the broadest "gestural" terms. Its very mysteriousness magnified the concerto's appeal, giving it an aura to which Stravinsky reacted as if to a religious revelation, declaring, "analysis as little explains a masterpiece or calls it into being as an ontological proof explains or causes the existence of God."[48] Then came the benediction that has been endlessly repeated in the literature on Carter: "There, the word is out. A masterpiece, by an American composer." A masterpiece exists as such even—or especially—when no one understands it, Stravinsky seems to imply. Difficulty—especially conspicuous in Carter's music of the 1960s and '70s, which had the most intricately detailed textures, the most complicated surfaces, and the most complex notation of any music of its time—was itself taken as an indication of masterpiece status.

Figure 34-13 Elliott Carter, age 100, at Carnegie Hall in New York, with James Levine, Daniel Barenboim, and the Boston Symphony Orchestra.

Carter's stature was further enhanced by sheer longevity, productivity, and intellectual brilliance. He continued writing large amounts of instrumental compositions (including two more string quartets) and vocal works, and as he neared the age of ninety, he even unexpectedly composed a one-act comic opera, *What's Next?* (1999). He was still composing at age 100. On his centennial birthday in 2008 two of his greatest champions, James Levine (b. 1943) and Daniel Barenboim (b. 1942), presented *Interventions*, a new work for piano and orchestra, with the Boston Symphony Orchestra at Carnegie Hall in New York City. A beaming Carter was in attendance (Fig. 34-13), as he was for numerous events that celebratory season. And through it all he continued to produce new music, always challenging if increasingly of a more lyrical quality. Sustained productivity at such a level in one's second century may be unique in the history of the arts.

Example 34-6 Elliott Carter, Double Concerto, p. 101 of the score

"Who Cares If You Listen?"

Much of the classical music of the twentieth century, unlike that of previous centuries, consistently encountered resistance from general audiences. But while Richard Strauss, Mahler, Debussy, Stravinsky, Bartók, Copland, Shostakovich, and many others may have initially faced varying degrees of opposition, in most cases it did not take long before their music was embraced by the concert-going public. Almost without exception the composers examined in this chapter, however, did not win such acceptance, nor did they seek it. Artistic resentment and alienation were Romantic attitudes that Modernists maximalized, particularly those working in the tradition of Schoenberg. Many composers after the Second World War, from Boulez and Stockhausen, to Cage and Feldman, to Babbitt and Carter, had other concerns and goals than courting the affection of audiences. Whether born of existential angst, of dreams of a scientific utopia, or of other motivations, these figures valued artistic autonomy and technical innovation. They wrote for history, largely unconcerned about communicating with society.

Many composers after the Second World War, from Boulez and Stockhausen, to Cage and Feldman, to Babbitt and Carter, had other concerns and goals than courting the affection of audiences.

The most candid and famous, indeed infamous, statement on the matter came in an impromptu talk Milton Babbitt gave in the summer of 1957 at the Berkshire Music Center at Tanglewood, the summer festival home of the Boston Symphony Orchestra. The lecture was transcribed from a tape and published the next winter in *High Fidelity*, a large-circulation magazine for record collectors and audio enthusiasts. Babbitt had titled his lecture "The Composer as Specialist," but a canny editor substituted a far more provocative one for publication: "Who Cares If You Listen?"[49]

Babbitt's little talk became one of the most widely reprinted and hotly discussed manifestos in the history of twentieth-century music. The article contains passages in which the author seems to be mocking the musical public (or what he calls "lay listeners"). "Imagine, if you can," one such passage begins,

> a layman chancing upon a [mathematics] lecture on "Pointwise Periodic Homeomorphisms." At the conclusion, he announces: "I didn't like it." Social conventions being what they are in such circles, someone might dare inquire: "Why not?" Under duress, our layman discloses precise reasons for his failure to enjoy himself; he found the hall chilly, the lecturer's voice unpleasant, and he was suffering the digestive aftermath of a poor dinner. His interlocutor understandably disqualifies these reasons as irrelevant to the content and value of the lecture, and the development of mathematics is left undisturbed. If the concertgoer is at all versed in the ways of musical lifemanship, he also will offer reasons for his "I didn't like it"—in the form of assertions that the work in question is "inexpressive," "undramatic," "lacking in poetry," etc. etc., tapping that store of vacuous equivalents hallowed by time for: "I don't like it, and I cannot or will not say why."

Before this passage, however, and using language shrewdly chosen for its scientific resonances, Babbitt had laid out the principles according to which the music that he and other composers of "contemporary serious music" were writing necessarily differed from music designed to appeal to general listeners, with their standard expectations. To appreciate the phenomenally complex new music, listeners must be specially trained, like their counterparts in physics or mathematics. Without such training, comprehension is impossible. Why, then, Babbitt asks rhetorically, "should the layman be other than bored and puzzled by what he is unable to understand, music or anything else?"

Babbitt had a solution in mind, and that was the "total, resolute, and voluntary withdrawal from this public world to one of private performance and electronic media, with its very real possibility of complete elimination of the public and social aspects of musical composition." This attitude clearly resonates with the premises of Schoenberg's Society for Private Musical Performances, advanced nearly forty years earlier. In Babbitt's view the university should take over patronage: "Such a private life is what the university provides the scholar and the scientist." The article ends with these ringing words:

> Granting to music the position accorded other arts and sciences promises the sole substantial means of survival for the music I have been describing. Admittedly, if this music is not supported, the whistling repertory of the man in the street will be little affected, the concert-going activity of the conspicuous consumer of musical culture will be little disturbed. But music will cease to evolve, and, in that important sense, will cease to live.

Babbitt's final sentence, his hymn to musical progress and evolution, caused quite a stir. Its presumption is indeed palpable. And yet in the decades that followed Babbitt's pronouncement one might argue the very opposite happened. Many composers made no secret that they cared about listeners and that in order for music to live it had to connect once again with people and with society.

Summary

The devastation of World War II had profound consequences for the arts, leading to a deep skepticism of the past and a wish to start over from scratch. This chapter explored various responses to this environment, including serialism, indeterminacy, and electronic music. Art music became increasingly separated from popular music. In his essay "Schoenberg Is Dead" (1952), Pierre Boulez (b. 1925) called for a rejection of the traditional elements of Schoenberg's music, including its expressivity. Looking instead to Webern as a model, Boulez proposed serializing four facets of music: pitch, duration, dynamics, and timbre. The result, "total serialism" or "integral serialism," which had precedents in works by Webern and Messiaen, became the dominant approach taught at the Darmstadt International Summer Courses for New Music, where many postwar composers were trained in styles associated in Cold War terms with the artistic freedom of "the West."

Another way forward after the war is represented by the works of the American composer John Cage (1912–92). Beginning in the 1940s, Cage was deeply influenced by Zen Buddhism, which focuses on eliminating ego and expectation. Cage began to create works based on the principle of chance or indeterminacy. In his *Music of Changes*, for example, the pitch, duration, and dynamics are derived by tossing the coins of the *I Ching*, an ancient manual of divination. Cage's works for "prepared piano" call for inserting metal screws and erasers into the piano, bringing all the timbres of a percussion orchestra to the keyboard player's fingertips (see *Bacchanale*). His *4′33″* calls for a performer to sit onstage silently while the audience listens to the sounds around them. These works pose questions about the very definition of music. Although indeterminacy contrasts with the predetermined structures of serialism, both serve to keep in check the personal wishes and preferences of the composer.

By the 1950s serialism had become such a potent force that two established composers, Copland and Stravinsky, began to write serial works while maintaining much of their individual style and sound. Stravinsky's *Requiem Canticles* (1966), for example, still makes reference to the octatonic scale, resulting in harmonies reminiscent of his early works. The preoccupation with mathematical procedures reached its height in works by composers such as Milton Babbitt (1916–2011), who spent his career at Princeton University. Babbitt believed that music should express objective, verifiable truth based on scientific principles. In one manifestation of this belief, Babbitt drew attention to a property of tone rows he called *combinatoriality*: One collection of pitches could be combined with a transformation of itself, such as in inversion or transposition, to create a row. Universities became the focus of this branch of the avant-garde and began offering doctorates in composition. Babbitt's 1957 lecture, published as "Who Cares If You Listen?," became one of the most hotly debated musical manifestoes of the twentieth century.

Seeking new sounds and increased precision, some composers turned to technology. Early composers of electronic music fell into two rival groups. *Musique concrete*, beginning in Paris in 1948, was created by taping and manipulating sounds from the real world, such as engines and phonograph records. Composers of *Elektronische Musik*, beginning in 1951 in Cologne, Germany, based their works exclusively on electronically generated sounds. The hub of electronic music in the United States was the Columbia-Princeton Electronic Music Studio, led by Babbitt along with Otto Luening (1900–96) and Vladimir Ussachevsky (1911–90). Composers soon began to combine taped sounds with live performers. A classic work from this period is Karlheinz Stockhausen's *Gesang der Jünglinge* (Song of the Youths, 1956), a combination of a boy's taped voice with electronically generated sounds. The orchestral works *Atmosphères* (1961) by György Ligeti (1923–2006) and *Threnody for the Victims of Hiroshima* (1960) by Krzysztof Penderecki (b. 1933) use conventional instruments to emulate the sound of electronic music.

The works of the American composer Elliott Carter (b. 1908) explore the simultaneous unfolding of time at different levels and use a technique known as "metrical modulation," in which changing time signatures bring about a transition from one meter to another. Although Carter followed neither the serialist nor the electronic trends of the twentieth century, his music is similar to other twentieth-century art music in its complexity, which challenges performers, audiences, and analysts.

Study Questions

1. Describe the views put forth by Pierre Boulez in his essay "Schoenberg Is Dead." Whose music did Boulez view as a model, and why? In what respects was this view of art rooted in nineteenth-century historicism (see Chapter 22), and in what ways was it a rejection of Romanticism?
2. What is total serialism? What were the first pieces to experiment with it? What social and political factors contributed to its emergence in the 1950s?

3. What was the importance of the Darmstadt International Summer Courses for New Music? Who were some composers associated with it, and what kinds of composition were emphasized?
4. Describe the musical philosophy of John Cage and the "chance," or aleatoric, procedures he used to create music. How do pieces such as *4′33″* challenge and expand traditional definitions of music? Compare and contrast Cage's music and philosophy to that of the total serialists.
5. What kinds of theatrical works, visual experimentation, and conceptual art grew out of Cage's philosophy? What kinds of innovations in music notation followed?
6. Describe Aaron Copland's and Igor Stravinsky's forays into serialism beginning in the 1950s. Why do you think they composed serial works, and how did they retain their individual styles and sounds?
7. Describe the aesthetic trends that gave rise to electronic music. What were some of the new musical instruments created through technology? What is the difference between *musique concrète* and *elektronische Musik?* Who were the main contributors to each genre?
8. How did composers like Mario Davidovsky, Krzysztof Penderecki, and György Ligeti incorporate techniques or sounds associated with electronics into music for conventional instruments?
9. What are some salient traits of Elliott Carter's music? Why do you think it was so well received by critics, despite its lack of a large audience?
10. Discuss the philosophy expressed by Milton Babbitt in "Who Cares If You Listen?" How was it rooted in nineteenth-century historicism?

Key Terms

aggregate
aleatoric music
combinatorial
Elektronische Musik
extended performance techniques
happenings
metrical modulation
musique concrète
ondes martenot
pitch class
prepared piano
synthesizer
theremin
total serialism
Zero Hour

35

Change in the Sixties and Seventies

As a catchphrase, "the sixties" refers to much more than the decade of the 1960s. Coined in nostalgia, in resentment, and, most of all, in retrospect, the phrase evokes disruption, a period of social division brought on by momentous societal transformations. First there was a newly militant drive for equality. The movement for the recognition of the civil rights of racial minorities scored an important victory in 1964 when the United States Congress passed a comprehensive Civil Rights Act. But much led to that watershed and much was to follow, both in America and abroad.

There was also a new impetus toward the assertion of equal rights for women, who sought greater control over their lives, including the right to compete as equals in the workplace and the right to control childbirth. New techniques in contraception, such as birth control pills, made family planning easier. There was a general loosening of sexual constraints, sometimes called the "sexual revolution." With this came a public questioning of the social stigma attached to homosexuality, which culminated in a riot at the Stonewall Bar in New York City in 1969, when a group of patrons forcibly resisted arrest in the name of "gay pride." Gay rights have ever since been an issue in legal contention, alongside women's rights and racial or ethnic minority rights. Events such as the Stonewall Riots and the earlier civil rights March on Washington in August 1963, at which Martin Luther King, Jr. (1929–68), gave his "I Have a Dream" speech, were examples of a new assertiveness in public protest that characterized the decade (Fig. 35-1). One of the era's signal accomplishments was to challenge the idea that American society was governed by a "mainstream" consensus, often symbolized by the metaphor of a melting pot.

The sixties also saw widespread opposition to America's unpopular war against communist expansion in Southeast Asia. What the government defended as a natural consequence of Cold War policies was increasingly perceived as reckless

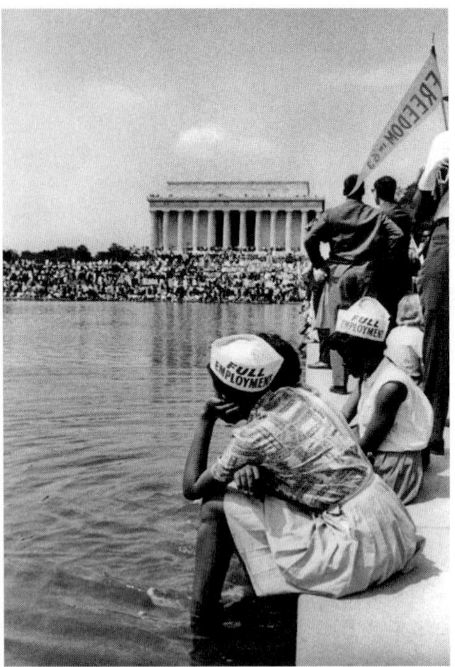

Figure 35-1 Demonstrators in front of the Lincoln Memorial during the civil rights March on Washington in August 1963.

intervention in the internal affairs of the "Third World," the technologically less advanced nations of Asia, Africa, and Latin America, many of them (like Vietnam, the site of the American war) newly liberated from colonial rule. Activists viewed the Vietnam War as a continuation of colonialist aggression under cover of Cold War politics as well as an unjustified threat to a generation of American men whose lives were thus placed at risk—a threat that, owing to inequities in the draft laws, put a disproportionate burden on the same minorities who were fighting for equal rights at home.

Opposition to the Vietnam War stimulated political militancy. Active resistance was mobilized by a self-proclaimed "New Left" of students, radicals, intellectuals, and politicians who questioned the authority of the government to impose its policies on an unwilling population. Others, who became known as hippies (from "hip," a slang word meaning aware or up to date), indulged in passive resistance, rejecting conventional bourgeois society and "dropping out." A utopian "counterculture" emerged devoted to the spontaneous expression of "free love" and to spiritual introspection, the latter often enhanced by the use of psychedelic (sensation-magnifying or mind-expanding) drugs like lysergic acid diethylamide (LSD). None of these phenomena originated entirely during the 1960s, nor did any come to an end with the decade's passing (Fig. 35-2).

Reference to "the sixties" in the collective memory also comes from a series of violent events that shocked American society. The most specific were the political assassinations: of President John F. Kennedy in November 1963; of Martin Luther King, Jr., in April 1968; and, a scant two months later, that of Robert F. Kennedy, the late president's younger brother, then campaigning for election as president himself on an antiwar platform. A more general and anonymous violence came that same spring of 1968 when student demonstrators occupied several buildings on the campus of Columbia University and were forcibly ejected by the police, who had been called in by the university administration. Pictures of bloody students filled the newspapers. In August there were violent confrontations between the Chicago police and antiwar demonstrators outside the Democratic National Convention. Worse was to come: In 1970 the Ohio National Guard killed four students on the campus of Kent State University, and some radical students known as the Weathermen accidently killed themselves while trying to make a pipe bomb in New York. The protests and violence were by no means limited to America—students took to the streets in May 1968 in France; Soviet tanks entered Czechoslovakia in August, ending an inspiring liberal flowering known as the Prague Spring.

Artistic controversies of the sixties mirrored larger societal debates. Some saw new opportunities for equality among the races, genders, and classes, a general expansion of the melting pot ideal of America as a land offering equal opportunity to all who were willing to shed their ethnic particularities and assimilate into the mainstream culture. Yet some vocally rejected that ideal as a myth ultimately protecting the interests of the existing white (and Christian and male) power structure. In its place, many now embraced the idea of "multiculturalism" or, in its more strident variants, cultural nationalism. Traditional high culture came under increasing fire as perpetuating an unjust status quo.

TIMELINE

1954 **Elvis Presley records his first album**
1955–75 Vietnam War
1963 Martin Luther King, Jr., "I Have a Dream" speech
1963 President John F. Kennedy assassinated
1964 **Terry Riley, *In C***
1967 **The Beatles, *Sgt. Pepper's Lonely Hearts Club Band***
1967 **Steve Reich, *Piano Phase***
1968 Student riots in Paris and New York
1969 Stonewall Riots inaugurate the gay rights movement

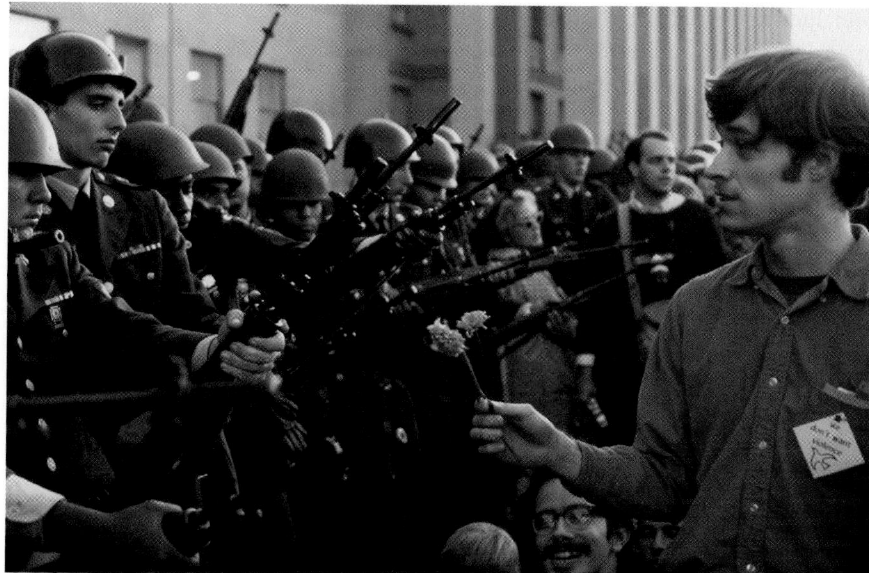

Figure 35-2 A peaceful anti–Vietnam War demonstrator holds up a flower to armed soldiers protecting the perimeter of the Pentagon, 1968.

The meaning and achievement of all this social unrest is still a matter of furious debate. Some look back on the decade of the sixties as a period of hedonism and irresponsibility that did lasting damage to the social fabric. Others, idealizing the optimism and social activism, view it as a period of eventually positive democratic change. What all must agree on and what the foregoing description has already tacitly disclosed is that the era was driven to an unprecedented degree by young people, primarily students. The counterculture was a youth culture and so was the activism of the period. Indeed one of the dominant terms of the time was "generation gap," referring to the massive increase of age-old generational tensions. Youth cultural and artistic expression took new turns, in no area more than in the music of the decade.

Now that we have named music, it must remain our focus. For the first time in this book we will trace in a bit more detail some of the history of "popular" music, music disseminated for commercial profit and not primarily through literate media. The popular music associated with the youth culture of the sixties became a transforming force affecting all other music. Seen in this way, popular music enacted a "revolution" similar to that ascribed to the period's activist culture and counterculture, for both of which it provided the indispensable soundtrack.

1969 **The Who, *Tommy***
1969 **Woodstock music festival**
1974 Watergate scandal results in President Richard Nixon's resignation
1970 **Miles Davis, *Bitches Brew***
1976 **Reich, *Music for 18 Musicians***
1976 **Philip Glass, *Einstein on the Beach***
1976 **Henryk Górecki, Third Symphony**
1977 **Arvo Pärt, *Tabula Rasa***

The Music of Youth: Rock 'n' Roll

The first music that was aimed expressly at a youth market was made by the so-called crooners of the 1940s, whose up-close, almost whispered style of singing appealed irresistibly to adolescent girls, the so-called bobby-soxers. The most successful of these male microphone singers was Frank Sinatra (1915–98; Fig. 35-3), who began his career as a big-band jazz singer but reached an early peak of popularity as a soloist singing soft, slow, intimate ballads. He modeled his style on that of Bing Crosby (1904–77), who in turn had appropriated some of his signature techniques from the performance practices of African American blues singers. Although Sinatra remained a popular singer and film star for the rest of his life, he gradually lost his appeal to a youth audience. That market was taken over by **rock 'n' roll**.

Far more than any previous popular music, rock 'n' roll made an exclusive appeal to youth. Indeed it is fair to say that it was, at least in part, a style calculated to irritate older generations and was often marketed expressly as a means of widening the generation gap. Unlike most previous popular music, rock 'n' roll was the opposite of family entertainment. It was socially divisive as well as socially uniting, and in its own way it could foster an elitism not so different from what we have seen many times within factions of classical music. As parents complained that what their children were listening to "was not music," the youth response was that old folks were too "square" and "just don't get it." A familiar slogan from the mid-1960s was "Don't trust anyone over 30."

Popular music enacted a "revolution" similar to that ascribed to the period's activist culture and counterculture, for both of which it provided the indispensable soundtrack.

The terms "rock 'n' roll" and "teenager" emerged at around the same time, a product of the postwar economic boom. The emerging youth culture was not only a social and political force but also a powerful economic one, the beneficiary of American affluence, something to be catered to or, depending on one's attitude, exploited. The two consumer areas directed most at young people were those of fashion and entertainment, chiefly music. Credit for coining the term "rock 'n' roll" was claimed by Alan Freed (1921–65), a Cleveland disc jockey. As the new medium of television usurped traditional radio programming in the 1950s, air time opened up what came to be filled with nonstop recorded music. Radio stations began pitching their musical offerings to niche markets. Freed had the inspired idea of playing recordings of what was being marketed as "**rhythm and blues**," or **R&B**. It was essentially blues and gospel singing enhanced by a driving percussive beat.

Given a name that further camouflaged R&B's African American origins in the blues, rock 'n' roll proved immediately marketable as dance music to white suburban teenagers. The successful spread of the new genre was facilitated by technology: cheap, highly portable transistor radios enabled fans to carry the music around with them everywhere. Freed played R&B recordings by black performers like Ray Charles (1930–2004) and "Chuck" Berry (b. 1926), while other stations tended to play "covers": remakes of R&B songs by white singers who toned down both their insistent rhythm and their sometimes frankly sexual lyrics. Racial associations, together with a rhythmic insistence that evoked a virtually irresistible physical (i.e., sexual) response, made the music controversial, whether designated R&B or rock 'n' roll and whether performed by blacks or by whites. The music became intertwined with the progressive politics of the civil rights movement. Never before on such a mass scale had a commercial music carried so much heavy cultural and political baggage.

Figure 35-3 Frank Sinatra (left) welcoming special guest star Elvis Presley home from the army on his TV variety show, 12 May 1960.

The most commercially successful rock 'n' roll performer was Elvis Presley (1935–77; Fig. 35-3), who made his first records in Memphis, Tennessee, in 1954, the year of the Supreme Court's landmark desegregation verdict in the case of *Brown v. Board of Education of Topeka, Kansas.* Presley achieved nationwide fame two years later, when his manager, "Colonel" Tom Parker, negotiated a major record contract and arranged the first of his three appearances on the nationally broadcast *The Ed Sullivan Show*, the leading television variety program of the day. More frankly than any previous white performer, Presley consciously cultivated a "black" style, which, although it played into offensive racial and sexual stereotypes (amplified by suggestive body movements that earned him the nickname "Elvis the Pelvis"), greatly magnified his allure. The third time Presley appeared on the program, the producers made a concession to parental unease and showed him only from the waist up. With his lower body cut off from view, Elvis may remind us of a modern-day castrato; he indeed inspired the subversive allure those manufactured uncanny beings had evoked two centuries before.

Politics, especially around issues associated with social protest movements, were also the subject in much of the new "folk" music from the time. The term is somewhat misleading. In the present context it designates not the work of actual folk singers (by definition unpaid amateurs) but, rather, that of professionals singing popularized arrangements of folk songs or composed folk-style songs. One pioneering group was the Weavers, a quartet of singing instrumentalists who came together in 1948. The best-known member, Pete Seeger (b. 1919), was the son of musicologist Charles Seeger, whose political engagement was alluded to in Chapter 33. The group fell victim to the anti-Communist blacklists of the McCarthy Era, but not before they had established a successful entertainment model that attracted imitators such as Joan Baez (b. 1941), Bob Dylan (b. 1941), Judy Collins (b. 1939), and Joni Mitchell (b. 1943). Except for Baez, these singers also sang songs they had written themselves, in effect blurring the line between folk and pop (Fig. 35-4).

The Kingston Trio (formed in 1957) and Peter, Paul, and Mary (formed in 1961) cultivated a clean-cut image, although their songs continued to broach social issues. The latter group identified strongly with the antiwar movement, included Pete Seeger songs in its repertoire, and cut a couple of hit records in 1963 that carried messages that were widely interpreted as radical. "Puff, the Magic Dragon" (1963), nominally a children's song, was read as a metaphorical endorsement of the emerging drug counterculture; and "Blowin' in the Wind" (1963) was a Bob Dylan song that could be read as an endorsement of the civil rights movement: "How many years can some people exist before they're allowed to be free?"

Figure 35-4 Bob Dylan and Joan Baez, 1965.

The British Invasion: The Beatles

The watershed, in terms both of musical content and of audience appeal, was the advent of the Beatles, the English rock 'n' roll group that first performed in America in 1964, soon to be followed by additional British invaders, such as the Rolling Stones, The Who, Pink Floyd, Cream, and Led Zeppelin. They now became the chief models for American pop performers. Unlike the earlier generation of rock 'n' roll performers, the British groups almost exclusively performed their own works. During the Beatles' second American tour, in the summer of 1965, they filled New York's Shea Stadium (capacity 55,600) with screaming girls, now called teenyboppers, and their less excited boyfriends. Appearances on *The Ed Sullivan Show* reached across America (Fig. 35-5). The Beatles began to emerge as the truly emblematic musical phenomenon of the sixties, with far-reaching consequences for music history, including the literate music history this book is tracing.

Two members of the group, rhythm guitarist John Lennon (1940–80) and bass guitarist Paul McCartney (b. 1942), were prolific songwriters who often collaborated. The lead guitarist, George Harrison (1943–2001), also wrote some influential songs, leaving only the drummer, Ringo Starr (b. 1940) confined for the most part to the role of performer. Drawing from the African American R&B antecedents of rock 'n' roll, the Beatles' early music conformed to what had become the standard instrumentation of amplified electric guitars and keyboards plus a "trap set," or one-man jazz percussion outfit. The British groups tended to be far more eclectic in their stylistic range than their American counterparts had been, and their creative aims were far more ambitious, emulating those of jazz and classical musicians, on whom they eventually had an influence. Building on a tradition of Anglo-Celtic folk music, mediated in part through the blues and the hymnody of the Anglican Church, their melodies displayed a modal character that conveyed both authenticity and exoticism, heightening the charm for Americans.

Lennon and McCartney had a nodding acquaintance with the jazz and classical repertoires, including the reigning avant-garde varieties. McCartney spent time in 1966 attending concerts of electronic music and listening to recordings of Karlheinz Stockhausen and Luciano Berio. Harrison added an exotic musical Orientalism stemming from his interest in non-Western music that led him to learn to play the

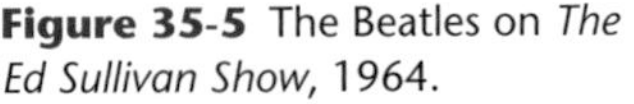
Figure 35-5 The Beatles on *The Ed Sullivan Show*, 1964.

Indian sitar under Ravi Shankar (b. 1920). The Beatles' legendary record producer, George Martin (b. 1926), was a conservatory graduate who crafted unusually rich arrangements for the band and also gave them technical and technological pointers that contributed greatly to their distinctive sound. Martin became known as the "Fifth Beatle." Lennon, McCartney, and Harrison, like virtually all pop musicians, worked exclusively by ear, none of them having been trained to read musical notation with any facility.

As the decade unfolded, the Beatles' music began to have qualities that could not be captured either in vocal score (produced, like most contemporary popular "sheet music," after the fact) or even in live performance. In a sense, they were no longer writing songs. Like some of the avant-garde icons of the day, the Beatles were creating collages, artifacts on tape, and they stopped touring. Their music continued to evolve during the sixties in ways that affected both its content and its musical range, and it continued to broaden its appeal to various audiences. Beginning with *Revolver* (1966) the Beatles produced "**concept albums**" in which the songs on a "Long Playing" (LP) record were coordinated, like the individual numbers in a Romantic song cycle, giving an overall impression that was unified through textual content and musical treatment. *Revolver* contained songs about social alienation and economic injustice, such as "Eleanor Rigby," a portrait of hopeless urban loneliness.

A New Challenge

The new conceptual and musical seriousness of *Revolver* was intensified the following year with *Sgt. Pepper's Lonely Hearts Club Band* (1967). The album cover showed the shaggy, bearded Beatles dressed like the imaginary vaudeville band of the title, standing amid a crowd of cutout portraits of their acknowledged models and mentors (Fig. 35-6). The assemblage included all-purpose saints and icons of modernity like Albert Einstein and Sigmund Freud. (Also there, for those who recognized him, was Stockhausen.) The music on the album was enhanced by whirling electronic effects that seemed to provide a sonic analogue to the visual hallucinations brought on by psychedelic drugs, already reflected in the work of visual artists then straddling the edge between avant-garde and commercial art and in the graphic designs of Peter Max (b. 1937), the ultimate visual embodiment of the sixties spirit (Fig. 35-7).

Figure 35-6 The cover of the Beatles' album *Sgt. Pepper's Lonely Hearts Club Band* from 1967.

The title song of *Sgt. Pepper* casts the album as a stage show given by an imaginary concert band. The album ends, or seems to end, with a reprise of the opening number. But it turns out that this musical recapitulation is not the end. There is a harrowing coda of commentary in the form of "A Day in the Life," the final number, which was very much a sign of the times on its release in the summer of 1967. This unusually long song of over five minutes was inspired in part by the violent death of Lennon's friend Tara Browne, a rich dilettante who savored the countercultural scene and who had crashed his sports car into a parked van, possibly under the influence of drugs. The lyrics consist in part of a surrealistic

Figure 35-7 Peter Max with some of his designs, 1968.

collage of glumly dispassionate newspaper reports—of Browne's death, of a story on potholes in a Lancastershire town, of a military victory (surely an oblique reference to Vietnam)—followed by an invitation to a drugged escape ("I'd love to turn you on . . ."), which led to a temporary ban of the song on British radio.

More ambiguous is the message delivered between the verses, by a sound effect borrowed directly from the avant-garde's bag of tricks. Forty London orchestral musicians were recruited for the recording sessions, which took place in early 1967, conducted by Martin and McCartney. The musicians were each given a chart consisting of a low note and a high note, and they were instructed to play gradually from the one to the other over a span of twenty-four bars, choosing the exact pitches at will, making no attempt at rhythmic coordination with the other musicians, and getting louder all the while. As McCartney knew, it was the kind of thing one expected in a score by John Cage, György Ligeti, or Krzysztof Penderecki; and Martin, who helped plan it, was delighted that the hired musicians reacted to the idea with the similar bewilderment as usually greeted those composers.

To conclude the album, a bit of "empty air" from the studio sessions was spliced on, which was not really empty but contained some low, incomprehensible background muttering and laughter from the members of the group. On the LP album as originally issued in England, this final component was recorded on the continuous inside groove, which meant that the sounds would continue until one chose to remove the needle from the record.[1] What did all this mean? What *could* all this mean? A large part of the album's reception took the form of endless speculation, explanation, and debate—unequivocally a reception accorded to "art" rather than to "entertainment." The group's conceptual experimentations continued in their later albums—*Magical Mystery Tour* (1967), *The Beatles* ("The White Album," 1968), *Yellow Submarine* (1969), *Abbey Road* (1969), and *Let It Be* (1970).

The reception of the Beatles from some quarters of the classical music world was unlike that for any other group. As early as 1963, William Mann, a distinguished critic of classical music for *The Times* of London, surprised his readers by naming Lennon and McCartney the outstanding new composers of the year. He gave a detailed technical analysis of their music, even comparing one song with Mahler's *Das Lied von der Erde*, about the loftiest comparison a critic could make in the heyday of the Mahler revival. He invoked a kind of nineteenth-century historicist thinking in his 1967 article "The Beatles Revive Hopes of Progress in Pop Music."[2] The usual thinking had been that pop music trafficked in the transient. (As the snobbish quip used to go, the nice thing about popular music is that it is not popular for very long.) Now, Mann observed, the Beatles were producing a music that did not fade so quickly, in part because they were growing up with their audience; reciprocally, their audience was staying loyal to them past the teenage years. Previously it had been expected that young people, at least ones of privilege and education, would outgrow their youthful passions and "mature" to appreciate classical music. The late 1960s was precisely the period in which sociological surveys stopped showing university students switching their taste allegiances to classical music. Increasingly young people kept on listening to the music they had grown up with, feeling little need to move on to the classical terrain.

Other critics and composers also joined in the chorus of praise. Leonard Bernstein hailed Lennon and McCartney as the greatest songwriters of the day. American composer Ned Rorem (b. 1923) argued that the Beatles marked a resurgence of genuine musical creativity after the long drought inflicted by the postwar avant-garde. Rorem was concerned less with the social aspects of the music than with the pleasure it gave. "Our need for them [the Beatles]," he insisted, "is neither sociological nor new, but artistic and old, specifically a *renewal*, a renewal of pleasure."[3] The secret of the Beatles, according to Rorem, was the secret of all good music: good tunes. He also admired the unexpected harmonies that spiced the music and often appreciated the words, including the "crushing poetry" of "A Day in the Life." Rorem was attempting to use the Beatles as a weapon in his own battle of revenge with the academic avant-garde. In effect, he was issuing an invitation to the concert-going public to defect from high Modernism, which is just what was happening at the time anyway.

The reception of the Beatles from some quarters of the classical music world was unlike that for any other group.

From the late sixties on, popular music was increasingly seen as part of an alternative culture to which not just hippies but educated people of all stripes could adhere. A growing alternative press covered the music in newspapers like *The Village Voice* and in new magazines such as *Rolling Stone* and *Crawdaddy!* Soon major magazines and newspapers were incorporating criticism on their culture pages. It took much more time for universities to admit popular-music studies as a legitimate branch of both musicology and cultural history, but that eventually happened as well. Academic articles, books, and dissertations slowly appeared that offered careful analysis of the music, not just of its cultural implications. This all challenged the notion that only classical music was worthy of serious musical analysis. As musicologist Joshua Rifkin, who as a Princeton graduate student had written a study on the Beatles, later remembered:

> The very passion that we conceived for them provoked troubling questions: How could these musically unlettered kids, operating more or less collectively, produce something that we could see as somehow coterminous with the products of those fearsomely learned individuals who alone, we imagined, could create "serious art"? Faced with such contradictions, we could either abandon the passion, try to reconcile it with the aesthetic and other paradigms to which we knowingly and unknowingly subscribed, or start to wonder about the paradigms themselves. We couldn't do the first; for a while, as my article attests, some of us tried the second; but ultimately, and perhaps inevitably, most of us wound up with the third.[4]

Rock 'n' Roll Becomes Rock

And so the great musical transformer of the 1960s became **rock** music, which was not merely an abbreviation of rock 'n' roll, although that was obviously its derivation. Rock now traced its lineage only indirectly to the working-class African American sources that had initially nourished rock 'n' roll. The counterculture was not listening to Elvis. Rock was a music created and performed by white musicians, largely for an audience that was white and bourgeois, however antibourgeois its posture.

It became a prime characteristic of British and American rock to produce grand statements, not just pop hits. In 1969, The Who released an album, *Tommy*, in which the songs—composed by lead guitarist Pete Townshend (b. 1945)—were linked in a continuous sequence describing the life of a "deaf dumb and blind boy" with a genius for playing pinball machines. Although it was in fact a narrative song cycle, *Tommy* was promoted as "the first rock opera," eventually adapted for stage and film productions. It became a milestone in the development of "**progressive rock**." That term was borrowed from the "progressive jazz" of the 1950s, an esoteric and artistically ambitious outgrowth of bebop, jazz's most esoteric and Modernist phase. Progressive rock bands such as the Velvet Underground (from 1965) and Blood, Sweat, and Tears (from 1968) often included members with jazz and classical training. Emerson, Lake & Palmer specialized in arrangements of favorite items from the classical repertoire, such as Musorgsky's *Pictures at an Exhibition* and Copland's *Fanfare for the Common Man*. By the 1970s, critics were discussing "art rock" and "avant-garde rock," associated with musicians such as Frank Zappa (1940–93), Robert Fripp (b. 1946), and Brian Eno (b. 1948) and with groups like Queen (from 1971) and Talking Heads (from 1976).

Figure 35-8 Promotional poster for the 1969 Woodstock Music and Arts Fair.

The influence of rock as a democratizing or leveling force on other kinds of music produced furious controversies. In particular, it inspired backlashes from those interested in insulating or protecting the "authenticity" of the nonpop genres from commercial contamination. Rock succeeded in overthrowing social hierarchies as expressed in music. It was a democratizing force that had strong repercussions within all other fields of musical production, influencing all of the genres (folk, jazz, and classical) that had formerly been considered alien or superior to the commercial pop scene.

Various popular currents came together at the most famous countercultural musical event of the 1960s: a free music festival held in August 1969 on a farm near Woodstock, New York—about a hundred miles north of New York City—and attended by upwards of half a million hippies and their sympathizers (Fig. 35-8). Amplification now allowed such mass events, which would only become more high tech in the decades that followed. Woodstock was a remarkable spectacle of nonviolence to offset the disturbing events of 1968 mentioned at the beginning of this chapter. The first day featured some folk musicians, including Joan Baez and Arlo Guthrie (b. 1947), and Ravi Shankar; the second day was devoted to rock, featuring Janis Joplin (1943–70) and the groups Santana, Grateful Dead, The Who, Sly and the Family Stone, and Jefferson Airplane; the third day (bleeding into a fourth) proved a mixture, with the group Crosby, Stills, Nash & Young and, later, Jimi Hendrix (1942–70).

Figure 35-9 Miles Davis, 1969.

Rock also fused with jazz in the later 1960s. Indeed this **jazz-rock fusion** caused some controversy because it involved both class and race. Again, it was the perceived defection of a universally acknowledged great that brought matters to a head. Miles Davis (1926–91; Fig. 35-9) was one of the leaders, in the late 1940s, in the rise of bebop. As such, he was conspicuous within the jazz faction most self-consciously concerned with the identity of their music as an art form, as distinct from entertainment. In the late 1960s Davis began to collaborate with accompanying artists who played electric keyboards and guitars and with drummers who backed his improvisations with a heavy rock beat. Two of his albums, *In a Silent Way* (1969) and *Bitches Brew* (1970), lit a fire of debate that even two decades later had not died down.

The integration of classical music with jazz also continued, becoming in many instances a negotiation on much more equal terms in the spirit of Duke Ellington, rather than the classical appropriation of jazz earlier attempted by Stravinsky, Copland, and others. One trend was called **Third Stream**, the brainchild of Gunther Schuller (b. 1925), a remarkably versatile musician who began his career as a French horn virtuoso and who composed prolifically, chiefly in a serial idiom. He became both a conductor and a major jazz historian interested in joining musical traditions that he felt could only profit from the confrontation. The liberal integrationist mentality of the times was reflected in Schuller's philosophy:

> It is a way of making music which holds that *all musics are created equal*, coexisting in a beautiful brotherhood/sisterhood of musics that complement and fructify each other. It is a global concept which allows the world's musics—written, improvised, handed-down, traditional, experimental—to come together, to learn from one another, to reflect human diversity and pluralism. It is the music of rapprochement, of *entente*—not of competition and confrontation. And it is the logical outcome of the American melting pot: *E pluribus unum*.[5]

Third Stream was envisioned as the confluence of two "mainstreams." "Western art music," in Schuller's view, "can learn a great deal from the rhythmic vitality and 'swing' of jazz, while jazz can find new avenues of development in the large-scale forms and complex tonal systems of classical music." In practice, Third Stream was the fruit of a collaboration between Schuller and jazz pianist John Lewis (1920–2001), who in 1952 had cofounded the Modern Jazz Quartet, which gained a reputation as a progressive ensemble.

The competitions, interactions, appropriations, and fusions between different kinds of music, between those traditionally considered high and low, artistic and commercial, literate and improvised or oral, became in the 1960s a source both of bitter contention and of musical innovation. The breaking down of boundaries and the mixture of styles, periods, and genres is fundamental to what came to be viewed as musical Postmodernism, which we will explore in the final chapter. Third Stream never aroused the antagonism that jazz-rock fusion inspired, perhaps because the music it sought to fuse—conservatory-style composition (in Schuller's case, twelve-tone) and progressive jazz—were both considered elite at the time. Jazz-rock fusion, on the other hand, was seen as part of a general encroachment of commercialism on art. The fusion of all these kinds of music as well as of non-Western music with classical music was praised by some and viewed as deeply threatening by others. We will see, however, that such fusions dominated the classical tradition in the late twentieth century and will thus dominate the conclusion of our story.

In music, commercial rock seemed to be swallowing up everybody's audience, and it appeared to traditionalists of all stripes as the common enemy, even as it was claiming the allegiance of many who would previously have "graduated" to one of the traditional elite genres. By the end of the 1960s, popular music accounted for more than 70 percent of all record sales, leaving jazz, folk, and classical to compete for the remainder. Since then the disparity has only grown. By the 1990s, classical music and jazz each commanded a measly 3 percent of record sales. They seemed like niche products, which in a sense they had always been, but there had never previously been such a mass culture with which they could be compared. Despite the fact that classical music had traditionally claimed a universal human appeal and indeed had based its sense of superiority to other genres precisely on this vaunted universality, it had never before been in competition with a global entertainment market for music, movies, and sporting events. Classical music was simply dwarfed by the sheer numbers represented by popular culture, in terms both of audience size and of money. When viewed from this new mass and global perspective, it seemed like a death sentence for classical music. The history of literate music in the last three decades of the twentieth century was in part a history of dealing with these new realities.

The Rise of Minimalism

The first identifiable group of composers in the literate tradition whose music not only exemplified but thrived on the blurring of socio-stylistic categories were the ones associated with a murky category known as **minimalism**. The term, as usual, was applied to the music after having been coined for other arts and may not be the best one for what it purports to describe. Of the alternatives that have been proposed over the years, "pattern and process music" might be the most neutrally descriptive. But as one of its major figures, Steve Reich (b. 1936), has observed, "Debussy resented 'Impressionism.' Schoenberg preferred 'pantonal' to 'atonal' or 'twelve-tone' or 'Expressionist.' Too bad for them."[6]

As will become clear in the discussion that follows, no single feature unites the music of all the composers to whom the term *minimalist* has been applied. Minimalist music in part comes out of an experimental tradition within classical music, but it owes a great debt as well to various kinds of popular music—jazz and rock—as well as to non-Western music. In its own right, some minimalist music has been commercially successful beyond the dreams of classical composers. Furthermore, minimalism has fused not only with other music styles but also with other arts to produce multimedia theatrical, operatic, dance, and visual works in a sort of Postmodern *Gesamtkunstwerk*, a total work of art.

Minimalism can thus neither be limited strictly to the classical sphere nor divorced from it. Its practitioners are as often listed and discussed in encyclopedias and dictionaries of "Popular Music" as they are in surveys of "Modern Music." Its existence and success have been among the strongest challenges to the separation of high and popular culture on which most twentieth-century aesthetic theorizing and artistic practice have depended. Brian Eno is normally classified as a rock musician (although a somewhat atypical one), while Philip Glass (b. 1937) is normally classified as a classical composer (although a somewhat atypical one). The distinction seems partly based on the kinds of training they received. Eno had an art-school education and is relatively untutored in traditional music theory, while Glass had an elite university education and a formal initiation into the literate tradition of music. But both create music for ensembles of amplified instruments. Both draw eclectically on many musical traditions (literate as well as nonliterate, Western as well as non-Western) formerly thought to be entirely separate if not incompatible. And both actively participate as performers of their works with their own groups, although neither is a virtuoso or a conductor. These traits are more characteristic of pop artists than of classical composers.

Underlying the attitudes of minimalist composers is their relationship to the recording technologies that set the twentieth century apart from all previous ones. They were the first generation of musicians who grew up taking those technologies and all their implications for granted. They received their formative musical experiences from records and broadcasts, and they founded their idea of the musical world on a wide range of experience to which those technologies gave access: a vast amount of music from diverse times and places. What had previously been an occasional opportunity for a few interested composers to hear popular music or "exotic" music from other countries or recordings of Medieval and Renaissance music now became a way of life for composers growing up in the age of the LP and the compact disc. Thanks to recordings, a composer could live, as Henry Cowell once put it, "in the whole world of music" in a way that had never previously been imagined.[7]

That much of the minimalist's initial ear-opening exposure to music, be it Medieval or Baroque, jazz or non-Western, came through records shows the way recording technology was redefining musical transmission in the twentieth century. Late-twentieth-century transmission was, in a word, "horizontal." All music past and present, nearby and far away, was simultaneously and equally accessible to any musician in the world. The way in which this horizontal transmission supplanted the vertical transmission of styles in chronological single file (the assumption on which all historicist thinking depends) was the genuine musical revolution of the late twentieth century, the full implications of which will only be realized in the twenty-first century.

Late-twentieth-century transmission was, in a word, "horizontal." All music past and present, nearby and far away, was simultaneously and equally accessible to any musician in the world.

La Monte Young

Calls for the sort of radical reduction that characterized minimalism had been heard before. The great Modernist architect Mies van der Rohe (1886–1969) had issued the battle cry "Less is more!" As early as 1948, the abstract expressionist artist Barnett Newman (1905–70) exhibited an oil painting, *Onement 1*, that consisted of a canvas of uniform red-brown color with a single narrow stripe of red-orange running down the middle. Mark Rothko, who so inspired Morton Feldman, won his greatest fame for enormous canvases divided into two or three floating rectangles of luminous color. In 1951, Cage's friend Robert Rauschenberg produced a series of paintings consisting of nothing but panels of white house-paint on unprimed canvas. A few years later, Ad Reinhardt (1913–67) did something comparable in black, while in France Yves Klein (1928–62) was producing monochrome blue canvases. By 1965, "minimal art," or "minimalism," had entered the standard vernacular of the art world, initially with pejorative connotations.[8]

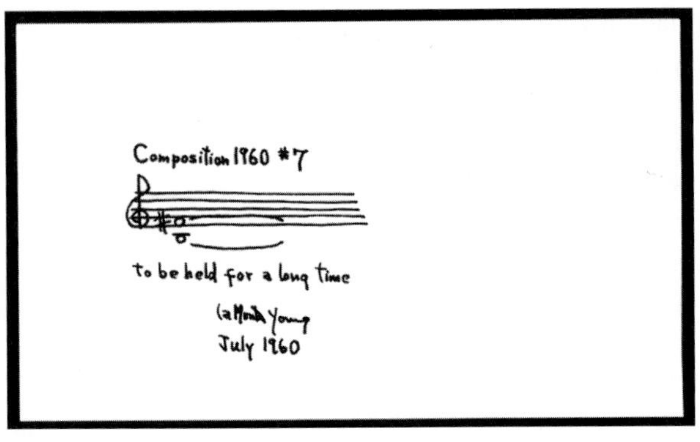

Figure 35-10 La Monte Young, *Composition 1960 #7.*

The term entered the vocabulary of music criticism in 1968, in an article about Cornelius Cardew by the English composer and critic Michael Nyman (b. 1944). What struck Nyman as minimal in this case was the process of composition rather than the result. The same goes for Cage's *4′33″*. Yet neither Cardew's *Scratch Music* nor Cage's piece fulfills the terms of musical minimalism, for such works are not "created with a minimum of means,"[9] nor do they "concentrate on and delimit the work to be a single event or object,"[10] defining characteristics according to La Monte Young (b. 1935), who might be considered the conceptual founder of American minimalism. His *Composition 1960 #7*, consisting in its entirety of a notated perfect fifth (B-F♯) and the direction "to be held for a long time," does fit the bill (Fig. 35-10).

The status of founder always commands an aura, and Young's is the name that shimmers in accounts of minimalism, even if most later minimalists pursued a style quite different from his. Young was connected with Fluxus, the loose association of artists and musicians on the fringe of the New York art scene who promoted happenings. Born in rural Idaho, he grew up listening to popular music on the radio and playing jazz saxophone. As soon as he got to UCLA, he was put on the same Schoenbergian compositional regimen as everyone else; he was particularly attracted by the sparseness he discovered in Webern's music. During the summer of 1958, just after graduation, he gave a neat minimalist spin to serialism: He composed a String Trio that started slowly, very slowly, by unfolding a single twelve-tone row—taking about eleven minutes (Ex. 35-1). Young's String Trio, which was never published, abounds in notational features unrelated to its actual sound in performance. There are tempo changes, for instance, that take place on rests (or in the middle of sustained tones) and syncopated entries made without any accentuation or surrounding pulse against which syncopations may be measured or even perceived by the ear. Taking things to unaccountable extremes immediately marked Young's work as avant-garde in the classical meaning of the word.

Example 35-1 La Monte Young, String Trio, opening

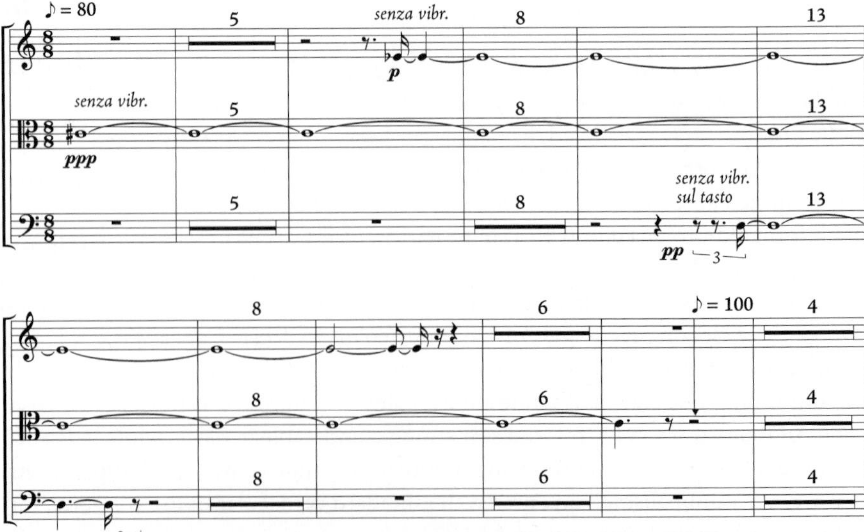

Example 35-1 (*continued*)

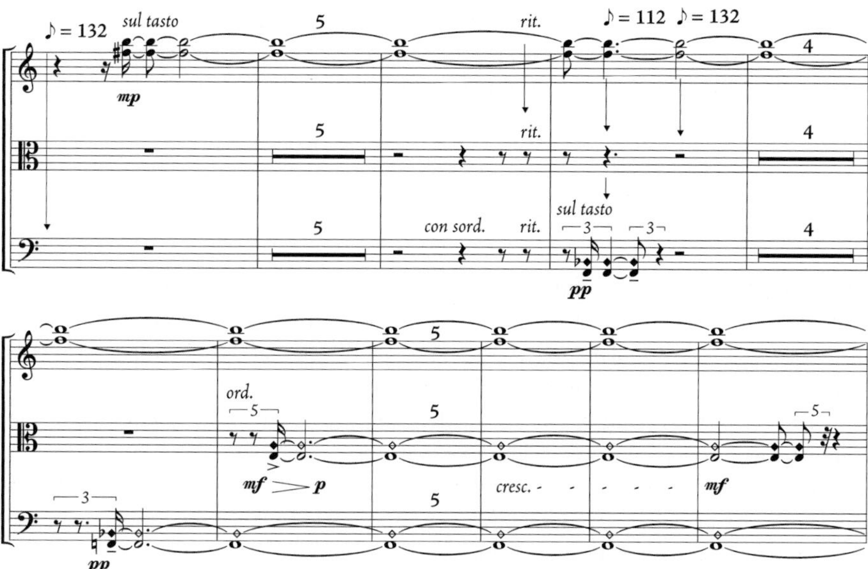

Young's String Trio came to be viewed as a spiritual exercise, reminiscent of the way Feldman's music is now also often interpreted. Raised a Mormon, he made a decisive turn in 1970 by becoming a disciple of Pandit Pran Nath, an Indian musician and spiritual guru. Already in the early 1960s, after moving to New York, he and his wife, artist Marian Zazeela (b. 1940), had founded the Theatre of Eternal Music (Fig. 35-11), an ensemble dedicated to the devout daily rehearsal and very occasional performance of his work, which consisted of several enormous, ongoing, and unfinishable compositions. Perhaps needless to say, these works no longer employ twelve-tone procedures. Pitch became the area to which Young applied the most

Figure 35-11 Members of the Theatre of Eternal Music (also known as the Dream Syndicate) perform in a private loft, New York City, 1965. *From left*: Tony Conrad, La Monte Young, Marion Zazeela, and John Cale.

rigorous restrictions, arriving finally at an approach based on natural acoustical resonance. Beginning in the mid-1970s, much of his composing and performing energy was devoted to *The Well-Tuned Piano*, a body of music to be played on a piano tuned in a system of just (or Pythagorean) intonation. Young's brand of musical minimalism became for him a form of esoteric religious practice, a discipline to be carried out by and in the presence of initiates rather than performed before the general public.

Terry Riley's *In C*

La Monte Young's behind-the-scenes role in the growth of minimalism played out largely through the musicians with whom he associated, a group that crosscuts the old boundary between popular and serious music. One of his early acquaintances, Welsh-born John Cale (b. 1942), went on to join songwriter Lou Reed (b. 1943) in forming the progressive rock band the Velvet Underground, and later collaborated with Eno. Young's most conspicuous early disciple was Terry Riley (b. 1935), the composer through whom minimalism first found a wide audience. A fellow graduate student at the University of California, Berkeley, Riley also rebelled against the forced diet of serial composition. Unlike Young, he managed to complete a master's degree in 1961, but only by writing a twelve-tone composition, immediately disavowed, to satisfy the degree requirement. What really interested Riley at the time was the composing he was doing to accompany a local modern dance ensemble. Like many others, he experimented with **tape loops**. One early piece that resulted was *Mescalin Mix*, named after a psychedelic drug that was popular among the San Francisco Beat poets and hippies. Through this association Riley made explicit the connection between the new avant-garde and the counterculture out of which progressive rock was about to emerge.

Riley followed up with a piece that transferred the looping technique to actual performers. From it came what he called "music that could be avant-garde and get an audience too,"[11] best represented by his most famous work: *In C* (1964). The complete score is given in Example 35-2. One is not likely to guess by looking at it that the composition lasts anywhere between half an hour and three full hours, to cite the range of documented performances. It is best known from a 1968 recording lasting forty-four minutes made at the State University of New York at Buffalo, a celebrated center for new music where Feldman later taught. Each of the fifty-three numbered "modules," which can be played by "any number of any kind of instruments" (including vocalizing singers), either at the notated pitch or at any octave transposition (and using either the notated time values or any arithmetic augmentation or diminution thereof), is to be looped—that is, repeated at the performer's discretion before moving on to the next. The piece is over when all performers, in practice usually somewhere between a dozen and thirty, have reached the last module. *In C* is not an aleatoric composition or a free-for-all; rather, it is controlled by a set of firm if loosely specified rules. Its unfolding is highly structured.

The extraordinary reception *In C* enjoyed at its 1964 premiere in San Francisco surprised everyone. Alfred Frankenstein, the esteemed critic of the *San Francisco Chronicle*, was bowled over. "At times," he wrote, "you feel you have never done anything all your life long but listen to this music and as if that is all there is or ever will be, but it is altogether absorbing, exciting, and moving, too."[12] He compared its slowed-down time scale, its gradual evolutionary unfolding, and its "climaxes of great sonority [that] appear and are dissolved in the endlessness" to the sublime effect of a

Bruckner symphony. But just as obviously, *In C* was a model of a very different kind of social behavior from that of a symphony orchestra under a dictatorial conductor, representing instead a model of cooperative behavior that was at the heart of the sixties counterculture. Also evident at a glance, and equally crucial to its immediate appeal, was *In C*'s relative ease of performance. It does not require highly trained professional musicians and lends itself equally well to all kinds of nonstandard ensembles. It received performances by rock bands and early-music groups, and among the instruments in its first performance were jazz saxophones, rock guitars, and recorders. The piece could be seen as proposing a more democratic, less hierarchical organization of society that might have appeared utopian in real life but that could be actualized directly in music. It all seemed to offer a lived experience of countercultural paradise.

Example 35-2 Terry Riley, *In C*, full score

For many listeners, the most characteristic and style-defining aspect of *In C* is the constant eighth-note pulse heard underlying all of the looping, and that seems, because it provides a constant pedal of Cs, to be fundamentally bound up with the work's concept. It may be surprising, therefore, to learn that this incessant pulse was an afterthought, adopted in rehearsal for what seemed at the time a purely utilitarian purpose: to keep the group together in lieu of a conductor. The idea was not even Riley's. It came from Steve Reich, who participated in the first performance playing an electric piano.[13]

"Classical" Minimalism: Steve Reich

Reich came from a background very different from the rural, working-class upbringing on the West Coast of Young and Riley. He was born into a wealthy, professional-class family in New York. He had traditional piano lessons, was exposed to what in later years he mildly derided as the "bourgeois classics," and attended Cornell University, where he majored in philosophy. Then came a year of private instruction in composition with Hall Overton (1920–72), a composer who combined classical and jazz idioms in a manner comparable to Third Stream. Reich next studied at the Juilliard School. Finally, lured by the presence of Berio on the faculty, he enrolled at Mills College in California for a master's degree, which he received in 1963. It was the sort of training that typically led to a career as an elite Modernist, obedient to tone rows and tenured at a university.

But as Reich had grown up being exposed to the great horizontal range of music to which technology gave access, he felt much more in sympathy with aspects of early and Baroque music, jazz, and rock than with serialism, chance music, or Coplandesque Americana. As a teenager he found himself particularly attracted to Stravinsky's *The Rite of Spring*, Bach's Fifth Brandenburg Concerto, and bebop, then the most avant-garde form of jazz. The obvious common denominator of what might otherwise seem the three unrelated styles that aroused his particular enthusiasm is the rhythmic spotlight on the strongly articulated subtactile pulse, the very thing that Reich contributed to *In C*. Baroque music has it, as does a lot of twentieth-century music, including Stravinsky and jazz, but the repertoire of nineteenth-century "bourgeois classics," such as Beethoven and Brahms, generally lacks it. Reich stated once in an interview: "Believe it or not, I have no real interest in music from Haydn to Wagner."[14]

Having discovered that subtactile "rhythmic profile," as he called it, Reich switched from piano lessons to lessons in drumming. He later encountered non-Western styles of percussion playing—West African drumming and Balinese gamelan—that effectively liberated his creative thinking from the assumptions of his traditional training. Eventually, he sought out native teachers in these traditions (to which end he spent time in Africa in 1970) to gain hands-on experience. The immediate effect on Reich, and on the many composers his work has stimulated, was to convince him that a truly valid late-twentieth-century music would be "a music that is essentially percussive and pulse-generated rather than melodic and phrase-generated," in the words of John Adams, one of the leading composers most influenced by Reich.[15]

After Mills, Reich decided to stay in the San Francisco Bay Area for a while, where he met Riley, whose tape pieces and *In C* inspired a pair of tape-loop compositions, his earliest compositions to achieve wide notice. *It's Gonna Rain* (1965; originally titled "It's Gonna Rain; or, Meet Brother Walter in Union Square after

Listening to Terry Riley") was based on just the three nominal words, spliced out of a recording of a gospel sermon about Noah and the Flood delivered by Brother Walter, a San Francisco street preacher. The implied warning of the title phrase, in the context of the scariest phases of the Cold War, was timely and topical. Reich's other tape-loop piece, *Come Out* (1966), had a political subtext related to the civil rights struggles of the time. The composer's original program note described both the occasion that inspired the piece and the distinctive technical process that made it a milestone in the emergence of minimalism:

> *Come Out* was composed as part of a benefit, presented at [New York's] Town Hall in April, 1966, for the retrial, with lawyers of their own choosing, of the six boys arrested for murder during the Harlem riots of 1964. The [recorded] voice is that of Daniel Hamm, then nineteen, describing a beating he took in the Harlem 28th precinct. The police were about to take the boys out to be "cleaned up" and were only taking those that were visibly bleeding. Since Hamm had no actual open bleeding, he proceeded to squeeze open a bruise on his leg so that he would be taken to the hospital—"I had to, like, open the bruise up and let some of the bruise blood come out to show them."
>
> The phrase "come out to show them" was recorded in both channels, first in unison and then with channel 2 slowly beginning to move ahead. As the phase begins to shift, a gradually increasing reverberation is heard which slowly passes into a sort of canon or round. Eventually the two voices divide into four and then into eight.
>
> By restricting oneself to a small amount of material organized by a single uninterrupted process, one's attention can become focused on details that usually slip by. A single repeated and gradually changing figure may well be heard as a composite of several figures. Finally, at any given moment, it is open to the listener as to which pattern within the pattern he hears.[16]

It's Gonna Rain and *Come Out* were planned from the start to exploit the **phasing** process, whereby musical material that begins in unison very gradually shifts out of phase. It was that process—inexorable and systematic—that mattered to Reich, because it gave the music a sense of purpose. The composer expounded his philosophy in a famous manifesto entitled "Music as a Gradual Process" (1968), which began "I do not mean the process of composition, but rather pieces of music that are, literally, processes." It then continued in short explosive paragraphs like planks in a political platform. Here are a few of them:

> The distinctive thing about musical processes is that they determine all the note-to-note (sound-to-sound) details and the overall form simultaneously. (Think of a round or infinite canon.)
>
> I am interested in perceptible processes. I want to be able to hear the process happening throughout the sounding music.
>
> To facilitate closely detailed listening, a musical process should happen extremely gradually.
>
> Performing and listening to a gradual musical process resembles:
>
> pulling back a swing, releasing it, and observing it gradually come to rest;
>
> turning over an hourglass and watching the sand slowly run through to the bottom;

> placing your feet in the sand by the ocean's edge and watching, feeling, and listening to the waves gradually bury them.
>
> Though I may have the pleasure of discovering musical processes and composing the musical material to run through them, once the process is set up and loaded, it runs by itself.[17]

Phase Music

Reich wondered whether the very gradual phasing technique that governed his tape pieces might be executed by live performers. After experimenting with his ensemble, he found the answer was yes: With enough practice, performers were able to reproduce the procedure. In *Piano Phase* (1967) for two pianos, a one-measure "basic unit" is subjected to the same phase process that he had first achieved by retarding the turning of a tape reel (Ex. 35-3). The two pianists begin by playing the figure in unison, the way the two tape recorders had begun in *Come Out*. While one pianist holds the tempo steady, the other very gradually gains on it, producing at first an enhanced resonance as the parts go slightly out of phase; eventually the second piano will be one sixteenth note ahead of the first. Here the two pianists are instructed to lock into the same tempo again, producing a sort of canon at the sixteenth note that establishes a new point of departure for the next phasing process. After twelve such processes, the original unison is regained.

Example 35-3 Steve Reich, *Piano Phase*, first "basic unit"

Reich's key work from the early period of his career was *Drumming* (1971), which can last up to nearly ninety minutes, depending on how many times the basic units are repeated (Fig. 35-12). It is scored for a percussion group plus a piccolo player and two women vocalists singing nonmeaningful syllables. Both the rhythmic patterning of the piece and the integration of voices into the ensemble were influenced directly by Reich's studies in Africa. The unfolding process is complex, combining the older phase technique with what Reich calls "rhythmic construction," a process that gradually replaces the rests in the basic unit with sound, as well as its opposite, "rhythmic reduction" (the gradual replacement of notes with rests). The piece achieves its impressive length through contrasts of tone color. The first of its four large sections is scored for tuned bongo drums; the second is scored for marimbas and voices; the third, moving into an unsingably high register, uses glockenspiels, with whistling and piccolo piping replacing the voices; the fourth combines all forces.

Drumming was a technical tour de force that served for several years as the staple of Reich's touring group, greatly increasing the number of his admirers, to the point where he began filling large halls, mainly on college campuses, and attracting imitators. A recording of *Drumming* and some other works was issued in 1974 by Deutsche Grammophon, the most prestigious European classical label. Its complexity

Figure 35-12 Steve Reich (in cap) performs *Drumming* with his ensemble, October 2006. Photo: Hiroyuki Ito for *The New York Times.*

notwithstanding, the euphoria *Drumming* produced in receptive listeners, more typical of popular music than of contemporary classical composition, made it newsworthy and, of course, controversial, not only because it challenged the basic definition of avant-garde art but also because listeners were obviously responding to more than just the beguiling sound patterns. There was the unstated but strongly implied social meaning that arose directly from its African antecedents. As with many of the pieces Reich wrote for his own ensemble, there was also a striking visual aspect to watching a ritualistic performance of *Drumming* that could seem to model a harmonious social interaction congruent with ideals of the sixties. John Adams remarked that

> performances of *Drumming* have the flavor of a ceremony, with the performers uniformly clad in white cotton shirts and dark pants, moving gradually during the course of the work from the bongos, to the marimbas, to the glockenspiels, and finally to all the instruments for the finale. The sense of ritualistic precision and unity is furthered by performers playing from memory and by their performing face-to-face, two on a single instrument.[18]

Reich's *Music for 18 Musicians*

In contrast to his austere early pieces, *Drumming* and *Music for Mallet Instruments, Voices, and Organ* (1973) offered rich sounds that pointed toward the piece many view as the masterwork of instrumental minimalism and what may be the most influential composition of the 1970s: *Music for 18 Musicians*. Reich wrote the hour-long piece for his ensemble between 1974 and 1976 and scored it for the typical Reichian percussion and keyboard instruments, presented in counterpoint with electronically amplified solo strings, winds, and voices.

Anthology Vol 3-56
Full CD VII, 28
Concise CD III, 44

Music for 18 Musicians represents a synthesis of all the techniques Reich had developed over the preceding decade to produce a kaleidoscope of evolving and interacting melodic patterns. The work opens with a slow-moving progression of eleven chords pulsating through the ensemble at a rate of fifteen to thirty seconds per chord and that ultimately structures the entire piece (Ex. 35-4). This opening harmonic sequence unfolds through "hairpin" (crescendo–decrescendo) dynamics corresponding to the length of a wind-player's breath. The introductory chords are then elongated at the rate of four to six minutes each to make up eleven "small pieces," mostly cast in simple ABA form. The change of harmony every five minutes or so amounts to a cleansing of the palate rather than a dramatic event. Some fifty minutes later, a relatively quick cruise through the original eleven chords brings the piece to its close.

Example 35-4 Steve Reich, *Music for 18 Musicians*, "cycle of chords"

I II III IV V VI VII VIII IX X XI

Compared with the monochromatic schemes of his early music, the varied timbres of *Music for 18 Musicians* are extravagant, even voluptuous. Reich acknowledged the change in a 1977 interview with Michael Nyman. The all-important process, he now allowed, was more his business than his audience's; he had become less concerned with people hearing the process and found his early pieces somewhat "didactic": "If some people hear exactly what's going on, good for them, and if other people don't but they still like the piece, then that's OK too." And then he named the thing that mattered most to him now: "What I was really concerned with in *Music for 18 Musicians* was making beautiful music above everything else."[19] These are no longer the words of an avant-gardist but, rather, those of an artist who feels his battle has been won. Such a sentiment may account for the joyous sense of celebration that fills *Music for 18 Musicians*.

Even within the minimalist concept, it now appeared, it was possible to achieve Milton Babbitt's ideal of "maximum complexity under maximum control," and beginning with *Music for 18 Musicians* Reich increasingly began to command the full respect of influential musicians, critics, and academics. At the same time, his music broadened its appeal to what became known as a "crossover" audience bridging classical and popular music. Reich's ensemble gave the premiere of *Music for 18 Musicians* at New York's Town Hall, primarily a classical venue, in April 1976. Two years later, his recording of the piece for ECM, a small German label founded by Manfred Eicher (b. 1943) that initially specialized in avant-garde jazz, sold 100,000 copies—obviously not just to the avant-garde audience—and the ensemble performed the piece before a packed audience at the Bottom Line, one of New York's most famous rock clubs. Add another few years, and Steve Reich and Musicians would be filling Carnegie Hall. He began to receive commissions and performances from major orchestras, including the New York Philharmonic and the San Francisco Symphony.

Reich continued to seek new sources of inspiration. His study of the chanting of Hebrew scriptures found expression in *Tehillim* (1981), one of his most euphoric pieces. In the 1980s he also produced a series of counterpoint compositions for solo flute (*Vermont Counterpoint*), clarinet (*New York Counterpoint*), and guitar (*Electric Counterpoint*) in which the soloist prerecorded a number of tracks on tape against which he played live in concert performance.

Philip Glass

In various ways Philip Glass's musical development paralleled Reich's. Early training in his native Baltimore was entirely conventional, as were his fledgling years as a composer. Glass (Fig. 35-13) majored in music at the University of Chicago, where he matriculated at the precocious age of fifteen. Next he went to Juilliard for his master's degree and then received a grant to become composer-in-residence to the Pittsburgh public schools, for which he turned out a quantity of simple functional music in a rather Americanist idiom. In 1963, he got a Fulbright Fellowship to pursue what remained a rite of passage for many American composers: study with the legendary and still-active Nadia Boulanger. He spent two years in France, unexpectedly finding his musical voice there as a result of a brush with non-European music. Glass took a job with Ravi Shankar (Fig. 35-14), notating from recordings the music the celebrated Indian musician had composed at his sitar to accompany a documentary film. Glass learned, as he put it, "how music may be structured by rhythmic patterning rather than by harmonic progression." He decided to go to India to study the music at its source.

Like Reich, who would learn similar lessons from African and Indonesian music, Glass realized that he would have to create his own performance opportunities. He adopted the amplified instruments of rock, putting the electric organ at the center of his sound world, and in 1968 he formed the Philip Glass Ensemble. For a while Reich and Glass, who had known each other superficially at Juilliard, were collaborators. Glass reencountered his old acquaintance shortly after returning from India, at a gallery concert in March 1967 at which Reich's *Piano Phase* was performed. He decided to strip down the style even further. He rigorously discarded the last trappings of dissonance and chromaticism from his music, these being the badges of Western harmonically driven Modernism, and rid his textures of all reference to conservatory-style counterpoint. Glass explored subtactile pulses at fast tempos and very loud volumes. For two years Glass and Reich performed in each other's ensemble, and each egged the other on toward ever more rigorous systematization of rhythm and duration, the musical dimensions they thought worthy of development. They even collaborated for a while as entrepreneurs: Chelsea Light Moving, consisting of two composers with strong backs and a van.

Figure 35-13 Philip Glass (left) and Robert Wilson, director of *Einstein on the Beach*. Portrait by Robert Mapplethorpe.

But the partnership between Glass and Reich became a rivalry, as each tried to outstrip the other's commitment to rigor and system. Matching Reich's

Figure 35-14 Ravi Shankar performing on the sitar, 1971.

achievement yet maintaining his creative individuality, Glass came up with his own procedure, distinct from Reich's phase technique, that reflected his involvement with Indian classical music. In place of Reich's progressive canons, Glass concentrated on what he called "additive structure," which could be applied to single musical lines played by solo instruments or by ensembles employing unison doubling or rudimentary homorhythmic textures in parallel or similar motion, something prohibited by the conservatory rulebook and therefore subversive.

The first embodiment of the process, *Strung Out* (1967) for solo amplified violin, was the most rigorous and radical. A twenty-minute barrage of relentless eighth notes employing only five pitches, it consists of a pentatonic module subjected to variations by increasing or decreasing its length by one note at a time. Each modification becomes a repetitive module in turn, so that the overall impression is one of constantly expanding and contracting phrases, a rigorously maintained undifferentiated rhythm that is continually and subtly reinterpreted metrically. *Two Pages for Steve Reich* (1968) was the first piece Glass composed for his Philip Glass Ensemble, and it applies the process of adding and subtracting notes to passages played in unison by the ensemble of electric keyboards and amplified wind instruments. In 1969, the title became *Two Pages*. The rivalry had turned unfriendly, and it remained so. Reich has attributed the falling-out to Glass's unwillingness to acknowledge his creative debts, but Glass's greater attraction to the theater, affinity for the rock scene, and commercial success seem likely contributors to the rift. Glass produced some huge instrumental works for his ensemble, most notably *Music in Twelve Parts* (1971–74), which lasts three and a half hours in the ensemble's recording. But increasingly he turned his attention toward opera and film, which made him internationally famous. Glass's music, in turn, had a strong and openly acknowledged influence on the art-rock of the 1970s and '80s.

Less openly acknowledged is the question of rock's influence on the development of Glass's music. That Glass, of all the pioneering minimalists, had the strongest ties to Anglo-American pop music has always been clear. While his music avoids the most obvious rock instruments (electric guitars and trap-set percussion), it is often amplified to the earsplitting level typical of rock bands. It is far more often played in rock clubs than is Reich's. Some recordings of Glass's music were issued by rock labels, and he began writing pieces that conformed in length and shape to the specifications of a rock single. By the 1980s he was collaborating with musicians like David Byrne (of the Talking Heads) and Paul Simon, and he served for a while as producer for a short-lived rock band called Polyrock. Joining the singers and players of his ensemble was a "sound designer" (audio engineer and mixer), Kurt Munkacsi, who had started his career as an electric bass player in a rock band and had previously worked alongside George Martin for the Beatles. He played a key role in cranking up the Philip Glass sound to a dynamic level standard in pop but unprecedented in classical music. By the 1990s, Glass was repaying the compliment rock musicians had paid him with works like his *Low Symphony* (1992), based on thematic material derived from a rock album, *Low* (1977), by Brian Eno and David Bowie.

Einstein on the Beach

Anthology Vol 3-57
Full CD VII, 29
Concise CD III, 45

Seven months after the premiere of Reich's *Music for 18 Musicians* came the other decisive moment in the great crest of the minimalist wave. On Sunday, 21 November 1976, *Einstein on the Beach*, an opera Glass composed in collaboration with the avant-garde theater director and stage designer Robert Wilson (b. 1941; Fig. 35-13), played to a packed Metropolitan Opera House in New York. (The piece had premiered in France and toured Europe the previous summer.) On this historic occasion, however, the wildly enthusiastic audience was not filled with traditional Met subscribers—indeed, the two performances were not even presented under the auspices of the august institution. Glass and Wilson had rented the hall and attracted aficionados from the alternative or so-called downtown New York arts scene—painters, conceptual artists, experimental theater enthusiasts, art-rockers and their fans. "Who are these people?" one of the Met's administrators supposedly asked Glass. "I've never seen them here before." As Glass tells the story, "I remember replying very candidly, 'Well, you'd better find out who they are, because if this place expects to be running in twenty-five years, that's your audience out there.'"[20]

By the time he wrote *Einstein on the Beach*, Glass had for years already been passionately involved with theater and film. His first wife, JoAnne Akalaitis, was a theater director, and he clearly thrived on the chance to collaborate, eventually working with writers such as Allen Ginsberg and Doris Lessing; theater and film directors Woody Allen, Errol Morris, and Godfrey Reggio; and popular musicians Leonard Cohen, Patti Smith, and Suzanne Vega as well as others already mentioned.

Einstein on the Beach is cast in four acts, each containing two or three scenes connected by musical joints that Robert Wilson called "knee plays" (Ex. 35-5). It was performed in a single nearly five-hour bout, without intermission, with the audience "invited to leave and reenter the auditorium quietly, as necessary."[21] The work was far from Robert Wilson's longest theatrical marathon. *The Life and Times of Joseph Stalin* (1973) lasted some twelve uninterrupted hours, and further theatrical pieces explored other larger-than-life historical figures, including Freud and Queen Victoria.

As might be expected in a Postmodern *Gesamtkunstwerk*, movement and dance also played a crucial role in *Einstein*, choreographed by Lucinda Childs (Fig. 35-15). The scenario and music, planned on the basis of a set of drawings by Wilson, revolve around three recurrent images: a train, a courtroom scene, and a spaceship. The title character occasionally wanders onstage as an onlooker, playing the violin. Although it has no plot to organize the visually striking tableaux, there are some recited texts with words by Childs, Samuel M. Jackson, an actor who spoke the role of judge and bus driver, and an eclectic assortment of prose poems by an autistic boy Wilson knew named Christopher Knowles. In addition to the solo violinist, the work is scored for the typical Glass ensemble of

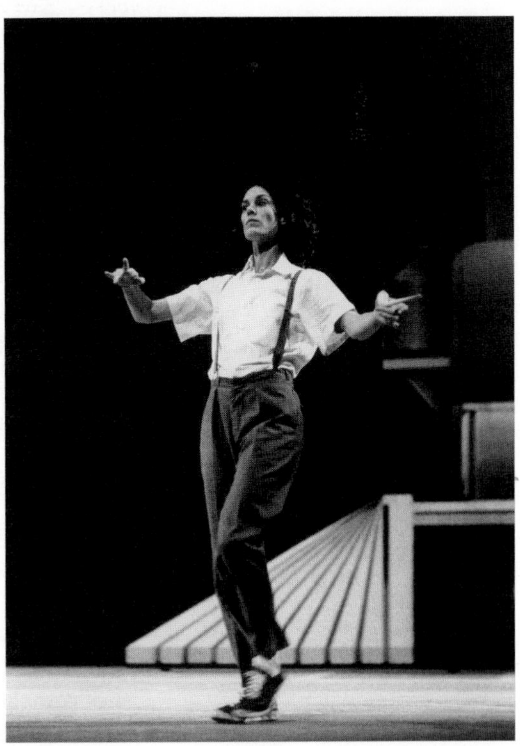

Figure 35-15 Lucinda Childs in *Einstein on the Beach* by Philip Glass and Robert Wilson, 1976.

amplified keyboards, winds, and soprano. The sixteen members of the chorus either count their notes (1, 2, 3, 4, etc.) or sing solfège syllables (do, re, mi, etc.). "When numbers are used," Glass has written, "they represent the rhythmic structure of the music. When solfège is used, the syllables represent the pitch structure of the music. In either case, the text is not secondary or supplementary, but is a description of the music itself."[22]

Example 35-5 **Philip Glass, *Einstein on the Beach*, first page of score**

Some audience members compared their experience of *Einstein on the Beach* to a dream, and it certainly recalled surrealism. Those with a Modernist frame of reference compared it to *Four Saints in Three Acts* of forty years before—another nonlinear, nonnarrative theatrical presentation in which the verbal component posed deliberate enigmas. The difference was that Virgil Thomson's ingratiating music, with its obvious references to folk and vernacular styles, made a less overtly avant-garde impression than Glass's resolutely abstract modules in their raw, rock-like timbres and loudness. The fact that Glass's music was consonant did little to lessen that impression of aggressive stylistic novelty. Particularly extraordinary was the visceral response that the music elicited, especially the finale—extraordinary, at any rate, to some classical musicians in attendance, who associated the visceral with the popular and therefore distrusted it. The response was, in fact, a calculated one. Glass told an interviewer: "I decided that I would try to write a piece that left the audience standing, and I've almost never played that music without seeing everyone leave his seat; it's the strangest thing, almost biological."[23]

For those sympathetic to Glass, such as music critic John Rockwell (b. 1940), who covered both classical and popular music for The *New York Times*, *Einstein* could be seen to represent a "genuine fusion music that can appeal effortlessly to fans of progressive rock, jazz, and even disco."[24] Those unsympathetic to minimalism worried about the manipulation of the audience. Elliott Carter warned that minimalists "are not aware of the larger dimensions of life. One also hears constant repetition in the speeches of Hitler, and in advertising. It has its dangerous aspects."[25] Yet we have seen that manipulation of desire had long been part of music, Wagner's *Tristan und Isolde* being a preeminent example, and the wish to write music that touched audiences increasingly became important to young composers.

Glass soon followed *Einstein* with two more conventional operas—at least in the sense that he wrote them for standard orchestra, chorus, and opera singers—based on the lives of other seminal figures. *Satyagraha* (1980) concerned the life and influence of Mahatma Gandhi, and *Akhnaten* (1984) was about the ancient Egyptian king believed to have introduced monotheism. By the end of the century Glass had composed more than a dozen operas and theater pieces as well as many film scores, both for experimental projects and big-budget Hollywood fare. In the end, as Glass had predicted, even the Metropolitan Opera commissioned an opera from him: *The Voyage* (1992), which commemorated the 500th anniversary of Columbus's journey to the New World.[26]

Game Changer

The music of Reich and Glass was transformative of classical music near the end of the twentieth century. There was no longer any point even in attempting to draw the line, formerly so sharp and well patrolled, between the high and low genres of music, at least where the impact of minimalism was concerned; nor was there any way of telling where the movement's impact had been greater. Musical minimalism turned out to be a great leveler, for which reason traditional Modernists regarded it as the direst of threats. Reich not only recognized but celebrated this fact, justifying his rejection of European Modernist styles by remarking that whereas "Stockhausen, Berio and Boulez were portraying in very honest terms what it was like to pick up the pieces of a bombed-out continent after World War II," the American experience had been different and demanded a different medium of expression. Reich continued that "for some Americans in 1948 or 1958 or 1968—in the real context of tail-fins, Chuck Berry

Musical minimalism turned out to be a great leveler, for which reason traditional Modernists regarded it as the direst of threats.

and millions of burgers sold—to pretend that instead we're really going to have the dark-brown angst of Vienna is a lie, a musical lie."[27]

In its seemingly indiscriminate, insatiable, world-devouring eclecticism, its live adaptation of musical techniques originating in the hardware-driven tape studio, and its tendency toward a kind of factory standardization (such as "mass-production" of repeated modules and equal pulses), minimalism exemplified the commodification, objectification, and exteriorization of the affluent postwar American consumer society, hailed by some as the economic salvation of the world and decried by others as the ultimate dehumanization of humanity. And as the values of this new American society spread, so did its musical embodiment. Minimalism has unquestionably been the most influential and worldwide of any literate musical movement born since the Second World War. It is the first (and so far the only) literate style born in the New World to have exerted a decisive influence on the Old. No wonder it has been controversial.

Some Europeans developed their own versions of minimalism. Dutch composer Louis Andriessen (b. 1939), for example, founded performing ensembles composed mainly of musicians with jazz and rock backgrounds. He drew from both Reich and Glass, particularly the latter's loudness, but fashioned his minimalist structures out of harmonies far more dissonant than those used by his American counterparts. One of Andriessen's greatest contributions has been as a teacher. Alone among the major minimalists, he occupies a distinguished academic position, and he has been a magnet to composers from many countries, including England and the United States. His American disciples have gone on to form groups or music festivals of their own, such as Bang on a Can and the Common Sense Composers' Collective.

The Holy Minimalists

From the beginning the minimalism of Young and Riley had a spiritual component, one that could be praised for its meditative qualities or be derided as an example of the shallowness of the so-called New Age phenomenon, marketed to people experimenting with relaxation techniques such as "transcendental meditation." The most important strain of European minimalism came independently from composers originating in Central and Eastern Europe who used minimalist techniques to evoke or induce a state of passive spiritual contemplation. The pioneering figure was the Estonian-born Arvo Pärt (b. 1935; Fig. 35-16). His Soviet-style education initially led him to compose in a neo-Romantic style and then in a Neoclassical manner, until he rebelled and embraced serialism. He managed to overcome a prolonged creative block thanks in part to his discovery of Medieval and Renaissance music. For Soviet musicians of the 1960s, early music offered a back door to religious experience, which was officially banned by the state.

Pärt's Symphony No. 3 (1971) is full of echoes of Medieval music, but within a few years archaisms became less overt. Thus he found his own route to the austerely reduced tonal vocabulary then being adopted, unbeknownst to him, by American minimalists. Pärt was also greatly influenced by the sound of bells—a sonic component of religious rituals in many traditions but particularly of the Russian Orthodox Church. The evocation of bell sounds became for him the sonic equivalent of an icon: a holy image that embodied mystical belief in material

Figure 35-16 Arvo Pärt at the London premiere of his Symphony No. 4, 2010.

form. His bell imagery ranged from obvious onomatopoeia—bell imitations, often achieved by using a prepared piano—to a unique harmonic idiom that he worked out during the early 1970s and called his "tintinnabular" style. A pitch produced by a tuned bell is an exceptionally rich composite of overtones, in which the fundamental can be all but overwhelmed by dissonant partials. To achieve a comparable sonic aura, Pärt accompanied the notes of a diatonic melody with "overtones" produced by the notes of an arpeggiated tonic triad in some fixed relationship to the melody notes.

Many of Pärt's compositions beginning in the early 1980s were set to Latin sacred texts. They are concert works not meant for actual liturgical use, but their purpose, as the composer envisions it, is sacred. ECM, the innovative record label that released Reich's *Music for 18 Musicians*, began to champion Pärt's music, thus introducing him to a large Western audience. Among his best-known works are a trio of instrumental compositions written in Estonia in 1977: *Fratres* (Brethren), *Cantus in memoriam Benjamin Britten*, and *Tabula Rasa*, composed to celebrate the composer's fresh start.

Anthology Vol 3-58
Full CD VII, 30
Concise CD III, 46

Tabula Rasa, which means a "clean slate," is the most extended work of this period and perhaps the most representative: a two-movement concerto grosso for two violins, string orchestra, and prepared piano. The first movement, called *Ludus* (Play), is marked *con moto* (with motion) and consists of progressively lengthening and loudening bouts of fiddling. In the second movement, *Silentium* (Silence), marked *senza moto* (without motion), the beats (M.M. = 60) conform to the ticking seconds on the clock. Its musical substance consists of a three-part lengthening mensuration canon in which the first violin solo, first violins, and cellos play identical scalar melodies at different speeds, with a proportional relation of 4:2:1 (Ex. 35-6). Wholly without chromaticism, infused with a steady pulse and a single omnipresent harmony, and played at a single subdued dynamic, the movement is a startlingly successful evocation of stillness, very easily read as religious quietism.

Example 35-6 Arvo Pärt, *Tabula rasa*, II (*Silentium*): mm. 1–3

The relationship between a radical reduction of means and wholeness of spirit is an ancient religious truth (the basis, to begin with, of monasticism). In conversation with conductor Paul Hillier, Pärt described his gradual arrival at tintinnabular music as a spiritual quest:

> In my dark hours, I have the certain feeling that everything outside this one thing has no meaning. The complex and many-faceted only confuses me, and I must search for unity. What is it, this one thing, and how do I find my way to it? Traces of this perfect thing appear in many guises—and everything that is unimportant falls away. Tintinnabulation is like this. . . . I work with very few elements—with one voice, with two voices. I build with the most primitive materials—with the triad, with one specific tonality.[28]

It is noteworthy that every one of the composers associated with radically reductive styles in the 1960s and '70s that we have discussed (except for Andriessen) has begun with or found his way to religious belief and has regarded his musical and spiritual quests as dual manifestations of a single impulse. Young, Riley, and Glass have all embraced some version of Asian religion: Young and Riley practice Yogic meditation, and Glass has been a devotee of Tibetan Buddhism since the mid-1960s. Reich, brought up in an agnostic household, found his way back to Orthodox Judaism in the mid-1970s. A leading English minimalist, John Tavener (b. 1944), formally converted to the Russian Orthodox faith—an unusual choice for an Englishman, but already connected, through Pärt, with austerely religious minimalism.

In addition to Pärt, several other European composers have associated reductive musical styles with resurgent Christianity in the 1970s. The greatest success—and an unusual case study of the crossover phenomenon between classical and popular music—came with the Polish composer Henryk Górecki (1933–2010). His Third Symphony (1976) consists of three movements, each a slow song of lamentation, for soprano soloist and orchestra. Strictly diatonic and highly repetitive, Górecki's setting was indeed akin to the music then being composed by Pärt and the Western minimalists, apparently unknown to him at the time. But in 1991, fifteen years after its first performance in Poland, a New York record executive heard a Polish recording of the work and realized its potential for capitalizing on the popularity that Pärt's music was generating. A new recording with American soprano Dawn Upshaw (b. 1960) as soloist was issued in 1992 and heavily plugged on radio stations normally devoted to pop music.

That recording of Górecki's Third Symphony sold over a million copies within three years' time, making it one of the best-selling classical albums ever, and the composer was assimilated retroactively to the ranks of the "holy" or "mystical" minimalists. This marketing term was cited in derision by Modernist skeptics, wary as ever of the affinities between minimalism and pop music and eager to write off the new phenomenon as a fad manipulated by the record industry. But such confrontational ways of thinking largely proved to be a last gasp of the Cold War. By the 1980s musical Modernism was pretty much dead, a very short twentieth century (after a very long nineteenth century) had ended, and a new eclecticism had emerged that brought the millennium to its end and that will bring our story to its conclusion.

Summary

This chapter explored musical trends that grew out of the social unrest of the 1960s and '70s, including the emergence of rock, minimalism, and a loosening of the boundaries between art music and popular music. The turbulence of the 1960s was attributable in part to the growing American involvement in the war in Vietnam and the movements for social equality among African Americans, women, and gays and lesbians. As young people exerted an unprecedented influence on American culture and politics, the cultural gap between generations was expressed through rock 'n' roll. The style had its origins in African American rhythm and blues but was appropriated by white performers and marketed to middle-class teens. Political dissent was expressed through the professionalized folk music of Bob Dylan and others. The first American tour of the Beatles, in 1964, marked the beginning of the "British Invasion," providing a model for American musicians to emulate.

The push for social equality was reflected in a blurring of the boundaries between "high" and "low" genres of music. Rock musicians began to incorporate features associated with art music and experimental Modernism. The Beatles, for example, based several "concept albums" on a central theme, in the manner of a Romantic song cycle. Some songs on *Sgt. Pepper's Lonely Hearts Club Band* incorporate avant-garde sound effects and collage techniques, closely related to contemporary electronic music. The Who's *Tommy*, an album of songs in a narrative sequence about a deaf, dumb, and blind boy, was promoted as the first rock opera. Progressive rock bands such as Emerson, Lake & Palmer further blurred the lines between art and popular music by producing arrangements of classical works. These same tendencies were evident in the Third Stream fusion between Western art music and jazz, advocated by Gunther Schuller.

The fusion of high and low genres was also an important trait of minimalism, a style based on repetition, a limited melodic vocabulary, and a simplified harmonic idiom. The composers who have contributed to minimalism have varied backgrounds and personal styles, incorporating influences of jazz, rock, and non-Western music. Although Steve Reich (b. 1936) had a background in Western art music, for example, he was also greatly influenced by his study of West African drumming and Indonesian gamelan. Terry Riley's (b. 1935) affinities lay more with the avant-garde; Philip Glass (b. 1937) studied music in India and collaborated with many film makers, theater directors, and popular musicians, usually resulting in a sound palette more similar to rock than other minimalists.

A common technique in early minimalism was to use prerecorded sounds to create and manipulate repeating patterns, often with tape loops, short segments of magnetic tape that could be manipulated as they were fed through a tape recorder. Many minimalist pieces replicate the same effect with live performers. Riley's *In C* (1964), for example, consists of fifty-three short, related motives that are played as many times as each performer wishes before moving on to the next segment. Reich's *Piano Phase* (1967) incorporates phasing technique, in which two players begin together and slowly get out of sync to produce a kind of canon.

A key feature of minimalism was its appeal to diverse audiences. Reich's *Music for 18 Musicians* (1976), for example, had successful performances both in classical and in rock venues, and Glass's theatrical work *Einstein on the Beach* (1976) drew unconventional audiences to the Metropolitan Opera. *Einstein on the Beach* exemplifies minimalism's close connection to Postmodernism: Its plotless text incorporates numbers, solfège syllables, and recited poetry by an autistic child, and the scenario involves recurring visual images such as a train and a spaceship. Another notable influence on minimalism was the heated political climate of the 1960s. Reich's *Come Out* (1966), for example, incorporates the recorded voice of a youth who was injured in the Harlem riots of 1964.

Europeans such as the Estonian Arvo Pärt (b. 1935) and the Polish composer Henryk Górecki (1933–2010) drew on the potential of minimalist musical materials to induce spiritual contemplation. Pärt's early works often mimic the sound of bells and a harmonic language based on a rich composite of overtones in a technique he called *tintinnabular*. Coupled with an influence of Medieval and Renaissance music, these features give his minimalism a distinctive flavor. Górecki's Symphony No. 3 also had a wide appeal to audiences outside of the classical mainstream.

Study Questions

1. Explain the political climate of the 1960s and the impact it had on popular and classical music.
2. How did the Beatles and subsequent progressive rock bands help to bridge the gap and blur distinctions between popular music and classical music? Why were *Sgt. Pepper's Lonely Hearts Club Band* and The Who's *Tommy* important in this respect?

3. Describe the various types of fusion between high and low genres of music that prevailed in the 1960s, as reflected in progressive rock, Third Stream, and minimalism. Why do you think the mixed aspects of these genres were so controversial? How did these controversies reflect larger social debates?
4. In what ways did minimalist composers mix popular and classical art forms? Which composers and works were influenced by jazz, popular, and non-Western music?
5. Explain the various ways that minimalism was influenced by the political culture of the 1960s. How do minimalist works such as Steve Reich's *Drumming* and *Music for 18 Musicians* reflect ideals about social hierarchy and interaction that were prevalent in the 1960s?
6. Minimalist composers were a part of the first generation of musicians that grew up with recording technologies. How did these technologies influence their attitudes and their music?
7. Describe Reich's views on musical process. How are these ideas reflected in his music?
8. In what respects is Philip Glass's *Einstein on the Beach* a Postmodernist work?
9. Describe the minimalist works of Arvo Pärt and Henryk Górecki and the prominent spiritual component in their music.

Key Terms

concept album
jazz-rock fusion
minimalism
phasing
progressive rock
rhythm and blues (R & B)
rock
rock 'n' roll
tape loops
Third Stream

36

"Many Streams": Millennium's End

The 1960s and '70s marked a time of political and cultural turmoil that had a profound impact on the arts. To conclude we will sketch various musical currents of the last decades of the twentieth century and the start of the new millennium, bringing the story close to the present day. Our survey of the twentieth century thus far has shown that an unprecedented variety of musical styles proliferated and became available to a worldwide audience, not just with respect to classical music, but even more explosively with popular music; this was complemented by a greater awareness of non-Western music. There was no single musical "mainstream." As John Cage put it: "We live in a time I think not of mainstream, but of many streams."[1]

One framing device that might help us begin to make some sense of the varied classical landscape at the end of the century would be to use a shorthand characterization based on the geography of the long, thin island of Manhattan: "uptown," "midtown," and "downtown" music. Although this scheme undoubtedly simplifies complex matters, by the 1980s these terms served as a kind of shorthand identification (and self-identification) for many musicians. The labels provide a convenient categorization for trends not just in New York City but throughout the Western world. Of course, many composers did not fit neatly into the tripartite division—and not just because they had little or nothing to do with New York. Other leading cities had their own markers of power, prestige, and influence, their own institutional structures, venues, prizes, and festivals. In any case, as the American composer and critic Kyle Gann (b. 1955) has observed, downtown music (and by extension uptown and midtown as well) represents a "state of mind" and can be written anywhere.[2]

Competing Visions

Uptown composers were (are?—as we confront recent history, tenses blur) the descendants of European composers, such as Schoenberg and his followers, most identified since the Second World War with high Modernism, serialism, computer music, and universities. The name comes from the location in upper Manhattan of Columbia University (and its alliance with Princeton University in nearby New Jersey). Many of the composers grouped under this label supported themselves as academics, and they often wrote the kind of "Ph.D. music" that we saw emerging in the 1950s. Their complex scores tended to be played before small audiences by ensembles specializing in new music. The academic and specialist mindset found its most potent expression in Milton Babbitt's "Who Cares If You Listen?" In many respects uptown music, associated with composers like Babbitt, Elliott Carter, and Roger Sessions and younger figures such as Donald Martino (1931–2005) and Charles Wuorinen enjoyed great prestige during the Cold War in America. For a while the composers in this camp won important awards, got tenure at leading universities, and were featured prominently in music history books.

According to the terms that arose in the mid-nineteenth century, uptown composers tend to be historicist in orientation, prizing history, research, and innovation over listeners, communication, and society. They believe they are the ones sustaining the progress of the hallowed mainstream tradition of Western music, the march of history we have traced in which a great composer of one generation bestows a benediction on a worthy successor in the next. By the 1980s, however, the uptowners' moment was fast fading, in part because, it turned out, very few people cared to listen to what they were doing, but even more so because combative debates about correct musical styles began to seem dated or, even to the most serious young musicians, irrelevant.

Moving on to midtown composers: They were geographically associated with Lincoln Center for the Performing Arts, home to the Metropolitan Opera, the New York City Opera, the New York Philharmonic, and other prominent institutions dedicated to the preservation and presentation of the museum repertory of the past. The city's premier conservatory, the Juilliard School, is located there as well. Nearby is Carnegie Hall, perhaps the most famous concert hall anywhere, where the most famous performers perform the most famous music of the past. There are similarly prominent "midtown" institutions all over the world, even if those in New York are unusually concentrated within a few city blocks. As custodians of museum culture, the midtowners, like the uptown composers, perpetuated the European tradition. The principal difference between them in this respect is that midtown composers won greater audience acclaim and engaged more with society in general.

Many leading midtown composers came of age in Stravinsky's Neoclassical and Copland's Americanist orbit, and they generally wrote in more or less conventional tonal idioms all through the period of stylistic revolution happening around them, uptown and downtown. A leading figure was the charismatic Leonard Bernstein, one of the most prominent conductors of the period, who was music director of the New York Philharmonic from 1958 to 1969. He perpetuated the nineteenth-century tradition of the composer/conductor, which had become much less common in the twentieth century. Uptown composers tended not to be performers at all, and most midtowners performed mainly their own music.

Anthology Vol 3-59
Full CD VII, 31

Bernstein's music frequently blurred boundaries between classical, jazz, and even rock. His popular Broadway musical *West Side Story,* with lyrics by Stephen Sondheim (b. 1930), updates Shakespeare's *Romeo and Juliet* as a contest between rival ethnic gangs on the West Side of New York (Fig. 36-1). Bernstein's vivid musical preserves something of the spirit of ethnic working-class families squeezed out by the gentrification of the city. Shortly after the 1957 premiere of *West Side Story,* seventeen blocks of neighborhood tenements where its fictional action took place were razed and thousands of families dispersed to make way for the elegant new Lincoln Center. Copland wrote *Connotations* (1962) for Bernstein to conduct with the Philharmonic to inaugurate their new concert hall there. Samuel Barber composed his second opera, *Antony and Cleopatra* (1966), for the opening of the newly relocated Metropolitan Opera.

Like Béla Bartók, Benjamin Britten, and others before them, some midtown composers gave evidence of their social commitment by introducing the public, especially young audiences, to the world of classical music. Copland's writings provided inspiring models that Bernstein complemented with his own superb introductory books *Joy of Music* and *Infinite Variety of Music* and which he took even further through the new medium of television. He reached vast audiences with the series of legendary Young People's Concerts (1958–72), which combined riveting explanations with orchestral performances by the New York Philharmonic. Television made Bernstein one of the most famous classical musicians in the world and also one of the great music educators of the century.

TIMELINE

1955–75 Vietnam War
1967 Jacques Derrida introduces the term "deconstruction"
1968 Martin Luther King, Jr., assassinated
1968 Student riots in Paris and New York
1968 **Luciano Berio, *Sinfonia***
1969 **David Del Tredici, *An Alice Symphony***
1970 **George Crumb, *Ancient Voices of Children***
1972 **George Rochberg, Third Quartet**
1972 President Richard Nixon visits China
1977 **Pierre Boulez founds IRCAM**
1979 **Sofia Gubaidulina, *In croce***
1981 **Laurie Anderson, *O Superman***
1981 **MTV debuts**
1983 **Alfred Schnittke, Third String Quartet**
1983 **Olivier Messiaen's *Saint François d'Assise* premieres in Paris**
1987 **John Adams, *Nixon in China***
1988 **Steve Reich, *Different Trains***
1989 Fall of Communism; Berlin Wall torn down
1991 Soviet Union dissolves
2000 **Kaija Saariaho, *L'amour de loin* premieres in Salzburg**
2001 Terrorists destroy the World Trade Center in New York City
2005 **Adams, *Doctor Atomic***

Some midtown composers, such as Copland, Barber, and Bernstein, enjoyed considerable popularity, writing music that was performed by leading orchestras, opera and theater companies, and chamber ensembles and instrumentalists. Audiences often embraced their music, or they certainly did not run screaming as they were wont to do when uptown music made it to a midtown concert hall. Yet one of the biggest challenges more traditional composers faced is exactly that they were competing with the museum repertory of Bach, Beethoven, and Brahms. They may have used an updated musical vocabulary, but the basic language and forms of their music was deeply rooted in the nineteenth century and earlier. From the historicist point of view espoused by contemptuous uptown Modernists, midtown composers, no matter how successful, were simply not historically significant. As late as 1979 the disdain was on full display in the opening paragraph of a textbook by uptown true believer Charles Wuorinen: "While the tonal system, in an atrophied or vestigial form, is still used today in popular and commercial music, and even occasionally in the works of backward-looking serious composers, it is no longer employed by serious composers of the mainstream. It has been replaced or succeeded by the 12-tone system."[3]

As for the downtown composers, they were most prominently associated by the 1980s with minimalists like Steve Reich and Philip Glass, descendants of the American experimental tradition stretching back to Charles Ives, Henry Cowell, and the ultra-moderns of the 1920s, now updated by influences from jazz, rock, world music, and the explosion of electronic media. The geographical association of lower Manhattan (including Greenwich Village) with an alternative cultural scene in art and politics stretches back to the early decades of the twentieth century and found expression as well in the visual arts and literature.

Kyle Gann, writing in the weekly newspaper the *Village Voice* in 1991, pointed to the tradition of American musical mavericks as generating "tremendous underground influence." The careers of these composers have tended to follow a pattern:

"He/she often works outside music (dry cleaning, insurance, and computers are popular), dies, gets canonized in the press, develops a cult."[4] These figures are often initially viewed, however, as innovative amateurs rather than as serious professionals. Morton Feldman, the posthumous beneficiary of one such downtown cult, himself commented on the phenomenon: "The real tradition of twentieth-century America, a tradition evolving from the empiricism of Ives, Varèse, and Cage, has been passed over as 'iconoclastic'—another word for unprofessional. In music, when you do something new, something original, you're an amateur. Your imitators—these are the professionals."[5]

During the 1970s and '80s the living legend of the experimental tradition was John Cage, who shared a downtown loft with his partner, Merce Cunningham, and whose music was more often encountered in art galleries, nontraditional performance spaces, and Europe than it was in the gloried midtown bastions of American cities. The dominant downtown movement by this time was minimalism, primarily tonal, rhythmically regular, blurring boundaries with jazz and rock, broadly accessible to audiences and becoming ever more so. Reich and Glass lived and worked downtown; they collaborated with experimental writers, filmmakers, choreographers, and theater groups. They were active performers who gave concerts with their own ensembles that were more likely to take place in an alternative venue like an art gallery or a rock club than in a traditional concert hall—at least at first. Both composers supported themselves primarily by performing and recording with their own groups and shunned academic affiliations (or were not offered them).

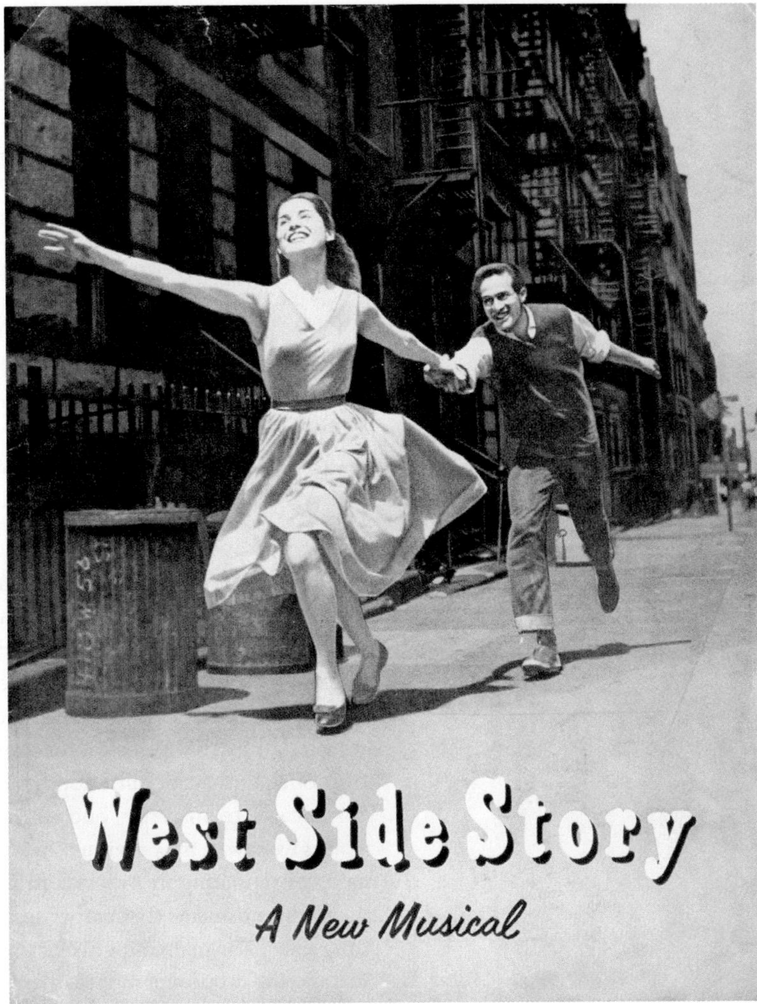

Figure 36-1 Program cover for Leonard Bernstein's *West Side Story*, showing the characters Maria and Tony outside the tenements near where Lincoln Center now stands.

The Cold War Ends

In retrospect, the fierce battles during the 1970s and '80s among these three compositional approaches (which nonetheless overlapped in certain respects) seem very much a cultural reflection of Cold War political debates. By the end of the millennium there was much less concern about what was progressive, what was conservative, and what was experimental, apparently signaling a fundamental ideological change. The loosening of Cold War thinking provoked the questioning of many old and ostensibly settled aesthetic issues, including whether commitment to historical progress was worth sacrificing the broader audience. Perhaps the midtown and downtown composers were right: Accessibility regained respectability.

Younger musicians, uninterested in the earlier musical polemics, were broadly tolerant of and receptive to many musical styles. New technologies and access to an incredible variety of music encouraged them to chart their own course and to combine disparate traditions, classical and popular, commercial and noncommercial, Western and non-Western. As Gann wrote in the *Village Voice* in 1995:

> Composers now graduating from college already see no incongruity in fusing techniques from MC Hammer and Luciano Berio. Music becomes more interesting when commercialism and intellectuality interpermeate each other than when they're neurotically separated. . . . [E]very week I hear a future in which High and Low Culture are no longer opposites but arbitrary points in a fluid continuum. . . . The aspirations of an entire generation are wrapped up in that much-maligned term: totalism. The word implies that we can put brain, body, and heart together and have it all, if the skeptics will just shut up and listen.[6]

As we have begun to see, the United States inherited musical leadership from Europe during the second half of the twentieth century. At first this was by default, a legacy of Adolf Hitler, because of whom by 1945 Schoenberg, Stravinsky, Bartók, Hindemith, Krenek, Korngold, and Milhaud, to name just some of the leading composers, had moved to America. The conditions that had stimulated the rise of the postwar European avant-garde associated with Darmstadt had been in part created and funded by the American occupying force. The considerable governmental, institutional, and academic support for avant-garde music lasted as long as the Cold War; it came to an abrupt end with German reunification in 1990.

As we saw in the previous chapter, minimalism was the first style of literate music making originating in America to have the kind of transformative impact on some European musicians that earlier European innovations had previously had on many Americans. The main impetus for the trends toward musical eclecticism, Postmodernism, and the rapprochement with commercial genres likewise came from the United States, having originated in American youth culture and the social turbulence of the 1960s. In this final chapter we will continue to see a fusion of musical approaches and styles in the wake of the Cold War. There are many parts to this story, but one consequence was that by the turn of the millennium, there was a noticeable blurring of some of the boundaries. Steve Reich and Philip Glass were selling out Carnegie Hall, Pierre Boulez was recording Bruckner's Eighth Symphony with the Vienna Philharmonic, and John Cage was giving the prestigious Norton Lectures at Harvard. New patronage led to a resurgence of ambitious opera and orchestral commissions that now seemed to take society and audiences into account. Young composers were using new technologies, charting new courses, and coming up with new answers. All of this was scarcely imaginable not long before, while a Cold War mentality had reigned.

It would be a mistake, however, a historicist error such as we have been trying to avoid, to say that music was somehow achieving a new synthesis. It is not a matter of reaching a better stage of music but, rather, of eclectically fusing different streams and creating new sounds with less concern for labels. Something of this spirit is captured in a photograph taken on 29 September 1999 (similar to a famous earlier image of jazz musicians gathered in Harlem in 1958) that shows a gathering of fifty-two prominent composers based in or around New York. One wonders what the conversations were like that day, as these former antagonists and allies assembled (Fig. 36-2).

Figure 36-2 A gathering of fifty-two composers, including Philip Glass, John Zorn, Joan Tower, Philip Lansky, and Wynton Marsalis, at the Alexander Hamilton U.S. Customs House in New York, New York in 1999. Milton Babbitt and Elliott Carter are the two figures closest to the camera. Photograph by Bruce Davidson.

The Postmodern Condition

For better or worse, helpfully or not, the label widely associated with much of the new art of the last third of the twentieth century is "**Postmodern**," a word we have already mentioned in passing a number of times. It was a predictable choice: What do you call the -ism that supplants Modernism? Why, Postmodernism, obviously (if you're in a hurry); and so the term became commonly used, first in connection with literature, in the 1960s, and it gained considerable currency in the 1970s, especially to describe trends in architecture. Like many labels that emerged in periods of uncertainty, it was a notorious catch-all that we will have to approach in various ways.

We might start by noting the distinction some commentators have made between Postmodernism as a historical condition, reflective of "late capitalism" at the end of the twentieth century, and Postmodernism as an aesthetic style. According to this argument, we live in the Postmodern age. Whether or not the art produced is also Postmodern, how so, what that really means, and whether the art is affirmative of the times or resistant to it—these are questions that only complicate matters. In a much-discussed essay from 1983, cultural critic Andreas Huyssen found the term *Postmodern* "at least for now, wholly adequate" to describe a "change in sensibility":

> The nature and depth of that transformation are debatable, but transformation it is. . . . [I]n an important sector of our culture there is a noticeable shift in sensibility, practices, and discourse formations which distinguishes a postmodern set of assumptions, experiences, and propositions from that of a preceding period. What needs further exploration is whether this transformation has generated genuinely new aesthetic forms in the various arts or whether it mainly recycles techniques and strategies of modernism itself, reinscribing them into an altered cultural context.[7]

What would these new "assumptions, experiences, and propositions" be, and how might they differ from Modernism? We have begun to see how the social movements of the 1960s led to greater opportunities for racial and ethnic minorities, women, and homosexuals that challenged the longstanding dominance of white heterosexual males. More voices and points of view were heard in politics and culture, a development often labeled as *multiculturalism*. Depending on one's background, interests, and ideological allegiances, these opportunities could be hailed as liberating or condemned as shallow "political correctness." With core values being reassessed, the issue became not just competition among different parties to assert the truth but, in some quarters, the assertion that there was no one truth. A radical skepticism refused to regard any proposition as inherently true or definitively proven, and a radical relativism refused to accept any hierarchy of values at all.

Many lost faith in history, in the idea that the human lot was improving. This dealt a further blow to the ideology of progress. The French philosopher Jean-François Lyotard (1924–98) questioned what he called the "master narrative," an assumption of cultural progress whose musical version can be seen in the historicist story promoted by the New German School and later by many high Modernists and uptown academics.[8] In the light of such critiques, new ways of thinking about politics, culture, philosophy, and history arose that seemed to many to mark a significant break with both Romanticism and Modernism. In France, the Cold War existentialism of Jean-Paul Sartre gave way to what is sometimes categorized by another catch-all term: *poststructuralism*. Loosely included in this group are the revisionist historical approaches of Michel Foucault (1926–84), the literary theories of Roland Barthes (1915–80), the psychoanalytic contributions of Jacques Lacan (1901–81), the philosophy of Jacques Derrida (1930–2004), and other influential currents of continental thought.

All this happened amid a rapidly changing global, economic, and technological context that had a decisive impact on the production, distribution, and consumption of music. Technology gave composers much more immediate contact with diverse music and a newly immediate sense of themselves as living in history, not only as direct recipients of a particular tradition but also as heirs to the sum total of musical culture. This access naturally spurred eclecticism as well as attempts at fusion. The Postmodern era reopened the old questions that had dogged Modernism, but these questions now elicited quite different answers: Who cares who listens? Who cares who did something first? Who pays for it all in any case? Who decides what is the best art (is there such a thing?) and on what grounds?

Collage and Pastiche

One of the defining features initially associated with Postmodern architecture was the eclectic juxtaposition of styles drawn from different historical eras and from different places around the world. A famous example of this **eclecticism** is Philip Johnson's AT&T Building, dating from the mid-1980s, which freely mixes traditional functionalist features with a "Chippendale" top, such as found in eighteenth-century English furniture (Fig. 36-3). The musical analogue to this was composers' increasing recourse to **collage** (a kind of artistic cutting-and-pasting) and **pastiche** (an imitation in the style of the past). As the earlier Neoclassical movement suggests, these approaches had a long history and therefore were not necessarily Postmodern. Like other Modernist techniques that became conventional, collage could be easily absorbed, in moderate doses, into the mainstream concert repertoire. Shostakovich's Fifteenth Symphony (1971), for example, makes ambiguous quotations, including from Rossini's *William Tell* Overture and to the "Fate" motive from Wagner's *Ring.*

We can perceive a more radical approach to collage coming from a leading figure of the European avant-garde, Luciano Berio (Fig. 36-4). He composed his *Sinfonia,* a sprawling composition for eight amplified solo voices and orchestra, in 1968, the year of great political turmoil in both America and Europe, on a commission from Bernstein and the New York Philharmonic. The idea of fusion and collage was embedded at *Sinfonia*'s core. The virtuoso vocal parts were composed for the Swingle Singers, an octet founded by Ward Swingle (b. 1927) to perform a crossover repertoire that encompassed everything from Renaissance madrigals to arrangements of current pop songs. The texts of *Sinfonia* form a wildly eclectic collage. Much of the time the singers vocalize on vowels or other sounds, in the fashion of some postwar avant-garde music. Against this background of primal lingual soup, the first movement pits readings from the eminent French anthropologist Claude Lévi-Strauss (1908–2009), whose subversively relativistic theories on the correspondences between modern thought and ancient myth had made him a hero of the New Left in the 1960s and a great influence on poststructuralist thinkers.

Anthology Vol 3-60
Full CD VII, 32

As its archaic title suggests, Berio's *Sinfonia* engages the eternal question of the relation between the present and the past, most explicitly in the third movement, based on the corresponding movement of Mahler's Second Symphony. This put *Sinfonia* in sync with the Mahler boom, of which Bernstein was the leading figure. The Mahler rediscovery was itself in sync with emerging Postmodern sensibilities, as musicians came to admire the mixture of high and low culture, collage effects, and eclecticism, all of which had initially bewildered many of the composer's contemporaries.

In *Sinfonia* the third movement of Mahler's Second Symphony unwinds virtually in its entirety as a background to a frantic projection of aural "graffiti," some in the form of spoken words (many drawn from Samuel Beckett's novel *The Unnamable*), others in the form of whispered solfège syllables, still others in the form of orchestral allusions to a panoply of repertoire items from Bach, Beethoven, Berlioz, and Brahms to Debussy, Ravel, Schoenberg, and Stravinsky (including Berio himself and other Darmstadt alumni). Words muttered or shouted by the singers are slogans ("Forward!" "We shall

Figure 36-3 The AT&T building (now called Sony Tower) in New York.

Figure 36-4 Luciano Berio, 1991.

overcome!") that Berio took down from the walls of Paris during the 1968 student riots as well as from musical performance directions from Mahler's score ("Keep going!"). Berio's collage, an overload of experience, offered a panorama of the historical disruption and unrest that so marked the 1960s.

The political background of *Sinfonia* is also evident in the second movement, "O King," a memorial to the slain civil rights leader Martin Luther King, Jr. Berio had first written it in 1967 as a tribute, and he decided, after King's assassination, to adapt the piece for *Sinfonia* and insert it as an addition that could serve both as a commemoration and as a rebuke to the Americans for their slow progress toward racial justice. It has an abstractly conceived pitch ostinato interacting and overlapping with an abstractly conceived rhythmic ostinato. Overlaid, meanwhile, on both of these is a series of vowel sounds enunciated by the singers. Near the end of the movement, these stately and impersonally interacting cycles build to a climax in which the vowels are permuted into a different order and equipped with consonants to articulate them, revealing that they are the constituent vowels of the phrase "O Martin Luther King."

Berio wrote *Sinfonia* when he was in his mid-forties. In some dozen solo instrumental works called *Sequenza*, composed between 1958 and 2002, he created a particularly impressive series that did not rely on earlier music. But from the period of *Sinfonia* to his death in 2003 he devoted considerable attention to creative transformations of past music. He orchestrated some early Mahler Lieder and creatively arranged folk songs. Particularly imaginative were his completions of other composers' unfinished works. He wrote an ending for Puccini's last opera *Turandot* that made use of the composer's draft materials but also worked in allusions to Schoenberg, Mahler, and the Beatles. *Rendering* (1989) calls on sketches that Schubert left for his final work, a Symphony in D Major (D. 936a). Berio orchestrated straightforwardly (that is, in the manner of the 1820s) those sections for which there were continuous sketches, such as the exposition to the first movement. But when Schubert left little or nothing, such as in the development section, Berio's music shifts to a strangely kaleidoscopic Modernist sound. The jarring juxtaposition is reminiscent of a Postmodern architectural trend in Europe in which partially bombed-out buildings, such as churches, were not restored to their original state but were instead newly rebuilt only where necessary, thus freely mixing, for example, original sixteenth-century designs and stained-glass windows with entirely new sections.

To explore further a cluster of ideas relating to collage, we can consider the music of George Rochberg (1918–2005). He began his career as an apparently untroubled academic composer, theorist, and professor at the University of Pennsylvania whose works were honored with coveted awards. In the 1960s he experimented with collage techniques. In *Music for the Magic Theater* (1965), for example, he juxtaposed a divertimento by Mozart, a symphony by Mahler, a slow movement from a late Beethoven string quartet, Webern's Concerto, Op. 24, Stockhausen's *Zeitmässe*, Varèse's *Déserts*, "Stella by Starlight" (a transcribed Miles Davis recording), and some of his own earlier pieces.

Anthology Vol 3-61
Full CD VII, 33

Nothing in the work of earlier collagists, however, prepared anyone for the premiere of Rochberg's Third Quartet on 15 May 1972 in New York's Alice Tully Hall. The first movement for the most part featured the dissonant fury that was by then an uptown staple. The shock came in the third movement, a set of variations marked

Adagio sereno, molto espressivo e tranquillo; pure (Ex. 36-1). Its three-sharp key signature means what it says: This is a work in a fully functional A major, confined to a style that in harmony, emotional affect, and treatment of the instruments is identifiably that of Beethoven's two most famous slow movements in his late quartets: the "Cavatina" from Op. 130 and the "Heiliger Dankgesang" (Sacred Hymn of Thanksgiving) from Op. 132.

Example 36-1 George Rochberg, Quartet No. 3: III, mm. 1–10

Coming as it does after two movements in an unspectacular but solidly identifiable Modernist style, the stylistic contrast is thus related to the collage techniques Rochberg had been employing for nearly a decade. The *Adagio*, however, was not a collage of actual earlier materials but, rather, a pastiche. This movement sounded remarkably like Beethoven, and the 1973 recording by the Concord Quartet quickly became a favorite item for "guess the composer" games. Rochberg was not quoting past composers but seeming as if he were channeling Beethoven himself.

A composition like this broke all the rules. There was little or no "distancing." The impression was one not of sophisticated irony but of disconcerting sincerity. Unlike the Neoclassicism of the 1920s, in which characteristics of obsolete styles were revived amid a syntax that was wholly contemporary, Rochberg's *Adagio* revived the syntax as well, treating Beethoven's style as if it were not obsolete at all, as if it were fine to write in the 1970s as if one were living in the 1820s. A rare precedent for such an approach, perhaps, was some of the untimely late works of Richard Strauss from the 1940s, but in Strauss's case he was channeling his own past, the kind of music he had written sixty years earlier. To compose in an obsolete style as if it were not obsolete was to challenge the whole idea of stylistic obsolescence and of progress in history. And to challenge that idea was to call into question the "necessity" of the twentieth century's stylistic revolutions, one of the most sacred of all Modernist dogmas.

To compose in an obsolete style as if it were not obsolete was to challenge the whole idea of stylistic obsolescence and of progress in history.

Aesthetics of Pastiche

An important question remains: Why evoke the styles of particular past masters rather than use the language of tonality in a way that might ultimately become one's own? Britten and Shostakovich were still alive in 1972 and composing in personal tonal idioms, as were many midtown American composers. Pastiche composition (as opposed to actual quotation) had rarely been used before for any purpose other than instruction or the formal demonstration of skill. To use it as a method for expression of personal emotion seemed a contradiction in terms.

In an essay on his Third Quartet, Rochberg claimed that one's personal emotions are never only that but are also part of the "physical-mental-spiritual web" that connects people.[9] The conviction that one had to speak in the recognizable voices of the past also emerged in the "Postscript" to the novel *The Name of the Rose* (1980) by Umberto Eco (b. 1932). The Italian writer and intellectual described the dilemma of "belatedness," a sense of coming after everything that mattered. Many artists and critics have identified that despairing sentiment as the distinguishing aesthetic frame of the late-twentieth-century mind. "I think of the postmodern attitude," Eco wrote,

> as that of a man who loves a very cultivated woman and knows he cannot say to her, "I love you madly," because he knows that she knows (and that she knows that he knows) that these words have already been written by Barbara Cartland [1901–2000, a famous romance novelist]. Still, there is a solution. He can say, "As Barbara Cartland would put it, I love you madly." At this point, having avoided false innocence, having said clearly that it is no longer possible to speak innocently, he will nevertheless have said what he wanted to say to the woman: that he loves her, but he loves her in an age of lost innocence. If the woman goes along with this, she will have received a declaration of love all the same. Neither of the two speakers will feel innocent, both will have accepted the challenge of the past, of the already said, which cannot be eliminated, both will consciously and with pleasure play the game of irony. But both will have succeeded, once again, in speaking of love.[10]

If Rochberg expressed his own heartfelt emotion "as Beethoven (Mahler, Schoenberg) would put it," he does so, according to Eco, because there was no other way of doing so at the fallen end of the twentieth century. Using an innocent language innocently—using tonality "in one's own way"—did not seem a serious option for most serious composers in the 1970s. The choice seemed bleak: Either renounce expression altogether or borrow a voice.

The implication is indeed depressing. Just as we can communicate artistically only through the studied imitations or "simulacra" of styles that were once spontaneous, so our emotions themselves have become imitations, likenesses without substance and authenticity. This became a pervasive theme in Postmodern fiction, theater, and film, for example, in Ridley Scott's *Blade Runner* (1982), which explored the very definition of the human being in relation to "replicants," artificially created people (Fig. 36-5). The quest to regain the full range of sincere emotional expression that had earlier been available to artists and everyone else before the horrors of the twentieth century thus seemed doomed to failure, but a noble failure because it faced the unhappy truth of contemporary life rather than retreating, as Modernism had done, into a self-satisfied, self-induced, socially isolated delusion of freedom. Postmodernism, in this view, meant resignation to (or making the best of) a state of diminished capacity.

Figure 36-5 Harrison Ford as Rick Deckard and Sean Young as Rachael in Ridley Scott's film, *Blade Runner*, 1982.

Since Rochberg's significance as an academic Modernist had been widely acknowledged, his Postmodern turn to pastiche was hard to ignore. A prominent figure had done the unthinkable: been at the vanguard and quit. Some hailed what he had done as liberating, others damned it. While former uptown colleagues felt betrayed, midtown composers were understandably put off for other reasons. Of the stir Rochberg's Quartet was making, Ned Rorem, an American traditionalist, wryly observed that it reminded him of how people who quit smoking gain a sort of praise that people who never smoked in the first place do not get, even though the latter are the more virtuous. As for Rochberg, he decried historicist thinking and set out to demolish it. No other century had been as style conscious as the twentieth, he complained. In no other century did the composer feel such a compulsion to "view his situation in terms of where he's been, where he is now, and where he must go."[11] These were the bedrock tenets of Modernism, so deeply ingrained that most composers were not even aware of alternatives.

Everyone had to deal with the dominant museum culture—every composer competed with Beethoven, not just midtown moderates. Rochberg confronted the old paradox that bedeviled all composers in the twentieth century: "The music of the 'old masters' was a living presence; its spiritual values had not been displaced or destroyed by the new music."[12] There was an inherent difficulty in a philosophy of history that compelled one to reject earlier styles, when the persistence of those same styles was a fact of every musician's daily life. Rochberg began to suspect that he had cut himself off from the expressive possibilities that enabled the older music to survive. He only later divulged a personal factor behind his change of style. In 1964 the composer experienced a personal tragedy when his twenty-year-old son, Paul, died of cancer. Rochberg found he had no vocabulary with which to mourn his loss or seek solace for it. In this light, his reversion to tonality was less about debating theories of history than about recapturing a lost expressive range.

So perhaps Postmodern responses were not so grim or cynical after all, especially among younger composers who grew up listening to everything. An eclectic recourse to the past and present, to classical and popular music, to the near and the far away, showed an openness toward whatever one considered sounded good, interesting, fun, engaged, or otherwise attractive. It became increasingly evident that eclecticism could be novel rather than just cynical or nostalgic. Juxtaposing historical references without respect for their chronology alters one's apprehension of them. Styles formerly thought of as part of an inexorable historical progression, such as "tonal" to "atonal," could be regarded as expressive rather than historical categories. All are equally available to artists of the present, whose "transhistorical" and "transgeographical" reach for that reason is all the richer in possibilities than that of any previous generation of artists.

Across Time and Space: George Crumb

Before turning to younger generations of musicians who lived their entire lives with such eclecticism and totalism, we will consider George Crumb (b. 1929; Fig. 36-6), Rochberg's longtime colleague at the University of Pennsylvania. For about a decade beginning in the mid-1970s he was one of the most frequently and widely performed of living American composers, although his music did not achieve as wide a popularity as did that of some of the minimalists emerging at the time. During the 1960s he composed various works to texts by the Spanish surrealist poet Federico Garcia Lorca (1898–1936), including *Night Music* (1963), *Night of the Four Moons* (1969, inspired by the Apollo moon landing that year), and *Ancient Voices of Children* (1970). Lorca's shocking imagery, full of nightmare visions and wild contrasts, aroused in Crumb "an urge to fuse various unrelated stylistic elements" so as to create similarly incongruous juxtapositions in his music.[13]

Anthology Vol 3-62
Full CD VII, 34–35
Concise CD III, 47

Crumb achieved his transhistorical reach through quotation of existing music. In *Ancient Voices of Children*, for example, the pianist plays an excerpt from Bach on a toy piano, and at the very end the oboist wanders slowly offstage while playing the closing "Forever" motif from Mahler's *Das Lied von der Erde*. The ingredients in Crumb's collages were chosen not as representatives of styles but as expressive symbols of "timeless" content. Quoting Bach and Mahler in the context of Lorca may be seen not as an exercise in incongruity but, rather, as an affirmation of the relevance of all to all. The striking thing about Crumb's collages is their uncomplicated form, their spare texture, and the loving way in which they gather up so much that had been expressly targeted for Modernist exclusion.

Crumb's transgeographical reach can be heard in his use of incongruously mixed timbres. Sounds of the American countryside are regularly combined with those of recognizably Asian percussion instruments like Tibetan tuned "prayer stones" or Japanese "temple bells." Altered timbres are obtained by sliding a chisel on piano strings, threading paper between the strings of a harp, fingering a violin or cello tremolo while wearing thimbles, tuning the unison strings on a mandolin a quarter tone apart, blowing into a flute while also singing, dipping a gong into a tub of water. Instrumentalists are required to sing, singers to play instruments. Crumb made timbre his primary creative preoccupation, varying it with great subtlety and resourcefulness while reducing the music's formal structure to simple repetitive or strophic designs and stripping its sound surface down to bare monodic or heterophonic textures. His music seemed virtually amnesiac, drawing on the music of divergent times and places as if it were all part of one undifferentiated here and now.

Figure 36-6 George Crumb, 2000.

Two other features of Crumb's music also attracted particular attention. One is the visual appearance of some of his scores (Ex. 36-2). The look of a page from *Ancient*

Example 36-2 George Crumb, *Ancient Voices of Children, III*

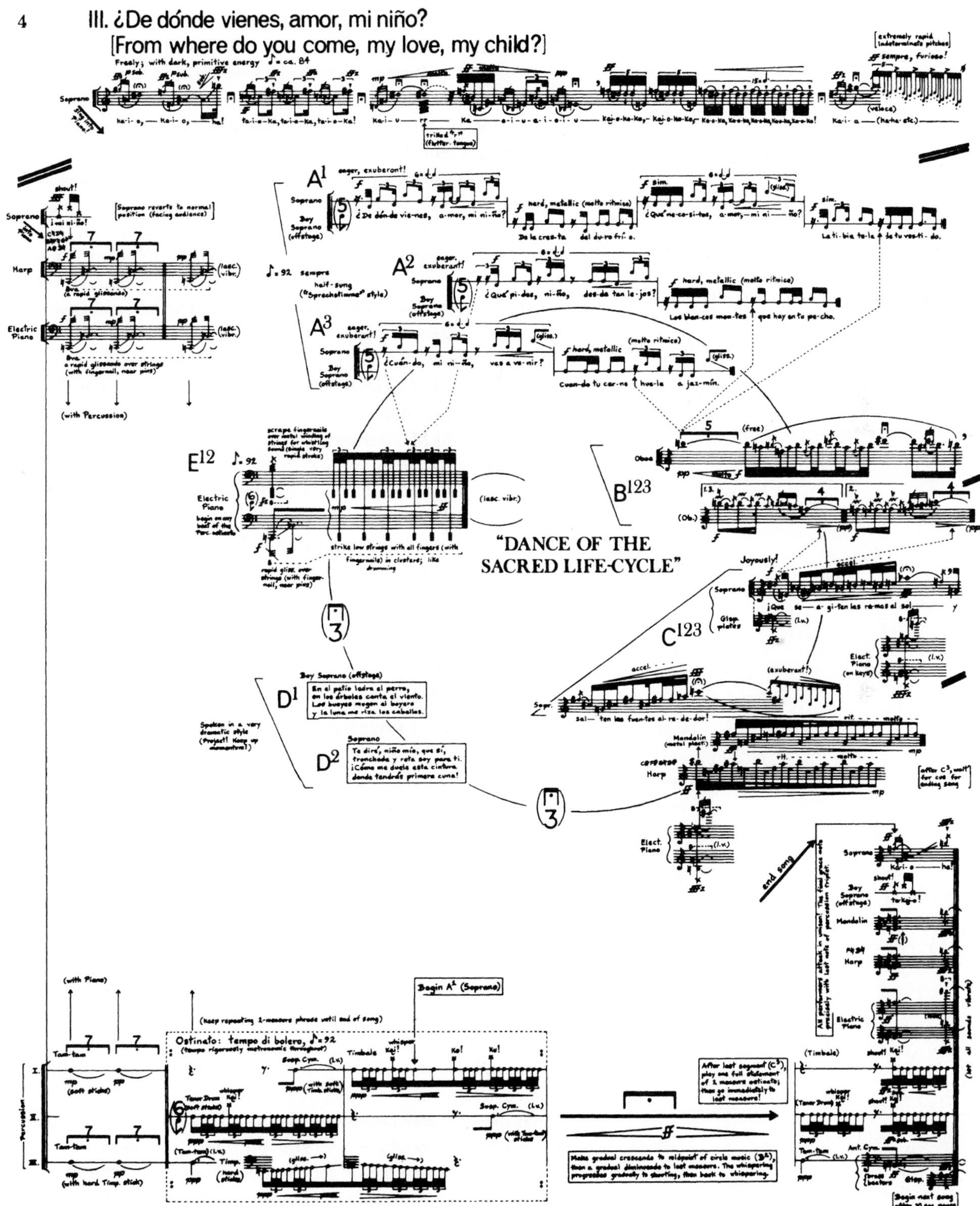

Voices of Children reinforces the idea of collage—an assemblage rather than an organic unity. Layouts that avoid the usual alignment of parts have the advantage of forcing performers out of their habits. Some works are notated on circular staves, others on spirals, still others in the shape of crosses. Secondly, Crumb joined with other composers of the 1960s and '70s in introducing elements of theater not only into vocal but also into instrumental compositions. In his widely imitated *Black Angels* (1970) for amplified string quartet, the players wear masks, are asked to chant unintelligible syllables and numbers in various languages, and lend a hand as percussionists playing maracas, tam-tam, tuned water goblets, and thimbles. Crumb composed the work at the height of the Vietnam War—the score is dated "Friday the Thirteenth, March 1970 (in tempore belli)," in time of war—and is subtitled "Thirteen Images from the Dark Land." The work repeatedly alludes to death, including references to the *Dies irae* chant and Schubert's "Death and the Maiden" String Quartet.

Once one renounces the idea of historical progress in the arts, then meaningful expression and connecting with present-day listeners become primary concerns.

Political engagement played a role in *Black Angels,* for its rituals enact a kind of surrealistic funeral to protest the killing. Political themes were also at the core of many works by Frederic Rzewski (b. 1938). Born in Massachusetts and educated at Harvard, he started his career as an avant-gardist living in Europe during the 1960s, at first in the orbit of Stockhausen, whose *Klavierstück X* Rzewski (a virtuoso pianist) premiered. The political upheavals later in the decade convinced him of the irreconcilable contradiction between the private games of the avant-garde and the social purposes to which he was dedicated as a communist.

Rzewski's outstanding work from the mid-1970s was *The People United Will Never Be Defeated* (1975), a virtuoso variation set for piano on the Chilean protest song "¡El pueblo unido jamás será vencido!" The thirty-six variations on the song look back in certain respects to two monumental keyboard sets: Bach's "Goldberg" Variations and Beethoven's "Diabelli" Variations. The piece opens with a simple, lyrical statement of the protest song (thus reminiscent of the "aria" that begins Bach's set) before embarking on a grand tour of a broad range of Modern and Postmodern styles, from the composer's earlier avant-garde idiom to improvisation to minimalism. As in the "Goldberg" Variations, the opening song returns to conclude the set.

Conversions in Reverse

Many composers of Rzewski's generation likewise defected from their Modernist training. We will recall that the big story of the early 1950s had been the conversion to serialism on the part of prominent figures like Stravinsky and Copland—a story that paid the highest tribute to, and considerably strengthened, the master narrative of uptown composers. By the 1970s the big story and the most convincing evidence that the historicist narrative was losing its grip were conversions that took place in the opposite direction. Uptown was moving downtown.

One prominent defector was David Del Tredici (b. 1937), who became best known for a series of works written between 1968 and 1996 based on Lewis Carroll, particularly his children's classic *Alice's Adventures in Wonderland* (1865), mostly scored for a solo soprano voice amplified to compete with a huge orchestra. These *Alice* pieces are only nominally about Alice. What they are really about is excess—glut, overindulgence, binging on voluptuous sonority and honeyed harmony—and these extravaganzas were welcomed by many orchestra audiences. Having been trained in high Modernist style, Del Tredici initially worried about what his uptown colleagues would think of him, probably either that he was an "idiot" or that he was selling out.[14] He came to appreciate, however, that "composers now are beginning to realize that if a piece excites an audience, *that doesn't mean it's terrible*. For my generation, it is considered vulgar to have an audience really, *really* like a piece on a first hearing. But why are we writing music except to move people and to be expressive?"[15] It was a sign of the times, the desire to engage listeners that we have already seen with Reich, Glass, Rochberg, and others. Midtowners like Rorem (like virtuous nonsmokers) may well have wondered what took Del Tredici so long to figure this out. Once one renounces the idea of historical progress in the arts, then meaningful expression and connecting with present-day listeners become primary concerns.

Most composers of Del Tredici's generation and the next had received a similar Modernist training, and many were coming to similar conclusions. Especially in America, virtually all the emerging talents in the final decades of the century were "**neo-tonalists**" (or "**neo-Romantics**," as critics tended to call them), by either upbringing or conversion. A short alphabetical list of them, confined to Americans, would include the following (where the asterisks denote winners of Grawemeyer and Pulitzer prizes, the most prestigious awards available to classical composers): *John Adams (b. 1947), *Stephen Albert (1941–1992), *William Bolcom (b. 1938), *John Corigliano (b. 1938), *John Harbison (b. 1938), *Jennifer Higdon (b. 1962), *Aaron Jay Kernis (b. 1960), Libby Larsen (b. 1950), *Peter Lieberson (b. 1946), Tobias Picker (b. 1954), *Christopher Rouse (b. 1949), *Joseph Schwantner (b. 1943), Conrad Susa (b. 1935), Michael Torke (b. 1961), *Joan Tower (b. 1938), *George Tsontakis (b. 1951), and *Ellen Taaffe Zwilich (b. 1939). It is worth noting, moreover, that composers born after the Second World War tended to be less equivocal about their embrace of a "tonal" composing grammar than those born before, and those born in the 1960s, who never went through a high Modernist stage, are the most straightforwardly tonal of all.

The justification for the recourse to tonal writing went beyond the personal and political reasons mentioned earlier. Some proponents attempted to offer more objective arguments, no longer content merely to play defense against the historicist line but, rather, wanting to go on the offensive as to why they believed they were pursuing the right path for music. For them, evidence could be brought forth based on science, comparative anthropology, historical studies, linguistics, and the natural physical properties of music that had been explored going back to Pythagoras and that included the much later discovery of the overtone series. It was around this time, in the 1970s, that the world's oldest existing melody—the Sumerian hymn dating from somewhere around 1200 BCE mentioned in Chapter 1 (see Ex. 1-1)—was deciphered and shown to use our familiar diatonic pitch set accompanied with harmonic intervals that we still classify as consonances.

Some of the most compelling arguments were based on findings of transformational grammar in linguistics and on gestalt and cognitive psychology, the latter explored in writings by music theorist Leonard B. Meyer (1918–2007). Particularly influential was the application to music of the theories of linguist Noam Chomsky (b. 1928), who had explored how people learn languages. Working with linguist Ray Jackendoff, composer Fred Lerdahl (b. 1943) published a study of tonal harmony that sought, on the Chomskian model, to uncover the psychological processes ("transformations") to which listeners intuitively subject chords and progressions of tonal music in order to perceive "meaningful" utterances. Borrowing directly from Chomsky's vocabulary, Lerdahl and Jackendoff called their book *A Generative Theory of Tonal Music* (1983). In a simpler and more popular form, Leonard Bernstein had made related arguments in the Norton Lectures he delivered at Harvard University in 1973 in a series entitled "The Unanswered Question," an allusion to an orchestral piece by Charles Ives that pitted traditional tonal writing against atonal interjections. The shared goal of these investigations was to understand how listeners make sense of music, how tonal music is hierarchically structured. In a controversial section near the end of their book, Jackendoff and Lerdahl argued that "post-tonal" music, which had no pitch or metrical hierarchy and avoided repetition, made structural listening impossible. The conclusion must be that, as far as unaided listeners are concerned (as opposed to analysts contemplating the written score), atonal music is cognitive noise.

We have already seen that some Modernist composers would have readily accepted such a characterization of their music, arguing that the issue of "understanding" was irrelevant. For them, it was simply the wrong question to ask and sought to define music in the wrong way. We may recall Stockhausen's sassy comment to Adorno in Darmstadt as to whether the esteemed professor was looking for a chicken in an abstract painting. The high Modernists held that the most important thing about music might not necessarily be to secure comprehensibility through hierarchy, tension and release, tonality, and so forth. Just as some visual artists felt representation was no longer necessary in painting, some composers continued to feel that music was not like a language, did not need to be understandable or have much to do with melody or tonality. Others believed that advanced listeners would one day learn to comprehend their advanced music.

But the new, linguistically informed theory suggested otherwise. Although Jackendoff and Lerdahl asserted they were not making aesthetic value judgments about musical works, their parting shot, with its deliberate allusion to Babbitt's notorious "Who Cares If You Listen?," asserted that their "theory is relevant to compositional problems, in that it focuses detailed attention on the facts of hearing. To the extent that a composer cares about his listeners, this is a vital issue."[16] By the late 1980s most young composers were persuaded, like Lerdahl, of the necessity for congruity between composing grammars and listening grammars, trying to be understandable and accessible to listeners, whether they wrote tonal music or not.

The End of Soviet Music

Cold War Modernist purity began to lose its hold in Europe and the Soviet Union as well. Two of the most prominent Central European avant-gardists, György Ligeti and Krzysztof Penderecki, made spectacular neo-Romantic swerves in the 1970s. Ligeti, who had moved to Western Europe after the 1956 Hungarian uprising, had a turnaround stimulated by hearing the early minimalist works of Terry Riley and Steve Reich, which influenced his *Clocks and Clouds* (1973) for women's chorus and orchestra. The second of his Three Pieces for Two Pianos (1976) is titled "Self-Portrait with Reich and Riley (and Chopin in the Background)." His opera *Le grand macabre* (1978) continued following the trend toward eclectic collage, now admitting rock. His Trio for Violin, Horn, and Piano (1982) was written as a companion piece to Brahms's trio for the same combination of instruments. He frankly described the work as his regretful acknowledgment that the avant-garde had run out of steam.

Penderecki's move may have been stimulated by the *Solidarność* (Solidarity) movement in Poland, an independent workers' initiative that helped lead to the fall of communism there. Seeing social solidarity rather than social alienation as the most progressive political and social force proved fatal to Penderecki's Modernism. It brought his music more in line with the other leading Polish figure, Witold Lutosławski, whose challenging scores had nonetheless never forgotten audiences.

Figure 36-7 Alfred Schnittke.

The Soviet Union likewise saw a growing and finally dominant eclecticism, the result of the decline in totalitarian power and greater access to music from Western Europe and America. There had been some liberalization following the death of Stalin in 1953. Official visitors came from abroad, as did smuggled scores and recordings. The brilliant Canadian pianist Glenn Gould (1932–82) made a Soviet tour in 1957, during which he gave an informal recital at the Moscow Conservatory, playing works by Berg, Webern, and Krenek and lecturing about the technique of serial music. The most spectacular such occasion came in 1962 with an eightieth-birthday-year visit by Igor Stravinsky, who performed his music, met with students, and was accepted thereafter in his homeland as a "Russian classic."

Two immigrants in Moscow also brought news of Western trends. Filip Gershkovich (1906–89), a Romanian-born composer and music theorist who had studied with Berg and Webern, fled from Nazi persecution to the Soviet Union in 1940. One of his students was Andrey Volkonsky (1933–2008), born in Geneva while his family was in exile from the Soviet Union. In 1956 he produced *Musica stricta,* the first twelve-tone composition by a Soviet citizen. Edison Denisov (1929–96), a protégé of Shostakovich's and another Gershkovich student, was especially energetic in promoting advanced Western techniques and aesthetic principles among his contemporaries. His apartment, like Volkonsky's, became a lending library for scores that he had procured from Boulez, Stockhausen, and other Darmstadters. Denisov made his debut as an avant-gardist with a twelve-tone cantata, *The Sun of the Incas* (1964), composed to a text by the Chilean poet Gabriela Mistral.

Denisov was one of the so-called Big Troika of late-Soviet nonconforming composers, regarded throughout Europe and America as major figures in contemporary music. The other two to emerge during the 1960s were Alfred Schnittke (1934–98; Fig. 36-7) and Sofia Gubaidulina (b. 1931; Fig. 36-8). Much of Gubaidulina's music shows religious influences; she has stated, "There is no more serious reason for composing music than spiritual renewal."[17] This is evident in a piece such as *In croce* (1979), the title of which refers to the crosswise relationship between the cello and the organ, the two main protagonists of the piece, as well as to the content of the music: "on the cross," a meaning that suggests its Christian subtext.

Anthology Vol 3-63
Full CD VII, 36

Schnittke was the son of a German-Jewish father and a Russian-born but ethnically German mother, whose first language was that of his parents. Plagued with health problems much of his life, he divided his time early on between writing utilitarian film scores for a livelihood and serious pieces "for the drawer." He was baptized as a Roman Catholic relatively late in his life (1982), and religious themes play an important part in many of his scores. Like so many composers in the 1970s, he abandoned serial technique out of a conviction that no single manner was adequate to reflect contemporary reality and that stylistic eclecticism—he called it "polystylistics"—had become mandatory. The watershed was his First

Figure 36-8 Sofia Gubaidulina, 2007.

Symphony (1972), the collage to end all collages, a riot of allusion and outright quotation, including self-quotation, in which Beethoven jostles Handel jostles Haydn jostles Mahler jostles Tchaikovsky jostles Johann Strauss II, and on into ragtime and rock. Here, too, the distinctive Schnittke orchestra announced itself, a huge machine in which the harpsichord is as essential as the electric bass guitar. All styles and genres are potentially and indiscriminately available to it. Rather than Postmodernism, the First Symphony may be thought to signify "post-ism," after-everythingism, it's-all-overism.

To say that Modernism "collapsed" in the last quarter of the twentieth century would be as misleading as the old claim that tonality had collapsed in the century's first quarter.

An ironic overlay is apparent in Schnittke's Concerto Grosso No. 1 (1977), his first composition to gain a big reputation in the West. The piece deploys three distinct stylistic strata: the highly disciplined, intensely fiddled neo-Baroque passagework promised by the title; an amorphous atonal sonic lava flow; and syrupy Soviet pop music at its stalest, banged out on a prepared piano sounding like a cross between Radio Moscow's signature chimes and the beating of ash cans. The Concerto Grosso established the pattern that would distinguish Schnittke's version of collage. No longer despairingly helter-skelter like the First Symphony, his polystylism now took shape through bald, easily read contrasts. Plush Romantic lyricism, chants and chorales and hymns, actual or invented historical passages (Neoclassical, neo-Baroque, even neo-Medieval), every make and model of jazz and pop—all of this and more are the ingredients. Schnittke's stylistic range is not quite so broad by the time of his Third String Quartet (1983), but its historical purview spans Renaissance composer Orlando di Lasso, through Bach, Beethoven, and Schubert, to his inspiring countryman Shostakovich.

Anthology Vol 3-64
Full CD VII, 37

With an unlimited stylistic range at one's disposal, one could construct contrasts of a previously inconceivable extremity. Out of them one could achieve a more vivid instrumental "dramaturgy" than anything previously attempted in Soviet music. Schnittke's polystylism reengaged with the grandest, most urgent, most timeless—hence potentially most banal—questions of existence, framed in the simplest way possible, as primitive oppositions. With a bluntness and an immodesty practically unknown since the First World War, Schnittke's music tackled life-against-death, love-against-hate, good-against-evil, freedom-against-tyranny, and I-against-the-world. In doing so, he recaptured the heroic subjectivity with which bourgeois audiences love to identify.

Senior Statesmen

To say that Modernism "collapsed" in the last quarter of the twentieth century would be as misleading as the old claim that tonality had collapsed in the century's first quarter. It is worth one last reminder that all so-called style periods are plural and that the dominance of certain trends is never as absolute or obvious as later historical accounts inevitably make them seem. At century's end, just to pick the most conspicuous American examples, Milton Babbitt (then age eighty-four) and Elliott Carter (age ninety-two) were both still impressively productive as composers. In Germany, Karlheinz Stockhausen was keeping up appearances as an avant-garde icon: In 1995, he made some headlines with a string quartet in which the players "phoned in" their parts from separate airborne helicopters. Pierre Boulez was honored in 2000, at the age of seventy-five, with the Grawemeyer Award for *Sur incises,* a work scored for three pianos, three harps, and three percussionists. These composers, all highly distinguished and quite loftily unaffected by recent trends, enjoyed the sort of critical adulation that always attends grand old men. Their styles remained Modern, but they were hardly new. They now represented a rearguard tradition seeking to retain the autonomy of music and fiercely opposed to the latest in Postmodernism and popular music. Whether serial (like Babbitt's and Boulez's) or not (like Stockhausen's and Carter's), their music identified them as senior composers, working in idioms that even their most respectful juniors, the writers of tomorrow's music, largely regarded as outmoded.

Some younger composers nonetheless worked in styles and media comparable to the grand old men. Two of them, Brian Ferneyhough (b. 1943) and Michael Finnissy (b. 1946), were English composers identified with a movement known as the "**New Complexity**," a term coined in direct and embattled reaction against the advancing minimalist and neo-tonal tides. Their music was, at least in appearance, even more complicated than that of the high Modernists in its attempt to notate virtually impalpable microtones, ever-changing rhythmic divisions and tiny gradations of timbre and loudness. Example 36-3, from Ferneyhough's String Quartet No. 2 (1980), shows clearly his device of "nested rhythms" (tiny sextuplets in the time of five sixteenths within medium triplets inside of big quintuplets, etc.) that motivated the notational extremities, plus the individual editorial attention given every single note (each with its own articulation mark and, usually, its own dynamic) and the "extended" playing techniques (trilled artificial harmonics, microtonal glissandos, etc.) that reflect the composer's determination to achieve timbral diversity. But despite the supposed progress it fostered in notational technology, the movement was obviously another rearguard action.

Example 36-3 Brian Ferneyhough, String Quartet No. 2

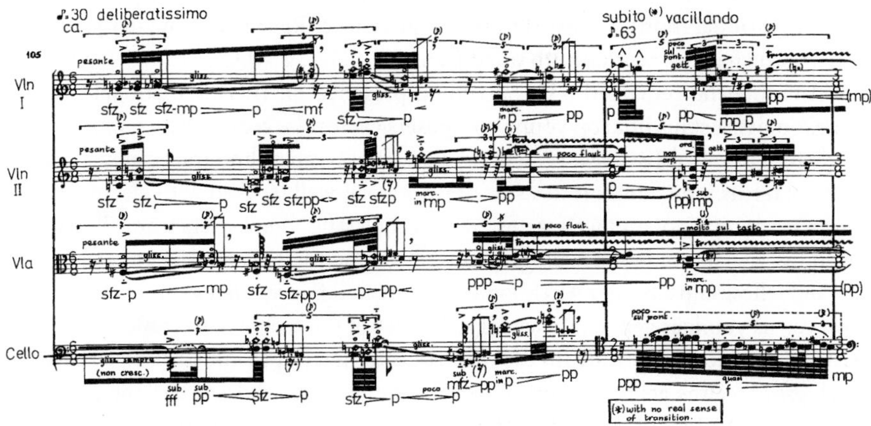

By and large the leading composers of the younger generation of English composers pursued an intellectually challenging but much more audience-friendly approach in their music. England has long loved child prodigies, either producing them herself (Henry Purcell) or embracing them from afar (Felix Mendelssohn). Oliver Knussen (b. 1952) conducted the London Symphony Orchestra in his First

Figure 36-9 Pierre Boulez at the IRCAM center (Institut de Recherche et Coordination Acoustique/Musique), in 1989.

Symphony at age fifteen. Nearly a generation later came Thomas Adès (b. 1971), who won a Grawemeyer Award for his orchestral composition *Asyla* and whose operas *Powder Her Face* (1995) and *The Tempest* (2004) enjoyed critical acclaim.

Much of the activity in France centered around **IRCAM** (Institut de Recherche et Coordination Acoustique/Musique), an electro-acoustical research institute the French government opened in 1977 under Boulez's direction (Fig. 36-9). The center not only offered the thrilling chance to work with the very latest technology but also inspired a group of French composers who wrote music on the basis of computer analyses and transformations of timbre. What is particularly interesting about these composers—figures such as Jean-Claude Risset (b. 1938), Gérard Grisey (1946–98), Tristan Murail (b. 1947), and Philippe Manoury (b. 1952)—is that their *musique spectrale* ("spectral" or "spectralist" music) is not typically computer music. It is neither (necessarily) composed nor performed with the aid of a computer and does not (necessarily) use electronic media. It is, rather, an approach to musical form, particularly to orchestration, that was inspired by computer music and would have been inconceivable without that precedent. Spectral music thus resembles earlier electronically influenced pieces, such as Ligeti's *Atmosphères,* with which it shares a predilection for long, slowly changing sounds.

Boulez was the driving force behind the establishment of IRCAM and retained the directorship until 1992, devoting much of his energy to its administration. He conducted its resident Ensemble Intercontemporain and at the same time increasingly led the world's great orchestras—conducting not just his twentieth-century specialties but standard Romantic repertoire as well, including the controversial centennial production of Wagner's *Ring* at Bayreuth in 1976. The few new pieces he composed tended to be based on older ones, as was the case with *Sur incises.* His largest work was *Répons,* which began in 1981 as a twenty-minute composition for chamber orchestra, six solo instruments, and live electronics; the next year it was extended to thirty-three-minutes, and in 1984 to a full-hour, "full evening" variant, which was taken on an international tour. The longer versions were developments, in the traditional motivic sense, of the original piece. *Répons* was further cannibalized in two chamber works, both titled *Dérive.*

Although he remained a commanding presence on the international musical scene, Boulez lost his hold on young composers even as he created new opportunities for them. He called IRCAM a "meeting place for scientists and musicians,"[18] and in practical terms it did amount to a sort of laboratory, well stocked with electronic and computer equipment and well staffed with technicians. Composers from all over the world (as well as some musicologists and music theorists) were invited for residencies and fellowships. Boulez was a somewhat isolated figure, even at his own institute, however, as younger generations emerged. Most of the technicians came from (or at least had significant exposure to) the world of commercial pop music, where at least as much progress was being made in audio technologies as in the world of the cloistered avant-garde. And while nobody thought that IRCAM was going to be hospitable to pop music, the differences in background and viewpoint of younger composers nevertheless showed up in attitudes toward technology, its applications, and its benefits.

Boulez was fervently committed to the conspicuous consumption of technology, and he had his own custom-built computer of enormous size, costliness, and complexity, which he used in *Répons* and other pieces. IRCAM's support staff, meanwhile, was more and more intrigued with the burgeoning "digital revolution," the commercial development of personal computers and software that miniaturized, standardized, and democratized technology. An English anthropologist even conducted a study of IRCAM built around this controversy, cast as a paradigmatic Modernist-versus-Postmodernist confrontation. Despite Boulez's opposition, the younger faction won.[19]

The Digital Revolution

Until the end of the twentieth century, the "high-tech" music that came out of places like IRCAM and the Columbia-Princeton Electronic Music Center depended on privileged access to expensive equipment housed in research institutions, industrial labs, and universities that enjoyed lavish subsidies. American composer Paul Lansky (b. 1944) estimated that "by 1979 you could probably get a good computer-music studio for $250,000, if you could raise it."[20] After twenty years, in other words, it was still something only elite institutions could afford. The new musical era that next emerged in the 1980s and '90s with the personal computer was a by-product of industrial innovation in pursuit of profits. It was directly created by capitalism and can stand therefore as a musical monument to the global triumph of the free market. The conversion from an industrial and service-based economy to an information-based one is standard economists' criterion of Postmodernity, and the possibilities that came from the personal computer are perhaps the most intrinsically entitled of all late-twentieth-century musical developments to the status of Postmodernist standard-bearer.

In its first phases, the musical possibilities of the personal computer relied heavily on MIDI technology. **MIDI** is an acronym for Musical Instrument Digital Interface. It was a set of technical specifications, or "protocols," agreed on by representatives of computer and synthesizer manufacturers in the early 1980s to standardize their products so that they could all interact. This development took place virtually simultaneously with the beginning of mass-produced desktop computers affordable for many households, soon followed by increasingly sophisticated, powerful, and inexpensive laptop computers. Two other developments similarly revolutionized the process of manipulating sound materials. One was the **sampler**, a device that stores and can variously manipulate recorded sounds of any kind. The other was the **sequencer**, a device that puts digitally stored sounds into a programmed order that can encompass thousands of individual units. With the sampler the "old promise of electronic music—that any noise could become available for musical use," as Lansky put it in 1989,[21] became a practical reality in a way that the pioneering composers of *musique concrète* could never have imagined in the late 1940s. The impact on popular music was also immense. Amplification had been crucial to the emergence of rock 'n' roll; now sampling and various electronic manipulations were integral to hip-hop and the new urban musics that were redefining popular culture.

What the digital revolution of the 1980s foreshadowed above all was liberation from the literate tradition.

Kyle Gann has suggested that "centuries from now, the years 1980 to 1985 may well appear one of the most significant watersheds in the history of music."[22] While it is of course too soon to gauge the ultimate accuracy of such a prediction, the world that many musicians inhabit at the time this text is being written certainly did come into being during those years. It is especially fitting that the implications of the digital age play such a crucial part in the concluding chapter of this book devoted to tracing the history of classical music in the West.

For the defining feature of that history, as emphasized from the very first page, has been the reliance on written transmission. What the digital revolution of the 1980s foreshadowed above all was liberation from the literate tradition.

Electronic music is the medium least dependent on notation. It can bypass both the pencil-and-paper phase of the creative process and the composer's need to communicate with performers. And no medium was more thoroughly transformed at the end of the twentieth century, thanks to the advent of personal computers. New technologies revolutionized every aspect of music making from composition (including nonelectronic composition) to performance, distribution, and consumption, especially once the Internet became central to everyday life. At every level the effect has been to simplify and democratize music. In the process these technological advances may well have dealt the literate musical tradition a slow-acting death blow.

Rather than the individual note, Gann has declared, the musical "atom" or minimal malleable unit became any sound complex that can be recorded and stored.[23] Observing that it is notation that creates the "note" (as opposed to the "tone"), he suggested that "the sampler frees composers from the habits inculcated by Western notation." Digital technology achieves what written texts seek to achieve—namely, the fixing of the unique artwork—even better than written texts can do: directly, like painting. "Text" and "work" can fuse under electronic conditions so as to produce a definitive work-object (phonograph record, tape, cassette, CD, and audio file) in a way that the intervention of human performers inevitably precludes.

An early "classic" of the new technology was Steve Reich's *Different Trains* (1988), which combines traditional notation and prerecorded sounds. It was commissioned by the Kronos Quartet, a San Francisco–based ensemble that dressed in trendy clothes, sported fashionable haircuts, and often included multimedia elements in its concerts. The ensemble presented a self-avowed Postmodern repertoire that mixed a range of twentieth-century pieces with transcriptions of early music, world music, jazz, and rock and that could justly boast of giving hundreds of premieres. In keeping with its adventurous spirit, Reich wrote a piece that pitted the live quartet against two prerecorded quartet tracks and a track of sampled sounds (train whistles, sirens) and voices. The words compare Reich's experience as a child in the early 1940s, shuttling back and forth across the continent between the New York and Los Angeles residences of his divorced parents, and the simultaneous experiences of Jewish children in Europe, who were being transported in "different trains" from the ghettos of Eastern Europe to the Nazi extermination camp at Auschwitz.

The live and recorded quartets play in a by-now-familiar minimalist style, only this time their chugging subtactile pulses symbolize the actual chug and clack of moving trains, evoked as well by periodic train whistles that in the piece's midsection are transformed into air-raid sirens as Reich's own childhood memories give way to the Holocaust nightmare. The sampled voices in the first section are those of the composer's childhood governess, Virginia, interviewed in later life, and a former train porter. In the middle section, the voices are those of Holocaust survivors, collected from oral history archives. To conclude, samples from the two sources are mixed. In the tradition of Leoš Janáček, the sampled words give shape to the instrumental lines as the musical phrases approximate their pitch and contour and dictate the music's tempos and tonal modulations. The understated climax comes in the third section, when the train porter's voice is heard matter-of-factly remarking, "Today, they're all gone." Remembering his voice from the first section, one knows that he was talking about the American transcontinental trains of the 1930s and '40s. But remembering the second section, one cannot help relating his comment to the Jewish children, too. Both a synthesis of the subject matter and an effective musical close, the moment is haunting. The coda adds another ironic and essentially Postmodernist stab: One of the survivors recalls the Germans' sincere love of music, preventing today's music-loving listeners from enjoying any complacent sense of moral superiority.

Since this breakthrough composition, Reich has used the voice-sampling technique in a series of multimedia compositions (or "documentary video operas"), including *The Cave* (1990–93) and *Three Tales* (*Hindenburg, Bikini,* and *Dolly*; 2002), both created in collaboration with his wife, the video artist Beryl Korot. Like *Different Trains,* they use collage techniques to address contemporary social and moral concerns.

Performance Art

At the same time as the digital revolution was transforming notated music, another approach emphasized ever since the first chapter also demands our attention: the persistence of the oral tradition. It has never been fully supplanted in Western classical music or anywhere else. The 1970s and '80s also saw the professional revival of age-old oral practices typically associated with folklore, giving rise to the genre that is known, for want of a better term, as **performance art**. The term conjures the multimedia combination of different art forms in performance. An early practitioner on the downtown scene, Japanese-born artist and musician Yoko Ono (b. 1933), was part of the Fluxus movement of the 1960s and collaborated with avant-garde figures such as Cage before her marriage to the Beatles' John Lennon in 1969.

Another leading figure in performance art, Meredith Monk (b. 1942), began her career as a lonely outsider. She created an eccentric music "corporeally," by training her own voice to do things no one within the traditions of her schooling had thought of doing before. Looking back on her early career she summed it up as "working with the solo voice as an instrument." She said:

> After classical voice training and experience as a folk and rock singer, I realized that I wanted to create vocal music that had the personal style and abstract (as well as emotional) qualities that come into play in the creation of a painting or a dance. My method began as one of trial and error: translating certain concepts, feelings, images and energies to my voice, seeing how they felt, how they sounded, and then refining them into a musical form. Over the years I have developed a vocabulary and a style designed to utilize as wide a range of vocal sound as possible.[24]

Monk became her own performance medium, producing music from within her own body. She tried to dispense with words without dispensing with expression. Most of her early compositions are solo songs, with simple piano accompaniments (usually ostinatos and grounds) that she played while producing an astonishing variety of nonverbal vocal sounds: sometimes invented syllables sung conventionally, sometimes more elemental sonorities—unusual wobbles and vibratos, nasal timbres, extreme registers, guttural breathing, vocalized inhaling. Monk, preempting a common reaction from listeners, called this "folk music from another planet."[25] Her ideal was a kind of musical abstract expressionism, which required the dethroning of words. Her early solo work, while fully composed (not improvised), was unwritten, since there was no need to communicate the music to any other performer. When she later began to write music for an ensemble it also remained unwritten, the product (like much rock) of intensive daily rehearsal and rote memorization.

Whether by accident or by design, many of the textures and structures Monk employed in her ensemble music recall the textures and structures of Medieval music. The first work she created after forming her own performing ensemble was the wordless *Dolmen Music* (1978), for six singers, a cello (played by one of the singers), and percussion (played by another). The title, derived from an old Breton word that refers to prehistoric cult monuments like Stonehenge (upright stones supporting a horizontal stone), evokes an imagined antiquity. The various movements—"Overture and Men's Conclave," "Wa-ohs," "Rain," "Pine Tree Lullaby," "Calls," "Conclusion"—seem to suggest the primordial rituals and practices out of which music emerged. At the very end of *Dolmen Music* all of the voices coalesce into a "composite" parallel organum (multiple fourths, fifths, and octaves) of the kind described—as we may recall from Chapter 1—in Medieval treatises. The contact made between twentieth-century musicians of the avant-garde and their ninth-century forebears dramatizes the idea of cyclic time, a notion that many in the late twentieth century found irresistibly attractive and used as a weapon for dismantling the idea of linear historical progress, which Monk among others has linked to patriarchy and "a very male point of view."[26]

Laurie Anderson (b. 1947; Fig. 36-10) was another leading performance artist to emerge in the 1980s and quickly became a widely known popular figure. In contrast to Monk's modestly scaled work, Anderson created one-woman multimedia shows that toured around the world and combined visual images, words, and music; performances could last four or five hours, sometimes split over two evenings. An Anderson concert rarely goes by without recourse to a wide array of digital hardware. The hardware includes samplers and sequencers that enable instantaneous manipulation (including looping) of sounds recorded on the spot; drum machines that synthesize percussion tracks; and voice-distorting machines like the vocoder (which blends the voice with keyboard-controlled harmonies so that one can "sing" whole chords) and the harmonizer, which radically transforms pitch and timbre, giving a user of either gender a potential range from the squeakiest soprano to the most booming basso (or what Anderson calls her "Voice of Authority"). Trained as a violinist, she rigged up an amplified fiddle with tape playback heads so that a bow strung with audiotape can play (and distort) intelligible words on it. The Anderson that performs is in effect a synthesized instrument herself, capable of simultaneously celebrating and mocking superhuman vocal and instrumental feats. She does it all with subtle humor, with a wink.

Figure 36-10 Laurie Anderson performing in 2010.

Self-parody is an essential part of her performances, which is another reason why some critics considered Anderson the Postmodern artist par excellence. Her breakthrough piece, *O Superman* (1981), is an excerpt from her multimedia presentation *United States*. Subtitled "For Massenet," on one level it is a straight parody of the aria "O souverain, ô juge, ô père" (O King, O Judge, O Father) from a once-popular grand opera *Le Cid* (1885) by French composer Jules Massenet. In the opera the title character sings the aria as he prays for victory on the eve of battle. Anderson's translation of the opening line, "O Superman, O Judge, O Mom and Dad," takes the elevated sentiment down many pegs, even as she identifies herself with a heroic operatic tenor.

The song begins with Anderson's voice, looped by the sampler into an unhurried "ha-ha-ha-ha-ha" that is sustained throughout the entire performance. Against this Anderson's voice is expanded by the vocoder into two alternating chords (C major and E minor) with two tones in common and the third differing by only a hypnotically reiterated half step. The song rocks gently back and forth between them like a babe in arms while the uncanny synthesized voice, joined gradually by small electric organ and a couple of winds, croons a dozy meditation, warm and comforting and matter-of-fact yet also somehow sinister:

> O Superman. O Judge. O Mom and Dad.
> Hi. I'm not home right now.
> But if you want to leave a message, just start talking at the sound of the tone.
> Hello? This is your mother. Are you there? Are you coming home? Hello? Is anybody home?
> Well you don't know me but I know you. And I've got a message to give to you. Here come the planes.
> So you better get ready, ready to go. You can come as you are, but pay as you go. Pay as you go.
> And I said: OK! Who is this really? And the voice said:
> This is the hand, the hand that takes. This is the hand. The hand that takes. Here come the planes.
> They're American planes, made in America. Smoking or nonsmoking? [. . .]
> So hold me, Mom, in your long arms. So hold me, Mom, in your long arms, In your automatic arms, In your electronic arms.
> So hold me, Mom, in your long arms, Your petrochemical arms,
> Your military arms,
> In your electronic arms . . .

A lullaby of annihilation? Of robotization? Of self-imprisonment? An Orwellian nightmare of sweetly instilled thought control? Or a demurrer at the election as president of the lullingly soft-spoken yet military-minded Ronald Reagan? The song seems to be about the potential horrors of technology, yet its medium is very high tech. Whether despite or because of its ironies and ambiguities, something in *O Superman* touched a nerve. Semiprivately released in a tiny edition, the song was played on the radio in Great Britain and shot briefly to the top of the pop charts in 1981. To fill the orders, Anderson signed a contract with Warner Brothers Records, a major pop label. Sales of *O Superman* grossed over a million dollars, lifting Anderson out of the New York downtown scene and into international popular culture.

That freakish, never-duplicated success is why Anderson's CDs are usually marketed as rock recordings, while those of Monk are found in classical bins. The arbitrariness of the classification is symptomatic of the nature of performance art, just as performance art is symptomatic of Postmodernism. Their superficial differences—Anderson highly verbal, openly political, and urbane; Monk pre- or postverbal, only implicitly political—are outweighed by their similarities, the most striking of which is the irreducibly oral/aural nature of their products. Translate their work into notes on a page and everything that counts is lost.

A slightly younger performance artist, Diamanda Galás (b. 1955), trained as a pianist, also employs extreme vocal techniques, theatrical sensibility, and a deep political commitment to create pieces of disturbing intensity. A Greek American born in California, Galás was shaped by the European avant-garde. In Europe, the Czech singer and violinist Iva Bittova (b. 1958) combines extreme vocal techniques pioneered by earlier performance artists with her Roma heritage, a Janáček-inspired concern with language, and considerable humor. Her wide range of collaborations with folk musicians, classical groups, and jazz and rock musicians is typical of Postmodern eclecticism. Although the Icelandic singer Björk (b. 1965) is more associated with commercial popular music, the similarity of some of her approach with that of the other figures we have been considering shows how unsatisfactory traditional categories (including "oral" and "literate") were becoming by the end of the century.

Performance art, as a site of female self-representation, found itself a natural ally of the feminist movement.

As is obvious from this brief discussion of performance art, the principal figures have been women. Musicologist Susan McClary observes, "Women's bodies in Western culture have almost always been viewed as objects of display."[27] It is the traditional role of women in the performing arts to be a "body set in motion for the pleasure of the masculine gaze." She quotes Anderson as corroboration: "Women have rarely been composers. But we do have one advantage. We're used to performing. I mean like we used to tap dance for the boys."[28] The difference, of course, is that these performance artists write their own scripts, not having to follow male ones.

Some performance artists have additionally espoused an aggressive feminism. Karen Finley (b. 1956), who performed acts of sexual degradation on herself, such as smearing her nude body with chocolate, became the object of a fierce controversy in 1990 when the National Endowment for the Arts withdrew a grant at the command of several enraged congressmen. Others, like Anderson, taking a less confrontational but still politically engaged approach, sought to mislead rather than rant. Anderson cultivated an androgynous persona with her "punk" hairstyle and unisex attire, deliberately downplaying her sexuality. Performance art is one way in which women have been able to wrest creative agency from its traditional custodians while maintaining, as Anderson whimsically suggests, their traditional "advantage" and without becoming authoritarian figures themselves. Performance art, as a site of female self-representation, thus found itself a natural ally of the feminist movement.

Performance art was primarily a downtown movement that expanded some of the approaches associated with Cage's earlier "happenings." A theatrical element has already been mentioned with respect to Crumb, to the ensembles of Reich and Glass, and to performances by the Kronos Quartet. The video operas by Robert Ashley (b. 1930) were another example of combining the musical, visual, and performative, usually employing a chant-like narration. Such activities seemed a natural consequence of composers performing themselves rather than writing for specialized groups as conservative and high Modernist composers did.

Downtown composers were ever-more influenced as well by popular culture. Glenn Branca (b. 1948) and Rhys Chatham (b. 1952) composed grand works for groups of electric guitars, with Branca writing more than a dozen symphonies and Chatham applying minimalist techniques to rock instrumentation. John Zorn (b. 1953) has been touted as "an archetypal example of the composer in the media age."[29] The composer himself admits that he has "an incredibly short attention span" and that his music is meant for listeners who, like him, grew up with television: "You've got to realize that speed is taking over the world. Look at the kids growing up with computers and video games."[30] This remark comes from the notes that accompany *Spillane* (1986), a twenty-five-minute collage balanced on the cusp between improvisation and composition, live performance and sample patchwork, that seemed determined to take eclecticism to its limit. In the early 1990s he founded a band called Masada in which he played saxophone and mixed Jewish traditions such as klezmer with jazz, pop, and experimental music.

Zorn first made his name as the leader of an improvising band that dazzled audiences with its quick style changes and a range of reference that recognized no boundaries, incorporating Josquin des Prez, TV jingles, Indian ragas, and every type of American pop. His self-proclaimed models were the soundtracks that accompanied the animated TV cartoons he grew up with (Bugs Bunny, Road Runner). Zorn's rapid-fire barrage jibed well with the emergence in 1981 of "Music Television" (MTV), where visual accompaniments were added to music tracks. Putting MTV on the map was the best-selling pop album of the century, Michael Jackson's *Thriller* (1982). The famous video of the title song was an enormous production number that combined music, dance, and visual effects; it had an operatic quality with respect to its relative length, general sense of spectacle, and Jackson's virtuosic vocal style which, as it happened, evoked the castrato tradition of unnaturally captivating artifice.

The Alleged Death of Classical Music

By the end of the twentieth century, uptown and downtown music were increasingly meeting midtown, where a rise in new patronage was in any case revitalizing the offerings of prestige institutions. This happened, however, amid endless predictions of the imminent demise of classical music. The traditional midtown audience, undermined by the decline in public music education and depleted by defections to pop, was said to be aging, indeed dying off. Record sales continued to decline; media coverage drastically diminished, as did the number of classical radio stations. Music publishers were less likely to take on new composers.

According to most reports all seemed dire. And yet some perspective is warranted, especially as we enter what is quite recent history. Laments about the decline of classical music have a very long history. The present age almost always looks back nostalgically to the past (usually to an imagined past). What the study of history makes clear, however, is that musical circumstances and culture are always adapting and changing. As the latest part of our story unfolds we therefore need to consider the implications of new concerns, technologies, markets, patronage, and talent. The rise of an eclectic musical Postmodernism meant that people listened to what they wanted: popular, classical, world music, whatever they liked. And not just what they wanted to hear but also when, where, and how they wanted. The Internet and digital players offered unprecedented choices. Technology meant that more people could hear a single live broadcast of a standard-repertory concert piece or opera than had ever heard the work in its entire history to that point. Composers and musicians could release their own self-produced scores and recordings. An explosion of interest

What the study of history makes clear is that musical circumstances and culture are always adapting and changing.

in Western classical music happened in other parts of the world, notably in Asian and South American countries, where governments cultivated extraordinary educational systems for training young musicians.

After the Cold War disconnect between high Modernist music and society, many Postmodern compositions displayed a cultural relevance that appealed to audiences. Opera, the genre that most elaborately combines the arts, enjoyed particular growth. New York's Metropolitan Opera, which had not presented a premiere since 1967, began to offer new operas, including *The Ghosts of Versailles* (1991) by John Corigliano; *The Voyage* (first performed on Columbus Day, 1992) by Philip Glass; and *The Great Gatsby* (1999) by John Harbison, based on the novel by F. Scott Fitzgerald. The Met and other prominent houses coproduced William Bolcom's *A View from the Bridge* (1999) and Tan Dun's *The First Emperor* (2006).

The San Francisco Opera commissioned several works, among them Conrad Susa's *Dangerous Liaisons*, after Pierre Choderlos de Laclos's eighteenth-century French epistolary novel; *A Streetcar Named Desire*, after Tennessee Williams's play, by André Previn (b. 1929); *Dead Man Walking* by Jake Heggie (b. 1961), based on a memoir by Sister Helen Prejean about her experiences with death-row prisoners, which had already been turned into a major Hollywood movie; and John Adams's *Doctor Atomic*, about Robert Oppenheimer and the development of the atomic bomb. The company also presented the American premiere of Olivier Messiaen's *Saint François d'Assise* in 2002. These were large and costly undertakings. Composers are unlikely to devote the time and resources necessary to write an opera without having concrete prospects for performance, but suddenly major opera houses in America and Europe seemed interested in offering new work, and audiences, for the most part, seemed eager to attend, often making them "hot tickets." Radio had long made opera available to large audiences, notably the Saturday afternoon broadcasts from the Met sponsored by Texaco. Live visual transmission from prominent opera houses, on TV, via the Internet, and in high definition to movie theaters, vastly expanded the audience for opera, while various kinds of subtitles now meant that everyone was much more likely to be able to follow the plot.

The resurgent interest in supporting classical compositions that audiences wanted to experience was evident in the concert hall as well. A notable case was John Corigliano's First Symphony, premiered in 1990 by the Chicago Symphony Orchestra and performed internationally by some hundred other orchestras. Along with its lavish orchestration, its rhetorical intensity, and its at-times-poignant use of collage, the symphony's topicality undoubtedly contributed to its initial success. In this memorial to victims of the AIDS epidemic, Corigliano dedicated each of the four movements to the memory of a deceased friend, giving public expression, as he says in the preface to the score, to his "feelings of loss, anger, and frustration," in alternation with "the bittersweet nostalgia of remembering."

In 2005 Joan Tower, who had previously written a series of pieces entitled "Fanfare for the Uncommon Woman" in an ironic nod to Copland's famous piece, composed *Made in America*, funded by the Ford Motor Company Fund and the National Endowment for the Arts. The work was performed by regional orchestras in every state in the country and uses "America the Beautiful" as its basic melodic material. Tower relates: "A musical struggle is heard throughout the work. Perhaps it is my unconscious reaction to the challenge of how do we keep America beautiful, dignified, and free."[31]

To commemorate the transfer of sovereignty of Hong Kong from the British empire to China, Tan Dun (b. 1957), a Chinese composer trained at the Beijing Conservatory and Columbia University, wrote *Symphony 1997 (Heaven Earth Mankind)* for orchestra, children's chorus, and an ensemble of Chinese temple bells. It contained a solo cello part fashioned for Yo-Yo Ma (b. 1955), a Paris-born American cellist of Chinese descent who had been making a specialty of crossover undertakings in which popular classical performers collaborated with artists from other walks of musical life. Ma also explored world music mixtures in what was called the Silk Road Project. Such pieces were suggestive of a new realization among composers and their patrons that contemporary classical music could (and perhaps should) have topical relevance, a view more commonly encountered in popular culture.

John Adams and *Nixon in China*

In 2002 the work that won the Pulitzer Prize in music was *On the Transmigration of Souls*, written to commemorate the first anniversary of the terrorist attacks on New York and Washington on September 11. Its composer was John Adams (Fig. 36-11), who had started his compositional career as a minimalist and who soon moved on to writing popularly successful operas and orchestral and choral music. Ten years younger than Reich and Glass, he enjoyed the benefits of the audience and critical acceptance they had opened up. His first big success, dating from 1977, was *Shaker Loops*, a string sextet. Adams was not only younger than his minimalist forefathers, but he also returned minimalism to its original West Coast geographical roots associated with Young and Riley. Born and raised in New England and educated at Harvard, he moved to San Francisco in the early 1970s and remained a prominent Bay Area presence.

Anthology Vol 3-65
Full CD VII, 38
Concise CD III, 48

Adams created his first opera, *Nixon in China* (1987; Fig. 36-12), in collaboration with poet Alice Goodman (b. 1959) and director Peter Sellars (b. 1957). It had been jointly commissioned by four houses: the Houston Grand Opera, the Brooklyn Academy of Music, the John F. Kennedy Center for the Performing Arts in Washington, D.C., and the Netherlands Opera. By the time of *Nixon*, Adams's music was set in what could be called a postminimalist style, in which the freely grouped and regrouped subtactile pulses and arpeggios of minimalism and the interesting textures obtained by pitting pulses at differing rates of speed in counterpoint were reconciled with a conventional harmonic idiom, naturalistic vocal declamation, a neat "numbers" format replete with entertaining choral and dance sequences, and references to popular music. A fairly standard orchestra was given a late-twentieth-century sonic edge by replacing the bassoons with a quartet of saxophones and by adding a pair of pianos and a keyboard sampler to the percussion section.

Figure 36-11 John Adams in rehearsal, 2002.

Nixon in China confounded expectations by being cast both as a farce and as a heroic opera that turned the title character as well as the Chinese leaders Mao Tse-tung and Chou En-lai into mythical representatives of their countries. The operatic mythologizing of Richard Nixon's most impressive diplomatic coup displeased a minority who objected to the way it helped turn memory away from the domestic scandal that ended his presidency. It disturbed others who objected to the way it cast the bloody Chinese Communist dictatorship, fresh from the excesses of the Cultural Revolution, in a possibly heroic light, although with a rather heavy layer of parody.

Figure 36-12 John Adams's opera *Nixon in China* directed by Peter Sellars at the English National Opera, London, in 2006, with Janis Kelly (Pat Nixon) and James Maddalena (Richard Nixon).

Music critic Alex Ross predicted that "a century from now audiences will still be fascinated by this opera, and that some listeners will have to double-check the plot summary in order to remember who Richard Nixon was."[32] Its value, like that of all great art, the critic implied, was independent of its relationship to external reality, and that value was its capacity to create mythic archetypes.

By the late 1990s Adams's orchestral music was the most often performed of any living classical American composer, both short orchestral curtain raisers such as *Short Ride in a Fast Machine* (1986) and large pieces such as *Harmonium* (1980–81) and *Harmonielehre* (1984–85). His music also garnered critical acclaim and prestigious prizes, including the Grawemeyer Award for his Violin Concerto (1994). The topicality of his operas continued with *The Death of Klinghoffer* (1991), based on the killing by Palestinian terrorists of an American Jew on board an Italian cruise ship in 1985, and *Doctor Atomic* (2005).

A New Spirituality

Peter Sellars, the dramaturgical mastermind of Adams's *Nixon*, *Klinghoffer*, and *Doctor Atomic* operas, pointed to another element beyond topicality that contributed to late-twentieth-century artistic success: "I think in this age of television and Hollywood film, if classical music is going to stick around, there'd better be a very good reason." Then he added, "We have to offer something that is not available otherwise. I think it is spiritual content, which is what's missing from the commercial culture that surrounds us." He was referring to another of his collaborations with Adams, a more overtly religious one: a nativity oratorio called *El Niño* (2000), commissioned by a consortium of illustrious international organizations: Théâtre du Châtelet in Paris, the San Francisco Symphony, Lincoln Center, London's Barbican Centre, and the British Broadcasting Corporation.

El Niño was one of a number of works of flamboyant "spiritual content" performed under prestigious auspices to solemnize the new millennium. Another, Philip Glass's Fifth Symphony (1999), was an oratorio in all but name, scored for five vocal soloists, mixed chorus, children's choir, and orchestra, with a text that draws on "a broad spectrum of many of the world's great 'wisdom' traditions," translated from Greek, Hebrew, Arabic, Persian, Sanskrit, Bengali, Chinese, Japanese, Tibetan, Hawaiian, Zuñi, Mayan, Bantu, and Bulu scriptures.[33] A further example was a cycle of four Passions—Matthew, Mark, Luke, and John—that the German choral conductor Helmut Rilling commissioned from four composers, one a German and three with conspicuously "multicultural" backgrounds. Luke went to Wolfgang Rihm (b. 1952), a neo-Expressionist German. Mark went to Oswaldo Golijov (b. 1960), an Argentinian-born Jew residing in the United States, who composed a lavish collage of Latin American, Afro-Cuban, and Jewish cantorial idioms. Matthew was assigned to Tan Dun and John to Sofia Gubaidulina, who by this time had left the Soviet Union and was living in Germany. The fact that Dun and Golijov were not Christian—the latter cheerfully admitting that it was only after receiving the commission that he looked into the New Testament for the first time—suggests that the impulse behind it was something other than religious in the customary or doctrinal sense of the word.

The new spirituality combined with the new topicality and multiculturalism to add further streams to musical life at the turn of the millennium. Dating from 2000 was a highly anticipated opera premiere: *L'amour de loin* (Love from Afar) by Finnish composer Kaija Saariaho (b. 1952; Fig. 36-13). Trained initially in her native Helsinki and then in Germany, Saariaho moved in 1982 to Paris, where she became involved with IRCAM. Although many of her early compositions had been vocal, in Paris she became interested in exploring tone color and seeing how electronics, tape, and computers could be exploited. Saariaho was thus identified to some extent with the Parisian spectralist composers, and by the 1990s her scores retained the textures and atmosphere characteristic of spectralism, but these were increasingly combined with lyricism and sections with rhythmic pulses.

Anthology Vol 3-66
Full CD VII, 39
Concise CD III, 49

Saariaho became attracted to the figure of the twelfth-century troubadour Jaufré Rudel, Prince of Blaye in Aquitaine, whose words she used in *Lonh* (1996) in preparation for writing an opera about the poet and the woman he loved from afar: Clémence, the Countess of Tripoli in Lebanon. Saariaho wrote *Lonh* for American soprano Dawn Upshaw, whom she heard sing the role of the Angel in a 1992 production of Messiaen's *Saint François d'Assise* at the prestigious Salzburg Festival. Messiaen's monumental opera in eight scenes, lasting some four hours, may be viewed as a descendent of Wagner's *Parsifal* and part of a tradition of theater pieces in which dramatic action is largely replaced by a series of tableaux with singers and chorus, more like an oratorio than an opera. Seeing Peter Sellars's imaginative staging of *Saint François* in Salzburg sparked Saariaho's desire to pursue something similar in collaboration with the director. *L'amour de loin* premiered in Salzburg in 2000, won the composer the Grawemeyer Award, and was soon taken up by opera houses internationally (Fig. 36-14).

Figure 36-13 Kaija Saariaho, 2004.

The Lebanese French writer Amin Maalouf wrote the libretto for the opera. It is set in twelfth-century Aquitaine, Tripoli, and

Figure 36-14 Scene from Kaija Saariaho's opera *L'amour de loin,* 2000.

aboard a ship traveling in between the two locations West and East. Besides the chorus, there are just three characters—the troubadour Jaufré, Countess Clémence, and "The Pilgrim," who acts as their intermediary. Jaufré, bored with his life, longs for a distant love, whom he extols in his poetry. While the chorus ridicules his wishes, The Pilgrim tells him of a woman far away who fulfills his dream. The Pilgrim returns to Tripoli and informs Clémence that Jaufré loves her and celebrates this "love from afar" in his songs. The Pilgrim goes back to Aquitaine, and Jaufré decides to undertake the voyage to meet Clémence. On the voyage he grows ill, and by the time he arrives he is dying. The two meet and profess their love as he dies in her arms. Clémence resolves to enter a convent. The opera ends in prayer, although a prayer ambiguously addressed to God and/or to her "love from afar."

While the subject matter of Medieval courtly love and the evocations of troubadour song situate *L'amour de loin* in a mythic past, the opposing settings in the West and East make possible an exploration of how the two different cultures influence one another, a topical subject at the start of the twenty-first century. In its subject matter Saariaho's opera draws on Wagner's *Tristan und Isolde,* Debussy's *Pelléas et Mélisande,* and Messiaen's *Saint François,* all set as well in the Middle Ages. The opera freely negotiates among Medieval, Modernist, and Postmodern musical styles, while its literary themes subtly address issues of national and gender identity as well as spirituality.

Such eclecticism, topicality, multiculturalism, and spirituality mark much of the music we have explored in this chapter. We will recall that American minimalists such as Reich and Glass as well as "Holy Minimalists" such as Pärt and Górecki were deeply involved personally with spiritual and religious matters. The list could be expanded to include many other leading composers. Such concerns may seem surprising in a largely secular, ironic, and Postmodern age. The burning question, however, is not the intent of the producers—the spirituality and faith of these composers—but, rather, why their music so appealed to audiences. Could the popular embrace of spirituality in general rather than of any religion in particular indicate the audience's desire for a way to return "aesthetically" to a world of "spiritual wholeness" without assuming the burdens of a genuine religious commitment, a commitment that many of the composers themselves practiced?

The literate tradition that we have traced in this book began about a thousand years ago, primarily in order to transmit and preserve sacred music. The invention of music printing some 500 years later (about 500 years ago) allowed for an enormous expansion of markets that facilitated a much broader dissemination of many more different kinds of music. Technological advances in the twentieth century represented another revolution, particularly by the end of the millennium, when the digital recording and distribution of music offered easy and nearly unlimited access to music of vastly disparate times and places. With the general recourse to fusion and eclecticism and with the globalization of Western music, an unprecedented variety of styles, approaches, and interests has come to distinguish the musical culture of our time. And so we must take leave of our story, without resolution. Our story ends, as it must, in the middle of things.

Summary

The variety of musical practice that proliferated in the later twentieth century has continued into the present time, even as the boundaries between different types of music have become less visible. This chapter surveyed several recent trends. In the 1970s and '80s, the terms "uptown," "midtown," and "downtown" had come to designate very different musical worlds. Although the terms are based on the locations of New York City neighborhoods associated with these styles, they can serve as general labels for American composers and their attitudes toward art and society. Uptown composers continued the academic legacy of Milton Babbitt. Midtown composers, associated with mainstream concert audiences, continued the tradition of Leonard Bernstein, Aaron Copland, and Samuel Barber. Downtown composers were associated with experimental trends, continuing the legacy of Charles Ives, John Cage, and the minimalists.

Since the late twentieth century, these categories have broken down, in part through the influence of Postmodernism. Postmodernism is an umbrella term that covers a group of interrelated intellectual, social, and artistic trends. In historical thought, Postmodernism involves a radical questioning of previous belief systems and values, including the idea of historical progress that has exerted such a powerful influence on Western art music. In the arts, Postmodernism is reflected in an increasing influence of multiculturalism and the dissolution of traditional boundaries between high and low art as well as the prevalence of stylistic collage and pastiche.

In response to the Postmodernist impulse, collage and pastiche became increasingly common in music in the 1960s and '70s. Collage is the simultaneous use of disparate musical elements, with no effort to unify them. *Sinfonia* (1968) by Luciano Berio (1925–2003), for example, combines vocalized sounds, quotations from the concert repertory, and readings from the anthropologist Claude Lévi-Strauss. George Crumb (b. 1929) has made particularly effective use of collage in sparsely textured works that incorporate disparate quotations to symbolize the inclusive relatedness of different times and places.

Many composers felt that the pressures to be innovative and the prohibition against composing in older styles had robbed them of the ability to be expressive. Increasingly they rejected the narrative of progress and began deliberately to compose in styles associated with older music, a process known as *pastiche*. George Rochberg (1918–2005), previously a Modernist, initially shocked his audience by writing the third movement of his Third Quartet (1972) in the style of Beethoven. David del Tredici (b. 1937) turned away from Modernism in the late 1960s and began to write works inspired by Lewis Carroll's *Alice's Adventures in Wonderland*, with a large, lush sound that has appealed to mainstream audiences. A long list of American composers followed in these footsteps. Embracing a return to tonality to various degrees, these composers have been labeled as "neo-tonalists" or "neo-Romanticists." Similar trends prevailed in Eastern Europe. In the 1970s, Modernist composers György Ligeti and Krzysztof Penderecki turned toward neo-Romanticism, and Alfred Schnittke (1934–98) turned to collage, returning to timeless grand themes, framed simply as contrasts, as in his Third String Quartet (1983). Sofia Gubaidulina (b. 1931) composed pieces such as *In croce* (1979) that showed her interest in spirituality.

At the same time that these composers rejected Modernism, some composers continued writing works in the Modernist vein, including Karlheinz Stockhausen, Elliott Carter, and younger advocates of the "New Complexity," such as Brian Ferneyhough (b. 1943). Much research in sound and technology was centered around IRCAM, an electro-acoustic music institute in Paris founded by Pierre Boulez in 1977.

The influence of technology on the musical experience—from creation to production and performance—newly engages questions of written and literate music. The ability to produce complex, intricate works without performers and notation has opened up the potential for a postliterate art music. A continuing influence of multimedia and physical presence is manifest in the genre known as *performance art*. The term incorporates a wide range of diverse practices, from the vocalizations of Meredith Monk (b. 1942) to the multimedia shows of Laurie Anderson (b. 1947). The common thread is that these performances cannot be reduced to notes on a page.

Since the later decades of the twentieth century, art music has experienced sagging CD sales and received far less attention in the American media. At the same time, new operas have had successful premieres. Many of these are on contemporary topics, such as *Nixon in China* (1987) and *Doctor Atomic* (2005) by John Adams (b. 1947), whereas others are settings of modern literary classics, such as *A View from the Bridge* (1999) by William Bolcom (b. 1938) and *The Great Gatsby* (2000) by John Harbison (b. 1938). The new millennium sparked an interest in spirituality, topicality, and multiculturalism among composers, evident in Kaija Saariaho's, opera *L'amour de loin* (2000).

Study Questions

1. Briefly explain the differences between uptown, midtown, and downtown composers, and give some examples of each. How are these categories useful, and why do you think they began to break down?
2. Explain Postmodernism. How does it differ from Modernism? How do collage, pastiche, performance art, and neo-Romanticism reflect a Postmodernist aesthetic?
3. Since the nineteenth century, historicism has been a defining feature of the Western musical narrative. How does Postmodernism pose a challenge to this narrative? Which composers and trends of this chapter best represent the ideals of historicism, and which pose the greatest challenge to it?
4. Describe the continuing influence of collage in the last four decades. Describe the approaches that Luciano Berio and Alfred Schnittke have taken to collage.
5. What is pastiche, and how is it reflected in the works of George Rochberg?
6. What is performance art? How do performance artists such as Meredith Monk and Laurie Anderson challenge traditional concepts of music and musical categories?
7. Explain and analyze the impact that technology has had on the culture and practice of art music.
8. Which genres of art music have been the most successful with audiences in the decades since 1990? Why do you think this is so?
9. In what ways does Kaija Saariaho's opera *L'amour de loin* reflect society in the new millennium?

Key Terms

collage
eclecticism
IRCAM
MIDI
neo-Romanticism
neo-tonalism
New Complexity
pastiche
performance art
Postmodernism
sampler
sequencer

Notes

Abbreviations

JAMS: *Journal of the American Musicological Society*, 1948–

MWW: *Music in the Western World: A History in Documents*, 2nd ed., eds. Piero Weiss and Richard Taruskin (New York, 2008).

NGDMM: *New Grove Dictionary of Music and Musicians*, 2nd ed., ed. Stanley Sadie and John Tyrrell (London, 2001).

SRMH: *Source Readings in Music History*, ed. Oliver Strunk, rev. ed., gen. ed. Leo Treitler (New York, 1998).

Chapter 1

1. Anne Draffkorn Kilmer, Richard L. Crocker, and Robert R. Brown, *Sounds from Silence: Recent Discoveries in Ancient Near Eastern Music* (Berkeley, CA, 1976).
2. The extant fragments of ancient Greek music have been collected and given new and authoritative transcriptions in Egert Pöhlmann and Martin L. West, *Documents of Ancient Greek Music: The Extant Melodies and Fragments* (New York, 2001). The translation and transcription here is from Thomas J. Mathiesen, *Apollo's Lyre: Greek Music and Music Theory in Antiquity and the Middle Ages* (Lincoln, NE, 1999), p. 150.
3. Plato, *Republic*, Book 3, trans. Paul Shorey (Cambridge, MA, 1930), 444B.
4. MWW, p. 34.
5. *SRMH*, p. 217.
6. Jacques Paul Migne, ed., *Patrologiae cursus completus, Series Latina*, Vol. 37 (Paris, 1853), p. 1953, trans. Gustave Reese in *Music in the Middle Ages* (New York, 1940), p. 64.
7. J. M. Hanssens, ed., *Amalarii episcope opera liturgica omnia*, Vol. 18 (Studi e testi, 140; Vatican City, 1950), p. 54. Translation adapted from that of Daniel J. Sheerin given in Ruth Steiner, "The Gregorian Chant Melismas of Christmas Matins," in J. C. Graue, ed., *Essays on Music in Honor of Charles Warren Fox* (Rochester, NY, 1979), p. 6.
8. The best translation of the preface to Notker's *Liber hymnorum* is Richard Crocker's, in *The Early Medieval Sequence* (Berkeley, CA, 1976), pp. 1–2. An adaptation of it can be found in *MWW*, p. 39.
9. Giraldus Cambrensis, *Descriptio Cambriae*, trans. adapted from that of Ernest H. Sanders in F. W. Sternfeld, ed., *Music from the Middle Ages to the Renaissance*, Vol. 1 from the History of Western Music series (New York, 1973), p. 264, by comparison with that in Shai Burstyn, "Gerald of Wales and the *Sumer* Canon," *Journal of Musicology* 2 (1983): 135, where the original Latin may also be found.
10. Barbara Haggh, "The Celebration of the 'Recollectio Festorum Beatae Mariae Virginis,' 1457–1987," *International Musicological Society Congress Report* 14 (Bologna, 1987), iii, pp. 559–71.

Chapter 2

1. St. Basil, *The Letters*, Vol. 4, trans. Roy J. Deferrari (London, 1934), p. 419.
2. Margarita Egan, trans., *The Vidas of the Troubadours* (New York, 1984), p. 28.
3. H. J. Chaytor, *The Troubadours* (London, 1912), pp. 38–9; the format of the dialogue has been adapted here to make it clearer.
4. *Les Chansons de Conon de Béthune*, ed. Axel Wallensköld (Paris, 1968).
5. Christopher Page, *Voices and Instruments of the Middle Ages* (Berkeley, CA, 1986), p. 77.
6. *MWW*, p. 52.
7. Craig Wright, "Leoninus: Poet and Musician," *JAMS* 39 (1986): 1–35.
8. An English translation is available: Johannes de Grocheio, *Concerning Music*, 2nd ed., trans. Albert Seay (Colorado Springs, 1974).
9. Grocheio, *Concerning Music*, p. 16.
10. Ibid.
11. Ibid.
12. Ibid.

Chapter 3

1. See Anna Maria Busse Berger, *Mensuration and Proportion Signs: Origin and Evolution* (Oxford, 1993), Chap. 2.
2. *SRMH*, p. 268.
3. Jacobus de Liège, *Speculum musicae*, Book VII, Chap. 43.
4. *De musica libellus* (Anonymus 7), in Coussemaker, *Scriptorum de musica medii aevi nova series*, Vol. 1 (Four vols., Paris, 1864–76), no. 7.
5. Kurt von Fischer, "'Portraits' von Piero, Giovanni da Firenze und Jacopo da Bologna in einer Bologneser-Handschrift des 14. Jahrhunderts?" *Musica Disciplina* 27 (1973): 61–64.
6. Craig Wright, "Dufay's *Nuper rosarum flores*, King Solomon's Temple, and the Veneration of the Virgin," *JAMS* 47 (1994): 395–441.
7. Giannozzo Manetti, quoted in G. Dufay, *Opera omnia*, ed. Heinrich Besseler, Vol. 2 (Rome, 1966), xxvii.

8. Quoted in James Haar, ed. *European Music 1520–1640* (Woodbridge, UK, 2006), p. 35.
9. Quoted in Bonnie J. Blackburn, *Composition, Printing, and Performance: Studies in Renaissance Music* (Burlington, UK, 2000), p. 269.
10. Cosimo Bartoli, *Ragionamenti Accademici* (1567), quoted in Jessie Ann Owens, "Music Historiography and the Definition of 'Renaissance,'" *MLA Notes* 47 (1990–91): p. 311.

Chapter 4

1. The phrase appears in le Franc's *Champion des dames* (ca. 1440); *NGDMM* 15:932.
2. Quoted in Bonnie J. Blackburn, *Composition, Printing, and Performance: Studies in Renaissance Music* (Burlington, UK, 2000), p. 269.
3. Michael Long, "Celestial Motion and Musical Structure in the Late Middle Ages," unpublished paper (1995), by kind courtesy of the author.
4. Charles Burney, *A General History of Music*, ed. Frank Mercer (New York, 1957), Vol. 1, p. 731.
5. See Craig Wright, *The Maze and the Warrior: Symbols in Architecture, Theology, and Music* (Cambridge, MA, 2001), Chap. 7, "Sounds and Symbols of an Armed Man."
6. See William F. Prizer, "Music and Ceremonial in the Low Countries: Philip the Fair and the Order of the Golden Fleece," *Early Music History* 5 (1985): 113–53.
7. Tinctoris, *De inventione et usu musice* (Naples, ca. 1482), ed. K. Weinmann: *Johannes Tinctoris und sein unbekannter Traktat 'De inventione et usu musicae'* (Regensburg, Germany, 1917), p. 31.
8. Bonnie J. Blackburn, "A Lost Guide to Tinctoris's Teachings Recovered," *Early Music History* 1 (1981): 45.

Chapter 5

1. Martin Luther, *Table Talk* (1538), quoted in Helmut Osthoff, *Josquin Desprez*, Vol. 2 (Tutzing, Germany, 1965), p. 9.
2. Quoted in Glenn Watkins, *Gesualdo: The Man and His Music* (Oxford, 1991), p. 96.
3. The phrase has been traced back to a seventh-century commentary on Horace's *Ars Poetica* by William Ringler in "*Poeta Nascitur Non Fit*: Some Notes on the History of an Aphorism," *Journal of the History of Ideas* 2 (1941): 497–504. It became commonplace in the sixteenth century.
4. L. Matthews and P. Merkley, "Iudochus de Picardia and Jossequin Lebloitte dit Desprez: The Names of the Singer(s)," *Journal of Musicology* 16 (1998): 200–26.
5. Letter from Gian di Artiganova to Hercules of Ferrara, 2 September 1502, in Osthoff, *Josquin Desprez*, Vol. 1 (Tutzing, Germany, 1962), pp. 211–12. For a translation of the full text of the letter, see *MWW*, p. 84.
6. Girolamo da Sestola (alias "il Coglia"), letter to Hercules of Ferrara, 14 August 1502, quoted in Lewis Lockwood, *Music in Renaissance Ferrara, 1400–1505* (Cambridge, MA, 1984), p. 203.
7. Gioseffo Zarlino, *Le istitutioni harmoniche*, Vol. 3 (Venice, Italy, 1558), p. 66.
8. Herbert Kellman, "Josquin and the Courts of the Netherlands and France: The Evidence of the Sources," in Edward E. Lowinsky and Bonnie J. Blackburn, eds. *Josquin des Prez* (London, 1976), p. 208.
9. T. Noblitt, "Die Datierung der Handschrift Mus. Ms. 3154 der Staatsbibliothek Munchen," *Die Musikforschung* 27 (1974): 36–56.
10. Gioseffo Zarlino, *Istitutione harmoniche* (Venice, 1558), Vol. 1, *Proemio*; quoted in Jessie Ann Owens, "Music Historiography and the Definition of 'Renaissance,'" *MLA Notes* 42 (1990–91): 314.
11. Zarlino, *The Art of Counterpoint* (*Istitutione harmoniche*, Vol. 3), trans. G. Marco and C. Palisca (New York, 1968), p. 289.
12. Ibid., p. 70.
13. Hermann Finck, *Practica musica . . . exempla variorum signorum, proportionum et canonum, iudicium de tonis, ac quaedam de arte suaviter et artificiose cantandi continens* (Wittenberg, Germany, 1556), quoted in George Nugent with Eric Jas, "Gombert," *NGDMM* Vol. 10, p. 119.
14. Letter from Cirillo Franco to Ugolino Gualteruzzi, trans. Lewis Lockwood, in *The Counter-Reformation and the Masses of Vincenzo Ruffo* (Venice, Italy, 1970), p. 129.
15. Trans. Lockwood, in *Palestrina, Pope Marcellus Mass* (New York, 1975), p. 26.
16. Ibid., p. 18.
17. Ibid., pp. 22–23.
18. Trans. Gustave Reese, in *Music in the Renaissance*, rev. ed. (New York, 1959), p. 449.
19. Trans. Lockwood, in *Palestrina, Pope Marcellus Mass*, p. 21.
20. Agostino Agazzari, *Del sonare sopra il basso con tutti gli stromenti*, trans. Oliver Strunk, in *SRMH*, p. 628.
21. Giuseppe Baini, *Memorie storico-critiche della vita e delle opera di Giovanni Pierluigi da Palestrina* (Rome, Italy, 1828), p. 216; trans. Lewis Lockwood, in *Palestrina, Pope Marcellus Mass*, p. 35.
22. Luigi Barzini, *The Italians* (New York, 1964), p. 308.
23. Quoted in Peter Le Huray, *Music and the Reformation in England, 1549–1660*, 2nd ed. (Cambridge, 1978), p. 9.
24. Richard Charteris, *Alfonso Ferrabosco the Elder (1543–1588): A Thematic Catalogue of His Music with a Biographical Calendar* (New York, 1984), p. 14.
25. Ferdinand Richardson, "In Eandem Thomae Tallisii, et Guilielmi Birdi Musicam," *Cantiones, Quae ab Argumento Sacrae Vocantur* (London, 1575), facsimile edition (Leeds, England, 1976), n.p.
26. See Joseph Kerman, "Old and New in Byrd's *Cantiones Sacrae*, in *Essays on Opera and English Music in Honour of Sir Jack Westrup*, ed. F. W. Sternfeld, N. Fortune, and E. Olleson (Oxford, 1975), pp. 25–43.
27. Joseph Kerman, *The Masses and Motets of William Byrd* (Berkeley, CA, 1981), p. 188.
28. Dedication of *Gradualia*, Book I (1605) to King James I, adapted from *SRMH*, p. 378.
29. See Joseph Kerman, "Byrd's Settings of the Ordinary of the Mass," *JAMS* 32 (1979): 416–17.

Chapter 6

1. This remark is reliably attributed to the English Methodist preacher Rowland Hill (1744–1833; see *The Oxford Dictionary of Quotations*, 3rd ed. [New York, 1979]), only by tradition to Luther. It is resisted by many modern Lutherans.
2. Trans. Ulrich S. Leupold, in *Luther's Works*, 53 (Philadelphia, 1965), pp. 323–24.
3. *D. Martin Luthers Werke: Tischreden*, ed. E. Kroker (Weimar, 1912–21), No. 968.
4. Martin Luther, preface to J. Walther, *Geystliches gesangk Buchleyn* (Wittenberg, 1524).
5. *The Spiritual Exercises of Ignatius Loyol*, Article XIII, trans. W. H. Longridge (London, 1908), p. 119.
6. St. Teresa of Avila, *Vida* (1565), in René Fülöp-Miller, *Saints That Moved the World* (New York, 1945), p. 375.
7. Adriano Banchieri, *Conclusioni nel suono dell'organo* (Bologna, 1609), in Frank T. Arnold, *The Art of Accompaniment from a Thorough-Bass* (London, 1931), p. 74.
8. Trans. Gustave Reese, in *Music in the Renaissance*, rev. ed. (New York, 1959), p. 449.
9. Baldesar Castiglione, *The Book of the Courtier*, trans. Charles S. Singleton (Garden City, NY, 1959), p. 60.
10. For the main revisionist account, see James Haar and Iain Fenlon, *The Italian Madrigal in the Early Sixteenth Century: Sources and Interpretation* (Cambridge and New York, 1988).
11. G. M. Artusi, *L'Artusi, ovvero, Delle imperfezioni della moderna musica* (Venice, Italy, 1600), in *SRMH*, p. 527.
12. Alfonso Fontanelli to Duke Alfonso II of Ferrara, 18 February 1594; in Glenn Watkins, *Gesualdo: The Man and His Music* (Chapel Hill, 1973), pp. 245–46.

Chapter 7

1. Quoted in Tim Carter, "The Concept of the Baroque" in James Haar, ed. *European Music 1520–1640* (Woodbridge, UK, 2006), p. 38.
2. Girolamo Mei, letter to Vincenzo Galilei (8 May 1572), trans. Claude V. Palisca, in *The Florentine Camerata: Documentary Studies and Translations* (New Haven, CT, 1989), p. 63.
3. Vincenzo Galilei, *Dialogo della musica antica e della moderna*, ed. Favio Fano (Milan, 1947), pp. 130–31; see translation in *MWW*, pp. 140–41.
4. Galilei, *Dialogo*, p. 162, *MWW*, p. 141.
5. Giulio Caccini, preface to *Le nuove musiche* (1601), ed. Angelo Solerti, in *Le origini del melodrama: Testimonianze dei contemporanei* (Turin, 1903), p. 56, trans. Piero Weiss in *MWW*, p. 143.
6. Ibid., p. 144.
7. Caccini, preface to *Le nuove musiche*, trans. John Playford, in *A Breefe Introduction to the Skill of Musick* (London, 1654), in *SRMH*, p. 611.
8. *SRMH*, pp. 660.
9. Marco da Gagliano, Preface to *La Dafne*, trans. Piero Weiss in *MWW*, p. 149.
10. Peri, Preface to *Euridice*, in Solerti, *Le origini del melodrama: Testimonianze*, p. 44.
11. Nino Pirotta, "Monteverdi and the Problems of Opera," in *Music and Culture in Italy from the Middle Ages to the Baroque* (Cambridge, MA, 1984), p. 248.
12. Claudio Monteverdi, *Tutte le opere*, ed. G. Francesco Malipiero, Vol. 10 (Vienna, 1929), pp. 69–72; *MWW*, p. 146.
13. The letter may be found complete, in English translation, in *The Monteverdi Companion*, ed. Denis Arnold and Nigel Fortune (New York, 1968), pp. 52–56, also in *MWW*, pp. 153–55.
14. See Ellen Rosand, "The Descending Tetrachord: An Emblem of Lament," *Musical Quarterly* 65 (1979): 346–59.
15. Percy A. Scholes, ed., *Dr. Burney's Musical Tours in Europe*, Vol. 1 (London, 1959), pp. 247–48.
16. Ibid., pp. 247–48.

Chapter 8

1. Quoted in Lorenzo Bianconi, *Music in the Seventeenth Century*, trans. David Bryant (Cambridge, 1987), p. 95.
2. Heinrich Schütz, letter to the Elector of Saxony (1651), trans. Piero Weiss, in P. Weiss, *Letters of Composers Through Six Centuries* (Philadelphia, 1967), pp. 46–51; abridged in *MWW*, pp. 157–59.
3. Ibid.
4. See *The Treatises of Christoph Bernhard*, trans. Walter Hilse, *The Music Forum*, Vol. 3 (New York, 1973); excerpts printed in *MWW*, pp. 159–61.
5. *NGDMM*, 22:31.
6. Anthony Newcomb, "Courtesans, Muses, or Musicians? Professional Women Musicians in Sixteenth-Century Italy," in *Women Making Music: The Western Art Tradition, 1150–1950*, eds. Jane Bowers and Judith Tick (Urbana, 1986), p. 103.
7. Quoted in Ellen Rosand, "The Voice of Barbara Strozzi," in *Women Making Music*, p. 174.
8. See Suzanne G. Cusick, "Thinking from Women's Lives: Francesca Caccini after 1627," *Musical Quarterly* 77 (1993): 484–507.
9. Jacques Bonnet, *Histoire de la musique*, Vol. 3 (Amsterdam, 1725), p. 322.
10. J. J. Rousseau, *Confessions* (New York, n.d.), p. 395; see also Rousseau's *Lettre sur la musique française* (1753), in *SRMH*, pp. 895–908.
11. Dan H. Lawrence, ed., *Shaw's Music: The Complete Musical Criticism in Three Volumes*, Vol. 1 (London, 1981), p. 559.

Chapter 9

1. Pier Francesco Tosi, *Observations on the Florid Song; or, Sentiments on the Ancient and Modern Singers*, trans. J. E. Galliard (London, 1742), pp. 128–29.
2. Quoted in Jean-Jacques Rousseau, *Dictionnaire de musique* (Paris, 1768), p. 452.

Chapter 10

1. Johann Joachim Quantz, *On Playing the Flute*, trans. Edward R. Reilly (New York, 1975), p. 341.

2. François Couperin, *L'art de toucher le clavecin (The Art of Playing the Harpsichord)*, ed. and trans. Margery Halford (Van Nuys, CA, 1974), p. 14.
3. See Susan McClary, "The Blasphemy of Talking Politics during Bach Year," in *Music and Society: The Politics of Composition, Performance and Reception*, eds. Susan McClary and Richard Leppert (Cambridge, 1987), and Michael Marissen, *The Social and Religious Designs of J. S. Bach's Brandenburg Concertos* (Princeton, NJ, 1995).

Chapter 11

1. John Brown, *A Dissertation on the Rise, Union, and Power, the Progressions, Separations, and Corruptions, of Poetry and Music* (London, 1763), p. 218; quoted in Howard E. Smither, *A History of the Oratorio*, Vol. 2 (Chapel Hill, NC, 1977), p. 255.
2. See Sedley Taylor, *The Indebtedness of Handel to Works by Other Composers* (Cambridge, UK, 1906); John Roberts, "Handel and Vinci's 'Didone Abbandonata': Revisions and Borrowings," *Music & Letters* 68 (1987), pp. 159–202; and Roberts, "Handel and Charles Jennen's Italian Opera Manuscripts," in *Music and Theatre: Essays in Honour of Winton Dean*, ed. Nigel Fortune (Cambridge, 1987).
3. Quoted in John Roberts, "Handel and Charles Jennen's Italian Opera Manuscripts," p. 192.
4. "Short But Most Necessary Draft for a Well-Appointed Church Music," in Hans T. David and Arthur Mendel, eds., *The Bach Reader*, rev. ed. (New York, 1966), pp. 120–24.
5. Joshua Rifkin, "Bach's Chorus," *Musical Times* 123 (1982): 747–54.
6. Burney, *A General History of Music*, ed. F. Mercer, Vol. 1 (New York, 1957), p. 21.
7. Carl Friedrich Zelter to Johann Wolfgang von Goethe (1827), quoted in Richard Taruskin, *Text and Act* (New York, 1995), p. 310.
8. Johann Adolph Scheibe, "Letter from an Able Musikant Abroad" (1737), in David and Mendel, *The Bach Reader*, p. 238.
9. Domenico Scarlatti, Preface to *Essercizi per gravicembalo* (London, 1738); quoted in Ralph Kirkpatrick, *Domenico Scarlatti* (Princeton, NJ, 1953), p. 102.
10. Thomas Twining, *Aristotle's Treatise on Poetry, Translated: With Notes on the Translation, and on the Original; And Two Dissertations, on Poetical, and Musical, Imitation*, 2nd ed. (London, 1812), p. 66.
11. Burney, *A General History of Music*, Vol. 2, p. 706.

Chapter 12

1. First reported (or invented) in Friedrich Rochlitz, "Karl Philipp Emmanuel Bach," *Für Freunde der Tonkunst*, Vol. 4 (1832), p. 308.
2. See Daniel Heartz, *Haydn, Mozart and the Viennese School: 1740–1780* (New York, 1995); and *Music in European Capitals: The Galant Style, 1720–1780* (New York, 2003).
3. F. W. Marpurg, *Der critische Musicus an der Spree*, No. 27 (Berlin, 2 September 1749), p. 215.
4. C. P. E. Bach, *Versuch über die wahre Art das Clavier zu spielen* (Berlin, 1753), p. 119.
5. C. P. E. Bach, *Versuch*, pp. 122–23, trans. Piero Weiss in *MWW*, p. 230.
6. C. P. E. Bach, *Essay on the True Art of Playing Keyboard Instruments*, trans. William J. Mitchell (New York, 1949), p. 430.
7. C. P. E. Bach to H. W. von Gerstenberg (1773); quoted in Eugene Helm, "The 'Hamlet' Fantasy and the Literary Element in C. P. E. Bach's Music," *Musical Quarterly* 58 (1972): 271.
8. C. P. E. Bach, *Versuch*, p. 121, trans. Piero Weiss, *MWW*, p. 230.
9. Burney, *A General History of Music*, Vol. 2, p. 866.
10. Ibid.
11. Quoted in Stephen Roe, "Johann Christian Bach," in *NGDMM* Vol. 2, p. 417.
12. Aristotle, *Poetics*, trans. Kenneth A. Telford (Chicago, 1961), pp. 10–29.
13. Denis Diderot, *Le Neveu de Rameau*, trans. Wye J. Allanbrook in "Comic Flux and Comic Precision," lectures delivered at the University of California at Berkeley in the fall of 1994, forthcoming as *The Secular Commedia: Comic Mimesis in Late Eighteenth-Century Music* (Ernest Bloch Lectures, Berkeley CA).
14. J. J. Rousseau, *Confessions* (New York, n.d.), p. 395; see also Rousseau's *Lettre sur la musique française* (1753), in *SRMH*, pp. 895–908.
15. Christoph Willibald Gluck, Preface to *Alceste*, trans. Piero Weiss in *MWW*, p. 255.
16. I. F. Edlen von Mosel, *Ueber das Leben und die Werke des Anton Salieri, k. k. Hofkepellmeister* (Vienna, 1827), p. 93; trans. Daniel Heartz in "Coming of Age in Bohemia: The Musical Apprenticeships of Benda and Gluck," *Journal of Musicology* 6 (1988): 524.
17. J. J. Rousseau, *Extrait d'une réponse du petit faiseur à son prête-nom, sur un morceau de l'Orphée de M. le chevalier Gluck* (Geneva, 1781).
18. Wye J. Allanbrook, *Rhythmic Gesture in Mozart* (Chicago, 1983), p. 16.
19. Immanuel Kant, "An Answer to the Question: What Is Enlightenment?" (*Beantwortung der Frage: Was ist Aufklärung?*, 1784), trans. James Schmidt, in *What Is Enlightenment? Eighteenth-Century Answers and Twentieth-Century Questions*, ed. James Schmidt (Berkeley, CA, 1996), p. 58.
20. Ibid., p. 59.
21. Leo Gershoy, *From Despotism to Revolution, 1763–1789* (New York, 1944), p. 105.

Chapter 13

1. Charles Burney, *The Present State of Music in Germany, the Netherlands, and United Provinces* (2nd ed., London, 1775), p. 95.
2. C. F. D. Schubart, *Ideen zu einer Ästhetik der Tonkunst* (Vienna, 1806), p. 130.
3. A. C. Dies, interview with Haydn, 15 April 1805; in A. C. Dies, *Biographische Nachrichten von Joseph Haydn* (Vienna, 1810), p. 17.
4. Georg August Griesinger, *Biographische Notizen über Joseph Haydn* (Leipzig, 1810), p. 17.

5. Ibid., p. 19; third paragraph follows Dies, *Biographische Nachrichten*, p. 48.
6. James Webster, *Haydn's "Farewell" Symphony and the Idea of Classical Style* (Cambridge, 1991).
7. H. C. Robbins Landon, *Haydn: Chronicle and Works*, Vol. 2 (Bloomington, 1978), p. 302.
8. Griesinger, *Biographische Notizen*, p. 60.
9. Quoted in H. C. Robbins Landon, *Haydn: Chronicle and Works*, Vol. 3 (Bloomington, 1976), p. 309.
10. Ibid., p. 308.
11. Ibid., Vol. 2, p. 283.
12. Donald Francis Tovey, *Essays in Musical Analysis*, Vol. 5 (London, 1937), p. 115.

Chapter 14

1. Leopold Mozart to his daughter, 16 February 1785; Emily Anderson, *The Letters of Mozart and his Family*, translated and edited by Emily Anderson (New York, 1985), p. 886.
2. Mozart to his father, 11 September 1778; ibid., p. 612.
3. Leopold Mozart to Lorenz Hagenauer, 30 July 1768; ibid., p. 89.
4. Maynard Solomon, *Mozart: A Life* (New York, 1995), p. 224.
5. Mozart to his father, 7 February 1778; Anderson, *Letters of Mozart*, p. 468.
6. Cliff Eisen, ed., *New Mozart Documents* (Stanford, CA, 1991), p. 78.
7. Franz Niemtschek, *Leben des K. K. Kapellmeisters Wolfgang Gottlieb Mozart, nach Originalquellen beschrieben* (Prague, 1798); quoted in Thomas Bauman, *W. A. Mozart: Die Entführung aus dem Serail* (Cambridge, 1987), p. 89).
8. Mozart to his father, 26 September 1781; Anderson, *Letters of Mozart*, p. 769.
9. Ibid.
10. Mozart to his father, 7 May 1783; ibid., pp. 847–48.
11. Ibid., p. 848.
12. Ibid.
13. *The Memoirs of Lorenzo Da Ponte*, trans. Elisabeth Abbott (New York, 1959), p. 232.
14. Mozart to his father, 3 July 1778; Anderson, *Letters of Mozart*, p. 558.
15. Mozart to his father, 28 December 1782; ibid., p. 833.
16. H. C. Robbins Landon, ed. *The Mozart Compendium* (New York, 1990), p. 386.
17. Haydn to Marianne von Genzinger, 20 December 1791; H. C. Robbins Landon, ed., *Joseph Haydn: Gesammelte Briefe und Aufzeichnungen* (Kassel, 1965), 269.
18. Wilhelm Wackenroder, *Phantasien über die Kunst, für Freunde der Kunst* (Hamburg, 1799); in Wilhelm Wackenroder, *Werke und Briefe* (Heidelberg, 1967), p. 254.
19. Leopold Mozart to his son, 18 October 1777; Anderson, *Letters of Mozart*, p. 331.
20. See Julia Moore, "Mozart in the Market-Place," *Journal of the Royal Musical Association* 114 (1989): 22.
21. Mozart to his father, 26 May 1781; Anderson, *Letters of Mozart*, p. 736.
22. Mozart to his father, 23 January 1782, ibid., p. 795.
23. Mozart to Michael Puchberg; 12 July 1789, ibid., p. 930.
24. Heinrich Christoph Koch, *Musikalisches Lexicon* (Frankfurt am Main, 1802), col. 354.
25. Carl Czerny, *Vollständiges Lehrbuch der musikalischen Composition*, Vol. 1 (Vienna, 1834), p. 159; see Jane R. Stevens, "Theme, Harmony, and Texture in Classic-Romantic Descriptions of Concerto First-Movement Form," *JAMS* 27 (1974): 47.
26. H. C. Koch, *Versuch einer Anleitung zur Composition*, Vol. 3 (Leipzig, 1793), p. 339; quoted in Stevens, "Theme, Harmony, and Texture," p. 91.
27. Quoted by Neal Zaslaw in *The Compleat Mozart: A Guide to the Musical Works of Wolfgang Amadeus Mozart* (New York, 1990), p. 305.
28. Mozart to his father, 22 January 1783; Anderson, *Letters of Mozart*, p. 837.

Chapter 15

1. *The Confessions of Jean-Jacques Rousseau* (New York, n.d.), p. 1.
2. E. T. A. Hoffmann, "Beethoven's Instrumental Music" (1813), in *SRMH*, p. 1193. Unless otherwise noted, all Hoffmann quotations in this chapter are drawn from that essay.
3. Edmund Burke, "A Philosophical Enquiry into the Origin of Our Ideas of the Sublime and the Beautiful," in Peter le Huray and James Day, eds., *Music and Aesthetics in the Eighteenth and Early Nineteenth Centuries* (Cambridge, 1981), pp. 70–71.
4. *Ludwig van Beethovens Konversationshefte*, Karl-Heinz Köhler, Grita Herre, eds. (Leipzig, 1972), Vol. 1, p. 235.
5. Carl Dahlhaus, *Nineteenth-Century Music*, trans. J. B. Robinson (Berkeley CA, 1989), p. 9.
6. Benedict Anderson, *Imagined Communities: Reflections on the Origin and Spread of Nationalism* (London, 1983).
7. Richard Wagner, "The Art-Work of the Future," in *Richard Wagner's Prose Works*, trans. W. Ashton Ellis, Vol. 1 (London, 1895), p. 123.
8. Stanley Hoffman, "Us and Them," *The New Republic*, 12 July 1993, p. 32.

Chapter 16

1. O. G. Sonneck, *Beethoven: Impressions by His Contemporaries* (New York, 1967), p. 10.
2. Elliot Forbes, ed., *Thayer's Life of Beethoven* (Princeton, NJ, 1967), p. 87.
3. Ibid., p. 115.
4. See Maynard Solomon, "The Creative Periods of Beethoven" in *Beethoven Essays* (Cambridge, MA, 1990), 116–25.
5. Quoted in Lewis Lockwood, *Beethoven: The Music and the Life* (New York, 2003), p. 58.
6. Wayne M. Senner, Robin Wallace, and William Rhea Meredith, *The Critical Reception of Beethoven's Compositions by His German Contemporaries*, Vol. 1 (Lincoln, NE, 1999), p. 164.
7. William Meredith, "*Bizarr* Beethoven," unpublished paper (2003), by kind courtesy of the author.

8. Senner et al., *The Critical Reception of Beethoven's Compositions*, p. 167.
9. Maynard Solomon, *Beethoven*, 2nd ed. (New York, 1998), pp. 146–47.
10. For the full text, trans. Piero Weiss, see *MWW*, pp. 277–79.
11. Quoted in *The Beethoven Companion*, Thomas K. Scherman and Louis Biancolli, eds. (Garden City, NY 1972), p. 124.
12. Senner et al., *The Critical Reception of Beethoven's Compositions*, p. 165.
13. Forbes, ed., *Thayer's Life of Beethoven*, pp. 348–49.
14. Quoted in Lockwood, *Beethoven*, p. 211.
15. Wayne M. Senner, Robin Wallace, and William Rhea Meredith, *The Critical Reception of Beethoven's Compositions by His German Contemporaries*, Vol. 2 (Lincoln, NE, 2001), p. 15.
16. Ibid., pp. 20, 35–38.
17. Forbes, ed., *Thayer's Life of Beethoven*, p. 285.
18. Ibid., p. 400.
19. Anton Felix Schindler, *Beethoven as I Knew Him*, Donald W. MacArdle, ed. (Mineloa, NY, 1996), p. 147.
20. Emily Anderson, ed. *The Letters of Beethoven*, Vol. 1 (London, 1961), p. 68.
21. *A Critical Study of Beethoven's Nine Symphonies by Hector Berlioz*, trans. Edwin Evans (Urbana, IL, 2000), p. 62.
22. Adolf Bernhard Marx, *Ludwig van Beethoven: Leben und Schaffen*, 6th ed., ed. and rev. Gustav Behncke, Vol. 2 (Berlin, 1908), p. 62.
23. See Johann Wolfgang von Goethe, *Versuch die Metamorphose der Pflanzen zu erklären* (Gotha, Germany, 1790).
24. E. T. A. Hoffmann, "Beethoven's Instrumental Music" (1813) in *SRMH*, p. 1195.
25. Lockwood, *Beethoven*, p. 226.
26. Forbes, ed. *Thayer's Life of Beethoven*, p. 436.
27. Anderson, ed. *The Letters of Beethoven*, I: 234.
28. Forbes, ed., *Thayer's Life of Beethoven*, p. 446.
29. Ibid., p. 448
30. Ibid., p. 446.
31. Senner et al., *The Critical Reception of Beethoven's Compositions*, Vol. 2, p. 49.
32. Goethe to Carl Friedrich Zelter, 2 September 1812; in *Beethoven: Impressions by His Contemporaries*, ed. O. G. Sonneck (New York, 1926), p. 88.
33. Ibid.
34. Anderson, ed., *Letters of Beethoven*, Vol. I, p. 384.
35. Solomon, *Beethoven*, pp. 207–46.
36. Forbes, ed., *Thayer's Life of Beethoven*, p. 780.
37. Schindler, *Beethoven as I Knew Him*, p. 231.
38. Forbes, ed., *Thayer's Life of Beethoven*, p. 762.
39. Quoted in Kristin M. Knittel, "Wagner, Deafness, and the Reception of Beethoven's Late Style" *JAMS* 51 (1998), p. 57.
40. Forbes, ed., *Thayer's Life of Beethoven*, p. 409.
41. Ibid., p. 586.
42. Quoted in ibid., pp. 897–98.
43. Quoted in ibid., p. 909.
44. Ibid., p. 909.
45. *Louis Spohr's Autobiography* (London, 1865), pp. 188–89.
46. Lockwood, *Beethoven*, p. 460.
47. Quoted in John Gingerich, "Ignaz Schuppanzigh and Beethoven's Late Quartets," *The Musical Quarterly* 93 (2010): p. 468.
48. Forbes, ed., *Thayer's Life of Beethoven*, p. 1044.
49. Joseph Kerman, *The Beethoven Quartets* (New York, 1979), p. 254.
50. Quoted in Christopher H. Gibbs, "The Performance of Grief: Vienna's Response to the Death of Beethoven," in *Beethoven and His World*, ed. Scott Burnham and Michael P. Steinberg (Princeton, NJ, 2000), p. 243.
51. Forbes, ed., *Thayer's Life of Beethoven*, p. 1043.

Chapter 17

1. Quoted in Richard Osborne, "Rossini," in *New Grove Dictionary of Opera*, Vol. 4 (London, 1992), p. 57.
2. Stendhal, *Life of Rossini*, trans. Richard N. Coe (Seattle, 1972), p. 80.
3. Ibid., p. 56.
4. Ibid., p. 407.
5. Edmond Michotte, "An Evening Chez Rossini, 1858," trans. Herbert Weinstock, *Opera* XVIII (1967): 955–58, condensed.
6. Giuseppe Verdi to Camille Bellaigue, 2 May 1898; *Verdi: The Man in His Letters*, ed. Franz Werfel and Paul Stefan, trans. Edward Downes (New York, 1973), p. 431.
7. Richard Storrs Willis and Augustus Morand, *Musical World*, Vols. 11–13, p. 89.
8. Quoted in Anthony Newcomb, "New Light(s) on Weber's Wolf's Glen Scene," in *Opera and the Enlightenment*, ed. Thomas Bauman and Marita McClymonds (Cambridge, 1995), p. 74.
9. *Richard Wagner's Prose Works*, trans. W. Ashton Ellis, Vol. 7 (London, 1898), p. 183.

Chapter 18

1. Goethe to Zelter, 21 December 1809; quoted in Eric Sams and Graham Johnson, "Lied (IV)," in *NGDMM*, Vol. 14, p. 672.
2. Quoted in Otto Erich Deutsch, ed., *Schubert: Memoirs by His Friends*, trans. Rosamond Ley and John Nowell (London, 1958), p. 10.
3. Schubert to Anselm Hüttenbrenner, 19 May 1819; Otto Erich Deutsch, ed., *The Schubert Reader* (New York, 1947), p. 117.
4. Ibid., p. 87.
5. Ibid., p. 175.
6. Schubert to Franz Schober, 14 August 1823; Ibid., p. 286.
7. Ibid., p. 338–40 (translation amended).
8. Ibid., pp. 740 and 375.
9. Moritz von Schwind to Franz Schober, 6 March 1824; ibid., p. 331.
10. See Gerald Abraham, "Finishing the Unfinished," *Musical Times* 112 (1971): 547–48.
11. *Hanslick's Musical Criticisms*, ed. and trans. Henry Pleasants (New York, 1978), p. 102.
12. Deutsch, *Schubert Reader*, p. 754.
13. Ibid., p. 756.

14. Manfred Willfort, "Das Urbild des Andante aus Schuberts Klaviertrio Es-Dur, D929" *Österreichische Musikzeitschrift* 33 (1978): 277–83; and Christopher H. Gibbs, *Life of Schubert* (Cambridge, 2000), pp. 157–60.
15. Deutsch, *Schubert Reader*, p. 764.
16. Quoted in Otto Erich Deutsch, "The Reception of Schubert's Works in England," *Monthly Musical Record* 81 (1951): 202–03
17. Quoted in Gibbs, *Life of Schubert*, p. 164.

Chapter 19

1. G. I. C. de Courcy, *Paganini: The Genoese*, two vols. (Normal, OK, 1957), I: 65.
2. O. E. Deutsch, ed., *Schubert: Die Erinnerungen seiner Freunde* (Leipzig, 1966), p. 261.
3. O. E. Deutsch, *The Schubert Reader* (New York, 1947), p. 773.
4. Stendhal, *Memoirs of Rossini* (London, 1824), p. 257.
5. F. J. Fétis, *Biographical Notice of Niccolò Paganini* (London, 1876; rpt. New York, 1976).
6. *Letters of Franz Liszt*, Vol. 1, ed. La Mara, trans. Constance Bache (rpt. ed., New York, 1968), pp. 8–9.
7. Ibid., p. 8.
8. Ibid., p. 8.
9. Liszt, "Concerning the Situation of Artists and Their Condition in Society" (*Gazette musicale de Paris*, 30 August 1835), trans. Piero Weiss, in *MWW*, pp. 311.
10. Quoted in "Ludwig Rellstab's Biographical Sketch of Liszt," introduced and translated by Allan Keiler, in *Liszt and His World*, Christopher H. Gibbs and Dana Gooley, eds. (Princeton, NJ, 2006), p. 351.
11. Franz Liszt, *An Artist's Journey: Lettres d'un bachelier ès musique 1835–1841*, ed. and trans. Charles Suttoni (Chicago and London, 1989), p. 144.
12. Eva Weissweiler, *The Complete Correspondence of Clara and Robert Schumann*, three vols. (New York, 1994), Vol. 1, 163.
13. Adrian Williams, *Portrait of Liszt by Himself and His Contemporaries* (Oxford, 1990), p. 106.
14. Quoted in Christopher H. Gibbs, "'Just Two Words: Enormous Success' Liszt's 1838 Vienna Concerts" in *Franz Liszt and His World*, p. 204.
15. Quoted in Alan Walker, *Franz Liszt*, Vol. 1: "The Virtuoso Years, 1811–1847" (New York, 1983), p. 365.
16. Ibid., p. 376.
17. Vladimir Stasov, *Selected Essays on Music*, trans. Florence Jonas (New York, 1968), p. 120.
18. Dezsö Legány, *Franz Liszt: Unbekannte Presse und Briefe aus Wien 1822–1886* (Budapest, 1984), pp. 96–97.
19. Quoted in Karin Pendle, *Eugène Scribe and French Opera of the Nineteenth Century* (Ann Arbor, MI, 1979), p. 50.
20. *Richard Wagner's Prose Works*, trans. W. Ashton Ellis, Vol. 5 (London, 1896), p. 39.
21. Ibid., Vol. 3, p. 96 (translation amended).
22. Eduard Bernsdorf, "K. Freigedank und das Judenthum in der Musik," in *Neue Zeitschrift für Musik*, Vol. 33 (1850), p. 168; quoted in Sanna Pederson, "Enlightened and Romantic German Music Criticism, 1800–1850" (Ph.D. diss. University of Pennsylvania, 1995), p. 258.

Chapter 20

1. Hector Berlioz, *The Memoirs of Hector Berlioz*, trans. and ed. David Cairns (New York, 1969), pp. 8–9.
2. Edward T. Cone, ed., *Berlioz: Fantastic Symphony* (New York, 1971), pp. 21–25.
3. *MWW*, p. 325.
4. Berlioz, *Memoirs*, p. 73.
5. Peter Bloom, *The Life of Berlioz* (Cambridge, 1998), p. 54.
6. Cone, *Berlioz: Fantastic Symphony*, p. 21.
7. Robert Schumann, "A Symphony by Berlioz," *Neue Zeitschrift für Musik*, 14 August 1835; trans. Edward T. Cone in *Berlioz: Fantastic Symphony*, pp. 246–47.
8. David Cairns, *Berlioz*, Vol. 2: *Servitude and Greatness* (London, 1999), p. 296.
9. Reviewing Mendelssohn's Piano Trio in D Minor, Op. 49, *Neue Zeitschrift für Musik*, 13 (1840), p. 198.
10. Berlioz to Liszt, 14–15 June 1855, Hector Berlioz, *Correspondance Générale* V: March 1855–August 1859, eds. Hugh Macdonald and François Lesure (1989).
11. Richard Wagner, Albert Goldman, and Evert Sprinchorn, *Wagner on Music and Drama: A Compendium of Richard Wagner's Prose Works* (New York, 1964), p. 55.
12. Ibid.
13. Alexander Fesca, "Robert Schumann, Review of Trios," and in *Schumann, Gesammelte Schriften*, Vol. 3, ed. Heinrich Simon (Leipzig, n.d.), p. 115.
14. Robert Schumann, *Tagebücher, Band 1*, ed. Georg Eismann (Leipzig, 1971), p. 151.
15. Quoted in Edward Lippman, "Theory and Practice in Schumann's Aesthetics," *JAMS* 17 (1964): 329.
16. Robert Schumann, *On Music and Musicians*, ed. Konrad Wolff, trans. Paul Rosenfeld (New York, 1946; rpt.1969), p. 125.
17. F. von Schlegel, "Fragments" (1798), quoted in Charles Rosen, *The Romantic Generation* (Cambridge, MA, 1995), p. 50.
18. Schumann, *Gesammelte Schriften*, Vol. 1, p. 39.
19. John Daverio, "Schumann's 'Im Legendenton' and Friedrich Schlegel's *Arabeske*," *19th-Century Music* 11 (1987–88): 151.
20. Clara Schumann, ed., *Jugendbriefe von Robert Schumann* (Leipzig, 1885), pp. 278, 302–03.
21. *Neue Zeitschrift für Musik*, 31 July 1835; Schumann, *On Music and Musicians*, p. 64.
22. Quoted in Rosen, *The Romantic Generation*, p. 93.
23. Joseph Wilhelm von Wasielewski, *Life of Robert Schumann*, trans. A. L. Alger (Boston, 1871, rpt. Detroit, 1976), p. 128.
24. John Daverio, *Robert Schumann: Herald of a "New Poetic Age"* (New York, 1997), p. 191.
25. Ibid., p. 360.
26. Schumann, *Gesammelte Schriften*, Vol. 1, p. 43.
27. Daverio, *Robert Schumann*, p. 301.

28. Quoted in Nancy Reich, "The Power of Class: Fanny Hensel," in *Mendelssohn and His World*, ed. R. Larry Todd (Princeton, NJ, 1991), p. 91.
29. Goethe to Felix Mendelssohn, 18 June 1825; *Felix Mendelssohn*, ed. G. Selden-Goth (New York, 1973), p. 34.
30. Beate Perrey, "Schumann's Lives, and Afterlives: An Introduction," in *The Cambridge Companion to Schumann*, ed. Beate Perry (Cambridge, 2007), p. 23.
31. Quoted in Nancy Reich, *Clara Schumann: The Artist and the Woman* (London, 1985), pp. 228–29.

Chapter 21

1. Robert Schumann, *On Music and Musicians*, ed. Konrad Wolff, trans. Paul Rosenfeld (New York, 1946; rpt. 1969), p. 126.
2. Jim Samson, *Chopin* (Oxford, 1996), p. 83.
3. Schumann, *On Music and Musicians*, p. 132.
4. Ibid.
5. Ibid., p. 140 (translation amended).
6. George Sand, *Un hiver à Majorque* (rpt., Palma, 1968), p. 60; trans. Thomas Higgins in *Chopin, Preludes, Op. 28* (New York, 1973), p. 5.
7. Hippolyte Barbedette, *Chopin: Essai de critique musicale* (Paris, 1861), p. 65; trans. Higgins, ibid., p. 92.
8. Schumann, *On Music and Musicians*, p. 143.
9. Karol Berger, "Chopin's *Ballade, Op. 23* and the Revolution of the Intellectuals," in *Chopin Studies 2*, eds. John Rink and Jim Samson (Cambridge, 1994).
10. Louis Moreau Gottschalk, *Notes of a Pianist* (Philadelphia, 1881), p. 33.
11. Quoted in Richard Jackson, "Gottschalk of Louisiana," Introduction to *Piano Music of Louis Moreau Gottschalk* (New York, 1973), p. v.
12. Quoted in Jeanne Behrend, "Postlude," in Louis Moreau Gottschalk, *Notes of a Pianist* (New York, 1964), p. 403.
13. Ibid., p. 402.
14. Gottschalk to his mother, undated fragment, ca. 1850; quoted in S. Frederick Starr, *Bamboula: The Life and Times of Louis Moreau Gottschalk* (New York, 1995), p. 50.
15. Lawrence W. Levine, *Highbrow/Lowbrow: The Emergence of Cultural Hierarchy in America* (Cambridge, MA, 1988).
16. Nikolai Gogol, "Peterburgskiye zapiski" (1836), in *Sochineniya i pis'ma N. V. Gogolya*, Vol. 7, ed. V. V. Kallash (St. Petersburg, Russia, 1896), p. 340.
17. Yanuariy Neverov, "O novoy opere g. Glinki 'Zhizn' za tsarya,'" quoted in David Brown, *Glinka: A Biographical and Critical Study* (London, 1974), pp. 112–13.
18. Neverov, "O novoy opere g. Glinki 'Zhizn' za tsarya,'" quoted in Tamara Livanova and Vladimir Protopopov, *Opernaya kritika v Rossii*, Vol. 1 (Moscow, 1966), part 1, p. 208 (italics in original).
19. Ibid., part 1, p. 207.
20. Mikhail I. Glinka, "Zapiski," in *Polnoye sobraniye sochineniy: Literaturnïye proizvedeniya i perepiska*, Vol. 1 (Moscow, 1973), p. 262.
21. "Tsirkulyarnoye predlozheniye G. Upravlyayushchego Ministerstvom Narodnogo Prosveshcheniya Nachalstvam Uchobnïkh Okrugov 'o vstuplenii v upravlenii Ministerstvom,'" quoted in Nicholas V. Riasanovsky, *Nicholas I and Official Nationality in Russia, 1825–1855* (Berkeley and Los Angeles, 1959), p. 73.
22. Ibid., p. 74.
23. *Entsiklopedicheskiy slovar'* Vol. 2 (Moscow, 1964), p. 542.
24. Quoted in Riasanovsky, *Nicholas I and Official* Nationality, p. 97.
25. Glinka, "Zapiski," p. 266.
26. V. F. Odoyevsky, "Pis'mo k lyubitelyu muzïki ob opere g. Glinki: Zhizn' za tsarya," in *Muzïkal'no-literaturnoye naslidiye*, ed. G. B. Bernandt (Moscow, 1956), p. 11.
27. Diary entry, 27 June 1888; quoted in Brown, *Glinka*, p. 1.
28. Quoted in ibid., p. 245.

Chapter 22

1. Franz Brendel, *Geschichte der Musik in Italien, und Deutschland Frankreich von den ersten christlichen Zeiten bis auf die Gegenwart*, 5th ed. (Leipzig, 1875), p. 594.
2. Georg Wilhelm Friedrich Hegel, *The Philosophy of History*, trans. John Sibree (New York, 1900), p. 19.
3. Karl Popper, *The Open Society and Its Enemies*, Vol. 2 (Princeton, NJ, 1966), p. 269.
4. Brendel, *Geschichte der Musik*, 4th ed. (Leipzig, 1867), p. 623; quoted in Carl Dahlhaus, *Esthetics of Music*, trans. William Austin (Cambridge, 1982), p. 57.
5. Franz Liszt to Freiherr Beaulieu-Marconnay, Intendant of the Court Theater at Weimar, 21 May 1855; *Letters of Franz Liszt*, Vol. 1, ed. La Mara (New York, 1968), pp. 241–42.
6. Liszt, "Berlioz and His 'Harold' Symphony," *Neue Zeitschrift für Musik*, 43 (1855); in *SRMH*, pp. 1166, 1169.
7. Lina Ramann, *Franz Liszt als Künstler und Mensch*, Vol. 3 (Leipzig, 1894), p. 69; quoted in Alan Walker, *Franz Liszt: The Weimar Years 1848–61* (Ithaca, NY, 1993), p. 336; Ramann's evidence was an 1875 letter from Princess Sayn-Wittgenstein herself.
8. *Neue Zeitschrift für Musik*, Vol. 50 (1859), p. 272, trans. Piero Weiss, in *MWW*, p. 328.
9. Arnold Schoenberg, "National Music" (1931), trans. Leo Black, in *Style and Idea: Selected Writings of Arnold Schoenberg*, ed. Leonard Stein (Berkeley CA, 1985), p. 170.
10. Tchaikovsky to Grand Duke Konstantin Konstantinovich, 2 October 1888; A. A. Orlova, ed., *P. I. Chaikovskiy o muzïke, o zhizni, o sebe* (Leningrad, 1976), p. 218.
11. The claim had previously been made in a more general context in Franz Brendel, "Die Aesthetik der Tonkunst," *Neue Zeitschrift für Musik*, 46 (1857), p. 186; trans. Martin Cooper in Bojan Bujic, ed., *Music in European Thought 1851–1912* (Cambridge, 1988), p. 130.
12. Joseph Joachim to Franz Liszt, 27 August 1857; quoted in Alan Walker, *Franz Liszt: The Weimar Years*, p. 347.
13. Quoted in Walter Niemann, *Brahms*, trans. C. A. Phillips (New York, 1929), pp. 77–78.

14. Bernhard Scholz, *Verklungene Weisen* (Mainz, 1911), p. 142; quoted in David Brodbeck, *Brahms: Symphony No. 1* (Cambridge, 1997), p. 96, n. 28.
15. Frederick Niecks, *Frederick Chopin as a Man and Musician* (London, 1988), p. 173.
16. *Letters of Franz Liszt*, Vol. 1, ed. La Mara, trans. Constance Bache (rpt. ed., 1968), p. 330.
17. Quoted in Hector Berlioz, *New Edition of the Complete Works*, Vol. 17 (Kassel, Germany, 2001), p. viii.
18. David Cairns, *Berlioz*, Vol. 2: *Servitude and Greatness* (London, 1999), p. 32.
19. Berlioz, *New Edition of the Complete Works*, Vol. 17, p. viii.
20. Ibid.
21. Ibid.

Chapter 23

1. Richard Wagner, *My Life* (New York, 1927), p. 234.
2. Wagner to Liszt, 5 July 1855; *Correspondence of Wagner and Liszt*, Vol. 2, trans. Francis Hueffer (New York, 1897), pp. 102–03.
3. *Richard Wagner's Prose Works*, Vol. 1, trans. William Ashton Ellis (London, 1892), p. 35.
4. Wagner, *Opera and Drama*, in *Richard Wagner's Prose Works*, trans. W. Ashton Ellis, Vol. 2 (London, 1893) p. 280.
5. Some of these examples are drawn from Deryck Cooke, *An Introduction to Der Ring des Nibelungen*, London Records, No. 443 581-2 (1995).
6. *Wagner's Prose Works*, Vol. 1, pp. 367–76, condensed.
7. Quoted in Tim Blanning, *The Triumph of Music* (Cambridge, 2008), pp. 147–48.
8. Richard Wagner, *Nachgelassene Schriften und Dichtungen* (Leipzig, 1895), pp. 163–64; trans. Piero Weiss in *MWW*, pp. 320.
9. Bryan Magee, *Aspects of Wagner* (New York, 1969), pp. 57–81.
10. Slogan attributed (or misattributed) not only to Adolf Hitler but to a wide variety of English writers, including D. H. Lawrence and Rudyard Kipling.
11. Quoted in Ernest Newman, *The Wagner Operas* (Princeton, 1991), p. 673.
12. Franz Werfel and Paul Stefan, eds., *Verdi: The Man in His Letters*, trans. Edward Downes (New York, 1973), p. 403–4.
13. Ibid., p. 392.
14. Quoted in John Rosselli, *Life of Verdi* (Cambridge, 2000), p. 166.
15. Giuseppe Mazzini, "Byron and Goethe," trans. A. Rutherford, quoted in David Kimbell, *Verdi in the Age of Italian Romanticism* (Cambridge, 1981), p. 12.
16. Ibid., p. 12
17. Ibid., pp. 16ff.
18. Quoted in Carlo Gatti, *Verdi*, Vol. 1 (Milan, 1931), p. 107.
19. Roger Parker, *Leonora's Last Act: Essays in Verdian Discourse* (Princeton, 1997), p. 33.
20. Alessandro Manzoni, "Lettre à M. C***," quoted in Piero Weiss, "Verdi and the Fusion of Genres," *JAMS* 35 (1982): 141.
21. George Steiner, "Maestro," *The New Yorker*, 19 April 1982, p. 171.
22. Verdi to Cammarano, 4 April 1851; quoted in Julian Budden, *The Operas of Verdi*, Vol. 2 (New York, 1979), p. 61.
23. Steiner, "Maestro," p. 171.
24. Quoted in Weiss, "Verdi and the Fusion of Genres," p. 152.
25. Verdi to Antonio Somma, 22 April 1853; quoted in Julian Budden, *The Operas of Verdi*, Vol. 1 (New York, 1973), pp. 483–84.
26. Werfel and Stefan, *Verdi*, p. 310.
27. Verdi to the mayor of Parma, 29 April 1891; ibid., p. 401.
28. Quoted in Julian Budden, *The Operas of Verdi*, Vol. 3 (New York, 1981), p. 425.

Chapter 24

1. František Bartoš, ed., *Bedřich Smetana: Letters and Reminiscences*, trans. Daphne Rusbridge (Prague, 1955), p. 59.
2. Ibid., diary entry, 23 January 1843, p. 5.
3. Ibid., pp. 24–26.
4. Quoted in Marta Ottlová, "Bedřich Smetana," in *NGDMM*, Volume 23, p. 539.
5. *Smetana: Letters and Reminiscences*, pp. 47–48.
6. Quoted in John Tyrrell, *Czech Opera* (Cambridge, 1988), p. 217.
7. Michael Beckerman, "In Search of Czechness in Music," *19th-Century Music* 10 (1986–87): 67, 73.
8. César Cui, "Muzïkal'nïye zametki: 'Prodannaya Nevesta', komicheskaya opera g. Smetanï," *Sankt-Peterburgskiye vedomosti*, 6 January 1871.
9. Anton Rubinstein, *Muka i yeyo predstaviteli* (Moscow, 1891), pp. 40, 83–84.
10. Stuart Campbell, *Russians on Russian Music, 1830–1880: An Anthology* (Cambridge, 1994), p. 65.
11. V. V. Stasov, "Slavyanskiy kontsert g. Balakireva," *Sankt-Peterburgskiye vedomosti*, May 1867; in Stasov, *Izbrannïye sochineniya*, Vol. 1 (Moscow, 1952), p. 173.
12. César Cui, "Pervye kompozitorskiye shagi Ts. A. Kyui," in Cui, *Izbrannïye stat'i* (Leningrad, 1952), p. 544.
13. Richard Taruskin, *Defining Russia Musically: Historical and Hermeneutical Essays* (Princeton, NJ, 1997), p. 69.
14. Musorgsky to Nikolai Rimsky-Korsakov, 30 July 1868; Musorgsky, *Literaturnoye naslediye*, Vol. 1, eds. A. A. Orlova and M. S. Pekelis (Moscow, 1971), p. 102.
15. Musorgsky to Vladimir Stasov, 13 June 1872; Musorgsky, *Literaturnoye naslediye*, Vol. 1, p. 132.
16. See César Cui, "Opernïy sezon v Peterburge" (1864); in Cui, *Izbrannïye stat'i* (Leningrad, 1952), p. 36.
17. Musorgsky to Rimsky-Korsakov, 23 July 1870; *Literaturnoye naslediye*, Vol. 1, p. 117.
18. Tchaikovsky to Nadezhda von Meck, 27 November 1877, P. I. Chaikovsky, *Perepiska s N. F. fon-Mekk*, Vol. 1 (Moscow, 1934), pp. 100–101.
19. Tchaikovsky to Nadezhda von Meck, 18 February 1880; Chaikovsky, *Polnoye sobraniye sochineniy: Literaturnïye proizvedeniya i perepiska*, Vol. 9 (Moscow, 1962), p. 56.
20. Tchaikovsky to Grand Duke Konstantin Konstantinovich, 21 September 1888; Chaikovsky, *Polnoye sobraniye sochineniy: Literaturnïye proizvedeniya i perepiska*, Vol. 14 (Moscow, 1974), p. 542.

21. Tchaikovsky to Nadezhda von Meck, 17 February 1878; Chaikovsky, *Polnoye sobraniye sochineniy: Literaturnïye proizvedeniya i perepiska*, Vol. 7 (Moscow, 1962), pp. 126–27.
22. Tchaikovsky to Sergey Taneyev, 27 March 1878; quoted in Modeste Tchaikovsky, *Life and Letters of Tchaikovsky*, Vol. 1 (New York, 1973), p. 294.
23. Tchaikovsky to Nadezhda von Meck, 17 February 1878; Chaikovsky, *Polnoye sobraniye sochineniy*, Vol. 7, p. 124.
24. Tchaikovsky to P. I. Jurgenson, 18 October 1893; *Life and Letters of Tchaikovsky*, Vol. 2, p. 722.
25. Tchaikovsky to P. I. Jurgenson, 12 August 1893 ibid., Vol. 2, p. 715.

Chapter 25

1. *Richard Wagner's Prose Works*, Vol. 1, trans. W. Ashton Ellis (London, 1895), p. 126.
2. Walter Frisch, *Brahms: The Four Symphonies* (New Haven, CT, and London, 2003), pp. 5–12.
3. Emil Naumann, *The History of Music*, Vol. 5, trans. F. Praeger (London, n.d.), p. 1194.
4. See William Weber, "Mass Culture and the Reshaping of European Musical Taste, 1770–1870," *International Journal of the Aesthetics and Sociology of Music* 8 (1977): 5–21.
5. J. Peter Burkholder, "Brahms and Twentieth-Century Classical Music," *19th-Century Music* 8 (1984–5): 81.
6. Ibid., p. 76.
7. Schumann, "Neue Bahnen," in *SRMH*, p. 1157.
8. Remark to Hermann Levi, October 1871, reported in Max Kalbeck, *Brahms*, Vol. 1 (Berlin, 1915), p. 165; quoted in David Brodbeck, *Brahms: Symphony No. 1* (Cambridge, 1997), p. 15.
9. Quoted in Brodbeck, *Brahms: Symphony No. 1*, p. 6.
10. Theodor Billroth to Brahms, 10 December 1876; *Johannes Brahms and Theodor Billroth: Letters from a Musical Friendship*, trans. Hans Barkan (Norman, OK, 1957), p. 41.
11. Eduard Hanslick, *Music Criticisms 1846–99*, trans. Henry Pleasants (Baltimore, 1963), pp. 82–83.
12. Carl Dahlhaus, *Between Romanticism and Modernism*, trans. Mary Whittall (Berkeley and Los Angeles, 1980), p. 41.
13. Ibid., p. 49.
14. Arnold Schoenberg, "Brahms the Progressive," in *Style and Idea: Selected Writings of Arnold Schoenberg*, trans. Leo Black, ed. Leonard Stein (Berkeley, CA, 1984), pp. 398–441.
15. Quoted in Leon Botstein, *The Complete Brahms: A Guide to the Musical Works of Johannes Brahms* (New York, 1999), p. 118.
16. Friedrich Nietzsche, *Untimely Meditations*, trans. R. J. Hollingdale (Cambridge, 1983), p. xxviii.
17. Clara Schumann to Joseph Joachim, 1 July 1862; quoted in Brodbeck, *Brahms: Symphony No. 1*, p. 10.
18. Quoted in Brodbeck, *Brahms: Symphony No. 1*, p. 98, n. 1.
19. *Richard Wagner's Prose Works*, Vol. 1, trans. William Ashton Ellis (London, 1895), p. 126.
20. The postcard is reproduced in facsimile in Brodbeck, *Brahms: Symphony No. 1*, p. 15.
21. Quoted in Kalbeck, *Brahms*, Vol. 3 (rpt. Tutzing, 1976), p. 109.
22. Brodbeck, *Brahms: Symphony No. 1*, pp. 68–69.
23. Friedrich Chrysander, performance review, *Allgemeine musikalische Zeitung* 13 (1878), col. 94; quoted in Brodbeck, *Brahms: Symphony No. 1*, p. 86.
24. *MWW*, p. 344.
25. Quoted in Brodbeck, *Brahms: Symphony No. 1*, p. 85.
26. *Richard Wagner's Prose Works*, Vol. 6 (London, 1897), p. 148.
27. Quoted in Carl Dahlhaus, *Nineteenth-Century Music*, trans. J. Bradford Robinson (Berkeley, CA, 1989), p. 271.
28. Hans-Hubert Schönzeler, *Bruckner* (New York, 1978), p. 65.
29. Benjamin M. Korstvedt, *Anton Bruckner: Symphony No. 8* (Cambridge, 2000), p. 4.
30. Deryck Cooke, "Bruckner," in *NGDMM*, Vol. 3 p. 364.
31. Eduard Hanslick, *Music Criticisms 1846–99*, p. 243.
32. Gian Francesco Malipiero, quoted in John C. G. Waterhouse, "Martucci," in *NGDMM*, Vol. 16, p. 10.
33. Quoted in Klaus Döge, "Antonín Dvořák," in *NGDMM*, Vol. 7, p. 779.
34. "Dvořák and Brahms: A Chronicle, an Interpretation" in *Dvořák and His World*, ed. Michael Beckerman (Princeton, NJ, 1993), p. 65, translation modified.
35. Quoted in Hans Hubert Schönzeler, *Dvořák* (London and New York, 1984), p. 181.
36. Josef Jan Kovařk to Otakar Šourek; quoted in Michael Beckerman, "The Master's Little Joke: Antonín Dvořák and the Mask of Nation," in *Dvořák and His World*, p. 135.
37. Michael B. Beckerman, *New Worlds of Dvořák: Searching in America for the Composer's Inner Life* (New York, 2003).
38. Quoted in John Clapham, *Antonín Dvořák: Musician and Craftsman* (London, 1996), p. 86.
39. Dvořák to Emil Kozanek, 12 April 1893; Otakar Šourek, *Dvořák in Letters and Reminiscences* (Prague, 1954), p. 158.
40. *New York Daily Tribune*, 17 December 1893, p. 7; quoted in Beckerman, *New Worlds of Dvořák*, p. 89.
41. Quoted in Adrienne Fried Block, *Amy Beach: Passionate Victorian* (New York, 1998), p. 103.
42. *Boston Herald*, 28 May 1893; quoted in Block, *Amy Beach*, p. 87.
43. Quoted in Brian Rees, *Camille Saint-Saëns: A Life* (London, 1999), p. 161.
44. See Vincent d'Indy, *César Franck*, trans. Rosa Newmarch (London, 1910), pp. 91, 171.

Chapter 26

1. See Edward W. Said, *Orientalism* (New York, 1978).
2. François-René, Vicomte de Chateaubriand, *Itinéraire de Paris à Jérusalem, et de Jérusalem à Paris* (Paris, 1812).
3. Ralph P. Locke, "Constructing the Oriental 'Other': Saint-Saëns's *Samson et Dalila*," *Cambridge Opera Journal* 3 (1991): 263.
4. Vladimir Vasilievich Stasov, "Dvadtsat' pyat' let russkogo iskusstvo: Nasha muzïka, *Vestnik Yevropï* (1882–83), in V. V. Stasov, *Izbrannye sochineniya v tryokh tomakh*, Vol. 2 (Moscow, 1952), p. 525.
5. Gabriele D'Annunzio, "Il capobanda," *Il Mattino* (Naples), 2 September 1892.

6. G. B., "Beseda s Chaikovskim," *Peterburgskaya zhizn'*, No. 2 (1892); in P. I. Chaikovsky, *Muzïkal'no-kriticheskiye stat'i*, 4th ed. (Leningrad, 1986), p. 319.
7. Julian Budden, "Puccini," in *New Grove Dictionary of Opera*, Vol. 3 (London, 1992), p. 1171.

Chapter 27

1. Richard Specht, *Johannes Brahms* (Hellerau, 1928), p. 382.
2. Claude Debussy, "L'influence allemande sur la musique française," in *Monsieur Croche* (Paris, 1971), p. 67.
3. Ezra Pound, "Arnold Dolmetsch" (1914), in *Literary Essays of Ezra Pound* (New York, 1968), p. 434.
4. Cited in Hermann Danuser, *Die Musik des 20. Jahrhunderts* (Laaber, Germany, 1984), p. 24.
5. Gustav Mahler to Anna von Mildenburg, 18 July 1896 (on his Third Symphony), *Selected Letters of Gustav Mahler*, ed. Knud Martner, trans. Eithne Wilkins, and Ernst Kaiser (New York, 1979), p. 190.
6. Mahler to Max Marschalk, 26 March 1896; Piero Weiss, *Letters of Composers Through Six Centuries* (Philadelphia, 1967), p. 393.
7. Quoted in Donald Mitchell, *Gustav Mahler: The Wunderhorn Years* (Berkeley, CA, 1980), p. 157.
8. Quoted in Karen Painter, ed., *Mahler and His World* (Princeton, NJ, 2002), pp. 292–93.
9. Ibid., p. 289.
10. Ibid., p. 286.
11. Quoted in Mitchell, *Gustav Mahler: The Wunderhorn Years*, p. 269.
12. Mahler to Marschalk, 26 March 1896; Weiss, *Letters of Composers*, p. 394.
13. Ibid., p. 393.
14. Henry-Louis de La Grange, *Gustav Mahler*, Vol. 2, *Vienna the Years of Challenge* (Oxford, 1995), p. 522.
15. Quoted in Constantin Floros, *Gustav Mahler: The Symphonies*, trans. Veron and Jutta Wicker (Portland, OR, 1993), p. 154.
16. Herta Blaukopf, ed., *Gustav Mahler–Richard Strauss: Correspondence 1888–1911*, trans. Edmund Jephcott (Chicago, 1984), p. 75.
17. Floros, *Gustav Mahler*, p. 214.
18. Deryck Cooke, *Gustav Mahler: An Introduction to His Music* (London, 1980), p. 106.
19. Leonard Bernstein, *Unanswered Question* (Cambridge, MA, 1981), pp. 312ff.
20. Ernst Krause, *Richard Strauss: The Man and His Work* (Boston, 1969), p. 160.
21. Richard Strauss, *Betrachtungen und Erinnerungen*, ed. Willi Schuh (Zurich, 1949), p. 184; trans. Piero Weiss *MWW*, p. 416.
22. Joseph Auner, *A Schoenberg Reader: Documents of a Life* (New Haven, CT, and London, 2003), p. 119.
23. Arnold Schoenberg, "How One Becomes Lonely" (1937); *Style and Idea: Selected Writings of Arnold Schoenberg*, trans. Leo Black, ed. Leonard Stein (Berkeley, CA, 1984), p. 36.
24. Arnold Schoenberg, "Criteria for the Evaluation of Music" (1946); in ibid., p. 132.
25. Schoenberg, "How One Becomes Lonely"; in ibid., p. 30.
26. Alban Berg, "Why Is Schoenberg's Music So Difficult to Understand?" (1924); in *Contemporary Composers on Contemporary Music*, eds. Elliott Schwarz and Barney Childs (New York, 1967), pp. 68–69.
27. Schoenberg to Wassily Kandinsky, 24 January 1911; *Arnold Schoenberg/Wassily Kandinsky, Letters, Pictures and Documents*, ed. Jelena Hahl-Koch, trans. John C. Crawford (London, 1984), p. 23.
28. Ibid., p. 23.
29. Schoenberg, program note to the first performance of *Five Orchestra Pieces*, Op. 16 (1909); Nicolas Slonimsky, *Music Since 1900*, 4th ed. (New York, 1971), p. 207.
30. Schoenberg, "Problems in Teaching Art" (1911) in *Style and Idea*, p. 365.
31. The term as such appears for the first time in "Opinion or Insight?" (1926); *Style and Idea*, p. 260.
32. Schoenberg, *Theory of Harmony* [*Harmonielehre*, 1911], trans. Roy E. Carter (Berkeley, CA , 1978), p. 384.
33. Schoenberg commented: "In this period I renounced a tonal center, a procedure incorrectly called 'atonality'," *Style and Idea*, p. 86.
34. Quoted in Auner, *A Schoenberg Reader*, p. 57.
35. Bram Dijkstra, *Idols of Perversity: Fantasies of Feminine Evil in Fin-de-siècle Culture* (New York, 1986).
36. Anton Webern, *The Path to the New Music*, trans. Leo Black (Bryn Mawr, PA, 1963), p. 51.

Chapter 28

1. Alan M. Gillmor, *Erik Satie* (New York, 1992), p. 10.
2. "La Musique Russe et les Compositeurs Français," *Excelsior* (9 March 1911); quoted in Malcolm H. Brown, "Modest Petrovich Musorgsky, 1881–1981," in *Musorgsky: In Memoriam 1881–1981*, ed. M. H. Brown (Ann Arbor, MI, 1982), p. 4.
3. Quoted in Edward Lockspeiser, *Claude Debussy: His Life and Mind*, Vol. 1: *1862–1902* (Cambridge, 1978), p. 208.
4. Ibid., 207.
5. Report by the Permanent Secretary of the Académie des Beaux-Arts, 1887; quoted in Stefan Jarocinski, *Debussy: Impressionism and Symbolism*, trans. Rollo Myers (London, 1976), p. 11.
6. Debussy, *Monsieur Croche Antidilettante*, trans. B. N. Langdon Davies; in *Three Classics in the Aesthetics of Music* (New York, 1962), p. 8.
7. Quoted in Lockspeiser, *Claude Debussy*, Vol. 1, p. 171.
8. Baudelaire, *Salon de 1859*; quoted in Jarocinski, *Debussy*, p. 29.
9. Debussy, "Why I Wrote Pelléas" (1902); in *Debussy on Music*, ed. François Lesure, trans. Richard Langham Smith (New York, 1977), p. 75.
10. Debussy to Ernest Chausson; *Debussy Letters*, eds. François Lesure and Roger Nichols, trans. Roger Nichols (Cambridge, MA, 1987), p. 62.
11. Debussy to Pierre Louÿs, 20 August 1894; in ibid., p. 72.
12. Debussy to Chausson, 2 October 1893; in ibid., p. 54.

13. Richard Strauss and Romain Rolland, *Correspondance; Fragments de Journal* (1951); quoted in Edward Lockspeiser, *Claude Debussy: His Life and Mind*, Vol. 2: *1902–1918* (Cambridge, 1978), p. 88.
14. Émile Vuillermoz, *Gabriel Fauré*, trans. Kenneth Schapin (Philadelphia, 1969), p. 75.
15. Ravel in conversation with M. D. Calvocoressi in 1931; quoted in *A Ravel Reader: Correspondence, Articles, Interviews*, Arbie Orenstein, ed. (New York, 1990), p. 477.
16. "Maurice Ravel's Opinion of Modern French Music," *The Musical Leader* (16 March 1911); in ibid., p. 410.
17. See Steven Baur, "Ravel's 'Russian' Period: Octatonicism in His Early Works, 1893–1908," *JAMS* 52 (1999): 376–77.
18. Linda Nochlin, "Why Have There Been No Great Women Artists?" (1971); in Nochlin, *Women, Art, and Power and Other Essays* (New York, 1988), p. 167.
19. Annegret Fauser, "*La Guerre en dentelles*: Women and the *Prix de Rome* in French Cultural Politics," *JAMS* 51 (1998), pp. 83–129.
20. Alexandre Benois, *Reminiscences of the Russian Ballet*, trans. Mary Britnieva (London, 1941), p. 372.
21. Alexandre Benois, "Beseda o balete," in V. Meyerhold, *Teatr* (St. Petersburg, 1908), 103.
22. Charles Hamm, "The Genesis of *Petrushka*," in *Igor Stravinsky, Petrushka*, ed. Hamm (New York, 1967), p. 12.
23. Edith Sitwell, "The Russian Ballet in England," in *The Russian Ballet Gift Book* (London, 1921); rpt. in ibid., pp. 187–88.
24. *The Russian Primary Chronicle*, trans. Samuel Hazzard Cross and Olgerd P. Sherbowitz (Cambridge, 1953), p. 56.
25. Debussy to Stravinsky, 5 November 1912; *Debussy Letters*, eds. Lesure and Nichols, p. 265.
26. *Le Figaro*, 29 May 1913; quoted in Thomas Forrest Kelly, *First Nights: Five Musical Premieres* (New Haven, CT, and London, 2000), p. 263.
27. Leonid Sabaneyev, "Vesna svyashchennaya," *Golos Moskvï*, 8 June 1913.
28. Stravinsky to Maximilian Steinberg, 3 July 1913; in *I. F. Stravinskiy: Stat'i i materialï*, ed. L. Dyachkova (Moscow, 1973), p. 474.
29. Louis Vuillemin, "Le Sacre du Printemps," *Comoedia* 7 (31 May 1913); in Truman C. Bullard, "The First Performance of Igor Stravinsky's *Sacre du Printemps*," Vol. 1 (Ph.D. diss., University of Rochester, 1971), p. 144.
30. Jacques Rivière, "Le sacre du printemps," *La Nouvelle revue française*, November 1913; Bullard, *The First Performance*, Vol. 3, pp. 271, 274.
31. Quoted in Léon Vallas, *Claude Debussy: His Life and Works* (New York, 1973), p. 276.
32. Quoted in Robin Holloway, *Debussy and Wagner* (London, 1979), p. 161.
33. Debussy to Jacques Durand, 12 September 1912; *Debussy Letters*, eds. Lesure and Nichols p. 263.

Chapter 29

1. Quoted in Glenda Dawn Goss, *Sibelius: A Composer's Life and the Awakening of Finland* (Chicago, 2009), p. 372.
2. Quoted in Andrew Barnett, *Sibelius* (New Haven and London, 2007), p. 103.
3. Quoted in Karl Ekman, *Jean Sibelius: His Life and Personality*, trans. Edward Birse (New York, 1938), p. 191.
4. Quoted in Goss, *Sibelius*, p. 343.
5. Quoted in Michael Kennedy, *The Works of Ralph Vaughan Williams* (Oxford, 1992), p. 37.
6. "Should Music Be National?" in Ralph Vaughan Williams, *National Music and Other Essays* (London, 1963), p. 10.
7. Quoted in Edward Lockspeiser, *Claude Debussy: His Life and Mind*, Vol. 2: *1902–1918* (Cambridge, 1978), pp. 257, 259.
8. Quoted in Benjamin Suchoff, *Béla Bartók: A Celebration*, p. 71.
9. Bartók and Kodály, *Mag Népdalok* (Budapest, 1906), Introduction; trans. Klára Móricz.
10. Bartók, "Autobiography"; *Béla Bartók's Essays*, ed. Benjamin Suchoff (New York, 1976), p. 410.
11. Quoted in Simon Broughton, "Bartók and 'World Music'," in *The Stage Works of Béla Bartók*, English National Opera Guide No. 44 (London, 1991), p. 17.
12. Quoted in Benjamin Suchoff, *Béla Bartók: Life and Work* (Lanham, MD, 2002), p. 61.
13. Quoted in Broughton, "Bartók and 'World Music'," pp. 16–17.
14. "The Influence of Peasant Music on Modern Music" in *Béla Bartók's Essays*, pp. 341–44.
15. Bartók, "The Folk Songs of Hungary" (1928); *Béla Bartók's Essays*, p. 338.
16. Suchoff, *Bartók: A Celebration*, p. 34.
17. Mirka Zemanová, ed., *Janáček's Uncollected Essays on Music* (London, 1989), p. 61.
18. Ibid., pp. 121–22.
19. Arthur Eaglefield Hull, *Scriabin: A Great Russian Tone-Poet* (1916), (2nd ed., London, 1927), p. 106.
20. Igor Boelza, "Filosofskiye istoki obraznego stroya 'Prometeya,'" *Razlichnïye aspektï tvorchestva A. N. Skryabina* (Moscow, 1992), p. 19.
21. See Geoffrey Block and J. Peter Burkholder, "Selected Reviews 1888–1951" in *Charles Ives and His World*, ed. J. Peter Burkholder (Princeton, NJ), p. 275–77.
22. Quoted in the liner notes to Leonard Bernstein's 1960 recording of Ives's Symphony No. 2 (Columbia records KL-5489).
23. Lawrence Gilman, "A Masterpiece of American Music Heard Here for the First Time," *New York Herald Tribune*, 21 January 1939, p. 9.
24. Ibid.
25. Vivian Perlis, ed., *Charles Ives Remembered: An Oral History* (New Haven, CT, 1974), p. 138.
26. Maynard Solomon, "Charles Ives: Some Questions of Veracity," *JAMS* 40 (1987): 453.
27. Charles Ives, *Essays Before a Sonata* (1920), in *Essays Before a Sonata and Other Writings by Charles Ives*, ed. Howard Boatwright (New York, 1964), pp. 72–73.
28. Ibid., p. 36.
29. Charles E. Ives, *Memos*, ed. John Kirkpatrick (New York, 1972), p. 84.

30. Henry and Sidney Cowell, *Charles Ives and His Music* (New York, 1955), pp. 144–45.
31. Draft of a letter to Paul Rosenfeld (1940), quoted in Jan Swafford, *Charles Ives: A Life with Music* (New York, 1996), p. 3.
32. Ives, *Memos*, p. 107.

Chapter 30

1. Quoted in Tony Judt, "The End of the World," *New York Times Book Review*, 27 June 1999, p. 12.
2. Aaron Copland, *The New Music 1900/60* (London, 1968), p. 72.
3. Ibid.
4. Igor Stravinsky and Robert Craft, *Expositions and Developments* (Garden City, NY, 1962), pp. 128–29.
5. Quoted in Scott Messing, *Neoclassicism in Music from the Genesis of the Concept through the Schoenberg/Stravinsky Polemic* (Ann Arbor, MI, 1988), p. 130.
6. Jacques Rivière, "Le Sacre du Printemps," *La Nouvelle Revue française*, 1 November 1913; trans. adapted from Truman C. Bullard, "The First Performance of Stravinsky's *Sacre du Printemps*," Vol. 2 (Ph.D. diss., Eastman School of Music, 1971), pp. 269–308.
7. Boris Asafiev, *A Book About Stravinsky*, trans. Richard F. French (Ann Arbor, MI, 1982), p. 99.
8. Ibid.
9. *Stravinsky: An Autobiography* (New York, 1936), pp. 83–84.
10. Prokofiev to Nikolai Myaskovsky, 5 March 1925; *S. S. Prokof'yev i N. YA. Myaskovskiy: Perepiska*, ed. M. G. Kozlova and N. R. Yastenko (Moscow, 1977), p. 211.
11. Prokofiev to Myaskovsky, 4 August 1925; ibid., p. 218.
12. Igor Stravinsky and Robert Craft, *Conversations with Igor Stravinsky* (Garden City, NY, 1959), p. 18.
13. Igor Stravinsky, "Some Ideas About My Octuor," *The Arts*, January 1924; reprinted in Eric Walter White, *Stravinsky: The Composer and His Works* (Berkeley and Los Angeles, 1966), p. 528.
14. Stravinsky, "Some Ideas," pp. 529–31; translation amended.
15. Schoenberg, "How One Becomes Lonely" (1937), trans. Leo Black, in *Style and Idea: Selected Writings of Arnold Schoenberg*, ed. Leonard Stein (Berkeley, CA, 1985), p. 53.
16. Heinz-Klaus Metzger and Rainer Riehn, eds., *Schönbergs Verein für musikalische Privataufführungen*, Musik-Konzepte 36 (Munich, 1984).
17. Schoenberg, "New Music, Outmoded Music, Style and Idea" (1946), in *Style and Idea*, p. 124.
18. Schoenberg, "How One Becomes Lonely" in *Style and Idea*, p. 52.
19. Paul Landormy, "Schönberg, Bartók, und die französische Musik," *Musikblätter des Anbruch*, May 1922; quoted in Messing, *Neoclassicism in Music*, p. 126.
20. Henrietta Malkiel, "Modernists Have Ruined Modern Music, Stravinsky Says," *Musical America*, 10 January 1925, p. 9.
21. H. H. Stuckenschmidt, "Zwölftöne-Musik," *Melos* 4 (1925), p. 520.
22. Schoenberg, "Schoenberg's Tone-Rows" (1936), in *Style and Idea*, p. 213.
23. Schoenberg, "National Music" (1931), in *Style and Idea*, p. 170.
24. Ibid., p. 171.
25. Ibid.
26. Ibid., p. 173.
27. Josef Rufer, *The Works of Arnold Schoenberg: A Catalogue of His Compositions, Writings, and Paintings*, trans. Dika Newlin (New York, 1963), p. 45.
28. Quoted in Alex Ross, *The Rest Is Noise: Listening to the Twentieth Century* (New York, 2007), p. 295.
29. Ibid., p. 207.
30. Leon Botstein, "Gustav Mahler's Vienna," in *The Mahler Companion*, ed. Donald Mitchell and Andrew Nicholson (Oxford, 1999), p. 38.
31. Theodor W. Adorno, *Alban Berg: Master of the Smallest Link*, trans. Juliane Brand and Christopher Hailey (Cambridge, 1991), p. 104.
32. Douglas Green, "Berg's De Profundis: The Finale of the *Lyric Suite*"; George Perle, "The Secret Program of the *Lyric Suite*"; both in the *International Alban Berg Society Newsletter*, No. 5 (April 1977).
33. George Perle, *Style and Idea in the Lyric Suite of Alban Berg* (New York, 2001), p. 35.
34. Ibid., p. 37.
35. Ibid., p. 33.
36. Anton von Webern, *The Path to the New Music*, trans. Leo Black (Vienna, 1963), p. 54.
37. Ibid., p. 56.
38. Ibid., p. 45.
39. Anton von Webern, "Analysis of the String Quartet, op. 28," trans. Zoltan Roman, in Hans Moldenhauer and Rosaleen Moldenhauer, *Anton von Webern: A Chronicle of His Life and Work* (New York, 1979), pp. 755–56.

Chapter 31

1. David Schiff, *Gershwin: Rhapsody in Blue* (Cambridge, 1997), p. 83.
2. Quoted in Stephen Walsh, *Stravinsky: A Creative Spring: Russia and France, 1882–1934* (New York, 1999), p. 264.
3. Darius Milhaud, *Notes without Music*, trans. Donald Evans (New York, 1953), pp. 136–37.
4. Maurice Ravel, "Contemporary Music," in *The Rice Institute Pamphlets*, Vol. 15 (1928); reprinted in *MWW*, pp. 482–83.
5. Aaron Copland and Vivian Perlis, *Copland: 1900 through 1942* (New York, 1984), p. 35.
6. Quoted in Anthony Tommasini, *Virgil Thomson: Composer on the Aisle* (New Work, 1998), p. 98.
7. Quoted in Howard Pollack, *Aaron Copland: The Life and Work of an Uncommon Man* (New York, 1999), p. 113.
8. Copland and Perlis, *Copland: 1900 through 1942*, p. 104.
9. Warren Storey Smith in *The Boston Post*, 21 November 1925; ibid., p. 121.
10. John Tasker Howard, *Our Contemporary Composers* (New York, 1941), p. 149.

11. Hugh C. Ernst, introduction to the Whiteman program book; quoted in Thornton Hagert, "Jazz Invades Aeolian Hall," liner insert to *An Experiment in Modern Music: Paul Whiteman at Aeolian Hall* (The Smithsonian Collection R 028, 1981).
12. George Gershwin, "The Relation of Jazz to American Music," in *American Composers on American Music*, ed. Henry Cowell (Palo Alto, CA, 1933), p. 187.
13. "Rhapsody in Catfish Row: Mr. Gershwin Tells the Origin and Scheme for His Music in That New Folk Opera Called *Porgy and Bess*," *New York Times*, 20 October 1935; quoted in Charles Hamm, "Toward a New Reading of Gershwin," in Wayne Schneider, ed., *The Gershwin Style: New Looks at the Music of George Gershwin* (New York, 1999), p. 9.
14. Quoted in Joan Peyser, *The Memory of All That: The Life of George Gershwin* (New York, 1993), p. 84.
15. *New York Herald*, 13 February 1924; quoted in Carol J. Oja, "Gershwin and American Modernists of the 1920s," *Musical Quarterly* 78 (1994): 653.
16. Samuel Chotzinoff (*New York World*); quoted in Peyser, *The Memory of All That*, p. 107.
17. George Gershwin to Isaac Goldberg; quoted in Peyser, *The Memory of All That*, pp. 80–81.
18. Alex Ross, *The Rest Is Noise: Listening to the Twentieth Century* (New York, 2007), p. 147.
19. Cf. Rudy Vallee Hour, broadcast 10 November 1932, on *Gershwin Conducts Excerpts from* Porgy and Bess, Mark 56 Records 667 (1974).
20. Quoted in the *Alexander Glazunov Society Quarterly Newsletter* 2 (July 1986): 12.
21. Quoted in Ross, *The Rest Is Noise*, p. 153.
22. Ibid.
23. Jean Cocteau, *A Call to Order*, trans. Rollo H. Myers (London, 1926), pp. 25–26.
24. Guillaume Apollinaire, "Parade," *Excelsior*, 11 May 1917.
25. Quoted in Ross, *The Rest Is Noise*, p. 106.
26. Darius Milhaud, *Notes without Music*, trans. Donald Evans (New York, 1953), pp. 122–23.
27. Darius Milhaud, "Polytonalité et atonalité," *Revue musicale* 4 (1923); trans. R. Taruskin in *MWW*, p. 473–74.
28. Kathleen Hoover and John Cage, *Virgil Thomson: His Life and Music* (New York, 1959), p. 157.
29. Virgil Thomson, program note for *The Seine at Night* (1947); quoted in ibid. p. 108.
30. Virgil Thomson, *Virgil Thomson* (New York, 1967), p. 90.
31. Virgil Thomson, "About 'Four Saints,'" liner note to Nonesuch Records, No. 79035-1 X (1982).
32. Quoted in Stephen Hinton, *The Idea of Gebrauchsmusik: A Study of Musical Aesthetics in the Weimar Republic (1919–1933) with Particular Reference to the Works of Paul Hindemith* (New York and London, 1988), p. 181.
33. Alban Berg, lecture on *Wozzeck* (1929); Hans Redlich, *Alban Berg: Versuch einer Würdigung* (Vienna, 1957), p. 327.
34. *Brecht on Theatre*, trans. and ed. John Willett (New York, 1964), p. 39.
35. *Brecht on Theatre*, pp. 44–45; quoted in W. Anthony Sheppard, *Revealing Masks: Exotic Influences and Ritualized Performance in Modernist Music Theater* (Berkeley, CA, 2001), p. 88.
36. Miklós Rózsa, *A Double Life: The Autobiography of Miklós Rózsa* (New York: 1982).

Chapter 32

1. Sergey Prokofiev, *Autobiography, Articles, Reminiscences*, trans. Rose Prokofieva (Moscow, n.d.), p. 50.
2. Joseph Stalin, Report to the XVI Congress of the Communist Party of the Soviet Union (Bolshevik); J. V. Stalin, *Works*, Vol. 12 (Moscow, 1952) p. 379.
3. Quoted from Yuriy M. Keldïsh et al., eds., *Muzïkal'naya èntsiklopediya*, Vol. 5 (Moscow, 1981), p. 226.
4. Quoted in Laurel E. Fay, *Shostakovich: A Life* (Oxford, 2000), p. 26.
5. Dmitri Shostakovich, "Moyo ponimaniye 'Ledi Makbet,'" in *Ledi Makbet Mtsenskogo uyezda: Opera D. D. Shostakovicha* (Leningrad, 1934), p. 6.
6. "Sumbur vmesto muzïki," *Pravda*, 28 January 1936.
7. "The Murders of Mtsensk," *Time*, 11 February 1935, p. 35.
8. "Moy tvorcheskiy otvet," *Vechernyaya Moskva*, 25 January 1938, p. 30.
9. Ibid.
10. Khubov, "5-ya simfoniya," p. 22.
11. Alexander Fadeyev, *Za tridtsat' let* (Moscow, 1957), quoted in *Dmitriy Shostakovich*, ed. G. Ordzhonikidze (Moscow, 1967), p. 43.
12. S. S. Prokofieff and N. Ya. Myaskovsky, *Perepiska* (Moscow, 1977), p. 455.
13. *Testimony: The Memoirs of Dmitri Shostakovich as Related to and Edited by Solomon Volkov*, trans. Antonina W. Bouis (New York, 1979), p. 183.
14. Malcolm Hamrick Brown, *A Shostakovich Casebook* (Bloomington, IN, 2004).
15. Christopher H. Gibbs, "'The Phenomenon of the Seventh': A Documentary Essay on Shostakovich's 'War' Symphony," in *Shostakovich and His World*, ed. Laurel E. Fay (Princeton, NJ, 2004), pp. 59–113.
16. Harlow Robinson, ed. and trans., *Selected Letters of Sergei Prokofiev* (Boston, 1998), p. 153.
17. Quoted in Simon Morrison, *The People's Artist: Prokofiev's Soviet Years* (Oxford, 2009), p. 14.
18. Prokofiev, *Autobiography, Articles, Reminiscences*, p. 114.
19. Alfredo Casella, "Neoclassicism in Italy," *Christian Science Monitor*, 7 January 1928, p. 12.
20. Luigi Dallapiccola, "The Genesis of the *Canti di Prigionia* and *Il Prigioniero*," *The Musical Quarterly* 39 (July 1953), p. 366.
21. Benito Mussolini, *Opera omnia* 41 (Rome, 1979): 424; quoted in Harvey Sachs, *Music in Fascist Italy* (New York, 1988), p. 17.
22. Ibid.
23. Quoted in G. Barblan, *Toscanini e la Scala* (Milan, 1972); Sachs, *Music in Fascist Italy*, p. 213.

24. See Igor Stravinsky, *Selected Correspondence*, Vol. 3, ed. Robert Craft (New York, 1985), pp. 267.
25. Arnold Schoenberg, "Two Speeches on the Jewish Situation" (1934), trans. Leo Black, in *Style and Idea: Selected Writings of Arnold Schoenberg*, ed. Leonard Stein (Berkeley, CA, 1985), p. 502.
26. Quoted in Benjamin Suchoff, *Béla Bartók: A Celebration* (Lanham, MD, 2004), p. 8.
27. Igor Stravinsky and Robert Craft, *Memories and Commentaries* (Berkeley, CA, 1981), p. 123.
28. Hans Moldenhauer and Rosaleen Moldenhauer, *Anton von Webern: A Chronicle of His Life and Work* (New York, 1979), p. 474 (reporting a conversation with Hans Erich Apostel).
29. Quoted in Günther Brosche, "The Concerto for Oboe and Small Orchestra (1945)" in *Richard Strauss: New Perspectives on the Composer and His Works*, ed. Bryan Gilliam (Durham and London, 1992), p. 178.
30. Quoted in Bryan Gilliam, *The Life of Strauss* (Cambridge, 1999), p. 166.
31. See Timothy L. Jackson, "The Metamorphosis of the *Metamorphosen*: New Analytical and Source-Critical Discoveries" in *Richard Strauss: New Perspectives on the Composer and His Works*, pp. 193–241.
32. Quoted in Michael Kennedy, *Richard Strauss: Man, Musician, Enigma* (Cambridge, 1999), p. 361.
33. Ibid., p. 359.

Chapter 33

1. Judith Tick, "Ruth Crawford's 'Spiritual Concept': The Sound-Ideals of an Early American Modernist," *JAMS* 44 (1991).
2. Michael Hicks, "Cowell's Clusters," *Musical Quarterly* 77 (1993): 428, 440.
3. Quoted in Fern and Ouellette, *Edgard Varèse*, trans. Derek Coltman (New York, 1968), p. 47.
4. *SRMH*, p. 1339.
5. *New York Times*, 15 February 1925; rpt. J. Peter Burkholder, ed., *Charles Ives and His World* (Princeton, NJ, 1996), p. 293.
6. Harry Partch, Introduction to *Photographs of Instruments Built by Harry Partch and Heard in His Recorded Music* (Champaign, IL, 1962).
7. George Gershwin to Isaac Goldberg; quoted in Joan Peyser, *The Memory of All That: The Life of George Gershwin* (New York, 1993), p. 80–81.
8. George Pullen Jackson, *White Spirituals in the Southern Uplands* (Chapel Hill, NC, 1933).
9. Edith Hale, "Author and Composer Blitzstein," *Daily Worker*, 7 December 1938; Barbara Zuck, *A History of Musical Americanism* (Ann Arbor, MI, 1980), p. 211.
10. Quoted in Howard Pollack, *Aaron Copland: The Life and Work of an Uncommon Man* (New York, 1999), p. 224.
11. Aaron Copland, "Dmitri Shostakovitch and the New Simplicity," unpublished lecture, notes to which are in the Library of Congress (loc.music/copland.writ0059).
12. See Beth E. Levy, "Frontier Figures: American Music and the Mythology of the American West, 1895—1945" (Ph.D. diss., University of California at Berkeley, 2002).
13. Quoted in Beth E. Levy, "'The White Hope of American Music'; or, How Roy Harris Became Western," *American Music* 19 (2001).
14. George Henry Lovett Smith, "American Festival in Boston," *Modern Music* 17 (October–November 1939): 44.
15. Leonard Bernstein to Aaron Copland, 27 May 1947; reproduced in facsimile in Aaron Copland and Vivian Perlis, *Copland Since 1943* (New York, 1989), p. 70.
16. Bernstein to Copland, 8 November 1948; quoted in ibid., p. 71.
17. Ibid.
18. Barbara B. Heyman, *Samuel Barber* (Oxford and New York, 1992), pp. 166ff.
19. Murray Schafer, *British Composers in Interview* (1963); quoted in Philip Brett, *Peter Grimes* (Cambridge, 1983), p. 190.
20. Peter Pears, "Neither a Hero Nor a Villain" (1946); Brett, *Peter Grimes*, p. 152.
21. Brett, *Peter Grimes*.
22. Donald Mitchell and Philip Reed, eds., *Letters from a Life: Selected Letters and Diaries of Benjamin Britten* (Berkeley, CA, 1991), p. 1189.
23. Benjamin Britten, *On Receiving the First Aspen Award* (London, 1964), p. 21.
24. Ibid., p. 7.
25. Ibid., p. 22.
26. Ibid., p. 14.
27. Ibid., p. 12.
28. Ibid., p. 15.
29. Ibid., p. 12.
30. Olivier Messiaen, *The Technique of My Musical Language*, trans. John Satterfield (Paris, 1956), p. 8.
31. Ibid., p. 13.
32. Olivier Messiaen, *Music and Color: Conversations with Claude Samuel*, trans. G. Thomas Glasow (Portland, OR, 1994), p. 26.
33. Rebecca Rischin, *For the End of Time: The Story of the Messiaen Quartet* (Ithaca, NY, 2003).
34. Messiaen, *Technique*, p. 21.
35. Messiaen, *Music and Color*, p. 79.
36. Rischin, *For the End of Time*, p. 130.
37. Ibid.
38. Ibid.
39. Ibid.
40. Anthony Pople, *Messiaen, Quatuor pour la fin du temps* (Cambridge, 1998), p. 64.
41. Quoted in John Canarina, *The New York Philharmonic: From Bernstein to Maazel* (Portland, OR, 2010), p. 177.
42. Messiaen, *Music and Color*, pp. 168–69.
43. Ibid., p. 249.

Chapter 34

1. Theodor W. Adorno, "Cultural Criticism and Society" in *Prisms*, trans. Samuel Weber (Cambridge, MA, 1981), p. 34.

2. René Leibowitz, *Schoenberg and His School*, trans. Dika Newlin (New York, 1949), p. xvi.
3. *New York Times Book Review*, 27 November 1949; quoted in Anne C. Shreffler, "Who Killed Neo-Classicism?: The Paradigm Shift after 1945," paper read at the Sixty-second Annual Meeting of the American Musicological Society, Baltimore, 8 November 1996.
4. Theodor W. Adorno, *Philosophy of New Music* (1948), trans. Anne G. Mitchell and Wesley V. Blomster (New York: Seabury Press, 1973), pp. 32–37.
5. Pierre Boulez, "Schoenberg Is Dead" in *Notes of an Apprenticeship*, trans. Herbert Weinstock (New York, 1968), p. 274.
6. Ibid., p. 275.
7. Theodor W. Adorno, "Das Altern der neuen Musik" (1954), trans. Susan H. Gillespie (as "The Aging of the New Music"), in T. W. Adorno, ed., *Essays on Music*, Richard H. Leppert (Berkeley, CA, 2002), pp. 197–98.
8. Boulez, "Schoenberg Is Dead," p. 275.
9. Olivier Messiaen, *Music and Color: Conversations with Claude Samuel*, trans. G. Thomas Glasow (Portland, OR, 1994), p. 47.
10. "German Music in the 1940s and 1950s," in Hans Werner Henze, *Music and Politics: Collected Writings 1953–81*, trans. Peter Labanyi (Ithaca, NY, 1982), p. 43.
11. Michael Kurtz, *Stockhausen: A Biography*, trans. Richard Toop (London, 1992), p. 36.
12. Alan Gillmor, "Interview with John Cage (1973)," quoted in David Revill, *The Roaring Silence. John Cage: A Life* (New York, 1992), p. 30.
13. John Cage, "The Future of Music: Credo," in *Silence: Lectures and Writings by John Cage* (Cambridge, MA, 1966), p. 4.
14. Ibid., p. 5.
15. Revill, *The Roaring Silence*, p. 84.
16. Ibid., p. 88.
17. Cole Gagne and Tracy Caras, *Soundpieces: Interviews with American Composers* (Metuchen, NJ, 1982); quoted in Richard Kostelanetz, *Conversing with Cage* (New York, 1988), p. 91.
18. Quoted in Revill, *The Roaring Silence*, p. 99.
19. John Cage, "History of Experimental Music in the United States," in *Silence*, p. 73.
20. Robert Rauschenberg, in "John Cage: I Have Nothing to Say and I Am Saying It," American Masters documentary directed and coproduced by Allan Miller, written and produced by Vivian Perlis; PBS broadcast 16 December 1990.
21. Morton Feldman, "Liner Notes," in *Give My Regards to Eighth Street: Collected Writings of Morton Feldman* (Cambridge, MA, 2000), p. 5.
22. Reproduced in Nyman, *Experimental Music: Cage and Beyond* (New York, 1974), p. 70.
23. Quoted in ibid., p. 74.
24. "Relations: Friends and Allies Across the Divide; Merce Cunningham and Nam June Paik," *New York Times Magazine*, 16 July 2000, p. 11.
25. Cornelius Cardew, "Introduction," in *Scratch Music*, ed. Cornelius Cardew (Cambridge, MA, 1974), p. 9.
26. *Scratch Music*, p. 62.
27. Feldman, *Give My Regards to Eighth Street*, p. 6.
28. Quoted in Nyman, *Experimental Music*, p. 45.
29. Feldman, *Give My Regards to Eighth Street*, p. 126.
30. "Rencontre avec Stravinsky," *Preuves* II, No. 16 (1952): 37.
31. Milton Babbitt, in Joel Chadabe, *Electric Sound: The Past and Promise of Electronic Music* (Upper Saddle River, NJ, 1997), p. 18.
32. Cage, *Silence*, pp. 3–4.
33. Ferruccio Busoni, *Sketch of a New Esthetic of Music*, trans. Theodore Baker, in *Three Classics in the Aesthetic of Music* (New York, 1962), p. 77.
34. *Panorama of Musique Concrète* (London/Ducretet-Thomson No. DTL 93090).
35. Charles Dodge, liner note to *Computer Music*, Nonesuch Records No. H-71245 (ca. 1970).
36. Edgard Varèse, "The Liberation of Sound," in *Perspectives on American Composers*, eds. Benjamin Boretz and Edward T. Cone (New York, 1971), p. 32.
37. Gunther Schuller, "Conversation with Varèse," *Perspectives on American Composers*, pp. 38–39.
38. Quoted in Fernand Ouellette, *Edgard Varèse*, trans. Derek Coltman (New York, 1968), p. 200.
39. Chadabe, *Electric Sound*, pp. 56–57.
40. Quoted in Paul Griffiths, *György Ligeti* (London, 1983).
41. Bernard Jacobson, *A Polish Renaissance* (London, 1996).
42. Elliott Carter, "Music and the Time Screen," in *Current Thought in Musicology*, ed. John W. Grubbs (Austin, TX, 1976).
43. Benjamin Boretz, "Conversation with Elliott Carter," *Contemporary Music Newsletter* 2, Nos. 7–8 (November–December 1968): 3.
44. Allen Edwards, *Flawed Words and Stubborn Sounds: A Conversation with Elliott Carter* (New York, 1971), pp. 91–92.
45. Ibid., p. 35.
46. Liner note to Nonesuch Records No. H-71249 (1970); reprinted in *Elliott Carter: Collected Essays and Lectures*, Jonathan W. Bernard, ed. (Rochester, 1997), 232.
47. Ibid., p. 233.
48. Igor Stravinsky and Robert Craft, *Dialogues and a Diary* (Garden City, NY, 1963), p. 49.
49. Milton Babbitt, "Who Cares If You Listen?," *High Fidelity*, February 1958; reprinted in *MWW*, pp. 532–34.

Chapter 35

1. Allan Kozinn, *The Beatles* (London, 1995), p. 159.
2. William Mann, "The Beatles Revive Hopes of Progress in Pop Music," *The Times*, 29 May 1967; in Elizabeth Thomson and David Gutman, *The Lennon Companion* (New York, 1987), p. 89.
3. Ned Rorem, "The Music of the Beatles," *New York Review of Books*, 18 January 1968; in Thomson and Gutman, *The Lennon Companion*.
4. Joshua Rifkin, "On the Music of the Beatles," in *The Lennon Companion*, pp. 113–14.
5. Gunther Schuller, "Third Stream Revisited," in *Musings: The Musical Worlds of Gunther Schuller* (New York, 1986), p. 119.
6. Edward Strickland, *American Composers: Dialogues on Contemporary Music* (Bloomington, IN, 1991), p. 45.

7. Michael Hicks, *Henry Cowell, Bohemian* (Urbana, IL, 2002), p. 145.
8. Richard Wollheim, "Minimal Art," *Arts Magazine*, January 1965, pp. 26–32.
9. La Monte Young, quoted in K. Robert Schwarz, *Minimalists* (London, 1996), p. 9.
10. La Monte Young, quoted in Keith Potter, *Four Musical Minimalists* (Cambridge, 2000), p. 48.
11. Ibid., p. 148
12. Alfred Frankenstein, "Music Like None Other on Earth," *San Francisco Chronicle*, 8 November 1964; quoted in Schwarz, *Minimalists*, p. 43.
13. Robert Carl, *Terry Riley's* In C (Oxford, 2009), p. x.
14. Strickland, *American Composers*.
15. John Adams, "Reich, Steve," in *New Grove Dictionary of American Music*, Vol. 4 (London, 1986), p. 23.
16. Liner note to Odyssey Stereo No. 32 16 0160 (1967).
17. "Music as a Gradual Process" (1968), in Steve Reich, *Writings on Music 1965–2000* (New York, 2002), pp. 34–36, condensed.
18. Adams, "Reich," p. 25.
19. Steve Reich, interviewed by Michael Nyman, *Studio International, November/December 1976*; quoted in Schwarz, *Minimalists*, p. 80.
20. Philip Glass, *Music by Philip Glass*, ed. Robert T. Jones (New York, 1987), p. 53.
21. Metropolitan Opera House program, 21 November 1976; reproduced in booklet accompanying Tomato Records No. TOM-4-2901 (1977), p. 6.
22. Philip Glass, "Notes on *Einstein on the Beach*," ibid., p. 10.
23. Cole Gagne and Tracy Caras, *Soundpieces: Interviews with American Composers* (Metuchen, NJ, 1987), p. 216.
24. John Rockwell, "Steve Reich and Philip Glass Find a New Way," *Rolling Stone*, 19 April 1979.
25. Quoted in Walsh, "The Heart Is Back in the Game," *Time*, 20 September 1982, p. 60, col. 3.
26. John Rockwell, "The Ups and Downs of Minimalism: *Broken Glass*," *The New Republic*, 10 April 2000, pp. 31ff.
27. Strickland, *American Composers*, p. 46.
28. Liner note to ECM Records New Series No. 1275 (1984).

Chapter 36

1. Alex Ross, *The Rest Is Noise: Listening to the Twentieth Century*, p. 341.
2. Kyle Gann, *Music Downtown: Writing from the Village Voice* (Berkeley, CA, 2006), p. x.
3. Charles Wuorinen, *Simple Composition* (New York, 1979), p. 3.
4. Gann, *Music Downtown*, p. 121.
5. Cited in ibid., p. 121.
6. Ibid., pp. 103–4.
7. Andreas Huyssen, "Mapping the Postmodern" in *After the Great Divide: Modernism, Mass Culture, Postmodernism* (Bloomington, IN, 1986), p. 181.
8. Jean-François Lyotard, *La condition postmoderne: Rapport sur le savoir* (Paris, 1979), p. 2. The English term "master narrative" was coined by Frederic Jameson in his foreword to the English translation of the book (Jean-François Lyotard, *The Postmodern Condition: A Report on Knowledge*, trans. Geoff Bennington and Brian Massumi [Minneapolis, 1984], p. xii) as a rendering of Lyotard's term *grand récit*.
9. Liner note to Nonesuch Records No. H-71283 (1973).
10. Umberto Eco, *Postscript to The Name of the Rose* (New York, 1984), pp. 67–68.
11. Liner note to Nonesuch Records H-71283 (1973).
12. Ibid.
13. Don C. Gillespie, *George Crumb: Profile of a Composer* (New York, 1986), p. 108.
14. John Rockwell, *All American Music: Composition in the Late Twentieth Century* (New York, 1983), pp. 82–83.
15. Paul Moravec, "An Interview with David Del Tredici," *Contemporary Music Review* 6, part 2 (1992): 21.
16. Fred Lerdahl and Ray Jackendoff, *A Generative Theory of Tonal Music* (Cambridge, MA, 1983), p. 301.
17. Liner notes to Sofia Gubaidulina, *Seven Words, Ten Preludes, De profundis*, ECM New Series No. 1775 (2008).
18. Tod Machover, "A View of Music at IRCAM," *Contemporary Music Review* 1, Part 1 (1984): 1.
19. Georgina Born, *Rationalizing Culture: IRCAM, Boulez, and the Institutionalization of the Musical Avant-Garde* (Berkeley CA, 1995).
20. Paul Lansky, "It's about Time: Some Next Perspectives (Part One)," *Perspectives of New Music* 27 (Summer 1989): 271.
21. Ibid., p. 271.
22. Kyle Gann, "Electronic Music, Always Current," *New York Times*, 9 July 2000, Arts and Leisure, p. 24.
23. Liner note to Meredith Monk, *Dolmen Music*, ECM Records No. 1-1197 (1981).
24. William Duckworth, *Talking Music: Conversations with John Cage, Philip Glass, Laurie Anderson, and Five Generations of American Experimental Composers* (New York, 1999), p. 359.
25. Geoff Smith and Nicola Walker Smith, *New Voices: American Composers Talk about Their Music* (Portland, OR, 1995), p. 192.
26. Susan McClary, *Feminine Endings: Music, Gender, and Sexuality* (Minneapolis, 1991), p. 138.
27. Quoted in ibid., p. 139.
28. Peter Niklas Wilson, "Zorn, John," in *NGDMM*, Vol. 27, p. 869.
29. John Zorn, liner note to *Spillane* (1987); quoted in Susan McClary, *Conventional Wisdom: The Content of Musical Form* (Berkeley, CA, 2000), p. 146.
30. Liner note to Joan Tower, *Made in America*, Naxos Records No. 8.559328 (2007).
31. Alex Ross, "The Harmonist," *The New Yorker*, 8 January 2001, p. 46.
32. Philip Glass, "A Bridge Between the Past, the Present, and the Future," booklet essay accompanying Glass, *Symphony No. 5: Requiem, Bardo, Nirmanakaya*, Nonesuch Records No. 79618-2 (2000).

Glossary

ABSOLUTE MUSIC instrumental music composed purely as music, and not intended to represent or illustrate something else as in program music.

A CAPPELLA Latin for "as in the chapel"; sung without accompaniment.

ACCOMPANIED KEYBOARD SONATA a type of keyboard sonata popular in the late eighteenth century in which the accompanying instrument or instruments (violin, sometimes flute, sometimes with cello) play a secondary role and could be eliminated if necessary.

ACCOMPANIED RECITATIVE a style reserved for special dramatic effects, in which the entire orchestra accompanies the singer.

AESTHETICS critical reflection on art, culture, and nature; the term also refers to a branch of philosophy dealing with the nature of beauty, art, and taste, and with the creation and appreciation of beauty.

AFRICAN AMERICAN SPIRITUAL Christian religious songs of the enslaved African peoples in the United States; although Antonín Dvořák considered this music a potential resource for American musical nationalism, the spiritual proved more useful to twentieth-century African American musicians.

AGGREGATE in serial theory, the complete set of all twelve pitch classes; a term coined by Milton Babbitt.

AGGREGATE HARMONIES "ultimate" chords, each containing all twelve pitches of the chromatic scale.

AGRÉMENTS French for "embellishments"; a crucial stylistic element of French Baroque music; an extensive series of ornaments that worked in tandem with the bass harmony to punctuate the lines and to enhance their rhetorical projection.

ALBERTI BASS a common pattern of the Classical style in which three-note chords are broken low-high-middle-high; the periodic phrases tend to be evenly balanced; those ending on the dominant, requiring continuation, are "antecedents"; their balancing "consequents" often begin like repetitions, creating "parallel periods."

ALEATORIC MUSIC music composed (or performed) to some degree according to chance operations or spontaneous decisions; a term used to describe the work of John Cage.

ALIENATION EFFECT from the German *Befremdung*, a characteristic of early twentieth-century German theater with a text and performance style designed to make its actions and workings as "strange" or "foreign" as possible, with the goal of focusing the audience on political rather than emotional responses; associated with the work of German playwright Bertolt Brecht.

ALLEMANDE a dance that originated in Germany, but by the time German composers borrowed it back from the French it had changed from a quick dance to a slower, stately movement in a broad quadruple meter.

ANSWER in a fugue, the entrance of the second voice that comes in playing the subject "at the fifth" (meaning a fifth up or a fourth down).

ANTIPHON a short prose sung sentence inserted before or after a psalm and sometimes between its individual verses, sung in alternation by two halves of the choir.

ARS NOVA Latin for "new art," the style represented by Guillaume de Machaut and composers of the fourteenth century.

ARS PERFECTA A term of appropriation employed by Heinrich Glareanus (*Dodecachordon*, 1547) to describe the music of Josquin des Prez as a "perfected art" to which nothing could ever be added.

ARS SUBTILIOR Latin for "subtle art"; a style that flourished from about 1370 to 1390, and employed Guillaume de Machaut's music to the employment of highly complex rhythmic and metrical relationships, sometimes with obscure notational devices. The term was coined in the 1960s.

ATONAL music that does not adhere to any system of key or mode.

AUGENMUSIK German for "eye music"; describes graphical features of scores that, when performed, are inaudible to the listener.

BALLAD the main narrative genre of Romantic folk poetry; a sung narrative poem, often one that included dramatic dialogue between humans and supernatural beings and that typically ended in disaster.

BALLADE French for a "danced song"; a genre of Medieval poetry and song that consists of three structurally identical stanzas each concluding with the same refrain line and each sung to the same music; one of three *formes fixes*.

BALLAD OPERA an English form of theatrical entertainment consisting of a spoken play (usually comic) with many interpolated short songs, the music for which was borrowed from popular songs of the day.

BALLATA from Italian *ballare*, "to dance"; Medieval Italian secular song in AbbaA form.

BALLET D'ACTION French for "pantomime"; a costumed ballet using gesture, dance, and instrumental music to tell a story without song or spoken text; while gesture functioned as recitative, set dances expressed emotional content as would an operatic aria.

BALLET DE COUR French for "court ballet"; an elaborate spectacle of dance, poetry, and decor in which the king himself occasionally took part (most famously Louis XIV); the overall effect represented the divinely instituted political and social hierarchy of the French monarchy.

BALLETS RUSSES a dance company directed by Sergey Diaghilev, based in Paris (1909–1929); many of its dancers and contributors came from the Imperial Ballet of Saint Petersburg and, after the Russian Revolution of 1917, from among the community of exiles.

BAROQUE a term used to encompass the music of the period from roughly around 1600 to 1750, that is, from the time of the first Italian operas to the death of J. S. Bach.

BASSO CONTINUO in Baroque music, an independent bass part written as one line but with shorthand numerical instructions (figures) to indicate the full harmony; a solo instrument performs the bass line while the harmony is realized on a keyboard instrument or lute.

BEL CANTO Italian for "fine singing"; a term to describe the Italian operatic style of the Romantic era, featuring virtuosic coloratura vocal parts that emphasized the upper registers and paralleled increasingly emotional scenarios and louder, more dramatic orchestral accompaniments.

BERGERETTE a fifteenth-century French song identical in structure with the *virelai*, but with only one stanza.

BINARY FORM a structuring of music into two related sections, each of which is repeated.

BLUE NOTE a note sung or played at a slightly lower pitch than that of the major scale for expressive purposes; typically the alteration is a semitone or less, but this varies among performers and genres; a blues singer will sing these notes sharp, so that they lie "in the crack" between the minor and the major third.

BLUES an African American folk genre with poorly understood latenineteenth-century origins; by the 1900s, a performance by a self-accompanying singer (with guitar or banjo) using a framework (commonly "twelve-bar," but not exclusively) over which the singer improvises a three-line poem on any subject—repeating the first line as the second line, with the third line rhyming with the other two; the expressivity of the blues style inspired American popular music around World War I, both in an urban setting (with piano and small band accompaniment) and as part of the early New Orleans jazz repertoire.

CABALETTA the concluding faster section of a two-part complex aria or duet in Italian opera.

CACCIA Italian for "chase"; a thirteenth-century type of madrigal, comprising two sections (terzetti, ritornello); the three-voice texture consisted of a cantus (running against itself in canon) over an untexted tenor; the subject matter often involved the hunt.

CADENZA an improvised or written-out ornamental passage played or sung unaccompanied by a soloist or soloists, often in a "free" rhythmic style, and allowing for virtuosic display; prominent in the vocal aria and the instrumental concerto.

CALL AND RESPONSE a technique in which a succession of two distinct phrases is played by different musicians, where the second phrase is heard as an echo of or a response to the initial phrase.

CAMERATA a group of humanists, musicians, poets, and intellectuals in late Renaissance Florence who gathered under the patronage of Count Giovanni de' Bardi to discuss and guide trends in the arts, especially music and drama.

CANON 1) a procedure in which a melodic part begins alone, then continues while a second part begins the same music on the same pitch (or in transposition), with the potential for more such entrances; the strictest form of imitative music; 2) an accumulating body of permanent masterworks that form the bedrock of a repertory.

CANSO Provençal for "song"; specifically the love song of the troubadour.

CANTABILE Italian for "song-like"; applied to instrumental chamber music.

CANTATA a Baroque vocal piece with instrumental accompaniment; originally for solo voice, later a liturgical work in several movements, often involving a choir.

CANTILLATION the chanting of a text by a soloist, associated with Jewish liturgical music.

CANTUS Latin for "song" or "melody."

CANTUS FIRMUS Latin for "fixed tune"; refers to the placement of a chant melody in the tenor part of a polyphonic piece.

CAPRICE a term meaning "according to the fancy of the performer"; used to designate a piece with sudden contrasts and unexpected effects.

CAPUT MASSES a group of Masses, many of which are anonymous, based on a cantus firmus, which unified all of the movements.

CASTRATO (pl. castrati) in the Baroque era, a male singer whose preadolescent vocal range was made permanent through castration; the resulting unique sonority produced internationally admired stars who sang in the difficult virtuosic style demanded by composers and audiences.

CAUDA Latin for "tail"; a polyphonic melisma, written in ligatures, on the penultimate syllable of a conductus.

CAVATINA A solo aria in one section, often connected with a character's entrance; in instrumental music a song-like movement (e.g. Ludwig van Beethoven's String Quartet in B♭, Op. 130).

CHACONNE before 1800, a moderately fast dance in variation form; after 1800, a severe set of variations over a ground bass, often interchangeable with the passacaglia.

CHANSON French for "song"; applicable to any French-language song from the Medieval era on; specifically, a lyric-driven polyphonic secular song, up to around 1600.

CHANSON DE GESTE French for "song of gesture"; a lyrical epic poem sung to short melodic formulas by the trouvères.

CHARACTER PIECE single-movement work for piano with a descriptive title.

CHORALE strophic unison Lutheran hymn based on Gregorian chant or original melody; also, the harmonization of such a hymn.

CHORALE CONCERTO a work for mixed instruments and voices based on religious texts; also called sacred concerto.

CHORALE PARTITA a large-scale multi-movement piece of music based on a chorale and written for a keyboard instrument; the first movement is a harmonization of the original chorale, while the subsequent movements are variations on the chorale melody and harmonization, using a variety of textures and figuration.

CHORALE PRELUDE a single-stanza setting with which the organist might cue the congregation to sing or to provide an accompaniment to silent meditation.

CHURCH MODE a scale type used in Gregorian and later music, assigned Greek names freely borrowed from Boethius by theorists; each mode has a final (the modal center), a hierarchy of secondary tones, and characteristic melodic turns; the original set of eight scales comprised the authentic modes, focused on the octave above finals D, E, F, and G (Dorian, Phrygian, Lydian, and Mixolydian, respectively) and the plagal modes, focused below and above the final (Hypodorian, Hypophrygian, Hypolydian, Hypomixolydian); Renaissance theorists expanded modal theory to polyphonic music and added the Ionian (final C) and Aeolian (final A) modes.

CIRCLE OF FIFTHS a geometrical representation of the relationships among the twelve tones of the chromatic scale, their corresponding key signatures, and the associated major and minor keys, based on the interval of a perfect fifth (ascending) or perfect fourth (descending).

CLASSICAL PERIOD a musical style that prevailed from around 1750 to the 1820s, embodied in the works of Franz Joseph Haydn, Wolfgang Amadè Mozart, and Ludwig van Beethoven.

CLAUSULA little discant sections inserted into Medieval polyphonic organum.

CLAVICHORD a keyboard instrument capable of dynamic gradations unavailable on the harpsichord, but with much softer dynamic range, best suited to intimate performances in small spaces.

COLLAGE the pasting together or superimposition of disparate styles, thus creating a unique whole; an eclectic approach akin to similar impulses in art and literature.

COLOR 1) in Medieval and Renaissance music, the repetition of a pitch sequence without regard to changing rhythmic values; 2) timbre.

COLORATURA elaborate melody, particularly in virtuosic vocal music.

COMBINATORIAL in serial theory, a term that describes how constituent hexachords can combine interchangeably to produce aggregates; a term coined by Milton Babbitt.

COMMERCIAL OPERA the presentation of opera in public theaters, rather than exclusively courtly auspices; the first such performance in an opera house took place in Venice in 1637.

COMMUNISM a left-wing sociopolitical movement that dominated much of Eastern Europe and Asia in the twentieth century; although Communist nations had much in common with governments based on fascist principles, its cultural impact led to ongoing battles between the notions of a unified, nonelitist state and individual artistic expression.

CONCEPT ALBUM a recording of nonclassical music in which the collection of pieces on a "long playing" (LP) album were coordinated, like the individual numbers in a Romantic song cycle, giving an overall impression unified through textual content and musical treatment.

CONCERTATO STYLE from the late Renaissance onward, an approach featuring alternation between different combinations of voices and instruments, with emphasis on short-range contrast; the music called for specific instruments, marking the beginning of the art of orchestration; an important concept throughout the Baroque era and which evolved into the concerto concept, with increased interest in long-range continuity and focus on a soloist or group of soloists.

CONCERTINO a group of soloists in a concerto grosso, alternating with the ripieno.

CONCERTO a musical work usually composed in three movements, featuring a solo instrumentalist (sometimes a group of soloists) accompanied by an orchestra.

CONCERTO GROSSO An instrumental concerto, most associated with the seventeenth and eighteen century, that pits a small group of soloistic players (concertino) against a full ensemble (ripieno).

CONCERT OVERTURE A piece of music in sonata form or in the style of an operatic overture intended for independent performance; a forerunner of the symphonic poem.

CONCERT SPIRITUEL the earliest significant European concert series, organized in Paris by Anne Danican Philidor in 1725 and lasting until 1790.

CONDUCTUS a Medieval genre of polyphonic music practiced at Notre Dame; a syllabic setting of a contemporary Latin poem, freely composed rather than chant-based, in a homorhythmic (note-against-note) texture.

CONSORT MUSIC in the sixteenth and seventeenth centuries, an early form of polyphonic instrumental chamber music, scored for a group of similar or mixed instruments, designed for domestic use.

CONTENANCE ANGLOISE French for "English manner"; a contemporaneous term for a fifteenth-century style of English polyphony, later influential on French composers, using full, rich sonorities based on the third and sixth (first inversion harmonies).

CONTRAFACTUM a vocal piece in which the original text is replaced by a new one.

CONTREDANSE a form of country dance, originating in the eighteenth century and related to the quadrille.

CONVERSATION BOOK a small notebook used by Ludwig van Beethoven in which people wrote out questions and comments to which he would respond orally.

COPULA an intermediate texture in Medieval organum during which the duplum sings usually two phrases in regular modal patterns over sustained tenor notes; the ratio of notes in the duplum to notes in the tenor in such sections becomes much smaller.

CORI SPEZZATI Italian for "split choirs"; the division of musical forces into distinct groups, both musically and sometimes spatially, in concertato style.

COUNCIL OF TRENT an emergency legislative body of the Roman Catholic Church that first convened in 1545 to stem the tide of the Protestant Reformation that was perceived as posing a threat to the Church.

COUNTER-REFORMATION the Roman Catholic reaction to the Reformation; resulting reforms to the Church involved structural reconfiguration, religious orders, spiritual movements, and political dimensions.

COUNTERSUBJECT the counterpoint with which the original voice accompanies the answer in a fugue.

COURANTE a grave triple-meter, notated in $\frac{3}{2}$ with many lilting hemiola effects caused by patterns cutting across the pulse.

CYCLIC FORM a unifying compositional device in which a theme, melody, or thematic material recurs in more than one movement of a multimovement work.

CYCLIC MASS a setting of the major unchanging elements of the Roman Catholic liturgy (the Ordinary) as a single musical unit, unified by a cantus firmus, modes, motives, or other compositional procedures; a leading musical genre of the fifteenth and sixteenth centuries.

DA CAPO ARIA an aria that is designed to go back "to the beginning," the form of which is ABA—two contrasting sections with a repetition (sometimes varied) of the first section to conclude the piece; found in opera, liturgical music, song, and in instrumental movements.

DECADENCE a term introduced by critics in the mid-1880s to criticize the fin de siècle culture of rarefied, artificial, esoteric, exacting taste and an acceptance of perversity; subsequently a favorite term of totalitarian authorities for uncooperative artists.

DEVELOPING VARIATION a musical process by which small motivic fragments are constantly evolving, not only in development sections but throughout a work; Arnold Schoenberg coined the term in association particularly with the music of Johannes Brahms.

DEVELOPMENT in sonata form, this section follows the exposition and typically develops one or more themes from the exposition through neighboring or remote keys before returning to the home key for the recapitulation of the exposition.

DIALECTIC the belief that human history develops according to a process in which a concept (thesis) inevitably gives rise to its opposite (antithesis); their subsequent interaction produces a resolution (synthesis) that in turn becomes the thesis to begin the process anew. Associated in particular with the German philosopher Georg Wilhelm Friedrich Hegel (1770–1831).

DIATONIC the field of pitches and pitch relationships reducible to a specific and functional arrangement of tones and semitones ("whole steps" and "half steps"); specifically, the major and minor scales recognized in Western music since the Baroque era.

DISCANT a technique of composition in Medieval organum in which one voice is added to a plainchant part, usually note against note and mostly in contrary motion.

DIVERTIMENTO Italian for entertainment music, which was usually scored for a combination of solo instruments and was light in approach.

DOMINANT the fifth scale degree of both diatonic scales.

DOUBLE RETURN the return of both tonic and the exposition thematic material after the development in a sonata form movement, following a harmonically and thematically freer development section; the double return creates one of the dramatic events of the sonata form.

DRAMMA GIOCOSO Italian for "humorous drama"; genre of opera common in the eighteenth century.

DUPLUM Latin for "in two parts"; originally, a Medieval composition for two voices; later, the second voice by itself, placed above the tenor.

ECLECTICISM a conceptual approach that does not hold rigidly to a single paradigm or set of assumptions, but instead draws upon multiple theories, styles, or ideas to create a unique interpretation of a subject or a particular work by whatever means are deemed necessary.

ELEKTRONISCHE MUSIK German for "electronic music"; music based on electronically altered (as in *musique concrète*) or newly synthesized sounds; for composers in the post–World War II Modernist orbit the neutrality of synthesized sound, its freedom from worldly associations, constituted its chief appeal.

EMPFINDSAMER STIL German for "sensitive style"; an early Classical compositional style developed in mid-eighteenth-century Germany, intended to express "true and natural" feelings and featuring sudden contrasts of mood.

EMPFINDSAMKEIT the German equivalent of sensibility; a musical aesthetic that aimed not at a more objective depiction of a character's feelings, as in an *opera seria*, but rather at the expression and transmission of varying human emotions.

EMULATION honoring a model through imitation; a simultaneous homage to and attempt to surpass that model, conforming to it while distinguishing itself from it in a conspicuous way.

ENDLESS MELODY a seamless stream of notes that continually avoids the finality of a cadence; associated with Richard Wagner.

EPISODE 1) a solo section for an instrument within a concerto; 2) a non-thematic section within a fugue.

ETHNOMUSICOLOGY the study of music outside of the Western classical tradition using fieldwork methods originally found in anthropology.

ETON CHOIR BOOK a richly illuminated manuscript collection of English sacred music composed during the late fifteenth century; one of the few collections of Latin liturgical music to survive the Reformation, it originally contained music by twenty-four different composers.

EXOTICISM a genre in which the rhythms, melodies, or instrumentation are designed to evoke the atmosphere of non–Western European cultures.

EXPOSITION the opening portion of the sonata form, in which the tonic and principal secondary keys and principal thematic material are introduced; originally framed by repeat signs.

EXPRESSIONISM an aesthetic movement of the early twentieth century, akin to similar literary and artistic movements; musical Expressionism concerned itself with the ruthless depiction of disturbing or distasteful emotions, often with a stylistic violence that could involve pushing ideas to their extremes or treating the subject matter with incisive parody; an outgrowth of late Romanticism, it was fully realized in the Modernist atonality of Arnold Schoenberg.

EXTENDED PERFORMANCE TECHNIQUES a collection of methods, including augmented ranges, novel sounds from traditional instruments and voices, and special fingerings to produce chords or "multiphonics" on woodwinds, used by specialist virtuosos in order to perform more experimental twentieth century works.

FABURDEN a late Medieval English technique of harmonizing melodies at sight by producing a series of parallel $^6_3$ chords with the melody note in the middle.

FANTASIA a musical approach characterized by structural freedom, improvisational in origin although later applied to composed music that emulated the rhythmic variability and increasing harmonic waywardness possible in this context.

FANTASY a musical piece of no fixed form, rooted in improvisation, in which the composer follows his imagination.

FASCISM an authoritarian and nationalistic right-wing system of government and social organization. Although it shared many aspects of the contemporaneous twentieth-century Communist movement (emphasis on a totalitarian single-party state, mass mobilization through indoctrination, physical education, and family policy), fascism's approach to musical censorship was based primarily on the principles of racial hatred.

FAUXBOURDON a choral technique of singing improvised polyphony in which a "false bass" a fourth below is added to the melody; in the fifteenth century this technique became compositional as well; easily confused with the faburden technique.

FAVOLA IN MUSICA Italian for "musical tale."

FIGURED BASS in basso continuo, an ongoing bass line played by a solo instrument; harmonies to be filled in by a keyboard or lute performer are indicated by little numbers (figures) representing intervals.

FIN' AMORS French for "refined love," or courtly love, the self-professed subject of the troubadour love song (*canso*).

FOLK SONG a "simple," "rustic," or "peasant" song; traditionally found in an oral tradition, but latterly applied to composed pieces that attain widespread popularity.

FORMES FIXES the three chief poetic forms used for late Medieval songs: the ballade, virelai, and rondeau, found in monophonic and polyphonic settings.

FRENCH OVERTURE in French Baroque opera, an orchestral introduction that consisted of a slow section with dotted rhythms, followed by a fast imitative section.

FROTTOLA syllabic, homophonic songs for three or more voices in Italian of a lighter character, popular around 1500; a predecessor to the Renaissance madrigal.

FUGUE from the Latin *fuga* (flight, fleeing); a texture in which a subject (theme) in one voice is followed by two or more voices entering successively and imitating the subject, thus "giving chase" to the preceding voice; in instrumental music, often a genre; with non-thematic episodes; in vocal music, a compositional procedure rather than a fixed structure.

FUTURISM an early twentieth-century movement encompassing the work of Italian artists (*futuristi*), notably poet Filippo Tommaso Marinetti and painter Luigi Russolo, who called for an "art of noises" and invented devices to produce sonic representations of the machine age; Russian composers were involved in their own futurist movement, which flourished immediately after the 1917 Revolution and involved extended instrumental techniques; their approach influenced American ultramodernists such as Henry Cowell.

GALANT from the French *galante*; an eighteenth-century aesthetic of decorative art and architecture that focused on pleasure and accessibility; in music, an emphasis on pleasant, easily absorbed melody with light accompaniment; a homophonic reaction to Baroque equal-voiced contrapuntal texture; found in the music of France, Italy, Germany, and England.

GEBRAUCHSMUSIK German for "music for use"; in early twentieth century German culture, music with a non-elitist, utilitarian purpose, especially that written for amateurs or students (*Hausmusik*), rather than professionals; associated with some works by Paul Hindemith.

GESAMTKUNSTWERK German for "total or united work"; a work of art, often operatic, that makes use of all or many media (e.g., music, theater, visual arts) as directed by a single creator; most often applied to the work of Richard Wagner.

GIGUE French for "jig" (Italian *giga*); an up-tempo dance with dotted rhythms imported from England and Ireland, usually in meter; in the Baroque, a standard movement of the instrumental suite.

GRAND OPERA a Romantic opera on a serious theme in which the entire libretto (including dialogue) is sung and the staging gives a dazzling sense of spectacle.

GREGORIAN CHANT the monophonic and traditionally unaccompanied music of Eastern and Western Christian liturgy, its texts are predominantly taken from psalm verses, along with other scriptural readings; named after Pope Gregory I (served 590–604).

GRUNDGESTALT German for "basic shape"; Arnold Schoenberg's term for a motivic complex presented at the beginning of a work that serves as a source for everything that follows, whether melodic, harmonic, or contrapuntal in nature; theoretically, their interrelationships could be discovered through analysis.

GUIDONIAN HAND a visual teaching aid from the Middle Ages showing the notes of the modes and their solmization syllables at specific points on the human hand.

HAPPENINGS in the mid-twentieth century, minimally planned performance events involving traditional or nontraditional media; forerunners of so-called mixed media and performance art.

HARMONIC RHYTHM the underlying rhythm articulated by changes of harmony within a given phrase or structure, often applied to the rate of change in chords.

HEXACHORD a six-note pitch segment recognized by Guido of Arezzo in the eleventh century, represented by the solmization syllables *ut, re, mi, fa, sol, la*; basis of musical theory through the Renaissance.

HISTORICISM in music, 1) the application of an older, recognizable approach to contemporary composition; 2) the notion of inevitability in stylistic development.

HUMANISM the study of ancient texts on linguistics and rhetoric that informed the ideals of the Renaissance.

HYMN a metrical song of praise derived from Greek pagan practice; the term is now usually applied to vernacular Christian songs for worship.

HYMNODY the repertoire of hymns within a specific tradition.

IDÉE FIXE French for "fixed idea"; a term invented by Hector Berlioz for a musical idea that recurs obsessively within a work, thus recalling an associated idea.

IMBROGLIO in comic opera, the moment of greatest plot confusion, prior to its inevitable disentanglement and resolution.

IMITATION MASS a Mass setting that borrows motifs, points of imitation, or two or more parts from a preexisting piece of music, such as a sacred motet or a secular chanson, as the basis for a new composition.

IMPRESARIO Italian for "entrepreneur"; a person who organizes and often finances concerts, plays, or operas; this individual used contacts and influence to hire composers and singers at the behest of theatrical organizations.

IMPRESSIONISM named after an influential school of late nineteenth-century French painters, a term first applied to the post-Wagnerian experiments of Claude Debussy in the 1890s; musical Impressionism encompassed calculated effects of spontaneity, fascination with subtle gradations in color and texture, and a greater interest in sensuousness than in psychology or strongly declared emotion.

IMPROMPTU structurally free character pieces that give the impression of white-hot improvisation.

INNIGKEIT German for poignant, intimate feeling.

INSTRUMENTAL RECITATIVE in instrumental works, passages in which melodic lines resemble vocal recitatives; a nonverbal communication from composer and performer to listener.

INTERMEDIO (Italian; pl. *intermedii*) short, musical-dramatic items performed between acts of a Renaissance theatrical performance.

INTERMEZZO Italian for "entr'acte"; 1) a short comic opera, often in two acts, presented between individual acts of a typical *opera seria*; 2) a short character piece for piano.

INVERSION the turning upside-down of a melody; in twelve-tone or serial music, the inversion of a row or series of notes.

IRCAM an acronym for Institut de Recherche et Coordination Acoustique/Musique (Institute for Research and Coordination of Acoustics and Music), opened by the French government in 1977 under Pierre Boulez's direction to provide opportunities to work with the latest electronic technology; the institute is now focused on computer music production and research.

ISORHYTHM term used by modern scholars to denote the use of recurrent nonsynchronous rhythmic and pitch patterns as a main structural component in late Medieval music.

JANISSARY an early example of musical exoticism, namely the imitation of Turkish wind and percussion bands in music of the Baroque and Classical periods.

JAZZ a musical style that originated at the beginning of the twentieth century in African American communities in the southern United States, a confluence of African and European music traditions that incorporated the outlines of late nineteenth- and twentieth-century American popular music; West African influence is evident in its use of blue notes, improvisation, polyrhythms, syncopation, and the swung (rhythmically altered) note; characterized by a spontaneity and vitality of musical production in which improvisation came to play a key role.

JAZZ-ROCK FUSION a popular genre mixing R&B rhythms, the amplification and electronic effects of rock, complex time signatures derived from non-Western music, and extended, typically instrumental compositions with a jazz approach to lengthy group improvisations; prevalent among late 1960s and 1970s-era jazz-rock bands.

JOGLAR (Provençal; French *jongleur;* English "juggler") a singer-entertainer of a lower class, later called a minstrel; quasi-troubadours who memorized the work of the noble poets and developed some creative facility, but who lacked courtly patronage and functioned as itinerant wits.

KLANGFARBENMELODIE German for "tone-color melody"; Arnold Schoenberg's term for a compositional technique in which a musical line or melody is distributed among several instruments, emphasizing its timbral and textural components; when applied to a single note, the potential for a compositional structure results.

KÖCHEL abbreviation for the standard thematic catalogue of the works of Mozart drawn up by the music historian Ludwig Köchel (1800–77) and revised several times.

KUCHKA Russian, from *moguchaya kuchka*, "mighty little heap"; translated as "the Five" or "Mighty Handful"; critic Vladimir Stasov's nickname for a circle of composers who met in Saint Petersburg during the years 1856–70 Miliy Balakirev, César Cui, Modest Musorgsky, Nikolai Rimsky-Korsakov, and Alexander Borodin; their goal was to develop a specifically Russian kind of art music that combined earlier Russian nationalist impulses with the Romantic doctrine of musical progress.

L'HOMME ARMÉ French for "The Armed Man"; an anonymous song used as the cantus firmus of or melodic resource for more than forty Masses by Renaissance composers from Dufay to Palestrina; applied on such a massive scale, these Masses represent a cross-section of 150 years of changing musical style.

LANDINI CADENCE a late Medieval phrase ending for two voices; while the lower voice moves from the second to the first degree, the upper voice starts on the raised seventh degree, drops down to the sixth degree before leaping up to the eighth degree to form a concluding octave.

LEITMOTIF the successor to the *idée fixe*, a recurring, recognizable musical idea representing a particular person, place, or idea in a narrative context; the music dramas of Richard Wagner exemplify the structural use of this technique.

LES SIX the nickname of six early twentieth-century French composers whose music was often seen as a reaction against German Romanticism and Impressionism; Georges Auric, Louis Durey, Arthur Honegger, Darius Milhaud, Francis Poulenc, and Germaine Tailleferre revered the work and attitude of Erik Satie, but shared little in common aesthetically.

LIBRETTO the text that is set in an extended musical work such as an opera, operetta, or musical.

LIED (plural: Lieder) German for "song"; in the Classical and Romantic periods, the setting of a lyric poem for voice accompanied (usually) by piano.

LIGATURE from Latin *ligare*, "to bind"; a single neume representing two or more pitches in Medieval chant and polyphony.

LITURGY the prescribed order for a religious service.

MADRIGAL 1) a fourteenth-century Italian secular song for two or three voices, setting poems comprising three-line stanzas with a melismatic upper part and a concluding ritornello (refrain); unrelated to 2) a part song for four or more voices sung a cappella, composed in a free style dictated by the text, sometimes set to elaborate counterpoint; refers primarily to English or Italian songs of the sixteenth and seventeenth centuries, intended for domestic use.

MADRIGALISM in Renaissance vocal music especially, the use of illustrative devices, notably word painting, to reflect musically the literal or figurative meaning of the text through pitch direction, texture, range, or other means.

MAGYAR NÓTA "Hungarian music," specifically urban popular music derived largely from Romani (gypsy) culture; misunderstood as indigenous Hungarian music by Franz Liszt, Johannes Brahms, and others; distinguished from *nepdalok* ("folk music"), the peasant music that Béla Bartók and Zoltán Kodály studied.

MARIAN ANTIPHON a devotional setting of a Latin prose text in praise of Mary; by itself, an antiphon (Greek *antiphōnon*, octave) precedes and succeeds the psalm setting in a service of the Divine Office.

MASQUE a form of festive courtly entertainment in sixteenth- and early seventeenth-century Europe, featuring music, dancing, singing, an acting (often by courtiers themselves), an elaborate stage design, and costumes; masks were used by the participants for disguises; as a theatrical genre, evolved into late seventeenth-century English dramas and semi-operas.

MASS the primary public worship service of Roman Catholic churches; also, a cyclical setting of the Ordinary of the Mass.

MASS SONG a choral song with lyrics designed to promote the Communist ideology, first in the Union of Soviet Socialist Republics (from the 1920s), later in Communist parties throughout the world.

MAXIMALISM a philosophical term applied to early twentieth-century music making, implying a radical intensification of means toward expressive ends; Gustav Mahler's symphonies, with their plurality of styles and extended dimensions, were the culmination of late Romantic aesthetics, while the unprecedented collage of resources in Charles Ives's works would come to be seen as the first significant Modernist form of maximalism.

MAZURKA a moderately fast Polish dance in triple time, the basis of Frédéric Chopin's musical nationalism.

MELODIC RECITATIVE a description of the vocal settings of Modest Musorgsky, characterized by strict one-note-per-syllable declamation, abundance of short repeated notes, mirroring of the intonational contour of the spoken language, and (after the opening) the absence of melodic repetitions; a concept related to Guiseppe Verdi's *parlando* and a major influence on Claude Debussy and Leoš Janáček.

MÉLODIE the French art song, lighter than a chanson, analogous to the German Lied.

MELODRAMA accompanied speech, spoken over an instrumental or orchestral background; on occasion a work of operatic length.

MENSURAL NOTATION in late Medieval and Renaissance music, a term referring to evolving (and not necessarily universal) systems that expressed rhythmic values through ligature interpretation, changing (sometimes simultaneous) meters, and a complex system of rhythmic levels; dependent on individual partbooks, mensural notation was superseded by score notation alongside the shift to metric uniformity in Baroque music and the addition of expression marks; note values were reduced to a single set of symbols related by a factor of two.

METRIC MODULATION a mid-piece pivot from one time signature (meter) and tempo to another, wherein a note value from the first is made equivalent to a note value in the second; associated with the practice of Elliott Carter, who favored the term "temporal modulation."

METRICAL PSALM a psalm translated into rhyming, strictly metrical verse in the vernacular, composed and sung as a hymn and collected in a psalter; developed for the worship services of John Calvin and his successors.

MICROTONALITY the use of pitch differences smaller than a half-step, already described in ancient theory; in the twentieth century, the basis for numerous experiments and tuning systems, notably by composers outside the American mainstream.

MIDI an acronym for Musical Instrument Digital Interface; a set of technical specifications or "protocols" allowing for free interaction between computers and synthesizers from the early 1980s on; a primary means of processing voices and instruments electronically.

MINIMALISM a term anticipated by twentieth-century art; initially, a post–World War II style of few pitches or pitch changes, long durations, and extensive use of silence (culminating in John Cage's 4′33″); from the 1960s, experimental music based mostly in consonant harmony, steady pulse, stasis or gradual transformation, and iteration of musical phrases or smaller units such as figures, motifs, and cells; this style, the popularity of which partly derives from similarities to various kinds of popular and non-Western musics, has featured in multi-media theatrical, operatic, and dance works.

MINNESANG German for "love song"; specifically, settings composed between the twelfth and fourteenth centuries, modeled on the troubadour courtly love songs.

MINUET AND TRIO the triple-meter form used in most third movements of the four-movement Classical symphony.

MODAL MIXTURE a tonally destabilizing technique that involves the infiltration within a major key of harmonies drawn from its parallel minor (or vice versa).

MODE 1) any scale, now applied to tone-centered Western music outside the major-minor axis and pitch sets used in non-Western classical music and music out of an oral tradition; 2) in Medieval theory, the rhythmic interpretation of mensural notation.

MODERNISM a commitment by artists of the nineteenth and twentieth centuries to find ways of reflecting the historical present and momentum toward the future; a revolt against late Romanticism and musical naturalism, initially characterized by the move toward atonality and the music of the Futurists, later by the stylistic distortion of Neoclassicism.

MODES OF LIMITED TRANSPOSITION a concept described by composer-theorist Olivier Messiaen (*The Technique of my Musical Language*, 1944), applying the concept of pitch invariance by means of symmetry; specifically, the invariance found in two scales—the whole-tone scale, which has only one possible transposition (by a half step) and the octatonic scale (alternating half steps and whole steps), which has only two; these scales had begun appearing in late nineteenth-century music.

MONODRAMA theatrical or operatic piece performed by a single actor or singer, using music and speech to portraying one character; although examples date back to the Classical period, Arnold Schoenberg's *Erwartung* (1909) help reestablish the genre as Modernist.

MONODY a style of song for one voice and basso continuo; the first characteristic Baroque genre and the basis of early opera.

MONOPHONY unaccompanied singing, solo or in unison.

MOTET 1) a genre of Medieval polyphonic vocal music that derived from the texting of upper parts in clausulae, starting in the thirteenth century; as the motet evolved, the tenor (chant) voice remained slower, while the (increasingly newly composed) polytextual upper parts focused on both religious or secular subjects, to be sung simultaneously and written in Latin, French, or occasionally both (macaronic). 2) in the Renaissance and Baroque, a nonliturgical sacred vocal work in the contemporaneous (or historical) style.

MUSEUM CULTURE a term for the idea, beginning in the early nineteenth century, that music needed to preserve the works of the past in the repertoire because of their being of permanent value; now applied to the present focus on music of the past, to the virtual exclusion of contemporary or even recent works, in performance.

MUSICA FICTA Latin for "false music"; refers to any accidentals (or chromatic alterations by the performer) that lie outside the notational system used in Medieval and Renaissance music; often a dilemma for present-day interpreters of this music.

MUSICA Latin for "music"; derived from Greek *mousike*, "art of the Muses"; a term, found in numerous treatises, such as those of Augustine of Hippo and Boethius.

MUSICAL or musical comedy, an English-language theatrical form (also found in film) that combines songs, spoken dialogue, and dance to convey a story or thematic idea; successor to such genres as the German Singspiel and the French and Austrian operetta.

MUSIC DRAMA the name given by Richard Wagner to his later operas.

MUSIQUE CONCRÈTE a form of electroacoustic music, first explored by Pierre Schaeffer in France in the late 1940s and made possible by the invention of the tape recorder; originally limited to the use of naturally occurring sounds (that is, not electronically generated) through electronic processing and cut-and-splice editing.

MUSIQUE D'AMEUBLEMENT French for "furniture music"; a genre invented and named by Erik Satie, described by Darius Milhaud as "background music that would vary like the furniture of the rooms in which it was played" and "that would not be listened to"; an inspiration for commercially recorded mood music to suit different environments, but ironically viewed by John Cage as a forerunner of works such as 4′33″—music that was *meant* for listening.

MYSTIC CHORD a complex six-note chord, scale, or pitch collection (C, F♯, B♭, E, A, D; all but A belong to the same whole-tone scale), which loosely serves as the harmonic and melodic basis for some late pieces by Alexander Scriabin; its lack of half-steps excludes that interval's role in the major/minor tonal system.

NATIONALISM a political ideology favoring the strong identification of a group of individuals with an ethnic or political entity, supported in part by that group's culture.

NEOCLASSICISM the conscious use of techniques, gestures, styles, forms, or media from an earlier period; a significant twentieth-century trend, particularly during the period between the two World Wars, in which composers sought to return to aesthetic precepts associated with the broadly defined concept of "classicism" (order, balance, clarity, economy, emotional restraint), but not limited to the Classical style; a reaction to both the giganticism of late Romanticism and the extreme emotional palette of Expressionist Modernism; ironically, two of its best-known exponents had composed in the very styles they were reacting to: Igor Stravinsky and Paul Hindemith.

NEO-ROMANTICISM a return, especially during the post-World War II era, to the emotional expression associated with nineteenth-century tonal musical style.

NEO-TONALISM a stylistic umbrella embracing musical composition in the twentieth and twenty-first centuries that is eclectic and unbound by "rules"; may incorporate atonality and tonality in the same score.

NEUE SACHLICHKEIT German for "new objectivity"; in post–World War I music, a desire for stylistic concreteness, alertness, sobriety, hard reality, and matter-of-factness, often couched in neo-Baroque modeling and eclectic use of popular music and jazz.

NEUME before late Renaissance notation, a written sign that represents a melodic turn such as might be sung in one breath. In chant notation, neumes first tracked the relative rise and fall of pitches, the approximate matching of note to text syllable, and rhythmic relationships; the system increased in precision before being replaced by score notation.

NEW COMPLEXITY a concept dating from the 1980s, principally applied to English composers whose work was often atonal, highly abstract, and dissonant in sound, its technical demands requiring complex musical notation; it has been interpreted both as a reaction to neo-Romanticism and minimalism and as a continuation of the highly abstract European avant-garde from the 1950s, notably the work of Karlheinz Stockhausen and Pierre Boulez.

NEW DEAL in response to the Great Depression, a series of economic programs implemented in the United States during the first term of President Franklin D. Roosevelt in the 1930s; in music, the Works Progress Administration gave jobs to numerous artists, including musicians, funded community orchestras, and supported the Archive of American Folksong at the Library of Congress, a major depository of ethnographic research.

NEW GERMAN SCHOOL a mid-nineteenth-century term applied to the circle of composers around Franz Liszt in Weimar; attached to Richard Wagner (who did not accept the appellation) and Hector Berlioz.

NOCTURNE French for "of the night"; a short character piece of a romantic or dreamy character, typically for piano.

NONRETROGRADABLE RHYTHM a rhythmic palindrome; an arrangement of note values that reads the same both forward and backward; used by Olivier Messiaen, it is more structural than audible.

OCCURSUS Latin for "meeting"; in two-part free organum, the ending on the same note (unison) by both parts.

OCTATONIC any eight-note musical scale, the most famous of which alternates half steps and whole steps.

OFFICE a cycle of eight daily prayer services in Catholic, Orthodox, and Anglican liturgy; Vespers, the evening service, was set most often in the polyphonic era.

OLD HALL MANUSCRIPT GB-Lbl *Add.57950*, earliest largely intact and decipherable English source of polyphonic church music (70 percent of it attributed); represents the state of English music ca. 1370–1420.

ONDES MARTENOT a monophonic electronic instrument, first demonstrated in 1928 by French engineer Maurice Martenot (1898–1980); in its final version, the performer may use a conventional keyboard or a ribbon that alters the pitch along a smooth continuum; its relatively small repertoire has been primarily created by French composers, most famously Olivier Messiaen.

OPERA BUFFA Italian for "comic opera"; applied first to Neapolitan-language works in the late Baroque, then to Italian works between 1750 and 1860 (Mozart, Rossini); characteristics include rapid-fire *secco* recitative, vigorous stage business, and a formally complex, often polytextural finale with dramatic confusion leading to peaceful resolution.

OPÉRA COMIQUE a type associated with Parisian theaters (the Opéra-Comique and Comédie-Italienne), where French ballad operas with spoken dialogue or recitative (*vaudevilles*) were performed (eighteenth-century Baroque); applied to French-language opera buffa of the Classical era; finally, a dramatic structure of arias alternating with spoken dialogue, prevalent after the French Revolution; the "comique" element became increasingly serious in tone, although happy endings remained; by Georges Bizet's time, an opera comique could be serious, even tragic in tone, as long as the dialogue was spoken, not sung.

OPÉRA LYRIQUE a nineteenth century musical genre combining the accompanied recitatives of grand opera with characterization of a less heroic group of individuals and with less grandiose if often tragic plots; makes use of attractive ("lyrical") melodies reminiscent of domestic songs and drama; unrelated to the Baroque *tragédie lyrique*.

OPERA SERIA the noble, "serious" style of Italian opera that dominated European music throughout the eighteenth century, with its standard alternation of recitative and aria and focus on larger-than-life characters.

OPERETTA French for "little opera"; a return to the less serious type of opéra comique, with its lighter music and subject matter; developed in the 1850s, this Parisian genre featured dancing, frivolous buffoonery, familiar tunes "borrowed" from other operas, and social and political satire; as absorbed by Austrian composers, the genre became increasingly sentimental; in this more serious form, it came to America in the early twentieth century; by the post-World War I era, it had been superseded by the musical.

ORATORIO a large-scale dramatic work based on a religious (usually biblical) topic, neither liturgical nor theatrical in intent, but performed in a concert setting.

ORDINARY the set of unchanging Mass texts sung at every service; the components of a cyclic Mass composition.

ORGANICISM the notion that all movements of a musical composition are thematically related, based on the work's opening measures; embodied by the Fifth Symphony of Ludwig van Beethoven.

ORGANUM the earliest form of Western polyphony, first described in the eleventh century; initially, a second voice improvised over a chant, then a more florid part over a slow moving, untexted chant line; by the thirteenth century, as many as three florid texted parts above the chant line, in modal rhythm.

ORIENTALISM the musical representation of non-European (generally Asian) cultures; before the nineteenth century, defined by the Janissary music of the Ottoman Empire; from the late nineteenth century on, resources expanded to Asia (the Javanese gamelan) and Africa (the expansion of timbres and complexity in percussion parts); only in the post–World War II period did Orientalism give way to the idea of world music.

PANTONAL a single transcendent, all-encompassing tonality; the term preferred by Arnold Schoenberg to describe his music, rather than the term "atonal," which he consider pejorative; characterized by the elimination of the tonal hierarchy of the scale, replaced by composition "with twelve tones [the chromatic scale] which are related only with one another."

PARAPHRASE 1) in late Medieval and Renaissance Mass composition, the transformation of an existing melody into a new cantus firmus; in the sixteenth century, use of this melody as thematic material for imitation and other contrapuntal techniques; 2) a virtuoso Romantic piano piece, usually based on operatic arias, in the spirit of a fantasia.

PARLANTE (parlando) singing in a speech-like or conversational manner, especially in Romantic Italian opera.

PART SONG typically a piece for four solo voices (or choral voices), with the melody in the highest voice (soprano or first tenor); in the nineteenth century, a genre geared toward domestic music making, most popular in Germany and England, for male, female, or mixed choruses.

PARTITA A Baroque suite, typically for a solo instrument or chamber ensemble.

PASSACAGLIA Italian translation of Spanish *passacalles*; an improvisational set of triple-meter variations on cadential patterns, developed by early Baroque guitarists; later composed for solo instruments or chamber ensembles; eventually interchangeable with the chaconne.

PASSION ORATORIO a Baroque setting of the Crucifixion story based on one of the four New Testament gospels; there are recitative parts for a narrator (the Evangelist) and various characters; arias reveal the Christian believer's reactions to the events; and the crowd, with its changing emotions, is represented by a chorus.

PASTICHE French for "imitation"; a musical piece parodying an earlier style; distinct from pasticcio (Italian, pastry), a single theatrical or instrumental work involving pieces by several composers.

PASTORELA Provençal for "pastoral"; a troubadour courtly song affecting a mock-popular style, depicting a conversation between a knight and a shepherdess.

PATTER SONG a comic aria in which a character has to enunciate a text at rapid-fire speed.

PERFORMANCE ART an umbrella for post–World War II actions that have been framed as works of art; such actions may be scripted or unscripted, random or carefully orchestrated, spontaneous or carefully planned, with or without audience participation; performance art may take place in any venue or setting, for any length of time, and involve an individual or a group; often but not necessarily multidisciplinary in nature.

PHASING a minimalist technique in which two players begin together and slowly get out of sync to produce a kind of canon; most associated with the music of Steve Reich in the 1970s.

PIANO DUET two people—four hands—playing at one keyboard; a form of domestic music making from the Classical era on, both practical and pedagogically useful.

PITCH CLASS in serial and atonal music theory, the set of pitches related by octave transposition and designated with a single letter name (twelve in all).

POINT OF IMITATION in contrapuntal music, an opening motif in one voice that is subsequently imitated by other voices; in fugal writing, this pattern may recur (in different keys) as needed; applicable to instrumental and vocal music.

POLONAISE French, from Polish *polonez*; a stately Baroque court dance in triple time; it had gained nationalist cachet by the Romantic era, culminating in the piano works of Frédéric Chopin.

POLYPHONY a compositional texture involving contrapuntally independent voices.

POLYTONALITY a vertical composite of two or more keys at once; a Modernist hallmark of the early twentieth century.

POPULAR FRONT a propaganda approach by Communist parties in the 1930s, de-emphasizing their connection to the USSR in an attempt to unite with the non-Communist left to fight the rise of German fascism; in music, a large number of song anthologies appeared, including volumes of mass songs.

POSTMODERNISM a late-twentieth-century concept and approach in the arts, architecture, and criticism that represent an anti-Modernist distrust of grand theories and ideologies as well as a problematical relationship with the notions of "art," "values," and "truth"; Postmodernism reveals a radical skepticism that may result in an inherent, even overwhelming, sense of irony.

PRELUDE an instrumental introduction to works ranging from fugues and suites to operas; sets of independent preludes began with Frédéric Chopin's Opus 24.

PREPARED PIANO drawing upon Henry Cowell's earlier experiments, an invention of John Cage in which he turned a grand piano into a multifarious percussion band by inserting metal screws, pencil erasers, and other objects between the piano strings to alter the timbre.

PRIMA PRATICA Italian for "first practice"; a term used in early seventeenth-century Italy to distinguish Renaissance polyphony from the new, more dissonant style (*seconda pratica*).

PRIMITIVISM a fascination by that which is least mediated by modern society; an exoticism based on notions of "savagery" and raw emotion; reflected in early twentieth-century music through the influence of African and Latin American percussion music mixed with unbridled rhythmic drive.

PROGRAM MUSIC a broad category of pieces with sometimes elaborate background stories or extramusical references.

PROGRESSIVE ROCK a subgenre of rock music that developed in the 1960s and 1970s, successor to the concept album; an attempt by rock musicians to increase musical depth by going beyond standard verse-chorus-based song structures, by exploring extended musical structures, intricate instrumental patterns and textures, and often esoteric subject matter; arrangements might draw from classical, jazz, and world music, and an increased role for non-texted instrumental pieces.

PROLATION the number of subdivisions (two or three) per mensural whole-note (semibreve).

PROPER the group of changing Mass texts according to a yearly cycle, as opposed to the Ordinary texts, which remain constant; chants based on Proper texts accompany specific actions of the liturgy.

PROTESTANT REFORMATION a series of challenges to Roman Catholic orthodoxy, becoming prominent in the sixteenth century; the resulting split in Western Christianity led to more than two centuries of war; in music it led to an inclination toward more homophonic music sung in the vernacular language.

PSALM A sacred song or hymn, with texts taken from the biblical Book of Psalms and used in Christian and Jewish worship; often collected in a book called a psalter.

PSALM TONE the chant formula for singing a psalm, in which melody is subservient to a medium for the exaltation of a sacred utterance. Eight psalm tones are used in the Latin liturgy, plus one called the *tonus peregrinus* ("migrating tone").

QUERELLE DES BOUFFONS French for "Quarrel of the Buffoons"; a philosophical battle between rival musical styles, in Paris between 1752 and 1754; specifically, the relative merits of French and Italian opera.

RAGTIME the highly syncopated African American music of great popularity between around 1890 and the end of World War I; a character piece exemplified by the piano music of Scott Joplin and influential on European composers.

REALISM a umbrella term for many arts in different eras, in which creators work within an aesthetic directed at producing works reflecting natural, "truthful" depictions of existence; in opera, a term applied to various styles: early Baroque recitative's attention to speech rhythms; Christoph Willibald Gluck's reform opera; early Romantic depictions of nature; Modest Musorgsky and others' setting of librettos in conversational prose to music mirroring actual tempos and contours; and late nineteenth-century Italian *verismo*.

RECAPITULATION in sonata form, the final section of the movement, in which the thematic material of the exposition is restated in such a way as to end in the tonic, often reinforced by a coda.

REFORM OPERA a type of opera, championed by Christoph Willibald Gluck, which embodied sensibility and aimed to be natural and true to real life, especially in accompanied recitative.

RESCUE OPERA a genre of opera in the late eighteenth and early nineteenth centuries that dealt with the rescue of a main character from danger, ending with a happy denouement in which lofty humanitarian ideals triumph over base motives.

RESPOND (RESPONSORY) in liturgical chant, a tripartite call-and-response structure a freely composed respond (begun by the cantor, then by the choir), a verse sung to a psalm tone (cantor), and a second respond (choir).

RETROGRADE the ordering backward of a row, especially in twelve-tone or serial music.

RHAPSODY a Romantic character piece that is episodic yet integrated, free-flowing in structure, featuring a range of highly contrasted moods, color, and tonality; often variation-like, but with an predominant air of spontaneous inspiration and improvisation.

RHYTHM AND BLUES (R&B) a genre of African American popular dance music that developed in the 1940s, mixing blues and gospel styles with a driving percussive swing beat; the source for Caucasian American rock 'n' roll of the mid-1950s.

RICERCARE a term first applied to rhapsodic lute preludes in the sixteenth century; became a contrapuntal instrumental genre modeled on the *ars perfecta* vocal style; in the Baroque, a kind of strict fugue with short thematic subjects.

RIPIENO the tutti group of the orchestra in a Baroque concerto, alternating with the concertino.

RISORGIMENTO the nineteenth-century political movement that sought and accomplished the unification and independence of Italy; Giuseppe Verdi became a symbol of the movement, and served in the chamber of deputies and the senate of the new nation.

RITORNELLO Italian for "return"; 1) a recurring passage in Baroque music heard in the tutti, serving as the structural framework in concertos and arias; 2) in the Medieval Italian caccia and madrigal, the concluding refrain, setting the same melody to the same text.

ROARING TWENTIES the era between the end of World War I and the onset of the Great Depression, an age of dynamic social change and contradictions, especially in urban centers; in popular music, the rise of jazz and urban blues; in art music, the flowering of the Neoclassical style.

ROCK term applied to 1960s rock 'n' roll as it shifted away from its rhythm-and-blues dance origins (the "roll") in style and, later, subject matter; centered in Britain and America, rock was intended for listening, not dancing; by the 1970s, its composers focused on the idea of "meaning" rather than its earlier utilitarianism.

ROCK 'N' ROLL a genre of American dance music that evolved in the United States from African American rhythm and blues, with elements of jazz as well as Caucasian American country and western music; unique in that it was socially divisive (between youth and parents) while being socially uniting (gradually breaking down color barriers).

ROCOCO a description of pre-Classical eighteenth-century aesthetics, originally pejorative; the emphasis on elegance, wit, and delicacy applies most closely to French solo and chamber music of the period; more or less equivalent to galant.

ROMANTICISM a movement in the arts and literature, originating in the late eighteenth century and carrying through to the early twentieth century, emphasizing inspiration, subjectivity, and the primacy of the individual.

RONDEAU a French Medieval round dance song setting; typically, a thirteen-line poem broken into three stanzas (5, 3, and 5 lines), set to only two musical phrases; the complex repetition pattern depends on the poem's length; the genre's popularity lasted through the fifteenth century; one of three *formes fixes*.

RONDO a Classical form in which a lively opening thematic section alternates with "episodes," then concludes with the theme (and often a coda); common in last movements of symphonies, concertos, and keyboard sonatas.

ROTA a short, circular canon at the unison or octave, normally for as many unaccompanied voices as its melody allows; each voice enters successively, then continues with the rest of the melody; equivalent to the modern-day round.

RUBATO Italian for "robbed" (*tempo rubato*, robbed time); originally, the altering of note values in a melody within a steady pulse to achieve expressive nuance; from around 1850, applying accelerando or ritardando to all parts freely, thereby achieving larger-scale expressivity.

SACRALIZATION OF MUSIC the Romantic elevation of the art form to a highly spiritual level, encouraging the belief that music could improve people and society aesthetically, ethically, and even politically.

SALON from the eighteenth century onward, a gathering of people in the home of a patron for the purposes of amusement and edification of its participants through conversation, readings, and chamber music making; as privileged as the small groups of invitees were, the prestige of the patron was even more at stake; gradually the salon became a increasingly competitive vehicle for the channeling of art patronage as well as the exchange of ideas, leading to the composition and commissioning of many new works.

SAMPLER a device that stores recorded sounds of any kind for the purposes of imitation or transformation into new forms.

SARABANDE a lively triple meter song-dance originating in New Spain (sixteenth century); brought to Europe, becoming a guitar genre with ostinato bass; later, harmonic patterns, characteristic rhythms, and a slower tempo led it onto the theatrical stage; by the middle Baroque period, sarabandes were standard in instrumental suites, becoming a virtuoso piece in J. S. Bach's chamber music.

SCENA any division of an act in Italian opera; an important set piece of several smaller pieces (finales), a scene with a self-contained dramatic trajectory focusing on the changing emotions of one or more characters.

SCHERZO Italian for "joke"; after 1800, a movement that replaces the slower minuet and trio in a four-movement work (symphony, sonata, string quartet); also a fast-moving independent composition.

SCHUBERTIADE a salon-like event centered around Franz Schubert, who performed his music and participated in party games such as charades; in modern times, any gathering devoted to that composer's work.

SECONDA PRATICA Italian for "second practice"; originally, Claudio Monteverdi's term of challenge to the conservative treatment of contrapuntal dissonance (*prima pratica*) favored by Gioseffo Zarlino and his followers; a promised treatise never appeared, and Monteverdi grew increasingly involved with the monodic style.

SECOND VIENNESE SCHOOL the circle of composers who studied with Arnold Schoenberg, notably Anton Webern and Alban Berg; the group paralleled the stylistic developments of their teacher in early twentieth century Vienna, first characterized by late-Romantic expanded tonality, later, a totally chromatic atonal Expressionism and eventually Schoenberg's serial twelve-tone technique.

SEMI-OPERA (DRAMATIC[K] OPERA) English Restoration–era entertainments that combined spoken plays with masque-like episodes employing singing and dancing characters.

SEQUENCE 1) the more or less exact repetition of a melody transposed to another level, higher or lower; 2) a type of Latin hymn that flourished from the ninth century to the sixteenth century, setting non-biblical texts syllabically to newly composed music; originally intended for specific feast days, sequences were gradually added to the Mass Proper to be sung after the Alleluia; in the mid-sixteenth century, the Council of Trent eliminated all but five from the Mass.

SEQUENCER a device that puts digitally stored sounds (or information about those sounds) into a programmed order, controlling any number of units within various parameters.

SERENATA in the Italian Baroque, a staged dramatic cantata intended for court or aristocratic homes.

SERIALISM a compositional technique in which the basic material is an ordered arrangement—row, set, or series—of pitches, intervals, durations, and, if desired, other musical elements; developed by Arnold Schoenberg.

SICILIANA a type of aria or instrumental movement of the Baroque period, in slow $\frac{6}{8}$ or $\frac{12}{8}$ time with lilting rhythms; also, a slow gigue for dancing.

SIMILE ARIA a Baroque aria in which the character compares his or her situation to some natural phenomenon or activity in the world at large, while the music provides appropriate illustration.

SINFONIA Italian for "symphony."

SINFONIA CONCERTANTE a Classical-era multimovement successor to the concerto grosso that features two, three, four, or more soloists who interact more with one another (like the earlier concertino) than with the larger ensemble (the latter-day ripieno); the term "symphony" applies more to the "sounding together" of parts, rather than symphonic form per se.

SINGSPIEL German for "singing play"; operatic works in German with spoken dialogue of the Classical and early Romantic eras; in substance, more like a ballad opera than a comic opera.

SOCIALIST REALISM the official arts doctrine of the Union of Socialist Soviet Republics (in fact a considerable departure from Marxist theory) in place from the 1930s on; this prescribed "a creative method based on the truthful, historically concrete artistic reflection of reality in its revolutionary development." Musical art was to derive from folklore or at least non-specialist styles familiar and meaningful to all; its texts were to show loyalty to the Communist Party and to conform with official doctrine; its application to music proved unpredictable and consequently threatened the lives and art of Russian composers.

SOCIÉTÉ NATIONAL DE MUSIQUE an association established in 1871 to promote works by French composers; its goals were to expand French awareness and production of orchestral music, and to provide resistance to contemporaneous German music; it gave numerous concerts in Paris through the mid-1880s.

SOCIETY FOR PRIVATE MUSICAL PERFORMANCES a concert series founded by Arnold Schoenberg in Vienna in 1918, to make carefully rehearsed Modern music available to general audiences; it was subsidized by subscriptions, by member contributions, and by occasional donations from wealthy patrons; its offerings were not advertised in the papers; critics were barred from attending; subscribers were not informed of the programs in advance to ensure regular attendance, and applause was forbidden. By 1921, the organization folded, having given 353 performances of 154 works in a total of 117 concerts.

SOGGETTO CAVATO DALLE PAROLE Italian for "a subject carved out of the words"; a pre-compositional technique of Josquin des Prez (and others), in which solmization syllables were mapped onto names to produce a cantus firmus theme; later examples include BACH (B♭ACB♮) and DSCH (DE♭CB♮, for Dmitry Shostakovich (both using German note spelling).

SOLMIZATION a mnemonic device in which intervals were associated with syllables to aid in the learning of melody. The name is derived from the Guidonian hand syllables (eleventh century).

SONATA DA CAMERA Italian for "chamber sonata"; four-movement sets of instrumental dances for domestic use; by 1700, essentially interchangeable with the sonata da chiesa.

SONATA DA CHIESA Italian for "church sonata"; four-movement sets of "abstract" instrumental pieces for use in place of sections of the Mass Proper; by 1700, essentially interchangeable with the sonata da camera.

SONATA FORM a structure that grew out of Baroque binary form; it eventually developed three distinct parts the first part moves from I to V (in major; to ♭III in minor), followed by a repeat sign; the second part features thematic fragments and rearrangements, in a tonally unstable setting, leading to the third part, signaled by a "double return" to the tonic key and the thematic content of the first part, and with any themes established in the V (or ♭III passages now in the tonic; in later theoretical terminology, these three parts were called "exposition," "development," and "recapitulation."

SONG CYCLE a set of songs grouped together by the composer, unified by a common theme, an accompanying narrative, or text authorship by one writer.

SONGS WITHOUT WORDS (translation from German, *Lieder ohne Worte*) Felix Mendelssohn's gently lyrical character pieces for piano, published in eight books and enormously popular.

SPEECH MELODIES short speech units recorded in music notation by Leoš Janáček, who believed that these revealed subliminal thoughts and emotions unexpressed by the words alone; the basis of his operatic vocal writing.

SPRECHSTIMME German for "speech voice"; referring to an Expressionist vocal technique between singing and speaking because it does not settle on a particular pitch (compare *parlando*); used by Arnold Schoenberg, his Modernist contemporaries, and later composers.

STABREIM German for "alliterative verse"; a technique in old Germanic verse (*Beowulf*, the Norse Edda) in which lines are divided in half, featuring internal stresses and unifying alliteration; the basis of Richard Wagner's attempt to create a speech-melody, combining heroic Medieval prosody with direct "natural" language.

STILE ANTICO Italian for "old style"; composing in the style of Palestrina, that is, acceptable to the Roman Catholic Church at the Council of Trent, and the model for subsequent papal chapel composers.

STILE CONCITATO Italian for "agitated style"; one of Claudio Monteverdi's *genere*, usually expressed by rapidly articulated repeated notes.

STILE RAPPRESENTATIVO Italian for representational "style"; a style of singing developed in early Italian monody, then transferred to the first operas; more expressive than speech, but not as melodious as song; a dramatic recitative style in which vocal lines move freely over a simple basso continuo.

STILE RECITATIVO a melody that imitated natural speech inflections; a term that became virtually synonymous with *stile rappresentativo*.

STRETTO from Italian, *stringere*, "to tighten"; a foreshortening device in a fugue in which the voices anticipate their predicted entries on the subject and answer.

STRING QUARTET a chamber ensemble of four string players —two violinists, a violist and a cellist; also, a piece written to be performed by this group.

STROPHIC a poem made of prosodically similar verse, set to a single more or less repeated musical stanza.

STURM UND DRANG German for "storm and stress"; an aesthetic movement with literary origins in the latter eighteenth century, in which Austrian and German composers aimed to depict violent emotional changes in the most dramatic way possible, sometimes leading to formal innovations.

STYLE HONGROIS French for "Hungarian style"; a nineteenth-century Viennese belief that the urban gypsy music it had imported was native to Hungary, rural, and exotic, none of which was true; however, the belief was widespread enough to result in numerous "Hungarian" pieces, notably by Franz Liszt and Johannes Brahms.

SUBJECT the single main theme of a fugue.

SUBLIME the notion, first articulated in the eighteenth century and accepted by the Romanticists, of the great and incomprehensible, even the painful and terrifying, being greater than the merely beautiful.

SUITE 1) an ordered set of instrumental or orchestral pieces, frequently based on dance movements, performed in a concert setting; 2) a set of extracts taken from a stage work, for concert performance, often intended to encourage performances of the entire work.

SURREALISM in music, the counterpart of contemporaneous movements in other arts (notably film); among its assigned qualities are the use of unexpected juxtapositions, improvisation, collage, and montage of broken pieces of the past; the result is meant to synthesize new meanings within a new aesthetic.

SYMBOLISM a literary movement of late nineteenth-century France, pursuing a way of seeing past the appearances of the lived world into the higher reality of the *au-delà*, the world "beyond" the senses; in music, the possible connection between musical elements and extramusical phenomena (words of a poem, a natural object, a person, an emotional state); Debussy, who disliked the term Impressionism, preferred an association with the Symbolist poetry of Stéphane Mallarmé (1842–98).

SYMPHONIC POEM a one-movement orchestral work, successor to the opera overture and concert overture, and developed by Franz Liszt; a form of program music that is an attempt to depict an event or a longer narrative, evoke an atmosphere (in nature or created by humanity) or mood, portray a personality, or contemplate the sublime; also called tone poem.

SYMPHONY from the Classical era forward, a substantial composition for full orchestra, typically (but not necessarily) in four movements, related tonally and often thematically; may be assigned programmatic meaning by the composer or an imaginative listener; Classical-era generic standards (begun with a sonata-form movement, a slow movement often in ABA form, a minuet and trio or scherzo, a lively finale in a choice of forms) loosened during the Romantic era, culminating in the lengthy, multimovement, programmatically driven works of Gustav Mahler.

SYNCOPATION assuming a steady meter, an accent in an unusual place, such as a weak beat or in-between beats, or lack of accent on a strong beat; also the delaying of contrapuntal resolutions, especially of non-chord tones, chromatic decoration, and rhythmic alteration.

SYNESTHESIA the equivalence and interchangeability of the five primary sense experiences; in music, primarily the relationship between pitch and color, explored in Alexander Scriabin's color organ concept.

SYNTHESIZER an electronic instrument capable of producing sounds by generating electrical signals of different frequencies, controlling a variety of parameters; originally produced analogically, synthesizer sound was revolutionized by voltage-controlled keyboards and, later, by computerization, allowing for greater precision and preparation (using samplers). Through MIDI and interactive programming, a live performer can now control and process sound through signals to the synthesizer.

TALEA Latin for "a cutting"; in Medieval and Renaissance polyphony, the repetition of rhythmic values without regard to pitches used.

TAPE LOOP a short segment of magnetic tape that could be repeated or manipulated when fed through a tape recorder continuously; the analog predecessor of digital sampling.

TEMPO DI MEZZO In nineteenth-century Italian opera, the transition between a cantabile and a cabaletta within a serious aria.

TEMPUS Latin for time; in mensural notation, the relationship between the note values breve and semibreve, a factor in determining the metric design.

TENOR from Latin *tenere*, "to hold"; the fundamental voice or chant-bearing part of organum and later polyphonic music, bearing a preexisting melody in long notes while another voice (or other voices) sings in more florid counterpoint; generally considered to have been performed instrumentally, this technique evolved until counterpoint of rhythmically equal parts became dominant (around 1500).

TENORE DI FORZA Italian for "strong tenor"; a nineteenth-century bel canto voice type stronger than the lyric tenor, in which the full, or chest, voice was maintained over the entire range; the even more powerful *tenore robusto* became the heroic voice of late Romantic opera, the equivalent to the German *Heldentenor* (heroic tenor).

TENORLIED a German Renaissance polyphonic setting of a song-like cantus firmus in three or more parts, less refined contrapuntally than the Italian madrigal; its melodies were often sources for Protestant chorales.

TENSO a debate-song in the troubadour and trouvère repertoire, characterized by a discussion about love and other subjects, depicted as an exchange between two or more participants; on occasion a joint composition by two or more poets.

THEMATIC TRANSFORMATION a variation technique whereby a theme is altered and placed in a new context, yet maintains a relationship to the original; with precedents in Ludwig van Beethoven and Hector Berlioz (*idée fixe*), this approach is most associated with the symphonic poems of Franz Liszt and the operas of Richard Wagner.

THEOSOPHY a Westernized form of the transcendentalist doctrines of South Asia, particularly Hinduism and Buddhism, through the filter of Gnostic revelation of divine knowledge; strongly associated with the late works of Alexander Scriabin.

THEREMIN the earliest electronic instrument still in use, invented by Russian physicist Lev Sergeyevich Termen in 1920; the disruption of an electromagnetic field (for example, a hand) would produced a pitch from a radio oscillator within a preset range; later models allowed for dynamic control.

THIRD STREAM a term coined in 1957 by Gunther Schuller to describe a synthesis of classical music and jazz, incorporating improvisation.

THROUGH-COMPOSED music that is relatively continuous, non-sectional, and/or non-repetitive; in song, a viable approach to both strophic and freely versified text.

TIN PAN ALLEY the collective name given to the preponderance of New York City music publishers and songwriters who dominated American popular music in the late nineteenth century and first half of the twentieth century.

TINTA Italian for "color" or "tone"; Guiseppe Verdi's term for underlying unifying factors in an individual opera.

TOCCATA from Italian *toccare,* "to touch"; after 1500, a virtuosic keyboard piece displaying dexterity and skill.

TONE CLUSTER a term devised by Henry Cowell for extended piano techniques he used, striking the keyboard with palms, fists, and forearms; known pejoratively as "elbow music" by its detractors, analytically as "secundal harmonies."

TONE ROW developed by Arnold Schoenberg, this term describes an ordering of all twelve chromatic pitches from which motivic and harmonic content will be derived; a major component of serialism.

TONIC the first and primary degree of the diatonic scale.

TONICIZATION compositionally or analytically, the treatment of a pitch other than the overall tonic as a "temporary tonic" by emphasizing the scale and harmonies of that key.

TOTALITARIANISM any government that concentrates political power in the hands of a ruling elite or even a single person; its goals are the application of an all-encompassing worldview, achievement of a completely controlled social and economic order, and the total mobilization of the population to further the interests of the state, excluding all civil rights and freedoms; the role of extreme censorship serves to restrict all artistic expression, repressing all contradiction and disagreement.

TOTAL SERIALISM a compositional technique that uses predetermined algorithms in order to generate duration, dynamics, and register in addition to pitch, associated with the post–World War II French avant-garde and Americans such as Milton Babbitt.

TRAGÉDIE LYRIQUE (TRAGÉDIE EN MUSIQUE) the French equivalent of Italian opera seria, with a similar seriousness of tone but with a focus on the preservation of the text when set to music and the frequent presence of dance interludes (the Paris Opéra required such "ballets" well into the nineteenth century).

TRAGICOMEDY a Renaissance genre of spoken drama with pastoral and heroic elements, later expanded to a mixture of comedy and tragedy.

TRANSCENDENTALISM in American culture, a belief in an ideal spirituality that "transcends" the physical and empirical, realized only through the individual's intuition, rather than through religious doctrine; this nineteenth-century philosophical movement, centered in New England, served as a direct source of inspiration and guidance for Charles Ives, Carl Ruggles, and others.

TRANSCRIPTION 1) the notation of music in any style by listening to a performance or recording, however complicated; 2) the transfer of music from one notational system to another; 3) a synonym for arrangement, specifically the Romantic-era translations of operatic excerpts into solo piano works.

TRIO SONATA a Baroque chamber music work written for two solo melodic instruments and basso continuo; thus three notated parts are normally realized by four performers.

TRIPLUM Latin for "in three parts"; originally, a Medieval composition for three voices; later, the third voice part itself, above the duplum and next but one above the tenor.

TROBAR CLUS from Provençal, "closed form"; difficult troubadour poetry of the twelfth century; the connoisseurship required to appreciate its technical prowess, its density of meaning, and the exclusive nature of its appeal led to its rapid demise as an art form.

TROPE especially in the ninth through twelfth centuries, an insertion of new text and corresponding music to Mass movements, specifically the Ordinary (except the Credo) and parts of the Proper (introit, offertory, communion); these additions served to amplify the original texts, making them "proper" to the liturgical calendar (feast days, Christmas, Marian worship); this practice was eliminated by the Council of Trent, with the exception of five sequences.

TROUBADOUR from Provençal *trobador,* "finder of words"; esteemed singer-poets active in what is now southern France during the eleventh through thirteenth centuries, composing highly formalized *cansos, tensos, sirventes* (satirical or political songs), *pastorelas,* and other genres in highly formalized styles.

TROUVÈRE esteemed singer-poets, equivalent to the troubadour but writing in Old French in northern France in the eleventh through fourteenth centuries, with a larger surviving repertory; trouvère genres matched those of the troubadour (*chanson d'amour, jeu-parti,* pastourelles), featuring religious and Crusades songs to a greater degree.

TWELVE-TONE TECHNIQUE the earliest form of serialism, in which all twelve chromatic scale notes have equal importance, leading to "pantonal" or "atonal" composition, as championed by Arnold Schoenberg.

ULTRA-MODERNIST incorporating ideas, styles, or techniques most recently developed or available; a pejorative term applied to such experimental art by its critics.

UNDERSCORING the use of background music to support the action and dialogue of a film; continuous, leitmotif-laden symphonic music is one possible result, drawn from late Romantic opera.

VERBUNKOS originally, Hungarian military recruiting music, drawn from native popular song, but performed in a gypsy manner; later incorporated into *style hongrois* dance music.

VERISMO Italian for "realism"; a late nineteenth-century Italian movement to make opera more immediate by rejecting traditional vocal virtuosity in the name of forceful emotional simplicity; by a radical reduction in scale and tone through which intensity took the place of grandeur; and by an increased interest in the lives of the lower classes, often in dialect; taking its cues from Giuseppe Verdi, the movement was embodied in the works of Giacomo Puccini and his contemporaries.

VIDAS brief troubadour and trobairitz biographies typically contained in their song collections (*chansonniers*).

VIRELAI a form of Medieval and early Renaissance song the music for which is in two clear sections (ABBA); one of three *formes fixes*.

VIRGINAL a smaller member of the harpsichord family, in which sound is produced by a plucking mechanism when a key is pressed down; the strings are plucked close to the middle of their sounding length, giving the instrument a distinctly plangent tone.

WHOLE-TONE SCALE a scale that excludes half-steps; there are only two complementary whole-tone hexatonic scales; their lack of leading tones eliminates all scalar functions.

ZARZUELA Spanish *zarza*, "bramble bush"; a popular Spanish theatrical "mixture" of spoken dialogue and music (song, dance) of a lighter quality, often in dialect, and with strong regional characteristics; freely applied to works akin to the *intermedio*, pastoral, ballad opera, opera buffa, opéra comique, operetta, and works of nearly operatic weight.

ZEITOPER German for "opera for the times"; early twentieth-century German topical theater concerning present-day issues, rather than enduring themes; the *Zeitoper* composer was acting as a citizen commentator, not a priest of art, and made free use of satire, both musical and narrative.

ZUKUNFTSMUSIK German for "music of the future"; a Wagnerian concept applied to his vision of the *Gesamtkunstwerk*; considered inappropriate to the aesthetics of other modern composers, the term was superseded by the collective term the "New German School."

Further Reading: A Checklist of Books in English

General Companions

Lippman, Edward A. *Musical Aesthetics: A Historical Reader.* Three vols. Stuyvesant, NY: Pendragon Press, 1991.

New Grove Dictionary of Music and Musicians. Rev. ed., New York: Oxford University Press, 2004.

New Grove Dictionary of Opera. New York: Oxford University Press, 2004.

Strunk, Oliver, ed., Leo Treitler, rev. gen. ed., *Source Readings in Music History.* Rev. ed., New York: W. W. Norton & Company, 1998.

Weiss, Piero, and Richard Taruskin. *Music in the Western World: A History in Documents,* 2nd ed., New York: Thomson Schirmer, 2007.

The Earliest Notations to the Sixteenth Century

Atlas, Allan. *Renaissance Music: Music in Western Europe, 1400–1600.* New York: W. W. Norton & Company, 1998.

D'Accone, Frank A. *The Civic Muse: Music and Musicians in Siena during the Middle Ages and the Renaissance.* Chicago: University of Chicago Press, 1997.

Haar, James. *European Music, 1520–1640.* Woodbridge, UK: Boydell Press, 2006.

Hoppin, Richard H. *Medieval Music.* New York: W. W. Norton & Company, 1978.

Knighton, Tess, and David Fallows. *Companion to Medieval and Renaissance Music.* Berkeley: University of California, 1992.

Pirrotta, Nino. *Music and Culture in Italy from the Middle Ages to the Baroque.* Cambridge, MA: Harvard University Press, 1984.

Strohm, Reinhard. *The Rise of European Music, 1380–1500.* Cambridge, UK: Cambridge University Press, 1993.

Wright, Craig. *The Maze and the Warrior: Symbols in Architecture, Theology, and Music.* Cambridge, MA: Harvard University Press, 2004.

Yudkin, Jeremy. *Music in Medieval Europe.* Englewood Cliffs, NJ: Prentice Hall, 1989.

The Seventeenth and Eighteenth Centuries

Bianconi, Lorenzo. *Music in the Seventeenth Century,* trans. D. Bryant. Cambridge, UK: Cambridge University Press, 1987.

Heartz, Daniel. *Haydn, Mozart and the Viennese School, 1740–1780.* New York: W. W. Norton & Company, 1995.

———. *Music in European Capitals: The Galant Style, 1720–1780.* New York: W. W. Norton & Company, 2003.

Hill, John Walter. *Baroque Music: Music in Western Europe, 1580-1750.* New York: W. W. Norton & Company, 2005.

Keefe, Simon P., ed. *The Cambridge History of Eighteenth-Century Music.* Cambridge, UK: Cambridge University Press, 2009.

Le Huray, Peter, and James Day, eds. *Music and Aesthetics in the Eighteenth and Early-Nineteenth Centuries.* Cambridge, UK: Cambridge University Press, 1981.

Pestelli, Giorgio. *The Age of Mozart and Beethoven,* trans. Eric Cross. Cambridge, UK: Cambridge University Press, 1984.

Ratner, Leonard G. *Classic Music: Expression, Form, and Style.* New York: Schirmer, 1985.

Spitzer, John, and Neal Zaslaw. *The Birth of the Orchestra: History of an Institution, 1650–1815.* New York: Oxford University Press, 2005.

The Nineteenth Century

Bent, Ian, ed. *Music Theory in the Age of Romanticism.* Cambridge, UK: Cambridge University Press, 1996.

Bujić, Bojan, ed. *Music in European Thought, 1851–1912.* Cambridge, UK: Cambridge University Press, 1988.

Hallmark, Rufus. *German Lieder in the Nineteenth Century,* 2nd ed., New York and London: Routledge, 2009.

Holoman, D. Kern, ed. *The Nineteenth-Century Symphony.* New York: Schirmer Books, 1996.

Rosen, Charles. *The Romantic Generation.* Cambridge, MA: Harvard University Press, 1998.

The Twentieth Century

Gann, Kyle. *American Music in the Twentieth Century.* New York: Schirmer, 1997.

Hitchcock, H. Wiley. *Music in the United States.* 4th ed., Englewood Cliffs, NJ: Prentice Hall, 1999.

Simms, Bryan R. *Music of the Twentieth Century: Style and Structure.* New York: Schirmer, 1996.

Slonimsky, Nicolas, and Laura Kuhn. *Music Since 1900.* 6th ed., New York: Schirmer Reference, 2001.

Watkins, Glenn. *Soundings: Music in the Twentieth Century.* New York: Schirmer, 1988.

Chapter 1

Atkinson, Charles. *The Critical Nexus: Tone-System, Mode, and Notation in Early Medieval Music.* Oxford, UK: Oxford University Press, 2009.

Berger, Anna Maria Busse. *Medieval Music and the Art of Memory.* Berkeley: University of California Press, 2005.

Crocker, Richard L. *An Introduction to Gregorian Chant.* New Haven, CT: Yale University Press, 2000.

Levy, Kenneth. *Gregorian Chant and the Carolingians.* Princeton, NJ: Princeton University Press, 1998.

Ong, Walter J. *Orality and Literacy (New Accents).* New York: Routledge, 2002.

Page, Christopher. *The Christian West and Its Singers: The First Thousand Years.* New Haven, CT: Yale University Press, 2010.

Treitler, Leo. *With Voice and Pen: Coming to Know Medieval Song and How It Was Made.* New York: Oxford University Press, 2003.

Chapter 2

Karp, Theodore C. *The Polyphony of Saint Martial and Santiago de Compostela.* Berkeley: University of California Press, 1992.

Page, Christopher. *Voices and Instruments of the Middle Ages: Instrumental Practice and Songs in France, 1100–1300.* Berkeley: University of California Press, 1987.

Wright, Craig. *Music and Ceremony at Notre Dame of Paris, 500–1500.* Cambridge: Cambridge University Press, 1990.

Chapter 3

Cumming, Julie E. *The Motet in the Age of Du Fay.* Cambridge, UK: Cambridge University Press, 1999.

Kirkman, Andrew. *The Cultural Life of the Early Polyphonic Mass: Medieval Context to Modern Revival.* Cambridge, UK: Cambridge University Press, 2010.

Leech-Wilkinson, Daniel. *Machaut's Mass: An Introduction.* Oxford, UK: Oxford University Press, 1992.

Robertson, Anne Walters. *Guillaume de Machaut and Reims: Context and Meaning in his Musical Works.* Cambridge, UK: Cambridge University Press, 2002.

Chapter 4

Bent, Margaret. *Dunstaple.* London: Oxford University Press, 1981.

Bernstein, Jane A. *Music Printing in Renaissance Venice: The Scotto Press (1539–1572).* New York: Oxford University Press, 1998.

Fallows, David. *Dufay.* London: J. M. Dent, 1982.

Higgins, Paula, ed. *Antoine Busnoys: Methods, Meaning, and Context in Late Medieval Music.* New York: Oxford University, 2000.

Lockwood, Lewis. *Music in Renaissance Ferrara, 1400–1505.* Cambridge, MA: Harvard University Press, 1985.

Chapter 5

Brett, Philip, Joseph Kerman, and Davitt Moroney. *William Byrd and his Contemporaries: Essays and a Monograph.* Berkeley: University of California Press, 2006.

Fallows, David, ed. *Josquin.* Turnhout, Belgium: Brepols, 2009.

Owens, Jessie Ann. *Composers at Work: The Craft of Musical Composition, 1450–1600.* New York: Oxford University Press, 1998.

Le Huray, Peter. *Music and the Reformation in England: 1549–1660.* New York: Oxford University Press, 1967.

Sherr, Richard, ed. *The Josquin Companion.* New York: Oxford University Press, 2001.

Stevenson, Robert. *Spanish Cathedral Music in the Golden Age.* Berkeley: University of California Press, 1961.

Chapter 6

Arnold, Denis. *Giovanni Gabrieli and the Music of the Venetian High Renaissance.* Oxford, UK: Oxford University Press, 1979.

Carter, Tim. *Music in Late Renaissance and Early Baroque Italy.* Portland, OR: Amadeus Press, 1992.

Feldman, Martha. *City Culture and the Madrigal at Venice.* Berkeley: University of California Press, 1995.

Fenlon, Iain. *Music and Patronage in Sixteenth-Century Mantua.* Two vols. Cambridge, UK: Cambridge University Press, 1980–82.

Leaver, Robin A. *Luther's Liturgical Music: Principles and Implications.* Grand Rapids, MI: Eerdmans Publishing, 2007.

Newcomb, Anthony. *The Madrigal at Ferrara, 1579–1597.* Princeton, NJ: Princeton University Press, 1980.

Chapter 7

Carter, Tim. *Monteverdi's Musical Theatre.* New Haven, CT: Yale University Press, 2002.

Heller, Wendy. *Emblems of Eloquence: Opera and Women's Voices in Seventeenth-Century Venice.* Berkeley: University of California Press, 2003.

Palisca, Claude V. *Humanism in Italian Renaissance Musical Thought.* New Haven, CT: Yale University Press, 1985.

Pirrotta, Nino, and Elena Povoledo. *Music and Theatre from Poliziano to Monteverdi*, trans. K. Eales. Cambridge, UK: Cambridge University Press, 1982.

Rosand, Ellen. *Opera in Seventeenth-Century Venice: The Creation of a Genre.* Berkeley: University of California Press, 1991.

Tomlinson, Gary. *Monteverdi and the End of the Renaissance.* Berkeley: University of California Press, 1987.

Wistreich, Richard, ed. *Monteverdi*. Farnham, UK: Ashgate Publishing Company, 2011.

Chapter 8

Cowart, Georgia. *The Triumph of Pleasure: Louis XIV and the Politics of Spectacle*. Chicago: University of Chicago Press, 2008.

Dill, Charles W. *Monstrous Opera: Rameau and the Tragic Tradition*. Princeton, NJ: Princeton University Press, 1998.

Dixon, Graham. *Carissimi*. Oxford, UK: Oxford University Press, 1986.

Glover, Jane. *Cavalli*. London: Batsford, 1978.

Frandsen, Mary E. *Crossing Confessional Boundaries: The Patronage of Italian Sacred Music In Seventeenth-Century Dresden*. New York: Oxford University Press, 2006.

Holman, Peter, ed. *Purcell*. Farnham, UK: Ashgate Publishing Company, 2011.

Silbiger, Alexander. *Keyboard Music before 1700*. New York: Schirmer, 1995.

Chapter 9

Feldman, Martha. *Opera and Sovereignty: Transforming Myths in Eighteenth-Century Italy*. Chicago: University of Chicago Press, 2007.

Freitas, Roger. *Portrait of a Castrato: Politics, Patronage, and Music in the Life of Atto Melani*. Cambridge, UK: Cambridge University Press, 2009.

Talbot, Michael, ed. *Vivaldi*. Farnham, UK: Ashgate Publishing Company, 2011.

Chapter 10

Boyd, Malcolm. *Bach*. 3rd ed., Oxford, UK: Oxford University Press, 2000.

Burrows, Donald. *Handel*. Oxford, UK: Oxford University Press, 2011.

Dreyfus, Laurence. *Bach and the Patterns of Invention*. Cambridge, MA: Harvard University Press, 1996.

Geck, Martin. *Bach*. Translated by Anthea Bell. London: Haus Publishing, 2003.

Vickers, David, ed. *Handel*. Farnham, UK: Ashgate Publishing Company, 2011.

Wolff, Christoph. *Bach: Essays on His Life and Music*. Cambridge, MA: Harvard University Press, 1991.

———. *Johann Sebastian Bach: The Learned Musician*. New York: W. W. Norton & Company, 2000.

Chapter 11

Boyd, Malcolm. *Domenico Scarlatti: Master of Music*. New York: Schirmer, 1987.

Chafe, Eric. *Analyzing Bach Cantatas*. Rev. ed., New York: Oxford University Press, 2003.

Harris, Ellen. *Handel and the Pastoral Tradition*. London: Oxford University Press, 1980.

———. *Handel as Orpheus: Voice and Desire in the Chamber Cantatas*. Cambridge, MA: Harvard University Press, 2001.

Kirkpatrick, Ralph. *Domenico Scarlatti*. Rev. ed., Princeton, NJ: Princeton University Press, 1983.

Leaver, Robin A. *Music as Preaching: Bach, Passions and Music in Worship*. Oxford, UK: Latimer House, 1982.

Chapter 12

Richards, Annette. *C. P. E. Bach Studies*. Cambridge, UK: Cambridge University Press, 2006.

———. *The Free Fantasia and the Musical Picturesque*. Cambridge, UK: Cambridge University Press, 2001.

Troy, Charles E. *The Comic Intermezzo: A Study in the History of Eighteenth-Century Opera*. Ann Arbor, MI: UMI Research Press, 1979.

Chapter 13

Grave, Floyd Kersey, and Margaret G. Grave. *The String Quartets of Joseph Haydn*. New York: Oxford University Press, 2006.

Landon, H. C. Robbins. *Haydn: Chronicle and Works*. Five vols. Bloomington: Indiana University Press, 1976–80.

Morrow, Mary Sue. *Concert Life in Haydn's Vienna: Aspects of a Developing Musical and Social Institution*. Stuyvesant, NY: Pendragon Press, 1988.

Schroeder, David. *Haydn and the Enlightenment: The Late Symphonies and Their Audience*. Oxford, UK: Clarendon Press, 1990.

Webster, James C. *Haydn's "Farewell" Symphony and the Idea of Classical Style*. Cambridge, UK: Cambridge University Press, 1991.

Wheelock, Gretchen A. *Haydn's Ingenious Jesting with Art: Contexts of Musical Wit and Humor*. New York: Schirmer, 1992.

Will, Richard. *The Characteristic Symphony in the Age of Haydn and Beethoven*. Cambridge, UK: Cambridge University Press, 2002.

Chapter 14

Abert, Hermann. *W. A. Mozart*. Edited by Cliff Eisen. Translated by Stewart Spencer. New Haven, CT: Yale University Press, 2007.

Allanbrook, Wye J. *Rhythmic Gesture in Mozart: Le nozze di Figaro and Don Giovanni*. Chicago: University of Chicago Press, 1983.

Heartz, Daniel, and Thomas Bauman. *Mozart's Operas*. Berkeley: University of California Press, 1990.

Hunter, Mary. *The Culture of Opera Buffa in Mozart's Vienna: A Poetics of Entertainment*. Princeton, NJ: Princeton University Press, 1999.

Solomon, Maynard. *Mozart: A Life*. New York: Harper Collins, 1995.

Steptoe, Andrew. *The Mozart-Da Ponte Operas: Cultural and Musical Background to Le nozze di Figaro, Don Giovanni, and Così fan Tutte*. Oxford; UK: Clarendon Press, 1988.

Zaslaw, Neal. *Mozart's Symphonies: Context, Performance Practice, Reception*. Oxford, UK: Oxford University Press, 1989.

———. ed. *Mozart's Piano Concertos: Text, Context, Interpretation*. Ann Arbor: University of Michigan Press, 1996.

Chapter 15

Burnham, Scott. *Beethoven Hero*. Princeton, NJ: Princeton University Press, 1995.

Dahlhaus, Carl. *Nineteenth-Century Music*, trans. J. Bradford Robinson. Berkeley: University of California Press, 1989.

Samson, Jim, ed. *The Cambridge History of Nineteenth-Century Music*. Cambridge, UK: Cambridge University Press, 2002.

Chapter 16

Cooper, Barry, ed. *The Beethoven Compendium: A Guide to Beethoven's Life and Music*. London: Thames and Hudson, 1991.

Kerman, Joseph. *The Beethoven Quartets*. New York: W. W. Norton & Company, 1979.

Kinderman, William. *Beethoven*. Berkeley: University of California Press, 1995.

Lockwood, Lewis. *Beethoven: The Music and the Life*. New York: W. W. Norton & Company, 2003.

Rumph, Stephen. *Beethoven after Napoleon: Political Romanticism in the Late Works*. Berkeley: University of California Press, 2004.

Solomon, Maynard. *Beethoven*. New York: Schirmer, 1977.

———. *Beethoven Essays*. Cambridge, MA: Harvard University Press, 1988.

———. *Late Beethoven: Music, Thought, Imagination*. Berkeley: University of California Press, 2003.

Chapter 17

Ashbrook, William. *Donizetti and His Operas*. Cambridge, UK: Cambridge University Press, 1982.

Osborne, Richard. *Rossini*. London: J. M. Dent, 1987.

Rosselli, John. *The Life of Bellini*. Cambridge, UK: Cambridge University Press, 1996.

———. *The Opera Industry in Italy from Cimarosa to Verdi: The Role of the Impresario*. Cambridge, UK: Cambridge University Press, 1984.

Warrack, John. *Carl Maria von Weber*. 2nd ed., Cambridge, UK: Cambridge University Press, 1976.

Chapter 18

Gibbs, Christopher. *The Life of Schubert*. Cambridge, UK: Cambridge University Press, 2000.

———. ed. *The Cambridge Companion to Schubert*. Cambridge, UK: Cambridge University Press, 1997.

Hanson, Alice M. *Musical Life in Biedermeier Vienna*. Cambridge, UK: Cambridge University Press, 1985.

Youens, Susan. *Schubert, Müller, and Die Schöne Müllerin*. Cambridge, UK: Cambridge University Press, 2006.

———. *Schubert's Poets and the Making of Lieder*. Cambridge, UK: Cambridge University Press, 1996.

Chapter 19

Charlton, David, ed. *The Cambridge Companion to Grand Opera*. Cambridge, UK: Cambridge University Press, 2003.

Gooley, Dana. *The Virtuoso Liszt*. Cambridge, UK: Cambridge University Press, 2004.

Metzner, Paul. *Crescendo of the Virtuoso: Spectacle, Skill, and Self-Promotion in Paris during the Age of Revolution*. Berkeley: University of California Press, 1998.

Walker, Alan. *Franz Liszt: The Virtuoso Years, 1811–1847*. New York: Random House, 1983.

Chapter 20

Berlioz, Hector. *The Art of Music and Other Essays (A Travers Chants)*, trans. Elizabeth Csicsery-Rónay. Bloomington: Indiana University Press, 1994.

———. *Evenings in the Orchestra*, trans. C. R. Fortescue. Baltimore, MD: Penguin Books, 1963.

———. *Memoirs*, trans. David Cairns. 3rd ed., New York: Random House, 2002.

Cairns, David. *Berlioz*. Two vols. Berkeley: University of California Press, 2000.

Daverio, John. *Robert Schumann: Herald of a "New Poetic Age."* New York: Oxford University Press, 1997.

Finson, Jon W. *Robert Schumann: The Book of Songs*. Cambridge, MA: Harvard University Press, 2007.

Reich, Nancy B. *Clara Schumann*. Rev. ed., Ithaca, NY: Cornell University Press, 2001.

Schumann, Robert. *On Music and Musicians*, ed. Konrad Wolff. New York: McGraw Hill, 1964.

Todd, R. Larry. *Fanny Hensel: The Other Mendelssohn*. New York: Oxford University Press, 2009.

———. *Mendelssohn: A Life in Music*. New York: Oxford University Press, 2004.

Chapter 21

Eigeldinger, Jean-Jacques. *Chopin: Pianist and Teacher*, trans. N. Shohet, K. Osostrowicz, and R. Howat. 3rd ed., Cambridge, UK: Cambridge University Press, 1986.

Frolova-Walker, Marina. *Russian Music and Nationalism: From Glinka to Stalin*. New Haven, CT: Yale University Press, 2007.

Fulcher, Jane. *The Nation's Image: French Grand Opera as Politics and Politicized Art*. Cambridge, UK: Cambridge University Press, 1987.

Gerhard, Anselm. *The Urbanization of Opera: Music Theater in Paris in the Nineteenth Century*, trans. Mary Whittall. Chicago: University of Chicago Press, 1998.

Samson, Jim, ed. *The Cambridge Companion to Chopin*. Cambridge, UK: Cambridge University Press, 1992.

Taruskin, Richard. *Defining Russia Musically: Historical and Hermeneutical Essays*. Princeton, NJ: Princeton University Press, 1997.

Chapter 22

Dahlhaus, Carl. *The Idea of Absolute Music*, trans. Roger Lustig. Chicago: University of Chicago Press, 1989.

Gibbs, Christopher, and Dana Gooley, eds. *Franz Liszt and His World*. Princeton, NJ: Princeton University Press, 2006.

Hanslick, Eduard. *On the Musically Beautiful*, trans. Geoffrey Payzant. Indianapolis, IN: Hackett Publishing, 1986.

Walker, Alan. *Franz Liszt: The Final Years, 1861–1886*. Ithaca, NY: Cornell University Press, 1997.

———. *Franz Liszt: The Weimar Years, 1848–1861*. Ithaca, NY: Cornell University Press, 1993.

Chapter 23

Abbate, Carolyn. *Unsung Voices: Opera and Musical Narrative in the Nineteenth Century*. Princeton, NJ: Princeton University Press, 1991.

Bailey, Robert, ed. *Richard Wagner: Prelude and Transfiguration from "Tristan und Isolde."* Norton Critical Scores. New York: W. W. Norton & Company, 1985.

Budden, Julian. *The Operas of Verdi*. Three vols. London: Oxford University Press, 1973–81.

Deathridge, John, P. Wapnewski, and U. Müller, eds. *The Wagner Handbook*. Cambridge, MA: Harvard University Press, 1991.

Grey, Thomas S. *Wagner's Musical Prose: Texts and Contexts*. Cambridge, UK: Cambridge University Press, 1995.

Kimbell, David. *Verdi in the Age of Italian Romanticism*. Cambridge, UK: Cambridge University Press, 1981.

Large, David C., and William Weber, eds. *Wagnerism in European Culture and Politics*. Ithaca, NY: Cornell University Press, 1984.

Millington, Barry. *Wagner*. Rev. ed., Princeton, NJ: Princeton University Press, 1992.

———. *The Wagner Compendium: A Guide to Wagner's Life and Music*. London: Thames and Hudson, 2001.

Phillips-Matz, Mary Jane. *Verdi: A Biography*. Oxford, UK: Oxford University Press, 1993.

Chapter 24

Emerson, Caryl. *The Life of Musorgsky*. Cambridge, UK: Cambridge University Press, 1999.

Kearney, Leslie, ed. *Tchaikovsky and His World*. Princeton, NJ: Princeton University Press, 1998.

Taruskin, Richard. *Musorgsky: Eight Essays and an Epilogue*. Princeton, NJ: Princeton University Press, 1993.

Tyrrell, John. *Czech Opera*. Cambridge, UK: Cambridge University Press, 1988.

Chapter 25

Avins, Styra, ed. *Johannes Brahms: Life and Letters*. New York: Oxford University Press, 1997.

Beller-McKenna, Daniel. *Brahms and the German Spirit*. Cambridge, MA: Harvard University Press, 2004.

Bonds, Mark Evan. *After Beethoven: Imperatives of Originality in the Symphony*. Cambridge, MA: Harvard University Press, 1996.

Beckerman, Michael. *New Worlds of Dvořák*. New York: W. W. Norton & Company, 2003.

Beveridge, David. *Rethinking Dvořák: Views from Five Countries*. Oxford, UK: Oxford University Press, 1996.

Jackson, Timothy L., and Paul Hawkshaw, eds. *Bruckner Studies*. Cambridge, UK: Cambridge University Press, 1997.

Chapter 26

Ainger, Michael. *Gilbert and Sullivan: A Dual Biography*. New York: Oxford University Press, 2002.

Crittenden, Camille. *Johann Strauss and Vienna: Operetta and the Politics of Popular Culture*. Cambridge, UK: Cambridge University Press, 2000.

Harding, James. *Folies de Paris: The Rise and Fall of French Operetta*. London: Chappell, 1979.

Huebner, Steven. *The Operas of Charles Gounod*. Oxford, UK: Oxford University Press, 1990.

Pasler, Jann. *Composing The Citizen: Music as Public Utility in Third Republic France*. Berkeley: University of California Press, 2009.

Phillips-Matz, Mary Jane. *Puccini: A Biography*. Boston: Northeastern University Press, 2002.

Wilson, Alexandra. *The Puccini Problem: Opera, Nationalism and Modernity*. Cambridge, UK: Cambridge University Press, 2007.

Chapter 27

Behr, Shulamith, David Fanning, and Douglas Jarman, eds. *Expressionism Reassessed*. Houndmills, UK: Palgrave-Macmillan, 1994.

Brand, Juliane, and Christopher Hailey, eds. *Constructive Dissonance: Arnold Schoenberg and the Transformations of Twentieth-Century Culture*. Berkeley: University of California Press, 1997.

Butler, Christopher. *Early Modernism: Literature, Music, and Painting in Europe, 1900–1914*. Oxford, UK: Clarendon Press, 1994.

Crawford, John C., and Dorothy L. Crawford. *Expressionism in Twentieth-Century Music*. Bloomington: Indiana University Press, 1993.

De la Grange, Henri-Louis. *Gustav Mahler: Vienna: The Years of Challenge (1897–1904)*. Oxford, UK: Oxford University Press, 1995.

———. *Gustav Mahler: Vienna, Triumph and Disillusion (1904–1907)*. Oxford, UK: Oxford University Press, 2000.

———. *Gustav Mahler: A New Life Cut Short (1907–1911)*. Oxford, UK: Oxford University Press, 2008.

Del Mar, Norman. *Richard Strauss: A Critical Commentary on His Life and Works*. Three vols. Ithaca, NY: Cornell University Press, 1986.

Floros, Constantin. *Gustav Mahler: The Symphonies*, trans. Vernon Wicker. Portland, OR: Amadeus Press, 1993.

Franklin, Peter R. *The Life of Mahler*. Cambridge, UK: Cambridge University Press, 1997.

Frisch, Walter. *The Early Works of Arnold Schoenberg, 1893–1908*. Berkeley: University of California Press, 1993.

Gilliam, Brian. *The Life of Richard Strauss*. Cambridge, UK: Cambridge University Press, 1999.

Mitchell, Donald. *Gustav Mahler: The Early Years*. Rev. ed., London: Boydell Press, 2003.

———. *Gustav Mahler: Songs and Symphonies of Life and Death. Interpretations and Annotations*. Rev. ed., London: Boydell Press, 2002.

———. *Gustav Mahler: The Wunderhorn Years*. 3rd ed., London: Boydell Press, 2004.

Schoenberg, Arnold. *Style and Idea: Selected Writings of Arnold Schoenberg*, ed. Leonard Stein, trans. Leo Black. Expanded ed., Berkeley: University of California Press, 1984.

Schorske, Carl. *Fin-de-siècle Vienna: Politics and Culture*. New York: Random House, 1980.

Smith, Joan Allen. *Schoenberg and His Circle: A Viennese Portrait*. New York: Schirmer, 1986.

Chapter 28

Cross, Jonathan, ed. *The Cambridge Companion to Stravinsky*. Cambridge, UK: Cambridge University Press, 2003.

Garafola, Lynn. *Diaghilev's Ballets Russes*. New York: Oxford University Press, 1989.

Huebner, Steven. *French Opera at the 'Fin de Siècle': Wagnerism, Nationalism, and Style*. Oxford, UK: Oxford University Press, 1999.

Lockspeiser, Edward. *Debussy: His Life and Mind*. Two vols. Cambridge; UK: Cambridge University Press, 1962.

Mawer, Deborah. *The Cambridge Companion to Ravel*. Cambridge, UK: Cambridge University Press, 2000.

Nectoux, Jean-Michel. *Gabriel Fauré: A Musical Life*, trans. Roger Nichols. Cambridge, UK: Cambridge University Press, 1991.

Orledge, Robert. *Satie the Composer*. Cambridge, UK: Cambridge University Press, 1990.

Roland-Manuel, Alexis. *Maurice Ravel*, trans. C. Jolly. London: Dennis Dobson, 1947.

Shattuck, Roger. *The Banquet Years*. New York: Random House, 1955.

Taruskin, Richard. *Stravinsky and the Russian Traditions*. Berkeley: University of California Press, 1996.

Trezise, Simon. *The Cambridge Companion to Debussy*. Cambridge, UK: Cambridge University Press, 2003.

Wilkins, Nigel, ed. *The Writings of Erik Satie*. London: Eulenburg Books, 1980.

Zank, Stephen. *Irony and Sound: The Music of Maurice Ravel*. Rochester, NY: University of Rochester Press, 2009.

Chapter 29

Baker, James. *The Music of Alexander Scriabin*. New Haven, CT: Yale University Press, 1986.

Beckerman, Michael. *Janáček as Theorist*. Stuyvesant, NY: Pendragon Press, 1994.

———. ed. *Janáček and His World*. Princeton, NJ: Princeton University Press, 2003.

Burkholder, J. Peter. *All Made of Tunes: Charles Ives and the Uses of Musical Borrowing*. New Haven, CT: Yale University Press, 1995.

Gillies, Malcolm, ed. *The Bartók Companion*. London: Faber & Faber, 1994.

Hicks, Michael. *Henry Cowell: Bohemian*. Urbana: University of Illinois Press, 2002.

Higgins, Dick, ed. *Essential Cowell: Selected Writings on Music by Henry Cowell, 1921–1964*. Kingston, NY: McPherson, 2002.

Hill, Peter, ed. *The Messiaen Companion*. London: Faber & Faber, 1995.

Hitchcock, H. Wiley. *Ives*. London: Oxford University Press, 1977.

Ives, Charles. *Essays before a Sonata, The Majority, and Other Writings*, ed. Howard Boatwright. New York: W. W. Norton & Company, 1970.

———. *Memos*, ed. John Kirkpatrick. New York: W. W. Norton & Company, 1972.

Laki, Peter, ed. *Bartók and His World*. Princeton, NJ: Princeton University Press, 1995.

Miller, Leta E., and Fredric Lieberman. *Lou Harrison: Composing a World*. New York: Oxford University Press, 1998.

Oja, Carol. *Making Music Modern: New York in the 1920s*. New York: Oxford University Press, 2000.

Schloezer, Boris de. *Skryabin: Artist and Mystic*, trans. Nicolas Slonimsky. Berkeley: University of California Press, 1987.

Tick, Judith. *Ruth Crawford Seeger: A Composer's Search for American Music*. New York: Oxford University Press, 1997.

Tyrrell, John. *Janáček: 1854–1914, The Lonely Blackbird*. London: Faber and Faber, 2006.

———. *Janáček: 1914–1928, Tsar of the Forests*. London: Faber and Faber, 2007.

Chapter 30

Andriessen, Louis, and Elmer Schönberger. *The Apollonian Clockwork: On Stravinsky*, trans. Jeff Hamburg. Oxford, UK: Oxford University Press, 1989.

Auner, Joseph. *A Schoenberg Reader: Documents of a Life*. New Haven, CT: Yale University Press, 2003.

Cocteau, Jean. *A Call to Order*, trans. Rollo H. Myers. London: Faber and Gwyer, 1926.

Messing, Scott. *Neoclassicism in Music from the Genesis of the Concept through the Schoenberg/Stravinsky Polemic*. Ann Arbor, MI: UMI Research Press, 1988.

Pople, Anthony. *Berg: Violin Concerto*. Cambridge, UK: Cambridge University Press, 1991.

Webern, Anton. *The Path to the New Music*, trans. Leo Black. Bryn Mawr, PA: Theodore Presser, 1963.

Chapter 31

Axsom, Richard H. *Parade: Cubism as Theatre*. New York: Garland Publishing, 1979.

Brett, Philip, ed. *Benjamin Britten: Peter Grimes*. Cambridge, UK: Cambridge University Press, 1983.

Carpenter, Humphrey. *Benjamin Britten: A Biography*. New York: Simon and Schuster, 1993.

Cook, Susan. *Opera during the Weimar Republic: The "Zeitopern" of Ernst Krenek, Kurt Weill, and Paul Hindemith*. Ann Arbor, MI: UMI Research Press, 1989.

Cooke, Mervyn. *A History of Film Music*. Cambridge, UK: Cambridge University Press, 2008.

Eisler, Hanns. *A Rebel in Music: Selected Writings*, ed. Manfred Grabs, trans. Marjorie Meyer. New York: International Publishers, 1978.

Gorbman, Claudia. *Unheard Melodies: Narrative Film Music*. Bloomington: Indiana University Press, 1987.

Harding, James. *The Ox on the Roof: Scenes from Musical Life in Paris in the Twenties*. London: Macdonald, 1972.

Hinton, Stephen. *The Idea of Gebrauchsmusik: A Study of Musical Aesthetics in the Weimar Republic (1919–1933) with Particular Reference to the Works of Paul Hindemith*. New York: Garland Publishing, Inc., 1989.

Marks, Martin Miller. *Music and the Silent Film: Contexts and Case Studies, 1895–1924*. New York: Oxford University Press, 1997.

Milhaud, Darius. *Notes without Music*, trans. Donald Evans. London: Dobson, 1952. Rev. ed. (titled *My Happy Life*), ed. Rollo H. Myers. London: Calder & Boyers, 1967.

Perloff, Nancy. *Art and the Everyday: Popular Entertainment and the Circle of Erik Satie*. Oxford, UK: Oxford University Press, 1991.

Pollack, Howard. *George Gershwin: His Life and Work*. Berkeley: University of California Press, 2006.

Watson, Steven. *Prepare for Saints: Gertrude Stein, Virgil Thomson, and the Mainstreaming of American Modernism*. New York: Random House, 1998.

Chapter 32

Applegate, Celia, and Pamela Potter, eds. *Music and German National Identity*. Chicago: University of Chicago Press, 2002.

Bartlett, Rosamund, ed. *Shostakovich in Context*. Oxford, UK: Oxford University Press, 2000.

Brown, Malcolm H., ed. *A Shostakovich Casebook*. Bloomington: Indiana University Press, 2004.

Fay, Laurel E. *Shostakovich: A Life*. New York: Oxford University Press, 1999.

———. *Shostakovich and His World*. Princeton, NJ: Princeton University Press, 2004.

Kater, Michael H. *Composers of the Nazi Era: Eight Portraits*. New York: Oxford University Press, 2000.

———. *The Twisted Muse: Musicians and Their Music in the Third Reich*. New York: Oxford University Press, 1997.

Levi, Erik. *Music in the Third Reich*. London: Macmillan, 1994.

Morrison, Simon. *The People's Artist: Prokofiev's Soviet Years*. New York: Oxford University Press, 2009.

Sachs, Harvey. *Music in Fascist Italy*. New York: W. W. Norton & Company, 1987.

Volkov, Solomon. *Testimony: The Memoirs of Dmitri Shostakovich as Related to and Edited by Solomon Volkov*. New York: Harper & Row, 1979.

Wilson, Elizabeth. *Shostakovich: A Life Remembered*. Princeton, NJ: Princeton University Press, 1994.

Chapter 33

Dingle, Christopher Philip, and Nigel Simeone. *Olivier Messiaen: Music, Art and Literature*. Farnham, UK: Ashgate Publishing, Ltd., 2007.

Levy, Alan Howard. *Musical Nationalism: American Composers' Search for Identity*. Westport, CT: Greenwood Press, 1983.

MacDonald, Malcolm. *Varèse: Astronomer in Sound*. London: Kahn & Averill, 2003.

Pollack, Howard. *Aaron Copland: The Life and Work of an Uncommon Man*. New York: Henry Holt & Co., 1999.

Shenton, Andrew. *Messiaen the Theologian*. Farnham, UK: Ashgate Publishing, Ltd., 2010.

Chapter 34

Bailey, Kathryn. *The Life of Webern*. Cambridge, UK: Cambridge University Press, 1998.

Boulez, Pierre. *Stocktakings from an Apprenticeship*, trans. Stephen Walsh. Oxford, UK: Clarendon Press, 1991.

Cage, John. *Silence*. Middletown, CT: Wesleyan University Press, 1961.

Cardew, Cornelius. *Stockhausen Serves Imperialism and Other Essays*. London: Latimer, 1974.

Cardew, Cornelius, ed. *Scratch Music*. Cambridge, MA: MIT Press, 1974.

Cott, Jonathan. *Stockhausen: Conversations with the Composer*. New York: Simon and Schuster, 1975.

DeLio, Thomas. *Circumscribing the Open Universe: Essays on Cage, Feldman, Wolff, Ashley, and Lucier*. Washington, DC: Rowman and Littlefield, 1984.

———. ed. *The Music of Morton Feldman*. Westport, CT: Greenwood Press, 1996.

Feldman, Morton. *Essays*, ed. Walter Zimmerman. Kerpen, Germany: Beginner Press, 1985.

Harvey, Jonathan. *The Music of Stockhausen*. Berkeley: University of California Press, 1975.

Henze, Hans Werner. *Music and Politics: Collected Writings, 1953–81*, trans. P. Labanyi. London: Faber & Faber, 1982.

Kaprow, Allan. *Assemblage, Environments, and Happenings*. New York: Abrams, 1966.

Kostelanetz, Richard, ed. *Conversing with Cage*. New York: Limelight Editions, 1987.

Kurtz, Michael. *Stockhausen: A Biography*, trans. Richard Toop. New York: Farrar, Straus and Giroux, 1993.

Nattiez, Jean-Jacques, ed. *The Boulez-Cage Correspondence*, trans. R. Samuels. Cambridge, UK: Cambridge University Press, 1993.

Peles, Stephen, et al., eds. *The Collected Essays of Milton Babbitt*. Princeton, NJ: Princeton University Press, 2003.

Pollack, Howard. *Harvard Composers: Walter Piston and His Students, from Elliott Carter to Frederic Rzewski*. Metuchen, NJ: Scarecrow Press, 1992.

Pritchett, James. *The Music of John Cage*. Cambridge, UK: Cambridge University Press, 1993.

Revill, David. *The Roaring Silence: John Cage, A Life*. New York: Arcade, 1992.

Steinitz, R. *György Ligeti: Music of the Imagination*. Boston: Northeastern University Press, 2003.

Toop, Richard. *György Ligeti*. London: Phaidon Press, 1999.

Van Solkema, Sherman, ed. *The New Worlds of Edgard Varèse: A Symposium*. Brooklyn, NY: Institute for Studies in American Music, 1979.

Wörner, Karl Heinrich. *Stockhausen: Life and Work*, trans. G. W. Hopkins. London: Faber & Faber, 1973.

Chapter 35

DeLio, Thomas, ed. *Contiguous Lines: Issues and Ideas in the Music of the Sixties and Seventies*. Lanham, MD: University Press of America, 1985.

Fink, Robert. *Repeating Ourselves: American Minimal Music as Cultural Practice*. Berkeley: University of California Press, 2005.

Frith, Simon. *Sound Effects: Youth, Leisure, and the Politics of Rock 'n' Roll*. New York: Random House, 1981.

Frith, Simon, and Andrew Goodwin, eds. *On Record: Rock, Pop, and the Written Word*. New York: Random House, 1990.

Gitlin, Todd. *The Sixties: Years of Hope, Days of Rage*. New York: Bantam Books, 1987.

Kostelanetz, Richard, ed. *Writings on Glass: Essays, Interviews, Criticism*. New York: Schirmer, 1998.

Marcus, Greil. *Mystery Train: Images of American Rock 'n' Roll Music*. New York: E. P. Dutton, 1975.

Mertens, Wim. *American Minimal Music*. New York: Alexander Broude, 1983.

Potter, Keith. *Four Musical Minimalists*. Cambridge, UK: Cambridge University Press, 2000.

Reich, Steve. *Writings about Music*. New York: Oxford University Press. 2002.

Schwarz, K. Robert. *Minimalists*. London: Phaidon, 1996.

Strickland, Edward. *Minimalism: Origins*. Bloomington: Indiana University Press, 1993.

Chapter 36

Attali, Jacques. *Noise: The Political Economy of Music*, trans. Brian Massumi. Minneapolis: University of Minnesota Press, 1985.

Austin, Larry, and Douglas Kahn. *Source: Music of the Avant-Garde, 1966–1973*. Berkeley: University of California Press, 2011.

Born, Georgina. *Rationalizing Culture: IRCAM, Boulez, and the Institutionalization of the Avant-Garde*. Berkeley: University of California Press, 1995.

Gann, Kyle. *Music Downtown: Writing from the Village Voice*. Berkeley, CA, 2006.

Gilmore, Bob. *Harry Partch: A Biography*. New Haven, CT: Yale University Press, 1998.

Goldberg, Roselee. *Performance Art: From Futurism to the Present*. Rev. ed., New York: Thames & Hudson, 2001.

Holmes, Thom. *Electronic and Experimental Music: Technology, Music, and Culture*. New York: Routledge, 2008.

Kornick, Rebecca H. *Recent American Opera*. New York: Columbia University Press, 1991.

Lochhead, Judy, and Joseph Auner, eds. *Postmodern Music/Postmodern Thought*. New York: Routledge, 2002.

Nyman, Michael. *Experimental Music: Cage and Beyond*. New York: Schirmer, 1974.

Art Credits

1-1 Nicholas Conard/HK Images
1-2 Cliché Bibliotheque Nationale de France
1-3 Lebrecht Music & Arts
1-5 Erich Lessing/Art Resource, NY
1-7 St. Gallen, Switzerland, Stiftsbibliotheck, MS St. Gall 359. From Willi Apel, Gregorian Chant, Bloomington: Indiana University Press, 1958, plate I facing p. 122. Reprinted with permission of Indiana University Press.
1-8 Lebrecht
1-9 Bayerische Staatsbibliothek München, Musikabteilung
1-10 Réunion des Musées Nationaux/Art Resource, NY
1-11 Staatsarchiv des Kantons Zurich, StaZ W I 3, 19, XXXV fol. 56r.
1-12 Erich Lessing/Art Resource, NY
1-13 © Arte & Immaginisrl/CORBIS
1-14 Cliché Bibliotheque Nationale de France
2-2 Cliché Bibliotheque Nationale de France
2-3 © Gianni Dagli Orti/CORBIS
2-4 Bibliotheque des Arts Decoratifs, Paris, France/Archives Charmet/The Bridgeman Art Library
2-5 akg-images/VISIOARS
2-7a Bridgeman Art Library
2-7b Bridgeman Art Library
2-8 Cliché Bibliotheque Nationale de France
2-9 Cliché Bibliotheque Nationale de France
2-10 Archivo de la Catedral de Santiago
2-11 akg-images/Catherine Bibollet
2-12a Courtesy of the New York Public Library
2-12b Reproduction from Biblioteca Medicea Laurenziana
2-13a Wolfenbuttel, Herzog August Bibliothek
2-13b Wolfenbuttel, Herzog August Bibliothek
3-3 Cliché Bibliotheque Nationale de France
3-4 Snark/Art Resource, NY
3-5 Cliché Bibliotheque Nationale de France
3-6 Palais des Papes, Avignon, France/Peter Willi/The Bridgeman Art Library
3-7 Palais des Papes, Avignon, France/Peter Willi/The Bridgeman Art Library
3-8 Medina, Bibliotech Estense
3-9 Réunion des Musées Nationaux/Art Resource, NY
3-10 Fulda, Landesbibliothek, MS D. 23, fol. 302.
3-11 Lebrecht Music & Arts
3-12 Vanni/Art Resource, NY
4-2 © British Library Board; All rights reserved
4-3 HIP/Art Resource, NY
4-5 Bridgeman-Giraudon/Art Resource, NY
4-6 Chateau de Versailles, France/The Bridgeman Art Library
4-7 Bibliotheque Nationale, Paris, France/The Bridgeman Art Library
4-8 Kimbell Art Museum, Fort Worth, Texas/Art Resource, NY
4-9 Courtesy of the Biblioteca Apostolica Vaticana
4-10 Courtesy of Napoli Biblioteca Nazionale
4-11 © Wallace Collection, London, UK/The Bridgeman Art Library
5-1 Lebrecht Music & Arts
5-2 Musée Condé, Chantilly, France/The Bridgeman Art Library
5-4 The Bridgeman Art Library
5-5 Scala/Art Resource, NY
5-6 Scala/Art Resource, NY
5-7 Scala/Art Resource, NY
5-8 Bayerische Staatsbibliothek München, Musikabteilung, Signatur: 2 Mus.pr. 10907, title page"
5-9 Scala/White Images/Art Resource, NY
5-10 Lebrecht Music & Arts
5-11a Scala/Ministero per i Beni e le Attività culturali/Art Resource, NY
5-11b Alinari/Art Resource, NY
6-2 bpk, Berlin/Hessisches Landesmuseum/Art Resource, NY
6-3 From Joseph Klug, Geistliche Lieder auffs new gebessert (Wittenberg, 1533); Stiftung Luthergedenkstätten in Sachsen-Anhalt, Lutherhalle, Wittenberg.
6-4 Scala/Art Resource, NY
6-5 Lebrecht Music & Arts
6-6 Plantin-Moretus Museum, Antwerp
6-7 Kunsthistorisches Museum, Vienna, Austria/Ali Meyer/The Bridgeman Art Library
6-8 Lebrecht Music & Arts

6-9	akg-images/Rabatti - Domingie
6-10	Prado, Madrid, Spain/The Bridgeman Art Library
6-11	Lebrecht Music & Arts
6-12	Lebrecht Music & Arts/TL
7-2	Lebrecht Music & Arts
7-3	Alinari/Art Resource, NY
7-4	Lebrecht Music & Arts
7-5	Library of Congress
7-6	Alfredo Dagli Orti/Art Resource, NY
7-7	Library of Congress
7-8	Leemage/Lebrecht Music & Arts
7-10	Courtesy of the British Library
8-2	Lebrecht Music & Arts
8-3	BPK, Berlin/Museo del Settecento Veneziano/Art Resource, NY
8-4	Museum of Fine Arts, Boston /Lebrecht
8-5	Lebrecht Music & Arts
8-6	bpk, Berlin/Art Resource, NY
8-7	Erich Lessing/Art Resource, NY
8-8	Lebrecht Music & Arts
8-9	Réunion des Musées Nationaux/Art Resource, NY
8-10	Lebrecht Music & Arts Photo Library
8-11	Réunion des Musées Nationaux/Art Resource, NY
8-12	Erich Lessing/Art Resource, NY
8-13	Lebrecht Music & Arts
9-2	Scala/Art Resource, NY
9-3	Lebrecht Music & Arts
9-4	Lebrecht Music & Arts
9-5	National Gallery of Victoria, Melbourne, Australia/Felton Bequest/The Bridgeman Art Library
9-6	Giraudon/Art Resource, NY
9-7	Music Division, NYPL for the Performing Arts; Astor, Lenox, and Tilden Foundations
9-8	Lebrecht/ColouriserAL
10-2	Lebrecht Music & Arts
10-3	Courtesy of William H. Scheide, Princeton, NJ.
10-4	Lebrecht Music & Arts
10-5	Hervé Champollion/akg-images
10-6	Centre Historique des Archives Nationales, Paris, France/Archives Charmet/The Bridgeman Art Library
10-7	Lebrecht Music & Arts
10-8	Paris: Ballard, 1793; Courtesy of the Sibley Music Library, Eastman School of Music, University of Rochester (New York).
10-9	Erich Lessing/Art Resource, NY
10-10	Lebrecht Music & Arts
11-1	Lebrecht Music & Arts
11-2	Tate, London/Art Resource, NY
11-3	Lebrecht Music & Arts
11-4	The Foundling Museum, London, UK/By permission of The William Salt Library, Stafford/The Bridgeman Art Library
11-5	Lebrecht Music & Arts
11-6	Lebrecht Music & Arts
11-7	Lebrecht Music & Arts
11-8	© DeA Picture Library/Art Resource, NY
12-1	Lebrecht Music & Arts
12-2	Lebrecht Music & Arts
12-3	Lebrecht Music & Arts
12-4	Lebrecht Music & Arts
12-5	Museo di Strumenti del Conservatorio, Naples, Italy/Giraudon/The Bridgeman Art Library International
12-6	Lebrecht Music & Arts
12-7	Lebrecht Music & Arts
12-8	Fitzwilliam Museum, University of Cambridge, UK/The Bridgeman Art Library International
12-9	Erich Lessing/Art Resource, NY
12-10	Erich Lessing/Art Resource, NY
12-11	Galleria Sabauda, Turin, Italy/Alinari/The Bridgeman Art Library International
13-1	V&A Images, London/Art Resource, NY
13-2	Lebrecht Music & Arts
13-4	Erich Lessing/Art Resource, NY
13-5	Erich Lessing/Art Resource, NY
13-6	Lebrecht Music & Arts
13-7	Getty Images
13-8	Erich Lessing/Art Resource, NY
13-9	Lebrecht Music & Arts
13-10	British Museum, London, UK/The Bridgeman Art Library International
13-11	akg-images
13-12	Lebrecht
13-13	Erich Lessing/Art Resource, NY
14-1	Scala/Art Resource, NY
14-2	Lebrecht Music & Arts
14-3	akg-images
14-4	Lebrecht Music & Arts
14-5	Lebrecht/ColouriserAL
14-6	Lebrecht Music & Arts
14-7	Erich Lessing/Art Resource, NY
14-8	Bibliotheque de l'Opera Garnier, Paris, France/Archives Charmet/The Bridgeman Art Library International
14-9	The Pierpont Morgan Library, New York, Dannie and Hettie Heineman Collection.
14-10	Alfred Publications
14-11	Culture images/ua/Lebrecht

15-1 Johann Nepomuk della Croce, Mozarteum, Salzburg, © Erich Lessing/Art Resource, NY.
15-2 Culture images/Lebrecht
15-3 Lebrecht Music & Arts
15-4 Lebrecht/ColouriserAL
15-5 A. Koch Interfoto/Lebrecht Music & Arts
16-1 Erich Lessing/Art Resource, NY
16-2 J. Massey Stewart/Lebrecht Music & Arts
16-3 akg-images/Beethoven-Haus Bonn
16-4 Lebrecht Music & Arts
16-5 Lebrecht Music & Arts
16-6 Lebrecht Authors
16-7 Lebrecht Music & Arts
16-8 Erich Lessing/Art Resource, NY
16-9 Scala/Art Resource, NY
16-10 Lebrecht/ColouriserAL
16-11 Lebrecht Music & Arts
16-12 Erich Lessing/Art Resource, NY
17-1 Museo Teatrale Alla Scala, Mailand© SuperStock/SuperStock
17-2 akg-images.
17-3 Bibliotheque de l'Opera Garnier, Paris, France/Archives Charmet/The Bridgeman Art Library International
17-4 akg-images
17-5 Scala/Art Resource, NY
17-6 Lebrecht Music & Arts
17-7 © Art Archive, The/SuperStock
17-8 Leemage/Lebrecht Music & Arts
17-9 Royal Academy of Music/Lebrecht Music & Arts
17-10 Lebrecht Music & Arts
17-11 Lebrecht Music & Arts
18-2 akg-images
18-3 © SuperStock/SuperStock
18-4 © SuperStock/SuperStock
18-5 Erich Lessing/Art Resource, NY
18-6 Erich Lessing/Art Resource, NY
18-7 Erich Lessing/Art Resource, NY
18-8 Erich Lessing/Art Resource, NY
18-9 akg-images
18-10 Erich Lessing/Art Resource, NY
19-1 Royal Academy of Music/Lebrecht Music & Arts
19-2 Scala/Art Resource, NY
19-3 Lebrecht/ColouriserAL
19-4 bpk, Berlin/Art Resource, NY
19-5 Lebrecht Music & Arts
19-6 Academie Imperiale de Musique, Paris, c.1855 (colour litho), Arnout, Louis Jules (1814–68)/Musee de la Ville de Paris, Musee Carnavalet, Paris, France/Archives Charmet/The Bridgeman Art Library International
19-7 New York Public Library, Jerome Robbins Dance Division; Astor, Lenox and Tilden Foundations.
19-8 akg-images
19-10 V&A Images, London/Art Resource, NY
19-11 Private Collection/Archives Charmet/The Bridgeman Art Library International
20-1 Scala/Art Resource, NY
20-2 Private Collection/Archives Charmet/The Bridgeman Art Library International
20-3 Giraudon/Art Resource, NY
20-4 Leemage/Lebrecht Music & Arts
20-5 Lebrecht Music & Arts
20-6 bpk, Berlin/Art Resource, NY
20-7 Lebrecht Music & Arts
20-8 Lebrecht/ColouriserAL
20-9 Réunion des Musées Nationaux/Art Resource, NY
20-10 Lebrecht/ColouriserAL
21-1 Lebrecht Music & Arts
21-2 Lebrecht Music & Arts
21-3 © SuperStock/SuperStock
21-4 Lebrecht Music & Arts
21-5 © DeA Picture Library/Art Resource, NY
21-6 National Portrait Gallery, Smithsonian Institution/Art Resource, NY
21-7 Tretyakov Gallery, Moscow, Russia/The Bridgeman Art Library International
21-8 Lebrecht Music & Arts
21-9 Culture images/Lebrecht
21-10 Lebrecht Music & Arts
22-1 National Archives of the Richard Wagner Foundation, Bayreuth.
22-2 bpk, Berlin/Art Resource, NY
22-3 Lebrecht Music & Arts
22-4 akg-images
22-5 © SuperStock/SuperStock
22-6 Lebrecht Music & Arts
22-7 Royal Academy of Music/Lebrecht Music & Arts
22-8 Tate, London/Art Resource, NY
23-1 Lebrecht Music & Arts
23-2 Lebrecht/ColouriserAL
23-3 Lebrecht
23-4 National Archives of the Richard Wagner Foundation, Bayreuth.
23-5 National Archives of the Richard Wagner Foundation, Bayreuth.
23-6 Lebrecht Music & Arts

23-7 akg-images
23-8 Lebrecht
23-9 Scala/Art Resource, NY
23-10 Lebrecht Music & Arts
23-11 Lebrecht Music & Arts
23-12 Leemage/Lebrecht Music & Arts
24-1 bpk, Berlin/Art Resource, NY
24-2 Lebrecht Music & Arts
24-3 Collection of the author.
24-4 n/a
24-5 Culture images/Lebrecht
24-6 Sammlung Rauch/Interfoto/Lebrecht Music & Arts
24-7 Lebrecht Music & Arts
24-8 Culture images/Lebrecht
24-9 Lebrecht Music & Arts
24-10 akg-images
25-1 JazzSign/Lebrecht Music & Arts
25-2 Erich Lessing/Art Resource, NY
25-3 akg-images
25-4 Erich Lessing/Art Resource, NY
25-5 © SuperStock/SuperStock
25-6 akg-images
25-7 Lebrecht Music & Arts
25-8 Library of Congress.
25-9 Courtesy of the Boston Public Library/Rare Books
25-10 Lebrecht Music & Arts
26-1 Lebrecht Music & Arts
26-2 akg-images
26-3 akg-images/Joseph Martin
26-4 Leemage/Lebrecht Music & Arts
26-5 Erich Lessing/Art Resource, NY
26-6 The Pierpont Morgan Library/Art Resource, NY
26-7 Lebrecht Music & Arts
26-8 Leemage/Lebrecht
26-9 Scala/Art Resource, NY
27-1 A. Koch Interfoto/Lebrecht Music & Arts
27-2 akg-images
27-3 Lebrecht Music & Arts
27-4 akg-images
27-5 Lebrecht Music & Arts
27-6 Lebrecht Music & Arts
27-7 Lebrecht Authors
27-8 Culture images/Lebrecht
27-9 Arnold Schoenberg Institute/Lebrecht
27-10 © 2011 Belmont Music Publisher, Los Angeles/ARS, New York/VBK, Vienna
27-11 © 2011 Belmont Music Publisher
28-1 Musee National d'Art Moderne, Centre Pompidou, Paris, France/© DACS/Giraudon/The Bridgeman Art Library
28-2 The Bridgeman Art Library
28-3 akg-images/André Held
28-4 Fair use
28-5 The Bridgeman Art Library
28-6 Lebrecht Music & Arts
28-7 Cliché Bibliotheque Nationale de France
28-8 Cliché Bibliotheque Nationale de France
28-9 akg-images
28-10 akg-images
28-11 Lebrecht Music & Arts
28-12 Lebrecht Music & Arts
29-1 Lebrecht Music & Arts
29-2 Arthur Reynolds Collection/Lebrecht Music & Arts
29-3 Lebrecht Music & Arts
29-4 akg-images
29-5 Lebrecht Music & Arts
29-6 Lebrecht Music & Arts
29-7 Lebrecht Music & Arts
29-8 bpk, Berlin/Art Resource, NY
29-9 akg-images
29-10 Charles Ives Papers, Yale University Music Library; © Peer International/Charles Ives.
30-2 Lebrecht Music & Arts
30-3 akg-images
30-4 Lebrecht Music & Arts
30-5 CNAC/MNAM/Dist. Réunion des Musées Nationaux/Art Resource, NY
30-6 Lebrecht Music & Arts
30-7 akg/Imagno
31-1 Getty Images
31-2 Rendered by A Good Thing, Inc.
31-3 Getty Images
31-4 Library of Congress.
31-5 Lebrecht Music & Arts
31-6 © Bettmann/CORBIS
31-7 Lebrecht Music & Arts
31-8 Lebrecht Music & Arts
31-9 Lebrecht Music & Arts
31-10 ©McNay Art Museum/Art Resource, NY
31-11 Getty Images
31-12 The Museum of Modern Art/Licensed by SCALA/Art Resource, NY
31-13 The Metropolitan Museum of Art/Art Resource, NY
31-14 akg-images/Joseph Martin

31-15 Getty Images
31-16 © Stiftung Archiv der Akademie der Kunste, Berlin, Bestandsbezeichnung
31-17 Metropolitan Opera Archives/Lebrecht Music & Arts
32-1 Lebrecht Music & Arts
32-2 Digital Image © The Museum of Modern Art/Licensed by SCALA/Art Resource, NY
32-3 Culture images/Lebrecht
32-4 akg-images
32-5 Lebrecht Music & Arts
32-6 akg-images
32-7 RIA Novosti/Lebrecht Music & Arts
32-8 Library of Congress.
32-9 akg-images
32-10 Lebrecht Music & Arts
32-11 Lebrecht Music & Arts
33-1 Courtesy of Judith Tick
33-2 © Bettmann/CORBIS
33-3 Courtesy of Judith Tick
33-4 © Bettmann/CORBIS
33-5 Courtesy of the Harry Partch Foundation, San Diego, CA
33-6 © Jerry Cooke/CORBIS
33-7 Photo © Christie's Images
33-8 Library of Congress.
33-9 akg-images
33-10 Harvard Theatre Collection, Houghton Library, Harvard University
33-11 Nigel Simeone, Private Collection
33-12 Nigel Simeone, Private Collection
34-1 © National Nuclear Security Administration/Science Faction/Corbis
34-3 © Karlheinz Stockhausen
34-4 Getty Images
34-5 Lebrecht Music & Arts
34-6 Getty Images
34-7 Rothko Chapel, Houston, Texas, photo by Hickey-Robertson.
34-8 Special thanks to the Computer Music Center for the use of these photos from the archives
34-9 Leo Theremin Playing Instrument © Bettmann/CORBIS
34-10 Special thanks to the Computer Music Center for the use of these photos from the archives
34-11 akg-images/Interfoto
34-12 Lebrecht Music & Arts
34-13 Photo by Chris Lee Photography
35-1 Interfoto/Lebrecht Music & Arts
35-2 © Bob Adelman/Corbis
35-3 Getty Images
35-4 Mirrorpix/Lebrecht Authors
35-5 Courtesy of Landov Images
35-6 Getty Images
35-7 Getty Images
35-8 Getty Images
35-9 JazzSign/Lebrecht Music & Arts
35-10 La Monte Young, Composition 1960 #7; Copyright © La Monte Young 1963, renewed 1991. All rights reserved.
35-11 Getty Images
35-12 Hiroyuki Ito/*The New York Times*/Redux
35-13 Mirrorpix/Lebrecht Authors
35-14 Copyright the Robert Mapplethorpe Foundation. Courtesy Art + Commerce.
35-15 Lelli & Masotti/Alinari/Lebrecht
35-16 Chris Christodoulou/Lebrecht Music & Arts
36-1 Lebrecht Music & Arts
36-2 Bruce Davidson/Magnum Photos
36-3 Getty Images
36-4 T. Martinot/Lebrecht
36-5 akg-images
36-6 Betty Freeman/Lebrecht Music & Arts
36-7 Victor Bazhenov/Lebrecht Music & Arts
36-8 Anne Purkiss/Lebrecht Music & Arts
36-9 T. Martinot/Lebrecht Music & Arts
36-10 Lebrecht Music & Arts
36-11 Lebrecht Music & Arts
36-12 Tristram Kenton/Lebrecht Music & Arts
36-13 Lebrecht Music & Arts
36-14 akg-images/Marion Kalter

Index